Handbook of Bureaucracy

PUBLIC ADMINISTRATION AND PUBLIC POLICY

A Comprehensive Publication Program

Executive Editor

JACK RABIN
Professor of Public Administration and Public Policy
Division of Public Affairs
The Capital College
The Pennsylvania State University—Harrisburg
Middletown, Pennsylvania

1. *Public Administration as a Developing Discipline (in two parts),* Robert T. Golembiewski
2. *Comparative National Policies on Health Care,* Milton I. Roemer, M.D.
3. *Exclusionary Injustice: The Problem of Illegally Obtained Evidence,* Steven R. Schlesinger
4. *Personnel Management in Government: Politics and Process,* Jay M. Shafritz, Walter L. Balk, Albert C. Hyde, and David H. Rosenbloom
5. *Organization Development in Public Administration (in two parts),* edited by Robert T. Golembiewski and William B. Eddy
6. *Public Administration: A Comparative Perspective, Second Edition, Revised and Expanded,* Ferrel Heady
7. *Approaches to Planned Change (in two parts),* Robert T. Golembiewski
8. *Program Evaluation at HEW (in three parts),* edited by James G. Abert
9. *The States and the Metropolis,* Patricia S. Florestano and Vincent L. Marando
10. *Personnel Management in Government: Politics and Process, Second Edition, Revised and Expanded,* Jay M. Shafritz, Albert C. Hyde, and David H. Rosenbloom
11. *Changing Bureaucracies: Understanding the Organization Before Selecting the Approach,* William A. Medina
12. *Handbook on Public Budgeting and Financial Management,* edited by Jack Rabin and Thomas D. Lynch
13. *Encyclopedia of Policy Studies,* edited by Stuart S. Nagel
14. *Public Administration and Law: Bench v. Bureau in the United States,* David H. Rosenbloom
15. *Handbook on Public Personnel Administration and Labor Relations,* edited by Jack Rabin, Thomas Vocino, W. Bartley Hildreth, and Gerald J. Miller
16. *Public Budgeting and Finance: Behavioral, Theoretical, and Technical Perspectives,* edited by Robert T. Golembiewski and Jack Rabin
17. *Organizational Behavior and Public Management,* Debra W. Stewart and G. David Garson
18. *The Politics of Terrorism: Second Edition, Revised and Expanded,* edited by Michael Stohl

19. *Handbook of Organization Management,* edited by William B. Eddy
20. *Organization Theory and Management,* edited by Thomas D. Lynch
21. *Labor Relations in the Public Sector,* Richard C. Kearney
22. *Politics and Administration: Woodrow Wilson and American Public Administration,* edited by Jack Rabin and James S. Bowman
23. *Making and Managing Policy: Formulation, Analysis, Evaluation,* edited by G. Ronald Gilbert
24. *Public Administration: A Comparative Perspective, Third Edition, Revised,* Ferrel Heady
25. *Decision Making in the Public Sector,* edited by Lloyd G. Nigro
26. *Managing Administration,* edited by Jack Rabin, Samuel Humes, and Brian S. Morgan
27. *Public Personnel Update,* edited by Michael Cohen and Robert T. Golembiewski
28. *State and Local Government Administration,* edited by Jack Rabin and Don Dodd
29. *Public Administration: A Bibliographic Guide to the Literature,* Howard E. McCurdy
30. *Personnel Management in Government: Politics and Process, Third Edition, Revised and Expanded,* Jay M. Shafritz, Albert C. Hyde, and David H. Rosenbloom
31. *Handbook of Information Resource Management,* edited by Jack Rabin and Edward M. Jackowski
32. *Public Administration in Developed Democracies: A Comparative Study,* edited by Donald C. Rowat
33. *The Politics of Terrorism: Third Edition, Revised and Expanded,* edited by Michael Stohl
34. *Handbook on Human Services Administration,* edited by Jack Rabin and Marcia B. Steinhauer
35. *Handbook of Public Administration,* edited by Jack Rabin, W. Bartley Hildreth, and Gerald J. Miller
36. *Ethics for Bureaucrats: An Essay on Law and Values, Second Edition, Revised and Expanded,* John A. Rohr
37. *The Guide to the Foundations of Public Administration,* Daniel W. Martin
38. *Handbook of Strategic Management,* edited by Jack Rabin, Gerald J. Miller, and W. Bartley Hildreth
39. *Terrorism and Emergency Management: Policy and Administration,* William L. Waugh, Jr.
40. *Organizational Behavior and Public Management: Second Edition, Revised and Expanded,* Michael L. Vasu, Debra W. Stewart, and G. David Garson
41. *Handbook of Comparative and Development Public Administration,* edited by Ali Farazmand
42. *Public Administration: A Comparative Perspective, Fourth Edition,* Ferrel Heady
43. *Government Financial Management Theory,* Gerald J. Miller
44. *Personnel Management in Government: Politics and Process, Fourth Edition, Revised and Expanded*, Jay M. Shafritz, Norma M. Riccucci, David H. Rosenbloom, and Albert C. Hyde
45. *Public Productivity Handbook*, edited by Marc Holzer
46. *Handbook of Public Budgeting*, edited by Jack Rabin

47. *Labor Relations in the Public Sector: Second Edition, Revised and Expanded*, Richard C. Kearney
48. *Handbook of Organizational Consultation*, edited by Robert T. Golembiewski
49. *Handbook of Court Administration and Management*, edited by Steven W. Hays and Cole Blease Graham, Jr.
50. *Handbook of Comparative Public Budgeting and Financial Management*, edited by Thomas D. Lynch and Lawrence L. Martin
51. *Handbook of Organizational Behavior*, edited by Robert T. Golembiewski
52. *Handbook of Administrative Ethics*, edited by Terry L. Cooper
53. *Encyclopedia of Policy Studies: Second Edition, Revised and Expanded*, edited by Stuart S. Nagel
54. *Handbook of Regulation and Administrative Law*, edited by David H. Rosenbloom and Richard D. Schwartz
55. *Handbook of Bureaucracy*, edited by Ali Farazmand

Additional Volumes in Preparation

Handbook of Public Personnel Administration, edited by Jack Rabin, Thomas Vocino, W. Bartley Hildreth, and Gerald J. Miller

Handbook of Public Sector Labor Relations, edited by Jack Rabin, Thomas Vocino, W. Bartley Hildreth, and Gerald J. Miller

Practical Public Management, Robert T. Golembiewski

ANNALS OF PUBLIC ADMINISTRATION

1. *Public Administration: History and Theory in Contemporary Perspective*, edited by Joseph A. Uveges, Jr.
2. *Public Administration Education in Transition*, edited by Thomas Vocino and Richard Heimovics
3. *Centenary Issues of the Pendleton Act of 1883*, edited by David H. Rosenbloom with the assistance of Mark A. Emmert
4. *Intergovernmental Relations in the 1980s*, edited by Richard H. Leach
5. *Criminal Justice Administration: Linking Practice and Research*, edited by William A. Jones, Jr.

Handbook of Bureaucracy

edited by

Ali Farazmand
Northern Kentucky University
Highland Heights, Kentucky

Marcel Dekker, Inc. **New York • Basel • Hong Kong**

Library of Congress Cataloging-in-Publication Data

Handbook of bureaucracy / edited by Ali Farazmand.
p. cm. — (Public administration and public policy; 55)
Includes bibliographical references and index.
ISBN 0-8247-9182-7 (alk. paper)
1. Bureaucracy. 2. Public administration. I. Farazmand, Ali.
II. Series.
JF1351.H266 1994
350'.001—dc20 94-15080
CIP

The publisher offers discounts on this book when ordered in bulk quantities. For more information, write to Special Sales/Professional Marketing at the address below.

This book is printed on acid-free paper.

Marcel Dekker, Inc.
270 Madison Avenue, New York, New York 10016

Current printing (last digit):
10 9 8 7 6 5 4 3 2 1

PRINTED IN THE UNITED STATES OF AMERICA

To
my mother, Keemya
my little son, Cyrus

Foreword

In the *Handbook of Bureaucracy*, Ali Farazmand has initiated and executed a massive project. The text is a major contribution to a body of literature that is already voluminous.

This collection of over 40 essays by nearly 50 authors is not the product of a preconceived framework for analysis, as it focuses on different aspects of the multifunctional role of public bureaucracies. Farazmand's mission was to stimulate participation by an impressive array of well-established experts in bureaucratic studies and then to organize their contributions in a coherent pattern for an encyclopedic compilation.

Because of this approach, it is not a volume likely to be read or studied chapter by chapter, from front to back. Rather, it offers a rich reservoir of materials on bureaucracy that can be tapped by different users for different purposes, with guidance from the arrangement of the text into seven distinct parts and from the comprehensive index. Thus, the *Handbook of Bureaucracy* can respond to the needs of an audience representing a variety of perspectives: historical, societal, political, policy, managerial, and geographical.

Professor Farazmand deserves commendation and thanks for his vision and persistence in bringing this enterprise to fruition. The publisher, Marcel Dekker, Inc., has now added another volume to its impressive list of contributions to the study of bureaucracy and public administration. Comparativists generally can find satisfaction in this additional evidence that a sustained and growing interest is leading to the enrichment of available resources in this field.

Ferrel Heady, A.M., Ph.D.
Professor Emeritus
School of Public Administration
The University of New Mexico
Albuquerque, New Mexico

Preface

The purpose of this encyclopedic handbook is to bring together original chapters that analyze the basic issues and major aspects of bureaucracy, bureaucratic politics and administrative theory, public policy, and public administration from American and international perspectives. The focus of this volume is on the multifunctional role of public bureaucracy in societies with various socioeconomic, political, cultural, and ideological systems and orientations. This multifunctional role can be studied in a variety of ways—at macro or micro level, either in a single nation or across national/regional levels.

The major themes and aspects of the study of bureaucracy include theoretical, analytical, philosophical, and historical perspectives and interpretations of bureaucracy and bureaucratization as they relate to: civilization, public administration/management, organization theory, politics and administration theory, debureaucratization, politics/public policy, political economy of public and corporate bureaucracies, global/multinational bureaucracies, system maintenance/regime enhancement, culture, representative bureaucracy, policy implementation, governance, national development, rural/agricultural/economic development, individuals, women, change and modernization, revolutions, alternatives to bureaucracy, democracy, political systems, environmental crisis management, ethics/accountability, public services, privatization, political responsiveness and administrative/managerial performance of bureaucracies across nations, and many other central issues/aspects of bureaucracy, administration, and management.

This encyclopedic volume covers all of these—and many more—approaches to the analysis of bureaucracy. The text also covers a wide range of functions, processes, and issues common to all bureaucracies across nations and the public, private, or nonprofit sectors (with an emphasis on the public and nonprofit sectors). These include: budgeting, personnel administration, policy analysis, organization and structural reorganization, local and national/central bureaucracies, intergovernmental functions, civil service, efficiency and effectiveness, service delivery, and bureaucratic domination and repression.

Multidisciplinary experts from around the world were invited to prepare chapters that would address and analyze bureaucracy and public administration and policy. While some chapters focus on specific countries or regions as case studies, others analyze countries and regions in comparative perspective. Still other essays address historical, analytical, and theoretical/conceptual perspectives on bureaucracy. The end result is a compendium by more than 45 experts, many of whom are of national and global distinction.

Together, these experts cover a broad scope of subject matter. Although many books are available on bureaucracy and in the fields of American and comparative/development public administration and management, none of them deals with the multidimensional aspects and issues of bureaucracy and bureaucratic phenomena so comprehensively.

This handbook is divided into seven parts, followed by a thorough index. Part I discusses historical perspectives on the development of public bureaucracy and administrative thought from ancient times. Here, two chapters deal with the development of administrative thought and the bureaucracy of the Spanish empire in the Americas. Part II focuses on the theoretical and conceptual perspectives on bureaucracy and bureaucratic politics. These six chapters analyze various aspects of bureaucracy and bureaucratization, the administrative state, bureaucracy and democracy, presidentialism vs. a parliamentary system, leadership, and organizational decline.

Part III covers a wide range of issues and subjects on bureaucracy, politics, and society. Here, ten theoretical and empirical chapters focus on such topics as: government reorganization, organization–environment, bureaucracy and environmental crisis, modernization, civil service, culture and management transfer, challenges to bureaucracy, ethical foundations of bureaucracy, and public service for the twentieth century. Part IV analyzes the relationship among bureaucracy, public policy, and administration/management. This is done in six chapters focusing on the international organizations under the new world order, comparative privatization and debureaucratization, bureaucracy and disaster management, local government training, conflict resolution, and productivity improvement.

Part V is a comprehensive treatment of bureaucracy and bureaucratic politics in North/Central/Latin American countries. Here, ten empirical chapters analyze a wide range of topics and issues, most of which deal with the United States. Part VI analyzes bureaucracy and bureaucratic politics in Europe and Australia. This is done in three chapters focusing on Australia and Britain in the Thatcher era.

Finally, Part VII discusses bureaucracy and politics in Asia, Africa, and the Middle/Near East. Here, six chapters analyze various aspects and issues of public bureaucracy in such diverse nations as Korea, the Philippines, India, Bangladesh, Turkey, and Iran.

This text is intended to serve students and instructors of American and comparative/international/development public administration, as well as comparative politics and policy, at both the graduate and undergraduate levels. It is also a comprehensive reference source for researchers as well as policy makers in the areas concerned. The contributors of this volume and I hope that this encyclopedic handbook will fill a major gap in the study of bureaucracy in American and comparative/global settings. We also hope that this project will trigger an undertaking of further studies on bureaucracy in the future.

This project could not have been accomplished without the assistance and generous cooperation of those involved. I would like to thank the contributors around the globe who, despite heavy research agendas, always responded promptly to my inquiries, demands, and memos. I am sure they all are pleased to see the volume published. I would also like to acknowledge the assistance of my former graduate research assistant at Northern Kentucky University,

Margaret Metzger, who helped me complete the project. My special thanks also go to the editors Hugh Haggerty, Sandra Beberman, and Thomas Finnegan at Marcel Dekker, Inc., and Jack Rabin, the series editor, whose cooperation and encouragement were much appreciated. I also extend my thanks to Professor Emeritus Ferrel Heady for his suggestions, moral support, and encouragement. Finally, I am grateful to my wife, Farideh, for her patience with me throughout the project.

Ali Farazmand

Contents

PART III: BUREAUCRACY, POLITICS, AND SOCIETY

PART IV: BUREAUCRACY, PUBLIC POLICY, AND ADMINISTRATION/MANAGEMENT

PART VI: BUREAUCRACY AND BUREAUCRATIC POLITICS IN EUROPE AND AUSTRALIA

PART VII: BUREAUCRACY AND POLITICS IN ASIA, AFRICA, AND THE MIDDLE/NEAR EAST

Contributors

Nolan J. Argyle Valdosta State University, Valdosta, Georgia

Gerald E. Caiden University of Southern California, Los Angeles, California

Raphael J. Caprio Rutgers University at Newark, Newark, New Jersey

Ledivina V. Cariño University of the Philippines, Diliman, Quezon City, Philippines

Adrian Carr University of Western Sydney, Nepean, Australia

James B. Christoph Indiana University, Bloomington, Indiana

Mark R. Daniels Memphis State University, Memphis, Tennessee

David L. Dillman Abilene Christian University, Abilene, Texas

Ali Farazmand Northern Kentucky University, Highland Heights, Kentucky

Lon S. Felker East Tennessee State University, Johnson City, Tennessee

Terri Susan Fine University of Central Florida, Orlando, Florida

Rita Giacalone Universidad de Los Andes, Mérida, Venezuela

Mary Ann Groves Manhattan College, Riverdale, New York

Arie Halachmi Tennessee State University, Nashville, Tennessee

John Halligan University of Canberra, Belconnen, Australia

Roger Handberg University of Central Florida, Orlando, Florida

M. Shamsul Haque National University of Singapore, Singapore

Richard Hartwig Texas A&M University—Kingsville, Kingsville, Texas

Lenneal J. Henderson University of Baltimore, Baltimore, Maryland and The Fielding Institute, Santa Barbara, California

Metin Heper Bilkent University, Ankara, Turkey

Jack W. Hopkins Indiana University, Bloomington, Indiana

R. B. Jain University of Delhi, Delhi, India

Harry M. Johnson University of Illinois at Urbana-Champaign, Urbana, Illinois

Mohammad Mohabbat Khan University of Dhaka, Dhaka, Bangladesh

Renu Khator University of South Florida, Tampa, Florida

Bun Woong Kim Dongguk University, Seoul, Korea

Michael Klausner University of Pittsburgh at Bradford, Bradford, Pennsylvania

Paul Knepper Northern Kentucky University, Highland Heights, Kentucky

Alexander Kouzmin University of Western Sydney, Nepean, Australia

Steven G. Koven Iowa State University, Ames, Iowa

Robert Leivesley University of Western Sydney, Nepean, Australia

Michael Lubatkin The University of Connecticut, Storrs, Connecticut

Kevin Mahoney University of Central Florida, Orlando, Florida

John G. Merriam Bowling Green State University, Bowling Green, Ohio

Momar Ndiaye The University of Connecticut, Storrs, Connecticut

Dorothy Olshfski Rutgers University at Newark, Newark, New Jersey

B. Guy Peters University of Pittsburgh, Pittsburgh, Pennsylvania

Fred W. Riggs University of Hawaii at Manoa, Honolulu, Hawaii

Hindy Lauer Schachter New Jersey Institute of Technology, Newark, New Jersey

David A. Schultz Trinity University, San Antonio, Texas

O. Glenn Stahl Arlington, Virginia

Ruth Ann Strickland Appalachian State University, Boone, North Carolina

Jorge I. Tapia-Videla Wayne State University, Detroit, Michigan

Stephen D. Van Beek San Jose State University, San Jose, California

Richard Vengroff The University of Connecticut, Storrs, Connecticut

Marcia Lynn Whicker Rutgers University at Newark, Newark, New Jersey

David E. Wilson United Nations Joint Inspection Unit, Geneva, Switzerland

Habib M. Zafarullah University of New England, Armidale, Australia

Daniel Zirker University of Idaho, Moscow, Idaho

1
Public Administration, Administrative Thought, and the Emergence of the Nation State

Nolan J. Argyle
Valdosta State University, Valdosta, Georgia

> It must be considered that there is nothing more difficult to carry out, nor more doubtful of success, nor more dangerous to handle, than to initiate a new order of things.
>
> Machiavelli

I. INTRODUCTION

The modern nation state emerged during a period of intense debate concerning the nature of the relationship between church and state, and in the context of great economic and commercial upheaval accompanying the Renaissance. With its emergence came the administrative structures needed to sustain the state. These structures built upon the feudal administrative apparatus centered around the Church—"clerk" is derived from "cleric"—to create a system in which the practice of government became a field of its own: public administration.

Study of this field of public administration is often presented as something new, with the passage of the Pendleton Act in 1883 or Woodrow Wilson's famous 1887 essay, "The Study of Administration," frequently seen as the genesis of the discipline in the United States. Indeed, 1983 saw the American Society for Public Administration celebrate the first century of the field. Over that century, the field has developed an extensive body of literature and a much less extensive body of knowledge concerning public administration. Leading texts in the field generally credit Max Weber with the role of founding father of the study of administration. Robert B. Denhardt is one of the few administrative theorists to address the question of an intellectual heritage for public administration, and he looks no earlier than the nineteenth century for that heritage, adding Karl Marx and Sigmund Freud to Weber as founding fathers of the discipline (Denhardt, 1984).

To some extent this myopic view of public administration is understandable. The past century has seen a great expansion in the scope and pervasiveness of organizations, both public and private. As organizations emerge as such a visible and incontestable part of daily life, it was only natural that we began to examine them, and, in examining them, to see them as something new.

Organization, however, is hardly new. Archeological evidence indicates that early man lived within organized units. While early hunters cannot be classified as "men in gray flannel suits," evidence indicates a high level of cooperation between them. With the dawn of the agricultural age about 6000 B.C., man developed villages, towns, and cities—and administrative apparatuses to coordinate the activities of those living within them. Our knowledge of these early people is limited, however, by a lack of written records. As Gladden points out, "Writing was not invented before the fourth millennium B.C. and obviously evidence of administration before this time is hard to come by" (Gladden, 1972, p. 1).

With the invention of writing came people who thought, and who wrote, about human behavior in an organizational context—organizational theorists. Collectively, these early voices provide public administration with a rich heritage, one that has been largely ignored. Ignoring this heritage damages the discipline of public administration in numerous ways. To the extent that these early voices reflect keen, accurate observation of human behavior in organizational contexts this neglect deprives the discipline of an impressive source of knowledge. Perhaps even more importantly, however, this neglect deprives the discipline, and its practitioners, of a sense of history—an understanding of who we are and how we arrived at where we are.

A key part of that sense of history can be found in the writings that underpinned the development of the modern nation state. The Renaissance and the Reformation brought great change to Europe, change that saw the end of the feudal system throughout Western Europe, and its replacement with the emergent nation state: an era that indeed witnessed the "initiation of a new order of things." This study will examine the concepts developed during this time, emphasizing the works of a few key individuals. It will begin by examining the link between Church and state preceding the rise of the modern nation state, then examine the impacts of the Renaissance and the Reformation on that linkage in Spain, England, and France. It concludes by examining the implications for the development of the administrative state.

II. CHRISTIANITY AND THE NATURE OF THE STATE

From its inception it has been impossible to separate Christian doctrine from political thought. Christ's statement that man should "render therefore unto Caesar the things which are Caesar's; and unto God the things that are God's" (Matthew 22:21) indicates a dual allegiance. Justification for the principle of divine right of government is clearly spelled out in Paul's letter to the Romans:

> Let every soul be subject unto the higher powers. For there is no power but of God: the powers that be are ordained of God. Whosoever therefore resisteth the power, resisteth the ordinance of God. . . . For this cause pay ye tribute also: for they are God's ministers, attending continually upon this very thing. Render therefore to all their dues: tribute to whom tribute is due; custom to whom custom; fear to whom fear; honor to whom honor. (Romans 13:1–7)

Trying to determine just how to apply Paul's admonition was not easy, however. The early Christians failed to produce a well-thought-out means of how one could "render therefore to all their dues." While Christ's advice to render unto Caesar that which is Caesar's and unto God that which is God's sounded simple enough, it left open the question of what was Caesar's and what was God's. In attempting to answer this question, the Christian fathers developed a view of society as a directed commonwealth [1], a view that is best presented in St. Augustine's *City of God.*

A. St. Augustine: The Theological Base of the Directed Commonwealth

Born in Tagaste in North Africa, Augustine (354–430) had a Christian mother and a pagan father. After a hedonistic youth, he converted to Christianity and entered the priesthood at the age of thirty-five. At forty-two he was appointed bishop of Hippo, a post he retained until his death.

Heavily influenced by Plato's *Republic*, Augustine mixed the concepts found in that volume with Christian theology, developing a view of society built upon man in a depraved state (dominated by desire) in search of the just community (commonwealth). Man is subject to "two cities," the earthly city of men and the city of God:

> For all the difference of the many and very great nations throughout the world in religion and morals, language, weapons, and dress, there exist no more than the two kinds of society, which, according to our Scriptures, we have rightly called the two cities. One city is that of men who live according to the flesh. The other is of men who live according to the spirit. Each of them chooses its own kind of peace and, when they attain what they desire, each lives in the peace of its own choosing. (St. Augustine, 1958, p. 295)

The two cities represent the forces of good and evil that each individual must contend with. The earthly city represents man in his fallen state, dominated by self-love. The city of God is dominated by the principle of love of God. The story of mankind, for St. Augustine, was the story of the struggle between the two cities; a struggle that would eventually end with the establishment of a Christian commonwealth. The state plays a role in moving man from the earthly city to the city of God. It can only do this, however, if it is a Christian state. Therefore, the state must be inferior to the Church, which alone could provide the guidance needed to move men from their fallen state to salvation. Only the Church, guided by God's reason and intelligence, could define the good community.

The primary function of the state was the maintenance of peace and order. The monarch (state) served as part of God's plan and was to be obeyed, even if the monarch were evil: "Nevertheless power and domination are not given even to such men save by the providence of the most high God, when he judges that the state of human affairs is worthy of such lords. The divine utterance is clear on this matter" (St. Augustine, 1958, p. 115).

St. Augustine provided a theological foundation for the view that government was necessitated by man's fall. He did not, however, go into great detail concerning how that government should be organized in order to move man back toward grace. As Europe moved from centralized Roman power to a feudal system, this question received more attention from the Christian fathers.

B. Regnum and Sacerdotium: The Two Swords Theory

With the fall of Rome in 476, centralized political power was replaced by the power of local lords operating in a feudal structure. Ostensibly bound through a series of reciprocal obligations, king and vassals theoretically operated under the dictates of God's law, with the Church serving as the final arbitrator of what that law was. In reality, central government was weak, with real power being exercised by local lords, who combined legislative, judicial, and administrative functions. Scott's description of the government of the Kingdom of Scotland during the late thirteenth century provides a typical view of feudal administrative structures:

> Such central government as existed was provided by the king and the officers of his household: the constable, the king's chief military officer, flanked by the marischal in special charge of the cavalry element; the chamberlain who provided for the costs of administration from the royal rents, feudal dues and other imposts; the chancellor, the keeper of the royal seal and Crown records who besides presiding over the king's chapel was virtually a secretary of state for all departments. . . . The fourth great officer was the steward responsible for the management of the royal household.
>
> Outside the household were the chief administrative and judicial officers of the Crown: the justiciar of Scotland north of the Forth and Clyde, the justiciar of Lothian and the justiciar of Galloway. Below them were the sheriffs, some thirty in all, who . . . were the sinews of the administration. (Scott, 1982, p. 7)

Any unifying framework that did exist was largely due to the influence of the Church, which, in a very real sense, emerged as the only centralized governing body in Europe. As Curtis points out, "in this unified but localized social structure, the Church pressed the idea of a universal Christian Commonwealth. In a period of barbarian kingdoms, the argument was put forward of a single society with two governments, each with separate powers" (Curtis, 1981, p. 158).

This argument was advanced under a series of Popes, beginning with Pope Gelasius I (492–496), who began what developed into the theory of the two swords. Church and state would become *sacerdotium* and *regnum*, two governments in a single Christian society. The civic ruler exercised delegated power over temporal affairs, but the Pope was supreme in authority and unchallenged in ecclesiastic matters. And, as the civic ruler needed the Church to obtain eternal life, he should heed the Pope's guidance.

This dual authority did not sit easy with either Pope or king. The feudal era saw increased tension concerning the nature of this relationship, with both king and Pope claiming supremacy. The papal claim was made most strongly by Gregory VII (1073–1085), who argued that the Pope could, through his exercise of ecclesiastic power, not only control the clergy but depose emperors. He used the analogy of the sun and the moon: ecclesiastic power was the power of the sun, and the Pope's light shone on the inferior satellite, the Emperor. The views of emperors and kings was somewhat different. This disagreement helped fuel changes that resulted in the emergence of the modern nation state.

III. THE EMERGENCE OF THE MODERN NATION STATE

The Renaissance played a key role in the emergence of the modern nation state. Economically, it saw new goods brought to Europe, which spurred a great demand for even more goods and created a new merchant class of those who succeeded in meeting those demands. As trade and commerce expanded, the need for a strong central power to protect and to regulate that commerce become increasingly apparent. Accompanying these rapid economic changes was a rebirth of ideas—Greek and Roman knowledge had been preserved in the Arab world and was being "rediscovered" in Europe.

The Reformation was another major force influencing the emergence of the modern nation state. Political and social change resulting from the Renaissance fostered change in the religious status quo. Two important trends emerged from this movement: the first from Protestant supporters of national monarchs such as Melanchton and more significantly Luther, the other from the extremists on both sides, including the Jesuits and Calvinists.

A. The Renaissance and Growing Nationalism

The Renaissance reshaped the face of Europe. Part of the decentralization following the fall of Rome had been economic. There were a few forces at work to keep alive the commercial legacy of the empire. Scandinavian seafarers circled Europe, and their traders moved through much of what is now Russia and Ukraine; the Eastern (Byzantine) Empire remained commercially active until its fall in the fifteenth century, and goods moved through it to Northern and Western Europe; the Islamic empires kept up active trade from one end of the Mediterranean to the other; and the Italian cities maintained a certain level of trade. Still, the feudal economic system that developed was largely agricultural, localized, and self-sustaining, with change coming slowly. The pace of economic change began to increase in the eleventh century, helping create the conditions needed for the rise of the nation state.

The consolidation of the German empire under the Saxon and Salian dynasties (925–1356) helped trade develop in an east-west flow from Northern Europe across Muscovy and on into Asia. This trade system emerged as a rival to that of the Italian cities, particularly Venice. Lubjeck, controlling trade between the Baltic and North Seas, became the key northern city in this network. It emerged as the seat of the Hanseatic League, which included a number of cities along Britain's North Sea coast, in what is now the Netherlands, and across the Baltic areas of northern Germany, Poland, and the Baltic States. The League took shape in 1259 and was formally constituted in 1358. It had connections with other cities from Spain to Egypt, until Egypt was conquered by the Ottomans in 1517.

The Hanseatic League and the city-states of Italy maintained a virtual monopoly on trade with Asia until the sixteenth century. As long as demand for Oriental goods remained relatively small, this monopoly was able to meet the needs of Europeans. However, forces were at work that resulted in a great increase in demand, forces that ostensibly had little to do with commerce and trade.

In 1095 Pope Urban II called for a Crusade to restore Asia Minor to Byzantium and to conquer the Turks. A series of ten Crusades ensued, running through 1291, with unanticipated consequences for European development. The stated objectives of the crusades ultimately failed, with the forces of Islam maintaining control of Asia Minor and the Holy Land. The crusaders, however, had been exposed to a culture far richer than Europe's, and to paraphrase the old song, it became impossible to keep them down on the farm after they had seen Damascus. The demand for Oriental goods exploded, straining the capacities of existing trade systems.

In addition to the demand for new goods created by the Crusades, Europe "rediscovered" Greek and Roman thought. While Platonic thought had been maintained through the works of the Christian Fathers, much of classical writing and knowledge had been lost to Europe. Eastern Orthodox churchmen and Arab scholars had maintained and added to this knowledge. Rediscovered works, particularly those of Aristotle, had major impact in Europe, fueling debate over the proper relations between church and state and between monarch and subject.

The expansion of commerce and the explosion of knowledge taxed the feudal system beyond its limits. The rising merchant class demanded strong central governments to protect and encourage trade. An emergent intellectual class, many of whose members were drawn from the Church, raised questions concerning what the nature of the state was to be. The concept of a universal Christian brotherhood under the guidance of a universal Christian Church lost ground to an emergent nationalism.

Domination of trade by Italian city-states and the cities of the Hanseatic League became increasingly intolerable to the rising monarchies of Western Europe, particularly those of the

Iberian states, which undertook major projects to find a way around the Italian and Hanseatic monopolies. When Portugal reached India in 1498, six years after Columbus reached America, a shift in trade patterns and power began, and Europe started to move to an Atlantic economy. The first modern nation states—Spain, France, and England—all benefitted from these developments.

B. The Reformation and the Nature of the State

The political and social change of the Renaissance was accompanied by religious change. The political questions concerning the relationship between church and state added fuel to the doctrinal disputes being raised within the Church. These disputes were to lead to the Protestant challenge to the Church, as well as to reforms within the Church.

Both Luther and Calvin, the two dominant Protestant reformers, asserted the right of the individual to establish a direct relationship with God, but the political implications of that assertion were very different for the two. Luther's arguments led to secular supremacy, with the ecclesiastic power clearly subordinated to the state. Calvin's arguments, on the other hand, led to an ecclesiastical association with the state in the form of theocracy. Both arguments became important for the nature of the nation state.

1. The Lutheran Protectorate

Luther (1483–1546) rejected the Pope as the interpreter of God's plan for mankind and argued for the supremacy of the Scriptures. Luther repudiated the Platonism of the Catholic Church's position that only a few were capable of understanding God's plan (natural law), and that those few must occupy positions of authority in order to impose obedience to God's plan upon others. Instead, he argued the more Aristotelian position that all men were capable of understanding God's plan through the Scriptures. The clergy were there to help explain and to administer the word of God, but it ranked no higher than lay persons.

While all men were inherently capable of understanding God's plan, Luther recognized that not all were true Christians. Indeed, man's fall left most people governed by self-interest. Mere baptism did not make one a Christian: the sign of a true Christian was a life lived in obedience to God's commandments. If everyone lived such a life, no organization—including the Church—would be necessary. The presence of these non-Christians, however, made organization necessary. The role of the state was to provide the coercive authority needed to control the nonbelievers.

The Church, Luther argued, could not use coercion. An individual's belief was solely a matter for that individual's conscience, and the state, as the legitimate wielder of force, could not assume any responsibility for enforcing any belief system. In making this argument, Luther did not anticipate the bewildering variety of belief systems his fellow citizens were capable of holding. He was shocked by the anarchism of the Anabaptists and by the Peasant Revolt in 1524. In response to these and other events, he wrote *An open letter to the Christian nobility*. In this and in his earlier *Secular authority: to what extent it should be obeyed*, he spelled out his political beliefs.

Anarchy, argued Luther, was the work of the Devil: "We must firmly establish secular law and the sword, that no one may doubt that it is in the world by God's will and ordinance" (Luther, 1981, p. 238). Pointing out that true believers "need no secular sword or law," he added:

> All who are not Christians belong to the kingdom of the world and are under the law. Since few believe and still fewer live a Christian life, do not resist the evil, and themselves do no evil, God has provided for non-Christians a different government outside the

> Christian estate and God's kingdom, and has subjected them to the sword, so that, even though they would do so, they cannot practice their wickedness, and that, if they do, they may not do it without fear nor in peace and prosperity. . . . (Luther, 1981, pp. 238–239)

Luther goes on to argue that "Christ himself describes the nature of temporal princes . . . when he says, 'The wordly princes exercise lordship, and they that are chief exercise authority' " (1981, p. 246). The prince's duty in exercising such authority is fourfold:

> First, that toward God consists in true confidence and in sincere prayer; second, that toward his subjects consists in love and Christian service; third, that toward his counselors and rulers consists in an open mind and unfettered judgement; forth, that toward evil doers consists in proper zeal and firmness. Then his state is right, outwardly and inwardly, pleasing to God and to the people. But he must expect much envy and sorrow,—the cross will soon rest on the shoulders of such a ruler. (1981, pp. 247–248)

If the ruler does not rule in accordance with these precepts, he is still to be obeyed. The only resistance Luther recognizes as legitimate is passive.

Under Luther's arguments, then, the prince's ministers (public administrators) draw their authority from the prince, not from God. They exercise the sword of the prince over all in the state, including the clergy, who are ministers of God's kingdom, a kingdom that, for Luther, is not of this world. This view was opposed by other reformers, most notably Calvin.

2. *The Directed Commonwealth of Calvin*

John Calvin (1509–1564) was born at Noyon, in Picardy, of a prominent family. Prepared by his parents for the priesthood, Calvin instead converted to Protestantism. Moving to Geneva in 1536, Calvin created one of the most successful Protestant movements. Unlike the nationalism that came to dominate Lutheranism, limiting its spread to the German and Scandinavian states, Calvinism had wide international appeal and rapidly spread throughout much of Europe.

Central to Calvin's arguments was the sovereignty of God in all matters. The state, then, had significance only to the extent that it furthered God's plan. Luther's distinction between secular and ecclesiastic power was rejected. The Church was a necessary intermediary to man's salvation, and thus princes, as agents of God, were subordinate to it. God was the origin of all good. Man, since Adam's fall, was evil and corrupt, born in sin, and afflicted with the curse of Adam's transgression. If man were to overcome this fallen state, both temporal and ecclesiastical discipline were required. The state provided the sword, but it was to be wielded under the guidance of the Church.

Under this view, civil ministers serve an ecclesiastic function: "Civil government is designed, as long as we live in this world, to cherish and support the external worship of God, to preserve the pure doctrine of religion, to defend the constitution of the Church, to regulate our lives in a manner requisite for the society of men, to form our manners to civil justice, to promote our concord with each other, and to establish general peace and tranquility" (Calvin, 1981, p. 225).

Civil ministers were to be involved in virtually all aspects of society. Where one lived could be determined by magistrates to ensure availability of religious instruction. The state could define standards of behavior and had a moral obligation to enforce them. Citizens had a moral obligation to obey the state,

> because the obedience which is rendered to princes and magistrates is rendered to God, from whom they have received their authority. . . . If there be anything in the public

administration which requires to be corrected, let them not raise any tumults or take the business into their own hands, which ought to be bound in this respect, but let them refer it to the cognizance of the magistrate, who is also authorized to regulate the concerns of the public. (Calvin, 1981, pp. 259–260)

Under Calvinist thought, public administration served a moral purpose. Public administrators were to lead society toward salvation, and they were to do so on the basis of authority that came from God. They were to define what the good commonwealth was to be, and they were to move society toward it. Terry Cooper's (1984) current view of public administrators as fiduciaries has similar overtones without the Calvinist base.

Where Calvinist governments were established, government became all-intrusive, and their ministers managed the affairs of society with the zeal of true believers. In England, the Puritan dictatorship of Cromwell imposed Calvinist dogma on a society that found itself unwilling to live with it for long. Still, Calvinism became a major force creating the modern nation state, and its influence remains strong in the American administrative state.

3. *Redefining* Sacerdotium *and* Regnum*: The Counter-Reformation*

The half-century following Luther's nailing of his Ninety-Five Theses on the church door at Wittenberg saw the rapid rise of Protestantism in Europe. For a time, it appeared that the Catholic Church could not save itself. In 1545 the Church convened the Council of Trent, inviting Protestant leaders to attend—an invitation they rejected. Three separate sessions of the Council took place from 1545 to 1563, and in these sessions the Church hammered out its response to the challenge mounted by the Reformation. Upon its adjournment in 1563, members were confident in the future of the Church. They had instituted a number of reforms and reaffirmed their basic doctrines: "This is the faith of the blessed Peter and of the Apostles," they stated. "This is the faith of the Fathers. This is the faith of the Orthodox. Anathema to all heretics!" (quoted in Snyder, 1967, p. 96).

The spearhead of the Counter-Reformation was the Society of Jesus. Founded in 1534 by a young Spanish nobleman, Don Iñigo de Oñez y Loyola, known as Ignatius Loyola (1491–1556), and given the official sanction of the Pope in 1540, the organization was established as a military order composed of spiritual soldiers fighting under the banner of Christ. Dedicated, in Loyola's words, to "the true Spouse of Christ, and our holy Mother, which is the Orthodox, Catholic, and Hierarchical Church" (Snyder, 1967, p. 97), the Jesuits' primary political argument was the assertion that kings cannot rightfully control spiritual affairs. The heart of their argument is found in the writings of Juan de Mariana (1536–1624), Francisco Suàrez (1548–1617), and Robert Bellarmine (1542–1621).

Mariana, in his *De Rege et Regis Institutione*, written in 1599, began with the venerable Christian argument that man once lived in a state of grace, but fell from that state as a result of the institution of private property. Man, in a state of grace, needed no government; fallen man, dominated by desire, does need government. Thus government does not originate in God, but in man's fall—it is a natural result of that fall. The people need a ruler to curb their desires for the benefit of society, and it is the people who establish government and who give the prince his authority. The prince is himself bound by the law; failure to obey the law justifies the removal and even the execution of the prince: "For it has been conceded that he is to be removed from office and even punished with death under exceptional circumstances. On the other hand, if he obeys of his own accord those laws which he himself has made . . . , no one should force him, against his will, or coerce him with sanctions." The way to ensure that the prince did, indeed, obey his own laws, was through education: "But above all the mind of the Prince should be trained from an early age to be convinced that he himself is more bound by the laws than the others who obey his rule" (Mariana, 1981, p. 286). Thus for Mariana, rule of law was key to a just state, but it was man's law, not God's law, that concerned the state. This left only a very limited role for the Church, a role that was stronger in the arguments of other Jesuits.

Both Suàrez and Bellarmine identified the Pope as the head of a universal Christian Church, making him the supreme arbiter of all spiritual questions. Asking "Is it possible—speaking solely with reference to the nature of the case—for men to command other men, binding the latter by [man's] own laws?" Suàrez concluded that "a civil magistracy accompanied by temporal power for human government is just and in complete harmony with human nature" (Suàrez, 1981, pp. 287–288). However, in spiritual affairs, the prince was to listen to the Pope: "For Christ the Lord gave to Peter and his successors the power to correct all Christians, even kings, and, consequently, the power to coerce and punish them when they are disobedient and incorrigible" (Suàrez, 1981, p. 297). "The Pope," Bellarmine adds, "by divine law has the power of disposing of the temporal affairs of all Christians in the order to the spiritual end" (Bellarmine, 1981, p. 299).

It was in the context of these arguments concerning the changing nature of the relationship between church and state, and in the context of great economic and commercial upheaval, that the modern nation state emerged. Calvinist thought inspired a number of movements, including those of the Huguenots in France and the Puritans in England. The theocratic nature of his arguments, however, found both states eventually rejecting Calvinism as a religious base for government. In England, Henry VIII ushered in Anglicanism, which, while maintaining much Catholic doctrine, borrowed from Luther in placing the Church under the authority of the state. In France as well as in Spain, the Counter-Reformation allowed Catholic clergymen to devote themselves to national service without undue influence from the Pope.

IV. ADMINISTRATIVE STRUCTURE IN THE EMERGING MODERN NATION STATE

As indicated earlier, the Renaissance and the Reformation created the need for stronger administrative structures. Public administrative practices such as that of Scotland's Alexander III, described earlier in this study, could no longer meet the needs of the developing nation state. England, Spain, and France led the way in developing the modern nation state and in creating the administrative structures needed to support it. This study will look at the administrative practices instituted by the Tudor "administrative revolution" in England, by Philip II in Spain, and by Cardinal Richelieu in France.

A. Tudor Administration

Henry VII (*reg.* A.D. 1485–1509) began the Tudor dynasty, a dynasty that saw England move from little more than a geographic to a national identity. Under his rule, ministers and advisers served the Crown; by the end of the reign of Elizabeth I (1558–1603) they served Crown and state. While the question of whether or not Crown and state were separate entities was not settled until the Glorious Revolution of 1688, the administrative system needed for that separation was well in place by the end of Elizabeth's reign.

The impact of both the Renaissance and the Reformation affected the development of Tudor administration. England's growing role as a world power—a role driven largely by a rising merchant class—and the ongoing tension between Church and state helped shape England's government during this period. The Anglo-Saxon Curia Regis, the king's great council consisting of the important persons of the realm, had led to a smaller edition of trusted councilors, and this smaller body had developed a clerk associated with the Privy Seal Office and a president to serve in the absence of the king under Henry VII. Despite a setback during the reign of Mary I (*reg.* 1553–1558), councilor government developed rapidly during the reigns of Henry VIII (*reg.* 1509–1547) and Elizabeth I (*reg.* 1558–1603) (Gladden, 1972, pp. 89–91).

1. *Henry VIII: Era of Reform*

The last of the great English clerical statesmen, Cardinal Wolsey, became a member of Henry VIII's Council in 1511, serving with considerable skill until 1530. Henry's well-documented problems with the Church, culminating in his break with Rome and his ascendancy to the head of the Church of England in 1535, deprived him of much of the effectiveness of the traditional "civil service"—the clergy. New administrative structures were needed to meet the growing demands made upon the central government, structures that required great skill to put in place. That skill was provided by Thomas Cromwell. If Machiavelli's statement that the "first impression that one gets of a ruler and of his brains is from seeing the men that he has about him" (1952, p. 114) is true, Cromwell ensured that anyone's first impression of Henry VIII was favorable.

Cromwell was, in many ways, a self-made man. Leaving a less than favorable home life at the age of eighteen, he distinguished himself in military and business affairs on the Continent, returning to England as a successful businessman and barrister. He attracted the attention of Cardinal Wolsey, who brought him into his administration as his personal secretary. Surviving Wolsey's fall, Cromwell gained Henry VIII's confidence and rose rapidly to high public office. He was made Privy Councillor in 1531, became Master of the King's Jewels in 1532, attained the status of Keeper of the Privy Seal in 1533, and became King's Secretary in 1536. "By sheer force of character," Gladden states, "he enhanced the offices to which he was appointed, and astutely widened his scope" to develop much more influence than he obtained from the formal offices themselves (Gladden, 1972, p. 96).

On August 10, 1540, councilor government was institutionalized when "his Highnes Pryvey Counsaill" came together to appoint a clerk and provide for the keeping of a register (Elton, 1953, p. 317). The Privy Council included nineteen men, dominated by Cromwell, and was a mixture of clerics and noblemen. A key part of this development was the removal of judicial functions from the council, allowing them to focus on executive and administrative tasks.

The Privy Council consolidated a number of administrative reforms taken earlier. In 1511, for example, significant steps were taken to reform the handling of finances with the appointment of two General Surveyors of Crown Lands, "thus freeing the greater part of the royal revenues for Exchequer control and redefining the manner in which these revenues were to be administered" (Gladden, 1972, p. 93). Still, finance did not become clearly a council function until Cromwell consolidated a number of functions under his own control, allowing him to act "both as collector of revenue and as paymaster." This consolidation allowed him to "approach the status of minister of finance" (Gladden, 1972, p. 93). His reforms transferred control of royal finances from the king's household (the Crown) to a number of administrative agencies (the state).

Cromwell may have continued administrative consolidation and reform, but his sudden fall in 1540 ended his brilliant administrative career. Yet efforts toward administrative reform continued for the rest of Henry VIII's rule, as well as through the reigns of Edward VI and Mary I. These efforts culminated in the reforms of 1554. The Lower Exchequer emerged as a true central treasury under the Lord Treasurer, who became a true minister of finance. The Lord

Treasurer developed a personal staff that grew into a treasury department. Similar patterns can be found in the other areas contained within the Privy Council. Elton summed up these developments by pointing out that "the reforms represented a remarkably efficient compromise between the highly speeded up administration of Thomas Cromwell and the safety of the old ways. They provided the government of Elizabeth with a workmanlike tool in its pursuit of solvency, and seventeenth century governments with a reasonably efficient basis for further reform in detail" (Elton, 1953, p. 258). That basis was further enhanced under the rule of Elizabeth I.

2. *Consolidating Reform: Elizabeth I*

Queen Elizabeth I consolidated and added to the reforms Cromwell had begun for her father. In this, she had the assistance of another able administrator: Sir William Cecil (1520–1598). Cecil served the Queen, with no responsibility to Privy Council or to Parliament; therefore he was not a prime minister in a modern sense, yet as the Queen's trusted aide, he clearly played a similar role.

Cecil had served under Lord Somerset and Lord Northumberland and had managed to survive as a Protestant in the administration of Mary I—not an easy feat. He served Elizabeth as a personal adviser, and as such he was involved in matters both domestic and foreign, as well as personal. He was made a peer in 1571, obtaining the title of Lord Burghley, by which he is best known. The conditions he served in, and the tasks he was given, were such that "only a diplomatic genius could have hoped to survive in office, as Cecil did, until his natural death" (Gladden, 1972, p. 101). Elizabeth I was a dominating—indeed, a domineering—monarch who involved herself in every aspect of her nation's life. The able assistance of Lord Burghley greatly contributed to the glory of her reign.

Lord Burghley operated largely behind the scenes. A key source of his power was his position as Master of the Queens Wards. An office created when Henry VIII confiscated Church lands, thus greatly increasing the amount of royal lands to oversee, this had become a major office in terms of power and patronage. Administering the Mastership was complicated by the local representatives' relationships with local nobility. The forty-five Feodaries, although appointed by the Crown (the Master), were often controlled more by local lords. This was further complicated by the somewhat conflicting objectives of the Mastership:

> Primarily it had been established (1) to preserve the interests of, and ensure the proper profit from the royal wardships to, [*sic*] the Crown, whose finances were organized very much on a personal basis, but (2) the interests of the wards themselves were to be cared for, though this was often overlooked by owners of wardships, and in addition, (3) the disposal of a wide range of royal patronage was involved; while, last but not least, (4) fees and personal profits were of first importance to the Master. (Gladden, 1972, p. 103)

Though his masterful use of objective (3)—the disposal of royal patronage—Burghley turned the Mastership into a source of great personal power. By using his personal power in the interests of his Queen—although this is not to say he did not also pursue self-interest—he ensured that he retained his position.

Burghley's use of the Mastership to solidify administrative reforms while advancing the power of his Queen illustrates the clear linkage between politics and administration. Woodrow Wilson (1887) would have done well to study Burghley before advancing his famous dichotomy between the two. This link between personal politics and administration was to become a high art form in the other two emerging nations covered in this study: Spain and France.

B. Spain and the Administration of Philip II

The nation of Spain resulted from the unification of Castile and Aragon in 1479, although both kingdoms retained their separate governments. At the time Philip II (*reg.* 1556–1598) ascended to the throne, he became the ruler of a vast, widely scattered territory, including Spain, the Netherlands, the Two Sicilies, and a rapidly expanding empire in the New World. He added Portugal to his kingdom in 1580, thereby bringing the entire Iberian peninsula under his control. Thus he was forced to administer three areas in Europe that were without land communication while building an empire at the end of a two- or three-month voyage from the seat of government. As Kennedy notes: "Although foreigners frequently regarded the empire of . . . Philip II as monolithic and disciplined, it was in fact a congeries of territories, each of which possessed its own privileges and was proud of its own distinctiveness" (Kennedy, 1987, p. 54). Administering such a state was a formidable task indeed.

On balance, Philip did not prove up to the task, but it was not from lack of preparation nor of trying. It may be that no one would have been up to that task. A precocious child, Philip demonstrated an early aptitude for mathematics and was able to read and write Latin at an early age. His father turned his education over to two key tutors, handpicked to prepare him for his future role. Evidence suggests that these tutors did an excellent job, and it is certain that Philip had a real interest in the administrative details of the state.

Philip's interest in administration was accompanied by a strong work ethic. He was personally pious, convinced that the Almighty had chosen him for the great work of defending the faith, and was capable of acting with complete ruthlessness. Spanish monarchs were determined to defend the true faith from both infidel Turks and apostate Protestants. Furthermore, after Charles V abdicated in 1556, passing the office of the Holy Roman Emperor, along with all Hapsburg possessions in Germany to Ferdinand, with Philip obtaining Spain, the Netherlands, and the Two Sicilies, the situation for Spain became worse. The Empire saw little need to assist Spain in its wars in Western Europe and overseas; Spain, on the other hand, feeling its responsibilities as the true defender of the faith, would come to the aid of the Empire against Turks and Protestants.

The Thirty Years War had been a major strain on the Hapsburg treasuries, and that strain continued for Philip as revolt flared into the open in the Low Countries. Forced to station 65,000 troops in Flanders and locked into a war of attrition with the Calvinist Netherlands, Philip saw one-quarter of his budget consumed by the Army of Flanders for decade after decade. Spain found itself constantly drained by warfare. As Kennedy notes:

> European conflicts in this period were frequent . . . , and their costs were a terrible burden upon all societies. But all other states—France, England, Sweden, even the Ottoman empire—enjoyed periods of peace and recovery. It was . . . Spain's fate to have to turn immediately from a struggle against one enemy to a new conflict against another. . . . During some awful periods, imperial Spain was fighting on three fronts simultaneously. . . . In contemporary terms, Spain resembled a large bear in the pit: more powerful than any of the dogs attacking it, but never able to deal with all of its opponents and growing gradually exhausted in the process. (Kennedy, 1987, pp. 48–49)

Such conditions called for a great statesman: someone who could see the big picture and could operate at the highest levels to build support for Spanish policy. Unfortunately for Spain, Philip was a clerk; he "quite literally liked undertaking the mundane activities of clerkship. He was never happier than when writing or dictating letters and consequently spent much of his time at the desk, from which, literally, he attempted to undertake the rulership of the world" (Gladden,

1972, p. 105). His passion for detail led Philip to ignore the larger picture. Coupled with his indecisiveness, Philip's managerial style was disastrous for Spain. Yet his attention to detail did result in a functional bureaucracy which served to bind a worldwide empire for a long period.

Many of Philip's—and Spain's—problems arose from the highly decentralized nature of the empire. Within Spain proper, Aragon, Catalonia, and Valencia had their own laws and tax systems; Portugal retained its separate system from its incorporation in 1580 to its independence in 1640; and Sicily had its own legislature and tax structure. Naples and Milan were under more direct control from Madrid, and the Americas became a major source of revenue for the Crown after 1560. Yet the only stable source of revenue for Philip was Castile, and even there he had to deal with a strong Cortes, which was willing to vote taxes only on items from which the landed gentry were exempt. Spain continued to be plagued by problems of overextension and an inability of the center to control the empire. This decentralization was a weakness that the next individual this study examines worked hard to eliminate, and his success helps explain why France replaced Spain as the dominant power on the Continent.

C. Cardinal Richelieu and Administrative Centralism

Richelieu (1585–1642) served France with two goals always in mind: he would make the power of the king supreme within France, and he would make France supreme within Europe. All of his efforts focused upon those goals. In accomplishing his goals, he created the strongest administrative structure of the emerging nations states. By education and temperament a priest, he proved himself an able administrator and a great statesman.

Richelieu was consecrated Bishop in his father's preferment at the age of twenty-two, an act that had required the special dispensation of the Pope. In 1614 he served as a clerical deputy to the last Estates General to be called before the French Revolution. He began his service at the court with Louis XIII's consort Anne before becoming secretary to the King. In 1622 he became Cardinal, and by 1624 he had achieved the status of chief minister, although he was not formally appointed such until 1629. In 1631 he received a dukedom. Thus, Richelieu emerged as a power in state, society, and church.

Richelieu built upon an administrative system begun during the reign of Henry IV (*reg.* 1589–1610). Henry had established a working council of five loyal followers to help administer the state. Realizing that administration was not his strong point, he had obtained the services of Maximilien de Bèthune Sully (1560–1641). Henry IV provided the statesmanship, Sully the administrative skill. A dedicated Calvinist, Sully devoted himself to serving his king for the benefit of France. He balanced the budget, paid off most foreign debts, eliminated illegal taxation, and built a substantial reserve. Sully strengthened French agriculture by reducing taxes on the peasantry, permitting exports, and providing peasant farmers with more protection from their noble overlords. Together Henry IV and Sully wrought "what amounted to a political, social, and economic revolution" (Snyder, 1967, p. 140).

Henry's assassination and the ineptness of Marie de' Medici destroyed much of what had been accomplished, however, leaving Marie's young son in a disastrous situation. The young Louis XIII, aware of Richelieu's great unpopularity among the nobility of the royal court, but also of his equally great administrative skills, turned to him for not only his own, but for France's salvation.

In Louis XIII, Richelieu served a monarch with the personal government, and the personal interest, of Philip II. All decisions were made in the name of the king, and very little power was delegated to any minister. Louis's interest in the details of administration meant that a great deal of attention had to be given to any document reaching him for his information or for his signature. Richelieu's competence as an administrator won him royal favor and allowed him to assume the role of intermediary between king and minister.

Richelieu set out to destroy the power of the nobility and to eliminate the division within France caused by the special status given the Huguenots by the Treaty of Nantes. To accomplish this latter goal, he opened a two-year war with the Huguenots in 1627, forcing them to give up their fortified cities and to relinquish their special military and political privileges. Once he achieved his aims against them, Richelieu ceased any further religious persecution. To destroy the power of the nobility, he established a royal executive whose loyalty was to him.

Much as Burghley had, Richelieu made masterly use of patronage to weld the administrative state to him. Members of the Conseil du Roi, or the royal executive, "frequently wrote to Richelieu acknowledging themselves outwardly and with affection as his 'creatures', a term widely used at the time which indicated a relationship between Richelieu and the other ministers very different from anything that exists today" (Gladden, 1972, p. 143).

Richelieu expanded the system of *intendants* begun by Sully, placing local government under the control of loyal citizens and royal civil servants and sending out royal officials to take over the actual administration of the provinces. The great nobles, who had reclaimed much of their former influence under the weak regency of Marie de' Medici, found their power severely curtailed by Richelieu. He used spies to identify nobles who might challenge the Crown, executing those he found particularly threatening. While the threat to central authority represented by the nobility was not to be completely eliminated until Richelieu's protégé, Cardinal Mazarin, put down the series of rebellions known as the Fronde (1648–1653), Richelieu did succeed in sharply curtailing regionalist tendencies.

The structure created by Richelieu on Sully's foundation was a highly personal one. From minister in the Conseil du Roi to local *intendant*, members of the emerging bureaucracy saw their loyalty as to Richelieu. Although his successor, Cardinal Mazarin, had been brought into government several years before Richelieu's death, he was not able to transfer that personal loyalty to himself. Instead, the bureaucracy began to develop a consciousness as an "administrative class"—a class whose loyalty was to the center, no matter who occupied the throne or who served as chief minister. Louis XIV was to build on this administrative consciousness, using it to solidify his position as absolute ruler.

Richelieu summed up his own life in these terms: "I employed all my energy to ruin the Huguenot faction, to humble the pride of the nobles, to reduce all subjects to their duty, and to exalt France to its proper position among foreign nations" (quoted in Snyder, 1967, p. 143). He was successful in each goal, but at a high price for his country's future. Upon his death the power of the monarchy was almost absolute within France and French influence and prestige had been raised abroad. Yet he left behind a state whose agriculture, trade, and industry had been seriously weakened, a country drifting toward bankruptcy. In the words of L. L. Snyder, Richelieu left "France outwardly resplendent, inwardly languishing" (Snyder, 1967, p. 143). In the process, however, he did form the base of a governmental bureaucracy.

V. SUMMARY

This study began by arguing that the writings that underpinned the development of the modern nation state can help students and practitioners of administration better understand contemporary public administration and, more importantly, provide them with a sense of history—an understanding of who we are and how we became what we are.

The emergence of the modern nation state transformed the relations among Church, state, and citizen and redefined public administration in the process. The feudal conception of a universal Christian brotherhood of man under the guidance of a universal Christian Church was replaced by an insurgent nationalism with the Church under the authority of the state. The position of the Catholic clergy as the de facto administrators of the state gave way to a growing de jure administrative class, an administrative class that was increasingly secular and whose first loyalty was to the Crown and state.

Each of the nations examined in this study saw the administrative class develop under the personal attention of the crown—the Tudors in England; the Hapsburgs in Spain, particularly Philip II; and the Bourbons in France. Under the Tudors, England developed councilor government, with key ministers developing a role that was to eventually result in that of Prime Minister. Philip II served as his own minister—indeed, as his own clerk—but he did establish lasting administrative structures. In France, Bourbon kings used a series of effective ministers who developed a strong, centralized administrative structure.

Developments during this period offer insights not only into the past, but into the present. Lord Burghley and Cardinal Richelieu's masterful use of patronage to strengthen their respective positions is certainly not a technique limited to their days. The problems of micromanagement by chief executives illustrated by Philip II can be seen in modern administration; indeed, it is a charge leveled against a modern "prince"—former President James Earl Carter. The arguments of Calvin, Luther, and others are reflected in the current debates concerning the proper relationships among Church, state, and public administrators over such issues as prayer in schools and abortion.

The intellectual origins of the administrative state are rich and varied. Examining this heritage enriches our understanding of current arguments, as well as providing us with a sense of history, an anchor upon which to fasten our understanding of the linkage between individual and state.

NOTE

1. The theoretical framework used in this chapter is developed in another chapter, "The Emergence of the American Administrative State: The Intellectual Origins."

REFERENCES

Bellarmine, R., *The Power of The Pope in Temporal Affairs*, in *The Great Political Theories* (M. Curtis, ed.), vol. 1, pp. 298–300, 1981.

Calvin, J., *Institutes of the Christian Religion*, in *The Great Political Theories* (M. Curtis, ed.), vol. 1, pp. 249–262, 1981.

Chandler, R. C., The Public Administrator as Representative Citizen, *Public Administration Review*, 44, 1984.

Cicero, *On the Commonwealth* (trans. G. H. Sabine and S. B. Smith) Bobbs-Merrill, New York, 1927.

Cooper, T. L., Citizenship and Professionalism in Public Administration, *Public Administration Review* 44:143–149 (1984).

Curtis, M., ed., *The Great Political Theories*, vol. 1, Avon, New York, 1981.

Denhardt, R. B., *Theories of Public Organization*. Brooks Cole, Monterey, Calif., 1984.

Elazar, D. J., *American Federalism: A View From the States*, 3rd ed., Thomas Y. Crowell, New York, 1984.

Elton, G. R., *The Tudor Revolution in Government*, Cambridge, London, 1953.

Fortesque, A Learned Commendation of the Political Laws of England, in *The Great Political Theories* (M. Curtis, ed.) Avon, New York, 1981, pp. 229–232.

Gladden, E. N., *A History of Public Administration*, vol. 2, Cass, London, 1972.

Gulick, L., Science, Values, and Public Administration, in *The Administrative Process and Democratic Theory* (L. C. Gawthrop, ed.) Houghton Mifflin, New York, 1970.

Harmon, M. J., *Plato Thought: From Plato to the Present*, McGraw-Hill, New York, 1964.

Kennedy, P., *The Rise and Fall of the Great Powers*, Random House, New York, 1987.

Luther, M., Secular Authority: To What Extent It Should Be Obeyed and an Open Letter Concerning the Hard Book Against the Peasants, in *The Great Political Theories* (M. Curtis, ed.) Avon, New York, 1981, pp. 238–249.

Machiavelli, N., *The Prince*. (C. Gauss, ed.) Mentor, New York, 1952.

Mariana, J., *The King and the Education of the King*, in *The Great Political Theories* (M. Curtis, ed.), vol. 1, pp. 280–287, 1981.

Sabine, G. H., *A History of Political Theory*, 3rd ed., Holt, Rinehart and Winston, New York, 1961.

Scott, F. M., *Robert the Bruce: King of Scots*, Peter Bedrick Books, New York, 1982.

Snyder, L. L., *The Making of Modern Man*, D. Van Nostrand, New York, 1967.

St. Augustine, *City of God*. Image Books, New York, 1958.

Suàrez, F., On Law and God the Lawgiver and a Defence of the Catholic and Apolistic Faith, in *The Great Political Theories* (M. Curtis, ed.), vol. 1, pp. 287–298, 1981.

Wilson, W., The Study of Administration, *Political Science Quarterly* 2:198–201, 209–214, (1887).

2
Administration of the Spanish Empire in the Americas

Jack W. Hopkins
Indiana University, Bloomington, Indiana

I. INTRODUCTION

States are what they were. This facile statement expresses the theme of this chapter: the legacies of the Spanish empire in the Americas were pervasive to such an extent that they probably have influenced fundamentally the nature of modern public administration and governance in Latin America. This essay consists of an analysis of the Spanish colonial apparatus in its peculiar context in time and space. The systems of colonial administration—that governed one of the world's longest-lasting empires—provided at least the foundation for public administration in the postrevolutionary independent states of Latin America. The importance of the imperial system in providing the base for national administration should not be minimized.

Obviously, no real system is as simple as the introductory statement suggests. We will see that the Spanish colonial system contained substantial inconsistencies, internal contradictions, and many conflicting elements. Some of these were so fundamental that they contributed to the eventual collapse of the empire. It is also clear that the system underwent constant change as the empire matured and confronted new challenges; the structure by no means remained static during the 300-odd years of Spanish rule. However, even with the vastness and complexity of the empire in the Americas, we can draw certain generalizations that may serve to explain the nature of administration during that period.

To the greatest extent practicable, the problem will be approached not simply historically, but rather as an analysis of the empire's administration seen as a set of complex management problems. Thus the focus will be upon major administrative and management aspects, tasks, and responsibilities. These include establishment of mission, territorial organization, delegation of authority, oversight, financial controls, accountability, auditing and reporting, and ethical considerations.

II. ABSOLUTE MONARCHY AND THE STATE TRADITION IN SPAIN

Just as the present-day system of public administration in Latin America can be understood best in relation to its colonial antecedents, administration of the Spanish empire should be related to the concept of absolute monarchy and the state tradition in Spain existent at that time.

The absolute rule of monarchs, though not a new concept, reached its zenith toward the end of the sixteenth century. The Spanish monarchs at that time—Ferdinand and Isabella, Charles V, and Philip II—were characteristic exemplars of the absolutist form. Consolidation of the kingdoms of Spain established the absolute monarchies as the source of "all authority, rights, and privilege," and it followed that the newly discovered lands in the Americas were in effect the exclusive property or patrimony of the Crown (Brown, 1982, p. 34).

As Madariaga observes, the concept of absolute monarchy was no "hasty and improvised construction"; rather the idea had been long in its development, and indeed was still being debated at the time of Charles V (Madariaga, 1947, p. 8). The monarch was a living symbol and a composite of long-evolved traditions, ecclesiastical pronouncements from church councils and the papacy, and efforts of kings to overcome the power of the feudal lords. Thus the resultant absolutism reflected, at least in part, shared interests with the people, the monarch's subjects. In its various manifestations, constantly evolving over many centuries, the absolute monarchy represented a continuing contest among all these elements, including the *fueros*, or local customs and corporate and guild rights, that stood in the way of centralizing tendencies as the sixteenth century ended. Absolute monarchy rested, in large part, on the ancient concept of the divine authority of kings, an idea that was undoubtedly self-serving, but also widely accepted. That divine authority extended even to the ruler's control over the Roman Catholic Church and to Church appointments, although this was a subject of fierce and protracted struggle between the Pope and secular rulers. Madariaga sums up the complexity of the system well:

> There was no rule of Spain. There was a congeries of kingdoms, three or four in Europe, three or four in the New World, governed by a complex system of powers among which: public opinion, which was far stronger than our modern vanity cares to admit; municipal home rule, which remained strong both in Spain and in the Indies; local passive resistance and even disobedience, a force of varying and sometimes overwhelming power—all forces acting in an autonomous way, which gave to each of the kingdoms a character of its own; and above them all a highly developed, complex and specialized Head, the King and his Councils (a Council for every kingdom) keeping a balance of interests amongst the kingdoms, and (with the exception of finance, ever in chaos) trying to instil as much religious and moral objectivity into practical affairs as the human nature of both governors and governed would allow. (Madariaga 1947, p. 22)

Domínguez describes the political culture of the Spanish empire as "neopatrimonial," a condition approaching Max Weber's notion of a patrimonial bureaucracy characterized by a "purely personal administrative staff" (Dominguéz, 1980, p. 13). The imperial system functioned in a highly interventionist style, with local officials acting on behalf of the Crown across a wide range of spheres, political, economic, social, and religious.

III. POLITICAL STRUCTURES: FORM AND REALITY

Every organization is purposeful; purpose is inherent, and it is expressed, either implicitly or explicitly, in the creation of organizations, even those as vast as empires. Indeed, purpose, as it is built into constructs such as organizations, is one of the prime distinguishing characteristics of artificial as opposed to natural organisms. The Spanish empire in America was no exception and, not surprisingly, debate over the mission and objectives of the imperial enterprise continued throughout its life.

A. Mission and Purpose

Many questions related to the establishment of mission or purpose remained unresolved throughout the history of the Spanish empire. There was scarcely any question about the sovereign and property rights of the Crown. The king was also clearly the political head of the dominions in America. However, the reach of the Crown was always problematical, and it varied considerably in different regions of the empire. The roles of the *adelantados*, the viceroys, and sundry other officials inevitably clashed with the rights of the sovereign. These conflicts affected the interpretation of royal policy as well as the implementation of that policy by colonial officials far removed from the court in Spain.

One of the most vexing issues in relation to organizational objectives was the matter of the nature and rights of indigenous people in America. Extended and impassioned debate on this issue, fueled by the eloquent arguments of Bartolomé de las Casas and others, continued throughout much of the colonial period. The legalistic policy that required the reading of the *Requerimiento* (a proclamation that demanded that the indigenous people acknowledge the supremacy of the Pope and the Castilian monarchs) did little to resolve the issue. Indeed, from the standpoint of the indigenous people, it must have been utterly baffling.

All in all, the Spanish enterprise in America evolved several principal policy objectives: the enrichment of the Crown in Spain through monopolistic industry and trade, the conversion of the indigenous inhabitants to the Christian (that is, Roman Catholic) faith, and the exclusion of rival colonial powers from the region. All of these objectives were premised on the fundamental assumption that "Spanish America should be regarded and treated as directly subject to the king" (Moses, 1898, p. 17). Each aspect of these overall objectives created certain problems for the Crown and the empire as it spread and developed over its 300-year duration.

Although the ends of imperial government shifted somewhat during the long course of the empire, its fundamental purpose became ever clearer:

> And, although law and theory still declared the primary purpose of government to be the provision of justice and the safeguarding of the common good—in America as well as in the metropolis—in practice it became more and more the exploitation of the colonies for the benefit of metropolitan interests (McAlister, 1984, p. 423).

B. Territorial Organization

Even though a major part of the early exploration and colonization of the Spanish empire in America was carried out by private entrepreneurs, these efforts were always considered to be state functions. The *adelantados*, as the early explorers and colonizers were often named, served by royal commission. Typically, their duties and responsibilities were stipulated in a *capitulación*, or contract, with the Crown. This agreement usually bestowed extensive military, executive, and judicial powers on the *adelantado*, who functioned as a royal deputy.

It would be misleading to suggest that the early assignments of authority, privileges, and territorial jurisdiction were precise or orderly. Despite the best efforts of the Crown and councils in Spain, the early years were simply chaotic in many areas. Haring observes how the *conquistadores* in Central America "fought with one another like feudal barons in a tropical wilderness" (Haring, 1947, p. 81).

The royal *capitulacón* or contract, because of the privileges and powers it entrusted to the *adelantado*, became a highly sought-after instrument. Typically, the contract could be exchanged or sold, and often its rights could be inherited, although few were actually transmitted to heirs (Haring, 1947, pp. 22–25). (As will be seen, the sale of public offices would create serious ethical problems during the later phases of the empire.)

Although the *adelantados* were important only during the early phase of exploration and colonization of the Americas—for some forty years after the first voyage of Columbus—the practice created certain patterns of governance and administration that proved to be persistent. The office of *adelantado*, an ancient one from medieval Castile, carried with it important benefits and powers. Generally, it conveyed the governorship of a territory, proprietary rights, a specified share of the territory's revenues, land grants (frequently of enormous, and sometimes of indeterminate, size), trading monopolies, and sundry other powers and controls. All in all, the *adelantado* was a powerful provincial official and an early key element in the Crown's control of the Spanish empire in America.

The contract between the *adelantado* and the Crown, in effect, was an exchange relationship that allowed the sovereign to achieve the early exploration, conquest, and colonization of the Americas at little direct cost to the Crown. The potential rewards for the *adelantados* were sufficient to attract many entrepreneurs, adventurers, and freebooters to the enterprise. Viewed in administrative terms, while the system provided many incentives for wide participation in the imperial venture, it also created many tensions and centrifugal tendencies that later contributed to the disintegration and collapse of the empire.

The Crown in Spain ruled the empire in America through a complex territorial organization. Jurisdictional boundaries changed as additional areas were conquered and settled, and the importance and prestige of regions correlated closely with the amount of wealth flowing from the region to the sovereign.

Two great political jurisdictions were created by the king as the conquest brought most of the American mainland under Spanish control. The Viceroyalty of New Spain, created in 1535 with its capital at Mexico City, encompassed all of the territory north of the Panamanian isthmus, as well as the Antilles and later the Philippine Islands. The Viceroyalty of Peru, centered at Lima, was established in 1544 and included most of the South American continent except the Portuguese territories in Brazil, the Guianas, and the Caribbean coast of Venezuela. Eventually, the expanding empire led to the creation of two additional viceroyalties in South America, the Viceroyalty of New Granada (1718) and the Viceroyalty of La Plata (1776). Subsidiary territorial and political organizations tended to follow a standard pattern, although substantial differences existed among the viceroyalties.

Below the viceregal level, subordinate territories were created as regions were gradually colonized and developed. The typical administrative arrangement included a governor as political head, supported by an *audiencia*, a judicial and administrative tribunal. (The role of the *audiencia* is discussed in the consideration of delegation of authority.) As the imperial system evolved, so did the subordinate territorial and administrative units. All the "kingdoms" within the viceroyalties were not equal in prestige or authority. In some cases, the viceroy exercised direct rule as governor; these units were referred to usually as *presidencias*. In other jurisdictions, in which the viceroy's authority was of a more general supervisory character, the area was called a captaincy-general. But these designations were by no means uniform; wide variations existed from region to region and from viceroyalty to viceroyalty. However, it is fairly accurate to generalize that the viceroy retained overall control of policy matters and subordinate officials were subject to his authority.

The lowest governmental unit in the administrative system of the empire was the *cabildo* or *ayuntamiento*, the local government. Evolving from a long tradition of local government in Spain, the *cabildo* was typically the very first organization created after the conquest of a region. It developed as virtually the only administrative unit with even modest autonomy in the tightly controlled, hierarchical imperial structure. It was also the only governmental institution in which *creoles* (Spanish persons born in the colonies) were able to participate fully. The *cabildo* in Spanish America represents an early form of city planning. Generally, the town was created and planned consciously, typically around a central plaza, a church, and the town hall. (*Cabildo* refers not only to the municipal council, but also to the town hall itself.) Typically, the municipal governments, or *municipios*, exercised jurisdiction not only over the urban nucleus of a settlement, but also over a wider area. Sometimes the area claimed was vast, and the imprecision of boundaries led frequently to disputes over jurisdiction among *cabildos* (McAlister, 1984, p. 136).

All in all, given the tremendous expanse of the newly colonized lands in America, the enormous difficulties of transportation and communication, the wide separation of the metropolis in Spain from the colonies, and the vague knowledge and appreciation of the geographical features of the New World, the degree to which governmental penetration and integration were achieved is remarkable.

C. Delegation of Authority

The viceroy, in effect the vice-king, was the supreme authority in his jurisdiction. His responsibilities included supervision of justice (although this was limited severely by the role of the *audiencia*), financial matters, and the secular functions of the Church, as well as the welfare of the indigenous people. "He is absolute in political, military, civil, criminal and financial affairs. He governs and decides everything as he thinks fit" (*Relación histórica*, 1748, pp. 51 and 53). (Although the powers of the viceroy were undoubtedly extensive, the author possibly overstated the degree to which the viceroy could act unilaterally, especially when the detailed limitations on his powers are considered.) Typically, the viceroy also served as president, governor, and captain-general. But the office of captain-general varied greatly by region. As Haring points out, the title primarily denoted a military rank, but usage differed: on occasion the title was given to a royal governor who was independent of the viceroy and reported directly to the king and council in Spain (Haring, 1947, pp. 77–78).

The lack of clarity in assignment of titles, offices, and responsibilities created serious administrative problems. Haring identifies two characteristic principles of Spanish government in the Americas: "a division of authority and responsibility, and a deep distrust by the crown of initiative on the part of its colonial officials" (Haring, 1947, p. 121). The fuzzy and often overlapping responsibilities of viceroys and captains-general exemplify those characteristics. The entire system was designed deliberately to ensure constant checks and balances on colonial officials in America. Duplicate assignments provided a useful device for preventing excessive accrual of power and prestige by colonial officials. However, some of the unclear and overlapping assignments probably reflected an imprecise appreciation of geographical boundaries as well as timing and communication difficulties between Spain and America.

The fast-paced expansion of the empire demanded improvisation by the Crown to manage the system. McAlister observes how the monarchs coped:

> Furthermore, conquest and colonization proceeded more rapidly than the resources of the crown could be mobilized. Isabella and her successors, therefore, proceeded diplomatically, often deviously, giving with one hand and taking with the other, retreating from confrontations and compromising when expedient. (McAlister, 1984, p. 186)

The office of captain-general, as a rule, had no fixed tenure. Time in office varied by incumbent, by his performance in the office, by region, and in other ways. Attempts to institute standard terms were generally ignored, although most captains-general served for several years.

But much blurring of responsibilities characterized the viceroy's duties as well as those of the other institutions of colonial administration. The *audiencia*, functioning as the highest court of appeals in a territory, possessed some legislative powers in addition to its judicial functions, and it also served as a council of state for the viceroy. The broad powers of the *audiencia* enabled it, if it so chose, to slow or hamstring the executive and administrative functions of the viceroy or captain-general. The earliest *audiencia*, that in Santo Domingo, was intended to provide a forum for discussion of and decision on public policies; it was designed clearly to check the power of the viceroy Diego Colón. That particular function appears to have been passed on to other *audiencias* in the New World, with different degrees of effectiveness.

Questions of authority and responsibility continued to plague the Crown as well as its subordinates in America throughout the empire's history. Disputes between viceroys and *audiencias* were common. Titles and assignments of supervisory and territorial authority were constantly in flux and as the empire developed, considerable confusion followed. Captains-general evolved, as time went on, into virtually little viceroys. The head of the *audiencia*, called president, was also the governor, and that role conferred substantial autonomy on him. Titles were assigned loosely and imprecisely. The official title of captain-general, for example, was "president, governor, and captain-general," and this inevitably led to confusion and conflict with the authority of *audiencia* presidents and viceroys who were also called governors. On top of this ill-defined structure, the captains-general were often given authority virtually independent of the viceroy, with direct responsibility to the Crown in Spain. A similar arrangement was established in 1776 in the northern provinces of Mexico, including present-day California, New Mexico, and Texas. These areas were placed under a Commandant-General of the Internal Provinces, who was independent of the viceroy in Mexico City and reported directly to the king.

IV. ADMINISTRATION OF THE EMPIRE: CONTROL AND CENTRIFUGAL FORCES

A. Limitations on the Power of Colonial Officials

Several factors and circumstances combined to limit the effective powers of viceroys and captains-general in America (Haring, 1947, pp. 120–121). First, the various officials in the colonies had the authority to correspond directly with the Crown's offices in Spain, and the viceroys and captains-general had little control over them. Second, the Crown and its councils in Spain chose to regulate and legislate to an incredibly detailed extent. Almost nothing was too insignificant to escape the minute regulations of the Council of the Indies. The net result, from the perspective of the viceroys and captains-general, was a severe restriction on their ability to carry out routine administration effectively. Third, virtually all major policy issues and decisions had to be referred to the Council of the Indies for approval. This inevitably introduced long delays into the policy implementation. Frequently, several months would elapse while approval from Spain was awaited. Finally, the necessity of sharing powers with the *audiencia* almost doomed the likelihood of expeditious decision and action by the viceroy or captain-general.

B. Centrifugal Forces Versus Centralized Control

Apparent centralization of power and authority, in unitary governments or in empires, may be illusory. As Riggs suggests, in his model of prismatic administration, extreme centralization of power for both policy-making and implementation may indicate a desperate attempt of the central government to hold on to power, rather than any real control (Riggs, 1964). Such may have been the case in administration of the Spanish empire.

Various factors and circumstances introduced centrifugal forces that counteracted the centralizing tendencies and institutional arrangements of the colonial system. These factors, in effect, often gave the colonial officials in America substantial independence from rigid Crown control. Distance strengthened their freedom. Viceroys and captains-general generally could stay the execution of directives from the king and council in the event of special circumstances in the region. Where the viceroy or captain-general could not or would not, for some special reason, execute a decree or policy, he could resort to the formula *Obedezco pero no cumplo* ("I obey but I do not comply") and request reconsideration by the Council in Spain. Distance and time worked in favor of the local colonial officials in such cases. In many respects, the situation exemplified the classic field-headquarters dichotomy, and the resultant dissonance, that affect so many aspects of policy and program implementation (Pressman and Wildavsky, 1979). Colonial officials in America undoubtedly took advantage of the situation in order to gain more administrative freedom in an overregulated, rigid bureaucratic system.

C. Oversight

Throughout the long course of the Spanish empire in America, the Crown struggled to maintain its control over the far-flung enterprise. An extraordinarily complex structure for oversight evolved from that effort. We have already discussed the complicated system of checks and balances built into the imperial apparatus.

Foremost among the oversight institutions in America were the *audiencias*. In addition to their strictly legal responsibilities, the *audiencias* functioned to provide judicial oversight of the local political and judicial authorities, including governors and *corregidores*. (The *corregidores* were commissioners, acting in the name of the king, who discharged a wide range of administrative, financial, and judicial functions to help cement the centralized rule of Spain.)

Another institution designed specifically for colonial oversight was the *residencia*, or judicial review of the conduct of officials upon termination of office. At first narrowly conceived to control the office of *corregidor*, the institution was expanded until it became a central oversight mechanism of royal government.

The king, through the Council of the Indies, designated special commissioners to conduct the *residencia*, which held all public officials strictly accountable for their acts while in office. The *tribunal de residencia* was open to anyone who wished to testify with complaints or to bring evidence. Normally, the official being reviewed was required to remain at his post until the *residencia* was completed. Typically the *residencia* resulted in very detailed reports on the stewardship of the public officials. Reports were transmitted to the Council of the Indies or to local *audiencias*, depending on the circumstances. Penalties for malfeasance in office, as a rule, were severe; some colonial officials found themselves forcibly returned to Spain in irons to face trial or imprisonment.

The negative effect of the *residencia* was to discourage colonial officials from taking the initiative on local matters. Faced with the possibility of damaging charges by a *tribunal de residencia*, colonial officers were often inclined to govern legalistically, following the letter of the law even where it did not fit local circumstances well. Haring observes how "a sort of creeping paralysis ultimately came to pervade the entire political structure of the Spanish empire in the New World" (Haring, 1947, p. 152).

A similar oversight mechanism was the *visita*. Corresponding roughly to a modern surprise inspection by a departmental inspector-general or a current program audit by the U.S. General Accounting Office, the *visita* might occur at any time during the term of a public official. *Visitas* could be either specific or general, depending on the type and scope of complaints received. Where the *visita* was general, virtually every act came within the purview of the *visitador-general*. In those cases, the *visitadores* came directly from the court in Spain and were often members of the Council of the Indies. The findings of *visitas* were reported to that Council, which decided on the action to be taken.

Several other institutions and offices were employed to oversee the colonial enterprise. Minor officials were subject to *visitas* by *pesquisidores* or *jueces de comisión*, who were appointed by the viceroy. Their role was similar to that of a modern auditor or special investigator, appointed for investigatory purposes and usually in response to a specific complaint.

All in all, the Crown possessed extensive legal institutions for oversight of the colonial structure in America. Check upon check, audit upon audit, characterized the empire, but the evident distrust of colonial officials on balance probably weakened rather than strengthened the system.

The monumental codification of the complex laws of the Indies, finally published in 1681 as the *Recopilación de leyes de los reinos de las Indias*, was a landmark in the development of the administration and jurisprudence of the Spanish empire.

> It reveals a patrimonial philosophy of government combining high idealism with pragmatic political considerations. If its laws were frequently disobeyed, evaded, or deliberately misinterpreted, it still guided the formation of American societies by establishing the limits of what could and could not be done. And it had great durability, for it strongly influenced the legal codes of the independent Spanish American republics. (McAlister, 1984, p. 436)

D. Financial and Economic Controls

There can be little doubt that an overriding motivation for the exploration, conquest, and control of the Spanish empire in America was the enrichment of the Crown in Spain. That driving purpose, in the context of the concept that the lands in America were the exclusive patrimony of the Crown, dominated much of the attention of the monarch and his councils. Primary among these councils was the Casa de Contratación, established in Seville in 1503 to oversee economic and trade matters.

In this role, the Casa (roughly equivalent to a powerful board of trade) controlled the Crown's (and Spain's) trade monopoly, granted licenses, equipped ships, and also exercised certain judicial and executive functions, in addition to performing more practical administrative functions. The Casa had, among its other officers, a *fiscal*, or solicitor, whose duties were described by Moses as

> the king's mouth in causes wherein he is concerned, a check upon these that manage the revenues, a spy upon those who embezzle it, an informer against those that defraud it, an agent to improve it, and lastly a two-edged sword in a civil and criminal capacity, to defend the patrimony of the crown. (Moses, 1898, p. 34)

The Casa's oversight of trade, shipping, navigation, and related matters included civil and criminal jurisdiction in cases rising from those activities. Its authority ranked second only to that of the Council of the Indies. The extent of detail by which the Casa controlled such matters was truly overwhelming. Moses describes the list of books kept as part of the regular business of the office. These included books of receipts and expenditures; books of revenue from the *cruzada* (a religious dispensation); books of the king's private revenue; books on warehouse commodity deposits; books recording all resolutions; books recording all property belonging to deceased persons; books recording fines and court expenses; books of passengers; books of letters; books filing orders, bills, and certificates; books filing commissions of Casa officials; books filing naturalization papers; books recording utensils and goods for the chief pilot and other officers; and books for the accounts of ship loadings (Moses, 1898, pp. 42–44).

Although such records were part of the normal business practices of such offices, when they are considered in the context of the manual record keeping of the times, their detail, scope, and volume are truly remarkable. The mountain of such records still existent in Seville attests vividly to the thoroughness of the control and oversight system that was characteristic of the Spanish empire. Moses describes the work of the Casa de Contratación as "the most rigid system of commercial restriction that was ever framed" (Moses, 1898, p. 50). Indeed, the economic and financial controls of the system were so detailed, extensive, and onerous that they severely retarded the development of the colonies and encouraged efforts to evade the requirements. In the long run, the bullionist theory (in which gold and silver bullion was considered to be the most important form of wealth) contributed substantially to the economic underdevelopment and impoverishment of Spain relative to the rest of Europe.

E. Ethical Problems

The patrimonial nature of the imperial system contributed to its ultimate disintegration and demise. Because the Crown could alter the system and its rules at its pleasure, serious inconsistencies in administration ensued. The absence of well-established, counterbalancing institutions led to personalistic abuses, arbitrary actions by the rulers, and widespread favoritism in the dispensation of public offices and commissions. The competence of appointees, frequently, was a very secondary concern. Compounding the problem of patrimonial administration was the practice of selling royal offices. Increasingly, as the treasury ran short of resources, the sale of offices was used as an important source of revenue. Rulers eventually sold offices openly to the highest bidders, who, not surprisingly, then considered those offices to be a concession to be exploited. Posts were available also to those who made donations or gifts to members of the royal court, a practice not unlike the award of ambassadorships to major contributors to U.S. presidential campaigns. The net effect, in any case, was a decline in the quality of the royal service in the Americas. As Parry observes:

> At the end of the century, the whole life of the empire seemed in danger of strangulation, not only by external enemies preying upon its trade and cutting its communications, but by the host of internal parasites preying upon the livelihood of its people. (Parry, 1966, p. 211)

F. The Breakdown of the Spanish Empire

By the end of the 1830s, Spanish rule in the mainland of the Americas was ended. But the fact that independence was achieved in very different ways in different parts of the empire emphasizes the great variations that characterized the overall system. As Domínguez points out, the colonies were markedly distinct in many respects—in the extent of political participation, in ethnic politics, in social mobilization, in local elite roles, and in other ways (Domínguez, 1980). Thus the process of independence followed different paths, unfolded at a slower or faster pace, led to various degrees of violence, and involved different kinds of local participation in different parts of the empire.

The proximate event that led to the outbreak of the wars for independence in the Americas was the Napoleonic invasion of Spain, followed by the abdication of Charles IV and his son, Ferdinand, in 1808. The Spanish war of independence that ensued sparked similar defiant acts in the colonies, and the irrevocable disintegration of the empire began. The attempts of the modernizing rulers at the end of the eighteenth century to develop more modern sectors had failed, and the system collapsed as the imbalances in it were overwhelmed by the spreading revolt.

G. A Concluding Note

A balanced assessment of the system of Spanish imperial administration in America must recognize both its negative (dysfunctional) and its positive aspects. The cumulative effects of the system were severe:

> Because of the Laws of the Indies were extraordinarily complex and detailed, and because of the centralized nature of the colonial system, administration became ponderous and tedious. The paternalistic system demanded frequent and extremely detailed reports from officials at all levels; these dealt with the minutest aspects of government. The cardinal virtues were order and orthodoxy, and eventually the incredible weight of law and regulation practically immobilized the colonial empire. Bureaucratic requirements smothered local initiative and the empire staggered under the burden. (Hopkins, 1991, p. 698)

For many reasons, the colonial structure provided "a frail foundation for the development of viable public administration after independence" (Hopkins 1991, p. 699). Yet, in many respects,

> much of the characteristic core, in terms of bureaucratic style, remains. The tenacity of those features, given the long history of attempted reform, governmental turnovers, foreign influences, and directed attempts at exogenous change, is truly remarkable. (Hopkins, 1991, p. 706)

Thus the persistent legacy. The past weights heavily on the present. Haring's overview eloquently expresses the colonial achievement:

> The colonial system of Spain did not greatly differ in essentials from that of other colonizing nations of that age. All of them met similar conditions with similar methods. But no European country had ever ruled so great an empire, and none could compare with Spain in the reach and exercise of royalty authority. The measures employed seemed to be the only possible ones at that time; they frequently brought good results; and Spain was not to be blamed if she could not foresee the future more clearly than her rivals. What must be remembered is that she maintained her empire undiminished for three centuries;

and if she lost it in the end, because unable to adapt herself to new methods and new conditions, it was no more and no less than happened to her great colonial rival, England, in the revolution of the North American colonies. Not only to have conquered such an empire, but to have held it so long, was an extraordinary achievement (Haring, 1947, p. 157).

REFERENCES

Brown, John Francis, *The Colonial World in Latin America*, Forum Press, St. Louis, 1982.

Domínguez, Jorge I., *Insurrection or Loyalty: The Breakdown of the Spanish American Empire*, Harvard University Press, Cambridge, Mass., 1980.

Haring, C. H., *The Spanish Empire in America*, Oxford University Press, New York, 1947.

Hopkins, Jack W., Evolution and Revolution: Enduring Patterns and the Transformation of Latin American Bureaucracy, in *Handbook of Comparative and Development Public Administration* (Ali Farazmand, ed.) Marcel Dekker, New York, 1991, pp. 698–707.

Madariaga, Salvador de, *The Rise of the Spanish American Empire*, Macmillan, New York, 1947.

McAlister, Lyle N., *Spain and Portugal in the New World 1492–1700*, University of Minnesota Press, Minneapolis, 1984.

Moses, Bernard, *The Establishment of Spanish Rule in America*, G. P. Putnam's Sons, New York, 1898.

Parry, J. H., *The Spanish Seaborne Empire*, Hutchinson, London, 1966.

Pressman, Jeffrey L. and Aaron Wildavsky, *Implementation*, 2nd ed., University of California Press, Berkeley, 1979.

Relación histórica del Viage a la América Meridional hecho de orden se S. MAG. para medir algunos grados de Meridiano terrestre etc, Por Don Jorge Juan etc. y Don Antonio de Ulloa, Impresa de orden del Rey en Madrid, año de MDCCXLVIII, Ch. III, Vol. II, pp. 51 and 63. Quoted by S. Madariaga *The Rise of the Spanish American Empire*, Macmillan, New York, 1947.

Riggs, Fred W., *Administration in Developing Countries: The Theory of Prismatic Society*, Houghton Mifflin, Boston, 1964.

3

Excessive Bureaucratization: The J-Curve Theory of Bureaucracy and Max Weber Through the Looking Glass

Gerald E. Caiden
University of Southern California, Los Angeles, California

I. THE J-CURVE OF BUREAUCRATIZATION

For some time, students of bureaucracy have been concerned with its apparent contradictions. On the one hand, its institutionalization of legal-rational authority makes it more productive than most alternative forms of human organization, especially on a large scale. Yet it manifests so many potential organizational deficiencies or bureaupathologies that it can become most unproductive. Can it be that there is in operation the same kind of process that economists and others have observed in respect to utility, namely a J-curve whereby with increasing resources, utility at first accelerates, then experiences diminishing marginal returns, and finally reaches a point of nonutility? With increasing bureaucratization, does productivity first accelerate, then experience diminishing returns, and finally reach a point of actual decline?

When, during the nineteenth century, industrializing societies experienced the increased productivity of bureaucratization, scholarship concentrated on the functionality of bureaucracy. Weber's ideal type analysis could be (and was often) interpreted as a justification and exhortation of bureaucratization, although he, like Durkheim and others, also noted its alienating effects on individuals and its other dysfunctional elements. As bureaucratization increased, so its dysfunctionalities became more apparent and attracted more and more attention during the first half of the twentieth century, and bureaucracy itself became subject to increasing criticism. But only in the second half of the century has research concentrated on the dysfunctional bureaucracy, suggesting that further bureaucratization may induce so many bureaupathologies that bureaucracy will become dysfunctional, productivity will decline, performance will be inhibited, and many of the already overbureaucratized organizations would be better off if they debureaucratized. So influential have these critics been that policymakers have begun to look for alternative ways of delivering public services other than through public bureaucracies, and responsive management has begun to experiment with debureaucratization to increase productivity.

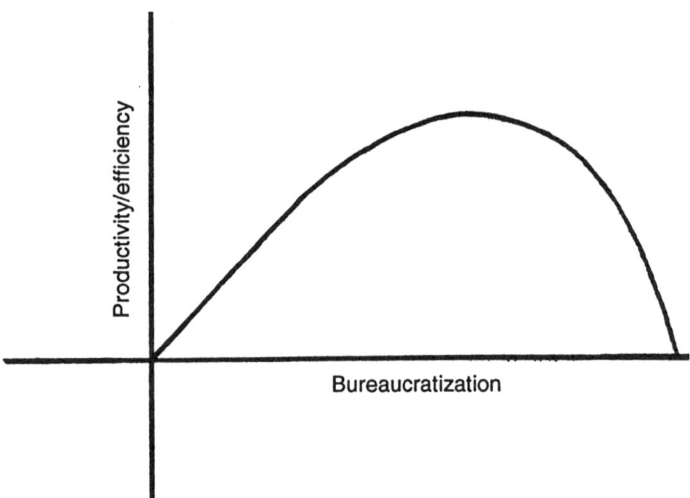

Figure 1 The J-curve of bureaucratization.

Studies of selected allegedly overbureaucratized organizations exhibiting bureaupathologies on an extensive scale (such as multinational corporations, armed forces, prisons, legal systems, mail services, welfare agencies) do suggest a J-curve effect (see Figure 1). They also indicate how the functional elements of bureaucracy—specialization, hierarchy, rules, managerial direction, impersonality, and professionalization—if overdone can turn dysfunctional and eventually unproductive. In combination the various dysfunctionalities alienate not only clients but also members/employees. Overbureaucratized organizations are not pleasant to deal with or comfortable to work in. They irritate more than they please. They add to rather than detract from life's daily trials. This paper sketches how the functional elements of bureaucracy when overdone become dysfunctional. The next step is to show how a J-curve of the bureaucratization process may be empirically verified.

II. MAX WEBER THROUGH THE LOOKING GLASS

No analysis of bureaucracy can avoid acknowledging the debt to Max Weber, whose conceptualization has yet to be surpassed. No only did he outline the advantages of legal-rational authority in organizing human activities, but he also referred to some of its disadvantages, increasingly so toward the end of his life when bureaucratization was fast becoming the norm of contemporary society. Despite his warnings, bureaucratization has almost been deified by organizational analysts who have preferred to blame its apparent shortcomings on the inability of people to adapt themselves to bureaucratization rather than delve into inherent shortcomings. The term "bureaupathology" should not be applied to organizational misfits, but, as the word would suggest, to the pathologies or sicknesses or shortcomings of the bureaucratic form of organization.

The virtues of bureaucracy are well known. It is my conviction that if the bureaucratization process is carried too far, if it is hastily pursued, and if it is misapplied, then the virtues turn into vices. Just where and when this occurs are matters of speculations, but it is my conviction again that through analysis and experimentation it is possible to discern the range when the functionality of bureaucratization becomes dysfunctional, just as when eating at first satisfies hunger but, if persisted in, becomes gluttony. There is a transition zone which will vary in happenstance and will differ from organization to organization. This transition zone can be likened to the downward sloping curve of marginal utility, save that in this case, it is the downward sloping curve of productivity, or to be much more exact and precise, organizational deficiency, for it is efficiency that will decline much before productivity, until further bureaucratization results in inefficiency then loss of productivity, and certainly dysfunctionality.

The analogy to eating and overeating is not all that far-fetched. What constitutes overeating will vary according to the size of individuals, their energy levels, their diets, their health, their habits, even their cultural perceptions as to build. For a long time the individual who overeats may not be aware of the fact and the consequences may be hidden. Nothing untoward may happen, but medically the body reacts and the eventual dysfunction may shorten life and certainly cause medical complications. So, too, what constitutes bureaucratic dysfunction will vary according to the size of organizations, their purposes, their structures, their tolerance of inefficiency, and even their perceptions of organizational health. Organizations may not be aware of what is happening slowly to them for there may not be any outward signs of bureaucratic dysfunction, but eventually they will suffer bureaupathologies which, if not treated in time or properly, will lead to their demise.

Care must be taken not to confuse symptoms with causes. It is not difficult to list and classify bureaupathologies, all the things that can and do go wrong in organizations. Indeed, it is an interesting exercise to remind ourselves how fallible we are and how many things can go wrong in our organizations. But listing them does not tell us what causes them or, better still, how we can cure them. The symptoms may have multiple causes requiring complex correctional actions, including drastic surgery, ongoing chemotherapy, and extensive (and expensive) convalescence. In the search for causes or some major causes, we do not have to go much beyond Max Weber's conceptualization of bureaucracy, for within each characteristic lay the seeds of its own decay. In short, if one overorganizes, if one overbureaucratizes, then the same virtues become vices, and if not reversed or corrected or compensated, they will result in self-destructive tendencies, which if not halted in time may eventually lead to organizational demise.

A. Specialization

The virtues of the division of labor have long been admired. The industrial society has carried the division of labor to its logical conclusion in the workplace. Industrial engineering has extended job differentiation, position classification, and simple task performance, epitomized by Charlie Chaplin in *Modern Times*. Now job fragmentation is universal, most employees in large organizations are required to do a very limited number of activities, using very little of their total abilities and potentialities. Their work is routinized, allowing almost no variation in performance and no scope for initiative. In many cases they are mere appendages of machines or machine minders. Very quickly their work becomes boring to them. It is the same thing over and over again, a boring ritual in which they are, for all intents and purposes, dehumanized. For them, the mechanics of work are soul-destroying. They are easily replaceable cogs, having no personal impact on the work they do.

Under such dehumanizing conditions, it is no wonder that few show any enthusiasm for their work, for the job they perform, for their place in the scheme of things. They are so divorced from the end product, so isolated in the total organization, so alienated from the industrial system that forces them into such servile labor, that they come not to care whether the work is done properly. They do their part, but if every so often they do it poorly, as imperfect beings must do occasionally, they carry on as if nothing untoward has occurred, hoping that in the pressures of the moment, nobody else will have spotted anything wrong. They are not going to draw attention to their own mistakes for they know when they do, they will be reprimanded, punished, and eventually replaced. So flawed products are detected only by a system of routinized checks and inspections, which, while more interesting to perform and allowing greater personal style, is not much more rewarding to perform well. It is difficult to generate interest in doing a good job.

Once people working under such a dehumanized, impersonal and mechanical system discover they can get away with occasional flawed work, they then test to find out how much flawed work they can get away with. Who notices? Can flawed work be traced back to the individual? Somebody eventually notices, but that may be well after the event or so far from the place of occurrence that nothing can be done. The organization as a whole has to live with flawed productivity, and in fact learns to accept a certain percentage or degree of failure. Flawed output is allowed for, written into the costs of production as returnable items or reprocessed services, and the work has to be done all over again, not necessarily by the original offenders. The responsible organization may never discover its culpability. Flawed products and services are suffered by members, clients, and customers who alone bear the loss simply because they do not know what to do or whom to complain to or believe that nobody will heed their complaints or, in the worst case, they are dead, victims of a flawed system of production and delivery.

Eventually people discover how much they can get away with undetected and untracable. They care not whether the work is done properly or at all. Theirs is a switched off, mindless existence on the job. Nothing more is required of them. They avoid becoming bored into insanity by thinking of interests off the job or by devising amusing games with or about work to provide some personal interest, or they resort to pure escapist thoughts and daydreaming. Their minds are not on their work. Their concentration lapses. They look for any excuse for a diversion or a break, and they skillfully manufacture interruptions in the routine. They work at half-pace, a gentle pace comfortable to all. Work norms are set well below capacity, which can be attained when they are sufficiently motivated or scared as the case may be, but which cannot be maintained for long without driving people to desperation. Thus, not only is performance flawed but the organization works somewhat below capacity unless machines replace human beings altogether.

For most caught in excessive division of labor, there is a detachment that cares not whether the jobs is spoiled, or targets are reached, or property is stolen, or the work is constantly disrupted. While they themselves may not deliberately act wrongly, they do not prevent others from doing so. They keep their minds on their own business, which is staying out of trouble. They do not inform on wrongdoing, which would be a breach of work etiquette in their position, and, when required by peer pressure and identification, they protect wrongdoers by covering up. They drift through life, or at least work life, in a dream, doing whatever is necessary to justify their continued employment and membership, but not much more. They do not believe—with reason—that anything they do will change their job situation. It will all be much the same wherever they go and whatever they do.

Here is a gigantic system which on the whole is the most productive but in the individual or the particular is actually quite unproductive. It wastes huge resources and potentialities. It enslaves most participants to mindless, soulless work, using a minute portion of their capabilities. It suffocates them, destroys their enthusiasm and initiative. It deadens them to pleas to do better, improve performance, produce more, contribute more of themselves. It destroys their enterprise. Common sense tells us that this excessive division of labor cannot be the most productive form of organization. At some point, it ceases to be functional. At the final stage, it promotes organizational sabotage by internal dissidents who have long given up on it and who take perverse joy in wrecking their own organizations.

B. Hierarchy

The virtues of hierarchy are well known. Hierarchy concentrates authority, provides direction, and ensures coordination. It enforces accountability through direct and clear lines of responsibility from top to bottom in a bureaucratic organization. It is simple and easily understood. Those in the upper reaches of hierarchy set the tone, give orders, and ensure that the lower reaches carry out the orders given them. Those in the lower reaches carry out the orders given them and report to their superiors on what they do. The bureaucratic organization moves with purpose, order, and discipline, with everyone pulling in the same direction and combining with everyone else to that end. If, however, hierarchy is carried too far, with layers upon layers of authority, something quite different results.

Excessive hierarchy encourages irresponsibility. Everyone below the apex has fixed jurisdiction, fixed authority, fixed duties and obligations, which are only fragments of the whole. Their vision is deliberately curtailed. They are warned not to exceed their bounds, not to invade somebody else's territory, not to concern themselves with matters outside their responsibility. So, apart from the apex, the interest of all becomes the interest of none. Nobody needs be concerned with the whole, only with his or her small part, and as long as that area seems to be doing well, it matters not that the whole may be jeopardized, although such subsystem optimization may work against the best interests of the whole system, which may require greater self-discipline and common sacrifices. The assumption is that the apex knows what is going on and looks after the interests of all. Should the apex fail to realize its responsibility to the whole, there is no way formally that the vacuum can be filled, and woe betide those who take upon themselves the task of filling apparent vacuums unless authorized expressly by the apex or some external overriding authority.

Unfortunately, excessive layers of hierarchy block the apex from knowing what really is going on far below it and jeopardize its ability to protect the interests of all against the interests of some. Each layer of authority tries to differentiate itself from immediately adjoining layers and to distance itself from them. Together they create both real and artificial or self-contrived barriers. Often only insiders know what distinguishes one layer from another, why one rank or title differs from another, and where one stops and another takes over. A complex organization resembles medieval jousting as each rank wards off challenges from inferiors and endeavors to encroach on the space of superiors. Such status seeking may decline into absurd symbolism as savage fights take place over who sits next to whom, who has the place closest to the window or door or fan or fireplace or the boss's office or—and Lord help the newcomer who mistakenly crosses the lines and provokes indignation well out of proportion to the incident. Strikes occur over trivial matters, trivial to outsiders but not to insiders. Such tribal warfare may well prevail over the interests of the whole organization, to say nothing of the public interest.

Warring factions impede the flow of information, knowledge, and communications vital to the smooth operation of the whole. Instead of passing information along, each layer filters and censors it, exaggerating its own importance and omitting detrimental items. The more layers the more distortions occur. What should be known by all is known only by a few, if any. Knowledge and the manipulation of knowledge constitutes power. When somebody knows something that somebody else should know but does not, the former can control the latter, who is thereby made dependent. Everyone soon finds this out and so joins the game. Those who know enjoy creating a mystique around their knowledge ("the aura of knowing") while cherishing secrecy and silence. Finding out what they should know is one of the major tasks of the middle levels of hierarchy.

Another major task of the middle layers of hierarchy is justifying themselves. What exactly do all the middle layers do? If the truth be known, they really manufacture work for themselves so that they can point to how much work they perform even if that work does not really advance the organization, and more importantly they manufacture work for lower layers, possibly needlessly. Actually their main job may be just to be there, to take the blame when things go wrong above and below them, and that alone may justify their existence within the organization. Taking the blame is an important organizational function that has to be performed by someone, but since no one likes to take the blame, least of all when he or she is not responsible for making the mistakes. People take pains to protect themselves; the art of self-protection in this case involves the needless manufacture of paperwork, or red tape in bureaucratic parlance.

Excessive red tape frustrates the hierarchial apex as much as it does clients of the organization. It further distances those at the very top from what is really going on. They are already isolated enough if they do not remove themselves altogether by indulging in the grosser forms of elite behavior. Having reached the top and being successful in their own eyes, they tend to self-indulge, to surround themselves with excessive privileges (the rewards of getting to the top) and act imperiously. The world they live in is so different from everybody else's: it is the world of the rich and famous. They are in danger of cutting themselves off even from their own organization. They do not wish to be reminded of what it used to be like lower down the hierarchy and may go so far as to kick the ladder away. In any event, they do not willingly descend. They do not want to dirty their hands again. If they do, it is largely for show and the more quickly they can get back to elite comforts, the better. In short, the two worlds at the top and bottom of the hierarchy have little in common; they could be on different planets. In their overprotected cocoon, the elite hear what they want to hear and they are told what it is supposed they want to be told. The picture they get of the organization is what *ought to be* going on, not what *is* going on. Calamity catches them by surprise, and their shock is real, not posed. They really do not know.

If the people at the apex do not know what is going on, who does? Nobody. This well-controlled, disciplined organization is headless. Leadership is diffused, power is fragmented and scattered. All people can do is insist on their authority because they probably lack commensurate power. In this amorphous state, things do fall between the cracks and things do get lost and misrouted. The surprise is not that excessive hierarchy works well (it does not), but that it works at all and works so well in the circumstances. It works so well because it is a very fluid organization in which he who wants to lead can lead. It gives ample scope for opportunism, entrepreneurship, and power plays to satisfy even the most manipulative. But this is a far cry from the usual picture of bureaucracy as restrictive, prohibiting, and unenterprising, and it is rather different from the way bureaucracies are supposed to work.

C. Rules and Regulations

We know why the rule of law is preferred to the rule of men; it is less capricious, arbitrary, discriminating. Rules and regulations do much to ensure equality, uniformity, equity, consistency, order. But if rules and regulations are carried too far, they can defeat their intent, to say nothing of the purposes of the organization. Rules have a habit of taking a life of their own, their purpose and origin forgotten. Having too many rules creates confusion, red tape, and indecision if rules include all formal policies, guidelines, laws, and written directions. Inevitably, with bureaucracy and rules playing such a commanding role in contemporary life, examples of the dysfunctions of excessive rule making are legion. I select two of my favorites.

1. *The Bus Company*

A large city was poorly served by its regional rapid transit agency. Buses were infrequent and service was erratic. No maps of the total route structure were available to the public. Bus stops gave no indication which buses stopped and what routes they took. Bus indicators gave only the final place of destination, and no route maps or timetables were available on buses. After much public protest, the bus company decided to systemize its route structure, standardize timetables, and publish route maps and timetables for the whole system and for individual bus routes. Actually very few bus maps and timetables were published and stocks were soon exhausted. Nonetheless, the bus company insisted on following its overall schedule, which, while standardizing the timetables, did not allow for daily fluctuation in traffic flow, number of riders, and weather conditions. Soon the rider public was protesting that the buses were not stopping at bus stops to pick up passengers. Investigation revealed that by picking up passengers, the drivers could not stick to the company's rigid timetable. So rather than fall behind the timetable, they did not stop.

2. *The Police Department*

Another large city was rocked by a police corruption scandal. To reduce the possibility of any repetition, the mayor insisted that the police department tighten up its rules and discipline. The department was ordered to codify all its policies, rules, regulations, guidelines, and practices, together with relevant legal and city council decisions on police work. In all, the code came to 1,600 pages, divided into four volumes. Every police officer was enjoined to know the code by heart. As legal decisions, mayoral instructions, council guidelines, and internal rules changed so often, the code was printed in looseleaf form, so that whenever changes were made, the relevant page was taken out and a new version substituted. Soon, so many changes were taking place that every day more and more pages had to be replaced, some several times a month. The police, who it must be admitted never really attempted to memorize the code, gave up consulting the code altogether and made paper airplanes out of the looseleaf replacements.

These two stories illustrate several dysfunctions of excessive red tape. The rules and regulations become captive of the legal profession, which writes them in such a way as to prevent court challenge and override. Unfortunately, only lawyers and judges can understand them. Nobody else has a notion what they mean. Being unable to comprehend them and realizing that rules cannot cover every conceivable situation anyway, the bureaucrats substitute their own group norms, which are based on common sense, experience, and prevailing notions of fairness. Such working group norms are not rules and they do not operate like rules. Furthermore, the written rules and the unofficial norms often clash. In following the latter, not the former, under peer pressure, bureaucrats run afoul of their hierarchial superiors, distort organizational policies, and corrupt the organization in the sense of deviating, deliberately and conspiratorally, from declared intentions. Dual standards exist. One is the publicly declared, official written declamations, and the other is the working practices. Bureaucrats disliked by peers, superiors, or both can be whipsawed as norms are put against rules, and they and their clients can be terrorized by their unrelenting oppressors. Once again, the actual working situation is quite different from an organization supposedly governed by rules, for the excessive use of rules can make for capricious, arbitrary, and discriminatory practices.

D. Management by Administrators

Bureaucracy requires the full-time employment of administrative generalists to manage the organization operated by technical specialists who produce and deliver its goods and services. This class of managers, which dominates the upper layers of the hierarchy, decides on major issues, raises and allocates the resources required by the specialists, sorts out jurisdictional disputes, ensures a smooth work flow, makes and revises the rules, and, in brief, performs all those tasks that have to be done to enable the organization to function and the specialists to get on with their jobs. The idea is that the administrators take care of all the extraneous factors to allow the specialists to concentrate on doing their work without having to worry over what to do and where to get the wherewithal to do it. The administrators service the specialists who carry out the real work of the organization. Of course, this is the concept of staff and line. The line fights the battles, while the staff decides where and when the battles will be fought by which fighting (line) units and services the line units, which can concentrate on fighting instead of being diverted by searching for billets, fashioning weapons, and foraging for supplies. This way, all is harmony, agreement, and efficiency.

When administrative rule is overdone, as is now so often the case in organizations, large and small, quite a different picture emerges. The administrative staff generalists are superimposed on the (line) specialists. They capture most of the top positions and take the lion's share of organizational privileges and rewards. The message is clear—if you want to go to the top, become an administrative generalist. Since most bureaucrats aspire to get to the top, they realize that sooner or later they must make a career switch. They must leave the ranks of the specialists and join the administrative/managerial class, or they will miss out. When they do, the organization probably loses the best of its line practitioners, the masters of their crafts, and gains uncertain, inexperienced, untutored administrators, whose performance is probably mediocre on work they perhaps do not enjoy and never quite master. At least this way they get some obnoxious ignoramus off their backs at last, even though they themselves become obnoxious ignoramuses to others. Fortunately, not all organizations misuse talent this way by exaggerating administrative rule, but too many ruled by administrative generalists do so at unknown cost to society and to their organizations, simply because they will not alter the reward structure or dogmatically believe in the superiority of the administrative class.

To enhance its appearance of superiority or "knowing," the administrative class has created a profession of its own, full of mystery to the uninitiated, with its own special jargon and terminology and emphasis on credentialism. One is not accepted unless recognized by other members of the club. But once they are accepted, the club is very protective of its members and will rarely admit to making a mistake or harboring the unworthy unless they run afoul of the law. Usually bad administrators are not dropped; they are passed on to another unsuspecting organization to start again. They may even be promoted but to circumscribed positions where the potential harm they can do is limited. Actually, it is difficult in complex organizations to determine how much impact they make, whether for good or bad. Rarely can specific outcomes be attributed to certain individuals. Rather, all is group effort, joint venture, collective decision making, not in a giant mosaic where individual pieces can be identified but in a spinning gyroscope where all is fused and confused.

The criterion of administrative performance is success, organizational success. Administrators do not see themselves in a support role, but in a leadership role. Organizational success is not due to line performance, but to their organizational leadership, not entirely of course, but it is leadership that counts. The ranks may fight the battles but the staff generals win the war. So the administrators must impress their organizational successes on the world. Marketing success is important to them, more important than achieving success. To them, everything is going well, things are looking up, problems are being resolved; they are enduringly optimistic. And well they might be, because they choose and determine the criteria of their organizational success, manipulate the criteria at will to project success, and suppress evidence to the contrary. They have their own organizational equivalents to the classic "the operation was a success but the patient died."

The two greatest deficiencies of administrative rule are the reluctance of administrators to admit their technical ignorance and their lack of proprietary interest. Administrators may be imposed on the specialists and have no technical knowledge at all other than what they pick up as they go along. Or they come from the ranks of the specialists and their administrative duties prevent them from keeping up with the specialists as they should. In any event, they are not as knowledgeable as the specialists on the details. Yet their leadership image impels them to decide technical issues which they are not properly qualified to judge. Professing knowledge and wisdom they lack, they make incredible technical blunders. Perhaps the story of the Sydney Opera House is as good an example as any. A design was selected that even the designer confessed he did not know how to construct, but the administrators proceeded anyway. After all, it was not their money at risk. They were playing with other people's money. Most administrators do, and by definition all administrators in bureaucratic organizations do. Administrative rule must take the major blame for the misuse and abuse of public monies by puffing up the self-importance of administrators who forget that they are supposed to serve others than themselves.

E. Impersonality

The virtue of bureaucracy and bureaucrats is that they are impersonal, act impartially, put aside all extraneous and personal considerations, and decide rationally. Presumably the rational decision is the right decision. But impersonality can be carried too far, especially in human service organizations where the aim is to assist deserving clients. Excessive impersonality turns clients into dehumanized objects—cyphers, symbols, cards, cases, files, numbers—and inevitably becomes quite insensitive even to genuine human plights. Bureaucrats have stood impassively by while terrible indignities have been inflicted on their fellow beings. Such impersonality has turned certain bureaucracies into fearful machines of human suffering, degradation, and murder, instruments of man's evil to man.

Even in welfare bureaucracies where humane treatment is the objective, the impersonality of the administration is dysfunctional as if the organization were itself uncaring, whereas that is not the case. The situation is terribly one-sided. An organization with resources to help confronts anxious potential clients who need help they can obtain nowhere else. Once accepted as clients they become dependent on it, scared that its help may be withdrawn at any time or without good reason or by mistake of uncaring bureaucrats. They need reassurance, a kind word and civility in their face to face dealings with the organization's representatives. They resent anonymity and impartiality, which they see as masking indifference (which could well be) and, worse, the petty manipulation of rules to make them servile, obedient, and uncomplaining clients. It is not too far-fetched in the guise of impersonality for mentally ill bureaucrats to exploit their organizational power and their clients' dependency to inflict cruelty (as in *One Flew over the Cuckoo's Nest*) or even to misuse bureaucratic procedures to kill clients (as in *The Hospital*).

Bureaucrats as well as their clients suffer from excessive impersonality. They are asked to be what they cannot be. They would not be human if they could put aside every extraneous and personal consideration. They are part and parcel of the society in which they live, and they know its values, prejudices, social structure, power relationships, and such like factors institutionalized by bureaucratization. They know their place in the social order and the behavior expected of them in the positions they hold. They hold these positions because they were attracted by the potential to help those less fortunate than they or to improve the lot of mankind. Impersonality grates on their helping hand outlook. They want to project their friendly personality, and they cannot be impartial to pain, suffering, poverty, cruelty. Excessive impersonality frustrates them, irks them, angers them, and eventually impels them to leave or to suffer that common bureaucratic disease in human service organizations of "burnout." Bureaucrats with burnout who go through the motions of the job without that spark of infectious enthusiasm which is so crucial for its successful performance are not much help to their clients in need and distress going through prolonged life crisis, and they can hardly be expected to fight indifference, discrimination, cruelty, injustice, vindictiveness, and other maladies perpetuated by bureaucracies on the underprivileged in society.

F. Careerism

Careerism certainly helps to attract and retain qualified and competent people to devote their working lives to bureaucratic organizations. Appointments are made on merit alone. Employees have guaranteed tenure as long as they do an acceptable job. And as a reward for their organizational loyalty, they receive a pension at retirement. Thus assured, they can devote themselves and their talents to advancing the interests of their employer and concentrate on doing a good job without worrying distractions. If carried too far, the concept of careerism can produce a quite different type of employee.

The career system is a closed system. Successful probationers stay with the same organization for the whole of their working lives. They know no other organization. They gain no other experience. They work with much the same people. The organization is incestuous. All who enter are socialized to conformity. Those who decide on promotion look for people much like them. The whole system is self-perpetuating. Its quality depends on whom it first attracts and whom it manages to retain. If it attracts quality, that quality will move through the organization, but if it fails to attract high quality people or high-quality people leave early, then mediocrity predominates.

As progression is assured (vacancies occur through expansion, retirement, or death), there are few incentives to excel. Employees can relax, knowing that sooner or later their turn will come. They do not have to exceed the comfortable norms set by the mediocre. If they miss their turn, they can safely serve out their time to retirement without exerting themselves beyond the doctrine of the minimum, that is, the minimum necessary to avoid being retired before time. An organization of mediocre time-servers is not quite what Max Weber had in mind when he enumerated the advantages of the bureaucratic form of organization.

III. IMPLICATIONS

Excessive bureaucratization can make for quite a different organization and quite different outcomes than Max Weber's analysis would lead one to expect. In time, it negates all that bureaucratization is supposed to promote. Excessive specialization may well result in uncaring, uninterested employees, working well below capacity and unwilling to stop the organizational saboteurs among them. Excessive hierarchy may well result in ignorant, powerless elites who are captives of bloated middle management busy manufacturing needless work for others. Excessive rules may well result in corruption and arbitrariness. Excessive impersonality may well result in insensitivity, indifference, petty manipulation of clients, and employee burnout. Excessive careerism may well produce a staff of mediocre time-servers. Together, these constitute quite a caricature of bureaucracy, but if we look around at the real world of organizations, one cannot be sanguine about the possibility that some large organizations, some autocratic organizations, and some secret fraternal organizations have already succumbed to excessive bureaucratization.

It is important for any organization to recognize, if possible, two points. One is where diminishing marginal efficiency (or output or performance) occurs and the other where marginal efficiency actually evaporates. This can only be done through complex and continued measurement of the operations of the whole organization. What is needed is the equivalent of the control room in a computerized production line. None now exists, and I hazard the guess that it will take many years to devise such organizational monitors. Even if it were technically feasible, the costs would be high, perhaps too high to be worthwhile, and the social ramifications of its deployment would cause serious problems in implementation.

But it is unnecessary to go to such lengths to profit from the foregoing analysis. Every organization can safeguard itself against overbureaucratization in simpler ways by directing close attention to each bureaucratic characteristic. Excessive division of labor is already being tackled by work integration, job rotation, mechanization of routinized operations, and a holistic view of members/employees. Even so, it will remain a fact that most people are overeducated for the work they do and if anything the spread of high technology will increase the gap. (Who will need to tell time or spell when machines do that already?) Work, not education, needs to be restructured to allow more active participation by those who perform it by increasing tasks and expanding decision-making responsibilities.

Unfortunately, excessive hierarchy prevents restructuring work in this way. Unnecessary layers, particularly at middle levels of the organization, need to be consolidated and the whole structure reduced, so that the distance between top and bottom is shortened. Similarly, excessive red tape and formalities need to be minimized and the gap between the formal rules and the informal group norms reduced, again by allowing line people to assume greater responsibility for deciding how to perform their tasks. Administrative rule does not have to be taken to such extremes, and reward structures should be arranged to permit line people to receive more than managers who exercise, at least on paper, authority over them, and steps should be taken to prevent the isolation at the apex.

Likewise, organizations should accept that the idea of impersonality is too demanding, particularly in welfare and human service bureaucracies. The personal touch may be desirable, as long as care is taken to prevent discrimination, prejudice, and arbitrariness. Work should not be structured as to demand perfect human beings to perform it, and greater attention should be paid to detecting and overcoming personal stress on the job and burnout. For this and other reasons, there should be greater freedom of entry and exit in the organization at all levels, without penalties imposed on promotion prospects or retirement benefits. Careerism has its place but not to the detriment of organizational performance. No one is owed a living and organizational generosity should not substitute for a proper social welfare system and adequate retraining facilities of members/employees who no longer pull their weight.

These are but samples of what can and should be done in dealing with overbureaucratization. The analysis still leaves open more serious questions as to where and when bureaucratization has been wrongly applied, how bureaucracy itself can be replaced by alternative schemes of human organization, and what refinements still need to be made in the bureaucratic form to make organizations more error-free, innovative, and adaptive. We do not have to stand Max Weber on his head. We just need to peer more closely at him through the looking glass.

4
Max Weber: Victim of Ethnocentric Mishandling, or How Weber Became a Management Consultant

Robert Leivesley, Adrian Carr, and Alexander Kouzmin
University of Western Sydney, Nepean, Australia

I. INTRODUCTION

Organization theory, from the late nineteenth century till perhaps the last two decades, has been in effect organization-design theory. It has carried both descriptive and normative freight; the normative element has been, on occasion, a conscious, deliberately rationalistic formula for organization formation and maintenance, but just as often implicit ideology embedded in metaphor or "scientific trappings." The cultural matrix of its origin has sometimes been recognized and the historical circumstances of its origins have often been routinely outlined. But the ethnocentricity of its formation has seldom been recognized, still less scrutinized, and the historical circumstances to which the theory has responded have largely been left unintegrated with the organization-design theory on offer. In consequence, such theory is present as a series of disembodied verities rather than as contextually specific ideological formations responding to contemporary social and, specifically, work situations. One is offered a packaged solution to problems, which should, in all commercial fairness, bear the stamp "Use by ______."

The more enlightened organization-design literature is superior to this precisely because it attempts to place such design in its cultural milieu, recognizing the presumptions, values, and contemporary problems or challenges by which organization responses are shaped.

It is understandable that, in the heyday of positivism, theory had ostensibly to be value-free, had to operationalize concepts, had to propose universality of application, and so on. It is not so comprehensible that organization textbooks are still being foisted on, and accepted by, tertiary institutions, texts which often do not offer any introduction to the philosophy of the social sciences and represent epistemologically naive mélanges of reading and analysis that give teachers no basis on which to assess the techniques and case studies before them [1].

Furthermore, attempts to understand and apply interpretive, hermeneutic, social constructivist, or broadly phenomenological approaches to organization study are comparatively rare. The attempt to cultivate cross-disciplinary approaches to the psychology, social psychology, or sociology of organizations is lost somewhere in the formalist, macro-micro abyss. Many texts are still offering so-called organization-process studies of leadership, communication, and conflict as if they were appendages to rationalistic design theory, or part of the unreal functionalist integration/Marxian conflict debate, instead of asking whether they are legitimate, unitary themes for study.

This chapter examines a few examples of organization theory which represent ethnocentrically anchored prescriptions masquerading as universal panaceas; distortions of classic thinkers in the name of pragmatic research or consultancy interest; and specimens of the mistranslation and misreading of Weber which have led to a pragmatic adulteration of his purposes.

II. WEBER ASSIMILATED TO PRESCRIPTION: A LATTER-DAY DESIGN CONSULTANT OR A VICTIM OF ETHNOCENTRICITY?

It should not be surprising that many a teacher of organization analysis claims Max Weber as his or her sociological forebear, nor that, as a consequence, the cry rises from every side "You've misunderstood Weber's ideal type analysis" (Donaldson, 1985, p. xi).

Perhaps all of us have misunderstood him, for the sweep of Weber's methodological thought is broad and not systematically complete. There have been many attempts at exploring his ideal typical procedure. And careful though one's research may be into the times and circumstances to which Weber addressed himself, one almost certainly does not have all the pieces of the methodological puzzle that he has bequeathed. There is no pretention in this chapter to explore the broad reaches of Weberian scholarship, nor is an historicist stance on Weber's work sought. But it is asserted that, while Weber's original text is often the source of subsequent creative discourse, it should not be reduced to a license to legitimate any work that is not, first, subject to the discipline of a hermeneutic that seeks to uncover something of the social milieu and circumstance which called forth that text. It is maintained that this principle holds not merely for Weber but for any social theorist whose work is to be comprehended. It is suggested that the best rendering, in English, of Weber's *ideal type* is a type-made-up-of-ideas, those ideas which are salient through their value-relevance to the heuristic enterprise at hand.

There are a number of reasons for adopting this as the most likely rendering of the term. Bendix and Roth's (1980) *Scholarship and Partisanship: Essays on Max Weber* is especially noted. They write: "Weber's typologies constitute the basic instruments of his comparative approach, which gradually emerged from his critique of organicist and evolutionary theories" (Bendix and Roth, 1980, p. 114). They continue:

> One of the standard misconceptions about Weber's work is that it provides the basic categories of social action but nothing comparable to larger systems analysis. In view of the methodological situation of his time, Weber insisted that interpretive sociology must start with the individual, not the group ["system"]. . . . Weber . . . avoided the term "system" because in his days it still reflected its older philosophical meaning as well as the organicist analogy. His terminological equivalent for "political system" is political organisation [*Verband*]. . . . The systems approach is in itself insufficient for historical analysis because of its level of abstraction. Here lies the well known difficulty of filling "empty boxes": the matrix fits every case irrespective of its historical context, whereas the historical dynamics remains elusive. (Bendix and Roth, 1980, p. 114–116)

Bendix and Roth (1980) argue from detailed analysis that, since for Weber there are no whole societies, unilinear developments, universal stages, or causal master keys, the varieties of historical structure were conceptualized by the ideal typical approach. Rather than search for a basic, timeless causal agent, he tried to rank factors in a given historical case. Faced with "the continuous stream of actual phenomena," an epistemological view of the world as an infinite manifold (Bendix and Roth, 1980, p. 45), Weber saw it as fruitful to reduce social reality to intelligible typological proportions. This was a nominalist position, in contradistinction to the notion that concepts and objects are intrinsically related.

Bendix and Roth (1980) also note Weber's indebtedness to Georg Jellinek (1892, 1914). From Jellinek's work on the theory of the state, Weber drew support for the notion of ideal types derived inductively through careful comparison of individual states. Weber wished to emphasize the abstracting and selective quality of all concepts, whereas Jellinek (1892, 1914) had suggested that types be constructed from phenomena with some historical relationship. Weber was prepared to build types from historically unrelated phenomena, since he was interested in the phenomena, not as historical object or historical cause, but as heuristic means for the formation of concepts in cultural theory (see especially, Weber, *Gesammelte Aufsätze zur Wissenschaftslehre*, p. 258, cited in Bendix and Roth, 1980, p. 262).

This emphasis on the heuristic and interpretive in the ideal type runs through many an introductory sociology text (Skidmore, 1979, p. 26; Campbell, 1981, p. 175; Swingewood, 1984, p. 147). It is a great pity that organization theorists appear to be less literate or more ahistorical in their pragmatic rush to universal truths about the work context. A review of the impoverished state of management applications of Weber in the Anglo-American college literature is revealing.

III. THE CONTINUING DEGRADATION OF WEBER'S "IDEAL TYPE" BUREAUCRACY

Discussing bureaucracy in the context of a wider examination of governance (*Herrschaft*) and of his typology of authority, Weber put forward his concept of ideal type bureaucracy. This, as Freund (1972, pp. 59–70) is careful to point out, Weber intends as a starting point for further research, a throw-away concept, neither true nor false, rather something to be evaluated as useful or useless (see also Lachman, 1972).

One of the clearest statements of Weber's intentions is that provided by Georgiou (1975, pp. 292–298), who deplores the ritual practiced by "sociologically-oriented organisational theorists [of] making obeisance to Max Weber's ideal type of bureaucracy before proceeding to a statement of their own work" and going on to reveal that "their idol has feet of clay." Georgiou adds, in respect to these writers, "The process of establishing and maintaining Weber as the godhead of organisational theory simultaneously produces *important distortions* of his work" (Georgiou, 1975, pp. 292–298, italics added).

An examination of this process which Georgiou so criticizes shows how a number of North American scholars have misinterpreted Weber, or built on the misinterpretations of others, until what reaches the, say, college student, via the invariably North American (and, more recently in Australia, locally adapted) management school textbook, bears little relation to the points Weber was making. Indeed he would turn in his so-called iron cage [2] (Weber, 1948, p. 181) and rise again to rattle the bars at his jailers (Dostoevsky, 1963, pp. 310–311).

Merton (1952, p. 361) opens his discussion of the dysfunctions of bureaucracy with a clear summary of the nature of bureaucratic organizations, acknowledging Weber's contribution to their formalistic analysis. However, in proceeding to highlight the shortcomings of bureaucracy

Merton (1952, pp. 364–371) implicitly criticizes those authors who, while extolling the "positive attainments and functions of bureaucratic organizations . . . almost wholly neglect . . . the stresses and strains of such structures." While perhaps not himself intending to attribute any shortcoming to Weber, it may be that Merton has here unwittingly set off a sequence of ill-directed and unscholarly criticism which has, over the intervening decades, left the features of Weber's concept unrecognizable for many ill-schooled scholars, its purpose forgotten [3].

Gouldner (1954) extensively discusses the validity of Weber's ideal type. First, conceding that Weber gives "unparalleled expression" to the discussion of bureaucracy in the context of "panoramic historical surveys of diverse administrative systems" (Gouldner, 1954, p. 15), Gouldner is quick to take Weber to task for a failure to distinguish between the origins of different classes of bureaucratic rules. He holds that Weber has disposed of a critical problem "in a surprisingly cavalier manner [and] tacitly . . . seems to have assumed that the cultural setting . . . would be neutral . . . toward different methods of initiating bureaucratic rules" (Gouldner, 1954, p. 15). Further, "Weber was silent on several other questions" such as to whom the rules had to be useful and whose goals they were to serve (Gouldner, 1954, p. 15). Limiting himself to the study of the "seemingly solidary government bureaucracy as an implicit model," Weber, in Gouldner's eyes, denied himself the insights that might have flowed from the study of bureaucracy in the factory situation, with its obvious stratification of the interests of supervisors and supervised (Gouldner, 1954, p. 15).

After some further discussion of Weber's shortcomings as a theorist, Gouldner takes issue with him again for "not providing sufficiently general analytical tools; for these we have to turn to the directives contained in Structural Functionalism" (Gouldner, 1954, p. 24) as formulated by Merton. While Weber has identified bureaucracy's manifest functions, his key shortcoming, for Gouldner (1954), has been his failure to take into account, along with its intended consequences, those that are unintended and not conventionally discussed. What Gouldner (1954), for his part, has quite ignored is that Weber never set out to explore these issues: the general sweep of his interest was elsewhere.

Selznick (1957, 1965) makes virtually no reference to Weber. He even appears to choose to ignore him when he writes retrospectively of his own earlier work in the preface to a subsequent edition of it, saying that it "stands in the tradition of Karl Marx, Gaetano Mosca, Robert Michels, Karl Mannheim and other critics of social myths and ideologies" (Selznick, 1965, p. iii). The omission of Weber is curious, but it does discharge Selznick from this current review and critique.

Simon's essay on organization decision making (1976) also, remarkably, contains no reference to Weber. His main target in his work is, no doubt, the administrative management school, just as it was that of his sponsor, Chester Barnard, when he chose the title *The Functions of the Executive* (1938) to put Gulick (1973, pp. 12–13) in his place [4], or so it would appear. Simon's avoidance of any references to Weber may reflect that insensitivity to the issue of values to which Banfield (1957) draws attention in his review of Simon's (1957) second edition of *Administrative Behavior*. Even so, the omission also makes it possible to exonerate Simon and to assume that it is March who was responsible, in their joint work on organizations (March and Simon, 1958, p. 36), for so inappositely labeling Weber as "not exceptionally attentive to the character of the human organism"—unless, of course, Weber's mistreatment here was the work of the helper mentioned in small type on their title page.

It is intriguing, therefore, to note that the authors of *Organizations* have key writers of the administrative management school in mind as they write, "Weber appears to have more in common with Urwick, Gulick, and others than he does with those who regard themselves as his successors" [5]. This is not to deny that March and Simon's (1958) chapter on the dysfunctions of bureaucracy has been a veritable mine of insights on the shortcomings of real life bureaucracy for those students who have been able to penetrate their turgid language. This means it is yet another example of serendipity in casual scholarship, ranking with the findings of the Hawthorne researchers [6].

Blau and Scott (1963, pp. 30–36) open their discussion of Weber's ideal type bureaucracy with an examination of his typology of authority, and of the characteristics he finds in bureaucracy. They describe ideal type bureaucracy as "an admixture of a conceptual scheme and a set of hypotheses" (Blau and Scott, 1963, p. 33). The first of these two points is not disputed; indeed by it they reinforce one of the key themes of this section, particularly when they say, "Such conceptual schemes provide important frameworks for analysis and research. . . . They are neither correct nor incorrect, only more or less useful in guiding scientific investigations." But they then slide inconsistently into a rejection of Weber's conceptual scheme on the grounds that it is "misleading" (Blau and Scott, 1963, p. 34). Claiming that he has been putting forward the characteristics of a "perfectly bureaucratised organization," they charge that he has failed to specify the criteria of bureaucratic perfection. Here, as elsewhere, one finds the confusion that arises from a widespread misunderstanding of the true thrust of the concept of ideal type. Apparently unaware of this, they claim to find "through a careful reading of Weber" that efficiency is his unspecified and implicit criterion of perfection (Blau and Scott, 1963, p. 34) [7]. On the contrary, perfection of performance has no place in Weber's ideal type, only perfection of conceptualization.

The same authors also criticize Weber for hypotheses which they find implicit in his writings on bureaucracy, ignoring completely the point they have already made that conceptual schemes are not subject to empirical testing. And, like Gouldner and others, they read into Weber their own preconceptions of what he must have intended, a point illustrated yet again when they say (Blau and Scott, 1963, p. 35) that "Weber's one-sided concern with the functions of bureaucratic institutions blinds him to some of the most fundamental problems in the study of formal organisations." To make quite clear that they have treated Weber as operating within the functionalist paradigm, they go on to refer approvingly to Parsons' and Gouldner's drawing attention to contradictions in Weber's conception of bureaucracy.

With Khandwalla (1977, p. 135) the degradation of ideal type of bureaucracy is well established. For him Weber is clearly providing a prescription for efficient organization. He attributes to Weber the conscious question "What is the organisational form that can service the increasingly more complex needs of an urbanizing, industrialising society?" and suggests that Weber has provided a list of the desirable features of such an organization, including "a non-bureaucratic, even charismatic head" to run it (Khandwalla, 1977, p. 135). He holds that Weber "insisted, on not very convincing grounds, that the administrative staff should not own the organisation in part or in full" (Khandwalla, 1977, p. 135).

He continues, "such a dictum, however, would rule out co-operatives, partnerships, proprietorships and firms in which the owner works as the manager" (Khandwalla, 1977, p. 135). Khandwalla (1977) has failed to grasp Weber's intention of focusing on the salient characteristics of governance in modern large-scale organization. He has taken him instead to be prescribing the features of the efficient organization. Weber would scarcely have presumed to lay down such a prescription without exhaustive and essentially heuristic investigation. In any case, such a point held no interest for him.

Contemporary business school texts, when discussing Weber in the context of formal organization, follow much the same inappropriate and disoriented line of discussion as

Khandwalla (1977) who claims that Weber wanted to understand how organizations could be designed to play a positive role in the larger society of the Western world, and, after a discussion of the needed characteristics, observes that Weber was "describing an ideal type of organisation." Khandwalla (1977) fails to specify the sense in which he interprets this (in English) patently ambiguous term [8] but goes on to demonstrate that he has totally misconstrued it, saying, "If Weber's ideas were adopted literally . . . the organisation would bog down under the weight of its own paper" (Daft, 1986, p. 175). There was, of course, no such literal intention in Weber's thinking; nor was Weber indicating a recommended design for organizations.

Dessler (1980, p. 25) adds his own measure of historical confusion and inaccuracy to the careless mutations prevailing in business school adaptations of organization theory by speaking of Weber as "writing during the 1920s," whereas Weber died in June 1920 (Gerth and Wright Mills, 1948, p. 23).

Robbins (1983, pp. 189–194) offers a lengthy discussion of Weber's bureaucratic "model" and carefully analyzes its significant features but, like so many others, throws no light on the sense in which it is "ideal." However, the implication is that Robbins (1983, p. 194) holds Weber to be prescribing a model of organization for managers to follow when, in his summary, he claims that "Weber's model *sought* to protect the rights of individuals" (italics added), with defined duties and avenues of redress.

Robey (1986, p. 34) distances himself from this company when he notes, "Weber himself was not interested in providing advice to managers. He was more concerned with developing a theory capable of explaining domination in society." And in a later passage, remarkable in the literature being examined here for its attempt, at least, to attain theoretical clarity, Robey goes on to point out that Weber's "concept of ideal bureaucracy connotes neither a desirable state nor an empirical reality"; he continues (1986, p. 101):

> Ideal means pure, as in a genetic strain [9] or in a Platonic sense [10]. The ideal need not actually exist in its pure form, but being able to describe it abstractly is an important analytical step [giving us] a basis for comparisons [so that Weber's] bureaucracy, therefore, is most appropriately thought of as the end of a continuum—a pure type against which most real organisations might be measured.

On the same page however, Robey, to a degree contradicting what he has already said, and without full regard to Weber's intentions, anachronistically claims that Weber uses the term "bureaucracy" to describe an ideal mechanistic structure.

A notable example of business school texts emanating from Australia, as usual adapting a North American work ignores the wider historical context of Weber's typology of governance when discussing his ideal type bureaucracy (Stoner et al., 1985, pp. 48–51). Weber is represented as needing to find a model of organization suited to twentieth-century conditions, first rejecting "charismatic" leadership for the business firm because the charismatic leader is not immortal and typically shies away from grooming a charismatic successor.

The authors indicate that Weber claimed "other organisations [in order to overcome the problems of instability associated with charismatic leadership] developed traditions and passed authority to clearly identified heirs. . . . Such organisations may be more stable but are often despotic, which in turn could be a major source of inefficiency" (Stoner et al., 1985, p. 48–51). They continue: "In his search for *more efficient ways* of managing organisations Weber developed an authority system based on what he called rational-legal authority" (Stoner et al., 1985, pp. 48–51; italics added).

They explain the rational element as providing machinelike efficiency based on logical design to produce, in Weber's own words, "precision, speed, unambiguity, knowledge of the files, continuity, discretion, unity, strict subordination, reduction of friction and of material and personal costs" (Roth and Wittich, 1978, p. 973). They observe that such an organization also "needs a legal system which formally defines explicit rules, relationships and procedures" (Stoner et al., 1985, pp. 48–51). If there is any doubt that this represents a greatly debased version of Weber's ideal type bureaucracy, it is dispelled in the following: "Weber offered the bureaucracy as an ideal form—*a model towards which managers should aspire*" (Stoner et al., 1985, pp. 48–51; italics added).

Stoner, Collins, and Yetton's (1985) work is no isolated case. Another North American work adapted for the Australian business school market (Milton et al., 1984, p. 244) represents Weber as claiming that bureaucracy is "the most efficient form of social organization," but in terms that do not do justice to the circumscribed manner in which Weber notes the "technical efficiency" of bureaucracy. Milton and his colleagues provide a list of the characteristics of bureaucracy which they attribute to Weber but derive specifically only from Dressler (1976, pp. 30–32), who is himself not basing his summary on Weber but using that of Hall (1962, pp. 295–308). One is not surprised, therefore, when the authors conclude by saying of this logical and rational organisation "Members must adopt its rationality as their own" (Milton et al., 1984, p. 244).

A third interpretation, again adapted for Australian use, leaves the critical reader at a loss in describing the final disfigurement of Weber's precise analysis. Bailey, Schermerhorn, Hunt, and Osborn (1986, p. 268) hold that Weber claimed bureaucracy to be "the best possible form of organisation, and bureaucrats were the people who made it work." After a short discussion of the major characteristics of what they dub Weber's "ideal bureaucracy," and of the dysfunctions associated with them, they bow out with the observation "It is important to understand the essence of Weber's ideal bureaucracy as a cornerstone concept of OB."

Lest it be imagined that too long a bow is being drawn on Australianized adaptations overseas management texts, one locally written text certainly serves to drive home the point. Hunt (1972, p. 47) paints the following canvas:

> In describing formal structures, Weber, Fayol, Urwick, Mooney and Reilly, Koontz and O'Donnell and Newman and Summer and a host of other "traditional" or prescriptive writers, predict, with some validity, that the lessons learned from observation provide a set of operating principles which can be transferred to other organisations.

At the end of this discussion one might even start looking in the second-hand bookshops for a text that claims Weber taught management in German business schools in the 1920s [11]! Certainly, contemporary German texts on organization and leadership, for example, overly rely on English-based liberties when outlining the content and function of the ideal-type bureaucracy (see Kübler, 1980, pp. 27–28).

The degradation of Weber's ideal type bureaucracy is not confined to countries on the Pacific rim. Pugh and Hickson (1976, pp. 2–4) draw on Weber to provide just two of the six key dimensions on which the whole structure of Aston empiricism is built. In an early chapter describing the setting up of the Aston program (Pugh and Hickson, 1968, pp. 374–396), they relate how they took "three influential writers, Fayol, Brown and Weber, as representative sources for [their] variables." The juxtaposition of these three names is fascinating, and the order even more so. Wilfred Brown does not feature prominently in current organization theory literature; the contrast between the intentions of Fayol and Weber makes them extraordinary company in this context, Fayol taking a position entirely distinct from Weber's, commending a specific model of the efficient organization [12].

Pugh and Hickson (1976, pp. 25–28) do not actually say that Weber is prescribing a model of efficiency, but one may infer that they are doing so. When one considers the minute portion of Weber's work they have appropriated [13], in contrast with the elaborate multidimensional statistical structure they proceed to erect, one may consider this yet another of those genuflections already mentioned toward a presiding, or rather legitimating, genius of sociology, such as Georgiou (1975) has identified. The extended discussion of how the Aston group make Weber one of the foundations of their West Midlands, United Kingdom, structure turns on the appropriation of just two variables: standardization of procedures and formalization of documentation, themselves uprooting Weber's ideal type characteristics in a most attenuated form.

IV. FURTHER REFLECTIONS ON CONTINGENCY AND IDEAL TYPES

As Mouzelis observes, Weber's ideal type bureaucracy has been the starting point and the main source of inspiration for many students of organization (Mouzelis, 1967, p. 38). At the same time the evaluation of Weber's writing on bureaucracy by others (Albrow, 1970, pp. 40–41) is somewhat confusing, especially from the perspective of Weber's critical contribution to methodology in social science, his ideal type formulation.

An irony lies in observing that, while Weber was concerned to place social analysis on a scientific basis, the very precision of concept achieved through ideal type methodology has provided the basis of a great deal of controversy about its value and use (Friedrich, 1973, pp. 28–29). Freund (1972, pp. 13–15) argues, for example:

> Weber was a pure analyst, whose sole concern was to gain a sound knowledge of historical data and to interpret them within verifiable limits . . . whose science was not to confirm or refute philosophical doctrine, but constructive in the sense that it contributes to the formation of the science of sociology which progresses on the basis of solid documentation, verified relationships and clear and precise relationships.

Apart from precision, however, Weber's methodology was also concerned with meanfulness of phenomena, meaningfulness in the sense that Weber saw the need to recognize that the same activity or institution may vary in time so that its meaning too may vary over time. There is, then, a duality in Weber's apparently contentious ideal type bureaucracy. As Mouzelis (1967, p. 50) says:

> On the one hand it contains empirical elements which were formulated in an inductive way by observing certain characteristics of concrete organisations. On the other, it contains assumptions about attributes of such elements, assumptions which were derived intuitively . . .

For Friedrich (1973, p. 29), "The construction of an ideal type seeks to distil an 'inner' rationality which the observer of a given reality imputes to the reality—a viewpoint which is philosophically rooted in a belief in an underlying rational order."

This empirical-evaluative dichotomy in ideal type method provides one reason for the inability of any one writer to resolve conclusively the methodological and substantive tension implicit in the ideal type methodology. Positivism, in the science of organizational behavior, has left a legacy which stresses the *abstracted empirical* rather than the *substantive and contextual* aspects of ideal type. Typically, the restatements that Georgiou (1968) refers to are empirical restatements, empirical readjustments, which employ the empirical characteristics of the ideal type by "adding, modifying or subtracting" certain of the Weberian characteristics according to the writer's analytical purposes and conception of bureaucracy (Mouzelis, 1967, p. 50).

It is these variously selected analytic purposes and conceptions of bureaucracy that the controversy about the ideal type turns on, for, contrary to Weber's construction and purpose for the ideal type bureaucracy, bureaucratic theory has become "predominantly ethnocentric, nonhistorical and microcosmic in orientation" (Delany, 1963, p. 459).

While the phenomenon of rationality in purposive instrumental action is highly congruent with positivist epistemology, method, and analysis, the ideal type as conceptual instrument is also problematic for positivist science in that it is a heuristic device whose qualitative nature is the antithesis of that phenomenon it attempts to explain. For Friedrich (1973, p. 30), the ideal type is problematic since "such an intuitionist basis is undesirable from a scientific point because there appears to be no way of settling disagreement by reference to scientifically ascertainable matter of fact or documentation." From a nonpositivist stance, ideal types can be seen as contingent or relativist tools which, by others, have been used in positivist fashion to further positivist knowledge about perceived unambiguous and formal collective action within organizations. The Parsonian formulation, to be referred to later in this chapter, is a case in point.

V. WEBER'S SCIENCE AND SCIENTIFIC METHODOLOGY

Aron (1967, p. 181) notes that Max Weber conceived sociology as being a comprehensive science of social action. The primary focus was on the subjective meanings that human actors attach to their actions in their mutual orientations within specific social and historical contexts (Coser, 1971, p. 217).

Of his categorizations of types of social action (Coser, 1971, p. 217), purposeful or goal-oriented rational action, in which both goal and means are chosen, preoccupies Weber as he further develops the question of the source of rationalization of the modern world (Mannheim, 1951, p. 52).

In tracing the predominance of rational application of means to ends over the forms of social action, Weber developed a methodology that was at once empirical and evaluative, one which emphasized the value-bound problem choices of the investigator and the value-neutral methods of research.

For Weber, the differences between natural and social sciences arise from differences in the *cognitive intentions* of the investigator and not from the inapplicability of the scientific and generalizing methods to the subject matter of human action (Coser, 1971, p. 219). Yet it is this cognitive intention of the investigator that remains hidden in overtly positivist methodologies in organizational analysis and which continues to obscure the tension between the empirical and the evaluative elements in Weber's ideal type bureaucracy. Freund (1972, pp. 6–7) discloses this tension:

> Weber's conception of science is governed by his idea of politics, namely, that the multiplicity and antagonisms of value and objectives find their parallel in the multiplicity and antagonism of the points of view from which a phenomenon may be scientifically explained. Despite its rigorous concepts and precise demonstrations, science is not free of rivalry among hypotheses and competition among theories, each based on a number

> of ascertained and ascertainable facts. . . . Weber's theory of science is a reflection of his theory of action, save that the first attempts to overcome the contradictions which are the life blood of the second.

Weber's view of the world and his distinctive methodology acknowledge the diversity, complexity, and uncertainty of both natural and social phenomena, so that generalizations about each, of necessity, involve *conditional, contingent, and probabilistic* constraints, obliterated in positivist analysis.

Complete systematization of phenomena, for Weber, was not possible since any attempt to generalize about such phenomena was an unending process contingent upon two sets of limitations. First, there exist the limitations of marshaling complete empirical evidence and, second, and more importantly in terms of qualitative analysis, generalizations are contingent upon the particular perspective or value orientation employed in marshaling and utilizing empirical evidence in order to make generic statements about social action.

Every statement, every coherent system of explanation only constitutes one vantage point, one facet of a complex conceptual prism through which to view a complex reality. Any science claiming universality and final validity was not only futile but antiscientific in content and purpose (Freund, 1972, p. 9). In this context, positivist science comes to be used for unscientific ends, becomes more dogmatic or doctrinaire than scientific, and does so because positivist science cannot readily operationalize the basic nature of empirical reality as "extremely and intensively infinite" (Freund, 1972, p. 7).

In a sense, Weber's ideal type methodology constitutes a contingency device being put to work some five decades before social science, employed in the realm of organization and administrative behavior, began to recognize the need for contingent strategies and theories of organization behavior. The notion of ideal type provided for Weber a means of overcoming the seemingly intractable scientific problem of stating causal significance at a level between the two extremes: that is, between generality which sacrifices the idiosyncratic, and the particular which sacrifices the value of comparative or more universal explanations.

In its function at the generalizing and particularizing levels, the role of the ideal type is to be a sensitizing factor mediating between the two levels of research and exposition. The construction of the ideal type enables one to make judgments involving causal imputation, not because the ideal types themselves are meant to serve as hypotheses, but because they allow one to "orient the forming of hypotheses" (Friedrich, 1973, p. 29), drawing upon an imagination enriched by experience and disciplined by methodology. By using this rationally devised, and in terms of content, utopian construct (Friedrich, 1973, p. 29) one is able to determine what is unique about a course of events by showing, in each particular case, to what extent reality departs from the unified and unreal analytical construct (Friedrich, 1973, pp. 68–69). Friedrich (1973, p. 69) states, "Being unreal, the ideal type has the merit of offering us a conceptual device with which we can measure real development and clarify the most important elements of empirical reality." It is this very unreality of construct which gives positivists such difficulty. As Friedrich (1973, p. 30) points out, "The intuitionist basis of the ideal type presents all the problems of the 'meaning of meaning.' "

To think about phenomena at two different levels, at the same time real and unreal, is to invoke Thompson's (1967, p. 10) observation that Western thought is unable to conceive at one and the same time of "something as half closed, half rational," a virtually countercultural notion. While the empirical dimensions of any construct are important, Friedrich (1960, p. 44) observes that, in keeping with Western cultural givens, there has been, in studies of administration, a predominant tendency to emphasize the "rational components" of organization means and designs. The intellectual fusion of elements of certainty (empirically real aspects) with elements of uncertainty (value-relevance), which are complex and infinite, is to incite anxiety for practitioners of positivist methodology.

Weber insisted that a value element inevitably entered into the selection of the problem an investigator chooses to attack; that there are no intrinsically scientific criteria for the selection of topics; the choice of subject matter or, more specifically, of the problem under analysis is not a value judgment (approval or disapproval of the chosen problem) but, rather, one's value orientation determines the questions one puts to reality. As Freund (1972, p. 54) suggests:

> Value orientation represents that arbitrary moment which precedes all scientific work and represents the limits of selection within which the scientist applies the regular procedures of investigation. . . . Differences in value orientation conditions the *points of view* from which reality can be examined. . . . Given the extensive and intensive infinity of empirical reality which no science can encompass, value orientation is seen to be that principle of selection which is the precondition for at least partial knowledge . . . it is the subjective factor which enables a scientist to acquire limited objective knowledge, *always provided that he is conscious of this inevitable limitation.* (italics added)

Freund (1972, pp. 55–56) goes on to provide a description of the role of value-orientation in scientific inquiry. All science proceeds by means of interpretation, the relativity of value orientations leading to different cognitive choices having nothing to do with questions of scientific validity. The uncertain, relative value-orientation which combines concrete empirical elements with unreal phenomena provides an imaginary picture of objectively possible action. The ideal type, critically contingent upon value-orientation, is not an empirical model or, in administrative studies, a conceptual approximation of formal organization. It is a statement of objective possibility about the organization phenomena under observation, purposeful or goal-oriented rational action.

To the extent that the ideal type combines aspects of the actual situation with abstractions, it creates the "mentally visual" means by which reasoned probabilities can be assigned to causal significance. For Weber, the function of the ideal type, as Shils and Finch (1949, p. 50) argue, "is a matter of constructing relationships which our imagination accepts as plausibly motivated and hence 'objectively possible' and which appear as adequate from the nomological standpoint."

In summary, an ideal type consists of a provisional synthesis of one's ideas about the nature of the phenomena under investigation and of the factors or variables appearing to be determinative of its character. An ideal type facilitates the task of comparison by isolating configurations of factors presumed salient to the purposes in hand. Simultaneously, then, factors are isolated for precise description and the analysis of possible relationships with other factors. For Freund (1972, p. 73), "in order to penetrate the real causal relationships we construct unreal ones."

It is in the context of positivist methodology, in which value-orientations are hidden, that the significant source of misunderstanding between Weber and the critics of his methodology can be framed: "The role of the category of objective possibility is thus not to form judgements as to the *necessary sequence of events* but to *weigh the significance* of the various causes of an event" (Freund, 1972, p. 76). Herein lies the methodological tension between description and evaluation, between the empirical and evaluative dimensions, that has plagued the analysis of formal organizations since Weber, and which has characteristically resulted in analysis of formal organizations in overtly empirical terms, ignoring the value-orientation of rationality that was so important for Weber.

The slide from value relevance to value neutrality in positivist sociological analysis of formal organizations, for whatever reason, has had the consequence, as in more managerial analyses of the productive enterprise,

> of taking "efficiency" as the problem and concentrating on explaining why organisations were or were not satisfying their goals. The content of this advice centred around areas which were readily comprehensible to them (leaders of enterprises)—formal organisational structure and the utilization of human and mechanical resources. (Silverman, 1970, p. 26)

In this way organization studies since Weber have tended predominantly toward a pronounced empirical character in which the focus of attention is not on the connection between organizations and the wider environment of the organization, but on the focal organization itself. As Mouzelis (1967, p. 49) says:

> Weber did not use the concept of bureaucracy for a microanalysis of the internal structure of an organisation. He used it in his cross-cultural general analysis, mainly in order to distinguish various types of *domination* and their corresponding administrative apparatus. (italics added)

Mouzelis's term "domination" will however be questioned in what follows.

VI. PARSONIAN MISAPPROPRIATION OF *HERRSCHAFT* AS *IMPERATIVE* CONTROL

Seminal thinkers, such as Weber, are typically at the confluence of the social thought and debates of their times. The very richness of their reflections makes them susceptible to contraction by lesser and simplifying minds. It is also the fate of seminal thinkers to be translated into numerous languages, well or poorly, and to be misinterpreted in various academic disciplines for diverse and perhaps nefarious purposes. In organization studies this has often meant that Weber's utilizers have felt free to wrest his ideal typical concepts from the matrix in which he located them and to deploy them for whatever institutional, commercial or other overextended purposes "felt good at the time." As we have seen, Weber has had to endure much at the hands of derivative and attenuated interpretation in college management texts. This wresting is acutely important when Weber is assimilated to the thought of a landmark theorist, such as Talcott Parsons. One particularly significant rendering of Weber in both translation and interpretation was that of Talcott Parsons who, at one time, was almost a monopolistic purveyor of Weber to a North American scholarly community; Weber's major oeuvres were not even "narrowcast" till the end of the Second World War even in English translation (Parsons and Henderson [1947a] chiefly) and still less available in the original German.

This fact made Weber susceptible to, perhaps innocent, ideological misappropriation by many Anglo-American writers on management and organization theory who accepted apparently plain English meanings for terms like *ideal type* when the German of Weber's time and matrix of his sociological and philosophical preoccupations might have suggested other connotations for the term. It has already been noted that North American college texts in management (and English and Australian versions of them) are replete with "ideal" as referring to a pattern of excellence, and, in the case of the rational-legal type of "authority," as a paragon or model of efficiency to be utilized in certain circumstances. But even the word frequently translated "authority" (*Herrschaft*) may be susceptible to innocent misappropriation. So the question of translation, and hence of understanding Weber's analytical intentions, is signally important to the illicitly overextended deployment of his concepts in management and organization thought. Weber's reflections on the rational-legal type of governance (*Herrschaft*) are delivered in a context of conceptual clarification of power relationships and governance and not, as commonly interpreted in college texts, as if they were an *Urquelle* on management theory and pragmatic management consultancy.

Hamilton (1983, p. 8), in a generally sympathetic overview of Parsons' work, remarks of one aspect of Parson's thought that "in terms borrowed from the philosophy of science, Parsonian systems theory appears now as an overturned *paradigm*, ousted from the centre of the sociological stage." Johnson's *Foreword* to Bourricaud (1984, p. vii) would see this announcement of Parsonian systems' demise as premature, and a number of influential others have developed a rapprochement with Parsonian structural systems (Habermas, 1987) or provide a contemporary elaboration of functionalism (Luhmann, 1982—Luhmann was a former student of Parsons but also, it must be said, critical of Parsons' action theory).

Bourricaud (1984, p. 1) claims that "central to Parsons' work is the aim—which, I might add, is not a simple one—of combining two intuitions of society, one 'active,' the other 'systemic'." Hamilton (1983, p. 80) notes that, throughout Parsons' *The Structure of Social Action* (first published in 1937) "the centrality of the concept of system is reiterated." Indeed Hamilton (1983, p. 83) further notes that the general analytical theory elaborated in *The Structure of Social Action* is gradually extended to embrace two main types of concept—social structure and function—and that "both elements were implicated in Parsons' initial elaboration of a voluntaristic theory of action and especially in his analysis of the theories of Weber and Durkheim."

It is this latter observation which is of concern here. Did Parsons (1937) assimilate Weber to his voluntaristic theory of action in particular ways that remain concealed in idiosyncratic translation of Weber? Have German terms like *Herrschaft* been abstracted from a Weberian matrix and replanted in a Parsonian one?

In what follows the term *Herrschaft* in Parsonian Weber is considered. Even careful but mistaken Parsonian scholarship can channel assumptions in subsequent management thought. Assumptions buried in the Parsonian translation of Weber and in his critical notes to English editions may lend immortality to Parsons's notions of social structure and function.

The German language, among Indo-European languages, is unquestionably a subtle one; terms accumulate meanings, connotations, nuances deriving from the period and in relation to the problematics in which they are employed. The accretion occurs not merely in an intellectual, logical, or conscious way but in an affect-laden, moral, evaluative, and ideological one. Terms like *Herrschaft* have a long and rich history stemming from medieval times. Its etymology points to a root meaning of *lordship*, equally rich in meaning and nuance in the English language. The term *Herrschaft* in Weber may well have been chosen by him for its capacity to carry meanings by its context or situatedness since his utilizing of the term ranges from methodological treatment (Roth and Wittich, 1978, chapter 1) to bureaucracy and society (chapter XI), to comparative cultural studies, including also the study of the city (chapter XVI).

As one might reasonably expect, Parsons appears to have translated those parts of Weber's *Economy and Society* that met his most immediate and later needs for social action theory. Chapter 1 in Weber (Roth and Wittich, 1978) is one that addresses basic conceptual and methodological issues and one that Parsons translated but whose critical notes were employed in Roth and Wittich's (1978) edition of *Economy and Society*, as well as for chapters 2 and 3. Roth and Wittich (1978, p. xxxii) note that "the broadest contribution to the reception of Weber's thought has clearly been made by Talcott Parsons' translation and writing." And Roth and

Wittich is still the most comprehensive English edition of Weber's major work. The possibility of a Parsonian hegemony among English-language-only readers is thus at least enhanced.

In Roth and Wittich (1978, p. 61) Parsons notes that *Herrschaft* has no satisfactory English equivalent but opts for a reading from Timasheff (1976) of "imperative control" which he claims, without any further justification, is close to Weber's meaning [14]. This rendering clearly bears a value-loading needing justification. An etymologically bland translation of *Herrschaft* (and, therefore, more generally useful) might have been "governance" or "rule," since even "lordship" in English has a somewhat antique flavor which projects the reader into a seigneural past. This rendering by Parsons as "imperative control" will clearly not satisfy other contexts (Roth and Wittich, 1978, chapter XVI on the city) in which Weber speaks of nonlegitimate governance (*nichtlegitime Herrschaft*) [15]. The choice of "imperative control" as the translation is odd unless Parsons is assimilating Weber to purposes of his own other than Weber may have intended. Parsons is at least ingenuous in asserting that he borrowed Timasheff's term in translation "for the most general purposes" (Roth and Wittich, 1978, p. 61).

But Parsons observes, in the same critical apparatus, that he later preferred the term "leadership." *Herrschaft* can quite legitimately be translated, according to context, dominion, mastery, control, power, government or governance, sovereign authority, command; manor, estate, domain; master and mistress, employers (of servants); person(s) of rank (Betteridge, 1957). This rich range of meanings suggests of course the various periods and contexts in which it has acquired its nuances. "Leadership," might, however, for general purposes, be more usually rendered by *Führerschaft* or *Leitung*.

Parsons then continues, "For more specific purposes . . . he used the term 'authority' " (Roth and Wittich, 1978, p. 61). Again, one should observe that Parsons is quite accurate in noting that, in Weber's German text, *Herrschaft* is followed by a then colloquial term (*Autorität*), but the subtlety of Weber's use of terms (borrowed from other languages) like *Autorität*, and *chance* appears lost on Parsons. As Roth notes, Weber's work "is full of irony, sarcasm, and the love of paradox; a deadpan expression may imply a swipe at the Kaiser, status-conscious professors or pretentious litterateurs" (Roth and Wittich, 1978, p. xxxiv). Weber appears to have used borrowed sociological terms when he was attempting to distance himself from terms conveying conventional understandings.

The assimilation of Weber of Parsons appears in the following critical apparatus of Parsons (Roth and Wittich, 1978, p. 61):

> In objecting to domination (as a translation of *Herrschaft*) . . . Parsons noted: It is true to be sure that the term *Herrschaft*, which in its most general meaning I should now translate as *leadership*, implies that a leader has power over his followers. But *domination* suggests that this fact, rather than the integration of the collectivity, in the interest of effective functioning (especially the integration of the crucial *Verband* or corporate group), is the critical factor from Weber's point of view. I do not believe that the former interpretation represents the main trend of Weber's thought. . . . The preferable interpretation, as I see it, is represented especially by his tremendous emphasis on the importance of legitimation. I should therefore wish to stick to my own decision to translate *legitime Herrschaft*, which for Weber was overwhelmingly the most significant case for general structural analysis, as authority (underlining added for emphasis, italics in original)

In this citation one can see the emergence at an early date in Parsons's scholarly work of the interest-driven, ideological suborning of the term *Herrschaft* to Parsons's integration of the social system which lies at the heart of his AGIL schema (that is, adaptation, goal attainment, integration, and latency) and which is reproduced in very similar terms in Parsons's joint work with Bales (1953: p. 64, in Bourricaud, 1984, pp. 85–86). For the reader's convenience, Bales's (1953) work is cited next so a comparison can be made with Parsons's preceding critical note:

> Such a system would have four main "functional problems" which were described, respectively, as those of adaptation to conditions of external situation, of instrumental control over parts of the situation in the performance of goal-oriented tasks, of the management and expression of sentiments and tensions of the members, and of preserving the *social integration of members with each other as a solidary collectivity*' (italics added)

One notes the striking similarity of terminology in these two citations. Bourricaud (1984) notes that responsibility "for the *control* function is borne by the *leader* of the group" (Bourricaud, 1984, p. 86; italics added). One can perhaps see, then, why Parsons's erratic translation of *Herrschaft* focuses on "leadership" with its control connotation.

Parsons continues in the same critical apparatus, "Sociologically, a *Herrschaft* is a structure of superordination and subordination, of <u>leaders</u> and led, rulers and ruled; it is based on a variety of motives and of means of <u>enforcement</u>" (Parsons, in Roth and Wittich, 1978, p. 62; underlining added). Parsons's critical notes on this key term *Herrschaft* indicates not just the range of meanings which have accreted to *Herrschaft* in various historical and cultural contexts but more importantly the "rereading" of Weber that has occurred at Parsons's hands for purposes of his own theorizing.

When one turns to Weber's definitions of *Macht* (rendered as "power" in Parsons's translation) and *Herrschaft* (rendered as "domination" despite Parsons's earlier protestations) one sees how the subtlety of Weber is lost by Parsons's tortuous critical apparatus. The definitions are reproduced next, with Weber's (Roth and Wittich, 1978, p. 53) German terms in place:

> Power (*Macht*) is the probability (*Chance*) that one actor within a social relationship will be in a position to carry out his own will despite resistance, regardless of the basis on which this probability rests.
>
> Domination (*Herrschaft*) is the probability (*Chance*) that a command with a given specific content will be obeyed by a given group of persons [16].

Herrschaft and *Macht* are both defined in probability terms because they are, in Weber's social action frame, relational and the outcome of relational transactions. Weber might have used the conventional and, in statistical contexts, more familiar term *Wahrscheinlichkeit*, that is, "probability," but he preferred the then and still colloquial "chance," implying the less-deterministic notion, the gambling analogy, the throw of the dice. The term "domination," which implies to the contemporary reader a static, given superordinacy, is a most uncomfortable, not to say unlikely, translation of *Herrschaft*, which in Weber's whole discussion of social action depends on action as social "insofar as its subjective meaning takes account of the behaviour of others and is thereby oriented in its course" (Roth and Wittich, 1978, p. 4). The parties to the transaction are free to obey, and so put themselves in a relationship of subordinacy, or not, as they choose. It is not, as Parsons suggests (Roth and Wittich, 1978, p. 59), just a case of higher and lower degrees of calculable probability but the "chance," the mere prospect, that they may so orient themselves in their relationships. "Governance lies in the prospect that" would be a more open interpretation of the relationships which are subsequently dealt with by Weber in chapter 3 (Roth and Wittich, 1978).

It is this sort of ideological mistranslation and misappropriation of Weber by Parsons that has also tinctured the treatment of traditional, charismatic, and rational legal governance, especially as they are handled in chapter 3 (Roth and Wittich, 1978). But here again Parsons, translator, interpreter, and supplier of critical notes, anticipates his reader and imposes his own hegemonic understanding on Weber, an infinitely subtler and more original thinker [17].

VII. THE PARSONIAN RENDERING OF *KULTUR*—CULTURE OR CIVILIZATION?

Already highlighted are some mistranslations or misappropriations by Parsons of Weber's work. In Parsons's translation of the word *Kultur* one again encounters a distortion of the social and historical context in which the meaning of the term arises.

Beilharz, in his biographical overview of Max Weber, commences by asserting:

> Of all the classical social theorists, it is probably fair to say that none have suffered such distortion as Marx and Weber (though this transformation is also a broader trend, including Freud and Durkheim). Marx and Weber have been turned into apologists for the very phenomena which they set out to criticise. (Beilharz, 1991, p. 224)

The German *Kultur* can be translated either "culture" or "civilization." Parsons's rendering of the translation was a clear preference for the word "culture." Weber's work, translated as *The Theory of Social and Economic Organization*, was largely written in the years 1911 to 1913 and published in German in 1920. The translation into English by Henderson and Parsons was completed in the mid-1940s and first published in 1947. At about the time Weber was working on this volume, Sigmund Freud was reflecting upon the development of civilization; 1908 saw the publication of *Die 'Kulturelle' Sexualmoral und Die Moderne Nervosität* (translated by Herford and Mayne, in 1924, as *"Civilized" Sexual Morality and Modern Nervous Illness*). He was later to take the central theme of that work—the antagonism between the demands of instinct and the restrictions of civilization—and consolidate it in a volume entitled *Das Unbehagen in Der Kultur*, translated by Joan Rivière into English and titled *Civilization and Its Discontents* (Freud, 1930). This dynamic and dialectical interplay is missing in the Parsonian treatment of culture as normative and essentially unitary.

Freud was knowledgeable and conversant in English (Gay, 1988, pp. 166, 325, 388–389; Ornston, 1992, p. 207) and it was he who actually approved of the English title (see editors' note, Freud, 1930). In *The Future of an Illusion*, Freud (1985a), in midsentence, indicates an awareness of the translation of the term *Kultur*: "Human civilization, by which I mean all those respects in which human life has raised itself above its animal status and differs from the life of beasts—and I scorn to distinguish between culture and civilization—, presents, as we know, two aspects to the observer" (Freud, 1985a, p. 184). This comment made, the editors in their preface to this work refer to "the tiresome problem of the proper translation of the German word *Kultur*" and announce that "we have usually, but not invariably, chosen *civilization* for the noun and *cultural* for the adjective" (editors' note, Freud, 1985a, p. 181). The distinction for Freud was not of great consequence because, underpinning his use of the term *Kultur*, often embedded in the same paragraph, and certainly reflected in the work as a whole, was an explication that made it clear that the term reflected a *process*. In *Why War* (1985c), an exchange of correspondence between Einstein and Freud, Freud asserts:

> For incalculable ages mankind has been passing through a process of evolution of culture (some people, I know prefer to use the term civilization). We owe to that process the best of what we have become, as well as a good part of what we suffer from.... The *psychial* modifications that go along with the process of civilization ... (Freud, 1985c, p. 361)

The editors, in their preface to the reprint of this correspondence, draw the readers' attention to what they viewed as an important issue: "Particular interest attaches to some further development here of Freud's view of civilization as a 'process', which had been brought up by him at several points in the latter work" (editors' note, Freud, 1985c, p. 344).

This emphasis by Freud upon civilization as a process is central to his conception of how the dynamics involved in civilization are really the same dynamics involved in the three provinces of the mind, only on a larger scale:

> I perceive even more clearly that the events of human history, the interactions between human nature, cultural development and the precipitates of primeval experiences are no more than a reflection of the dynamic conflicts between the ego, the id and the super-ego, which psychoanalysis studies in the individual-are the very same processes repeated upon a wider stage. (Freud, 1986, p. 257)

It was this parallel relational dynamic that led Freud to suggest, in both *The Future of an Illusion* (Freud, 1985a, p. 226) and *Civilization and Its Discontents* (Freud, 1985b, p. 338), that the elements of civilization may be open to psychoanalytic reflection. Could, he asked, "some epochs of civilization—possibly the whole of mankind—have become neurotic? An analytic dissection of such neuroses might lead to therapeutic recommendations" (Freud, 1985b, p. 338).

The distinction between the terms "culture" and "civilization" has, at different times, been seen as of great consequence, and even politicized. During the Second World War, Hitler referred to the French as having civilization but not culture—the term "civilization" being used in a pejorative sense and the term "culture" as unambiguously good at a moment in history. One dictionary defines civilization as including "the act of civilizing or the process of becoming civilized," whereas it defines culture as "a specific stage in the development of a civilization" and "the condition thus produced" (Funk and Wagnall, 1985, pp. 115, 155). Parsons's rendering of the term *Kultur* as "culture" rather than "civilization" is really to make it an *object*—a reification that gives an impression of a state of existence that can be taken as a given and treated in a positivistic manner. This would not have been Weber's intention, as we will now argue.

Weber is rendered by Parsons as advocating that, in order to understand self and society, one must understand the individual—in particular the subjective meanings that appear "adequate" to the individual (Weber, 1947a, pp. 88–110; Greenfield, 1979, p. 102). Thus the tasks of sociology are "interpretation" of human meanings and showing how these meanings are derived and their consequences for the individual and for others. This point is well captured in a later published work in which Weber argues:

> Interpretive sociology considers the individual and his action as the basic unit, as its "atom".... In this approach, the individual is also the upper limit and the sole carrier of meaningful conduct.... In general, for sociology such concepts as "state," "association," "feudalism," and the like, designate certain categories of human interaction. Hence it is the task of sociology to reduce these concepts to "understandable" action, that is, without exception, to the actions of participating individual men. (Weber, 1958, p. 55)

The irony is that Parson engorges Weber's warning against an organic analogy in relation to society, using his own functional terminology:

> This functional frame of reference is convenient for purposes of practical illustration and for provisional orientation . . . at the same time, if its cognitive value is overestimated and its concepts illegitimately reified it can be highly dangerous. (Weber, 1947a, p. 103)

The non-determinate and asymmetrical social relationships has been noted by other writers who have addressed themselves to Weber's work. Silverman, for example, asserts:

> Weber had already noted, many years previously, that in social relationships the parties may (and to some extent always do) attach different meaning to their interaction. . . . It is certainly true that interaction may involve shared values (Weber gives the example of a father-child relationship), but very frequently the meanings involved may not be shared and the relationship will then be, as he puts it, "asymmetrical." (Silverman, 1970, p. 137)

Silverman, in a footnote, continues with his analysis of Weber's "asymmetrical" notion, drawing the readers' attention to key passages of Weber:

> The subjective meaning, Weber notes, need not necessarily be the same for all the parties who are mutually oriented in a given social relationship. . . . "Friendship," "love," "loyalty," "fidelity to contracts," "patriotism," on one side, may well be faced with an entirely different attitude on the other. In such cases the parties associate different meanings with their actions and the social relationship is insofar objectively "asymmetrical" from the points of view of the two parties. . . . A social relationship in which the attitudes are completely and fully corresponding is in reality a limiting case. (Silverman 1970, p. 145; quotes from Weber 1947a, p. 119)

It would seem that Parsons chose to render *Kultur* in Weber as "culture," because such a rendering was no doubt more in keeping with Parsons's functionalist emphasis and "need" in that context, for the "abstraction of the individual and the translation from person into 'action' " (Carr, 1989, p. 24; Carr, 1992, p. 11). To be able to reify intention, interaction, and meaning as social facts—a state of being—enables Parsons to ascribe conformity and predictability to the individual as a integrated component or "unit" of a social system. Silverman (1970) also notes this hyperintegration when he argues:

> Parsons may, therefore, be criticised for having adopted a "over-socialised conception of man" which overlooks the fact that role-expectations are not just given by society but arise from and depend upon on-going human interaction. Social order is, therefore, problematic. A more complete analysis would need to take account of the range of motives underlying conformity to the expectations of others, and to pay attention to the possible role of coercion in imposing a normative definition of the situation on others. (Silverman, 1970, p. 137)

Schmid (1992) notes that Parsons's conceptualization of culture is posited on the assumption that culture can be regarded as a logically and semantically consistent system; that social order and solidarity will immediately occur if the rules of symbolic usage are consistently formulated and shared by all actors; that Parsons cannot, because of his functionalist stance, conceive of the cultural code (rules and standards) as functioning without its being consistent and mutually shared; that the commonality of consistent collective (cultural) symbols suffices to ensure societal solidarity. Indeed, Atkinson similarly notes "Parsons' struggle to suppress the Weberian formulation of social action, the principle of subjectivity entailed in it, and that margin of 'choice' which he allowed in his earliest work" (Atkinson, 1971, p. 36). Parsons was effectively putting forward a view *about* human agency but not *of* human agency (Carr, 1989, p. 2), turning a *process* into an *object*. Adorno, in proposing his thesis to understand how it is that the individual responds to society, one must draw insights from both psychology and sociology, singles out Parsons's understanding (or lack of understanding) of psychoanalysis as an example of a "primitive notion of a single universal science" (Adorno, 1967, p. 69; see also Parsons, 1950; and Adorno, 1968). He then asserts:

> While Parsons . . . discerns the inadequacy of many of the usual psychological explanations of societal phenomena, he does not suspect behind this incompatibility any real clash between the universal and the particular, any incommensurability between the objective life-process, the "in itself" and the individual that is merely "for himself." (Adorno, 1967, p. 69)

The denial of the more interactive formation of the individual as social being in Weber's work left Parsons with a problem. Wright Mills's celebrated paraphrase of Parsons's work *The Social System* (1951), which was published shortly after Parsons's translation of Weber, encapsulates Parsons's incapacities:

> There are "social regularities," which we may observe and which are often quite durable. Such enduring and stable regularities I shall call "structural." It is possible to think of all these regularities within the social system as a great and intricate balance. That this is a metaphor I am now going to forget, because I want you to take as very real my concept: The social equilibrium. . . .
>
> One point does puzzle me a little: given this social equilibrium, and all the socialization and control that man it, how is it possible that anyone should ever get out of line? This I cannot explain very well, that is, in the terms of my Systematic and General Theory of the social system. And there is another point that is not as clear as I should like it to be: how should I account for social change—that is for history? About these two problems, I recommend that whenever you come upon them, you undertake empirical investigations. (Wright Mills, 1959, p. 32–33)

The irony is that, if Parsons had truly sought to understand the manner in which Weber used the term *Kultur*, then Parsons himself would have been less puzzled by the conceptual holes in his own notion of "the social system"!

VIII. CONCLUSION

The scope and richness of Weber's endeavors, and the brokenness too of his academic career, have left a legacy that will be variously interpreted to the continual enriching of the sociological tradition. There is no argument with that. The plea to be entered is that Weber be approached with some greater sensitivity to his sociological purposes, and to the subtlety of his Germanic philosophic and linguistic tradition. He has been misappropriated by monolingual positivists hell-bent on rendering him into the archetypal management consultant, and mistranslated and misread by landmark theorists driven by grand, overarching designs of their own.

Organization-design prescriptivists should pursue legitimacy without wantonly adulterating Weber. Perhaps then Weber's interpretive legacy can be freed to be explored without ethnocentric pragmatism obscuring his insight. Perhaps too organization theory and even the understanding of the bureaucratic imperative might be enhanced (Ritzer, 1975; Satow, 1975)!

NOTES

1. The authors gratefully acknowledge the analysis of university texts by Nicholas Scott in a previous paper by Leivesley, Scott and Kouzmin, published as 'Australian Organisation Theory: A Garbage Can?' in Kouzmin and Scott (1990, pp. 367–391). The authors also wish to thank Hortense Klein, Ph.D. candidate at the Hochschule für Verwaltungswissenschaften Speyer, for her valuable comments and suggestions on an earlier draft of this paper.
2. Parsons has rendered Weber's *Ein stahlhartes Gehäuse* (Weber, 1947, p. 203) inadequately as 'iron cage' (Weber, 1948, p. 181). It is better rendered 'a steel-hard casing,' or, as Mitzman says, 'housing hard as steel' (Mitzman, 1970, p. 172), since the German has a significance beyond the phrase 'iron cage' used by Parsons. The original reference is to the reified institutional cosmos evolved from puritan voluntary asceticism. Weber elsewhere refers to *Gehäuse der Hörigkeit* which Swingewood, after Parsons, renders loosely as 'iron cage of bondage' (Mitzman, 1970, p. 188).
3. This is no historicist quibble, but a deliberate attempt to preserve sociological insight against ill-founded reinterpretation and prescription which work to the detriment of both scholarship and teaching.
4. It should not pass unobserved that Gulick's famous acronym POSDCORB occurs in a passage headed "Organizing the Executive," which proceeds to examine the "executive function." Gulick continues, "This brings us directly to the question, 'What is the work of the chief executive? What does he do?' " (1973, pp. 12–13). Barnard's work (1938) is oriented to show that the work of the executive goes far beyond the cycle of activities encompassed by that acronym.
5. No doubt referring to those American sociologists discussed in the first part of this section, from whom Weber might wish to dissociate because of their misinterpretation of his concepts.
6. Wren (1972, pp. 279–280) characterizes the Hawthorne findings as a remarkable illustration of the principle of serendipity.
7. Readers will recall Albrow's discussion (1970, pp. 61–66) of the care Weber took not to be misunderstood on the distinction he was making between rationality and efficiency.
8. In Weber's German, the term *Idealtypus* leaves scant room for such misinterpretation.
9. Even this attempt at explanation does not bear rigorous scrutiny in terms of the literature on the concept of *ideal type*.
10. One is constrained to point out that Robey is here stretching Plato's concept of "forms" (Taylor, 1952), which is by no means the same as Weber's ideal type.
11. The authors have taken the liberty of suggesting a title for this mythical work. Such a Ruhr-ideal could be listed as Weber, Maximilian (1928), *Ein Elementarbuch für deutsche Industrielle*, Stahlmann and Bauer, Mönchen-Gladbach.
12. Might one not also find here an echo of Urwick's (1947, p. 126) enthusiasm for Taylor, Gantt, and Gilbreth as "the three points of the triangular foundation on which the full science of management was built?"
13. Even centralization they might perhaps have drawn from him, under its Weberian form of hierarchy, but they preferred to attribute it to Fayol (Pugh and Hickson, 1968, pp. 375–376).
14. Timasheff (1976) actually employs the term "imperative co-ordination." But no doubt "control" suits Parsons's purposes in this context better.

15. Wittich (Roth and Wittich, 1978, p. 1234) notes that *nichtlegitime Herrschaft* refers to what was for Weber the decisive feature of the Occidental city "its breach with the ruler's traditional legitimacy, and the substitution of Herrschaft based on various types of usurpatory consociations of the *ruled.*" It is interesting that Wittich, uses "ruler" and "ruled" quite comfortably in this context also. "Governance" or "rule" is a general-purpose rendering and one consistent with Weber's purposes.
16. One should consult Winckelmann's (1976) definitive critical editing, commentary, and textual notes; see Weber (1976a, 1976b).
17. Scaff (1989 pp. ix–x) notes: "I began to doubt that the 'social science' of our own age, either in form or content, had much to do with Weber's version of *Wissenschaft* or with the problems *he* had in mind. It appeared that even our best authorities had put together a peculiarly domesticated rendition of his ideas. (The outstanding case in point is surely Talcott Parsons, a 'theorist' who violated Weber's most cherished views about 'theory', while nevertheless claiming the Weberian patrimony as his own.) . . . My interest, then, is in that 'other' Weber, the man we have known . . ."

REFERENCES

Adorno, T., Sociology and Psychology, Part 1 *New Left Review*, 46:79–96 (1967).

Adorno, T., Sociology and Psychology, Part 2, *New Left Review*, 47:67–80 (1968).

Albrow, M., *Bureaucracy*, Macmillan, London, 1970.

Aron, R., *Main Currents in Sociological Thought*, vol. 2, Basic Books, New York, 1967.

Atkinson, D., *Orthodox Consensus and Radical Alternative*, Heinemann Books, London, 1971.

Bailey, J. E., Schermerhorn, J. R., Hunt, J. G., and Osborn, R. N., *Managing Organizational Behavior in Australia*, Wiley, Brisbane, 1986.

Bales, R. F., The Dimensions of Action-Space, in *Working Papers in the Theory of Action*, Free Press, Glencoe, Ill., 1953.

Banfield, E. C., The Decision Making Schema, *Public Administration Review* 17(4), 278–285 (1957).

Barnard, C., *The Functions of the Executive*, Harvard University Press, Cambridge, Mass., 1938.

Beilharz, D., Max Weber, in *Social Theory: A Guide to Central Thinkers* (P. Beilharz, ed.), Allen and Unwin, Sydney, 1991, pp. 224–230.

Bendix, R. and Roth, G. *Scholarship and Partisanship*, University of California Press, Berkeley, 1980.

Betteridge, H. T., *Cassell's New German Dictionary*, Cassell and Company, London, 1957.

Blau, P. M. and Scott, W. R., *Formal Organizations: A Comparative Approach*, Routledge and Kegan Paul, London, 1963.

Bourricaud, F., *The Sociology of Talcott Parsons* (trans. A. Goldhammer, Foreword by H. M. Johnson) University of Chicago, Chicago, 1984.

Campbell, T., *Seven Theories of Human Society*, Clarendon Press, Oxford, 1981.

Carr, A., *Organisational Psychology: Its Origins, Assumptions and Implications for Educational Administration*, Deakin University Press, Geelong, Victoria, 1989.

Carr, A., Towards an Indigenous View of School Administration, *The Australian Administrator*, 13(3 and 4):1–9 (1992).

Coser, L. A., *Masters of Sociological Thought: Ideas in Historical and Social Context*, Harcourt Brace Jovanovich, New York, 1971.

Daft, R. L., *Organization and Management*, Prentice-Hall, Englewood Cliffs, N.J., 1986.

Delany, W., The Development and Decline of Patrimonial and Bureaucratic Administrations, *Administrative Science Quarterly*, 7(1), March: 458–501 (1963).

Dessler, G., *Organization and Management*, Prentice-Hall, Englewood Cliffs, N.J., 1976.

Dessler, G., *Organisation Theory: Integrating Structure and Behavior*, Prentice-Hall, Englewood Cliffs, N.J., 1980.

Donaldson, L., *In Defence of Organization Theory*, Cambridge University Press, Cambridge, 1985.

Dostoevsky, F. M., *The Brothers Karamazov*, Progress Publishers, Moscow, 1963.
Friedrich, C. J., Organizational Theory and Political Style, *Public Policy*, 10:44–46 (1960).
Friedrich, C. J., *Man and His Government: An Empirical Study of Politics*, McGraw-Hill, New York, 1973.
Freud, S., Die "Kulturelle" Sexualmoral Und Die Moderne Nervosität, *Sexual-Probleme*, 4(3) (March): 107–129 (1908). (The English translation of this paper appears in S. Freud, *Civilization, Society and Religion*, vol. 12, Pelican Freud Library, 1985, pp. 33–55).
Freud, S., *Civilization and Its Discontents* (trans. J. Riviere), Hogarth Press and the Institute of Psycho-Analysis, London, 1930.
Freud, S., The Future of an Illusion, in *Civilization, Society and Religion*, vol. 12, Pelican Freud Library, 1985a, pp. 183–241.
Freud, S., Civilization and its Discontents, in *Civilization, Society and Religion*, vol. 12, Pelican Freud Library, 1985b, pp. 243–340.
Freud, S., Why War, in *Civilization, Society and Religion*, vol. 12, Pelican Freud Library, 1985c, pp. 345–362.
Freud, S., An Autobiographical Study: Postscript, in *Historical and Expository Works on Psychoanalysis*, vol. 15, Pelican Freud Library, 1986, pp. 256–259.
Freund, J., *The Sociology of Max Weber*, Penguin, Harmondsworth, 1972.
Funk and Wagnall, *Standard Dictionary*, vol 1, Harper and Row, New York, 1985.
Gay, P., *Freud: A Life for Our Time*, Macmillan, London, 1988.
Georgiou, P., Weber's Ideal Type of Bureaucracy and Its Critics, *Melbourne Journal of Politics*, 1:22–28 (1968).
Georgiou, P., Weber's Ideal Type of Bureaucracy and Its Critics, in *Public Policy and Administration in Australia: A Reader* (R. N. Spann and G. R. Curnow, eds.), Wiley, Sydney, 1975, pp. 291–310.
Gerth, H. H. and Wright Mills, C., eds., *From Max Weber: Essays in Sociology*, Routledge and Kegan Paul, London, 1948.
Gouldner, A. W., *Patterns of Industrial Bureaucracy*, Free Press, New York, 1954.
Greenfield, T., Organisation Theory as Ideology, *Curriculum Inquiry*, 9(2): 97–112 (1979).
Gulick, L., Notes on the Theory of Organization: With Special Reference to Government in the United States, in *Papers on The Science of Administration* (L. Gulick and L. Urwick, eds.), A. M. Kelley, New York, 1973, pp. 1–45.
Habermas, J. *The Theory of Communicative Action—Systems and Lifeworld*, vol. 2, Beacon Press, Boston, 1987.
Hall, R. H., Intra-organizational Structure Variation: Application of the Bureaucratic Model, *Administrative Science Quarterly* 7 (3), September:295–308 (1962).
Hamilton, P., *Talcott Parsons*, Ellis Horwood, Chichester, 1983.
Hunt, J. W., *The Restless Organisation*, Wiley, Sydney, 1972.
Jellinek, G., *System der Subjektiven Öffentlichen Rechte* (as cited in Roth and Wittich, 1978, p. 659), 1892.
Jellinek, G., *Allegmeine Staatslehre*, 3rd ed., Hàring, Berlin, 1914.
Kouzmin, A., and Scott, N., *Dynamics in Australian Public Management: Selected Essays*, Macmillan, Melbourne, 1990.
Khandwalla, P. N., *The Digest of Organizations*, Harcourt Brace Jovanovich, New York, 1977.
Kübler, H., *Organization und Führung in Behörrden:- Band 1 Organisatorische Grundlagen* (4 Auflage), Verlag W. Kohlhammer, Stuttgart, 1980.
Lachman, L. M., *The Legacy of Max Weber*, Heinemann, London, 1972.
Leivesley, R., Scott, N., and Kouzmin, A., Australian Organisation Theory: A Garbage Can? *Dynamics in Australian Public Management: Selected Essays*, Macmillan, Melbourne, 1990, pp. 367–391.
Luhmann, N., *The Differentiation of Society* (trans. S. Holmes and C. Larmore), Columbia University Press, New York, 1982.
Mannheim, K., *Man and Society in an Age of Reconstruction*, Harcourt Brace Jovanovich, New York, 1951.
March, J. G. and Simon, H. A., *Organizations*, Wiley, New York, 1958.
Merton, R. K., Bureaucratic Structure and Personality, in *A Reader in Bureaucracy* (R. K. Merton et al., eds.), Free Press, New York, 1952, pp. 361–371.

Milton, C. R., Entrekin, L., and Stening, B. R., *Organizational Behaviour in Australia*, Prentice-Hall, Sydney, 1984.

Mitzman, A., *The Iron Cage*, Knopf, New York, 1970.

Mouzelis, N., *Organization and Bureaucracy: An Analysis of Modern Theories*, Routledge and Kegan Paul, London, 1967.

Ornston, D., ed., *Translating Freud*, Yale University Press, New Haven, Conn., 1992.

Parsons, T., *The Structure of Social Action*, vol. 1 and 2, Free Press, New York, 1937.

Parsons, T., Psychoanalysis and the Social Structure, *Psychoanalytic Quarterly*, 19(3):371–376 (1950).

Parsons, T., *The Social System*, Free Press, New York, 1951.

Pugh, D. S. and Hickson, D. J., The Comparative Study of Organisations, in *Industrial Society* (D. Pym, ed.), Penguin, Harmondsworth, 1968, pp. 374–396.

Pugh, D. S. and Hickson, D. J., *Organisational Structure in Its Context: The Aston Programme I*, Saxon House, Westmead, 1976.

Ritzer, R. M., Professionalization, Bureaucratization and Rationalization: The View of Max Weber, *Social Forces*, 53(4), June:627–634 (1975).

Robbins, S. P., *Organization Theory: The Structure and Design of Organizations*, Prentice-Hall, Englewood Cliffs, N.J., 1983.

Robey, D., *Designing Organizations*, Irwin, Illinois, 1986.

Roth, G. and Wittich, C., eds., *Max Weber: Economy and Society*, vols. 1 and 2, University of California Press, Berkeley, 1978, pp. 88–120 (1978).

Satow, R. L., Value Rational Authority and Professional Organizations: Weber's Missing Type, *Administrative Science Quarterly*, 20(4), December:526–531 (1975).

Scaff, L. A., *Fleeing the Iron Cage: Culture, Politics, and Modernity in the Thought of Max Weber*, University of California Press, Berkeley, 1989.

Schmid, M., The Concept of Culture and its Place Within a Theory of Social Action: A Critique of Talcott Parsons' Theory of Culture, in *Theory of Culture* (R. Münch and N. J. Smelser, eds.), University of California Press, Berkeley, 1992, pp. 88–120.

Selznick, P., *Leadership in Administration: A Sociological Interpretation*, Row Peterson, Evanston, 1957.

Selznick, P., *TVA and the Grass Roots*, University of California Press, Berkeley, 1965.

Shils, E. A. and Finch, H. A., *Max Weber on the Methodology of the Social Sciences*, Free Press, Glencoe, Ill., 1949.

Silverman, D., *The Theory of Organisations*, Heinemann, London, 1970.

Simon, H., *Administrative Behaviour*, Free Press, New York, 1976.

Skidmore, W., *Theoretical Thinking in Sociology*, Cambridge University Press, Cambridge, 1979.

Stoner, J. A. F., Collins, R. R., and Yetton, P. W., *Managing in Australia*, Prentice-Hall, Sydney, 1985.

Swingewood, A., *A Short History of Sociological Thought*, Macmillan, London, 1984.

Taylor, A. E., *Plato: The Man and His Work*, Methuen, London, 1952.

Thompson, J. D., *Organizations in Action: Social Sciences Bases of Administrative Theory*, McGraw-Hill, New York, 1967.

Timasheff, N. S., *An Introduction to the Sociology of the Law*, Greenwood Press, Westport, Conn., 1976.

Weber, M., *The Theory of Social and Economic Organization* (trans. A. Henderson and T. Parsons), Free Press, New York, 1947a.

Weber, M. *Gesammelte Aufsätze zur Religionssoziologie: 1* (4 Auflage), J. C. B. Mohr, Tübingen, 1947.

Weber, M., *The Protestant Ethic and the Spirit of Capitalism* (trans. T. Parsons and R. H. Towney) Unwin University Books, London, 1948.

Weber, M., *Gesammelte Aufsätze zur Wissenschaftslehre* (2nd ed. revised J. Winckelmann), J. C. B. Mohr, Tübingen, 1951.

Weber, M., *From Max Weber: Essays in Sociology* (trans. by H. Gerth and C. Wright Mills), Oxford, New York, 1958.

Weber, M., *Wirtschaft und Gesellschaft, Grundriss der Verstehenden Soziologie*, Fünfte Revidierte Auflage, Halbband I, II (Text Kritischen Erläuterungen herausgegeben von J. Winckelmann), J. C. B. Mohr, Tübingen, 1976a.

Weber, M., *Wirtschaft und Gesellschaft, Grundriss der Verstehenden Soziologie*, Fünfte Revidierte Auflage, Erläuterungsband von J. Winckelmann, J. C. B. Mohr, Tübingen, 1976b.
Wright Mills, C., *The Sociological Imagination*, Oxford Press, New York, 1959.

5
Getting at the Essence of the Administrative State

Gerald E. Caiden
University of Southern California, Los Angeles, California

Administration is the core of modern government.
—Carl Friedrich

Public administration to me is the study of the state in action, that is, the *administrative* state as contrasted with the political, economic, or social aspect of the state as institutionalized collective power. A theory of public administration would entail a theory of the administrative state, something more than a theory of government but less then a theory of collective action. More likely, it would be a refined theory of governance that would reach further back than the modern bureaucratic state, which is barely two hundred years old, that would be broader in scope than any idiosyncratic form of institutionalized collective power found in contemporary nation-states [1] and that would have to take into account the international superstructure that binds the community of nations into a real world network. Although this form of governance has been growing at an increasingly accelerating pace, particularly in the latter half of the twentieth century, there is still no global theory of the administrative state and few related to it, despite its obvious centrality in contemporary society and its clear staying power.

Could there be any universal elements on which a global theory of the administrative state could be based? In conducting research into administrative reform, I have been struck by universal ideas about the nature of public maladministration. Take this comment of the then–Prime Minister of India on December 28, 1985, in Bombay about his public bureaucracy:

> We have government servants who do not serve but oppress the poor and the helpless . . . who do not uphold the law . . . but connive with those who cheat the state and whole legions whose only concern is their private welfare at the cost of society. They have no work ethic, no feeling for the public cause, no involvement in the future of the nation, no comprehension of national goals, no commitment to the values of modern

> India. They have only a grasping mercenary outlook, devoid of competence, integrity and commitment. . . .

Clearly, he had in mind a picture of how public officials should behave, and that ideology of public service would be little different, one suspects, from codes of ethics for public employees paraded in many countries from one part of the world to another. Such public service norms would be the reverse of what Prime Minister Rajiv Gandhi was criticizing in India. From this, I conclude that it should be possible to generalize and theorize about the administrative state, a universal feature of modern governance, and elements of such a theory should be the basis on which a global theory of public administration could be constructed.

I have sought to identify such elements that are not time specific or culture bound, that are truly universal, and that are common throughout the world in all systems of governance. They had to be based on reality, that is, how public administrators think, behave, and act and how others view their conduct and disposition. At the same time, they had to reveal the de facto value base not found elsewhere and also the ideological foundations of public administration norms. They had also to cut across public professions, functions, and specialties. Despite such a demanding agenda, I claim to find at least twenty-five such elements or pieces of the much bigger puzzle. Some go back thousands of years. Notions of public trust and integrity, of public responsibility and accountability, predate the earliest recorded civilizations and the earliest surviving written records of public business. Others are relatively new and are very much contemporary concerns bolstered by the realization that the power of the administrative state is so enlarged that it can do both great good and great harm. A few are still evolving and are not yet fully articulated, let alone universally accepted. So what follows is very much a preliminary map; a rough, hasty, incomplete, and fuzzy sketch of the terrain that has to be traversed before a global theory of the administrative state and public administration can be formulated.

Work in these twenty-five fertile patches could in time combine several and link all. Some may be integrated; others may have to be split. There is no telling at this early stage what may develop. The aims of such an endeavor are clear: It is to ground public administration on a firm theoretical foundation, to establish its intellectual value, and to guide research. It is to help practitioners understand the ideological dimensions of their activities and to provide a clear value base with universal guidelines as to what is and is not permissible conduct. It is to provide a more concentrated focus to theoretical explorations in public administration and to link widely divergent public administration postulates. It is to go beyond the rather culture-bound limitations of previous attempts, such as the Blacksburg Manifesto, to unite theoretical endeavors that emphasize the positive side to collective action, government intervention, public entrepreneurship, and communal initiatives.

I. RAISING SIGHTS

Despite increasing internationalization of the world's economy, politics, and culture, the nation-state has more than held its own in this century against the battering of regionalism and supranationalism. The number of states has more than trebled and is likely to increase still further. Once again, the state as the major potent and autonomous organizational actor in contemporary society has become the focus of political analysis (Evans et al., 1985), and clearly the state in question is the administrative state, not so much Hobbes's tyrannical Leviathan or the heartless totalitarian state, but the caring, interventionalist welfare state, the *superfamilia* (Chodak, 1989) advancing the general interests of all members. This has all come about because of the global advances made in public policy and administration since 1789 when the new American Constitution and the French Revolution transformed public perceptions of society, government, and official public conduct and the bureaucratic revolution transformed the state's ability to harvest public resources and deliver public goods and services.

The discipline of public administration has concentrated on the emergence of the administrative state, virtually ignoring anything that preceded it. In the absence of global analysis, studies have been fragmented into the studies of individual or specific administrative states and the theories that have been developed have largely been and continue to be idiosyncratic. Since the field has been dominate by American scholars, what mostly is available are theories about public administration as practiced in the United States as if they were universal, whereas in fact the peculiarly American administrative state has little in common with public administration in other parts of the world. The field still resembles a Tower of Babel where scholars and practitioners bent on a common task speak different languages and have great difficulty in comprehending the grand design. Even current attempts to reformulate American public administration theory despite their recognition of the global nature of the field still tend to be insular and myopic (Goodsell, 1983; Rohr, 1986; Minnowbrook II, 1989; Wamsley, 1990; Kass and Catron, 1990; *International Journal of Public Administration*, 1990) as they update Dwight Waldo (Waldo, 1948) rather than Fritz Morstein Marx (Marx, 1957). They take the American scene (pluralism, capitalism, democracy, constitutionalism, rule of law, guaranteed basic human rights, administrative due process, public service, professionalism, and so on) too much for granted and assume all their readers are as familiar and versed in American public administration theory as they are, which is not the case.

Nowhere is this more apparent than in the struggle toward a valid theory of the administrative state. No universal theory exists. There are theories about the idiosyncratic forms that the administrative state has taken in particular countries, and there are theories about public administration or rather American public administration or Western-style public administration but little of global dimensions. Laments about the failure to construct a truly universal or international discipline go back at least fifty years (Dahl, 1947), but attempts by international agencies to impose universalistic doctrines have been thwarted time and time again by aid recipients as being culturally imperialistic, intellectually suspect, and operationally impractical. Perhaps this indiscipline has been fortunate in fostering originality and innovation, but in higher education cadres it has given the appearance of scholars who did not know what precisely they were about, unable to see the wood for the trees, and lacking academic class, and in the field it has divided practitioners from scholars, the former tending to see the latter as barely tolerable parasites and the latter tending to be frustrated at their remove from the cutting edge of action. Both sets have been carried away by fads and fancies, whim and chance, that have taken public administration first in one direction and then in another without any apparent logic or reason. Even the buzz words change rapidly. Of course, other social sciences suffer similar defects, but at least they do have a common core of universally recognized theory, a shared foundation which has stood the test of time and enabled them to progress intellectually. In contrast, the study of public administration seemingly stumbles along, largely descriptive, often polemical, less frequently analytical and introspective, rarely theoretical, "rather peripheral to the facts of political and administrative behavior, and to the forces which shaped social change" (Self, 1986a, p. 329), and proceeding "from order to chaos" (Lundquist, 1985). The fault is largely the failure to explore the essence of the administrative state.

To understand the administrative state does mean joining forces with political theorists who have been exploring the nature of the (political) state. For half a millennium, they have been clearing a track. They have described its origins and evolution, the different forms it has taken, the roles it has played, the powers accredited to it, its legitimacy, its employment by rulers and acknowledged authorities, its strengths and weaknesses, and even its psyche. It would take a lifetime to cover the literature on the subject, and still that survey would not be complete. Suffice to say that the state is not just a collection of governmental instruments or the institutionalization of collective decision making or the repository of the collective force of its citizens. It is more than its concrete manifestations. It embodies sets of abstractions concerning government, law, legislation, and law enforcement; concerning the legitimate use of coercion, power, authority, and persuasion; concerning social inequities, injustices, indecencies, indignities, and inhumanities; concerning the ambitions, dreams, desires, and ends of mankind; concerning human conduct, behavior, relations, and expectations. No wonder it means different things to different people and so much thinking about the state is embedded in ideology. It is a matter of belief whether the state is seen as being necessary at all, whether it is too big or too small, whether it is doing too much or not enough, whether it has too much or too little power, whether it is under too much or too little control, whether it is worthwhile and provides value for money or not.

Yet when it comes to the administrative state, that part of the state that is responsible for getting done what the state wants done, ideology and belief have taken a back seat. The proof has been in the doing, in the end product or outcome, in the results. What works has been recognized as an art form reducible to scientific study, bereft of subjectivity. It has all too glibly been assumed that public administrators have taken their cues from political actors and seen as their task the best (meaning most economical, productive, efficient, and effective) ways of getting done what they have been told has to be done. The real world has never been quite this simple. The public administrators have had their own beliefs, traditions, self-interests, and professional norms that have impacted not only how things have gotten done but what has been judged feasible to attempt, thwarting political intentions. Deep down, there has been a professional belief system or ideology governing the administrative state among its practitioners, rarely articulated. Indeed, one is struck by the remarkable absence of ideology at least overtly in the practice of public administration, how rarely ideology has contributed to its pragmatic development, and even theorists have shied away from ideological concerns. At least, the principal actors have taken pains to emphasize public policy needs and pragmatic considerations and to downplay any ideological foundations or implications.

Yet if one tries to get at the essence of the administrative state, one quickly becomes enmeshed in an ideological thicket. This is best seen in examining progress in theoretical building blocks or infrastructure for the edifice of the administrative state, each of which is capable of being universalized or globalized or internationalized.

A. A Theory of Collective Action and Human Organization

The administrative state constitutes possibly the largest organization in any country if one includes the whole machinery of government, together with public enterprises, military and police forces, parastatals and quasiautonomous nongovernmental organizations (QANGOs), official overseas representation, and neighborhood associations, however ill knit. This huge assembly constitutes collective action encountered primarily with public as opposed to private concerns. It forms part of the even greater entity of human organization and collective action that transcends the individual person which is so inclusive as to challenge generalization. Theories abound—indeed, so many that they defy simple classification. Attempts to integrate and consolidate them were evident in the early issues of *Administrative Science Quarterly* and Bertram

Gross's encyclopedic effort (Gross, 1964) after the *International Encyclopedia of the Social Sciences* had rather glossed over the subject even though the entry under "Organizations" was one of the longest. Since the 1960s, little attempt has been made to find a universal theory covering all human organizations and all collective nonprivate action. Theories in this area continue to proliferate, and they are expressed in increasingly obtuse and difficult language beyond the comprehension (and knowledge) of most practitioners.

B. A Theory of the Public Interest

The state, and certainly the administrative state, is to operate in pursuit of the common good, the general welfare, the overall quality of life for present and future generations, the collective realization of social values and rights: that is, those factors which affect all more or less equally and in the same way. For public administrators, it is a moral obligation to achieve what is good for society as a whole, not the welfare of any particular class including their own, "a good which enhances common life and is shared by all" (Cochrane, 1974, p. 330), not just the greatest good of the greatest number of the aggregation of individual and group interests. Plato and Aristotle were quite clear on this, as were the authors of *The Federalist Papers*. Echoes of this sentiment can be heard from the earliest days of recorded history in many diverse cultures. It remains a basic tenet of American public administration theory (Wamsley, 1990), despite its carping critics. It is the bureaucratic equivalent to exhortations to rulers to be just and to act justly, and needless to say it is a normative, ethical, and dynamic concept to guide practitioners in what they do and how they proceed.

C. A Theory of Bureaucracy

Since the predominant form of organization within the administrative state is bureaucracy, so an essential ingredient in understanding its essence is a theory of bureaucracy. For the past century that has meant Max Weber's theory of bureaucracy, which is timeless and universal, hardly surprising given its origins. But the Weberian model is incomplete, and ever since his work was translated from German, scholars have been busily filling in the gaps. Although it is not yet complete, this aspect of the administrative state is among the best understood and the most widely propagated. As a result, attention has switched to organizational alternatives to bureaucracy and the nonbureaucratic delivery of public goods and services.

D. A Theory of Public Trust, Responsibility, and Accountability

Because the administrative state was all too prone to misuse its authority and resources and to deviate from its pursuit of the public interest, so it cannot be trusted to be unsupervised; it has to be held publicly answerable for all its actions through external political, legal, hierarchical, and professional accountability, to which recently has been added moral accountability (Dwividi and Jabbra, 1988) and accountability for managing the diverse expectations generated within and outside public organizations (Romzek and Dubnick, 1987). In short, to be accountable is to answer for one's responsibility and for the trust reposed in one; to report, to explain, to give reasons, to respond, to assume obligations, to render a reckoning, and to submit to outside or external judgment. For too long, the debate between Carl Friedrich and Herman Finer in the early 1940s dominated theory in this area without being resolved while it became apparent that public officials could not be trusted to police themselves and public watchdogs were ill equipped to perform effectively. All measures are dumbfounded by political incompetents, corrupt officials, an authoritarian ethos, bureaucratic inertia, anonymity, and government that is unconstitutional, secret, special interest, bureaucratic, collaborative, discretionary, independent, contracted, professional, and privileged. None of this excuses any public official from being morally responsible "for an outcome insofar as (1) the official's actions or omissions are a cause of the outcome; and (2) these actions or omissions are not done in ignorance or under compulsion" (Thompson, 1980). And this is where theory stands with its obvious universal implications.

E. A Theory of Government Intervention and Regulation

The justification for the exercise of authority to protect people from others and themselves need not be repeated simply because the raison d'être of the state is grounded in its protection of its members from external attack and its maintenance of order. Nobody quite envisaged their evolution into the garrison state or warfare state or the police state or their assumption of totalitarianism and tyranny, and ever since the state has taken on these features, theorists have been keen to define limitations to state intervention and regulation and to justify revolts, that is, disobedience against intolerable interference with individual privacy. This in turn has led to disputes over what is *public* or rather what should be public. In pursuit of the general welfare, the administrative state has enlarged its functions from personal and group security and survival to concerns about food and water supplies, sanitation and sewerage, communications and trade routes to the provision of (full) employment, guaranteed safety nets, environmental protection, preservation, and equal opportunity. Indeed the administrative state has been asked to do so much that current fears are that it has been asked to do too much, that it is overloaded, that it has assumed functions it cannot perform at all or as well as other institutions, that it does not have the capacity to perform adequately: in short, that it should shed some of its activities, especially its commercial activities and possibly its underfinanced welfare activities and other "gray" areas of government which could be performed by the private sector and nongovernmental organizations.

While there are clear ideological motives related to the nature of capitalism, competition, private property, individualism, and markets, the growth of administrative state activities has been forced/argued by the logic of the situation, that is, sheer necessity or unavoidability due to the failure of private initiative and enterprise, natural calamities, population pressures, democratization, decline of religion, the nature of industrialization and urbanization. Similarly the shedding of state activities has ideological overtones, but it is largely being decided pragmatically with respect to the availability of alternative suppliers willing and able to assume cast-off state activities, cost-effectiveness, public funding, policy unevenness, and mismanagement. Often theory has followed practice very much as the state had to exist before the concept of the state could become accepted. So too it is likely that the administrative state has to be settled before theories about it are formulated. Right now, the boldest attempt to formulate such a theory after the fact is Chodak's study of the etatization of Western societies consisting

> of a complex intertwining of economic, organizational, social, value, and other changes advancing differently . . . but generating even more state control and regulation . . . a process in which growth, change, and multiplying interactions and conflicts are molded by the state's newer functions. (Chodak, 1989, p. 2)

Eight processes are discerned in etatization:

1. Multiplication of state functions
2. Monopoly control over economic management, education, and other selected areas of social activity

3. A new stage of social development: old and new interpretations of development
4. State responses to social and economic problems, including services for the populace at large and welfare systems for the needy and unemployable
5. Transformation of the stratification structure
6. Emergence of two-sector mixed economies and systems of direct and indirect regulatory practices
7. Spread of a bureaucratic mentality and appearance of a new double morality
8. Change in the conflict structure of society (Chodak, 1989, p. 13)

Chodak sees etatization as inevitable and predicts the eventual emerging of existing state models into a common administrative state model politically Left of today's Western societies but Right of Communist (or rather the former Communist) regimes. In it, all organizations will be public because they will be under public authority and within the reach of government interference but short of Orwellian totalitarianism, their purpose to free human energies, not restrict them, in the service of collective not individual ends. This is different from those who see government intervention as the result of interest groups' struggling among themselves to maximize the benefits of their members or the sheer irresistible dynamics of Keynesianism or the many failures of capitalism rather than political reaction to rapid technological, economic, and social changes (Self, 1986b), although Chodak tries to combine all these explanations.

F. A Theory of Public Policy

Public policy, like public administration, still lacks an all-encompassing theory per se and is the product of several different theoretical perspectives concerning the goals of state activities and efforts to develop knowledge relevant to public policy-making. In trying to provide a theoretical basis for the study of public policy, Yehezkel Dror identified many different models, including rational comprehensive theory, economic rational model, satisficing theory, sequential decision model, incremental model, systems theory, elitism, group theory, institutional model, optimal qualitative model, and extrarational model (Dror, 1968), all of which are oriented toward the improvement of policy-making, its outcomes and processes, its modes of inquiry and access to relevant information, its quality and efficacy, its responsiveness and morality. Clearly, there is such a need as etatization proceeds, and Dror has sketched out an optimal framework for the policy sciences that has still to be filled in. Its philosophical basis is largely neoutilitarian, scientism, and rationality, and it still leaves open several "metaproblems" (Nagel, 1989).

G. A Theory of Public Goods and Services

Although Adam Smith acknowledged the need for public goods and services, only in the 1950s was a structured theory formulated by Paul Samuelson based on Pareto optimality and market failure, and by Tiebout's case for local public goods (Batina, 1990, p. 389). Private goods were fully rival and excludable, whereas public goods were not. Nonexcludability was the crucial factor in determining which goods should be publicly provided. Then the public choice theorists explored "impure public goods," goods that were not public or private but characterized by excludable benefits which could be provided by nongovernmental suppliers if an exclusion mechanism could be installed at a reasonable price (Cornes and Sandler, 1986). This notion further expanded the list of public goods that could be privately provided. From a different direction, the externalities of social costs of private goods was expanded to market failure and public goods. Simply put, the mere existence of an externality was not sufficient cause for government intervention as bargaining or liability assignments could provide nongovernmental means for neutralizing externalities. Corrective means included private as well as governmental action. Furthermore, as governments could fail just as markets could, public goods and services should be competitively provided to prevent the pitfalls of monopoly. Unfortunately, many government functions cannot mimic free market concepts, particularly not those public goods and services from which society as a whole benefits; immediate gratification is not possible, and the long-term overall community needs cannot be assessed.

H. A Theory of Public Initiatives and Enterprise

Keynes maintained that governments should not do things which individuals were already doing (even if it could do them better) but do those that were not done at all, that is, to fill in the gaps left by private enterprise and initiative. Against this, collectivists have wanted to do away with most private provision, market forces, and private property in favor of government or collectivist provision. Both approaches admit the existence of state owned enterprises, public corporations, and government controlled corporations, in which surpluses accrue to the public, decisions rest on social as well as commercial criteria, and accountability is held to government and consumers: that is, public elements are mixed with enterprise elements. How states assume such public enterprises varies, as illustrated in the case of railways, where they have been nationalized for ideological, economic (natural monopoly), developmental, military, technological (unification), financial (bankruptcy), and national (reduction of foreign ownership) reasons. The rationale for public enterprise can be reduced to five arguments, namely (1) ideology—state ownership as an end in itself and a transfer of wealth producing assets from private to public sector, (2) nationalism—an end to imperialist or foreign domination and external dependency and ensuing local supply, (3) power—an end of dominance of certain interest groups and their special privileges or deliberate exploitation of the public sector for consolidating their political position, (4) pragmatism—a shift in public opinion, promotion of development and employment, encouragement of competition and influence on markets, and mitigation of hardship, and (5) natural monopolies—preference for ownership over regulation. Whatever their origins, governments are concerned about their performance and Australasia has taken the lead recently to define principles governing their operations and spell out concrete performance measures to which they must conform or face termination.

I. A Theory of Parastatals

Unlike the deliberate efforts at nationalization (or privatization), parastatals have just grown over the years, largely unobserved and certainly unstudied, to form the hidden public sector composed of some twenty-four different types of PGOs (paragovernment organizations), a chameleon concept (Hood, 1984). Are they part of government, or are they, as private bodies, constitutionally irresponsible like President Roosevelt's National Recovery Administration, as the U.S. Supreme Court ruled? They are too common to be considered aberrations, and they conduct activities essential to the administrative state. Just where do they fit? So far, it has been virtually impossible to generalize about this menagerie other than to say that they muddy the waters when it comes to public-private distinctions, accountability, governmental coordination, and legitimacy. They need the attention of theorists.

J. A Theory of National Planning and Utilization of Resources

Although distinctly out of favor with the worldwide failures of national planning and resource utilization and the discredit of bureaucratic centralism, the East Bloc euphemism for national planning, theories were once popular to justify government intervention in the economy to overcome market failures, mobilize and conserve natural resources, and boost national development prospects. Planning lays out a course of action that can be followed to lead to desired goals. It implies order, logic, and rationality and also regulation, control, and loss of freedom. It puts administrative efficiency above pluralist democracy, expertise over popular choice, bureaucracy over participation, secrecy over openness, conformity over variety, although several theorists argue that all these are compatible with the right choice of planning system (Bowden, 1978; Mannheim, 1965). Most countries have some form of national planning, and even those which do not have resorted to it during emergencies (Graham, 1976). The World Bank used to advocate national planning but now seems to have lost all faith in it, at least in economic matters, at a time when there is increasing support for international planning in environmental matters.

K. A Theory of Social Welfare and Equity

The prophets urged rulers to promote justice and govern justly, to do right and to act correctly, to rule humanely and to help the needy. Philosophers ever since have agreed, but they have had difficulty formulating what is socially right, although in the contemporary world all states are welfarist. As a result several different concepts of social welfare, social justice, and social good have been fashioned into different forms of the welfare state to do away with want. Should the administrative state attend to every need of its members or only selected needs? Should it distribute them equally, equitably, or differentially according to what criteria and with or without respect to ability to pay, social position, and employability? What does natural justice, fairness, suggest? What is efficient? As Titmuss has pointed out, for many so-called welfare benefits are really partial compensations for disservices, for social costs and social insecurities that are the product of a rapidly changing society; "They are part of the price we pay to some people for bearing part of the costs of other people's progress" (Titmuss, 1976, p. 155), but those not in want are reluctant to pay the price and for those who receive it, it may undermine their need to save and their will to work. The welfare state rests on the certainty that everyone someday will need the help of others (Logue, 1979, p. 87).

L. A Theory of Public Conduct

Governments should act ethically, for they set the standard and style to the governed. Likewise public officials are expected to act ethically, to observe a common code of right conduct. It has been easier to define wrongdoing and forbid its practices than to spell out and justify right doing. Hence the quest for professional codes of ethics, not least by the American Society for Public Administration, accompanied by a burgeoning literature in which theorists are having a field day.

M. A Theory of Public Maladministration

Public maladministration is another area where theorists are having a field day, and before long this building block should be in place (Caiden, 1991).

N. A Theory of Public Value and Worth

Not so in this area of public value, where there is fundamental disagreement whether or not the public sector is worth its keep and whether or not investment in it is valuable. Do the outputs justify the inputs? The fact that the argument is usually put in these terms and reduced to Pareto optimality or value-for-money, cost-benefit analysis is testimony to the hegemony of the liberal conception of the administrative state as an unfortunate necessity, valuable only in providing the conditions under which freedom (i.e., the individual pursuit of utility) can flourish (e.g., protecting against invasion and crime, enforcing contractual obligations, and guarding against fraudulent weights and measures). Its value and worth should be measured by the extent to which it enables people to pursue life, liberty, happiness, and property. Against this view of the liberal administrative state has been both revolutionary and evolutionary socialism with their stress on the value of the public goods and services, public property, equal access, fair shares, and societal enrichment and community to offset social disintegration and atomization. The jury is likely to be out for a long time yet on this one.

O. A Theory of Bureaucratic Growth

By any measures, the administrative state, more popularly known as the public bureaucracy, has grown enormously over the last two hundred years. It is only in the past decade that attempts have been made to reverse this situation—and then more by mirrors—making for a pause in growth. What accounts for such bureaucratic growth? One theory suggests bureaucratic aggrandizement, empire building, and self-interest. Another attributes it to the enlargement of the public sphere as society grows more complex and complicated: that is more public authority is necessary to superintend the modern industrial and postindustrial society, and Big Government has to offset Big Business. Yet another blames democratization, public demands, and rising public expectations. Growth is attributed largely to the nature of warfare and welfare together. Others point to frequent crises requiring government intervention (Higgs, 1987). And so it goes.

P. A Theory of Public Investment and Employment

Keynes has come the closest to a general model of public sector investment and employment which assumes that the administrative state plays a continuous role in securing economic stability and growth, including the notion that the state is an employer of the last resort and an instigator of infrastructure investment. Another, quite different theory sees the administrative state as pure spoils for whoever commands it. Because of the obvious deficiencies of the spoils system, economists, planners, and accountants have ventured to depoliticize public investment and employment in favor of more rational, logical, and scientific ways of managing public resources based on more objective criteria and leaning heavily on management sciences. Labor leaders have urged public employers to be model employers, to set the example to the public sector, and to innovate in industrial relations, working conditions, and social values (equal pay, nondiscrimination, equal opportunity, redeployment).

Q. A Theory of Public Laws

Outside English-speaking countries, public administration is studied under the umbrella of public law. The administrative state is or has been largely seen as the instrument for implementing public law as authorized by legitimate governmental authority rather than as an instrument for implementing public policy and a political actor in its own right. Recent political analysis has begun to redress the balance and contrast the different views of the state vis-à-vis society and other social institutions. Thus at least eight different concepts of the state have been identified in Germany over the past two centuries, namely, ***Obrigkeitsstaat*** (authoritarian), ***Beamtenstaat*** (bureaucratic), ***Rechtsstaat*** (rule of law), ***Parteienstaat*** (party), ***Fuehrerstaat*** (dictator), ***Bundesstaat*** (federal), ***Sozialstaat*** (social), and ***Wohlfahrtstaat*** (social welfare) (Kristad, 1989, p. 99), all with different implications for the theory of public law and the constitutional basis for administrative law.

In comparison, public and administrative law have been relegated to the study of public administration in the English-speaking countries and left largely to lawyers to ponder. Philip Cooper and David Rosenbloom have kept the subject alive in the United States with a strict constitutional law approach (Cooper, 1988; Rosenbloom, 1983). As yet, there is no philosophy of law that clearly delineates the areas of government intervention but has developed criteria which should prevail when intervention occurs—due process and equal protection assured by rule making and judicial review—and has contributed the most to the protection of individual rights.

R. A Theory of Collective and Individual Rights and Obligations

The Bible did not stress rights but obligations or duties to God, and it was logical to switch them to the state instead. But what were the obligations of the state in return? Protection certainly, and a protection that was to extend to the protection of fundamental or basic human rights of individuals per se derived from the fact that they are human beings, as spelled out by Thomas Paine and various bills of rights. When someone has rights, against whom are these rights to be enforced and who is to provide for these rights? Clearly, the administrative state, which must not only protect those rights but also enforce those rights against itself. In time, those rights have been extended to include what society is deemed obligated to do for the individual, and those obligations have grown from legal and civil rights to economic, social, and even cultural rights. For this reason the United Nations Declaration on Human Rights 1948 is now deemed too narrow.

S. A Theory of Collectivist/Administrative Limitations

Rights against the state are only one aspect of limitations on the administrative state. The debate has been reopened in recent years on what the state should or should not do, determined ideologically or empirically. It is now recognized that even with the best will, the state is incompetent to perform some activities and its overall performance is inhibited by sheer lack of resources, time, capacity, experience, and organization. The administrative state also suffers from unavoidable bureaupathologies. Size has its problems, entropy others. Public organizations, just like any others, come and go, appear and disappear, according to their ability to solve social problems and internal malfunctioning, despite their persistence. Definite limitations have been spotted by Marshall Meyer (Meyer, 1985) and Christopher Hood's case for the imperfectability of public administration (Hood, 1976).

T. A Theory of Public Service

The issue whether public administration should be administration *of* the public or administration *for* the public seems to be resolved clearly in favor of the latter. The administrative state is an instrument for furthering the general interest, and its officials are servants of the public. The ideology of public service has been drilled into public officials for centuries, if not thousands of years, and the penalties for substituting self-interest and utilizing public office for serving the self-interest of private careers have also been well established. On the basis of this well-known ideology, lists of "dos" and "don'ts" for public servants have been elaborated. This building block is almost complete.

U. A Theory of Citizenship and Public Participation

The role of the citizen is another building block which is rapidly being completed, after much neglect. The *public* in public administration has at last begun to receive as much attention as the *administration*. The citizen is not a cipher or recipient or consumer or object or resident, that is, something passive being manipulated, molded, shifted, influenced, acted upon by the administrative state, but a contributor, a participant, a giver, a resource, a doer, a mover and shaker, notions that go back at least as far as the idealization of Athenian democracy and updated to prevent the bestiality of totalitarianism. The question has shifted away from whether citizens should participate to what forms ensure their greatest impact.

V. A Theory of Public Sector Productivity and Effectiveness

Because of the harsh criticism of public sector parasitism, the need to prove beyond any shadow of doubt the worth and value of public sector activities has prompted scholars and researchers to produce indisputable measures of public gain and something that could act as a general indicator as profits do for business. Right now, theorists are off in all directions, but eventually they should consolidate and integrate their findings, and *Public Productivity Review*, for instance, serves as a useful mechanism for locating indicators on a standard grid. Eventually we might achieve objective W, a theory of public sector management.

W. A Theory of Public Sector Management

Formulating a theory of public sector management is work very much in progress.

X. A Theory of Human Responsibility toward Nonhumans and Future Generations

The building block of human responsibility is still in the making.

Y. A Theory of the Good Society (Utopia?)

Ever since the dawn of civilization, philosophers have strived to describe the perfect society, the ideal state, the utopia to which all should aspire and by which present societal arrangements should be judged. In this utopia, would there be privilege, property, discrimination, injustice, sloth, indifference, war, crime, immortality? Of course not. The Good Society is the ideal for which public officials should work. It would presumably provide the highest quality of life for all, and it would maximize individual potentialities. Presumably it would be a democracy, not just any democracy but a truly participative democracy in which happiness would result from the sheer joy of achievement and virtue and everyone would enjoy the good life. However visionary, a theory of the Good Society is an indispensable building block, for without it public administrators are tempted to forget the ends of the state and lower their sights too much.

When rounded out, these twenty-five elements or building blocks, each of which is capable of being internationalized, should be integrated into a general theory of public administration.

Some pieces of this intellectual jigsaw puzzle are already at hand. But too many are still missing or wrongly shaped to fit into a coherent pattern. We cannot show the way to people trapped in cruel, crippling, and corrupt administrative states if we ourselves cannot properly justify our ideas of public administration and convince even our own politicians to heed us. We cannot assume that the political marketplace will buy our wares unless we have worthwhile products to sell and parade them more attractively than we do. But first we have to agree among ourselves that our enterprise of theory building should be given a higher priority in our own value system.

ACKNOWLEDGMENTS

This chapter is a revised version of a paper originally presented at the Fourth Annual Symposium of the Public Administration Theory Network, Marvin Center, George Washington University, Washington, D.C., March 21, 1991.

NOTE

1. Hereafter called the state because the association of nation with state has always been fuzzy. The state appeared long before the nation, and states do not coincide with nations. Most states are multinational. Whereas a reference to membership in a state is accurate, one to membership in a nation is not.

REFERENCES

Batina, R. G., Public Goods and Dynamic Efficiency: The Modified Samuelson Rule, *Journal of Public Economics, 41*:389–400 (1990).

Bowden, G. T., Planning—Yes, but by Whom? in *Planning, Politics and the Public Interest* (W. Goldstein, ed.), Columbia University Press, New York, 1978.

Caiden, G. E., *Administrative Reform Comes of Age*, Walter De Gruyter, Berlin, 1991.

Chodak, S., *The New State: Etatization of Western Societies*, Lynne Reinner, Boulder, Co., 1989.

Cochrane, C. E., Political Science and "The Public Interest," *Journal of Politics, 36*:327–355 (1974).

Cooper, P. J., *Public Law and Public Administration*. Prentice-Hall, Englewood Cliffs, N.J., 1988.

Cornes, R. and Sandler, T., *The Theory of Externalities, Public Goods, and Club Goods*, Cambridge University Press, Cambridge, 1986.

Dahl, R. A., The Science of Public Administration: Three Problems, *Public Administration Review, 7*:1–11 (1947).

Dror, Y., Grand Policy Analysis, APPAM Annual Research Conference, San Francisco, Calif., October, 1990.

Dror, Y., *Public Policymaking Reexamined*, Chandler Publishing Company, Scranton, Penn., 1968.

Dwividi, O. P., and Jabbra, J. G., *Public Service Accountability: A Comparative Perspective*, Kumarian Press, West Hartford, Conn., 1988.

Evans, P. B., Rueschemeyer, D., and Skocpol, T., *Bringing the State Back In*, Cambridge University Press, Cambridge, 1985.

Goodsell, C. T., *The Case for Bureaucracy: A Public Administration Polemic*, Chatham House Publishers, Chatham, N.J., 1983.

Graham, O., *Toward a Planned Society*, Oxford University Press, New York, 1976.

Gross, B. M., *The Managing of Organizations*, Free Press, New York, 1964.

Higgs, R., *Crisis and Leviathan*, Oxford University Press, New York, 1987.

Hood, C. C., *The Limits of Administration*, John Wiley and Sons, London, 1976.

Hood, C. C., *The Hidden Public Sector: The World of Para-Government Organization*, Studies in Public Policy, No. 133, Centre for the Study of Public Policy, University of Strathclyde, Glasgow, 1984.

International Journal of Public Administration, Special issue on administrative theory *13*(6) (1990).

Kass, H. D. and Catron, B. L., eds., *Images and Identities in Public Administration*, Sage, Newbury Park, Calif., 1990.

Kristad, G. O., Radicals and the State: The Political Demands on West German Civil Servants, in *The Elusive State: International and Comparative Perspectives* (J. A. Caporaso, ed.), Sage, Newbury Park, Calif., 1989.

Logue, J., The Welfare State: Victim of Its Success, Special issue on "The State," *Daedulus, 108*:69–88 (1979).

Lundquist, L., From Order to Chaos: Recent Trends in the Study of Public Administration, in *State and Market* (P. Lane, ed.), Sage, London, 1985.

Mannheim, K., *Freedom, Power, and Democratic Planning*, Routledge & Kegan Paul, London, 1965.

Marx, F. M., *The Administrative State: An Introduction to Bureaucracy*, University of Chicago Press, Chicago, 1957.

Meyer, M. W., *Limits to Bureaucratic Growth*, Walter de Gruyter, Berlin, 1985.

Minnowbrook II, Changing Epochs of Public Administration, *Public Administration Review, 49*:101–227 (1989).

Nagel, S. S., Five Great Issues in Public Policy Analysis, in *Handbook of Public Administration* (J. Rabin, W. B. Hildreth, and G. J. Miller, eds.), Marcel Dekker, New York, 1989.

Rohr, J. A., *To Run a Constitution: The Legitimacy of the Administrative State*, University Press of Kansas, Lawrence, Kan., 1986.

Romzek, B. S. and Dubnick, M. J. Accountability in the Public Sector: Lessons from the Challenger Tragedy, *Public Administration Review, 47*:227–238 (1983).

Rosenbloom, D. H., *Public Administration and the Law*, Marcel Dekker, New York, 1983.

Self, P., What's Gone Wrong with Public Administration? *Public Administration and Development, 6*: 329–338 (1986a).

Self, P., *Political Themes of Modern Government: Its Role and Reform*, Allen and Unwin, London, 1986b.

Thompson, D., Moral Responsibility of Public Officials: The Problem of Many Hands, *American Political Science Review, 74*:905–916 (1980).

Titmuss, R. M., Welfare State and Welfare Society, in *Welfare: Readings in Philosophy and Social Policy* (N. Tines and D. Watson, eds.), Routledge & Kegan Paul, London, 1976.

Waldo, D., *The Administrative State: A Study of the Political Theory of American Public Administration*, The Ronald Press, New York, 1948.

Wamsley, G. L., ed., *Refounding Public Administration*, Sage, Newbury Park, Calif., 1990.

6

The Bureaucracy–Democracy Conundrum: A Contemporary Inquiry into the Labyrinth

Steven G. Koven
Iowa State University, Ames, Iowa

> We must expressly recall at this point that the political concept of democracy, deduced from the "equal rights" of the governed, includes these postulates: (1) prevention of the development of a closed status group of officials in the interest of a universal accessibility of office, and (2) minimization of the authority of officialdom in the interest of expanding the sphere of influence of "public opinion" as far as practicable. . . . Thereby democracy inevitably comes into conflict with the bureaucratic tendencies which, by its fight against notable rule, democracy has produced. (Weber, 1982, p. 226)

> The ruled, for their part, cannot dispense with or replace the bureaucratic apparatus of authority once it exists. For this bureaucracy rests upon expert training, a functional specialization of work, and an attitude set for habitual and virtuoso-like mastery of single yet methodically integrated functions. If the official stops working, or if his work is forcefully interrupted, chaos results, and is difficult to improvise replacements from among the governed who are fit to master such chaos. This holds for public administration as well as for private economic management. (Weber, 1982, p. 229)

I. INTRODUCTION

According to Max Weber, tension and conflict are inherent between principles of democracy and principles of bureaucracy. Democratic interests lie in preventing the establishment of a closed group of officials and in minimizing the authority of unelected officials. Principles of democracy support the notion of rule by the majority. The essence of democracy is conceptually antagonistic to the idea of creating an elite governing body.

A basic paradox exists in governance of modern societies. Robert Michels (1915) observed, long ago, that power was likely to be concentrated, even in organizations (such as socialist-democratic parties) whose stated aim was the struggle against inequality. Michel's famous iron law of oligarchy contended that all organizations no matter what their aims eventually come to be ruled by a group of self-perpetuating elites. This represents an inherent and continuous problem for democratically based societies. On the one hand, democracies subscribe to the ideal of rule by the consent of the governed. On the other hand, the existence of a body of technicians who are removed from popular control seems to be a requisite of modern societies. Nonelected administrators may owe allegiance to their craft, profession, or organization rather than some vague notion of the common good. Administrators may also undergo a "profound metamorphosis" whereby they suddenly forget their commitment to democratic principles and become part of the established elite (Etzioni-Halevy, 1983, p. 22).

The dangers of bureaucracy have been documented in both classical and contemporary writing. Michels viewed bureaucrats, especially lower ranking ones, as enemies of individual liberty and initiative. It was claimed that their dependence on superior authorities suppressed individuality, corrupted character, and engendered moral poverty. Michels viewed bureaucrats to be not only corrupting society, but also as exercising an arrogance toward inferiors that transformed them into masters rather than servants of the people (Etzioni-Halevy, 1983, p. 19). Such characteristics of bureaucrats were noted by contemporary scholars such as Nobel Prize–winning economist Milton Friedman and politicians such as former president Ronald Reagan.

Much of the recent political rhetoric in the United States has in one manner or another centered around the issue of the size, scope, and responsiveness of the bureaucracy. Populists such as Ronald Reagan, George Wallace, and Jimmy Carter gained notoriety through unabashed bureaucracy bashing. While Jimmy Carter was able to reduce some of the trappings of the "imperial" presidency, little success appears to have been made in constraining the size (as a percentage of gross national product) of the governmental apparatus. This chapter will review the historical growth of public sector bureaucracies in the United States, explore the roots of bureaucracy, examine contemporary issues related to the bureaucracy-democracy nexus, and offer some concluding observations.

II. GROWTH OF PUBLIC SECTOR BUREAUCRACIES IN AMERICA

Growth of bureaucratic structures in the United States has been well documented (Woll, 1963; Waldo, 1984; Meier, 1987; Wilson, 1975; Dodd and Schott, 1986). When the nation was formed, the bureaucratic apparatus of the government was minuscule. The first national administration under President George Washington included a bureaucratic network of Thomas Jefferson as Secretary of State, Alexander Hamilton as Secretary of Treasury, Henry Knox as Secretary of War, and Edmund Randolph as Attorney General. These agencies, in essence, made up what we term today the executive branch of government, acting as agents of Congress, capable only of carrying out "executive details" (Woll, 1963, p. 29).

Over time, the executive branch of the government expanded significantly from its initial threshold. The growth of the bureaucracy is commonly attributed to an array of factors. Wilson (1975, p. 62) contended that *client oriented politics*, or the rewarding of benefits to distinct interests in society, produced an enlarged bureaucracy in the latter half of the nineteenth century. The Departments of Agriculture, Labor, and Commerce are examples of bodies which were formed in order to address the interests and aspirations of particular groups. Previously, federal departments were formed exclusively around specialized governmental functions such as foreign affairs and finance.

A second factor in the growth of the public sector has been termed *cooperative federalism*. Cooperative federalism became more pronounced with passage of the Sixteenth Amendment to the Constitution in 1913, which permitted the federal government to levy an income tax on citizens of the United States, which in turn greatly increased the revenue raising capacity of the federal government. Access to the incomes of American citizens coincided with greatly expanded federal aid to state and local governments. Between 1914 and 1917, federal aid to states and localities increased by a magnitude of one thousand. Federal aid comprised one-tenth of all state and local spending in 1948 and over one-sixth of such spending in 1970 (Wilson, 1975, p. 64).

Regulatory activity represents a third explanation for growth of public sector bureaucracies. Woll (1963, p. 31) asserted that having fostered large industries with subsidies of various kinds, both the national and state governments had to contend with the dangerous externalities of social inequality, deceptive business practices, economic instability, and the growth of monopolies. Government officials were faced with demands by small businesses, labor, agriculture, and general consumers. These clients demanded that government take steps in controlling the potential excesses of big business; specifically, clients demanded that government begin to control monopolies that had evolved in the oil, steel, public utilities, and transportation industries. Limited government control of the economy was established through creation of regulatory bodies.

The Interstate Commerce Commission (ICC) was created in 1887 as the first agency of the federal government established for purposes of regulating a national industry. The creation of this body is perceived to be a historic step in the development of the American bureaucracy (Cushman, 1941). With the creation of regulatory agencies, government began to move away from the laissez-faire perspective of classical economics and began to assume responsibility in management of the marketplace. Following the creation of the Interstate Commerce Commission other regulatory commissions were formed to address various problems in other sectors of the economy. These regulatory agencies included the Federal Reserve Board (1913), the Federal Trade Commission (1914), the Federal Power Commission (1920), the Federal Deposit Insurance Corporation (1933), the Securities and Exchange Commission (1934), the National Labor Relations Board (1935), the Maritime Commission (1936), the Civil Aeronautics Board (1938), the Atomic Energy Commission (1946), and the Equal Employment Opportunity Commission (1964). Commissions were mandated to regulate banking, advertising, energy, stock transfers, radio and television, labor relations, shipping, use of atomic energy, and other activities.

The phenomena of client oriented politics, cooperative federalism, and regulatory activity represent only a partial explanation for bureaucratic growth. War and economic depression intercede periodically as stimulants for public sector spending (Dodd and Schott, 1986). Ott and Ott (1965, p. 40) documented that in American history, wars have pushed federal spending up sharply. With the return of peace, expenditures fall but never return to prewar levels. This is attributed, in part, to the wars' left-over heritage of interest expense and veterans' payments. The Great Depression of the 1930s and the Keynesian response to subsequent recessions also contributed to spending growth.

In the 1980s federal spending continued to rise despite the presence of the conservative Reagan administration. Three reasons have been cited to explain the most recent increase in federal spending: higher net interest payments (attributed to large deficits), higher defense costs, and programmed increases in entitlement programs (Schick, 1982, p. 291). Between 1980 and 1990 spending for national defense, Social Security, and net interest grew by 120 percent, 113 percent, and 183 percent, respectively (Koven, n.d.). By 1990 these three categories alone accounted for approximately 58% of total government expenditures.

Bureaucracy no doubt was aided by the external factors of war, economic travail, clientele pressure, and other forces. Bureaucracy also has a rich and deep intellectual tradition. The roots of administrative thought can be traced as far back as the Bible (Wildavsky, 1989). The antecedents of modern American bureaucracy, however, have been influenced by more recent work such as that of Woodrow Wilson and Max Weber.

III. ROOTS OF BUREAUCRATIC THOUGHT

Woodrow Wilson is widely assumed to be the founder of the academic study of public administration in the United States (Van Riper, 1983, p. 478; Van Riper, 1989, p. 8). Some controversy, however, surrounds the view that public administration is a purely American invention. Martin (1987) noted that virtually every significant concept that existed in American public administration literature by 1937 had already been published in France by 1859, and most had been published by 1812. Wilson, however, is reaffirmed as the formulator of a normative model of administration that still should hold fascination for those who work in large bureaucratic agencies of the public sector (Martin, 1988).

Other authors also contributed to the development of the discipline of public administration in the United States. Frank Goodnow (1900) further discussed the politics/administration dichotomy developed by Wilson in 1887. Leonard White (1926) published in the first textbook entirely devoted to the field of public administration. In the 1920s and 1930s W. F. Willoughby (1927), Luther Gulick and Lyndall Urwick (1937) introduced what has been termed the "principles of administration" school of thought. This period has been termed the "high noon" of administrative orthodoxy (Henry, 1987). Orthodoxy declined as the principles outlined by Gulick and Urwick began to be challenged by critics such as Chester Barnard (1938) and Herbert Simon (1947). Later, works by March and Simon (1958), Cyert and March (1963), and Thompson (1967) helped to move public administration into the domain of administrative science/ management. The late 1960s movement toward "the new public administration" attempted to focus the discipline on values, ethics, morals, and the relation of the client to the bureaucracy. Advocates of the new public administration questioned the responsiveness of government in general. These individuals were critical of pluralism, believing that electoral interest-group democracy favored particular groups, thereby reducing the achievement of greater social equity (Marini, 1971).

More recent emphasis in public administration has concentrated on the development of "a pure science of administration." Progress is perceived to have been made toward this goal in the subfields of organization theory and information science. Specific foci of emphasis in public administration today includes issues of state and local government, executive management, administrative law, and the definition of the public interest (Henry, 1987).

Public administration appears to have gone through many permutations since Woodrow Wilson's time. In terms of delineating purely bureaucratic thought, perhaps the German scholar Max Weber was most influential. Weber indicated that bureaucracy refers to the exercise of control by means of a particular kind of administrative staff. Weber maintained that bureaucrats should be neutral servants of their political master, echoing Wilson's perception that administrators should be only responsible for execution of the law, uninvolved in the political process of making law. Weber considered bureaucracy to be a major element in the rationalization of the modern world and the most important of all social processes (Fry, 1989). Characteristics of what

Weber termed the most rational form of bureaucracy or the "ideal-type" bureaucracy are as follows:

I. The principle of fixed and official jurisdictional areas, which are generally ordered by rules
II. A firm ordered system of hierarchy in which there is supervision of the lower offices by the higher ones
III. Written documents (files) which are preserved in their original or draft form
IV. Specialized office management which presupposes thorough and expert training
V. The full working capacity of officials
VI. The following of rules, which are more or less stable, more or less exhaustive, and teachable

In addition to the enumeration of general characteristics of an ideal-type bureaucracy, Weber delineated a set of characteristics which were recommended for officials within the organization. Positions within bureaucratic organizations were to be structured in the following manner:

> I. Office holding would be a vocation. This is shown in the requirement for a prescribed course of training demanding the entire capacity of workers for a long period. Office holding would not be considered a good to be exploited for pay, as was normally the case during the Middle Ages.
> II. Personal positions of officials would be patterned so that
> A. Officials would strive for and usually enjoy a distinct social esteem as compared with the governed. The possession of educational certificates would usually be linked to qualifications for office and enhance the status of officials.
> B. Bureaucratic officials would be appointed rather than elected. Officials elected by the government are not purely bureaucratic figures since they do not derive their positions from the hierarchical chain of command but from the wishes of the people. Because elected officials do not depend upon superior authorities in the official hierarchy, it is expected that officials who are appointed would function more exactly, from a technical point of view. All other circumstances being equal, it is more likely that purely functional points of consideration and qualities would determine selection and advancement of these appointed officials.
> C. The positions of officials normally would be held for life. When such legal guarantees against arbitrary dismissal or transfer are developed, they act to guarantee objective discharge of office duties which are free of personal considerations.
> D. Officials would receive monetary compensation in the form of a normally fixed salary, and security in old age would be ensured by a pension. The officials' income in addition to the rewards of social esteem would make public offices sought after positions.
> E. Officials would be trained for a career within the hierarchical order of the public service. Officials would move from lower, less important to higher positions. The average official would expect a mechanical fixing of the conditions for promotion determined by either seniority or a system of expert examinations (Weber, 1982, pp. 196–204).

Weber believed that bureaucratic mechanisms represented the most rational and efficient organizational form devised by man. Bureaucracies were perceived to be efficient as a result of their precision, speed, clarity, continuity, unity, strict subordination, and reduction of interpersonal friction. Weber's perception of the ideal-type bureaucracy was summarized by the notion that the purely bureaucratic type of administrative organization is, from a technical point of view, capable of attaining the highest degree of efficiency (Fry, 1989, p. 32).

Weber is recognized in American public administration for his great contribution to bureaucratic thought. He is also credited with recognizing the limitations to his model. He expressed such reservations that were based upon the perception that bureaucracies could create a new elite and control elected leaders through their effective use of expertise. A central problem identified by Weber was the conflict between the ethos of bureaucracy and democracy (Lutrin and Settle, 1985, p. 27). On the one hand, bureaucracies were perceived to be technically superior and essential for modern societies. At the same time, however, bureaucracies were antagonistic to democratic ideals and the notion of popular sovereignty. This conflict is long standing and can be observed today in contemporary debates over issues such as the image of bureaucrats, affirmative action, and patronage.

IV. CONTEMPORARY ISSUES

A. Image of the Bureaucrat

The phenomenon of bureaucracy bashing and decline of trust in governmental institutions has received a good deal of attention in recent years (Goodsell, 1983; Gormley, 1989; Cigler, 1990; Volcker Commission, 1990). Goodsell (1983) noted that countless politicians run for office on platforms that blame society's problems on the burdensome rules, wasteful extravagance, and social experimentation of bureaucrats. Candidates promise to clean up the mess of bureaucracy, yet after the election neither bureaucrats nor problems disappear. Ironically, bureaucracy has come to symbolize the opposite of Weber's conceptualization. Instead of optimal rationality in organizations, bureaucracy today is more commonly associated with waste, inefficiency, excessive rules, and an inability to respond.

John F. Kennedy's inaugural address in 1961 had urged Americans, "Ask not what your country can do for you. Ask what you can do for your country." Kennedy's challenge not only justified the existence of government in the utilitarian sense but challenged Americans to sacrifice for the common good. This challenge framed government service as a noble calling, worthy of citizen loyalty. In recent years numerous politicians have jumped on the anti-bureaucracy bandwagon. George Wallace's 1968 presidential campaign asserted that bureaucrats were overpaid, arrogant, nonresponsive, lazy, and even pointy-headed. In 1976, Jimmy Carter successfully campaigned on the promise that he could cleanse the immortality of Washington and Watergate.

Vietnam, failure of Lyndon Johnson's Great Society, Watergate, and the perceived ineptitude of the Carter administration succeeded in tarnishing the image of public service. The apotheosis of bureaucracy bashing was observed in the rhetoric of Ronald Reagan. In his inaugural address Reagan stated, "Government is not the solution to our problem. Government is the problem." As Reagan's fans cheered wildly, it was apparent that attitudes toward government had come full circle in twenty years. Thus, by the 1980s Americans were ready to embrace, once more, the message of limited government and the free market. Laissez-faire principles of lower taxes and less government regulation were sanctioned, as the rallying cry to "get government off the backs of the people" gained acceptance. Numerous books and articles supporting the position of limited government suddenly began to appear. Arguments were raised supporting the view that major societal problems such as poverty, economic growth, and drug related crime were actually caused by government (Murray, 1984; Gilder, 1981; Nadelmann, 1989; Szasz, 1992).

By the mid-1980s a number of individuals were becoming concerned with the thrust of the antigovernment rhetoric. As a result of this concern, a small number of leaders in 1986 convened the conference, "A National Public Service for the Year 2000." This conference was jointly sponsored by the Brookings Institution and the American Enterprise Institute and expounded the view that action was necessary in order to reverse a "quiet crisis" that existed in the public sector (Volcker Commission, 1990, p. xviii).

Following the conference in 1986 a small group of organizers recruited Paul Volcker (keynote speaker at the conference) to chair a proposed commission on public service. The commission's thirty-six members included men and women with broad experience in government and private life, such as a former president and vice-president of the United States, senators, representatives, cabinet level officers, ambassadors, corporate executives, university presidents, and leaders of national nonprofit organizations.

The Volcker Commission's report was issued in 1989 and made specific reference to problems arising from the negative perceptions of public service in the United States. The report noted that although distrust of politicians and government power was a perennial feature of American culture, attacks on the federal government and "bureaucrat bashing" had recently become particularly virulent. Public attitudes of distrust toward government represented one of three main threats to the health of the public service. Additional deficiencies were noted in the areas of political leadership and the international management system. These deficiencies had the negative effect of eroding the ability of the government to function at the same time that demands on government were rising.

The Volcker Commission revisited some of the same issues of previous commissions: the Taft Commission (Commission on Economy and Efficiency, 1912), the Brownlow Commission (President's Committee on Administrative Management, 1937), and the two Hoover Commissions (Commission on Organization of the Executive Branch of Government, 1949, 1955). The Volcker Commission argued that attracting and retaining high-quality personnel to the public sector were necessary and crucial to the future of the nation:

> For all the glories of Adam Smith, somebody has to set the rules and adjudicate disputes. Somebody has to defend the country and explore space. Somebody has to keep the air clean and the environment safe for the next generation. Somebody has to respond to those more mundane, but nonetheless sometimes quite challenging, assignments of keeping government working effectively and efficiently if self government is to work at all. (Volcker Commission, 1990, p. 4)

Commission member Walter Mondale reinforced the view that the role of the public sector was vital to American society and that the erosion of bureaucratic competencies was a cause for concern:

> Is "OK" enough for those who direct the next shuttle mission? After Three-Mile-Island and Chernobyl, what levels of competence do we want inspecting our nuclear plants? The next time you take an air flight, do you tell your family not to worry, the controllers aren't the best but they are OK? (Volcker Commission, 1990, p. 3)

The Commission cited specific evidence for a gradual, almost imperceptible erosion in the image and competencies of the public sector. Among the evidence collected by the Commission were the findings that (1) a very small proportion (13%) of senior executives interviewed by the General Accounting Office would recommend that young people start their careers in government, (2) a smaller proportion (2%) of engineering students from three outstanding universities (Massachusetts Institute of Technology, Stanford University, and Rensselaer Polytechnic Institute) took jobs in government at any level, (3) half the respondents to a recent survey of federal personnel officers said that recruitment of high-quality personnel for government service had become more difficult over the past five years, and (4) a large majority (75%) of specially recruited and trained personnel (presidential management interns) stated that they would leave government within ten years (Volcker Commission, 1990, p. 3).

The Commission recognized that restoring pride in the public service rested in large measure on the public's willingness to trust its own government. One can ask whether a democracy can survive for long if popular distrust of "the government of the people, by the people and for the people" runs rampant. According to the Commission Report, distrust is derived from scandals such as Watergate and Pentagon procurement, from wasteful government programs, and from campaign rhetoric. The Commission stated: "Such distrust, if continued, may undermine the democratic process itself. It most certainly acts as a disincentive to potential recruits who too often associate public life with frustration or breaches of integrity." In other periods attitudes toward the public sector were more supportive. The words of John F. Kennedy reflected an earlier era of optimism and faith in the public sector:

> Let the public service be a proud and lively career. And let every man and woman who works in any area of our national government, in any branch, at any level, be able to say with pride and with honor in future years: I served the United States government in that hour of our nation's need. (Volcker Commission, 1990, p. 9)

Kennedy's words not only serve as a reminder of optimism and trust in government of an earlier era, but provide a contrast to the bureaucracy bashing of the 1980s and early 1990s. The broader issue of the inherent conflict between administrative and democratic values is reflected in the words of Ronald Reagan and John Kennedy. Balance between competing ethos of democracy and administration remains an enduring question. It is troubling from the administrative perspective that bureaucrats find themselves under constant assault by elected leaders. One must ask first, how can structure in democracy survive if popularly leaders find it necessary to attack the very system necessary to implement their plans? Second, how can democracy survive without its administrative structure? From the democratic perspective, the idea that governmental ineptitude can be used as a tool of demagoguery is also troubling. One must ask first, whether a "strong man" will be able to gain enough popularity and support to "fix the mess" in Washington? Second, will the enhanced efficiency of fixing "the mess" come at the expense of American freedom? Bureaucracy bashing represents only one arena where the conflict between bureaucratic and democratic values is observed today. Other issues where these tensions between these ethos can be observed include representative bureaucracy and patronage.

B. Representative Bureaucracy and Patronage

The issues of representative bureaucracy and patronage also play a prominent role in identifying the parameters of conflict between bureaucratic and democratic values. Many questions are raised: Does representativeness correspond to responsiveness? Where is the proper balance between principles of social equity and principles of efficiency? Do patronage appointments erode technical capacities in the public sector? Is patronage a necessary evil in order to control public agencies that may be unsympathetic to popular views? A general understanding of the concepts of representative bureaucracy and patronage is necessary in order to begin to address some of these questions.

The concept of representative bureaucracy relates to the issue of the balance between principles of bureaucracy and the ethos of democracy. Representative government is advocated by its supporters because of its perceived ability to enhance the legitimacy of the state. It is contended that a public sector consisting of administrators with characteristics that roughly mirror those of its population will be representative and have tighter linkages with the populace.

According to representative bureaucracy advocates, issues of legitimacy supersede other issues such as efficiency and power. Power of the bureaucracy may or may not be a threat to individual freedom and liberty. More relevant than the degree of power exercised is the issue of the manner in which power is used. Power may be used to implement popular policies which are in great demand by the populace. Power may also be used for the advantages of a small elite to the great detriment the vast majority. Democracy is enhanced by the former and denigrated by the latter. The greatest threat to principles of democracy therefore is not perceived to be power, by itself, but power that is unrepresentative of popular sentiment (Krislov and Rosenbloom, 1981, p. 22).

In light of the dangers of unrepresentative power, efforts to increase representation assume great importance. Various methods of enhancing representation exist and have been postulated, including enhancing representation by composition of personnel, enhancing representation by type of administrative organization, and enhancing representation by increasing citizen participation (Krislov and Rosenbloom, 1981).

The idea that public bureaucracies can be transformed into representative institutions through the composition of their work force is not radical or new. It was advanced in early America by Presidents Thomas Jefferson and Andrew Jackson. In more recent years, the idea of increasing representation through a more diverse work force has been debated within the context of affirmative action/racial quota programs. These programs have been highly controversial and continue to evolve in American public policy.

A number of Supreme Court cases have set the parameters of the affirmative action debate. In *University of California Regents v. Bakke* the Court, in one regard, ventured beyond the earlier statutory letter of the law by permitting use of race as one factor in selection decisions. Statutory justification for the Court's action is found in Title VII of the Civil Rights Act of 1964 as amended by the Equal Employment Act of 1972. Title VII of the Act prohibited discrimination in employment on the basis of race, color, religion, gender, or national origin. The *Bakke* case, however, has been interpreted as a victory by both sides in the affirmative action controversy. The Court's decision that utilizing race as the sole criterion for admission to medical school violated the 1964 Civil Rights Act was interpreted as a victory for advocates of a "color-blind" set of laws. Although race could not be the sole criterion for admission, according to the rules, it could still be considered among other factors. This was hailed as a victory for advocates of expanding the scope of affirmative action. The Court, in this complex ruling, upheld the principle of equal opportunity defined as color-blind law, but also left the door open for programs that sought to redress former injustices.

In *Kaiser Aluminum and Chemical Corporation and United States Steelworkers v. Weber* the Court upheld voluntary affirmative action by private sector employers. Kaiser and the United States Steelworkers decided to sponsor a training program in which 50 percent of the slots were reserved for blacks, until black representation in the skilled trades reached 39 percent, the percentage of blacks in the community. The training program was interpreted by the Court as a case of a private-sector employer's engaging in remedial affirmative action to correct problems in society for which the employer was not directly responsible. The majority of the Court in Weber held that the Kaiser program was a private voluntary program of limited duration. The program therefore was considered to fall within the acceptable parameters of the 1964 Civil Rights Act. In the case of *Johnson v. Transportation Agency, Santa Clara County* (1987), the court applied the Weber principle of reasonable voluntary programs to a case in which a woman wa promoted over a male worker whose overall rating was higher than hers. The Court argued that both candidates were certified as well qualified in an initial assessment and that the difference separating them in terms of ratings was negligible. Furthermore, denial of a promotion in this case would not preclude denial in the future.

In recent years the court has imposed some limits on affirmative action type behavior. In the case of *Firefighters' Local 1784 v. Stotts* (1984) the firefighters union filed suit on behalf of white firefighters who were laid off in a budget cutting plan of the city of Memphis, Tennessee. The city chose to lay off newly hired firefighters in alphabetical order but not to lay off recently hired black firefighters with the same seniority as others who were terminated. The firefighters union charged reverse discrimination in their suit. The Court subsequently ruled that it was inappropriate to deny an innocent employee the benefits of seniority in order to remedy the misdeeds of the organization. The Court reaffirmed the protections due to innocent members of the majority in *Wyant v. The Jackson Board of Education*. The Court struck down a layoff plan which called for proportional layoffs so that the percentage of black teachers would not fall below their proportion before the layoff. In its reasoning the Court maintained that societal discrimination alone was not sufficient justification for race conscious remedies, it insisted on some showing of prior discrimination by the governmental unit involved before allowing use of racial classifications in order to remedy discrimination (Sylvia, 1989, p. 81).

The Court recognized in *Wygant v. Jackson Board of Education* that innocent third parties may have to bear some of the burden of race-conscious relief but that the Court was more likely to approve of relief when the burden of the remedy was diffuse and not borne by particular individuals.

The issue of racial quotas has also been addressed in recent Supreme Court decisions such as *United States v. Paradise*, in which the decision dealt with discrimination in an Alabama police department. The District Court had found the Alabama Department of Public Safety guilty of intentional discrimination and recalcitrant in complying with subsequent decrees. The District Court then ordered a one-for-one promotion quota which the United States, supported by the Department of Public Safety, claimed violated the Equal Protection Clause of the Fourteenth Amendment. The Supreme Court upheld the District Court order of a promotion quota to be enforced on the Alabama Department of Public Safety. This ruling, however, was far from being universally endorsed. Justice O'Connor was joined by Chief Justice Rehnquist as well as Justices Scalia and White in her dissenting opinion. O'Connor argued strongly against quotas because of their impact on innocent nonminorities. While O'Connor was part of the minority opinion in *United States v. Paradise*, the sharp five-four split in the Court reflects deep divisions over the issues of quotas.

The lack of consensus on the Supreme Court is reflective of fundamental disagreements over the scope of affirmative action/quota programs in American society. Eloquent arguments have been raised on both sides of the issue. In the Supreme Court case of *Regents of University of California v. Bakke*, Justice Thurgood Marshall enunciated one of the perspectives:

> This Court's past cases establish the constitutionality of race-conscious remedial measures. . . . There is thus ample support for the conclusion that a university can employ race-conscious measures to remedy past societal discrimination, without the need for a finding that those benefited were actually victims of that discrimination. . . . It is because of a legacy of unequal treatment that we now must permit the institutions of this society to give consideration to race in making decisions about who will hold the positions of influence, affluence, and prestige in America.

Others such as the former Democratic congressman from Massachusetts Father Robert Drinan reaffirmed Marshall's perspective:

> Affirmative action recognizes that society must attempt to do something to correct the monumental mistakes made by generations of Americans toward blacks and women. This calls for a sensitivity to the institutional prejudices whose existence cannot be denied. What this country did in tolerating slavery from 1619 to 1865 has distorted reality for millions of Americans. What it did by requiring segregated schools up to 1954 has further confused that reality. Affirmative action, however, ambiguous and nebulous, is one answer to all of the many misconceptions that Americans have about blacks and women. (Drinan, 1991, p. 125)

The perspective enunciated by Marshall and Drinan was vigorously opposed by a host of critics. Nathan Glazer, professor of education and philosophy at Harvard University, summarized many of these arguments. Glazer stated that opponents of the affirmative action/quota approach contend that programs would arouse resentment among those not included among the "affected classes"; that affirmative action/quota programs would encourage other groups to demand the same protection, putting the government in the business of determining who belongs to which racial ethnic group; and that such programs may offend what many have believed to be the main thrust of liberalism in America, the primacy of individual rights (Glazer, 1991, p. 22).

Former president of Brandeis University and former member of the U.S. Commission on Civil Rights Morris Abram also identified his misgivings about modern attempts to end discrimination:

> In the absence of any neutral decision making mechanism, the attempt to end discrimination through color-conscious remedies must inevitably degenerate into a crude political struggle between groups seeking favored status. Once we have abandoned the principles of fair procedure, equal opportunity, and individual rights in favor of the advancement of a particular group, we have opened wide the door to future abuses of all kinds. . . . What the social engineers fail to perceive is that societies that depart from color-blind, neutral decision making do so at their own peril. The history of societies that have adopted this approach in order to reach substantive social goals more quickly has been a history not of liberation but of crippling oppression. (Abram, 1991, p. 40)

The general issue of representation through personnel is far from an arcane matter. The issue of affirmative action not only is relevant to the bureaucracy-democracy debate but to working men and women who are impacted by government mandated personnel policies. The salience of the affirmative action/quota issue is evident from observation of recent American elections.

In North Carolina's 1990 senatorial race, Jesse Helms raised the issue of affirmative action/quotas in a highly charged appeal to nonminority, nonprotected individuals. Commercials used by Jesse Helms appeared to replicate the success of the infamous Willie Horton commercials used in the 1988 presidential race. Both campaigns were said to include highly negative as well as racist inferences (Strickland and Whicker, 1992). The Helms commercial skillfully played on the fears of nonminorities by showing a white man sitting at a table with a letter in hand. The camera moved to a closeup of white hands as they crumple a job rejection notice while a voice intones, "You needed that job and were the best qualified. But they had to give it to a minority because of a racial quota. Is that really fair?" The message goes on to add, "Harvey Gantt says it is. Gantt supports Ted Kennedy's racial quota law that makes the color of your skin more important than your qualifications."

The nature of the Helms commercials as well as the cautionary statements of Morris Abram alluded to previously suggest that affirmative action/quota programs indeed can have a divisive effect on populations. In California, the Republican gubernatorial nominee, Pete Wilson, also raised the issue of affirmative action, however, in a less blatant manner than the case in North Carolina. Both Helms and Wilson won tough elections. Their success indicates that affirmative action/quota programs remain highly charged issues that can be employed by politicians for electoral advantage.

From the perspective of recent elections, it appears that the voice of the people in the democratic structure may be less concerned about the dangers of an unrepresentative technocracy than they are about unfair advantage being assigned to one particular group or another. Tensions between perspectives of fairness persist. On the one hand, it is argued that specific groups should be given preference in hiring because of prior injustices and the desire for representation in the public sector. On the other hand, it is contended that equity requires the establishment of uniform "color-blind" standards to be applied to all. No group should be assigned special privilege and rewards should be allotted on the basis of merit. The issue of representation versus merit is further discussed later from the perspective of patronage.

Patronage has long been considered to be one of the treasured prizes of elective office. "To the victor go the spoils" was a catechism in what was characterized as the "machine era" of American politics. The needs for democratically elected leaders to shape and direct administrative units under their jurisdiction was offered as a rationale for the practice. Patronage, however, became associated with the appointment of political "hacks" to government positions. The real job of these officials was to "get the vote out" at election time. Between elections many of these officials were reputed to hold "no show" jobs, pull down generous governmental salaries, and cavort with their political allies at places such as the local race track. The reform era of the early 1900s was aimed at eliminating these abuses through the adoption of professionalism and competencies within the structure of government. Civil service, merit hiring, and the city-manager form of government were all innovations aimed at replacing the patronage system with a structure based upon efficiency and neutral competence.

The issue of patronage also has been raised in recent years. The Volcker Commission (1990) identified problems with the current system of political appointment. In its *Report of the National Commission on the Public Service* the Commission stated:

> Each President brings into his Administration a substantial number of people committed to him and to his philosophy of government. These political appointees constitute an essential democratic link with the electorate. This link ensures that the permanent bureaucracies that carry out the policies of the U.S. government will be led by people who are committed to the policies and priorities of each new President. This "in-and-outer" system also brings into the government fresh ideas and new blood to try them out. . . . But the huge agencies and complex programs of the government cannot be run entirely by these in-and-outers. The permanent processes and ongoing programs of the U.S. government need the continuity and expertise of specialized bureaucracies. (Volcker Commission, 1990, p. 219)

A cohesive working relationship between the two basic components of the executive system (officials who are committed to the elected leader's philosophy of government and others who constitute the knowledge base of the permanent bureaucracy) was viewed as essential by the Volcker Commission. A section of the Commission (The Task Force on the Relations between Political Appointees and Career Executives) headed by former cabinet member Elliot Richardson concluded that the executive system was not working at peak efficiency, that the infrastructure of the federal government was deteriorating, and "perhaps more important" that the problem involves the interaction between the two essential components (presidential appointees and career bureaucrats) of the executive leadership system.

Reasons for the "disturbing developments" in the system of executive leaderships were cited and discussed. The rising turnover in the political ranks (the average tenure of Senate-confirmed political appointee has been decreasing and was only two years in 1984), an increased layering of political appointees (robbing the career executives of opportunities for more demanding responsibilities), the increased number of political appointees at lower ranks (placing minimally qualified individuals in important posts that previously were filled by those with many years of specialized experience), the "brain drain" in career ranks (from 1979 to 1983 40 percent of Senior Executive Service [SES] personnel left government employment, producing a "talent hemorrhage" at the top), the falling morale in the career service (attributed in a survey to poor career-political working relations), the erosion of executive compensation (a commission on salaries reported that between 1969 and 1985 the purchasing power of executive level salaries in the federal bureaucracy had decreased by 39 percent, making it difficult to recruit the best and brightest at the entry level or retain good people for their career), and the decrease in institutional memory that will occur if career civil servants are more and more excluded from policy development are each discussed in the Volcker Commission's report.

Numerous authors have discussed the negative impact that patronage appointments have had on the public sector in recent years (Van Riper, 1983; Ingraham, 1987; O'Toole, 1987; Pfiffner, 1987; Koven, 1992). Pfiffner argued that recent presidents have come to office with distrust and hostility toward the career bureaucracy and that this attitude has been reflected in their appointments. The Reagan administration is cited for taking the trend toward increased control and politicization to the extreme by insisting on White House clearance of each noncareer appointment in the government (Pfiffner, 1987, p. 59). He further contended that the effectiveness of the government was being strained by the trend toward increasing numbers of political appointees and that reversing the number of political appointees would increase the capacity of the government to function without sacrificing political accountability or responsiveness.

The trend toward increasing politicization of the federal bureaucracy can be observed through a comparison of cabinet level presidential appointments of the Carter and Reagan administrations. Carter's appointments of Blumenthal (Treasury), Califano (HEW), Schlesinger (Energy), Vance (State), Adams (Transportation), and Brown (Defense) were believed to "emote an air of efficiency and pragmatism." Carter repeatedly used the phrase "tough, competent managers" when introducing his cabinet (*Time*, 1977). In contrast to this hiring strategy Reagan's appointments were said to reflect attention to politics and ideology. In 1981, Reagan appointed a strong proponent of developing federal land (Watt) to the Department of Interior, a conservative black attorney (Pierce) to the Department of Housing and Urban Development, a free market farmer (Block) to the Department of Agriculture, an individual with no apparent qualifications (Edwards) to the Department of Energy, and a supply-side loyalist (Stockman) to the Office of Management and Budget. Each of these appointments was perceived to be more heavily influenced by ideology than the ethos of neutral competence (*Newsweek*, 1981).

It has been proposed that political patronage even may have impaired America's ability to compete successfully in the international economy. In the late 1980s political appointees accounted for only 150 positions in Great Britain, 60 in West Germany, and practically 0 in Japan compared to approximately 3,000 jobs in the United States. This is said to contribute to a condition in the United States bureaucracy of "weak institutional conscience (and memory), poor coordination of macro and micro objectives, and widespread amateurism in policy implementation" (Hale, 1989, p. 32).

V. CONCLUSIONS

Bureaucratic and democratic structures peacefully coexist in the United States, yet this arrangement should not be confused with compatibility. Fundamental assumptions of these belief sets differ. Bureaucracy prioritizes hierarchy, chain of command, and a top down approach to problem solving. Democracy, on the other hand, values input from all stratums of society as a guide to proper action. An inherent fault line therefore runs through all modern democratic societies. Periodically, this fault line is exposed, revealing populist antipathy toward bureaucratic structures and government officials.

Conflict between bureaucratic and democratic principles is revealed in the contemporary controversies over affirmative action/quotas and patronage. In theory, affirmative action/quotas respond to abuses of the past and help to assure the representation of the public sector. Representation in turn acts to suppress the creation of a ruling class of technocrats, a class that would act as masters rather than servants to the people.

In theory patronage acts to prevent an autonomous group of officials from becoming a power unto themselves. If this occurred, government officials, over time, could shape policy according to their own desires regardless of the wishes of the people. Patronage acts to eliminate this threat by allowing elected leaders to place their own people in positions of importance in the public sector hierarchy. Controls over the career officials are secured by such appointment strategies. In theory, patronage appointments answer directly to the elected leader; thus the linkage between the government agencies and the representatives of the people remains intact.

Issues of affirmative action/quotas and patronage expose the conflict between bureaucratic and democratic values. These conflicts are not likely to be resolved in the near future and threaten to divide protected and nonprotected groups in American society further. Resolution of these conflicts will depend upon a number of factors. The degree of economic growth may influence, to a large extent, popular opinion. A zero-sum society of slow growth and gains for one group at the expense of another is likely to produce deep divisions and invidious comparisons of protected and nonprotected classes of citizens. In contrast, higher levels of growth are likely to assuage conflicts over hiring as more citizens from both protected and nonprotected classifications partake in the American dream.

Similarly, the quality of the educational system in America may impact upon the balance between bureaucratic and democratic values. In theory, there does not have to be a tradeoff between quality of personnel and representation of personnel in the public sector. Both can be achieved: one does not have to be sacrificed at the expense of the other. In theory, technical skills and capacities can be learned by all, by nonprotected as well as protected categories of citizens. These same skills can deteriorate in all citizens over time. Therefore, what appears to be essential in fostering a competent bureaucracy that is also representative of the demographic composition in the nation is a sound and effective educational system.

Affirmative action/quotas issues have been shrouded in controversy not only from nonprotected groups claiming reverse discrimination but also from minorities. Affirmative action is said to produce a bifurcation within protected groups as a small stratum of minorities achieves middle class and upper middle class status while the vast majority of others remain trapped in conditions of abject poverty. Furthermore, the question of whether affirmative action will produce a bureaucracy whose views are representative of all citizens in society is unclear. Bureaucracies have been known to inculcate personnel and capture the allegiance of their work force. Blacks, Hispanics, and native Americans who have benefited from affirmative action policies and achieved middle class status may no longer represent attitudes prevalent in the lower socioeconomic stratum of American society. If this is the case, then affirmative action may not provide the mechanism for a more representative form of government. Some black activists argued that the black Chairman of the Joint Chiefs of Staff, Colin Powell, did a far better job of representing the views of the military establishment than he did of representing the views of the average black American.

Policies of affirmative action/quotas were introduced as a mechanism for achieving greater justice in American society. Justice in turn would act as a firm pillar for affirming the legitimacy of the state. Legitimacy, however, is undermined if the majority of the citizens perceive the cure to be discriminatory, unfair, and punitive. In such a scenario, the remedy of assigning sinecures of office can have a debilitating and destabilizing effect on society. Opportunity for advancement and achievement of different stations in life has been a hallmark of American society. Assignment of position based on special characteristics, no matter how good the original intent of the plan appears to be antagonistic to this ideal. One is advised to remember the cliché "The road to Hell is paved with good intentions."

Patronage represents another point of contention between the competing principles of bureaucracy and democracy. Patronage, in theory, protects average citizens against the potential abuses of a nonaccountable "fourth branch" of government. Recent studies, however, have been critical of the degree to which patronage has been applied to the federal bureaucracy. One needs to ask whether the average citizen will benefit from a destruction of the competencies acquired over the years by bureaucratic agencies.

Classical theorists such as Mosca (1939), Michel (1915), and Weber (1974) all have commented extensively on the inherent tension that exists between democracy and bureaucracy. The issues discussed in this chapter suggest that the debate between bureaucratic and democratic principles is far from being resolved in the United States. Perhaps the very nature of democracy mandates that debate on key issues be ongoing. A termination of real debate and discussion of critical issues may in fact indicate that democracy has died and bureaucratic values have triumphed.

REFERENCES

Abram, Morris, Fair Shakers and Social Engineers, in *Racial Preference and Racial Justice* (R. Nieli, ed.), Ethics and Public Policy Center, Washington, D.C., 1991, pp. 29–44.

Barnard, Chester, *The Functions of the Executive*, Harvard University Press, Cambridge, Mass., 1938.

Cigler, Beverly, Public Administration and the Paradox of Professionalization, *Public Administration Review, 50*(6):637–653 (1990).

Cushman, Robert E., *The Independent Regulatory Commission*, Oxford University Press, New York, 1941.

Cyert, Richard and March, James, *A Behavioral Theory of the Firm*, Prentice-Hall, Englewood Cliffs, NJ, 1963.

Dodd, Lawrence C. and Schott, Richard L., The Rise of the Administrative State, in *Current Issues and Public Administration* (F. Lane, ed.), 3rd ed., St. Martins, New York, 1986.

Drinan, Robert, Affirmative Action Under Attack, in *Racial Preference and Racial Justice* (R. Nieli, ed.), Ethics and Public Policy Center, Washington, D.C., 1991, pp. 117–125.

Etzioni-Halevy, Eva, *Bureaucracy and Democracy*, Routledge & Kegan Paul, London, 1983.

Fry, Brian, *Mastering Public Administration*, Chatham House, Chatham, N.J., 1989.

Gilder, George, *Wealth and Poverty*, Basic Books, New York, 1981.

Goodnow, Frank, *Politics and Administration*, Macmillan, New York, 1900.

Goodsell, Charles, *The Case for Bureaucracy*, Chatham House, Chatham, N.J., 1983.

Gormley, William, *Taming the Bureaucracy*, Princeton University Press, Princeton, N.J., 1989.

Gulick, Luther, and Lyndell Urwick, eds., *Papers on the Science of Administration*, Institute of Public Administration, New York, 1937.

Hale, D., Must We Become Japanese? *National Review*, October 27:30–32 (1989).

Henry, Nicholas, The Emergence of Public Administration as a Field of Study, in *A Centennial History of the American Administrative State* (R. Chandler, ed.), Free Press, New York, 1987, pp. 37–85.

Ingraham, Patricia, Building Bridges or Burning Them? The President, the Appointees, and the Bureaucracy, *Public Administration Review, 47*(5):425–435 (1987).

Johnson v. Transportation Agency, Santa Clara County, 55 L.W. 4379 (1987).

Kaiser Aluminum and Chemical Corp. and the United States Steelworkers v. Weber, 443 U.S. 193 (1979).

Koven, Steven, Budgetary Policy in the Post Cold War Era, in *Post-Cold War Policy* (W. Crotty, ed.), Nelson-Hall, Chicago, 1992 (n.d.).

Koven, Steven, Base Closings and the Politics-Administration Dichotomy Revisited, *Public Administration Review, 52*(5) (1992).

Luttrin, Carl, and Settle, Allen, *American Public Administration*, 3rd ed., Prentice-Hall, Englewood Cliffs, N.J., 1985.

March, James, and Simon, Herbert, *Organizations*, John Wiley & Sons, New York, 1958.

Marini, Frank, ed., *Toward a New Public Administration: The Minnowbrook Perspective*, Chandler, Scranton, Penn., 1971.

Martin, Daniel, Deja Vu: French Antecedents of American Public Administration, *Public Administration Review, 47*(4):297–303 (1987).

Martin, Daniel, The Facing Legacy of Woodrow Wilson, *Public Administration Review, 48*(2):631–636 (1988).

Michels, Robert, *Political Parties*, (trans. E. Paul and C. Paul), Jarrold & Sons, London, 1915.

Mosca, Gaetano, *The Ruling Class*, (trans. H. D. Kahn), McGraw Hill, New York, 1939.

Murray, Charles, *Losing Ground*, Basic Books, New York, 1984.

Nadelmann, Ethan, Drug Prohibition in the United States: Costs, Consequences, and Alternatives, *Science*, 245:939–947 (1990).

Nalbandian, John, The U.S. Supreme Court's 'Consensus' on Affirmative Action, *Public Administration Review*, 49(1):38–45 (1979).

Newsweek, January 5, 1981, p. 18.

Ott, David and Ott, Attiat, *Federal Budget Policy*, The Brookings Institute, Washington, D.C., 1965.

Pfiffner, James, Political Appointees and Career Executives: The Democracy-Bureaucracy Nexus in the Third Century, *Public Administration Review*, 47(1):57–65 (1987).

Schick, Allen, Incremental Budgeting in a Decremental Age, in *Current Issues in Public Administration*, 276–299 (1982).

Simon, Herbert, *Administrative Behavior: A Study of Decision-Making Processes in Administrative Organization*, Macmillan, New York (1947).

Strickland, Ruth Ann, and Whicker, Marcia Lynn, Comparing the Wilder and Gantt Campaigns: A Model for Black Candidate Success in Statewide Elections, *PS: Political Science & Politics*, XXV(2):204–212 (1992).

Sylvia, Ronald, *Critical Issues in Public Personnel Policy*, Brooks/Cole, Pacific Grove, Calif., 1989.

Szasz, Thomas, *Our Right to Drugs: The Case for a Free Market*, Praeger, New York, 1992.

Time, January 3, 1977, p. 40.

United States v. Paradise, 94 L Ed 203 (1987).

University of California Regents v. Bakke, 438 U.S. 265 (1978).

Thompson, James, *Organization in Action*, McGraw-Hill, New York, 1967.

Van Riper, Paul, The American Administrative State: Wilson and the Founders—an Unorthodox View, *Public Administration Review*, 43(6):477–490 (1983).

Van Riper, Paul, The American Administrative State: Wilson and the Founders, in *A Centennial History of the American Administrative State* (R. Chandler, ed.), The Free Press, New York, 1989, pp. 3–36.

Volcker Commission (National Commission on the Public Service and the Task Force Reports to the National Commission on the Public Service), *Leadership for America Rebuilding the Public Service*, Lexington Books, Lexington, Mass., 1990.

Waldo, Dwight, *The Administrative State*, Holmes & Meier, New York, 1984.
Weber, Max, Some consequences of bureaucratization, in *Sociological Theory* (L. Coser and B. Rosenberg, eds.), 4th ed. Macmillan, New York, 1976.
Weber, Max, Bureaucracy, in *Max Weber: Essays in Sociology* (H. H. Gerth and C. Wright Mills, eds.), Routledge & Kegan Paul, London, 1982.
White, Leonard, *Introduction to the Study of Public Administration*, Macmillan, New York, 1926.
Wildavsky, Aaron, What is Permissible So That This People May Survive? Joseph the Administrator, *PS Political Science & Politics*, XXII:779–788 (1989).
Willoughby, W. F., *Principles of Public Administration*, The Johns Hopkins Press, Baltimore, 1927.
Wilson, James Q., The Rise of the Bureaucratic State, in *Public Administration Concepts and Cases* (R. Stillman, ed.), 3rd ed., Houghton Mifflin, Boston, 1975.
Woll, Peter, *American Bureaucracy*, W. W. Norton, New York, 1963.
Wygant v. Jackson Board of Education, 90 L Ed 2nd 260.

7
Bureaucracy: A Profound Puzzle for Presidentialism

Fred W. Riggs
University of Hawaii at Manoa, Honolulu, Hawaii

I. CONTROLLED OR DOMINANT BUREAUCRACY

Modern states need a system of public administration that is capable of implementing its policies well enough to satisfy its citizens and also to retain the support of its bureaucrats. When uncontrolled public officials are not paid adequately or lack the security and status they consider fair, they often revolt, stage a coup d'état, and create a *bureaucratic polity* (i.e., a political system dominated by bureaucrats and led, in every case, by military officers) [1].

In order to sustain effective public administration, bureaucrats must be empowered enough to utilize their expert knowledge, experience, and good judgment in solving the innumerable complex and interrelated problems generated by industrialized or postindustrial societies. However, when bureaucrats become politically dominant, as they are by definition in a bureaucratic polity, they typically run wild: they become corrupt, lazy, and oppressive because no political institution is strong enough to discipline and guide them, to set policies and norms and exercise effective control over public officials. A critical issue for every modern state, therefore, is how to empower officials enough to assure good public administration without permitting them to become dominant.

A. Dispersed Power

Different constitutional systems vary in their ability to accomplish this difficult task. In general, the concentrated power found in *parliamentary* systems, where cabinet government links the executive and legislative authority, has a much greater potential for controlling and guiding the state bureaucracy than does any *presidentialist* regime [2]. In the latter, the separation of powers has two profoundly dysfunctional consequences for the regime: first, political division and the resulting inability to provide coherent guidance for the bureaucracy weaken the system and render it vulnerable to overthrow by a coup d'état; second, lack of coordination at the top generates dispersal of power below [3]. Resulting intrabureaucratic cross-pressures hamper public administration and provoke both public and bureaucratic dissatisfaction. Thus presidentialist regimes are inherently vulnerable to disruption because of both their essential inability to maintain effective control over the state bureaucracy and the maladministration that unavoidably results.

Actually, all presidentialist regimes experience breakdowns—typically by a coup d'état and the seizure of power by public (mainly military) officials [4]—except for the United States. If we assume that the typical case is to be expected, then we need not explain what this generalization predicts. Heady makes the same point, though more cautiously: "Despite the popularity of the American Constitution as a model, its staying power has not been matched elsewhere" (1987, p. 14).

B. The U.S. Exception

What needs to be explained, therefore, is the exceptional case: why has the U.S. constitution never been suspended? During the Civil War and some other grave national crises, the American Constitution has indeed been severely tested and elected Presidents have even exercised unconstitutional authority, but they have never suspended the Constitution nor discharged Congress [6]. Although the balance of power has fluctuated, Congress has always retained the power to block American Presidents by refusing to enact the laws or policies they propose.

I believe that a variety of important (and sometimes essentially undemocratic) practices are largely responsible for the exceptional ability of the U.S. constitutional system to survive (they are examined at length in Riggs, 1993b) [5]. One aspect of the subject that has hitherto been ignored involves the relative lack of power of the American bureaucracy. Had the U.S. bureaucracy been as powerful as are the bureaucracies found in virtually all other democracies—both presidentialist and parliamentary—it would probably, during a severe crisis, have seized power.

In order to explain this exception, we need to understand four factors that affect the power position of the U.S. bureaucracy; (1) the creation of a *nonpartisan professionalized career system*, (2) continuing reliance on *politically appointed transients and nonpartisan consultants*, (3) the influence of *federalism*, and (4) the impact of *private enterprise* as manifested in the use of nongovernmental organizations to implement many public policies. Analysis of these features in a comparativist perspective helps us to reassess the relations between politics and administration in America. It will also demonstrate, I believe, the value of using a comparative approach to enhance our understanding of the American constitutional system. Only when we abandon the notion that comparative politics and comparative administration apply only to the study of foreign governments can we gain a deeper understanding of our own system.

II. THE BUREAUCRATIC DESIGN

Two variable dimensions of the bureaucratic design profoundly affect both the extent of bureaucratic power and the administrative capabilities of a bureaucracy: duration in office and the qualifications of officeholders. Combining them produces a fourfold matrix of long-termers (with and without technical qualifications) and short-termers (also with and without qualifications). We can visualize these possibilities as shown in Table 1.

The terms used here are somewhat arbitrary but they should help us discuss these basic variables and their significance, for both bureaucratic power and administrative performance. In general, *duration affects power* and *qualifications affect performance*. The more the bureaucrats

Table 1 Bureaucratic Design Variables

	No Qualifications	With Qualifications
Long-term	Retainers	Careerists
Short-term	Politicos	Consultants

in a polity are long-termers (whether as careerists or as retainers), the more capable they are of exercising power; and the more qualified they are, the more effective are they as administrators [7].

Empowered officials are better administrators than powerless ones, provided they cannot become politically dominant. This statement implies a four-degree scale of bureaucratic power: from the top down it ranges from dominant to powerful to semipowered to powerless. Both extremes produce maladministration [8].

Careerists link long-term service with qualifications. This is the ideal combination provided—and this is basic—the state can maintain effective control over them. When such control cannot be maintained, careerists can seize power (through a coup) and bureaucratic domination ensues, leading not only to autocracy but also to maladministration. Presidentialist regimes are fragile: they typically cannot maintain long-term control over a powerful bureaucracy. Eventually, during severe crises, either the bureaucrats or the President seizes power—both presidential and bureaucratic autocracies, however, are equally fragile and both are, therefore, likely to collapse. By contrast, most (though not all) parliamentary regimes are able to sustain their control over a powerful bureaucracy indefinitely, and thereby both to ensure effective public administration and continuing support for the regime.

A relatively stable semipowerful bureaucracy has emerged in the United States during the last century as a result of its exceptional mixture of short-termers and professionalized careerists. This mixture has enhanced the regime's administrative capabilities while curtailing bureaucratic power. The proposition that a presidentialist regime can persist only if its bureaucracy is semipowered rests primarily on the exceptional experience of the United States by contrast with that of all other such regimes.

A. Some Misperceptions

It is only possible to recognize and explain the exceptional qualities of the American experience when it is compared, explicitly with that of other countries committed to the same constitutional formula. Without such a context, American writers on Public Administration often treat the prevalence of patronage during the first decades of the Republic and the subsequent development of the spoils system as either a lamentable aberration or the result of the failure of the Founding Fathers to recognize the need for effective public administration or a professional career service when they drew up the Constitution [9].

If the Founding Fathers had, indeed, prescribed a career bureaucracy in the written Constitution, it would have made the system unworkable. Actually, they simply took for granted the viability of the only system they knew about—the retainer system they inherited from their former British overlords [10]. Fortunately, this system survived for only forty years. How and why it was then changed proved crucial for the maintenance of the American republic.

B. The Ubiquity of Patronage

All presidentialist regimes originating before the twentieth century inherited patronage-based bureaucracies from the imperial powers that administered them before they acquired their independence. Their bureaucrats had been recruited by kings as favorites and protégés; subsequently they become long-term retainers. When independent successor republics came into existence, the only way they could imagine to staff their bureaucracies was based on patronage. Retainers still prevail in all of them, except the United States.

By contrast, patronage has been largely eliminated in contemporary parliamentary regimes in favor of careerist bureaucracies. This reflects both the superior willingness and the capacity of such regimes to carry out this fundamental reform, and also their ability to maintain effective control over the powerful bureaucracies produced by their reforms. The inability of presidentialist regimes to accomplish this transformation resulted, I believe, from both the resistance of powerful retainers and the reluctance of Presidents to abandon patronage: without it they would have been unable to maintain the power of their office in balance with that of an elected Congress.

The executive power in parliamentary systems is exercised by cabinets that are, in fact, organs of a parliament—they last only so long as they retain a parliamentary majority and their members are, normally, elected members of that body. This compels them to act as a unified body and gives them powerful political support. The resulting fusion of executive/legislative powers enables them both to carry out bureaucratic reforms and to maintain control over powerful bureaucracies composed exclusively of careerists.

Any President who appointed members of Congress to a cabinet while permitting them to retain their seats would jeopardize the executive's autonomy in relation to Congress [11]. Similarly, a President cannot name career officers to the cabinet or to other high level positions without risking domination by the bureaucracy [12]. In order to retain power and initiative in the executive office, therefore, every President must recruit individuals from outside Congress and the career bureaucracy to fill most cabinet positions. Moreover, Presidents are not obliged to retain their cabinet members—they may be discharged at any time. Actually, therefore, they are top level transient bureaucrats. A cabinet composed of career bureaucrats would easily dominate the President, making that position untenable.

Moreover, the unavoidable links between Congress and key bureaucrats in a regime based on divided power fundamentally undermine presidential authority. Hence, I believe, all Presidents in presidentialist regimes need a substantial number of personal protégés in office in order to maintain the constitutional separation of powers. This necessity combines with the persistence of traditional patronage systems to compel all Presidents in presidentialist regimes to maintain and depend heavily on political appointees.

The President's direct need for patronage is also reinforced, indirectly, by the political needs of members of Congress. Consider that, to maintain its autonomy within a presidentialist system, every Congress has to tackle a huge agenda. It cannot merely accept or reject governmental initiatives as does a parliament, where party discipline requires that, in order to keep its cabinet in power, majority members must normally vote for every government measure. Consequently, MPs typically have neither the incentive nor the capacity to influence bureaucratic appointments.

By contrast, to handle its large agenda, every Congress must delegate significant decision-making powers to its members and the committees in which they serve. This normally entails personal autonomy in their voting behavior [13]. As a result, Presidents typically find that, to secure the congressional votes needed to gain approval of their own policies, they must use patronage (and support local, "pork barrel" projects). Thus members of Congress have both the interest and the power to influence a President's patronage appointments when they choose to demand posts for their own political protégés—especially those who helped them win their seats [14].

C. Congressional Relations

Put differently, the structural inability of Presidents to rely on party discipline—even when their own party has a majority in Congress—generates strong pressures to trade jobs for votes. By appointing the nominees of members of Congress, a President can win votes for his or her policies. Reciprocally, members of Congress need patronage to reward supporters who helped them win at the polls. Consequently, the minimum number of political appointees needed to staff a presidentialist bureaucracy is magnified by every President's need to win the support of fractious members of Congress [15].

Unfortunately, such trade-offs only win short-term benefits for a President. Members of Congress are likely to think of these bargains as mere indulgences: after they have supported a bill or two favored by the President, will they not ask for new favors in exchange for more votes? At least, this seems to be a ubiquitous phenomenon in presidentialist regimes.

If all patronage appointees were well qualified to administer government programs and to implement public policies, heavy reliance on patronage under presidentialism might prove administratively acceptable. However, as everyone knows, although friends and supporters are sometimes well qualified for a post, it often happens that they are not. The maladministration that frequently results from patronage appointments not only hampers the performance of specific tasks but, cumulatively, erodes the ability of any government to achieve its own goals, undermines the confidence of citizens in the capacity of representative government to meet their needs, and simultaneously destroys the morale and loyalty of public officials themselves. Ultimately, when and if a presidentialist regime is overthrown by a military coup group, few citizens rally to its defense: indeed, they often hail the usurpers as saviors.

As the American case shows, a presidentialist regime does not need to depend exclusively on transient appointees. Indeed, all contemporary regimes rely heavily on long-term bureaucrats, whether they be retainers or careerists. Since careerists can administer more effectively than retainers, they are better able to uphold the credibility of the regimes they serve. However, they are also more likely to dominate them. The unique quality of the American system is that it, alone, stumbled upon a way to establish a relatively weak career bureaucracy linked with transient appointees. By contrast, the retainer bureaucracies that other presidentialist regimes have never been able to replace are both politically powerful and administratively ineffectual. We need to know why this is so. Since American Public Administration still lacks an accepted term for the concept, its significance has been overlooked. Actually, retainers still play decisive political/administrative roles in all presidentialist regimes except the United States—and even in the Unites States, they have been important.

III. RETAINER POWER

Although retainers lack tenure (i.e., they have no contractual basis for keeping their posts), they are typically able to generate political power. At first, they may rely on individualistic expedients to remain in office [16]. Eventually, however, they create networks ("informal organizations" or trade unions) designed to safeguard their interests and resist efforts to discharge them from the public service. Merely because bureaucrats are appointed as political protégés and lack legal tenure in their jobs does not mean that they cannot exercise political power. As the statistics indicate (see [5]), retainer bureaucracies in all of the pre-twentieth-century presidentialist regimes (except the United States) were able to stage successful coups.

A. Dependency in Modern Bureaucracies

To explain the motives as well as the capacity of modern retainer bureaucracies to seize power, we need to understand that all modern bureaucrats (both merit-based career officers and patronage-based retainers) have a common feature: namely their dependence on salaries and the perquisites of office. The fundamental differences between premodern (traditional) bureaucracies and modern (salaried) bureaucracies are not well understood. Contrary to a widespread assumption, the basic distinction is not based on the replacement of patronage officials by careerists nor the substitution of a merit system for political favoritism—this belief is rooted, I think, in the unique history of the American system.

Actually, many modern bureaucracies, like that of the United States and all other presidentialist regimes, still rely heavily on patronage, while some premodern bureaucracies established the merit principle, utilizing examinations and lifelong tenure as a basis for staffing the government. Chinese dynasties provide the most notable examples, but in other empires, such as the Ottoman, similar principles prevailed.

The most important difference between traditional and modern bureaucracies, I believe, involves the dependence of the latter on salaries as the main, if not exclusive, basis for income security. By contrast, premodern bureaucracies were *prebendary* in the sense that they could, quite legitimately, augment whatever stipends they received from the government by contributions (gifts, commissions, fees, rents—not really bribes) offered by those who benefited from their services. No doubt, corruption is endemic in all governments and we can scarcely claim that modern officials always live exclusively on their legal income. Nevertheless, as a gross comparison, modern bureaucrats are primarily salary-dependent whereas premodern (prebendary) officials were not [17].

The significance of this difference becomes apparent when we remind ourselves that officials, like everyone else, have their own interests to defend, their expedient needs to satisfy. However, their control over public offices and resources gives them weapons of power (especially in the armed forces) not available to other citizens. Consequently, modern bureaucrats—and only bureaucrats—can seize power through a coup d'état led by a cabal of military officers. Military coups are a recurrent feature of many states in the third world today, especially in presidentialist regimes. According to the data I collected in 1985, 111 third world republics had been established. Of these, 49 (44%) had broken down because of coups. Of the 111, 33 had presidentialist constitutions and all but 3 (91%) had experienced coups [18]. By contrast, of 35 states with single-party authoritarian regimes, only 6 (17%) had experienced coups, see [5] and Riggs (1993a).

Such coups are a modern phenomenon—premodern bureaucrats did not stage coups although, of course, they often exercised great power within traditional monarchies (Riggs, 1991a, pp. 491–492). Even badly run governments, so long as they relied on traditional bureaucracies, had little to fear from revolts by appointed officials [19].

Although we conventionally think of these coup-based regimes as "military dictatorships," they typically gain the full support of civil servants who hope, thereby, to assure the maintenance of their positions, income, and other perquisites as public employees. Civil servants frequently share power in the cabinets created by a military junta or council. They often have the "technocratic" expertise required to run a government that military officers lack. Rank and file civil servants, although not active participants in a coup, typically remain passive in order not to "make waves" and to assure their continued job security—indeed, they rarely offer any resistance to a coup. After all, they usually have no reasons to support an ousted government that has, in fact, treated them harshly. Thus contemporary appointed officials have all become political actors in the broadest sense [20], but this is especially true of the retainers found in presidentialist regimes.

B. Expansion of Retainer Bureaucracies

In order to understand the special grievances of retainers, we need to recognize that, although modern bureaucrats are salary-dependent, those in career services can normally expect their income and status to improve with seniority, but retainers, by contrast, often experience losses due to the tendency for retainer bureaucracies to grow. To the degree that careerism prevails (whether in its traditional or modern forms) the problem of bureaucratic expansion is not a major problem: the regime can appoint only as many officials as are needed to fill vacancies when they occur.

By contrast, the thirst of all presidentialist regimes for patronage generates bureaucratic expansionism when rotation is not practiced—that is, when retainers are, indeed, able to stay in office. Every new President and every member of Congress seeks to appoint new officials. If former appointees could be discharged according to the principle of rotation in office, the bureaucracy would not need to grow. However, because of their dependence on salaries and their eagerness to protect the security, status, and fringe benefits associated with public office, most hold-over incumbents are resentfully willing to accept the shame of being superseded in order to keep their posts despite, typically, diminished real income and reduced status. Thus the self-interest of retainers plus their capacity to exercise power enable them to cling, desperately, to their deteriorating positions. Moreover, demoralized and underpaid officials, especially when they are poorly qualified or inappropriately posted, do unsatisfactory work. By lowering the quality of public administration they augment popular discontent and, eventually, erode their own job security, that, after all, depends on effective tax administration and salary management.

So long, therefore, as a President cannot impose rotation on incumbent bureaucrats, presidentialist bureaucracies are bound to expand. Moreover, since new patronage appointees bump the retainers whom they replace, it is predictable that downgraded retainers will not only swell the ranks of an expanding bureaucracy but also become demoralized and increasingly ineffective as public servants. As a result, the payroll grows and real income declines (perhaps by inflation) while tax burdens mount. The grievances that drive popular insurrections cumulate as do the discontents that provoke military coups.

The only way to overcome these basic dysfunctions involves reducing the number of patronage appointments. This might be done by accepting the right of retainers to keep their offices while curtailing the number of new patronage appointees. As retainers gain experience, they may learn to administer more effectively—but the corruption of office by retainers is also an incurable problem and if they cannot be discharged when they administer ineffectively, sinecurism and incompetence will increase and newly elected Presidents will be helpless to remedy the situation. When Presidents insist on their patronage powers but cannot compel incumbents to resign, no real solution is possible. Clearly, the remedy involves discharging incumbents (i.e., enforcing a policy of rotation) [21].

C. Bureaucratic Retention Versus Rotation

If we assume that incumbents will strive to retain their posts and that, collectively, they can exercise significant power, we may conclude that presidents will normally experience great difficulty when they try to rotate officials out of office. Indeed, the capacity of incumbents to hold on to their offices is truly intimidating (see [16]). Presidents soon discover that it is much easier to make patronage appointments when incumbents are allowed to retain their jobs than it is to try to oust them.

A good solution to the problem of patronage and bureaucratic expansionism is available to parliamentary regimes that can more easily establish a ubiquitous merit-based career system. This is clear from the case studies, but it is also evident on theoretical grounds: (1) cabinets enjoying parliamentary support have enough undivided political power to control a large entourage of career officials, and to given them reasonably unified direction, without much need for patronage; (2) the continuous risk of a cabinet's discharge by a parliamentary vote of no confidence offers little incentive for qualified outsiders to accept indefinite and necessarily precarious positions in government; and (3) members of Parliament, depending for their election on party backing more than on individual supporters, have neither the power nor the motive to press for patronage appointments. For somewhat different reasons, it is also possible for autocratic monarchies, a single ruling party, and even a military dictator to maintain a viable career (or retainer) system in the public bureaucracy while minimizing patronage appointments.

By contrast, presidentialist regimes cannot afford to abandon patronage, but they need not insist that all public offices be filled by protégés: they can, in principle, accept a compromise under which many if not most bureaucratic posts are staffed through a merit-based career system. No doubt they will always need patronage positions, although it is not easy to determine how many are really necessary. However, establishing a merit system permits a presidentialist regime to improve its administrative capabilities, and it limits the growth of bureaucracy by restricting the number of positions to those necessary for effective public administration—provided, however, that it can first establish the principle of rotation in order to discharge unnecessary retainers.

The greatest obstacle to the introduction of a merit system, I believe, involves the powerful forces that sustain the principle of retention—incumbents ordinarily have both the incentive and the power to hold on to their jobs even when they experience demotions, humiliations, and demoralization. Moreover, so long as the government is greatly overstaffed, it can ill afford to recruit additional officials through a merit system. It can afford to introduce or expand the merit system only when it can, at the same time, create vacancies by discharging retainers.

Presidents and members of Congress often find themselves in a double-bind: approving a merit system of career appointments reduces their ability to use patronage both to enhance their power positions and to deal with the separation of powers, but without a merit system, the quality of public administration deteriorates so much that it undermines public confidence in the regime. In this dilemma, retention of patronage appears unavoidable: so long as they cannot discharge incumbents, they really cannot afford to develop a merit-based careerist bureaucracy—its size and costs (political and economic) simply become insupportable.

If these arguments are valid, then it seems to me that it is impossible for any presidentialist regime to establish a merit-based career system without first establishing its right to discharge incumbents, that is, to institutionalize a policy of rotation. The "in-and-outers" must really be *amphibians*, willing to go out [22]. In most presidentialist regimes, however, retainers strive (like *fish*) to stay in—to lose the security of government jobs is, virtually, to die. Divided governments, based on the separation of powers, understandably lack the fused authority needed to control retainer power effectively.

IV. PRESIDENTIALISM: THE FIXED TERM

Although the separation of powers is usually viewed as the fundamental principle of presidentialism (by contrast with the fusion of powers inherent in the parliamentary form of government), a basic rule is needed to maintain the separation of powers: namely the requirement that *the head of government must be elected for a fixed term in office*. This rule is a necessary—though not a sufficient—basis for the maintenance of the constitutionally prescribed separation of powers: it is possible, I believe, for the separation principle to be eroded or nullified even though the fixed term election rule is adhered to. Moreover, although the concurrent power of a judicial system may vary substantially, I believe all presidentialist regimes need a court system with enough authority to restrain elected officials who seek to violate the separation of powers. Despite these caveats, we may treat the fixed term rule as definitive for presidentialism.

The Founding Fathers debated the length of the President's term and eventually accepted four years, with the option of reelection, but they never considered the possibility that a President (as head of government) could be removed from office for political reasons by a simple vote of Congress—impeachment was to be only for "high crimes and misdemeanors," not policy differences. They could scarcely have considered this idea because parliamentary regimes had not yet become institutionalized and they were unable, by themselves, to invent the concept. The American founders would surely have opposed the rule as giving Congress too much power: it could undermine the sense of national unity that they hoped to create among the citizens of thirteen contentious and self-consciously "sovereign" states by establishing the President as the head of state, a surrogate for the King. The distinction between heads of state and of government had yet to be made.

A. The Puzzle of Separated Powers

Let us assume that bureaucrats will only stage a coup when they are truly provoked—they need motives in addition to ambition for power. The main reason why retainers establish political networks reflects their desire to protect their jobs. Severe provocations are also needed to generate the incentives for collective political action in support of a coup.

Such provocations arise in every presidentialist regime because of the cross-pressures on bureaucracy generated by the separation of powers: see section I.A and [1]. The constitutional teaching that sovereignty resides ultimately in the people, while a superb legitimizing myth, provides little concrete help for a government that needs the support of a powerful and effective bureaucracy but lacks a concentrated fulcrum for the exercise of executive authority.

The founders of modern Public Administration theory in America have long wrestled with the dilemmas posed by the presidentialist formula. Frank J. Goodnow (1900) proposed a pseudo-parliamentary fusion of the powers exercised by President and Congress, to be achieved by means of a unified political party that could dominate both branches and thereby correct the problems arising from divided government. Were such a fusion achievable, Goodnow argued, we would be able to separate clearly the expression of the will of the state from its execution. The "executive" function (not that of the President only but that of the President and Congress acting in concert) would then be implemented by three types of authorities: the judicial authorities who apply the law in individual cases, the executive authorities who supervise the execution of the will of the state, and the administrative authorities who implement its details [23].

A more realistic scheme for understanding and accepting the principles of governance in America was proposed by W. F. Willoughby (1927). He distinguished between the executive and administrative functions: the former, he claimed, centers in the office of the chief executive, whereas the latter can be located in Congress. "The administrative function," he wrote, "resides in the legislative branch of the government," and the executive function "is vested by constitutional provisions in the chief executive" (10, pp. 10–11) [24].

According to Herbert Kaufman's more contemporary data, this corresponds to the American reality. We should remember, he tells us, that the legislators "can write a specific mandate or prohibition or authorization into a law, or reduce the funds available for a particular program or part of a program, or inquire into an individual action" (1981, p. 164) [25]. Louis Fisher, a respected American scholar and staff member of the Congressional Research Service, has written "The constitutional and political responsibilities of Congress require its active and diligent participation in administrative matters" (1981, p. 40) [26]. It is important to recognize, of course, that although these powers are sometimes exercised by a Congress acting in plenary sessions, more usually individual members, committees, and subcommittees, acting independently—though with the consent of their colleagues and the assistance of their appointed staff members and government agencies—make the crucial decisions that actually guide the day-to-day operations of government agencies in America.

Conventional American Public Administration theory has reacted against this reality, promoting the idea that exclusive authority over the national bureaucracy ought to be exercised by the President as chief executive. Congressional involvement in public administration is viewed as an abuse to be corrected. Leonard D. White's classic text on Public Administration deplores the excesses of legislative intervention in the conduct of public administration and, under the norm of unity of command, supported the efforts of President Franklin D. Roosevelt's Committee on Administrative Management in 1936 to establish three overhead management agencies and six executive assistants who would empower the President to implement his constitutional obligation to "see that the laws are enforced" (White, 1939, p. 69).

A widely help opinion links the executive and administrative functions as a comprehensive responsibility of the President to be accomplished through both politically appointed and career officials, acting independently of a Congress that, in principle and subject to presidential veto powers, should focus its energies exclusively on its legislative functions. All of these positions, I think, reflect the essentially unresolvable problems of trying to rationalize the structure of authority over bureaucracy in a regime unnecessarily burdened with the constitutional separation of powers.

B. The Bureaucratic Implications of Divided Government

No doubt American Public Administration will continue to wrestle with the logical contradictions implicit in the presidentialist formula, while both bureaucrats and politicians will have to cope as best they can with the unfortunate consequences. These consequences need to be assessed from two contrasting points of view.

At the administrative level, they generate acute cross-pressures: presidential authority can lead (ideally) to emphasis on the managerial values of efficiency and effectiveness; congressional demands generate insistence on political responsibility and responsiveness; and judicial decisions often give priority to standards of legality and the protection of citizens' rights versus bureaucratic abuse of power (Rosenbloom, 1983). When bureaucratic demoralization and confusion result, administrative performance suffers. As noted, bad public administration generates popular discontent and may even fuel revolutionary movements. However, the cross-pressures that undermine administrative effectiveness in presidentialist regimes also motivate bureaucratic responses, that is, political action. At the political level, such responses involve much more than the efforts of individual officeholders to safeguard their jobs. More significantly, they generate efforts to transform the political system. Confused and frustrated officials support concerted efforts to magnify their own authority and even, in extreme cases, to seize power through a coup d'état.

In the United States bureaucratic protest is only marginally evident, by contrast with what is often found in other countries. One example is the *Blacksburg Manifesto*, that, although an academic document, proclaims the "ultimate responsibility" of public administrators to the constitutional order and asserts that, in this context, they "may have to incline their agencies' responsiveness toward the president at one point and toward Congress at another, or at other times toward the courts or interest groups that are likely to serve the long-term public interests as the agency sees it" (Wamsley et al., 1990, p. 49). In this perspective, the Manifesto asserts, "The Public Administration needs to assert, but also to be granted, its propriety and legitimacy as an institution," so that civilian public administrators, "like judges before them or like their military colleagues today, could question a directive of their political superiors and have the question regarded as a sober second thought rather than as an act of bureaucratic sabotage" (p. 43) [27].

In most other presidentialist regimes, by contrast, bureaucratic grievances mount and reinforce popular discontents fueled, in part at least, by the constitutionally based confusions that hamper public administration and produce disastrous results that, in turn, provoke popular resistance movements. The fact that public officials are retainers rather than professionally qualified careerists in most of these cases contributes both to administrative failures and to the anxieties felt by public officials. Cumulatively, these forces drive the rebellions that, under military leadership, lead to coups and bureaucratic domination accompanied by suspension of the constitution and the voiding of electoral politics.

V. THE AMERICAN EXCEPTION

The fact that, despite severe crises—including a major civil war, a devastating depression, and two world wars—there has never been a coup d'état or other catastrophic collapse of the American presidentialist polity gives us a basis for testing some of the hypotheses advanced in the foregoing discussion. Several approaches may be followed.

One approach would accept a popular interpretation that attributes American "exceptionalism" to its distinctive historical, geographic, cultural, economic, and social environment. I do not dismiss this mode of explanation, but I prefer to start from an analysis of the distinctive rules and practices that, on the one hand, have permitted the American presidentialist polity to function more or less well and, on the other, to produce a bureaucracy that, for various reasons, lacked the motivation and the capacity to seize power. The persistence of these distinctive practices, however, also needs to be explained and so, following the logic of circular causation, we must eventually return to the environmental factors.

A. The Exceptional Environment

One such factor involves the psychosocial basis of the motives and behavior of appointed officials. At the risk of oversimplification, consider how Abraham Maslow's explanation of the hierarchy of human needs might help us [28]. Let us suppose that all bureaucrats, everywhere, share some fundamental human needs for livelihood and security: their expediency needs. In addition, at a higher level, they seek self-actualization through achievement, ideally expressed by achieving the goals of the public agencies in which they are employed or their professional norms: their principled needs. To the degree that they find that their expedient needs are not met, however, these basic requirements take priority over the principled goals.

Stable political regimes provide enough security of income and status to permit their bureaucrats to focus their energies on accomplishing organizational objectives, and these normally include political as well as administrative functions. They will strive to secure adequate resources and to clarify and implement their goals so that they can succeed in their official duties. By contrast, in poor countries, deplorable working conditions and insufficient material rewards have a destructive effect on the morale of public officials, inclining them to stress their unsatisfied expedient needs.

Admittedly, it is easier to satisfy the expedient needs of public officials in relatively affluent industrialized democracies than it is in poverty-stricken third world countries. However, we should remember that a century or two ago, Western countries were not much better off than those of the third world today. Nevertheless, coups were rare in all the Western countries before they became industrialized. Perhaps some historical differences may explain this disparity.

The countries that experienced few or no military coups made the transition to modern bureaucracy before experiencing a radical proliferation in the number of salaried officials. Although traditional monarchs did rely on patronage and their appointees usually become retainers, they were unlikely to replace them with new incumbents every few years. Moreover, as these kingdoms evolved into parliamentary systems—whether they took the form of constitutional monarchies or republics—merit-based career officials eventually replaced retainers while bureaucracies expanded slowly, in parallel with the growth of the state's income.

Moreover, bureaucratic expansion during the nineteenth century occurred rather slowly, in parallel with the process of industrialization. This meant that, on the whole, the expedient interests of public officials were well cared for—many no doubt felt that their situations were actually improving as regular salaries replaced prebendary income. The presidentialist regimes, for the most part, also evolved slowly during the nineteenth century and their salaried bureaucracies expanded concurrently with the industrial revolution. Consequently, despite revolutionary struggles and civil wars, few coups occurred during these formative years.

By contrast, in the twentieth century, following the industrial revolution and the establishment of a world capitalist system, all the bureaucracies of the third world had traumatic experiences when they gained their independence. New and inexperienced political regimes replaced the entrenched imperial authorities who had created colonial administrations as instruments of domination and economic exploitation. These new states inherited large-scale and costly postindustrial bureaucracies that they could not afford to support at preestablished salary levels. Because of inflationary pressures, the real income of many officials declined. Consequently, regardless of regime type, the new states often could not satisfy the basic needs of their bureaucrats, who, in turn, supported coups to replace constitutional regimes with military authoritarianism.

Since the presidentialist regimes experienced military coups more frequently than did the new states that acquired parliamentary systems or single-party rule, I conclude that there must have been some additional factors in presidentialist systems that compounded the typical difficulties experienced by all the new states of the twentieth century. The dynamics of bureaucratic expansionism in all these countries was surely part of the problem. The persistence of retainer bureaucracies in most presidentialist systems led to the growing frustrations described in section IV.B.

The dynamics of bureaucratic dissatisfaction was, of course, compounded by the deep problems inherent in presidentialism that I have already mentioned—see [4]. Collectively, these problems are so acute that we should expect every presidentialist regime to break down and experience military rule from time to time. Since military (bureaucratic) authoritarianism also has profound structural weaknesses, these polities will also soon collapse and be replaced, either by a new coup group or by a regime based, again, on constitutionalism and representative government—typically repeating the fragile presidentialist design (Riggs, 1993a).

No doubt some presidentialist regimes (e.g., in Costa Rica, Colombia, Chile, Venezuela) have been more stable than others. However, all of them—except for the United States—have experienced at least one breakdown followed by military (bureaucratic) rule. To account for this exception, we need to look at the U.S. experience more closely.

B. The Constitutive System

Every modern regime contains two major components: a constitutive system and a bureaucracy. I use the term "constitutive system" to refer to a complex of institutions found in every contemporary state where popular sovereignty (rather than monarchic absolutism) provides a basis for political legitimacy (Riggs, 1969, pp. 243–246). *Every constitutive system has at its core an elected assembly (Parliament, Congress, Soviet, Legislature), an electoral system (including an electorate), and a party system, plus a head of government.* Differences between the constitutive systems determine the properties of parliamentary, presidentialist, and single-party regimes.

The separation of powers, usually viewed as a distinctive feature of presidentialist regimes, is actually a result of the rule that the head of government is elected for a fixed term and, hence, is not accountable to the parliament (see section IV). By contrast, of course, the head of government in parliamentary regimes may be discharged by a parliamentary vote of no confidence. This difference governs relations between the two major components of a constitutive system, creating the basic features of presidentialism as distinguished from parliamentarism.

Every presidentialist regime, consequently, is less able to control a powerful bureaucracy than is a parliamentary system. The reasons are discussed in section I.A. To explain the ability of the United States, exceptionally, to survive without a breakdown we need to understand two important facts: first, how the American constitutive system has managed to function despite its inherent flaws (See [5]) and, second, why the American semipowered (see [8]) bureaucracy has been unable or unwilling to stage a coup. The first topic is examined in Riggs (1993b). Here my focus is on the second.

C. A Semipowered Bureaucracy

From its inception, the U.S. bureaucracy has been semipowered and this has greatly facilitated the exercise of control over it by a relatively weak constitutive system. Four basic factors contribute to this outcome: *federalism, privatization, rotationism*, and *functionism* [29].

1. *Federalism*

Federalism in the United States was explicitly incorporated into the Constitution and is as important as the presidentialist design. I believe federalism is a necessary though not a sufficient condition for the survival of presidentialism for two reasons: it hampers domination by a single political party [30], and it weakens the central bureaucracy.

Only the effects of federalism on bureaucracy will be discussed here. Clearly, when a bureaucracy is fragmented geographically among a great number of autonomous states and municipalities, the size of the central bureaucracy becomes so small, relative to the total number of public officials, that its power potential is seriously reduced. However, when the armed forces are centralized, this factor may not be decisive. In the U.S. case, a long tradition of localized militias and scattered military bases has greatly reduced the relative power position of the armed forces based in Washington. Elsewhere, more typically, the armed forces are concentrated in the capital city, greatly facilitating coups.

2. *Privatization*

Privatization refers to the practice of contracting with private organizations (both nonprofit and profit-making) to carry out functions that in other countries are normally administered by public officials. Ira Sharkanski has estimated that "more people work for private firms under contract to the U.S. government than work for the government directly" (1979, p. 5). The implications are evident: the more public functions are performed by nonofficials, the fewer the number of officials. Without privatization, the federal bureaucracy would be at least twice as large as it is or has been; thus privatization greatly reduces the U.S. bureaucracy's power potential.

Two intrinsic properties of the U.S. bureaucracy that may be even more significant remain to be analyzed: namely rotationism and functionism. Together, they explain both the rise and significance of bureaucratic professionalism in the U.S.

VI. BUREAUCRATIC PROFESSIONALISM

When Andrew Jackson became President in 1829 he found a host of retainers in office. Leonard D. White tells us, "The spirit of the Federalist system favored continuity of service from the highest to the lowest levels. . . . No property right in office was ever established or seriously advocated, but permanent and continued employment during good behavior was taken for granted" (White, 1951, p. 369). The rotation system changed all of that: it was established during the Jacksonian period. White reports that President Andrew Jackson (1829–1837) "did not introduce the spoils system," but he did "introduce rotation into the federal system" (1954, pp. 4–5) [31].

A. The Rise of Professionalism

We normally associate the Jacksonian era with the rise of the spoils system, but it was the introduction of rotation that, historically, expanded the practice of spoils, encouraged the routinization (bureaucratization) of the public services, and paved the way for bureaucratic professionalization [32]. How radical the Jacksonian transformation was for all later American Presidents (plus American governors and mayors) becomes apparent only in a comparativist perspective: in other presidentialist regimes, the retention of incumbents has remained the norm, despite the ability of successive Presidents to make new appointments. They typically displace and anger incumbents but do not replace them [33].

1. *Rotationism*

The immediate cause of the Jacksonian "revolution" was the access to power of a populist President during the wave of a substantial expansion in the electorate, both geographically and socially [34]. No doubt the tremendous surge of populist support for Jackson, as a vigorous man of the people, also empowered him to attack existing officeholders who were widely unpopular as upper-class elitists—indeed, most of them were gentlemen, that is, men of property and education. Rotation was also facilitated by the many attractive opportunities offered by the growing private sector and the new settlement opportunities found within a rapidly expanding geographic frontier. Whatever the reasons, the principle of rotationism soon became well established and enabled American presidentialism to abort the development of a retainer bureaucracy that would have become powerful enough to jeopardize its survival.

Retainer power evolves gradually but inexorably. Hold-over officials—especially if they have been downgraded by new patronage appointees—are peculiarly vulnerable to "corrupting" influences. Having lost status and income, they are easily moved to establish self-protective networks (whether as "informal organizations" or "formal unions"). Moreover, they form unethical alliances with private interests and political parties and use these connections both to enhance their influence in the Congress and to secure benefits for their clients [35]. So long as retainers can prevent rotation, they can also block the introduction of a merit system: both are viewed as threats to their own job security. Perhaps above all, when the political (constitutive) system fails to govern acceptably, angry retainers can use their established networks to mobilize support for a military coup group conspiring to overthrow the regime.

By contrast, transients subject to rotation cannot form long-term alliances with outsiders or members of Congress. They have little to lose by the introduction of a merit system and they may even hope that their experience would qualify them for reentry into the government's new career system. The growing public anger at bureaucratic corruption and inefficiency that drove the American reformers, after a long and bitter political struggle, to secure the adoption of the Pendleton Act in 1883 was made possible, I believe, by the absence of significant bureaucratic resistance [36].

The highly partisan rotation policy, therefore, paved the way for the civil service reform movement by degrading the quality of public administration so much that widespread popular dissatisfaction made reform a major political issue. "For more than thirty years," Van Riper tells us, the introduction of the merit system was viewed as "the most essential governmental reform" (Van Riper, 1958, p. 83). A widespread perception of abuse was expressed, typically, by an observer who wrote in 1841 that "performance of official duty was far less requisite to a tenure of office than electioneering services. Hence the offices had become for the most part filled with brawling offensive political partisans of a very low moral standard—their official duties performed by substitutes, or not performed at all" (White, 1954, p. 310).

2. *Nonpartisan Careers*

The provisions of the Pendleton Act that resulted from the reform movement actually laid the foundations for a truly unique type of career system. Most notably, it made tenure in office conditional on a "nonpolitical" (i.e., nonpartisan) pledge. Remember that partisan transients typically received their appointments as a reward for services performed during previous campaigns—to remain in office they were often, if not normally, constrained to support future campaigns, not only by being activists but by paying assessments (White, 1954, pp. 332–343). Now, career officials would be immune from pressure to support party campaigns, either financially or by partisan services—a right most careerists were eager to protect [37].

This stipulation reflected the reality that, to gain political support for the establishment of a merit system, it was necessary to insist that all careerists refrain from supporting any political party [38]. The notion both reflected and promoted the myth of a dichotomy between politics and administration: the evils of the rotation system were attributed to "politics," and the proposed career service was seen as a "nonpolitical" device.

The reform effort could scarcely have succeeded, therefore, without widespread acceptance of the idea that public administration could be separated from (party) politics—that is, that career officials could be isolated from political parties and would not become activists in partisan campaigning [39]. Although the dichotomy myth was born of political expediency, it has come to be accepted as both a normative and an empirical truth. Some of its far-reaching implications for bureaucratic politics and the study of public administration are discussed in section VI.D.2.

Although the "classified services" established under the Pendleton Act continued to grow at the expense of positions reserved for "political appointees," the system of rotation in office remained entrenched and several thousand new appointees are still named by each incoming President [40]. Rotation and careerism have, therefore, coexisted in an uneasy and often embattled relationship to the present day [41]. In order to evaluate the significance and interdependence of careerists and transients in American government we need to understand that these careerists are all functionaries rather than mandarins, and that the necessary role of mandarins has to be played, however imperfectly, by transient political appointees.

3. *Functionism*

The underlying dynamics for the rise of professionalism in the American bureaucracy may be attributed, quite unintentionally, to several provisions of the Pendleton Act that made functionism the norm. Most importantly, it stipulated that the exams should be practical, a provision with far-reaching implications. It also rejected the notion that only young people should be recruited for entry-level tenured careers; rather, positions were to be open and available to qualified candidates, regardless of age. Finally, recruitment was to be apportioned on the basis of population so that candidates from all the states would have equal opportunities for government jobs [42]. A completely new kind of career system evolved, exceptionally, in the United States as a result of these specifications.

To understand how exceptional the American system was, we need to be clear about the properties of the classical mandarin system manifested in the original Chinese model, as it was adapted to the needs of the Indian Civil Service and the British administrative class [43]. It was the starting point for the debates that led to the Pendleton Act but resulted in a very different kind of bureaucratic system. A mandarinate is recruited by academic, not practical, exams; recruitment is closed, not open; and it leads to a status-based, not a position-based, career system. Put differently, academic exams (philosophical, literary, historical, mathematical, etc.) paved the way for young university graduates to enter a generalist career service in which personal rank, not positions to be filled, is emphasized [44].

A generalist mandarin class or cadre has two properties of fundamental importance: first, it is powerful, and second it can coordinate programs at a macropolicy level. Its members identify themselves with the bureaucracy as their primary frame of reference and source of self-esteem. Consequently, mandarins easily establish close bonds or intrabureaucratic networks that enhance their power position. They lack "professional standing" in the sense that they do not have university degrees in a particular field of expertise such as medicine, law, education, or agriculture. However, their experience (rather than their university training) gives them genuine managerial competence and an ability to look at the overall needs of a government. They understand how diverse and often competing programs can be coordinated, and they can achieve administrative excellence without formal preentry training in Public Administration.

The provisions of the Pendleton Act precluded the development of a mandarinate in America. Instead, a highly diversified set of functionally specialized career officers came into being, each oriented to specific jobs, program areas, policies, and ultimately, professions. A foundation had been laid by the Morrill Land-Grant College Act of 1862, that was intended to help finance institutions that would "teach agriculture and the mechanic arts" and enhance the opportunities of "the industrial classes in the several pursuits and professions in life" (Edmund 1978, pp. 15–16). Apportionment among the states provided an impetus for the new land grant colleges to strengthen and develop their training programs so as to equip their graduates to take the "practical" civil service examinations. Strangely, a substantial and growing literature on the characteristics and problems of the profession pays little or no attention to the linkages between bureaucratic appointments and professional status; see Moore (1970) for a good example of this literature.

The traditional liberal arts college (especially the Ivy League schools) were effectively bypassed by the authorizing legislation, for both geographic and substantive reasons. The new state universities were able to strengthen their burgeoning professional schools by adding academic departments. They gradually evolved into great state universities well equipped to train an increasingly professionalized career bureaucracy in the United States. The convergence of these factors produced a higher level of professionalism in the U.S. bureaucracy than any to be found in other countries, regardless of their constitutional design [45].

B. The Consequences of Professionalism

Although the rise of a professionalized career bureaucracy was neither the intention nor the immediate result of the Pendleton Act, it was a long-term consequence. The practical exams were gradually transformed into tests of professional knowledge and capabilities. Open recruitment permitted experienced professionals, not only recent university graduates, to enter the public service, thereby facilitating the professionalization of the U.S. career bureaucracy. Initially, I believe, many professionals were reluctant to accept the controls imposed by a bureaucratic hierarchy, but eventually they found that they could influence administrative policies and they began to exert pressures through their own organizations to create conditions favorable to their professional standards and norms, including recognition of professional standing (degrees and certificates) as requirements for specific categories of bureaucratic posts (Willbern, 1954, p. 15).

Bureaucratic professionalization had several important consequences that can be described systematically by reference to two variables: positive/negative and intrinsic/extrinsic. By the first I refer to evaluation of the results as good or bad; by the second, to the immediate or direct effects of something versus the indirect or feedback effects. Circular, not linear, causation is taken for granted in this discussion—if A causes B, it is assumed that by a feedback effect, B also influences A. When circular causation has a negative effect, we often speak of it as a vicious cycle. To refer to a positive effect, we may speak instead of a benign circle. Professionalism in the U.S. bureaucracy is implicated in both vicious and benign cycles. One could discuss these interdependent relations in any order, but I will look at the positive effects before the negative, and under each heading, the intrinsic before the extrinsic. However, because of circular causation each aspect has implications for the others.

C. Positive-Intrinsic Consequences

Bureaucratic professionalism has surely enhanced the level of administrative performance within specific niches. Engineers, for example, are qualified and motivated to perform well within the domain of their special competence. Their motives are complex, however. Although subject to hierarchic intrabureaucratic and political constraints, they also respond to norms established by the professional associations in which they participate. No doubt their early socialization in professional schools lays the foundation for the sensitivity to professional norms that is reinforced throughout the life of a professional by continuous involvement in interest networks that link the schools with officials and private sector practitioners [46].

Medical and legal associations are familiar to all, but parallel organizations can be found in every professional domain. All three branches of the presidentialist regime are also implicated insofar as professionalism has penetrated both Congress and the courts. By a feedback effect, for example, court decisions affecting bureaucratic conduct and criteria have increased the need for and influence of lawyers in many government agencies. Decisions affecting health benefits, safety standards, environmental safeguards, and so on, have similarly enhanced the role of physicians, engineers, and natural scientists.

A useful distinction is needed between standing and standards. Professional standing is acquired by certification upon completion of required training programs in a school, but professional standards become internalized as behavioral norms that are continuously reinforced by associates and reference groups. By stressing "practical" tests, the Pendleton Act enabled professional standing to become, gradually, a major criterion or prerequisite for personnel recruitment. The consequence has been that professional standards (often in conflict with each other as well as with governmental rules and political goals) have become the basic guidelines for administrative performance by innumerable American career officials (Wilson, 1989, p. 60) [47].

D. Positive-Extrinsic Consequences

The prevalence of professional standards in American public administration has produced two important results: it has facilitated the survival of American presidentialism and it has motivated the rise of Public Administration in America.

1. *Regime Survival*

The first consequence was unintended and is still unmeasured: namely, a significant reduction in the power position of the American bureaucracy reduces the possibility of a coup d'état. This can be explained as a feedback effect of the provisions of the Pendleton Act. Most bureaucracies—whether anchored in a top echelon of mandarins or based on retainers—generate a powerful sense of intrabureaucratic loyalty and identity. Of course, mandarins, like professionals, have standards, but these are bureaucratic standards—they relate to the esprit de corps or morale of officials as officials, and they reflect a strong sense of loyalty to the state. The familiar term administrative state is quite appropriate when referring to mandarin-powered regimes, and it helps us understand why notions of the state are so prevalent in most parliamentary systems. By contrast, I believe it is an imprecise term to characterize the United States, which might more precisely be called a network state.

As for presidentialist systems outside the United States, bureaucratic solidarity assuredly evolves among retainers, but it becomes self-serving to the degree that status anxiety motivates the development of informal organizations or networks dedicated to the preservation of bureaucratic privileges and security. Intrabureaucratic networks among retainers as well as mandarins, however, can generate high levels of solidarity and power.

Whenever a regime fails to adopt policies that confront its great problems effectively and, therefore, aggravate its major crises, a powerful bureaucracy is likely to support a coup. To the degree that parliamentary regimes are politically effective, mandarin bureaucracies are unlikely to become disaffected enough to back coup attempts. Moreover, their experience and loyalty to the state enable them to administer effectively enough to permit the regime to implement its policies, thereby dissolving the motives for a revolt.

By contrast, whenever a regime is severely hampered in its efforts to cope with crises, the risks of a coup are enhanced. A vicious circle comes into effect: retainers lack the qualifications and standards needed to administer well and, as performance of the state declines, they become more disaffected. At critical junctures, their power position enables them to support successful coups.

The American exception reflects the fact that its professionalized bureaucrats lack the solidarity to support a military coup. Moreover, their professional competence helps them carry out relevant policies and programs within their niches, that is, when they are compatible with the professional standards formulated by the associations in which they are active. These associations help link many American bureaucrats with private sector constituencies and the legislative committees (with their staffs) that form the broader interest networks in which they participate. The personal satisfaction experienced by professionals who are able to satisfy their standards means that they do not want to seize power. Moreover, because of their semipowered status as a bureaucracy, they could not succeed even if they were to support a coup attempt.

Moreover, functionaries, in ambivalent alliance with members of Congress and powerful lobbies, buttress the capacity of that overloaded body to handle a vast agenda of public policy issues and to maintain its autonomy as a separate branch of government. Well entrenched professionals in the bureaucracy, working with supportive members of Congress and their own staff professionals, also cooperate to maintain the system of seniority that helps incumbents win elections and retain cherished committee assignments (Riggs, 1993b). The resulting autonomy of government agencies permits different and even conflicting norms and policies to flourish and coexist. It enables a host of governmental functions to become relatively autonomous and stable—they can survive successive elections regardless of which political party happens to be in power. The main functions of government have become self-perpetuating and they help the regime as a whole to work, even while frustrating successive Presidents who find that they cannot guide or coordinate a massive infrastructure of highly autonomous bureaus.

2. *Public Administration*

A second *positive-extrinsic* effect of bureaucratic professionalism involves the development of Public Administration as an academic field. Clearly, Public Administration was not a recognized profession nor were "practical" exams created to test administrative capabilities for almost half a century after the Pendleton Act. Gradually, however, the need for explicit training in Public Administration gained recognition, textbooks were prepared and professional training in this area came into existence. A management exam was established for M.P.A. graduates. Although many professionals in the bureaucracy recognized the need for additional training and knowledge to help them administer more effectively, no professional role as a line administrator has evolved in the American bureaucracy. At best, some of the staff fields of Public Administration have gained such recognition—that is, one can be a professional in personnel, budgeting, accounting and auditing, planning, or office management, but it is difficult to find positions earmarked for "professionals" in general Public Administration.

A notable aspect of Public Administration as a field of teaching and research—if not as a profession—is its disposition to avoid politics. This attitude is rooted in the Pendleton Act's stipulation that careerists should be nonpartisan, neither supporting financially nor working in an electoral campaign. Actually, careerists were delighted with this stipulation, which overcame an onerous burden that patronage appointees (both retainers and transients) had long carried. The dichotomy between politics and administration may have been an important consideration driving the reform effort, but I suspect that it was also a weighty consequence of the legislation.

The new training programs that arose chose to focus on preparing civil servants for entry to the nonpartisan career services. Military officers already had their own training programs, including those at West Point and other military academies and staff colleges. Partisan appointees were typically politicos whose party services were being rewarded—professionally oriented training programs could scarcely reach them. Given these constraints, Public Administration evolved necessarily as a "nonpolitical" (i.e., nonpartisan) activity intended primarily for future and present civil servants. As a fragile new academic project, training in "Public Administration" could not survive bureaucratic opposition—quite the reverse, it needed (nonpartisan) bureaucratic support in order to assure graduates of career appointments.

Under these conditions, the study of government as a unified focus of teaching and research became subdivided into two contrasting and even antagonistic fields: Public Administration programs eschewed politics, turning to business management and all the social sciences except politics for inspiration, while political science systematically downplayed public administration as either unworthy of serious study or even an essentially "nonpolitical" activity (Waldo, 1968, pp. 7–8) [48]. The negative consequences of this orientation are discussed in section VI.F.2.

E. Negative-Intrinsic Consequences

Professionalization produces American bureaucrats who cannot manage and coordinate programs that cut across the interests of many government agencies—turf warfare and intrabureaucratic struggles are inescapable. Even within the same agency, when several different professional fields are involved, conflicts proliferate.

All presidentialist constitutions, by definition, generate an overriding problem of power dispersion in the bureaucracy by creating three centers of legitimacy (executive, legislative, and judicial), each of which impinges directly, and with conflicting normative and action implications, on the bureaucracy. The adoption by Congress, under the Pendleton Act, of a functionist mode for institutionalizing the career bureaucracy reinforced this divisive force, especially by paving the way for the emergence of bureaucratic professionalism, leading to the proliferation of powerful interest networks. When viewed from the perspective of would-be integrators who seek to reconcile divergent forms and overlapping jurisdictions, the combined pressures for the dispersal of power are overwhelming. Career officials, especially the professionals, build their own power base and often appropriate policy-making powers from Congress. Krislov and Rosenbloom tell us that "the bureaucratic agency may actually organize a constituency in order to assure an adequate level of support for its activities. . . . Policymaking is largely transferred from the elected branches of government to bureaucratic agencies" (1981, pp. 82–83) [49].

In this context, predictably, successive American governments have struggled in vain to find a workable strategy for achieving coordination. As Seidman (1980) writes, "The quest for coordination is in many respects the twentieth-century equivalent of the medieval search for the philosopher's stone. If only we can find the right formula for coordination, we can reconcile the irreconcilable, harmonize competing and wholly divergent interests, overcome irrationalities in our government structures, and make hard policy choices to which no one will dissent" (p. 200). Willbern (1954), by contrast, has pointed out that at the intergovernmental level, professionals may well serve a positive coordinating function, helping to link activities that would otherwise remain uncoordinated (p. 17). Nevertheless, it has seemed unfortunate to many that the British model of a generalist administrative elite was not established in the 1880s. However, when the power potential of any mandarinate is understood, it becomes clear that if the United States had embraced that model, it would almost surely have succumbed to bureau power.

1. *The Senior Executive Service*

In the absence of any understanding of this relationship, it is not surprising that efforts were made from time to time to create an American mandarinate that could coordinate the far-flung and highly dispersed apparatus of governance in America. A project to establish a cadre of generalist civil servants became one of the strong recommendations of the second Hoover Commission in 1955. The proposal was long resisted by Congress, however. Its members saw that "rotation of career administrators would break up long-standing and mutually profitable relationships between congressional subcommittees and career officials in the line agencies and bureaus of the executive branch" (Mackenzie, 1981, p. 127). Resistance to a youthful British style class of future mandarins proved invincible. A compromise that was finally accepted appeared in the form of a senior mandarinate to be created by recruiting established functionaries. After an intense struggle led by President Jimmy Carter, Congress endorsed the idea and the Senior Executive Service (SES) was established through the Civil Service Reform Act of 1987. So far, however, the SES has not displayed the properties of a genuine "mandarin" class nor became a cadre of "super-bureaucrats" (Campbell and Szablowski, 1979, p. 217).

The SES has not even impressed its incumbents as a highly prestigious or financially attractive career goal—something that would truly astonish anyone familiar with the power and high status of the "mandarins" in parliamentary regimes [50]. In both the Chinese and British prototypes, authentic mandarins were recruited as young nonprofessionals and spent their entire careers as generalists—perhaps this is the only way a true mandarinate can be formed (Dogan, 1975, p. 4); see [42].

In the American case, outstanding professionals who might have been recruited for the SES already had well established networks and standards that could not easily be reconciled with those of a mandarinate. The essential failure of the SES project, however, is fortunate for the survival of American presidentialism: a genuine mandarin system would have undermined the power positions of both the President and the Congress, creating a kind of "meritocracy" reminiscent of Plato's Guardians. Admittedly, this is a speculation since we have no example of a viable presidentialist regime with an established mandarinate of generalists, but the logic of the scenario seems pretty persuasive [51].

2. *The Patronage Alternative*

By default, the best mechanism available to an American President in the attempt to coordinate the host of competing professionalized bureaucratic agencies is reliance on patronage appointments. Unfortunately, perhaps because of the dichotomy myth and their preoccupation with careerists, students of American Public Administration have failed to pay serious attention to both the need for and the costs of employing a large number of transients as public administrators, including members of the Cabinet.

Political scientists have, of course, studied this subject but in a political context that directs attention to the problems of the presidency and Congress rather than the bureaucracy. The cabinet and the office of the White House offer contemporary Presidents their main opportunity to create a governing apparatus that can modify the diverse priorities of professionals in the career bureaucracy so as to align them with the popular "mandate" given by the electorate. Traditionally this was done by appointing *politicos*, persons without professional commitments of their own whose primary loyalty was to the President and policies endorsed by the winning party.

Increasingly, however, amphibians or technopols rather than politicos are employed to staff the executive entourage or "sacerdotal collegium" (Newland, 1987, pp. 49–52). The term *amphibian* has been used to characterize in-and-outers who find themselves equally at home inside and outside the government service [52]. Typically, departmental secretaries and their assistants are broad-gauge professionals whose personal networks reach extensively into the constituencies served by government departments and agencies. Instead of helping the President coordinate diverse overlapping programs and policies, amphibians, I suspect, often share the professional standards and norms of career officers under their authority. By contrast, cabinet members in a parliamentary regime are primarily politicians without professional commitments. The fact that they must stand or fall as a collectivity provides an external sanction to reinforce their intention to coordinate diverse policy goals in the interest of the state.

Presidential cabinet members are subject to no such constraints. They stand or fall as individuals, each vulnerable separately to the President's preferences and their ability to command support from members of Congress, especially as expressed by relevant committees. Increasingly, the executive office of the President, rather than the cabinet, has become the locus of political coordination in the American system. Ultimately, of course, the President must almost stand alone as the person finally responsible for coordinating the deeply dispersed structures of power (Newland, 1987; Pfiffner, 1987; Durant, 1990; Moe, 1991) [53].

Despite their vast patronage powers, American Presidents can never really dominate the careerists nor assure coordination among them. As Wamsley tells us: "The political appointee . . . does not stride in the door of the government organization as the powerful proconsul of an emperor but more like a tentative and lonely ambassador appointed to a beleaguered foreign outpost. . . . Their fortunes lie more in the hands of Congress, particularly its committees and subcommittees, and of interest groups than the president or White House staff" (Wamsley, 1990, p. 136).

The proper role of transients (both politicos and amphibians) in the American government remains a lively theme of debate. Without them, the dispersed orientations of a professionalized and semipowered bureaucracy would almost threaten chaos. Although patronage appointees cannot truly coordinate or reconcile intrabureaucratic conflicts, the problem would surely be much greater without them. They provide a completely inadequate solution to the problem of coordination, yet without them, malcoordination would become so great a problem that it alone would threaten the collapse of the system—not because of a coup but rather *through* internecine strife [54].

F. Negative-Extrinsic Consequences

Bureaucratic professionalism in the United States has reinforced the myth of a political/administrative dichotomy. The importance of the dichotomy myth as a reform slogan is familiar to all students of American Public Administration, and much has been written on the validity/invalidity of the dichotomy. However, its consequences need more careful analysis. The professionalization of the American bureaucracy which underpins its semipowered status owes much to this myth. At least, it supplemented the other factors that can be attributed to the Pendleton Act, as explained in sections VI.A.2 and VI.A.3.

Moreover, the separation of Public Administration as an academic field of study and teaching from the study of politics can easily be attributed to the myth—see section VI.D.2. If careerists were to be "nonpolitical" civil servants, it seemed to follow that they should study only nonpolitical subjects such as those taught in all professional schools. When the project to establish professional schools of "Public Administration" emerged, it accepted the need for a nonpolitical orientation.

Consequently, the phenomena that generated American Public Administration theory as a distinctive and important field of research and teaching also hampered the analysis of the power potential of appointed public officials. Had a Comparative framework been used, students of American government would have noticed how exceptional its bureaucracy is. No doubt the parochialism of a mode of analysis that focussed attention exclusively on the truly unique situation in the United States hampered any serious effort to go beyond the stereotypes generated by the dichotomy myth [55].

1. *Bureaucratic Power*

Quite clearly, all bureaucracies in democratic regimes are significantly more powerful than the semipowered U.S. bureaucracy. Moreover, all the governments of the industrialized democracies are able to control and use powerful bureaucracies effectively for administrative purposes. The United States alone among presidentialist regimes has been able to avoid a regime breakdown—and it is the only such regime that has a semipowered bureaucracy. Surely if, like others, it had a powerful bureaucracy, it would also have experienced one or more catastrophic breakdowns during a time of major crisis.

Paradoxically, the relative lack of power of the American bureaucracy and the continuity of the U.S. regime combined to render the idea of a dichotomy between politics and administration plausible. In other countries—and especially in (undemocratic) bureaucratic polities—appointed officials (military and civil) are powerful enough to block serious analysis of their operational methods, and their characteristic preentry training requirements call for legal, humanistic, or even scientific education but not for a professional education in Public Administration—unless, sad to say, the approach has been denatured by the omission of its political aspects [56].

Bureaucratic professionalism, then, has been a major factor in the explanation of the relative weakness of American civil servants while also providing a context in which the creation of training programs for public administrators could flourish. Although "Public Administration" never gained full recognition as a profession within the U.S. bureaucracy, it did acquire marginal respect both for its contributions to various career staff roles and for its capacity to help line administrators enhance their own careers. These advantages have actually induced many contemporary American administrators to support Public Administration as a useful and nonthreatening activity. Their willingness to collaborate in organizations like ASPA (American Society for Public Administration) and NAPA (National Academy of Public Administration) provides evidence of this attitude, by contrast with the situation in most other countries, where public officials and academics teaching Public Administration typically distrust each other and avoid contact in such associations.

2. *A Myth Perpetuated*

This cooperative attitude facilitates Public Administration as an academic field, provided—we may speculate—that the myth of a dichotomy between politics and administration is sustained. So long as serious inquiry into the phenomena of bureaucratic power is avoided, Public Administrationists are protected from threatening scrutiny by officials and officials are not menaced by scholarly inquiry. As for American political scientists, who might have been expected to look critically at the power position of career officials, we find that they have largely ignored the subject. Perhaps this is so because they accept the myth uncritically or because their penchant for specialization has led them to focus on the components of constitutive systems and to relegate the study of bureaucracy to specialists in Public Administration.

Although the dichotomy myth still prevails in America, there are exceptions which deserve attention. For example, Nachmias and Rosenbloom remark that "all developed nations are thoroughly dependent upon a body of highly specialised and hierarchically organized administrators. . . . Bureaucrats have sometimes been considered a (new) ruling class" (1978, p. 10). Heady (1991) has explained that "comparative public administration is linked closely to the study of comparative politics, and must start from the base provided by recent and current developments in the comparative study of whole political systems" (p. 6). Scholars like these may eventually lead both public administrationists and political scientists in America to see how bureaucracy inescapably links politics and administration.

The dichotomy myth by itself, admittedly, would not have led to the emergence of Public Administration as an important focus of attention in America. Among the other contributing factors we must include the specifications of the Pendleton Act—practical exams; open recruitment for positions, not ranks; and apportionment among the states—all of which reinforced each other to generate the forces that led to the emergence of professionalism in general, and to the field of Public Administration as an unsuccessful candidate for professional status.

The negative aspect also needs to be recognized: careerism could never displace the need for transients as political appointees in the United States. They scarcely recognize Public Administration as a relevant field for preentry training, while Public Administration specialists tend to ignore transients as an irrelevant and undesirable remnant of the spoils era. Whenever political scientists study political appointees, they usually treat them in the context of the presidential institution rather than of bureaucracy and public administration.

To summarize, an important negative-extrinsic consequence of professionalism in the U.S. bureaucracy involves its contribution to the rise of Public Administration as a specialized and very insular field rooted in the politics/administration dichotomy myth. The time has come, I believe, to transcend this limitation: comparative analysis can now reveal the highly political causes and consequences of professionalized bureaucracy in the United States.

VII. COSTS OF PRESIDENTIALISM: A SUMMARY

The manifest purpose of the function-oriented merit system reforms rooted in the Pendleton Act was *administrative* rather than *political*: it produced a growing body of bureaucratic specialists whose institutional memory and professionalism enabled them to implement public policies with some consistency and efficiency despite changes in the presidency. However, these improved administrative capabilities had profoundly important political implications: the creation of stable interest networks based on increasingly entrenched relationships between professionals in public service, congressional subcommittees, and interested private associations or groups (e.g., the "military-industrial complex") meant that most governmental functions would be performed with minimal intervention from the White House and with the active participation of Congress and the court (Riggs, 1988a, pp. 363–365). Moreover, the dispersal of bureau power which resulted meant that a bureaucracy which was politically weak because of its heavy reliance on transients remained weak (or semipowered), thereby overcoming the risk of a coup d'état inherent in all contemporary presidentialist regimes.

A. The Need for Comparativism

The comparative study of presidentialist regimes is needed to clarify these relationships—they remain obscure so long as American government is studied in isolation. All presidentialist regimes originating before the middle of the twentieth century (except the United States) relied heavily on patronage without rotation, leading to the emergence of retainer dominated bureaucracies. Such bureaucracies are both politically powerful and administratively ineffectual. This combination is potentially explosive: it undermines popular support for the regime and provokes bureaucratic disloyalty. During crises, retainer bureaucracies have the power and the motives for revolting and seizing power, after a coup d'état led by military officers.

The United States exception is based, in part at least, on a significant historical difference. Administrative performance by "gentlemen" retainers during the first forty years was probably above average and, during this short period, bureau power could not develop, although abuse of power by some officials fueled the Jacksonian revolution. During the half century which followed, under the rotation system, transients dominated the bureaucracy but were inherently incapable of mobilizing enough power to overthrow the regime, even though their administrative performance was so bad that it alienated many citizens. The reform movement which led to enactment of the Pendleton Act in 1883 initiated the growth of a careerist system dominated by specialists, many of whom were, in time, replaced by professionals.

Because of the external orientation of professionals—and their participation in powerful interest networks which link officials with lobbyists, members of Congress, and associations responsible for the maintenance of professional standards—the reshaped American bureaucracy has remained semipowered. Its political weakness is reinforced by a superstructure of in-and-outer politicos and amphibians, as well as by federalism and heavy reliance on private organizations to implement many governmental functions. This historical sequence was not replicated elsewhere: all of the older presidentialist regimes acquired predominantly retainer bureaucracies that could not be replaced by careerist systems despite noble reform efforts. Two major exceptions are the regimes of South Vietnam and South Korea, whose preexisting mandarin traditions enabled their bureaucracies to replace republican government after one presidency. A third exception is that of the Philippines, where, despite a half-dozen coup attempts following a period of presidential authoritarianism, presidentialism survives. In this case, a specialist career bureaucracy established during the long period of American domination was simply incapable of seizing power.

B. Political Competence

The motivation for any coup stems, I believe, not primarily from the ambitions or greed of government officials, but rather from the inability of a regime to adopt appropriate policies and maintain effective control over the bureaucrats charged with responsibility for their implementation. No doubt any government, during critical times, may find that it cannot cope with severe challenges. However, a great structural difference radically limits the effectiveness of all presidentialist regimes by contrast with parliamentary ones. The constitutional separation of powers in these regimes assigns authority to three branches of government and gives each of them approximately equal powers over the bureaucracy. As a result, not only is it difficult for the regime to formulate adequate policies, but a confused and cross-pressured bureaucracy is often unable to implement effectively the policies that are promulgated. By contrast, the fusion of powers characteristic of parliamentary regimes enables them to formulate and implement policies much more easily. The fact is that all of the industrialized democracies except the United States have parliamentary forms of government and display no intention to switch to presidentialism [57].

The retention by the United States of a constitutional design that was invented in the eighteenth century before any country had established a parliamentary system can be attributed in part to its reluctance to abandon some antiquated but fundamental practices that were rejected as undemocratic by the newer presidentialist republics. However, I believe that even so, the American regime would have broken down during major crises, such as the Civil War, two world wars, and a major depression, had its bureaucracy not been both relatively weak (semipowered) and reasonably effective. The professionalization of its career services since the end of the nineteenth century, as augmented by federalism, privatization, and the persistence of transient political appointees in the upper reaches of the bureaucracy, continues to account for this remarkable exception.

C. Basic Reform

Despite its survival and obvious strengths, a growing sense of frustration and disillusionment with government is apparent in contemporary America (Dionne, 1991). Talk about "gridlock" and the evils of "divided government" is rife, especially during presidential campaigns. Almost universally, however, this discourse takes for granted the viability and persistence of a presidentialist constitution. Nevertheless, in a comparativist perspective, we can easily see that this constitutional design is essentially flawed and its maintenance imposes a heavy burden on the American people. We are, therefore, confronted with a profound dilemma. Comparative analysis of many viable democracies, all subscribing to some kind of parliamentary system, might clarify the options whenever consensus could be reached on the need for basic amendments to the existing U.S. Constitution.

Because parliamentary systems vary widely among themselves, and some work much more successfully than others, it will not be easy to reach consensus on any single alternative to the existing constitutional design in the United States. Moreover, the very survival of the regime for two centuries provides the basis for a powerful argument that it is safer to tinker with and sustain a flawed system that works than to accept the far greater risks involved in seeking consensus on an alternative design.

No doubt it would be wildly irresponsible to promote any radical restructuring of the persisting Constitution in the United States before undertaking a deep analysis, based on extensive comparisons with experience elsewhere, in order to learn more about the fundamental dynamics of alternative systems and the requisite strategies for gaining consensus on possible options. Any such analysis ought to pay serious attention to the role and problems of public bureaucracy, including both its power potential and its administrative capabilities.

The focus of such a continuing enterprise ought to be on the conditions needed for representative government to survive, to be viable. No matter how idealistic may be the procedures and goals of a constitution, democratic values are easily sacrificed whenever autocratic and authoritarian systems destroy a fragile democracy. We now need to mobilize all relevant resources—research, education, mass information, and political action—in a coordinated effort to understand the requisite conditions for the maintenance of viable constitutionalism.

NOTES

1. Despite the normal assumption in American Public Administration that bureaucrats are "nonpolitical" administrators, in fact all modern bureaucracies have their own expedient interests and both the will and ability to exercise political power. The widespread incidence

of coups throughout the third world reflects not just military power but, more generally, bureaucratic dissatisfaction and influence—many civil servants support and work for the military juntas that spearhead the seizure of power because they also feel threatened by political anarchy and recognize that their security and income depend on regime maintenance. A cabinet composed mainly of career officials (both civil and military) is typical of all bureaucratic polities, reflecting the triumph of bureaucratic power (Riggs, 1966 and 1981). (Interestingly, the original concept of a bureaucracy was that of a polity dominated by appointed officials (Riggs, 1979).

The seizure of power by armed officials in many third world countries is only the tip of an iceberg. In fact, in every contemporary state the ability of the regime to maintain control over its bureaucracy and to share power with it in the development and implementation of public policy is problematic. Parliamentary systems are inherently better equipped to exercise such control than presidentialist regimes because the concentration of power in a cabinet that is also a majority-based ruling committee of the parliament provides a framework within which a state bureaucracy (composed almost exclusively of careerists, including mandarins) can be prevented from dominating the polity. Put more positively, only parliamentary regimes can maintain effective long-term control over a mandarin bureaucracy (Dogan, 1975, pp. 3–24), while permitting them to exercise great de facto power as policy "advisers."

In presidentialist regimes, by contrast, the dispersal of power between the executive and legislative branches weakens the capacity of governments to constrain the bureaucracy, rendering them vulnerable to the seizure of power by appointed (mainly military) officials. So vulnerable are such regimes to bureaucratic power that, I believe, only a politically weak bureaucracy—as found in the United States—can be kept under control in a presidentialist system.

2. Both parliamentary and authoritarian regimes are often called presidential regimes because they elect—substantively or tokenistically—their heads of state. In this sense all republics are presidential by contrast with monarchies. In this article I shall discuss only one kind of presidential regime, one in which the President is really elected (not just confirmed in office) to serve as the head of government as well as the head of state. To emphasize this point, I shall use the admittedly awkward terms presidentialist and presidentialism for this concept. Presidential is used only to characterize the office of the President, and this word is capitalized to distinguish the head of a presidentialist regime from other kinds of presidents.
3. It is important to discriminate between the geographical and functional distribution of power. The word centralization is often used for both. Here I shall use it only for the geographic distribution of power between central and local governments. Both parliamentary and presidentialist regimes may be centralized or localized so this concept does not distinguish between them. However, the localization of power, as in a federal system, probably contributes (though not always) to the survival of presidentialism.

By contrast, the concentration or dispersion of power, by functions, varies with our regime types. All presidentialist regimes must disperse power because each of the three main branches exercises autonomous authority based on rather crudely distributed "functions"—executive, legislative, and judicial. By contrast, power in parliamentary systems is concentrated since cabinets unite the "executive" and the "legislative" functions in a single structure. It is much easier, therefore, for parliamentary bureaucracies to follow coherent and coordinated policies based on cabinet rule than it is for presidentialist bureaucracies, who are always cross-pressured by three competing sources of authority—unity of command is an empty phrase for them.

4. Every presidentialist regime confronts serious difficulties that are inherent in the separation of powers among the executive, legislative, and judicial branches of government, leading sometimes to gridlock or stalemate. Such difficulties also seriously hamper the operations of every President and Congress, viewed as separate institutions, and they usually ruin political parties and the party system while also bewildering the electorate and corrupting the electoral system (details are presented in Riggs, 1993b).
5. As of 1965, more than thirty countries had adopted American-style presidentialist constitutions and all of them had experienced breakdowns, usually (91%) through a coup d'état whose leaders scrapped the constitution and ruled autocratically. By contrast, the capacity of parliamentary regimes to resist breakdown was much greater than that of presidentialist systems. Only 31% of the forty-three new states that established parliamentary forms of government experienced such collapses (Riggs, 1993a). Although an updated recoding will no doubt lead to some revision of these findings, the difference is so dramatic that it raises insistent questions about the problems with presidentialism.

A variety of important, though often essentially undemocratic, practices have enabled the United States to deal with these problems more effectively than its counterparts in other presidentialist regimes, where, as we have seen, breakdowns have universally occurred. These practices—which I call paraconstitutional because of their importance for the survival of any presidentialist regime—include federalism, single-member-district majoritarianism, nonvoting by many eligible citizens, senioritism, lobbyism, and relatively unregulated capitalism. My first effort to examine the relation of these "isms" to the survival of presidentialism in the United States can be found in Riggs (1988b). Subsequently, I found confirmation that the absence of these practices in other presidentialist regimes contributed to their breakdown. Many of these practices are so patently undemocratic that they have been rejected and replaced in the newer presidentialist democracies. Although their retention by the older U.S. regime has been severely criticized (the Electoral College symbolizes many such relics), their importance for the survival of representative government in the United States remains largely unrecognized.

Several scholars now recognize the inherent obstacles to the success of presidentialism, but they have not analyzed the reasons for the American exception. Juan Linz, for example, has written most perceptively, "Presidentialism is ineluctably problematic because it operates according to the rule of 'winner-take-all'—an arrangement that tends to make democratic politics a zero-sum game, with all the potential for conflict such games portend" (1990, p. 56). By contrast, he argues, it is possible for even small political parties in parliamentary systems to win seats in the legislature and even to join coalition governments. Clearly, Linz is thinking mainly of the President's ability to promulgate policies which will, assuredly, alienate defeated partisans who are committed to different outcomes.

However, in the American case, a powerful Congress seriously limits the President's authority and thereby dampens the impact of the winner-take-all game. Moreover, the President's patronage powers are seriously moderated by Congress, and the presence in contemporary America of an overwhelming number of careerists has radically reduced the President's authority over appointments. Consider, also, that bureaucratic fragmentation due to federalism, and the great power of capitalism and free enterprise in the United States inhibits the number of government-financed benefits—health, education, social security, welfare—over which the President can exercise control.

A vigorous capitalist market system in the United States also offers innumerable job opportunities in the private sector that, for most people, are more attractive than public office. This also reduces the costs of the winner-take-all syndrome. By contrast, in other presidentialist countries, the demand for government jobs is disproportionately large because of the relative weakness of the private sector. Such factors as these have simply lowered the stakes of the zero-sum game in the United States (Riggs, 1993b).

6. When a constitutional crisis leads a President to usurp power, the Congress is discharged and the constitution suspended. Clearly a constitutional stipulation authorizing the executive and legislative branches to exercise independent authority by no means assures the survival of such a system. In any test of strength, a President can normally quash the Congress. The basic rule sustaining a presidentialst regime is the requirement that the head of government be elected for a fixed term, not subject to dismissal by a legislative vote of no confidence. Impeachment is not such a vote since it is a judicial procedure designed to oust Presidents guilty of "high crimes and misdemeanors" and does not automatically lead to a change of government, but only to the replacement of the President by someone (e.g., a vice president) of the same political persuasion.

   Although Congress sometimes overshadows the President in presidentialist regimes, I do not know of any case in which a Congress has usurped power and abolished the presidency. When a presidentialist regime confronts a deep crisis, therefore, the typical scenario involves crushing the Congress and suspending the constitution, occasionally by the President with military support, but much more often by the military acting alone.

7. Although retainer is normally used for family servants, it has also been employed to mean "civil service retainers" (W3), and I shall use it only in this sense, to identify patronage (political) appointees who retain their posts—to be distinguished clearly from merit-based careerists, whose tenure in office is assured by a legally binding contract with the state. Historically, a king's retainers become officials and the word was long used to refer to them. Although the word has fallen out of use in democratic regimes, I see no reason not to use it to refer to patronage appointees who retain their offices on a long-term basis (cf. section III, Table 1, p. 99, and [16]).

8. The familiar dichotomy between powerful and powerless does not enable us to distinguish adequately between significant levels of bureaucratic power. The four-level scale from powerless through semipowered to powerful and dominant is discussed in Riggs (1992)—when precise measurement is needed, a numerical scale could be used. Following a coup, public officials in a bureaucratic polity are politically dominant and, by contrast, nonparty officials in a single-party regime are typically powerless. Democratic regimes typically have powerful bureaucracies, whether they be presidentialist or parliamentary in character. The United States is exceptional among such democracies because its bureaucracy is only semipowered, a property that contributes significantly, I believe, to the survival of this regime.

9. Article II of the U.S. Constitution prescribes, "The Executive Power shall be vested in a President." A useful analysis of what the founders meant by the executive powers can be found in Cronin (1989, pp. 180–208). American writers on Public Administration usually claim that the administrative functions are implied by the President's executive powers, but others admit that all three branches of government in a presidentialist system have authority over bureaucrats. The classic explanations offered by Goodnow and Willougby, for example, assign the "executive/administrative" functions to different branches—see [23] and [24].

   Still others claim that the Constitution is silent on public administration. Thus, Stillman, a contemporary, writes that the Constitution leaves "a blank slate involving 'administration' as something to be filled in and defined by later Americans" (Stillman, 1991, p. 20). Clearly, he views administration as something different from the executive function, something that still needed to be created after the Constitution had been established. He even argues that, during the first century, American public administration—if it existed—was determined by the regime's statelessness (i.e., the lack of a career bureaucracy). Genuine public administration, he asserts, arose only as and after the creation of an American (administrative) state following the introduction of the career system.

I differ from Stillman about the first American century when, I think, we did have a state, but it was clearly not an administrative state possessed of a career bureaucracy. We might call it a civic state in which citizens, through "republican" institutions, could manage their own affairs and the limited apparatus of government—Webster's dictionary gives "attendant on citizenship" as the original meaning of civic. The Jacksonian ideal of amateurs in government seems to fit this model, as does the Athenian model of a city state in which officeholders were selected by lot (Waldo, 1980, p. 84). Surely administrative functions are performed in a civic state even though it lacks a professional career service.

No doubt the quality of American public administration was radically changed after the establishment of career services, a transformation that also led to the development of Public Administration as a subject field. (Following Waldo's example, I shall use public administration for the function and Public Administration for the subject field that studies this function [1980, p. 6n]). In this field, the administrative function is often understood as part of or even identical with the "executive" function. Borrowing from business administration, the President may be said to have powers similar to those of the "CEO" of a private corporation, that is, someone responsible for "managing" the whole federal bureaucracy. Indeed, management is often used—instead of the "administrative" or "executive" function—to talk about the President's role, viewing Congress and the courts as interlopers who have no legitimate right to shape bureaucratic behavior.

Some writers in Public Administration go even further, claiming that the career bureaucracy ought to be recognized as a fourth branch of government with its own inherent authority—see section IV.B and [27]. In this perspective, the administrative function is seen as different from that of all three branches of a presidentialist regime. Bureaucratic agencies should possess separate authority coequal with that of the three other branches.

My own opinion is that neither the Founding Fathers nor modern writers on Public Administration have made a clear distinction between the administrative and the executive functions (or even management). Although the Constitution clearly assigned the "executive function" to the President (as "Chief Executive"), all three branches of any presidentialist regime are inextricably involved in the administrative function as they cross-pressure the bureaucracy to accept norms that are often in conflict with each other (Rosenbloom, 1983). Trying to institutionalize public administration as a fourth autonomous function cannot really work.

The apparent dilemmas of Public Administration in America are inherent in the basic rules of any presidentialist regime within which no integrated structure of authority is possible and all efforts to generate a consistent and coherent view of the administrative function in such regimes are bound to fail. In short, the institutionalization of separated powers sets a context within which powerful and administratively competent bureaucracies cannot be managed effectively: only a fragmented, and hence semipowered, bureaucracy can be long sustained. This constraint, rather than any specific constitutional provision, severely limits the kind of bureaucracy that can be tolerated by any presidentialist regime—see Riggs (1994).

10. Actually, the founders could scarcely have imagined the concept of bureaucratic careers based on examinations and the merit system. Although the idea had been invented by the Chinese two thousand years earlier, it became established in Europe only after the American Constitution was promulgated; see [43].

    The system they knew was one in which patronage appointees, under autocratic European rulers, held their positions for a long time as a result of seniority, inertia, and family obligations—indeed, they sometimes inherited posts as a family possession for many generations, a remnant of feudalism. Although they were originally viewed as family retainers, they also served the state which was ruled by their masters, the royal families and the aristocrats. The royal bureaucracy and arbitrary government against which the Declaration of Independence protested ("swarms of Officers to harass our People and eat out their substance") was, indeed, rule by retainers.

    The founders had no alternative vision of a better way to recruit and maintain the administrators of a republic, but they did expect that officials appointed by the President would help implement the laws passed by Congress and that they would stay in office unless discharged for good reasons. Alexander Hamilton, for example, refers to "the assistants or deputies" of the President who "ought to derive their offices from his appointment, at least from his nomination, and ought to be subject to his superintendence." Thus he presupposed political patronage, and he favored the retention principle over rotation: writing about the propensity of "every new President to promote a change of men to fill the subordinate stations," he alleged that such a practice "could not fail to occasion a disgraceful and ruinous mutability in the administration of the government" (Hamilton, 1788, in *Federalist Papers*, 1961, no. 72, p. 436—see also [31]).
11. The Founding Fathers realized this when they specified, (Art. I, Sec. 6), that "no person holding any office under the United States shall be a member of either house during his continuance in office." When members, like Richard Cheney or Les Aspen, accept cabinet positions, they must vacate their seats in Congress.
12. Note that bureaucracy often refers only to careerists, by contrast with retainers or transients, generally presupposing the qualities Max Weber attributed to his "ideal-type." When Durant writes about "helping appointees and bureaucrats to understand their different motivations," he clearly uses "bureaucracy" to refer only to careerists (Durant, 1990, p. 321). This usage makes sense, of course, in parliamentary systems where virtually all appointed officials are careerists, so that "bureaucrat" is a comprehensive term for all nonelected public officials, military and civil. However, the identification of bureaucracy with careerists (and especially with civil servants but not military officers) handicaps the American understanding of public administration because it mistakes a part for the whole—like using apples to mean fruit or Yankees to mean Americans.

    In his discussion of the "intellectual crisis" in American Public Administration, Vincent Ostrom tells us that "Wilson rejected a theory of *democratic* administration while propounding a theory of *bureaucratic* administration as the one rule of 'good' administration for all governments alike" [emphasis added] (Ostrom, 1989, p. 65). In this usage, bureaucrat refers to career civil servants, only a part of the total set of appointed federal officials, and a tiny part when Wilson wrote.

    To make sense in comparative analysis, bureaucracy has to include transient political appointees (and military officers) as well as career civil servants. This understanding would impair the neat hierarchic stereotype of civil service careerists that Ostrom apparently had in mind when speaking of Wilson's "bureaucratic administration." No doubt, in the context of presidentialist (by contrast with parliamentary) regimes, many if not most bureaucrats are not "careerists"—at best they are "retainers." However, in the United States, the top layer of bureaucrats actually consists of "transients," short-term presidential political appointees. Although a small minority within the bureaucracy, they exercise great power (Newland, 1987).

In a comparativist context, therefore, we simply cannot use bureaucracy to refer only to merit-based career officials, even though that concept fits most nonpresidentialist regimes. In order to make comparisons with presidentialist systems (especially that of the United States), we need to use bureaucrat generically to include all nonelected officials: (i.e., transients and retainers as well as careerists). Fortunately, my usage is not idiosyncratic: for example, Aberbach and colleagues write of their survey, "Nearly half of the American 'bureaucrat' sample are non-career appointees" (1981, p. 44 and p. 94).

Many administrators, of course, are elected in the United States, especially in local government, and I would exclude them from the category of bureaucrats. The fact is that both appointed and elected officials can and do perform political and administrative functions in every country. We simply need to be able to distinguish officials, structurally, on the basis of mode of selection (election or appointment) and, functionally, on the basis of what they do (political and/or administrative).

Note that in this usage, official is not a synonym for bureaucrat. Rather, it includes both elected and appointed officeholders. Although all elected officials are necessarily "politicians," they are also often "administrators." Similarly, although all appointed officials are administrators, they can also be politicians.

In view of the decisive political role played by military officers in many countries—notably after a group of them has seized power in a coup d'état—we must constantly remind ourselves that the category of bureaucrats includes not only civil servants but also the armed forces. Our analysis will be greatly sharpened if we always remember to use bureaucracy to include all the appointed officials in a government's executive branch—both military officers and civil servants—without assuming that they perform only "administrative" roles. In fact, many perform important "political" functions also.

13. Over forty years ago I found that local/regional and committee priorities often prevail over party loyalties as determinants of U.S. congressional voting behavior (Riggs, 1950, pp. 170–192). In a few presidentialist regimes, exceptionally—Chile is an example—strong party discipline reduces the voice of individual members of Congress. However, I believe that in these cases also the winning parties demand posts for important supporters.
14. When the effective powers of Congress are vitiated, we might speak of a quasi-presidentialist rather than a genuinely presidentialist system. Presidents who bypass Congress may rely, instead, on their enhanced popular, partisan, or military influence, and on the use of executive or emergency orders. Although this strategy weakens Congress temporarily, it eventually undermines the President's authority by diminishing the ability of the executive power to gain legislative legitimacy for its policies, and it fails to eliminate the interest of members of Congress in patronage.

Hartlyn describes this problem in Colombia: a "President had massive appointive powers, whose significance was augmented by the importance of spoils and patronage to the clientelist and brokerage oriented parties and by the absence of any meaningful civil service legislation. Presidents could appoint cabinet ministers without congressional approval" (Hartlyn, 1989, p. 13). The effect of the growing power of the President was "to marginalize Congress further from major decisions, reducing its functions to ones of patronage, brokerage and management of limited pork barrel funds" (Hartlyn, 1989, p. 21).

Although the usurpation of powers by a President is an important cause of congressional weakness, I believe an even more basic reason involves the party system—a hegemonic party, as found in Mexico, is a recipe for congressional weakness (Riggs, 1973). To sustain a viable Congress and hence the separation of powers, a competitive party system is needed, and the exercise of influence over presidential patronage seems to be unavoidable as a price for the maintenance of party competition.

15. Mainwaring reports that, in Brazil, "The only glue (and it is a powerful one at times) that holds the President's support together is patronage—and this helps explain the pervasive use of patronage politics. . . . Both Vargas and Kubitschek pressed for reforms that would strengthen the merit system and protect state agencies from clientelistic pressures, but they were defeated by a Congress unwilling to relinquish patronage privileges" (Mainwaring, 1989). A similar dynamic prevails, I believe, in all presidentialist systems—although, as we shall see, its force has been mitigated in the United States by the development, exceptionally, of a nonpartisan merit system.
16. The inherent insecurity of all retainers who, by definition, lack legally protected tenure in office, leads them to adopt a variety of expedients to protect their positions and optimize their prospects for indefinite retention of office. One that is well known is that of the *workhorses*, persons who, by hard work, make themselves indispensable. Any bureaucracy that relies solely on transients would experience a rapid collapse. The availability of workhorses provides some protection for an otherwise endangered presidentialist system because it enables the regime to perform necessary tasks with at least minimal success. Because of their invaluable contributions, workhorses are usually retained, though often in subordinated and ignominious positions.

    Retainers who are not workhorses may, nevertheless, resist discharge by other means. Some, whom I would call *turtles*, are well protected by their external alliances—friends and relatives in high places, especially in the Congress and among wealthy landowners, business men, and the social elite. Such external patrons provide a protective shell to help the turtles survive even though they treat their posts as sinecures and do little or no work, moving slowly, like turtles.

    A third category of retainers survive by their wits and by corruption: they might be called *foxes*. Unscrupulously, they are willing to indulge in blackmail, bribery, deceit, and trickery in order to perpetuate their precarious hold on public office. The presence of many turtles and foxes among the retainers in a bureaucracy undermines its viability as a tool of public administration and generates much public anger.
17. In earlier work, I mentioned interdependence and tenure as additional variables distinguishing traditional from modern bureaucracies. I now believe that only income (the salary/nonsalary distinction) clearly marks this distinction. Modern bureaucracies are usually more complex and interdependent than traditional ones, but this variable does not provide a sharp distinction between them. As for "tenure," I now see that it is not a clear differentiator: patronage prevailed in premodern bureaucracies, but the retention of office by incumbents and merit-based careerism also developed, notable in the Chinese case. Although careerism prevails in most modern bureaucracies, patronage is common in some, notably those found in all presidentialist regimes (Riggs, 1991a, pp. 487–490).
18. Of the three Asian presidentialist regimes created in the twentieth century, two inherited powerful career bureaucracies. These two, South Vietnam and South Korea, experienced coups immediately after the terms of their first elected presidents. A third, the Philippines, broke down when its elected president, Ferdinand Marcos, seized power in 1972 and ruled

autocratically until 1986, when presidentialism was restored under President Corazon Aquino. Six unsuccessful coup attempts marred her rule. Their failures, I believe, can be attributed to the relative weakness of the Philippine bureaucracy, which, alone among presidentialist systems, had been established under American rule, following the merit system principles imposed by the United States during its administration of that conquered country.

19. Because much if not most of the income of traditional officials was secured from extra-governmental sources, bureaucrats lacked the incentives found in modern polities for seizing power and we find no examples of a real coup d'etat in these societies, with the possible exception of the Mamlukes in Egypt (Riggs, 1991a, pp. 491–492).
20. The historical reasons for this phenomenon are elaborated in Riggs (1993a). Most importantly, the new states typically inherited well entrenched modern bureaucracies, whereas the institutions of representative government required to control them were established only as independence approached. Not surprisingly, when and if these newborn institutions failed to solve serious problems, especially those involving public finance and domestic security, threatened officials were willing to support a coup that promised to stabilize their own status and incomes.
21. A costly alternative to rotationism was developed in Chile, where civil servants could retire "with fifteen years service and a relatively good pension. Agency heads, however, would retire with what was known as la perseguidora—a pension that kept pace with the salary of the current occupant of the post retired from. . . . Agency heads were thus appointed as a culmination of their careers and could be persuaded to retire to allow a new President to make new appointments" (Valenzuela, 1984, p. 262). Another common bureaucratic practice in Chile deprived officials of significant functions while respecting their job security: "The huesera (or common grave), a series of offices for individuals with no official responsibilities . . . became a feature of many agencies" (Valenzuela, 1984, p. 264). In Chile, moreover, to overcome resistance from entrenched bureaucrats, "new agencies . . . that could carry forth new program initiatives of the new administration were brought into existence without having to abolish older ones. Even the conservative and austerity-minded Jorge Alessandi added 35,000 new employees to the public sector during his tenure in office" (Valenzuela, 1984, p. 263).

    Similarly, in Brazil, Presidents often expanded the apparatus of government by creating new state agencies in order to enhance their power and overcome congressional resistance (Mainwaring, 1989, p. 15). As in Chile, this practice enabled the President to make patronage appointments without discharging incumbent officials. The point to remember is that, although rotationism was avoided, a high political and economic cost was not. Thus some of the political benefits of rotationism were achieved, but only at immense cost. Meanwhile bureaucratic expansionism persisted.
22. It is useful to distinguish between two kinds of "in-and-outer," on the basis of the roles they play when they go "out." In the nineteenth century American spoils system, getting a government job was often crucial for an incumbent and being forced out of office by rotation was highly traumatic. Like a fish out of water, a discharged spoilsman truly suffered, longing for the security of the old-fashioned retainer system, as it had been inherited from Europe and maintained by the Federalists and Jeffersonians before Jackson launched the rotation principle.

    By contrast, those who easily reenter private life after a period of public service are more like amphibians—a well-chosen term already in use (Campbell, 1986, p. 200). Campbell makes an overlapping distinction between *politicos* and *amphibians*: the former includes campaign workers who claim a reward for having helped bring a President to power, whereas the latter have no special partisan claim for a reward, but they can offer their experience and "expertise within a substantive policy field" (Campbell, 1986, p. 200). Virtually all the fish were and are politicos. The difference between my treatment and Campbell's is that I think we need to consider the postemployment prospects of transients in addition to their preemployment records: contrasting the poor fish with the more fortunate amphibians.

Hugh Heclo has this phenomenon in mind when he refers to *technopols* as "people with recognized reputations in particular areas of public policy. . . . There are subordinate and superordinate positions through which they climb . . . but these are not usually within the same organization." Upward mobility is determined by "the assessments of people like themselves concerning how well, in the short term, the budding technopol is managing each of his [or her] assignments in and at the fringes of government" (Heclo, 1978, p. 107). Such people are mobicentrics and they will become increasingly powerful and prevalent in American society.

Campbell also speaks of career officials who are sometimes tapped by a President to serve as temporary political appointees. This normal practice in parliamentary systems is usually traumatic for incumbents in presidentialist America: like the amphibians, they can easily move from career to transient roles and may even feel honored by a "promotion," but like the fish, they cannot return home. Once "politicized," they lose their welcome in the career services and usually have to reenter private life after a stint as a political executive. The infrequency with which career officials take political appointments in the United States may well reflect their reluctance to accept such a "terminal" invitation as much as it does executive indifference to their talents. However, as mobicentricity increases, we may find that many careerists become amphibions, accepting political appointments as a stepping stone to new and more lucrative roles outside government.

23. John Rohr explains, "This threefold way of executing the will of the state is crucial for understanding Goodnow's book." A careless reading, he says, would equate the "will of the state" with the President's authority as chief executive, and then "equate both of these with Public Administration" (Rohr, 1986, p. 86).
24. Willoughby's notion of the executive function corresponded to Goodnow's: he expected the President to integrate and control the whole bureaucracy as its members sought to implement the laws adopted by Congress. He would rely mainly on his patronage appointments—from cabinet officers on down, including thousands of in-and-outers—to accomplish this function. Willoughby also emphasized, however, that the administrative function per se belongs mainly to Congress as performed by the nonpartisan career officers who work primarily with its members and committees.
25. Congressional decisions impact on political appointees as well as careerists, often compelling them to relate more closely to Congress than to the President; see [46]. Herbert Kaufman studied six American bureau chiefs, half careerists and half transients. He reports that all of them "were constantly looking over their shoulders . . . at the elements of the legislative establishment relevant to their agencies. . . . The legislative relations of administrative agencies consist largely of contacts with the chairmen, members, and staffs of the committees and sub-committees that have jurisdiction over the administrators" (Kaufman, 1981, pp. 47–48). By contrast, he tells us, their contacts with the presidency often seemed to be quite marginal. Nevertheless, in a presidentialist regime, each of the three separate branches of government can and must play an important role in guiding and controlling appointed officials (members of the bureaucracy). By contrast, of course, direct intervention by any parliament in the

management of government programs is more limited—again, because of the fusion of powers inherent in the design of parliamentary systems.

26. Despite the appointment of career officials to most of the positions to which congressional patronage previously applied, complaints against the abuse of power by members of Congress are often heard in the United States, especially from critics on the Republican right. A good example can be found in the Heritage Foundation's book *The Imperial Congress*, which asserts that "America faces a constitutional crisis stemming from two causes: the congressional failure to observe traditional limits on its power, and the acquiescence of the other two branches of government in the resulting arrogation of power" (Jones and Marini, 1988, p. 1). In countries where extensive patronage continues to prevail, this kind of "arrogation" of congressional power may be even more prevalent.
27. Elaborating on the frustrations of American bureaucrats, the *Blacksburg Manifesto* tells us, "Public Administrators were the persons in no-man's land who were left with ambiguities and a discretion that was viewed, on the one hand, as a threat to them (and to others) and, on the other, as a challenging opportunity to keep the constitutional process from becoming a stalemate in which the public interest would be the ultimate casualty" (Wamsley et al., 1990, p. 45).

    In response, we should claim that "the popular will does not reside solely in elected officials but in a constitutional order that envisions a remarkable variety of legitimate titles to participate in governance." Accordingly, Public Administration ought "not to cower before a sovereign legislative assembly or a sovereign elected executive. . . . Rather the task of The Public Administration is to share in governing wisely and well the constitutional order that the framers of the Constitution intended as an expression of the will of the people who alone are sovereign" (p. 47). "This means . . . that the Public Administrators may have to play the role of balance wheel in the constitutional order, using their statutory powers and professional expertise to favor whichever participant in the constitutional process needs their help at a given time in history to preserve the purposes of the Constitution itself" (p. 49).
28. A sophisticated analysis of the psychology of interpersonal relationships and human needs as they arise in different organizational contexts can be found in Shepard (1965, pp. 1125–1127), including a description and critique of Abraham Maslow's theory. A shrewd application of this theory to public administration can be found in Howard McCurdy (1977). For details, see Maslow (1962).
29. The awkward neologism *functionism* is used here to signify the principle that careers should be oriented to specific programs, policy areas, or "functions." Incumbents whose careers are based on this principle are called *functionaries*. Ideally, functionism is also functional (i.e., conducive to system survival), but we cannot use *functional* as a synonym for *functionism* without risking ambiguity. Some nonfunctionist principles are, actually, quite functional. The two terms, in short, designate two different concepts. Professionalism in the U.S. bureaucracy has flourished because of functionism, but clearly not all functionaries are professionals.
30. A two-party system is probably strengthened by a federal structure that hampers the emergence of a national hegemonic party. Opponents of any party in power at the center can rally to opposition parties locally, thereby creating power bases from which to campaign for power nationally. By contrast, in a centralized polity, once a party becomes entrenched in power, it can more easily defeat all efforts by opposition parties to replace it.

    This principle may only work, however, for a centripetalized party system where many citizens do not vote and the rival parties seek the support of moderate or centrist forces.

When a centrifugalized party system is combined with federalism, as in the Brazilian case (Mainwaring, 1988), federalism may well have a negative impact on the survival of presidentialism. For further comments on this point see Riggs (1993b).

31. Leonard White comments that Jackson "may well be criticized for failing to see the consequences of the theory of rotation . . . [but] he can hardly be criticized for the purposes he sought to achieve—to destroy the idea of property in office, to cut down an officeholding class, and to give all citizens an equal opportunity to enjoy the privilege of participating in the task of self-government" (White, 1954, p. 5). White also tells us that "the requirements of party machines for the sinews of war, the doctrine that citizens generally should have a turn at the business of government, and the anxiety of thousands of citizens for the privilege of office, all conspired to build a nation-state-local party organization" and "to break down the stable, permanent, politically inactive type of career [i.e., retainer] system that had grown up during the first four decades of the Republic (White, 1954, pp. 12–13). By establishing rotation in office, Jackson was able to replace many (though fortunately not all) retainers with spoilsmen.

    It is important to distinguish between two types of patronage appointees: those who are able to keep their jobs (the retainers) and those who are forced out of office so that newcomers can take their places (the transients). When White wrote that Jackson did not introduce "spoils," he was commingling retainers with transients—both are recruited by patronage. In other presidentialist regimes, by contrast to that of the United States, powerful retainers were able to block rotationism and, as a result, to prevent the rise of careerism. A retainer bureaucracy is both politically powerful and administratively inept.

    Nineteenth-century transients were often called *spoilsmen*, whereas their contemporary counterparts are the *in-and-outers*. Despite significant differences, it is important to identify their shared properties as transients. No doubt transients are pervasive in all presidentialist systems at the higher levels of governance. However, at middle and lower levels, retainers prevail in all presidentialist regimes with nineteenth century origins except that of the United States, where careerism at these levels has become institutionalized.

32. Ironically, Jackson can also be credited with the bureaucratization of the American public services which he accomplished by making agencies more impersonal and subjecting them to formal rules and regulations (Crenson, 1975, pp. 131–139). We should not equate bureaucracy with career services but, rather, with formal hierarchies of office governed by rules and regulations, regardless of how the offices are filled. The retainer system which Jackson restricted depended heavily on the personal idiosyncracies of its long-term incumbents rather than on formally prescribed rules and regulations.

33. Although the Jacksonian revolution had remarkable effects, we should not exaggerate its extent. Probably no more than 10% of incumbents (certainly less than 20%) were actually removed from office during the Jackson administration (White, 1954, p. 308). Throughout the following decades, "a hard core of experienced men . . . remained steadily at work" despite "the clamor for removals and partisan appointments to resulting vacancies" (White, 1954, p. 349). In short, despite the conspicuous role played by transients, a substantial number of retainers were able to maintain the essential functions of public administration. After 1829, "two personnel systems were thus in operation. . . . The patronage [transient] system held the public attention, but it was primarily the career [retainer] system that enabled the government to maintain its armed forces, to collect its revenue, to operate its land system, to keep its accounts and audit its expenditures. . . . The adjustment of the two systems remained even a century later an object of concern" (White, 1954, p. 362).

The reform movement was driven, of course, not only by the flagrant abuses of power indulged in by partisan transients, but also by the irresponsible behavior of the retainers whom I have called "turtles" and "foxes" (see [16]). Although experienced and indispensable "workhorses" were often good public administrators, as White claimed, they were largely invisible and could scarcely protect the status quo from its critics.

34. The aggregate vote in the presidential election of 1824 was only 356,000; by 1836 it had risen to 1,500,000 and in 1849 to 2,400,000. Although population growth was undoubtedly a factor, the major reasons were the elimination of property restrictions, especially in the new western states, and a growing interest in politics (Nevins and Commager, 1956, p. 175). In his first annual message to Congress (December 1829) Jackson declared: "More is lost by the long continuance of men in office than is generally to be gained by their experience. . . . Where offices are created solely for the benefit of the people no one man has any more intrinsic right to official station than another" (Hofstadter, 1954, p. 51). The successful establishment of rotation reflected the emergence of mass politics at an early period in U.S. history—by contrast, elsewhere, entrenched property rights and the seeming stability attributable to government by retainers have persisted to the present day.
35. In Brazil, where the retention of patronage-based offices prevails despite energetic reform projects (see [15]), Mainwaring tells us, "The political class has been acutely aware of the overshadowing of the legislature by the bureaucracy and has responded by expanding their influence within the bureaucracy . . . [with] catastrophic consequences upon the efficacy of the state apparatus" (1988, p. 24). Clearly, powerful networks composed of private interests, bureaucrats, and political parties, working with legislators, are able to secure particularistic concessions for themselves. Although superficially similar to the "iron triangles" found in America, these networks are more amenable to particularistic interests and less likely to promote universalistic policies and programs as a result of the pervasiveness of retainers. As triangles, they are "soft" (not iron), representing retainers rather than careerists, and rich families or corporations rather than functionally organized interest networks associated with large numbers of voters.
36. I can only hypothesize about this relationship because I cannot find concrete documentation for it. Van Riper emphasizes the importance of the civil service reform movement led by "a small group of predominantly wealthy and politically conscious easterners with a philanthropic turn of mind, aided by an aroused public opinion" (Van Riper, 1958, p. 80). A more detailed profile of the reformers is given by Hoogenboom: "The civil service reform movement was essentially conservative. . . . Reformers wished to return to the good old days before Jacksonian democracy and the industrial revolution—days when men with their background, status, and education were the unquestioned leaders of society." They "attacked the hated spoilsman's conspicuous source of strength in the civil service" (Hoogenboom, 1961, p. 197). See also White (1958, pp. 278–302).

In the American case, transient spoilsmen could scarcely have organized enough political support to present any significant opposition to the reformers—they lacked the power that entrenched retainers could offer in other countries. Evidence of such resistance can be found in the many obstacles to postwar merit-system reform encountered by American and United Nations public administration advisers in Latin America (Ruffing-Hilliard, 1991).
37. The Pendleton Act forbade career employees "to coerce the political action of any person," and penalties were prescribed for "political assessments of or by competitive employees, or by any other federal officials" (Van Riper, 1958, p. 99). In 1939 and 1940, responding to President Franklin D. Roosevelt's efforts to discipline recalcitrant Democrats in Congress by

means of patronage, the Hatch Acts were enacted. The first act extended the prohibition against partisan activities to unclassified employees (except those in top policy determining posts), and the second strengthened the terms of this prohibition by extending it to all state and local employees paid in full or in part by federal funds. Officials violating this proscription could be removed from office (Van Riper, 1958, pp. 340–341). No doubt career officers were happy to comply with laws which enabled them to avoid onerous partisan tasks and financial assessments.

38. The provisions of the Pendleton Act, perhaps unintentionally, were not hostile to the long-term interests of transient appointees. Some, already out of office, may have hoped to reenter the public service as careerists, beneficiaries of the act's open recruitment policy. Even transients, still in office but facing discharge because of rotation, may have supported merit system reforms in the hope that they could be "blanketed" into a position. The American "rank-on-the-job" tradition—by contrast with the "rank-in-the-man" system prevalent in most parliamentary regimes—has enabled some Presidents, almost clandestinely, to convert their transient appointees into retainers by "covering" their positions into a classified service. This probably could not have been done in any rank-in-the-man system where overt changes in personal status would have been far more conspicuous. Although transients in the bureaucracy could not exercise collective power, no doubt some of them individually supported the reform movement from which they may have hoped to benefit.

39. The nonpartisanship of American careerists may be contrasted with the bureaucratic partisanship typically found in other presidentialist regimes. Consider, for example, the situation in Chile, where merit systems and partisanship have been commingled. According to Valenzuela, "The Chilean civil service was recruited and promoted through a Chilean version of the spoils system: party recommendations, and legislative support, in addition to formal credentials, were important in gaining entry and crucial in rising to higher office. The civil service was fragmented . . . by strong partisan loyalties that prevented the development of institutional loyalties" (Valenzuela, 1984, p. 271).

Because of its American colonial heritage, the Philippine presidentialist regime has installed an examination-based career system. However, according to Carino (1989), its "career" officials were often openly partisan. She reports, for example, that "a third of middle-level bureaucrats in a survey mentioned helping in an electoral campaign—against civil service rules. Another third acknowledged nurturing political ambitions. . . . Civil servants also sometimes played off the executive against Congress, claiming the ability to get appropriations despite the absence of the President's support" (pp. 12 and 14). In addition to the career officials, of course, there were always a substantial number of presidentially appointed "agency heads and such aides as could be justified as 'policy determining, highly technical or primarily confidential' " (p. 10).

This was the "normal" pattern of bureaucratic politics in the Philippines before the advent of the dictatorship of President Ferdinand Marcos in 1972. He sought to institutionalize an intermediate, highly politicized, and well paid layer of political appointees, the "Career Executive Service," to serve as the cadres of his authoritarian regime and to help him perform functions of the dissolved Congress. When President Corazon Aquino came to power in 1986 and sought to reestablish a democratic presidentialist regime, she imposed sweeping bureaucratic replacements, purges of many officials, and tumultuous reorganization schemes. The partisanship involved in this highly traumatic and often unsuccessful effort to "de-Marcosify" the bureaucracy are summarized in Carino (1989) and described in more detail in her earlier monograph (1988).

The Philippines and Chile are sometimes mentioned as good examples of presidentialist regimes (in addition to that of the United States) where the merit system has been successfully installed. Closer scrutiny suggests, however, that they have developed modernized retainer systems. Without the politics/administration dichotomy myth and strict enforcement of nonpartisanship in its professionalized bureaucracy, the American regime might also have broken down, as all the other presidentialist regimes have.

40. In 1947, 92% of all federal bureaucrats in the continental United States were career officials—that is, some 8% were political appointees. According to a recent report, there are now about 3,000 political appointees as compared with 2.1 million civilian federal employees—about 0.15% (Lynch, 1991, p. 54). This transformation is remarkable: the overwhelming majority of appointed federal officials in the United States are now nonpartisan careerists. Nevertheless, the patronage appointees, despite their small number, play politically and administratively essential roles that cannot be ignored.

41. The supporters of careerists in America are sometimes referred to as bureauphiles, by contrast with their opponents, the bureauphobes, who favor transients in office. A bureauphobic call for more reliance on political appointees was issued by Lynch (1991), himself an experienced in-and-outer, when he complained that the Volcker Commission "has created an image of political appointees that seriously misunderstands modern government operations." Instead of cutting back on political appointees, Lynch tells us, "more responsive government today requires substantial increases in their numbers." He thinks that "the executive should have enough political positions to provide adequate staff for its policy, public affairs, congressional affairs, general counsel and intergovernmental relations divisions. . . . Responsive government requires a close link between the political ideas that win elections and the policies of government." Because the Volcker Commission sought to isolate "government operations from winning political ideas," Lynch concludes, "those recommendations deserve to be shelved. . . . They violate the most basic notions of democratic government" (pp. 54–55). Specialists in American Public Administration, he thinks, ignore this point of view at their peril.

A bureauphilic perspective is offered by James Pfiffner, who deplores "the present trend toward increasing numbers of political appointees. Reversing this direction would increase the capacity of the government to function efficiently and effectively without sacrificing political accountability or responsiveness" (Pfiffner, 1987, p. 64). Similarly, Dwight Waldo says, "We are now witnessing a devaluation of neutral competence; some would say, a frontal attack on neutral competence. There has been a substantial invasion of political appointees, many of whom I judge to be willfully ignorant of government and woefully insensitive to public norms" (Brown and Stillman, 1986, p. 145). Neither the bureauphobes nor the bureauphiles seem to be aware of the constitutional causes and consequences of the phenomena they deplore.

42. Since apportionment opened the door for favorable treatment of applicants from all the states—a nineteenth-century counterpart to contemporary "equal opportunity" rules—graduates of the new, widely dispersed land grant colleges where "practical" courses were taught became eligible for appointments, displacing graduates of the older liberal arts colleges. This laid the foundation for professionalism in the American bureaucracy, precluding the development of an American generalist cadre or mandarin system. Ex-transients, having been appointed for partisan reasons from all the states, were also beneficiaries of the apportionment principle.

43. The British empire extended to Canton, China, where agents of the East India Company were deeply impressed by the effectiveness of the exam-based mandarin bureaucracy in ruling the world's largest empire over long periods. Later, when the company began to experience severe difficulties administering the growing Indian empire from London (the tendency of British retainers in India to become Indianized prebendaries [nabobs], going into business on their own account, compelled London to realize that drastic measures were needed to reassert imperial control over its far-flung and distant possessions), they decided to borrow the Chinese design. Glimpses of the indiscipline prevailing among Englishmen in India in the eighteenth century can be found in Spear (1963, pp. 80–94). By the midnineteenth century, the successful Indian (Chinese) mandarin system was extended to England, where only youthful graduates of the most prestigious universities (Oxford and Cambridge) were entitled to take classical and literary exams through which an elite corps of generalists—the "administrative class"—joined the government service and became its ruling cadre (Teng, 1943).
44. Was there a kind of culturally determined egalitarianism in America that prompted rejection of the British model of an elitist administrative class? Paul Van Riper has suggested that this rejection rested on a deep-seated aversion to the elitism inherent in the recruitment of graduates from prestigious universities to serve as future mandarins (1958, p. 101); however, he also tells us that the congressional debate thoroughly explored "the likely effects of the proposed legislation upon the constitutional position of the President and Congress, upon the party system" (1958, p. 97). Whether consciously or not, members of Congress may have sensed that careerists, rooted in functionism, would be more responsive to legislative committees and more dependable as political allies than would an elite core of bureaucratic generalists (Riggs, 1988a, pp. 363–365, and 376, n. 40).
45. Aberbach and Rockman (1988) characterize the bureauphilic view that "a professionalized bureaucracy . . . elevates the effectiveness of government" as "the 'mandarin' perspective—a term that resonates, for historical reasons, better in Europe than in the United States" (p. 606). We need to understand the reasons for this historical dissonance, and to recognize the basic difference between a professionalized bureaucracy and a mandarinate.

    Mandarins, following the European (parliamentary) model, include generalist (cross-cutting) elite cadres who can, indeed, become a "ruling class," gaining widespread acceptance of their autonomous authority. By contrast, in the U.S. (presidentialist) system, a different model of policy-oriented (corner-fighting) specialists, climbing intraagency career ladders, should be referred to as *functionaries*, a far less potent or authoritative class of bureaucrats than the mandarins. Many, if not most, of them are professionals whose extra-bureaucratic standards and reference groups differ strikingly from the orientations typical of mandarins.

    It does, therefore, convey a misleadingly "European" notion to speak of American careerists as mandarins. Fortunately, we can use the broader term, *careerists*, to refer to all merit-based officials regardless of whether they are generalists or specialists—mandarins or functionaries. Remember, however, that retainers are not careerists, and most bureaucrats in presidentialist regimes (except in the United States) are retainers. For more details, see Riggs (1988a, pp. 364–365, 376, n. 40). In America, virtually all careerists are functionaries, and many of them are now also professionals.

    According to Aberbach and Rockman, bureauphobes argue that only officials appointed by the elected political authorities (i.e., the transients) ought to have "discretionary authority within the administrative apparatus"—they are exponents of the "mandate" perspective

(1988, p. 606). This perspective gains its importance in the American context from the power of professionals in the career bureaucracy. In order to compel them to give more weight to the politically based priorities of elected politicians, especially the President, transients appointed by each successive administration are charged with a mandate to oversee and direct the careerists, compensating for their professional "biases."

Concerning the change from the British closed mandarin model to the American open functional model, Paul Van Riper tells us, "We thoroughly adapted [the British model] to the American political and social climate" (Van Riper, 1958, p. 100). This cultural explanation needs to be amplified by consideration of the structural (constitutional) implications of the substitution of functionaries for mandarins in the American polity.

46. Francis Rourke tells us that the "closed [iron triangle] system is long gone, a casualty of the 'glastnost' that swept over American government beginning in the 1960's" (Rourke, 1991, p. 119). Among the causes that he identifies are the growing scrutiny of bureaucratic conduct by legislators and interest groups; the growth of grass-roots political activism; the increased extrabureaucratic expertise found in think tanks, congressional staffs, and research agencies; and the rise of "issue networks," that is, interactive public interest groups and professionals armed with expert knowledge. Rourke's more recent thinking on this subject can be found in his APSA paper (1992).

The "iron triangles" metaphor is admittedly too rigid to characterize the American political system as a whole, but the phenomenon itself has not disappeared. Rather, it has become absorbed in a larger and more comprehensive structure of interest networks. In addition to the traditional triangles, we find "issue networks" that link bureaucratic professionals with professional schools, private practitioners, and a host of nonprofit research and action organizations. I would add, also, the golden webs formed by in-and-outers, beneficiaries of the "revolving door" which incumbents use to establish intricate networks of collaboration among officials, consultants, and private organizations, again cutting across all three branches of the presidentialist regime, and penetrating a vast number of autonomous regulatory agencies, boards, and commissions.

Taken as a collectivity, interest networks constitute a gargantuan and complex system of interests, issues, and norms that sustain the highly dispersed structure of policy planning and implementation in vast reaches of American public life. I believe that these networks actually ease the burdens carried by American Presidents, and make the executive office more viable. By contrast, no doubt, some observers view this infrastructure as an impregnable monster on which the President cannot really impose his will. After outlining three available but equally unsatisfactory options open to a President who seeks to dominate and direct the executive establishment, Heclo concludes that there is no "neat way out of this trilemma." Instead, he thinks, the President "is bound to become a creature of the issue networks and the policy specialists" (Heclo, 1978, p. 122).

The Heritage Foundation, a conservative think tank, offers another perspective on this phenomenon. For example, we read in Jones and Marini's *The Imperial Congress* about how the ("Democrat-controlled") Congress has usurped presidential powers and undermined the presidentialist Constitution's prescribed separation of powers. A chapter by "H. A. Mellor" (pseudonym for a former DOD official and congressional aide) details some of the practices whereby interested members of Congress intervene in the appropriations and policy-making processes of the Defense Department to achieve very costly and unfair results through "micromanagement" that seriously undermines the powers of the presidency. Mellor concludes, "The final irony in the struggle between Congress and the executive branch is that, were Congress to more evenly share its responsibilities, treating the executive as a coequal, rather than as a servant, many of these problems would disappear" (Mellor, 1988, p. 129).

Nevertheless, from a comparativist perspective, American Presidents are more fortunate than their counterparts in polities where the interest networks are not so well developed or have highly personal and particularistic priorities. Outside the United States, I believe, Presidents must personally intervene in more current issues or face more public fiascos and disasters than does the American President: at least, this is a hypothesis that deserves to be investigated.

47. "A professional," according to Wilson (1989), is "someone who receives important occupational rewards from a reference group whose membership is limited to people who have undergone specialized formal education and have accepted a group-defined code of proper conduct. . . . In a bureaucracy, professionals are those employees who receive some significant portion of their incentives from organized groups of fellow practitioners located outside the agency" (p. 60). Here Wilson stresses professional standards. A cause-effect relation is implicit: when recruitment is limited to persons with professional standing, we may expect them to adhere to professional standards.
48. In 1968, Waldo observed, "The attitude of political scientists [toward Public Administration] . . . is at best one of indifference and is often one of undisguised contempt or hostility" (p. 8). He also claimed that "it is now unrealistic and unproductive to regard public administration as a subdivision of political science" (p. 7).
49. The rotation and functionist merit system reforms which have enabled the American government—exceptionally, I believe—to fend off the dangers inherent in bureaucratic power and dissatisfaction have lulled most American academies into a misplaced confidence in the essential durability of presidentialism as a constitutional design. This perception has spread to other countries, where some reformers see presidentialism as a more stable political system than parliamentarism. Prindle (1991) claims that a widespread preference in the third world for presidential regimes suggests they are more viable than parliamentary systems (p. 62). This perception may reflect a failure to distinguish between frequent cabinet changes and regime collapse. Admittedly, a highly polarized multiparty parliamentary regime is very likely to experience many cabinet crises. Such crises, however, occur within a constitutional regime—they do not necessarily generate a regime breakdown.

    An interesting test case is provide by Nigeria, which began its life as a new state in 1960 with a British-style parliamentary government. Following the coups of 1966 and 1975, a presidentialist constitution was promulgated in 1978. In 1985 another coup occurred. The military regime under General Ibrahim Babangida which followed promised to reconstitute representative government through a five-year process launched in 1987, leading to a revised version of the 1978 constitution. The Nigerian case is exceptional, however: for the most part, representative governments reconstituted after a phase of bureaucratic domination have recreated the basic structure of their precoup regimes. The empirical evidence mentioned in [5] clearly shows that presidentialist regimes are much more likely to break down as a result of a coup than are the parliamentary regimes.
50. As reported by Ventriss (1991), a recent survey found that "only 13 per cent of Senior Executive Service (SES) managers would recommend a governmental career to young people" (p. 275). The enthusiasm generated by direct recruitment of junior mandarins from the universities (as in the United Kingdom) cannot, apparently, be replicated when senior officials are wrenched out of their long-term functionary (or professional) roles and secure interest networks to become nouveau "mandarins" in a bureaucratic stratum lodged

precariously between suspicious political appointees and envious former colleagues in the career civil services.

More practical considerations added to the demoralization of the SES: Bonafede (1987), for example, reports that more than half of the career members of the SES have "left the government and at least 1,000 'simply retired' because of disagreements over the pay cap, the limitations on bonuses, the inadequate relocation allowances and other points of conflict" (1987, p. 135—quoting Blair Childs, executive director of the Senior Executives Association). Former executives who retired from the SES are reported to have "increased their annual salaries by an average of $17,800 in the private sector," and about 46% of current SES members "are thinking of leaving because of inadequate salary" (Bonafede, 1987, p. 136).

One might add that in a parliamentary system financial incentives for top civil servants need not be tied to those of legislators: by contrast, in the United States, "the pay link bonding the salaries of executive level personnel with those of members of Congress is generally condemned and is widely regarded as the cause of the inability to set fair and equitable government salaries" (Bonafede, 1987, pp. 136–137). The point, of course, is that Congress incurs so much public wrath when it tries to raise the salaries of its own members that it compensates by supplementing its own income from outside sources (essentially "prebendary" in character) while penalizing the executive branch by setting pay limits that restrict official salaries to no more than their own. Ironically, the weakness and low morale of the SES may, perversely, enhance the viability of presidentialism in the United States—notably by not really undermining it (see [54]).

51. Had the British model been adopted without significant revisions, a youthful cadre of future mandarins, recruited from elite universities, would have rotated among government programs, acquiring a generalist (cross-cutting) orientation that could have taken them to the top of the executive branch as powerful superbureaucrats. One of their early goals would have been to reconcile turf battles between rival bureaus in the same department but, eventually, they would have intervened in interdepartmental struggles to help secretaries resolve their own intracabinet conflicts. It is important to remember that a presidentialist cabinet—unlike its parliamentary prototype—has no motive for solidarity. "In the day to day work of the Cabinet member, each man fends for himself without much consideration of Cabinet unity" (Fenno, 1959, p. 247). If mandarins ("superbureaucrats"—see Campbell and Szablowski, 1979) became top advisers or "undersecretaries," they would seize the opportunity to counteract the dispersing pressures of the presidentialist format. For a lucid account of the way different American Presidents have attempted to work with and coordinate their cabinets members see Campbell (1986, pp. 37–57).

Ultimately, I imagine, they would also be able to curtail the powers of Congress, perhaps through a constitutional amendment to set limits on the terms of office of all elected officials and to require congressional committees to elect their leaders—such an attack on "senioritism" would be eagerly supported by liberal reform leagues (the common cause and public citizen lobbies) and even the Republican right. Thomas G. West, a resident scholar at the Heritage Foundation, reminds us, "In the 1968 election, 98 percent of House incumbents who ran for reelection won. . . . Until this pattern of automatic reelection changes, senators and congressmen have no incentive to change" (1988, p. 311). No doubt the new superbureaucrats would find eager allies on both the right and the left to join in a major reform campaign to "democratize" the American government.

If such strategies were to succeed, the American President would be reduced to a purely symbolic head of state, national parties would wither as effective political organizations, while their volunteer and PAC supporters would lose interest in them: the superbureaucrats would constitute a kind of "college of cardinals" to nominate future Presidents gifted with the prestige and pliability needed to serve as national figureheads. A pliable Congress would continue to legitimize the government's decisions, but its frequently rotating members would find themselves dependent on mandarin officials for the information needed to ratify "sound" legislation.

No doubt this futurist vision of the power potential of a mandarinate sounds far-fetched, yet it could inspire a British science-fiction novel: *The Rise of the Meritocracy, 1870–2033* (Young, 1958). Actually, the concentrated and politically entrenched cabinet in a parliamentary system is far better equipped to manage and control such a mandarinate than is any dispersed and fragile presidentialist regime, including that of the United States. No doubt British cabinets are not as cohesive as we imagine: Colin Campbell tells us that "executive harmony does not come as readily to British governments as Americans expect" (1986, p. 27). Nevertheless, despite the impression given by "Yes, Minister," the power potential of British executives surely exceeds that of American Presidents.

52. Discussing the consequences of the rise of issue networks, Heclo observes "Instead of party politicians, today's political executives tend to be policy politicians. . . . Their reputations among those 'in the know' make them available for presidential appointments. Their mushiness on the most sensitive issues makes them acceptable. Neither a craft professional nor a gifted amateur, the modern recruit for political leadership in the bureaucracy is a journeyman of issues" (Heclo, 1978, p. 106). Although the President can make many final choices, he/she is constrained to select amphibians who are acceptable to competing issue networks rather than to reward politicos who supported the winner's electoral campaign.

Moreover, the President is also constrained by the unwillingness of many highly qualified persons to undergo the costs of accepting (and retaining) political appointments: for example, relatively low salaries, painful questioning in the Senate, elaborate and time-consuming clearances. Commenting on "The Quiet Crisis" growing out of the inability of the U.S. government to attract qualified personnel, Bonafede (1987) writes of "the dilemma over fixing government salaries comparable to those in the private sector, and the resulting controversy created by the issue," plus the "harm to the quality of government caused by the exodus of public officials" (p. 134). He discusses the grueling experience of nominees facing Senate confirmation hearings and hostile reporters, the red tape and delays associated with security and conflict of interest clearances, plus such factors as "petty aggravations, low pay, high cost of living, inadequate expense allowances, long hours, and the surrender of much of their personal privacy" (p. 139).

Such perceptions clearly identify some of the significant costs of maintaining a viable presidentialist system of government, but without a comparativist framework, it is difficult to understand its constitutional basis: we are left to deal with the symptoms rather than the underlying causes of these problems.

53. Anyone who counts on the judicial branch to facilitate the coordination of government programs will, I suspect, be disappointed. Although the effects of court proceedings on public administration have received a good deal of attention, I do not know of any discussion of their implications for the dispersal/coordination of bureaucratic activities. My guess is that judicial decisions actually intensify the dispersal of power in American bureaucracy, compelling agencies to employ more lawyers, to rely more on administrative law and procedure, to establish their own quasi-judicial processes, and to compel administrators to become ever more specialized in their knowledge not only of program policies and methods but also of the laws and precedents affecting their implementation.

This might, perhaps, engender even more specialization, boundary maintenance, and rigidity, which, in turn, justify the intrusion of more political appointees to promote coordination, flexibility, and political sensitivity. The proliferation of judicial and congressional staff services and their associated technical requirements and procedural limitations also reinforces these processes. Although public administration may suffer as a result, the resilience of the constitutional system is enhanced. However, admittedly these are speculations and I cannot defend them with any self-assurance.

54. Durant's stimulating discussion of "appointee-careerist relations" provides ample evidence of the conflicts and accommodations generated by the fundamental cleavage within the American polity between bureaucratic transients and careerists. What his analysis leaves out, however, is any explanation of why this cleavage is necessary for the survival of democratic presidentialism, even though it produces fundamental problems, both political and administrative, of great magnitude (Durant, 1990). Similarly, Paul Light tells us, "Presidents and their appointees must move quickly to succeed. In responding to that pressure, careerists must be sensitive to the dynamic nature of the policy process" (Light, 1987, p. 173). Light's analysis, based on the data collected in the 1985 Presidential Appointee Project of the National Academy of Public Administration, is rooted solely in the American experience and offers no comparisons to suggest the truly exceptional character of this situation.

Actually, of course, the appointee-careerist dichotomy oversimplifies the American reality, where, for example, there exist many independent regulatory agencies, which, collectively, are often viewed as a "headless fourth branch" of government. It is impossible to discuss this phenomenon here. Its critics allege that by delegating legislative/executive/judicial powers to these autonomous agencies, the effective powers of both President and Congress have been seriously eroded—a strong attack on them is offered by Nolan Clark, currently an official of the Federal Trade Commission, who writes that "almost without exception, independent regulatory agencies have failed to promote the public interest" (Clark, 1988, p. 271). I can only speculate about the extent to which comparably autonomous bodies have been created in other presidentialist polities, but I suspect that, despite their many flaws, they facilitate the survival of American presidentialism by reducing the burdens placed on both the President and the Congress, and reducing the stakes in the winner-takes-all electoral sweepstakes identified by Juan Linz.

Both the bureauphiles and the bureauphobes seem to think that we are free to choose a very different design: they would increase the ratio and enhance the power of career officers (and independent commissions) or subject them to more stringent control by transient appointees. The "realpolitik" model—or Heclo's "conditional cooperation" (Heclo, 1977, p. 193)—accepts the status quo, however, and offers a formula for trying to make unavoidable confrontations manageable in a system that cannot survive without both careerists and transients. However, I suspect that the realpolitik formula might be strengthened if it explicitly recognized that maintenance of the American constitutional system actually depends on the cleavage, thereby rebutting the more extreme views of both the bureauphobes and bureauphiles.

55. The noncomparativist way of viewing American Public Administration still hampers our ability to understand public administration anywhere, and especially in the United States. Had students of American government paid attention to the tragic experiences of all the countries that emulated the American presidentialist design, they would have seen that constitutive systems in presidentialist regimes are typically unable to control their bureaucracies and coups have taken place in almost all of them.

They might also have seen that although the exceptional survival of the U.S. regime can be explained, in part, by the relative workability of its constitutive system (attributable in large measure to the persistence of some undemocratic practices), a fuller explanation must also take into account the relative (political) weakness of its bureaucracy. This weakness is due to such factors as federalism, privatization, and transience of political appointments combined with a professionalized career bureaucracy. The capacity of this mixed bureaucracy to administer well in specialized program areas also reduces the incentive for military coups.

Comparative analysis might also have led to the conclusion that parliamentary regimes are typically able to control more powerful and administratively effective bureaucracies, and that generalist administrators (mandarins) can well coordinate complex interagency programs (health care or drug enforcement, for example) that cannot be managed by the American professionalized bureaucracy. The cultivation of a top cadre of mandarin administrators in the United States, however, would seriously undermine its presidentialist regime. Reliance on transient political appointees is an unavoidable necessity for regime survival in the United States, despite their inability to help the President achieve effective coordination in a highly dispersed (and professionalized) bureaucratic system.

Viewing American bureaucrats as essentially nonpolitical actors has also blinded Americans working in the third world to the vast incongruity between powerful bureaucracies and weak constitutive systems in many of these countries. They could not see, therefore, how projects designed to enhance the administrative capacity of these bureaucracies would further strengthen them politically, contributing thereby to the likelihood of coups and bureaucratic domination, with accompanying deterioration of administrative capabilities.

56. The political realities that enabled Public Administration to emerge as an important field of study in the United States have remained invisible to analysts who assumed they could ignore politics as a factor relevant to their analysis. They remained unaware of the exceptional political weakness of American career officials which enabled them to cultivate Public Administration as a nonpolitical subject. Paradoxically, bureaucratic rulers who display, in an extreme form, the unity of politics and administration are quite tolerant of university programs in Public Administration, whereas they look askance at departments of political science. Precisely because the former, under American inspiration, are viewed as nonpolitical, they are seen as nonthreatening, whereas the latter are feared as potential troublemakers for the ruling group.
57. The French Fifth Republic has been cited as an exception, but I believe it is at most semipresidential. As the Chirac interlude (1986–1988) indicated, the need for parliamentary support compelled a Socialist President to nominate a Gaullist prime minister. Moreover, the basic structure of the French bureaucracy and the government's capacity to control it resemble the situation found in parliamentary regimes much more than what we see in any presidentialist system. Of course, it remains to be seen whether or not the 1986 experience will be replicated. An alternative scenario, of course, might be the creation of a Sixth Republic, but we can only speculate on what its properties might be.

REFERENCES

Aberbach, Joel D., Putnam, Robert D., and Rockman, Bert A., *Bureaucrats and Politicians in Western Democracies*, Harvard University Press, Cambridge, Mass., 1981.

Aberbach, Joel D., and Rockman, Bert A., Mandates or Mandarins? Control and Discretion in the Modern Administrative State, *Public Administration Review*, 48(2):606–612 (1988).

Bonafede, Dom, Presidential Appointees: The Human Dimension, in *The In-and-Outers, Presidential Appointees and Transient Government in Washington* (G. C. MacKenzie, ed.), Johns Hopkins University Press, Baltimore, 1987, pp. 120–140.

Brown, Brack, and Stillman, Richard J., II, *A Search for Public Administration: The Ideas and Career of Dwight Waldo*, Texas A & M University Press, College Station, Tex., 1986.

Campbell, Colin, *Managing the Presidency*, University of Pittsburgh Press, Pittsburgh, 1986.

Campbell, Colin, and Szablowski, George J., *The Superbureaucrats: Structure and Behavior in Central Agencies*, Macmillan, Toronto, 1979.

Carino, Ledivina, *Bureaucracy for a Democracy: The Struggle of the Philippines Political Leadership and the Civil Service in the Post-Marcos Period*, Occasional Paper no. 88-1. University of the Philippines, College of Public Administration, Manila, 1988.

Carino, Ledivina, A Dominated Bureaucracy: An Analysis of the Formulation of, and Reactions to, State Policies on the Philippine Civil Service, Unpublished paper (1989).

Clark, Nolan E., The Headless Fourth Branch, in *The Imperial Congress* (Jones and Marini, eds.), Pharos Books, New York, 1988, pp. 268–292.

Crenson, Matthew A., *The Federal Machine: Beginnings of Bureaucracy in Jacksonian America*. Johns Hopkins University Press, Baltimore, 1975.

Cronin, Thomas E., The President's Executive Power, in *Inventing the American Presidency* (Thomas E. Cronin, ed.), University Press of Kansas, Lawrence, Kan., 1989, pp. 180–208.

Dionne, E. J. Jr., *Why Americans Hate Politics*, Simon & Schuster, New York, 1991.

Dogan, Mattei, The Political Power of the Western Mandarins, in *The Mandarins of Western Europe: The Political Role of Top Civil Servants* (Dogan, ed.), John Wiley & Sons, New York, 1975, pp. 3–24.

Dogan, Mattei and Kazancigil, Ali, eds., *Comparing Nations: The Pendulum Between Theory and Substance*, Basil Blackwell, London, 1993.

Durant, Robert F., Beyond Fear or Favor: Appointee-Careerist Relations in the Post-Reagan Era, *Public Administration Review*, 50(3):319–331 (1990).

Edmond, J. B., *The Magnificent Charter: The Origin and Role of the Morrill Land-Grant Colleges and Universities*, Exposition Press, Hicksville, N.Y., 1978.

Farazmand, Ali, ed., *Handbook of Comparative and Development Public Administration*, Marcel Dekker, New York, 1991.

Fenno, Richard F., *The President's Cabinet*, Harvard University Press, Cambridge, Mass., 1959.

Fisher, Louis, Congress and the President in the Administrative Process: The Uneasy Alliance, *The Illusion of Presidential Government* (Heclo and Salamon, eds.), Westview Press, Boulder, Colo., 1981, pp. 21–43.

Hamilton, Alexander, Madison, James, and Jay, John, *The Federalist Papers* (Clinton Rossiter, ed.), New American Library, New York, 1961.

Goodnow, Frank J., *Politics and Administration: A Study in Government*, Russell and Russell, New York, 1900.

Hartlyn, Jonathan, Presidentialism and Colombian Politics, Paper for Georgetown University Symposium on Presidentialism, 1989.

Heady, Ferrel, American Constitutional and Administrative Systems in Comparative Perspective, *Public Administration Review*, 47(1):9–16 (1987).

Heady, Ferrel, *Public Administration: A Comparative Perspective*, 4th ed., Marcel Dekker, New York, 1991.

Heclo, Hugh, *A Government of Strangers: Executive Politics in Washington*, Brookings Institution, Washington, D.C., 1977.

Heclo, Hugh, Issue Networks and the Executive Establishment, in *The New American Political System* (Anthony King, ed.), American Enterprise Institute, Washington, D.C., 1978, pp. 87–124.

Heclo, Hugh, and Salamon, Lester M., eds., *The Illusion of Presidential Government*, Westview Press, Boulder, Colo., 1981.

Hofstadter, Richard, *The American Political Tradition and the Men Who Made it*, Vintage Books, New York, 1954.

Hoogenboom, Ari, *Outlawing the Spoils: A History of the Civil Service Reform Movement, 1865–1883*, University of Illinois Press, Urbana, Ill., 1961.

Jones, Gordon S. and Marini, John A., eds., *The Imperial Congress: Crisis in the Separation of Powers*, Pharos Books, New York, 1988.

Kaufman, Herbert, *The Administrative Behavior of Federal Bureau Chiefs*, Brookings Institution, Washington, D.C., 1981.

Krislov, Samuel and Rosenbloom, David H., *Representative Bureaucracy and the American Political System*, Praeger, New York, 1981.

Light, Paul C., When Worlds Collide: The Political-Career Nexus, in *The In-and-Outers* (Mackenzie, ed.), Johns Hopkins University Press, Baltimore, 1987, pp. 156–173.

Linz, Juan, The Perils of Presidentialism, *Journal of Democracy*, 1(1):51–69 (1990).

Lynch, Edward J., No, We Don't Have Too Many Political Appointees, *Government Executive*, 23(4):54–55 (1991).

Mackenzie, G. Calvin, The Paradox of Presidential Personnel Management, in *The Illusion of Presidential Government* (Heclo and Salamon, eds.), Westview Press, Boulder, Colo., 1981, pp. 113–146.

Mackenzie, G. Calvin, *The In-and-Outers: Presidential Appointees and Transient Government in Washington*, Johns Hopkins University Press, Baltimore, 1987.

Mainwaring, Scott, Brazilian Party Underdevelopment in Comparative Perspective, Revised version of paper presented at the International Political Science Association Congress, 1988.

Mainwaring, Scott, Presidentialism in Latin America: A Review Essay, *Latin American Research Review*, 25(1):157–179, 1989.

Maslow, Abraham, *Towards a Psychology of Being*, Van Nostrand, Princeton, N.J., 1962.

McCurdy, Howard E., *Public Administration: A Synthesis*, Benjamin/Cummings, Menlo Park, Calif., 1977.

Mellor, Herman A., Congressional Micromanagement: National Defense, in *The Imperial Congress* (Jones and Marini, eds.), Pharos Books, New York, 1988, pp. 107–129.

Moe, Terry M., The Politicized Presidency in *The Managerial Presidency* (James P. Pfiffner, ed.), pp. 135–157. Reprinted from John E. Chubb and Paul E. Peterson, eds. *The New Direction in American Politics*, The Brookings Institution, Washington, D.C., 1985.

Moore, Wilbert E., *The Professions: Roles and Rules*, Russell Sage Foundation, New York, 1970.

Nachmias, David and Rosenbloom, David H., *Bureaucratic Culture: Citizens and Administrators in Israel*, Croom Helm, London, 1978.

Nevins, Allan and Commager, Henry Steele, *The Pocket History of the United States*, Pocket Books, New York, 1956.

Newland, Chester, Public Executives: Imperium, Sacerdotium, Collegium? *Public Administration Review*, 47(1):45–56 (1987).

Ostrom, Vincent, *The Intellectual Crisis in American Public Administration*, University of Alabama Press, Tuscaloosa, Ala., 1989.

Pfiffner, James P., Political Appointees and Career Executives, *Public Administration Review*, 47(1):57–67 (1987).

Pfiffner, James P., *The Managerial Presidency*, Brooks/Cole, Pacific Grove, Calif., 1991.

Prindle, David F., Head of State and Head of Government—in Comparative Perspective, *Presidential Studies Quarterly*, 21(1):55–72 (1991).

Rabin, Jack and Bowman, James S., *Woodrow Wilson and American Public Administration*, Marcel Dekker, New York, 1984.

Riggs, Fred W., *Pressures on Congress*, King's Crown Press, New York, 1950.

Riggs, Fred W., *Thailand: The Modernization of a Bureaucratic Polity*, East-West Center Press, Honolulu, 1966.

Riggs, Fred W., The Structures of Government and Administrative Reform, in *Political and Administrative Development* (Ralph Braibanti, ed.), Duke University Press, Durham, N.C., 1969, pp. 220–324.

Riggs, Fred W., Legislative Structures: Some Thoughts on Elected National Assemblies, in *Legislatures in Comparative Perspective* (Allan Kornberg, ed.), McKay, New York, 1973, pp. 30–93.

Riggs, Fred W., Shifting Meanings of the Term *Bureaucracy, International Social Science Journal*, 314: 563–584 (1979).

Riggs, Fred W., Cabinet Ministers and Coup Groups: The Case of Thailand, *International Political Science Review*, 2(2):159–188 (1981).

Riggs, Fred W., Bureaucratic Politics in the U.S.: Benchmarks for Comparison, *Governance*, 1(4):343–379 (1988a).

Riggs, Fred W., The Survival of Presidentialism in America: Para-Constitutional Practices, *International Political Science Review*, 9(4):247–278 (1988b).

Riggs, Fred W., Bureaucratic Links Between Administration and Politics, *Handbook of Comparative and Development Public Administration*, Marcel Dekker, New York, 1991a, pp. 485–509.

Riggs, Fred W., Public Administration: A Comparativist Framework, *Public Administration Review*, 51(6):473–477 (1991b).

Riggs, Fred W., Coups and Crashes: Lessons for Public Administration, Paper presented at APSA conference in Chicago, Sept. 1992.

Riggs, Fred W., The Fragility of the Third World's Regimes, *International Social Science Journal*, 136:199–243 (1993a).

Riggs, Fred W., Presidentialism: An Empirical Theory, in *Comparing Nations: The Pendulum between Theory and Practice* (Mattei Dogan and Ali Kazancigil, eds.), Basil Blackwell, Oxford, 1993b.

Riggs, Fred W., Bureaucracy and the Constitution, *Public Administration Review*, (in press, 1994).

Rohr, John A., *To Run a Constitution: The Legitimacy of the Administrative State*, University Press of Kansas, Lawrence, 1986.

Rosenbloom, David H., Public Administrative Theory and the Separation of Powers, *Public Administration Review*, 43(3):219–227 (1983).

Rourke, Francis E., American Bureaucracy in a Changing Political Setting, *Journal of Public Administration: Research and Theory*, 1(2):111–129 (1991).

Rourke, Francis E., Politics and Professionalism in American Bureaucracy, Paper presented at the American Political Science Association conference in Chicago, 1992.

Ruffing-Hilliard, Karen, Merit Reform in Latin America, in *Handbook of Comparative and Development Public Administration* (Ali Farazmand, ed.), Marcel Dekker, New York, 1991, pp. 301–312.

Seidman, Harold, *Politics, Position, and Power: The Dynamics of Federal Organization*, Oxford University Press, New York, 1980.

Sharkanski, Ira, *Wither the State?* Chatham House, Chatham, N.J., 1979.

Shepard, Herbert A., Changing Interpersonal and Intergroup Relationships in Organizations, in *Handbook of Organizations* (James March, ed.), Rand McNally, Chicago, 1965, pp. 1115–1143.

Spear, Thomas G. P., *The Nabobs: A Study of the Social Life of the English in Eighteenth Century India*, rev. ed., Oxford University Press, London, 1963.

Stillman, Richard J. II, *Preface to Public Administration: A Search for Themes and Direction*, St. Martin's Press, New York, 1991.

Teng, Ssu-Yu, Chinese Influence on the Western Examination System, *Harvard Journal of Asiatic Studies*, 7:267–312, (1943).

Valenzuela, Arturo, Parties, Politics and the State in Chile: The Higher Civil Service, in *Bureaucrats and Policy Making* (Ezra N. Suleiman, ed.), Holmes & Meier, New York, 1984.

Van Riper, Paul A., *History of the United States Civil Service*, Row, Peterson, Evanston, Ill., 1958.

Ventriss, Curtis, The Challenge of Public Service, *Public Administration Review*, 51(3):275–279 (1991).

Waldo, Dwight, Scope of the Theory of Public Administration, *Annals* (James C. Charlesworth, ed.), Monograph #8, ASPSS, Philadelphia, 1968.

Waldo, Dwight, *The Enterprise of Public Administration*, Chandler & Sharp, Novato, Calif., 1980.

Wamsley, Gary, et al., Public Administration and the Governance Process: Shifting the Political Dialogue, *Refounding Public Administration* (Wamsley et al., eds.), Sage, Newbury Park, Calif., 1990, pp. 31–51.

West, Thomas G., Restoring the Separation of Powers, in *The Imperial Congress* (Jones and Marini, eds.), Pharos Books, New York, 1988, pp. 309–329.

White, Leonard D., *Introduction to the Study of Public Administration*, rev. ed., Macmillan, New York, 1939.

White, Leonard D., *The Jeffersonians*, Macmillan, New York, 1951.
White, Leonard D., *The Jacksonians*, Macmillan, New York, 1954.
White, Leonard D., *The Republican Era*, Macmillan, New York, 1958.
Willbern, York, Professionalization in the Public Service: Too Little or Too Much, *Public Administration Review*, 14(1):13–21 (1954).
Willoughby, W. F., *Principles of Public Administration*, Brookings Institution, Washington, D.C., 1927.
Wilson, James Q., *Bureaucracy: What Government Agencies Do and Why They Do It*, Basic Books, New York, 1989.
Young, Michael D., *The Rise of the Meritocracy, 1870–2033*, Penguin Books, Harmondsworth, England, 1958.

8
Mal-Leaders and Organizational Decline

Marcia Lynn Whicker, Dorothy Olshfski, and Raphael J. Caprio
Rutgers University at Newark, Newark, New Jersey

Ruth Ann Strickland
Appalachian State University, Boone, North Carolina

I. INTRODUCTION

This chapter identifies mal-leadership as a force contributing to organizational decline. Several types of mal-leader are identified: the absentee leader, controller, busybody, hedonist, enforcer, street fighter, and bully. Stages of response by rational employees to mal-leaders are trust and cooperation, disappointment and disillusionment, outrage and contempt, covert game playing, open warfare, siege mentality, and isolation and alienation. Strategies for reversing organization decline range from expanding the organizational resource base to removing the mal-leader, restructuring the organization, and abolishing the organization.

II. REPEATED CALLS FOR STRONG LEADERSHIP

As the United States confronts considerable challenges in the future, politicians, policymakers, pundits, and popularizers have repeatedly called for strong leadership (Maccoby, 1981; Nanus, 1989; Kotter, 1990). Many problems await on the national agenda that require healthy organizations to meet these challenges. Among these national challenges are the following needs (Reich, 1991; Kennedy, 1987; Whicker and Moore, 1988; Phillips, 1990):

To revise our educational system
To integrate diverse ethnic and religious minorities and immigrants successfully, tapping the creative energies of each
To integrate the U.S. economy into the global economy
To address the increasing disparity between the rich and the poor
To develop a viable health delivery system at a reasonable cost in terms of share of GNP
To restore our technological edge in manufacturing
To return the United States to the cutting edge in new technologies

To increase exports and address the balance of trade
To contain if not lower the federal deficit and national debt
To develop long-term capital and human investments to assure future economic growth

These complicated, challenging, and difficult tasks can only be achieved if organizations in all sectors—public, private, and nonprofit—are healthy and performing to capacity (Kouzes and Posner, 1987; Cribbin, 1981; Hunt et al., 1984; Yukl 1989; Bryman, 1986). Public bureaucracies, in particular, are crucial to the attainment of these national goals (Wilson, 1989; Doig and Hargrove, 1987). Leadership is crucial to the effective functioning of social institutions. Its presence is not always appreciated yet its absence is keenly felt.

Scholars in the field have struggled to define the elusive elements of leadership (Burns, 1978; Cronin, 1984; Jones, 1989; Rost, 1991). The ambiguity of leadership qualities, however, sometimes leaves confusion between effective leadership that produces socially desirable goals and equally effective leadership that produces socially undesirable outcomes.

Most scholars focus upon the desirable qualities and types of leadership that lead to high organizational and institutional performance (Jacques and Clement, 1991; Crosby, 1990; Lundy, 1986; Koestenbaum, 1991; Batten, 1989; Maccoby, 1988; Hunt et al., 1988; Badaracco and Ellsworth, 1989). An emphasis upon leadership effectiveness and techniques, however, does not promote distinctions between good leadership and bad leadership, both of which in the short run might be equally effective. For lack of a better term, here we call such socially desirable leadership that promotes goals beneficial to society *moral leadership.*

Less attention has been devoted to leaders who undermine social goals and the well-being of the people who follow them, some of whom are quite effective in achieving socially and organizationally deleterious objectives (Bennis, 1989; Kets de Vries, 1984; Mant, 1983; Doob, 1983). We call this negative but nonetheless sometimes killed in the short run leadership *mal-leadership.*

Despite their craftiness and short-run effectiveness, mal-leaders drive our organizations into decline. Moral leaders are needed to maintain their health and productivity. But what do moral leadership and mal-leadership look like in human flesh? What are their defining characteristics? This chapter compares and contrasts the two types of leadership. Both moral leaders and mal-leaders are of different types, which will be briefly identified. We explore the impact mal-leaders have upon organizations as well as individual responses to mal-leaders. Finally, organizational strategies for coping with mal-leaders are discussed.

III. MAL-LEADERSHIP AS ANTITHESIS TO RATIONALITY

Much of the literature that examines individuals in public and private administration assumes rationality. In the happy world of effective management literature, governments, public agencies, nonprofits, and businesses are all populated by rational managers dealing with rational superiors and subordinates. However, most of us who have consulted, worked, or taught in public or private sector organizations, know from experience that not everyone working in organizations, including institutions of higher education, is rational. There are some maladjusted, neurotic, emotionally unstable, perverse personalities out there in the workplace. These irrational managers have received only scant attention in the literature, both academic and popular (Kets de Vries and Miller, 1984; 1985; 1987; Bernstein and Rozen, 1992; 1988; Bing, 1992; Kets de Vries, 1989).

Identifying these maladjusted managers is problematic. Top management knows that something is seriously wrong in a department or bureau when the absentee and turnover rates begin to climb and productivity takes a nose dive. However, if the cause is a maladjusted manager, it is better for the organization to address the problem directly before the entire work unit is harmed and organizational productivity is severely threatened. The model presented here aims to help identify problems before the entire team retreats from the field or open warfare makes productivity impossible. Our model of employee responses to a maladjusted manager is speculative: it begins in a manner similar to the phases of the grieving (or working through) process but shifts midway to a separate path because ultimate acceptance of the mal-leader as the new reality (the end phase of grieving) is an unsatisfactory outcome. We conclude by examining organizational responses to maladjusted, irrational leaders in management.

IV. MAL-LEADER DEFINED

"Mal-leader" is the term used here to connote the maladjusted manager. The mal-leader is defined through two key criteria identified by leadership research: task competence and human relations skills (Hershey and Blanchard, 1984; Blake and Mouton, 1984; Likert, 1967; Misumi, 1985; Fleishman and Harris, 1962). But unlike the importance associated with the presence of these skills in the leadership literature, in the case of the mal-leader, these positive skills are conspicuous by their absence.

Mal-leaders employ destructive or inept interpersonal relations and counterproductive task skills. But it is not only the deficiencies in human relations and task skills that define the mal-leader; as Bass (1985) defined transformational leaders in terms of the leader's positive effect on followers, mal-leaders also transform their followers in terms of negative effects. Mal-leaders attempt to displace task accomplishment with maneuvering in pursuit of non-task-related ends and replace cordial, supportive human relations activities with unpleasant, self-protecting personal interactions. Mal-leaders may differ from each other stylistically, but in general they lack task and human relations skills, pursue goals other than those sanctioned by the organization, and display a malicious streak that brings out the worst in subordinates.

V. TYPES OF MAL-LEADERS

On the surface, mal-leaders (MALs) may seem charming, cordial, helpful, and even sympathetic. Especially initially, the baser characteristics of the MALs may not be readily apparent. Therefore, it may require close observation and time to discover their real motives and intentions. Across time, however, the discrepancy between the rhetoric of a mal-leader and the reality of his behavior and decisions becomes apparent. This discrepancy is rooted in the sense of personal inadequacy, selfish value system, and deceit that characterizes all mal-leaders. Eventually, many or all of these MALs will emerge, even if disguised initially.

Further complicating the quick and ready identification of mal-leaders is their diversity. Mal-leaders are of several different varieties, each with its own peculiarities and obsessions. Seven types are identified here. Mal-leadership is really a continuum, however, rather than a series of finely graduated categories. This continuum ranges from mal-leadership that is most benign toward others to that which is most personalized and malicious toward others. Thus the seven types may be arranged along this continuum. The most benign is the absentee leader; the most malicious is the bully. The other types fall along the continuum between the absentee leader and the bully.

Of the seven types of mal-leaders, four operate primarily at level three of Maslow's hierarchy, concerned about social standing in the group and desperately but secretly craving belonging. These four types are the absentee leader, the controller, the busybody, and the hedonist. The remaining three operate primarily at level two of Maslow's hierarchy. They are the enforcer, the street fighter, and the bully. The seven mal-leadership types and their basic drives are discussed in the sections that follow.

A. The Absentee Leader

The absentee leader is a disengaged, remote mal-leader who is only tangentially involved in organizational decisions, manipulates symbols more than substance, and doesn't mind the organizational store. This mal-leader is more mindless than malicious, but eventually creates chaos and malaise from the turmoil and infighting that are perpetrated by underlings who are malevolent and who sense a leadership vacuum.

B. The Controller

The controller is a rigid mal-leader with an overdeveloped sense of tradition, perfectionism, and need to control others predominantly through the control and miscontrol of information. Unlike the street fighter, this mal-leader lacks the charisma to attract huge crowds and followings and controls by elaborate use of bureaucratic rules restricting and directing information.

C. The Busybody

The busybody is an indecisive, ineffective mal-leader who craves affection, is fearful of alienating others, and specializes in rumor mongering. This mal-leader sets himself up as the center of a communications network so that others must constantly turn to him to "tattle" on others and, by failing to make decisions to resolve conflicts among subordinates, assures that the flow of complaints and information about conflicts and therefore the attention he receives will be continuous.

D. The Hedonist

The hedonist is a mal-leader obsessed with the pleasures of sexual conquests, often also excessive with alcohol, money, and ostentatious consumption. This mal-leader defines self-worth in terms of sexual exploits, frequently denies responsibility for his own behavior, and therefore, in the long run has difficulty leading and inspiring an entire organization.

E. The Enforcer

The enforcer is a subservient, often second-in-command mal-leader who needs hierarchy, certainty, and money, and who echoes the mal-leadership styles of those to whom he attaches himself and supports. This mal-leader rarely achieves dominance in an organization but is instrumental to the success of others, especially street fighters, bullies, and absentee leaders.

F. The Street Fighter

The street fighter is an egotistical, often charismatic mal-leader with a "king of the mountain" attitude who is driven to dominate through gang politics. This mal-leader operates on gut level survival instincts and the principle of rewards and punishments for loyalty to his "gang," rather than to the organization as a whole. Street fighters can be generous to those who show loyalty to their own faction, but vicious, exacting swift retribution against those who do not.

G. The Bully

The bully is a very angry, pugnacious mal-leader who is mad at the world, is jealous of others who outperform him, and is driven to invalidate and tear others down in any setting, including and especially work. This mal-leader is bitter about past failures and tears others down to feel less like a failure himself. Bullies control through a variety of means, including and especially inappropriate angry personalized outbursts that lash out with the force of an emotional tidal wave.

In theory, mal-leaders may be male or female since the presence of X chromosomes does not necessarily render one immune to the psychological sense of inadequacy and inferiority that produces mal-leadership, nor to its behavioral manifestations. However, in reality, most leadership positions, especially top positions with enough power to spin a whole organization into decline, are still occupied by men. Thus, statistical accuracy, not a refutation of feminist concerns about gender neutral pronouns nor an affinity for male conspiracy views, causes us typically to use the pronoun "he" rather than "she" when referring to mal-leaders.

VI. MAL-LEADER-INDUCED ORGANIZATIONAL DECLINE

All of the seven types of mal-leaders have a distorting and eventually debilitating impact on the organization they govern. If they are unchecked, or reinforced by rather than rejected and rebuked by others, this impact can become devastating. When an organization falls under the influence of mal-leaders, a downward spiral of decline begins. Organizations may be "turned around" at each stage of decline, but the further down the spiral an organization has proceeded, the more difficult well-intentioned rescue becomes.

Organizations in decline are marked by plummeting productivity as well as malaise and low morale. Seven stages of organizational decline will be discussed briefly in this book. Each is wrenching to the employees involved and results in ever lower levels of productivity. With each stage, employees become less focused on the true mission of the organization and devote ever greater degrees of energy to surviving in what has become an organizational morass.

For an organization that has spiraled downward to the last stages of decline, most likely more than one type of mal-leader is at work. Even relatively benign absentee leaders can cause precipitous decline, however, by allowing and implicitly encouraging other types of mal-leaders at lower organizational levels to wreak havoc on organizational functioning and productivity. Once a cycle of decline and a culture conducive to mal-leading are established, they tend to be self-sustaining and even to attract other types of mal-leaders. How this occurs and how it eventually might be ended are the themes of this book.

Mal-leadership is not the only pressure generating organizational decline. Economic conditions also have a significant impact. A shift from favorable to unfavorable economic conditions and an increase in environmental uncertainty will increase pressure on organizations and the likelihood that some or all of the stages of organizational decline will emerge. The shift in economic conditions may come from several sources: general recession, an increase in foreign competition resulting from globalization of markets, or threat of a hostile takeover. In each instance, stress within the organization mounts, and the flaws of mal-leadership, once acceptably disguised, become more apparent and even exacerbated under the resulting strain.

Organizations that were performing at an excellent level under favorable economic conditions drop to mediocre lackluster performance when economic conditions become harsh. Similarly, organizations that were performing at barely acceptable levels in good times will likely spin into decline as conditions become more competitive and less favorable. These organizations will limp along as internal relations deteriorate along with the external environment. Some will barely endure and others will not survive.

When confronted with harsher and uncertain economic conditions, organizations with moral leadership will rise to meet the demands of the harsher environment through innovation, resolution, and greater team spirit, while those with mal-leadership will waste precious time, resources, and energies fighting internally rather than strategizing and implementing new survivable, and even superior futures. An organization in decline is like a train barreling out of control: bad economic conditions provide the rails that allow the organization to slip readily into decline, but mal-leadership provides the engine that drives it downward.

Like any sickness, organizational sickness resulting from mal-leadership, perhaps confounded by a downturn in economic conditions, can be overcome in most instances. But as with any sickness, first, the patient must fight the sickness and become well before confronting tasks of greater magnitude and returning to work in full force. Thus, an organization that has fallen into decline must "heal itself" by several strategies to be discussed later if decline is not too advanced. Then it must meet the challenges that constitute its raison d'être—the reasons it exists in the first place.

Our entire economy is but a complex mosaic of overlapping and many faceted organizations. Most of our work is conducted in organizations. When any of these organizations suffers decline from mal-leadership, we may momentarily feel superior, especially if our own organization is thriving and our current workplace is healthy and blessed with moral leadership. But the reality is when any of these organizations, especially large ones, suffers decline from mal-leadership, we all suffer directly or indirectly a loss in quality of life.

And no one is immune. The probability is high that throughout a lifetime of work, most people will run into a case of mal-leadership that will cause them personal pain, affect their own career, and plunge their organizations into lower productivity and dysfunction. The lucky ones will experience this only once.

VII. INDIVIDUAL RESPONSES TO MAL-LEADERSHIP

One of the key problems in responding to mal-leaders is the assumption of rationality that most managers and employees bring to the analysis of organizational problems. Whereas rational responses to rational individuals and situations are varied and broad ranging, rational responses to nonrationality are severely limited. Thus, problems or situations irrationally defined are not solved by rationally determined solutions. A paranoid manager who believes that everyone is withholding information from him is not placated by a new, improved information management system. Consequently, appropriate individual responses to the mal-leaders are very limited. Table 1 details the alternatives.

Most of the prescriptions offered by the management literature assume rationality and therefore fall in the upper left cell: rational managers dealing with rational employees is a situation where the broad range of managerial practices and techniques is applicable. Most prescriptive and descriptive management literature falls into this category.

The cell that holds the unpredictable managers dealing with unpredictable subordinates presents an impossible situation for the rational manager. If given the choice, the manager observing from the outside is best advised to leave the situation alone. In a limited time, the two maladjusted individuals will undermine each other. If the situation threatens the broader organization, the supervising manager might consider reallocating the tasks to a functioning unit until the irrational unit self-destructs.

Table 1 Individual Responses to Maladjusted Coworkers

		MANAGER	
		Rational	Irrational
EMPLOYEE	Rational	Refer to Management Literature	Quit Shot in the Back
	Irrational	Employee Assistance Programs Counseling Fire/terminate	Unmanageable

The situation of the rational manager dealing with the unpredictable, irrational employee offers only two options. First, if the employee is irrational and unpredictable because of drugs or alcohol, or if he has mental or emotional problems, the manager should first attempt to get the employee straightened out: that is, restore the employee to psychological health, using employee assistance programs or work-sponsored counseling. If this does not work within a reasonable amount of time, the problem employee should be terminated. In the public sector it is not easy to fire an employee but it is possible.

Consider the alternative. The unpredictable employee does not respond to therapy, firing is difficult, so the employee is transferred, maybe even promoted to relieve the manager of the stress of dealing with the problem at that time. Now the problem comes back to haunt in the form of the mal-leader situation. The maladjusted manager has been promoted or transferred so often that he is now a supervisor. The original derelict manager now finds himself working for a mal-leader because no supervisor or manager took the trouble or had the courage or persistence to fire the maladjusted employee. (This is the strongest case for firing maladjusted workers that we can muster.)

Next consider the cell housing the rational employee working for a nonrational, unpredictable mal-leader; here the rational employee has only two options. The most direct and effective response is to get out. Transfer, if that is possible, if not, then quit. It may not be practical or easy, but getting out is the only safe option available. Sticking it out may seem a viable alternative but in most cases it is not. Mal-leaders can cause extensive emotional, and sometimes even physical, damage to subordinates. Rational employees will try all the techniques and ideas from the literature and their experience (cell one of the chart) to make the situation better, but these suggestions and techniques do not work, because we are outside the bounds of rationality. Nothing seems to work because in fact nothing does work. Rational employees trying to succeed in this environment can only fail and carry that feeling of failure and frustration home to their families. Over time all those close to the manager, family and friends, will find the employee's reaction to the stress imposed by the mal-leader intolerable and will distance themselves from the beleaguered employee.

The second alternative in this category is very risky, because most of those who try it go down with the mal-leader. If the employee feels that quitting is not possible then there is only one strategy left: shooting the mal-leader in the back, metaphorically speaking, of course. Historically, all military leaders, from Greek and Roman times up to the Vietnam era, have known that if they put their troops in situations that cause unwarranted risk to their personal safety, they run the risk of getting shot in the back by their own troops. In Vietnam it was called fragging, named after the fragmentation grenade that was used to take out careless or unresponsive officers. Mal-leaders are organizationally fragged by being placed by their subordinates in situations where they look bad to their superiors. The goal of the fragging is to have the mal-leader demoted or dismissed.

We now examine the last situation: rational employees responding to a mal-leader. Recognizing early that a mal-leader problem exists will save the subordinates and the organization from having to deal with the adverse effects. We have adapted the phases of the grieving processes, also called the working though process, to characterize the rational employee's response to the mal-leader. The key differences here is that normally coming to grips with a change or a loss results in acceptance of the new reality as the final stage. However, accepting a mal-leader as a new reality is an unacceptable option so the process cannot proceed normally.

VIII. STAGES OF INDIVIDUAL RESPONSE TO MAL-LEADERSHIP AND ORGANIZATIONAL DECLINE

We propose that individuals respond to a mal-leader in a manner similar to the way they deal with personal loss or trauma, at least in the beginning stages. The process of working through a major trauma encompasses four phases: First, the individual is shocked, angry, and numb. Next, the individual refuses to believe that this bad thing has happened, and is saddened. Third, the individual discards the old patterns of behaving, thinking, or feeling and begins to redefine himself and the situation. Finally, the new situation is accepted.

Although the stages of individual response to a mal-leader parallel the first two stages of working through a trauma, the final stages of the working through process are never reached. It is simply not a satisfactory solution for the rational organization members to accept the mal-leader as the new reality. From the individual perspective, the mal-leader produces major stress and inflicts emotional and physical harm to subordinates, and from the organizational level of analysis, the mal-leader disrupts productivity and causes serious personnel problems. Because of the harm these mal-leaders inflict, it is important that we begin to pay some systematic attention to the process of identifying such managers. The seven stages of response to a mal-leader are presented to help us recognize, analyze, and begin to develop strategies for identifying and coping with mal-leaders in public and private organizations.

Each of the stages outlined here has characteristics that make it identifiable to an outsider, although those living through the decline associated with a mal-leader may be so swept up in the dysfunctional games and strategies, so overcome with anxiety, and so emotionally distraught, angry, and fearful that clear analysis of the stages may evade them.

A. Stage 1: Trust and Cooperation

At first glance the organization appears healthy. The flaws of the mal-leader have been masked or are not yet apparent. Employees work in an atmosphere of trust and cooperation. There is sharing of information among individuals and face-to-face interactions are cordial and friendly.

Since trust is the operative mode of employee and manager interaction, there is no need to document every aspect of decision making. Nor is there any perceived gap between rhetoric and reality, communications are taken at face value, and employees believe that the goals of the working unit support the overall goals of the organization.

B. Stage 2: Disappointment and Disillusionment

The mal-leader's malicious behavior, task problems, and goal displacement become apparent. Employees privately respond to the mal-leader's dictates with disbelief and incredulity. They express disappointment in the performance and decisions of the mal-leader. Although public and open dismay is not yet present, the gap between reality and the mal-leader's rhetoric is increasingly clear.

As employee disillusionment and disenchantment grow, so do anxiety and skepticism. Employees cease sharing information for fear that it will be used inappropriately by the mal-leader. Communications are written to ward off blame in the event of a misunderstanding or unfortunate event. As the free exchange of information and ideas is curtailed, so too decision making slows down. Indecisiveness is a reflection of the employees' growing uncertainty and anxiety. Employees must increasingly exert efforts to verify information and document choices. This stage is comparable to the first stage in the grieving process: the employees are shocked and beginning to be angry.

C. Stage 3: Outrage and Contempt

Employees who have bought into the goals of the organization and try to accomplish those goals, as stated in their job descriptions or the published agency policy, become outraged as the mal-leader pursues alternate goals and objectives. The unit begins to break into factions, with the common breaking point between supporters and opponents of the mal-leader. Each side beings to accuse the other of having misinterpreted or displaced organizational goals.

Meetings cease to function as avenues for exchanging information and begin to resemble boisterous debates where the competing groups present their interpretations of the causes and sources of the malaise. The rift is now obvious and the mal-leader's actions are met with outrage and contempt from those who feel that the organization's goals have been displaced with self-serving, vindictive, or malicious goals.

Some individuals respond here by refusing to believe that this is happening, the second stage of grieving, and it may take a while before they feel outrage and contempt. Others, finding the situation increasingly uncomfortable, begin to look for other work. The number of requests for transfers increases beyond what would normally be expected.

D. Stage 4: Covert Game Playing

The factions that began organizing in stage three are more unified. Members of each side disguise and conceal true motives. Communication is characterized by the positioning of an event or situation in order to present one side of the conflict in a complimentary light. Truth becomes relative and the art of putting a positive spin on negative information is frequently practiced. All sides begin to reinterpret the statements of others to assess true rationales.

Secret meetings are called to compare notes, strategize, and discuss options. Public and private criticism of organization members becomes customary. Formal meetings are more numerous and take on the character of combat. The mal-leader tries to use the meetings to control the employees and the situation. Fear makes attendance mandatory. An absence might become an issue on an employee's personnel record, or failure to be present might mean that the employee would not be able to protect himself and his work from abuse or criticism.

As the fighting continues, little attention is devoted to the actual work of the organization or department. Policy becomes a tool to punish enemies, not an aid to pursuing organization goals. Rules and regulations are combat weapons for all sides.

Those who report to the mal-leader are now quitting in greater numbers. Transfer requests increase. The stress causes many to call in sick or take personal days off to avoid having to face the situation at work.

E. Stage 5: Open Warfare

Covertness and pretense are dropped as relations become more hostile. Open warfare breaks out. More and more employees are dragged into the fray as the conflict spills into the open. Few employees can maintain neutrality because both sides will interpret their non-involvement as disloyalty.

Both sides publicly and privately discredit and disparage each other. The mal-leader attempts to take resources away from the opposing side and often succeeds, at least temporarily. Strategizing and struggling over resources intensify. Neither the copier, fax machine, travel support, computer accounts, nor secretary's time is too small an item to generate passion. Perquisites become a carrot for the mal-leaders; personnel evaluations become the stick.

Charges of incompetence become commonplace; these changes are very threatening to many managers because management positions are rarely subject to strict objective evaluative measures. The mal-leader's attacks become frontal, overt, and personal. The entire unit is now preoccupied with the conflict, and work is interrupted. Managers outside the warring unit are entreated to take sides in the conflict. All organizational actions and behaviors are not interpreted through the filter of the conflict.

This is the stage where the stressed-out rational managers begin to implement fragging strategies. The number of those leaving the unit increases significantly at this stage.

F. Stage 6: Siege Mentality

Normal practices and norms are violated. Lines of authority are breached as higher levels are inveighed to join the conflict. Outsiders are lured into the conflict even when enlisting their support is inappropriate or unethical. Customers, clients, supporters, consultants, and tangentially linked persons are involved by one or another faction. Threat of legal consequences for character defamation or other vague, unspecified reasons are implied.

There does not seem to be any hope that the situation can be rectified. Paranoia reigns. Productivity plummets. Rumors of trouble and turmoil spread beyond the organization, making outsiders leery of working with or even being associated with the contentious department. Yugoslavia comes to mind.

G. Stage 7: Isolation and Alienation

If the situation continues to this stage, most members of the unit are isolated and alienated. All employees, battle worn and scarred, experience emotional exhaustion. Hopelessness and cynicism prevail. Many withdraw emotionally from work and cease to care about the organization. Communication breaks down almost totally. Meetings that were highly charged earlier are now poorly attended. Effort and time spent on work are reduced to the bare minimum.

IX. ORGANIZATIONAL STRATEGIES FOR COPING WITH MAL-LEADERS

Individual strategies for dealing with mal-leaders are cumbersome, threatening, and difficult. Designing organizational strategies for identifying and coping with mal-leaders, before too much individual and organizational damage is done, might be a better course of action. In terms of goal accomplishment, competitiveness, reputation, effectiveness, and efficiency, a mal-leader can severely damage an organization, especially if he occupies a position at the upper levels of the hierarchy.

What can be done to reverse mal-leader induced organizational decline? Must organizations that start on the downhill slide into decline go through all the stages to hit rock bottom? What happens then if they do?

Several strategies can be used to halt and reverse organizational decline. The strategies may be ranked in terms of impact on the organization itself and on its employees. The strategy with the least impact is *expanding the organizational resource base.* The second least severe strategy for most employees in the organization is *removing the mal-leader.* The third strategy in terms of gravity and size of impact is *restructuring the organization.* The most severe strategy with the greatest impact is *abolishing the organization.* The following factors determine which strategy is most appropriate:

1. How long has decline gone on? The longer decline has continued, the more severe the strategy that will need to be employed. If decline has persisted for a long time, then dysfunctional behaviors have become habit and are deeply ingrained. More severe strategies will be needed to reverse long-standing behavior patterns.
2. How far, through how many stages, has decline proceeded? The more stages of decline the organization has passed through, the more severe the strategy that will be needed to combat organization dysfunction successfully. An organization that has begun the descent into dysfunction need not necessarily go through all the stages to hit rock bottom, but the further down the organization has slid, the more severe the strategy that will be needed to pull it out of malaise and to restore productivity.
3. How many mal-leaders are there? If an organization has only one or two mal-leaders who are causing havoc with their behavior and making the organization dysfunctional, then less severe strategies to combat decline may be adequate. If, however, the organization has many mal-leaders, more severe strategies are needed.

   If decline has persisted for some time, the likelihood is great that the number of mal-leaders will increase, for mal-leaders attract each other. Moral leaders drive mal-leaders out, by virtue of acting on a higher moral plane and maintaining high standards of productivity, if not by specific actions. Mal-leaders, however, benefit from and feed off each other's dysfunctional behavior.
4. Are mal-leaders layered in several successive levels in the organizational hierarchy, or are they dispersed? If mal-leaders are layered, severe strategies are needed. Merely removing one mal-leader will not solve the problem of organizational dysfunction when mal-leaders are stacked up several layers deep. Remaining mal-leaders will work to see that the replacement is no better than the one who was removed.

   Even if a moral leader is selected, he will immediately be stiffed and attacked by the even more threatened mal-leaders who have observed one of their own being stripped of authority. If, however, the mal-leaders are relatively dispersed and can be organizationally isolated, less severe remedies may work.

Here are the strategies that may be used to counter and combat organizational decline. Each has advantages and disadvantages.

A. Expanding the Organizational Resource Base

This strategy involves giving dysfunctional units more resources in an attempt to migrate the infighting that invariably becomes worse when resources are tight. Thus, mal-leaders and their factions are "bought off" by giving them less reason to fight, and by making them feel relatively successful and more secure.

This strategy is more likely to be employed in times of economic plenty than in times of economic scarcity, so its actual use may depend as much on conditions external to the organization as those internal to it. Expanding the resource base as a strategy for combating decline has the advantage of leaving organizational arrangements intact, thereby preventing the turmoil that will inevitably result when organizational arrangements are changed.

This strategy also has several major disadvantages. It rewards units that by their dysfunction have been less productive, sending a message to other units and organizations that the way to get more resources is to fight internally, rather than to produce more. It may actually increase the power of the mal-leader by giving him more resources with which to reward supporters and penalize opponents. Thus it may not work. Finally, it may not be a rational, efficient allocation of resources overall.

B. Removing the Mal-Leader

This strategy entails removing the mal-leader from his position of authority. The mal-leader may either be forced out of the organization or pushed into a role peripheral to decision making that affects the whole organization. This strategy has the advantage of removing the immediate problem and source of decline.

Removing the mal-leader also has disadvantages. If the mal-leader is not forced out of the organization—and in some settings this may not be possible or even desirable—the disgruntled and angry mal-leader may become a totally destructive force, even without formal power, sabotaging whenever possible all efforts to restore the organization to health. If decline has been pronounced is quite advanced, then the bitterness from infighting may not be addressed or solved merely by replacing the mal-leader.

But the most crucial problem, since most likely removed mal-leaders can be neutralized to some degree, is finding an adequate replacement. If economic conditions are harsh, then recruitment of a replacement from outside the organization may be hampered or not possible. If recruitment must occur internally, then the mal-leader has likely trained no one to replace him and has worked hard, in fact, to assure the reverse. If decline is severe, most likely the mal-leader has already attracted other mal-leaders, limiting the pool of moral leaders available internally.

C. Restructuring the Organization

This option is more severe than merely replacing the mal-leader. It involves everyone in the organization. Dysfunctional units are restructured. The dysfunctional unit may be merged with more healthy units. Pieces may be removed and shifted to other divisions. Other pieces may be combined in an attempt to mitigate infighting and neutralize mal-leaders. In the process one or more mal-leaders in the unit may have their authority reduced. Mal-leaders may also be replaced. The unit continues as a whole but looks very different from its original configuration.

This strategy is more likely to work as an antidote to organizational decline in a larger unit. The bigger the unit, the greater the flexibility for restructuring, and the greater the likelihood that moral leadership talent exists within the unit and can assume control. It is less likely to work for small units and organizations, for there are few logical options for restructuring subunits into new combinations.

This strategy has the advantage of retaining the organization's identity. Organizations across time tend to take on a life of their own and do not die easily, even when afflicted with the virus of mal-leadership and showing the sickness of organizational decline. Even if organizational health is eventually restored by restructuring, however, the new structure may not initially increase productivity. Productivity increases may take some time to materialize and may do so only after new working arrangements are established. Restoring employee self-esteem and allowing for development of skills of employees who have not had such opportunities or who have been discouraged from taking advantage of such opportunities will also take time.

D. Abolishing the Organization

In the most extreme cases of decline, the only feasible option may be to abolish the organization. If the dysfunction is occurring in a division within a larger organization, pieces of the organization may be split up and spun off to healthier divisions. If the whole organization is sick, pieces may be sold to other corporations, in the private sector. In the public sector, pieces may be moved to other departments or agencies. In some instances, the whole organization may be swallowed up by a larger organization, as in the case of mergers and hostile takeovers.

The most extreme option is to disband the organization totally. This happens in cases of bankruptcy in the private sector, college closings, and abandonment of public sector agencies. While ostensibly the reason for some of these organizational abolitions is economic, each likely experienced a preceding period organizational decline.

E. Preventing Decline in the Future

How might organizations stay healthy in the future and prevent the agony and ultimate defeat of mal-leadership? Both the process of decline and the remedies for correcting it are painful, and if both can be avoided, then everyone associated with an organization, as well as the economy as a whole, will be better off. Are there any "preventive medical strategies" that will stop decline before it grows?

Strategies to prevent decline are easier to discuss than to implement. Following are some employee actions that may help prevent decline or survive it if prevention is not possible:

1. Employees must be aware that mal-leadership is a real threat to organizational health and be vigilant in watching for the first signs of it.
2. When the presence of one or more mal-leaders becomes obvious, rational employees should talk with the mal-leaders in as nonthreatening a fashion as possible to convey their awareness of dysfunctional mal-leader behavior.
3. If mal-leaders continue to act dysfunctionally, employees may begin to seek support and redress through the organizational hierarchy, following appropriate chains of command, expressing concerns about what is going on.
4. An unfortunate but realistic aspect of rational employees' operating under mal-leaders is that the former should put everything in writing to develop documentation that may be needed later.

5. Rational employees should try to identify moral leaders who are genuinely concerned about the health of the organization and the welfare of its employees and reach out to these leaders with their concerns.
6. Rational employees should be firm at every step, refusing to engage in dysfunctional behavior just because others are doing it.
7. Despite impediments to productivity, rational employees should try to maintain output and return collective attention to productivity at every possible juncture.
8. While difficult to do in an atmosphere of decline, rational employees should take a long-run view of petty slights and actions, ignoring them whenever possible.
9. Rational employees refuse to participate in secret meetings and agreements that cannot be revealed publicly, for closed environments are a part of creating a culture of decline.
10. Rational employees should persist in the view that mal-leaders are fundamentally flawed and will eventually self-destruct.

Organizational decline, like any sickness, is dynamic, not static. A sick organization will eventually get better or die. In either event, mal-leaders will be replaced. The greatest antidote to mal-leadership and the organizational decline it foments is moral leadership.

REFERENCES

Badaracco, Joseph L., Jr., and Ellsworth, Richard K., *Leadership and the Quest for Integrity*, Harvard Business School Press, Boston, Mass., 1989.

Bass, B. M., *Leadership and Performance Beyond Expectations*, Free Press, New York, 1985.

Batten, Joe D., *Tough-Minded Leadership*, AMACON, New York, 1989.

Bennis, Warren, *Why Leaders Can't Lead: The Unconscious Conspiracy Continues*, Jossey-Bass, San Francisco, 1989.

Bernstein, A. and Rozen, S. C., *Dinosaur Brains*, John Wiley and Sons, New York, 1988.

Bernstein, A. and Rozen, S. C., *Neanderthals at Work*, John Wiley and Sons, New York, 1992.

Bing, Stanley, *Crazy Bosses*, Morrow, New York, 1992.

Blake, R. R. and Mouton, J. S., *The Managerial Grid*, Gulf, Houston, Tex., 1964.

Bryman, Alan, *Leadership and Organizations*, Routledge and Kegan Paul, London, 1986.

Burns, James MacGregor, *Leadership*, Harper and Row, New York, 1978.

Cribbin, James J., *Leadership: Strategies for Organizational Effectiveness*, AMACON, New York, 1981.

Cronin, Thomas E., Thinking About Leadership, *Presidential Studies Quarterly*, 14(Winter):22–34 (1984).

Crosby, Philip B., *Leading: The Art of Becoming an Executive*, McGraw-Hill, New York, 1990.

Doig, Jameson W. and Hargrove, Erwin C., *Leadership and Innovation: A Biographical Perspective on Entrepreneurs in Government*, Johns Hopkins University Press, Baltimore, 1987.

Doob, Leonard W., *Personality, Power and Authority*, Greenwood Press, Westport, Conn., 1983.

Fleishman, E. A. and Harris, E. F., Patterns of Leadership Behavior Related to Employee Grievances and Turnover, *Personnel Psychology*, 15:4–56 (1962).

Hershey, P. and Blanchard, K. H., *The Management of Organizational Behavior*, 4th ed., Prentice-Hall, Englewood Cliffs, N.J., 1984.

Hunt, James G., Hosking, Dian-Marie, Schriesheim, Chester A., and Stewart, Rosemary, eds., *Leaders and Managers: International Perspectives on Managerial Behavior and Leadership*, Pergamon Press, New York, 1984.

Hunt, James G., Baliga, B. Rajaram, Dachler, H. Peter, and Schriesheim, Chester A., eds., *Emerging Leadership Vistas*, Lexington Books, Lexington, Mass., 1988.

Jaques, Elliot, and Clement, Stephen D., *Executive Leadership: A Practical Guide to Managing Complexity*, Basil Blackwell, Cambridge, Mass., 1991.

Jones, Bryan D., ed., *Leadership and Politics: New Perspectives in Political Science*, University of Kansas Press, Lawrence, 1989.

Kennedy, Paul, *The Rise and Fall of the Great Powers*, Random House, New York, 1987.
Kets de Vries, Manfred F. R., ed., *The Irrational Executive: Psychoanalytic Explorations in Management*, International Universities Press, New York, 1984.
Kets de Vries, Manfred F. R., *Prisoners of Leadership*, John Wiley and Sons, New York, 1989.
Kets de Vries, M. and Miller, D., *The Neurotic Organization*, Jossey Bass, San Francisco, 1984.
Kets de Vries, M. and Miller, D., Narcissism and Leadership: An Object Relations Perspective, *Human Relations*, 38:583–601 (1985).
Kets de Vries, M. and Miller, D., *Unstable at the Top*, Mentor, New York, 1987.
Koestenbaum, Peter, *Leadership: The Inner Side of Greatness*, Jossey-Bass, San Francisco, 1991.
Kotter, John P., *A Force for Change: How Leadership Differs from Management*, Free Press, New York, 1990.
Kouzes, James M., and Posner, Barry Z., *The Leadership Challenge: How to Get Extraordinary Things Done in Organizations*, Jossey-Bass, San Francisco, 1987.
Likert, R., *The Human Organization: Its Management and Value*, McGraw-Hill, New York, 1967.
Lundy, James L., *Lead, Follow, or Get Out of the Way*, Avant Books, San Diego, Calif., 1986.
Mant, Alistair, *Leaders We Deserve*, Martin Robertson, Oxford, England, 1983.
Maccoby, Michael, *The Leader: A New Face for American Management*, Simon and Schuster, New York, 1981.
Maccoby, Michael, *Why Work: Motivating and Leading the New Generation*, Touchstone Books, New York, 1988.
Misume, J., *The Behavioral Science of Leadership: An Interdisciplinary Japanese Research Program*, University of Michigan, Ann Arbor, Mich., 1985.
Nanus, Burt, *The Leader's Edge*, Contemporary Books, Chicago, 1989.
Phillips, Kevin, *The Politics of Rich and Poor: Wealth and the American Electorate in the Reagan Aftermath*, Random House, New York, 1990.
Reich, Robert B., *The Work of Nations: Preparing Ourselves for Twenty-First Century Capitalism*, Alfred A. Knopf, New York, 1991.
Rost, Joseph C., *Leadership for the Twenty-First Century*, Praeger, New York, 1991.
Whicker, Marcia Lynn and Moore, Raymond A., *Making America Competitive*, Praeger, New York, 1988.
Wilson, James Q., *Bureaucracy: What Government Agencies Do and Why They Do It*. Basic Books, New York, 1989.
Yukl, Gary A., *Leadership in Organizations*, 2nd ed., Prentice-Hall, Englewood Cliffs, N.J., 1989.

9
Government Reorganization: A Theoretical Analysis

B. Guy Peters
University of Pittsburgh, Pittsburgh, Pennsylvania

I. INTRODUCTION

Reorganization and reform are among the most common of governmental activities, but often are undertaken without adequate theoretical or practical guidance. This paper investigates several alternative families of models for understanding reorganization. It evaluates each according to its theoretical claims and utility. The three families of models are purposive models from economics and political science, environmental models largely from organizational sociology, and institutional approaches. The analysis favors the institutional approach, but points to the need for an enhanced understanding of change processes within public administration.

The reform and reorganization of their administrative structures are among the most common activities of contemporary governments. Indeed, governments have invested a great deal of time and energy in reform efforts for as long as there have been governments. This extensive concern with reform and reorganization may appear paradoxical to the dispassionate observer. Much of the literature—both that contributed by practitioners and that written by scholars—argues that reform is largely ineffective and often has significant unintended negative consequences on the efficiency and effectiveness of government. Reading evaluations of major public reform efforts from a number of national settings appears to indicate that a finding of no significant results is often the indicator of a reform "success," while a "failure" often is characterized by serious negative side effects. The preceding description of reforms in the public sector is probably excessively cynical, but it does point to the persistence of reform in the face of evidence that no one should expect a great deal of return from the investment in time and energy.

A second notable element that leads the observer to question the real administrative utility of reform efforts is the dominance of fad and fashion in the reforms. Not only do reorganization efforts appear to be proposed in clusters or waves, but the same remedies appear to be proposed regardless of the preexisting structures of the governments being reformed. For example, in the 1980s there was a plethora of reorganization and reform efforts, many of them derived from the conservative political philosophies of political leaders such as Margaret Thatcher and Ronald Reagan. These reforms all involved an ostensibly diminished role for the state in social and economic affairs, and a reduction of the power and influence of the career civil service in the policy process. Also, rather extreme patterns of devolution of authority within government appear to have been a major component of this dominant reorganization pattern. The best known example of this type of deconcentrating reform is the "Next Steps" initiative in the United Kingdom (Kemp, 1990). This program seeks to devolve the policy executing role of ministries to several hundred executive agencies. A similar reform creating agencies is being undertaken by a center-right government in the Netherlands. Interestingly, however, very similar patterns of change have occurred in France and Australia under Socialist and Labour governments, respectively, and the most extreme deconcentrating reform of all occurred under a Labour government in New Zealand (Scott et al., 1990).

It would be extremely easy to dismiss most reform and reorganization efforts as the result of either fads or political needs to respond to problems without having any real policy remedies. Despite all those problems, reforms are important phenomena in the study of public administration and public policy. They do happen, and some are more successful than others. In addition, the fact that the reforms do occur in clusters across time indicates that there is either a diffusion of ideas about good public administration or a *Zeitgeist* that leads governments to common diagnoses of the problems of the public sector and therefore to relatively common prescriptions for remedying the problems discovered. Further, the prevalence of reforms, and of certain types of reform at one time, may indicate as much about fad and fashion in administrative science as it does about fads in governments (Astley, 1985). It may be that the professional advisers responsible for the changes in the public sector are more culpable if time and resources are being wasted than are the politicians. Thus, we need to understand as analysts the possible roots of reform, and something about their possible success in producing real policy change.

II. THEORETICAL APPROACHES TO REFORM

There are at least three alternative theoretical positions useful for understanding reform and reorganization efforts in the public sector. In at least one approach discussed later it may be stretching the claims of the position itself to refer to it as being theoretical, but even that more descriptive and commonsense approach does appear to have an implicit theory residing at its foundation. We will describe briefly these three fundamental positions, along with the various subsets contained within each. We will discuss how each of the approaches might be applied, and how we might decide among them as ways of understanding what has happened in public administration. There may even be a case to be made for the ability of several of the approaches to predict what might transpire in any future prospective reforms of government. One of the major weaknesses in most public administration literature, and indeed the political science literature taken more broadly, is the inability to predict logical outcomes of emerging situations and opportunities in government. As a consequence, analysts postdict, rather than predict, outcomes in the public sector. What will be discussed here are by no means full-blown predictive models, but there are at least some inklings of movement in that direction.

As we discuss theories in reorganization, we will need to be extremely careful to distinguish the theories (implicit or explicit) that have guided practitioners who constructed the reorganizations from those theories which political scientists and other organizational analysts have utilized in their attempts to understand, ex post facto, the changes imposed. In some instances the two bodies of theory may be synonymous, while in other cases there are marked differences. Several of the more abstract theories of the analysts may in fact be useful for informing practical reform efforts, but few appear to be consulted as governments cycle through their progression of reform and then reform again. We should point out here that we will be looking at changes that could be considered either as reorganizations—structural changes—or as reforms—procedural or relational changes (Ingraham and Peters, 1988). These two categories are at times difficult to separate and the motivations underlying them tend to be very similar. Therefore, we will deal with these as synonymous for the purposes of this chapter.

A. Purposive Models of Reform

The first major set of approaches to reform are broadly purposive in their perspective on the process. That is, these analyses assume that one or more actors in the process have a particular end-state in mind when they propose the reform or reorganization. They further assume that the actor(s) involved are sufficiently powerful or skillful to have the reform adopted and implemented. These models consider the perceived problems and motivations of political actors—including organizations within the public sector themselves—and seek to comprehend why reorganization decisions are taken, given those motivations. Many of these approaches focus more on the implicit theories of the reformers themselves than on supply analytic frameworks of their own to understand the process. At least one (the economic approach), however, is able to provide a powerful (if somewhat simplistic for most purposes) theoretical analysis of bureaucratic policy-making. There are several different approaches to reform contained within this broader category.

1. *Administration as Usual*

The first alternative approach to understanding reorganization in government is the one most commonly used in the real world, and to some extent also most commonly used (at least over time) in academic studies of public administration. In this approach, reorganizations occur because of the perceived political needs to produce a change in the administrative structure, and the perceived inadequacies of existing arrangements. Pollitt (1984) refers to these studies as the "traditional, pragmatic" approaches to the machinery of government, and therefore to changing the machinery. Dealing specifically with the British literature (Chester and Willson, 1968; Chapman and Greenaway, 1980; Johnson, 1976), Pollitt points to the tendency of writers in this tradition to ascribe reform to a "need" for change, without their ever specifying whose need, or the operational definition of such a need. In reality the need is usually the one perceived by a political leader (a prime minister) who wants to achieve a set of goals (including perhaps greater efficiency) through the public sector. That leader may see the existing administrative structures as impediments to achieving those goals and therefore attempt to restructure government. This tendency toward attributing vague political causes for reform is not confined to Britain, and a good deal of writing on administrative reform in the United States and elsewhere has the same characteristics (Seidman and Gilmour, 1986; Anderson, 1981; Caiden, 1970; 1984). Skowronek (1982) refers to this pattern of pragmatic and ad hoc reorganization as "patchwork" in the context of the United States.

This traditional mode of analysis is not, however, without its value. In the first place, it is often descriptively much richer than is more theoretically motivated research on organizational change, and a reader can understand the logic in action justifying the changes in government. Further, this writing generally approaches more closely the understandings of practitioners actually involved in government about what happened in a reorganization and why it happened.

The politicians and administrators involved in reform rarely think about their activities in the theoretical terms which fill the political science literature. Finally, although there may not be a theory explicitly stated in the work, there is often one underlying the description of change, and that theory is one based on a nuanced understanding of organization politics. The difficulty is that the theory may not be comprehensible to anyone who has not lived through the same set of experiences as the formulator of the "theory."

2. *Overload and Governance*

Pollitt (1984, pp. 170–172) discusses a second category of reforms (again largely in Britain) under the category of "political science," but the concerns are more general than the bounds of a single academic discipline. This approach to reform emphasizes the impact of overall governmental change on public administration, and especially those changes produced by a sense of "overload" and "ungovernability" that began in the late 1970s (Rose, 1978; Rose and Peters, 1978) and has persisted to the present (Snellen, 1985; Chubb and Peterson, 1989). In administrative terms, these diagnoses of the condition of modern governments have produced a panoply of reform efforts. At perhaps the simplest level, some of these have been called "cutback management" and concern the need of some managers in government to reduce the size of their own departments or agencies in order to meet externally imposed budgetary ceilings (Levine, 1978; Dunsire and Hood, 1989). The "cutback management" approach has emphasized the managerial need to produce reductions in programs and personnel without excessive disruption. Some disruption is inevitable, but the managerial question is how to reduce the human and organizational impacts of change.

The cutback approach in some ways presaged subsequent events in the public sector, which in turn required even greater managerial changes. Most of these changes were associated with the conservative governments elected in the aftermath of economic slowdowns and apparent mushrooming of the public sector; Reagan, Thatcher, and Mulroney are well known examples of the breed. Associated with these political regimes have been a host of reforms and reorganizations, most directed toward reducing the size and influence of government and having more services managed privately. Privatization has been one of the dominant themes in these reforms, as has the decentralization of administrative authority to autonomous or quasi-autonomous organizations (Peters, 1990a). Even less conservative political leaders have found it fiscally advantageous to reduce direct public employment and to use privatization and deregulation as means of reducing their levels of expenditure in the face of rising costs and increasing taxpayer resistance to big government. In fact some of the most extreme versions of administrative reform have occurred under the leadership of Labour governments.

As in the traditional approach to reorganization, there is a theory implicit in this approach to governmental reform. The theory is more evident in the reforms themselves than in most of the scholarship which has been applied to them. One strand of the "theoretical" thinking has been rather simplistic bureaucracy bashing, based upon a naive belief that most if not all of the problems of modern government are largely a function of inefficiencies inherent in large complex public bureaucracies (Goodsell, 1985; Milward and Rainey, 1983). This approach has generated a number of attempts to make the public sector look more like the private sector, and some have used private sector executives to implement those ideas (Metcalf and Richards, 1984; Kelman, 1985; Wilson, 1988). These hymns of praise to private sector management have been raised while government has been called in to save a number of failing steel mills, automobile factories, and financial institutions.

A more complex version of the same idea about reform parades under the banner of managerialism (Aucoin, 1990; Gray and Jenkins, 1986). The idea put forward here is that the civil service has been too much concerned with policy advice and insufficient attention has been directed toward managing organizations within government. The second part of the thesis is that most if not all of the perceived inefficiencies of government are a function of poor management rather than more fundamental problems or policy design. Therefore, it is argued that the formulation of policy ideas should be left to political leaders, and civil servants should be directed simply to manage their organizations, or to oversee the management of the newly created decentralized quasi-private organizations. This approach to the public sector can be justified as good democratic practice, with the politicians elected by the public responsible for policy and program ideas and the unelected civil servants responsible for their administration.

In a peculiar way, much of the academic literature on policy implementation (Pressman and Wildavsky, 1973; Mazmanian and Sabatier, 1983) shares the view of the politicians responsible for pushing managerialism onto the public sector. It could be argued (Linder and Peters, 1987) that the implementation literature works from the underlying premise that most of what malfunctions in government is largely a function of faulty administration. Therefore, if the systems of implementation are designed properly, there will be fewer policy failures and better government. Little blame for failure is placed at the doorstep of the designers of programs, other than their failure at times to consider the implications for implementation of the programs they have formulated. The implementation literature does not share the manifest ideological distaste for, and suspicion of, the career bureaucracy, but its diagnosis of the policy problems of government is in many ways similar to the more ideological strand of thought about the public sector.

3. *Economics and Rational Actors*

It may appear internally contradictory to lump economic models of administrative change into a larger section containing primarily political models of change, but there is a close theoretical connection if the two classes are considered from the appropriate vantage point. Just as the political models tend to look at the motivations of political (largely elective) actors to make things work properly in government and thereby to meet campaign promises and satisfy ideological supporters, the economic models look at the motivations of officials (largely nonelective although often the two types are conflated) to maximize their own utilities. These models then assume the impacts of those motivations on the structure and performance of administrative institutions. All of these models, therefore, assume individual purposive actions to generate structural and procedural changes, and all assume that the institutions themselves are largely responsive to those internally generated and rationalistic (within different frameworks of rationality) assumptions about the appropriate shape of the organizations.

The economic models of public administration that have become very familiar (Niskanen, 1971; Breton and Wintrobe, 1975; Bendor, 1989) all assume that the individual bureaucrat is a rational actor seeking to maximize his or her personal utility through involvement in the administrative process. In most of these models, the utility of the individual bureau chief is linked with the size of the bureau's budget and/or personnel allocation. In another variant of the model, Downs (1967) has the bureau chief identify more with collective goals of the organization so that maximizing the size of the organization is a means of protecting it against any future cuts imposed by politicians. Expanding the size of the bureau by adding new functions—one of several possible strategies—is a means of protecting the "heartland" of the organization from cuts. Therefore, in any of these models, the bureau chief has an interest in making the organization as large as possible, and reform would be seen as a means of improving the competitive position of the organization in the budgetary process.

The fundamental problems with these economic models of bureaucracy have been discussed any number of times (Jackson, 1982; Blais and Dion, 1992), and we will not repeat that labor here. Rather, we will point to a few specific problems for the models which arise in the context of examining contemporary reform efforts in the public sector. The most obvious problem is that most contemporary reform efforts involve efforts to reduce the size of the bureaucracy rather than constituting a means through which even an aggressive bureaucratic entrepreneur might be able to maximize the size of his or her organization. Given the generally tautological nature of these economic models, it is almost impossible to prove that a bureau chief did not act rationally in a reform—we do not know what sort of damage might have been done without the use of a rational economic strategy. Unless one is willing to accept a highly convoluted version of the model, these models simply do not appear applicable in decremental times (Tarschys, 1985). Following from that, most economic models of bureaucracy are largely silent about structural change, although structure is a crucial feature of any bureaucracy. In fact, these economic models are largely silent about strategies other than suggesting simply that organizations should disguise their true production functions, and that communications patterns have an effect on the ability of organizations to achieve their goals through the policy process (Tullock, 1965).

Another problem with this literature as it relates to the reform and reorganization of government is that it is ill suited to predict for the scholar, or advise the practitioner, what types of reforms might be most efficacious. The concentration of the size of the budget as virtually the (posited) sole concern of the bureau chief does not permit any nuanced or subtle discussions of strategies. Indeed, the major help in that regard comes from other political scientists who have commented on these economic models and sought to elaborate their meaning for the real world of government (Dunleavy, 1985; Goodin, 1982). This latter discussion has included an analysis of the types of expenditures which would be most beneficial to a bureaucratic entrepreneur, and the right types of personnel and programs to pursue if indeed the goals are to grow as large as possible. In this analysis, "bureau shaping" rather than sheer size is the goal for the rational administrative politician. Unfortunately, the advice rendered by those scholars has little or nothing to do with the type of models which most scholars using the economic approach have developed.

4. *Assessment*

The preceding models of change in the public sector all assume a particular purpose of a reform advocated by one or a few actors. These reforms are generally rationalistic, with a clear means-ends connection assumed between a diagnosis of a problem and the remedy. Both the diagnoses of problems and the remedies proposed may be related to common ideological and/or professional beliefs about good government and good administration, but there will be a basic belief that the actors in government themselves are central to identification, selection, and implementation of administrative changes.

It is easy to criticize these approaches to administrative reform. They all involve placing at times a very simplistic template over organizations and attempting to force them all into something like a common pattern. Diversity tends to be endemic, and important, within the public sector, and the promoters of simple volitional models tend to press toward uniformity. Further, they often make unrealistic assumptions about the capacity of public organizations, or organizations in general, to change in response to hierarchical directives. These approaches apparently fail to understand the informal aspects of organizations, and the need to modify not only formal structures but operating patterns if a reform is to be successful. Finally, most are based on assumptions about efficiency in organizations which, as Miles (1977), Salamon (1981) and others have argued, is often a very fleeting value in the study of public organizations. These problems are perhaps exaggerated in the economic models of bureaucracy, but they to some degree exist in all the approaches identified in this section.

B. Environmental Dependency

The second major grouping of approaches to administrative change tends to be the antithesis of the first in that the changes which do occur are posited to be a function of the relationship of the administrative structures to their environment. Again, that environment may be conceptualized as being either political or economic, but the underlying logic of the several approaches in this grouping is very similar. This logic is that over time structures adapt, or perhaps whole groups of structures adapt, to the environment and construct patterns of organizations that are functional for the fulfillment of their collective goals. This pattern of adaptation is in large part a function of the resources and challenges posed by the environment rather than more conscious choices by organizational leaders. While the first group of models depends upon the volition of individual political actors, these models appear to function more automatically, and any individuals involved appear to be in the role of transmitting environmental forces to the organization rather than necessarily making independent decisions on their own. Further, the organizations themselves do not appear to have any collective volition or will to survive but are relatively passive recipients of the messages from the environment.

1. *Political Science Approaches*

The first models of the political science types are again derived from political science/public administration and are based on the reactions of government to innovations in their relevant environments. Phrased simply, if government observes a new form of economic or technological activity, or a new opportunity for social change, its tendency is to create new organizations that can exploit the opportunity or control the potentially destructive anomaly. This will be true whether the pressure for change is generated internally within the public sector or is a function of political pressures coming from the society. In this model, reactions to changes in the environment tend to be more in the form of the creation of new organizations than of the reorganization of existing government organizations.

The major work in this area has been done by Grafton (1984), who has argued that reorganization and the creation of new organizations within the federal government could be explained by the occurrence of changes in the environment. In particular, he argued for the importance of "SET" anomalies requiring governmental innovations. This term refereed to *s*ocial, *e*conomic, or *t*echnological changes that may occur in the environment and that may require new organizations or reorganization of existing ones to manage them effectively. An example of a social change might be the civil rights movement of the 1950s and 1960s, which generated a variety of structural changes in the public sector. The economic changes of the Depression created a huge variety of new or changed government organizations (Skowronek, 1982; Skocpol and Feingold, 1982). Finally, the increased technical demands on government could be seen in the creation of NASA in the 1960s and in a variety of energy and environmental organizations during the 1970s and 1980s.

The difficulty with using these types of models of change is that it is not clearly stated in operational terms when an innovation is an innovation. That is, the environment of the public sector is changing constantly. When is the change sufficiently large enough to trigger a change in the organizational structures of government to compensate for it, or to take advantage of it? As has been stated of incremental models: when is an increment an increment (Dempster and Wildavsky, 1980)? These models appear to provide no answer to that question but can only say, ex post facto, that the change must have been sufficiently large since something did happen to the organizational structures.

In a less formalized way, much of the political science literature on public administration stresses the environmental dependency of public organizations. In any democratic model of public administration, administrative organizations are responsible and accountable to their political masters (Redford, 1969; Day and Klein, 1987). Likewise, if those organizations have an idea about improving policy it must be accepted by political institutions before it can be put into effect; this activity frequently falls under the rubric of "bureaucratic politics" (Allison, 1971; Downs, 1967) as organizations attempt to have their policy ideas accepted (Heymann, 1988). The budgetary process also stresses the dependent nature of public organizations and their vulnerability to the desires of politicians. For a public organization, gaining the latitude to change, whether its policies or even its own internal structure, involves recognizing its dependence upon external political forces.

2. *Contingency Approaches*

Perhaps the most familiar of the environmentally driven approaches to organization and reorganization is contingency theory (Lawrence and Lorsch, 1969; Galbraith, 1977). The logic of this approach is that the internal structuring of organizations will, over time, come to reflect the characteristics of the task environment of the organization. There are a number of different versions of this approach. The Aston group and related British researchers (Pugh and Hickson, 1976) sought to relate the structure of organizations to characteristics such as task specialization and technological intensity of the environment. Perrow (1986) has related the internal structure and functioning of organizations to the degree of variation of the raw material being processed and the degree of certainty about causal processes being utilized within the organization. A variety of other contingency models for organizational structure also have been developed to attempt to demonstrate that internal organizational features depend upon the nature of the environment within which the organization functions.

The problem with all these contingency models of organizations is that they do not work very well to predict organizational structure or behavior. This is largely true for the private sector, despite some successes (Pugh and Hickson, 1976), and is even more true for the public sector. For example, several British studies have applied contingency theory to both subnational governments and the departments of central government (Greenwood et al., 1975a; 1975b; Pitt and Smith, 1981). The results in both applications were disappointing, to say the least. It appears rather that, much as was pointed out when discussing the numerous public sector reforms of the 1980s and 1990s, fad and fashion may have as much to do with organizational formats as does the nature of their task environments. Governments adopt either the organizational format with which they are most familiar (hierarchical, ministry forms) or fashionable formats (decentralized "agencies" during the 1990s) rather than planning some systematic connection between the environment and the tasks of the newly formed, or reformed, organization. As in other settings, there appears to be an "iron cage" (DiMaggio and Powell, 1983) which drives organizations toward a single structural format, or at most a limited range of formats, rather than the highly differentiated structures dependent upon tasks or resources posited in contingency theories. Whether that conformity is a result of mimicry or of legal requirements is of little consequence, although if similarities result from learning from successes it may indicate that the environment is more uniform than assumed in the contingency approaches.

Another problem with contingency theory as a means of understanding the structures of public administration is measurement. That is, public administration as yet does not have a very good vocabulary for describing the structure of formal organizations in the public sector (but see Hood and Dunsire, 1981). Also, we lack a very effective vocabulary for describing policy problems and the characteristics of those policy problems which might be related to the need for alternative structural forms in the public bureaucracy. Some scholars have attempted to provide instruments for categorizing public bureaucracies and their structures (Hood and Dunsire, 1981; Darbel and Schnapper, 1969), and for categorizing organizational forms more generally (McKelvey, 1982), but as yet this work remains rather rudimentary. The scholarship still does not appear capable of bearing the load which contingency theories might impose on it for elaborate structural categories to be associated with differentiated environmental factors. The work on categorizing policy areas appears even more rudimentary and seems to have progressed little beyond Lowi's (1973) familiar four types of policy. That categorization has been seminal in many ways but as yet also lacks the ability to bear the weight of the needs of a fully developed contingency theory.

3. *Population Ecology Approaches*

A third family of models attempting to explain the nature of organizations in terms of their relationship with the environment are population ecology models (Aldrich, 1979; Carroll, 1984; Peters and Hogwood, forthcoming). The basic premise of this family of models is that analysts should look less at the existence, performance, and structure of individual organizations than at the characteristics existing within whole populations of organizations. Just as in studying biological organisms, this approach argues that the best way to understand the birth, death, and survival of organizations is to comprehend them as whole "ecosystems" and to look at the evolution of the entire population of organizations. The population ecology approach is environmentally deterministic in the extent to which it assumes that the success (measured largely in terms of survival) of an individual organization is a function both of its relationships with other organizations in the environment as well as of its relationships with the environment conceptualized more in terms of resources and challenges. Phrased more formally, the environment of the organization is conceptualized in terms of the available niches within which it can survive, including the availability of funding sufficient for its survival in the case of a public sector organization, as well as the existence of predators seeking to destroy it.

Given the volitional character of most descriptions and analyses of decision making in the public sector, it is not surprising that this family of ecological models has been applied relatively infrequently to public organizations (but see Peters and Hogwood, 1991; Casstevens, 1980; Kaufman, 1976; 1985; Brudney and Herbert, 1987). Further, the tendency of ecological models to reify organizations, for example, to assume that they will react to the availability of niches as would biological entities, also causes many scholars concerns about the utility and desirability of this approach in the public sector. Unlike market and private sector organizations, public sector organizations appear to involve conscious decisions, often in the face of significant opposition. Despite these concerns, the ecological approach does appear to have substantial utility for understanding observed changes within groups of organizations, including organizations within the public sector.

The utility of the ecological approach becomes especially evident when we consider the evolution of larger, inclusive structures over time, and the generation of niches for different type of organizations within those larger ecological systems (Freeman and Hannan, 1983; McKelvey and Aldrich, 1983). So, for example, reorganization efforts within government can be analyzed in terms of the exploitation of new niches created by social and/or technological change, or of responses to the creation of new niches through a changing ideological conception of how the public sector should be structured or managed (Zammuto and Cameron, 1985). Torstendahl (1990), for example, points to the creation of large numbers of public organizations in Sweden in response to social and economic changes. Our own research (Peters and Hogwood, 1988) points to the large number of organizations created in the United States in response to "opportunities" created by the Depression. Likewise, the models of Grafton (1984) with public organizations exploiting SET changes in the environment can be reconceptualized as governments simply responding to the appearance of the new environmental niches by creating new organizations. The organizations occupying those niches need not be entirely new themselves, but rather simply may be reformulations (Hogwood and Peters, 1983) of previously existing organizations redesigned better to exploit a changed environment.

One of the more interesting applications of this family of models involves linking ecology models with some concepts emerging from strategy in management theory (Hrebiniak and Joyce, 1985; Zammuto, 1988; Burgelman, 1990). The idea of blending ecological and strategic choice approaches is that organizations usually are unable to find niches on their own, as biological organisms might be able to do. Rather, organizations must be led to find those niches, and their managers are the strategists and entrepreneurs within the organization charged with exercising leadership in searching out new or underutilized niches. These organization leaders have several alternative strategies available to them. These strategies are to some degree based on the nature of the niches which appear to exist within the environment. Theorists working within the ecological models have described niches in terms of their width. A narrow niche is one in which only a limited type of organizations can survive, while wide niches would be hospitable to a wide range of organizational types. At the broadest possible level, the distinction is made between generalist and specialist organizations that might fit into those niches. This is a familiar distinction in reference to individual civil servants, but some of the same logic can be applied to organizations. Do organizations choose to allocate resources toward a narrow range of goals and with a narrow repertoire of policies, or do they attempt to meet a wider range of policy goals with a more extensive repertoire of policies? One set of strategies might be successful if the niches are relatively wide and varied, while the other might be successful in more tightly defined environmental situations.

Another characteristic of the environment important for understanding governmental reorganization is the grain of the environment (Freeman and Hannan, 1983). By *grain* we mean the existence of different types of niches, and hence the opportunities for different types of organizations to survive simultaneously. A fine-grained environment would have most niches of the same type, while a coarse-grained environment might have a variety of different niches existing simultaneously. We have already noted that the public sector tends toward fine-grained environments, with most organizations tending toward relatively common forms, such as agencies in the United States or ministries in most other democracies. Some attempts at reorganization and reform have tended toward making that grain even finer, for example, "quango-bashing" in Mrs. Thatcher's Britain to eliminate a number of nondepartmental bodies (Hood, 1981). On the other hand, some reforms have tended toward increasing organizational diversity, as the numerous reforms decentralizing and deconcentrating administration in the 1980s did.

Perhaps especially for the public sector, we need to look at the grain of the environment over time as well as at any single point in time (Tucker et al., 1990). As different organizational fashions sweep through the public sector, different vestigial structures may remain and continue functioning for years with the result that the grain may actually appear coarser than it is at any one time. In particular, the process of forming new organizations may function as if the grain were very fine, and limited structural options may be considered for new organizations (but see Egeberg, 1988). In the United States, for example, during the Roosevelt era, the pattern was to create numerous small and relatively autonomous bodies headed by a single entrepreneurial administrator. The fashion during the Eisenhower administration changed to consolidating many of those organizations into larger organizations, especially cabinet departments. The Kennedy/Johnson years returned to the Roosevelt pattern, with more consolidation under Nixon and Carter. Some similar patterns appear to have occurred in Western Europe (Torstendahl, 1990).

A final factor to be considered in the relationship of organizations to their niches is the role of the density of the population of existing organizations (Brittain and Freeman, 1980). When a niche is being opened for the first time, there is little necessity of competition among the entities involved (whether organizations or biological organisms) for resources, and efficiency is not particularly valuable given the comparatively easy access to resources. As more entities begin to crowd into that niche, competition for resources will increase and efficiency in the use of available resources will become important for survival. These factors lead to the idea of two types of organizational strategies for dealing with the environment—labeled r and k strategies. An *r strategy* involves rapid exploitation of new niches and rapid reproduction of new organizations or organisms to fill the available space. A *k strategy*, on the other hand, involves generating the staying power for an organization to occupy the niche and hold off competitors over the long run, usually through relative efficiency in the use of resources.

In terms of organizations within the public sector, the formation of r organizations may be seen in the rush of creation of new organizations when there is some sort of perceived crisis in government, or the identification of a new opportunity. These may be Grafton's SET opportunities. The creation by Franklin Roosevelt of so many new organizations during the first year of his administration is a classic example of adopting the *r* strategy. Likewise, the rapid creation of social service and poverty agencies during the Johnson administration, and the apparent inefficiency of many of them, is an indication of rapid exploitation of new niches. In some instances, however, the nature of the policy itself may dictate that a single large-scale organization be vested with responsibility for the policy (Schulman, 1980), as has been the case for NASA with space travel. On the other hand, the numerous attempts of governments to produce greater efficiency by consolidating apparently similar organizations in a single large organization may be implicit recognitions of the need for *k* strategies for coping with survival in the long run. This does imply that such large-scale reorganizations of government are always, or even usually, successful but rather that those reforms do recognize the need to match the space in a niche with a number of organizations. Of course, the practically minded advocates of these reforms rarely, if ever, discuss concepts such as density dependent selection models of public organizations.

The impact of the availability of niches and the ecological effects on populations of organizations can also be seen as a form of collective learning about effective administration and organizational structure. To the extent that a specific organizational format is successful in producing desired outcomes, the population of organizations should shift in its favor (DiMaggio and Powell, 1983). In this model of organizational change, individual organizations do not adapt to the changing environment, but over time the entire collection of organizations does (Carroll, 1984). As with the other ecological conceptions of reform and reorganizations, however, the mechanism through which the pressure for change is transmitted from the environment to an organization is not specified clearly.

C. Institutional Models of Organizational Change

The final family of models of organizational change is a product of the increased interest in the "new institutionalism" evident in political science (March and Olsen, 1984; 1989; Smith, 1988) and to some extent in the other social sciences as well (DiMaggio, 1988; Bromley, 1989). These institutional models begin with rather different assumptions about the behavior of organizations, and about their ability to absorb readily necessary changes in their structures and operations. The most fundamental differences are between these models and the volitional models discussed first. In the volitional models, the individuals within organizations are purposive and therefore may attempt to alter organizations to conform to their own goals, whether those goals are political (e.g., Chapman and Greenaway, 1980) or personal (e.g., Niskanen, 1971). In institutional models, however, the goals pursued by an organization are more collective than individual and do not necessarily represent purposive, maximizing behavior by any individual. Rather, the behavior of an organization might be understood better as the attempt to match its actions with some standards of "appropriateness" derived from the history and collective values of the organization, or even from a broader social foundation.

Organizational reform from an institutionalist perspective is a less mechanical proposition than it might appear from the other perspectives. Rather than requiring only the wishes of an organizational leader, or significant changes in the environment, to occur reform in this mode of analysis requires to some extent altering the internal values of the organization. It therefore requires modifying the operative values of organizational members as well. Thus, an institutional approach to reorganization and reform is somewhat similar to an approach relying on the concept of organizational culture (Ott, 1989). One significant difference might be the extent to which the organizational culture literature, given its roots in business management, assumes that those cultures are highly mutable and can be manipulated by managers to produce greater efficiency (but see Peters, 1990a). The institutionalist literature, on the other hand, tends to stress the durability of organizational values, or cultures, and therefore the extreme difficulty that may be encountered in attempting to produce any rapid or significant changes in performance through reorganization. Olsen (1991) refers to this as "bounded power" in producing the reform of organizations. This viewpoint therefore is not dissimilar to that of much of the traditional literature in public administration pointing to the difficulties of producing efficiency by reorganizations (Miles, 1977; Salamon, 1981). Further, the impetus for reorganization would appear much more effective if it were endogenous in the organization and recognized its fundamental values rather than being imposed from outside.

The institutional approach is also capable of providing a more differentiated viewpoint of the nature of an organization, and therefore of organizational change. Most of the approaches we have discussed to this point tend to treat an organization as an integrated entity, speaking with a single voice. Further, the presumed integration of values within an organization tends to be a "top-down" rather than a "bottom-up" conception. This permits relatively little possibility for discussion or conflict over the nature of the organization or of its mission. From an institutionalist perspective, there does not have to be such an integration of values. Internal conflicts over the definition of organizational mission, and even over the deeper meaning of the organization itself, are more an integral part of organizational life than in other approaches. A goal of development within the organization may be an integrated value perspective, but that perspective cannot be assumed a priori as it is in, for example, economic models of organizations. This approach then permits the operation of organizational subcultures as do some approaches to organizational culture (Siehl and Martin, 1987).

The recognition of internal differences within organizations, in turn, means that organizational reform can be more internally generated, if there is agreement on the need and nature of reform. Further, the existence of alternative viewpoints within the organization may mean that reform pressures arise naturally inside the structure itself. The existence of alternative visions also means that attempting to implement from above a reorganization or reform plan that is not acceptable to most members of the organization would not be judged to be very likely of success by an analyst operating from this perspective.

Although we can think of the internal differentiation of institutions as offering sources of innovation, institutions can also be extremely conservative and attempt (knowingly or not) to preserve their stable routines and structures (March, 1981a; 1981b). Organizations may themselves initiate change, but the processes used for change tend to be stable, even if the actual outcomes are not. Institutions develop routines and defenses that make the imposition of change difficult, and permit the perpetuation of routines and procedures whose utility has long been exhausted. Further, any apparent innovations in an institution may be adapted to look as much as possible like old routines as they are being implemented (Browning, 1968). Another of the more important of these defenses for organizations is the competency trap, in which an organization appears to be competent at what it does and institutionalizes certain means of achieving its ends. By doing so, however, it also ignores the possibilities to respond in other ways that might be more efficient or effective. Thus, a public sector organization that has always relied on economic instruments for policy intervention will tend to staff itself with economists who will, in turn, also see economic instruments as the best means of intervening (Linder and Peters, 1989). Once a successful pattern of functioning is established, it becomes difficult for an organization (institution) to reform itself. This persistence of organizational styles and values is closely related to the literature on the life cycles of organizations (Kimberly and Miles, 1980; Winter, 1990).

Another of the virtues of the institutional approach is that for it the essentially random and ad hoc aspects of much of organizational change is no mystery. Changes may be initiated by a rational process, but once in train the process becomes largely unpredictable. If there is an assumption that history is efficient and teleological, then this randomness creates a severe problem (see March and Olsen, 1989, pp. 54–56). On the other hand, if it is assumed that individuals and institutions respond poorly to many efforts to induce change and that the outcomes are therefore unpredictable, any notion of the efficiency of history and of the positive developmental aspects of organizational responses becomes untenable. Therefore, much of organizational change becomes a "garbage can" model of choice. The outcomes which emerge are not really planned or perhaps even explicable by rational processes, but rather represent the confluence of a number of streams of thought and action within the organization.

Finally, it must be pointed out that as much as they represent the search for efficient administration, the administrative institutions of a government also represent important social and even cultural values. Groups want organizations to provide benefits, as symbols of their social significance and their political muscle. As a consequence, reform and reorganization efforts may be understood as much more significant political events than their advocate sometimes perceive when they initiate the process of change. The rationalistic advocates of reform may assume that its effects can be contained within the narrow organizational or policy area bounds within which it appears to apply, but the effects of even seemingly minor reforms can be profound. Institutionalist models may not enable us to predict the nature of those consequences very well, but they do at least alert the practitioner (and the analyst) that they are likely to occur. By so doing, these models interject a healthy skepticism into any attempts to generate meaningful organizational change by simple fiat and reorganization plan.

III. CONCLUSION

This paper has attempted to demonstrate the impact that several alternative conceptions of reform and reorganization might have on the analysis of organizational change in the public sector. None of these alternative views is necessarily completely right or completely wrong, but each adds a different dimension to the understanding of the analyst. The purposive models discussed as the first alternative add a great deal of realism and detail to the discussion, but many of them (especially the economically based ones) depend upon a number of premises about organizational change that appear untenable in the real world of government. Those several models positing dependence of organizations on their environment collectively make an important point about such dependence, but each lacks any clear explanation of the dynamics of organizational adaptation to the environment. In essence the first group of models depend too much on the will of individual political and administrative actors, while the second group tends to rely excessively on invisible hands to do the work of forcing change. Neither extreme appears particularly viable.

If we had to make a choice among these alternative models of reorganization, we would place our money on the institutional models discussed previously as the third approach. This approach in many ways combines the strengths of the other two approaches. Because of its concern with the meaning and values of organizations, the institutional approach places great weight on understanding the details of organizations and therefore on understanding the precise (and generally largely unpredictable) impact of proposed changes on the organization. Even stable and well-integrated organizations may not be able to manage the effects of change. By virtue of its recognizing the cultural and ideational aspects of organizations, the institutional approach can move the discussion of reorganization and reform beyond a strictly mechanical or political level to a more cultural level of understanding of organizations and the involvement of their members. In this approach the preferences of the individuals are not exogenous, but are in part a function of the organization itself and its collective values. This role of collective values makes change at once more understandable and more difficult to predict. The institutional approach to organizational change also acknowledges the relationship of an organization to its environment, and, although not dependent totally on the environment, an organization is not conceptualized as capable of being effective if its values are incompatible with its own environment. In this approach, the environment may be conceptualized substantially more broadly than in the ecological approaches, but much of that same logic is applicable.

Even with the utility we find in institutional analysis, some very fundamental questions remain unaddressed in all of these approaches to reorganization. In essence most of public administration operates with an implicit theory of routine, and we do not as yet have very good ideas about the types of events that would produce disequilibrium sufficient to move away from that routine. It would appear that one central task in attempts to cope with reorganization and reform is to understand the trigger mechanisms for change. This may be especially difficult for institutional analysis because of its focus on the internalized values of organizations that may function as impediments to any significant change. Focusing more explicit attention on the phenomenon of change will also be important for linking this type of organizational inquiry more directly into political science and its concern about political change. This is therefore a crucial direction in which to take some of our subsequent research on administrative reform and reorganization.

REFERENCES

Aldrich, H. E., *Organizations and Environments*, Prentice Hall, Englewood Cliffs, N.J., 1979.

Allison, G. T., *The Essence of Decision*, Little, Brown, Boston, 1971.

Astley, W. G., Administrative Science as Socially Constructed Truth, *Administrative Science Quarterly 30*:497–513 (1985).

Aucoin, P., Administrative Reform in Public Management, *Governance 3*:115–137 (1990).

Bendor, J. Formal Models of Bureaucracy, in *Public Administration the State of the Discipline* (N. Lynn and A. Wildavsky, eds.), Chatham House, Chatham, N.J., 1989.

Blais, A. and Dion, S., *The Budget Maximizing Bureaucrat*, University of Pittsburgh Press, Pittsburgh, 1992.

Breton, A. and Wintrobe, R., The Equilibrium Size of a Budget-Maximizing Bureau, *Journal of Political Economy 83*:195–207 (1975).

Brittain, J. W. and Freeman, J. H., Organizational Proliferation and Density Dependent Selection, in *The Organizational Life Cycle* (J. R. Kimberly and R. H. Miles, eds.), Jossey-Bass, San Francisco, 1980.

Bromley, D. W., *Economic Interests and Institutions*, Basil Blackwell, Oxford, 1989.

Browning, R. P., Innovation and Non-innovation Decision Processes in Government Budgeting, in *Public Budgeting and Finance* (R. T. Golembiewski, ed.), Peacock, Itaska, Ill., 1968.

Brudney, J. L. and Herbert, F. T., State Agencies and Their Environments: Examining the Influence of Important External Actors, *Journal of Politics 49*:186–206 (1987).

Burgelman, R. A., Strategy-Making and Organizational Ecology: A Conceptual Integration, in *Organizational Evolution: New Directions* (J. V. Singh, eds.), Sage, Newbury Park, Calif., 1990.

Caiden, G. E., *Administrative Reform*, Aldine/Atherton, Chicago, 1970.

Caiden, G. E., Reform and Revitalization in American Bureaucracy, in *Problems in Administrative Reform* (R. Miewald and M. Steineman, eds.), Nelson-Hall, Chicago, 1984.

Carroll, G. R., Organizational Ecology, *Annual Review of Sociology 10*:71–93 (1984).

Casstevens, T., Birth and Death Processes of Government Bureaus in the United States, *Behavioral Science 25*:161–165 (1980).

Chapman, R. A. and Greenaway, J. R., *The Dynamics of Administrative Reform*, Croom-Helm, London, 1980.

Chester, D. W. and Willson, F. M. G., *The Organisation of British Central Government, 1914–1964*, 2nd ed., Allen & Unwin, London, 1968.

Chubb, J. E. and Peterson, P. A., *Can the Government Govern?* The Brookings Institution, Washington, D.C., 1989.

Darbel, A. and Schnapper, D., *Les agents du système administratif*, Mouton, Paris, 1969.

Day, P. and Klein, R., *Accountabilities*, Tavistock, London, 1987.

Dempster, M. A. H. and Wildavsky, A., On Change, Or There Is No Magic Size for an Increment, *Political Studies 28*:371–389 (1980).

DiMaggio, P. J., Interest and Agency in Institutional Theory, in *Institutional Patterns and Organizations* (L. G. Zucker, ed.), Ballinger, Cambridge, Mass., 1988.

DiMaggio, P. J. and Powell, W. W., The Iron Cage Revisited: Institutional Isomorphism and Collective Rationality in Organizational Fields, *American Sociological Review 48*:147–160 (1983).

Downs, A., *Inside Bureaucracy*, Little, Brown, Boston, 1967.

Dunleavy, P., Bureaucrats, Budgets and the Growth of the State, *British Journal of Political Science 15*:299–320 (1985).

Dunsire, A. and Hood, C., *Cutback Management in Public Bureaucracies*, Cambridge University Press, Cambridge, 1989.

Egeberg, M., Organizing Competing Decision Principles into Governmental Structures, paper prepared for Scandinavian Symposium on Organizational Research, Hemsedal, Norway, June 13–15, 1988.

Freeman, J. H. and Hannan, M. T., Niche Width and the Dynamics of Organizational Populations, *American Journal of Sociology 88*:1116–1145 (1983).

Galbraith, J. R., *Organizational Design*, Addison-Wesley, Reading, Mass., 1977.

Goodin, R. E., Rational Politicians and Rational Bureaucrats, *Public Administration 60*:23–41 (1982).

Goodsell, C. T., *The Case for Bureaucracy*, Chatham House, Chatham, N.J., 1985.

Grafton, C., The Creation and Reorganization of Federal Agencies, in *Problems in Administrative Reform* (R. Miewald and M. Steinman, eds.), Nelson-Hall, Chicago, 1984.

Gray, A. and Jenkins, W. I., Accountable Management in British Central Government: Some Reflections on the Financial Management Initiative, *Financial Accountability and Management* 2:171–185 (1986).

Greenwood, R., Hinings, C. R., and Ranson, S., Contingency Theory and the Organisation of Local Authorities. Part I. Differentiation and Integration, *Public Administration 53*:1–23 (1975a).

Greenwood, R., Hinings, C. R., and Ranson, S., Contingency Theory and the Organisation of Local Authorities. Part II. Contingencies and Structures, *Public Administration 53*:159–190 (1975b).

Heymann, P. B., How Government Expresses Public Ideas, in *The Power of Public Ideas* (R. B. Reich, ed.), Harvard University Press, Cambridge, Mass., 1988.

Hogwood, B. W. and Peters, B. G., *Policy Dynamics*, Wheatsheaf, Brighton, England, 1983.

Hood, C., Axeperson, Spare that Quango . . . , in *Big Government in Hard Times* (C. Hood and M. Wright, eds.), Martin Robertson, Oxford, 1981.

Hood, C. and Dunsire, A., *Bureaumetrics, the Quantitative Comparison of British Central Government Agencies*. University of Alabama Press, University, Ala., 1981.

Hrebiniak, L. G. and Joyce, W. F., Organizational Adaptation: Strategic Choice and Environmental Determinism, *Administrative Science Quarterly 30*:336–349 (1985).

Ingraham, P. W. and Peters, B. G., The Conundrum of Reform: A Comparative Analysis, *Review of Public Personnel Administration 8*:3–16 (1988).

Jackson, P. M., *The Political Economy of Bureaucracy*, Philip Allan, Oxford, 1982.

Kaufman, H., *Are Government Organizations Immortal?* The Brookings Institution, Washington, D.C., 1976.

Kaufman, H., *Time, Chance and Organizations: Natural Selection in a Perilous Environment*, Chatham House, Chatham, N.J., 1985.

Kelman, S., The Grace Commission: How Much Waste in Government? *The Public Interest 78* (1985).

Kemp, P., Next Steps for the British Civil Service, *Governance 3*:186–196 (1990).

Kimberly, J. R. and Miles, R. H., *The Organizational Life Cycle*, Jossey-Bass, San Francisco, 1980.

Lawrence, P. R. and Lorsch, J. W., *Organization and Environment*, Richard D. Irwin, Homewood, Ill., 1969.

Levine, C. H., Organizational Decline and Cutback Management, *Public Administration Review 38* (1978).

Linder, S. H. and Peters, B. G., A Design Perspective on Policy Implementation: The Fallacy of Misplaced Precision, *Policy Studies Review 6*:459–475 (1987).

Linder, S. H. and Peters, B. G., Instruments of Government: Perceptions and Contexts, *Journal of Public Policy 9*:35–58 (1989).

Lowi, T. J., Four Systems of Policy, Politics and Choice, *Public Administration Review 32*:298–310 (1972).

March, J. G., Decisions in Organizations and Theories of Choice, in *Perspectives on Organizational Design and Performance* (A. Van de Ven and W. Joyce, eds.), Wiley, New York, 1981.

March, J. G., Footnotes to Organizational Change, *Administrative Science Quarterly 26*:563–577 (1981b).

March, J. G. and Olsen, J. P., The New Institutionalism: Organizational Factors in Political Life, *American Political Science Review 78*:734–749 (1984).

March, J. G. and Olsen, J. P., *Rediscovering Institutions*, Free Press, New York, 1989.

Mazmanaian, D. A. and Sabatier, P. A., *Implementation and Public Policy*, Scott, Foresman, Glenview, Ill., 1983.

McKelvey, B., *Organizational Systematics*, University of California Press, Berkeley, 1982.

McKelvey, B. and Aldrich, H., Populations, Natural Selection and Applied Organizational Science, *Administrative Science Quarterly 28*:101–128 (1983).
Miles, R., Considerations for a President Bent on Reorganization, *Public Administration Review 37*:155–162 (1977).
Milward, H. B., Don't Blame the Bureaucracy, *Journal of Public Policy 3*:149–168 (1983).
Niskanen, W., *Bureaucracy and Representative Government*, Aldine/Atherton, Chicago, 1971.
Olsen, J. P., Modernization Programs in Perspective: Institutional Analysis of Organizational Change, *Governance 4*:133–157 (1991).
Perrow, C., *Complex Organizations: A Critical Essay*, Random House, New York, 1986.
Peters, B. G., Administrative Culture and the Analysis of Public Organizations, *Indian Journal of Public Administration*, (forthcoming).
Peters, B. G., Changing Government in an Era of Retrenchment and Commitment, in *Handbook of Comparative and Development Administration* (A. Farazmand, ed.), Marcel Dekker, New York, 1990b.
Peters, B. G. and Hogwood, B. W., Births, Deaths and Metamorphoses in the U.S. Federal Bureaucracy, 1933–1983, *American Review of Public Administration 18*:119–134 (1988).
Peters, B. G. and Hogwood, B. W., Applying in Population Ecology Models to Public Organizations, in *Research in Public Administration* (J. L. Perry, ed.), JAI, Westport, Conn., 1991.
Pitt, D. C. and Smith, B. C., *Government Departments: An Organizational Perspective*, Routledge and Kegan Paul, London, 1981.
Pollitt, C., *Manipulating the Machine: Changing the Pattern of Ministerial Departments, 1960–83*, Allen & Unwin, London, 1984.
Pressman, J. L. and Wildavsky, A., *Implementation*, University of California Press, Berkeley, 1973.
Pugh, D. S. and Hickson, D. J., *Organisation Structure and Its Context: The Aston Programme*, Saxon House, Farnborough, England, 1976.
Redford, E. S., *Democracy in the Administrative State*, Oxford University Press, New York, 1969.
Rose, R., *Ungovernability: Is There Smoke Behind the Fire?* University of Strathclyde Centre for the Study of Public Policy, Glasgow, 1978.
Rose, R. and Peters, B. G., *Can Government Go Bankrupt?* Basic Books, New York, 1978.
Salamon, L. M., The Question of Goals, in *Federal Reorganization: What Have We Learned?* (P. Szanton, ed.), Chatham House, Chatham, N.J., 1981.
Schulman, P., *Large-Scale Policymaking*. Elsevier, New York, 1977.
Scott, G., Bushnell, P., and Salle, N., Reform of the Core Sector: New Zealand Experience, *Governance 3*:138–165, 1990.
Seidman, H. and Gilmour, R., *Politics, Power and Position*, 4th ed., Oxford University Press, New York, 1986.
Siehl, C. and Martin, J., The Role of Symbolic Management, in *Leaders and Managers* (J. G. Hunt, C. A. Schreisheim, and R. Stewart, eds.), Pergamon, New York, 1987.
Skocpol, T. and Feingold, K., Political Responses to Capitalist Crises: Neo-Marxist Theories and the Early New Deal, *Political Science Quarterly 97*:255–278 (1982).
Skowronek, S., *Building an American State*, Cambridge University Press, Cambridge, 1982.
Smith, R. M., Political Jurisprudence, the "New Institutionalism," and the Future of Public Law, *American Political Science Review 82*:89–108 (1988).
Snellen, I. T. M., *Limits of Government: Dutch Experiences*, Kobra, Amsterdam, 1985.
Tarschys, D., Curbing Public Expenditures: Current Trends, *Journal of Public Policy 5*:23–67 (1985).
Torstendahl, R., *Bureaucratisation in Northwestern Europe, 1880–1985: Domination and Governance*, Routledge, London, 1990.
Tucker, D. J., Singh, J. V., and Meinhard, A. G., Founding Characteristics, Imprinting and Organizational Change, in *Organizational Evolution: New Directions* (J. V. Singh, ed.), Sage, Newbury Park, Calif., 1990.
Tullock, G., *The Politics of Bureaucracy*, Public Affairs Press, Washington, D.C., 1965.
Wilson, V. S., What Legacy? The Nielsen Task Force Program Review, in *How Ottawa Spends, 1988/89* (K. A. Graham, ed.), Carleton University Press, Ottawa, 1988.

Winter, S. G., Survival, Selection and Inheritance in Evolutionary Theories of Organizations, in *Organizational Evolution: New Directions* (J. V. Singh, ed.), Sage, Newbury Park, Calif., 1990.

Zammuto, R. F., Organizational Adaptation: Some Implications of Organizational Ecology for Strategic Choice, *Journal of Management Studies 25*:105–120 (1988).

Zammuto, R. F. and Cameron, K. S., Environmental Decline and Organizational Response, *Research in Organizational Behavior 7*:233–262 (1985).

10
Organizational Strategy for Coping with External Environments: Reducing Work Load as One Approach

Roger Handberg
University of Central Florida, Orlando, Florida

I. INTRODUCTION

Across modern societies, a wide variety of organizational structures have been developed in order to process myriad human problems. Indeed, such organizations usually characterized as bureaucracies operate in environments which are normally stressful (that is, events which significantly disrupt the organization's routine constantly occur), but regardless of those continual disruptions, the bureaucracy is expected to respond successfully to those matters occurring within its defined jurisdiction (Downs, 1957). Successfully here means the agency acting quickly and effectively to deal with the problem presented to it for processing and solution. Failure by the agency to respond successfully only increases the stress levels as "outsiders" intervene to redress what they perceive as an imbalance in performance. Outsiders can truly be from outside the organization's boundaries or else be higher echelons within the larger organization. The Federal Emergency Management Agency's inability, for example, to respond to several natural disasters led to such an intervention after the Hurricane Andrew disaster when President Bush established a special cabinet level task force to coordinate the federal relief effort.

This chapter focuses on one aspect of bureaucratic behavior, the shedding or reduction of caseload, as a systematic strategy for coping with this organizational stress. The intent of the caseload reduction here is not simply to reduce overall work load but, in fact, by such action to improve or maintain agency responsiveness to meet its own goals and the expectations of significant outsiders first. Public agency support for privatization efforts is one manifestation of that effort. By shedding work load, the agency is able to concentrate its efforts and divert potential criticism to the new private providers.

Here we will delineate some preconditions for such work load reduction efforts and examine their implementation and implications within the context of a peculiar set of semibureaucratic structures, criminal trial courts (Feeley, 1973). The primary empirical emphasis here will be upon the criminal courts, but the analysis will be briefly extended to encompass civil courts, where the access issues are similar through perceived as less intense by outsiders. The principles identified here are applicable across the bureaucratic spectrum, although the context there is usually pejorative (e.g., comments such as "bureaucratic inefficiency" and "incompetence").

II. ENVIRONMENTAL PRESSURES

Bureaucracies often operate within work environments subject to drastic fluctuations in their case- or work load. These fluctuations frustrate efforts by the organization to plan and organize its routine activities to cope best or manage its work load. Predicting future work load, the essence of the problem, is a very inexact process subject to unanticipated external events outside the organization's control. Obviously, many organizations currently operate in what they perceive as very stable work environments; that current stability though is usually the product of earlier initial periods of change. Anthony Downs spoke of this situation earlier in his discussion of the "life cycles of bureaus" (Downs, 1967).

But, for other organizations, the work load crisis can be inherent or built into their environment. For example, an organization concerned with environmental protection can be confronted by an accident creating a large oil spill, effectively polluting a large ocean area or stretch of environmentally sensitive coastline. For example, major tanker accidents have occurred in Alaska and the English Channel, pumping millions of gallons of oil onto coastlines. Predictive models have been developed to estimate the future probabilities of such traumatic events, but the models are usually average-value-driven, which means such extreme events are missed or the prediction is so general as to be effectively useless in pinpointing location. Knowing that an oil spill is likely to occur somewhere does not effectively guide agency policy given the vast areas over which the accident could occur. Everyone knows where the major shipping lanes are located along with the most treacherous passages, but that information in itself is insufficient for successful prediction.

Such calculations constantly confront disaster relief organizations dealing with natural disasters such as earthquakes or hurricanes. Prepositioning cleanup equipment or other supplies becomes a calculated gamble, as likely to fail as succeed. For example, Hurricane Andrew in South Florida in August 1992 completely disrupted the state of Florida's budget and organizational structure by inflicting severe losses upon the state's infrastructure and, more critically, its future revenue base, the tourist industry. In effect, a double whammy hit the state. Such a singular catastrophic event had been predicted in Florida for the preceding twenty-five years, but its actual arrival still constituted an unanticipated and only partially planned for occurrence. Elaborate evacuation plans of residents were in place and largely successful in threatened coastal areas; actual relief operations after the storm's passage were more problematic, given the inherent uncertainties about physical damage and road disruption. More critically, the disruption caused by the hurricane spread to other agencies and areas of the state as resources were collected and sent south. Thus, even apparently unaffected agencies can be disrupted by a distant crisis.

Such disruptions, while more common (although obviously less dramatic and drastic than a hurricane's impact) than thought, are not the usual problem for most organizations. Instead, more organizations likely confront an environment in which their work load continues to rise, even escalate dramatically, while available fiscal and personnel resources stagnate or even go backward relative to inflation and the real cost of doing business. Over time, tasks have become increasingly complicated, requiring more resources to complete each individual case, a fact often unrecognized or ignored by the agency's budgetary authority. Therefore, any surplus or slack resources within the organization are eventually exhausted, stressing the organization's total capacity and leading to a breakdown in its normal service and a general decline in efficiency.

Coping with this ongoing organizational stress becomes a primary objective of the organization's leadership. Several strategies can be pursued in this effort. One, much discussed but often difficult to realize in practice, the organization can attempt to operate more efficiently by lowering per unit processing costs, increasing employee productivity, or creating some combination thereof. Employees often resist such efforts either overtly or covertly—a fact which further disrupts the organization's routine since the resistance is often subtle and difficult to confront or correct. Also agencies often discover that what purports to be heightened efficiency is in fact a reduction in real performance, especially the quality aspect. That hidden cost (a decline in quality of service) may or may not be acceptable in the long term although recognition of its existence may take some time to penetrate the agency's image of itself.

Quality is often for bureaucracies an intangible issue measured largely by speed of case disposition and client satisfaction ratings. The first may be irrelevant (speed does not necessarily correlate to quality of decision; the relationship is more complicated), while the second is often heavily influenced by whether the client received what he or she wanted. If the request is denied, then the client satisfaction rating is likely low even though from the agency's perspective the "right" outcome was achieved (e.g., the client was denied benefits not authorized under the rules). Given this strong relationship between client satisfaction and individual outcomes, agencies often develop an internal value structure downplaying client satisfaction as an evaluative criterion, looking more inward toward their own internal evaluation of performance (this is one definition of professionalism). Such a strategy is most viable when the clients have low social status (e.g., welfare recipients, the unemployed, and criminal defendants), less viable when the clients have high status (e.g., physicians in Medicaid programs) and are able to mobilize others if aggrieved. The difficulty for outsiders evaluating the agency is that the routine processes of most organizations are usually so tightly structured and well established that becoming more efficient is effectively impossible. The agency's standard operating procedures have to be completely revamped, an action that, if successful, probably requires a major purge of existing personnel (an action unlikely to occur, given civil service and other political constraints). As Graham Allison has demonstrated, agency repertories of possible actions are constrained by their internal procedures and traditions (Allison, 1971). Therefore, in good budgetary times, the option is often to create a new agency, supplementing the older one. Only in the severest budgetary crisis do old agencies truly disappear. Rather, multiple layers of government handling the same problem develop over time.

Second, the organization can acquire an increase in resources which expands or reinflates or just simply maintains its existing capacity to handle its work load. This is very difficult to implement since there are usually many other resource competitors also injured by possible or past cutbacks. Their fiscal claims are likely just as reasonable as the agency's request in the eyes of higher authorities. If the claims are successful, though, branch offices can be reopened or expanded in their scope of operations. Service functions dropped earlier as a result of resource shortages can in theory be reinitiated although usually not at the same earlier level of effort. This latter goes back to the quality argument: declines in service quality are rarely recaptured even when budgets return. New patterns of behavior have been established, preempting earlier concerns. The new generation of workers and managers are unaware of the old practices except as the nostalgic stories of the old-timers (a dubious source to the newcomers).

Third, the agency can deliberately narrow the scope of its operations by, for example, changing its access rules or by rigidly enforcing its existing access rules, with the practical effect of reducing work load only in terms of size, not necessarily of complexity. The strategy pursued here is not one motivated by sloth and inefficiency (the usually charge made against bureaucracy) but an attempt to retain or recapture agency efficiency and effectiveness. This latter bureaucratic strategy and its implications are the subject of the reminder of this paper.

III. COPING BY EXCLUSION: A STRATEGY FOR AGENCY SURVIVAL

Again, one must remember that the intent of the efforts described later is not merely to evade work but to cope with a work load otherwise seen as out of control. The envisioned reduction is to be done in such a manner as to make the organization in some overall sense more responsive in achieving its socially important goals. This rationale legitimizes what would otherwise be seen simply as a shirking of work or an avoidance of responsibility. Bureaucracies (especially in the public sector) are always suspected of such nonproductive practices so that practitioners of this particular strategy tend to conceal its existence under a rhetoric claiming other rationales as justification. Such an approach has been used by a number of organizations, but the most visible and successful practitioners can be found within the courts. This approach permeates the entire court system from the highest appellate level to the initial and lowest trial courts.

At the most rarified level, for example, the United States Supreme Court has engaged in a continuing struggle to gain complete control over litigant entry onto its docket. By the mideighties, the Court finally achieved a basically completely discretionary docket [1]. That is: for all practical purposes, the Court has complete control over what cases it considers. By contrast, until the Judges Bill of 1925, well over half the cases dealt with by the Court were cases over which it had no effective docket control. From the Court's perspective, most such cases were trivial (involving individual claims of injury such as workmen's compensation insurance and railroad worker cases), a waste of scarce judicial resources, especially time. The ostensible politically neutral motivation behind the justices' unrelenting pressure to eliminate such cases was to allow the justices to deal only with those major cases dealing in socially significant issues.

The practical effect of these changes has been further to lessen access of weaker, less prestigious parties to the Court. This policy result has occurred because the Court concomitantly has more rigidly applied its existing rules concerning issues of litigant standing and justiciability, thus making access for certain types of litigants even more problematic. Such heightened access difficulty is consistent with some justices' contention that there are certain issues to which the Court is unable to provide acceptable or viable judicial answers; therefore, it should in practice withdraw from the field. The debate is continually framed in the context of jurisdictional disputes while the real issues are in truth substantive ones.

For example, beginning in the forties Justice Felix Frankfurter argued for such restrictive access until his retirement in the early sixties. Although the judicial rhetoric was neutral in wording, the effects are not. Politically and economically disadvantaged groups are further damaged by this lack of access since it means the law continues to favor already dominant groups (Galanter, 1974). The Supreme Court is in one sense a poor example because its decisions are so politically visible and important with consequences heatedly debated. But the rhetoric of reducing work load in order to improve the quality of court performance is almost clearly articulated at that level. Other agencies must be more circumspect and discrete in their rhetoric but the reality is the same there.

IV. TRIAL COURT STRATEGIES: ELIMINATING OR SHEDDING CIVIL CASES

When one shifts the level of analysis to focus upon trial court systems, the heavy use of caseload reduction strategies in order to cope and remain effective as an institution becomes even clearer without the overt political overtones, although such strategies do have real consequences in terms of outcomes for certain groups. Trial courts, both criminal and civil, confront case dockets that have drastically grown in size and procedural complexity. Court cases now require more handling than previously, so as case numbers go up, the actual work load escalates exponentially rather than linearly. How to cope becomes the issue since additional resources are unlikely to come to the courts. Courts are comparatively obscure institutions whose workings are hidden by conscious court practices and public indifference.

A definitional note before we proceed further: trial court systems here refers to the trial court itself plus the ancillary organizations and individuals that intersect with that institution, such as law enforcement agencies, clerks' offices, prosecutors, legal counsel (both private attorneys and public defenders), litigants and defendants, bondsmen, and corrections organizations. A number of studies have found that despite their informal appearance in terms of structure, such courts are organized in a bureaucratic manner with a standardized processing of cases in a manner at times only marginally dissimilar to that practiced in standard bureaucratic agencies (Feeley, 1973; 1979). The judge, although nominally the central decision maker, is often peripheral to much of the organization's operations (thus emphasizing the ongoing reality of routine processing and disposition of most cases), although judges can heavily influence the expectations held by the various other participants if they act to assert their legal authority much as a new agency manager does. Evidence as to the judge's often marginal role in the trial court's normal operations is the amount of disruption that occurs when a judge in fact becomes an active (and erratic from the perspective of others) participant. Newly appointed or elected judges are normally socialized into a pattern of relative inactivity, letting the others process the work load. The judge may set a new punishment schedule for certain criminal offenses, but that change is rapidly assimilated into the ongoing operations (Eisenstein and Jacob, 1977). Individual judge's quirks become fodder for the machine.

Consistently, trial courts have sought various procedural mechanisms by which to eliminate cases either prior to formal court processing (the best option) or with only minimal pro forma court action. In a manner analogous to the earlier described United States Supreme Court efforts at docket control, the intent is not directly to evade work but rather to enhance individual judge effectiveness by significantly reducing if not totally eliminating inconsequential cases. The quality of judge decision making is presumed to decline as caseload escalates. The extent of the decline is in fact unknown since decision quality is such a murky and ambiguous concept. Actually rising caseload is presumed to decrease the quality of performance in all components of the trial court system of which the effects on the trial judge are only the most visible manifestation.

At the trial court level, this reduction effort is seen as especially critical given the large volume of cases at this level. If one can reduce the formally and completely processed cases to include only the most important ones, those truly deserving of significant expenditure of judge time, then a great social good has been achieved (from the perspective of proponents) rather than having the system buried in the mundane and the trivial. There is political content here too (although much more muted) since the important civil cases in the judges' views tend to correlate highly with corporate and business status and individual cases get shorter shift.

A variety of methods have been developed by which to reduce the civil courts' formal caseload (Stumpf and Culver, 1992). We present only a few selected examples. One method attempts explicitly to divert civil disputes from the court system by increasing the use of arbitration and mediation as alternative dispute resolution procedures (Cooley, 1986). Such approaches are in principle less formal and costly than regular court processes; plus they have the advantages of allowing the decision maker explicitly to split the difference if that is the appropriate outcome. Normal trial processes conducted before a judge must arrive at a decision point where one litigant or the other must clearly win or lose. The abruptness and finality of such a public loss, it is thought (by advocates of this approach), inflame passions and do not always truly settle the real issues. Property and money may be distributed efficiently through a lawsuit, but the underlying causes may linger on, festering into but another in a series of lengthy disputes. Therefore, such alternative methods also reduce social divisiveness. Mediation and arbitration allow the parties to continue to interact within a more positive framework.

More critically, such less formal procedures have the virtue in theory of saving the litigant much time and expense, not inconsiderable issues when normal civil cases can take three to five years to reach the trial stage (Harrington, 1985). This delay is endemic to the civil court process since there are no "speedy trial" mandates for such cases and criminal cases take precedence because of such time-sensitive disposition rules. Participation in such alternatives to formal courts has been made mandatory in some circumstances. For example, some federal district courts have required that arbitration efforts be considered, while medical malpractice claims in Florida must undergo such processes prior to formal institution of litigation. The effectiveness of such efforts has been mixed since litigants are at times reluctant to accept adverse decisions without going before the judge. A less coercive procedure but one increasingly used by civil courts is the use of mandatory pretrial conferences with the judge. The intent is to use this more informal setting in order to reduce the broad scope of the pending litigation or at least isolate the areas of disagreement. Thus, disposition by the judge can be more efficiently achieved. Pretrial settlement is constantly urged as an inherent part of the process although judges vary in their individual assertiveness in urging such solutions (Ryan et al., 1980).

Simplified trial procedures have also been developed in conjunction with the push for pretrial conferences. For minor civil disputes, small claims courts have been developed in a two-headed effort to create greater access for litigants whose financial claims do not economically justify an attorney's services and, at the same time, divert such disputes from the regular courts. Small claims courts feature simplified procedures and relatively informal trial processes, although the reality in many such courts is dominance by debt holders (credit companies, retail businesses, and landlords) and their attorneys, who economically justify their work through an assembly line processing of multiple claims at a single hearing (Sarat, 1976).

In part because of the rhetoric concerning the litigation explosion, efforts have more consistently moved in the direction of reducing individual grounds for litigation and shortening the interval available in order to sue (the statute of limitations). Such arguments are rationalized as efforts to reduce frivolous and unnecessary litigation, allowing the courts to deal with the important issues. Related to this reduction process is the increased difficulty in appealing adverse lower court decisions especially for individual litigants (usually the plaintiffs in personal injury and medical malpractice litigation). The overt intent is to reduce unnecessary clutter in the appellate court dockets, again allowing judicial concentration on more critical issues and cases.

Across the spectrum of the civil trial court process and the later appellate stages, the overt goal is caseload reduction in order to ensure that more critical issues are heard and given fuller deliberation. These efforts, commendable in theory, often in practice have the effect of favoring one set of litigants as opposed to another. Repeat players, especially corporate and institutional litigants, have a continuing advantage in this context. Arguments have recently been made, most notably by former vice president Dan Quayle, that such restrictions are essential in order to restore the United States' industrial competitiveness, a claim hotly disputed but indicative of the issues embedded in the controversy (Hensler, 1992).

V. TRIAL COURT STRATEGIES: CASE REDUCTION IN CRIMINAL COURTS

Criminal courts are even more interesting in this context since their actual operations so clearly conflict with strongly held societal norms of law and order. The theory from the public's perspective is that criminal cases flow automatically into the legal system because some criminal act has occurred and (most critically) been detected by law enforcement. Most crime detection occurs as the result of public reporting of the offense rather than any proactive efforts by the police (Wilson, 1968). Regardless, the operative assumption is that when a crime has been reported and a criminal apprehended, then the system slowly and relentlessly moves to impose punishment. The reality of criminal prosecution is indeed more complex than that simplistic notion, but the critical fact here is that the entire court process is imbued with the notion that effectiveness and responsiveness can only be achieved through a shedding of caseload (Blumberg, 1967).

Caseload reduction can be overt and public or, more usually, indirect and discrete. For example, a publicly visible reduction in criminal prosecutions in a particular area can be achieved through judge and jury actions consistently finding defendants not guilty, reducing charges if found guilty, or dismissing charges. Prostitution and recreational drug use have achieved de facto decriminalization in many jurisdictions as police and prosecutors find convictions difficult to achieve or the resulting sentences, if defendants are convicted, are nominal. Consequently, those offenses are no longer routinely prosecuted.

Such cost-benefit calculations occur in all bureaucracies as the organization struggle to maximize its effectiveness with only finite resources. Minor—even major—offenses can be legally decriminalized, but that decision is often too publicly controversial or fraught with other problems. Euthanasia, for example, represents one of those offenses whose proposed decriminalization causes some social trepidation even though in fact such acts occur daily in medical settings with no intervention by the authorities.

Criminal justice systems also discourage prosecution of certain trivial offenses by displaying very nominal official attention to complaints. Telephone reports are taken of household burglaries in some jurisdictions—sufficient response for insurance purposes (a police report is necessary to initiate a claim) but inconsequential in terms of actual crime detection or possible arrest. Police departments, according to James Q. Wilson's classic study (1968), systematically vary in their willingness to handle certain types of offenses so that many such crimes are either unreported or underreported. But, despite such discouragement, crime rates and commensurately caseloads continue to climb both in raw numbers and on a per capita basis with the result that the criminal court systems are overrun with cases. Given continued public anxieties concerning the crime problem, caseload reduction efforts, regardless of their apparent "good" motivations, must be handled discretely. Therefore, any solutions must be effective but relatively invisible to the general public.

One must bear in mind that these more proactive case reduction or shedding strategies are deemed necessary in order that the organization can achieve or maintain some semblance of control over its operational environment, especially the work load component. Otherwise, the organization is overwhelmed with cases and lapses into coherence and ineffectualness as a consequence of the inability to choose what is important to deal with or at least to make such choices without a significant investment of scarce organization time and energy. For example, certain stages in criminal case processing take the same amount of time and energy regardless of the individual case's importance and complexity. A murder in that sense is equivalent to a minor marijuana possession case in the early stages. Judges deal in forms and procedures which must be pushed to completion once begun. Elimination of what are seen as comparatively unimportant cases thus becomes a critical step in freeing up the courts to deal with more important controversies.

One caveat must be expressed, though: the courts do not wish to encourage openly the thought that certain crimes are essentially "free," that is, without punishment, even if literally caught in the act. The hope is to help the courts cope with this dilemma, freeing up resources by reducing caseloads without being perceived as encouraging even more crime. This balancing process remains largely both secret and sophisticated, creating a gap between official rhetoric and behavior. Citizens in the abstract assume punishment will follow as a matter of course, although they are realistic about the chances of apprehension (low). To illustrate this point, a brief case study is sketched out here using the Florida criminal courts as the locus of research [2].

Florida, like many states, confronts a problem in that crime has proved to be a major, continuing social and political issue, an issue without ready solution given the strong drug-crime linkage. What makes the problem even more difficult for the criminal justice system is that resources (financial and personnel) have clearly not kept up with the crime problem. In fact, in recent years, the budget available for such efforts has actually receded through budget rescissions in order to maintain a state constitution–mandated balanced budget. As the state's fiscal crisis escalates, prosecutor and public defender offices have as a consequence closed for half or a whole day during the workweek. State prisons already completed have not opened because of the lack of funding. This latter situation is especially important given the persistent prison overcrowding characteristic of Florida, which has meant that convicted felons now serve on average around a third or less of their expected sentence. In addition, local jails confront similar caps on capacity, meaning that less and less bed space is available for housing "minor" offenders (Handberg and Holten, 1992; Holten and Handberg, 1990).

Confronted by this continuing crisis of system capacity in both the courts themselves and the associated corrections component, a number of options which attempt to reduce or divert work load from the court system have been pursued. Most of the strategies involve elimination of cases at the initial stages, where the cost and time savings are greatest (Handberg, 1990; Feeley, 1979). For example, some courts increase the emphasis upon disposition of the accused at first appearance. Especially useful for misdemeanor cases, the defendant who is only being initiated into the court system is persuaded by example to plead guilty to time served (that is, the incarceration period between arrest and first appearance in court for possible pretrial release). The benefit to the defendant is immediate release, although this creates an official record of deviance, a conviction record. Persuasion by example simply refers to the fact that experienced defendants plead out first and receive the usual minimal sentence. This act encourages others less experienced in the process to follow that example since the judge by his first sentences establishes the prevailing tariff for that offense. This disposition is normally restricted to minor offenses, but up to a half of the potential docket can be released through such a program. In effect, the defendant and the court reach a tacit bargain: you plead guilty and I will release you with effectively no additional punishment while I shed a portion of my work load.

The social consequences are not entirely clear but over the long term raise questions concerning misdirected police effort in apprehending such individuals. Many such offenders are status offenders such as vagrants, alcoholics, addicts, and others seen as socially disreputable, the homeless in a generic sense. In the context of Florida, with its strong tourist industry, such arrests help maintain the public appearances seen as critical in sustaining the industry, an escape from one's day to day reality. By removing disreputable individuals and encouraging their departure from the locality (usually to another city in Florida), the courts and police are being responsive to the demands of an important clientele group, the local business community.

Another coping method involves releasing individuals from jail on the basis of minimal and often unverified information and at no cost to the accused. Arrested individuals are rapidly processed for release through the pretrial release processes. In one county, for example, individuals were let go on the basis of having no residential address except a "General Delivery" postal address. No significant effort was made to verify identities or any other critical information about the individual. The implicit expectation was that the individuals would leave town, removing themselves from further significant processing by the courts.

This lack of concern about the defendant's nonappearance could also be seen in the use by many counties of letters sent to the offender's last known address as the only official effort made to return them to custody or to court. Arrest warrants for a failure to appear in court were routinely issued, but no apparent effort was made at actual enforcement. Individuals subsequently running afoul of the law for other unrelated reasons might be arrested on the basis of the warrant, but that was a secondary effect rather than a proximate cause of the police contact (the officer was not actively seeking the individual). In addition, individuals so arrested were rarely if ever prosecuted for their failure to appear, and the charge was dropped. Individuals apprehended out of state on the basis of a warrant are rarely returned for prosecution even on the original charge. Such a return is too expensive and not worth the cost of incarceration when the state's jails and prisons are already overcrowded with readily available offenders.

Other mechanisms for work load reduction include the police's issuing a street summons (a "Notice to Appear") to appear in court rather than arresting the individuals for misdemeanor offenses. The appearance rates for individuals so cited are usually low, with comparatively little follow-up to locate those who fail to show up in court. A more nebulous but real police response is the de facto decriminalization of certain offenses such as marijuana possession for personal use. This particular approach preserves the public appearance of stability in the formal law while allowing the law enforcement agencies to involve themselves in more important matters. Leaving such laws on the books makes them available for invocation later if deemed necessary. For example, an individual arrested for other reasons may be charged with these additional offenses by the prosecutor for plea bargaining purposes. The arsenal of crime fighting weapons remains in place even though certain ones have been effectively deactivated.

One must bear in mind that the underlying intent here is not merely an evasion of work (at least from a systematic perspective) but rather a clearing away of the underbrush to allow concentration upon more important crimes and, in theory, the root causes. Thus, one supposedly focuses upon major drug dealers rather than street dealers, who are readily replaceable if arrested and confined. Even among felons, efforts are focused upon violent offenders rather than on all felony offenders equally. Habitual felony offender sentencing statutes punish some more severely but also have the added bonus of eliminating a major source of future court work load since such offenders consistently produce a disproportionate share of crime and the accompanying work for the courts.

Given the context within which criminal courts operate along with their low visibility and relatively low budgets, the strategies identified here may be the most logical response. Balancing aggregate case inclusiveness versus effectiveness is a painful process. Therefore, the clear choice to reduce cases is made by most courts. In a world of finite resources, one produces finite or limited policies. Recognition of this reality is more likely to occur at the operational or agency level than at the legislative, where the problems are more remote and hypothetical in nature.

VI. CONCLUSIONS

The argument pursued in this chapter moves along two distinct tracks. One track argues that agencies routinely move to control their work environment, and an important component of that effort is the bureau's caseload. By reducing access or eliminating cases once received, the agency is able to achieve that goal. Devices used in pursuit of that strategy include difficulties in client access in terms of hours of operations and physical location, complicated forms and contradictory or complex regulations, rigid application of eligibility rules and headlines, systematic patterns of delay in file processing so that the client becomes discouraged, and failures to respond in a timely manner to queries as to whether the client wishes to continue as a means of quickly closing a file. Through such devices, cases are routinely deleted from the agency's work load. Those cases are usually classified as "closed" with no real indications as to why and with what result. Such tactics reenforce the image of public bureaucracy as unresponsive and in fact hostile to citizen demands. Not all bureaucracies pursue such strategies, but enough do so that the public is disillusioned with their work.

One must recognize, though, that agencies through these devices often reflect the decisions of others in control of the agency's destiny. During Clarence Thomas's nomination hearing for the United States Supreme Court, for example, testimony showed that the Civil Rights Commission during his tenure had slowed down its processing of discrimination claims. It was alleged that Mr. Thomas acted on behalf of the Reagan administration, which rejected the validity of such claims despite the legal mandate that they be pursued.

The other argument track postulates the same desire by the agency to control its work environment, but the attributed intention is different. Reducing work load is not the goal in itself but rather a step in the struggle to improve or, more realistically, maintain agency performance levels against the escalating pressures of rising case volumes. The conceptual difficulty lies in the fact that separating the two motivations is not necessarily easy since agency motivations in most situations are mixed. Organizations are confronted by open-ended agendas which they attempt to tailor to fit by eliminating what are termed the least important cases. The problem is that the weakest players are the most likely to be eliminated from agency consideration or have their access drastically reduced. That outcome creates public dissatisfaction, which undermines the agency's credibility. Thus, most such efforts are made covertly and incrementally. In Lindblom's phraseology, bureaucracies "muddle through" to the most optimal solution possible (Lindblom, 1959). Rather than rationally and openly confronting such questions as work load effect upon the quality of bureau performance, agencies move surreptitiously to do good (as they see it) against a backdrop of public indifference, even hostility, to such efforts. Getting the job done properly may be the most difficult task for a bureaucracy, a goal ardently strived for but rarely achieved in practice given the obstacles.

NOTES

1. See Title 28, Sections 1254 and 1257, *United States Code Annotated*, for the relevant positions.
2. The research reported here on the Florida criminal courts is based on a series of studies conducted over the past decade in various jurisdictions within the state (Handberg, 1991; Handberg, 1990; Handberg and Holten, 1985; Holten and Handberg, 1990; Handberg and Holten, 1992).

REFERENCES

Allison, Graham, *The Essence of Decision*, Little, Brown, Boston, 1971.

Blumberg, Abraham, *Criminal Justice*, Quadrangle, Chicago, 1967.

Cooley, John W., Arbitration vs. Mediation—Explaining the Differences, *Judicature 60*:263–29 (1986).

Downs, Anthony, *Inside Bureaucracy*, Little, Brown, Boston, 1967.

Eisenstein, James and Jacob, Herbert, *Felony Justice*, Little, Brown, Boston, 1977.

Feeley, Malcolm M., Two Models of the Criminal Justice System: An Organizational Perspective, *Law & Society Review* 7:407–426 (1973).

Feeley, Malcolm M., *The Process Is the Punishment*, Russell Sage Foundation, New York, 1979.

Galanter, Marc, Why the 'Haves' Come out Ahead: Speculations on the Limits of Legal Change, *Law and Society Review* 9:95–160 (1974).

Handberg, Roger, *The Impact of Failure to Appear upon Florida's Criminal Justice System*, Florida Bail Bond Regulatory Board, Department of Insurance, Tallahassee, 1990.

Handberg, Roger, The Florida Courts: Change and Adaptation, in *Government and Politics in Florida* (Robert Huckshorn, ed.), University of Florida Press, Gainesville, 1991.

Handberg, Roger and Holten, Gary N., *The Impact of Florida's Sentencing Guidelines on the Processing and Disposition of Criminal Cases*, Florida Sentencing Guidelines Commission, Tallahassee, 1985.

Handberg, Roger and Holten, Gary N., *Something for Nothing: Criminal Justice Policy in Florida in the Eighties*, paper presented at Annual Meeting of the Academy of Criminal Justice Sciences, Pittsburgh, March, 1992.

Harrington, Christine B., *Shadow Justice: The Ideology and Institutionalization of Alternatives to Court*, Greenwood, Westport, Conn., 1985.

Hensler, Deborah R., Taking Aim at the American Legal System: The Council on Competitiveness's Agenda for Legal Reform, *Judicature* 75:44–48 (1992).

Holten, N. Gary and Handberg, Roger, Florida Sentencing Guidelines: Surviving—but Just Barely, *Judicature* 73:259–267 (1990).

Lindblom, Charles E., The Science of 'Muddling Through,' *Public Administration Review 29*:79–85 (1959).

Ryan, John Paul, Ashman, Alan, Sales, Bruce D., and Shane-DuBow, Sandra, *American Trial Judges*, Free Press, New York, 1980.

Sarat, Austin, Alternatives in Dispute Processing: Litigation in Small Claims Courts, *Law & Society Review 10*:339–375 (1976).

Stumpf, Harry P., and Culver, John H., *The Politics of State Courts*, Longman, New York, 1992.

Wilson, James Q., *Varieties of Police Behavior*, Harvard University Press, Cambridge, Mass., 1968.

11
Bureaucracy and the Environmental Crisis: A Comparative Perspective

Renu Khator
University of South Florida, Tampa, Florida

Environmental degradation has reached a point of global and universal crisis. Since the formal recognition of the problem in the early 1970s, most nations have tried to respond to its urgency by adopting new laws and establishing independent bureaucracies. Between 1972, the time of the first United Nations Conference on Human Environment, and 1992, the time of the Earth Summit in Rio, the number of nations with environmental bureaucracies increased by ten times—from 11 to over 150. Thanks to the pioneering work of the United Nations Environment Program (UNEP), most nations today have some form of national policy for the protection of the environment. Interestingly, most of three environmental policies are regulatory in nature. Since bureaucracies are the prime institutions for regulatory control and monitoring, they are automatically at the center of all activity—winning praise and taking blame. The near-global and universal emergence of environmental bureaucracies raises an important question for the scholars of comparative public administration: Do these bureaucracies perform comparably? Is their performance tainted by their contexts?

In comparison to public administrationists, policy analysts and political scientists have paid greater attention to the need for compassion. The literature in these fields focuses on the issue of comparability, or rather noncomparability, and the factors that force the environmental performance of one system to be different from that of another (Kamieniecki and Sanasarian, 1990; Lundqvist, 1980; Kelman, 1981; Knoepfel et al., 1987; Reich, 1984; Solesbury, 1976; Enloe, 1975; Siegel and Weinberg, 1977; Kelley et al., 1976; Brickman et al., 1985). Several of the studies identify the determining role of administrative systems in explaining policy performance across nations. Others find political-cultural factors to be of greater significance. A pioneering work in this area came from David Vogel (1986), who, after comparing the American and British styles of regulation, concluded that the administrative culture of the United States fostered an incompetent image of the U.S. Environmental Protection Agency even when its overall performance was not significantly different from that of its British counterpart.

While administrative structures have always been a favorite explanatory variable among political scientists and policy analysts in comparative models, comparative studies on environmental administrative systems—studies that use administrative systems as a dependent variable—are not many. There is a dearth of comparative work that includes non-Western systems. Non-Western systems are assumed to be either noncomparable or irrelevant for cross-learning purposes. Kamieniecki and Sanasarian (1990) cite a number of factors that serve as stumbling blocks in this area, particularly accuracy of data, comparability of language usage, differences in political systems, and dependency on foreign assistance. Scholars try to reduce this void by offering periodic "overview" analyses of a group of case studies from the non-Western world (Lehman, 1992). Although these overviews are precious, an effort should be made to develop a common intellectual nexus and learn from cross-comparisons (Kamieniecki and Sanasarian, 1990).

The objective of this study is to put environmental bureaucracy in a global context, an approach being demanded by several scholars in the environmental policy field (Guirmaraes, 1991; Goodman and Redclift, 1991; Barrett and Therivel, 1991). The idea is to use environmental bureaucracy as a dependent variable, as an entity that does not exist in a vacuum and cannot be deemed effective or ineffective on its own. Bureaucracy is being perceived as an entity that is affected by forces outside its own parameters. It is an entity that is neither monolithic nor static; an entity that has a definite form and character—for without any form and character of its own it cannot be said to meet the first two conditions. In prior studies, bureaucracy served as an explanatory variable—a variable that was assessed to see why things did not work, why outcomes were different in different settings, and how they affected other institutions.

In this study, we first explore the form and character of three different environmental bureaucracies: American, Hong Kong, and Indian. The selection of these three bureaucracies is important. They offer not only three different political settings (liberal democratic, bureaucratic-authoritarian, and controlled democratic, respectively), but also three different economic settings (industrialized, newly industrialized, and yet-to-be industrialized) and three different global settings (leading, responding, and relatively closed). The selection of the cases sets the stage for using the global and comparative approach advanced by Garcia-Zamor and Khator (1994) in *Public Administration in the Global Village*. They argue that the administrative system should be viewed within the parameters of its external systems, including political, economic, and global systems. They suggest that the degree and nature of penetration from external systems can offer a common ground of comparison. They specifically raise three questions: (1) To what degree is a system capable of functioning in the global context? (2) To what extent is an administrative system able to correspond to the social and cultural norms of the society? (3) To what extent is an administrative system congruous to its political setting? These criteria significantly enlarge the scope of administrative systems and public administration. The administrative system stretches beyond the Weberian boundaries of rationality, hierarchy, neutrality, and role orientation and relies upon international pressures, social expectations, and global responsibilities as its driving forces. Administrative systems are viewed on a continuum, ranging from complete integration to complete disjointment (Figure 1). A completely integrated system is assumed to be in full harmony with outside forces (global, social, and political)—depending upon them and responding to them. On the other hand, a completely disjointed system is in constant conflict with these forces. We shall be returning to this model again in the concluding section of this chapter.

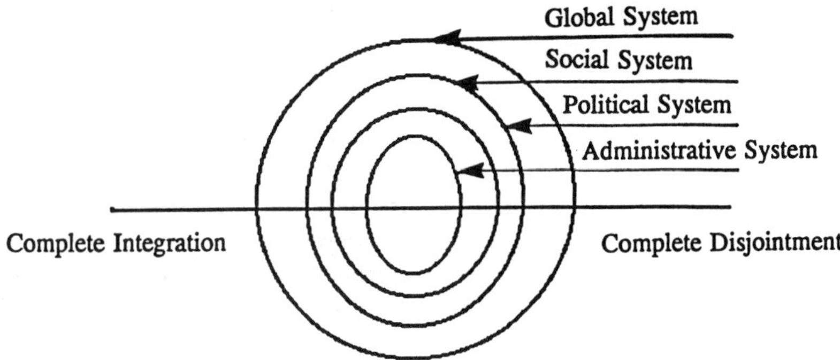

Figure 1 Classification of administrative systems based on penetration continuum.

I. INDIA: ENVIRONMENTAL BUREAUCRACY IN A SOCIAL SYSTEM

The Indian bureaucracy has historical roots. It bears the marks of its precolonial heritage and the signs of the British colonialism of over 200 years. Commenting on its evolution, Jain (1991, p. 44) says:

> On attainment of independence, India inherited from the British a monolithic, strictly hierarchical administrative structure, with the line of command running unimpeded from the Viceroy and Governor-General in Delhi to the farthest village, albeit conforming to certain well-established traditions. The purpose of such a system was to keep the interest of British power in India dominant, ensure that the government secured the revenue it needed, maintained law and order to serve the cause of peace and security.

In its modern form, the environmental bureaucracy manifests the British traditions and values brought to India during colonization. At the same time, its functioning is a product of the country's social fabric woven with delicate threads of religion, caste, and cultural beliefs. Hindu religion, practiced by 82% of the Indian population, defines the relationship between human beings and their physical environment as interdependent (Dwivedi and Tiwari, 1987). The inherent dependency of human beings on their surroundings does not leave room for environmental degradation, yet degradation of the environment is severe in India. Natural resources such as rivers, ocean, and trees are all glorified as forms of god, yet dams are built on rivers, toxins are dumped into the ocean, and trees are constantly chopped for fuel, fodder, and construction. Today, only 11% of the land surface in India is covered with adequate tree cover, 70% of all available water is polluted, and most major cities are choking with severe air pollution (Agarwal and Narain, 1985).

The first signs of environmental regulation in India came in the late nineteenth century, when the British government declared forests as the property of the state. In an 1878 law, the government classified forests in three categories: village, community, and restricted. People were allowed to use only "village forests" for their fuel and fodder needs. To monitor this policy, a forest bureaucracy was necessary. This forest bureaucracy eventually set the stage for the coming environmental bureaucracy (Khator, 1989). For the next 90 years, the federal government remained mostly silent; only individual states made some sporadic attempts to regulate the environment.

The next real attempt to shape the environmental bureaucracy was in 1972, when then–Prime Minister Indira Gandhi established the National Committee on Environmental Planning and Coordination. This action came in direct response to a United Nations call to prepare a report on the status of the environment for its scheduled conference in the same year (Caldwell, 1972). The task of the committee was basically exploratory; it was not granted any regulatory or advisory functions. In later years, however, this committee proved to be a precursor of a full-fledged regulatory bureaucracy. The government, alarmed by the committee's report, passed a trend- setting law in 1974 to curb water pollution. The Water (Prevention and Control of Pollution) Act of 1974 created a centralized, cohesive bureaucracy in the form of Water Boards, which were set up as a network, with the Central Board accountable to the central government at the top and state boards answerable to individual state governments as well as to the Central Board at the second layer. The task of the boards was predominantly regulatory: regulating businesses on the one hand and municipalities on the other. The boards were the point of gravity because, unlike in the United States, the Indian public did not have the right to take an offending party (business or municipality) to court without the consent of the boards. All public complaints were required to go through the boards, even though the boards could process only 5% of such complaints (Khator, 1991). The revenue of the boards came partially from their respective governments and partially from the fees collected from offenders through a law passed in 1977 (Cess Act of 1977). Since their inception, the Water Act and the Water Boards both have been subjected to serious criticism and controversy: scholars have called them inefficient and ineffective (Lalvani, 1985; Agarwal and Narain, 1985; Puri, 1987).

In 1980, the Indian government realized the complexity and multiplicity of environmental issues. It responded to the situation by creating the Department of Environment, which later was transformed into a full-fledged ministry: the Ministry of Environment and Forests (MEF). Today, the environmental bureaucracy consists of water boards (which also implement air pollution control laws), Environmental Committees at the state level, and a Central Water Board and a Ministry at the federal level. The federal layer has grown considerably in strength—from an exploratory committee of 15 in 1972 to over 1200 personnel in 1990. It has 18 divisions, including Conservation and Survey, Forest Conservation, Wildlife Conservation, Impact Assessment, and Education and Information. The members of the environmental bureaucracy are selected through a common Civil Services Examination. They are permanent civil servants (their positions are secured by the Constitution of India), and they are expected to perform their tasks in a hierarchical organization with full neutrality. Their primary task is to implement the laws passed by parliament.

The environmental bureaucracy in India performs regulatory and nonregulatory functions. Its regulatory functions follow the same procedure as in the United States: the source of the problem is identified; standards are set; compliance is monitored; and noncompliance is punished. Its nonregulatory functions are unique, and important—because they assume a proactive role of the bureaucracy in distributing and redistributing the use of natural resources (Khator, 1989). One such program is social forestry. Under social forestry, the government offers seeds and saplings of forests plants to villagers to be planted on river banks and unused property. It is hoped that these artificially grown forests will fulfill the fuel and fodder needs of the forest-dependent peoples and will protect the natural forests from unnecessary assault (Fernandes and Kulkarni, 1983).

The functioning of the environmental bureaucracy is riddled with many problems. To begin with, developmental priorities of the country undercut the position of the environmental bureaucracy; it finds its task of promoting the environmental cause difficult, particularly in times of fiscal austerity. Often, the task of the environmental bureaucracy is not only to regulate the business, but more importantly to regulate other bureaucracies (transportation, development, agriculture, industry) that may overlook the environmental aspect in their plans. Without the unwavering support of the people and that of the government, the environmental bureaucracy finds itself in an awkward position.

Second, the overarching influence of business in Indian politics makes it difficult for the environmental bureaucracy to implement laws. Harowitz (1989, p. 201), while discussing the general capacity of governments in developing societies, points out that they lack the penetrative capacity necessary for effective implementation. The lack of penetrative capacity in India is the result of corruption and monopoly. Corruption can, more often than not, offset the cost-benefit ratio of compliance. If an offender is able to buy off a regulator at a cost substantially lower than the cost of compliance, regulation is not likely to take place.

Similarly, the near-complete monopoly of the Congress Party in India also hinders the ability of environmental groups to articulate the interests of their constituencies efficiently. The ruling Congress Party in India is closely aligned with business, making it difficult for nonbusiness or antibusiness groups to find any meaningful representation in the government. Lack of constituency weakens the position of environment groups.

I have argued elsewhere that the local policy culture—the surroundings in which local bureaucrats must function—is not favorable for bureaucratic functioning in India (Khator, 1992). In the pollution control field, for instance, local elite—who need to be regulated for creating pollution—have a strong hold on local affairs. Regulators lack the ability to break their hold and force them to comply with regulation. These local elite almost always have connections in the higher echelons of the bureaucratic machinery; in cases of conflict with local regulators, they are capable of reaching bureaucratic superiors to pressure the local regulators. In a hypothetical case, let us say a regulator finds the waste discharge from a given industry is beyond the permissible limits. He is offered a bribe to ignore it or to delay the process. Now he has a choice of either accepting the bribe and benefitting from his authority or rejecting the bribe and bearing the consequence of being demoted by his higher-ups. A rational regulator will make a rational choice. Local policy culture offers no protection to regulators to force compliance. A case in point is social forestry, where, under the government's plan to distribute free seedlings, it was found that most of the benefits went to the higher-caste farmers, who have significant clout in the local area. The effectiveness of the policy was undermined in this case because the recipients of seeds/saplings planted them for profit. The resulting crop of eucalyptus could not provide fuel and fodder to the poor and thus could not reduce the strain on natural forests.

Why are the regulators weak? Some scholars blame social circumstances (Jain, 1991). As a result of strong social bonds, regulators in India perceive themselves first as the members of their social, ethnic, and religious groups and then as members of the bureaucratic machinery. In particular, systems such as social caste (which divides the country in social hierarchical categories), sons of the soil (which promotes regionalism), and ethnoexpansionism tend to have harmful effects on bureaucratic functioning. Aside from promoting corruption, the prevalence of these practices taints the image of the bureaucracy, which in India is perceived to be corrupt and dysfunctional (Dwivedi and Jain, 1985). This hurts the cause of building a constituency. Jain (1991, p. 8) argues that the social structure of India has shaped its bureaucracy and has given rise to bureaucratic dysfunctionalism.

Overall, the environmental bureaucracy in India suffers from serious contradictions. Its tone is decisively regulatory, yet its authority comes from advisory and consultative capacities. There are serious loopholes in the implementation network. The environmental bureaucracy has a built-in flexibility (it does not offer time schedules and strict standards), yet the bureaucratic culture is full of rigidity and rule-bound orientation. Another contradiction occurs in political-bureaucratic relations. While there is a close alliance between business and the ruling Congress Party, there is little evidence that this alliance is used to build a cooperative culture for decision making. Policy-making is closed and one-sided, with little consideration for what is feasible and reasonable. Scholars describe the current system of environmental standard setting as "non-participative, non-consensual, and non-transparent" (Reich and Bowonder, 1992, p. 655). The approach used is a "fire-brigade" approach, focusing all energy on crises and making decisions in a panic-stricken environment. Maneka Gandhi, former Minister of the Environment, pushed the Public Liability Act after the Bhopal tragedy (Reich and Bowonder, 1992). The process of passing the act did not involve any consultation with the industry, who, in the act, is forced to provide Rs.25,000 (approximately US $1,000) compulsory insurance to people handling hazardous waste. Understandably, the law is yet to be implemented.

The most serious contradiction is between the desired image and the available image of the bureaucracy itself. While the government passes blame on to the people, evidence continues to mount against the government itself. On several occasions, this contradiction has proved embarrassing. Justice Krishna Iyer, while giving his judgment on an environmental controversy (the 1980 *Ratlam Municipality vs. Virdhi Chand and Others* case, in which Virdhi Chand had sued Ratlam Municipality for not providing adequate protection), said:

> One wonders whether our municipal bodies are functional irrelevancies, banes rather than boons and "lawless" by long neglect, not leaders of the people in local self government. It may be a cynical body minus the people and plus the bureaucrats are the pathetic vogue—no better than when the British were here. (Varandani, 1987, p. 122)

When it comes to the integrity of the bureaucracy, scholars and analysts also raise questions:

> The municipal organizations today, which are required to enforce existing provisions against pollution, are themselves the major polluters. Their own outdated methods of solid waste management, the crude dumping grounds, the inadequate drainage systems which carry raw sewage along the siltage, polluted water sources, inadequate administrative machinery are some of the glaring examples as to how the controlling authorities help spread pollution in cities. (Puri, 1987, p. 288)

In brief, the environmental bureaucracy in India suffers from both inadequate horizontal relations (with other bureaucracies) and superficial vertical relations (with regulators and the public). It is a misfit in the compartmentalized structure of the bureaucracy. Its role is all-encompassing, multilayered, and complex. Because of the inherent contradictions, it faces a barrier that is proving to be insurmountable.

II. ENVIRONMENTAL BUREAUCRACY IN HONG KONG

In contrast to India's parliamentary, federal, and democratic setting, Hong Kong offers a bureaucratic-authoritarian, colonial, and city-state setting for its bureaucracy. The two countries are also on the opposite ends of the economic growth continuum. While India is a poor country with per capita income of less than $300, Hong Kong is a newly industrialized country with a per capita income of $10,000. Socially and culturally, the two countries are comparable: both harbor a family-oriented and tradition-rich social culture. While the Hong Kong society is not segregated into social classes, such as observed in the Indian caste system, the philosophical underpinnings of Confucianism still divide the society based on gender and age. Once known only for its amiability to Chinese refugees, Hong Kong is now acclaimed in the world for its ultramodern commercial and financial infrastructures. The miraculous economic growth of Hong Kong is the result of the economic strategy that integrates the territory's economy with the global economy.

As a British colony, Hong Kong is naturally attracted to the British ideals and paradigms of public administration: merit-based, hierarchical, neutral, and rational bureaucracy. Peter Harris (1988) describes Hong Kong bureaucracy as politically apathetic and ideologically detached. Yet it is the bureaucracy in Hong Kong that is at the nexus of all political activity. Its power and legitimacy come from its practice of seeking wide public consultation on political issues. Its authority and legitimacy are rarely questioned. The job of the bureaucracy is simple: it is expected to provide a conducive environment for economic growth. The process of public administration is described as a two-stage process: "First, policy is made and second, monies are authorized" (Rabushka, 1976, p. 35). The job of public administrators is described by Peter Harris (1988, pp. 70–71) as follows:

> In Hong Kong, officials dominate where they must—though they prefer the "market" to take care of the decision-making process. Their objective is not to distort the market process, but rather to provide the conditions to make the process more effective. . . . Where it is inefficient, it is not necessarily a question of will, but lack of will.

The environmental bureaucracy of Hong Kong is part of this larger setting. The Hong Kong policy on the environment is still in its infancy. While water distribution and land use laws have been on the books for several decades, environmental degradation control laws are new to the territory. As in India, formal interest in the environment appeared in Hong Kong in 1972, when the Governor of Hong Kong appointed an advisory committee on environmental pollution on land and water (commonly known as EPCOM). This committee was established in response to the United Nations' call to prepare a report on the status of the environment in the territory. The report of this committee prompted the Hong Kong government to appoint another exploratory committee in 1974 to review and suggest measures to rectify the problem of environmental degradation (Bidwell, 1988). The team was instructed specifically to suggest actions that would not "interfere with the industry or otherwise impair the potential economic growth; and it should not add to the cost of government" (Bidwell, 1988, p. 19).

Recommendations of the review team set the tone of environmental bureaucracy. The review team suggested emphasis on planning rather than control, on consensus rather than conflict, on economic noninterventionism rather than active interference, and on administrative flexibility rather than uniformity (Khator, 1990). More specifically, the team asked that several ordinances on pollution control be passed and a permanent environmental agency to coordinate the efforts be established. The result was the Environmental Policy Unit (EPU), founded in 1977. It consisted of one Environmental Protection Adviser (appointed by the Governor, himself an appointee of the British government) and four Environmental Protection Officers, one each for waste, air, water, and noise (also appointed by the Governor). Its task was to advise the government on planning.

Interestingly, the government retained EPCOM although its composition changed significantly. Its members were now drawn from various public and private sectors. It was chaired by the Secretary of Environment and provided permanent representation to three main industrial organizations: the Chinese Manufacturers Association, the Federation of Hong Kong Industries, and the Hong Kong General Chamber of Commerce. It also secured seats for environmental groups as well as other governmental departments. EPCOM was meant to become a unique forum for public consultation. However, it was a delicate arrangement, because of the ever-existing possibility that the industrial lobby would take over the committee.

The environmental bureaucracy finally found its ground in 1980 when the first ordinance, the Water Pollution Control Ordinance, was enacted. Ordinances on air control and noise control followed in 1983 and 1988, respectively. In order to centralize all environmental activities, the government also granted the environmental bureaucracy agency-level status. The newly created Environmental Protection Agency grew in staff and budget strength. However, its implementation powers were still limited, as they were dependent on persuasion and consultation. It was only in 1986 that it received full implementation powers, its status raised to department level and its name changed to the Environmental Protection Department (EPD). The economic agenda of the territory provided extreme challenges to the infant environmental bureaucracy. Its home was shifted from one policy area to another; first placed under the Secretary for Home Affairs, it was subsequently shifted to the Administrative and Environmental Affairs Branch, then to the Health and Welfare Branch, and then to the Lands and Works Branch, until finally, in 1989, it found its home in the Planning, Environment, and Lands Branch.

The environmental bureaucracy now performs regulatory functions. Its regulatory policy follows the usual pattern of permit-monitor-prosecute. Interestingly, despite the territory's mature capitalism, the Hong Kong government does not prefer market-oriented mechanisms to check environmental degradation. Several reasons account for it, the most important of which is the unwillingness of the government to alter its competitive edge in the international market. The territory's dependency on the international market economy may explain its less-than-forthright approach to environmental problems. In the following section, I explore the effects of the global economy on Hong Kong's environmental policy.

The Water Pollution Control Ordinance as passed in 1980 and implemented in 1987 had two unique features: leniency and flexibility. In the name of environmental pollution control, the ordinance not only allowed the continuation of the existing level of emission discharge into the colony's waterways, but, to the environmentalists' dismay, permitted a 30% increase over the current levels. On the basis of the ordinance, industries received a quota that was 30% higher than their current level of discharge. This meant that the water pollution from industrial discharge was going to increase in the future. To make matters worse, industries could also request a waiver from this already lenient policy. Second, to prevent sudden shocks to the system, the ordinance allowed an implementation strategy that was both flexible and gradual. The ordinance required the establishment of several pollution control zones slowly over an extended period. The Tolo Harbor Zone was considered to be the area most severely hit by water pollution; thus the first water zone was in this area. After a year-long pause, the second zone was declared in the Southern region, including Repulse Bay, a prime tourist area. Two more came into existence during the following year.

Thus, the environmental policy in Hong Kong had an industrial overtone: it protected industry, it fostered industry, and it made sure that industry was equipped to compete in the world market. Hong Kong relies primarily on small-scale, family-oriented industries that operate on minimum profit margins. Sheltering these industries is almost essential for the territory's economic survival. How, then, does the "government of bureaucrats," as the Hong Kong government is called, reconcile the differences between economic growth and environmental protection? Hong Kong has developed an industrial approach to environmental protection. The environmental bureaucracy, acting as caretaker and decision maker, has invented several mechanisms to caress industrial growth while pushing a parallel environmental agenda. Other than regulating, it performs two very critical tasks: (1) it serves as a depository of information, relieving industry from the burden of singlehandedly investing in research and development; and (2) it functions as a consensus builder, searching for a middle ground on which economic and environmental interests can be reconciled. The second function is performed by its EPCOM unit; the first function is accomplished, to a large extent, by the Hong Kong Productivity Council (HKPC) unit. HKPC was established in 1967 to promote industrial productivity in Hong Kong. Realizing the significance of an environmentally friendly technology in the future, the council expanded its scope by establishing an environmental wing. This wing advises small and medium industries on pollution control methods. Its task goes so far as to design individualized treatment instruments for house-based, tin-shade, small family operations. Usually its customers are referred to it by environmental regulators; however, several opt to knock on its doors of their own free will. The council is financed by annual governmental subvention (HKPC, 1989, p. 48).

The environmental bureaucracy in Hong Kong suffers from the usual criticism and controversy (Lam, 1987; Downey, 1987), but these are within the parameters of "open feedback." Charges of corruption are never made and questions regarding the integrity of the regulators are rarely raised. In fact, the majority of the criticism is against the policy rather than the implementors. Evidence indicates that, unlike the Indian environmental bureaucracy, the Hong Kong bureaucracy maintains a good image of neutrality and sincerity. In a survey of environmental regulators in 1990, researchers found that only 5% of the street-level regulators belonged to environmental interest groups and more than half refused to call themselves environmentalists (Khator et al., 1992). In the same survey, more than 80% of them applauded the cooperative attitude of business. Interestingly, by an overwhelming majority, the regulators cited Hong Kong's dependency on the international economy as the single most important barrier in the territory's slow environmental progress.

III. ENVIRONMENTAL BUREAUCRACY IN THE UNITED STATES

The United States offers another interesting political, social, economic, and international setting for our study. An industrialized democracy with per capita income of over $25,000, the United States enjoys leadership status in the world. Its political system with a presidential form of government and federalism offers a complex context for bureaucracy. In fact, Fred W. Riggs (1994) goes so far as to say that the political setting of the United States is responsible for producing a semipowered bureaucracy—bureaucracy that is highly professional and yet is extremely disconnected.

A vast amount of literature on the failures of the American environmental bureaucracy already exists. Comparative studies, in particular, paint a dreary picture of the abilities of the environmental bureaucracy. It is often compared with European counterparts. The findings, more often than not, ridicule the American environmental policy, and consequently the bureaucracy, as inefficient, ineffectual, and outright irresponsible. What are the reasons for such flawed performance? The reason for the failure generally lies in the political setting. In a comparative study, Lundqvist (1980) compared the performance of the American clean air policy with that of the Swedish clean air policy: the former reflected the hastiness and unreliability of the "loser hare" while the latter reflected the slow and steady run of the "winner tortoise." He claimed that this was, in part, due to the conflict-oriented, nationalized, and litigant style of decision making in America. In contrast, the Swedish style of decision making was consensus-oriented, localized, and voluntary. Lundqvist's findings were echoed by those of many other studies (Vogel, 1986). Several case studies undertaken in America on individual program performance also seem to assign the burden of program failure to political factors. There are other scholars, however, who defend the American performance by offering success stories. Rosenbaum (1989, p. 234) says in defense:

> Taken uncritically, this tacit consensus about program failures would seem a damning indictment of bureaucracy's role in federal environmental protection and a discouraging omen for the future. Yet there is empirical evidence that some programs, in some instances, have worked reasonably well—or, at least, that the environment has improved when the programs were operating.

A careful examination of the American political setting is warranted at this point. The tone and direction of the environmental policy and environmental bureaucracy in the United States were set in the National Environmental Policy Act (NEPA) of 1969. In particular, two features of the act defined the scope and nature of the environmental bureaucracy. The first was an "action-forcing" provision included in Section 102 of the act. This provision required the Environmental Protection Agency to perform certain acts within a given period and in a given manner. This style of implementation was kept alive in the legislation that followed in the 1970s. For instance, the Clean Air Act of 1970 required the Environmental Protection Agency to propose a set of national standards on air quality within 30 days, to adopt state plans within 1 year, and to develop technology standards for auto emission within 5 years. This was a strategy of "speculative augmentation" that was bound to put an excessive burden on the bureaucracy and consequently was bound to fail (Jones, 1975).

According to Rosenbaum (1989), action-forcing provision (or "hammer clauses") had serious implications for the environmental bureaucracy, which, at that time, included three presidential staff agencies, twelve cabinet departments, and a few other independent agencies. They set strict time tables, assigned specific guidelines, and left the bureaucracy open to litigation. This meant that the bureaucracy had to stay constantly on the defensive. Collectively, these provisions challenged the traditional modes of administrative behavior by making the bureaucracy directly accountable to the public and by giving it an "untrustworthy and unreliable" image. These provisions put a considerable burden on the bureaucracy for setting uniform standards, producing fast results, and working in an open environment. This ran contrary to the British and Swedish administrative styles, which relied on discretion and flexibility.

The second feature of NEPA defining the nature of the environmental bureaucracy was the provision for environmental impact assessment (EIA). This provision placed the burden of identifying environmentally sensitive projects, assessing their impact on the environment, and eventually using the environmental criteria in decision making about the agency. This put the environmental bureaucracy further on the defensive, for it was the bureaucracy that had to do the justifying. The act, with its EIA provision, also pitted the environmental bureaucracy against the developmental bureaucracy and allowed the critics to label the environmental bureaucracy as an antidevelopment and antigrowth. A glaring example of this conflict occurred in June 1993, when a federal court passed a judgment requiring the Clinton administration to prepare an environmental impact study on the North American Free Trade Agreement (NAFTA) before sending it to Congress for approval. Critics immediately called this requirement antigrowth, for the resulting delay of several months may likely hurt the economies of Mexico, the United States, and Canada.

Furthermore, the task of environmental impact assessment places a heavy burden on the environmental bureaucracy. The EIA provision is based on the assumption that the bureaucracy possesses the scientific ability to conduct such studies. Furthermore, it is based on the assumption that accurate costs and benefits can always be determined. Paradoxically, these assumptions that place trust in the bureaucracy eventually make the bureaucracy more vulnerable—vulnerable to litigation and to the whims and fancies of the scientific community. The EIA decisions of the bureaucracy have been and continue to be challenged, in the courts by industry for being too harsh, and by the public for being too soft. The process of litigation itself, regardless of the outcome, weakens the bureaucracy by tarnishing its image, splitting its clientele, and making it a topic of media-led investigations. This entire process creates unnecessary adversity and promotes the image of the bureaucracy as ineffective and often even antidemocratic.

Today, the United States has one of the world's most complex and comprehensive environmental bureaucracies. The genesis of the consolidated environmental bureaucracy dates back to the early 1970s, when President Nixon reorganized it by bringing several federal programs under the umbrella of the Environmental Protection Agency (EPA). Since then, more than 20 new agencies dealing with environmental issues have been created to implement more than 150 new laws passed during the last 20 years alone. The EPA's network now includes 10 regional offices, with a staff of over 15,000 and a budget of $4.9 billion. This reflects the doubling of staff and a tenfold increase in budget since 1972 (a large amount of this increase amounts to waste treatment grant money committed for Superfund and local governments). Along with the EPA, several federal agencies—including the Department of Interior, Bureau of Land Management, National Parks Service, Forest Service, OSHA, Council on Environment Quality, Nuclear Regulatory Commission, and Department of Energy—work in the environmental cause.

The American environmental bureaucracy faces many problems, including fragmentation, politicization, and excessive public and media exposure. The fragmented nature of the bureaucracy is evident from the fact that there are some eighteen hundred subunits engaged in overlapping activities. Barry Rabe (1986) argues that the nature of the bureaucracy—highly professionalized and greatly specialized—is the main source of institutional fragmentation. Commenting on the level of fragmentation, he notes that "federal control of all exposures from the manufacture, use, and disposal of vinyl chloride would have required the participation of five federal agencies and involvement of 15 separate laws" (1986, p. 14). Fragmentation leads to duplication, unnecessary turf fighting, and wastefulness. Although there are some scholars who find merit in fragmentation (Clarke and McCool, 1985), in general most consider this to be a liability. They also agree that the fragmentation results from the unique American political setting. This setting is built around the principles of the separation of powers, interest group lobbying, and federalism.

Environmental issues in the American setting are highly politicized. Even though such issues enjoy a certain degree of bipartisan support in the legislature, party politics is evident in many other areas. During the Reagan years, for instance, the Republican Party worked under the principles of the new federalism. New federalism and its emphasis on decentralization affected the environmental cause adversely. The budget and staff of the EPA were slashed, assistance to state and local governments was reduced, and national priorities were redefined in favor of economic growth (Kraft and Vig, 1990). Similarly, during the Bush years, the focus on competitiveness hurt the environmental cause and continued the trend begun during the Reagan years. The fragility of Bush's support of the environmental cause was exposed during the 1992 Earth Summit in Rio. The presidential elections of 1992, which put a Democrat in the White House, may promise better support for environmental groups. Environmentalists are hopeful that the election of Al Gore as vice president will produce a more conducive setting for environmental decision making. However, while the Clinton administration promises to be environment friendly, proof of such friendliness is yet to surface.

IV. EXPLAINING DIFFERENCES: A GLOBAL APPROACH TO COMPARISON

In the three cases studied here—India, Hong Kong, and the United States—we find that environmental bureaucracy suffers from the image of being ineffective, inefficient, and insensitive. Some common reasons account for this image: one, environmental issues are complex, and managing them is a daunting task. Two, there is much ambiguity about the long-term impact of these issues. Three, the logic of environmental management is threatening; it aims at changing those very fundamental values and priorities of modern societies so precious to us. Four, environmental administration often involves costs that are immediate and appear to be exceeding the long-term benefits. Costs are costs, whether in the form of cleanup projects or technological investments.

Beyond these common barriers, however, are areas where differences mount as a result of administrative settings and strategies. When we compare the three bureaucracies on a common continuum of penetration, we realize that while all of them are being penetrated by their external systems (political, social, and global), they are not being invaded by the same set of factors and to the same degree. In other words, the settings pose unique problems for individual bureaucracies. If the problems are unique, then the solutions must also be unique. The quest for uniqueness, however, involves a painful process of separating factors that are not so unique, or, in other words, are standard. This is where comparative analysis is most useful, because it is only through comparison that we can separate the unique from the "standard."

In our study, the Indian environmental bureaucracy is found to be most severely restricted by its social system (see Figure 2a). The effect of the global system, although present, is minimal. In fact, the forces of the global system (in the form of foreign aid and imported technologies) are undermined by the local culture—the culture which, in the end, defines the functioning scope of the bureaucrats. Bureaucrats are bound by their social identities, which offer them greater security and solace than their administrative positions. Administrative positions in this context become the means of social mobility. The political system in India, although resting on the assumption of a neutralized bureaucracy, fails to protect the bureaucrats from the pulls and pushes of the social system. It eventually becomes a counterproductive organization.

In fact, the Indian environmental bureaucracy conflicts with the interests of the political system while maintaining a harmonious relationship with the social system. Global forces also have a role to play. They influence the political system by changing the political agenda (the United Nations Conference on Human Environment tilted the agenda in favor of environmental issues); however, they are incapable of penetrating the social system. Since the penetrative capabilities of the political system are inept, the eventual effect of the global system (which tries to influence the administrative system through the political system) is minimal. New laws are passed, new programs are enacted, but the same practices continue.

The Hong Kong case is the direct opposite to the Indian case. The Hong Kong bureaucracy shows the greatest degree of vulnerability to the global system. Economic growth through international trade and competition is clearly the top priority of the territory. This priority is the driving force behind the political system and the political system is in full harmony with the global system. We have observed that in India the lines of communication between the political system and the global system were, at best, blurred as a result of the overarching role of the social

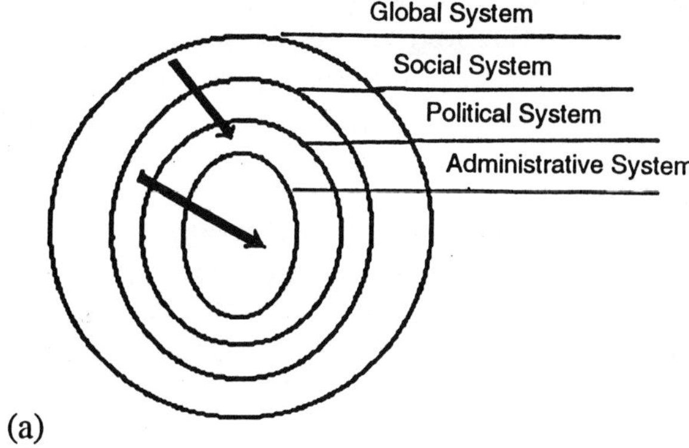

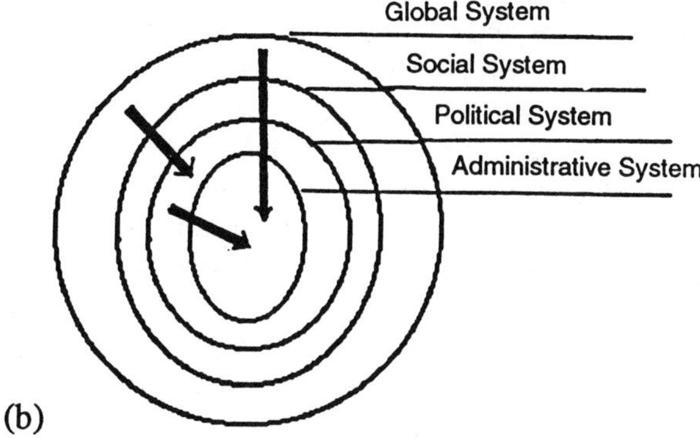

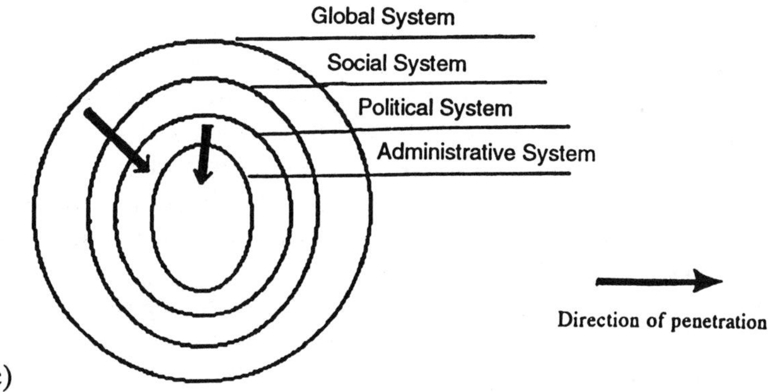

Figure 2 Environmental bureaucracy in (a) India, (b) Hong Kong, (c) the United States.

system. In the case of Hong Kong, the reverse is true. Similar to Indians, Hong Kong people are also bound by countless social traditions and rituals. However, this does not hamper the functioning of the political system and consequently the administrative system. Interestingly, the global forces are unable to penetrate the social system of Hong Kong (just as we observed in India); however, unlike in India, the "unpenetrated" social system does not become a stumbling block for the effective functioning of the political system.

The Hong Kong bureaucracy thus functions in a context which is global (Figure 2b). Its role is to support the political system so it can effectively steer the economy in the global system. Particularly because the political system itself is subservient to the global system, the task of the bureaucracy is to see that the system of Hong Kong remains competitive and in harmony with the global system. It is due to this special demand that the environmental bureaucracy in Hong Kong appears less regulatory and more consensus building than other bureaucracies in our study.

The Weberian characteristics of bureaucracy—clear lines of authority and neutrality—are most carefully preserved in Hong Kong. This is essential to maintain coordination. Local regulators are reluctant to define and shape policies even when the flexibility to do so exists (Khator, 1992). Very little tension and frustration seem to appear in the lower echelons of the bureaucracy. On the other hand, top level bureaucrats, who in Hong Kong are the decision makers, function within the parameters of the global economy. While they may realize the need for environmental protection, they are unlikely to engage in promoting it unless other competitors in the international arena also do so. It would not be surprising to see Hong Kong turn into a champion of the environmental cause if this would benefit its position in the international market. It is capable of reorienting its economy to international shifts. Such a shift would be painfully slow for India to make.

Unlike the Indian and the Hong Kong bureaucracies, the American bureaucracy is most easily penetrated by the political system. While the global role of the United States is undisputed, this does not, to a great extent, affect the bureaucracy. With a few exceptions, environmental politics in the United States is very much a local game fought in the local arena with local interests. In fact, global and social forces are absorbed by the political system, which ultimately defines the functioning scope of the bureaucracy (see Figure 2c).

Separation of power, an important precondition of presidential regimes, puts the American bureaucracy under the service of more than one master. Since a great proportion of interpretive power is vested in the bureaucracy, it becomes a ground for direct lobbying by interest groups. More often than not, intense lobbying fragments the bureaucracy. Over the years, it leads to an organization that is relatively independent and yet is undesirably fragmented. The independence of the bureaucracy results from an apparent lack of cohesiveness within the political system (in parliamentary systems, cohesiveness is automatic). The fragmentation of the bureaucracy arises from the high level of professionalism within its own ranks.

Overall, the political system in the United States makes it largely impossible for the environmental bureaucracy to be anything other than regulatory. Moreover, the political arrangements require that its regulatory powers be closely scrutinized. A fear of too much administrative discretion is shared by all parties concerned—the executive branch, the legislature, the judiciary, and the public. They also dread bureaucratic professionalism, for such is again a source of independence and authority. Binding the environmental bureaucracy with hammer clauses and scientific norms is a sign of mistrust as well as apprehension.

Thus, our study shows that a different context exists for each of the three bureaucracies: the Indian functions in a social setting, the Hong Kong in a global setting, and the American in a political setting. Their unique settings are hardly matters of choice: on the contrary, the three systems are captives of their history, culture, and forced priorities. While the three bureaucracies face the same monumental task—that of making their economic growth environmentally-friendly—they each must rely on different mechanisms to alter the status quo. In India, the primary need is to develop a harmonious relationship between the social and the political system. This means a far more sweeping agenda for change than has been identified so far. In Hong Kong, the factors are global and economic. The strategy there must be to strengthen the hands of the supportive bureaucracy rather than introduce a regulatory bureaucracy, because regulations are self-defeating for the territory. In the United States, the factors are political, and efforts must be made to find a harmonious political setting for the environmental bureaucracy.

From a general point of view, this study suggests that the positing of bureaucracy as a dependent variable is useful. Since bureaucracy does not exist in a vacuum, the space around it must be as carefully examined as the bureaucracy itself. A global and comparative approach will help us build new generalizations and, at the same time, will help us better understand our own problems and settings.

REFERENCES

Agarwal, Anil and Narain, Sunita, *The State of India's Environment, 1984–85: The Second Citizens' Report*, Centre for Science and Environment, New Delhi, 1985.

Barrett, Brendan F. D. and Therivel, Riki, *Environmental Policy and Impact Assessment in Japan*, Routledge, London, 1991.

Bidwell, R., 15 Years of Progress: Environmental Institution Building in Hong Kong, in *Pollution in the Urban Environment* (M. W. H. Chan et al., eds.), POLNET, Hong Kong, 1988.

Brickman, R., Jasanoff, S., and Ilgen, T., *Controlling Chemicals: The Politics of Regulation in Europe and the United States*, Cornell, Ithaca, New York, 1985.

Caldwell, Lynton K., *In Defense of the Earth: International Protection of the Biosphere*, Indiana University Press, Bloomington, 1972.

Clarke, Jeanne Nienaber and McCool, Daniel, *Staking out the Terrain: Power Differentials Among Natural Resource Management Agencies*, State University of New York Press, Albany, 1985.

Downey, M. J., Law and Control of Hong Kong Environment, *Hong Kong Engineer 15*:17–23, 1987.

Dwivedi, O. P. and Jain, R. B., *India's Administrative State*, Gitanjali, New Delhi, 1985.

Dwivedi, O. P. and Tiwari, B. N., *Environmental Crisis and Hinduism*, Gitanjali, New Delhi, 1987.

Enloe, Cynthia, *The Politics of Pollution in a Comparative Perspective: Ecology and Power in Four Nations*, David McKay, New York, 1975.

Fernandes, Walter and Kulkarni, Sharad, *A New Forest Policy: People's Rights and Environmental Needs*, Indian Social Institute, New Delhi, 1983.

Garcia-Zamor, Jean-Claude and Khator, Renu, eds., *Public Administration in the Global Village*, Praeger, Westport, Conn., 1994.

Goodman, David and Redclift, Michael, eds., *Environment and Development in Latin America: The Politics of Sustainability*, Manchester University Press, Manchester, England, 1991.

Guimaraes, Roberto P., *The Ecopolitics of Development in the Third World: Politics and Environment in Brazil*, Lynne Reinner, Boulder, Colo., 1991.

Harris, Peter, *Hong Kong: A Study in Bureaucracy and Politics*, MacMillan, Hong Kong, 1988.

HKPC, *Annual Report*, Hong Kong Productivity Council, Hong Kong, 1989.

Horowitz, D. L., Is There a Third World Policy Process? *Policy Sciences, 22*:197–212 (1989).

Jain, R. B., Inter-Relationships Between Sociopolitical Structure and Public Administration in India, in *Administrations and Industrial Development* (Hartmut Elsenhans and Harald Fuhr, eds.), National Book Organization, New Delhi, 1991.

Jones, Charles O., *Clean Air: The Policies and Politics of Pollution Control*, University of Pittsburgh Press, Pittsburgh, Penn., 1975.

Kamieniecki, S. and Sanasarian, E., Conducting Comparative Research on Environmental Policy, *Natural Resources Journal, 30*:321–329 (1990).

Kraft, Michael and Vig, Norman J., Environmental Policy from the Seventies to the Nineties: Continuity and Change, in *Environmental Policy in the 1990s* (Norman J. Vig and Michael E. Kraft, eds.), Congressional Quarterly, Washington, D.C., 1990.

Kelley, D. K. Stunkel and Wescott, R., *The Economic Superpowers and the Environment: The United States, the Soviet Union and Japan*, W. H. Freeman, San Francisco, 1976.

Kelman, S., *Regulating America, Regulating Sweden: A Comparative Study of Occupational Safety and Health Policy*, MIT Press, Cambridge, Mass., 1981.

Khator, Renu, *Forests: The People and the Government*, National Book Organization, New Delhi, 1989.

Khator, Renu, Bureaucracy, Environmentalism, and Industrial Policy in Hong Kong, in *Bureaucracy in the Third World* (H. K. Asmerom, H. Hoppe, and R. B. Jain, eds.), Free Press, Netherlands, 1990.

Khator, Renu, *Environment, Development, and Politics in India*, University Press of America, Lanham, Md., 1991.

Khator, Renu, State Autonomy and Environmental Challenge in India, *The Political Chronicle* November–December, 1992.

Khator, Renu, Ng, Kathleen, and Chan, Hon S., Environmental Management and Street-Level Regulators: A Cultural Trap? *Public Administration and Development, 12*:387–397 (1992).

Knoepfel, P., et al., Comparing Environmental Policies: Different Styles, Similar Content, in *Comparative Policy Research: Learning from Experience* (M. Dierkes, H. Weiler, and A. Berthoin, eds.), St. Martin Press, New York, 1987.

Lalvani, G. H., Law and Pollution Control, in *India's Environment: Crises and Responses* (J. Bandopadhyay et al., eds.), Natraj, Dehradun, 1985.

Lam, K. C., Consultative Mechanisms for Environmental Legislation in Hong Kong, *Green Productivity*, December:14–23 (1987).

Lehman, Howard, The Political Economy of Comparative Environmental Policy, *Policy Studies Journal, 20*:719–732 (1992).

Lester, James P., *Environmental Politics and Policy*, Duke University Press, Durham, N.C., 1989.

Lundqvist, Lennart J., *The Hare and Tortoise: Clean Air Policies in the United States and Sweden*, University of Michigan Press, Ann Arbor, 1980.

Puri, K. K., Environment Pollution: Policies and Programmes, in *Environment Management in India* (R. K. Sapru, ed.), Ashish, New Delhi, 1987.

Babe, Barry, *Fragmentation and Integration in State Environmental Management*, The Conservation Foundation, Washington, D.C., 1986.

Rabushka, Alvin, *Value for Money: The Hong Kong Budgetary Process*, Hoover Institution Press, Stanford, Calif., 1976.

Reich, Michael R., Mobilizing for Environmental Policy in Italy and Japan, *Comparative Politics, 16*: 379–402 (1984).

Reich, Michael R. and Bowonder, B., Environmental Policy in India: Strategies for Better Implementation, *Policy Studies Journal, 20*:643–661 (1992).

Riggs, Fred W., Bureaucracy: A Profound Puzzle for Presidentialism, in *Handbook on Bureaucracy* (Ali Farazmand, ed.), Marcel Dekker, New York, 1994.

Rosenbaum, Walter A., The Bureaucracy and Environmental Policy, in *Environmental Politics and Policy* (James P. Lester, ed.), Duke University Press, Durham, North Carolina, 1989.

Siegel, R. and Weinberg, L., *Comparing Public Policies: United States, Soviet Union, Europe*, Dorsey, Homewood, Ill., 1977.

Solesbury, S., Issues and Innovations in Environmental Policy in Britain, West Germany, and California, *Policy Analysis, 2*:1–38 (1976).

Varandani, Gursharan, Judicial Approach to Environmental Pollution, in *Environmental Management in India* (R. K. Sapru, ed.), Ashish, New Delhi, 1987.

Vogel, David, *National Styles of Regulation: Environmental Policy in Great Britain and the United States*, Cornell University Press, Ithaca, N.Y., 1986.

12
Bureaucracy and Modernization

Harry M. Johnson
University of Illinois at Urbana-Champaign, Urbana, Illinois

Although Max Weber regarded bureaucracy as more effective for certain tasks than earlier forms of organization and provided a classical "ideal type" description of it (1968, vol. III, pp. 956–1005), he is one of the originators of negative stereotypes about "bureaucracy" and the modern world in general. His extremely negative and pessimistic view (1930, pp. 180–183) has been taken as gospel by many other critics. Bureaucracy in the modern world is said to have become dull and inappropriately routinized. Closely related is the thesis that modern bureaucracy has stifled if not actually killed individuality and creativity. The distortion that modern organizations have created human robots and crushed out individualism was taken up in a recent "Point of View" essay in *The Chronicle of Higher Education.* In "The Persistence of Individualism" (1993), Michael McGerr, a professor of history at Indiana University, is skeptical. He ends his one-page op-ed piece as follows: "Our nation may well be exceptional not for the power of organization, but for the persisting sense of human agency. We need to explain why."

No author that I know of provides a better answer to Mr. McGerr's questions than Talcott Parsons (1902–1979), known mainly as a sociologist. This chapter is little more than a secondary work on Parsons. All I can claim for myself is that my interpretations of his theory have not been obvious to most of his critics and that I have interwoven ideas from many works by Parsons in order to bring out how modern formal organizations are interdependent with other important phenomena in modern societies. No one of Parsons's papers on bureaucracy does this.

"Modern" societies have qualitative characteristics different from those of "traditionalist" societies. All societies in all evolutionary stages have tradition and traditional aspects, structural and processual. But modern societies, as compared with traditionalist, are not to the same extent "stuck" in tradition.

Parsons saw grounds for cautious hope in the "struggle" now objectively going on between an increasingly complex and difficult world, on the one hand, and our far greater functional capacity, at present as compared with the past, to cope with complex problems, in both cognitive and moral respects. Of course, no theory of progress can make overall judgments of inferiority/superiority; many individuals understandably prefer to live in a relatively "backward" social environment. A scientific theory of sociocultural evolutionary progress must have relevant criteria that in principle can be objectively applied in the relevant scientific community. As far as Parsons's theory is concerned, I do not think that enough potentially qualified people have yet made a serious attempt to understand it. My impression is that many social scientists have rejected it on the basis of secondhand errors.

Two errors about Parsons should be forestalled, if possible, from the outset. First, his "functional" theory does not imply "perfect" internal ordering, integration, or solidarity in social systems. Parsons *was* interested in the question of what we might mean by a perfectly integrated action system, but (following in particular Freud and Durkheim as models here) he regarded an integrated action system as a theoretical limiting case, heuristically useful for functional analysis of the more or less malintegrated cases we meet with in actuality—that is, cases involving various sources, kinds, and rates of deviant behavior, orientational confusion (anomie), alienation, and more or less debilitating conflict (as well as the quite-to-be-expected incomplete consensus to be found in all societies).

The second error or set of errors would be to assume that Parsons's refusal to be totally pessimistic about the prospects for "modernity" in the late twentieth century and beyond means that he was insensitive to the terrible costs and dangers involved in modernization. Parsons was acutely aware of tragedy in human life and regarded as virtually inevitable for some time to come a great deal of agonizing suffering. He regarded the distant future of the human species, however, as uncertain and impossible to predict. He was also aware of strong ideological tendencies to romanticize the past. The masses of people until quite recently, even in relatively advanced societies, have been slaves, serfs, or peasants, illiterate, living short lives in hovels without conveniences such as fresh running water, electricity, and public sanitation.

Parsons describes and analyzes more explicitly than most people do what we vaguely mean when we speak of relatively "advanced" societies as compared with "underdeveloped" or "developing" ones. The latter have varying approximations to modernity in some respects, while the relatively advanced societies on the whole exhibit closer approximations.

Some of the developing societies have so far done little more than acquire some of the more superficial trappings of modernity, such as highly destructive weapons, while still clinging to such outmoded features of the traditionalist past as largely ascriptive social structures, as in Somalia; the attempt to make relatively specific religiously based law prescriptive for the society as a whole, though the society may have several religious groups and varying degrees of "secularized" belief/unbelief/disbelief within it; and governments that refuse to permit more than one political "party" while pretending to command virtually total political support.

"Modern" social structure is indeed relatively recent in important respects, is difficult to establish, and in no society is fully established and universally supported. Further, it is possible for any society to regress under various circumstances.

(Whenever possible I shall refer to four of Parsons's collections: 1967, 1969, 1977, 1978. The separate chapters were originally published at different dates. It is better to use the collections, however, because Parsons gives valuable additional introductions to each collection and to parts. For the best overall view of Parsons's work, see 1977 and 1978. Parsons stretches the mind with his kind of analytical theory. A reader previously unacquainted with it may have to read this brief article more than once.)

According to Parsons, there is no known society that does not have at least one religion, one language, one kinship system, and a rather impressive amount of technology. These and possibly a few other "true universals" are starting points for evolutionary development.

An important conception is what Parsons calls "evolutionary universals" (1967, chapter 15). These are cultural and social innovations so important for further development and for the functional "potential" of societies that they have been "hit upon" and institutionalized several times and in quite different, largely independent traditions: but they are not strictly universal even now. There are six, in temporal order in three pairs, as follows: social stratification of kinship lineages (a "breakthrough" at first but profoundly transformed later) and cultural legitimation of political authority (inherently hierarchical), bureaucratic organization and the development of money and markets, and generalized norms (law) and democratic associations.[1]

One of the two criteria for sociocultural evolutionary advance is, in Parsons's term, "enhanced adaptive capacity," for which we can read "enhanced *functional* capacity"—that is, *potential* ability to handle or cope with any one or any combination of the types of functional problem with which all societies must cope. Evolutionary change is judged in part with reference to a complete list of four abstractly stated invariant types of problem, which make meaningful comparison possible—comparison between societies of the past and societies of the present and between societies in the same period of time.

The second criterion of evolutionary advance is actually implied in the first: the change must be institutionalized to some extent in some actual society. This criterion is implied in the first because we must be able to compare societies with the change with those without it. To put it another way, progress is not merely a matter of speculative arguments: there must be evidence that steps of change can actually work and work better than alternatives in the same field. Thus the ultimate test, for example, between state-owned and controlled "economic" enterprises and "privately" owned enterprises is comparison of actual performance. Such comparison is inherently complex, however, and takes time. Hence the "case" for the view that such and such a structural arrangement is on the whole better than another can be strengthened by plausible arguments explaining why the structural arrangement might well work better. Parsons presents empirical evidence mixed with analysis.

(For brief discussions by Parsons of scientifically fundamental analogies between biological systems and action systems, on the one hand, and between the biological sciences and the sciences of action, on the other, see Parsons 1977, chapters 4, 5, 11. For deeper discussion of action evolution and many references to empirical studies, see Parsons, 1966; 1971; 1977, chapter 11; and V. Lidz and Parsons, 1972.)

Parsons divides evolutionary history (of action systems) into three broad stages, the rationale for which I will not go into here. The third or modern stage, in a loose sense, began when universalistic law began to emerge in several parts of the world, to a great extent independently. But modernity began "in earnest," so to speak, when a society (or a large part of it) institutionalized a disciplined, activist "this-worldly" orientation under the legitimation of "supernatural" religion. In other words, Parsons took over, developed, and subtly modified Max Weber's Protestant-ethic thesis, without Weber's ambivalence toward modernity if not total pessimism about it. "This-worldly activism" refers to the Calvinists' commitment to contribute toward "building the Kingdom of God *on earth*." The expression goes back to the "Lord's Prayer" in the New Testament. Jesus is said to have instructed his disciples to pray to God the Father as follows (in part): "Thy Kingdom come [we pray that it may come], thy will be done [we should do God's will], on earth as it is in Heaven." This prayer implies, of course, that human societies are imperfect and need to be improved. The Roman Catholic emphasis, however, had been on the salvation of individual souls, their entering into Heaven after their life and death in this world. An important part of the plan of salvation was administration of sacraments to the laity of ordained priests (a mode of attaining salvation that Weber refers to as a form of "magic"—certainly an extension of that term as it is used in anthropology). The word "ascetic" in "ascetic Protestantism" means self-disciplined, strict, as opposed to characterized by repeated cycles of self-indulgent "sinning" followed by repentance. Characteristically, however, Parsons emphasizes that through the centuries the Roman Catholic Church in effect had prepared for the individual responsibility emphasized in the Reformation, by strongly emphasizing morality as well as trust in the sacraments. Furthermore, the early Christian Church had of course taken over the emphasis on morality from Judaism.

We often forget massive facts. Parsons points out that the Roman Catholic Church in the Middle Ages was a true bureaucracy in a time when the general social structure had become so strongly based on ascription that there was a decline from social models provided by the Roman Empire. The Church was able to have a bureaucratic structure of offices because of the celibacy of the clergy. Members of the clergy could not have legal heirs to inherit their offices. Moreover, Parsons also points out that the Church preserved the system of Roman law; and there is a direct filiation between the legal system of the Church and the civil codes of many European countries.

It should be emphasized that, with or without the so-called magical sacraments, there is, *today*, little or no difference between Protestants and Catholics with regard to this-worldly activism (see Tiryakian, 1975). Several Popes have engaged in it. Moreover, as Parsons points out, in the eighteenth-century Enlightenment, Jews were emancipated from the ghettoes of Northern Europe and at the same time emancipated from the rather extreme traditionalistic Orthodoxy that informed those ghettoes. From then on, as everyone knows, Jews have made outstanding contributions in the "modern" sense. Ironically, their emphasis on literacy and learning for all men and women, which had been devoted to understanding and debating the subtleties of the complex traditionalistic Law, was now turned to advantage in all the "modern" pursuits, as modern universalism slowly and gradually put anti-Semitism in question and opened up new opportunities for emancipated Jews. Anti-Semitism still exists but in greatly reduced forms, and the drastic and terrible period of the Nazi movement was a reaction against modernity, not an aspect of it, except of course in the sense that failure to adjust smoothly to modernization could not occur, logically, without the prior occurrence of modernization (see Parsons, 1969, chapters 3–6; Gerhardt, 1993).

A somewhat extended quotation from Parsons (omitting four footnotes) will serve to illustrate the systematic incisiveness and "realism" of his functional and evolutionary analysis (1967, chapter 15, pp. 517–518, dealing with the sixth evolutionary "universal"):

> Especially, though not exclusively, in national territorial states, the stable democratic association is notoriously difficult to institutionalize. Above all this seems to be a function of the difficulty in motivating holders of immediately effective power to relinquish their opportunities voluntarily despite the seriousness of the interest at stake—relinquishment of control of governmental machinery after electoral defeat being the most striking problem. The system is also open to other serious difficulties, most notably corruption and "populist" irresponsibility, as well as *de facto* dictatorship. Furthermore, such difficulties are by no means absent in private associations, as witness the rarity of effective electoral systems in large trade unions.
>
> The basic argument for considering democratic association a universal, despite such problems, is that, the larger and more complex a society becomes, the more important is

> effective political organization, not only in its administrative capacity, but also, and not least, in its support of a universalistic legal order. Political effectiveness includes both the scale and operative flexibility of the organization of power. Power, however, precisely as a generalized societal medium, depends overwhelmingly on a consensual element, i.e., the ordered institutionalization and exercise of influence, linking the power system to the higher-order societal consensus at the value level.

The vote, says Parsons, is a unit of power (since it must be counted and, along with the other votes in the aggregate, is binding); and equality of the franchise is functionally important for linking up the power and effectiveness of formal organizations, including of course bureaucracies, with societal solidarity, through equal access to occupational employment on the basis of universalistic standards.

The Calvinist movement was especially significant because it crystallized and integrated all six "universals" "in earnest," as I have put it. The six evolutionary "universals," you will remember, are stratification, cultural legitimation of authority, bureaucracy, money and markets, universalistic law, and democratic associations. The Calvinist movement enhanced all six.

The Calvinist unplanned "breakthrough" to ascetic this–worldly activism was not an evolutionary universal but a "unique" advance because other promising starts of this kind had not been adequately institutionalized. For instance, Islam made a promising beginning and did contribute to modernity with such cultural achievements as the Arabic numerals, including the zero, and contributed to the Renaissance in the West by hiring Jewish and Christian scholars to translate and thus recover many of the literary treasures of Greece and Rome. (For a brilliant essay, Weberian-Parsonsian in inspiration, tentatively accounting for the Islamic lapse into traditionalism, see Bellah, 1970, chapter 8; see also occasional remarks in Parsons, 1937, the section on Weber; Parsons, 1978, chapter 9.)

On the functional superiority of bureaucratic organization, Parsons, as usual, is very much to the point:

> The basis on which I classify bureaucracy as an evolutionary universal is very simple. As Weber said, it is the most effective large-scale administrative organization that man has invented, and there is no direct substitute for it. Where capacity to carry out large-scale organized operations is important, e.g., military operations with mass forces, water control, tax administration, policing of large and heterogeneous populations, and productive enterprise requiring large capital investment and much manpower, the unit that commands effective bureaucratic organization is inherently superior to the one that does not. It is by no means the only structural factor in the adaptive capacity of social systems, but no one can deny that it is an important one. Above all, it is built on further specifications ensuing from the broad emancipation from ascription that stratification and specialized legitimation make possible. (1967, chapter 15, p. 507)

Stratification of kinship lines permitted innovations by the lines with most prestige, but of course restricted access to higher positions by all those, the great majority, who were not in the "right" line. Today, of course, even large-scale business firms that were formerly ruled at the top by heirs of successive generations are usually run by people with no known kinship descent from the founders.

Officials in some earlier bureaucracies were often slaves. As Parsons points out, however, this practice was not an example of open access to high positions; as members of the emperor's household, high officials who were also his slaves represented him and shared in the prestige of his household. They were not exactly ascribed to their positions, but neither were they appointed from the population at large. A related fundamental point is that service in a modern formal organization is voluntary. In the United States this is true even of military service, though at "need" the government could of course resume conscription.

Among the most important differences between traditionalistic formal organizations and modern ones are the vastly greater importance and variety of professional roles in the modern organizations. "Professions" should not be taken as just any occupations. Professional roles require a great deal of formal specialized training and commitment to relatively high moral standards in carrying out their fiduciary responsibilities.

The increased professionalization of roles in modern formal organizations goes along with a decrease in the use of magic. It is rare indeed to hear about executives who consult astrologers even in their personal lives, but in their official activities they are certainly expected to base their decisions, as far as possible, on scientific and derived technological knowledge, on controlled statistical surveys, and on other more or less rational procedures.

Another big change is the greatly reduced importance of the "labor" role, in the sense of occupational positions requiring relatively little specialized training. This reduced importance of the labor role is not simply the other side of professionalization. It is also due to automation and, in relatively advanced modern societies, to the shifting of low-paying jobs to "developing" countries. Everyone by now is familiar with the growing demand in the United States not only for improved education but for greater equalization of access to it. (The best single paper on the diversity of modern formal organizations, and its rationale, is Parsons, 1968, "Le Breton.")

With regard to the ideological distortions of "bureaucracy" as excessively routinized and as crushing individuality and creativity, we should note, in passing, that both automation and professionalization have exactly the opposite tendencies. Even in modern armies (the proverbial site of stereotypical bureaucracy) practically every participant must be able to cope with a great deal of discretion, in the sense of independent judgment in carrying out his or her duties.

Traditionalist bureaucracies, with ascribed heads, have been an obstacle to the development of money and relatively open and impersonal markets because hereditary heads are afraid to relinquish tight control over productive enterprises. Here again it may be suggested that the Protestant ethic helped to break down this barrier by emphasizing the need to improve the system and the belief in the essential equality and dignity of all individuals. Parsons was convinced that the way to the Industrial Revolution was prepared by the Reformation. (For an extremely subtle but quite cogent functional analysis of the importance of money and markets, see Parsons 1967, chapter 15, pp. 507–510. This essay is perhaps the most important single work referred to in this chapter because of its compact functional defense of the social institutions of a "modern" society. Reading of it, however, is greatly facilitated if one has some previous knowledge of the four-function schema and the generalized symbolic media, such as I attempt to provide.)

On the importance of generalized universalistic law and the seventeenth-century "break-through" Parsons says, in part:

> Although it is very difficult to pin down just what the crucial components are, how they are interrelated, and how they develop, one can identify the development of the general legal system as a crucial aspect of societal evolution. A general legal system is an integrated system of universalistic norms, applicable to the society as a whole rather than to a few functional or segmental sectors, highly generalized in terms of principles and standards, and relatively independent of both the religious agencies that legitimize the normative order of the society and vested interest groups in the operative sector,

> particularly in government. . . . Although many of the elements of such a general normative order appeared in quite highly developed form in earlier societies, in my view their crystallization into a coherent system represents a new step, which more than the industrial revolution itself, ushered in the *modern* era of social evolution. (1967, chapter 15, pp. 510–511, emphasis in original)

Modern formal organizations of all types are controlled by two or three or even more levels of formal law. One level, of course, consists of the internal rules of the organization as a collective "unit" in its "home" society and in any foreign societies in which it may have branches. Although these organizational units include many we call "private" organizations, actually they are all "public" in the functionally important sense that their internal legal systems must be consistent with the law of the "state" (in the United States, with federal law and "state" law, both). Further, in the United States or Canada or any other modern society with two or more levels of public law, these levels "control" (regulate) the internal-organizational level. The enforcement agencies at the public levels will at need enforce the internal rules of any organization, provided that these internal rules are indeed consistent with the public law. This means, in effect, that the internal rules become "public" also.

But a so-called private formal organization is indeed private in the important sense that its internal policy and operating decisions with regard to its subcollectivity goals are made by its own executives and staff. The specific content of these decisions is not determined by public officials.

All these levels, from constitutional law all the way down to the level of "internal" rules, in modern societies more and more closely approximate the ideal of attainable universalism (equal treatment under the law); however, the rich still have an advantage in that they can afford to pay highly skilled, specialized lawyers, rather than rely on the run of the mill.

In the earlier period, Calvinism was notoriously oppressive, but Parsons emphasizes that liberalization took place within the Calvinist tradition itself—that is, did not await development elsewhere which could then be taken over. Two of the most fundamental aspects of modernity, namely, the institutionalization of a more this-worldly and more highly generalized and diversified legal system and the institutionalization of scientific research, occurred or began even before the gradual liberalization of Calvinism. (The well-known persecution of Galileo indicates, of course, that scientific research was not institutionalized in his day. On the developments in science and technology in seventeenth-century England, see Merton, 1970; and on the Puritan influence on law, see Little, 1969.)

In any case, what is sometimes called the rule of law, the most important foundation of a "modern" society, can hardly be "complete" or fully realized, as a principle and a basic factor in practice, without the "separations" of law from direct religious morality, of executive authority from religious ascription, and of the law itself from executive powers. These three "separations" are examples of what Parsons called differentiation, one of the four fundamental aspects or overlapping phases of evolutionary process. The four evolutionary processes are called, in Parsons's technical terms, value generalization, integration or inclusion, differentiation, and adaptive upgrading. This series of somewhat overlapping processes is an example of Parsons's famous four-function schema, and the order of terms in the series is significant as a hierarchy of control and conditioning.

Among the changes Parsons made in Weber's account of the Reformation was to emphasize the "deposit" or "residue," so to speak, that stern, dogmatic Calvinism left behind it in the later religious stage of what Parsons calls "unbelief." He distinguishes between *unbelief* and *disbelief.*

Disbelief is what a modern person might feel about ancient Aztec religion, with its ritual sacrifices of human beings, although of course many modern scholars have been interested in analyzing Aztec beliefs and practices for their internal coherence and their functions and dysfunctions for Aztec society. *Unbelief is far from affective indifference.* Many people who go to church or synagogue or whatever, today, do not believe "literally" in the Incarnation and the Resurrection (to take Christian examples), but that does not mean that such religious symbolism and its implications no longer have any resonance. Parsons is not the only commentator to point out the important difference, sometimes, between "belief that" and "belief in." You may not believe that God in a burning bush appeared to Moses, but you may still believe in some of the Ten Commandments. (On belief, etc., see Parsons, 1979, chapters 11, 13, 15.) The deposit these churchgoers still have faith in is one of "sacred" values—in the Christian case of interest here, the value of individual activism in making a "better" society, the sacredness of the individual, the inalienable responsibility of the individual for his or her own moral decisions, the doctrine that "love thy neighbor" summarizes the Jewish Law and the Prophets (where "neighbors" now include, in principle, all human beings everywhere). Thus, "Christians" today may or may not believe in an afterlife in Heaven, but even if they do, they are very much interested in life in this world before death and take it for granted that social structure (whatever they may call it) can and certainly should be improved. They may also be interested in money, preferably a large amount, but that does not necessarily mean that they are interested in money alone.

Durkheim, of course, brilliantly analyzed the positive functional significance of religious beliefs and rituals for the periodic renewal of societal solidarity (1954). In a memorable passage he asks rhetorically whether the holidays and rituals of the French revolutionaries differed in any essential respect from the ritual dances and impersonations of his Australian aborigines. Of course, there are evolutionary differences, but Durkheim was making an important point and was anticipating the concept of civil religion. The by now "classical" reference, however, for the civil religion of the United States at least, is Robert Bellah's brilliant analysis (1970, chapter 9). The importance of this, it seems to me, is that it is possible for a modern society to have "the best of both worlds." That is to say, a modern society can have both religious heterogeneity and freedom, on the one hand, and the unifying, "effervescent" symbolism of "sacred" ceremonies on the other. This is possible because the civil religion does not depend directly on any one of the potentially divisive heterogeneous religions. Both "fundamentalists" and highly secularized "unbelievers" can participate. Besides participating in the national holidays of the American civil religion, I have had the good fortune to participate more than once in the solemn yet festive ceremonies of the First of August toward nightfall in Switzerland, a special example in the West of a religiously, ethnically, and linguistically heterogeneous society indeed. Even as a foreign visitor, I have been deeply moved by the public reading of the compact of the original Confederation (1292), the lanterns, the unpretentious speeches, the communal meals outdoors, the citizens seated at long wooden tables, and the common view, from a mountain slope, of many other bonfires lighting up the same rituals in many other local communities.

The term "secularization" has quite diverse meanings, of which the following are among the most important:

1. Paul and the other early Christian missionaries to the Roman "pagan" world were too weak to challenge the Roman god-emperor directly, and they gave unto Caesar what was Caesar's, but in rejecting the sacredness of the Emperor and of the social order of the pagan Roman Empire, they were secularizing the social structure of "this world" (of their time, of course).
2. When the much later Calvinists set out to "build the Kingdom of God on earth," they were secularizing the Gospel itself by putting a new emphasis on transforming the social structure

of this world in accordance with God's will as they saw it, while not, of course, giving up their hope of paradise and resurrection.
3. The (much later) separation of church and state was a secularization of the state.
4. When people give up "supernatural" religion, or even supplement it with such doctrinal systems as Stoicism, Epicureanism, or "godless" Communism, they are following, at least in part, secular faiths.

(On the historical background of the Reformation in sociological terms, and on secularization, see Parsons, 1967, chapter 12; 1978, parts III and IV. For excellent defenses of Weber against the many attacks on his Protestant-ethic thesis, see Eisenstadt, 1968, pp. ix–lvi; Nelson, 1973; Little, 1969. Parsons, 1937, argues that Weber's series of studies on the religions of India, China, ancient Israel, and Christianity was in effect the rough equivalent of a controlled experiment.)

Instead of thinking vaguely about functional needs, exigencies, conditions for survival, or problems (take your pick of terms), or attempting to make a detailed list of specific functional needs (a hopeless task), Parsons developed a logical and exhaustive classification. It was a fundamental move, beautifully simple. This scheme is known as the *LIGA paradigm*, after the initial letters of the four general types of function: *L* for Latent pattern-maintenance and tension-management, *I* for Integration, *G* for Goal attainment, and *A* for Adaptation (see Parsons, 1961, vol. I, pp. 30–79). This functional scheme applies to subsystems of larger systems, to structure, to process, and to what Parsons came to call generalized symbolic media, to which I turn now.

In societies or other social systems a great many action decisions implicitly make use of one or more of four ways in which it is possible for one "unit" to seek to guide, control, or make specific the action decisions of others with whom he, she, or it is interacting. A social "unit" in the relevant sense may be an individual in his or her capacity as a role "occupant" or may be a collective unit—a subcollectivity such as a formal organization, which acts through individuals whose particular roles in the subcollectivity are authorized to represent in certain ways the subcollectivity as a whole.

The "four ways" are cross-classified according to *channel-type* and *sanction-type*. There are two channels, one situational and one intentional. Using a situational channel, an actor offers or threatens to change the situation of the other. Using the intentional channel, the actor tries to direct the other's motivation without offering or threatening to change the other's situation. Each channel has a positive and a negative possibility. Thus, through cross-classification we arrive at "four ways" or four *generalized symbolic media* by which an actor may hope to affect another's action decisions.

The four media symbolize or stand for four social values, which in turn are implemented (to varying extents) by the four functional subsystems of social systems, beginning with societies. These media, values, and functional subsystems together constitute one complex application of the famous four-function scheme, which can be applied to all types of action system, including, for instance, personalities.

(For a more detailed treatment of the complexities of social generalized symbolic media, see Parsons, 1967, chapter 9; 1969, part IV.)

I am now going to approach the American societal value system indirectly through a bit more attention to the generalized symbolic media of social systems. It should be understood that the American societal value system is a variant of modern societal value systems.

Societal values are normative conceptions of what a society should be, as far as its members have been able to formulate (largely implicitly or latently) such a grand conception.

The four generalized symbolic media in the social system symbolize, respectively, from the "top" down, that is, from the broadest in scope to the most specific, the four social values corresponding to the four functional requirements, exigencies, or "needs" of social systems, as follows: value commitments (L) stand for integrity, the value of the *pattern maintenance* subsystem (or, in the social-system case, the fiduciary system); influence (I) stands for solidarity, the value of the *integrative* subsystem of social systems, which is called the societal community; power (G) stands for collective effectiveness, the value of the *goal attainment* subsystem of social systems, which is called the polity; and money (A) stands for utility, the value of the *adaptation* subsystem of social systems, called the economy.

It should be obvious that these generalized symbolic media can be abused. In all social systems, they are "controlled" to some extent by institutionalized normative patterns, which Parsons, following some but not all usage, calls social institutions. These are normative patterns, not organizations, although Parsons does occasionally use the term "institution" (as perhaps most people do) to mean a social organization—the usual meaning in such phrases as "institutions of higher learning," "cultural institutions." In Parsons's writing, the context will enable the reader to decide which usage is meant, provided he or she is aware of Parsons's basic usage, as in "the institution of the family," "the institution of authority," "the institution of contract." Social values such as utility, collective effectiveness, solidarity, and integrity are too broad, have too little specificity, to be adequate guides to conduct. Societies must have more specific patterns defining, for instance, fraud, undue influence, abuse of power, property rights, which contracts will be valid and which not in a court of law. It should almost go without saying that the degree and extent of institutionalization of such patterns vary widely from one society to another, as does the complexity or elaboration of custom and law with regard to any one area such as authority or contract or freedom of the "press" (meaning essentially all "mass media" such as newspapers, radio, television, and movies).

Social values, in modern societies especially, are often stated pretty explicitly, but, as Parsons points out, in earlier evolutionary stages the two levels of values and norms or social institutions are more likely to be "fused" rather than "differentiated," so that the value system must be inferred, much as an anthropologist "reconstructs" the culture and social organization of some remote tribe he or she is studying by using what he hears from the members of the society as evidence. They are competent informants in the same sense that native speakers of a language are "competent" speakers. This "fusion" in traditionalist societies contributes to their being stuck in tradition.

Formal organizations are at one level of social structure. As Parsons conceives of normative social structure as a whole, it has four levels—in order of decreasing generality and increasing specificity of normative control: societal values and their specifications; social institutions; subcollectivity structure, including the rules of specific formal organizations and the more or less taken-for-granted, sometimes routine, mutual expectations that prevail in particular households; and, finally, the structure of social role-types that are found in many specific subcollectivities—for example, corporation chief executive officer, accountant, member of a maintenance crew.

Parsons's term "cybernetic hierarchy of control and conditioning" is appropriate, in part, because the normative order constitutes a series of levels of control, as in a cybernetic system designed by an engineer. As in such information-processing systems, so in human action systems there are also feedback and more or less successful correction of errors and deliberate departure from the controlling codes (1977, chapter 8). Any LIGA series—of subsystems, structural elements, processes, or media—constitutes a cybernetic hierarchy of control and conditioning. A good illustration is the series of levels and components of normative social structure: social values, social norms or institutions, the structure of subcollectivities, and the structure of social roles. The two higher or controlling levels of function, L and I, or Latent pattern maintenance and Integration, give direction or guidance to the two lower levels, G and A, or Goal attainment and Adaptation. The higher levels control but do not determine; actors making decisions in their varying specific situations must interpret for themselves how the guidelines apply. In complex societies, lawyers are often called upon, of course, to help in this process; and lawyers represent both the interests of their clients and the integrity of the legal system; they mediate through interpretation of the law and through persuasion and influence, as well as by strategy and tactics in behalf of the client.

Actually all the levels are both controlling and conditioning, but the higher levels do control the lower levels. From another perspective, all the levels are conditions that must be fulfilled to "solve" the problem of order in social systems. All hierarchies of control and conditioning in the theory of action are in terms of declining scope and increasing specificity, not in terms of functional importance. In the LIGA series of levels and components of normative social structure, social roles are at the more conditional end, in the A position, yet everything that gets done in any social system is ultimately done by individuals-in-roles. At the same time, in the limiting case of integration, every role includes in its normative content "components" from the controlling levels above it. Hence we speak of levels and components of normative social structure. Where all elements in a series are necessary for certain outcomes (here, value implementation and fulfillment of functional requirements, exigencies, or "needs"), then it would make no sense to say that any one of the elements is generally more important than any other. The four elements in this case, as in others in action systems, are important in different ways, make different but interdependent functional contributions. Since action systems, like any other type of empirical system, can fail or give out, it is of course just as important, in a functional analysis, to note the lack or inadequate supply of any type of contribution as to note evidence of presence and relative adequacy.

Despite the fact that formal organizations are at the third level in the LIGA hierarchy of control and conditioning, we must also reckon with the fact, as Parsons notes, that some formal organizations are much more important than others. This is obvious for certain business firms in a given industry, or for certain universities in the academic world.

We could even arrange formal organizations themselves in a rough LIGA hierarchy. No one "church" is at the top, but, in the aggregate, organized religious groups, as guardians of values social and personal, are clearly in the L position. The traditional "three branches" of government—judicial, legislative, and executive—all have formal organizations, of course. In Parsonsian terms, the Supreme Court and the lower courts are partly L, concerned with the integrity of the law; partly I, in that—in the Supreme Court, for instance—the members try to persuade one another toward a consensus; and partly G, in that their decisions are binding. Congress—to use an American example—is to a large extent a democratic association using influence, but the aggregate of its votes have power in the technical sense, subject to approval by the courts and to veto by the President. The executive branch is primarily G, concerned with collective-goal attainment, but the President in particular, like all top executives in modern formal organizations, spends most of his time trying to persuade—that is, using influence—though he or she may also offer implicit "deals" to obtain votes (here using power, technically). University departments of government or political science understandably pay a great deal of attention to the mass media, which to a certain extent (in their editorial policy) are using influence (I) and to that extent "control" the collective-goal attainment process but are not directly a part of it. There is mounting pressure to change the rules for funding political campaigns—quite understandably since, although "pressure groups" are quite legitimate as users of influence properly speaking, it is not consistent with democratic process that pressure groups should be able to buy legislation, as to a certain extent they are now able to do by being allowed to contribute and distribute campaign funds. Finally, university departments of government or political science understandably pay a great deal of attention to one of the most important bearers of all four media—commitments, influence, power, and money—namely, the electorate. The electorate in one sense is not part of government in that most of its members are not full-time officials in any one of the three branches. In another sense, however, the citizen's right to vote does make him or her a member of two branches directly and sometimes of courts as well (where citizens vote for judges). In fact, Parsons remarks that in this sense citizens with the right to vote are officials. These points show clearly the analytical nature of Parsons's functional analysis. Technically, for example, the use of power involves "private" organizations, as well as to varying extents the branches of government, in collective-goal attainment (G). But all formal organizations are involved in all four types of process—LIGA.

A somewhat different hierarchy of formal organizations is constituted by the series modern full-scale universities, professional associations, and labor unions, with universities clearly close to the top of this hierarchy of control and conditioning (see especially Parsons and Platt, 1973).

The graduate schools are certainly among the most "progressive" agencies in a modern society, with their emphasis on research of all kinds, notably in the sciences. They train most of the future professionals—lawyers, medical doctors, engineers, and not least future members of the academic profession itself.

Both graduate and undergraduate training must be enormously important for advancing freedom and equality of religion in a modern society. In private universities, most theologians and clergymen and -women receive their training, and in the faculties of religion that have the greatest prestige—whether Protestant, Catholic, or Jewish—what Parsons calls "extended ecumenism" is a strong influence; that is, the faculties include representatives of not only the Jewish, Christian, and Islamic traditions but frequently of the other religions of India, Hinduism and Buddhism in particular, as well. In the great public universities, there is of course no direct training of theologians and clergy as such, but instead there are religious studies programs, which put a strong emphasis on objective scholarship, on the study of all religions (in principle), and on respect for all religions.

Both graduate and undergraduate programs provide training in the arts, including performance skills in music, painting, writing, theater, and dance.

The undergraduate programs, with their "distribution" requirements, help to create a relatively well-informed leadership among citizens, including creative and critical leadership with regard to "ideology" in one of its senses—the vital moral and intellectual activity of planning and comparing social goals and programs for the future. Insofar as undergraduates participate in the religious studies programs, they are also likely to be relatively enlightened citizen supporters of religious pluralism.

Finally, Parsons strongly defends what he calls "the bundle," by which he refers to the inclusion of all these graduate and undergraduate activities—pursuit of science and the humanities, theoretical and more directly practical training, book knowledge and the performing arts—in the same organization, the full-scale university. He points out that this inclusiveness tends to spread the influence of rationalism as far as the various activities allow it, and tends to provide prestige to all these diverse activities and respect for them all (see Parsons, 1978, Chapter 7).

Instead of trying to eliminate self-interest, as some utopian dreamers would like to do, the best we can realistically hope for and work toward, Parsons contended, is to harness self-interest so that it will tend to improve the functioning of social systems, indirectly benefiting other "selves" as well as any particular role occupant's "self" or set of role occupants' "selves." This means we must have institutionalization, as structure and process.

For *full* institutionalization, first of all there must be normative ideas or patterns definite enough to become objects for consensus. These are the four levels and components of social structure. Second, the normative content must be internalized in the personalities of those to whom it applies. Third, as a backup there must be sanctions, both positive and negative. Fourth, the normative content must help to define which interests are socially acceptable and which are not, and full institutionalization will have been reached only when some actual existing interests are defined as acceptable and are righteously defended and successfully defended—in other words, institutionalized interests become "vested interests." Social structure by definition is therefore to some extent conservative.

We must keep in mind that even "deviant" or revolutionary groups must have the equivalent of institutionalization within them; such groups, of course, have special problems in coping with the larger society, and vice versa.

Some degree of institutionalization is necessary to the very survival of social systems. Following Emile Durkheim (1960), Parsons distinguished between the internal environment of a social system (le milieu social) and its external environment or environments (e.g., natural, biological, psychological).[2]

The very personalities of a social system's members or participants are in large part analytically external to the social system itself. The subcollectivities and roles that compose the social system are, analytically, only those parts or aspects of the total action of all the personalities involved which are defined, by more or less institutionalized normative rights and obligations, as conforming, deviant, or rebellious actions in the system. It is obvious enough that a formal organization must worry about having customers or supporters, and therefore must worry about external competing organizations, but, as Parsons says, the most immediate environment of a formal organization is made up of those aspects of its own members' personalities that are not part of the organization itself.

From the point of view of a participating "unit" (subcollectivity or social role), the normative order of a social system, abstracted from concrete individuals, is an internal environment in a double sense. First, the internal environment enables the acting unit to do things he, she, or it would otherwise not be able to do; acting units can adapt it to their own purposes to some extent, creatively. Second, in a more general sense acting units must adapt to it in order to gain social approval and necessary social support from others and in order to avoid suffering negative sanctions. Without the internal environment or milieu social, acting units vis-à-vis one another would not be able to act rationally because they could not depend on it that the purposes of others would harmonize with their own purposes. The "problem of order," as Parsons calls it, is to some extent "solved" then, by this shared or institutionalized internal environment. From this it follows that the internal environment makes some degree of solidarity possible (see Parsons 1937; 1968; 1977, chapter 8).

One of the ways in which the internal environment functions for the social system is to provide its leaders with already accepted rules and procedures by which they can realistically hope to mobilize consensual motivation for new specific collective projects—directed to external environments and the relation of the system to these. Thus internal and external are intimately interrelated.

Parsons mentions, in two or three places, the simple but fundamental point that whatever satisfactions social and cultural systems can provide, they ultimately can be enjoyed only by individuals, especially human individuals. Perhaps the central idea of this theory is expressed in the term "institutionalized individualism," which conveys that individuals enjoy or do not enjoy social systems (the systems as such are incapable of enjoying anything); that it is largely because, and to the extent that, institutionalized social structure exists, that human individuals can enjoy much of anything; and that social systems "work" or "function" largely by helping to shape or "control" individuals' interests through socialization, controlled by social institutions, which themselves are made more effective to the extent that they are legitimized by social values.

Two value orientations in advanced modern societies seem to be about as generalized as it is possible for values to be—consequently as sweeping in their latent possibilities or potentialities as one might wish. These values, of course, are freedom and equality—for "units" of social systems, including subcollectivities and roles and, ultimately, for concrete individuals. Since, as we have seen, some constraints and inequalities are functionally necessary, obviously the "ideal" modern society would have some complex balance between freedom and equality, on the one hand, and inequalities and normative constraints, on the other.

(Another of Parsons's best papers is 1977, chapter 12, in which he shows how equality/inequality and freedom/constraint relate to the four types of functional problem. One effect of modernization is to differentiate values more clearly from the three "lower" levels of social structure. Thus we can see that a modern society has six highly generalized values: four for the media anchored in four functional subsystems, and two values related to the four in ways that Parsonsian theory makes plain. The six values are not given equal weight or the same relative weight, however, in the value systems of all modern societies.)

Values are more effective than we may realize. For example, most black or African-American leaders and educated African-American voters put their faith in the so-called American dream of equality and freedom and respect activists such as Thurgood Marshall and Martin Luther King, Jr., both of whom accomplished progressive change basically by appealing to American social values and working to mobilize political support under the rule of law. Mahatma Gandhi was a British-trained lawyer and at the same time the charismatic leader, white-robed like a mendicant mystic, of the largely illiterate Indian masses. When he mounted his nonviolent campaign for Home Rule or independence for India, he knew that he could rely on British values of freedom and democracy to get him a large measure of support in Great Britain itself, and he was correct. Parsons points out that Harold Laski (one of his old professors at the University of London), among other Marxists or neo-Marxists, had confidently maintained "that no 'ruling class' would ever relinquish its position peacefully" (1967, chapter 15, 517n., emphasis in original), yet when the British Labour Party let India go free, the British Conservatives did not rise up and revolt; they submitted to the rule of law, the values underlying it, and the procedures of democracy that partly implement them.

Implicit in these examples of the practical importance of values are suggestions to the effect that value implementation in progressive change must overcome often-formidable impediments, of which crude vested interests are not necessarily more important than deep-rooted ideological distortions, held to in good faith as if they were sacred principles. I will illustrate this point with American examples, familiar to people who attempt to keep up with "the news."

Closely allied to the dogma of unregulated markets is "The less government, the better." Yet Durkheim was closer to the truth (which Parsons accepted) that the more complex and highly differentiated modern societies are, the more government is required to help integrate the diversity and to achieve approximations to such basic modern values as equality of opportunity.

Absolutely unavoidable inequalities in occupational achievements and status mean, among other things, that, statistically speaking, some children have an enormous "headstart" in life because they are being socialized by parents who are unusually well educated, have had broader occupational experience, and have "better" social connections. This will be so no matter how "democratic" the society is. If the relatively disadvantaged children are going to have even rough "equality of opportunity," then costly government services and regulations are necessary, such as public schools at all levels, health care, and minimum standards of "welfare." This is so no matter how "irresponsible" or "misguided" poor parents who have children for whom they cannot provide may be. Government services are also needed in the maintenance of highways, harbors, sanitation systems, and environmental protection—the more so, the more populations grow and are concentrated in urban centers.

In the United States certainly, but perhaps no more than in many other societies, the movement toward equality of opportunity is impeded by gross ideological distortions about "race," ethnicity, and "country of origin": for example, the grossly ignorant beliefs that it is "race" that determines the quality or level of a people's culture and social organization and that skin color is an indicator of *innate* capacities, strong or weak.

Regardless of "race" and ethnicity, it is another serious ideological distortion and impediment to implementation of American values to think that high occupational achievement or high income (not necessarily closely related) is the result of such factors as great innate ability and hard work only. Such pleasant self-flattery is an ideological distortion because it ignores massive facts. No one in a modern society especially, but in any society actually, makes significant achievements without the help of social values and social institutions. No one in a modern society could get along without the great assistance provided by government services, among others.

With such impediments to overcome as those just mentioned, it is perhaps evidence of the strength of institutionalized values that we make any progress at all toward full implementation and integrity of the value system. There is no reason to suppose that other modern societies are essentially different from the United States in this respect, though the specific ideological distortions may differ. (Many references could be given, but see especially Parsons 1967, chapter 13, in which he distinguishes between *assimilation* and *inclusion* and discusses the handicaps of certain ethnic or religious groups.)

NOTES

1. The three direct quotations from Parsons in this article all come from "Evolutionary Universals in Society," which was originally published in The American Sociological Review (June 1964), vol. 29, number 3. I am grateful for permission to use these quotations.
2. Technically, what I call the internal environment of societies is the internal environment of the "general system of action." However, explications of this concept would exceed acceptable space limits of this article. The difference is important for full appreciation of Parsonsian theory but not for most readers who are mainly interested in "bureaucracy" and "modernization."

REFERENCES

Bellah, Robert N., *Beyond Belief: Essays on Religion in a Post-Traditional World*, Harper & Row, New York, Evanston, and London, 1970.

Durkheim, Emile, *The Elementary Forms of the Religious Life*. Allen & Unwin, London, 1954.

Durkheim, Emile, *The Division of Labor in Society*, Free Press, Glencoe, Ill., 1960.

Eisenstadt, S. N., ed., Introduction, in *Max Weber on Charisma and Institution Building*, University of Chicago Press, Chicago, 1968, pp. ix–lvi.
Gerhardt, Uta., ed., *Talcott Parsons on National Socialism*, Aldine de Gruyter, Hawthorne, N.Y., 1993.
Lidz, Victor M. and Parsons, Talcott, eds., *Readings on Premodern Societies*, Prentice-Hall, Englewood Cliffs, N.J., 1972.
Little, David, *Religion, Order, and Law*, Harper Torchbooks, New York, 1969.
McGerr, Michael, The Persistence of Individualism, *The Chronicle of Higher Education*, Feb. 10, A48 (1993).
Merton, Robert K., *Science, Technology and Society in Seventeenth-Century England*, Howard Fertig, New York, 1970.
Nelson, Benjamin, Weber's Protestant Ethic: Its Origins, Wanderings, and Foreseeable Futures, in *Beyond the Classics: Essays in the Scientific Study of Religion* (Charles Y. Glock and Phillip E. Hammond, eds.), Harper & Row, New York, Evanston, San Francisco, London, 1973, pp. 71–130.
Parsons, Talcott, *The Structure of Social Action: A Study in Social Theory with Special Reference to a Group of Recent European Writers*, McGraw-Hill, New York and London, 1937.
Parsons, Talcott, An Outline of the Social System, in *Theories of Society* (Parsons, Edward Shils, Kaspar D. Naegele, and Jesse R. Pitts, eds.), The Free Press of Glencoe, a Division of Crowell-Collier, New York, 1961.
Parsons, Talcott, *Societies: Evolutionary and Comparative Perspectives*, Prentice-Hall, Englewood Cliffs, N.J., 1966.
Parsons, Talcott, *Sociological Theory and Modern Society*, The Free Press, New York, 1967.
Parsons, Talcott, Components and Types of Formal Organization, in *Comparative Administration Theory* (Preston P. LeBreton, ed.), University of Washington Press, Seattle and London, 1968a.
Parsons, Talcott, Order as a Sociological Problem, in *The Concept of Order* (Paul G. Kuntz, ed.), University of Washington Press, Seattle, 1968b.
Parsons, Talcott, *Politics and Social Structure*, The Free Press, New York, 1969.
Parsons, Talcott, *The System of Modern Societies*, Prentice-Hall, Englewood Cliffs, N.J., 1971.
Parsons, Talcott, *Social Systems and the Evolution of Action Theory*, The Free Press, New York, 1977.
Parsons, Talcott, *Action Theory and the Human Condition*, The Free Press, New York, 1978.
Parsons, Talcott and Platt, Gerald M., *The American University*, Harvard University Press, Cambridge, Mass., 1973.
Tiryakian, Edward A., Neither Marx nor Durkheim—Perhaps Weber, American Journal of Sociology *81*:1–33 (1975).
Weber, Max. *The Protestant Ethic and the Spirit of Capitalism*, Charles Scribner's Sons, New York, 1930.
Weber, Max, *Economy and Society*, 3 vols., Bedminster Press, New York, 1968.

13
The Role of Efficiency in Bureaucratic Study

Hindy Lauer Schachter
New Jersey Institute of Technology, Newark, New Jersey

Efficiency, conventionally defined in terms of optimizing output/input or benefit/cost, has always been a key criterion in evaluating public and private bureaucracies. (For example, see Blau and Meyer, 1987; Downs and Larkey, 1986; or Wilson, 1989.) Weber (1946) argues that bureaucracies are a crucial aspect of modern life because their organizational characteristics such as specialization and hierarchy engender greater efficiency than other organizational forms. Considerable organizational theory literature centers on designing units to maximize efficiency.

Contemporary public administration textbooks (e.g., Gordon, 1986, p. 45, or Rosenbloom, 1989, pp. 15–16) sometimes describe a classical era where efficiency was the principal criterion used to evaluate bureaucratic performance. This period begins with Frederick Taylor's work on scientific management (1895; 1947a; 1947b), encompasses the municipal reform and early twentieth-century governmental reorganization literature, and is supposed to close with Luther Gulick and Lyndall Urwick's (1937) *Papers on the Science of Administration.* Its seeming reliance on a monochromatic conceptual perspective is contrasted with modern concern with bureaucratic responsiveness, equity, and efficiency with inevitable trade-offs among these variables precluding optimal performance on all counts (Wilson, 1973). For some analysts, the new, more variegated perspective means less keenness for efficiency at least in the short run (Frederickson, 1971).

Contemporary arguments against attempts to maximize efficiency can be interpreted either as an increase in analytic sophistication or as an underreliance on a concept that really explains what people want from bureaucracies. Knowledge of historical use of efficiency as a paradigmatic concept is necessary to make a choice. It is important to know how earlier scholars conceptualized the construct—whether as a stand-alone goal or in relation to other values such as responsiveness. In particular we should want to know whether they posited relationships between efficiency and other values that did not involve trade-offs but rather where high output/input was seen as a prerequisite to responsiveness or equity.

This essay analyzes some of the ways that efficiency has been used as a conceptual underpinning to bureaucratic study. The thrust of the argument is that the classical era actually contains two approaches to understanding efficiency, one primarily managerial and the other political. The first literature, which stretches from Taylor to Gulick and Urwick, examines the internal mechanisms of public and private organizations with an eye toward increasing output/input. The second, written by turn-of-the-century political Progressives, focuses on ways to improve efficiency by strengthening the links between bureaucrats and their stakeholders. This literature anticipates and deflects many of the modern concerns about relating efficiency to responsiveness and equity. It provides a socially responsive dimension to the efficiency concept. The issue then becomes how modern analysts can appropriate its insights to expand the usefulness of efficiency in bureaucratic study.

The first three sections of the chapter provide an overview of the classical era. The first section identifies how Frederick Taylor's work inaugurated a concern for organizational efficiency. The second examines the main tenets of the principles of management literature. The third explores the role of efficiency in municipal reform writings.

Two challenges to this early work are then examined. The first challenge, exemplified by the writings of Herbert Simon (1947), critiques specific approaches to optimizing efficiency. The second, proposed by "new" public administration and by critical theory, challenges the importance of efficiency itself.

The final section of the chapter discusses the impact of these critiques on contemporary bureaucratic management. The major thrust of this section is to use insights from the municipal reform literature to propose a revitalized way of conceptualizing efficiency that answers some of the problems raised by new public administration and critical theory.

I. FREDERICK TAYLOR AND SCIENTIFIC MANAGEMENT

The turn-of-the-century engineer and management consultant Frederick Taylor is often credited with inaugurating both business and scholarly concerns with bureaucratic efficiency (e.g., Wren, 1979). Taylor (1895) delivered his first paper at an American Society of Mechanical Engineers meeting, a forum where managers had been discussing productivity improvement for at least nine years (e.g., Metcalfe, 1886; Towne, 1886). The decisive innovation of his contribution was to argue that organizations could optimize output/input by creating a work science applicable to even the most routine tasks.

For Taylor (1947a, p. 21), the art of management required knowing what an organization or unit should do and then meeting this goal in the best and cheapest way. The effective manager creates information, applying new data to solve old problems, particularly through time study, where engineers deconstruct work into elementary components and analyze the time it takes to do each under varying contingencies.

Taylor was an early proponent of the idea that a new approach to studying work required a more specialized organizational structure, particularly the development of a planning department (Taylor, 1947a, pp. 94–148). He argued that organizations should leave the military form of command and create functional hierarchies where each worker received orders and help from multiple supervisors each with a separate expertise and function.

Taylor's ideas were extensively debated in the first two decades of the twentieth century with hundreds of articles published on his work in Europe and America. Almost everyone writing on efficiency credited his ideas as an influence although Taylor did not always agree with the optimizing strategies proposed by various of his contemporaries (e.g., Schachter, 1989).

The most well-known literature that emerged from the drive to create new information involved an attempt to systematize internal principles of management to improve efficiency in any organization, public or private. With demand for efficiency spilling over from the business to the public sector (e.g., Weber, 1919), a second (somewhat less cited) literature appeared centering on how increasing output/input could spark a renaissance in citizen activity. This second literature is somewhat more parochial, concentrating only on American public agencies, but it offers links between efficiency and other valued goals. Each literature will be examined in turn.

II. ADMINISTRATIVE PRINCIPLES

On demographic variables, Harrington Emerson (1912a; 1912b), Henri Fayol (1937; 1949), Luther Gulick (1937a; 1937b), and Lyndall Urwick (1938; 1944) compose a good cross section of principles proponents. Emerson, Fayol, and Urwick came from the business world, while Gulick wrote about public agencies; Emerson and Gulick were Americans, Fayol was French, and Urwick came from Great Britain.

To these writers, such background differences would be inconsequential because their concern lay in finding organizational similarities. Efficiency was the paramount goal or "axiom number one" (Gulick, 1937b) for all organizations regardless of any other purposes they might have. Indeed, Emerson (1912a, p. 373) went so far as to say, "The ideal of the . . . Efficiency Principles is waste elimination. . . . The mere purpose for which waste is to be eliminated is not important."

A key belief was that the same structural principles would enhance public and private efficiency in all cultures. Fayol (1937, p. 101) wrote, "All undertakings require planning, organization, command, co-ordination and control, and . . . all must observe the same general principles. We are no longer confronted with several administrative sciences but with one alone, which can be applied equally well to public and to private affairs."

While these writers differed on the exact number of principles that undergirded the science of administration, three issues that all saw as important were division of labor, authority, and span of control. All four authors posit that specialization increases efficiency because it makes better use of the varying skills of different workers and eliminates the time lost when people turn from one job to the next. Gulick (1937a, pp. 9–10) writes, "The efficiency of a group working together is directly related to the homogeneity of the work they are performing." Urwick (1944, p. 48) calls specialization "the way of progress in human organisation."

Because specialization requires coordination, bureaucracies create hierarchies to manage work and amalgamate specialized tasks. All four writers insist that the authority of each person on the chain of command be commensurate with responsibility. Top management must define responsibility precisely and allocate enough authority to accomplish each task.

In an interlocking hierarchy reaching from the chief executive to entry-level workers, unity of command is crucial. Fayol (1949) and Gulick (1937a) explicitly criticize Taylor's advocacy of functional supervision because this violates the principle of one command locus for a given worker.

The principles literature also posits the need for each manager to have a relatively tight span of control, that is, a small number of people under his or her direct supervision. Gulick (1937a) argues that the best span will vary, depending on the executive, the time required to complete the task, and the spatial arrangement of the enterprise. Urwick (1938, p. 8) adds numbers to the relationship, asserting that no manager can supervise more than five or six people whose work interlocks.

One difference that does appear among the four authors is their relative sophistication in apprehending the difficulties in applying these principles to specific cases. The three private-sector writers give unconditional loyalty to the principles, and Urwick (1944, p. 9) even argues that going against them amounts to an antisocial act in the same sense as forgery or murder. Gulick, on the other hand, explicitly notes the difficulties involved in applying the principles to various contingencies (e.g., 1937a, p. 8). He even cautions that structural change alone may prove insufficient to produce effective operations (1937a, p. 37). (For a discussion of this aspect of Gulick's thought see Hammond, 1990.) Because of this nuancing, Gulick's work serves as a bridge between the classical era and some of the modern critics.

III. MUNICIPAL REFORM LITERATURE

While the principles literature concentrates on establishing correct internal relations in public and private bureaucracies, the municipal reform literature uses the drive to efficiency as a way of stimulating greater citizen interest in government. William H. Allen, Henry Bruere, and Frederick Cleveland, all associated with New York's Bureau of Municipal Research, argue that collecting new management data to improve efficiency in local agencies can change the relations of governors and governed. Their search for greater output/input is not simply a plea to clean more streets; its importance lies in the fact that citizens will take a larger role in guiding government action when additional data are collected and made available to show them what works and what does not. It is part of an attempt to get both a more assertive and a more democratic government.

New York's Bureau of Municipal Research, established in 1906, was a privately funded organization that was often critical of local government (Dahlberg, 1966; Schachter, 1989). Its director, William Allen (1907), was a stalwart proponent of increasing output/input, but for him the most important ingredient of efficiency was the data collection on which it was based. Communities wanted certain accomplishments in areas such as education. In a traditional system, citizens had little information on current or optimal school performance and thus could not interact effectively with executives, legislatures, and administrators and get responsive government (Allen, 1912). Only when agencies began to collect needed data could the relations between governed and governers change. The new information would allow people to critique governments that did not give them what they wanted.

Allen (1949/1950, p. 525) once objected to a state law that exempted New York City from filing certain reports. His complaint was "That's as undemocratic as can be. It's against efficiency." Contemporary writers might say the law aided efficiency by allowing bureaucrats to concentrate on task fulfillment, but for Allen, efficiency was inextricably linked with information exchange.

Cleveland also saw information as the key to more responsive legislatures (1912) and more active citizens (1913). His writing laments the waste of money in cities run by grafters and bosses (1915) and blames the problem on the paucity of scientific information on municipal work. The people want high output/input but will only be able to get it through more data on how much cities should spend to reach certain levels of lighting or street paving.

Bruere joined Allen and Cleveland in seeing efficiency as important because it helps meet want satisfaction. He observed (1912b) that building a new school at least cost is not very useful if the location is one that the community does not desire. A police department's efficiency has to be directed to the purposes for which the community erected it (Bureau of City Betterment, 1906, p. 3). Bruere (1912a) explicitly differentiates his use of the efficiency concept from that of private-sector engineers. Construction engineers may consider New York's East River bridges quite efficient, but he labels them inefficient because they were not designed to meet the needs of the mass transit population.

The Bureau writers also relate efficiency to social equity because the poor were the ones most likely to suffer in its absence (e.g., Allen, 1907, p. vii); slum dwellers had the most to lose from waste in public health care or education. (It would be difficult to overemphasize the indignation at class hypocrisy that pervades this literature. At one point, Allen [1907, pp. 198–199] says that readers should ask themselves, "Am I doing things that would be considered crimes or misdemeanors if done by residents of the slums? Am I indifferent to wrongs committed by the government? Am I infinitely more interested in suppressing flagrant vice than in preventing flagrant injustice?")

The key difference between the principles and municipal reform literatures is that the former assumes efficiency is a stand-alone bureaucratic goal and concentrates on internal changes to promote it. The latter regards efficiency as a strategy to promote the goal of bureaucratic responsiveness and concentrates on explaining how this aids equity and citizen participation.

A. Linking Principles and Municipal Reform

Some highly regarded public administration literature of the twenties and thirties relies on both the principles and municipal reform traditions. White's 1926 public administration textbook begins by considering efficiency in relation to political goals. The author notes that the immediate objective of public administration is efficient use of resources, but the broader goal is to perform the functions of the state itself (e.g., maintain order, secure justice). It is in that context that White places heavy emphasis on how to structure units to increase efficiency.

Pendleton Herring (1936) writes that a democratic state requires efficiency to accommodate the needs of the community. Efficient administrators try to eliminate friction between them and the community so that they can readily learn what they must accomplish.

Marshall Dimock (1936) argues that while many people define the concept as a synonym for economy, he insists that true efficiency means securing the optimum social and human results that are possible with given resources. To implement social programs in the way that helps the most people, administrators must learn the general principles of management such as unity of command. But this is done simply as a strategy. Dimock (1937, p. 39) notes, "We do not want efficiency for its own sake; we want it for the sake of our democratic form of government."

The wisdom of this literature is that bureaucracies are efficient for a purpose. The principles are a tactic to aid what is itself only a strategy.

IV. CRITIQUE OF THE PRINCIPLES LITERATURE

The earliest critiques of the efficiency concept concentrate on demonstrating problems with these tactics, the principles, without attacking the importance of efficiency itself. The most influential of such critiques is Herbert Simon's *Administrative Behavior* (1947). (For an account of its impact on textbooks, see Dunn, 1988.) Simon is squarely in the tradition of those who accept efficiency as the guiding criterion in bureaucratic design; his protest is against regarding the principles as immutable guides in concrete situations.

The principles literature offers to tell practicing executives how to maximize output/input, and Simon argues that the advice is not very useful on a case-by-case basis. Division of labor is a key precept in the principles literature, but the manager's problem is not simply whether to specialize but how to decide the basis for dividing labor. The principles do not say whether cuts by function, place, process, or client are preferable.

In addition, the principles conflict with each other. If unity of command means that only one person can give orders to a given worker, then it is incompatible with specialization because a worker may need advice from different experts. Span of control conflicts with keeping to a minimum the number of hierarchical levels through which information must pass before a decision maker acts on it. When all workers in a health department report to one person, that executive has a large span of control; if the agency appoints assistant managers for some clinics, then people may complain of red tape as it takes a long time for information to move through the newly created layers (Simon, 1947, p. 27).

Simon did not urge managers to forgo the principles but rather to take a more tentative approach to structural questions. Although Simon was not the first to urge a tentative stance (both Gulick and Dimock [1938] did this in the thirties), understanding Simon's 1947 presentation is important because after his work appeared many writers took a less dogmatic tack in bureaucratic analyses. For example, the fourth edition of Leonard White's (1955, pp. 20–21) public administration textbook adopts a more nuanced perspective when the author adds to his usual introduction that managers may not always know the one best way of designing organizations.

Since 1947, the principles have been undermined from many angles. Motivation theorists (e.g., Hertzberg et al., 1959) now question the relationship between specialization and efficiency, arguing that wholistic, challenging assignments stimulate some workers to better performance. This argument has led private and public organizations to implement job enlargement and enrichment, amalgamating tasks that were once rigidly divided.

A need for flexibility has caused some organizations in volatile environments to forsake rigid hierarchies and unity of command. These organizations implement matrix teams where employees are simultaneously members of a functional department and a project team (Griffin, 1990, pp. 322–324). The argument is even made (Landau, 1969) that early attempts to prevent duplication may have hurt efficiency because redundancy can aid reliability (as in a conversation where people repeat words to prevent misunderstandings).

The principles literature tried to present an easy path to efficiency. The work of Simon and others convinced managers that the road to high output/input was more difficult to traverse.

V. NEW PUBLIC ADMINISTRATION

The assault on efficiency itself is identified with the "new" public administration of the late sixties and seventies (Marini, 1971; Waldo, 1971a), although the equity concerns of this literature also appear in the works of economists advocating a stakeholder view of corporate responsibility. Participants in these literatures cast themselves as rebels and announce that efficiency should not necessarily be the foremost organizational goal.

The most popular approach is to stress that agency activity is a zero-sum game with inevitable trade-offs between efficiency and other values. H. George Frederickson (1971; 1980) asserts that the contest is between high output/input and responsiveness to the poor; although Frederickson sees efficiency as a value with some usefulness, he prefers greater deference to the wishes of low-income communities.

Orion White (1969, p. 35) casts the struggle as between efficiency and client freedom, arguing, "The degree of efficiency . . . is simply a lower-level framing of the question of how much freedom the client wishes or may have to yield in the name of the general order." For White, the efficiency criterion causes bureaucracies to husband resources and choose how much to invest in a given case; he prefers a client-centered organization with an unequivocal mandate to help people—even hopeless cases.

Economist Arthur Okun (1975) sees a trade-off between efficiency and equal rights. To achieve maximum output/input organizations must concentrate resources and authority in a few hands, but this leads to inequity because the central players have better access to legal advice and more forums to disseminate their views. No blanket solution to the dilemma exists because some disparity in income will always be necessary in our sociopolitical system.

The trade-off metaphor is not the only one offered for reconsidering maximum output/input. Goodin and Wilenski (1984) assert that efficiency is not a stand-alone goal but simply an instrumental means to obtain want satisfaction. They see this interpretation as a stronger check on efficiency than the trade-off metaphor where no theoretical reason exists to prefer responsiveness or client freedom. In Goodin and Wilenski's scenario, efficiency (a surface principle) has to yield to want satisfaction (a metaprinciple that gives it meaning). Goodin and Wilenski (1984, p. 513) argue that bureaucracies must override the need for efficiency if people want particular arrangements that make decision making "less efficient in some sense."

The new public administration writers share two characteristics. First, like so many of their predecessors from Taylor on, they combine scholarship with a call to action. They want improvement as well as understanding. Second, they tend to see their concern for responsiveness and want satisfaction as a challenge to traditional theory. They make scant reference to the municipal reform literature and its analogous concerns.

Perhaps because these writers do not grapple with earlier attempts to relate efficiency and responsiveness, their critique is somewhat amorphous. It is not clear whether these analysts are actually against high doses of efficiency or simply regret the uses for which bureaucrats invoke high output/input as an icon. One problem seems to be that these writers have a limited view as to where efficiency might be a pertinent concept. They envision high output/input as a variable in allocating goods and services but not in distributing chances to participate. If we tie the concept to want satisfaction, however, and we find that a considerable portion of a community wants more opportunity to participate in some public agency activity, then a key administrative question becomes how to implement a system that offers such opportunities with maximum efficiency. If a community wants to increase social equity, then the task is to do this efficiently; surely, we prefer to spend $2,000,000 and raise equity by *X* than to spend $6,000,000 and change the equity ratio by 1/3*X*.

Savage (1971) is one of the few new public administration writers to see that input/output questions are actually crucial to the social agenda. He argues that the problem with contemporary bureaucracies is that they do not ameliorate social justice efficiently.

This is the position of the municipal reform literature. The Bureau writers considered efficiency a prerequisite to responsiveness and equity, not a trade-off with them. The old writers would have agreed with Goodin and Wilenski's argument about want satisfaction, but they would have envisioned a broader notion of the wants that organizations should satisfy efficiently. For example, Goodin and Wilenski (1984, p. 514) argue that efficiency and equity clash in job training programs; it is more cost effective to train middle class people, but equity considerations may cause a community to work with the truly disadvantaged. The municipal reformers would reply that if a community wants job training for the poor, then the key question becomes how to implement such programs efficiently. If the public wants training for the disadvantaged, opening programs for middle class people can never be efficient, just as the most skillfully constructed bridges are inefficient if they do not meet the needs of mass transit riders. For the municipal reformers, high benefits/least cost gains the respected name of efficiency only in the service of responsive action. The municipal reform literature celebrates efficiency because it holds high output/input to be a prerequisite for realizing the value of responsiveness. On the issue of efficiency the new public administration and its allies might have engaged the older literature in dialogue.

VI. CRITICAL THEORY

The most radical attack on output/input comes from critical theory, which sees the analytic deference given this value as a way of preserving existing power relations. Critical theorists stress that every bureaucracy consists of a controlling entity and subordinates; the powerful select goals for the organization and define actions as rational if they help meet those objectives (Denhardt, 1981; Fischer and Sirianni, 1984; Forester, 1983). Traditional bureaucratic studies focus on the quest for better performance, neglecting the tension created when lower-level employees do not consider goal attainment rational in terms of their own interests.

Denhardt (1981, p. 43) uses critical theory to argue that a concern with efficiency leads scholars to neglect the inner lives of the workers—their search for meaning—and to concentrate "on the outer world of behavior, performance and accomplishment." He asserts that a critical focus means reprioritizing scholarly interest toward processes that favor individual growth rather than efficient production. For him the central question "*is no longer how the individual may contribute to the efficient operation of the system, but how the individual may transcend the system*" (Denhardt, 1981, p. 131, emphasis in original).

Focusing on the need for people to find meaning through work does not necessarily place critical theory out of alignment with other writing on bureaucracies. The bulk of the postwar motivation literature puts great stock on increasing autonomy and responsibility throughout the chain of command. Critical theorists are not even the first to assign innate importance to the psychological state of individual bureaucrats. As early as 1936, Dimock argued that employee satisfaction was a good in its own right.

Use of critical theory is at odds with earlier work for two other reasons. First, from Taylor on, previous writers always assumed that the interests of organizations and workers were (or through technique could be made) compatible. Critical theory assumes that interests are opposed; structures of organized actions make legitimate, uncoerced discourse between workers and executives difficult to achieve. Critical theory emphasizes the elitist character of modern bureaucracies.

Second, critical theory is one of several attempts in the 1970s and 1980s to make inner life a pivot of organizational analysis, to define organizations as something more than instruments for task accomplishment. (For other attempts see Hummel [1982] and White and McSwain [1983].) Almost every person mentioned in the early sections of this chapter (Taylor, the principles exponents, the municipal reformers, Simon, etc.) would show dismay at an emphasis on consciousness at the expense of concrete objectives.

This may mean that traditional theory neglected a key aspect of agency life. But problems emerge in using the search for personal meaning as an ultimate criterion. Over time no person can ever be certain of his or her own inner feelings much less those of a comrade; emotions constantly shift, an insight used brilliantly by Dostoevsky in creating fictional characters with the ring of truth. Arendt (1963, p. 91) puts the matter clearly in noting that

> not only is the human heart a place of darkness which, with certainty, no human eye can penetrate; the qualities of the heart need darkness and protection against the light of the public to grow and to remain what they are meant to be, innermost motives which are not

> for public display. However deeply heartfelt a motive may be, once it is brought out and exposed for public inspection it becomes an object of suspicion rather than insight . . . unlike deeds and words which are meant to appear . . . the motives behind such deeds and words are destroyed in their essence through appearance.

Trading insights about personal growth is often laced with hypocrisy. Ultimately, we must validate a person's assertions of having found meaning by examining that person's deeds; subjective feelings are measured against outcomes. John Jones can scream that he has found his inner soul until he is blue in the face, but if he treats clients and fellow bureaucrats exactly as he did before the inner breakthrough—who cares? Indeed, if clerk Jones works with welfare clients or the homeless or the terminally ill, to put his consciousness rather than their services at the center of analysis is to care more for the relatively privileged member of the relationship. The rationale for doing that has to focus on future action. The scholar relates concern for the bureaucrat's psyche to a belief that an agency that fosters legitimate internal discourse provides better services or that an organization that builds barriers to internal communication will not know how to have legitimate discourse with clients.

Analysis of alienation is important for understanding what happens in organizations, but such a focus has maximum impact only if it links up with how consciousness affects delivery of products and services. In 1977 Denhardt cautioned that scholars did not know whether the new approach would prove useful in enhancing actions relating to public service, but it seemed that much might be gained in pursuing it. By 1985 Forester argued that critical theory had practical implications for planning departments; its focus on distorted communication helps bureaucrats anticipate and correct for effective design review and implement more democratic planning. Matters are handled more economically because open information exchange reduces unnecessary disruption of the planning process.

For scholars who are not themselves critical theorists, interest in this approach can be sustained by the belief that its psychological insights relate to service delivery, that less alienated entry-level personnel perform their tasks in a preferable way, or that an organization that engages the agendas of its entry-level workers will be more responsive to the public-at-large. For such analysts, critical theory is important precisely because its arguments suggest new approaches to old questions about efficiency; the emphasis is on using insights from this approach to help individuals contribute to better provision of services.

VII. CONCLUSIONS

The quest for more efficient organizations has been a staple of bureaucratic study throughout the century. Looking for an easy path to efficiency, some of the earlier writers tried to enunciate immutable principles of bureaucratic structure. Today, writers on public and private organizations stress that no one structural ideal exists; the most useful patterns depend on circumstances. Managers are taught to take a contingency approach to structure; they appreciate that appropriate design depends on many variables. Traditional bureaucratic characteristics such as specialization and hierarchy may be useful in one instance, dysfunctional in the next.

Since the late sixties, the worth of the efficiency concept itself has come under fire from people with concerns for responsiveness and equity. The conflict is articulated most vividly in public-sector writing, but it also appears in debates about how to make businesses more socially responsive. People with a broad concept of corporate performance want to judge private bureaucracies on their impact on customers, employees, and neighbors as well as on shareholder profits. Some people say it may even be right to see less output/input in the short run to further responsiveness to outside parties, but generally even those who take a broad view of corporate performance stress that socially responsible companies should not lose in the profit ratings over long periods (for example, see the discussion in Hampton, 1986, pp. 119–120).

These corporate innovators face a dilemma that appears in any assault on efficiency: it is difficult to disregard high output/input as a value in practice. Waldo (1971b) notes that even people who criticize efficiency are not so blunt as to say that they prefer inefficiency.

Indeed, Dwight Waldo's career is a case in point. In *The Administrative State* (1948) he cautions against considering efficiency an ultimate value. But by 1986 he notes, "[I]n the beginning I came at efficiency with the instincts or biases of the humanist. . . . Along the way, so to speak, I had second thoughts. . . . I concluded that considerations of efficiency were relevant to the attainment of liberal or humane values" (Brown and Stillman, 158). Efficiency is a criterion in programs to increase civil rights, feed the hungry, or house the poor.

One way of dealing with this trade-off dilemma is to make it explicit at the definition level that actions are inefficient unless they are responsive to relevant publics. In a 1912 article, William Prendergast, New York City's Progressive comptroller, explicitly rejected "results/expenditures" as a definition for efficiency. He preferred defining the concept as doing what the public wants done as well as possible at least expense. While this definition begs the question of defining "public" or saying how its wants are to be measured, it does announce that efficient action requires responsiveness—a relationship that the municipal reformers recognized.

Modern use of this expanded definition would link the concepts of output/input and responsiveness in the public and private sectors. It would make explicit that "efficiency" is not a synonym for "least cost" and that the word has no meaning in relation to projects that do not meet a relevant public's wants. (Indeed, efficient action may require greater costs if this leads to even larger benefit ratios.)

To denigrate efficiency is to turn away from a value that common sense tells us is crucial to all endeavors. More useful for bureaucratic analysts is to identify the range of responsive outcomes for a given organization or unit and to be explicit about what efficiency calculations can and cannot be made for each.

The conventional wisdom assumes that efficiency is easier to measure than other values. However, ease of calculation only attends such measurements for the production of goods. In other cases, analysts may actually find it easier to calculate equity rather than output/input. (For example, it is easier to calculate whether a school system has spent the same amount of resources to imbue each child with an appreciation of art than to know how much genuine appreciation it gets per dollar of expenditure.)

The difficulty of measuring output/input in "soft" areas leads analysts to restrict efficiency calculations to a sparse number of goals. This, in turn, yields a perception that efficiency is irrelevant to the satisfaction of other wants. Managers who produce goods consider output/input in planning their strategies and tactics. When promoting other goals—such as political accountability—managers do not subject their idealism to rigorous appraisal of what a public gets for a given expenditure.

Once the full list of desired outcomes is associated with efficiency analysis, discussion can begin on how to measure cost/benefit outside the provision of goods, how to calculate maximum output/input for securing honesty, say, or accountability. Present-day analysts calculate how much energy a railroad gets from the expenditure of X dollars on various fuels. Why not discuss how much honesty we are likely to get from the work done passing a code of ethics or putting restrictions on the ability of public servants to receive gifts from those with whom they work?

Even if the original calculations are crude, the attempt indicates that the analyst is aware of the full range of outcomes that the public wants from a given bureaucracy. The approach also suggests that simply writing an ethics code or restricting gifts is not enough; the important matter is to learn how such innovations influence the incidence of honest behavior.

Using the expanded definition may open a Pandora's box of problems in defining relevant publics (particularly in the private sphere), but it also leads analysts to consider output/input in relation to a host of genuine wants. By doing this, it enhances the value of the efficiency concept. Such an approach shows that efficiency remains a useful construct to a socially informed study of bureaucracies as it constitutes an aid to understanding in those cases where profit and/or delivery of tangible goods are the only benefits people seek from organizations.

REFERENCES

Allen, William, *Efficient Democracy*, Dodd, Mead, New York, 1907.

Allen, William, How May a Community Learn Its Unmet School Needs? Paper presented to the National Education Association, Division of Superintendence, St. Louis, 1912.

Allen, William, Reminiscences, vol. 4, Unpublished manuscript in Oral History Collection, Columbia University, 1949/1950.

Arendt, Hannah, *On Revolution*, Viking, New York, 1963.

Blau, Peter and Meyer, Marshall, *Bureaucracy in Modern Society*, 3rd ed., Random House, New York, 1987.

Brown, Brack and Stillman, Richard II, *A Search for Public Administration: The Ideas and Career of Dwight Waldo*, Texas A&M University Press, College Station, 1986.

Bruere, Henry, Efficiency in City Government, *Annals 41*:1–22 (1912a).

Bruere, Henry, *The New City Government*, D. Appleton, New York, 1912b.

Bureau of City Betterment, *The Police Problem in New York City*, Citizens Union, New York, 1906.

Cleveland, Frederick, The Application of Scientific Management to the Activities of the State, Paper presented at Dartmouth College, New Hampshire, 1912.

Cleveland, Frederick, *Organized Democracy*, Longmans, Green, New York, 1913.

Cleveland, Frederick, *Chapters on Municipal Administration and Accounting*, Longmans, Green, New York, 1915.

Dahlberg, Jane, *The New York Bureau of Municipal Research*, New York University Press, New York, 1966.

Denhardt, Robert, The Continuing Saga of the New Public Administration, *Administration and Society 9*(2):253–261 (1977).

Denhardt, Robert, *In the Shadow of Organization*, The Regents Press of Kansas, Lawrence, Kans., 1981.

Dimock, Marshall, The Criteria and Objectives of Public Administration, in *The Frontiers of Public Administration* (John Gaus, Leonard White, and Marshall Dimock, eds.), University of Chicago Press, Chicago, 1936.

Dimock, Marshall, The Study of Administration, *American Political Science Review XXXI*(1):28–40 (1937).

Dimock, Marshall, Administration as a Science, *National Municipal Review XXVII*(4):265–266, 288 (1938).

Downs, George and Larkey, Patrick, *The Search for Government Efficiency*, Temple University Press, Philadelphia, 1986.

Dunn, Delmer, The Impact of *Administrative Behavior* on Public Administration Textbooks, *Public Administration Quarterly 12*:369–384 (1988).

Emerson, Harrington, *Efficiency as a Basis for Operation and Wages*, Engineering Magazine Press, New York, 1912a.

Emerson, Harrington, *Twelve Principles of Efficiency*, Engineering Magazine Press, New York, 1912b.

Fayol, Henri, The Administrative Theory in the State, in *Papers on the Science of Administration* (Luther Gulick and Lyndall Urwick, eds.), Institute of Public Administration, New York, 1937.

Fayol, Henri, *General and Industrial Management*, (trans. Constance Storrs), Sir Isaac Pittman, London, 1949.

Fischer, Frank and Sirianni, Carmen, Organization Theory and Bureaucracy: A Critical Introduction, in *Critical Studies in Organization and Bureaucracy* (Frank Fischer and Carmen Sirianni, eds.), Temple University Press, Philadelphia, 1984.

Forester, John, Critical Theory and Organizational Analysis, in *Beyond Method: Strategies for Social Research* (Gareth Morgan, ed.), Sage, Beverly Hills, Calif., 1983.

Forester, John, Critical Theory and Planning Practice, in *Critical Theory and Public Life* (John Forester, ed.), MIT Press, Cambridge, Mass., 1985.

Frederickson, H. George, Towards a New Public Administration, in *Towards a New Public Administration* (Frank Marini, ed.), Chandler, Scranton, Pa., 1971.

Frederickson, H. George, *New Public Administration*, University of Alabama Press, University, 1980.

Goodin, Robert and Wilenski, Peter, Beyond Efficiency: The Logical Underpinnings of Administrative Principles, *Public Administration Review 44*(6):512–517 (1984).

Gordon, George, *Public Administration in America*, 3rd ed., St. Martin's Press, New York, 1986.

Griffin, Ricky, *Management*, 3rd ed., Houghton Mifflin, Boston, 1990.

Gulick, Luther, Notes on the Theory of Organization, in *Papers on the Science of Administration* (Luther Gulick and Lyndall Urwick, eds.), Institute of Public Administration, New York, 1937a.

Gulick, Luther, Science, Values and Public Administration, in *Papers on the Science of Administration* (Luther Gulick and Lyndall Urwick, eds.), Institute of Public Administration, New York, 1937b.

Gulick, Luther and Urwick, Lyndall, eds., *Papers on the Science of Administration*, Institute of Public Administration, New York, 1937.

Hammond, Thomas, In Defense of Luther Gulick's "Notes on the Theory of Organization," *Public Administration 68*(2):143–173 (1990).

Hampton, David, *Management*, 3rd ed., McGraw Hill, New York, 1986.

Herring, Pendleton, *Public Administration and the Public Interest*, Russell and Russell, New York, 1936.

Hertzberg, Frederick, Mausner, Bernard, and Synderman, Barbara, *The Motivation to Work*, 2nd ed., Wiley, New York, 1959.

Hummel, Ralph, *The Bureaucratic Experience*, 2nd ed., St. Martin's Press, New York, 1982.

Landau, Martin, Redundancy, Rationality and the Problem of Duplication and Overlap, *Public Administration Review 29*:346–358 (1969).

Marini, Frank, ed., *Towards a New Public Administration*, Chandler, Scranton, Pa., 1971.

Metcalfe, Henry, The Shop Order System of Accounts, *American Society of Mechanical Engineers Transactions* 7:440–448 (1886).

Okun, Arthur, *Equality and Efficiency: The Big Tradeoff*, Brookings, Washington, D.C., 1975.

Prendergast, William, Efficiency Through Accounting, *Annals 41*:43–56 (1912).

Rosenbloom, David, *Public Administration: Understanding Management, Politics, and Law in the Public Sector*, 2nd ed., Random House, New York, 1989.

Savage, Peter, Contemporary Public Administration: The Changing Environment and Agenda, in *Public Administration in a Time of Turbulence* (Dwight Waldo, ed.), Chandler, Scranton, Pa., 1971.

Schachter, Hindy, *Frederick Taylor and the Public Administration Community: A Reevaluation*, State University of New York Press, Albany, N.Y., 1989.

Simon, Herbert, *Administrative Behavior*, Free Press, New York, 1947.

Taylor, Frederick, A Piece-Rate System Being a Step Towards Partial Solution of the Labor Problem, *American Society of Mechanical Engineers Transactions 16*:856–883 (1895).

Taylor, Frederick, *Shop Management*, Harper and Brothers, New York, 1947a.

Taylor, Frederick, *The Principles of Scientific Management*, Harper and Brothers, New York, 1947b.

Towne, Henry, The Engineer as an Economist, *American Society of Mechanical Engineers Transactions* 7:428–432 (1886).

Urwick, Lyndall, *Scientific Principles and Organizations*, American Management Association, New York, 1938.

Urwick, Lyndall, *The Elements of Administration*, Harper and Brothers, New York, 1944.

Waldo, Dwight, *The Administrative State*, Ronald Press, New York, 1948.

Waldo, Dwight, ed., *Public Administration in a Time of Turbulence*, Chandler, Scranton, Pa., 1971a.

Waldo, Dwight, Some Thoughts on Alternatives, Dilemmas and Paradoxes in a Time of Turbulence, in *Public Administration in a Time of Turbulence* (Dwight Waldo, ed.), Chandler, Scranton, Pa., 1971b.

Weber, Gustavus, *Organized Efforts for the Improvement of Methods of Administration in the United States*, D. Appleton, New York, 1919.

Weber, Max, *From Max Weber: Essays in Sociology* (trans. H. Gerth and C. Wright Mills), Oxford University Press, New York, 1946.

White, Leonard, *Introduction to the Study of Public Administration*, Macmillan, New York, 1926.

White, Leonard, *Introduction to the Study of Public Administration*, 4th ed., Macmillan, New York, 1955.

White, Orion, Jr., The Dialectical Organization: An Alternative to Bureaucracy, *Public Administration Review 29*(1):32–42 (1969).

White, Orion, Jr., and McSwain, Cynthia, Transformational Theory and Organizational Analysis, in *Beyond Method: Strategies for Social Research*, (Gareth Morgan, ed.), Sage, Beverly Hills, Calif., 1983.

Wilson, James, The Bureaucracy Problem, in *Urban Politics and Public Policy* (Stephen David and Paul Peterson, eds.), Praeger, New York, 1973.

Wilson, James, *Bureaucracies: What Government Agencies Do and Why They Do It*, Basic Books, New York, 1989.

Wren, Daniel, *The Evolution of Management Thought*, 2nd ed., Wiley, New York, 1979.

14
The Thatcher Agenda, the Civil Service, and "Total Efficiency"

David L. Dillman
Abilene Christian University, Abilene, Texas

In a 1966 article entitled, "The Political Economy of Efficiency," Aaron Wildavsky compares "pure efficiency" (meeting objectives at the lowest cost) and "mixed efficiency" (altering the objective to suit available resources) with "total efficiency." "Both pure and mixed efficiency are limited in the sense that they take for granted the existing structure of the political system and work within its boundaries." The "total efficiency" advocate, on the other hand, "may discover that the most efficient means for accomplishing his ends cannot be secured without altering the machinery for making decisions. He not only alters means and ends (resources and objectives) simultaneously but makes them dependent on changes in political relationships" (p. 307).

Margaret Thatcher, the reformer, is by this definition a total efficiency advocate. Like the decision-making techniques that Wildavsky describes and analyzes, the Thatcher agenda is rooted in the language of political neutrality yet "pursues efficiency to the heart of the political system" (Wildavsky, 1966, p. 307). This chapter will review the role that "efficiency" has played in past civil service reform efforts, describe the Thatcher reform agenda, and critically examine some of the characteristics and implications of that agenda.

I. ADMINISTRATIVE REFORM IN THE FABRIC OF POLITICS

Civil service reform in Britain has been rooted historically in the political process. While efficiency and economy have long been goals of reform, they have competed with notions of representatives, accountability, political responsiveness, administrative ethics, and other values for prominence during reform debates. It was unthinkable "that a single value, however, important, could triumph over other values without explicit consideration being given these others" (Wildavsky, 1966, p. 335). While one value might receive emphasis, competing values were never totally neglected. And though agreement about which values should be emphasized has sometimes been tenuous, there has been substantial consensus about the purpose and function of government and about the value of a unified, politically neutral career civil service (Kaufman, 1969).

When the famous report issued by Northcote and Trevelyan in 1854 found patronage to be the root cause of inefficiency and waste, the proposed remedy was to "supply the public service with a thoroughly efficient class of men" who were selected by open competitive academic examinations and then separated into a "higher division" composed of "intellectual" tasks and a "lower division" composed of "mechanical" tasks; "to encourage industry and merit" through the use of probation and promotion based on merit; and to unify the appointment process with a central examination board (Northcote-Trevelyan, 1853, p. 118). While Trevelyan's effort to secure more efficient administration stands out throughout that reform period, other participants were pursuing different goals. Many in Parliament, particularly the Parliamentary Select Committee on Miscellaneous Expenditure, were more interested in simply achieving economies in public expenditure through lowering salaries and reducing the number of positions. Others, notably W. E. Gladstone, were less interested in economy and efficiency than in securing political advantage by bringing together the interests of the aristocracy and the middle class. The emerging middle class saw in the reforms an opportunity for increased access to government and more jobs. Leading civil servants were more interested in the administrative convenience that the reforms would bring. by the time Gladstone issued his Order in Council in 1870 to implement the proposals, seventeen years after the Northcote-Trevelyan Report appeared, a political consensus had emerged to support the reforms.

The consensus was built upon the understanding that the reforms were consistent with the nineteenth-century liberal philosophy that assumed limited government activity but, at the same time, prescribed internal efficiency through reason and competition. Furthermore, reform leaders reflected the liberal political ideals of the late 1800s, "namely the political supremacy of the House of Commons, ministerial responsibility to Parliament, and electoral politics determined by issues rather than vested interest." In this context, the aim of Northcote and Trevelyan, Gladstone, Thomas Macaulay, Benjamin Jowett, J. S. Mill, Charles Dickens, and other reformers was broadly "the purification of *political* life, in particular the heightening of the tone of Parliament and the conduct of elections, and the furthering of meritocratic as opposed to hereditary values" (Chapman and Greenaway, 1980, p. 16). Thus, the report, in its opening paragraphs, asserts that "the Government of the country could not be carried on without the aid of an efficient body of permanent officers, occupying a position duly subordinate to that of the Ministers who are directly responsible to the Crown and to Parliament, yet possessing sufficient independence, character, ability, and experience to be able to advise, assist, and to some extent, influence, those who are from time to time set over them" (p. 108). During this reform period, the pursuit of efficiency, though significant, was ultimately subordinated to the need to address ongoing social and political changes. Administrative reform served the purposes of strengthening democratic institutions and furthering democratic accountability.

It is also important to note that efficiency was a qualitative concept. Packed into the notion of efficiency were elements of economizing and competence, but it also included character traits such as honesty, energy, initiative, and the attitude of political responsiveness. Furthermore, efficiency was not touted as a technique which would expunge politics from administration. While the Northcote-Trevelyan project was, in large part, to abolish patronage, it also recognized a policy-advising role for permanent officials. In due course, as patronage became insignificant, "politics was conceived principally as the activity of 'policy-making' " (Thomas, 1978, p. 22). Thus in the British context, politics and administration are fused rather than separated.

Rosamund Thomas's examination of British administration concludes that through the early years of the twentieth century efficiency continued to be construed primarily in qualitative terms. Even with the advent and growing influence of scientific management ideas, particularly in America, British administrative thinkers continued to "relate organisational goals to the attainment of virtue, excellence and the good life, as well as to efficient output and administration. The result was that efficiency assumed not a *quantitative* but a *qualitative* character" (Thomas, 1978, p. 195). Furthermore, while efficiency tended to be an all-consuming value in American public administration, in Britain even the qualitative view of efficiency was balanced with, if not subordinate to, other social and political objectives. Early twentieth-century efforts to increase efficiency and productivity took as given existing administrative-political conventions (such as ministerial responsibility) and structures (with characteristics such as unity and central control) (Chapman and Greenaway, 1980, chapter 2). The view that efficiency needs to be balanced and limited essentially remained unchallenged until the end of the Second World War.

II. THE FULTON COMMITTEE: A FLIRTATION WITH TOTAL EFFICIENCY

Though Great Britain emerged victorious from World War II, its civil service was not unscathed. The war and its aftermath brought a weakened economy and the loss of empire, a democratized educational system, and a broad social malaise and self-criticism. Anthony Sampson aptly notes that "the old fabric of the British governing class, while keeping its social and political hold, has failed to accommodate or analyse the vast forces of science, education or social change which (whether they like it or not) are changing the face of the country" (Sampson, 1962, p. 638).

The civil service, particularly the higher civil service, took the brunt of the criticism for Britain's postwar problems. The basic elements of the British administrative system for over a hundred years—the primacy of the policy advising role for senior administrators, the dominance of the "amateur" or "generalist" over the specialist, the anonymity of civil servants, and the notion of collective and, ultimately, ministerial responsibility—were perceived widely to be no longer representative of postwar attitudes and adequate for postwar needs. For many citizens the civil service epitomized all that was wrong with Britain.

In groping for solutions many critics turned to science and technology in hopes that they would provide an escape from Britain's economic and social malaise. Harold Wilson's often repeated campaign theme in 1964 was that the "white heat of the scientific revolution" would be harnessed by Labour to serve Britain. Scientific and business management techniques applied to public administration were seen by many as a cure for bureaucratic sluggishness and inefficiency. New decision-making techniques for achieving economic efficiency being used in the United States such as cost-benefit analysis, systems analysis, and program budgeting were attracting much attention in Britain. The Fulton Committee published its report in 1968 at the height of this faith in science and business management, a faith shared by key committee members.

The Fulton Committee found that "the Home Civil Service today is still fundamentally the product of the nineteenth-century philosophy of the Northcote-Trevelyan Report" despite the economic and technological challenges that it faces in the second half of the twentieth century (Fulton Committee, 1968, p. 9). In order to modernize the civil service the committee produced 158 recommendations which were wide-ranging but often ambiguous and conflicting. Overall, however, the committee's report placed a clear emphasis on managerial, quantitative techniques to achieve a more efficient, professionally competent administration. Attempting to apply new standards of performance to the civil service, the committee adopted the language of business and the techniques of economic rationality.

The Fulton Committee chose as its "guiding principle" for the future development of the civil service the concept "Look at the job first" (p. 13). The civil service, in other words, must do better at staffing and implementing the tasks it is called upon to perform. In large part this involves, the Fulton Report argued, staffing senior positions with "men and women who are truly professionals" (p. 16), defined as specialists—accountants, engineers, and economists and administrators trained in subject area specialties—all further trained in the principles and techniques of modern management. In addition, professionalism could be enhanced by more "late entrants" and "secondments" from industry and commerce. The committee found that structure also matters and called for new institutional arrangements to secure efficiency. "Accountable management," a term which seemed to be synonymous with efficient management, meant establishing accountable units "where output can be measured against costs or other criteria, and where individuals can be held personally responsible for their performance" (p. 51). "Efficiency audits" (p. 55), long-term planning (p. 57), and "hiving-off" central government work to autonomous public corporations (p. 61) were all advocated as means to reach the goal of organizational efficiency. The Wilson government accepted three recommendations immediately—the creation of a new Civil Service Department, the establishment of a Civil Service College, and the abolition of classes within the civil service. Many other recommendations were accepted later, at least in principle.

Though often criticized for their radical attack on the civil service, in most respects the Fulton proposals were well within traditional boundaries. As if to ensure that the committee would not challenge the basic structures and conventions of the civil service, it had been given by the government limited terms of reference prohibiting an explicit examination of fundamental structural relationships, particularly the relationship between the civil service and Parliament or ministers. Prime Minister Wilson did not need to worry since many of the committee's recommendations "merely confirmed developments which were going ahead in the Civil Service quite independently of [the Fulton] enquiry" (Public Administration, 1968, p. 368). For example, the service had already made management improvements in the use of specialist staff, training programs, and recruitment procedures. Thus, in underrating the changes that had already occurred, the proposals of the committee, as one member reflected later, were "broadly conservative" (Dunnett, 1976, 372).

Nonetheless, some of the Fulton proposals did strike at the underpinnings of traditional conventions. For example, the committee sought to replace informed judgment with positivist techniques, liberally educated generalists with technically trained "professionals," and collective responsibility with individually accountable managers.

Some critics argue that these proposals for fundamental change were sabotaged by civil servants in order to protect their own self-interest (Kellner and Crowther-Hunt, 1980; Sedgemore, 1980). Civil servants and union representatives on a National Whitley Council implementation committee were, after all, charged with implementing the Fulton recommendations (Fry, 1985, p. 38). However, Thomas suggests that

> a more plausible reason is likely to be an instinctive concern by officials that the long-standing administrative tradition of the British Civil Service, often admired by other countries, should not be reformed too drastically, at the risk of losing the good qualities of the generalist administrator, such as his forte as a co-ordinator, his skills in ministerial

> and parliamentary affairs and the continuity, stability, and lack of corruption associated with his tradition. (Thomas, 1984, p. 246)

That some civil servants saw their task of securing efficiency in qualitative terms is supported by the view of Sir (later Lord) William Armstrong, head of the new Civil Service Department (CSD) and the Whitley implementation committee, that one of the tasks of the CSD is "to carry out a programme of reforming the Civil Service, with the object of improving its efficiency, and its humanity . . . both humanity as between the Civil Service as a whole and the public which it serves, and humanity as between the management of the Civil Service and the civil servants who are managed" (1971, p. 319).

Yet more than a broader, humanistic concept of efficiency was at stake for many participants. Civil servants like Armstrong were keenly aware that in the details of implementation resided numerous and difficult questions. In thinking about these administrative issues Armstrong advises that

> it would be quite wrong to view these problems solely as a question of finding the most efficient form of organization, on the assumption that what is wanted is a managerial system comparable to that found in a large private enterprise or group of such enterprises, or for that matter in a place like the Inland Revenue. In the field in which we operate, political considerations can never be excluded; the disposition of managerial authority is also the disposition of political power; and these institutions reflect not simply the desire to produce an efficient Government machine, but also the need to keep it under democratic control. (Armstrong, 1971, p. 329)

In other words, managerial techniques and structural changes advocated by the Fulton reformers had the potential to undermine democratic political safeguards. Armstrong, mindful of the dangers inherent in such total efficiency, advocated a limited efficiency perspective of working within existing political relationships. Perhaps the irony of civil servants acting as guardians of democratic government should be noted.

For all its emphasis upon efficiency the Fulton Committee never explicitly defined the term. Unlike in earlier reform efforts, there seemed to be little concern with economizing in government spending. Efficiency did seem to include some concern for maximizing objectives with a given amount of inputs, hence an emphasis upon recruiting more specialists. Primarily, however, efficiency seemed to be identified with management "accountability" and "control." To the extent that the reformers made efficiency dependent upon changes in the traditional accountability mechanisms, the Fulton reformers were pursuing total efficiency. That these reformers were prevented from inflicting radical change rests not in their concept of efficiency but in their inability to develop a strong enough consensus to implement such changes. The Thatcher Government knew no such restraints.

III. THE EVOLVING THATCHER AGENDA: FROM "PURE" TO "MIXED" EFFICIENCY

Mrs. Thatcher took office in 1979 with well-practiced political skills, a strong working majority in the House of Commons, and a weakened Opposition—all ingredients for policy success. Her convictions with regard to the civil service were clear: she was personally hostile to its prominent features, particularly the policy role of senior civil servants, their denigration of management work, and the inability to hold civil servants individually responsible. "With its security of tenure, assured salary arbitration, and inflation-indexed pensions, the higher bureaucracy she inherited was almost the antithesis of the Thatcher ideals of the individual work ethic, hard-paced competitive striving, and performance-based rewards" (Christoph, 1992, p. 166). Moreover, she held an unswerving commitment to the ideology of economic liberalism and "as a proclaimed anti-statist, she had strong ideological reservations about the centrality of bureaucracy in modern society" (Christoph, 1992, p. 164). It is not surprising, then, that Mrs. Thatcher was determined to change the administrative culture, which she believed preferred consensus to principle and caution to action.

An efficiency strategy became a key component in this effort. The prime minister "took office determined to improve the efficiency of the civil service, to eliminate waste and to promote methods of administration which enable and encourage staff to give the best possible value to the taxpayer" (Cmnd.8293, 1981, p. 1). In practice, at least through 1983, the government's "focus was overwhelmingly on saving inputs—particularly public-sector manpower—and there seemed to be little faith or enthusiasm for increasing efficiency through changes in the macro-structures of government departments" (Pollitt, 1984, p. 121). Yet by 1987, even though economizing and increasing value for money were still prominent goals, institutional changes that are in tension with fundamental elements of the political system were being implemented.

Working within the constraints of the political system, the Thatcher Government set out first to establish a "financial framework" consisting of "cash limits" and "manpower targets" designed to create incentives for governmentwide economy and efficiency (Cmnd.8293, 1981, p. 2). To secure savings the government pledged to reduce the civil service by over 100,000 jobs to 630,000, by April 1984. By December 1984, the number of civil servants had fallen to 617,000, more than meeting the target, and allowing Mrs. Thatcher to claim £700 million a year in savings. Some of this reduction in size was achieved through "natural wastage," more through streamlining jobs or procedures, transferring jobs and agencies to the private sector, and eliminating activities and functions altogether (Management and Personnel Office, 1986, p. 3). While the wisdom of pursuing such a strategy has been questioned by civil servants, unions, some members of Parliament, and academic critics, these actions lie squarely in the tradition of securing economy gains within the existing decision-making structures.

A second component of the government's efficiency strategy is to focus on specific actions to secure "better value for money," action which "demands a continuing process of critical examination of activities, functions, and policies, with particular regard to cost and need" (Cmnd.8293, 1981, p. 2). What has come to be called the New Public Management (NPM) began in 1979 with "Rayner scrutinies," whereby a small team of management advisers from the Prime Minister's Efficiency Unit helps departmental officials identify cost savings and productivity improvements and then monitors implementation of the recommendations accepted by the minister (Efficiency Unit, 1985). Metcalfe and Richards argue that significant financial savings have been realized but, more importantly, department officials have been given a framework to carry out their own scrutinies (1990, pp. 10–12).

More important still, in terms of the efficiency strategy, the Rayner scrutinies paved the way for more complex and comprehensive management programs that would provide a basis for "lasting reforms"—the third efficiency component—through which the government is attempting to "tackle the underlying obstacles to efficiency by creating the right conditions for managers to manage, and by bringing on and rewarding those who are successful" (Cmnd.8293, 1981, 2). Scrutinies led to the development of management information systems such as the Management Information System for Ministers (MINIS) in the Department of the Environment (Metcalfe and Richards, 1990, chapter 3). Likewise, the scrutiny program laid the groundwork for the

Financial Management Initiative (FMI) launched in 1982, a major governmentwide effort to bring about fundamental reforms in the management and control of public spending. "FMI aimed to give managers a clear view of their objectives, measures of performance, well-defined responsibility over their resources, information about costs, and adequate training" (House of Commons, 494-I, 1988, paragraph 6; also see Cmnd.8616, 1982, paragraph 13). To achieve these objectives it emphasized (replicating Fulton terminology) accountable management in which authority and responsibility are delegated to individual civil servants and performance measures are applied to operational activities. In line with these developments, performance-related pay systems were introduced to motivate individuals to improve their work on the job. Taken together, these techniques have resulted in a "notable advance in cost awareness and in the procedures of general resource management" (Gray and Jenkins, 1991, p. 56).

They are not, however, free of value judgments. While Rayner scrutinies and their more complex developments are promoted as techniques to secure economies and efficiency, they are, as Wildavsky noted in reference to benefit-cost analysis, full of "political and social value choices and surrounded by uncertainties and difficulties of computation" (Wildavsky, 1966, p. 314). For example, as Gray and Jenkins point out, the emphasis now being placed on justifying expenditures (as opposed to strategic objectives, priorities, and effectiveness) "has enhanced the role of economic rationality in the management of services" (p. 56). As Fry says more bluntly, "The Financial Management Initiative is the economic liberal gospel as applied to the Civil Service" (Fry, 1988b, p. 5). In other words, Rayner scrutinizes and FMI are based on a political theory of economic liberalism in which priority is given to individual autonomy, the primacy of the free market, and the rights of private property. In this theory, "the economy is to serve the individual's consistent preferences revealed and rationally pursued in the market place. Governments are not supposed to dictate preferences nor make decisions" (Wildavsky, 1966, p. 310). Thus, rather than being politically neutral and value-free, scrutiny techniques secrete a political ideology.

Objectives are not often "given" and managers who determine the organization's objectives are engaging in value choices. Sometimes stated objectives are ambiguous, conflicting, resistant to quantification; or they "may be expressed in an apparently precise but potentially meaningless fashion" (Chapman, 1991a, p. 15). Performance measures, for example, may have perverse consequences, resulting in behavior which is easily measured but which neglects the agency's primary goals. Also, as James Q. Wilson observes, even when operating goals are clear, they are not the only goals an agency is expected to serve. "In addition it must serve a large number of contextual goals—that is, descriptions of desired states of affairs other than the one the agency was brought into being to create" (1989, p. 129). Many of these goals are procedural in nature; others are prompted by political motives to favor certain interests over others. Given the value-infused and complex nature of objectives, Gray and Jenkins identify three ways in which efficiency techniques "have changed the internal politics of the department rather than eradicated them." First, "the budgetary process is now more favourable to those with discrete and measurable activities, particularly if costs can be matched with outputs." Second, "tensions arise between the quantitative and qualitative, between those activities that can be easily expressed in the language of the FMI systems and those which cannot." Third, "a system designed, however imperfectly, for informing choices can be used selectively as a political control" (1991, pp. 52–53).

The Thatcher program moved from the "pure efficiency" techniques of the Rayner scrutinies and MINIS to the "mixed efficiency" FMI. Even FMI appears capable of working within the existing British political structure. While these approaches may contain implicit challenges to fundamental conventions, they do not necessarily require changes in the conventions of the British constitution. However, as Fry points out, if the Conservative government wished to break out of these confines and "press forward with what some saw as 'revolutionary' changes in the civil service, then the reconstructions both of government departments and of the service were logically *The Next Steps*" (1988a, 429).

IV. "THE NEXT STEPS" INTO "TOTAL EFFICIENCY"

True believers in the efficiency strategy are now putting their hopes in "The Next Steps" program, the latest offspring of Rayner scrutinies. Inaugurated in a 1988 report, *Improving Management in Government: The Next Steps*, issued by Sir Robin Ibbs, Rayner's successor at the Efficiency Unit, the Next Steps initiative was designed to create a series of autonomous executive units or agencies, each headed by a manager or chief executive with personal and direct responsibility for operational matters and expanded independence to decide how to meet objectives. The rationale for giving agency heads the "freedom to recruit, pay, grade and structure in the most effective way" is to—moving beyond economizing—"strengthen operational effectiveness" (Efficiency Unit, 1988, paragraphs 21–23). According to the Ibbs report, "the aim should be to establish a quite different way of conducting the business of government. The central Civil Service should consist of a relatively small core engaged in the function of servicing Ministers and managing departments, who will be the 'sponsors' of particular government policies and services. Responding to these departments will be a range of agencies employing their own staff . . . with clearly defined responsibilities" (Efficiency Unit, 1988, paragraph 44). In May 1991 Sir Angus Fraser, the new prime minister's adviser on efficiency, handed John Major an assessment of the Next Steps effort, *Making the Most of the Next Steps*, that continued to recommend increased managerial discretion and independence for agency heads. The creation of independent agencies has, indeed, continued apace. At the end of 1988 there were three Next Step agencies; by May 1992 there were seventy-two agencies in existence, employing 290,000, or half of all civil servants. And more agencies have been promised by the government.

It is perhaps surprising that in the Next Steps literature, which advocates more rational approaches to public service delivery, there appears to be little or no analysis of the costs—beyond direct economic costs—involved in implementing the proposed changes. While advocates of the Next Steps have stressed calculations of cost savings, their calculations virtually have ignored unanticipated and noneconomic costs. Ideally, analytic techniques used to aid decision making will make some contribution to making implicit judgments explicit and subject to analysis. That the Next Steps has not done this should not be surprising given its ideological underpinnings. Calculating economic costs is difficult enough. But it is the failure to include the noneconomic costs of changing organizations and political relationships which suggests the triumph of total efficiency over other values. To illustrate the types of values which have either been omitted from or undervalued in Next Steps calculations, two organizational and two political changes are examined.

First, there has been little explicit consideration given to the possible consequences of the loss of a unified civil service. The assurance of Sir Robin Butler (head of the Home Civil Service) that the Next Steps does not imply "a fragmentation of the Civil Service or the end of the Civil Service as a unified Service" (House of Commons, 348, 1989, para. 320) has been eroded by Sir Angus Fraser's view that "a 'unified civil service' really is not compatible with the way we are going" (quoted in Theakston, 1992, p. 9). O'Toole (1989) and Chapman (1992) agree that the unity of the service is being eroded. Chapman argues, for example, that "the fact that about half the civil service now works in agencies or other organizations operating on Next Steps lines, which are being positively encouraged to develop their own team spirit and loyalties" is undermining the unity of the civil service (Chapman, 1992, p. 3). Theakston, too, raises the point that the Next Steps may be leading to increased privatization of the British civil service in the form of either selling some agencies, such as HMSO, the Passport Office, or the Ordinance Survey, or government by contract. According to Theakston,

> A White Paper in November 1991, *Competing for Quality* (Cm 1730), suggested that "public services will increasingly move to a culture where relationships are contractual rather than bureaucratic," and indicated that contracting-out in Whitehall will move beyond cleaning or catering functions to areas "closer to the heart of government," involving clerical and executive operations and many professional and specialist services. (Theakston, 1992, p. 14)

The civil service staff under the Next Steps program will increasingly confront each other in contractual and competitive relationships. The American experience suggests that privatization approaches such as contracting out do not consistently result in cost savings (see, for example, Goodsell, 1985, chapter 3 and pp. 156–160). Beyond this, however, Chapman concludes that "conscious efforts are now made to stimulate feelings of enterprise and initiative in [the new agencies] and there can be no doubt that these have resulted in a fundamental change from an ethos that was previously admired, and which contributed to the identity of the civil service" (Chapman, 1992, p. 3). Elements of this civil service ethos which may be weakened include a sense of unity, team spirit, concern for the wider service and broader public interest, and self-restraint. It is these noneconomic values that need to be more explicitly and broadly debated.

Second, changes in the methods of recruitment and selection for the civil service as a result of the Next Steps program may result in weakening the principles that have guided recruitment in British civil service since the Northcote-Trevelyan era, including the efficient use of modern personnel methods and the subordination of recruitment procedures to the values and practices of the political system (Chapman, 1981; the remainder of this paragraph is summarized from Chapman, 1991b and 1992). In 1991, under the Next Steps initiative, the Civil Service Commission, which formerly was responsible for recruiting and testing candidates on a servicewide basis, was reorganized into a small office servicing the Civil Service Commissioners and an executive agency, the Recruitment and Assessment Agency (RAS). The RAS contracts to do recruitment for departments, while responsibility of the Office of Civil Service Commissioners is reduced to monitoring the departments and agencies which are directly responsible for 95% of all civil service recruitment. Departments and agencies may either use the services of the RAS, do their own recruitment, or contract with a private personnel consulting firm. These structural changes along with Civil Service Order in Council 1991, which greatly enhances the power of the Prime Minister and the Treasury Department in civil service selection and other matters, at a minimum end the unified system of recruitment and selection. Richard Chapman, who has made the most detailed and thoughtful study of the implications of Next Steps for civil service recruitment, suggests three consequences. First, it seems unlikely that the numerous recruitment agencies will be any more economical—perhaps they will be less so. Second, neither is it likely that decentralized agencies will be "able to maintain the high standards previously expected and achieved by the Civil Service Commission, and so much admired in other countries" (Chapman, 1992, p. 3). Third, it seems likely that there will be more opportunity for political influence over appointments. "Candidates recruited to the higher civil service are being increasingly selected from those with privileged social and educational backgrounds, and present political leaders seem to be playing a more positive role in choosing top officials" (Chapman, 1988, pp. 179–180). Surely these are organizational costs that should be included in Next Steps decision making. Some of them may indeed be difficult or impossible to quantify, but thoughtful decisions cannot be made without weighing these types of considerations.

The Next Steps calculus appears to exclude important values in a second broad area called by Wildavsky, system politics. System politics is distinguished from partisanship and arguments about particular policies. Clearly much of the efficiency strategy was motivated by partisan concerns and by preferences for particular policies. It appears that the Next Steps program was initiated in part to influence reelection chances and effect policy change. More importantly, however, Next Steps was motivated also by a desire to change decision-making structures and constitutional conventions, namely, system politics.

Next Steps is an explicit attempt to change the culture of the civil service. Few would disagree that economies and productivity gains are desirable and achievable. However—to choose one goal on the cultural change agenda—the effort to inculcate within senior civil servants managerial attitudes and values has important implications for system politics. One concern is whether changing the patterns of behavior to make civil servants more businesslike will not undermine the qualities that have been fundamental in the British civil service for more than one hundred years—qualities such as integrity, public service, nonpartisanship, and judgment. If indeed these are qualities that citizens have come to regard as political safeguards and qualities that are perceived to be diminishing, then the legitimacy of the political system may be threatened. Furthermore, creating a managerial culture and delegating decision-making power to managers in the ways envisioned by Next Steps raise questions about political accountability, the fourth undervalued cost incurred by Next Steps.

The tension between increasing agency autonomy in a managerial culture and accountability is made clear by the evidence given to the Treasury and Civil Service Committee in 1988 (see Flynn et al., 1988). Among the concerns raised was that

> the creation of agencies would mean that ministers would be able to deny to an even greater extent that they were responsible for an action, while a minister and chief executive could shuffle responsibility for a decision between them. There would also be difficulties in distinguishing between the policy decisions of ministers and the operational ones of agency managers which would make the lines of responsibility even hazier. This ambiguity could have adverse effects on those trying to gain redress for grievances. (Flynn et al., 1988, 443)

These concerns suggest that the doctrine of ministerial responsibility—one of the most important features of the British constitution and under attack since the Second World War—may be in jeopardy. Ironically, an unintended consequence of the Next Steps program may be to increase the power of managers whether they are in the civil service or in autonomous agencies.

V. CONCLUSION

Taken together, the implications of the Next Steps as articulated by its advocates in the Efficiency Office and some in Parliament strike at the heart of the British political system. There is general consensus that the Next Steps program is producing lasting change in the civil service. Some, such as Metcalfe and Richards, are hopeful that there is emerging a new type of civil service whose senior members, having mastered high-level management skills, will take individual responsibility for its performance. Others are not so sanguine. As this review and analysis suggest, the steps toward "total" efficiency appear to be undermining the ideals of British politics and administration.

The elements of this current debate—economy, efficiency, legitimacy, accountability, administrative ethics, and public service values—again remind us that civil service reform is fundamentally concerned with defining the nature of responsible administration. At least since the 1830s in Britain a variety of values have competed for prominence in efforts to secure responsible public bureaucracy. It was not until the 1980s that the value of efficiency was pursued so single-mindedly and with such success. To close where we started—indebted to Wildavsky (1966, p. 335)—it would be tragic if economic rationality were allowed to swallow up political values—but it will do so, unless the importance of political values for democracy is asserted by adept defenders.

NOTE

1. Early studies of the economic performance of new agencies, suggest that even Next Steps economic calculations may be wanting. For example, after analyzing the performance in productivity, employment, and financial ratios of the new agencies, Dunsire, Hartley, and Parker have found that there is no clear relationship between changing organizational status and improved performance (Dunsire et al., 1991).

REFERENCES

Armstrong, Sir William, The Civil Service Department and Its Tasks, in *Style in Administration* (Richard A. Chapman and A. Dunsire, eds.), George Allen and Unwin, London, 1971.

Chapman, Richard A and Greenaway, J. R., *The Dynamics of Administrative Reform*, Croom Helm, London, 1980.

Chapman, Richard A, Recruitment to the Higher Civil Service in Britain: The Situation in 1981, paper presented to the Eleventh Annual Conference of the Public Administration Committee of the Joint University Council for Social and Public Administration, University of York, 1981.

Chapman, Richard A, The Changing Administrative Culture of the British Civil Service, in *Organizing Governance, Governing Organizations* (Colin Campbell and B. Guy Peters, eds.), University of Pittsburgh Press, Pittsburgh, 1988.

Chapman, Richard A, Concepts and Issues in Public Sector Reform: The Experience of the United Kingdom in the 1980s, *Public Policy and Administration 6*:1–19 (1991a).

Chapman, Richard A, Editorial: New Arrangements for Recruitment to the British Civil Service: Cause for Concern, *Public Policy and Administration 6*:1–6 (1991b).

Chapman, Richard A, The End of the Civil Service? *Teaching Public Administration 12*:1–5 (1992).

Christoph, James B, The Remaking of British Administrative Culture, *Administration and Society 24*: 163–181 (1992).

Dunnett, Sir James, The Civil Service: Seven Years After Fulton, *Public Administration 54*:371–378 (1976).

Dunsire, Andrew, Hartley, Keith, and Parker, David, Organizational Status and Performance: Summary of the Findings, *Public Administration 69*:21–40 (1991).

Efficiency in the Civil Service, Cmnd.8293, HMSO, London, 1981.

Efficiency and Effectiveness in the Civil Service, Cmnd.8616. HMSO, London, 1982.

Efficiency Unit, *Making Things Happen: A Report on the Implementation of Government Efficiency Scrutinies*, HMSO, London, 1985.

Efficiency Unit, *Improving Management in Government: The Next Steps*, HMSO, London, 1988.

Efficiency Unit, *Making the Most of the Next Steps: The Management of Ministers' Departments and Their Executive Agencies*, HMSO, London, 1991.

Flynn, Andrew, Gray, Andrew, Jenkins, William, and Rutherford, Brian, Implementing 'The Next Steps', *Public Administration 66*:439–445 (1988).

Fry, Geoffrey K., *The Changing Civil Service*, George Allen and Unwin, London, 1985.

Fry, Geoffrey K., Outlining 'The Next Steps', *Public Administration 66*:429–439 (1988a).

Fry, Geoffrey K., The Thatcher Government, the Financial Management Initiative and the 'New Civil Service', *Public Administration 66*:1–20 (1988b).

Fulton Committee, Committee on the Civil Service, *The Civil Service*, Cmnd.3638, vol. 1. HMSO, London, 1968.

Goodsell, Charles T., *The Case for Bureaucracy*, Chatham House, Chatham, N.J., 1985.

Gray, Andrew and Jenkins, Bill, The Management of Change in Whitehall: The Experience of the FMI, *Public Administration 69*:41–59 (1991).

House of Commons Treasury and Civil Service Committee, Eighth Report, *Civil Service Management Reform: The Next Steps*, HC 494-I, HMSO, London, 1987–1988.

House of Commons Treasury and Civil Service Committee, Fifth Report, *Developments in the Next Steps Programme*, HC 348, HMSO, London, 1988–1989.

Kaufman, Herbert, Administrative Decentralization and Political Power, *Public Administration Review 29*:3–15 (1969).

Kellner, Peter and Lord Crowther-Hunt, *The Civil Servants*, Macdonald General Books, London, 1980.

Management and Personnel Office, *Reforms at Work in the Civil Service*, Cabinet Office (Management and Personnel Office), London, 1986.

Metcalfe, Les and Richards, Sue, *Improving Public Management*. Sage, London, 1990.

Northcote-Trevelyan Report, *Report on the Organisation of the Permanent Civil Service*. Reprinted in *The Civil Service*, Cmnd.3638. vol. 1, app. B. HMSO, London, 1853.

O'Toole, Barry J., 'The Next Steps' and Control of the Civil Service: A Historical Perspective, *Public Policy and Administration 4*:41–52 (1989).

Pollitt, Christopher, *Manipulating the Machine*, George Allen and Unwin, London, 1984.

Public Administration, Editorial, *46*:367–374 (1968).

Sampson, Anthony, *Anatomy of Britain*, Hodder and Stoughton, London, 1962.

Sedgemore, Brian, *The Secret Constitution*, Hodder and Stoughton, London, 1980.

Theakston, Kevin, Keeping Up with the Next Steps: A Review, *Teaching Public Administration 12*:6–15 (1992).

Thomas, Rosamund M., *The British Philosophy of Administration*, Longman Group, London, 1978.

Thomas, Rosamund M., The Politics of Efficiency and Effectiveness in the British Civil Service, *International Review of Administrative Sciences 50*:239–251 (1984).

Wildavsky, Aaron, The Political Economy of Efficiency, *Public Administration Review 26*:292–310 (1966).

Wilson, James Q., *Bureaucracy*, Basic Books, New York, 1989.

15
Culture and Management: Are Western Management Styles Transferable?

Richard Vengroff, Momar Ndiaye, and Michael Lubatkin
The University of Connecticut, Storrs, Connecticut

The replicability of Western management models in non-Western settings has been the subject of diverse interpretations by scholars in the fields of both development and development administration. For years, many leading analysts have argued that Western management models are relevant to the conditions of developing nations such as those of Africa (Hickson, 1974; Leonard, 1977; Hage and Finsterbush, 1985).

The work of Mintzberg (1973) is indeed central to what is known today in the comparative management literature as "the universality hypothesis." This hypothesis suggests that Western management theories, particularly organization theories, are applicable worldwide regardless of culture or historic experience of a society (Mintzberg, 1973; Hickson, 1974; Leonard, 1977; Drentch, 1985; Hage and Finsterbush, 1985; Montgomery, 1985a,b,c; Vengroff, 1988). Implicit in the universality perspective is the idea that at some basic level, people in organizations think and act similarly, and that these similarities can be the basis for a generic theory of organization development (Bjur and Zomorrodian, 1986).

Mintzberg (1973) argues that managers' jobs are remarkably similar from one setting to another and that the work of all managers can be usefully described by common sets of behavior and roles. The traditional concept of managerial work which has dominated the management vocabulary since the time of the French industrialist Henri Fayol (1916) tells us little about what managers actually do (Mintzberg, 1971a; 1971b; 1973).

Using the "structured observation" method, Mintzberg closely monitored the activities of chief executives of five medium to large organizations. He also examined some of the available studies on how managers in the United States, Canada, Sweden, and Great Britain spend their time. A synthesis of those studies along with the findings from his own research enabled him to define all managerial work as consisting of three main categories of roles: interpersonal roles, informational roles, and decisional roles.

The relevance of Mintzberg's managers' role model, however, has been the subject of a great deal of discussion among academicians in the field of development management and organization theory. Lau, Newman, and Broedling (1980), conducted an extensive study on the nature of managerial work in the public sector in the United States. They drew a sample of executives in the federal government (N = 370) who were to describe their job content using Mintzberg's framework and description of managerial roles. The basic finding was that the responses yielded by these executives confirmed Mintzberg's universality hypothesis. Alexander (1979), similarly, undertook an empirical study employing survey research on a sample of 225 managers in the United States. The overall goal was to examine the effect of both manager's level in the hierarchy and functional area on the extent to which Mintzberg's managerial roles are required by managerial jobs. The basic finding, here also, suggests that the managerial functional area has a strong significant effect on the extent to which Mintzberg's roles are required.

Hickson (1974), Leonard (1977), and Hage and Finsterbush (1987) argue that culture plays a minor role in the applicability of Western organization theories to the conditions of non-Western countries, especially Third World countries. In fact, they assert that irrespective of culture, bureaucratic organizations operate the same way regardless of where they are located. Their research, by noting that many organizational relationships are stable across societies, is consistent with the culture-free hypothesis.

There is also among the universalists a subgroup of convergence theorists, who, while accepting the proposition that culture has an important but limited impact on management, suggest that the impact varies inversely with the level of economic development. Hyden (1983), for instance, states that cultural differences in management, although of some importance today in Africa, will disappear progressively as countries develop. In other words, with increasing industrialization the influence of economic and technological factors will become stronger than the impact of culture. This argument, known as the "convergence hypothesis," is strongly supported by authors like Clausen (1968) and Lauter (1969).

Extensive research on the issue of management training needs and the replicability of Western models in the African context was completed by Montgomery in 1984 and Vengroff et al. in 1988. The nine countries of the Southern African Development Co-Ordination Conference (SADCC), Angola, Botswana, Lesotho, Malawi, Mozambique, Swaziland, Tanzania, Zambia, and Zimbabwe, recognizing the key role that management plays in their prospects for sustained development and growth, cooperated in a large-scale study to assess management problems and training needs in their region. The SADCC study team, led by John Montgomery, covered not only the public and private sectors but also various intermediate hybrids, parastatals, and public enterprises or statutory enterprises (Montgomery, 1985a; 1985b; 1985c; 1986a; 1986b; 1986c). Respondents were asked to report on and rate their daily activities (management events) in terms of importance and time.

Building on the SADCC study, Vengroff (1988) undertook an extensive study under the auspices of the United States Agency for International Development (USAID) to assess the extent of management needs in the Central African Republic (CAR) (Vengroff, 1988, 1990; Vengroff, Belhaj, and Ndiaye, 1991). A series of structured interviews with a large sample of public sector managers was conducted. The questionnaire basically replicated the same management events generated by the SADCC research. Overall, the findings in both the SADCC and the CAR studies are consistent with Mintzberg's model, although some nuances directly related to the African milieu were identified.

I. THE CULTURE-SPECIFIC THEORY OF DEVELOPMENT MANAGEMENT

Hofstede (1980) states that theories—including Western management theories—indeed reflect the cultural environment in which they are developed. If this is true, according to Hofstede, Italian, British, German, French, and American theories reflect the culture of Italy, Britain, Germany, France, and the United States of their day. The question is then, To what extent do theories developed in one country and reflecting the cultural boundaries of that country apply to other countries? More specifically, do American management theories apply to other countries? Hence, Hofstede suggests that culture be explicitly addressed when one's research deals with the replicability of theories from one setting to another setting.

Over a period of six years (1967–1973), Hofstede undertook an extensive study based on a value survey module (VSM) among employees, including managers, at all levels of a U.S. multinational corporation operating in forty countries to determine empirically the main criteria by which their national cultures differed. He found four such criteria, which he labels dimensions: power distance, uncertainty avoidance, individualism-collectivism, and masculinity-femininity (Hofstede, 1980, pp. 45–46).

Using these four dimensions, Hofstede, on the basis of responses of employees on a number of key questions, was able to assign an index value to each country on each dimension. Overall, Hofstede's findings suggest that, given their various cultural differences, countries in the sample can be grouped in clusters. His finding support a contingency theory that devises culture cluster categories, Latin, Anglo-Saxon, and so on, that are characterized in terms of organization (centralization versus decentralization, bureaucratic control, power distribution, etc.). In a later study focused on Asian managers, an additional cultural dimension, "Confucian dynamism," was added to the list (Hofstede and Bond, 1984).

Hofstede's theoretical perspective on the impact of cultural differences on management is reinforced by other scholars who argue for the existence of broad clusters of cultures among nations. Laurent (1985), for instance, hypothesized that "the national origin of European managers significantly affects their views of what proper management should be." On the basis of data gathered from 817 respondents from ten different Western countries (nine European countries and the United States) attending the various executive development programs between 1977 and 1979 at INSEAD in France, he developed an ecological factor analysis technique to evaluate the impact of national cultures on the respondents' managerial ideologies. The findings suggest that, overall national culture strongly affects popular conceptions of management.

Similarly, Crozier and Friedberg (1980), Riggs (1973), and Bourgoin (1984) posit a management function that is directly responsive to culture. Heady (1984), in particular, contends that Western management styles are not applicable to developing nations, for these models are based on the Weberian ideal model of bureaucracy, which, in large part, is neither stressed nor internalized by managers in developing countries. Bjur and Zomorrodian (1986) suggest that given existing environmental—including cultural—traits and differences, there is a need for a context-based framework for administrative theories, "for one should not assume that there is any trans-cultural consensus about societal values." The contingency perspective on the impact of cultural differences on management is also supported by Neghandi's argument that, indeed, (a) "there is no one-way of doing things"; (b) "there is no universal applicability of either authoritarian or participating-democratic management styles"; and (c) "there are enough similarities and differences among the managers around the world" (Neghandi, 1985, p. 75).

Some authors (Kiggundu, 1989; Nzelibe, 1986) contend that the underlying principles of management in Africa are quite different from those which apply in the West. For example, the central elements of modern African management, they argue, revolve around traditionalism, communalism, and cooperative teamwork. The inclusion of such elements from African management thinking in day to day operations indeed constitutes a serious problem in indigenous management capacities. Ahiauzu (1986) suggests that recent studies are beginning to show that attitudes and behavior of African industrial workers are different in many aspects from those of their counterparts in the West. The influences that shape the Africans' actions and thought system in the workplace, this author contends, are likely to emanate from a historical, cultural base. In a 1988 study of culture and management in Eastern Africa, Warwick (1988) also contends that to be successful program designs and organization must integrate indigenous collective attitudes and local pressures. In an observation similar to Warwick's, Deny (1990) also contends that the socioeconomic and cultural environments of development programs have a decisive impact on economic development. Most (if not all) Western-initiated projects, he contends, are based on premises about desirable cultural change, without sufficient attention either to the prospects that such changes will occur, or to how this might be achieved. Projects, he concludes, must then involve some compromise among accommodations, rather than trying to change prevailing cultural traits.

It is the feeling of these authors that the differing views expressed in the literature on cultural contingencies and their impact on institution norms (behavior and performance) are far from being resolved. Yet, the culture factor, in any case, has yet to be readily captured and its influence on management performance evaluated thoroughly. In spite of evidence of "cultural consequences" suggested in many recent development studies, there is yet no conclusive set of research findings "to show the relative importance of cultural variables (e.g., values, social relations) and noncultural variables (e.g., technology, structure) in explaining management process and organizational performance at both the operating and the strategic management levels" (Kiggundu, 1989, p. 29). If culture plays a minor role in determining the relevance of Western organization theories to the conditions of non-Western countries, the question becomes, Why do others (Africans, for example) fail to assimilate Western norms? Is it because of differences of (role) perceptions, differences of values/judgments in the content of employee/manager schemas and behavioral scripts, or the extent to which individuals process information in an automatic or controlled manner (Shaw, 1990)? Are such differences of perceptions and values culturally determined, as indicated by Hofstede (1980)? The literature of the last two decades remains inconclusive on this issue.

II. HYPOTHESIZED MODEL: CONCEPTUALIZATION AND KEY VARIABLES

The theoretical model elaborated later was developed by the authors to assess the impact of culture on organizational performance in the context of Third World countries, those of Africa in particular.

The proposed research model examines the relationships among national culture and organizational cultures, organizational roles, decision processes, and organizational effectiveness. The purpose of this research model is to address empirically the following issues:

1. What are those management roles or groups of roles—as identified by Mintzberg (1973); Montgomery (1985a,b,c); Montgomery (1986a,b,c); Vengroff (1988); and others—which are common to managers in developing country bureaucracies?

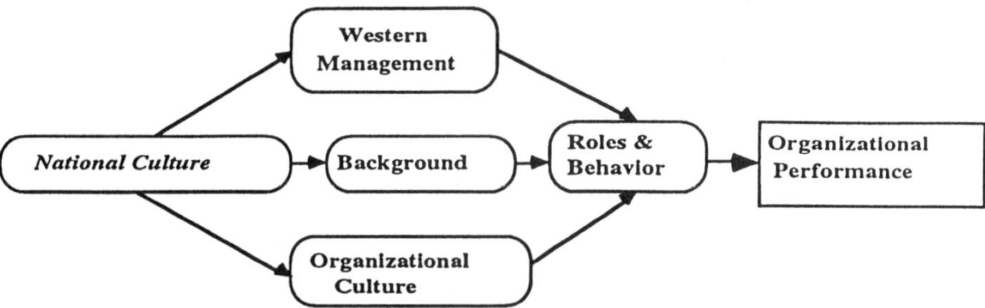

Figure 1 Culture and management model.

2. In what ways, if any, do these roles differ in the context of the Third World from patterns of management roles in Western countries?
3. What differences exist between the performance of Third World and Western managers?
4. To what extent can these differences be attributed to the effects of culture on management roles and functions?

A. Key Hypotheses

The idea that national cultures in developing countries may vary among themselves and from Western (U.S. and Western European) norms leads to the following basic hypotheses:

1. *Hypothesis 1*

The variance along the cultural dimensions between countries (and regions with similar cultural and historical experience) will be greater than the variance within countries.

2. *Hypothesis 2*

Western management roles are universally applicable.

Culture could also be considered to be but one of many factors which have an influence on management roles in a society. Economic conditions, physical resources, and historical factors may all be equally or relatively more influential than culture. Hence, hypothesis 3 could be suggested.

3. *Hypothesis 3*

The local culture of a developing country acts as a limited contingency; it modifies the nature of management roles and the applicability of Western management roles in a given country.

If hypothesis 3 is correct, greater variation in management roles should be found between countries than within countries. The amount of variance in management roles accounted for by cultural variables, however, will be relatively modest. Furthermore, it can be expected that the impact of culture on management will have a differential effect on different types of managers (public sector versus private sector).

Given the greater familiarity of private sector managers with the value systems of their counterparts and colleagues from other countries, especially in the context of large multinational corporations (MNCs), they are more likely to accept these values than are their public sector colleagues. Since these organizations are driven more by profit than by the political and social pressures of their societies, their managers are less subject to local cultural influences than are their public sector counterparts and the organizations in which they work. The possible moderating influence of sector is formally expressed in the following corollaries to hypothesis 3.

4. *Hypothesis 3a*

The impact of culture on the role perceptions of public sector managers will be greater than the impact on private sector managers in the same country.

5. *Hypothesis 3b*

The disparity in management roles between public sector managers in different countries (or in different cultural regions) will be greater than the disparity between private sector managers in different countries.

Finally, culture may indeed be the dominant factor in determining the status of management roles in a nation. If this is the case, it is expected that there will be significant variation between countries in the types of management roles which are deemed most important. In addition, management roles are likely to be more uniform within a society, regardless of sector (public or private), than between societies.

6. *Hypothesis 4*

The local culture of a country acts as a dominant contingency; it determines the degree of applicability, if any, of Western management roles.

7. *Hypothesis 4a*

The variance in management roles between countries will be greater than the variance within countries.

8. *Hypothesis 4b*

The differences in management roles between public and private sector managers within a country will be less than the differences between management roles found in comparable organizations in other countries.

The proposed model suggests a contingent relationship between national culture and organizational performance. Specifically, the performance of an organization and the associated level of commitment, cooperation, and satisfaction with the organization by employees depend upon the degree to which they perceive that management practices are compatible with the characteristics of their own value system (i.e., local culture). Whereas the three previous hypotheses relate to the applicability of Western management roles, they do not directly address the associated performance implications for different cultural settings. The point of the proposed model is not to test for schematic differences across cultures, but rather to recognize their influence when measuring behavioral responses to management roles and, hence, organizational performance. This idea leads to the final set of competing hypotheses.

9. *Hypothesis 5*

Western management roles are universally acceptable and applicable.

10. *Hypothesis 5a*

The most effective organizations are those which adopt these roles regardless of the local (national) culture.

11. Hypothesis 6

The local (national) culture acts as a limited contingency; it modifies somewhat employee responses to Western management roles.

12. Hypothesis 6a

The most effective organizations are those which adapt the Western norms to their specific cultural needs.

13. Hypothesis 7

The local (national) culture acts as a dominant contingency.

14. Hypothesis 7a

The variance in employee responses (and organizational performance) to Western management roles will be largely explained by cultural differences between nations.

B. Key Variables

The key variables in this model are built upon the works of Hofstede (1980), Hofstede and Bond (1984), Montgomery (1985), Mintzberg (1973), and many other scholars involved in cross-national studies of culture and management. These variables can be grouped into categories.

1. Independent Variables

Organizational culture provides the direct link between national culture and the other aspects of management and organizational performance. This key variable (organizational culture) in the basic research model is operationalized in terms of a set of Likert-type items which address various aspects of the broader concept. The specific measures (twenty-seven items) which serve as the core of the analysis of the impact and mediating role of organizational culture are based on questions which have been successfully employed in other relevant studies (Hofstede, 1980; Hofstede and Bond, 1984).

C. Intervening Variables

Two groups of intervening variables are involved.

1. Group 1: Skills/Activities

Forty-five variables have been developed from previous studies (e.g., Montgomery, 1986; Vengroff, 1988). Each activity/skill will be rated in terms of its occurrence at the workplace by the respondent. The rating is based on a four-point Likert scale. The key intervening variable is management roles, or at least the perception of management roles which permeates a particular nation or culture. The management roles included in this study are based on a set of empirically derived roles, identified in the work of Mintzberg (1973) and Lau, Newman, and Broedling (1980). These roles are identified with various skills associated with the performance of the management function (Montgomery, 1985a,b,c). The relationship between these skills and the various management roles was further delineated by Vengroff, Belhaj, and Ndiaye (1991). On the basis of these findings, a set of forty-five items was developed for inclusion in this research model as measures of the role perceptions of the interviewees. Validity checks, using a panel of experts and a test population of respondents, were run and items were modified, dropped, or added consistent with these findings and the goals of this study.

2. *Group 2: Values*

Values reflect a) the respondent's perceptions of "how things appear at the organization" and b) "how he or she feels things ought to be (done)." Twenty-seven such items have been developed from earlier studies. The respondents will rate each item from the perspective of the organization (to reflect his or her perception of the organization's culture) and from the perspective of his or her own perception of how things ought to be done.

D. Dependent Variables

Dependent variables are primarily measured in terms of the respondents' perception of their organization's performance. The respondents' ratings (using the relevant criteria) cover items that may vary from public, to parastatal, to private organizations and may include issues such as (a) short-term profitability in terms of ratio of revenues to costs, (b) long-term profitability in terms of long-term return on present investments, (c) productivity (effectiveness) in terms of production per employee (services rendered per employee), (d) management's (administrator's) ability to make timely decisions, (e) organization earnings in terms of revenues from sales of goods and/or remuneration from services provided to the clientele, and organization's attainment of its goals/objectives, (f) the organization's ability to increase its share of the market, (g) the organization's ability to satisfy its clientele.

The model is being tested in Senegal using a structured questionnaire to interview representatives of large- and medium-size enterprises and government officials from various ministries. Among other questions, respondents are given the opportunity freely and extensively to describe their jobs, monitor their daily activities, and give their own opinions as to what they think are the managerial areas or skills that fundamentally affect and explain job performance. These perceptions will be compared with those of managers in the United States and Western Europe.

III. THE UNIVERSALITY OF ORGANIZATION THEORY: THE CASE OF AFRICA

Many development administration theorists advocate institutional development and the strengthening of indigenous skills from a Western management development perspective as the ways to ensure economic development and growth. The prime implication is that Western management models and the skills required to operate them effectively are directly relevant for Africa. According to this argument, Africa has performed less well than other regions primarily because of the incapacity of indigenous leaders and managers to apply modern (i.e., Western) management style to the problems of development. "Policy reformists" suggest structural reforms in the way Third World governments, including those of Africa, conduct their affairs. For these, including the International Monetary Funds (IMF) and the World Bank, the relevance, hence the transferability, of Western management experience is not a question which is open to debate.

From a strictly managerial standpoint, structural adjustment has intentionally aimed at promoting a comprehensive restructuring and coordination of Third World countries' public, parastatal, and private sector organizations so as to make them individually and collectively more productive and to contribute more effectively, on a sustainable basis, to their development goals (Kiggundu, 1989). A rapid review of the current literature on management development administration in Africa suggests that despite the good intentions, structural adjustment has generally fallen short of its expectations. Generally, when structural adjustment reforms are introduced, it is assumed that they will contribute to solutions to the combination of a lack of business initiatives and a lack of modern management skills. It is assumed admittedly that a policy reorientation toward private sector development and more exposure to Western management experience are (part of) the solution.

A few development strategists (Moore, 1987) argue, however, that the successful implementation of policy reform is limited in part by the absence of a clear understanding of the institutional and administrative requirements for sustained and sustainable reform efforts. Moore, in fact, contends that (today) the failure in the search for efficiency and effectiveness resides in "the limited groundwork that has been done with regard to a realistic understanding of the complexity of the institutional, political, and economic impact that inhere in policy reform" (Moore, 1987, p. 4). For example, large-scale economic reforms including the development of the private sector require a strong state role to improve, for instance, monitoring capabilities or policy analysis capabilities. Yet, the number of sectors involved directly or affected indirectly by reform initiatives will depend—above all—on the government's readiness to coordinate the capabilities within government's own institutions. Therefore, there is a need to focus explicitly on the issue of implementation, which involves the task of a strategic mapping or tracking exercise, to provide a means for preempting the potential bottlenecks—including culture contingencies—in implementing reform. Such an exercise, these authors also believe, would help sort out key factors or variables (including environmental factors, of which culture would represent an important one) that would affect the implementation of any policy.

After several years of experimentation with attempts to "Westernize" African bureaucracies, result at the macrolevel (economic growth) and at the microlevel (public and private organizations) are not all encouraging. Thus the transferability of Western models has been brought into question, for "the issues of applicability, transferability, and utility of advanced management know-how and practices have remained cloudy, if not controversial" (Neghandi, 1985, p. 71). In sub-Saharan Africa, in spite of heavy investments in training through the creation of large numbers of national and regional management schools to teach Western management skills, the continent's global economic performance has continued to be unimpressive. Some studies have indicated that practices have not been as effective and efficient as possible or necessary, while others contend that management behaviors in these countries differ from those in Western countries because of culture differences—and should hence be acted upon cautiously.

IV. CONCLUSIONS

The impact of culture as an important contingency on the applicability of Western management to developing countries remains an important empirical question in the development management literature. While it is not possible at this juncture to define the nature of the relationship, substantial advances have been made in conceptualizing the problem, identifying the key variables, operationalizing those variables in a replicable format, and providing new empirical data and analysis. Although it is all too common to suggest that additional research is necessary, in this case it is clearly called for. These authors firmly believe that the scholars concerned with development management are on the verge of a breakthrough in identifying not only the impact of culture on management in particular societies/nations but the dynamics of change in this relationship and the sources of such change.

The African milieu is identified here as a key testing ground for the propositions raised in the literature from both theoretical and applied perspectives. The failure of African managers to address critical development issues successfully makes Africa a laboratory in which, if culture does exert a significant influence, that influence can be expected to be maximal. While the work of collecting empirical data from a number of African countries continues, additional work is indicated in a variety of other world regions, particularly the states of the former Soviet Union and Eastern and Central Europe.

A number of positive outcomes of studies using the model elaborated here are expected:

1. Advancing management theory: While many useful research projects exist on the separate topics of culture, management practices, and organizational effectiveness, a theory linking these factors into an overall contingency framework applicable to both the public and private sectors has not yet been developed.
2. Improving the design and implementation of management training programs by strengthening their theoretical underpinnings: Further investigation would be useful for developing more effective management training programs for public and private sector organizations. These programs, up to the present, may not have achieved their fullest potential or intended success because they are primarily based on Western models of management (Heady, 1984).
3. Contributing to the successful growth and development of international business alliances, such as joint ventures: Further investigations will provide suggestions for improving joint business ventures between developed and developing countries and between developed countries with significant cultural differences.

REFERENCES

Ahiauzu, A. I., The African Thought-System and the Work Behavior of the African Industrial Main, *International Studies of Management & Organization 16*(2):37–58, 1986.

Alexander, D. Larry, The Effect Level in the Hierarchy and Functional Area Have on the Extent Mintzberg's Roles Are Required by Managerial Jobs, *Academy of Management* 186–189 (1979).

Berg, Robert J. and Whitaker, Jennifer S., *Strategies for African Development*, University of California Press, Berkeley, 1986.

Bryant, Coralie and White, Louise G., *Managing Developing in the Third World*, Westview Press, Boulder, Colo., 1982.

Bjur, Wesley E. and Zomorrodian, Asghar, Towards Indigenous Theories of Administration, *International Review of Administrative Sciences 52*:393–420 (1986).

Bourgoin, Henry, *L'Afrique Malade du Management*, Paris, Ed. Jean Picollec.

Clausen, J. A., Perspectives on Childhood Socialization, in *Socialization and Society* (J. A. Clausen, ed.), Little, Brown, Boston, 1968, pp. 153–167.

Crozier, Michel and Friedberg, Erhard, *Actors and Systems, the Politics of Collective Action*, The University of Chicago Press, Chicago, 1980.

Deny, Ian, The Failure of Success and the Success of Failure: The Youth Polytechnic Programme in Kenya, *Public Administration and Development 10*:179–198 (1990).

Hage, Herald and Finsterbush, Kurt, *Organizational Change as Development Strategy: Models and Tactics for Improving Third World Organizations*, Lynne Rienner Publishers, 1987.

Heady, Ferrel, *Public Administration: A Comparative Perspective*, Columbia University Press, New York, 1984.

Hickson, D. J., The Culture-Free Context of Organization Structure: A Trinational Comparison, *Sociology 8*:59–81 (1974).

Hofstede, Geert, Motivation, Leadership, and Organization: Do American Theories Apply Abroad? *Organizational Dynamics* Summer (1980).

Hofstede, Geert, *Culture's Consequences*, Sage, 1984.

Hofstede, Geert and Bond, Michael Harris, The Confucius Connection: From Cultural Roots to Economic Growth, *Organizational Dynamics 16*(4):4–21 (1988).

Hyden, Goran, *No Shortcuts to Progress: African Development Management in Perspective*, University of California Press, Berkeley and Los Angeles, 1983.

Kiggundu, Moses N., *Managing Organizations in Developing Countries*, Kumarian Press, Hartford, Conn., 1989.

Lau, Alan W. and Broedling, Laurie, The Future of Managerial Work in the Public Sector, *Public Management Forum*, September/October:513–520 (1980).

Laurent, André, The Cultural Diversity of Western Concepts of Management, in *Managing in Different Cultures* (Pat Joynt and Malcolm Warner, eds.), Universitetsforlaget AS, Oslo, 1985, pp. 41–56.

Lauter, G. P., Socio-Cultural and Legal Factors Impeding Decentralization in Developing Countries, *Academy of Management Journal 12*:367–378 (1969).

Leonard, K. David, *Reaching the Peasant Farmer: Organization Theory and Practice in Kenya*, The University of Chicago Press, Chicago, 1977.

Mintzberg, Henry, The Manager's Job: Folklore and Facts, *Harvard Business Review 53*(4):49–61 (1971a).

Mintzberg, Henry, Managerial Work: Analysis from Observation in *The Great Writings in Management and Organizational Behavior* 2nd ed., (Boone, E. Louis and Bowen, Donald D., eds.), Random House, Harper and Row, New York, 1971b.

Mintzberg, Henry, *Managerial Work*, Harper and Row, New York, 1973.

Montgomery, John, *Improving Management in Southern Africa*, final report to the Regional Training Council of Southern African Development Co-ordination Conference, National Association of Schools of Public Affairs and Administration (NASPAA), Washington, D.C., 1985a.

Montgomery, John, *Probing Managerial Behavior: Image and Reality in Southern Africa*, paper prepared for the Annual Meeting of the African Studies Association, Madison, Wisc., Madison, October 29–November 1, 1986, 1985b.

Montgomery, John, The African Manager, *Management Review XXVI*(2):82–111 (1985c).

Montgomery, John, Life at the Apex: The Functions of Permanent Secretaries in Nine Southern African Countries, *Public Administration and Development 6*:211–221 (1986a).

Montgomery, John, Bureaucratic Politics in Southern Africa, *Public Administration Review 46*(5):407–413 (1986b).

Montgomery, John, Levels of Managerial Leadership in Southern Africa, *Journal of Developing Areas 21*:15–30 (1986).

Montgomery, John, How African Managers Serve Development Goals, *Comparative Politics Review* April:347–360 (1987).

Moore, Richard J., Unpublished. Management Requirements of Policy Reform: A Strategic Mapping of Implementation Bottlenecks, The American University, Washington, D.C., December 9–10, 1988.

Neghandi, Anant R., Management in the Third World, in *Managing in Different Cultures* (Pat Joynt and Malcolm Warner, eds.), Universitetsforlaget AS, Oslo, 1985, pp. 69–97.

Nzelibe, C. O., The Evolution of Management Thought, *International Studies of Management and Organization 16*(2):6–16 (1986).

Riggs, W. Fred, *Prismatic Society Revisited*, General Learning Press, Morristown, 1973.

Shaw, James B., A Cognitive Categorization Model for the Study of Intercultural Management, *Academy of Management Review 15*(4):626–645 (1990).

Vengroff, Richard, *Rural Development, Policy Reforms and the Assessment of Management Training Needs in Africa: A Comparative Perspective*, paper prepared for Delivery at the Annual Meeting of the African Studies Association, Chicago, October 27–30, 1988.

Vengroff, Richard, *Senegal M.A.P.S. Formal Sector Survey*, paper prepared for Labat Anderson Incorporated, Arlington, Va., 1990.

Vengroff, R., Belhaj, M., and Ndiaye, M., The Nature of Managerial Work in the Public Sector: An African Perspective, *Public Administration and Development 11*:95–110 (1991).

Warwick, Donald P., Culture and the Management of Family Planning Programs, *Studies in Family Planning 19*(1):1–18 (1988).

16
The Emerging Challenges to Bureaucratic Accountability: A Critical Perspective

M. Shamsul Haque
National University of Singapore, Singapore

I. INTRODUCTION

The hallmark of public bureaucracy is its accountability to the public for its policies and actions. Without the realization of such accountability, public bureaucracy loses its identity of publicness, surrenders its public legitimacy, and may relegate itself to the fetish of self-seeking private interests. It is the very abstraction of public interest into the generalized will of the polity and the conscious surrender of public resources for the actualization of the state policies that justify the need for bureaucratic accountability [1] or accountability of the state bureaucracy to the public. On the other hand, it is public accountability that largely constitutes the ethical foundation of the practical public service as opposed to that of the private market and provides the intellectual norms of academic public administration in contradistinction with those of business administration.

Accountability has been a common concern in all societies, although because of the cross-national diversity in the philosophy, ideology, and historical formation of the state, there were always differences in its conceptual meaning, institutional structures, and procedural mechanisms [2]. Even within the same societal context, the connotation of accountability changes [3]. However, it is quite well known that both the academic concepts and theories and the practical institutional mechanisms of bureaucratic accountability in most societies are increasingly being articulated within and have become mere reflections of the Western ideological framework of capitalist liberalism (Smith 1988, p. 37; Smith, 1991, p. 99). Although the globalization of such ideological orientation and institutional structures of accountability took place during the colonial and postcolonial periods, it has been reinforced and expanded further in recent years as a result of the worldwide propagation and adoption of liberal capitalist democracy.

Given such sociohistorical context, however, it has increasingly been realized that the existing institutions of public accountability are under challenge, the effectiveness and credibility of various mechanisms of accountability are in question, and bureaucracy has become more unresponsive and unaccountable (Jagannadham, 1978, p. 372; O'Loughlin, 1990, p. 275; Carey-Jones et al., 1974, pp. 85–86). There is common agreement and concern among practitioners and academics that the degree of bureaucratic accountability has declined in both developed nations and Third World countries (Subramaniam, 1983, p. 450; Harris, 1990, p. 76; Peters, 1984, p. 179).

Many critics suggest that various mechanisms of bureaucratic accountability [4] have become increasingly ineffective for various reasons: the difficulty in gathering information by elected political representatives, the routine nature of the roles of legislative committees, and the expansion of government functions (see Subramaniam, 1983; Caiden, 1988). Accountability is also constrained, according to some critics, by the adverse characteristics of bureaucracy itself [5]. For others, accountability has become difficult to ensure because of certain extrabureaucratic phenomena, such as the activities of employees' unions, the constitutional protection of public servants, and the informal influence of some powerful people on public officials (see Mukhopadhyay, 1983, pp. 483–485).

However, these obstacles to bureaucratic accountability identified by many critics are mostly instrumental in nature: in general, their focus is either on the negative features of bureaucracy (such as rigidity, corruption, inefficiency, and centralization) or on the incapacity of political representatives in terms of their information limitation, lack of expertise, and excessive responsibility for too many policy issues. These arguments rarely relate the problems of bureaucratic accountability to the question of bureaucratic power within the context of overall social power structure, although it is this structure of power that allows bureaucracy to be irresponsible and corrupt, incapacitates political representatives to control bureaucracy, and weakens the public power to influence bureaucratic decisions and actions. Since power is the essence of the state bureaucracy and the power structure constitutes the foundation of bureaucratic power (Etzioni-Halevy, 1983; Denhardt and Denhardt, 1979, p. 107), it must be the central focus in studying bureaucracy (Sheriff, 1976), including the question of bureaucratic accountability.

In short, on the one hand, it has been commonly recognized that bureaucratic accountability has come increasingly under challenge. On the other hand, the interpretations of such challenges remain inadequate because of the relative exclusion of power structure as a determining factor for accountability from the existing discourse. The main purpose of this study, thus, is to examine the nature of the contemporary challenges to bureaucratic accountability from the perspective of social power structure.

II. THE CONTEMPORARY CHALLENGES TO BUREAUCRATIC ACCOUNTABILITY

There are different sources or bases of social power [6] in different societies, which, in their mutual interaction and confluence, constitute the composition or structure of power [7]. The positions of various social groups, classes, and institutions in this power structure fundamentally determine the degree of their mutual interdependence, autonomy, and control: thus, they eventually shape the dynamics of how, to what extent, and to whom public bureaucracy is accountable. The contention here is that the current challenges to bureaucratic accountability in different societies are posed by the recent changes in power structure composing of three main components: the state bureaucracy, the elected political representatives, and the common people.

In most societies, the recent transition in power structure involves the following three trends: (1) the increasing power of public bureaucracy over people or the decreasing power of people over bureaucracy; (2) the increasing power of bureaucracy over elected political representatives or the decreasing power of political representatives over bureaucracy; and (3) the increasing power of political representatives over people or the decreasing power of people over political representatives [8]. In the current literature, this triangular dialectic of power between bureaucracy and politicians, between bureaucracy and people, and between people and politicians has been examined, but mostly in piecemeal manner and less in relation to the issue of bureaucratic accountability. In this study, however, these existing arguments are synthesized and utilized to present a critical discourse on accountability.

A. The Increasing Power of Bureaucracy over People as a Challenge

Bureaucratic accountability and bureaucratic power are negatively correlated: as the power of bureaucracy increases in relation to the power of people and their representatives, the realization of accountability becomes more difficult (see McKinney and Howard, 1979, pp. 26–31). However, in most modern societies, the power of bureaucracy has significantly increased for various reasons, such as the expansive state intervention in socioeconomic affairs, the growing importance of bureaucratic expertise in relation to increasing specialization of government functions, and the continuing expansion of bureaucratic control over strategic information (Etzioni-Halevy, 1983, pp. 37–60; Thynne, 1983, p. 81; Fischer and Zinke, 1989, p. 846; Dwivedi, 1987, p. 38; Peters, 1984, pp. 31–32). Some of these major factors that have contributed to the overwhelming power of bureaucracy, and thereby created obstacles to accountability, are discussed later.

First, bureaucratic power has significantly increased with the rise and expansion of the administrative state, which affects almost every aspect of life in modern societies [9]. The all-encompassing infiltration of the state bureaucracy into social institutions and functions has increased public dependence on bureaucratic organizations, eroded or replaced the autonomous sphere of public life, and thus strengthened bureaucratic power and weakened the power of people. In the case of socialist countries (many of which have radically changed), contradicting the Marxian rhetoric of the eventual withering away of the state, the state bureaucracy expanded in all directions and subordinated individual citizens to its power and domination (Sethi, 1983, p. 526; Mosher, 1982, p. 7). According to Abrahamsson (1977, p. 26), in the former Soviet Union, the Bolshevik bureaucracy "had appropriated the political power which had slipped from the hands of the working class; and it stood above all social classes and was politically independent of them all."

Even in advanced capitalist countries, since the Great Depression the scope of the administrative state has expanded significantly. Two of the main indicators of such expansive capitalist states are the percentage of labor force and the percentage of Gross Domestic Product (GDP) engaged in the public sector. During this century, the number of government employees has significantly increased in major capitalist nations: the government sector employs almost 20% of the national labor force in France, 25% in the United States, 32% in the United Kingdom, and 40% in Sweden (see Harris, 1990, pp. 21–31; Pempel, 1984, p. 100; Davies, 1988, p. 75). On the other hand, public expenditures involve a significant part of the GDP: almost 35% percent of the GDP in the United States, 45% in the United Kingdom, 57% in Sweden, and 60% in Italy (see Peters, 1984, p. 18; Davies, 1988, p. 75; Dye and Ziegler, 1986, p. 271; Harris, 1990, p. 27). In Third World countries, on the other hand, although the public sector's share in the labor force is below 6% on average (Robinson, 1991), mostly because of a large agricultural sector, in terms of expenditure public service is quite expansive [10].

Several sociohistorical factors have contributed to the proliferation of the state and state bureaucracy in capitalist nations and Third World countries. For instance, in capitalist countries the scope of state intervention expanded to overcome market crises through fiscal and monetary means, to control political uprisings through law enforcment agencies, and to resolve poverty and juvenile delinquency by creating more welfare agencies and mental hospitals (Sjoberg et al., 1973, pp. 68–69). In Third World countries, on the other hand, the state bureaucracy expanded overwhelmingly during the postcolonial period mainly to initiate and implement development plans and programs, which led to the bureaucratization of major socioeconomic sectors.

This expansion of state bureaucracy has significantly enhanced bureaucratic power over people by increasing state ownership and bureaucratic control of the various means and processes of production and distribution. It is not only in Third World countries that the state bureaucracy has become extremely powerful, exercising domination over the powerless peasants and workers by controlling the flow of resources [11]. In advanced capitalist societies as well, although the affluent classes can afford to purchase goods and services from the open market, the less affluent classes, who constitute the majority of the population, are dependent on goods and services provided by the state bureaucracy (Smith, 1986, p. 22). In the United States, for instance, "The urban underclass is increasingly dependent on public subsidies such as income transfers, food stamps, and rent and housing subsidies, and thus increasingly dependent on the state service bureaucracies that administer those programs" (Ferguson, 1983, p. 312). Thus, the increasing bureaucratic control over resources and the bureaucratization of social functions have reduced the self-reliance of common people, made them dependent on bureaucratically managed goods and services, and thus weakened their power to influence bureaucracy to make it accountable (Jacoby, 1973, p. 1; Mukhopadhyay, 1983, p. 473).

Second, another major source of modern bureaucratic power that makes the actualization of accountability difficult is the rise of scientism and technicism in state policies, which has increased the demand for specialized technical knowledge possessed by bureaucratic experts and thus enhanced their power [12]. In modern capitalist societies, the integration of scientific and technical knowledge with capitalist production has led to the rise of superspecialization and the displacement of political and normative questions by instrumental technical interests (Balbus, 1975, pp. 326–327; Denhardt, 1984, p. 171). In this societal context, the rationale and validity of capitalist state policies have become increasingly based on instrumental rather than practical reason, scientific rather than human considerations, and reductionist-quantitative rather than holistic-qualitative criteria.

This transformation of both the nature and the basis of state policies has made specialized technical knowledge essential and inevitable and thus has increased the power of a "new class" of bureaucrats claiming the monopoly of expert knowledge (Balbus, 1975, pp. 326–327). Even in many Third World countries, during the 1980s, the technocratic nature of public bureaucracy was intensified as their governments increasingly recruited technical and professional experts (including foreign experts) in the higher civil service, sometimes under the pressure of international lending agencies (Grindle and Thomas, 1991, p. 97).

The introduction of expert knowledge, specialized techniques, and mathematical models has strengthened the professional monopoly of bureaucratic experts, enhanced their independence from external political constraints, and increased their power over the general public, who are less able to comprehend such knowledge, techniques, and models (for details, see Jagannadham, 1978; Rainey and Backoff, 1982; Dye and Zeigler, 1986; O'Loughlin, 1990; Peters, 1984). Thus, as a result of the scientization and instrumentalization of state policies in most modern states, it has become increasingly difficult for ordinary citizens to influence bureaucracy and make it accountable for carrying out those policies which they can hardly comprehend.

Third, related to the rise of the expert power of bureaucracy is the increasing bureaucratic control over information about various state policies. On the one hand, because of the specialized and technical nature of state policies, relevant empirical and quantitive information has become so essential that by increasing the control over such information bureaucracy has gained more power. On the other hand, the volume and complexity of such information have multiplied to the extent that people can hardly understand it: it is also written in complex and secret language that is incomprehensible to the public (Ferguson, 1983, p. 314). Moreover, in the name of public interest, information on many government activities, such as national security, intelligence gathering, defense research, diplomatic relations, corporate tax records, and police intelligence, is not available to the public (see Caiden, 1988, p. 29). Thus, the growing complexity and secrecy of policy-related information and its increasing control by bureaucracy make people incapable of understanding, assessing, and influencing bureaucratic decisions.

Fourth, the power of common people to influence and monitor bureaucracy through direct participation in bureaucratic decisions is limited by the monopolization of bureaucratic access by the social elites. The idea of direct public participation in the administrative process through means such as citizens' committees, decision-making boards, administrative appeals, and consultations (Kernaghan, 1986, p. 10; Mukhopadhyay, 1983, p. 483) emerged in North America and Western Europe in the 1960s with a view to ensuring administrative responsiveness, need-based public policies, and opportunities for the underprivileged to express their views (see Kernaghan, 1986, pp. 9–10; Berry et al., 1989, p. 209). In reality, however, it is mainly the upper-class elites who can have an impact on bureaucratic decisions by dint of their ability and knowledge of how to manipulate bureaucratic organizations, while the "general public" remains outside the process since they have little knowledge of the rules of the bureaucratic game [13].

In many postcolonial states, such incapacity of the common people to influence bureaucracy through participation is perpetuated further by the residue of colonial institutions, the colonial mentality of master-servant relations, and the gap between the mass culture and bureaucratic subculture (Attwood et al., 1988, p. 2; Mathur, 1986, p. 139). Thus, in both developed capitalist nations and Third World countries, the participatory mechanisms of bureaucratic responsiveness and accountability remain relatively ineffective for the majority, the common masses.

Finally, the lack of representativeness in the very composition of bureaucracy often leads to an unequal structure of bureaucratic responsiveness and accountability to different groups and classes of people. The assumption is that the administrators tend to serve their own socio-economic groups or classes better: thus, if the composition of the bureaucracy is not proportional to the class, gender, and racial composition of society, it will be less responsive and accountable to the needs and desires of underrepresented classes and groups (see Clegg, 1983, p. 20; Peters, 1984, pp. 74–75; Romzek and Hendricks, 1982, p. 75; Mukhopadhyay, 1983, p. 482).

In this regard, although the class, gender, and racial representation in the overall public service has increased in some countries, the economic underclass or the disadvantaged groups are represented mostly at the relatively powerless lower echelons of the bureaucratic hierarchy and are highly underrepresented in the higher civil service, where real administrative power lies. Even in Western democracies, the majority of top administrators come from the dominant socio-economic groups or classes and this tendency reinforces the unequal social structure and leads to the colonialization of the public service by the social elites (see Peters, 1984, p. 82; Hetzner, 1985, p. 100; Sjoberg et al., 1973, p. 62). In terms of gender, it has been shown by Peters (1984, p. 103) that the percentage of women in higher civil service is only 1.8% in Australia, 2.9% in Canada, 6.5% in Italy, 2.3% in the Netherlands, 4.8% in Sweden, 0.8% in Switzerland, 3.5% in the United Kingdom, and 4.2% in the United States (see Peters, 1984, p. 103). Similarly, in terms of racial representation, it is the dominant racial groups that often dominate higher civil service in both Third World countries and developed nations (see Harris, 1990; Peters, 1984).

Such class, gender, and racial underrepresentation in higher level bureaucracy is the outcome of not only the legal discrimination of the past, but the elitist recruitment process that continues to exist in many countries, including democratic nations [14]. Furthermore, elitism in civil service is rooted in the education system itself: in many countries, the institutions, structure, and content of education are highly elitist (Johnson, 1988; Peters, 1984, p. 91). Whatever may be the reason, even in developed nations like Britain and France, the underrepresentation of the underclass or the underprivileged in the composition of bureaucracy leads to its relative isolation from the common people (see Hetzner, 1985, p. 114; Suleiman, 1984, p. 110).

In addition, the structures and norms of bureaucracy and the socialization and life-style of higher-level bureaucrats are such that they are often incapable of understanding the needs, norms, and subcultures of their lower-class clients (Sjoberg et al., 1973, pp. 64–65). In short, as a result of this elitism and upper-class bias in the composition, structure, and norms of higher bureaucracy, it is difficult for the common people to communicate with bureaucrats [15], to have access to bureaucratic organizations, to participate in bureaucratic decision making, and to make bureaucracy responsive and accountable to their needs and desires. Thus, bureaucratic accountability remains class accountability or accountability to the dominant groups and classes of society.

B. The Decreasing Power of Political Representatives over Bureaucracy as a Challenge

From the perspective of liberal democracy, bureaucratic accountability depends, to a great extent, on the power of elected political representatives to guide, direct, and control bureaucracy and actualize its compliance on behalf of the citizens [16]. The question is not whether the representatives always use such power, but whether they have it or not (see O'Loughlin, 1990, p. 276). However, even in advanced democratic nations such as the United States, the United Kingdom, and Japan, power has shifted from politicians to bureaucrats: bureaucracy has become increasingly dominant over political representations in the formulation of public policies (Hetzner, 1985, p. 100; Malbin, 1980, pp. 84–87; Pempel, 1984, p. 78). The British, German, and Japanese bureaucrats themselves have agreed that "it was they, rather than the elected politicians, who were solving the country's general policy problems" (Pempel, 1984, p. 86). The major reasons for this decreasing power of politicians over bureaucracy are explained in the following discussion.

One of the main reasons for decreasing power of political representatives over bureaucracy is the expansive administrative state and its bureaucracy, as discussed previously. In many Western nations, bureaucratic functions and organizations have proliferated to such an extent that they have become difficult to comprehend and manage, and thus the elected representatives have no choice but to introduce very generic and vague laws, leaving the main decision-making power to bureaucracy (Dye and Zeigler, 1986, p. 270; Meier, 1979, pp. 48–55). Thus, in the United States, the federal bureaucracy has emerged as the most powerful "fourth branch" of government (McKinney and Howard, 1979, p. 411) and become "largely independent of Congress, the president, the courts, and the people themselves" (Dye and Zeigler, 1986, p. 269). In addition, the unprecedented volume and complexity of enormous government policies have also incapacitated the political representatives to deal with every policy in detail: thus, it has increased the discretionary power of bureaucracy, shifted power from political representatives to bureaucratic administrators, and made the conventional means of accountability ineffective (Subramaniam, 1983, pp. 451–452; McKinney and Howard, 1979, pp. 410–411; Maheshwari, 1983, p. 466).

Second, in modern societies, the incorporation of specialized techniques and professional jargons into government policies (discussed earlier) has reduced the power of political representatives over bureaucracy in formulating and validating such policies since the social and political reason of politicians has been replaced by the technical reason of bureaucratic experts. As very few legislators and their committees possess specialized expert knowledge to deal with technical details of specific policy issues, they have become increasingly dependent on bureaucracy. According to Subramaniam (1983, p. 453), the political representatives have become "ignorant prisoners" in the hands of bureaucratic experts.

On the other hand, the expert-bureaucrats have become more responsive to their respective professional communities, which provide the professional legitimacy of their decisions and actions, although many of these bureaucratic decisions might contradict the policy stance of political representatives. Today, under the facade of technoscientific validity and professional ethics, bureaucratic experts can easily avoid the influence of politicians who are supposed to control bureaucracy to ensure its accountability. Thus, although the emergence of professionalism and technicism in policy matters has increased bureaucratic efficiency to some extent, it has also reduced the power of political representatives and led to the rise of an administrative machine without accountability (Etzioni-Halevy, 1983, p. 55; McKinney and Howard, 1979, p. 24).

Third, in regard to the bureaucratic control over information, although the political representatives try to create their independent sources of information, such as the Congressional Budget Office in the United States and the Central Policy Review Staff in the United Kingdom, "the bureaucracy retains a central role in the development and dissemination of policy-relevant information and thereby retains a powerful position in policy making" (Peters, 1984, p. 182). Modern public bureaucracy with its greater access to and expertise in storing and processing vital information possesses significant bureaucratic power (Smookler, 1988, p. 42; Meier, 1979, pp. 55–66), particularly over politicians who need such information for formulating and validating public policies.

In addition, such control over information enables the bureaucracy to conceal facts that are embarrassing, to use selective information for creating favorable public opinion, to mask the true costs of government services, and to trade information for influence on policy choices (see Miewald, 1978, p. 66; Peters, 1984, p. 188). In short, the growing bureaucratic control over information has increased the dependence of political representatives on bureaucracy, weakened their capacity to examine secret bureaucratic malpractices, and thus reduced their ability to ensure bureaucratic accountability.

Fourth, specifically in regard to postcolonial states, while the power of political representatives remains less articulated and institutionalized, the state bureaucracy, with its inherited colonial structure, is highly organized, integrated, and, thus, powerful. In many of these countries, extrabureaucratic political institutions such as parliament, political parties, and interest groups are too weak to encounter the overwhelming power of bureaucracy (see Riggs, 1971, pp. 331–351; Crouch, 1985, p. 311; Peters, 1984, pp. 56–57). Moreover, colonial bureaucratic structures, norms, and attitudes continue to perpetuate bureaucratic power through the process of selection, socialization, and organization [17] and thus constrain the development and empowerment of representative political institutions needed for ensuring the accountability of this powerful bureaucracy. This powerlessness of politicians is evident in, and further accentuated by, continuous political instability and fragmentation in many countries [18].

Finally, in many Third World nations, the power and control of political representatives over bureaucracy become extremely limited as a result of frequent military interventions, which often dismantle political parties, imprison or assassinate elected political leaders, install military rule, and thereby deinstitutionalize the process of bureaucratic accountability [19]. In recent years and in line with the worldwide propagation of liberal democracy, some Third World countries have experienced the replacement of military regimes by elected governments; however, under the facade of such democratic rule, one might discover covert military power [20]. The main source of military power is the possession of destructive arms, which continues to mount in many postcolonial states: this power of coercion has enabled military bureaucracy to intervene in politics and establish dictatorial regimes which are neither responsive to public needs nor accountable to public representatives (see Mirsky, 1981; Ball, 1981, p. 580).

C. The Increasing Power of Political Representatives over People as a Challenge

In liberal democratic system, the elected political representatives are supposed to ensure bureaucratic accountability on behalf of people [21]. In this framework, the institutional set-up of politics is such that the effective control of politicians over bureaucracy is not sufficient to ensure "public" accountability if politicians themselves are not accountable to people or their public representativeness itself is in question. In other words, the validity of the indirect public accountability of bureaucracy through politicians cannot be established without authenticating the representativeness of politicians on the one hand and the power of people to make them accountable on the other. However, as discussed later, both the genuineness of political representation and the power of the common people to influence their representatives have declined recently for various reasons [22].

First, the increasing commoditization of politics and commercialization of election campaigns through privately owned and profit-oriented mass media in advanced capitalist countries (Johnston, 1986, pp. 186–187; Kroker et al., 1990, p. 453) have led to a situation in which it is unthinkable for the economically disadvantaged groups or the underclass to participate actively in political process, compete for party candidacy, and win any political position. Despite the rhetoric of democracy in these countries, the powerful political positions remain the monopoly of the upper-class elites [23], and very few elected representatives can be found who have lower-class background. Similar underrepresentation in politics also exists in terms of race and gender: very few top political positions are held by women and racial minorities [24].

For this lack of positional representation of the underprivileged segments of the population, there is no guarantee that the elected political representatives would not adopt state policies that are favorable mainly to the upper-class (which they themselves belong to) but irrelevant, or even detrimental, to the interests of the underclass [25]. In fact, in the current context of commercialized politics in Western democracies, the political parties and leaders have become more dependent on industrial and business corporations for financing their media-based political campaigns and thus have become more responsive to corporate interests than to the interests of the common masses who actually elect them.

Second, in modern societies, the political parties have become highly bureaucratized in terms of rigid party hierarchy and the incorporation of professional experts and technical advisers into politics. Such bureaucratization of the political system has reduced the accessibility of the general public to their own elected political representatives. Moreover, there have emerged varieties of intermediaries between people and politicians who not only increase the distance between the two but also pursue self-interest at the expense of public interest. For instance, the number of private lobby groups in Washington, D.C., increased to 1,700 in 1980 (see Page, 1992) which are actively involved in influencing political policies. The point here is that since the common masses have become increasingly distanced from their own elected representatives through the bureaucratized, mediated, and thus relatively inaccessible system of party politics, people cannot exercise power over their political representatives. Therefore, it becomes less meaningful to people whether these representatives have control over bureaucracy or not.

Third, in Western capitalist democracies, the public power over politicians has also declined as a result of the depoliticization of people through capitalist norms and means. For instance, the norms of hedonistic utilitarianism and individual self-interest that pervade capitalist societies have instigated the desire for economic gains, created an atmosphere of intensive competition, and weakened the public belief in political power through social solidarity [26]. Gradually, society has become a composition of mutually isolated self-seeking individuals who, although legitimize the power of politicians through elections, are depersonalized into powerless numerical figures.

Such processes of social atomization and depoliticization have been accentuated further by institutionalizing consumerism through all forms of commercial media. As Garnham (1990, p. 111) points out, politicians use media advertisements to appeal to potential voters not as rational beings, but "as creatures of passing and largely irrational appetite, whose self-interest they must purchase." In the process, people have become indifferent to mutual political discourse and reflection, and thus depoliticized and powerless. Thus, people have voting rights individually to legitimize the power of politicians through elections, but they have little power collectively over these politicians to influence their political decisions.

Fourth, public power has diminished because of the erosion of civil society [27] and the displacement of the public sphere [28] by mass media as the ground for rational political discourse and the formation of public opinion. In modern societies, the scope of civil society has diminished because of the increasing level of state intervention in the realm of private life, regulation of autonomous social activities, and control of public goods and services on which many people depend [29]. Civil society is also affected by the increasingly monopolistic capitalist market that has commoditized social life, ranging from the patterns of consumption to the modes of entertainment, from the culture industry to knowledge production [30]. Thus, civil society that constitutes the social basis of the public sphere, within which free public discourse takes place to assess state policies and actions and to form public opinion, has been largely taken over by the expansive state and the monopolistic market.

However, at least in appearance, public opinion is necessary in liberal capitalist states to legitimize state policies and to let the people feel that they have freedom of expression. This dual role is accomplished by the modern mass media, which allow selected individuals to express their views and present them as the views of the general public and conduct statistical opinion polls to legitimize state policies. Thus, for Carpignano et al. (1990), the mass media themselves have become the public sphere that has degraded the public life through the commodification of politics and replaced rational discourse by communicating emotionally charged images. For Denhardt (1984, p. 169), in recent times the scope of the public sphere has diminished to the extent that it is mainly the interests of the business and professional elites which are voiced through the mass media.

In this context of weakening civil society and the eroding public sphere, political leaders have more power to manipulate the depoliticized voters, mold the opinion of a fragmented public, and create support for their favored policies through the use of the mass media [31]. Thus, the accountability of bureaucracy to politicians becomes less meaningful to the common people, who have lost power over the politicians themselves.

Finally, in many Third World countries, since a significant number of voters never exercise their votes or are apathetic toward elections, the representativeness of politicians is in question and they are hardly responsible to the people (Subramaniam, 1983, p. 453). Moreover, in the past, there have been fraudulent elections, suppression of opposition parties, and coercion of illiterate peasants and workers to vote for certain candidates (Clark, 1978, p. 81). In such situations, one must question the usefulness of bureaucratic accountability to political institutions, because the domination of political elites over the powerless common masses has not yet been overcome.

III. CONCLUSION: OVERCOMING THE CHALLENGES TO ACCOUNTABILITY

In the preceding discussion, it has been explicated how the formation of an unequal power structure composing the power relations among bureaucracy, politicians, and people has posed challenges to the realization of public accountability of the state bureaucracy. Given the diverse politicoeconomic and sociohistorical contexts of advanced capitalist nations and Third World countries, there is an overall increase in bureaucratic power in relation to the diminishing power of political representatives and the growing powerlessness of people for which it has become increasingly difficult to ensure bureaucratic accountability. At this point, it is necessary to provide some concrete suggestions to overcome these challenges to accountability. It is necessary, however, to assess the existing recommendations for resolving accountability problems.

A. Existing Recommendations and Their Limitations

The nature of academic prescriptions for resolving the problems of bureaucratic accountability usually reflects the way such problems are perceived or understood. Hegel understood the problem of selfish and expansionist tendencies in bureaucracies, and his solution was to educate bureaucrats in both the moral and the functional mission so that control would come from within each bureaucrat (see Jackson, 1986, p. 149). Such a moralistic or ethical solution to bureaucratic accountability can be found in different religious and cultural traditions as well. But in the real-life social context, administrative ethics are often compromised for gaining bureaucratic power and domination to satiate bureaucratic self-interest at the expense of general public interest. This internal moral constraint within bureaucracy is difficult to develop, particularly in capitalist societies, where the norms of individualistic competition, profit, and accumulation have largely replaced the collective moral basis of society. Even if it is achievable, such a normative solution is inadequate to address the reality of the unequal structure of power that poses a great challenge to accountability.

Suggestions also have been made in the past to resolve the problem administratively, by expanding the scope of bureaucratic discretion so that bureaucracy could be more responsive, and politically, by improving the quality of political parties and elections [32]. More recently, some scholars have recommended the reduction of bureaucratic scope and power to enhance accountability: by making bureaucracy more dependent on external economic and political forces, expanding public participation in politics, curtailing government expenditure and financial control, introducing administrative decentralization, and using legislative committees more intensively (see Abrahamsson, 1977; Subramaniam, 1983).

However, although these recommendations address some manifest instrumental problems of bureaucratic accountability, they have some serious shortcomings. For instance, the administrative discretion of lower-level bureaucracy becomes less feasible because of the centralized intrabureaucratic structure of power in many countries. Such discretion also becomes less effective in responding to the needs of the underclass when the influential social elites divert public goods and services to their own benefit. In regard to the dependence of bureaucracy on political and economic forces, such subordination might benefit mainly the political and economic elites without empowering the grass-roots politicians and the economic underclass. Similarly, the reduction of government functions and expenditures (through privatization) may mainly increase the economic power of the business elites unless state resources are transferred directly to the general public.

Finally, the extensive use of legislative committees may increase legislative control over bureaucracy but, as discussed, may not ensure bureaucratic accountability to the powerless masses, particularly the poorer classes, who are highly underrepresented in and have very limited access to the legislature itself. Thus, in the ultimate analysis, the question of power structure must be taken into consideration in making recommendations for resolving the challenges to bureaucratic accountability: "Accountability and the empowerment of people are mutually supportive" (McKinney and Howard, 1979, p. 421).

B. Proposed Strategies for Bureaucratic Accountability

From the preceding critical review, it can be concluded that although it is essential to increase the power of the common masses in relation to both bureaucracy and politicians to overcome the crisis of accountability, the existing recommendations are not adequate to realize such an objective. Hence, the following propositions are made with a view to overcoming the current challenges to bureaucratic accountability.

First, to increase people's power over bureaucracy, it is necessary to reduce the scope of the administrative state by restructuring and curtailing state functions and expenditures and by transferring those functions and resources to the masses through representative local institutions. Such a transfer of bureaucratically controlled public functions and resources would reduce the size and power of bureaucracy, decrease public dependence on government goods and services, and thus increase the self-reliance and power of people. It would also increase the power of national-level political representatives over bureaucracy since the diminishing scope and role of the state would reduce the volume of policy issues, increase the capacity of these representatives to engage more intensively in policy, and thus enhance their influence over the policy-implementing bureaucracy. It is necessary to remember, however, that the transfer of government functions and expenditures is to be made mainly to local representative organizations of the common masses, not to business corporations through the existing strategy of privatization. This is because the profit-oriented corporations are also bureaucratic in structure, less responsive to the needs of the underclass, not accountable to the general public, and often allies of the state bureaucracy itself [33].

Second, it is also necessary to rescue public policies from the existing domination of instrumental reason, quantitative techniques, and technical language that gives too much power to bureaucratic experts. At a macrolevel, most of the policy issues are political and normative questions since they involve the interests and values of different social groups and classes: for instance, the policy choices between the production of nuclear weapons and the provision of basic needs for the poor or between the investment in space program and that in housing for the homeless. These macrolevel policy choices do not require much expert knowledge and quantitative skill: such policy issues should be interpreted in common public language and made accessible to the general public for public discourse, critique, and scrutiny. By ripping off the instrumental reason and complex technical language from this macrolevel policy debate, the power of bureaucratic policy experts would diminish since it is the use of specialized techniques and complex vocabulary in interpreting major policies by these experts that increases their power while it decreases the power of both people and politicians.

However, at a microlevel, the use of expertise and techniques is unavoidable, particularly in this era of highly scientific and technical means of production, distribution, and exchange. But it should be remembered that these microlevel policy matters that require the expertise of bureaucracy are only instrumental to the actualization of macrolevel policies already undertaken by the public and politicians. For instance, before studying the technical feasibility of various alternatives for upgrading nuclear weapons (based on expert opinion), it is necessary first to decide whether scarce resources should be utilized for upgrading defense capability or should be spent on producing food for the hungry (based on public opinion). Thus, by subordinating microlevel instrumental and technical issues (bureaucratic concerns) to macrolevel normative and political questions (public concerns), the power of bureaucracy would diminish in relation to that of the general public and politicians. To make policy-making truly democratic, such primacy of public values and needs over those of bureaucratic policy experts is essential (DeLeon, 1992, pp. 125–129).

This public accessibility to and discourse on macropolicy decisions would also weaken the relevance and rationale of another instrument of bureaucratic power: that is, bureaucratic secrecy and control over information. Establishing the primacy of politiconormative public discourse on macropolicies (based on public interest, reason, and interpretations) over information-based technical decisions would reduce the power of the bureaucratized information stock and make the bureaucratic rationale for secrecy less relevant. However, most bureaucratic information, except some extremely sensitive information that might jeopardize the collective social interest itself, must be made available for public consumption and evaluation.

Third, the overall increase in public power over bureaucracy by the preceding strategies, however, may not ensure bureaucratic responsiveness and accountability to all social groups and classes unless bureaucracy itself represents them in its personnel composition. Thus, it is necessary to ensure that the underclass and the underprivileged are sufficiently represented not only in lower-level public service (as found in the United States), but also in the higher civil service. In this regard, even a strong affirmative action program might be inadequate without a fundamental shift in selection criteria (from the elitist university degree to common job-related qualifications) and without a basic transformation of the whole education system (from an elitist system to equal representation of all groups and classes). By adopting appropriate social, educational, and recruitment policies, the representativeness of bureaucracy can be increased, and thereby bureaucratic accountability to different social groups and classes can be ensured more effectively.

Fourth, on the political front, the existing structure of liberal capitalist democracy must be changed to enhance people's power over elected political representatives. For this purpose, the accessibility of the general public to political representatives has to be increased by debureaucratizing the party system, reducing the party hierarchy, and eliminating various intermediaries (interest groups and lobbies) that inhibit the ability of the public voice to be heard by politicians. But the barrier to public access created by private interests cannot be eliminated as long as there is scope for politicians to gain economically from such vested interests and as long as the political process is based on commercialized and privately financed political campaigns. In this regard, there should be a provision for regular assessment of the status and sources of wealth and income of top politicians to discourage their financial attraction to corporate interests.

On the other hand, to overcome the commercialization of election campaigns, it is essential to make all private contributions to election campaigns illegal. Rather, there should be a provision for allocating an equal amount of public funds to all parties and party candidates to carry out their election campaigns. This would decrease the dependence of politicians on big corporations for financing elections, while it would increase their dependence on the general public, the real voters. Constraints on commercial campaigns would also increase people's capacity to evaluate parties and candidates more objectively.

Fifth, related to the previous point, it is also necessary to regulate the commercial mass media, specifically in regard to political campaigns. In modern societies, the profit-oriented media play a significant role in commoditizing and packaging politics, selling candidates like other commodities, mediating between politicians and people, and depoliticizing people by overemphasizing apolitical issues. Such a media role should be replaced by face-to-face encounters between people and politicians, by direct political debate on crucial social issues, and by more direct assessment of politicians by the critical public. If the media are to be used at all for political campaigns, they should be equally accessible to all parties and candidates through government financing and should emphasize serious debates and discussions on major public concerns rather than the sale of commercialized political images through advertisements. The replacement of media politics by the politics of people would definitely increase people's power over politicians, who would be less able to impress or convince voters simply by using commercially packaged images, messages, and speeches.

Sixth, this replacement of the intermediary role of the mass media in molding public opinion and influencing the election process, however, has to be complemented by the revival of civil society. Because of the erosion of civil society in advanced capitalist nations caused by the all-pervasive penetration of the state and monopoly market (discussed earlier), there is a relative absence of critical public consciousness. Civil society needs to be strengthened in these countries to repoliticize, unite, and empower the existing depoliticized, fragmented, and powerless public.

For constructing such a civil society, it is necessary to curtail the scope of state intervention in society and economy, to regulate the oligopolistic corporations which tend to monopolize the market, and, above all, to eliminate the role of the commercial mass media in structuring and forming public opinion. The construction of this civil society is necessary to maintain an autonomous public sphere where people would become engaged in open critical debate on state policies, form opinions either supporting or rejecting such policies, and thus, exercise significant power to influence the actions of both bureaucrats and politicians.

Finally, the preceding propositions for realizing bureaucratic accountability might become less effective in societies characterized by extreme economic inequalities, because bureaucratic accountability depends on the political power structure, which in turn is inseparable from basic economic structure. Thus, without minimum economic equality in society, the transfer of state functions and resources to local institutions might be monopolized by the local economic elites, the simplification of policy process might transfer power from bureaucratic elites to other social elites, and the public discourse in civil society might be dominated by the economically powerful industrial and business elites. As a result of economic powerlessness, the low-income population or the underclasses would have little access to representative political institutions, limited capacity to acquire higher education to enter the higher civil service, and minimal ability to participate in civil society and its public sphere [34]. Thus, some form of income redistribution through various policies, such as drastic land reforms and highly progressive taxation policies, should complement other strategies of empowering the public. The current challenges to bureaucratic accountability are rooted not only in politicoadministrative institutions but also in socioeconomic structures. Thus, to overcome these challenges, the strategies need to encompass both the politicoadministrative and socioeconomic spheres of society.

NOTES

1. Bureaucratic accountability is commonly understood as the answerability of public servants to the "public" for their actions or inactions, for which they are subject to external or internal sanctions (Oakerson, 1989, p. 114; Mertins and Hennigan, 1982, p. 6; Romzek and Dubnick, 1987, p. 228; Caiden, 1988, p. 25).
2. For instance, the liberal capitalist notion of accountability is inconceivable and unacceptable in China because of the ideological nature of the state (Harris, 1988, pp. 227–249).
3. According to Tashiro (1988, pp. 216–217), in Japan, the meaning of accountability changed: it was accountability to feudal lords during the feudal period, to the emperor during the pre–World War II period and to the people and their representatives during the post–World War II period.
4. Different authors have presented different classifications of the mechanisms of accountability. For details, see Sethi (1983, pp. 527–528), Dwivedi and Jabbra (1988, p. 5), Romzek and Dubnick (1987, pp. 228–230), Maheshwari (1983, pp. 460–461), Henry-Meininger and Lebreton (1988, pp. 56–62), Oakerson (1989, p. 119), and Smith (1991, p. 97). However, from these existing taxonomies, one can classify the mechanisms of accountability into the following four major categories: (1) formal-external mechanisms, including the legislative means (e.g., legislative committees, parliamentary questions, and budgetary means), executive means (e.g., control of political executives over personnel matters and internal investigation), judicial means (exercised by both regular and administrative courts), and others (e.g., advisory committees and ombudsmen); (2) formal-internal mechanisms, such as internal bureaucratic hierarchy, performance evaluation, official rules, and codes of conduct; (3) informal-external mechanisms, including public hearings, interest groups, opinion polls, and media scrutiny; and (4) informal-internal mechanisms, such as organizational culture and norms, professional ethics, and peer pressure.
5. Bureaucracy is often critiqued for its ignorance, incompetence, negligence, and authoritarian temper (Mukhopadhyay, 1983, p. 474). According to Jabbra (1988, pp. 185–195), the main obstacle to accountability in Lebanon, Egypt, and Saudi Arabia is the obsolete, overcentralized, expansive, untrained, rigid, irresponsible, and corrupt nature of bureaucracy.
6. Power, according to Georgiou (1977, p. 253), is the realization of one's intention through the behavior of others, or "the ability to impose one's will on others despite their resistance." There are various sources or bases of power, such as the control over scarce resources; ownership of technology or other means of production; control over information, expertise, and knowledge; possession of organizational position or formal authority; command of informal groups or organizations; and possession of charisma, symbolism, and meaning (see Morgan, 1986, pp. 159–185; Cavanaugh, 1984, pp. 3–17). One can add another important source of power: the possession of arms, which makes the military so powerful in Third World societies. By possessing these sources in various degrees , an individual, group, or class can influence other individuals, groups, or classes who either depend on those sources (e.g., economic resources) or are afraid of being harmed by them (e.g., military weapons).

7. Power is a social phenomenon: it exists only in the context of interpersonal, intergroup, or interclass relations, and it requires structure for its stability and continuation (Ryan, 1984). The composition of the power structure depends on both the nature of the sources or bases of power (e.g., land ownership in a feudal society, capital ownership in capitalist society) and the patterns of ownership of those sources (e.g., different patterns of capital and land ownership that lead to variations in power structure among different countries). Beyond the Marxian economic interpretation of power structure as a reflection of production relations, there are other noneconomic sources of power, such as the possession of information, expertise, and organizational position, which provides a significant amount of power to the state bureaucracy and should not be simply reduced to the economic sphere.
8. Aberbach, Putnam, and Rockman (1981, p. 1) suggest that in the advanced Western nations during the period 1870–1970, the power of both permanent bureaucrats and professional party politicians increased significantly. However, it needs to be mentioned here that this power structure composed of bureaucracy, politicians, and people is vertical in nature: each of these three components is considered in its totality as an independent unit without analyzing horizontal class or group composition within it. For instance, there are horizontal relations of power between classes within the state bureaucracy, within political parties, and within the public. This horizontal class dimension of power itself is a complex issue, and thus requires a separate study. Here, the consideration is limited mainly to the power relations among bureaucracy, politicians, and people.
9. The scope of the administrative state has expanded significantly in socialist countries, because of the monopolistic role of the state; in capitalist countries, as a result of state initiatives to overcome market crises and perform welfare functions; and in Third World countries, through the government's role in developmental and nation-building activities (see Subramaniam, 1983, pp. 450–451). The power of public servants has significantly increased with this increasing role of the state in almost every sphere of society (Dwivedi and Jabbra, 1988, p. 1).
10. For instance, the public sector accounts for almost 15% of GDP in Colombia, 21% in Kenya, 18% in India, 46% in Peru, and 60% in Venezuela (Peters, 1984, p. 18; Harris, 1990, p. 88, Kasza, 1987, p. 860).
11. Bunker explains (1983, pp. 182–207) that in East Africa, the economic dependency of peasant producers increased the domination of state bureaucracy.
12. As Aberbach, Putnam, and Rockman (1981, p. 3) point out, "Western civil services have become increasingly specialized, highly professionalized, and unquestionably powerful—a cadre of experts in the running of the modern state." It is also exactly the case in socialist countries, where the emergence of a technical and managerial class has led to more centralization of power (Preston, 1967, pp. 216–219).
13. For details, see Pateman (1970, p. 104); Kearney and Sinha (1988, p. 571); Meier (1979, p. 182); Sjoberg, Brymer, and Farris (1973, p. 66); and Thompson (1983, p. 60).
14. In the United Kingdom, for instance, of all the university graduates who joined the higher civil service during the 1970s, almost 50% came from the two elitist universities, Oxford and Cambridge (see Rose, 1984, p. 144; Hetzner, 1985, p. 106). In Japan, almost 70% of the senior bureaucrats graduated from the University of Tokyo (Pempel, 1984, pp. 90–92; Koh and Kim, 1982, p. 292). Such elitist criteria of selection also exist in Germany (Mayntz, 1984, p. 181).

15. In a study of the Australian federal bureaucracy, it has been found that the higher-level bureaucrats, because of their elitist backgrounds, life-styles, and attitudes, are largely separated from the general public (Boreham, Michael, and Michael, 1979).
16. As Dubhashi (1983, p. 518) explains, in a parliamentary democracy, the administrative executives are accountable to the political executives, political executives are accountable to the parliament, and the parliament represents the people.
17. For instance, according to Ankomah (1983, pp. 286–297), the higher civil servants in Africa carry the colonial heritage and attitude, support the remains of the colonial influence, and often use their official power to actualize personal interests. Similarly, in the case of India, transfer of power from London to New Delhi hardly changed the elitist structure of the higher civil service (Misra, 1983, p. 443; Jain, 1990, pp. 31–47).
18. Even in some Western nations, political fragmentation has strengthened the power of bureaucracy. According to Robert D. Putnam (1975), "The fragmentation of the Italian political class has allowed and encouraged the bureaucracy to 'rise above politics,' responsible to no higher authority and fundamentally unresponsive" (quoted in Cassese, 1984, p. 35).
19. From a survey of 112 Third World countries, Clark (1978) shows that in more than 40% of these countries, the legislative branch was dismissed, dissolved, or suspended indefinitely. He also found that "a coup or attempted coup occurred once every four months in Latin America (from 1945 to 1972), once every 7 months in Asia (1947 to 1972), once every three months in the Middle East (1949 to 1972), and once every 55 days in Africa (1960 to 1972)" (Clark, 1978, p. 99). During the period 1920–1985, 40% of 143 Third World regimes (including monarchical, one-party, parliamentary, and presidential) were overthrown by military coups (Riggs, 1993, p. 5).
20. In many of the African states, civilian governments rule the country on the basis of their security forces (Hutchful, 1985, p. 61). In some newly emerging democracies in Asia, such as Pakistan and Thailand, the military still plays a significant role in political process (Smith, 1991, p. 101). In addition, this military power and the power of civilian bureaucracy are often mutually complementary. For instance, in Nigeria, the military rule has increased the power of civil bureaucracy (see Phillips, 1989, pp. 423–445).
21. In both presidential and parliamentary forms of government, bureaucracy is supposed to be accountable to elected political representatives, who in turn are to be accountable to the people. In the presidential systems, the president is directly accountable to the public, and in parliamentary democracies, government is accountable to people through the elected members of the legislature (Greenberg, 1991, p. 120).
22. According to B. Ginsberg and A. Stone (1986), the traditional accountability loop between "the people" and elected officials in America has been weakened by the influence of money, the image selling of candidates, and the apathy of voters (see Fox and Cochran, 1990, p. 250).
23. For instance, most of the U.S. presidents, vice–presidents, and secretaries have had an upper-class background (see Parenti, 1988, pp. 196–212).
24. Women are poorly represented in Western parliamentary democracies, ranging from only 4% in Britain and Italy to 14% in the Netherlands (Aberbach, Putnam, and Rockman, 1981, p. 47).
25. As Post (1982, p. 63) suggests, the basic concerns in public policy-making are how policy is related to power, who exerts power and influences policy, and to what extent a policy expresses the ideas of the powerful. In capitalist societies, it is the economic power of

corporate elites rather than the voting rights of economically powerless people which has significant influence on the elected political leaders.

26. Even the provision of public goods and services can weaken social unity: since these "benefits are distributed to individuals, not to groups, perceptions of common interests are blurred and the existence of a shared situation is disguised" (Ferguson, 1983, p. 314).
27. For Hegel, civil society is a complex system of interaction that provides benefits to its members (such as unions, cooperatives, and municipalities), which not being a part of the state, facilitate the free realization of personality (see Jackson, 1986). Since Hegel's interpretation, significant diversity has developed in conceptualizing civil society. For instance, civil society has been understood as anything that does not belong to the state or exists in opposition to the state; as the private sphere, which involves interindividual and interassociational relations and exists between individuals and the state (the public); as an economic drain of exchange which interacts with the state through the public sphere; and so on (see Sales, 1991, pp. 295–312). However, the various interpretations of civil society examined by Sales (1991, p. 309) can be synthesized and articulated further in the following manner: civil society consists of social entities within which various forms of mediation and integration occur between individuals, groups, and institutions; within which the public discourse takes place and critical public opinion is formed; and which, thus, constitutes a basic component of democracy.
28. Fraser (1990, p. 58) has critically examined the conceptualization of the public sphere by Jurgen Habermas. Habermas interprets the "public sphere" as a body of "private persons" assembled for discussing issues of the "general interest" or the "public concern": it exists as an intermediary between society and the state and holds the state accountable to society by critically scrutinizing state activities, forming public opinions, and transmitting these opinions to the state via free speech and the free press. Similarly, according to Kamniski (1991, p. 339), "The public domain grows out of the private, and through the medium of discourse, bargains, and compromises, transforms private concerns into public goals while influencing in turn the private domain by the way collective needs are met."
29. For Jurgen Habermas, the public sphere has diminished, particularly as a result of state-society cohesion with the emergence of the welfare state (see Fraser, 1990, p. 59).
30. Although in capitalist states, there are many professional associations, clubs, and unions, which apparently constitute parts of civil society, many of them are either initiated by the state or are organized for profit or private gain.
31. Thus, according to Kroker, Kroker, and Cook (1990, pp. 458–459), American presidential candidates have come to realize that "TV is the real world; where 'public opinion' can be stampeded electronically by instant TV polling." In this regard, Childers (1990, p. 15) also mentions that democracy is at risk in those societies where it has been converted into "teledemocracy."
32. In the early 1940s, an extensive analysis of these administrative and political solutions was made notably by C. J. Friedrich and H. Finer (for further details, see Jos, 1990, pp. 230–231).
33. According to Farazmand (1989, pp. 190–191), in the United States, privatization policies have discriminatory impacts: minority and female personnel have lost their jobs, while the political appointees, in collaboration with business corporations, have become engaged in corruption.
34. In this regard, some scholars are less comfortable with the idealization of the liberal public sphere by Jurgen Habermas, because it excludes the issue of gender, class, and ethnicity, and

originally this liberal idea of the public sphere excluded women, the lower-class population, and ethnic minorities from the public discourse (see Fraser, 1990, pp. 59–61).

REFERENCES

Aberbach, Joel D., Putnam, Robert D., and Rockman, Bert A., *Bureaucrats and Politicians in Western Democracies*, Harvard University Press, Cambridge, Mass., 1981.

Abrahamsson, Bengt, *Bureaucracy or Participation: The Logic of Organization*, Sage Publications, Beverly Hills, Calif., 1977.

Ankomah, Kofi, Bureaucracy and Political Unrest in Africa, *Indian Journal of Public Administration, 29*(2):284–298 (1983).

Attwood, Donald W., Bruneau, Thomas C., and Galaty, John G., Introduction, in *Power and Poverty: Development and Development Projects in the Third World*, Westview Press, Boulder, Colo., 1988, pp. 1–11.

Balbus, Ike, Politics as Sports: An Interpretation of the Political Ascendency of the Sports Metaphor in America, in *Stress and Contradiction in Modern Capitalism* (Leon N. Lindberg et al., eds.), Lexington Books, Lexington, Mass., 1975, pp. 321–336.

Ball, Nicole, The Military in Politics: Who Benefits and How, *World Development, 9*(6):569–582 (1981).

Berry, Jeffrey M., Portney, Kent E., and Thomson, Ken, Empowering and Involving Citizens, in *Handbook of Public Administration* (James L. Perry, ed.), Jossey-Bass Publishers, San Francisco, 1989, pp. 208–221.

Boreham, Paul, Cass, Michael, and McCallum, Michael, The Australian Bureaucratic Elite: The Importance of Social Backgrounds and Occupational Experience, *Australian and New Zealand Journal of Sociology, 15*(2):45–55 (1979).

Bunker, S. G., Dependency, Inequality, and Development Policy: A Case from Bugisu, Uganda, *British Journal of Sociology, 34*(2):182–207 (1983).

Caiden, Gerald E., The Problem of Ensuring the Public Accountability of Public Officials, in *Public Service Accountability: A Comparative Perspective* (Joseph G. Jabbra and O. P. Dwivedi, eds.), Kumarian Press, West Hartford, Conn., 1988, pp. 17–38.

Carey-Jones, N. S., Patankar, S. M., and Boodhoo, M. J., *Politics, Public Enterprise and the Industrial Development Agency*, Croom Helm, London, 1974.

Carpignano et al., Chatter in the Age of Electronic Production: Talk Television and the 'Public Mind,' *Social Text, 25/26*:33–55 (1990).

Cassese, Sabino, The Higher Civil Service in Italy, in *Bureaucrats and Policy Making: A Comparative View* (Ezra N. Suleiman, ed.), Holmes & Meier, New York, 1984, pp. 35–71.

Cavanaugh, Mary S., A Typology of Social Power, in *Power, Politics and Organization: A Behavioral Science View* (Andrew Kakabadse and Christopher Parker, eds.), John Wiley and Sons, New York, 1984, pp. 3–17.

Childers, Erskine B., The New Age of Information—What Kind of Participation? *Development, 2*:11–16 (1990).

Clark, Robert P., *Power and Policy in the Third World*, John Wiley and Sons, New York, 1978.

Clegg, Stewart, The Politics of Public Sector Administration, in *Public Sector Administration: New Perspectives* (Alexander Kouzmin, ed.), Longman Cheshire, Melbourne, 1983, pp. 1–36.

Crouch, Harold, The Military and Politics in South-East Asia, in *Military-Civilian Relations in South-East Asia* (Zakaria Haji Ahmed and Harold Crouch, eds.), Oxford University Press, Singapore, 1985, pp. 287–317.

Davies, Morton R., Public Accountability in the United Kingdom, in *Public Service Accountability: A Comparative Perspective* (Joseph G. Jabbra and O. P. Dwivedi, eds.), Kumarian Press, West Hartford, Conn., 1988, pp. 72–85.

DeLeon, Peter, The Democratization of the Policy Sciences, *Public Administration Review, 52*(2):125–129 (1992).

Denhardt, Robert B., *Theories of Public Organization*, Brooks/Cole Publishing, Pacific Grove, Calif., 1984.
Denhardt, Robert B. and Denhardt, Kathryn G., Public Administration and the Critique of Domination, *Administration and Society, 11*(1):107–120 (1979).
Dubhashi, P. R., Public Accountability and Ethics in Administration, *Indian Journal of Public Administration, 29*(3):518–524 (1983).
Dwivedi, O. P., Ethics, the Public Service and Public Policy: Some Comparative Reflections, *International Journal of Public Administration, 10*(1):21–50 (1987).
Dwivedi, O. P. and Jabbra, Joseph G., Public Service Responsibility and Accountability, in *Public Service Accountability: A Comparative Perspective* (Joseph G. Jabbra and O. P. Dwivedi, eds.). Kumarian Press, West Hartford, Conn., 1988, pp. 1–16.
Dye, Thomas R. and Ziegler, Harmon, *American Politics in the Media*, 2nd ed., Books/Cole Publishing, Monterey, Calif., 1986.
Etzioni-Halevy, Eva, *Bureaucracy and Democracy: A Political Dilemma*, Routledge and Kegan Paul, London, 1983.
Farazmand, Ali, Crisis in the U.S. Administrative State, *Administration and Society, 21*(2):173–199 (1989).
Ferguson, Kathy E., Bureaucracy and Public Life: The Femininization of the Polity, *Administration and Society, 15*(3):295–322 (1983).
Fischer, Frank and Zinke, Robert C., Public Administration and the Code of Ethics: Administrative Reform or Professional Ideology? *International Journal of Public Administration, 12*(6):841–854 (1989).
Fox, Charles J. and Cochran, Clarke E., Discretion Advocacy in Public Administration Theory: Toward a Platonic Guardian Class? *Administration & Society, 22*(2):249–271 (1990).
Fraser, Nancy, Rethinking the Public Sphere: A Contribution to the Critique of Actually Existing Democracy, *Social Text, 25/26*:56–80 (1990).
Garnham, Nicholas, *Capitalism and Communication: Global Culture and the Economics of Information*. Sage Publications, London, 1990.
Georgiou, Petro, The Concept of Power: A Critique and an Alternative, *Australian Journal of Politics and History, 23*(2):252–267 (1977).
Greenberg, Jeff, Accountability in the Context of the Changing Role of Government, in *The Changing Role of Government: Management of Social and Economic Activities* (Brian C. Smith, ed.), Management Development Programme, Commonwealth Secretariat, London, 1991, pp. 119–131.
Grindle, Merilee S. and Thomas, John W., *Public Choices and Policy Change: The Political Economy of Reform in Developing Countries*, Johns Hopkins University Press, Baltimore, 1991.
Harris, P., China: The Question of Public Service Accountability, in *Public Service Accountability: A Comparative Perspective* (Joseph G. Jabbra and O. P. Dwivedi, eds.), Kumerian Press, West Hartford, Conn., 1988, pp. 201–213.
Harris, Peter, *Foundations of Public Administration: A Comparative Approach*, Hong Kong University Press, Hong Kong, 1990.
Henry-Meininger, Marie-Christine and Lebreton, Jean-Michel, Accountability in the Public Service: France, in *Public Service Accountability: A Comparative Perspective* (Joseph G. Jabbra and O. P. Dwivedi, eds.), Kumarian Press, West Hartford, Conn., 1988, pp. 55–71.
Hetzner, Candace, Social Democracy and Bureaucracy, *Administration and Society, 17*(1):97–128 (1985).
Hughes, Steven W. and Mijeski, Kenneth J., *Politics of Public Policy in Latin America*, Westview Press, Boulder, Colo., 1984.
Hutchful, Eboe, Disarmament and Development: An African View, *IDS Bulletin, 16*(4):61–67 (1985).
Jabbra, Joseph G., Public Service Accountability in the Arab World: The Cases of Lebanon, Egypt, and Saudi Arabia, in *Public Service Accountability: A Comparative Perspective* (Joseph G. Jabbra and O. P. Dwivedi, eds.), Kumarian Press, West Hartford, Conn., 1988, pp. 181–200.
Jackson, M. W., Bureaucracy in Hegel's Political Theory, *Administration and Society, 18*(2):139–157 (1986).
Jacoby, Henry, *The Bureaucratization of the World*, University of California Press, Berkeley, 1973.
Jagannadham, V., Public Administration and the Citizen: How Far Public Administration Can Be Public, *Indian Journal of Public Administration, 24*(2):355–373 (1978).

Jain, R. B., The Role of Bureaucracy in Policy Development and Implementation in India, *International Social Science Journal, 42*(2):31–47 (1990).

Johnson, Anthony P., The Protestant Ethic and the Legitimation of Bureaucratic Elites, *Politics, Culture, and Society, 1*(4):585–597 (1988).

Johnston, R. J. and Taylor, Peter J., Introduction: A World in Crisis? in *A World in Crisis?* Basil Blackwell, New York, 1986, pp. 1–11.

Jos, Philip H., Administrative Responsibility Revisited: Moral Consensus and Moral Autonomy, *Administration and Society, 22*(2):228–248 (1990).

Kaminski, Antoni Z., Res Publica, Res Privata, *International Political Science Review, 12*(4):337–351 (1991).

Kasza, Gregory J., Bureaucratic Politics in Radical Military Regimes, *American Political Science Review, 81*(3):851–872 (1987).

Kearney, R. and Sinha, C., Professionalism and Bureaucratic Responsiveness: Conflict or Compatibility? *Public Administration Review, 48*(1):571–579 (1988).

Kernaghan, Kenneth, Evolving Patterns of Administrative Responsiveness to the Public, *International Review of Administrative Sciences, 52*(1):7–16 (1986).

Koh, B. C. and Kim, Jae-On, Paths to Advancement in Japanese Bureaucracy, *Comparative Political Studies, 15*(3):289–313 (1982).

Kroker, Arthur, Kroker, Marilouise, and Cook, David, Panic USA: Hypermodernism as America's Postmodernism, *Social Problems, 37*(4):443–459 (1990).

Maheshwari, Shriram, Accountability in Public Administration: Towards a Conceptual Framework, *Indian Journal of Public Administration, 29*(3):452–472 (1983).

Malbin, Michael J., Congress, Policy Analysis, and Natural Gas Deregulation: A Parable About Fig Leaves, in *Bureaucrats, Policy Analysts, Statesmen: Who Leads?* (Robert A. Goldwin, ed.), American Enterprise Institute for Public Policy Research, Washington, D.C., 1980, pp. 62–87.

Mathur, Krishna Mohan, Value System in Administration, *Indian Journal of Public Administration, 32*(1):104–146 (1986).

Mayntz, Renate, German Federal Bureaucrats: A Functional Elite Between Politics and Administration, in *Bureaucrats and Policy Making: A Comparative View* (Ezra N. Suleiman, ed.), Holmes & Meier, New York, 1984, pp. 174–205.

McKinney, Jerome B. and Howard, Lawrence C., *Public Administration: Balancing Power and Accountability*, Moore Publishing, Oak Park, Ill., 1979.

Meier, Kenneth J., Politics and the Bureaucracy: Policy Making in the Fourth Branch of Government, Duxbury Press, North Scituate, Mass., 1979.

Mertins, Herman and Hennigan, Patrick J., *Applying Professional Standards and Ethics in the '80s: A Workbook and Study Guide for Public Administration*, American Society for Public Administration, Washington, D.C., 1982.

Miewald, Robert D., *Public Administration: A Critical Perspective*, McGraw-Hill, New York, 1978.

Mirsky, Georgy I., The Role of Army in the Sociopolitical Development in Asian and African Countries, *International Political Science Review, 2*(3): (1981).

Misra, B. B., Evolution of the Concept of Administrative Accountability, *Indian Journal of Public Administration, 29*(3):435–445 (1983).

Morgan, Gareth, *Images of Organization*, Sage Publications, Beverly Hills, Calif., 1986.

Mosher, Frederick C., Public Administration, in *Current Issues in Public Administration* (Frederick S. Lane, ed.), St. Martin's Press, New York, 1982, pp. 4–13.

Mukhopadhyay, Asok, Administrative Accountability: A Conceptual Analysis, *Indian Journal of Public Administration, 29*(3):473–487 (1983).

Oakerson, Ronald J., Governance Structures for Enhancing Accountability and Responsiveness, in *Handbook of Public Administration* (James L. Perry, ed.), Jossey-Bass Publishers, San Francisco, 1989, pp. 114–130.

O'Loughlin, Michael G., What is Bureaucratic Accountability and How Can We Measure It? *Administration and Society, 22*(3):275–302 (1990).

Page, Edward C., *Political Authority and Bureaucratic Power: A Comparative Analysis*, 2nd ed., Harvester Wheatsheaf, New York, 1992.

Parenti, Michael, *Democracy for the Few*, 5th ed., St. Martin's Press, New York, 1988.

Pateman, Carole, *Participation and Democratic Theory*, Cambridge University Press, Cambridge, 1970.

Pempel, T. J., Organizing for Efficiency: The Higher Civil Service in Japan, in *Bureaucrats and Policy Making: A Comparative View* (Ezra N. Suleiman, ed.), Holmes & Meier, New York, 1984, pp. 72–106.

Peters, B. Guy, *The Politics of Bureaucracy*, 2nd ed., Longman, New York, 1984.

Phillips, Claude S., Political Versus Administration Development: What the Nigerian Experience Contributes, *Administration and Society, 20*(4):423–445 (1989).

Post, Ken, The Politics of Developing Areas and the 'Son of a Bitch' Factor, in *Rethinking Development* (Bas de Gaay Fortman, ed.), Institute of Social Studies, The Hague, 1982, pp. 49–64.

Preston, Nathaniel S., *Politics, Economics and Power: Ideology and Practice Under Capitalism, Socialism, Communism and Fascism*, Macmillan, New York, 1967.

Rainey, Hal G. and Backoff, Robert W., Professionals in Public Organizations: Organizational Environments and Incentives, *American Review of Public Administration, 16*(4):319–336 (1982).

Riggs, Fred W., Bureaucrats and Political Development: A Paradoxical View, in *Political Development and Social Change* (Jason L. Finkle and Richard W. Gable, eds.), 2nd ed., John Wiley and Sons, New York, 1971, pp. 331–351.

Riggs, Fred W., Bureau Power in Southeast Asia, *Asian Journal of Political Science, 1*(1):3–28 (1993).

Romzek, B. S. and Dubnick, M. J., Accountability in the Public Sector: Lessons from the Challenger Tragedy, *Public Administration Review, 47*(3):227–238 (1987).

Romzek, Barbara S. and Hendricks, J. Stephen, Organizational Involvement and Representative Bureaucracy: Can We Have It Both Ways? *American Political Science Review, 76*(1):75–82 (1982).

Rose, Richard, The Political Status of Higher Civil Servants in Britain, in *Bureaucrats and Policy Making: A Comparative View* (Ezra N. Suleiman, ed.), Holmes & Meier, New York, 1984, pp. 136–173.

Ryan, Margaret, Theories of Power, in *Power, Politics and Organization: A Behavioral Science View* (Andrew Kakabadse and Christopher Parker, eds.), John Wiley and Sons, New York, 1984.

Sales, Arnaud, The Private, the Public and Civil Society: Social Realms and Power Structure, *International Political Science Review, 12*(4):295–312 (1991).

Sethi, J. D., Bureaucracy and Accountability, *Indian Journal of Public Administration, 29*(3):525–538 (1983).

Sheriff, Peta, The Sociology of Public Bureaucracies, 1965-75, *Current Sociology, 24*(2):1–171 (1976).

Sjoberg, Gideon, Brymer, Richard A., and Farris, Bufford, Bureaucracy and the Lower Class, in *Bureaucracy and the Public: A Reader in Official-Client Relations* (Elihu Katz and Brenda Danet, eds.). Basic Books, New York, 1973, pp. 61–72.

Smith, Brian C., Access to Administrative Agencies: A Problem of Administrative Law or Social Structure? *International Review of Administrative Sciences, 52*(1):17–25 (1986).

Smith, B. C., *Bureaucracy and Political Power*, St. Martin's Press, New York, 1988.

Smith, Thomas B., The Comparative Analysis of Bureaucratic Accountability, *Asian Journal of Public Administration, 13*(1):93–104 (1991).

Smookler, Helene V., Accountability of Public Officials in the United States, in *Public Service Accountability: A Comparative Perspective* (Joseph G. Jabbra and O. P. Dwivedi, eds.), Kumarian Press, West Hartford, Conn., 1988, pp. 39–54.

Subramaniam, V., Public Accountability: Context, Career and Confusions of a Concept, *Indian Journal of Public Administration, 29*(3):446–456 (1983).

Suleiman, Ezra N., From Right to Left: Bureaucracy and Politics in France, in *Bureaucrats and Policy Making: A Comparative View* (Ezra N. Suleiman, ed.), Holmes & Meier, New York, 1984, pp. 107–135.

Tashiro, Ku, Accountability in the Public Service: A Comparative Perspective in Japan, in *Public Service Accountability: A Comparative Perspective* (Joseph G. Jabbra and O. P. Dwivedi, eds.), Kumarian Press, West Hartford, Conn., 1988, pp. 214–226.

Thompson, Elaine, Democracy, Bureaucracy, and Mythology, in *Public Sector Administration: New Perspectives* (Alexander Kouzmin, ed.), Longman Cheshire, Melbourne, 1983, pp. 57–77.

Thynne, Ian, Accountability, Responsiveness and Public Service Officials, in *Public Sector Administration: New Perspectives* (Alexander Kouzmin, ed.), Longman Cheshire, Melbourne, 1983, pp. 78–100.

17
A Public Service for the Twenty-First Century

O. Glenn Stahl
Arlington, Virginia

No simpler or more eloquent statement of the purposes of the Government of the United States has ever been expressed than these words in the preamble of the Constitution: "to form a more perfect union, establish justice, insure domestic tranquility, provide for the common defence, promote the general welfare, and secure the blessings of liberty to ourselves and our posterity. . . . "

Every time I read this noble introduction, I wonder how many citizens remember studying these objectives in school—or if they ever had any exposure to them at all. I wonder how many teachers have taken the time to pore over these words in their classes, to examine the meaning and implications of each phrase as it has been interpreted and elaborated upon in the actions of the government over our two-hundred-year history. How many dissect the full meaning of justice, analyze the ramifications of welfare, explore the significance of liberty, realize the variants on how we secure it, ponder the futuristic connotations of our posterity? What examples of current functions of government flow from or are explained by any one of these phrases? I am not alluding here to all the fine points of constitutional law but simply to the elementary fact that this preamble alone is the foundation of so much that has developed in two centuries, of so much that profoundly affects the daily lives of all of us.

And I also wonder what emphasis is placed on the opening phrase: "We the people. . . . " It should remind us that government is not only something that serves and controls our very existence but also is an instrument of all of us, a means that our forebears established and that we

---

This essay is reproduced, with minor adaptations and by permission of the author and publisher, from Chapter VIII, of the same title, in STANDING UP FOR GOVERNMENT: CHALLENGES FOR AMERICAN CITIZENSHIP by O. Glenn Stahl (New York: Vantage Press, 1990). The essay should be read with the understanding that it is part of an intensive critique of recent U.S. political leadership and of the failure of so many American citizens to appreciate their communitywide responsibility in a democracy and to express that responsibility adequately through the machinery of government, the only instrument they all have in common.

are expected to treasure, bring to fruition, and from time to time shape and refine—in short, that we are a democracy.

The thirst for democracy among long-repressed peoples of the world demonstrates how precious a concept it is. We Americans dare not take it for granted. We must equip ourselves to make it work and work in the interest of all. Our good fortune in having democracy as our heritage must not be wasted. We must savor it and nurture it.

Each age brings different threats to democracy and therefore different challenges to our citizenry. We cannot risk actions on the part of ourselves or of our leaders that threaten our joint interest together or the interest of those who follow us in the next and succeeding centuries. We dare not focus on short-term issues or goals and ignore ultimate effects—whether it be our security from military attack, from the threats to our public health, from environmental despoilment, from undermining of the economy, from failure to develop and cultivate the constructive talents of all our people, or from degradation of the human spirit. As Franklin Delano Roosevelt put it, our government must not only guarantee freedom of speech and freedom of religion—it must secure freedom from fear and freedom from want.

The overarching theme in these pages is that the preservation and enrichment of democracy require duties from all of us. It means that we cannot treat our privilege of voting lightly, that our sad record, among Western democracies, of the lowest proportion of eligible voters who exercise the privilege must be changed. It means that we must keep informed on public issues and not just in the superficial sense of scanning headlines or listening to the evening news. It means that we must be conscious of respecting the expenses of government as much as we respect our personal needs for food, clothing, shelter, and amusement. It means that we need to understand and give support to those who toil in the halls and remote outposts of government as much as we respect our own private interests and our own personal acquaintances. And it means that we must prepare our children and our grandchildren to do better than we have in living up to these civic responsibilities.

I. THE FOUNDATION FOR A STRENGTHENED PUBLIC SERVICE

When the twenty-fifth anniversary of the founding of the Peace Corps was celebrated in 1986, Public Television commentator Bill Moyers, a former Peace Corps Deputy Director, expressed this penetrating reminder:

> The Peace Corps was born after a long season during which young Americans had been spiritually unemployed. Now, once again, a generation of Americans is tempted to live undisturbed, buying tranquility on credit while hearts atrophy, quarantined from any great enthusiasm but private ambition. [1]

Moyers felt it was time to get a little more nobility into our aspirations—an objective that relates closely to the subject of this chapter. It is a challenge to all of us, not just the young—for all of us in a democracy are responsible for how our young are developed and educated. It is a challenge especially to our public schools and universities.

A discouraging characteristic in our nation's public life is not demagoguery by so many unprincipled leaders who prey on the body politic, but by the number of otherwise intelligent people who are so susceptible to it, so ripe for exploitation. It is a sad commentary that after two centuries of practicing politics—by which I mean concern for public policy—we still have no definitive plan for preparing citizens to examine public issues, to take part, to vote, or even to be interested. It is too much a thing apart. It is not one of the essences of civilized life for so many of us. It is not an essential part of our life curriculum. We have concentrated instead on schooling ourselves to"make a living," to interpret freedom as devoting our full energies to our own private pursuits and welfare. How can a nation that prides itself on freedom, pays periodic respect to its flag, boasts of its supposed superiority, and throws its weight around the world give so little attention to preparation for citizenship?

A. The Role of Education

Much of the answer lies in the educational system. Something is missing. The long separation of public schools from the rest of government, the preoccupation with keeping them "nonpartisan," are conditions that have contributed to insulation, to making them "unpartisan"—and, consequently, uninterested. There is an insensitivity to the fact that education itself is a part of government, that teachers are bureaucrats, that the very grist of education is vital to citizenship. Education cannot escape a major share of the responsibility for the decline of interest in public affairs and for the shameful levels of illiteracy and "functional illiteracy" among our population.

The major elements of educational curricula from secondary school through graduate study still appear to be: the arts, language and literature, science and mathematics, business and finance, physical fitness, and an elusive field with various labels that embraces history and social studies (under which government and politics is a stepchild subsidiary). Even at university level such subjects as political science, government, political affairs, political philosophy, and public administration are usually minor wings at most campuses. Where they exist, their funding and enrollments have declined in recent years. They remain the enthusiasm of only an isolated few.

There was an awakening early in this century to the need for the governmental aspect of a truly broad, liberal education, with the establishment of specialized schools and departments in many universities, including the landmark pace-setters such as the Maxwell School of Citizenship and Public Affairs at Syracuse and later the Kennedy School of Government at Harvard. But the sparkle of their founding has faded, and, most important, there never has been a recognition that at least some of their subject matter needed to be a part of the curricula in all branches of the university, just as such facilitative subjects as writing, mathematics, and science are woven into so many of the specialized schools' curricula. By its very nature, a matter concerning all citizens equally in a democracy, citizenship and government ought to be a required part of the curricula for engineers, business students, doctors, lawyers, nurses, teachers, scientists, and every other field of study directed toward living in a career-oriented society.

Considering its central importance in our lives, understanding of government and public affairs ought to be a major division of educational purpose—ranking alongside science, literature, and the arts. Why, for example, if we have National Endowments for the Arts and for the Humanities, is there not a National Endowment for Citizenship and Public Affairs? Is it possible that the reason politics is held in such low repute is because it has declined as a basic part of our educational system and as a pursuit of our intelligentsia? Could this be a reason that it seems to attract so many persons of venal instinct and that it is looked upon by so many as an avenue for exploitation? Does it fit too neatly as a companion piece with our overemphasis on profit and material success? Is the feebleness of education in the field a cause for our lack of a public philosophy that ought to permeate every citizen's inner fiber, ranking along with his religion, his sense of morals, his sense of human values?

Important as it is, to work in government or be associated in some substantial way with public affairs is only one part of this educational need. But, in my zeal to broaden appreciation for the responsibility of all citizens in a democracy, I do not mean to slight it.

B. Public Service as an Occupation

There are so many ways in which individuals can devote all or major parts of their lives to public service that it is impossible to catalog them all. Participation in political campaigns for office or causes and entrance into careers in government departments are the most obvious avenues for public service. But the gradual increase of associations and enterprises of a nonprofit character, pursuing professional or public issue agendas, adds greatly to these opportunities. Of course, we should consider all branches and forms of education as a public service, which is all the more reason that public-service education should be a part of it everywhere.

The relationship of this obligation on the part of education to the needs of the public service is highlighted by the National Commission on the Public Service in four of its recommendations:

- The President and Congress must ensure that federal managers receive the added training they will need to perform effectively;
- The nation should recognize the importance of civic education as a part of social studies and history in the nation's primary- and secondary-school curricula;
- America should take advantage of the natural idealism of its youth by expanding and encouraging national volunteer service;
- The President and Congress should establish a Presidential Public Service Scholarship Program targeted to 1,000 college or college-bound students each year, with careful attention to the recruitment of minority students [2].

As a means toward all these purposes, the Commission also urged that schools of public affairs enrich their teaching with opportunities for practical experience for their students. To this end, it suggested a Public Service Fellows Program, modeled on successful programs already in existence for White House, Congressional, and Judicial fellowships.

Occupational choice is ordinarily neither totally random nor predetermined. It is, however, often heavily influenced by circumstances beyond the individual's control. It depends on where one was born and raised; the parents' occupations, interests, and economic status; educational choices; entertainment or other extracurricular experiences; and the like. We prefer to think that physical appearance, ethnicity, or sex has nothing to do with choices, but undeniably such may have a decided impact, especially in some environments. Of course, personal inclinations, preferences, and aptitudes can influence choices markedly.

Regardless of all other influences, at some point fairly early in one's life, an individual begins to think about what he or she would like to do—what activity or subject matter he finds interesting, challenging, or even exciting, something for which the individual senses a talent, something he feels he can master. It has been my observation that this attraction to an occupation, skill, or field of knowledge is by far the most potent force directing the person's choices. I reject the prevailing mythology—so casually articulated by people who do not even analyze their own motivations—that mankind is driven entirely by prospects for financial reward.

Therefore, this is the most malleable point for influence by public officials, educators, parents, friends, and citizens in general. This is why the "climate" for a particular employment area is all important. Personnel policies of government agencies and the attitudes of counselors in school and college can make or break a young person's intuitive desire for identification with one activity or another. Mere information may not be enough. A detection of sincerity and enthusiasm, or lack thereof, on the part of the advisor may tip the decision one way or the other.

This is also why there is hope in the forthright assessment and recommendations of the Volcker Commission. This is why it is heartening to hear the opening comments of a recent appointee to the directorship of the U.S. Office of Personnel Management at her Senate confirmation hearing. Constance B. Newman informed the Senate Government Affairs Committee that she was proud to be returning to "an honorable profession—one that allows its members to work for the common good, one that charges its members with preserving the democratic form of government, and requires that its members serve the public with excellence." She reminded them that this was the profession where "its members have won almost two-thirds of the Nobel prizes for medicine and physiology in the last twenty-five years." Noting, however, that the efforts of public servants are often not appreciated, she concluded:

> This situation leads to the challenge of convincing the public that there is a difference between public service and public servitude and only the former can be expected of any person. One challenge of the director of the Office of Personnel Management then is to communicate to America about the dignity and worth of public servants. [3]

Would that this insight could have been expressed earlier in the decade of the 1980s. It is certainly grounds for hope that the methods and financial support will be forthcoming to enable OPM to play the role that Ms. Newman envisages.

II. THE "NATIONAL SERVICE" IDEA

The most exciting idea on the horizon for turning the nation's attitudes around is the proposal advanced from several quarters to provide, as a natural part of the development of every young man and woman in America, a period during which he or she could serve in some junior capacity in civilian, military, or foreign posts, working for the government. Modeled in part on conscription for military service in time of war but even more pointedly on the magnificent Peace Corps experience begun over a quarter of a century ago, it would at one and the same time enlarge young people's appreciation for public service and also provide extra hands and minds to perform at modest expense the many public chores for which there appears always to be a shortage of funds.

Certainly the Peace Corps already proved that altruistic motivations could be counted on to get jobs done in some of the most poverty-stricken corners of the world and with only token compensation. But the rewards in developing civic and altruistic awareness were testified to by practically every participant. Of course, the prospects for all national service opportunities might not be as exotic or entail as much exciting travel. Nevertheless, they would all share in teaching value and in exposing the "cadets" to the public service atmosphere and to the satisfactions of performing needed and worthwhile duties. An extraordinarily high proportion of Peace Corps graduates, incidentally, wound up becoming civil servants later in their careers. In fact, the promise of a more enduring and life-sustainable job could be one of the lures attached to service in such a national service corps.

It may take some time to work out all the debatable issues that arise in planning a national service program. Most proposals suggest voluntary enlistment, but some argue for making it mandatory, although the latter would probably be prohibitive in cost unless it were for very short periods. Duration is another issue, with ideas ranging from six months to two years. Then comes the question whether service must be limited to the young only. The Peace Corps was not confined to young people, so that more and more older persons enlisted as the program developed. (Many will recall that a then-future President's mother was among them—Lillian Carter.) Likewise, some feel that some proposals place too much emphasis on military service, while others would confine it to civilian endeavors. The actual amount that would be practicable for compensation remains to be worked out. A particularly intriguing idea is for linkage with student aid, whereby an individual could pay off a loan to get a college education by spending a specified period in national service.

Several organizations and private groups are promoting the basic idea for national service. In a comprehensive book on the subject, Charles C. Moskos proposes a voluntary, decentralized program that links civilian and military service to foster civic participation and commitment through engagement in crucially needed social and human services. Hailed as a pregnant notion of shared responsibility for society that must once again be instilled in young people and a call to America to restore civic vision, the Moskos book is a significant contribution [4]. Among the variants on the basic idea is the suggestion that the locales of national service might well include nonprofit charities and foundations, as well as governmental organizations.

Certainly, proposals of this caliber are worth a try. They would provide a splendid supplement to a beefed-up program of instilling greater civic awareness and sense of societal obligation in and by our educational institutions themselves. The National Service Act of 1993, initiated by President Clinton, is a modest but valiant step to meet this objective.

III. RESTORING THE PUBLIC SERVICE

To energize the public service to cope with the anticipated problems of the twenty-first century will require implementing not just the recommendations of the Volcker Commission, not just the ideas of several professional associations and academies, not just the suggestions in this and several other books of recent years, but many proposals yet to come as America regains its sense of civic consciousness. A few admonitions and urgings from my other writings deserve reemphasis or amplification here because they relate so intimately to the "rebuilding" of the public service:

1. Above all, the climate for public administration needs to be improved dramatically. If this means more changes in our basic educational system and more attention to civic virtue on the part of the general population, then we must muster the fortitude to face up to it and begin action.

2. The government personnel system and organization require a host of modifications, especially a regirding of the principle of merit in public employment, a drastic reduction in the use of political appointees and a systematic improvement of their caliber, giving careerists more clout in policy debates, making greater use of training opportunities (including the Executive Exchange program for career and private sector top people, and expanded orientation of new political appointees), substantial increases in government salaries, and more rational definitions of ethical performance.

3. More urgent study is called for, with a view to early action, on the idea of a system of national service, especially for young people. The present status of this intriguing idea is too academic and leisurely. (See above, concerning recent progress.)

4. More forthright attention should be given to the fundamental problem of how public policy is affected by the inordinate influence of money from special-interest groups in financing candidates' campaigns for legislative and executive posts in government. None other than former President Jimmy Carter in mid-1989 published this bit of information, going back to his own administration:

> In November 1979, the U.S. House of Representatives rejected hospital cost containment legislation that the U.S. Senate had passed by a 3-to-1 margin. Two hundred and two of the House members who voted "nay" had accepted an average of more than $8,000 from the American Medical Association, plus additional sums from the American Hospital

> Association. A number of these members of Congress acknowledged to me that the bill would have saved patients at least $10 billion annually, that hospital costs had been rising 50 percent more than the national inflation rate and that the legislation was good for our country. However they were obligated to vote against it. The "obligations" were to generous medical doctors and hospital owners and operators in their home districts. The bill was defeated. Americans lost. Greed triumphed. [5]

Carter than reminded us of the more recent experience with the relaxed controls "bought" by defense contractors, savings-and-loan operators, and others. The only solution on the horizon for ridding the body politic of this scourge is public financing of all political campaigns for Federal office.

5. To give some continuity to creating a greater American awareness of the importance of restoring prestige and performance quality to our public service, one more recommendation of the Volcker Commission deserves citation: "The President and Congress should establish a permanent independent advisory council, composed of members from the public and private sector, both to monitor the ongoing state of the public service and to make such recommendations for improvement as they think desirable" [6]. The Commission felt that, since the "quiet crisis" problems are many and complex and have been long in the making, corrective action must be part of a coherent and sustained long-term strategy. Actions of a permanent body would help ensure that the state of the public service remains high on the national agenda.

IV. CONCLUSION

It is arguable whether the dispositions of so many victims of mythology about government can be readily changed. Ingrained prejudices and long nurtured habits of thought may be too solid to tolerate alteration. It is surprising, however, that sometimes people en masse, whole cultures of human beings, can display remarkable resilience that seemed impossible under different conditions.

I remember how quickly attitudes changed during the Great Depression from a period of antipathy and suspicion about government to one of warm embracing of government's deep involvement in so many aspects of daily living. I remember how readily people adapted to collaborative efforts during the two World Wars. And I witness now what is happening in so many countries around the globe—where totalitarianism and repression had stifled dissent and independent thinking for generations—once exposure to new ideas and some novel facts of life occurred. Miraculously, even in the citadels of communism, when shackles were relaxed even slightly, there was an outpouring of new thinking and fresh expression that had been assumed impossible a scarce few years before.

In the United States, our problem is somewhat different. Being a free society, we have such a plethora of information and openness that we tend to ignore all except what pleases us. Our very freedom leaves us susceptible to the easy way out—relying on prevailing myths, shibboleths, and prejudices to substitute for study and reflection in formulating our opinions about conditions around us.

Yet, in our nation, too, we can free ourselves of such habits as mindless trashing of government programs and personnel—programs that a majority of our representatives voted to put in place, and personnel who have been trying valiantly to bring them to a realization of their objectives. We have the advantage of being accustomed to free speech and to opportunities to express and vote our preferences. What we have to guard against is succumbing to distortions of reality that inhibit us from acting in our own best interest collectively as a society.

Respect for our symbols of patriotism—the flag, the pledge of allegiance, the Constitution—is a vital part of our civic life. But it is superficial and without depth of meaning if at the same time we demean our governmental institutions and discourage good people from devoting personal energies and resources to their maintenance at optimum levels.

Fourth of July fireworks, commemorative parades, and strident shouting at political rallies about the flag and freedom (in the abstract) are scarcely the full content of patriotism and freedom. Patriotism is a reverence for the laws that ensure freedom and give it meaning, for the rights of others, for the general collective welfare, and for the institutions that promote these values. Freedom is exercising the right to vote, to keep informed, to put our civic responsibilities high on our life's agenda [7].

This is the message that younger generations most need to remember. This is the message that public servants and those who are considering the public service for employment most need to remember. In a speech in Washington in 1989, a distinguished career public servant with vast experience at home and abroad, Ambassador Robert M. Sayre (later Assistant Secretary for Management of the Organization of American States), observed that the world is approaching a stronger consensus on the proper relationship between the people and government. He also reminded Americans of the increasing interdependence of nations, with consequent impingement on sovereignty and national independence. The public servant of the twenty-first century, he concluded, will be expected to have a broader perspective and be more knowledgeable of relationships with and among our neighbors.

Our immediate obligation as a society is to imbue more young people with a selfless vision, with the excitement and satisfaction that derives from most governmental activity. Recruits in all fields—engineers, technicians, social scientists, even clerical workers—must be infused with a sense of mission, an ethical passion for the public interest. Dedication to such ideals should be among the criteria for judging performance and according recognition. For, this is how we support democracy.

NOTES

1. Bill Moyers, as reported by Saundra Saperstein in "Peace Corps Honors Its Living Ideals," *The Washington Post*, September 22, 1986, p. A4.
2. *Leadership for America: Rebuilding the Public Service*. The Report of the National Commission on the Public Service, Paul A. Volcker, chairman, 1989, p. 7.
3. Constance B. Newman, testimony at confirmation hearing, U.S. Senate Committee on Government Affairs, June 6, 1989.
4. Charles C. Moskos, *A Call to Civic Service*, The Free Press, New York, 1988.
5. Jimmy Carter, "Congress for Sale," *The Washington Post*, June 12, 1989, op. ed. page.
6. *Rebuilding the Public Service*, p. 8.
7. One of government's most senior and respected practitioner/scholars, Dr. Marshall E. Dimock, eloquently presented the significance of citizenship in a democracy in a brilliant article: "The Restorative Qualities of Citizenship," *Public Administrative Review*, January/February 1990, pp. 21–25.

18
Ethical Foundations

O. Glenn Stahl
Arlington, Virginia

Problems of ethical attitudes and behavior in a public service are not easily divorced from the society and culture in which the bureaucracy exists. This was notoriously true in American history and especially evident during the latter decades of the twentieth century.

Disdain by large portions of the population for matters governmental goes hand-in-hand with lower ethical standards in politics and public administration. The root of the condition particularly in the United States has been longtime exaggeration and exaltation of the profit motive in American culture. The drive for personal gain has been given too much credit for American economic success and has, in addition, handicapped objective consideration of ethical issues in both public and private sectors. A brief examination of this condition is in order as background.

I. STIMULUS OF THE PROFIT MOTIVE

Profit in the form of monetary reward is not the only fuel that energizes the engines of modern life. The assumption that energetic and devoted people are motivated primarily by the desire for wealth has been one of the too-infrequently-challenged canards for many, many years. From the standpoint of any relative evidence, it is a gross exaggeration, to say the least. On the basis of ample evidence, it is (to borrow a phrase from a 1930s president of the University of Wisconsin, Dr. Glenn Frank): "meretricious ballyhoo and demagogic claptrap."

This essay is reproduced, with minor adaptations and by permission of the author and publisher, from Chapter VI, "The Ethical Dimension," in STANDING UP FOR GOVERNMENT: CHALLENGES FOR AMERICAN CITIZENSHIP by O. Glenn Stahl (New York: Vantage Press, 1990). The essay should be read with the understanding that it is part of an intensive critique of recent U.S. political leadership and of the failure of so many American citizens to appreciate their communitywide responsibility in a democracy and to express that responsibility adequately through the machinery of government, the only instrument they all have in common.

This rather limited motivation that is given so much weight by some economists and publicists is seldom analyzed for its implications for ethics or for its potential for abuse. Nor is it evaluated as a force in history or in the development of our own civilization. A look at the record suggests that, at the very minimum, it must be tempered by many substantial qualifications and reservations:

1. Every survey of employee attitudes in both industry and government that I have ever seen indicates that workers rank money well down the list of reasons they work at the jobs or for the employer with which they are involved. Admittedly these surveys do not often include top executives but rather focus on the rank-and-file workers, including many professionals and technical people, who develop and produce the organization's product or service.

2. If profit-making were the prime cause for human effort, then how do we explain the major advances and discoveries in history—up to this very day—that came from educational institutions, nonprofit organizations, dedicated scientists, and, not the least of these, governmental agencies such as the National Institutes of Health, the Tennessee Valley Authority, and the National Aeronautics and Space Agency? At this very moment, thousands of determined scientists and engineers are laboring intensively in remote government and semipublic establishments on health therapies, environmental issues, astronomical explorations, new product designs, and many other fascinating endeavors that will shape the future of ourselves and our children. Few of them take the time to think about their remuneration, so long as they are not reduced to a state of deprivation.

3. If profit-making is such an indispensable element in our economy, then how do we explain the choices and the contentment of so many millions upon millions of workers all over the world engaged in charities, religious groups, overseas missions, health services, school teaching, research, civil services, military careers, and the like? Have we ever measured their happiness and job satisfaction against those who are stimulated only by the prospect of amassing wealth?

4. Profit may make a difference in many parts of the economy where there are few other criteria for success, but it has always had to be kept within bounds wherever it works; it is highly susceptible to abuse; and it discounts mankind's most noble, less self-serving instincts too cavalierly. Profit is a delicate and dangerous force. Like the surgeon's scalpel, it can be a boon when applied with skill and restraint, but, in the wrong hands, it can be a lethal weapon. I am realistic enough to suspect that "wrong hands" are forever lurking in the shadows.

5. Profit, in any event, seldom motivates people down the line in any enterprise. As we have previously noted, success in creating a better product or providing a better service cannot often be attributed to the ambitions of financiers, stockholders, or even corporate executives—who generally are the only or major ones who stand to gain from profit margins. Business success is largely due to the creativity and hard work of those at lower and intermediate levels in the enterprise—who enjoy their work and do it for the satisfaction of performing at their best. Rarely would they expect to become owners or partners of the business by doing their jobs well. They may aspire to promotion or bonus awards (and may deserve to), but such possibilities may be uncertain and are certainly beyond their personal control.

So, if profit is the principal driving force of economic behavior, how is it that so many persons responsible for success are content to work for a salary or wage?

6. The most negative aspect of the profit issue is the strong incentive it creates for unethical performance. The association between money-making and corruption is too striking to overlook. We have already seen that programs intended to help the less fortunate in our society—such as housing for low-income families—seem to be prime areas for greedy men and women to operate. As one former careerist in the housing field has observed, reliance on real-estate developers to use

government funds wisely for moderate-priced housing is inherently flawed because the temptation is too great for private real estate magnates to make a killing by raking off exorbitant fees and other "cream" from the government subsidies. After many years of experience, he concludes that the only sure protection against this practice is to keep it out of the hands of developers and return to direct government ownership for any housing built with public money.

Examples could, of course, be cited in many areas of activity where the pressure of the profit motive instigates corruption in the use of public funds.

7. Finally, a doubt about the superiority of the profit motive is found in the contrast between public or semipublic nonprofit operation and private operation of a service essential to modern urban existence. Three examples come immediately to mind, each from a different period in our history:

- Government operation of the nation's railroads during World War I, when a first-rate instance of good public administration was demonstrated;
- The Tennessee Valley Authority's electric-rate yardstick beginning in the mid-1930s that easily outdistanced private electric utilities in providing electric power, brought rates down all over the country, and made the famous Manhattan Project possible for building the atomic bomb during World War II (when otherwise there would have been a power shortage); and
- The phenomenal success of the Public Television network (nonprofit and partially funded by government) that has shown America what good television can be like and has shamed commercial networks into improving the quality of their programming.

The public yardstick has often served as a brake on too much dependence on the profit-making sector.

All of these reservations about the pervasiveness and benevolent power of the profit motive in many segments of society suggest ethical implications. We need to examine the contrasts in this respect between the public and private spheres.

II. ETHICS AND THE PUBLIC INTEREST

Sensitivity to the public interest is the most fundamental ethical obligation of the public official and the one most often lacking among novices or venal men and women, especially those appointed for partisan reasons to key posts. The ideal public servant, of which there are many, is one who thinks in terms of the general welfare, the overall good, the long-range effect an action might have. He resists the temptation to respond just to the group or individual pressing a case before him; he must, first of all, be well enough informed to be aware of other interests and to make certain that all interests are taken into consideration in any decision-making. It was more than forty years ago that a distinguished Federal official and scholar declared in a classic book on ethics that "virtuous performance" requires "attempting to inject some increased allowance for the more public interest and some increased concern for those citizens not immediately present or heard" [1]. The advice is as relevant today as then.

To the average citizen, ethical performance in public positions means merely avoidance of overt corruption involving money—such as the acceptance of bribes in return for dispensing some favor or for exemption from some requirement or penalty, or some action that advances the official's own financial interest. These are indeed breaches of the public trust, as emphasized on various past occasions.

But this is not all there is to standing up for the public interest. There are policy issues, too, that invoke ethical considerations. And they are often more significant (and more elusive or harder to identify) than the money-related kinds of violations. Dwelling only on the financial corruption misses some even more common, subtle, and serious ethical flaws in political and administrative behavior.

Chances are that men and women in public life are more likely to succumb to their prejudices, ideologies, and limited perspectives than they are to the prospect of monetary gain, dangerous as the latter may be. One member of Congress, a thoughtful and public-minded veteran of twenty-four years in the House of Representatives who has had much responsibility on issues of ethics, confessed that when he was a young idealistic newcomer: "I had the idea that public decisions which deny decent shelter to today's poor and steal from the living standards of tomorrow's families in order to continue the fiction that wealthy people are overtaxed are at least as unethical as . . . [some of the personal and financial peccadilloes of which his colleagues or nominees for cabinet posts were then being accused]" [2].

In other words, a persons' wrong-headed or self-centered prejudices or misconceptions are the source of "public-interest corruption" as distinguished from money-related crimes. Another much-respected member of Congress, Claude D. Pepper, has been quoted as explaining (some years before his death in 1989 at age 88) that his philosophy "rejects the notion that those who are underprivileged have earned their fate, that hard work inexorably leads to success." Pepper held that:

> the health, economic security, and—to the degree possible—happiness of its people is a proper concern of government. It acknowledges the value—indeed the necessity—of individual worth and effort. But it diverges sharply from conservatism by recognizing what should be clear to all: that in a complex twentieth-century free society, no one and nothing is big enough, powerful enough and universal enough to make life bearable for the masses of its citizens. [3]

To be sure, relatively selfless people of goodwill can differ over the means and methods for government to sustain the "general welfare," as the Constitution ordains; this is the everyday stuff of politics and public policy debates. But the extremes of these positions, such as what we witnessed during the Reagan years, are as immoral as they are unwise. And it is interesting that this kind of immorality seems to go hand-in-hand with overt financial corruption—probably because the fountainhead of both kinds of evil are the old-fashioned human failings of greed and acquisitiveness.

Society loses plenty from bribery and financial manipulation, but it loses even more from extremism and just plain irresponsibility for our fellow man's welfare, for man's inhumanity to man. The old English rhyme puts it well:

> The law locks up both man and woman
> Who steals the goose from off the common,
> Yet lets the greater felon loose
> Who steals the common from the goose. [4]

In addition to financial and policy corruption, there is "the corruption of incompetence," as one former Federal official once expressed it. Irresponsibility, in the choice of presidential appointees on down to selection methods within the career service, is a profound constraint on virtuous public administration. Two of the most devastating evils of the Reagan administration were the astounding low caliber of so many political appointees and the partly successful efforts to subvert the merit system of employment in the career service. It is a disgusting blot on the American escutcheon that, by the spring of 1988, 113 senior Federal appointees, including some agency heads and deputies, had to be indicted or otherwise forced to resign for legal or ethical violations. And there were scores more about whom suspicions were raised.

III. THE DOUBLE STANDARD

There is a failure on the part of the general public to appreciate that a public service can not rise very far above the level of its environment and that it derives most of its temptations for wrongdoing from that environment. Perhaps this explains why the overwhelming proportion of mischief in government stems from temporary political appointees from the outside and almost never from the millions of career people who have had the discipline and motivation of public service built in to their experience. Perhaps it also explains the striking and unfortunate contrast between what the public expects of government officials and what it expects of those engaged in private pursuits.

Informed and fair-minded persons will surely concede that we demand higher standards of conduct from public servants that we do from businessmen. Except in nonprofit organizations and a few other pursuits, there seems to be little opportunity outside of government for practice in the rigorous objectivity and impartiality required of government workers. In practically all commercial and industrial enterprises the principals can buy and sell where they wish, can play favorites without fear of punishment, can disclose or conceal information on their operations largely as they please, can accept gifts without question of impropriety, and need seldom worry about conflicts of interest. (In those occasional instances when they must consider such constraints, it is almost invariably the result of a law against it, an act of government.) Obviously, when any of the activities just cited are committed by public servants, we are shocked, if not enraged, at such behavior—even though it may be commonplace in the business world.

The incongruity is evident when we consider the marked difference in moral behavior within and outside government service. First of all, there is a clear relation with motivation. Many persons are attracted to government in the first place—just as they are to religious pursuits, charitable causes, and other service-oriented endeavors—by a genuine zeal for identification with a larger good than some narrow economic, sectional, or self-serving interest. In addition, when the facts are examined, we unquestionably find more people dedicated to the broad public interest within the public service than we do outside. A finding expressed well by a Senate Subcommittee on Ethical Standards more than forty years ago is remarkably relevant today:

> We . . . believe that the ethical standards of public officials are probably higher than those prevailing in business and other walks of life. On this point . . . there was persuasive testimony from men of experience in both Government and business and from observers of both. Public officials apparently are more conscious of the problem of moral standards. The resentment which public officials sometimes show when subjected to public criticism may be explained in part by their awareness of the fact that some of their critics would be even more vulnerable to criticism if the same standards were applied. [5]

One might add that similar findings by leaders with experience both in and out of government have been reported repeatedly year after year.

The point bears repeating: so much depends on what motivates people. The contrast in ideals between public functions and some private-sector work can be quite marked. Can one imagine a stock speculator on Wall Street being concerned with national park development? A corporate takeover financier in promotion of the public health? A real-estate manipulator in the conservation of forests, in wildlife management, in the explorations of soil scientists? These may be examples of the extremes, but they are very real contrasts in motivation. Can there be any doubt about which activities benefit mankind and which prey upon it?

In the last analysis, society as a whole must bear the responsibility for ethical conduct in public affairs. Those who complain of corruption but busy themselves with seeking special benefits not available to the general public are the basic corruptors. The relentless pressure of special, single-issue, or parochial interests, and conflicts over symbols instead of substance in public debate, are hardly indicators that we have arrived at a stage meriting the appellation "the good society."

Whenever the medical doctor mistakes his own prosperity as synonymous with the status of the public health, whenever an association of manufacturers resists legislation for the general welfare of workers or consumers, whenever the labor leader places the sanctity of his union structure ahead of protection of all citizens, whenever a veterans' organization exploits patriotism for class legislation, whenever the voter views his representative to Congress as an errand boy, as a channel to get favors or special consideration, we fall short of the goal of the highest public ethics. A wise senator many years ago made an insightful forecast: "Until the citizen's own moral code prevents him from debasing himself by procuring corruption of public servants, the problem of corruption and morality in public life will remain very real and earnest" [6].

Americans must learn this elementary truth—that the onus for good government is not just on those in public employment, it is on every citizen. I suggest that such learning begin in public schools.

A self-indulging society that glorifies the amassing of obscene private wealth, to the exclusion of other values, and is obsessed with protecting its wealthiest citizens from the heaviest taxation does not set the best example. Also, a society is not morally worthy in the highest sense if it undervalues its service-minded members—its teachers, its police, its scientists, its civil servants—because they do not worship at the altar of money-making.

To some persons whose prime ambition is to get rich, it is apparently inconceivable that there can be others who are so deeply involved in some field of work, so fascinated with some challenging endeavor, so dedicated to achievement in whatever they do that monetary rewards are far down on the list of their lifetime aspirations. There is a surprising concentration of such work-oriented people in the public service—more than in any other sector of society. It is this kind of motivation that is more readily converted into serving the public interest than are motivations centered on rewards. As I have insisted before, this statement does not say that only a few work-centered, other-oriented individuals enter into the ranks of private organizations. They are everywhere. But I do contend that there is a different attitude among the bulk of professional and ministerial careerists throughout government from that found elsewhere. It is certainly among the reasons I am so completely skeptical of the moves toward privatization.

IV. WHAT CAN BE DONE ABOUT ETHICAL PERFORMANCE

I am not one to advocate more laws or penalties regarding ethical conduct. In fact, I think some on the books miss the mark and create too legalistic an atmosphere for the problem rather than developing a philosophical base for attention to the public interest, stimulating an awareness of it, and focusing on such concepts as policy ethics and competence ethics. Following are a few approaches that could move us in this direction. Some are important because of their indirect impact on moral performance, although they serve other purposes as well.

1. We need more emphasis and support for the career service. It is a very fundamental imperative for an ethical environment. A proud public servant is a good public servant. Efforts should be directed toward building and maintaining that pride.

2. Coincident with this objective is making better use of the career service, with all its expertise, institutional memory, and discipline in serving the public interest. The concept of a responsive bureaucracy was reduced during the Reagan years to one of a submissive bureaucracy. Many of the policy missteps and moral lapses at that time could have been avoided if career people had been given a chance to participate. Not only were alternatives or warnings by careerists ignored, for the most part they were suppressed. Knowledgeable professionals were often kept in the dark, with work planning frequently confined to woefully unqualified amateurs. An open, healthy exchange between inside experts who safeguard institutional memory and integrity and outside appointees who ostensibly represent a president's overall policy is absolutely essential both to effective government and ethical government. Moreover, the art as well as the science of governance demands assimilation of all relevant points of view before final decisions are made. Multiple participation in decision-making is the only rational methodology in public administration.

3. Less stress on ethics as such and more emphasis on selection of personnel would help reach the fundamental problem of wrongly motivated people. This applies both to promoting the quality of presidential and other political appointments and to fostering rigorous application of merit principles for entry and advancement in the career service.

4. A good deal of awakening has already occurred to the inadequacy of rules relating to individual financial holdings and restrictions on employment subsequent to government service. For example, requiring appointees to divest themselves of corporate stock or real estate before entering on public job focuses too much on the appearance or prospect of wrongdoing without taking into account the impact on recruiting or retaining the best candidates. Likewise, too mechanistic or legalistic limitations on employment after leaving government may create impossible situations for professionals who might not be able to pursue their lifelong expertise at all outside government if they so desire. This, too, dissuades competent people from accepting public employment.

It would be naive to remove all penalties for misdeeds that might grow out of too cozy a relationship between outside financial interests and public policy-makers or to lift all restrictions on the "revolving-door" mentality that pervaded the Reagan administration. But some of the more absurd and badly drawn proscriptions require modification, lest recruitment of qualified people be severely handicapped.

A more sensible emphasis might be on machinery (a) to investigate more fully in advance a candidate's personal history and sense of ethical behavior; (b) to provide for continuous review, by multimembered panels of experts inside government, of conditions that lend themselves to wrongdoing; and (c) to make ethical performance a major ingredient of executive training for both career and noncareer appointees. This may cost a little more in government personnel operations, but it would pay for itself a thousand times over.

5. Since so much depends on the ethical climate outside government, we cannot overlook the importance of building more understanding of the political world and more civic consciousness among the general population.

6. Because of its direct relationship to morality in government, more insistent attention must be given to reform of the ways in which political campaigns for office are financed, including both the presidency and the Congress. Studies and programs of the public-interest organization Common Cause are one of the best sources for enlightenment and action on this subject. Ultimate

success in removing the strong connection between campaign gifts and decisions by elected officials, in my judgment, will not come until we provide a neutral and nonpartisan financial source for conducting campaigns. It is well known that lavish gifts to political campaigns provide the contributor with access to members of Congress and the Executive Branch that is not so easily available to other citizens. The spillover effect from a congressional office to a cabinet member or other key official is obvious. The system itself is corrupt. The ultimate solution is public financing for all campaigns, but with stringent controls on spending limits for any one candidate and restrictions on the number of candidates for any one office. In my judgment, it would be worth the extra cost to government, even if it means more taxes, but it is nowhere near as expensive as the current loss to all citizens in the unwarranted influence procured by political action committees, corporations, and wealthy individuals. It is not only the best way to insulate government from corruption but the only way ultimately to ensure the democratic process, under which all voters have equal access.

V. CONCLUDING OBSERVATIONS ON ETHICS

The foregoing ideas are no panacea. Matters of ethics are too complex and human frailties are too pervasive for anyone to expect that his prescriptions will bring us to the millennium. But we have to try.

In an unpublished statement made in January 1987, retired General of the Army Andrew J. Goodpaster summed up the scope of unethical performance in the government in this way: "When poorly qualified people are given office, when weak institutional procedures and organizational designs are permitted to exist, when decisions reflect ideologies rather than objective evaluation, trust and confidence . . . must suffer." In his judgment, corruption is not just the use of public office to make a fortune for oneself or others. It covers a much broader field. Says Goodpaster: "It remains one of the highest duties of national leadership—and of national leaders—to inspire and nurture the growth of public trust—to the end that those who receive it work ever harder to deserve it, and those who grant it do so ever more generously and willingly, in order that our country may be best served."

I cannot help but contrast this true patriot's conception with that of some of our recent political leadership, such as parlaying the prestige of the presidency itself into munificent lecture fees. Referring to former President Reagan's two-million-dollar deal to play master of ceremonies for a Japanese company's week-long arts festival, columnist William Safire commented: "For a former president with a hot agent and no sense of sleaze, the profit opportunities are endless." And, when a freewheeling owner of a recently seized savings-and-loan institution was asked if his generous campaign contributions bought him influence with key politicians, he replied: "I want to say in the most forceful way I can, I certainly hope so" [7].

The contrast between sensitivity to the public trust and a complete absence of it is not only sad, it is alarming!

The comments in this essay are not to disparage good work and good people in the private sector of the American economy but to counteract the reverse psychology—the short-sighted, senseless, ill-informed, and sometimes diabolical propaganda to curtail government, to deprecate it, to cripple it, all in the name of an ideology that foolishly maintains that all of mankind's success and future welfare depends on the unfettered profit motivation.

It just isn't so.

NOTES

1. Paul H. Appleby, *Morality and Administration in Democratic Government*, Louisiana State University Press, Baton Rouge, 1952, p. 176.
2. David R. Obey, a Democrat from Wisconsin, as quoted by Haynes Johnson, "Is Congress Misjudged?" *The Washington Post*, May 26, 1989, p. A2.
3. As quoted: Ray Stephens, "Recalling Pepper," *American Association of Retired Persons Bulletin*, June–August 1989, p. 14.
4. Anonymous. From Edward Potts Cheyney, *Social and Industrial History of England*, 1901, introduction.
5. U.S. Senate Committee on Labor and Public Welfare, Subcommittee on Ethical Standards, *Ethical Standards in Government*, 82nd Congress, 1st session, 1951, p. 12.
6. Sen. Estes Kefauver, Democrat from Tennessee, in *Ethical Standards in American Public Life*, Annals of the American Academy of Political and Social Science, March 1952, p. 7.
7. Both the statements of Mr. Safire and of the savings and loan owner (Charles H. Keating) cited in this paragraph, appeared in separate boxes on pages 41 and 42, respectively, in *Common Cause Magazine*, July/August 1989.

19
Bureaucracy in International Organizations: Building Capacity and Credibility in a Newly Interdependent World

David E. Wilson*
United Nations Joint Inspection Unit, Geneva, Switzerland

The emergence of international organizations has been a notable development of the twentieth century. This process has been stimulated by recognition of the many political, economic, and social issues which are global and interdependent; the tripling of the number of nation-states since World War II; and the "global village" created by new telecommunications and transport technologies.

These trends have produced a tremendous increase in the number and purposes of international organizations. At present, there are literally thousands of international organizations and associations of diverse types: public or private; administrative, political, professional, or special interest; global, regional, or subregional; with or without supranational power (Union of International Associations, 1991). The approximately 175 organizations of nation-states may be defined as those that "possess institutional structures based on treaties which bind together several or many nation-states in long-term agreements designed to foster cooperation with each other, in specified ways, and for the promotion of general or particular political and/or social goals" (Miller, 1972, p. 5).

This study provides a brief overview of the best-known and most universal of these international organizations, the United Nations system, or, as it is informally known (positively to its admirers, disparagingly to its detractors), "the world organization." More specifically, the emphasis is on the operations of the secretariats of the United Nations system, and the challenges, problems, constraints, and successes that have shaped their bureaucratic development.

The study proceeds from the very useful and incisive framework established by Miller (1972, pp. 3–19). International organizations have a characteristic duality. In creating them, member states made only a small step toward giving up their sovereign rights to decide when,

---

*Mr. Wilson is Senior Research Officer of the United Nations Joint Inspection Unit in Geneva, Switzerland. The views expressed here are his own and do not necessarily reflect those of the United Nations.

where, and how to act in the international arena. On the other hand, international organizations do permit relatively more transnational "government" to be introduced than existed before. In this process, relations between states may alter, and the structure and functioning of the international system itself, or a part of it, may be transformed. Thus, international organizations are very conservative in their conception, but radical in their potential.

The United Nations system, as the only organizational structure created to deal with all types of international issues worldwide, continuously encounters this basic tension in its goals, organizational approaches, and two broad functions of managing conflict and advancing human welfare. It is part of an enormously complex process of international social interaction. It also embodies a cooperative/integrative duality, existing uneasily somewhere along a continuum from total international anarchy at one end to a fully integrated international community at the other.

The following brief history and analysis reveal a provocative progression. The League of Nations failed dismally, but provided useful lessons for operating an international bureaucracy. The United Nations system struggled during the long Cold War period from about 1945 to 1989. It had to cope with a vast increase in nation-states; widespread political confrontation; haphazardly built, cumbersome, and increasingly fragmented organizational structures; and an uneasy mix of negotiating, research, and operational functions.

In the late 1980s, however, a confluence of political, economic, social, and technological factors suddenly revived possibilities for significant international cooperation. The 1990s give the United Nations system (and other international organizations) unexpected new opportunities to achieve their basic goals but raise as well the question of whether their bureaucratic systems and political support are up to the task.

I. LEAGUE OF NATIONS, 1919–1939

During the nineteenth century, activities involving many states, such as communications and the treatment of prisoners of war, were increasingly entrusted to international regulatory organizations like the International Telegraph Union and the Red Cross. By the time World War I began, there were over thirty such international organizations in operation. Joint efforts were also undertaken to settle disputes between countries, and to discuss issues such as disarmament, at international conferences. These initiatives showed growing awareness that the world needed new institutions whose authority would cut across national boundaries.

The Treaty of Versailles of 1919 led to the establishment of the League of Nations. After the devastation caused by World War I, the league sought to provide an organ of collective security, whose members would help each other repel aggression and would arbitrate their own disputes. The league, based in Geneva, had a General Assembly which met annually and an Executive Council originally intended to be composed of the five great powers (France, Great Britain, Italy, Japan, and the United States) plus four elected members. It also had a Secretariat involved in labor, economic, trusteeship, and other functions.

Despite high hopes, the league failed. The United States never joined, and the Soviet Union did not join until 1934, when Brazil, Germany, and Japan had already withdrawn. The interwar period was extremely unstable, characterized by many boundary disputes, ethnic struggles, the Great Depression, the collapse of liberal democracies, and the rise of new dictatorships and totalitarian states. The League of Nations worked hard to settle the many international disputes, but its authority and machinery were too limited. By the late 1930s, World War II loomed ahead, and the League of Nations faded into obscurity.

The league did achieve some successes in its two decades of operation. It held health conferences and helped control international drug traffic. It stimulated national programs and agencies in fields such as nutrition. The International Labour Organisation launched initiatives to improve working and living conditions. And although early human rights activities made little progress, a High Commissioner for Refugees was created and worked to mitigate significant refugee problems in Eastern and Central Europe (Claude, 1971; Miller, 1972).

The league's two decades of experimentation also established the basic shape and functions of the international bureaucracy that have continued generally to the present day (Jenks, 1943; Purves, 1945; Royal Institute, 1944). The key need, of course, was to recruit, develop, and effectively employ staff of a high caliber. These staff were found to need certain special qualities: an international outlook and awareness, loyalty to the organization rather than to a national government, a high level of skill and imagination to deal with complex international policy matters, and fluency in both spoken and written French and English (the working languages of the league) plus an understanding of several other major languages.

These considerations eventually led to the establishment of a permanent international civil service. But controversy arose, and has long continued, over the extent to which this core staff should be supplemented or even overshadowed by national officials seconded for assignments of several years or specialists brought in to perform short-term tasks.

Establishing a personnel management system proved difficult. First and foremost, a principle of "national representation" required that posts be equitably distributed among staff from all member countries. However, there were major problems in assessing candidates with widely differing academic credentials, skills, and experience. Maintaining national balances in various small units, service categories, and grade levels was a constant struggle. Recruits had to be accepted from countries with very modest administrative and professional standards as well as from countries with very high ones. Staff had persistent concerns that these complicated balancing acts, and subsequent promotions and assignments, were decided too often by considerations of nationality rather than merit.

In addition, although salary and benefit levels varied enormously from country to country, the league's salary scales had to be sufficient to attract the best talent available. Under the "Noblemaire principle," they were established at the level of the highest national civil service (then the British, now the United States). The risks of international civil service also became evident. Staff were giving up stable, familiar careers in their home countries and becoming true expatriates cut off from established family, friendship, and cultural ties.

Secretariat substantive work also presented special problems. The League staff was small, but it had to deal with many diverse global issues. As a result, many small technical, specialized units were established and gradually formed themselves into watertight compartments. This situation greatly hampered overall recruitment, career advancement, rotation, training, and transfers. It also led to recognition that unified or common personnel, administrative, and support systems should be established if possible among the various international organizations of the future.

Although league budgets were modest, financial headaches arose and have continued to the present day. The budgets depended on the whims of nationally minded appropriations committees in dozens of countries. Arguments began over how much, and by what criteria, each country should pay. Budget resources were always tight, and budgetary procedures became quite rigid. There was much quibbling over small amounts of expenditure and difficulty in collecting annual assessments, as the league struggled to respond to the diverse political interests, financial practices, and disputes among its many member states.

Leadership and management were also identified as critically needed skills. Senior Secretariat officials were not just administrative officers. They needed consistently to present a world outlook and concrete policy proposals to policy-making bodies as the basis for negotiations and discussions by member states. This required a sharp awareness of changing global conditions and very constructive statesmanship. At the same time, a weakness was identified in the middle ranks. Many league staff were a combination of political negotiator, diplomat, technical specialist, and academician but had relatively little sense of, or experience in, practical administration. It was hoped that this would change as international organization size and administrative functions expanded, by providing diverse field assignments and establishing some kind of staff college for international officials (Jenks, 1943, pp. 93–96, 102).

Despite these many complications, the league and its related bodies did move forward. Health, drug, nutrition, labor, and refugee initiatives have been noted. Also noteworthy was the establishment of efficient machinery for the handling of international conferences: technical secretariats, documentation, interpreters, translators, reporters, and publication units. The League Secretariat slowly grew into a potentially useful tool, but the political turbulence of the times did not permit its further evolution.

II. THE UNITED NATIONS AND THE COLD WAR YEARS, 1945–1989

During World War II, a group of nations resolved to join together to maintain international peace and ensure social progress in the future. An international conference, held in San Francisco in 1945, adopted the United Nations Charter. Conferences were also held to set up specialized agencies to deal with other global problems. The United Nations came into being in October 1945, with fifty-one original member countries and a small Secretariat headquartered in New York.

The United Nations is an organization of independent, sovereign states: it has no sovereignty of its own. Its function is to harmonize, encourage, and initiate. Its basic purposes, as stated in the Charter, are to maintain international peace and security; develop friendly relations among nations; cooperate in solving international economic, social, cultural and humanitarian problems, and in promoting respect for human rights; and to be a center for harmonizing the actions of nations toward those common goals (United Nations, 1986a, pp. 3–10).

The assets, property, and some functions of the League of Nations were transferred to the new United Nations, along with the general overall organizational structure. The administrative processes of the new Secretariat also drew heavily on the league's experience. However, over the 1945–1989 period the new United Nations system grew haphazardly to an organizational size and complexity that dwarfed its original concept and have led to many administrative and operational problems.

While a full listing of all the system's components would cover many pages, a listing of at least the major elements is useful to suggest the scope and diversity of this unwieldy structure. The United Nations proper has six principal organs: the General Assembly, the Security Council, the Economic and Social Council, the Trusteeship Council, the International Court of Justice, and the Secretariat. In addition, the General Assembly has over time created a score of other programs, councils, and commissions, with varying degrees of financial and administrative autonomy. The following are the major ones:

UNCTAD—United Nations Conference on Trade and Development
UNDP—United Nations Development Programme

UNEP—United Nations Environment Programme
UNFPA—United Nations Population Fund
UNHCR—United Nations High Commissioner for Refugees (Office of)
UNICEF—United Nations Children's Fund
UNRWA—United Nations Relief and Works Agency for Palestine Refugees in the Near East
WFP — World Food Programme

Further, there are sixteen specialized agencies and two autonomous organizations (GATT and IAEA) associated with the United Nations by formal agreement. These agencies were all independently established, and they all have their own governing bodies, secretariats, and budgets. Four of these organizations—the "Bretton Woods" institutions—are somewhat separate from the others, by virtue of their international financial character: the World Bank, International Finance Corporation (IFC), International Development Association (IDA), and International Monetary Fund (IMF). The other fourteen agencies (with year of establishment in parentheses) are the following:

FAO	Food and Agriculture Organization of the United Nations (1945)
GATT	General Agreement on Tariffs and Trade (1948)
IAEA	International Atomic Energy Agency (1957)
ICAO	International Civil Aviation Organization (1947)
IFAD	International Fund for Agricultural Development (1977)
ILO	International Labour Organisation (1919)
IMO	International Maritime Organization (1958)
ITU	International Telecommunication Union (1865)
UNESCO	United States Educational, Scientific and Cultural Organization (1946)
UNIDO	United Nations Industrial Development Organization (1986)
UPU	Universal Postal Union (1874)
WHO	World Health Organization (1948)
WIPO	World Intellectual Property Organization (1970)
WMO	World Meteorological Organization (1950)

The activities of the system have grown enormously over the years. United Nations membership had more than tripled from the original 51 member states to 178 by mid-1992. Almost all these countries maintain permanent missions in New York, and many have missions at other United Nations headquarters' sites in Geneva, Vienna, and Nairobi. Many nongovernmental and other intergovernmental organizations also maintain offices in these cities as well. The specialized agencies have similar situations. All of these missions and representatives engage in literally thousands of governing body, committee, conference, and expert group meetings on a year-round basis throughout the system and around the world.

The secretariats have grown equally rapidly. The United Nations system employs some fifty thousand people: about twenty thousand professionals, including five thousand development experts in the field, and thirty thousand secretarial and clerical staff. The staff are located at headquarters, regional offices, and in more than one hundred countries where several or many agencies maintain field offices. The General Assembly uses six official languages for its deliberations and documents (Arabic, Chinese, English, French, Russian, and Spanish). English and French are the working languages of the Secretariat. The specialized agencies follow similar patterns, and in some regional offices staff use other working languages as well.

The system spends about $U.S. 6 billion a year (excluding the capital lending of the financial institutions). About one-third comes from mandatory assessments for "regular budgets," with twenty states paying about 80% of the total cost. The other two-thirds comes from voluntary contributions from member states to many diverse "extrabudgetary" programs and trust funds.

The United Nations system is thus a loose confederation, with the United Nations Organization at the hub. Concerns about the unwieldy structure have led to continuous attempts to improve coordination and prevent overlap and duplication, while retaining a decentralized system and respecting the areas of specialization of the various agencies. The Economic and Social Council (ECOSOC) and the Administrative Committee on Co-ordination (ACC), composed of the heads of the agencies and chaired by the United Nations Secretary-General, help the General Assembly to coordinate the system's work (United Nations, 1986b).

Over the years, the United Nations system organizations have developed four broad functions:

1. Their intergovernmental conferences and meetings negotiate many international technical standards, conventions, treaties, agreements, and resolutions. This work has proved quite important in building structures of agreed international behavior, policies, and interaction in many economic, social, and technical fields.

2. Technical cooperation programs, which help developing countries to enhance and manage their institutions and human resources, have grown from almost nothing in the early 1950s to an effort that now involves over half the system's total resources. Despite the many inherent difficulties and controversies of the economic and social development process, the agencies have made some significant contributions.

3. The agencies all conduct many expert group meetings and prepare extensive research in support of the preceding two functions. This has led to many global information networks which have greatly furthered the spread of knowledge and international cooperation.

4. The United Nations Secretariat has unique and high-visibility functions of its own, such as those related to decolonization, refugees, disaster relief, disarmament, human rights, and peacekeeping. Progress in the last three areas was painfully slow and frustrating during the Cold War period.

In all these functions, the United Nations system is expected to provide an international perspective and neutral services and policy advice to governments, rather than the biased and self-interested activities which other governments and organizations have to offer.

In national governments, leadership and decision making are provided by presidents, prime ministers, ruling committees, and cabinets. In international organizations, however, proposals come from many less-authoritative individual government representatives or groups and are filtered through combative legislative proceedings. International secretariats can influence or reshape the organizational policies and decisions to some extent, but their operations, and the obstacles they face, are often much different from those in national governments (see Claude, 1971; Loveday, 1956; Luard, 1966; Padelford and Goodrich, 1965; Waters, 1967).

The United Nations system has proved to be very complex. Some observers have described it as possibly the most complicated organization in the world. Further, its member states, and their cultural and geographic blocs, support it only tentatively: sometimes for genuinely altruistic reasons; more often for reasons of narrow national prestige, protection, or immediate advantage. Inertia is strong, and the existing structures resist any change.

Too often, the United Nations system organizations have been battlegrounds for publicly fighting out disputes among various member countries, rather than independent organizations with a cooperative spirit and decision-making powers of their own. In effect, these many separate, competing political units manipulate global interdependence in a continuing process. While one can always hope for more, the situation is a confirmed and continuing reality.

This tension puts extra pressure on international civil servants in their day-to-day work. They must deal with shifting negotiations and treaties, not enforce laws. They are caught between the demands of international and national loyalty and in extreme cases may even be strongly penalized by their home country if they support the interests of the former over the latter. The financing of their programs (and salaries) is also plagued by chronic deficit, liquidity, and withholding problems, as many recalcitrant or tardy member states give their funding obligations low priority or feel that one or another United Nations system program does not adequately reflect their interests.

Within the broad functions of furthering international cooperation and economic and social welfare, international staff have six tasks. They support the work of legislative bodies. They provide worldwide information and research services. They carry out technical cooperation programs. They conduct important diplomatic, political, and operational tasks in refugee, disaster, peacemaking and peacekeeping programs. They administer and support field operations, and they also attempt to coordinate the system's many activities.

All these tasks occur against a shifting and contentious political background. In the early years, for instance, socialist countries sought to restrict international bureaucratic power and initiatives, while Western countries tried to strengthen them. During the 1970s and 1980s, however, new member states placed a very strong emphasis on efforts to solve their economic and social development problems and on field-level operations worldwide, while Western countries sought also to emphasize other global policy issues.

These political and cultural factors carry over into international personnel policy (see Finger and Mugno, 1974; Mailick, 1970; Maron, 1977; Reymond and Mailick, 1985; Young, 1958). Although agency heads are given independence in selecting staff, member governments often press and succeed in having their favorite candidates appointed. Appointment is expected to be based on merit, but an elaborate system of "geographic distribution" also operates to maintain a balance among nationalities in most units and at higher management levels.

Arguments continue over the proper proportion of career staff versus shorter-term staff. Another critical area is staff quality: while many staff are argued to be outstanding, others are criticized as mere political favorites or people running away from home-country problems. In addition, the system must struggle with a cumbersome salary and adjustment system among its many duty stations, slow progress in establishing job classification and career development systems, and other issues such as limited advancement opportunities for women.

International civil servants also face unique cultural problems. For instance, the General Assembly has continually stressed language training for staff to achieve "linguistic balance," to the detriment of management, career development and other training. United Nations system staff, coming from some 150 countries and working in almost as many, must cope with three different systems of self-definition: their "home" culture, that of their international organization, and that of the country where their particular organizational office is located. In fact, these staff are the forerunners of a significant modern phenomenon: millions of people in government, business, and other organizations whose careers and family lives are caught up in defining new relationships in an international "no-man's land" which straddles many cultures.

Finally, operations and management present special problems. Executive heads of international agencies must be resourceful power brokers. They must seek opportunities for action while working in very vague policy frameworks and with legislative bodies that are both cautious and combative. Program managers and staff must also be sensitive to these hazards, as well as to linguistic and cultural misunderstandings. They become frustrated with negotiations and program debates that may drag on for years without resolution. The United Nations system has made considerable progress in establishing program planning, budgeting, evaluation, and reporting systems to improve performance since the mid-1970s. However, these processes do not yet cover all parts of the organizations, and they are not yet fully accepted and used by managers and staff.

The haphazard growth of United Nations system programs, dealing with almost every field of human activity, has led to persistent efforts at reform. The United Nations Secretariat alone experienced major reform attempts in 1953, 1961, 1966, 1969, 1975, 1982, 1986 and 1992. The best known reform, the "Capacity Study" (United Nations, 1969, p. iii), found the United Nations system to be polycentric, highly decentralized, and uncoordinated. It concluded bluntly that it was an "unmanageable" machine; "unwieldy, like some prehistoric monster"; and so disorganized that neither member states nor top officials could possibly control or direct it. The study's proposals to remedy and streamline this structure, however, were not widely implemented.

The many reform efforts do provide some further insights about United Nations system dynamics. First, reform has always been highly politicized rather than merely technocratic. Industrialized countries (the "North") have generally stressed the need for better management, operations, and control, while developing countries (the "South") have often been suspicious of such initiatives as attempts to reduce funding and cut programs. Second, the continuous quest for incremental management reform in the system is much easier to pursue than broader questions of structural change (how better to organize the programs?) or institutional change (what are the real purposes of international cooperation efforts?). Third, the resulting reform proposals have been too timid and too generalized to succeed, especially when exposed to the corrosive scrutiny of the many intergovernmental bodies and diverse constituencies found throughout the system.

These general characteristics of United Nations system bureaucracy, and the system established by the United Nations Charter of 1945, remained fairly stable throughout the 1945–1989 period. The two most significant changes were increasing complexity, due to the many new member states and the many new programs and organizations, and the emergence of technical cooperation for development and humanitarian programs as the dominant activities of the overall system.

However, in the United Nations system a major wave of optimism and success arose in the 1970s, only to decline again in the 1980s. The system benefitted from strong support for new multilateral approaches to international affairs during the 1970s (Commission on International Development, 1969). This trend was greatly enhanced by interest in the "limits to growth," "spaceship Earth," and other urgent problems cutting across national borders (Brown, 1972). The system held ground-breaking special conferences between 1972 and 1984 on environment, food, shelter, science and technology, women, energy, least-developed countries, aging, population, and other issues, and determined efforts were made to discuss and launch a "New International Economic Order" (NIEO). Although the NIEO foundered badly in drawn-out and acrimonious North-South debates, the other conferences led to significant consciousness raising and useful new international and national programs and initiatives.

In the 1980s, however, this multilateral impulse faded again. Cold War attitudes revived, worldwide economic growth slowed (especially in the poor countries), and a period of international "issue fatigue" set in. Analyses of United Nations system performance had long been polarized between enthusiastic tributes (Joyce, 1984) and biting criticisms of muddled functioning and misdirection (Pines, 1984). Yet other analyses, particularly a very thorough study by Elmandjra (1973), provided perceptive insights into the functioning of the United Nations system (Bhagwati and Ruggie, 1984; Feld et al., 1983; Franck, 1985; Hill, 1978).

Even the sharpest critics acknowledge significant accomplishments. The smaller, more technical specialized agencies have done much to establish essential global systems in fields such as telecommunications, civil aviation, maritime transport, and postal services. WHO's work to eradicate smallpox, spread basic health care, and combat new scourges such as AIDS is widely respected, as is UNICEF's work with and on behalf of children worldwide.

UNHCR and WFP work in very difficult conditions to aid refugees, and "blue helmet" soldiers and staff carry out dangerous peacekeeping assignments under United Nations auspices. The larger specialized agencies have strengthened government programs and capacities in such fields as agriculture, education, and labor relations and have helped build essential global research and information networks in these fields. And the system has helped establish international dialogue, agreements, and policies to advance human rights, settle territorial disputes, and draft treaties and standards for national or international adoption.

But, appropriately, other organizations emerged during the 1980s to carry out these tasks as well. The World Bank and regional development banks have expanded from capital lending to dominate the technical cooperation efforts which the United Nations system formerly monopolized. International and national nongovernmental organizations (NGOs) have greatly increased their participation in development and humanitarian programs. They also do high-quality research work on global problems and mobilize public opinion, support, and participation on important issues. And multinational or "transnational" corporations, largely beyond the influence of multilateral organizations, are very powerful actors in the global economy. In the political sphere, the annual "Group of Seven" economic summits of the major industrial countries, and regional political bodies in the Americas, Europe, Africa, and Southeast Asia, have provided significant alternatives or supplements to United Nations system efforts.

These complicating factors—Cold War revival, slow economic growth, issue fatigue, competition—were accentuated by yet another financial crisis, as the major United Nations system donor country (the United States) and many smaller ones became more and more tardy in providing their annual assessed contributions. At the "fortieth birthday" celebration of the signing of the United Nations Charter in 1985, the United Nations Secretary-General cited a "crisis of confidence" that threatened the very functioning of the system.

The fortieth anniversary stimulated a burst of new assessments of the system's condition. Critiques came from many diverse sources (Dicke and Hüfner, 1987; Forsythe, 1989; ILO, 1987; Ramcharan, 1987; Renninger, 1989). Many of them emphasized the crisis aspect of the situation (Ghebali, 1988; Harrod and Schijver, 1988; Stanley Foundation, 1987; Williams, 1986), while others stressed the need for new management initiatives and greater operational effectiveness (Beigbeder, 1987; Cassen and Associates, 1986; Collins, 1987; Pitt and Weiss, 1986; United Nations Association, 1987). But they were in general agreement that the United Nations system suffered from a severe malaise. Notwithstanding its past progress and achievements, it seemed a cumbersome organism that had lost a great deal of its dynamism and sense of direction.

Even the study of international organizations had foundered (Rochester, 1986). The League of Nations had produced initial, optimistic research on international institution building. After World War II and many early studies of the new United Nations, however, the "realist" school of international relations shifted to an emphasis on national power, military strategy, diplomacy, and the nature of national interests. As United Nations system influence declined in this harsh Cold War environment, international organization studies shifted again. Research in the 1960s concentrated on "regional integration" (especially the European Community). Research in the 1970s reflected "globalist" views of international relations and "interdependence," in which the United Nations system was considered to be only one, lesser participant. The early 1980s brought a resurgence of Cold War power politics and an emphasis on "regimes." By the late 1980s, the

United Nations had "fallen on hard times," and its study had almost disappeared within the larger study of international politics.

III. 1990 AND BEYOND

When the Berlin Wall came crashing down in November 1989, the superpower confrontation between the United States and the Soviet Union, which had dominated international relations for so long, suddenly faded. A "new world order" (still to be defined or even understood) emerged. All kinds of global economic and political initiatives suddenly seemed possible, and the United Nations system was pushed back out to center stage as a tool for achieving them.

The most dramatic openings came in the long-enfeebled political and conflict management functions of the United Nations. The new atmosphere provides great hopes, and equally great dangers, for mankind and for United Nations efforts.

1. Superpower nuclear arsenals are dropping rapidly, but the unchecked proliferation of nuclear, chemical, and other weapons among many states is a new threat. There was substantial progress toward a new United Nations treaty and organization to stem the spread of chemical weapons in early 1992, but the risks of nuclear confrontation and nuclear terrorism are increasing.

2. There is a strong new emphasis on democracy and popular participation in many countries, but democracy is proving to be a complex, messy, and not readily transferable process. The United Nations had great success in supporting elections in the new nation of Namibia, but subsequent experience in Haiti, Western Sahara, and Cambodia suggests that other cases may be far more difficult.

3. A change in many countries to market economies could eventually bring widespread global prosperity, but it will require a wrenching period of transition and social hardship, at a time when the global economy is already strained and new development funding is difficult to obtain. United Nations system efforts are hampered by the lack of models for such drastic economic transformation, the system's traditional ties to existing governments, and the shortage of new funds.

4. International affairs should benefit from the absence of superpower struggles. The United States Conference on Environment and Development ([UNCED], or "the Earth summit"), held in Brazil in June 1992, may eventually represent a transition as significant as the Industrial Revolution. But is also clearly showed that great disputes remain about the problems, policies, and remedies of "sustainable development," and especially about who should pay and how. This experience suggests that "global management" will be as contentious a process in the future as in the past.

5. The new global order could lead to stronger efforts at peacemaking and peacekeeping through the United Nations Security Council. The Gulf War of 1991 constituted a massive military action under United Nations auspices, but other conflicts—as in Cambodia, Somalia, Liberia, and the former Yugoslavia—are a sobering reminder that such interventions may be an unending and tremendously difficult task.

6. The Gulf War also provided an important precedent for the international community to override "national sovereignty" to protect minorities within a country. But the volatile and bitter ethnic conflicts that have erupted in so many countries suggest that this task too will require enormous determination and resources.

7. Finally, the nation-state is under siege: the United Nations Secretary-General has estimated that the United Nations of the future might have three hundred member states. This

presents considerable global problems in terms of small, fragmented economies; a need for new regional or subregional federations; and the risks of even more muddled "world government."

The dominant economic development work of the United Nations system has not been forgotten in the new era. One of the most extensive studies ever made of the system's development operations was issued in 1991 (Nordic). It stressed the need for system agencies to reform and strengthen operational quality and impact, focus on areas of comparative advantage, make governing body oversight much more responsive and pragmatic, and create more dynamic leadership and staff resource management. A 1992 system report (United Nations JIU) shows that the agencies are responding to these challenges with new policies and innovative programs. But they will need to accelerate this pace in order to maintain and enhance their development role.

A March 1992 *UN Chronicle* article (United Nations) serves as a reminder that while member states call for the performance of heroic new tasks, the existing constraints on the system have not gone away. The outgoing Secretary-General noted with pride that, after being "virtually immobilized" for four decades, the United Nations was completing a "most productive" period with the "enthusiastic participation" of the major powers and moving again "to near the centre of international relations." However, another article stated that the United Nations was owed $1 billion by member states and that the latest financial crisis was "very, very serious." (By May 1992 new peacekeeping operations had raised this deficit to about $2 billion, or double the normal annual United Nations budget. Further, only 14 of the 178 member countries had fully paid their assessments.)

Similarly, the outgoing Secretary-General cited reform efforts involving "meticulous . . . self-analysis" and streamlining that had produced a "rejuvenated" United Nations. But the very next article reported on a plan developed by twenty-two countries (and subsequently implemented in 1992) to remedy the Secretariat's "top-heavy" administrative structure and "ad hoc" operations.

The dramatic changes in international relations are nevertheless producing new ideas for drastic change in United Nations system operations. For example:

- Bertrand (1989) analyzed the basic defects of past operations and called for a "third-generation" world organization based on well-organized, high-level summit meetings on global issues and carefully chosen action programs to help solve them.
- Toffler (1991, pp. 456–460) and many others have observed that the present United Nations system is a "trade association of nation-states," which may have to admit NGO groups, transnational corporations, and religious groups in order to build broad support for action in the new cross-national, heterogeneous world order of the future.
- UNDP's Human Development Report (1992, chapter 5) argued that the present "weak, ad hoc and unpredictable" framework of global governance should be replaced by an ordered, fair, and effective system that would represent not just the rich and powerful, but all the peoples of the world and the powerless and vulnerable developing countries.
- And several sources have observed that the many developed and developing countries with bloated defense budgets could regularly commit a small portion of these funds to joint peacekeeping and development efforts. This action could finally give the United Nations system a stable funding and programming base in these fields. It could also help to prevent the intense human suffering, and subsequent heavy economic relief and reconstruction burdens, which unchecked civil strife now imposes on individual countries and on the international community.

Coping with such sweeping changes will require strong new leaders. One of the most persuasive thinkers of the new era, President Václav Havel of Czechoslovakia, called in a widely publicized speech in March 1992 for overcoming the ponderous and paralyzing technocratic approaches, control systems, institutions, and other political "machinery" of the Cold War period. He argued that future issues will be those of survival rather than geopolitical security and that only the new ideas, experiences, and actions of many individuals, plus responsibility, courage, and compassion, can lead to a transforming new politics. In a parallel view, Urquhart and Childers (1990) stated that changes in the selection of top United Nations system officials are urgently needed. Governments should systematically seek out the best possible men and women worldwide to lead the system, with far greater attention to the nature of the jobs to be done and the qualifications needed to do them.

At present, the United Nations system is still imprisoned in the past. The need for global actions has never been greater, but the requisite resources, capacity, and political will are still lacking. Will the United Nations system muddle along? Fight through to new levels of effectiveness? Or be replaced by totally new global institutions?

Some new model of global order may emerge, or a period of increasing disorder and stress may evolve: it is far too early to tell. Whatever the outcome, the peoples and problems of the world will be ever more closely entwined in the twenty-first century. International organizations and civil servants, in whatever form, will become more and more central in determining how well or how poorly mankind copes with the urgent global challenges of the future.

REFERENCES

Beigbeder, Yves, *Management Problems in United Nations Organizations: Reform or Decline?* Frances Pinter, London, 1987.

Bertrand, Maurice, *The Third Generation World Organization*, Martinus Nijhoff, Dordrecht, The Netherlands, 1989.

Bhagwati, Jagdish and Ruggie, John G., eds., *Power, Passions and Purpose: Prospects for North-South Negotiations*, MIT Press, Cambridge, Mass., 1984.

Brown, Lester, *World Without Borders*, Vintage, New York, 1972.

Cassen, Robert, et al., *Does Aid Work? Report to an Intergovernmental Task Force*, Oxford University Press, Oxford, 1986.

Claude, Inis L., *Swords into Plowshares: The Problems and Progress of International Organizations*, 4th ed., Random House, New York, 1971.

Collins, Paul, ed., Special Issue: The Administrative Reform Process in International Organizations, *Public Administration and Development,* 7(2): (1987).

Commission on International Development, *Partners in Development: Report*, International Bank for Reconstruction and Development, Pall Mall, London, 1969.

Dicke, Klaus and Hüfner, Klaus, eds., *Die Leistungsfähigkeit des UN Systems: Politische Kritik und wissenschaftliche Analyse*, DGVN, UN-Texte: 37, UNO Verlag, Bonn, 1987.

Elmandjra, Mahdi, *The United Nations System: An Analysis*, Faber and Faber, London, 1973.

Feld, Werner J., Jordan, Robert S., and Hurwitz, Leon, *International Organizations: A Comparative Approach*, Praeger, New York, 1983.

Finger, Seymour M. and Mugno, John, The Politics of Staffing the UN Secretariat, Ralph Bunche Institute, City University of New York, New York, 1974.

Forsythe, David P., ed., *The United Nations in the World Political Economy*, Macmillan, London, 1989.

Franck, Thomas M., *Nation Against Nation: What Happened to the U.N. Dream and What the U.S. Can Do About It*, Oxford Press, New York, 1985.

Ghebali, Victor-Yves, *La crise du système des Nations Unies*. No. 4854, La Documentation Française, Paris, 1988.

Harrod, Jeffrey and Schrijver, Nico, eds., *The UN Under Attack*, Institute of Social Studies, The Hague, The Netherlands, Gower, Aldershot, England, 1988.

Hill, Martin, *The United Nations System: Coordinating Its Economic and Social Work*. Cambridge University Press for UNITAR, Cambridge, 1978.

International Labour Office, *Reflections on the Future of Multilateral Co-Operation: The ILO Perspective: Report of the Director-General, Part I*, Geneva, 1987.

Jenks, C. Wilfred, Some Problems of an International Civil Service, *Public Administration Review 3*:93–105 (1943).

Joyce, James Avery, *One Increasing Purpose*, Christopher Davies, Llandybie, Wales, 1984.

Loveday, Alexander, *Reflections on International Administration*, Oxford University Press, London, 1956.

Luard, Evan, ed., *The Evolution of International Organizations*, Thames and Hudson, London, 1966.

Mailick, Sidney, ed., A Symposium: Toward an International Civil Service, *Public Administration Review 30*:206–263 (1970).

Maron, Theodor, *The United Nations Secretariat: The Theory and the Practice*, Lexington, Lexington, Mass., 1977.

Miller, Lynn H., *Organizing Mankind: An Analysis of Contemporary International Organization*, Holbrook Press, Boston, 1972.

Nordic UN Project, *The United Nations in Development: Reform Issues in the Economic and Social Fields: A Nordic Perspective: Final Report*, Almqvist & Wiksell International, Stockholm, 1991.

Padelford, Norman J. and Goodrich, Leland M., eds., *The United Nations in the Balance: Accomplishments and Prospects*, Praeger, New York, 1965.

Pines, Burton Y., ed., *A World Without a UN: What Would Happen If the UN Shut Down*, Heritage Foundation, Washington, D.C., 1984.

Pitt, David and Weiss, Thomas G., eds., *The Nature of United Nations Bureaucracies*, Croon Helm, London, 1986.

Purves, Chester, *The International Administration of an International Secretariat*, Royal Institute of International Affairs, Oxford University Press, London, 1945.

Ramcharan, B. G., *Keeping Faith with the United Nations*, Martinus Nijhoff and UNITAR, Dordrecht, The Netherlands, 1987.

Renninger, John P., ed., *The Future Role of the United Nations in an Interdependent World*, UNITAR Moscow Roundtable, Martinus Nijhoff, Dordrecht, the Netherlands, 1989.

Reymond, Henri and Mailick, Sidney, *International Personnel Policies and Practices*, Praeger, New York, 1985.

Rochester, J. Martin, The Rise and Fall of International Organization as a Field of Study, *International Organization 40*(4):777–813 (1986).

Royal Institute of International Affairs, *The International Secretariat of the Future*. Oxford University Press, London, 1944.

Stanley Foundation, *The United Nations and the Future of Internationalism*, The Stanley Foundation, Muscatine, Iowa, 1987.

Toffler, Alvin, *Powershift: Knowledge, Wealth and Violence at the Edge of the 21st Century*, Bantam, New York, 1991.

Union of International Associations, ed., *Yearbook of International Organizations 1991/92*, 28th ed., K G Saur, München, 1991.

United Nations, *A Study of the Capacity of the United Nations Development System*, vols. I, II, DP/5, United Nations, Geneva, 1969.

United Nations, *Everyone's United Nations*, 10th ed., Department of Public Information, New York, 1986a.

United Nations, *Image and Reality: Questions and Answers About Management, Finance and People*, Department of Public Information, New York, 1986b.

United Nations, *UN Chronicle*, March:6–10 (1992).

United Nations Association of the USA, United Nations Decision-Making Project, *A Successor Vision: The United Nations of Tomorrow: Final Panel Report*, United Nations Association of the USA, New York, 1987.

United Nations Development Programme, *Human Development Report 1992*, Oxford University Press, New York, 1992.

United Nations Joint Inspection Unit, 1992. *United Nations System Co-Operation with Multilateral Financial Institutions*, part I, *Performance and Innovation Challenges*, part II, *Examples of Fresh Approaches*, JIU/REP/92/1, United Nations, Geneva, 1992.

Urquhart, Brian and Childers, Erskine, 1990. *A World in Need of Leadership: Tomorrow's United Nations*, Dag Hammarskjöld Foundation and Ford Foundation, Uppsala, Sweden, 1990.

Waters, Maurice, *The United Nations: International Organization and Administration*, Macmillan, London, 1967.

Williams, Douglas, ed., *The Specialized Agencies and the United Nations: The System in Crisis*, Hurst, London, 1986.

Young, Tien-Cheng, *International Civil Service: Principles and Problems*, International Institute of Administrative Sciences, Brussels, 1958.

20
Privatization and Debureaucratization: A Comparative Analysis of Bureaucratic Alternatives

John G. Merriam
Bowling Green State University, Bowling Green, Ohio

Privatization, a global phenomenon, has major implications for bureaucratic role and scope, especially in state-dominated political systems. With privatization the bureaucracy forgoes policy-making in the very areas turned over, wholly or in part, to the private sector, whether domestic or foreign, or a combination thereof. The case will be made that bureaucracy is nevertheless persistent and pervasive, even in countries that are not considered command economies. Although the downsizing of the state apparatus is often considered threatening to bureaucrats, it may be argued that with it, efficiency increases not decreases, thus providing role enhancement and continued justification for their existence. Furthermore, while the bureaucratic role and operational level may change with privatization, the reconfigured bureaucracy may take on new tasks such as regulation of what is now the private sector. Therefore, net staff reductions may not be as large as expected.

I. PRIVATIZATION DEFINED

The purpose of privatization is to subject administrative activities to the disciplines (and presumably the benefits) of the marketplace, usually globally as opposed to merely domestically. The fact of nominal ownership may be less important than the actual function: Do economic activities occur on a user-pays basis, free of close political control and subject to genuine competition? If so, then privatization has effectively taken place (de Ru and Wettenhall, 1990, p. 8).

The unmistakable act of selling off government-held assets readily comes to mind when attempting to define privatization. Delion would agree but would add that privatization may involve "deregulation" or the removing of public rules from specific private sector activities. Another interesting reverse-flow reform is "the application of private-sector management methods or criteria to the public sector" (Delion, 1990, p. 64).

The privatization phenomenon is in fact complex, regardless of the form that it takes, as it is all too often partial rather than complete. Although in cases where the basic definition applies and the government relinquishes day to day management and the unwelcome financial burden, it may be compelled to take on regulatory responsibilities to mitigate unwanted, socially negative side effects, for privatization is not a panacea. Then, too, privatization may be accompanied by rebureaucratization as civil servants take on new roles, though often at the regional or local level. The call for new or at least updated economic and technical expertise, as is true of all change, may translate into gains for some and losses for others.

II. SELECTED EXAMPLES OF PRIVATIZATION

The United States merits study, to begin with, as it has the world's largest economy, even though it also has the world's largest private sector. President Reagan's Commission on Privatization, according to Seidman's study on which this selection is based, was viewed as a reaction to "big" government and an overgrown bureaucracy, although, comparatively speaking, federal civilian government has remained "relatively static" (Seidman, 1990, p. 15).

The stated rationale for private management and service delivery is that it is more efficient than government and may better serve the public interest. Less frequently stated is the need for what the utilities would call "load shedding," in this case removing demands on the overstretched federal budget and with it the pressures for additional, political unpopular taxes. The sale price of private products or services may encompass a more politically acceptable hidden tax.

To make possible the benefits of privatization by providing services while not producing them subject to pressures for cost-effectiveness, the federal government has set goals for the following (Seidman, 1990):

1. Contracting for management and operation of government-owned facilities, systems management and technical supervision, and delivery of goods and services
2. Guaranteeing and underwriting loans made by private financial institutions
3. Financing programmes by user charges rather than by general tax revenues
4. Chartering quasi-private and quasi-government enterprises to achieve public purposes
5. Distributing purchasing power to eligible consumers by vouchers which enable them to buy designated goods and services on the open market (Seidman, 1990, citing Seidman and Gilmour, 1986, p. 119)

In the United States, however, privatization is not a major issue. The most significant development is not privatization but rather the blending of the governmental and the private and the growth of quasi-governmental and quasi-nongovernmental institutions resulting in "degovernmentalization" (Seidman, 1990, citing Seidman, 1988).

Great Britain is a most appropriate example often cited by countries recently attempting privatization. As a mature, industrialized country that made a major policy commitment to socialism and a massive public sector after World War II, Britain under Prime Minister Margaret Thatcher marked a major policy turn.

Was this shift accompanied by a downsizing of the central government bureaucracy? Whitehall could point to fewer than 600,000 (1985), in contrast with nearly three-quarters of a million in 1976: a worthy example of "cutback management" (Dunsire and Hood, 1989, pp. xiii, 18).

Public pressures for expanded services in contrast with calls for reducing "bloated" bureaucracy and "ruinous" taxes made reduction of expenditures more difficult for the Thatcher government. (The authors cite the astute French observer Alexis de Tocqueville, who saw a connection between rising government expenditure and democracy in America.)

Wagner's "law" posits that the increasing complexity of modern industrial states causes public expenditure to rise faster than national output (Dunsire and Hood, 1989, p. 5). Certainly new bureaucratic skills are required as the kinds of tasks or scope have expanded in Britain and elsewhere; and new survival skills are needed in a time of cutback management if inventive officials are to assure their superiors they are cutting staff or expenditures.

France under François Mitterand made an even more abrupt policy shift from nationalization policies in 1981 to denationalization (privatization) from 1986 onward. With the elections of May–June 1981 came the decision to nationalize twelve major industrial groups—five of them by means of Public Law of February 11, 1982, under which the majority of the remaining private banks were also nationalized. The result was 800,000 more on the public payroll, bringing the public work force to a total of 2.4 million. The share of gross domestic product (GDP) rose from 12 percent (1981) to 17 percent.

Undercapitalization and bad management made even worse by the unwillingness of the public authorities to take into account economic realities resulted in poor performance and outright loss. Although some reforms preceded the March 1986 elections, the new government put through the Public Law of July 2, 1986, which provided for the privatization of sixty-four publicly owned establishments, that is, all of the banks and insurance companies, and the larger part of the industrial public sector groups.

Nevertheless, in contrast to that in Great Britain, the public enterprise sector remains substantial, employing some 2 million people, and comprising the major public service enterprises, plus major banks, insurance companies, and industrial groups. With 9 percent of the labor force, it contributes 14 percent of the GDP (Delion, 1990, pp. 66–67).

The public sector therefore remains large, but it has learned its lesson and now does a better, more pragmatic job of applying managerial expertise.

State corporations have a role to play, as an examination of privatization in Canada and specifically the province of Quebec by Pierre Fournier illustrates. He urges a cautious approach to privatization, arguing "Quebec cannot rely solely on the private sector or on market forces to ensure its economic development."

In Fournier's view, free enterprise advocates uncritically rely on "myths" about the inherent superiority of private management and market forces to ensure national development. Is it not the "shortcomings" of the private sector, its inability to deal with key economic problems, to take necessary risks, that brought about an enlarged state role in the first place? And then there is the commitment of the provincial government to further the interests of the francophone companies and entrepreneurs.

The state corporations continue to play an essential role, "reorganizing traditional and technologically deficient sectors . . . by supporting the development of key industries . . . by creating or attracting new economic activities . . . and [playing] a vital restructuring role." In addition, they have played a defensive role, says Fournier, safeguarding local firms against foreign encroachments (Fournier, 1990, pp. 106–107,115).

Hungary has been a bellwether in the privatization process for Eastern Europe, although other countries might compete for the title. Along with Hungary, Czechoslovakia and Poland are considered "vanguard countries" in the forefront of market reforms. For its part, Hungary has pursued a policy of "reform from above," of "enlightened absolutism," maintain the authors, by gradually abolishing the central planning system, adopting significant elements of the market mechanism, and opening the way for private sector activities.

Aided by a favorable climate following Gorbachev's 1985 introduction of perestroika (economic reform), the government of Hungary established an Economic Reform Commission in 1988–1989, of which the authors have been an active part, and out of that a Blue Ribbon Commission. The goal: successful reintegration into the global marketplace.

In keeping with these goals the Hungarian government has sought to reform the state enterprises and cooperatives, pursue a policy of "reprivatization," act as a facilitator for the reappearance and development of private entrepreneurship, and encourage domestic private and also foreign capital investment in the restructured enterprises. Hungary provides an excellent example of what I would term "defensive privatization."

The Hungarian government recognized that "termination of the party-state" was an essential prerequisite to economic reform (Belassa et al., 1990, pp. 33, 36–37). Such a momentous event, the logical outcome of glasnost (democratization) in the Soviet Union*, if perestroika is to succeed is only now being played out in the wake of the failed hard-liner coup of August 19, 1991.

Can Hungary be a model for the Soviet Union? Is the "stagnant socialist economy" of the former USSR on the verge of collapse? Production levels are declining with the dismantlement of the command economy and dramatic fall in the value of the ruble. Privatization would mean the end of "administrative price-setting" (Saburov, 1991, p. 19). State-owned as well as a growing number of private businesses would be able to purchase raw materials and sell finished products in keeping with economic realities. A drop of close to 50 percent in oil production could be halted by economic reform and, in particular, much overdue technical modernization. But even Boris Yeltsin, the popularly elected president of the Russian S.S.R., which contains 80 percent of the crumbling empire's mineral resources, may not yet have formed an economic game plan.

Two other points need to be made. Hungary is a much smaller entity than the Soviet Union or, for that matter, some of its sizable constituent republics. Also, Hungarians have the "memory" of a private sector which is much less true of the Soviets.

Much of the privatization initiative in the Soviet Union will rest with the republics, but Mikhail Gorbachev in the period since the abortive putsch has called for a seven point agenda which includes "full privatization—including of land—and a rapid shift to a market economy," proposals he was unwilling or unable to advocate before the fateful date of August 19, 1991.

Meanwhile, the now discredited command economy, for all practical purposes, is now viewed as "dead." Yet the market is nowhere in sight. Moreover, Grigory Yavlinsky, a deputy prime minister and a reform economist, says inflation is running 2% to 3% a week. Compounded, such hyperinflation could work out to 365% in a year. Nongovernmental observers conclude that the economy is on the point of collapse (*Economist*, September 28, 1991, p. 73), not an auspicious time for the very reforms that are so desperately needed.

Perhaps the Soviet leadership is taking its cue from the Hungarian experience in recognizing the need for social protection for the unemployed and pensioners in the difficult period of transition to a market economy (Sneider, 1991, pp. 1, 2). Republican governments will regain a role as they tax those who benefit from economic rationalization.

In the recent period former Soviet bloc countries have been more interested in political control than economic efficiency. Now privatization may be seen as a means to wresting control from the center. The question is, Will decentralization merely mean reassertion of bureaucratic oversight at the republic level?

*The Soviet Union, of course, collapsed in 1991. However, many of the Soviet–style top heavy bureaucratic structures are far from being dismantled particularly in some of the more conservative Central Asian Republics.

The question posed may not be particularly applicable to a smaller, unitary state like Hungary. Its government, in keeping with the states examined elsewhere, will continue to play a national role as implementor by administering the process of privatization. Restructuring of ownership will include not only privatization but public limited companies with mixed ownership and a new role for state and regional authorities. Joint venture deals are examples of partial privatization in terms of ownership and management. That is to say, the ownership will be divided according to some formula, but private sector management practices may permeate the entire venture.

State companies entering into such arrangements need to have a clear understanding of their obligations with regard to such basic matters as shipments and payments. Foreign investors will want a favorable and workable legal climate. Hungary will presumably have less difficulty in standardizing its regulations than Moscow and the republics, which presently have on the books a jumble of contradictory laws. Again the state has a role to play as umpire.

The government of Hungary, to pursue this particular example, as well many other Eastern and Central European governments, is well aware that it needs to monitor socially disruptive differences in wealth and income and the dangers that managers will become owners of former state property (Belassa et al., 1990, pp. 43, 51). While civil servants will continue to play a redefined role, a new generation will more likely move into the more rewarding private sector. Whether the public sector will shrink through a policy of layoffs or more gradually through attrition remains to be seen. I would hazard a guess that, lip service to the contrary, many of the former Soviet bloc countries will move in the direction of bureaucratic-authoritarian regimes, in which the state bureaucracies will handily survive.

Developing countries look once again to the more advanced industrialized economies as models to be followed in the privatization process. The Soviet Union with its (historical) commitment to forced draft industrialization is no longer a viable mentor. At the same time the movement away from state-directed growth and the government as the major employer is likely to meet with resistance when there is a lack of a well-developed modern large-scale private sector (as opposed to the primitive capitalist stall-type economy that abounds). Bureaucrats the world over do not like losing jobs and the security that goes with them. To defend themselves they will adopt obstructive tactics that will undermine privatization initiatives where possible.

What needs to be underscored is that there are political and administrative limits to bringing about privatization in developing countries, despite the fact that much of the literature attributes slow change to economic constraints. Therefore, as Cook and Minogue show, political and administrative processes are a crucial part of understanding what in fact happens to state economic policies in the implementation process. However, they find substantial variation among India, Pakistan, Thailand, and Sri Lanka, their chosen examples (Cook and Minogue, 1990, pp. 389 et seq).

Why has there been an "implementation gap" despite donor (World Bank, IMF, etc.) pressures? In Pakistan bureaucratic reactions went from reluctance to outright hostility. Issues ranged from battles over turf (under whose jurisdictions would the implementation process take place?) to a fear of loss of influence as private investors joined the board of fully or semi-privatized enterprises. In India public enterprises have been a source of "black money" funneled to political parties. Economic reform, it goes without saying, has to take into account the political climate.

Public sector unions in some developing countries are well organized with considerable political clout enabling them to articulate fears of loss of collective bargaining, job security, or even the right to organize.

In India (Egypt would be another excellent example) the public sector provides a welfare function of jobs for many of the thousands of graduates pouring out of educational institutions. If privatization takes place, is economic efficiency the guiding rationale? As a matter of political reality can massive layoffs take place as the work force is streamlined? Or are private owners obligated to take on welfare organizations? Plant closings may raise questions of regional and ethnic sensitivity.

Sri Lanka illustrates that an oversized industrialized public sector which is generally agreed to be "riddled with inefficiency" may nevertheless be politically rational. Can private sector disciplines be introduced into enterprises that remain under state control? If a program of divestiture is to be implemented, is the prior development of a large-scale capital market essential? This call for preconditions raises the classic chicken versus egg controversy.

Keen observers note the widespread existence of a "spoils system." The dispensing of political patronage by such means as public enterprise jobs and contracts makes privatization an intensely political matter. Grindle (1984) provides something of a classic study on why the best laid plans for reform come to naught if the political environment is not taken into account.

A case study of public transportation in Belo Horizonte, Brazil, described later illustrates the horns of a dilemma on which advocates for privatization or conversely nationalization may find themselves (de Azevedo and de Castro, 1990, pp. 19–26). The applicable reasons here for privatization readily come to mind: inefficient public sector administration, low quality of service, visibly deteriorating bus fleet, not to mention the prevalence of nepotism in staff hirings and high deficits caused by subsidized fares.

Public needs can actually aggravate what I would call the "pathology" of public sector management. But large numbers of low-income people may have a desperate need for access to affordable government-supported transport to outlying areas that works against purely economic considerations of profit maximization.

METROBEL, the public agency created in the 1980s to deal with the problem, was a mixed success. The population at the outset welcomed the improvement in the chaotic urban transportation. Private franchises were eliminated, but the new system functioned by contracting out to private firms. The fleet was modernized and service improved by the specialized, highly motivated planners. Financial equilibrium was achieved in the fare system by having medium-distance, wealthier neighborhoods and the downtown area subsidize the long-distance service used by many of the poor. The welcomed net results were a revenue surplus and a rate decrease for the masses.

So, what went wrong? The state government intervened, undermining agency autonomy. Fares were held down and not readjusted over time, while deficits and dependence on state subsidy reduced effective service. In a short space of time, the agency became a political scapegoat. De Azevado and de Castro argue that this specific agency could have been a preferable solution to either a short-sighted socially unresponsive private sector, on one hand, or dysfunctional government oversight on the other (1990, p. 25).

The major problem for Brazil is being the Third World's largest debtor, compounded by an oversized and seemingly unchangeable bureaucracy. President Fernando Collor de Mello announced drastic measures to trim the public sector deficit (about 8% to 9% of GDP when he came into office March 1990) which included downsizing the administration and privatizing state concerns.

However, a temporary freeze on private sector prices and a momentarily contemplated nonrepayment of debt might discourage all but the most intrepid foreign investors from sinking money into privatization schemes. The government has managed to dismiss 30,000 workers, but 46,500 laid-off civil servants continue at home to receive their salaries, secure in populist-inspired constitutional guarantees (*Economist*, May 18, 1991, pp. 48, 50; September 14, 1991, pp. 47–48).

Privatization efforts were recently halted momentarily when left-wing militants pelted would-be investors outside Rio de Janeiro's stock exchange and angrily questioned the legality of auctioning off $980 million worth of shares in Usiminas, the country's largest steel maker. Nervous government officials called off the sale. Yet the collapse of the sale—set up to be the first of twenty among Brazil's two hundred-odd state enterprises—marked a defeat for President Fernando Collor de Mello's commitment to privatization as the key to modernizing Brazil's troubled state-dominated economy (Michaels, 1991, p. 7).

Pakistan in particular has, according to Ziauddin Khan, ostensibly pursued a policy of denationalization since 1977, thus supposedly reversing the 1970 government policy of nationalizing major industries, banks, insurance companies, and agro-based industries. "Growing disenchantment" with public servants, in particular those at the senior level, has been caused by a departure from Weberian expectations of "integrity, impartiality, and neutrality" for the all too familiar Third World practices of "corruption, favouritism, and nepotism" (Khan, 1989, p. 185).

Enter privatization. It should be noted that the government actually encouraged privatization before 1970, stepping in only when private entrepreneurs would not make the necessary financial commitments. The nationalization period that followed ended with the 1977 coming to power of the military.

Reprivatization and restoration of private sector confidence have been slowed by the bureaucratic consequences of nationalization. Large public sector liabilities deter private party financial commitment. Vehement employee opposition (textile mills are an example) paralyzes reformers. Nationalized banks report declining efficiency, fraud, and approval of unsecured loans, with the result that with the exception of a few foreign banks not one Pakistani has been allowed to set up a private sector bank.

Privatization, warn Pakistani observers, should not mean government abnegation of responsibility. Private institutions require proper regulation if society at large is to benefit. Collection of taxes now farmed out to local authorities in both urban and rural areas needs to be rationalized to preclude the "growing ineptitude and malpractices of the collection staff." Bureaucrats have a redefined role to play. Privatization should not be viewed, concludes Khan, as a form of escapism. The goal should be to "achieve an administration without bureaucratization" (1989, pp. 192, 196).

A country attracting little recent attention, says Hainsworth, is Indonesia. Under their fifth five-year plan (Repelita V, 1989–1993) economic takeoff is to be achieved by greater reliance on the private sector. Reform efforts include substantial deregulation of trade and investment, improved effectiveness of banks and other financial institutions, and a reduction in the intrusion of the government in the economy—a marked departure for such a highly centralized and bureaucratized state.

Moving away from outmoded import substitution strategies, the government now encourages foreign investment by allowing up to 90% foreign ownership for export-oriented investments, while joint ventures with 75%-plus Indonesian equity are permitted to market their products in Indonesia itself.

Falling oil revenues, inadequate foreign aid flows, and staggering debt service payments have put the proponents of Thatcherism and Reaganism on the defensive. Deregulation to its critics means increasing the power of private monopoly and more pollution, a socially harmful externality. "Privatization," a term generally avoided by Indonesian bureaucrats, can come to mean giving "freer rein to greed and opportunism in societies already marked by wide and blatant inequalities" (Hainsworth, 1990, p. 124).

To protect the economy from private and foreign exploitation, reregulation is appropriate, not only for protection of infant industries but for sustainable development policies and thoughtful assessment of the societal impact of strategies ostensibly designed to achieve "profitability, liquidity, and solvency." Meanwhile, burdensome regulations inhibiting foreign investment and powerful opposition from domestic interests remain (Hainsworth, 1990, p. 134).

The Republic of Korea is significant for two reasons. One is that state policy is to intervene positively to foster growth, recalling Japan's Ministry of International Trade and Industry (MITI), or, for that matter, France's outspoken prime minister, Edith Cresson. Both believe in the positive aspects of state intervention while not necessarily endorsing nationalization. That the state, properly motivated, can assist the private sector in dealing with global competitors flies in the face of the present-day conventional wisdom to which many would ascribe.

The second highly speculative reason is that someday the two Koreas may be reunited. While not exactly parallel with the present public sector morass in Eastern Germany confronting the Treuhandanstalt reprivatizers, lessons learned from the privatization experience adumbrated later may be suggestive.

State-induced growth in Korea, avers Shin, has created "economic distortions." State intervention has not proved to be the positive economic force it was promised to be. This reform does not leave the government without purpose, however. To restore economic equilibrium, the government role in privatization or financial liberalization is as necessary as it was in directing national resource allocation for development (Shin, 1990, p. 79). The government, I would add, becomes the enabler, implementor, or if you will, midwife.

Shin, using commercial banks as a case in point, advocates the development of a "market-driven" banking system as government intervention in the banks' management of assets and daily operations has worked against operational efficiency and innovation. Foreign banks provide, it could be added, a "demonstration effect." Privatization would reduce distortion on capital allocation and lending rates. Liberalization would benefit and stimulate small and medium industries in particular and Korea's underdeveloped financial markets in general.

Simultaneous reform across all sectors, to judge from experiences in Argentina, Brazil, and Chile, will result in chaos, not the sought-after increased economic efficiency. Success requires a "gradual" course of government action. Government pervasiveness needs to be replaced, it is concluded, by prudent guidance (Shin, 1990, p. 87).

III. LESSONS LEARNED

A global movement toward decentralized planning and privatization appears to be in process. Great Britain and France, both nominally socialist democratic economies, have led the way, but Eastern European central command economies have also taken the cue. In turn, Third World countries aspiring to rapid "forced draft industrialization" have become disillusioned with the unrewarding socialist model. In all parts of the globe, whether First and Second World or Third World (if these somewhat obsolete terms coined by the French demographer Alfred Sauvy may be used), leaders have recognized the necessity of achieving political legitimacy by economic performance.

State leaders may be driven by grand economic imperatives, but the growth of the politically relevant strata in all countries means that popular pressures have to be taken into account. It may be noted that dissatisfaction with private sector performance may have necessitated the "reform" of nationalization in the first place. In developing countries large-scale indigenous private enterprises may not have existed. In any case, beneficiaries of government ownership may be reluctant to let go. Loss of wages, benefits, or even position translate into recalcitrant and hostile behavior. Leaders are reluctant to make major cuts in the ranks of the bureaucrats for fear of adverse domestic political consequences. Nevertheless, reduction can take place over time though attrition in the work force. Virtual guarantees of government employment for the Third World countries in which almost half the youthful population is or will be seeking first-time career positions amounts to co-optation of potential political discontents. Thus, political considerations come before economic realities.

Private and public sectors alike can either benefit workers and staff through enlightened policies or cruelly exploit them. Neither the one nor the other is a panacea. Today's problem may have been yesterday's solution. If the trend is toward privatization, then the question is, How is it to be achieved? And what will be the end result? The means affect the ends.

Is privatization good social (as well as economic) policy? Eaton examines expectations raised by the two models:

1. Government has the responsibility to make sure that all production, sales, and service enterprises meet minimum social utility standards. The expectation of maximum profit must be curbed by minimum wage standards, safety measures, product warranties, and many other social goods.
2. All enterprises are expected to operate efficiently. They should serve the public at a price reasonably related to the actual cost of the raw materials plus an add-on based on the value of the required manpower and capital, plus a profit that is reasonable rather than excessive. (1989, p. 469)

The rationale for privatization is more rapid response to market signals, fewer political constraints, and the introduction of employee incentives that might be proscribed by uniform but unimaginative personnel policies. Unspoken may be the welcome if one-time substantial infusion of cash from the proceeds of a public sector sale to fill the empty state coffers.

Private enterprise, it may be remarked, has always existed in some form in all economic systems, but the size and viability of the sector vary considerably. There is something amounting to ideological fervor for privatization. Yet, the public sector not the private entrepreneur has often been viewed as the more socially responsible despite the current wave of criticism. The paradox remains how to achieve efficiency with social commitment.

There are many paths to privatization, which run the gamut from the total sale of all publicly held assets, to partial sale, to contracting *out* a service, to contracting *in* the private management of a public enterprise.

One useful alternative which might have application in some instances, says Eaton, is the "populist management method" whereby the public service is sold to a cooperative which makes decisions on a one person–one vote basis. The sale itself would allow employee purchase of stock under a wage level–determined Employee Stock Ownership Plan (ESOP) (Eaton, 1989, pp. 470–471).

The employees will assume a vested interest in their firm's survival. Some crucial decisions would have to be made with regard to the ratio of wages to reinvestment. Guarantees of government support for, or at least the promise of no competition with, the populist enterprise would be important. Restrictive government control of private sector purchases of raw materials and product sales, domestic or overseas, can make or break any business.

Concludes Eaton, a government role continues with privatization. The government needs to maintain performance standards, positive fiscal controls, and realistic wages and benefits. Who controls the organization and how well it is run are most important. Neither one is a cure-all. "There is no shortage of evidence of 'Carnage, Chaos and Corruption' in both governmental and privatized public services" (Eaton, 1989, p. 491).

Third World countries are entering another development phase. The reaction by the newly independent polities against the former Western colonial powers that followed World War II was understandable. Furthermore, rapid industrialization was considered imperative. The USSR for these two paramount reasons became the model. But the model has failed and, to make matters worse, Soviet subventions can no longer be counted on.

Countries with underdeveloped capital markets now look to the West and Japan. Yet, the urge to economic liberalization of which privatization is a key part threatens "bureaucratic fiefdoms." It may be true, as Grimstone says, that "privatization can deepen as well as widen a country's capital market" (1989, pp. 107, 113). But that remains to be seen in countries that are not sufficiently advanced and therefore do not have the absorptive capacity to move to higher stages of economic development. And it should be added that some key public sector industries may not be suitable for privatization.

IV. CONCLUSION

Does privatization lead to debureaucratization? That is the central question. Over time the answer is probably affirmative. Yet numerous authors cited here indicate the need, indeed, the duty, of governments to provide protective regulation even as they relinquish ownership. Then, too, governments need to regain at least partial access to revenues through taxation. How fortuitous to have the benefits of private profits without the onerous burden of public subsidies!

When all is said and done, bureaucrats have a definite claim to continued participation in the decision-making process. There have been a few examples of civil servant layoffs in such widely diverse countries as Great Britain recently under Margaret Thatcher and Brazil under Fernando Collor de Mello, but they are few and far between. Bureaucratic structures, reconfigured no doubt, will inevitably reemerge with unmistakable claims to new responsibilities, albeit at possibly different operational levels.

One is tempted to refer to the much-maligned nineteenth-century seer Karl Marx. He thought the sin of capitalism—the pursuit of profit and the inevitable accompaniment of worker exploitation—would be removed with the termination of private ownership. It was not.

Now a twentieth-century prophet is needed to ascertain whether more privatization and less bureaucracy will erase the sins of gross inefficiency inimical to national interests in an increasingly global economy. Whatever the predicted synthesis, bureaucrats, as I have maintained in an earlier work, will persist (Merriam, 1990).

REFERENCES

Balassa, A., Berend, I., and Vertes, A., The Transformation of the Hungarian Economic System, in *The End of Central Planning?* (D. M. Kemme and C. E. Gordon, eds.), Westview Press, Boulder, Colo., 1990.

Brazil: Out of Style, *Economist*, May 18 (1991).

Brazil: Big Country, Big Constitution, *Economist* September 13, pp. 47–48 (1991).

Cook, P. and Minogue, M., Waiting for Privatization in Developing Countries: Towards the Integration of Economic and Noneconomic Explanations, *Public Administration and Development 10*(4):389–403.

de Azevedo, S. and de Castro, M. M., State Management of Public Transportation as an Alternative to Both Privatisation and Nationalization of Bus Service: A Case Study of Belo Horizonte, Brazil, *Public Administration and Development 10*(10):19–26 (1990).

Delion, A., Public Enterprises: Privatization or Reform? *International Review of Administrative Sciences 56*:63–78 (1990).

de Ru, H. J. and Wettenhall, R., Progress, Benefits and Costs of Privatization: an Introduction, *International Review of Administrative Sciences 56*:7–14 (1990).

Dunsire, A. and Hood, C., *Cutback Management in Public Bureaucracies: Popular Theories and Observed Outcomes in Whitehall*, Cambridge University Press, Cambridge, 1989.

Eaton, J. W., Bureaucratic, Capitalist and Populist Privatization Strategies, *International Review of Administrative Sciences 55*:467–492 (1989).

Fournier, P., Privatization in Canada: A Critical Evaluation of the Situation in the Province of Quebec, *International Review of Administrative Sciences 56*:105–123 (1990).

Free Fall: While Its Economists Debate, the Soviet Union Faces a Catastrophic Slump, *Economist* September 28, p. 73, 1991.

Grimstone, G., Privatisation: Macroeconomics and Modalities, in *Privatisation in Developing Countries* (V. V. Ramanadham, ed.), Routledge, London and New York, 1989, pp. 103–132.

Grindle, M. S., *Politics and Policy Implementation in the Third World*, Princeton University Press, Princeton, N.J., 1984.

Hainsworth, G. B., Indonesia: On the Road to Privatization? *Current History 89*:545:121–124, 134 (1990).

Khan, Z., Simplification and Reduction of Procedures and Controls and Deregulation: Experiences of Pakistan, *International Review of Administrative Sciences 55*:183–197 (1989).

Merriam, J. G., Bureaucrats as Agents of Development in the Middle East, in *Handbook of Comparative and Development Public Administration* (A. Farazmand, ed.), Dekker, New York, Basel, and Hong Kong, 1990, pp. 273–285.

Michaels, J., Brazil Stumbles in Effort to Sell White Elephants, *The Christian Science Monitor*, September 27, p. 7 (1991).

Saburov, Evgeny F., Boris Yeltsin's Economic Strategy, *The Christian Science Monitor*, August 27, p. 19 (1991).

Seidman, H., Public Enterprise Versus Privatization in the United States, *International Review of Administrative Sciences 56*:15–28 (1990).

Shin, R. W., The Paradox of Privatization as a Public-Policy Instrument: The Case of Korean Commercial Banks, *International Review of Administrative Sciences 56*:79–88 (1990).

Sneider, Daniel, Soviets Assess Future of Union, *The Christian Science Monitor*, August 27, pp. 1, 2 (1991).

21
Managing Human and Natural Disasters in Developing Nations: The Multidimensional Bureaucratic Role

Lenneal J. Henderson
University of Baltimore, Baltimore, Maryland and The Fielding Institute, Santa Barbara, California

I. INTRODUCTION

Managing human and natural disasters represents a pervasive and complex challenge to the public bureaucracies of developing nations.* Ironically, natural and human disasters are often perceived as sporadic, episodic, and occasional by many comparative administration scholars and analysts (Bryant and White, 1982; Farazmand, 1991; Heady, 1982). Consequently, the management of emergencies or disasters is often characterized as adjunct to "more routine" bureaucratic functions such as planning, financial management, human resources management, and economic development.

This chapter proposes emergency, or disaster, management as a basic and critical dimension of comparative and international management, particularly in developing nations. The pervasive vulnerability of such nations to risks of natural and technological disasters is an artifact of the following factors (Lohman, 1992):

1. The unusually high exposure of populations in developing nations to disaster risk resulting from widespread conditions of poverty, poor health care, illiteracy/low educational attainment and poor housing
2. Hyperurbanization of the population, i.e., the overpopulation and overbuilding of cities, which challenges effective governmental response to human need
3. Aging and inferior physical infrastructures such as roads, dams, bridges, telecommunication systems, irrigation facilities, and buildings

*The terms *bureaucracy, administration,* and *management* are used interchangeably in this chapter. The terms *disaster* and *emergency* are also used interchangeably.

4. Public bureaucracies that are often underfinanced, poorly trained, inappropriately organized, and generally overmatched by the scale, immediacy, and intensity of disaster events and the resulting social, economic, and political impact
5. The need for massive coordination of both internal governmental and nongovernmental agencies and multiple international disaster relief and assistance agencies

Indeed, routine and emergency management are frequently characterized as opposite ends of the public management continuum. Emergencies suspend "normal" operations and impose extraordinary imperatives. Conversely, routine management "stabilizes" bureaucracies by avoiding crisis behavior. However, in developing nations, the line between emergency and routine management is often blurred: the adequacy of routine management is immediately reflected in the quality of emergency management. And emergency management response often conditions public policies and administrative procedures in more day-to-day bureaucratic functions (Denhart, 1993).

Schneider (1992) observes that disasters result in conflicts between "bureaucratic norms" and "emergent norms." Emergent norms transcend bureaucratic norms as the disaster event and its impact unfold. Immediate, widespread, and unusual challenges face bureaucracy in a disaster. Resort to "emergent norms" is often impeded by the severity of the disaster, disruption of normal lines of information and resources, and the often frenzied and extreme expectations citizens impose on bureaucracy during and following a disaster. Beyond family and place of worship, government is regarded as the resource of first resort in emergency contexts.

II. THE DISASTER CONTEXT

The multidimensional role of public bureaucracy in disasters reflects the varied nature of disaster contexts. Disasters vary in type, time frames, intensity, locus, and human impact (Figure 1). The disaster event proceeds on a time frame from very sudden and immediate to emergent. Earthquakes, explosions, volcanic eruptions, power plant accidents, and toxic and hazardous releases resulting from train, ship, or airplane accidents usually occur suddenly and without much warning (Comfort, 1989). Tsunamis, hurricanes, floods, and typhoons provide some warning time, both as seasonal occurrences and through increasingly more sophisticated weather forecasts. Other disasters proceed in slower time frames, such as drought, famine, desertification, and insect or rodent infestations. Epidemiological disasters such as cholera, yellow fever, HIV infection, and malaria proceed in time frames determined by the nature and frequency of human interaction. Although not always labeled disasters, the more endogenous conditions of poverty, malnutrition, infant mortality, water contamination, and lower life expectations are disaster embedded in the socioeconomic conditions of developing nations and characterized by time frames associated with the overall development of affected populations. Thus, the varied time frames of disasters provide varied temporal dimensions for administrative response (Waldo, 1970).

The intensity of a disaster is its combined impact on human life, property loss, physical infrastructure, geographical location, and institutional function. The catastrophic earthquake in Iran on June 21, 1990 killed 40,000 people and on December 7, 1988, in northwestern Armenia, another earthquake killed 25,000 people and destroyed billions of dollars in property. Hospitals, clinics, and educational facilities suffered most from the earthquake. Roads, bridges, and tunnels were destroyed, and hundreds of buildings collapsed. The work of 47 international rescue and medical teams from more than 35 nations was essential in locating and rescuing survivors trapped in the debris (Solomaine, 1988). The intensity of this event, combined with its sudden occurrence, posed formidable challenges for former Soviet officials, local administrative agencies, and many

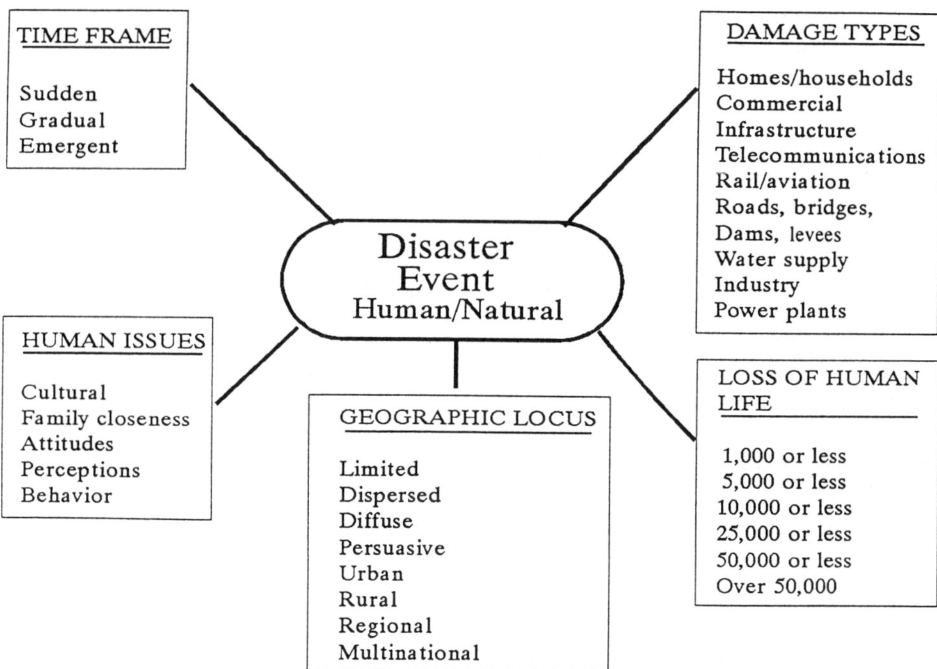

Figure 1 Matrix of figure characteristics.

international relief authorities. In the summer of 1989, another massive earthquake struck northern Iran. Measuring over 8 on the Richter scale, it left in its wake a loss of over 100,000 lives, towns destroyed, and villages swallowed whole.

The intensity of disaster often represents the intersection of human and natural disaster. Conditions of poverty, poor housing, lack of information about disaster risk, poor telecommunications, and inadequate physical infrastructures, including bridges or roads, frequently exacerbate natural disasters such as floods, earthquakes, hurricanes, and volcanic eruptions. Evacuations of large populations is complicated by low-capacity infrastructure or family or cultural impediments.

In addition to the temporal and intensity issues in emergency management, the geography of disaster often represents another challenge to bureaucratic response. The locus of the disaster event can be local, regional, national, or international. Famine, malnutrition, and war has gripped the entire nation of Somalia between 1991 and 1994, with no legitimate government in place to respond (De Waal and Omaar, 1993). The Bhopal chemical release in India killed more than 2500 persons in a local community. In contrast, the release of radiation from the Chernobyl nuclear power plant in Ukraine has reached several nations. The 1992 earthquake in Cairo, Egypt, was confined to a relatively small, but densely populated, part of the metropolis. There is often a coincidence of disaster locus and the national or subnational levels of government expected to respond. However, some nations invoke emergency powers and suspend all but national authority to respond even to the most local disaster.

However, it is the combined impact of disaster on human life that evokes the most profound expectations for bureaucratic response. The significant loss or damage of human life, the dislocation of families and individuals, the widespread homelessness following disaster, food, and water shortages, the disruption of information systems, and widespread and profound uncertainties usually occur in the wake of a disaster (Comfort, 1990). Louise Comfort (1991) observes that "the complexity of disaster environments poses an extraordinary burden on human decision-makers to take timely, appropriate action in uncertain conditions." It is this direct and observable impact on both human victims and decision-makers that focuses most disaster relief and emergency management efforts.

III. THE EMERGENCY MANAGEMENT CONTEXT

Once disaster occurs, the quality of the national emergency management system becomes evident. Four distinct but interrelated phases of emergency management involve public bureaucracies, particularly in developing nations: mitigation, preparedness, response, and recovery (Figure 2). Mitigation involves decisions by government to prepare and to preposition its emergency management resources to minimize or reduce the multiple impact of anticipated disasters. The stockpiling of emergency supplies, the training of medical, security, and transportation personnel, and the conduct of drills or disaster simulations are examples of mitigation activities.

Closely connected to mitigation is disaster preparedness. Preparedness includes efforts to put in place organizational response systems involving various types, levels, and skills of governmental, nongovernmental, and international organizations likely to be involved in responding to a disaster. Preparedness also includes public notification and warning on the most appropriate ways and means of preparing for natural disasters and preventing or responding to human-induced disasters (Petak, 1985; Siegel, 1985; Steiner, 1985). As Figure 2 indicates, mitigation and preparedness are two predisaster roles that, when pursued effectively by emergency managers, not only reduce the adverse impacts of disaster but also facilitate postdisaster response and recovery management.

The immediate response to a disaster includes a situation assessment, allocation of critical resources to the disaster locus and population, and the command and control of both governmental and nongovernmental actions, money, equipment, and information by administrative agencies designated by political leaders to coordinate the immediate response to the disaster event (Wailace and DeBalogh, 1985). The response phase is disaster-immediate and usually frenzied and chaotic, and often requires the most patient, composed, and competent capabilities of administrative officials. Time frames are rapid, the context is intense, and the potential for complete breakdowns of organizational and information systems is omnipresent. Bureaucracy

			Intergovernmental/Organizational/Stakeholders							
			Central Government	State/ Provincial Government	Local Government	Regional Organizations	Corporate Sector	NGO Sector	Military Sector	Global Sector
Disaster Phases	Pre-Disaster	Mitigation								
		Preparedness Planning and Warning		Roles and responsibilities of developing bureaucracies in managing human-induced and natural hazards, risks and disasters						
	Post-Disaster	Response								
		Recovery								

Figure 2 Administrative matrix for emergency management in developing nations.

must coordinate and orchestrate many actors very quickly and very effectively to minimize both loss of life and loss of control at disaster sites.

Finally, the postdisaster recovery phase includes longer-term reconstruction of human, financial, and physical infrastructure, the restoration of order and information flow, and the slow and tortuous rebuilding or relocation of communities at, or from, disaster sites. Bureaucracy is often called upon to calculate household, commercial, industrial, and public sector financial recovery needs. The public sector is also expected to provide, or to coordinate, relief from the homelessness, hunger, dislocations, and death and injury wrought by disaster in the recovery phase, particularly in developing nations. Often, recovery is incomplete: physical devastation and human dislocation remain months and years after the disaster event. However, the effective management of the recovery phase is linked with both the mitigation and preparedness phases. Mitigation, preparedness, response, and recovery each has its own information requirements and decision-support systems (Wallace and DeBalogh, 1985).

Moreover, as Figure 2 suggests, these four phases of emergency management involve all levels of government and various nongovernmental sectors such as the corporate, religious, and international sectors. Among the essential roles expected of bureaucracy in each of these phases are information management, the application of varied expertise to and within each phase, organizational coordination, logistical support, and the identification of natural and technological risks.

Rae Zimmerman (1985) observes that many of the issues normally facing bureaucracy become accelerated and more complex when disaster mitigation, preparedness, response, or recovery is involved. Management choices often involve emergency procedures that temporarily suspend, or alter, organizational hierarchies, division of labor, or more routine public mandates. Political leaders will often deploy military forces to disaster sites both to provide security at the site and to enforce temporary emergency management mandates. Such a choice is often not popular with those in, or affected by, the disaster site. The return to "normalcy" often includes the suspension of such temporary emergency measures and the return to more familiar and normal administrative patterns. However, within and between mitigation, preparedness, response, and recovery are a profusion of bureaucratic tasks involving training, information dissemination, coordination, regulation, financial management, media control, technology use, and direct service delivery to the wounded, relatives of the deceased, and others affected by disaster events (Siegel, 1985). Even when these phases of disaster management are executed and even when international response to disaster has been substantial and generous, serious damage to human and infrastructural life can occur. Commenting on the 1985 Mexican earthquake, Comfort (1986) suggested that "comparatively weak ratio of results achieved to assistance extended compels a reconsideration of the international disaster assistance process."

IV. THE ENVIRONMENT OF EMERGENCY MANAGEMENT IN DEVELOPING NATIONS: THE CONCEPT OF PERVASIVE RISK

Whether national, regional, or local bureaucracies or international relief and assistance agencies, emergency management in developing nations confronts a complex and unique administrative environment. Five interrelated dynamics constitute this environment (The World Bank, 1991):

1. The demographic and socioeconomic characteristics of developing nations
2. The varied cultural and institutional contexts in which mitigation, preparedness, and recovery tasks are pursued in developing nations

3. The direct and indirect economic of disasters on the often fragile economic systems of developing nations
4. The impact of disaster on household, village, urban, regional, and national infrastructures
5. The establishment or extension of emergency management capabilities in developing nations

Taken together, these five dynamics challenge any routine or emergency action or decision of public bureaucracies. Ongoing human challenges in developing nations are amplified and complicated by disasters. The disaster aftermath only sustains and aggravates already tragic human conditions. These nations are continually exposed to hazards and risks. *Hazards* may be broadly defined as threats to humans and what they value—life, well-being, material goods, and a sound environment. *Risk* is the probability that a particular technology, activity, or existence will lead to a specified adverse consequence over time (Kasperson and Pijawka, 1985). A key hypothesis in the analysis of emergency management in developing nations is that *embedded or endogenous demographic, socioeconomic, cultural, infrastructural, and administrative problems aggravate human exposure to hazards and result in pervasive risk to human populations and systems when disasters occur.* Pervasive risk is a continuing challenge to the capacity of operation of public bureaucracy.

First, demographic and socioeconomic characteristics of human populations in developing nations contribute to pervasive risk. More than 70% of the world's population resides in the developing world. Population projections through the year 2020 suggest that even more of the world's population will reside in these nations. Population growth rates, attributable to both fertility and immigration rates, are conspicuously higher in the developing world (Mosely and Cowley, 1991). Another key demographic attribute of the developing nations is the larger proportion of the population in the 0–14 age group and the smaller proportion in the age group 65 and over. Young populations not only are more susceptible to injury or death during and following disaster, but are often more difficult to evacuate or relocate following disaster. Their availability as part of the instant human resource response capability is also limited.

Three additional demographic and socioeconomic characteristics of developing nations challenge emergency managers. First, developing nations are experiencing, and will continue to experience, higher rates of urban population growth, poverty, and density (Tien et al., 1992; Kreimer and Munasinghe, 1992). Whether human or natural disaster, these patterns of urbanization make disaster risks more pervasive. Second, higher rates of poverty in the populations of developing nations not only provide fewer resources for the poor to reduce their exposure to both hazards and risks but they also prolong disaster recovery. Third, junior and middle-level public servants and administrative officials are often very young, not well trained, and lacking in emergency management experience and skills. They are often closely connected to family, village, or neighborhood populations who constitute their priority in a disaster.

In addition to these demographic and socioeconomic dynamics, varied cultural and institutional contexts challenge emergency managers. These contexts can either enhance or impede emergency management. Disaster prediction may include traditional ways of calculating when an event will occur and its likely intensity and impact. Local forecasting methods may be nontechnological but may be quite complex—for example, the reading of animal behavior and weather patterns, the cycle of calamities as recorded in religious collections, or the predictions of a local soothsayer (Rahmato, 1987). Warning systems may include local channels of alert such as spreading the news of flood by word of mouth or through religious organizations. Village elders in the Indian state of Andhra Pradesh assess potential needs and capabilities within the community in the event of a hurricane and make their own indigenous contingency arrangements. At the recovery level, family and kinship relationships often provide mutual assistance and social contact, which play different functions in periods of stress and disaster. Mutual aid and self-help groups represent other methods of social adjustment mechanisms. Leadership arrangements also establish explicit lines of obligation as in the traditional *patron* relationship in Latin America. During periods of hardship, particularly following a disaster, the *patron* will materially assist the workers (Kieffer, 1977; Kreimer and Munasinghe, 1992).

Moreover, religious or traditional beliefs and values; the uneven and often inadequate socialization of populations by national or local schools; communal institutions; local, regional, or national bureaucracies; and such nongovernmental organizations as business, agricultural cooperatives, and factories constitute an institutional network in developing nations. This network must often be quickly and effectively contacted and orchestrated by public bureaucracies in each of the four phases of emergency management. Often, these institutions routinely compete or are engaged in conflict with public bureaucracies. They are skeptical about the scope, priorities, or adequacy of emergency response or recovery or opposed to some, or all, international relief efforts. Local institutions may oppose or criticize national preemption of authority in disaster response or recovery and may insist on sustaining the intergovernmental system of the nation (Hopkins, 1990). Clearly, whether supportive or critical of emergency managers, indigenous cultural and institutional dynamics must be incorporated into the strategic operations of emergency management.

Another essential dynamic of the disaster context is its economic impact. The United Nations Disaster Relief Organization (UNDRO) has urged that the effects of disasters by viewed not only in humanitarian and broad social terms but also—and primarily—in economic terms. Albala-Bertrand (1993) has observed that a slowly developing disaster, such as a drought, by affecting agricultural capital in a gradual and cumulative rather than instantaneous way, may have more important and longer-lasting economic effects than a "sudden" disaster. Whether short, near, or long term in effects, the macro- and microeconomic effects of natural or human-induced disasters are often disruptive to developing economies. They damage or render useless essential economic input such as land, trained labor, or capital assets. They make imperative the diversion of foreign exchange and public finance to disaster response and recovery. Combined with demographic and socioeconomic challenges already endemic to the nation, they may retard local, regional, or national economic development projects such as housing, power plants, environmental protection systems, industrial plants, or public works projects.

Economic dislocations induced by disaster often result in severe damage to household, village, urban, regional, or national infrastructures. Bridges, tunnels, roads, power plant facilities, dams, rail lines, airports, water treatment plants, and water and gas mains are costly fixed-capital investments that are either managed or regulated by public bureaucracies. The World Bank (1991) has observed that 1.3 billion people in the developing world already lack access to clean and plentiful water, and nearly 2 billion people lack an adequate system for disposing of their feces. Even without disaster events, pervasive risk resulting from inadequate public facilities and infrastructures is evident. When disaster occurs, damaged or destroyed infrastructures not only cease to function but become major secondary hazards to the population. Broken dams release rampaging floodwaters; damage to power lines and plants precipitates fires and electrocutions; water treatment plants and reservoirs become contaminated; and collapsing buildings trap, maim, or kill hundreds of persons.

Disaster mitigation and preparedness assign a large and significant role to physical infrastructures. Mitigation measures may include the storage of emergency generators, flashlights, water supplies, and rescue vehicles. Preparedness warnings may urge the population to avoid disaster locations, be wary of damaged power lines, or refrain from drinking or using contaminated water. The construction of temporary roadways, railways, and airstrips may be necessary in the disaster response and recovery phases. Louise Comfort (1986, 1991) has emphasized the need for a strong and adaptable information system in every phase of emergency management.

Consequently, the concept of *pervasive risk* offers unique and complicated challenges to the public bureaucracies of developing nations. Many of these challenges are embedded in endogenous demographic, socioeconomic, institutional, and infrastructural conditions in the nation. Some are the result of the cumulative impact of recurrent environmental degradation resulting from inadequate economic development, poorly managed infrastructure, misuse of technology, or rapidly expanding industrialization (Kreimer and Munasinghe, 1992; Khator, 1991). Therefore, the fifth, and most critical dynamic in the disaster context is the continuing development of emergency management capability in developing nations.

V. THE DEVELOPMENT OF EMERGENCY MANAGEMENT CAPABILITY

The continuing development of emergency management capability in developing nations is inseparable from the ongoing general development and reform of the public sector (Jain, 1976; Asmerom, 1993; Nunberg, 1990). Four foci of development and administrative reform enhance emergency management:

1. Continued *decentralization of disaster mitigation and preparedness* capability at regional and local levels of the nation. Given the wide variations in the demographic, socioeconomic, cultural and infrastructural conditions within the regions and local areas of a nation, local and regional levels of government should be encouraged and supported to extend their roles in the mitigation of disasters, disaster prevention, and the preparation of local and regional populations for disaster.
2. Continued *integration of disaster response and recovery management* at the national level of management. Although the entire intergovernmental system should be involved in disaster response and recovery, the national administrative system should be the focal point for both the coordination of subnational emergency management capability and international or multinational relief, assistance, and reconstruction activities. *National emergency management is the essential pivot for international, national, and subnational disaster response and recovery.*
3. Emergency management should be carefully interconnected with more routine administrative systems. Points of bureaucratic interconnection are determined by "issue networks" (Heclo, 1978; Palumbo, 1988). These issue networks interrelate emergency management with environmental management, national security, urban policy, social services policy, public works, energy policy, and other issue areas. *The incorporation of emergency management into these policy issue networks will also facilitate the integration of emergency and other bureaucracies in developing nations.*
4. The development of emergency management capability is integral to overall administrative reform (Caiden, 1969, 1976). Such reform efforts focus on the role of bureaucracy in managing as effectively as possible most of the four phases of emergency management within the nation. In mitigating risk, urging preparedness, responding to disaster events, and orchestrating recovery, bureaucracies gain experience and insight that can contribute to emergency management reforms. Moreover, widespread emphasis on "structural reform" by the World Bank and other multilateral agencies urges a bureaucratic reform and rationalization that will facilitate a vigorous economic and financial climate in developing societies (Asmerom, 1993). Included in reform is the increasing privatization of bureaucratic activity and decentralization of

overcentralized administrative systems. ***Emergency management contributes experience to administrative reform through experience with disaster response and recovery, through interaction with private national, subnational, and international relief, assistance, and cultural agencies and through the raising of continuing issues about routine administrative operations and systems.***

These four issues underscore the continuing need of administrative systems throughout the world to participate in emergency management technology transfer, both directly and through multilateral organizations such as UNDRO. Human and natural disasters will continue to challenge the most adept administrative systems. They are likely to continue to be a particularly troublesome nemesis to the bureaucracies of developing nations.

ACKNOWLEDGMENTS

I would like to express robust gratitude to Louise K. Comfort, University of Pittsburgh; Ali Farazmand, Northern Kentucky University; and Diane Aull of the University of Baltimore for their generous assistance in the preparation of this chapter.

REFERENCES

Albala-Bertrand, J. M., Natural Disaster Situations and Growth: A Macroeconomic Model for Sudden Disaster Impacts, *World Development, 21*(9):1417–1435 (1993).

Asmerom, H. K., The Impact of Structural Adjustment Policy on Administrative Reform and Strategy, paper presented at the International Conference on Policy-Making, Bureaucracy and Structural Adjustment in Developing Societies, University of Delhi, February 25–27, 1993, p. 9.

Bryant, C. and White, G., *Managing Development in the Third World,* Westview Press, Boulder, Colo., 1982.

Caiden, G., Development Administration and Administrative Reform, *International Social Science Journal, 21*(9):9–29 (1969).

Caiden, G., Implementation: The Achilles Heel of Administrative Reform, in *The Management of Change in Government* (A. F. Leemans, ed.), Martinus Nijhoff, The Hague, 1976, pp. 142–164.

Comfort, L. K., International Disaster Assistance in the Mexico City Earthquake, *New World: A Journal of Latin American Studies, 1*(2):12–44 (1986).

Comfort, L. K., The San Salvador Earthquake, *Coping with Crises: The Management of Disasters, Riots and Terrorism* (U. Rosenthal, M. T. Charles, and P. 'THart, eds.), Charles C Thomas, Springfield, Ill. 1989, pp. 323–338.

Comfort, L. K., Turning Conflict into Cooperation: Organizational Designs for Community Response in Disasters, *International Journal of Mental Health, 19*(1):89–108 (1990).

Comfort, L. K., Designing and Interactive, Intelligent, Spatial Information System for International Disaster Assistance, *International Journal of Mass Emergencies and Disasters, 9*(3):339–354 (1991).

Denhart, R. B., *Theories of Public Organization,* 2nd ed., Wadsworth Publishing, Belmont, Calif., 1993.

De Waal, A. and Omaar R., Doing Harm by Doing Good? The International Relief Effort in Somalia, *Current History,* May 1993, pp. 198-202.

Farazmand, A., ed., *Handbook of Comparative and Development Administration,* Marcel Dekker, New York, 1991.

Heady, F., *Public Administration: A Comparative Perspective,* 3rd ed., Marcel Dekker, New York, 1982.

Heclo, H., Issue Networks and Executive Establishment, in *The New American Political System* (A. King, ed.), The Enterprise Institute, Washington, D.C., 1978, pp. 27–51.

Hopkins, J. W., Intergovernmental Relations in Mexico and the United States, *International Review of Administrative Sciences, 56*(3):403–420 (1990).

Jain, R. B., *Contemporary Issues in Indian Administration,* Vishal Publications, Delhi, India, 1976.

Kasperson, R. E. and Pijawka, K. D., Societal Response to Hazard Events: Comparing Natural and Technological Hazards, *Public Administration Review, 45*:7–19 (1985).

Khator, R., *Environment, Development and Politics in India,* University Press of America, Lanham, Md., 1991.

Kieffer, M., *Disasters and Coping Mechanisms in Cakchiquel, Guatemala: The Cultural Context,* Dallas, Tex., 1977.

Kreimer, A. and Munasinghe, M., *Environmental Management and Urban Vulnerability,* The World Bank, Washington, D.C., 1992.

Lohman, E. J. A., Policies, Institution-Building and Legislation for Land-Use Management in Disaster-Prone Countries, *United Nations Disaster Relief Organization News,* May–June 1992, pp. 8–11.

Mosley, W. H. and Cowley, P., The Challenge of World Health, *Population Bulletin, 46*(4):3 (1991).

Nunberg, B., *Public Sector Management Issues in Structural Adjustment Lending,* The World Bank, Washington, D.C., 1990.

Palumbo, D. J., *Public Policy in America: Government in Action,* Prentice-Hall, Englewood Cliffs, N.J., 1988.

Petak, W., Emergency Management: A Challenge for Public Administration, *Public Administration Review, 45*:3–6 (1985).

Rahmato, D., *Famine and Survival Strategies: A Case Study from Northeast Ethiopia,* Addis Ababa University, Institute of Development Research, 1987.

Schneider, S. K., Governmental Response to Disasters: The Conflict Between Bureaucratic Procedures and Emergent Norms, *Public Administration Review, 52*(2):135–145 (1992).

Siegel, G. B., Human Resource Development for Emergency Management, *Public Administration Review, 45*:107–117 (1985).

Solomaine, N., International Solidarity for Armenian Quake Victims, *United Nations Disaster Relief News,* Nov.–Dec. 1988, pp. 4–7.

Tien, H. Y. et al., China's Demographic Dilemmas, *Population Bulletin, 47*(1) (1992).

Waldo, D., et., *Temporal Dimensions of Development Administration,* Duke University Press, Durham, N.C., 1970.

Wallace, W. A. and DeBalogh, F., Decision Support Systems for Disaster Management, *Public Administration Review, 45*:134–146 (1985).

The World Bank, *The Reform of Public Sector Management: Lessons from Experience,* Washington, D.C., 1991.

Zimmerman, R., The Relationship of Emergency Management to Governmental Policies on Man-Made Disasters, *Public Administration Review, 45*:29–39 (1985).

22

Providing Services to Service Providers: Local Government Training Issues in Constrained Budgetary Times

Terri Susan Fine and Kevin Mahoney
University of Central Florida, Orlando, Florida

Ronald Reagan's "New Federalism" had a profound impact on the ability of local governments to deliver public services efficiently and effectively. In his 1983 budget message before Congress, Reagan stated the following:

> I am proposing a major effort to restore American federalism. The key to this program is that the states and localities make the critical choices. . . . A major sorting out of Federal, state and local responsibilities will occur, and the Federal presence and interaction in state and local affairs will gradually diminish. (Quoted in Ladd and Yinger, 1989, p. 286)

Reagan's simplification efforts were meant to decentralize government administration, increase government accountability, cut administrative costs, encourage program experimentation, and offset budget reductions by increasing and targeting flexibility (Waugh and Streib, 1990, p. 27). Many argued that this strategy would fulfill Reagan's political goal of keeping federal spending down (Ladd and Yinger, 1989). At the same time, the dynamics of these new intergovernmental relationships created undue burdens on state and local authorities. The new federalism placed additional stressors on governments that were already experiencing difficulties distributing those resources available to them in a manner consistent with public expectations. Federal efforts aimed at downsizing government resulted in added responsibilities being shouldered by overencumbered subnational entities. In short, local governments were forced to do more with less.

The role of local governments as providers of public services has changed since the 1930s. At that time, the collapse of many local governments led to the "era of nationalization" in which the federal government grew in size and influence. Local governments, whose primary responsibility had been administering local programs, became responsible for managing national programs locally.

The period between 1945 and 1970 brought the "era of capacity building." During this time, restructuring local government administration was emphasized. A stress on efficiency as a means to assure that local government could function at its optimal capacity evolved. Local government had to be professionalized in order to promote efficiency. Further, structures had to be established to ensure that a professionalized public administration could function effectively (Anton, 1988, p. 164).

Since 1970, local, state, and national obligations have been less clearly defined. The responsibility for providing public services is more integrated across all levels of government than it was (Anton, 1988). One example of this integrated relationship is a general revenue sharing approach that forges a direct financial connection between the national government and local authorities (Anton, 1988, p. 158).

According to Ladd and Yinger (1989), the 1980 election hastened the already rapid diminution of federal aid to American central cities. By 1982, federal aid to central cities had declined to just over 18% of own-source revenues. Two years later, this proportion was just under 15%, and by 1986 federal general revenue sharing was eliminated. Aid reductions have not been coupled with regulatory detachment, however. Expectations of local government performance by state and federal authorities grew during this same period. A decrease in general revenue sharing by the Reagan administration resulted in decreased funding to subnational governments and increased autonomy. Local governments now take greater responsibility for program administration yet remain concerned about their ability to finance these programs (Waugh and Hy, 1988).

The present system is, then, one in which state and national governments play a more active role in influencing how, and under what conditions, the provision of public services occurs at the local level. At the same time, the resources made available to local governments from these same entities have declined in an effort to reduce the size of the federal government. Put another way, "The Reagan administration has meant reduced revenues, diminished authority and greater state government authority" for local governments (Anton, 1988, p. 168).

These stressors on local government are derived from higher-level institutions. One other set of pressures springs from the public. Local government is most beholden to the American polity because of its proximity to the citizenry. Local governments must not only deal with new intergovernmental relationships and an integrated financial and regulatory system, but must also contend with changing citizen expectations of local government services in the 1990s.

The nature of public services has changed significantly since the 1930s. Government plays a more integral role in a society where technological advances influence social and political response (Ladd, 1991). Public expectations about the nature and delivery of government services have changed as well. The public is keeping a more watchful eye on how well local governments are spending their resources. Concerns about inefficiency and waste have resulted in declining public trust in government's ability to spend its diminishing resources wisely and appropriately (Ostrowski et al., 1984; Lorenz and Rogers, 1987). One way that diminishing trust has been expressed is public support for spending limitations.

Support for spending reductions with such initiatives as California's Proposition 13 suggest that the public believes that its tax burden is too large for the services that it receives (Sears and Citrin, 1985). Miller and Miller (1991) find that public evaluations of government services differ from those normally held for similar services provided by the free market. Because a free enterprise system competes for consumer patronage, the absence of market competition for government means that public scrutiny will increase because of its inability to decide whether certain services are provided and to calculate the price of those services.

Many argue that dissatisfaction with public services has led to a nationwide tax revolt that has caused local governments to undertake management improvements (Ladd and Yinger, 1989). Thus, one consequence of tax revolts is an increased emphasis on the efficiency of service delivery. Local governments that are obliged to abide by diminishing tax bases must at the same time respond to the increased public scrutiny that produced the initial concern about government spending practices (Ostrowski et al., 1984).

Citizen initiatives placing limits on the public sector's taxing authority are not the only means available for the public to express their concern that government is not spending wisely. The selection of public officials also provides an indirect opportunity to communicate public preferences on which programs should be created and how they should be administered. For example, "voting the rascals out" is a strategy whereby the public decides that the present makeup of government should be terminated. Thus, spending decisions are

> determined by the complex interaction between citizens' demands for public services and the political and institutional environment of the city. Citizens' demand for public services reflects the same economic tradeoffs as the demand for private goods and services but is articulated in different ways. (Ladd and Yinger, 1989, p. 216)

A bureaucrat's performance in this environment requires a unique combination of skills. The bureaucracy is the primary liaison between the public and its elected officials. Public opinion about the provision of government services is reflected in its voting behavior. Elected officials are, then, held accountable for policy administration by the public (Anton, 1988, p. 151).

Elected officials determine the laws that public agencies are responsible for enforcing as well as the resources that these offices receive for policy administration. In the past, the primary skill needs of the public administrator emphasized the technology of service delivery, the analytical skills of administration, and a top-down management strategy. Today, the hazy boundaries dividing public institutions mean that public administrators must improve their mediation and negotiation skills (Rutter, 1980).

Administrative values also play an important role in bureaucratic conduct. Because of their expertise in policy implementation, public administrators often participate in the policy formulation process by communicating to elected officials their concerns about enforcement (Yates, 1988, p. 76). One would expect that an apolitical stance emphasizing value neutrality is the most appropriate because appointed officials are removed from the electoral process and receive civil service protection. Their detachment from the electoral process allows bureaucrats to make recommendations based on their policy expertise without fear of public reprisal. Yet constrained budgetary environments can lead to fierce competition for diminishing resources. Value neutrality may be compromised in an effort to maintain present funding levels.

The diverse and growing literature suggests that local governments must simultaneously heed fiscal and regulatory pressure from their parent governments and fulfill changing public expectations of the administration of government services. Both pressure points impose two performance standards on local governments: "Local government performance is the extent to which public officials in a community are able to achieve stated economic, social, or environmental conditions with a minimum of expenditure of resources" (Rapp and Patitucci, 1977, p. 4). First, local governments are compelled to be effective in their administration; they must possess the necessary skills to implement their programs. Second, by operating in a restrictive financial environment under an ever watchful public eye, the must be able to accomplish their mission efficiently (Downes, 1987, p. 185; see also Anton, 1988, p. 151).

Public administration is a diverse profession sandwiched between two equally needful pressure groups: a public expecting that services will be delivered in an appropriate fashion and elected officials who seek public approval for overseeing the provision of these services (Yates, 1987, pp. 78-82; Rutter, 1980, pp. 142-144). One method of improving efficiency and effectiveness is by updating skills through training.

In the present study, local government efficiency and effectiveness are explored in the context of how local-level public administrators view training needs for agency personnel. One of the ways that local governments strengthen their service delivery is by providing civil servants with opportunities to improve their performance. Updating skills so that new technologies can be utilized, educating workers on the impact of new legislation, and developing ways to deal with changing political environments all contribute to better service delivery. Thus, training gives bureaucrats the opportunity to improve their performance.

Preliminary findings suggest that efficiency and effectiveness are both viewed by local governments as important, yet additional assistance is required in order to achieve these goals. Further, in relative terms, training opportunities that would improve efficiency are considered more important than those that would improve effectiveness. The evidence suggests that local governments recognize that resource allocation patterns will not likely change in the near or far distant future. Thus, local authorities must continue serving the public despite constrained fiscal times.

Efficiency and effectiveness are not mutually exclusive. By demonstrating to their funding sources that they are functioning at a high degree of efficiency, local governments can expect that they will be better regarded by higher authorities. As a result, local governments may view improved efficiency as a precursor to greater effectiveness.

Training is often made available to local governments though university-based institutes. American universities are modeled on three general obligations: teaching, research, and public service. The public service role is often implemented through ongoing relationships between governments and universities. In this way, knowledge advanced by academicians is incorporated into the practice of public administration.

Whorton, Gibson, and Dunn (1986) studied the attitudes and opinions of users and providers of university public service. They argue that both universities and governments benefit from an arrangement that employs university expertise in public service. Yet academicians and practitioners differ in their needs, goals, and values.

> The academic environment fosters developing theory and understanding of a field, with much discretion for defining areas of effort and flexible time parameters for accomplishing one's largely self-defined tasks. Practitioners do not usually have the luxury of time, and they seek answers to pressing public sector problems, regardless of their theoretical relevance. They may not find the services offered by academicians relevant or timely; academicians may not see the problems of practitioners as challenging, interesting, or congruent with the definition of their current tasks. (Whorton et al., 1986, p. 38)

A mutually beneficial arrangement is, then, hindered by one's role orientations. Advancement within each field requires that different skills and talents be developed.

As a means to understand the differences between academicians and practitioners better, Whorton et al. sought to identify whether, and to what extent, shared values exist between users and providers of university public service. A national sample of city and county managers, state officials, and directors of university-based service institutes was surveyed in 1984. The results suggest that providers perceive technical assistance and consulting as the most important services, whereas users indicate that training holds highest priority (Whorton et al., 1986, p. 40).

Whorton et al. suggest that the absence of shared values between academicians and practitioners can be confronted if universities and governments forge a more symbiotic interaction. An improved linkage based on a shared understanding of individual needs will benefit both sides of the relationship. They advise that "universities and practitioners . . . reach agreement on (1) the type of assistance that state and local units need and (2) the mode of delivery that public service units would use in providing that aid" (Whorton et al., 1986, p. 46).

Whorton and colleagues' study, because it was based on a national sample, does not gauge the views of those users and providers engaged in the same relationship. Thus, to follow these researchers' advice requires that university service providers elicit the views of their users in order to understand the training needs of the practitioners in their service delivery area. One such needs assessment was commissioned by the University of Central Florida (Orlando) Institute of Government.

Many of the political and economic conditions being experienced in central Florida are also being felt in other municipalities across the nation. Budgetary constraints, environmental issues, changing financial structures, and technological advances all influence a local government's ability to serve its constituency. Therefore, the needs assessment discussed here builds on Whorton and associates' promotion of more symbiotic university-government relationships. At the same time, the budgetary and programmatic issues raised by the public administrators chosen for the survey are likely felt by those serving in similar capacities in local governments nationwide.

I. BACKGROUND RESEARCH

The opinions of public administrators responsible for providing public services have been tapped for many reasons. Among these are role orientation and skill assessments, perceptions of the impact of higher-level authorities on local government autonomy, and occupational stress.

Mitchell (1991, p. 433) analyzed the skill assessments of public authority executives (government owned transportation service). He found that executives considered financial analysis and budgeting the most important skills among those listed for managing a public authority; in contrast, bargaining and negotiating methods were found to be the least relevant. To some extent, authority directors believed that detached technical abilities were more important than subjective people-oriented skills.

Public administrators frequently operate in an environment where competing demands exist. They must often choose from among several possible roles. Newell and Ammons (1989), in an analysis of the role emphases of mayors, mayoral assistants, city managers, and assistant city managers, found that a more substantial portion of time is spent by city officials on management concerns than on political or policy roles. This finding is consistent with Streib and Waugh's conclusion that municipal executives emphasize management capacity issues (1991).

Streib and Waugh (1991) analyzed the results of a national survey of county administrators and executives in which local government perceptions of state and federal authorities were addressed. Streib and Waugh argue that increased state leadership is needed because of the vulnerable position that the counties were put in by the new federalism. The counties and states have an important relationship, and it is impossible to discuss improving county management without considering the role that the states play in providing the counties with the funding and authority for self-governance (Streib and Waugh, 1991, p. 380).

Waugh also compared the occupational considerations of county authorities and executives. They found that professional development is less important than intergovernmental relations and management capacity (1991, p. 390). Nonetheless, these administrators recognize that the job performance of their personnel is critical to good public service: the "retention of quality employees and rewards for professional employees generate a great deal of concern among county leaders, more than a number of key issues in the areas of management capacity and professional development" (1991, pp. 392–393).

Hinton and Kerrigan (1989) studied those political issues that public administrators believed were most important to confront. On the basis of their analysis of a 1987–1988 survey, they suggest that a primary concern of public administrators is understanding the "causes underlying major urban problems, human relations, and values motivating behavior" (1989, p. 157). Further, increasing public expectations that government play a more active role in stimulating the economy are not lost on those responsible for policy implementation: "A general pattern seems to be getting clearer with regard to economic development issues: local communities and state governments will become increasingly active on a wider range of economic development issues" (Annison, 1987, p. 325).

Public administration is frequently concerned with providing adequate services while keeping government expenditures down. Local agencies are responsible for administering service departments; enforcing laws and ordinances; providing pertinent information to councils, commissions, and boards; and managing the operation and financial conditions of their units of government (Rutter, 1980, p. 142). Requirements such as these can often be accompanied by conflict and ambiguities that often lead to job frustration and stress. Available public resources, citizen views about local government, and job pressures are many of the prevalent factors causing frustration among local government managers (Rutter, 1980, p. 119). City and county managers, though confronted with public pressure, must maintain standards of professional and personal integrity. "Most often their professional worth is determined by an ability to negotiate with conflicting interests and to operate in complex political environments" (Rutter, 1980, p. 142).

Waugh and Streib (1990) examined the attitudes of county officials toward expanding state and local responsibilities. Assessments of state responsiveness to local government needs were also analyzed. Responses to a 1984-1985 survey of county officials indicate that 70% did not believe that states give as much financial support to local government programs as they can, while half believe that state governments are responsive to local government needs. More than half argue that state governments have failed to fulfill their proper fiscal obligations to maintain public services at the local level (Waugh and Streib, 1990, p. 35). Waugh and Streib conclude that "a sizable number of respondents felt that the state's proper fiscal obligations fell short of their capacities for local government financial support" (1990, p. 37).

As a result of the new federalism, the local government administrators's decision-making capacity has been questioned. A survey of the directors of state associations of county governments attempted to gauge their perceptions about whether counties are able to make relatively independent decisions (Waugh and Hy, 1988). Further, state willingness to expand powers and responsibilities to lower-level authorities was also queried.

Waugh and Hy (1988, p. 30) conclude that county association directors perceive that counties have the administrative capability for newly inherited programs, yet lack sufficient political and financial capabilities. The importance of the need for county governments to raise revenues with as few restrictions as possible was also identified. Counties cannot assume any additional fiscal responsibilities while requiring fiscal control over the ability to deliver services (1988, p. 31). "Subtle fiscal and administrative controls allow counties to search for creative ways to cut expenditures, deliver services, increase revenues, and raise capital" (Waugh and Hy, 1988, p. 31).

These research efforts demonstrate that a public administrator's worldview influences a multitude of behaviors including decision making and management. One common theme that persists in these endeavors is that public administrators often find themselves frustrated by a lack of human and financial resources. Training provides administrators with the opportunity to invest in their human resources, thereby making the use of financial resources, the bulk of which provide direct services to the public, more effective.

II. METHODOLOGY

Five hundred local government public administrators who hold decision-making authority over personnel training in the University of Central Florida Institute of Government's eleven-county service delivery area were surveyed during June 1991. All members of this population received a self-administered questionnaire. The response rate was 33% (N = 165).

The questionnaire focused on assessing the needs of the institute's constituents and identifying the ways to meet those needs. Three general issues were addressed in the survey: preferred seminar offerings, program support, and budgetary concerns.

The first part of the questionnaire elicited information indicating the kinds of seminars that would garner the greatest interest and the highest enrollment. This section consisted of twenty seminar topics that the respondents were asked to rate on the basis of their interest and likelihood of participation. A five-point scale ranging from very low to very high was used as the response set for all of the questions concerned with seminar offerings.

The seminar topics focused on efficiency and effectiveness. Seminars that the institute would offer that focus on efficiency included communication skills, financial management, cultural diversity, meeting management, team building, supervisory skills, senior management skills, ethics, downsizing, and strategic planning.

Programs that would improve effectiveness included in the survey are media relations, labor relations, customer service, government in the sunshine, affordable housing, economic diversity, water/wastewater management, transportation, alternative revenue sources, and growth management. The respondents were then asked in an open-ended format to identify programs that they preferred that were not listed on the survey instrument.

The second section dealt with the reasons why respondents would not support available programs. These questions ranged from identifying the reasons why one would not attend seminars to evaluating similar offerings provided by private organizations.

As a university-based entity, the Institute of Government is itself subject to public funding. Thus, it competes with private organizations for public agency training dollars. By learning about how administrators view the institute, programming preferences can be understood in terms of the quality that users accord training seminars. Further, these administrators were asked whether they had attended any seminars themselves. Those who had attended were asked whether they believed that seminar participation benefitted them in fulfilling their responsibilities.

Finally, budgetary concerns were addressed. Respondents were asked about the general and specific issues surrounding training allocations in the overall budgetary process. Training expenditures are often regarded as one component of the budget that can be cut without reducing service delivery. Therefore, in an era of fiscal constraint, one must determine the impact of general budget reduction on training expenditures because reduced budgets may affect training

Table 1 The Impact of Budgetary Concerns on Training Expenditures

	What impact do budget reductions have on your seminar participation? (Percentage)	What impact do reduced training budgets have on employee training expenditures? (Percentage)
1. Very low	2	1
2. Low	9	5
3. Moderate	30	32
4. High	33	41
5. Very high	26	21
	100%	100%
N	164	165
Mean	3.7	3.8
Standard Deviation	1.02	.87

	How much of a factor is seminar price in employee and your seminar participation? (Percentage)	How much of a price increase would not affect seminar participation?	(Percentage)
1. Very low	1	1. $12 per seminar	1
2. Low	10	2. $3–5 per seminar	10
3. Moderate	33	3. $6–9 per seminar	33
4. High	39	4. $10–15 per seminar	56
5. Very high	17		
	100%		100%
N	164		148
Mean	3.6		2.7
Standard Deviation	.93		.98

allocations that may then influence seminar participation. Two questions addressing these issues were included in the questionnaire.

Questions about the provision of preferred services are included because reduced budgets mean that funds allocated for training must be spent efficiently. Questions pertaining to seminar price determined the extent to which program cost was a factor in participation. Tolerance of price increases and the extent to which participation would be affected was also elicited. Price elasticity is the relationship between price and consumption where one increases as the other decreases. The price elasticities of private and public goods are not identical (Green, 1992). When comparing the two, "the [price] elasticity of private/economic goods is considerably greater than the elasticity of public/political goods" (Green, 1992, p. 133). Pricing questions can determine both the willingness and the ability to pay for particular programs while allowing the institute to decide which seminars can be feasibly offered.

The bureaucrat provides public goods and purchases private goods in the form of institute seminars. Even though the institute is funded with public monies, its need to compete with private training providers forces it to behave as a private good. Therefore, the institute must behave according to its competitive position even though it is a public agency.

III. DATA ANALYSIS

Several interrelated issues are addressed here. First, we recognize that administrators are feeling financial pressure because of changing intergovernmental relationships and citizen concerns about government spending practices. Second, the bureaucrat's distinct position as the primary link between the public and its elected officials means that personnel are scrutinized by both. Thus, agencies are compelled to function effectively at a high degree of efficiency in order to earn positive regard from each. Operating at the greatest efficiency and effectiveness requires that training opportunities be made available to civil servants when the need arises.

Confounding the demand for improved service delivery is the view of local governments that training allocations provide the opportunity for reducing one's operating budget. Unlike many elements of a budget, training does not provide a direct service to the public. Therefore, those responsible for allocating training resources may be forced to redirect these funds to direct public service. This situation leaves training allocations more vulnerable to cutbacks than other components of an agency budget. When public administrators decide to commit training resources for themselves and their employees, they must do so in a manner that is consistent with agency needs and resource availability.

The results of the survey were analyzed accordingly. The role that budgetary issues play in spending decisions for training was first addressed. The programmatic issues that held the foremost priority among respondents and those programs that garnered the least interest and likelihood of participation were then analyzed. Finally, the impact of budgetary considerations on program issues was examined.

The data summarized in Table 1 demonstrate that budgetary issues are an important consideration when training resources are considered. In general terms, an agency's financial situation has a strong impact on the monies allocated for training. Nearly three-fourths of the respondents rated budget reductions as high or very high when asked about the impact of possible budget reductions on training expenditures. Only 6% deemed these issues unimportant, thereby suggesting that training budgets may be considered an expendable luxury in austere times.

The University of Central Florida Institute of Government conducts seminars as the primary means of providing training to local government employees. Accordingly, responses to specific questions geared toward those seminars offered by the institute were then analyzed. Reactions are consistent with those conveyed earlier. Budgetary issues are a high priority when considering training allocations. Nearly equal proportions maintained that reduced training budgets had a moderate or high impact on seminar participation. Seminar price was also an issue when making training determinations. More than one-half of the respondents expressed the view that seminar price was either a high or a very high factor in seminar participation.

Enrollment decisions can take two forms. First, the administrator must decide whether any employee will be attending a given seminar. The question then becomes how many employees will be allowed to attend that seminar from a particular agency. The data in Table 1 suggest that training allocation decisions may be made on the basis of price rather than benefit to the agency. Further, fewer employees will likely attend training seminars in the future.

In the next part of the analysis, efficiency questions were addressed. As discussed earlier, efficiency focuses on an agency's ability to function in a manner that emphasizes appropriate use of resources when providing public services. Each respondent was asked about his or her interest and willingness to participate in a series of seminars with an efficiency-oriented focus.

Interest in and willingness of participation were elicited separately because the former suggests that the administrator finds a seminar important and relevant to the functioning of that particular agency. The participation question alludes to whether agency employees would participate in a seminar of this type given the budgetary considerations presented in Table 1. An alternative view suggests that, despite its overall importance, expressing interest in a program that one would not participate in indicates that the skill levels at that agency are deemed sufficient in this particular area.

Interest in those skills that would foster improved internal efficiency is generally higher than is willingness to participate in these programs (see Table 2). Organizational skills are stressed. Interest and participation are highest for senior management skills, strategic planning, supervisory skills, and team building. Developing these skills promotes improved internal efficiency by ensuring that the organization is being managed well. Or, one could argue that these responses are biased toward those holding administrative positions because the respondents are administrators.

An emphasis on agency organizational operations does suggest that administrators do not anticipate that their present situation will change significantly in the near future. This interpretation is also borne out by the degree of importance and relative ranking of cultural diversity and downsizing, two programs that may require personnel and/or organizational changes.

Consistency across interest and participation ranks is demonstrated in all cases (see Table 3). Each program was ranked according to its position in relation to the other efficiency-based seminars. If one compares each set of rankings of the interest and participation responses, no one program differs by more than one rank. Public administrators view efficiency programs as both worthwhile and beneficial to their organization as demonstrated by the comparable interest and participation levels across relative ranks.

External effectiveness was then investigated. As discussed previously, effective performance is exhibited through relationships with outside organizations (see Table 4). The greater an agency's effectiveness, the higher will be the positive regard that it receives from outside institutions such as parent governments and the mass media that are crucial to good public service delivery. If an agency is in good standing with these organizations, its ability to educate those who determine their authority and level of resources will be improved.

Table 2 Interest in Programs That Would Improve Efficiency

	Mean	Standard Deviation	Rank	Correlation
Communication Skills	3.38	1.04	5	0.13
Cultural Diversity	2.19	1.14	10	0.10
Downsizing	2.84	1.27	8	0.00
Ethics	3.28	1.18	6	0.18
Financial Management	3.08	1.31	7	0.11
Meeting Management	2.74	1.05	9	–0.01
Senior Management Skills	3.97	1.00	1	0.09
Strategic Planning	3.64	1.27	3	0.18
Supervisory Skills	3.60	1.14	4	0.06
Team Building	3.69	1.11	2	0.10

Table 3 Likelihood of Participation in Progress That Would Improve Efficiency

	Mean	Standard Deviation	Rank	Correlation
Communication Skills	2.84	1.26	6	0.01
Cultural Diversity	1.94	1.18	10	0.02
Downsizing	2.44	1.35	8	–0.02
Ethics	2.88	1.38	5	0.19
Financial Management	2.78	1.39	7	0.15
Meeting Management	2.36	1.16	9	–0.01
Senior Management Skills	3.63	1.23	1	0.10
Strategic Planning	3.25	1.27	3	0.15
Supervisory Skills	3.10	1.40	4	0.03
Team Building	3.30	1.24	2	0.07

Table 4 presents administrative responses to questions gauging interest and likelihood of participation in programs promoting effectiveness. The results indicate that programs aiding personnel with legislative change and financial constraint hold the highest priority. Further, those programs that would require additional funding for implementation, such as affordable housing and economic diversity, receive the lowest interest and likelihood of participation. Local administrators may have recognized this financial reality when answering these questions.

The program that garners the strongest interest and likelihood of participation is alternative revenue sources. Central Florida governments, like other municipalities facing economic difficulties produced by new intergovernmental financial and legislative relationships, must develop ways to address their diminishing resource base. Thus, the relatively strong regard granted this program, in both interest and likelihood of participation, is as expected (see Table 5).

Two of the remaining high-priority items, growth management and government in the sunshine, are issues germane to Florida. Growth management was mandated by the state legislature in 1985. The legislation requires that

> local governments . . . maintain adequate service levels . . . that are consistent with state requirements. Local governments must maintain the service levels they choose and cannot approve development that would reduce those levels. . . . Local governments . . .

Table 4 Interest in Programs That Would Improve Effectiveness

	Mean	Standard Deviation	Rank	Correlation
Affordable Housing	2.36	1.41	10	0.04
Alternative Revenue Sources	3.56	1.30	1	0.18
Customer Service	3.46	1.20	2	0.05
Economic Diversity	2.58	1.35	9	0.07
Government in the Sunshine	3.08	1.28	4	0.17
Growth Management	3.40	1.28	3	0.12
Labor Relations	2.78	1.34	6	0.13
Media Relations	2.09	1.10	5	0.06
Transportation	2.71	1.31	8	0.08
Water/Wastewater Management	2.73	1.43	7	0.15

Table 5 Likelihood of Participation in Programs That Would Improve Effectiveness

	Mean	Standard Deviation	Rank	Correlation
Affordable Housing	1.99	1.24	10	0.04
Alternative Revenue Sources	3.28	1.38	1	0.13
Customer Service	2.93	1.34	3	0.02
Economic Diversity	2.31	1.33	9	0.09
Government in the Sunshine	2.65	1.38	4	0.28
Growth Management	2.98	1.35	2	0.08
Labor Relations	2.42	1.43	7	0.05
Media Relations	2.33	1.25	8	0.06
Transportation	2.43	1.35	6	0.01
Water/Wastewater Management	2.51	1.45	5	0.09

must plan for assurance of adequate and available capital facilities. . . . (Juergensmeyer, 1988, p. 103)

Local government service level adherence to state requirements, otherwise known as concurrency, is deemed by many to be the most important element of the growth management law because all decisions made at the local level must agree with those determined by higher authorities. If there is a discrepancy between them, state guidelines must be followed. Local governments must plan within the context of state law.

The difficulty being experienced in enforcing these provisions is demonstrated by the relatively high interest levels that growth management receives. Likelihood of participation is not nearly as high, suggesting that local agencies do not view the need for this program to be as important as they do other seminars.

Government in the sunshine is the second seminar that is pertinent to Florida. The government in the sunshine law, so named because of Florida's sunny locale, requires that all meetings of government officials be open to the public. Interpreting this law can prove difficult because of the informal communication that often occurs among elected and appointed officials.

The difficulties caused by urban growth that are facing municipalities nationally and the increasing concern among the public about the conduct of government suggest that similar laws will be adopted elsewhere. The interest of those who must operate within these guidelines suggests that local administrators recognize the need for programs of this type in light of their need to be more effective.

Unlike the previous analysis of the efficiency curriculum, the comparable ranking is not consistent across programs. Here, there is a much greater interest than likelihood of participation in media relations programs. Public administrators may view these programs as a luxury that, given the choice, will not likely take precedence over others.

Two important phenomena are revealed by these response patterns. First, support for programs that would foster improved efficiency is favored over support for those promoting more effectiveness. Second, program interest is higher than is likelihood of participation for all programs. Either agency administrators are pleased with their skill levels and those of their employees or they recognize that it is unlikely that, because of budgetary constraints, they can provide their employees with these training opportunities.

Finally, the impact that budgetary constraints have on program interest and participation was explored. Each response was cross-tabulated with the question asking whether seminar price was a factor in participation (see Table 1). These results are presented in Table 3. There is a consistently weak impact of seminar price on participation in any program. Those correlations that are stronger suggests an emphasis on efficient and highly regarded public service in times of budgetary austerity. Seminar price had the strongest impact on participation in programming dealing with ethics, alternative revenue sources, government in the sunshine, and strategic planning.

The challenges facing local government public administrators are becoming ever more complex. Their self-defined training needs exhibit a high priority for efficient public service. A recognition that local bureaucracies must respond effectively to changing legislative and financial environments is also demonstrated.

IV. CONCLUSION

In this paper, we have discussed the way that local government administrators view training needs and the budgetary concerns associated with those needs. The findings suggest that improving an agency's internal operations will improve its reputation, thereby creating an environment that enables public officials to receive positive regard from outside forces. The electorate will be pleased with the services that it receives, and public approval will be reflected in voting behavior. Further, elected officials who recognize high-quality service delivery will use those tools available to them to try to provide these agencies with adequate funding levels necessary for efficient public service.

On a broader scale, concerns expressed by those responsible for training decisions on a local level reflect the impact of the new federalism. Local governments do have more independence, yet they must improve the efficiency of their operations in order to contend with the reduced funding levels that accompany their new autonomy.

Finally, we see one other facet of the university-government relationship. The needs assessment on which this article is based is unique because previous efforts did not survey the users and providers involved in the same relationship. Here, the scope of the present study allows the concerns of users to be known to the providers of university-based training programs.

ACKNOWLEDGMENTS

The authors wish to thank Ms. Marilyn Crotty, director of the University of Central Florida Institute of Government, who provided the idea for the study and the necessary office support and office space that allowed the study to be implemented.

REFERENCES

Annison, Michael H., New Economic Development, *Economic Development Quarterly 1*:325 (1987).

Anton, Thomas J., The Political Economy of Local Government Reform in the United States, in *The Dynamics of Institutional Change: Local Government Reorganization in Western Democracies* (Bruno Dente and Francesco Kjellberg, eds.), Sage Modern Politics Series, vol. 19, Sage, London, 1988.

Busson, Terry and Coulter, Philip, eds., *Policy Evaluation for Local Government*, Greenwood Press, Westport, Conn., 1987.

Dente, Bruno and Kjellberg, Francesco, eds., *The Dynamics of Institutional Change: Local Government Reorganization in Western Democracies*, Sage Modern Politics Series, vol. 19, Sage, London, 1988.

Downes, Brian T., The Effects of Fiscal Stress and Cutback Management on Local Government Performance, in *Policy Evaluation for Local Government* (Terry Busson and Philip Coulter, eds., Greenwood Press, Westport, Conn., 1987.

Dunn, Delmer, Gibson, Frank K., and Whorton, Joseph W., University Commitment to Public Service for State and Local Government, *Public Administration Review 45*(4):503–509 (1985).

Frederickson, H. George, ed., *Ideal and Practice in Council-Manager Government*, International City Managers Association, Washington, D.C., 1989.

Green, Donald Philip, The Price Elasticity of Mass Preferences, *American Political Science Review 86*(1):128–148 (1992).

Hinton, David W. and Kerrigan, John E., Training the Changing Knowledge and Skill Needs and Service Attitudes of Public Managers, in *Ideal and Practice in Council-Manager Government* (H. George Frederickson, ed.), International City Managers Association, Washington, D.C., 1987.

Juergensmeyer, Julian Conrad, The Development of Regulatory Impact Fees: The Legal Issues, in *Development Impact Fees* (Arthur C. Nelson, ed.), Planners Press, Chicago, 1988.

Kellar, Elizabeth, ed., *Ethical Insight, Ethical Action: Perspectives for the Local Government Manager*, International City Managers Association, Washington, D.C., 1988.

Ladd, Everett Carll, *The American Polity: The People and Their Government*, W. W. Norton, New York, 1991.

Ladd, Helen F. and Yinger, John, *America's Ailing Cities: Fiscal Health and the Design of Urban Policy*, Johns Hopkins University Press, Baltimore, Md., 1989.

Lorenz, Frederick O. and Rogers, David L., Impact of Federal Government Grants on Local Government Capacity, in *Policy Evaluation for Local Government* (Terry Busson and Philip Coulter, eds.), Greenwood Press, Westport, Conn., 1987.

Miller, Thomas I., and Miller, Michelle A., Standards of Excellence: U.S. Resident's Evaluations of Local Government Services, *Public Administration Review 51*(6):503–514 (1991).

Mitchell, Jerry, Education and Skills for Public Authority Management, *Public Administration Review 51*(5):429–437 (1991).

Nelson, Arthur C., ed., *Development Impact Fees*, Planners Press, Chicago, 1988.

Newell, Charldean and Ammons, David N., Role Emphases of City Managers and Other Municipal Executives, in H. George Frederickson, ed., *Ideal and Practice in Council-Manager Government*, International City Managers Association, Washington, D.C., 1989.

Ostrowski, John W., White, Louise G., and Cole, John R., Local Government Capacity Building: A Structured Group Process Approach, in *Administration and Society 16*(1):3–26 (1984).

Rapp, B. W. and Patitucci, F. M., *Managing Local Government for Improved Performance: A Practical Approach*, Westview Press, Boulder, Co., 1977.

Rutter, Laurence, Committee on Future Horizons of the Profession 1978–1979. The Essential Community: Local Government in the Year 2000, in *Municipal Management Series*, International City Managers Association, Washington, D.C., 1980.

Sears, David and Citrin, Jack, *Tax Revolt: Something for Nothing in California*, Harvard University Press, Cambridge, 1985.

Streib, Gregory L. and Waugh, Jr., William A., Probing the Limits of County Reform in an Era of Scarcity: A National Survey of County Administrators and Executives, in *Public Administration Quarterly 15*(3):378–395 (1991).

Waugh, Jr., William C. and Hy, Ronald John, The Administrative, Fiscal, and Policymaking Capacities of County Governments, in *State and Local Government Review 20*(1):28–31 (1988).

Waugh, Jr., William C. and Streib, Gregory, County Officials Perception of Local Capacity and State Responsiveness After the First Reagan Term, in *Southeastern Political Review 18*(1):27–50 (1990).

Whorton, Jr., Joseph W., Gibson, Frank K., and Dunn, Delmer D., The Culture of University Public Service: A National Survey of the Perspectives of Users and Providers, in *Public Administration Review 46*(1):38–47 (1986).

Yates, Jr., Douglas T., Hard Choices: Justifying Bureaucratic Decisions, in *Ethical Insight Ethical Action: Perspectives for the Local Government Manager* (Elizabeth Kellar, ed.), International City Managers Association, Washington, D.C., 1988.

23
Organizational Conflict

Michael Klausner
University of Pittsburgh at Bradford, Bradford, Pennsylvania

Mary Ann Groves
Manhattan College, Riverdale, New York

I. THE NATURE AND INEVITABILITY OF ORGANIZATIONAL CONFLICT

Conflict is extremely common within organizations. A sample of managers surveyed indicated that they spend approximately a quarter of their time dealing with various forms of organizational conflict (Thomas and Schmidt, 1976). This finding should not be surprising given the widespread occurrence of conflict both within and among societies, coupled with the fact that organizations can be viewed as microcosms of the broader society of which they are a part.

Organizational conflict may occur at different levels; that is, it may be *interpersonal* (occurring between individuals within the organization), *intergroup of interdivisional* (transpiring among two or more groups or units within the organization), or *interorganizational* (involving two or more organizations). Since this paper focuses upon conflict within organizations, we shall discuss the causes and consequences of interpersonal and intergroup conflict.

The concept of conflict denotes some type of incompatibility, disagreement, and opposition among members or groups within an organization. Conflict can stem from disagreements and opposition involving cognitions, emotions, behaviors, and goals and the means to achieve them. For example, members of an organization can perceive situations or ideas quite differently. Interpersonal conflict can stem from opposing emotions. In addition, conflict can result from reactions to behaviors perceived as offensive, out of order, or counterproductive. Finally, members or groups can have opposing goals or can disagree on the desirable means for achieving agreed-upon goals [1].

Why is organizational conflict inevitable? As Charles Ferguson (1986, p. 20) argues, "Varying life experiences have equipped all of us to see, feel, and appraise things more or less differently, inevitably producing conflict." In addition, we should expect the consequences of decisions and policies within organizations to affect various groups and subunits within an organization in different ways, thus producing opposing positions of the various groups.

Consequently, some conflict within organizations is to be expected. What varies is the amount of conflict which exists and which is expressed.

Of course power relationships within an organization affect the degree to which the conflict is expressed, and the ways in which it is expressed. As conflict theorists point out, even when there is little conflict within an organization, one cannot assume consensus: maybe members of the organization do not dare express disagreement or opposition, because of fear of punishment from management. As Kolb and Bartunek (1992) note, conflict within organizations is often hidden or suppressed. Workers may choose to avoid interaction with those with whom they disagree, or they may employ strategies of "passive resistance" (rather than open disagreement or conflict) against their supervisors or coworkers. Furthermore, managers may employ manipulative strategies (such as the use of praise or humanitarian gestures to pacify persons with complaints) in order to suppress conflict within an organization.

II. THE CAUSES OF ORGANIZATIONAL CONFLICT

> While much conflict in organizations is undoubtedly an interpersonal phenomenon—two people in competition, or with incompatible personalities, lacking in ability to empathize with another—a theory of organizations, rather than one of individual interaction, should be able to accommodate group conflict. Theory should see conflict as an inevitable part of organizational life stemming from organizational characteristics rather than from the characteristics of individuals. (Perrow, 1986, p. 132)

As the preceding statement indicates, the factors that cause organizational conflict are not only psychological or interpersonal; they also can be social structural, stemming from organizational features or the social context in which the organizations operate.

A. Psychological Factors

Psychological factors involve various aspects of an individual's personality, such as traits and behavioral dispositions which are irritating to others. In extreme cases some form of psychopathology or severe personality disorder may be present and may produce poor interpersonal skills or strategies. However, in this chapter we are not examining psychological causes of organizational conflict; instead, we shall focus on social structural and social interactional factors, only mentioning intrapsychic variables if they are relevant to our understanding of the ways in which social interactional and social structural factors contribute to organizational conflict.

B. Social Interactional Factors

There are many factors which can affect interactional patterns, styles, and strategies within organizations and which can produce organizational conflict. They include the following: misattributions of motives or behavior, faulty communication patterns, prejudice and discrimination toward individuals holding certain ascribed statuses, negative residues of past experiences with specific people (grudges), erroneous causal accounts or explanations for behavior, dissimilarity of persons, destructive criticism, and perceptions of unfairness or inequity (Baron, 1990, p. 202; Bies et al., 1988).

Misattributions of motives occur because people make errors in trying to explain and interpret each other's behavior. For example, there is a strong tendency for individuals to overemphasize the part that personality characteristics play in causing other people's behavior and to underestimate the influence of situational factors (Ross, 1977). Also "conspiracy" theories sometimes emerge within organizations, with persons suspecting ulterior motives of others.

An empirical study by Bies, Shapiro, and Cummings (1988) found that a boss's "causal account" (or explanation) for refusing the request of a subordinate lessened or intensified conflict, depending on two factors: the adequacy of the reasoning the boss uses, and his/her perceived sincerity in stating the causal account. Those conclusions were the result of a survey of 121 employees from different business organizations who were enrolled in an evening M.B.A. program. The resulting "conflict" resulting from various situations was measured by the amount of anger it produced in the employees, whether or not they perceived the boss's decision as fair, the extent to which they disapproved of the boss, and the extent to which they complained about the boss's action to higher authorities within the company. Consequently, this study illustrates how causal accounts, communication methods, and perceptions of equity can affect amounts and degrees of organizational conflict.

Conflict is best viewed as a process rather than a static phenomenon. Kenneth Thomas (1976, pp. 894–910) describes the process through which conflict between two members of an organization proceeds. Each member experiences these four stages: frustration, conceptualization, behavior, and outcome. At first each person is frustrated because one of his/her goals is not being realized. "Conflict episodes might stem from: disagreement, denial of a request, violation of an agreement, insult, active interference with performance, vying for scarce resources, breaking a norm, diminishing one's status, ignoring one's feelings, etc." (Thomas, 1976, p. 895). Then each party conceptualizes the situation, defines it as an "issue," and considers action alternatives and their outcomes. After frustration and conceptualization, the parties determine their conflict behaviors. Figure 1, taken from Thomas (1976, p. 900), illustrates five possible behavioral orientations that may be taken (competitive, collaborative, avoidant, accommodating, and

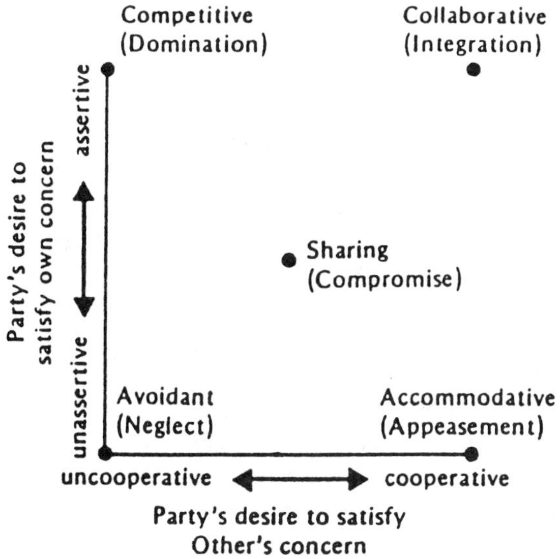

Figure 1 Five conflict-handling orientations (from Thomas, 1976, p. 900).

sharing) in relation to two dimensions: the extent to which the party is assertive or unassertive (the vertical axis) and the extent to which the party is cooperative or uncooperative (the horizontal axis). Thomas describes each behavioral orientation in the following ways:

1. the *competitive* orientation represents a desire to win one's own concerns at the other's expense, namely, to dominate.
2. an *accommodative* orientation focuses upon appeasement—satisfying the other's concerns without attending to one's own.
3. The *sharing* orientation . . . is a preference for moderate but incomplete satisfaction for both parties—for compromise.
4. the *collaborative* orientation fully represents a desire to satisfy fully the concerns of both parties—to integrate their concerns.
5. The remaining orientation, *avoidance*, reflects indifference to the concerns of either party. (Thomas, 1976, p. 901)

The last stage in Thomas's process model involves the outcome of the conflict episode. He notes that only the integrative agreement represents a true resolution of the issue; the other forms of agreements (domination, neglect, compromise, and accommodation) are all likely to leave some residual frustration in one or both parties. Therefore, the specific outcome which is reached is likely to affect subsequent conflict situations. Some research has found that subordinates see conflict as being handled most constructively when they perceive supervisors as using collaborative or accommodative tactics (and most destructively when they use competitive or avoidant tactics) (Burke, 1970; Thomas, 1971).

Kenneth Thomas also noted important factors that affect the types of behaviors persons will exhibit in conflict episodes (see Figure 2). Each party's behavior is influenced by personality factors (or "behavioral predispositions"), by social pressures (e.g., group norms and sanctions), by the incentive structure in their work environment, by the rules and procedures within the organization, and by the other party's behaviors toward them. Thus organizational conflict is a complex processual phenomenon which involves a multiplicity of causal factors. The models by Kenneth Thomas are very helpful in our understanding and analysis of conflict episodes within work organizations.

Conflict arises in interaction patterns within organizations. As Robert Kahn (1979) notes, organizational conflict can result when *one* person (for example, a supervisor) places incompatible pressures on a worker; Kahn calls this "*intra*-sender conflict." *Inter*-sender conflict occurs when contradictory messages from *two or more* persons are sent to a worker (for example, when opposing messages are coming from superiors and subordinates). A middle manager could experience his/her supervisor as pressuring him/her to stick strictly to rules and rigid production schedules while the subordinates desire weak supervision and high levels of autonomy. *Person-role* conflict results from conflict between a worker's role requirements and his/her personal values.

Kahn found that *role conflict* was common among workers he studied. An example of role conflict would be when a worker experiences contrary demands from two or more roles, as when a research scientist serves as a manager of a research group and feels conflicting pressures from being committed to the role of scientist (which would encourage innovation and creative projects) and, at the same time, as a manager feels pressure to discourage creative research projects that might be risky for the company (Greenberg and Baron, 1993, p. 230). As Kahn notes (1979, p. 207), there are emotional costs of the role conflict: stress, low levels of job satisfaction, and low confidence in the organization. Conflict and tension also can result from *role overload* (when one role has so many demands that they are difficult to meet.

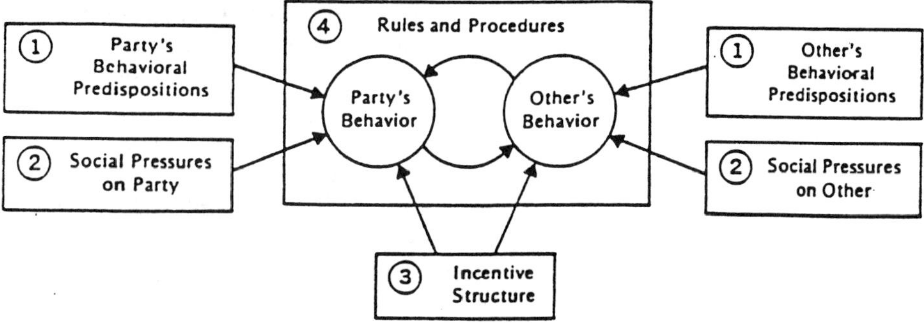

Figure 2 Structural model of dyadic conflict (from Thomas, 1976, p. 912).

C. Social Structural Factors

There is a tendency for many people, including managers, to attribute organizational conflict to personality factors and clashes among members of the organization. There are several reasons for this type of "psychological reductionism."

First, unlike organizational structure, which is intangible and invisible, individuals are both tangible and visible and thus easier to refer to when searching for the causes of organizational conflict. We cannot "see" social structure, and we often are not aware of structural influences. Second, in our society there is a strong propensity to "psychologize" or "individualize" behavioral phenomena. The philosophical and cultural roots for this are deep and pervasive. We place a strong value on individualism and stress the control that individuals have over their own behaviors and destiny. We are unlikely to see how social structural influences operate. Third, conflict manifests itself via individuals. It is individuals, not organizational structures, whom we see arguing, disagreeing, threatening, and fighting with each other.

Sociological research has shown the effects of the structure of work organizations on the behaviors, and even personality patterns, of the workers (Kanter, 1977). Kanter found that structures of opportunity, power, and numerical proportions of categories of workers shaped the behaviors of men and women in the corporation she studied. Bouza (1991), drawing upon his thirty years of experience in a wide range of roles in three law enforcement agencies, argues that the structure of police agencies, their subcultures, and especially the demands the police role comprises result in significant personality and attitudinal changes in police personnel. He notes that the background checks of potential law enforcement personnel are thorough in the extreme and that the recruits, who are initially idealistic and enthusiastic, undergo a personality and mind-set transformation. Thus the personality and attitudinal transformations that occur are the result of a combination of organizational and subcultural variables, role demands, and experiences on the job. Therefore, we must consider structural factors that could help us to explain the amounts and kinds of conflict within organizations.

The term "social structure" refers to the way an organization is "set up," the conditions under which it operates, and the relationships existing among the different units, positions, and roles within the organization. Structural factors would include the hierarchical or authority relationships, the division of labor, the span of control, the communication patterns, the degree of centralization within the organization, statuses with their role requirements and demands, and decision-making patterns. Kilmann and Thomas (1978, pp. 62–63) used the term "structural factors" to refer to conditions "outside of the individual," including conflict of interest between the goals of conflict parties, and procedures, such as frequency of contacts, barriers to openness, formality, and sequencing of issues within the organization. Structure thus refers to the underlying conditions that shape events within a work organization. The way that the product, service, or technology is produced and used affects the organizational structure, which in turn may either facilitate or impede the development of conflict.

Hierarchical authority structures within an organization can create a fertile soil for conflict. In addition to differences in power, prestige, perks, status, and salary, all of which may engender feelings of jealousy and envy which may lead to conflict, the time perspectives associated with each level are different and are likely to be conflict-producing. Executives who may have long-range time horizons may clash with other managers with shorter-range time orientations (Gibson et al., 1991).

In addition, another cause of organizational conflict rooted in the authority structure is the feeling among subordinates that they are being too closely monitored by their superiors. If they feel that they are not being given sufficient leeway in performing their jobs as they see fit, conflict may result.

If the hierarchical structure within an organization is very rigid and if workers have little power and autonomy, "hidden rebellion," rather than open conflict, may emerge. Workers may engage in work slowdowns, do inferior work, or attempt to undermine the organization in subtle ways.

Scarcity of resources and conditions of competition can produce organizational conflict (Baron, 1990, p. 200). Since organizations have a limited amount of resources available to allocate to the various units, and the workers in each division want as large a slice of the resource pie as possible, conflict among units is likely. A zero-sum situation may exist in which any increase in resources for a given department results in a corresponding decrease for one or more of the other. Feelings of jealousy, injustice, and unfairness are almost inevitable as members of the various departments believe they have been shortchanged. This phenomenon is promoted by the fact that their perceptions of their own and other departments' personnel and contributions are likely to be biased. As a result, they perceive the "norm of distributive justice" to have been violated and experience anger which may manifest itself in a variety of ways (Homans, 1974).

Competition and conflict over scarce resources have a tendency to exacerbate differences in power: "Scarcity has a way of turning latent or disguised conflict into overt conflict. Two scientists who don't get along very well may be able to put up a peaceful front until a reduction in laboratory space provokes each to protect his domain" (Johns, 1983, p. 418).

Reward structures and incentives of certain types are more likely to be conflict-generating than others. "Intergroup conflict is more likely to occur when the reward system is related to individual group performance rather than to overall organizational performance" (Gibson et al., 1991, p. 304). For example, if a company's sales force is rewarded for sales increases and the credit department is rewarded for its effectiveness in minimizing losses due to inappropriate credit approvals, a situation of conflict may emerge between the sales and credit departments because of the company's reward structure. In this situation, in order for one group to succeed, another group has to lose.

Goals and philosophies of each division of an organization are related to its specific functions, and the distinctive values, norms, and mind-sets differ. Thus the sales, credit, and manufacturing divisions of an organization have members who have developed different priorities, outlooks, and orientations, primarily as a result of their distinctive goals. In many cases the goals of one division conflict with those of another. For example, the goal of the sales department is to sell as many of the organization's products as possible. Doing so will result in higher salaries for members of the sales force and positive recognition by the president. The goal of the credit department is to make certain that potential customers who are poor credit risks do not become actual customers. Thus they may not approve the sale of the company's products to customers they deem to be poor credit risks. Similarly, the marketing/sales department may pressure the manufacturing division to modify a particular product to suit a customer's changed specifications and to do so in what the manufacturing executives view as too short a time frame.

These and similar situations among other organizational subsystems are all likely to engender conflict, yet the conflict is not due to personality differences among members, but to their different agendas and goals. As members of the different divisions pursue the goals of their division, they are likely to lose sight of the overall mission of the organization of which their unit is a part. They may be focused on defending their turf and pursuing their unit's goal even if doing so may be detrimental for the organization as a whole.

> Decision-makers in various organizational roles tend to perceive problems in terms of the goals and functions of their department rather than from the view of the organization as a whole. Giving top priority to the goals of one's subunits (as against overall organizational goals) occurs quite frequently in organizations. (Kochan, 1976, p. 534)

Kochan's research also indicates that organizational conflict is most likely to occur when there is perceived goal incompatibility among organizational subunits that are interdependent (Kochan, 1976, p. 529).

Even when there is agreement about goals, there can be conflict over the desired means to achieve those goals. As Tjosvold and Chia (1989, p. 236) note, although conflict results in situations of opposing interest, it also can occur "when interests overlap and goals are common." Cooperative goals, not just opposing goals, can cause organizational conflict. Tjosvold and Chia found that cooperative goals do not ensure "constructive" conflict within an organization, but that they make it more likely than if the goals were competitive rather than cooperative.

A case study from the New York City Police Department illustrates the point that a major source of conflict within organizations occurs when members have sharply divergent philosophies of organizational management and mission. The consequences of conflicting organizational philosophies are most likely to affect policy when they are held by high-ranking organizational members.

This is exemplified by the sharply contrasting philosophies and conceptions of policing that were held by two senior police executives in the New York City Police Department, Anthony V. Bouza, Bronx borough commander, and Mike Codd, commissioner. Bouza remarks, "Although Codd had always taken an avuncular and affectionate posture toward me personally, philosophically we were worlds apart. . . . We differed totally in our view of the police mission" (Bouza, 1990, p. 101). Bouza describes their sharply contrasting philosophies of policing:

> His view was conservative, gradual, cautious, consolidating, and traditional. Words like "orthodox" and "precedent," "centralization" and "structure" were favorites of his. Police work was narrowly defined as enforcing the law, preserving the peace, protecting life and property, detecting and arresting offenders and the prevention of crime. No need to go further afield than this. Ideas that threatened change were sent down for "further study." Pilot programs started by previous administrations were simply perpetuated: nothing was eliminated and nothing was initiated. The department was frozen in place, an iceberg adrift. (Bouza, 1990, p. 101)

According to Bouza, Codd's view was that police work meant maximizing the number of people in patrol, in uniform, doing simple police routines. Suggestions of staff support, specialized units or functions, or any kind of experimentation were discouraged. Codd argued that police officers should not serve as social workers, teachers, or "community relations types." He saw anything that took them away from bare-bones police work as weakening the department.

In stark contrast to this philosophy of managing a police department and view of the functions and mission of police work was Bouza's:

> My view envisioned a very expansive role for the police: wide experimentation; solid staff support; decentralized authority and responsibility; research; participative management and the use of modern administrative techniques; aggressive proactive and freewheeling law enforcement policy (that had the Bronx forces making more arrests and issuing more summonses than their counterparts in other boroughs); community relations programs that had cops teaching ghetto kids to swim and a host of other projects and programs that sought to bring the police closer to the people they served. My programs were seen as straying from "police work" and my methods were labeled "laissez-faire management" that supposedly had my subordinates fending for themselves while I lay back designing graphs and measuring the results. (Bouza, 1990, pp. 101–102)

Bouza's notion of the police function was, in part, affected by his knowledge that in certain sections of the Bronx, "the only semblance of daily government resided in the police" (1990, p. 102). The void had to be filled, and because the police were visible and had the most contact with residents, they became the logical candidates to do so. Implementation of this view resulted in turning "station houses into community meeting halls and our police officers into community advocates for cleaner streets, higher water pressure, more and better concerts, tree plantings, street lighting, youth sports and senior citizen programs" (1990, p. 102). Many of these activities could not be defined as "police work" in the traditional sense, yet if they had not been implemented, the crime rate undoubtedly would have been markedly higher because these basic functions would not have been filled.

Since Bouza's philosophy of policing and its implementation were at odds with those of the top brass, the question arises as to why they let him translate his views into policy and actions. He answers this question by noting, "The clear signal from headquarters was that my methods were anathema. My Spanish origins and the presence of half a million Hispanics in the Bronx had kept me reasonably safe for the last three years from bureaucratic slaughter" (1990, p. 102).

In addition, Bouza had support and encouragement from two politically important people were not part of the police department: Bob Abrams, the Bronx borough president, and Mario Merola, the Bronx district attorney. Moreover, Commissioner Codd's aversion to "rocking the boat" ironically worked in Bouza's favor. Bouza stated, "Also I had a kind of tenure. I had been there almost a year by the time Codd had been appointed, and he wasn't one for rapid or violent personnel moves. I could stay; but I wasn't to be copied, and I'd better produce. The message was clear" (Bouza, 1990, p. 102). Thus the natural conservatism of the commissioner, coupled with the inertia that exists in most large organizations, served to keep Bouza from being ousted, even though his philosophy and actions were strongly incompatible with those of the top brass in the department.

This case study illustrates organizational conflict resulting from distinct differences in organizational philosophies, missions, and the means to attain them among key organizational members. It also shows how the presence of particular circumstances may serve to restrain a powerful organizational member from dismissing a key subordinate who has a philosophy and approach sharply at odds with his own.

Degree and type of interdependence of work units can promote conflict (Baron, 1990, p. 201). Three separate kinds of task unit interdependence can exist: pooled interdependence, sequential interdependence, and reciprocal interdependence (Thompson, 1967). The type that is likely to promote the least conflict among units is "pooled interdependence," whereby each unit does not require any interaction with other units in order to accomplish its tasks. The aggregation of each unit's work, however, is pooled and affects the performance of the whole organization. A WalMart store in Oshkosh, Wisconsin, is not interdependent with a WalMart store located in Bakersfield, California, yet the profits of those two units, and hundreds of others, when pooled together, determine the success or failure of the WalMart Corporation as a whole.

The result of "sequential interdependence" among units of an organization is that one unit can start its task only after another unit has finished it. It involves a situation in which the output of one unit serves as the input for another one. For example, the staff in a hospital laboratory must complete a patient's blood analysis before doctors can make a diagnosis and prescribe treatment. Sequential interdependence is likely to set the stage for some conflict within organizations since if the personnel in one unit do not perform their tasks in a timely fashion, or if their output is of low quality, the persons working in the unit dependent on that output will experience problems.

"Reciprocal interdependence" exists when the output of each of the unit within an organization provides the input for other units, when all units depend upon the others. An example would be the reciprocal interdependence of the various groups needed to run an operating room in a hospital (Gibson et al., 1991). The surgical staff, the nursing staff, the anesthesiology staff, and other workers are dependent upon one another and must coordinate their efforts in order to accomplish the necessary work during surgical procedures. In such instances the potential for conflict is high. If one of the organization's units does not perform its task adequately, the organization's major goal may not be attained, or be attained only at a high cost.

The majority of organizations have some degree and combination of pooled, sequential, and reciprocal interdependence among their units. As a result, the potential for conflict among such units is always present.

Strength of ties among groups affect the entire organization, Granovetter (1973) suggests. Reed Nelson (1989) conducted an empirical study of the network structure of twenty organizations (including manufacturing, public-sector, private-sector, and service entities). He measured the strength of ties within and between groups in the twenty organizations, which were classified as either high-conflict or low-conflict organizations. Nelson found that *low-conflict organizations* were more likely than high-conflict organizations to have *strong ties between groups* within the organization. (Frequent contacts between workers indicated the strong ties.) Frequent contact between groups enables workers to resolve issues as they arise, thus preventing the build-up of grievances. Furthermore, his research suggested that "conflict is less probable when one dominant group mediates between all other groups and when a hierarchy links groups serially" (Nelson, 1989, p. 397).

Innovations in organizations generate conflict when responses to innovations proposed or enacted within organizations are negative. A case in point is the conflict that ensued in the New York City Police Department in 1975 when its commissioner, Mike Codd, at the urging of Anthony V. Bouza, commander of police forces in the borough of the Bronx, required that all police officers wear name tags. At that time, badge numbers were the only means by which citizens could identify police officers. Badge numbers, however, were often difficult to read, and Bouza argued that the police uniform made its occupant almost faceless and unidentifiable

(Bouza, 1993). Bouza felt that the nameplate requirement would be a relatively noncontroversial policy change. Therefore, he was surprised when the proposal met vigorous opposition from the police officers and their union. The rank and file officers feared harassing phone calls and retribution from the persons they arrested and harassment if they had unusual names. After much debate and acrimony, the name plate innovation was adopted and implemented. This innovative procedure increased the accountability of the police officers and humanized them in the public's eyes. Now the name plate requirement has been adopted by police departments throughout the United States, while before 1975, it was vigorously resisted.

Ambiguity produces conflict when organizational members desire and need a clear delineation of their job responsibilities, lines of authority, and performance expectations. When these are ambiguous, stress and conflict may result (Greenberg and Baron, 1993, p. 230). For example, a sales manager who has been encouraged to develop advertising strategies may experience feelings of hurt and anger if his suggestions are not implemented because they were vetoed by the company's advertising department. Similarly, regarding authority jurisdiction, another sales manager may become upset when she learns that the personnel director or the vice president for marketing, not she, has the authority to fire a salesperson. Vague performance criteria may also engender conflict. For example, a manager may believe that he has been doing a fine job because sales in the region under his jurisdiction have increased 15% since he has been hired. Yet the president of the company may be dissatisfied with the sales manager's performance because she as president had expected sales for this region to increase by 30%.

Specialization of roles within an organization make it more likely that conflict will occur among those performing the roles. This is because specialization produces differences in goals, outlooks, time perspectives, priorities, and judgments. When an organization comprises members who possess highly specialized knowledge, "their areas of expertise are likely to lead them to different conclusions about the same matter" (Hague, 1974, pp. 101–124). For instance, in a waste disposal company it is very likely that the lawyers, public relations personnel, sales, and technical people will differ about whether a particular area should be selected for the location of a new landfill. These persons will be assessing the issue through their individual perspectives. As a result different factors will have differentially salience to each of them. The salespeople, for example, will be concerned about whether or not there are waste-producing organizations nearby. The public relations people will focus on whether there is likely to be much opposition to locating the landfill in the proposed location. The lawyers will focus on state regulations. Consequently, the chance that those persons will reach different conclusions is high. It is less a matter that one person is right and the others wrong than that each is sensitive to different types of issues and has divergent agendas and priorities.

Subcultures which develop within organizations can provide the basis for conflict. Moreover, in addition to organizational subcultures that emerge within organizations, "memberships and identification with social groupings that transcend organizational boundaries are carried into organizational life" and may generate conflict (Trice and Beyer, 1993, p. 226).

The potential for conflict among members of different organizational subcultures arises from the same factors that contribute to the emergence of the subcultures in the first place. These factors include selective interaction which leads to the formation of different perspectives, shared experiences among members of different groups, and similar personality orientations. All of these factors tend to produce similar interpretations of segments of reality and help form a shared identity (Trice and Beyer, 1993). As the sense of solidarity among members of organizational subcultures increases, so does the potential for conflict with other subcultures. The values, norms, and behavior of people belonging to other subcultures may be viewed as wrong or inappropriate;

as a result, feelings of threat and hostility may emerge. Trice and Beyer note, "Decisions about such matters as the allocation of resources, future goals, change in practices, and criteria used to evaluate performance seem especially likely to promote conflict because they can be seen as affecting the relative welfare of groups" (Trice and Beyer, 1993, p. 228).

Conflict among organizational subcultures is most likely to occur "when organizations must apparently choose among different subcultural beliefs, values, or norms as the basis for action that the differences become salient and subcultural conflicts surface" (Trice and Beyer, 1993, p. 229).

III. THE CONSEQUENCES OF ORGANIZATIONAL CONFLICT

We have seen that some degree of conflict within organizations is inevitable, and that it is caused by a wide variety of social structural and social psychological factors. Now we shall address the consequences, or effects, of organizational conflict.

There is a tendency to view conflict as negative or destructive. This may be the case in many instances; however, conflict may also result in a variety of positive outcomes within an organization. For example, a survey of the deans and directors of 194 departments of social work in the United States conducted by Carol Singleton and Alan B. Henkin (1989–1990) found that the administrators were more likely to view conflict positively than negatively (especially if the levels of organizational conflict were low). Singleton and Henkin (1989–1990, pp. 7–8) delineated five possible "positive" functions of conflict for organizations:

1. Unifying function (getting members involved and building trust, team building, and commitment)
2. Preserving function (involving the confronting of issues, curtailment of hostility, airing of minor antagonisms, and venting of frustrations)
3. Integrative function (involving the creation of norms, distribution of power, promotion of accommodations between groups, job satisfaction)
4. Growth function (involving creative ideas, innovation, initiative, and job performance)
5. Problem-solving function (focusing attention on problems, increasing the number of alternative solutions considered, increasing the exchange of information required for problem solving, and improving the quality of the problem-solving process).

Singleton and Henkin reported the following results of their survey:

1. The function that received the *most positive responses* by the deans and directors was the *problem-solving function*. That is, 65% of the deans and directors surveyed either agreed or strongly agreed that the conflict they had experienced in their departments had fulfilled the problem-solving function (that is, had focused attention on problems, had increased the number of alternative solutions considered, and had increased the exchange of information required for problem solving).
2. Positive perceptions of conflict appeared to be confined to positive consequences *for the organization* as a whole, rather than for the members of the organization or for their interpersonal relationships. For example, only 13% of the deans and directors said that conflict built trust among department members; only 22% perceived that conflict improved job satisfaction; only 30% saw conflict as resulting in the airing of minor antagonisms; and only 30% said that the conflict curtailed hostility within the departments. In contrast, concerning organizational issues, more than 60% of the respondents said that conflict caused the confronting of issues (the preserving function), that it resulted in the creation of norms (the integrative function), that it produced creative ideas and innovation (the growth function), and that it focused

attention on problems and solutions and enhanced the exchange of information (the problem-solving function).
3. In response to questions measuring the degrees of conflict within the departments, the majority of the deans and directors reported low to average amounts and intensity of departmental conflict. "The most conflict by frequency within setting was related to differences over goals, differences over means to attain goals, and differences over the allocation of resources. Respondents reported lower incidences of conflict between levels of personnel, between groups with interdependent functions and over the allocation of personal rewards" (Singleton and Henkin, 1989–1990, p. 9).

Other social scientists (Coser, 1957; Wilson and Jerrell, 1981) have also described positive consequences of conflict. In commenting on the propensity to view conflict solely in negative terms, Wilson and Jerrell (1981, p. 105) note, "A more strategic or long-range perspective would judge the worth of the process form the nature and quality of the social ends that are gained, rather than in terms of the benefits and costs of the process itself." They further state that the labeling of processes as evil or unproductive has little merit, especially when those processes are inevitable aspects of human nature.

Of course, whether or not a particular episode of conflict within a particular organization produces positive, negative, or neutral outcomes is an empirical question, and it also depends upon whose perspective is being taken. "Positive" for whom? For certain members of the organization, and not for others? For the organization as a whole? For particular units within the organization, and not for others? For the clients of the organization? In addition, particular consequences may appear to be positive in the short term, but negative in the long-term, or vice versa. A given conflict may be beneficial for a particular unit or subgroup within the organization but not for the organization as a whole. Conversely, the conflict may be disadvantageous to a specific unit but beneficial to the organization in general. When we refer to positive or negative consequences of organizational conflict, we shall mean positive or negative for the organization as a whole, unless otherwise stated. In this section we shall discuss the potential consequences of organizational conflict and illustrate our points with a case study (the Motorola Corporation).

What are the consequences of organizational conflict? There are many possibilities, including the following:

1. Creation of organizational change. (Such changes may take a variety of forms many of which are discussed in this chapter.)
2. Problem-solving: facilitation of the visibility, discussion, and resolution of problems and increased emphasis on task orientation (thus allowing the attainment of organizational goals), *or* impeding the attainment of goals and impeding communication. Conflict can cause grievances to be aired, although in some situations it may result in decreased communication among groups. A danger is that intense conflict among organizational units may make winning, rather than the attainment of the organizational goals, the primary objective of each group. The conflict can lead to constructive problem solving, or it can drain the energy and time of the members of the organization and divert their attention from the important problems which need to be solved.
3. Facilitation of creativity and innovation within the organization.
4. Reinforcement of organizational culture and norms.
5. Increased stereotyping of organizational members occupying certain positions and possible distorted perceptions. Conflict among groups can generate distorted, inaccurate perceptions about one's own group as well as other groups. "Each group sees itself as superior in performance to the other and as more important to the survival of the organization than other

groups" (Gibson et al., 1991, p. 309). A dysfunctional cycle can be created as distorted perceptions lead to anger and jealousy, which, in turn, can reinforce the distorted perceptions. As Gibson and associates (1991, p. 309) note, "The members of each group see fewer differences within their unit than actually exist and greater differences between the groups than actually exist."

6. Increased authoritarian styles of behavior. Depending upon the severity of the conflict and what is at stake, group members may become tolerant of an autocratic style of leadership, when they want a leader who will do whatever is necessary to give their group the edge in its conflict with other groups (Gibson et al., 1991).
7. Impede the coordination of organizational units
8. Improve *or* damage the morale of the members of the organization. Conflict can increase job stress and can cause either an increase or a decrease in morale among the workers. When people within an organization have deep-seated beliefs, ideas, and mind-sets that are job-related and in conflict with one another, the seeds for the emergence of a perpetual state of tension, resentment, and stress may be sown. If the beliefs have been deeply internalized, they may be equated, by those holding them, with their core self or identity; consequently, an attack on those beliefs may be perceived as an attack on the persons holding them.
9. Increased solidarity within groups. Conflict between units of an organization can increase solidarity and cohesiveness within the units. This can be positive, in that morale may improve within the groups, but it can be negative if stereotypes and discrimination develop and are used against persons in other groups within the organization. When there are conflict and competition between groups, group members are likely to put aside their differences in order to mobilize their resources for battling the "enemy." Introducing an outside enemy (i.e., a competitor organization) can draw together the various groups within the organization (Coser, 1957).

As groups become more cohesive, there may be increased social pressures for conformity. Pressure to conform to group norms increases when groups are in conflict. There may be a decrease in tolerance for deviance within the group and an increased emphasis on loyalty to the group. "Group goals take precedence over individual satisfaction as members are expected to demonstrate their loyalty. In major conflict situations, interaction with members of 'the other group' may be outlawed" (Gibson et al., 1991, p. 308).

Organizational conflict can be the catalyst for a variety of favorable changes that range from better working conditions to increased productivity, sales, or morale. There are several ways by which conflict may promote positive changes. First, it may impel management to reconsider current procedures, policies, and structures. Such a reexamination may lead to improved efficiency, better morale, and increases in productivity. Conflict can serve as a stimulus for innovation and adaptation to changing conditions. A good example of how a large corporation intentionally encouraged conflict for this purpose is that of Motorola, which will be discussed in detail.

A second way in which conflict may benefit an organization is *by stimulating members to do their best* and *to produce creative ideas*. Conflict also can serve as a *safety valve for pent-up frustrations*. Semistructured conflict sessions may function to let organization members air their complaints, and as a result sources of irritation will be addressed (of course the venting of frustration does not necessarily have positive consequences). Organizational conflict may produce interest and excitement among members of the organization. The following case study of the Motorola Corporation illustrates how conflict can stimulate creative ideas, lead to innovation within an organization, and enable it to adapt to a rapidly changing environment. This case study also mentions some negative consequences of conflict that emerged within the Motorola Corporation.

A. The Case of Motorola Corporation

Unlike some corporations which have lost their market share and their competitive edge because of their size and failure to sot and act upon new market trends and technological innovations, Motorola Corporation [3] has been thriving.

Motorola is an international leader in the design, development, manufacture, and distribution of cellular phones, pagers, two-way radios, and microprocessors. It has been extraordinarily successful in opening up previously closed Japanese markets for its products and in beating Japanese companies in manufacturing higher-quality consumer electronic products at lower prices. A key factor in its success has been its ability to lower its defect rate in manufacturing by 99% in five years (from 1987–1992). This amazing achievement has resulted in saving approximately $900 million this year, and $3.1 billion cumulatively (Hill and Yamada, 1992, p. A1).

Throughout its history Motorola has excelled at something that most large, highly bureaucratized companies fail to do well: anticipating changes in technology, markets, and customer needs. This ability to anticipate changes and to act accordingly did not develop without the creation and implementation of specific strategies. "Anticipation is a religion at Motorola, codified in the culture in a number of ways and designed to keep critical information flowing quickly to the top" (Hill and Yamada, 1992, p. A14). Motorola, for example, has an "intelligence department" whose purpose is to ferret out from trade and technical journals conferences, and "scuttlebutt" the most recent technological developments and determine how the company's strategy should be modified in light of those developments.

According to Hill and Yamada, however, the key ingredient that has enabled Motorola to be nimble and successful, despite its ponderous size and bureaucratic structure, is its encouragement, cultivation, and constructive use of conflict and dissent within the company. Indeed, Motorola creates a "cult of dissent and open verbal combat" (1992, p. A14):

> Each employee is entitled to file a "minority report" if he feels his ideas aren't being supported. The reports are read by bosses of the team's bosses. Unlike other firms that have such devices, retribution at Motorola is considered "unmacho" or craven. Engineers say they are encouraged to dispute their superiors and one another vigorously at open meetings. (Hill and Yamada, 1992, p. A14)

The intensity and outward manifestation of conflict can be shocking. One employee, an applied mathematician with a Ph.D. degree, notes, "It gets wild. I was amazed when I got here. The discussions get violent—verbally fortunately" (1992, p. A14).

The institutionalized conflict at Motorola serves several important functions. It "quickly identifies and fixes mistakes, unmasks and kills weak or illogical efforts, keeps top managers fully informed and sometimes unearths enormous opportunities" (1992, p. A14). Motorola's computer microprocessor—the 68000 series—came into being as a consequence of a minority report and a dispute with top corporate people. "The engineering concept behind the 68000 wasn't supported by division chiefs, but it was agreed that a group could work on it independently" (1992, p. A14). As a result, those who were in favor of it "went off into a corner of the lab until they proved their principles" (1992, p. A14). The 68000 series chips went on to become "the brains of Apple Computer's MacIntosh line" (1992, p. A14).

The company's most costly project also emerged from a dissenting minority report. The project, code-named "Iridium," was designed to "by 1997 girdle the earth simultaneously receiving and transmitting cellular-phone communication anywhere in the world" (1992, p. A14). Initially the idea was rejected by its originator's superior as being too inexpensive. Moreover, it was noted that a plethora of regulatory obstacles worldwide would necessitate the cooperation of many countries and cost over $3 billion. Yet because the initiator of the idea was allowed to plead his case for the project enthusiastically in front of top executives, the project received the go-ahead.

The culture of conflict, however, has its negative consequences, too, such as stress and burnout of some workers. At Motorola "infighting has sometimes resulted in confusion and mistakes, including delays that cost the company most of the market for personal-computer microprocessors and high-speed microprocessors for workstations" (1992, p. A1). Moreover, jealousy between workers' teams can cause one subgroup to reject an idea from a newly emerging subgroup, even though the idea may have merit. A case in point was when in 1986 a

> chip team in Austin, Texas, designed a high-speed workstation microprocessor called the 88000, many times more powerful than Motorola's by-now successful 68000 line. But the 68000 group lobbied against the new chip and tried to persuade customers to ignore it. The conflict led to delays and to a critical decision by a potential customer, Sun Microsystems, Inc., to design its own chip after initially leaning toward the 88000. . . . Motorola officials have conceded that the 88000 was late to market and that "jealousy" was a factor. (1992, p. A14)

The Motorola case study illustrates several points about the consequences of conflict. First, it clearly shows that conflict can be *deliberately* structured and incorporated within an organization's culture with the aim of producing certain desired results. Second, it exemplifies the fact that such conflict can serve to motivate employees to realize their fullest potential and not be deterred by those opposing their ideas even if the opposition originates form their superiors. Finally, it tells us that no matter how positive the consequences of conflict are, it is almost inevitable that these favorable outcomes will be accompanied by unfavorable ones.

IV. CONCLUSION

Just as conflict in various forms pervades societies, so does it pervade organizations. This should not be surprising since organizations can be viewed as microcosms of the larger society of which they are a part. Thus all of the processes and structures that are endemic to societies also are endemic to organizations but on a much smaller scale. Conflict within organizations can stem from psychological, social interactional, and structural factors, both individually and in combination. Conflict within organizations, like conflict within society, has consequences. These consequences may be viewed as positive or negative, or, as is most likely to be the case, some combination of both. Whether the consequences are viewed as positive or negative depends upon the perspective of the person doing the viewing.

All of the causes of organizational conflict suggest policy implications. While it probably is not possible (or desirable) to eliminate organizational conflict, it undoubtedly can be managed so that it does not escalate to the point of being destructive to the organization and its members. Moreover, conflict may be developed consciously and structured with the purpose of bringing about positive outcomes while minimizing negative ones.

NOTES

1. Tjosvold and Chia (1989, p. 236–245) note that cooperative goals, not just opposing goals, can cause organizational conflict. Persons can agree upon goals but disagree on the desirable means

for achieving them. They found that cooperative goals do not ensure constructive conflict within an organization, but that they make it more likely than if the goals were competitive rather than cooperative.

2. The "social pressures on party," "social pressures on other," "incentive structure," and "rules and procedures within the organization" components of Thomas's model shown in Figure 2 would involve the influence of *roles* on the behavior of members of organizations.
3. This case study is based on G. Christian Hill and Ken Yamada, "Motorola Illustrates How an Aged Giant Can Remain Vibrant," *The Wall Street Journal*, December 9, 1992, p. A1.

REFERENCES

Baron, R. A., Conflict in Organizations, in *Psychology in Organizations: Integrating Science and Practice* (Kevin R. Murphy and Frank E. Saal, eds.), Lawrence Erlbaum and Associates, Hillsdale, N.J., 1990, pp. 197–216.

Bies, Robert J., Shapiro, Debra L., and Cummings, Larry L., Causal Accounts and Managing Organizational Conflict, *Communication Research, 15*(4):381–399 (1988).

Bouza, A. V., *Bronx Beat: Reflections of a Borough Commander*, Office of International Criminal Justice, University of Illinois, Chicago, 1990.

Bouza, A. V., *The Police Mystique*, Plenum, New York, 1991.

Bouza, A. V., Accountability, Unpublished paper, 1993.

Burke, R. J., Methods of Managing Superior-Subordinate Conflict: The Effectiveness and Consequences, *Canadian Journal of Behavioral Science, 2*:124–135 (1970).

Coser, Lewis, *The Functions of Social Conflict*, Free Press, Glencoe, Ill., 1957.

Ferguson, Charles K., Ten Cases from an OD Practitioner's Experience: Coping with Organizational Conflict, *Organization Development Journal, 4*(4):20–30 (1986).

Gibson, J. L., Ivancevich, J. M., and Donnelly, J. H. Jr., *Organizations: Behavior, Structure, Processes*, Irwin, Homewood, Ill., 1991.

Granovetter, Mark, The Strength of Weak Ties, *American Journal of Sociology, 78*:1360–1380 (1973).

Greenberg, Jerald and Baron, Robert A., *Behavior in Organizations, Understanding and Managing the Human Side of Work*, 4th ed., Allyn and Bacon, Boston, 1993.

Hague, Jerald, *Communications and Organizational Control*, Wiley, New York, 1974.

Hill, G. Christian and Yamada, Ken, Motorola Illustrates How an Aged Giant Can Remain Vibrant, *Wall Street Journal* December 9, p. A1, (1992).

Homans, George C., *Social Behavior: Its Elementary Forms*, Harcourt Brace, New York, 1974.

Johns, G., *Organizational Behavior*, Scott Foresman, Glenview, Ill., 1983.

Kahn, Robert L., Stress from 9 to 5, in *Socialization and the Life Cycle* (Peter I. Rose, ed.), St. Martin's Press, New York, 1979.

Kanter, Rosabeth Moss, *Men and Women of the Corporation*, Basic Books, New York, 1977.

Kilmann, Ralph H. and Thomas, Kenneth W., Four Perspectives on Conflict Management: An Attributional Framework for Organizing Descriptive and Normative Theory, *Academy of Management Review 3*:59–68 (1978).

Kochan, T., Cummings, L. C., and Huber, G., Operationalizing the Concept of Goals and Goal Incompatibility in Organizational Behavior Research, *Human Relations 29*(6):527–544 (1976).

Kolb, Deborah M., and Bartunek, Jean M., eds., *Hidden Conflict in Organizations: Uncovering Behind-the-Scenes Disputes*, Sage, Newbury Park, Calif., 1992.

Nelson, Reed, The Strength of Strong Ties: Social Networks and Intergroup Conflict in Organizations, *Academy of Management Journal, 32*(2):377–401 (1989).

Perrow, Charles, *Complex Organizations*, Random House, New York, 1986.

Ross, L., The Intuitive Psychologist and His Shortcomings: Distortions in the Attribution Process, in *Advances in Experimental and Social Psychology* (L. Berkowitz, ed.), vol. 10, Academic Press, New York, 1977.

Singleton, Carol, and Henkin, Alan B., Conflict As An Organizational Utility: Perceptions of Social Work Department Executives, *Journal of Applied Social Sciences 14*(1):1–21 (1989–1990).

Thomas, K. W., Conflict-Handling Modes in Interdepartmental Relations, unpublished doctoral thesis, Purdue University, Lafayette, Indiana, 1971.

Thomas, Kenneth, Conflict and Conflict Management, in *Handbook of Industrial and Organizational Psychology* (M. Dunnette, ed.), Rand-McNally, Chicago, 1976, pp. 889-935.

Thomas, K. W. and Schmidt, W. H., A Survey of Managerial Interests with Respect to Conflict, *Academy of Management Journal 19*:315–318 (1976).

Thompson, J. D., *Organizations in Action*, McGraw-Hill, New York, 1967.

Tjosvold, Dean and Chia, Lai Cheng, Conflict Between Managers and Workers: The Role of Cooperation and Competition, *The Journal of Social Psychology, 129*(2):235–247 (1989).

Trice, H. and Beyer, J. M., *The Culture of Work Organizations*, Prentice-Hall, Englewood Cliffs, N.J., 1993.

Wilson, J. A. and Jerrell, S. L., Conflict: Malignant, Beneficial or Benign, *Reprint Series #387*, University of Pittsburgh, Pittsburgh, 1981.

24
Improving Productivity Through Demographic Literacy

Arie Halachmi
Tennessee State University, Nashville, Tennessee

The way an agency interfaces with its environment influences its productivity. Strategic planning and stakeholder analysis are examples of analytical approaches for studying how organizations interface with their environment. They may be promising approaches for understanding the complex web of interrelationships among variables within and outside a given public agency. Still, to get the most out of what these analytical techniques can offer, decision makers must deal with the reality/environment that is relevant to the mission of the agency. They need to develop the capacity to resist the temptation of dealing with trivial issues that can be studied more easily than the more important ones that call for more work.

The thesis of this chapter makes three basic assumptions: First, improving the productivity of a public sector agency requires an optimal interface between the agency and the human dimension of its environment(s). Second, optimization requires each government agency not only to search for the best way to carry out its mandate(s) (from technical, legal, economic, political, or ethical points of view) but to consider the consequences of its actions for various subgroups of the population. Third, by studying the demography of a target area (or the geographic distribution of a target population), an agency has a chance of finding out what other organizations are active in the target area (or trying to affect a target population) before charting a course of action. Thus, the agency may be able to avoid some of the problems resulting when the activities of one organization interfere with what another organization is trying to achieve.

The thesis of this chapter is that optimizing the work of a public agency requires its administrators to consider not only the short-term results of their actions for society as a whole but the long-term influences on other than the initial target population. Through demographic literacy, that is, an understanding of the relationship among different kinds of data about human ecology, public administrators may be in a better position to decide what the relevant reality (or environment) is for determining what the agency needs to do to carry out its mission and what the best way of doing it may be.

The chapter begins by addressing the inability of many managers to get information out of data and the need to improve the information literacy of public administrators. After briefly defining the importance of demographic awareness for responsive and efficient decision making in the public sector, the chapter proceeds to examine some of the implications for management and training.

I. INFORMATION LITERACY AND NEW INFORMATION TECHNOLOGY

Public agencies spend large sums of money getting the hardware, the software, and the data they think are necessary in order to be responsive to public needs. At the federal level alone, agencies spent in 1992 about $20 billion on computer systems (DeSilva, 1992) and requested another billion dollars for data collection (Stanfield, 1991).

There is already a consensus that managers must be computer literate. They must know how to turn a personal computer on, how to connect to a mainframe, how to use electronic mail and various applications, and how to save and edit what they see on the screen for future use. However, most managers are still without information literacy. As noted by Peter Drucker (1992), few executives in the public or the private sector know what information they need, when they need it, in what form, from whom to get it, and to whom they owe it. Fewer still know what new tasks they can accomplish with the information they can extract from new data, which of the old tasks should be abandoned or be done differently. Many administrators do not realize that unlike other materials organizations consume as they produce goods and services, the quantity and quality of the data they use remain the same. Some of them forget that the right and wrong information can be obtained from the same data and that the data they use do not improve (deplete or deteriorate) just because they are being used. Similarly, many administrators do not realize that the value of a given set of data (and thus any information that is based on it) for subsequent decisions changes over time. The difference is not due to a metamorphosis of the data. Rather, it is the result of changes in the human environment of the organization after government decisions, the economy, or ecology.

Changes in demography make data obsolete. Thus, data may lose their value because of developments in the environment, not because they are (or are not) being used; the purpose for which they are being used; the way they are being used; how they are being collected, stored, shared; or how they are being analyzed. Many decision makers are not clear about the nature of the fixed and variable costs of using information resources. They may be concerned about the huge investment in hardware and software but may overlook the cost of inferior decisions, as a result of using the wrong information or data base.

New information technology provides the means for mobilizing more, and better quality, information for decision making. Advances in the development of hardware and software allow presentation of data in different ways. Geographic information systems (GISs), for example, have important promise for improving government responsiveness and the quality of its decision making by merging data with geographic mapping. Such maps can summarize important information, such as where the concentrations of elderly people are in relation to existing routes of public transportation. Such information, which can be crucial for successful planning of social services, for example, may be lost when presented in verbal or numerical fashion.

Yet, managers can be overloaded with information. Administrators can waste precious time dealing with the wrong kind of data about insignificant issues. Worse, they may get wrong ideas from the data; that is, they may get the wrong information out of it. The case of *Workforce 2000* and its federal counterpart *Civil Service 2000* can help us illustrate this point. The two reports were released by the Hudson Institute in 1987 and 1988, respectively, and were to be used as a basis for human resource management (HRM) planning within and outside the federal government. The reports suggested that slow population growth will cause a labor shortage after the turn of the century. In addition most of the new jobs will require advanced skills and most new workers will be women and minorities. In a reaction to the two reports, Mishel and Teixeira (1991, p. 39) say, "This account of the near future is, in most respects, either wrong or misleading—wrong in that 'key' factors are contradicted by available data, misleading in that key predictions are more wishful thinking than logical explanations of existing trends." Reporting about possible problems with the report, *Government Executive* (October 1991, p. 8) wonders whether "federal personnel experts [are] spending a lot of time and money preparing for a labor shortage that isn't going to happen?" (Government Executive, 1991). The Government Accounting Office (GAO) investigation of the issue acknowledges some weaknesses of the two reports. In its report to Congress (*The Changing Workforce*, 1992), GAO concludes first that labor economists and experts do not agree that labor shortages and skill gaps are likely to occur by the year 2000. Second, they conclude that the demographic composition of the labor force has changed and will continue to change. Third, many of these work force changes are, in GAO's view, more prevalent in the federal work force than in the nonfederal sector. Fourth, they believe that federal work force planners should not assume that labor shortages and skills gap will occur. Fifth, they caution that in addressing these demographic changes, work force planners should also consider the specific needs of the work force and the organization. In other words, GAO does not dispute the data collected for the two reports by the Hudson Institute but the information that was extracted from the data.

Information literacy is understanding the intricate and dynamic relationships among data, information, and intelligence. Without information literacy, managers cannot improve the quality of their decisions. In particular, managers must have a better understanding of the nature of demographic data and the reliability of the various sources that produce them. For example, given the questions about the 1990 census (Stanfield, 1991), administrators need to know what precautions to take when using demographic data. They have to discern the need to compensate for possible intended or unintended omissions or other misrepresentations of the data about the different groups they serve.

II. THE NEED FOR DEMOGRAPHIC AWARENESS

Gronhaug and Falkenberg note, "The basic idea behind strategic management is that a firm needs to match its capabilities to its ever changing environment if it is to obtain best performance" (1989, p. 349). This chapter, like the work of Gronhaug and Falkenberg, acknowledges that the strengths and weaknesses of an organization cannot be assessed in a vacuum but goes on to correct some of the misconceptions and faulty arguments surrounding this subject.

Gronhaug and Falkenberg conclude that strengths and weaknesses "are relative, as the firm's offerings in the marketplace will be compared with those of its competitors" (1989, p. 349). However, as demonstrated by the American automotive industry in the 1970s, comparison with the competition may not be enough. To the dismay of U.S. car manufacturers, their American competition was also oblivious to important changes in the environment. As it turned out, each of the manufacturers was paying too much attention to competitors and not enough attention to its other stakeholders. Postwar obsession with competition may have been the reason for the development of the myopic vision in Detroit. Because of this obsession, "the environment" became a synonym for "the competition," even though the latter is only one component of the environment car manufacturers should have considered. If, as Gronhaug and Falkenberg conclude, "it is of crucial importance to develop *relevant* capabilities, and to *use* these capabilities in the best possible way" (1989, p. 350), organizations cannot limit the study of the environment to the study of competitors. In the same vein, it is unlikely that an organization will develop "relevant capabilities" without understanding the makeup of the population that interacts with various parts of the organization as employees, clients, or stakeholders. As pointed out by Farooq and MacKellar (1990) in development planning, special attention should be paid to the ways in which demographic factors affect not only the quantity but also the quality of the human resources base. Thus, they claim, "the implications of demographic changes must be integrated into developmental planning if social and economic objectives are to be achieved at all levels of planning, i.e., overall macro planning, sectoral planning (for education, health, agriculture, etc.) and regional and local planning" (Farooq and MacKellar, 1990, p. 309).

In sum, since changes in demography alter the relevant environment of an organization, understanding demographic trends can focus the strategic planning effort on critical issues. While this assertion holds true for all organizations, it is particularly important in the case of public agencies. The reason is that an analysis of the environment, or the context in which the strategic public planning unit (SPPU) operates, is the first critical phase of the strategic management process (Montanari and Bracker, 1986, p. 253).

III. THE PROMISE OF DEMOGRAPHIC ANALYSIS

Heretofore, the cumbersome access to demographic data has seriously constrained its widespread use in strategic planning efforts. Robert Woods describes how the nature of, and access to, population data has constrained the process of demographic analysis in the past (Woods, 1979, p. 19). And Plotnick cites the shortage of state-level data on poverty as one reason for federal intervention in programs that deal with poverty (Plotnick, 1989). However, dramatic advances in information technology have changed the nature and potential benefits of demographic analysis.

New information technology facilitates faster, cheaper, and easier retrieval, storage, sharing, and dissemination of data. This alleviates many of the earlier constraints which hindered demographic analysis. In addition, relational data bases and improved querying facilities allow managers to use simple language, rather than a formula or a statistical notation, to generate information about the characteristics of subgroups, to conduct complex analyses of the general and target populations, and to improve their forecasting capacity.

As a result of these advances, a large volume of data is readily available about localities and salient subgroups of people. After the 1990 Census, the Bureau of the Census, for example, released data on tape and in print about general population characteristics for states, counties, and communities of 1,000 or more inhabitants. The information dealt with such factors as race, sex, age, household relationship, marital status, and ethnic origin. Other reports from the bureau deal with the social and economic characteristics of other kinds of communities, such as metropolitan areas or specific groups, such as Native Americans. The U.S. Department of Commerce has a network of state data centers that serves as a clearinghouse for public and private data banks.

To learn about the possible implications of any change in the execution of a given program, managers can import such data directly into their computer simulations and spreadsheets. The results can then be presented numerically, as a graph or as an overlay for a map of the area under study.

New information technology provides managers with better means for studying the human ecology in the area they want to effect. It improves their ability to convey to stakeholders, both within and outside the organization, why and where they see a need for action or no action. For administrators who develop the necessary skills, the study and communication of demographic data, for example, through the use of GIS and computer mapping, are now more appealing than ever.

The importance of understanding and being familiar with basic demographic trends increases as a result of the availability of supplementary information from nongovernmental sources. Without the knowledge and understanding of demography, a manager cannot retrieve and make efficient use of ancillary data for specific communities. This, in turn, makes it hard for organizations to fine-tune operations, to be responsive to changing needs, and, thus, to enhance productivity.

Important intelligence with a direct bearing on the demand for government services (as provider or regulator) can be derived from a prudent analysis of credit bureau reports, airline frequent-flier programs that track individual travel behavior, bar-code scanners that track supermarket purchases, and purchase histories that credit-card companies maintain (Morrison, 1990, p. 14). Such data may reveal service preferences, expectations about level and quality of service, and willingness to pay for various levels of service. These data may indicate the predispositions and expectations of a given community (or subgroup) toward government services as well. In the case of public services that may be contracted out, data about consumers' behavior in a given community may reveal what individuals are willing to pay for various levels of service.

However, to harness this ability for the purpose of improving planning and decision making, managers must be able to relate this information to relevant demographic data. Now, computer technology and modeling techniques allow the interested manager to examine such linkages. The relationship between demographic characteristics and individual behavior can then be examined at various levels of aggregation, from single households to a whole nation, and over different periods of time. By controlling for specific demographic variables, a manager can learn how an observed trend at the system level (e.g., a state or a country) relates to developments in a given subsystem (e.g., a city or a neighborhood). The interested manager can now study and present to others, like a TV weather report and forecast, the existing and future demographic conditions of a community in the context of general population trends. Such insights, we assert, are a precondition to a proactive approach to planning.

Demographic analysis provides a new type of input to the planning process. A major premise of such analysis is that organizations do not exist detached from the communities they serve or from those in which they operate. For example, in order to compare alternative responses to a given issue, an agency may want to conduct a fiscal impact analysis (FIA). The value of the analysis, however, depends on the accuracy of assumptions about the impact of each alternative course of action (e.g., on who will move in or move out) as a result.

Public agencies interact with individual households, groups, and other public and private organizations. In the process, they affect and are affected by them (Rogers, 1981, p. 168). To deal adequately with the human ecology of their environment, organizations must have a better understanding of the forces and factors that shape this ecology. The ability to identify, define, and describe the environment precisely is necessary for proper identification of key stakeholders and for development of successful strategies for dealing with them. As Martine and Faria have noted, "More data/better data and more research/better research will guarantee . . . more 'adequate' or 'rational' policies" (Martine and Faria, 1988, p. 57).

The question is, How much and what data are relevant to the mission of an organization in the public sector? To answer this, managers must ponder whether it is realistic (or desirable) to examine markets for public goods and services by using the same market-oriented approach that guides organizations in the private sector. To be effective they must find new ways to tailor government services to meet the needs of specific subgroups. Current legislation that mandates the mainstreaming of schoolchildren, affirmative action employment policies, or the necessary arrangements to accommodate disabled employees indicates a trend. Such legislation suggests that the polity expects public agencies to address the needs of specific publics as a preferred way for meeting its need as a collective. For example, to address the needs of children in foster homes, administrators must know about other children who are raised in their natural families. To comply with such mandates public administrators, like marketing experts in the private sector, must know about each subgroup and the broader population from which the subgroup is derived.

Understanding demographic trends and the demographic reality is necessary if an agency is to be responsive to actual needs and demands for service. Because the public marketplace has many similarities to private markets in terms of the competition for resources and support (i.e., market share), understanding demographics is a condition for effectiveness and efficiency. Without this understanding an agency may retain programs to meet old needs beyond their usefulness and ignore new needs that are growing in importance. In the private sector, the study of demographic trends is a way of learning about prospective demands for goods and services, availability of an adequate labor force, and geographic location of markets. It is a way of getting a better understanding of the future characteristics of an important environmental component—the population. The logic that justifies the use of demographic analysis in strategic planning for the private sector seems to be as applicable in the public sector, because a profile of the population is equally important in determining the results.

IV. STRATEGIC MANAGEMENT AND UNITY OF PERSPECTIVE

Strategic planning is the primary element, but not the essence, of strategic management. The other components of strategic management include implementation and evaluation. Derkinderen and Crum (1988) suggest the past decade has seen a focus on strategic management as a leading factor in advancing managerial capabilities for two reasons. First, strategic management focuses attention on making decisions that are consistent with whatever information is available at the time. Second, decisions can be made that position the organization most effectively to meet future challenges of the environment (Derkinderen and Crum, 1988, p. 29). As noted by Bryson and Roering, "Strategic planning focuses on achieving the best 'fit' between an organization and its environment" (1987, p. 11).

However, there may be a different reason for improved performance after the introduction of strategic management. As pointed out by Halachmi (1992), a common orientation throughout the organization creates favorable conditions for improved performance. The reason is that involvement in the implementation of a strategic plan that was sanctioned by top management facilitates the development of a shared (and a verifiable) perspective by all the decision makers. The strategic plan directs all members of the organization to consider the implications of any decision on the basis of the interface of the organization with its environment in toto. As such, it contributes to a shared out-in perspective. Also, since the strategic logic of each decision can be verified by reference to the strategic plan, organization members are encouraged to consider the implications of such decisions on the basis of the interface between the environment and other members, that is, to use an inside–inside-out perspective. The outcome, according to Halachmi

(1992), is that the common strategic orientation of all decision makers results in what Charles Lindblom refers to as "parametric adjustments" (Lindblom, 1965, pp. 35–43) across the board.

Without the strategic orientation that emphasizes the importance of looking from both the outside in and the inside out, some decision makers may ignore certain aspects of the interface of the organization with its environment. As shown by Halachmi and Taylor (1978), staff units whose mission it is to regulate other units or agencies tend to use in their decision-making process a "domestic" (i.e., inside-inside) perspective, which focuses only on interorganizational implications. This perspective usually disregards the implications of decisions that are meant to affect the inner workings of the organization for the way the agency interfaces with the environment. In short, the strategic posture enhances management ability because it facilitates a common frame of reference and a joint perspective—the interface with the environment. These, in turn, foster coordination and consistent decision making, freeing managers to concentrate on the environment instead of spending their energies resolving interdepartmental conflicts.

While embracing the interface with the environment as the common perspective has the promise of improving organizational performance, organizations can do more. This author asserts that when employees share a common understanding of demography and relevant demographic trends, the organization can refine the shared perspective about its interface with the environment. The result can be a greatly enhanced strategic management process.

Gronhaug and Falkenberg (1989) draw on earlier writers to develop the argument for replacing an "inside-out" with an "outside-in" perspective. They start their discussion by reminding the reader that organizations consist of individuals with only so much cognitive capacity. They reiterate the claim of organization theorists that environments are not given realities but are created through a process of attention and interpretation and that the human actor does not react to the environment but instead enacts it (1989, p. 350). Gronhaug and Falkenberg go on to point out that factors such as organizational structure, structure of information systems, and activities conducted by the organization are important determinants in the organizational enactment process. Because of cognitive limitations and biased information, subjectively constructed environments may be more or less biased. To underscore this point they argue that since managers and employees are all members of the organization, "They are embedded in an organizational structure: they share values and information; they communicate; they perform actions and compare with the past. Thus the firm's perception of its own strategy will be subject to an inside-out perspective" (1989, p. 350). Such a perspective tends to ignore changes in the environment and thus the need to alter strategies in order to cope with the new reality.

The study and understanding of demographic trends by all members of the organization have the promise of helping the organization gain a common outside-in perspective. Such perspective may develop even if the members are not involved in the implementation of a specific strategic plan. The reason is that the analysis of demographic characteristics of a given community is less open to subjective bias due to tunneled vision or wishful thinking than are the other data the organization may collect about the environment. Independent data and analysis provided by demographers not affiliated with the organization serve as a safeguard against subjective perceptions. A common understanding of one component of the environment is therefore the first step toward the sharing of a common outside-in perspective throughout the organization.

V. DEMOGRAPHY AND THE STRATEGIC MANAGEMENT PROCESS

Though many factors can be examined in an analysis of the environment, organizations are limited, by practical considerations, from analyzing too many variables in depth. Hence, as part of the metastrategic planning effort (the planning of the strategic planning process) organizations must decide which factors and/or what dimensions are likely to be more critical for the interface of the organization with the environment.

To get the most out of the strategic planning effort, a demographic study of the target community or target area should take place. Only with the results of that study in hand can the organization be in a position to proceed with the strategic planning process. The reason is that a better understanding of the present and future profile of the population, in both the immediate and remote environments, can help the identification of other strategic forces/factors in the environment.

Unlike the private sector, public agencies tend to use a reactive rather than a proactive approach to planning. The result is that rational analysis associated with the study of demography is often missing. While the use of a reactive rather than a proactive approach in the public sector can be explained, it is hard to find a convincing excuse for the limited use of demographic analysis by public administrators. In the private sector, projected demographic trends are a prime consideration. The present makeup of the population is secondary in importance. In contrast, public administrators base their decisions on the proven or expressed demand for goods or services, which may be related to the immediate past or present demography. Projected demand, which must be based on a study of demographic trend, is used only as a secondary argument in support of decisions. In making decisions public agencies tend to use short-term considerations that coincide with the electoral cycle. For example, in the public sector the decision to build a new school will be influenced by the fact that the people living in a new development demand such a service. The locality is likely to underwrite the cost of a school building that could last fifty years, even though in fifteen years there may not be enough students in the new development to keep it open. A private entrepreneur would make such an investment only when demographic data about the future, not the present, suggest growth that would guarantee full or satisfactory utilization.

VI. ENVIRONMENTAL INFORMATION AND DEMOGRAPHIC CONSIDERATIONS

Most strategic planning designs do not address the issue of demographic analysis directly. Instead, they provide room for demographic analysis as part of a broader study that is typically labeled the "environmental assessment" (Duchane, 1985, p. 33), "environmental scan" (Sorkin et al., 1982, p. 28), "situation audit/analysis" (Steiner, 1979, p. 122), or "internal/external analysis" (Fisher, 1990, p. 4).

However, demographic analysis need not be formal or systematic. In fact, much of the demographic analysis which occurs in organization is done "off process," that is, in an informal way. In the words of Steiner (1979, p. 124):

> The situation audit is not something that can or should be completed in the planning process solely on a formal basis. A very important part, if not the most important part, of the situation audit is done continuously in the personal surveillance of environments by individual managers. This type of environmental scanning is performed in a variety of ways from methodically reading business journals to casually conversing with fellow managers at lunch.

When it comes to "situation audit" in the broadest sense, Steiner's observation is well taken. However, it is not hard to see that the said observation leaves the issue of studying and understanding demography to chance. Issues involving demographic analysis might be overlooked by the manager, undermining the quality of the strategic plan. This possibility increases when one considers the fact that managers increasingly rely on information they obtain from subordinates, and on informal reports, than on formal reports and outside sources (Augilar, 1967, pp. 69–70; Stevenson, 1976). Thus, strategic planning designs that do not call for demographic analysis as a distinctive part of the formative stage of the planning may lead to defective strategic plans.

VII. IMPLICATIONS FOR MANAGEMENT AND TRAINING

Since the geopolitical changes in Eastern and Western Europe, we have been moving faster toward a global village. Under these circumstances a minimal understanding of sweeping demographic trends across national, regional, state, and local boundaries is a must. The global village means, among other things, that coupled with the closing in of the world which brings nations closer to each other there is a growing global exchange of information in real time. Another result of the emergence of a global village is that demands for goods and services in one place can have an immediate effect on the demand and/or supply of the same in other places. As is the case for a single country, the global demand of goods and services is influenced by demography. Yet, information on how demographic changes at one level (e.g., a continent) are related to matter of public policy at other levels (e.g., individual countries) is limited. What is available is currently used only by professional demographers, and managers are not trained to look for it. Even on Wall Street, where the name of the game is anticipating supply and demand for goods and services, the use of demographic data is not as common as might be expected (Dunn, 1992).

Many administrators find the professional literature of demographers to be too intimidating and nontechnical reports on critical demographic trends not readily available. This underlines the need to expand computer literacy to include information literacy and to make demographic education a formal step in preparing the work force that is going to be involved in developing a strategic plan.

Demographic models and theories can shed light on the possible interconnectiveness of what seem to be unrelated demographic trends. Understanding demographic modeling and theory is essential for establishing the correct framework and selecting appropriate variables for an organization-specific demographic analysis. Indeed, precisely because managers rely on subordinates for insights, demographic education should not be limited to upper-level employees. An educated work force, one that understands the importance of demography, may identify important trends for the organization even before they are observed and reported by professional demographers.

In order to educate and maintain such a work force, organizations may need to secure the services of professional demographers. Such demographers should work in close proximity with, and with easy access to, managers who authorize and develop strategic plans. According to Martine and Faria (1988), demographers are destined for a greater role in the organization. They believe that it would be reasonable "to expect that demographers should interact with other analysts, other pressure groups, and other sectors of the society to negotiate solutions which will benefit a wider segment of the population" (Martine and Faria, 1988, p. 59).

Last, but not least, is the need to increase the use of the data from the national census by increasing public awareness of its availability. By law, the federal government collects and compiles a new amalgam of data about regions, communities, subgroups, and households every ten years. The data from the national census (as well as demographic data from other sources) can now be accessed if one knows where to look for them. Yet, most managers in both the public and the private sectors do not know where to look for such data or even what data are available. The primary goal of the national census is to provide the numerical basis for reapportionment of electoral districts. However, it seems to us that the public would get a better return on the tax monies that were used for the census if its results were used for decision making on other matters. From a societal point of view, the incremental cost of educating managers about the data that become available after each census will be justified by better planning and improved responsiveness.

REFERENCES

Augilar, Francis J., *Scanning and Business Environment*, Macmillan, New York, 1967.

Bryson, John M. and Roering, William D., Applying Private-Sector Strategic Planning in the Public Sector, *Journal of the American Planning Association, 53*(1):11 (1987).

Bryson, John M. and Roering, William D., Initiation of Strategic Planning by Governments, *Public Administration Review*, November/December, p. 995 (1988).

The Changing Workforce, Government Accounting Office, Washington, D.C., report no. GAO/GGD-92-38, March 1992.

Cleveland, Harlan, *The Knowledge Executive*, Truman Talley Books, New York, 1985.

DeSilva, D. Richard, A Confederacy of Glitches, *Newsweek*, September 21, pp. 70–71 (1992).

Derkinderen, Frans G. J., and Crum, Roy L., The Development and Empirical Validation of Strategic Decision Models, *International Studies of Management and Organization, XVIII*(2):29 (1988).

Drucker, Peter F., Be Data Literate—Know What to Know, *The Wall Street Journal*, December 1, p. A16 (1992).

Duchane, Steve M., *Designing Strategic Management Planning in Municipalities*, Michigan Municipal League, Ann Arbor, Mich., 1985.

Dunn, William, The Demographics of Wall Street, *American Demographics 14*(7):42–46 (1992).

Dychtwald, Ken, Age Wave, Bantam Books, New York, 1990.

Farooq Gazi M., and MacKellar, F. Landis, Demographic, Employment and Development Trends, *International Labor Review, 159*(3):301–315 (1990).

Ferris, Abbot L., The Uses of Social Indicators, *Social Forces 66*(3):601 (1988).

Finkelstein, Clive, Together at Last, *Computerworld*, December:91–94 (1991).

Fisher, Lowell, *A Strategic Planning Workbook for A.E.I.*, A.E.I. Minneapolis, Minn., 1990.

Freeman, R. E., Strategic Management: A Stakeholder Approach, Pitman, Boston, 1984.

Geographic Information Systems, U.S. General Accounting Office, GAO/IMTEC-91-72FS, September, 1991.

Green, Sebastian, Understanding Corporate Culture and Its Relation to Strategy, *International Studies of Management and Organization XVIII*(2):6 (1988).

Gronhaug, Kjell and Falkenberg, Joyce S., Exploring Strategy Perceptions in Changing Environments, *Journal of Management Studies 26*(4):249–259 (1989).

Halachmi, Arie, Strategic Management and Productivity, in *Public Productivity Handbook* (Marc Holzer, ed.), Marcel Dekker, New York, 1992.

Halachmi, Arie, Strategic Planning and Management? Not Necessarily, Public Productivity Review *40*:35 (1986).

Halachmi, Arie and Holzer, Marc, Toward Strategic Perspectives on Public Productivity, in *Strategic Issues in Public Sector Productivity* (Marc Holzer and Arie Halachmi, eds.), Jossey-Bass, San Francisco, 1986, pp. 5–14.

Halachmi, Arie, and Taylor, George, "How Agencies and Regulate Agencies, Paper presented at the 1978 Annual Conference of the American Society for Public Administration (ASPA), Phoenix, Arizona (1978).

Is the Coming Labor Shortage a Myth? *Government Executive 23*(10):8 (1991).

Johnston, William B., The Changing Workforce—and Its Tug on Your Bottom Line, *Financial Executive* March/April:9 (1990).

Kaufman, Jerome L. and Jacobs, Harvey M., A Public Planning Perspective on Strategic Planning, *Journal of the American Planning Association, 53*(1):23 (1987).
Konda, Suresh L., Stewman, Shelby, and Belkin, Jacob, Demographic Models for Manpower Planning and Policy, *Policy Sciences 13*(3):297–343 (1981).
Lindblom, Charles, *The Intelligence of Democracy*, New York Free Press, New York, 1965, pp. 35–43.
Martine, George and Faria, Vilmar, Impacts of Social Research on Policy Formulation: Lessons from the Brazilian Experience in the Population Field, *Journal of Developing Areas, 23*(1):59 (1988).
McNicoll, Geoffrey, Population and Development: A Structuralist Approach, *Population and Development*, Frank Cass, London, 1978, p. 79.
Mercer, James L., Improving Local Options Through Strategic Planning, *Florida Municipal Review*, October:9 (1986).
Mintzberg, Henry, The Machine Bureaucracy, in *The Strategy Process* (Henry Mintzberg, James Brian Quinn, and Robert M. James, eds.), Prentice Hall, Englewood Cliffs, N.J., 1988, pp. 547–558.
Mishel, Lawrence and Teixeira, Roy A., *The Myth of the Coming Labor Shortage*, Economic Policy Institute, Washington, D.C., 1991.
Montanari, Arthur and Bracker, Jeffrey S., The Strategic Management Process at the Public Planning Unit Level, *Strategic Management Journal*, July:7, 1986, pp. 251–265.
Morrison, Don A., *Strategic Planning: A How-to Guide for Local Government*, Sound Resource Management, Seattle, 1988.
Morrison, Peter A., Applied Demography: The Growing Scope and Future Direction, *The Futurist*, March–April:14 (1990).
Naisbitt, John, *Megatrends: Ten New Directions Transforming Our Lives*, Warner Books, New York, 1982.
Naisbitt, John and Aburdene, Patricia, *Megatrends 2000: Ten New Directions for the 1990's*, William Morrow, New York, 1990.
Plotnick, Robert D., Poverty and Income Transfer Policy at the State Level, *Growth and Change, 20*(4):41 (1989).
Rogers, Thomas H., Strategic Planning: A Major OD Intervention, in *Organization Development* (Wendell French, Cecil Bell, and Robert A. Zawacki, eds.), Business Publications, Plano, Texas, 1983, p. 168.
Saaty, Thomas L., *The Analytical Hierarchy Process*, McGraw-Hill, New York, 1980.
Saaty, Thomas L., Axiomatic Foundation of the Analytical Hierarchy Process, *Management Science 32*(7):841–855 (1986).
Sorkin, Donna L., Ferris, Nancy B., and Hudak, James, *Strategies for Cities and Counties: A Strategic Planning Guide*, Public Technology, Washington, D.C., 1982.
Stanfield, Rochelle L., Statistics Gap, *National Journal* April 13, pp. 844–854 (1991).
Steiner, George A., *Strategic Planning: What Every Manager Must Know*, The Free Press, New York, 1979.
Stevenson, Howard H., Defining Corporate Strengths and Weaknesses, *Sloan Management Review 17*, Spring: 51–68 (1976).
Vogel, Ronald K., and Swanson, Bert E., Setting Agendas for Community Change: The Community Goal-Setting Strategy, *Journal of Urban Affairs, 10*(1):41 (1988).
Wechsler, Barton and Backoff, Robert W., The Dynamics of Strategy in Public Organization, *Journal of the American Planning Association, 53*(1):34 (1987).
Wikle, Thomas A., Computer Mapping and Education, *T.H.E. Journal 19*(5):51–54 (1991).
Woods, Robert, *Population Analysis in Geography*, Longman Group, New York, 1979.

25
The Emergence of the American Administrative State: The Intellectual Origins

Nolan J. Argyle
Valdosta State University, Valdosta, Georgia

> Men by their constitutions are naturally divided into two parties. I. Those who fear and distrust the people, and wish to draw all powers from them into the hands of the higher classes. 2ndly those who identify themselves with the people, have confidence in them, cherish and consider them as the most honest and safe, altho' not the most wise depository of the public interests.
>
> Thomas Jefferson

I. INTRODUCTION

This study argues that to understand the role of government and of public administration, it is necessary to go back to our intellectual heritage. We need to examine the differing views of man and state held by the founders of this nation, how those views were developed, and how they affect the way we see the administrative state of today. Such an understanding of the discipline's past can also aid in the development of a sense of professionalism. As Michael Nelson points out, when economics, history, and other disciplines sought to establish themselves as "professions," they drew upon their past to set a foundation. Yet when political scientists (and public administrators) attempted to define their profession, they went back not to the cave of Plato but to the 1880s of Woodrow Wilson (Nelson, 1979, p. 269).

The American administrative state is often portrayed as a creation of the last century. Indeed, the American Society for Public Administration celebrated the centennial of American public administration in 1983, using the Pendleton Act as "the beginning" of American public administration. A few political scientists and public administrative theorists have looked at earlier experiences. Matthew Crenson (1975) argues that American public bureaucracy took shape during the Jacksonian era. Marshall E. Dimock, arguing the need to "become more historically minded," sets the origins of public administration at "around the end of the 16th century," with the development of nation-state—and the development of the American colonies (Dimock, 1983, p. 99). Stillman (1990) also looks to the sixteenth century, noting the influence of Tudor institutional practice on the development of the American administrative state. Yet as Gladden points out, available evidence makes it apparent that "the [public] official ranked early among the first professionals," predating written history. Indeed, Gladden refers to public administration as the oldest profession (Gladden, 1972, vol. 1, p. 6). Thus the American administrative state draws upon an intellectual heritage that may be as old as mankind itself.

The American administrative state developed during an era of intense questioning of the relationship between church and state, between *sacerdotium* and *regnum*, questions that dominated much of early American administrative development. It also reflected arguments concerning the proper relationship of the state to the individual, arguments that were peaking as we became an independent nation. These were and remain ongoing debates, and the founders of the American state were well versed in them. As Lynton Caldwell indicates, "The architects of . . . [the American administrative state] sought to construct a new political system unconstrained by the past; but their ideas and arguments bore the stamp of history" (Caldwell, 1976, p. 477). And that "stamp of history" shaped the development of the American administrative state from the first colonists through the adoption of the Constitution.

II. INTELLECTUAL ORIGINS OF THE ADMINISTRATIVE STATE

Central to any organization theory is its view of man. This view is often implicit in the theories advanced by any individual, but it remains the key to understanding and, more importantly, evaluating the theory. Douglas McGregor (1960), a contemporary theorist whose work has taken on "classical" status of its own, recognized the importance of this, relating how a view of man affects any given theory of organization. Calling two contrasting views of man "Theory X" and "Theory Y," McGregor illustrates the consequences of views for management in modern organization.

At the most basic, a view of man is built upon a belief about human nature—what makes man behave as he does. In a dichotomous sense, man may be viewed as either a creature differentiated from other creatures, and thus distinguished from them, by his ability to reason; or a creature whose reason is subordinate to desire. In the first view, *reason* becomes the most dominant characteristic of humanity, and any explanation of human behavior must take this into account. In this view, man is a rational creature, who recognizes that his needs are caught up in the needs of society. The contrasting view, while not denying man's ability to reason, places less faith in his ability to use and rely on it. The dominant force in man is not reason, but *desire*. This desire may be for security, for power, or whatever; it is always selfish and egocentric, outweighing man's use of reason, preventing him from always recognizing his true interests. This view of the dominant force in man, reason or desire, becomes the first factor in a framework to evaluate various contributions to organization theory.

The second element in the framework is the way a theorist views society. Again, a dichotomy is found. Some theorists emphasize the individual as an independent actor, an emphasis which leads some to emphasize the difficulty of understanding human behavior in organizational contexts. Others discount an emphasis on the individual, arguing instead that individual action only has meaning in a group setting. This first view might be labeled *individualistic*; the latter view, *communal*. Using these two factors, a framework for analysis can be developed as shown in Figure 1.

View of Man	View of Society: Individualistic	View of Society: Communal
Dominated by Reason	Marketplace	Responsive Commonwealth
Dominated by Desire	Protectorate	Directed Commonwealth

Figure 1 Framework for analyzing organization theories.

This framework provides us with four cells, each representing a way of viewing human society and organization. Borrowing in part from Daniel Elazar (1984), these views can be labeled as either *marketplace* (emphasis on individual, dominated by reason), a *protectorate* (emphasis on the individual, dominated by desire), *responsive commonwealth* (emphasis on community, dominated by reason), or *directed commonwealth* (emphasis on community, dominated by desire). Each of these views sees organizations differently, in terms of both the way individuals behave in organizations and the role organizations play in society, and each has influenced the development of the American administrative state.

Those adopting a marketplace view would be more comfortable with McGregor's "Theory Y" man. Man will behave rationally in the organization, either in the sense of the classic "economic man" or in the sense of Simon's (1957) "administrative man," whose rationality is limited, thus forcing him to "satisfice." He will have a desire to cooperate, understanding how his contribution advances the good of all, including himself. The value of the individual remains paramount, and organizations can be judged normatively in terms of how they treat the individual. Furthermore, these organizations come into being as a result of demands made by individuals, and they can be judged in terms of how well they respond to those demands. This is true whether the organization is governmental or private.

The protectorate view, while emphasizing the individual, finds that individual somewhat wanting. Rather than behaving rationally in the organization, this individual, dominated as he is by desire, seeks selfish goals, goals that may in the long run prove self-defeating. Therefore, these few in society who are dominated by reason must in turn dominate the organization, protecting the majority from themselves. McGregor's "Theory X" describes the organizational man of this view. Organizations come into being to protect the individual from himself; they must often curb the demands made by individuals. Organizations can be judged normatively in terms of how well they maintain order in a society by limiting and channeling individual desires for the good of society, and thus for the good of the individuals that society comprises. Strong, hierarchical structures are necessary for this, and those structures must concentrate power at the upper levels. Private organizations may play this role, but they must be linked and controlled by a central power—government—in order to prevent them from working at cross-purposes.

The responsive commonwealth view sees man as dominated by reason, and as developing fully only within society. The isolated individual is a pathetic figure; man becomes worthy only through interaction with others—through organization. Therefore, the community becomes greater than the sum of the individuals that it comprises. Being reasonable, man recognizes this and seeks out organizational relationships that promote the common good; these organizations may be judged normatively in terms of how well they do so. As man is capable of determining this through reason, these organizations should respond to that reason. Structurally, they must provide features which will allow individual reason to be aggregated into a common will.

The directed commonwealth view agrees that the isolated individual is a pathetic creature; it does not agree, however, that man will recognize this and seek organizational relationships to promote the common good. Man, dominated by desire, is incapable of determining the common good. Therefore, those few in society who are dominated by reason must create the commonwealth and, once they have created it, must direct it to the betterment of man. Power must be concentrated at the top of organizations, enabling those organizations to lead man toward a common good. Normatively, these organizations may be judged by the same standard as those in the responsive commonwealth. Structurally, however, they are quite different. As most men are incapable of determining what the common good is, organizations cannot respond to an aggregate common will. Rather, they must develop a mechanism to identify those few in society dominated by reason and then bring them into the organizational hierarchy. Organizations, therefore, must be tightly connected, enabling them to work in unison to direct society toward the common good.

These disparate views concerning the relationships among individuals, society, and organizations provide fertile ground for developing theories concerning the behavior of man in organizational contexts. And each of these views has impacted the intellectual origins of the American administrative state.

A. The Directed Commonwealth: *Sacerdotium* and *Regnum* Revisited

The directed commonwealth can be traced back to the writings of Plato. Like that of all the ancient Greeks, Plato's focus was on the total community, with man becoming meaningful only through participation in the civic community, the polis. This community was natural, more so than any of its components, including the individuals who composed it. For Plato, the community could be divided into distinct classes, with the majority of the citizens belonging to a lower, artisan class dominated by desire. The state must be ruled by those few, dominated by reason, who constituted the upper class. They, according to Plato, were reluctant to rule but would do so from a sense of obligation (1971, p. 29): "They must be forced to consent [to rule] under threat of penalty; . . . [a]nd the heaviest penalty for declining to rule is to be ruled by someone inferior to yourself."

The directed commonwealth view dominated the thought of the Christian Fathers, who saw the clergy, and in particular the Pope, as the best interpreter of natural law, law that ultimately rested on God's authorship. This argument was advanced under a series of Popes, beginning with Pope Gelasius I (492–496), who outlined what eventually was to develop into the theory of the two swords. Church and state would become *sacerdotium* and *regnum*, two governments in a single Christian society. The civic ruler was superior to the Pope in temporal affairs, but the Pope was supreme in ecclesiastic matters. And, as the civic ruler needed the Church to obtain eternal life, he should heed the Pope's guidance.

This dual authority did not sit easy with either Pope or king. By the time the colonies that were to become the United States were being developed, this conflict was being resolved in favor of the king. Rising nationalism and the emergence of the modern nation-state led to growing subordination of ecclesiastic power to temporal power. An exception to this was found in the structural arrangements developed by followers of John Calvin.

Central to Calvin's arguments was the sovereignty of God in all matters. The state, then, had significance only to the extent that it furthered God's plan. The Church was a necessary intermediary to man's salvation, and thus princes, as agents of God, were subordinate to it. God was the origin of all good. Man, since Adam's fall, was evil and corrupt, born in sin, and afflicted with the curse of Adam's transgression. If man were to overcome this fallen state, both temporal and ecclesiastical discipline was required. The state provided the sword, but it was to be wielded under the guidance of the church.

Under this view, civil ministers serve an ecclesiastic capacity:

> Civil government is designed, as long as we live in this world, to cherish and support the external worship of God, to preserve the pure doctrine of religion, to defend the constitution of the Church, to regulate our lives in a manner requisite for the society of men, to form our manners to civil justice, to promote our concord with each other, and to establish general peace and tranquility. . . . (Calvin, 1981, p. 225)

Both church and state were to be controlled by those few in society with the capability of understanding God's purpose. Society was to be a directed commonwealth.

The directed commonwealth view was best expressed in England by Thomas Hobbes, and was brought to America by some of his contemporaries: the Puritans. Puritan leaders saw man as a being in a fallen state, whose carnal nature must be controlled for the good of the commonwealth by strong magistrates operating under God's laws. The England of Hobbes and of the Puritans certainly lent credence to the view of man dominated by desire. The civil strife within England of this period illustrated man at his worst. The Puritan view, however, did not take root in England. As Huntington (1981, pp. 154–158) has indicated, England underwent a Puritan revolution without creating a Puritan society; America created a Puritan society without undergoing a Puritan revolution.

The works of two American Puritan leaders illustrate the nature of the directed commonwealth in America: John Cotton and John Winthrop. These two men were the most prominent leaders of church and state during the formative years of the Puritan commonwealth in Massachusetts. Cotton was by far the most prominent minister in Massachusetts, deriving his extraordinary influence from his achievements as a scholar and his gifts in the pulpit (Polishook, 1967, p. 14). John Winthrop served as governor during most of the early years. Together, these two men were called upon to describe and to defend the system of political government and its relationship to the church in forming the commonwealth. Although Winthrop is usually recognized as the chief spokesman for Puritan theocracy, he consulted Cotton often on these matters, as well he might, since he was a member of Cotton's church. Furthermore, it was Cotton who played the major role in answering the charges leveled against the relationship between church and state by Roger Williams.

The attacks by Roger Williams stand in sharp contrast to the quieter internal struggle which is most characteristic of this debate. While many of the opponents of Cotton and Winthrop are known, including such men as William Pynchon, Israel Stoughton, and Thomas Hooker, most opponents remained anonymous, and few people directly attacked either Cotton's or Winthrop's ideas.

These men came to Massachusetts less to establish a "New England" than to establish a "New Zion." In his sermon "A Modell of Christian Charity" (probably delivered on board the flagship *Arabella* during the crossing) Winthrop told the people, "Wee must Consider that wee shall be as a Citty vpon a Hill, the eies of all people are vppon us. . . . " (Winthrop, 1869, p. 32). The Puritans considered themselves an elect people who had entered into a covenant with God;

they were to serve as a model for the entire Christian world. Fourteen years after the first Puritans established themselves in Massachusetts, Governor Winthrop wrote, "England is a state of long standing, yet we haue had more positive & more holesome Lawes inacted in our shorte tyme, than they had in many hundred years" (Winthrop, 1869, p. 446).

Church and state, in this model, were to be separate but complementary institutions, tied together to preserve peace in the commonwealth and to promote the virtue of the citizenry. As Cotton stated (Polishook, 1967, pp. 73–74):

> If it were true, that the magistrate has charge only of the bodies and goods of the subject, yet that might justly excite to watchfulness against such pollutions of religion as tend to apostasy. For if the church and people of God fall away from God, God will visit the city and country with public calamity, if not captivity, for the church's sake.
>
> Did ever God commit the charge of the body to any governors to whom he did not commit (in His way) the care of souls also? . . . The truth is, church governors and civil governors do herein stand parallel one to another.

Church governors and civil governors "stand parallel one to another," then, in a joint effort to secure peace in the commonwealth and to ensure that the laws of the commonwealth are in accord with the laws of God. The extent to which civil authority was to parallel religious authority can be seen from one representative sample of Cotton's *An Abstract, or the Lawes of New England as They are now established*, a document Winthrop called "a model of Moses his judicials, compiled in an exact method," which stated that no one is to be permitted to live more than a mile from a church meeting house, for "all civil affairs are to be administered and ordered so as may best conduce to the upholding and setting forward of the worship of God in church fellowship" (Emerson, 1965, pp. 144–146).

Political participation was limited to those in good standing in the church. Residents who were not members of a church—and some 80% of the population were not—were guaranteed their rights under law, but could not participate either in choosing the magistrates or in defining the laws. Members of the churches were considered freemen of the commonwealth and could participate in civic affairs. For both Cotton and Winthrop, however, this did not mean that they could determine those affairs. Democracy, for Cotton, was not "a fit government either for church or commonwealth. If the people be governors, who shall be governed?" (Scott, 1959, p. 8). In his "Little Speech on Liberty," Winthrop defined the role of the governor and governed (Scott, 1959, p. 19): "The covenant between you and us is the oath you have taken of us, which is to this purpose: that we shall govern you and judge your causes by the rules of God's laws and our own, according to our best skill."

Thus public administration was directed from the top. Civil ministers were to enforce the will of God, as interpreted by an elite. All aspects of community life were under the watchful eye of the state, and rules and regulations were strictly enforced in order to enable the citizens to live in accordance to God's laws. "Thus stands the cause between God and vs," Winthrop stated, "wee are entered into Covenant with him for this worke, wee haue taken out a Commission, the Lord hat giuen vs leave to drawe our owne Articles wee haue professed to enterprise these Accions . . . " (McGiffert, 1969, p. 31).

The elect people, then, had been given leave to draw their own articles of government. Thus, while close cooperation was called for between church and state, the Puritans insisted that they were separate institutions—the old argument of concerning the nature of *sacerdotium* and *regnum*, begun by Gelasius I as a means of strengthening papal influence over temporal affairs, had been recast as a system in which the same individual exercised both powers, but with civil authority serving to buttress religious power. This relationship is stated in Articles 58 through 60 of the *Massachusetts Body of Liberties* (Scott, 1959, p. 14):

> 58. Civil authority hath power and liberty to see the peace, ordinances and rules of Christ observed in every church according to his word. So it be done in a civil and not in an ecclesiastical way.
>
> 59. Civil authority hath power and liberty to deal with any church member in a way of civil justice, notwithstanding any church relation, office, or interest.
>
> 60. No church censure shall degrade or depose any man from any civil dignity, office, or authority he shall have in the commonwealth.

Civil authority and religious authority were to be bound together for the betterment of the commonwealth. Rejecting Roger Williams's arguments in favor of freedom of religious expression, Cotton argued that it would be unreasonable to suppose that God would condone the existence of competing religious philosophies within one state. As Miller points out, "Moses and Aaron, the priest and the statesman, were equally the vice-regents of God, and the notion that one could contaminate the other was insanity" (McGiffert, 1969, p. 46).

If religious and civil leaders "were equally the vice-regents of God," it would follow that the civil leader must hold impeccable credentials as a follower of His word, and this is the position taken by Winthrop and Cotton. Church membership was the essential prerequisite for the magistery. Traditional or hereditary leadership was not totally rejected but was made subordinate to standing in the church. High birth carried with it the right of preeminence in society, but not in government. While persons of high birth would be given preference in elections to the magistery, they could qualify for such positions, according to Cotton, only if they were "godly men, who are fit materials for church fellowship, . . . For the liberties of the freemen of this commonwealth are such as require men of faithful integrity to God and the state, to preserve the same" (Scott, 1959, p. 12).

Magistrates were to be guided by God's laws, not by the dictates of the people. The freemen of the commonwealth did have a check on the exercise of authority by the magistrates in the yearly election at the General Court each May. It was a check that was seldom utilized, however, and few freemen bothered to exercise their franchise. Winthrop's argument that God "will also teache his ministers the Judges what sentence to pronounce, if they will allso observe his worde, & trust in him," and that "Judges are Gods upon earthe" (Scott, 1959, p. 448) was not seriously challenged. The only time the General Court voted to remove a governor occurred in 1637 when Governor Vane was removed, and that removal was based on Vane's stance on religion. Elections were seen by the freemen not so much as a method of choosing a leader, but "as an emergency safeguard, as a means, short of revolution, for removing those rulers whom they found unacceptable" (Breen, 1970, p. 53).

Yet even in this early period, the views of Cotton and Winthrop did not go unchallenged. The seeds of a more democratic view of the commonwealth, a responsive rather than a directed commonwealth, were sown during this period. By the time the colonies were starting to break with England, this directed commonwealth view, held by such intellectual descendants of Cotton and Winthrop as Jonathan Mayhew and Daniel Leonard, was being modified by the responsive commonwealth, and by individualistic views of the state.

B. The Responsive Commonwealth

The responsive commonwealth can be traced back to the ancient Greeks, with Aristotle serving as its best proponent. He agreed with the general Greek view of nature and society. The polis—the civic community—was both natural and the highest expression of humanity. Aristotle makes this clear in the *Politics* (1979, pp. 6–7):

> We thus see that the polis exists by nature and that it is prior to the individual . . . all individuals are so many parts all equally depending on the whole [which alone can bring about self-sufficiency]. The man who is isolated—who is unable to share in the benefits of political association, or has no need to share because he is already self-sufficient—is no part of the polis, and must therefore be either a beast or a god.

Man, for Aristotle, is a social creature defined by his ability to reason. He is a seeker of the good community; he strives for justice, for himself and for others. He seeks moral perfection, even though he has thus far fallen short. Yet, even falling short, man succeeds through his striving for the good community.

Cicero helped bring this view forward through history. The key to the responsive commonwealth, he felt, was found in education. This would allow a natural aristocracy to arise, one which could respond to the collective reason of the community and create the good state. "And when men have felt . . . that, to the powers of mind received from nature and developed by experience in public affairs, they should add also scholarly interests and a richer acquaintance with life, such men must be universally conceded to be superior to all others" (1927, p. 198). In what could serve as a motto for the administration state, he adds (1927, p. 216), "What, indeed, can be more glorious than the union of practical experience in great affairs with an intelligent enthusiasm for the liberal arts?"

As the impact of the Enlightenment spread to America and linked to the colonial experience, some inheritors of Puritan thought adopted similar arguments. John Wise, writing in 1717, rejected Cotton and Winthrop's arguments concerning the relationship between governed and governors. Civil government, he argued, "must needs be acknowledged to be the effect of human free-compacts and not divine institution: it is the produce of man's reason" (1959, p. 30). This free compact, for Wise, was a natural state: man needed to "maintain a sociableness with others, agreeable with the main end and disposition of human nature in general" (1959, p. 31).

In making his arguments, Wise was influenced by the growing "natural law" school of thought, a school that tended to stress the Lockean view of the individual. Although Wise continued to emphasize the communal nature of society, other thinkers began to stress the individual as the key. One of the most significant of these thinkers was John Adams.

The communal view of the state placed an emphasis on securing virtue; the growing individualistic emphasis was on securing individual rights. Adams, in his writings, mixed both. In his "Thoughts on Government . . . ," written in 1776, Adams argues that "the happiness of man, as well as his dignity, consists in virtue" (1959, pp. 102–103). He goes on to cite such communal theorists as Zoroaster, Socrates, and Mahomet to support his contention. Yet he next draws on Locke, Milton, and others who emphasize the individual. He does this, as Webking (1983, p. 3) points out, "without indicating an awareness of the tension between the two sets of principles."

Adams's lack of clarity reflects the ambiguity of much of American political thought (see Hartz, 1955, for an excellent examination of this). This ambiguity is reflected in those who do explicitly focus on the individual.

C. The Protectorate

A focus on the individual is more modern in the development of the intellectual origins of the administrative state. One of the first to focus on the individual, Niccolò Machiavelli, saw that individual as dominated by desire and wrote a classic treatise on how to govern in this context.

Machiavelli rejected the natural, communal state, arguing instead that the state had no reality apart from the individuals it comprised. He also rejected the idea that these individuals were themselves governed by natural law determined through reason. Instead, he argued that "[t]here is no inherent purpose in the state. Any direction it may receive must be imposed upon it by the ruler" (1952, p. 16). This ruler must understand human nature and manipulate it to rule effectively.

The protectorate view did not become a dominant view in colonial America. While some observers have placed many of the Federalists, notably Alexander Hamilton, in this category, this study will argue that the individualist view in colonial America fits within the marketplace view of man and state.

D. The Marketplace

A key marketplace theorist for the American experience was John Locke. His writings, particularly his *Letter on toleration* and his *Second treatise of government*, greatly influenced political discourse in both England and the English colonies that were to become the United States. Yet Locke was only one of many sources of British political thought that influenced the development of a marketplace view. English opposition thought of the last half of the seventeenth and first half of the eighteenth centuries was crucial in shaping the American mind.

Among the most effective opposition writers were those who associated themselves with the republican theorists of the Civil War period—writers who traced their thoughts from Milton and Harrington through Neville, Sidney, and Locke—particularly John Trenchard and Thomas Gordon. For Americans, states Bailyn, their writings "ranked with the treatises of Locke as the most authoritative statement of the nature of political liberty and above Locke as an exposition of the social sources of the threats it faced" (Bailyn, 1967a, p. 35). In addition to these writings of the left a number of writings from the right also influenced American thought, particularly the writings of Lord Bolingbroke. "The people of the colonies," wrote Burke (1968, p. 57) at the start of the war in 1775,

> are descendants of Englishmen. England . . . is a nation which still, I hope, respects, and formerly adored, her freedom. The colonists emigrated from you when this part of your character was most predominant; and they took this bias and direction the moment they parted from your hands. They are therefore not only devoted to liberty, but to liberty according to English ideas and on English principles.

Key among these English principles as developed by opposition theorists was the concept of a mixed constitution: a government that would balance monarchy, aristocracy, and democracy. Whereas Locke's arguments led to legislative supremacy, with the ministers under the control of the legislature, opposition theorists sought to balance the legislative, executive, and judicial powers and thus argued that ministers should be accountable to more than one power. Indeed, it was their belief that too much power was being concentrated in a ministerial plot, resulting in a growing imbalance of power that made their arguments so appealing to Americans faced with an increased use of executive power.

Unlike Cotton and Winthrop, who saw civil ministers and churchmen in a cooperative arrangement to lead society forward, opposition writers exhibited a marked distrust of the magistery. Writers of the left and right were in agreement on this. Civil ministers, wrote Trenchard and Gordon, "will endeavor to bribe the electors . . . so to get a council of their own creatures; and where they cannot succeed with the electors, they will endeavor to corrupt the deputies after they are chosen" (Bailyn, 1967b, p. 44). Such corruption, Bolingbroke added, "was a natural enough phenomenon. Public ministers naturally 'lie under great temptations, through the infirmities and corruption of human nature, to prefer their own *private interests* to that of the *community*' " (Bailyn, 1967b, p. 46). For these writers, then, the reality of the ministerial plot was both unquestionable and inevitable. The struggle for power was constant, and only through equally constant vigilance could free men hope to remain free.

The legacy of seventeenth- and eighteenth-century opposition thought for Americans was the conviction of the need to maintain a mixed state, and to ensure that the magistrates of such a state did not become a threat to individual liberty. The English tradition of liberty had been developed in America as the natural birthright of man. Whenever liberty had been achieved—in the Roman republic of Cicero or under the mixed constitutionalism of English law—it had been lost when the moral and political virtues of the societies decayed. These views were presented in the emerging nation by a number of people; this study focuses upon Thomas Jefferson and Alexander Hamilton. Of the two, Jefferson dealt more with theory—although he certainly understood practical politics—and Hamilton more with the pragmatic application to the affairs of government.

Jefferson has often been identified as the most Lockean of the Revolutionary era leaders. Locke's *Second treatise of government* found its colonial expression in Jefferson's authorship of the *Declaration of Independence*. Jefferson agreed with Locke's emphasis on the individual, dominated by reason. Like Locke's, however, Jefferson's faith in man's reason seemed to lessen with time. In a letter to Henry Lee, written in 1824, he reaffirmed his belief in the individual, while tempering it by indicating the limits of their wisdom (Caldwell, 1964, p. 113):

> Men by their constitutions are naturally divided into two parties. I. Those who fear and distrust the people, and wish to draw all power from them into the hands of the higher classes. 2ndly those who identify themselves with the people, have confidence in them, cherish and consider them as the most honest and safe, altho' not the most wise depository of the public interests.

Jefferson, while not always convinced of the wisdom of the people, still believed them the best guide for the state to follow. "In a government like ours," he stated, "it is the duty of the Chief Magistrate . . . , to endeavor, by all honorable means, to unite in himself the confidence of the whole people" (Caldwell, 1964, p. 107). To staff this government, Jefferson argued in favor of selecting the best and brightest among society. In a letter to John Adams, he wrote: "I agree with you that there is a natural aristocracy among men. The grounds of this are virtue and talents. . . . " The best government, then, is that "which provides the most effectually for a pure selection of these natural aristoi into the offices of government" (Peterson, 1977, pp. 534–535).

Jefferson, basically an egalitarian, "was coincidentally an individualist, loving men as persons, cherishing them collectively in the abstract, but distrusting them to the point of fear when massed together in cities" (Caldwell, 1964, p. 105). Some of this same mixture of "loving men as persons" while not completely trusting them in particular was shared by his contemporary and political rival Alexander Hamilton.

Hamilton, like Jefferson, dealt in theory, but his true emphasis was on the pragmatic affairs of government. "How widely different the business of government is from the speculation of it," he wrote, "and the energy of the imagination dealing in general propositions from that of *execution in detail*" (Flaumenhaft, 1976, p. 145).

Hamilton saw the individual as dominated by reason: "The supreme being gave existence to man, together with the means of preserving and beautifying that existence. He endowed him with rational faculties, by the help of which to discern and pursue such things, as were consistent with his duty and interest . . . " (Flaumenhaft, 1976, p. 175). This reason, for Hamilton, was universally shared. Hamilton was one of a handful of people anywhere in the European world of his day to state that blacks were equal in facilities—and rights—to whites (Flaumenhaft, 1976, pp. 177–179).

Like Jefferson, Hamilton felt that the administrative state was best served by attracting the service of those qualified by reason. He argued that most men, if properly trained and educated, could serve quite well—a view later echoed by Andrew Jackson. Hamilton was among the first to address the link between the emerging technology and administration, the first to address the potentials and problems of technocracy. Hamilton stressed such organizational features as division of labor, training and development, and planning for diversifying and improving the supply of labor. He argued for what contemporary administrators would call job enrichment, basing his argument on the different capacities of man, and on man's need for personal development. "It is a just observation," he argued, "that minds of the strongest and most active powers for their proper objects, fall below mediocrity, and labor without effort, if confined to uncongenial pursuits" (1959, p. 163).

In making his arguments, Hamilton sounds modern; he links an active, creative mind with practical experience to present clear and compelling arguments concerning the proper way to organize human behavior. His contributions make it clear that, by the dawn of the nineteenth century, the basic ideas that were to underpin the American administrative state were firmly in place.

III. DEVELOPING AN ADMINISTRATIVE STRUCTURE

Those who developed the administrative structure of the new nation drew on three primary sources: the laws and history of England, their own colonial experiences, and classical and modern political theory. Burke's argument that Americans were "devoted to liberty . . . according to English ideas and on English principles" (1968, p. 57) was accurate. Yet it failed to account for the fact that Americans were no longer English. It ignored the implications that stemmed from the colonies' settlement in part by those whose cause had been lost in England. While Americans argued English ideas and English principles, they were ideas and principles that, while dominant in America, were held by only a minority in England. Rossiter may be correct in arguing that their English heritage "gave direction and impetus to their struggles for liberty," and that "it is a decisive fact of American history that until 1776 it was a chapter in English history as well" (1953, p. 6), but 1776 was, as Kohn indicates, "a civil war comparable to that of the seventeenth century" as well (Kohn and Walden, 1970, p. 14). Americans no longer shared the view of man that was dominant in England.

The two dominant views of man represented by the Founding Fathers were the directed commonwealth view drawn from their Puritan heritage, modified by some movement toward the responsive commonwealth view, and the marketplace view emerging in the eighteenth century. Each of these views sees a different role for public administrators. The marketplace view, in particular the arguments of Locke, dominated the Declaration of Independence and the Articles of Confederation; the *Constitution* drew more heavily upon English opposition thought, particularly Trenchard and Gordon's *Cato's Letters*, influenced by the Puritan legacy.

Both the responsive commonwealth view and the protectorate view played lesser roles in the intellectual origins of the American administrative state. While an argument can be made that many Americans—and certainly some current managers—operate on the protectorate scheme, it played only a small role in developing the origins of the administrative state.

The directed commonwealth view of the state played an important role in developing American views of the administrative state and continues to be a factor in current debates over the nature of that state. The directed commonwealth view argues that those few in society who are dominated by reason must create the commonwealth and, once they have created it, must direct it toward the betterment of man. Power must be concentrated at the top of organizations, enabling those organizations to lead man toward a common good. As most men are incapable of determining what the common good is, organizations cannot respond to an aggregate common will. Rather, they must develop a mechanism to identify those few in society dominated by reason, and then bring them into the organizational hierarchy. Organizations, therefore, must be tightly connected, enabling them to work in unison to direct society to the common good.

The intellectual heirs of the Puritans are found among members of the Reagan and Bush administrations as well as among today's fundamentalists; in those who believe in absolute truth and who evidence a distrust of democracy as damaging to the national morality and spirit. The administrative state, and the career administrators who compose it, are to follow not only the laws of the state, but the laws of God. They would agree with Cotton that this is a Christian nation, whose government is ordained by God.

The other key view of man, the marketplace view, was dominant in the period leading up to the Revolutionary War. Those adopting a marketplace view believe that man will behave rationally in the organization. He will have a desire to cooperate, understanding how his contribution advances the good of all, including himself. The value of the individual remains paramount, and organizations can be judged normatively in terms of how they treat the individual. Furthermore, these organizations come into being as a result of demands made by individuals, and they can be judged in terms of how well they respond to those demands. This is true whether the organization is governmental or private. In this view, government is to respond to the articulated needs of the people. It should be staffed by those who, using reason, can help meet these needs and direct the affairs of state in the interest of the individuals that it comprises. Those with this view would agree with the current school of thought exemplified by Chandler's argument that administrators are more representative of the public than are legislators (Chandler, 1984).

The intellectual origins of the American administrative state are rich and varied. This study has only scratched the surface of what they offer the contemporary student of administration in the United States. An examination of this heritage can enrich an understanding of current arguments, as well as provide a student of the administrative state with a sense of history, an anchor upon which to fasten his or her understanding of the linkage between the individual and the state.

REFERENCES

Adams, J., Thoughts on Government Applicable to the Present State of the American Colonies, in *Political Thought in America* (A. M. Scott, ed.), Holt, Rinehart & Winston, New York, 1959.

Aristotle, *The Politics of Aristotle* (trans. Ernest Baker), Oxford University Press, London, 1979.

Bailyn, B., *The Ideological Origins of the American Revolution*, Harvard University Press, Cambridge, Mass., 1967a.

Bailyn, B., *The Origins of American Politics*, Vintage Books, New York, 1967b.

Breen, T. H., *The Character of the Good Ruler*, Yale University Press, New Haven, 1970.

Burke, E., On Conciliation with America, in *Edmund Burke on Revolution* (R. A. Smith, ed.), Harper & Row, New York, 1968.

Caldwell, L. K., *The Administrativc Theories of Hamilton and Jefferson*, Russell and Russell, New York, 1964.

Caldwell, L. K., Novus Ordo Seclorum: The Heritage of American Public Administration, *Public Administration Review 36*:476–488 (1976).

Calvin, J., Institutes of the Christian Religion, in *The Great Political Theories*, (M. Curtis, ed.), Avon, New York, 1981.

Chandler, R. C., The Public Administrator as Representative Citizen, *Public Administration Review 44* (1984).

Cicero, *On the Commonwealth* (trans. George Holland Sabine and Stanley Barney Smith), Bobbs-Merrill, New York, 1927.

Cotton, J., A Letter to Lord Say and Sele, in *Political Thought in America* (A. M.Scott, ed.), Holt, Rinehart and Winston, New York, 1959.

Crenson, M. A., *The Federal Machine: Beginnings of Bureaucracy in Jacksonian America*, Johns Hopkins, Baltimore, 1971.

Dimock, M. E., Centennials, Continuities, and Culture, *Public Administration Review, 43*:99–107, 1983.

Elazar, D. J., *American Federalism: A View from the States*, 2nd ed., Thomas Y. Crowell, New York, 1972.

Emerson, E. H., *John Cotton*, Twayne, New York, 1965.

Flaumenhaft, H., Jr., Alexander Hamilton on the Foundation of Good Government, *The Political Science Reviewer 6*:143–214 (1976).

Gladden, E. N., *A History of Public Administration*, vols. 1–2, Cass, London, 1972.

Hamilton, A., Report on Manufacturers, in *Political thought in America* (A. M. Scott, ed.), Holt, Rinehart & Winston, New York, 1959.

Harmon, M. M., Normative Theory and Public Administration: Some Suggestions for a Redefinition of Administrative Responsibility, in *Toward a New Public Administration: The Minnowbrook Perspective*, (Frank Marini, ed.), Chandler, Scranton, Pa., 1971.

Hartz, L., *The Liberal Tradition in America*, Harcourt, Brace and World, New York, 1955.

Huntington, S. P., *American Politics: The Promise of Disharmony*, Harvard University Press, Cambridge, Mass., 1981.

Kohn, H. and Walden, D., eds., *Readings in American Nationalism*, Van Nostrand Reinhold, New York, 1970.

Locke, J., *Two Treatises of Government*, (Peter Laslett, ed.), Cambridge University Press, New York, 1960.

Machiavelli, N., *The Prince* (trans. Christian Gauss), Mentor, New York, 1952.

McGiffert, M., ed., *Puritanism and the American Experience*, Addison-Wesley Publishing, Reading, Mass., 1969.

McGregor, D., *The Human Side of Enterprise*, McGraw-Hill, New York, 1960.

Nelson, M., What's Wrong with Political Science, in *Inside the System* (C. Peters and N. Lehman, eds.), 4th ed., Holt, Rinehart and Winston, New York, 1979.

Peterson, M. D., ed., *The Portable Thomas Jefferson*, Penguin Books, New York, 1977.

Plato, *The Republic of Plato* (trans. Francis MacDonald Concord), Oxford University Press, London, 1971.

Polishook, I. H., *Roger Williams, John Cotton and Religious Freedom*, Prentice-Hall, Englewood Cliffs, N.J., 1967.

Rossiter, C., *Seedtime of the Republic*, Harcourt, Brace & World, New York, 1953.

Scott, A. M., ed., *Political Thought in America*, Holt, Rinehart and Winston, New York, 1959.

Simon, H., *Administrative Behavior*, 2nd ed., McMillan, New York, 1957.

Stillman, R. J. III, The Peculiar "Stateless" Origins of American Public Administration and the Consequences for Government Today, *Public Administration Review 50*:156–167 (1990).

Webking, R., Virtue and Individual Rights in John Adams' *Defense*, panel conducted at the Meeting of the Western Social Science Association, Albuquerque, New Mexico, 1983.
Winthrop, J., A modell of Christian charity. In *Political thought in America*, 1959.
Winthrop, J., Little Speech on Liberty, in *Political Thought in America* (A. M. Scott, ed.), Holt, Rinehart & Winston, New York, 1959.
Winthrop, R. C., *Life and Letters of John Winthrop*, vols. 1–2, Little Brown, Boston, 1869.
Wise, J., A Vindication of the Government of New England Churches, in *Political Though in America* (A. M. Scott, ed.), Holt, Rinehart & Winston, New York, 1959.

26
Three Efforts at Managing Crises from FDR's White House

Stephen D. Van Beek
San Jose State University, San Jose, California

Franklin Delano Roosevelt, during his more than twelve years in the White House, redefined and solidified the role of the presidency in American government. The new mantle of enhanced presidential power arose in response to two national crises, the Great Depression and later the United States' involvement in World War II. While managing the nation's foreign affairs and protecting national security were universally acknowledged to be primarily in the president's domain, the events of the 1930s and 1940s, and Roosevelt's responses, ensured that subsequent presidents also would have the responsibility for maintaining the nation's economic health. With this legacy in mind, the importance of the Roosevelt presidency has been widely recognized and discussed. Given little attention, however, were the means FDR used to respond to, prevent, and manage crises directly from the White House.

This chapter examines the work of three organizations: the National Recovery Administration (NRA), the National Resources Planning Board (NRPB), and the Office of War Mobilization (OWM). Roosevelt created them to bring the nation out of Depression, prevent long-term threats to the economy, and manage the nation's domestic affairs during wartime. The managerial role for the presidency Roosevelt thought implicit in their creation would become strained and more distant with his successors, who would face great challenges on their time based in part on the wartime precedents of economic and military leadership. Roosevelt himself hoped to lead and, at the same time, stay on top of the bureaucracies he had created. The successes and failures of these efforts and the operations of the agencies inform efforts by Roosevelt, and later by his successors, to fulfill public and presidential expectations of a more active presidency.

The first agency, the National Recovery Administration, came into existence when the president signed the National Industrial Recovery Act (NIRA) into law on June 16, 1933. The NIRA's stated purposes were "to encourage national industrial recovery, to foster fair competition, and to provide for the construction of certain useful public works. . . . " As Title I of the NIRA, the National Recovery Administration had the goal of pulling the nation out of the

Depression and finding employment for its idle workers. To bring relief to the beleaguered economy, the NRA devised a set of codes or agreements with industry to curtail cost-cutting competition and curb the tensions between business and labor. This experiment in corporate capitalism was Roosevelt's attempt to micromanage the industrial economy, a strategy completely foreign to the national government at the time and one necessarily devised from scratch [1].

Roosevelt believed that government could also head off potential economic dislocations by using the vast resources at its disposal to increase demand. The vehicles he employed were a series of planning agencies, the most prominent of which was the National Resources Planning Board. The functions of the NRPB included analyzing how best the nation could utilize and conserve its national resources (natural, human, and otherwise); serving as a clearinghouse for planning activities of the government; monitoring economic conditions; reviewing existing national policies; and predicting future trends and needs in society [2]. Although the concept of "planning" was and is susceptible to several definitions, the role of these agencies was to advise Roosevelt on how best the government could intervene in the economy so as to mitigate economic down cycles and thereby improve the standard of living of its citizenry [3]. This coordinating role in FDR's White House did not last beyond his third term, as the operations of the NRPB were terminated in 1943.

The Office of War Mobilization was the last in a series of agencies charged with administering the wartime economy. Created on May 27, 1943, the OWM specifically was designed to simplify the chaos generated by hundreds of domestic agencies, characterized by overlapping agency jurisdictions and mandates, in making decisions related to the war effort. While the OWM's predecessors were involved in both the carrying out of policy and coordination, the objective of the OWM, in contrast, was to centralize decision making and decide disputes among the operational agencies. By delegating such widespread authority to a single agency, Roosevelt could concentrate more fully on the foreign aspects of the war effort.

What is most striking about all three agencies is that they are all now footnotes in the history of public administration and presidential management. The common philosophy of each—to centralize administration and give the presidents the means for managing—has since largely been abandoned in favor of a more piecemeal approach to management.

I. GOVERNMENT RESPONSIBILITY PRIOR TO 1933

While prior to 1933 the national government did have the responsibility to regulate certain sectors of the economy, it had neither the mandate nor the wherewithal to affect or control the entirety of the American marketplace. Within his own narrow base of authority and limited vision of the presidency, Herbert Hoover tried to respond to the calamities of the late 1920s and early 1930s. Included in his efforts were pleas for voluntary cooperation between business and labor, the establishment of agricultural cooperatives designed to stabilize prices, a revision in tariffs that turned into the disastrous Hawley-Smoot Tariff Act of 1930, and the Reconstruction Finance Corporation, which provided $1.4 billion in capital mainly to large banks, trust companies, and savings and loans in the hope that increasing the availability of capital would fuel greater consumption (Campagna, 1987, p. 95). As Hoover himself summarized his administration's efforts, "In these measures we have striven to mobilize and stimulate private initiative and local and community responsibility. There has been the least Government entry into the economic field, and that only in temporary and emergency form" (Hoover, 1976, p. 583). Unfortunately for Hoover, his policy of limited intervention fell far short of success in the midst of a profound lack of consumer confidence, poor and contradictory economic advice, and the failed monetary policy of the Federal Reserve.

Roosevelt's subsequent landslide victory over Hoover in the 1932 election did not constitute a public blessing for a specific and sweeping package of reforms, for the Democrat ran his presidential campaign without a clear program to address the economic problems of the nation. The American electorate, it appeared, simply demanded a clear change from the failed Hoover economic policies. Voters hoped that a new occupant of the White House would be able to deliver them swiftly from the disastrous state of the American economy. Roosevelt's task upon taking office was formidable: one in four heads of household were unemployed in an age without the "safety net" of today, the price of finished manufactured goods had dropped by half, and 1 to 2 million people were wandering the nation looking for work. The crisis was deep and visible, affecting each region and nearly every family in the land.

II. NATIONAL RECOVERY ADMINISTRATION

When Roosevelt signed the NIRA, creating the NRA, he said, "History probably will record the National Industrial Recovery Act as the most important and far-reaching legislation ever enacted by the American Congress." His goal for NIRA truly was ambitious: to promote industrial recovery and put the unemployed back to work. The idea behind the NRA had its origins during the First World War. Some economists believed that direct economic planning by the government had been vindicated by the experiences of the War Industries Board (WIB). The WIB, directed by Bernard Baruch, had stimulated industrial cooperation and pushed the nation's resources into needed areas, developing the productive capacity that armed America and its allies. In the early 1930s, General Hugh Johnson—a former aide to Baruch at the WIB—was one of Roosevelt's advisers who believed that a similar relationship between business and government was needed to boost the peacetime economy. Johnson and others saw the root of the economic problem in the continual pressures to cut costs, which diminished workers' wages and decreased their purchasing power to buy goods from other manufacturers. This unchecked competition, they believed, precipitated many of the country's economic problems by producing alternate swings of prosperity and depression. In short, wartime-type planning applied to the industrial sector could help the nation out of its peacetime crisis.

Sharing this belief were various representatives of big business, including leaders from the Chamber of Commerce and the National Association of Manufacturers, who urged that businesses be permitted to form associations under public supervision. These groups argued for antitrust exemptions so that they could meet to discuss and fix prices. The goal, according to a resolution adopted by the Chamber of Commerce in May 1931, was to implement "a rational program of production and distribution to be initiated by business itself" (Beard, 1932, p. 196). Such associations were not unprecedented. During the 1920s, Republican presidents, through the Federal Trade Commission, had enabled many such associations to form.

An otherwise improbable ally of big business were leftist planners like Charles Beard and Rexford Tugwell who felt that the whole system of private enterprise was flawed. They were wary, however, of solely entrusting business with the operation of the economy. Rather, these planners believed that business itself was responsible for the Depression by oversaving, providing inadequate wages to workers, and limiting production. All of the economy's participants, in their view, should have an equal voice in government planning which would set and then implement national goals. Industrial councils would be formed, consisting of workers, farmers, consumers, and businessmen, who would work in concert to control prices and profits and to set limits on production.

The NIRA was thus a compromise among the planners, big business, and organized labor. To build his coalition, Roosevelt appeased the planners by specifying minimum and maximum hours together with salary guidelines; for business, he provided antitrust exemptions that allowed prices and profits to be set; and to address labor's concerns, he gave protections to organize and bargain collectively without the threat of competing company unions. The heart of the program was Title I, which authorized the president or his designee to set up administrative agencies to monitor and assist with formulating "codes of fair competition." These codes, in effect, were legalized cartels, voluntary agreements among businesses within particular industries or associations. Participation was far from voluntary, however. All business falling under a code's guidelines had to abide by the provisions of the agreement. According to the codes, business had to conform to the minimum and maximum hour guidelines and permit the protections for labor. By giving businesses the ability to set price policies through the codes, the administration hoped that the vicious cost-cutting would stop and that the wages for workers would stabilize and later rise.

Administratively, the NRA was set up as an independent agency that was to report directly to FDR, not through the channel of an existing departmental agency like Commerce. The president or his designee, in most cases Hugh Johnson, NRA's director, had to approve all code agreements. In the absence of an agreement or if abuses of an existing code were discovered, the president was authorized to draft a new code or rewrite an old one. This latter authority, Roosevelt rightly feared, would be ruled unconstitutional by the Supreme Court if a challenge were brought. Because of this legal problem, Roosevelt stayed away from bringing suit against recalcitrant industries during implementation, instead relying on moral exhortation and ambiguous threats to achieve compliance.

While the codes were being negotiated, FDR decided to encourage employer hiring immediately through his Reemployment Agreement. It specified maximum weekly hours (forty or thirty-five depending on the industry), and minimum wages (forty cents) and forbade unwarranted price increases. The latter was necessary to head off any building up of inventories at old prices before individual agreements were signed. In an herculean effort between July and October, Roosevelt, Johnson, and a collection of his NRA deputy administrators were able to bring all of the parties together to sign the specific code agreements. To convince industries to fall into line they used Roosevelt's popularity, threats to write codes for the industries, and the omnipresent symbol of the Blue Eagle. Affixed with the motto "We Do Our Part," the Blue Eagle was a sign to customers indicating which businesses cooperated, and which opposed, the popular president's program to lift the nation out of Depression. Reluctant businesses faced enormous economic pressure from the public to comply or face the consequences. The pressure worked; by October, all major industries had codes governing their operations and, by 1934, over five hundred industries fell under the NRA's purview.

Although official optimism was prevalent in October, problems with the NRA quickly became apparent. Because the act was unclear about how the program would be administered, vague guidelines were set up for the administrators charged with bringing the various industries and labor groups together. Lacking standard operating procedures and legal mandates, deals on codes were often shaped by dominant industries and personalities. These same industries governed their own codes, requiring scores of government auditors and enforcement personnel. By June 1934, out of four hundred codes examined, only 11% contained provisions for handling complaints (Lyon et al., 1935, p. 454). Codes were routinely violated and ignored by industry, with little threat of discovery or punishment.

Particularly vexing was the shortage of an administrative cadre that had yet to be trained to assist business with self-regulation and the monitoring of compliance (Skocpol and Finegold, 1982, pp. 266–268) [4]. In August 1933, the NRA had a staff of just four hundred people to manage the codes and enforce the thousands of pages of regulatory language they contained (Lyon et al., 1935, pp. 29, 30). Administrators were also not always honest brokers, as many were trained by business itself; few represented the interests of labor or of the consumer. Later, when NRA administrators became more experienced, conflict emerged between businesses and the regulators, who by that time were acting more impartially by representing a wider set of interests. These administrative staffers, however, did not have Roosevelt's clout; hence when disputes arose the industries were hesitant to follow the dictates of deputies who represented the NRA [5].

Key supporters of the NRA, including the American Federation of Labor and leftist planners like Beard and Tugwell, were dissatisfied with the agency. Increasing wages, not fixed prices, they believed, was the linchpin to economic recovery. Despite complaints to NRA officials about high prices, businesses kept them up, thereby preventing any appreciable rise in consumers' purchasing power. As head of the Special Industrial Recovery Board, Tugwell had urged Johnson to force lower prices so that the purchasing power of workers would increase and thus fuel expansion. Johnson did not budge, however, concluding that the root of the problem lay in low wages rather than high prices. Consumers, represented by the head of the Consumer Advisory Board, also were unhappy. The board continually inveighed against high pricing practices, but they too found Johnson an unreceptive ear.

While the economy did grow modestly between 1933 and 1935, few attribute much of the improvement to the NRA. Economists have explained the failures of the NRA to stimulate demand by the high prices allowed for by the codes. Lofty prices overwhelmed any increase in wages provided for by the labor sections in the agreement, and thus workers (at the same time consumers) were unable to increase their demand for goods. Also responsible for the NRA's failure was inadequate implementation of Title II of the NIRA, which provided for the administration of public works. Managed by Harold Ickes, the Public Works Administration proved slow in releasing the $3 billion authorized under the act. A more aggressive expenditure of capital would have employed more idle workers and stimulated greater demand for capital goods in heavy industry.

The *Schechter* decision, handed down by the Supreme Court on May 27, 1935, declared that Title I of the NIRA unconstitutionally regulated interstate commerce [6]. By this time, the NRA was in administrative disarray and faced an uphill battle to have its two-year authorization renewed. The NRA codes did not promote cooperation as they had originally been intended to do. Instead, the codes worsened natural tensions among the different sectors of the economy, all of whom were represented in the administration by separate spokesmen. These pluralistic battles falsely suggested that the problem with the NRA was political when, in fact, it was economic. Without a strong coalition of interests advocating its reauthorization, no attempt was made to circumvent the *Schechter* decision so that its operations could be continued in another form. This is not surprising since as Anthony Downs suggests in his work, if a young agency loses the support of its clientele, as the NRA did with business through its later tendency to play the role of honest broker, it makes itself particularly vulnerable to termination (Downs, 1967, p. 10). Save for wartime, the NRA represented the government's last attempt at planning industrial production through a centrally directed, top-down bureaucratic apparatus.

III. THE NATIONAL RESOURCES PLANNING BOARD

Whereas the NRA was Roosevelt's device to get the nation out of a short-term industrial crisis, the functions of the various planning agencies were directed toward heading off long-term threats to the economy. While the NRA was directly designed to augment FDR's authority, the NPRB was created to increase the effectiveness of already existing presidential authority. Harold Ickes, who in the summer of 1933 was administrator of Public Works, issued an order establishing the National Planning Board (NPB) as an advisory panel for his agency. Later, extolling the virtues of planning, the NPB recommended that a permanent planning board be created as a cabinet-level committee, with its director reporting to the president. Thus, the National Resources Board (NRB) was instituted in 1934. Serving on the NRB were the secretaries of the Departments of Interior (Chair), War, Agriculture, Commerce, and Labor, together with the Federal Emergency Relief Administrator and three presidentially appointed members. The name changed again after the NRB's statutory authority was invalidated along with that of the NRA in the *Schechter* decision. The Emergency Relief Appropriation Act of 1935 provided the statutory basis for the new National Resources Committee (NRC). On the basis of the subsequent recommendations of the Brownlow Commission, planning was institutionalized (albeit briefly) as part of the Executive Office of the President on July 1, 1939, and the NRC officially became the NRPB [7].

Distinct from the NRA's grandiose scheme for a private-public partnership to direct the economy, the objective of FDR's planning agencies was to use the nation's public resources as a means to stimulate the economy. Government already constructed projects, bought goods from suppliers, leased public lands, and otherwise influenced the market. The new goal was to make those decisions comprehensively, in such a way as to provide the maximum benefit to the economy. The president lacked a staff based in the White House to help him centrally manage the administrative agencies and make long-range plans for the future. Designed to give the administration a neutrally competent managerial work force, the NRPB was removed from the values and norms of departmental agencies. The mission was akin to the more familiar Bureau of the Budget (BOB), which centralized year-to-year budget decisions. Originally housed in the Treasury Department, the BOB—like the NRPB—was moved to the Executive Office of the President (EOP), following the recommendations of the Brownlow Commission.

Throughout the ten-year history of Roosevelt's planning agencies, the permanent staffs remained small. The numbered between 5 at the inception of the National Planning Board to a total of 154 when the operations of the NRPB ceased in 1943 (Clawson, 1981, p. 77). Each of the agencies relied largely on temporary employees, outside consultants, and work details from other government agencies. The NRPB, and its predecessors, were catalysts in bringing government talent together to study or to coordinate policy in a given area. For example, in its report on consumer income and spending behavior, the NRC utilized its own staff, along with representatives from the Bureau of Labor Statistics, Treasury, and Agriculture. The study itself was funded by the Works Progress Administration (Clawson, 1981, p. 149). The idea was for the agencies to tap into the existing personnel and expertise available. Not only was this more cost-effective, but it also fostered a sense of cooperation across the federal agencies and down to regional, state, and local governments. Today, this type of arrangement, albeit in a more ad hoc form, is reflected in the operation of cabinet-level committees that promote interagency cooperation on issues such as the environment.

When Roosevelt first came into office, there was no routine information available that gave him an indication about the economy's performance. If a president was to intervene effectively and rationally in the economy, he needed to have some idea about the distribution of income and the spending patterns of the public. The NRC collected this information, as well as data about the composition and distribution of the industrial and agricultural work forces. In addition, established within the NRC was the Fiscal and Monetary Advisory Board, which was shifted to the Department of Treasury in 1939. Armed with more information, FDR would know better what areas of the economy needed stimulus, where employment needed to be generated, and how public works spending should be timed. This "economic adviser" function represents one of the few areas of operation created during the New Deal that was emulated by subsequent administrations. The Council of Economic Advisers, created by President Truman in 1946, still provides this expertise.

Establishing better criteria for public works spending and developing inventories of the nation's natural resources were two impetuses behind the formation of FDR's planning agencies and remained an area of their concern through their existence. Too often, Roosevelt felt, decisions on how and where to spend public works money were made without substantial concern for their effects on the general state of the economy. To maximize the benefits, the NRC recommended that more utilitarian criteria be used in decision making (to create expenditures that would maximize benefits to the most people). They suggested that the flow of money should increase during times of poor economic performance and decrease when the economy was prosperous. The NRC report argued that the national government could use grant-in-aid money as a device to encourage state and local governments to withhold projects until an economic slump made infusions of money necessary and most effective.

Later reports by the NRPB went beyond natural resource and public works planning to include social policy. In this latter capacity, the NRPB provided the outlines of a postwar Keynesian economic strategy. Its 1942 report, *After the War—Full Employment*, recommended that the government step in at the first sign of an economic slowdown and pump large amounts of money into the economy, even if a public debt was required for financing. Another example of this work in the social policy arena was a series of recommendations produced by the interagency Committee on Long-Range Work and Relief Planning entitled *Security, Work and Relief Policies*. Among the committee's recommendations were proposals for a government guarantee of employment if work was unavailable in the private sector and a system of social insurance. These objectives, precursors to the modern "safety net," became a legacy of the New Deal and part of the postwar liberal agenda of the Democratic party. They also were part of an economic philosophy holding that without certain necessary services, society could not maintain enough consumer demand to keep the nation prosperous. Some of the most heated criticism of the NRPB came over these reports, which some proclaimed bordered on socialism. Ideology aside, in this capacity the NRPB was acting as a developer of ideas, and as a policy planner at a more general level, a task impractical and inconceivable in any single departmental agency.

In analyzing the activities of Roosevelt's planning agencies it is difficult, if not impossible, to measure the influence they wielded within the government. The fact that the federal government *did* move into the areas of public policy mentioned in the reports, however, means either that they had some impact or that the NRPB's analysts were unusually prescient in their recommendations. By all accounts the agencies performed well in policy development areas [8]. Their reports generally provided good quality information to the president that he was unlikely to receive from other sources. The coordinating role of the NRPB appears at first glance to be less successful. Recommendations to bring order to the allocation of public works were no doubt thwarted by client-style politics, in the case of public works through such groups as the Rivers and Harbors Congress and the Army Corps of Engineers. In other areas, too, such as wartime planning, the NRPB detailed problems and proposed viable solutions, only to see its recommendations ignored. Sometimes the suggestions collided with political forces; other times their voices were just too small to be heard among the cacophony of voices and directives issued by other federal agencies.

Labeling FDR's planning agencies a failure, however, would be unjust given the brief period they were tried and the complexity of their operations. History has shown that without significance presidential backing, no agency is capable of overcoming the turf battles and conflict built into an administrative apparatus that contains a multitude of agencies with overlapping jurisdictions. These disputes are inherently political, not just administrative, requiring resolution at the highest level. No single planning agency can triumph over departmental agencies backed by members of Congress and interest groups without possessing clear presidential support. The very vested interests that weakened Roosevelt's planning agencies, however, remain the justification for a source of independent advice within the White House. Roosevelt, in fact, wanted administrators to compete with each other and viewed the planning agencies as unique sources of information from which he could draw economic information, long-range policy planners, and evaluators of public programs.

Congress disliked the NRPB so much that by the time of the 1944 budget debate, there was little opposition raised against terminating it. Many members of Congress opposed its forays into social planning and interference in what they saw as congressional prerogatives on allocating public works monies. Others claimed that the NRPB merely duplicated the work of other departmental agencies. With a relatively small staff, many of whom were detailed from other agencies, the NRPB lacked the strong, identifiable institutional interest that has characterized other agencies in the history of public administration (Downs, 1967, pp. 21–23). This fact, together with Roosevelt's preoccupation with the war effort, contributed to the agency's demise.

IV. THE OFFICE OF WAR MOBILIZATION

The enormity of the war effort precipitated another effort to establish a central planning source to assist the president that would be removed from existing bureaucracies. In the case of creating the Office of War Mobilization, the objective was to have a White House office manage the array of administrative bodies with control over the domestic war front. Executive Order 9347, issued on May 27, 1943, spelled out the sweeping mandate of the new agency:

> To develop unified programs and to establish policies for the maximum use of the nation's natural and industrial resources for military and civilian needs . . . ;
>
> To unify the activities of Federal agencies and departments [related to the war effort] . . . except those to be resolved by the Director of Economic Stabilization . . . ; and
>
> To issue such directives on policy of operations to the Federal agencies and departments as may be necessary to carry out the programs developed.

The OWM was not merely a source of ideas or an agency to bring together parties for discussions: it would be the locus of administrative decision making in matters of war policy. This was a sweeping consolidation of power in a White House office, but one supported by Congress, which for many years had pressed for just such a body. To advise and consult with the director of the OWM, a War Mobilization Committee was put together consisting of the secretaries of War and Navy, the chairmen of the Munitions Assignment Board, and the War Production Board, and the director of the Office of Economic Stabilization. The first director of the OWM delegated daily control over domestic policy was James Byrnes, who, in an extraordinary move, stepped down from the U.S. Supreme Court to become what many dubbed the "Assistant President" [9].

Prior to establishment of the OWM, Roosevelt's domestic wartime administrative apparatus went through a series of design and functional changes. Before the United States entered the war, Roosevelt relied on several advisory bodies, most prominently the National Defense Advisory Commission (NDAC). Split into seven divisions—industrial production, industrial materials, employment, farm products, transportation, price stabilization, and consumer protection—the NDAC's structure presaged the design of later wartime agencies, dividing interests into separate divisions. In typical Roosevelt fashion there was no chair of the commission, encouraging conflict-ridden issues to percolate up the chain of command.

In fall 1940, as U.S. entry into the European conflict seemed increasingly inevitable, Congress began pressing Roosevelt to consolidate decision making in a single powerful domestic agency. FDR continued to resist, preferring that various executive agencies battle it out over questions of policy. This diffused decision making strategy, consistent with the recommendations of some administrative theorists who criticize the hierarchical model, helped to assure that Roosevelt would retain ultimate authority over policy (Redford, 1969, pp. 70–82). Such a strategy is very time-intensive, however, sometimes leading to inadequate attention to the preparation for war. Even at this point, the president's time was stretched and increasingly dedicated to foreign affairs. Nevertheless until 1943, a number of wartime agencies were devised, each with only partial control over policy, meaning that conflicts continued to be waged between labor and management, consumers and business, and civilians and the military [10].

The War Production Board (WPB), the predecessor of the OWM that ran the war effort from January 1942 to July 1943, experienced a number of administrative problems that directly led to the more streamlined OWM design. Among the WPB's difficulties were an unwieldy large staff of eighteen thousand employees; the delegation of powers away from the WPB by its chairman, Donald Nelson; separate control by the military over procurement decisions; and the fact that the agency had operational and planning responsibilities, coordinating other agencies while itself possessing control over production decisions. This latter problem caused the WPB to be seen as a competitor by other agencies and not simply as a coordinator. As a result, decisions were challenged and the president, in turn, was forced to make many of them himself. Considering Roosevelt's multiple responsibilities, the situation was intolerable.

In contrast to Nelson, Byrnes at the OWM moved quickly to assert his authority. One of his first actions upon assuming office was to write to the heads of the procurement agencies of the Army and Navy, informing them that he had every intention of reviewing all of their programs and policies. Byrnes established procurement review boards consisting of civilian and military personnel, with an OWM representative on each board to direct any problems back to him. When the Navy initially proved reluctant to go along with the OWM directive, instead relying on their special connection to Roosevelt (formerly a Navy assistant secretary), Byrnes contacted the president complaining of the Navy's obstinacy. Although there is no record that Roosevelt forced the Navy to comply, the Byrnes message apparently was heeded. Two months later, the Navy reported that a reappraisal of Navy procurement programs had saved the government $2 billion (Somers, 1950, pp. 121, 122).

The issue of manpower provides an example of the OWM effectively acting as a coordinator of domestic policy. During Nelson's tenure, the WPB had delegated policies relating to manpower to the War Manpower Commission (WMC). From the beginning, the WPB and the WMC clashed over the allocation of labor to the nation's industries, all of which were complaining of shortages. Each agency devised its own recommendations, but neither was able to compel the other to comply. Accordingly, Byrnes used Bernard Baruch and his deputy John Hancock as mediators in the interagency dispute, and they devised a plan clarifying the jurisdictions of the agencies. As the Bureau of the Budget concluded a short time later, the OWM plan provided the impetus for the agencies to bring production schedules in line with the availability of labor (Somers, 1950, p. 153).

Another example of OWM's adjudicative role arise in response to a dispute waged between the Office of War Information (OWI) and the Army. The OWI claimed that the Army was withholding photographs that detailed some of the war's more graphic aspects. Byrnes wrote to the Army reiterating that OWI's mission was necessary to maintain support for wartime sacrifices. The Army subsequently complied with the director's request and released the photos (Somers, 1950, p. 61). Unlike the NRPB, Congress showed its support for the OWM and the methods of Byrnes by reauthorizing the activities of the OWM on a statutory basis and renaming it the Office of War Mobilization and Reconversion (OWMR). The additional duties granted by Congress to OWMR consisted of contract termination, disposition of surplus property, human demobilization, and relaxation of wartime controls. Congressional willingness to delegate power was traceable to its concern over reconversion, founded on the memory of the problems with demobilization that had followed World War I, and the review of wartime operations by the Truman Committee.

The exigencies of reconversion added to the burden of OWM's responsibilities. A greater range and scope of issues also stimulated more planning and involvement with the operations of other agencies. To handle the extra work, the OWMR increased its staff size and its degree of specialization by hiring statisticians and economists. It still operated predominantly as a coordinator, reviewing the work of other agencies and making use of interagency committees to foster cooperation among the agencies involved with operations. With its wider mandate the OWMR did stimulate greater conflict with other agencies, but it was an important factor in the relatively smooth transition following the war. When its responsibilities were fulfilled, this superagency, which gave President Roosevelt (and later President Truman) a central coordinator and policymaker, was terminated in 1946.

The OWM(R) proved successful in fulfilling its role as a coordinator of domestic economic policy. One reason for its success was that Roosevelt had gained experience with what did not work, namely the WPB. Another was the national unity stimulated by the war effort. The most important factor, though, may have been the prestige of its first director, James Byrnes, who had served in all three branches of the federal government. Over the course of twenty-five years as a member of Congress from South Carolina, Byrnes had gained the confidence of both political parties and was known as a shrewd and diplomatic politician, skilled in winning over critical legislative votes for Roosevelt. Signaling the degree of influence Byrnes commanded, Roosevelt provided him with an office in the East Wing of the White House, giving him direct access to the Oval Office.

Like Roosevelt, Byrnes had learned from the failings of Nelson and the WPB. Unlike the large and unwieldy bureaucracy Nelson faced, the OWM was deliberately kept small by Byrnes. After a year of operations the staff numbered only 10; even after the increase in duties assigned to the OWMR, the agency never numbered more than 146 (Somers, 1950, p. 83). The small staff ensured that the agency could not be involved in low-level administrative squabbling and contributed to its eventual demise since there was not a powerful institutional interest clamoring for its continuation and/or redefinition of function (Downs, 1967, pp. 21–23). The OWMR simply did not have the resources to intervene, serving to maintain the position of Byrnes as the final arbiter on matters of policy. Had he chosen to become entangled in operational decisions, other agency heads would have been encouraged to go to Roosevelt for a final decision. Lastly, having a small staff and limiting the scope of the agency's function guaranteed that Byrnes would be the one making final decisions, rather than a subordinate who did not have the credibility or the power to instruct the directors of other agencies.

Despite his prestige and the favorable administrative design set up for Byrnes, all of these advantages would have been for naught had he decided to delegate authority as Nelson had or to let other agencies, such as the Navy, assert control over OWM policy granted by executive order. By intervening immediately, and by remaining detached from operational matters, Byrnes solidified the role of the OWM as a "Court of Appeals" and retained his reputation as the Assistant President.

V. THE LEGACY OF THE AGENCIES

The experience of the NRA has soured prospects for a planning agency charged with directing almost the entirety of the American manufacturing sector. Roosevelt and his successors learned from this failed attempt at micromanaging the economy, instead deferring by and large to the private markets and to the "invisible hand." Governmental responsibility, of course, has not ceased. Presidents have increasingly relied upon macroeconomic policies such as fiscal and monetary policy. While the control of the latter is indirect and inexact, presidents (with the cooperation of the Congress) have used the former strategy consistently, running budget deficits to pump-prime the economy. When dealing with specific industries, Congress and presidents have deliberately delegated their authority to regulatory agencies and independent agencies and commissions. None of these, however, has the wide scope of control over different industries the NRA had.

The NRPB, and its predecessors, had a more limited and a longer-term role to play than did the NRA and OWM. Their purposes were geared more toward planning for the future. To their credit, these agencies provided economic statistics and data to FDR; they produced reports that inventoried our natural resources for the first time; they formulated and elaborated on what would become the dominant postwar economic philosophy; and they stimulated planning that would later prove beneficial to promoting orderly growth in state and local communities. Perhaps most importantly, the NRPB provided President Roosevelt with a special body, separated from the departmental agencies, within the White House whose energies were directed toward long-term policy development and to facilitation of cooperation among the departmental agencies [11]. Since the termination of NRPB's operations in 1943, presidents have lacked such an asset primarily because they have little incentive to focus on policy development and evaluation that may be most relevant several years down the line. But such continuity between administrations, provided by such an agency, may have headed off some of the failures of government policy in the postwar period.

Roosevelt used the OWM for an altogether different purpose than he did the NRPB, namely to disengage himself from the bureaucratic morass necessary to mobilize the nation for World War II. Like the NRA, the agency had a wide mandate, but, with few exceptions, it was not involved in daily operational decisions. It took a series of trials and errors before FDR came up with the optimal organizational structure and the best-suited director. Only a body like the OWM, which maintained a strict coordinating role, could act with the authority necessary to arbitrate disputes among the multitude of domestic agencies. The fortune of the OWM(R) seems to parallel the war effort; when the war was over, Truman again decided it was the responsibility of the president to manage the federal bureaucracy. Had the OWM(R) been retained as a White

House agency, it is possible that presidents today would be more removed from the daily operation of a bureaucracy they seem less able to control [12]. Whether or not presidents would have provided the unambiguous support Byrnes and OWM received, however, remains a very open question.

Since the time of the OWM(R) and the NRPB, presidents have utilized more ad hoc arrangements for influencing economic decisions by the bureaucracy: no agency or office, with the limited exception of the OMB, is charged with bringing together what the lines of administrative jurisdiction separate. The closest parallel, perhaps, is the National Security Council, created in 1947 to unify advice to the president on issues related to the nation's security.

The three agencies discussed in this chapter (the NRA, the NRPB, and the OWM) all had distinct functions. What all had in common was their intent, and sometimes their ability, to provide Roosevelt with the means for responding to different economic challenges and crises. Their legacies not only are lessons in understanding presidential leadership and public administration, but also offer opportunities to future reformers of the American presidency and bureaucracy.

NOTES

1. The government did have more experience in planning agricultural policy, which was reflected in the greater success of the Agricultural Adjustment Administration. Planning was also incorporated into the Tennessee Valley Authority, an experiment in regional planning and development.
2. For specific information regarding the NRPB's responsibilities see Executive Order 8248, promulgated September 8, 1939.
3. For an interpretation of these three agencies as experiments in government planning see Graham, *Toward a Planned Society*.
4. The authors point out that the Agricultural Adjustment Act (AAA), designed as that industry's counterpart for recovery, had the benefit of an experienced crop of administrators from the Department of Agriculture and its connection with the land grant colleges that helped to develop consistent guidelines. These experienced personnel were in a better position to resist the demands of client groups.
5. Roosevelt was made aware of these problems through his National Emergency Council (NEC). The NEC's purpose, similar to that of the NRPB and the OWM in later years, was to provide the president with a channel of input independent of NRA's bureaucracy. Although it tried to coordinate work of departmental agencies like the OWM, the NEC did not have the consistent presidential support necessary and quickly fell into disuse. For more on the work of the NEC see Seligman and Cornwell, *New Deal Mosaic*.
6. *A.L.A. Schechter Poultry Corp. v. U.S.* 295, U.S. 495.
7. Excellent descriptions of the planning agencies' activities are found in Philip W. Warken, *A History of the National Resources Planning Board 1933–1943* and Marion Clawson, *New Deal Planning*.
8. For a summary of the various evaluations see Clawson, *New Deal Planning*, especially pp. 255–263.
9. The best history of the OWM and its successor the Office of War Mobilization and Reconversion is Herman Somers, *Presidential Agency OWMR*.
10. Among the most important of these agencies were the Office of Production Management, the Supply Priorities and Allocations Board, and the War Production Board, created January 1941, August 1941, and January 1942, respectively.

11. For a description of the usefulness of a NPRB-type body, see Charles Merriam, "The National Resources Planning Board."
12. For an argument that the responsibilities of a president are inconsistent with the public expectations and abilities of the office, see James S. Young, "The Troubled Presidency."

REFERENCES

Beard, Charles A., ed., *America Faces the Future*, Houghton Mifflin, Boston, 1932.

Byrnes, James F., *All In One Lifetime*, Harper & Brothers, New York, 1958.

Campagna, Anthony, *U.S. National Economic Policy 1917–1985*, Praeger, New York, 1987.

Clawson, Marion, *New Deal Planning*, The Johns Hopkins University Press, Baltimore, 1981.

Downs, Anthony, *Inside Bureaucracy*, Little, Brown, Boston, 1967.

Graham, Otto L., *Toward a Planned Society*, Oxford University Press, New York, 1976.

Gulick, Luther, War Organization of the Federal Government, *American Political Science Review 40*: 1166–1179 (1944).

Hawley, Ellis W., *The New Deal and the Problem of Monopoly*, Princeton University Press, Princeton, N.J., 1966.

Hoover, Herbert S., *Public Papers of the Presidents of the United States*, Government Printing Office, Washington, D.C., 1976.

Lyon, Leverett et al., *The National Recovery Administration*, The Brookings Institution, Washington, D.C., 1935.

Merriam, Charles E., The National Resources Planning Board, *Public Administration Review 1*:116–121 (1941).

Redford, Emmette S., *Democracy in the Administrative State*, Oxford University Press, New York, 1969.

Roos, Charles F., *NRA Economic Planning*, Principia, Bloomington, Ind., 1937.

Schlesinger, Arthur M. Jr., *The Coming of the New Deal*, Houghton Mifflin, Boston, 1959.

Seligman, Lester G. and Cornwell, Elmer E. Jr., *New Deal Mosaic*, University of Oregon Press, Eugene, 1965.

Skocpol, Theda and Finegold, Kenneth, State Capacity and Economic Intervention in the Early New Deal, *Political Science Quarterly 97*:255–278 (1982).

Somers, Herman Miles, *Presidential Agency OWMR*, Harvard University Press, Cambridge, Mass., 1950.

Stein, Herbert, *Presidential Economics*, Simon and Shuster, New York, 1984.

Warken, Philip W., *A History of the National Resources Planning Board, 1933–1943*, Garland, New York, 1969.

Young, James Sterling, The Troubled Presidency, *New York Times* December 7, p. 23 (1978).

27
Supreme Court Articulation of the Politics/Administration Dichotomy

David A. Schultz
Trinity University, San Antonio, Texas

To the victor belong only those spoils that may be constitutionally obtained.
—Justice Brennan, *Rutan v. Republican Party of Illinois* 110 S.Ct. 2729 (1990)

I. INTRODUCTION

In 1990 the Supreme Court held in *Rutan v. Republican Party of Illinois* 110 S.Ct. 2729 (1990) that the state of Illinois could not consider political affiliation when hiring, transferring, or promoting individuals because such a consideration violated the First Amendment rights of individuals applying for government employment [1]. *Rutan* was not an aberration or an isolated judicial attack on spoils; instead it represented a continuation and extension of a series of patronage decisions over the last twenty years in which the Court has attempted to place limits upon the ability of governmental units to employ the spoils system in the staffing of the bureaucracy [2]. In addition to these patronage cases, since 1947, the Court has ruled in two cases that congressional legislation (i.e., the Hatch Act) aimed at limiting the political activity of federal employees was reasonable and not a violation of their First Amendment rights [3].

When the patronage and Hatch Acts cases are examined together the Court might appear inconsistent, in that the Court is saying in the patronage cases that the First Amendment protects federal workers against politics when hiring, while in the Hatch Acts cases the First Amendment does not protect their right to engage in certain types of political activity that might affect their job performance. What will be argued is that these Supreme Court decisions are not as contradictory as they seem. Instead, the decisions are guided by a "neutral competence" ideology or rhetoric seeking to separate the politics of governing from the neutral functions of administrative behavior. This politics/administration dichotomy, or neutral competence ideology as it came to be called in the Progressive Era, was labeled as a major reform of government that would place limits upon political corruption, the spoils system, and the abuses of patronage found in the Boss Tweed era.

The claim is that neither the Hatch Acts nor patronage cases are novel or recent attempts by the Court to regulate the political action of the bureaucracy. Instead, they represent the Court's generally overlooked attempt to enforce neutral competence, and this enforcement dates back to the Progressive Era. In effect, the Court has been crucial in the (re)enforcement of this ideology, and particular justices have appealed to this ideology in rendering decisions over the last 100 years.

The first section of this chapter will outline the history and main tenets of neutral competence ideology. Next will be a discussion of the Court's pre–Hatch Acts enforcement of neutral competence where it dealt with the role of money and political assessments in the maintenance of the spoils system. The third part addresses the Hatch Acts adjudication, while the fourth and fifth sections examine the patronage cases that commenced in the 1970s.

The final section will be a prediction of future trends in judicial enforcement of the politics/administration dichotomy. The claim will be that while up to now the Court has been an important articulator of neutral competence ideology, this support has been mixed. Moreover, given recent shifts in Court personnel, there are signs that several current justices are less than supportive of this ideology and would perhaps be willing to relax recent patronage employment bans.

II. THE SOURCES OF THE NEUTRAL COMPETENCE IDEOLOGY

The ideological impetus for neutral competence can be traced to the late nineteenth century civil service reform movements that were directed at rooting out the corruption and spoils that had emerged in Andrew Jackson's time and which fully blossomed during Lincoln's and Grant's administrations. Political patronage and spoils, which during the Jacksonian era were heralded as a reform movement to improve political accountability, strengthen political parties, and improve the representative quality of the federal bureaucracy, had by the 1850s become viewed as corrupt practices that undermined the moral integrity of the government. Thus, starting as early as the 1840s, some in Congress sought to establish competitive examinations for some positions, and by 1856 there were demands for a professionalized civil service (Hoogenboom, 1961). After the Civil War, Congress, and especially Representative Thomas Jenckes from Rhode Island, began pushing for civil service exams and other reforms. While claims that spoils were inefficient were articulated, the primary focus of these early reformers was moralistic and aimed at the purification of federal employment, which was tainted by politics (Maranto and Schultz, 1991).

The first serious movement toward reform of spoils came in 1871 when Congress issues a joint resolution authorizing President Grant to create a Civil Service Commission (CSC) (Maranto and Schultz, 1991). This commission classified some positions, issued guidelines for competitive examinations, and also recommended a ban on political assessments (the practice in which employees paid yearly fees in return for continued federal employment). Unfortunately, the commission died in 1873 for lack of funding. However, the Grant Commission had created many regulations and terminology that would eventually become the basis for the 1883 Pendleton Act, which was the first major federal civil service reform act (Maranto and Schultz, 1991).

Further action toward the reform of the civil service took place throughout the 1870s. In 1873, for example, Grant issued an executive order forbidding civil servants from holding state or local offices (Rosenbloom, 1971). Although the order did not preclude campaigning, it did place some limits upon the individual's own political career. In 1877 President Hayes issued an order limiting the political activities of federal employees by banning their involvement in the management of political organizations, caucuses, conventions, and elections, although their right to vote or speak out on issues was not affected (Rosenbloom, 1971). This order, while laudable, was not enforced vigorously.

The 1883 Pendleton Act represented a first, small triumph over spoils and the articulation of the position that political control of administration did not further democratic ideals but instead threatened the neutral administration of justice, the moral integrity of government, and the efficiency of administration. Three years subsequent to its adoption, President Cleveland strengthened earlier efforts toward political neutrality by issuing an order that reiterated the ban on political activity by federal employees (Rosenbloom, 1971).

After the Pendleton Act's passage the civil service reform movement underwent several important changes. First, passage of the act was not a complete remedy for all the social and political ills facing the federal government. There were still other problems, and the Pendleton Act could not address them because the act covered only a very small percentage of the positions in the federal government (entry level and clerical positions in urban centers and where customhouses were located). Also, the reform spirit somewhat lapsed on the federal level after 1883 and some hostility against the act developed in Congress, leading to unsuccessful efforts to repeal it.

However, neither did the desire for reform die nor did the demand to take politics out of administration subside. George William Curtis, an important civil service reformer, indicated that the aim of his movement was "to take the whole non-political public service out of politics" (Rosenbloom, 1971). Indeed reformers at this time believed that the only way to eliminate spoils was to depoliticize the civil service. Hence, the reform movement changed in a couple of important ways. First, starting in the late 1890s and into the early twentieth century, there was a new focus to reform. Partly as a result of the Populist movement, reformers became preoccupied with efforts to reconcile the operation of the federal bureaucracy with the basic political values of Madisonian democracy and popular government. Reformers asked how a politically neutral merit system and a tenured civil service could operate within a political system that respected representative democracy and the public accountability of public officeholders through competitive elections. One solution to this problem would be to try to distinguish politics from administration and push the goal of neutral competence.

A second chance that would preoccupy reformers developed in the early twentieth century. While early reformers stressed rooting out moral corruption as the impetus for reform, the Progressives became increasingly more concerned with efficiency and economy as goals of bureaucratic reform. During the early twentieth century, the federal government sought to professionalize the civil service and adopt many business practices to improve the efficiency and organization of the bureaucracy. Early civil service reformers, thus, were united by the need to take corruption out of administration, but few gave much thought to how to reconcile the power of an unelected civil service with the larger political goals of American democracy that placed, at least in theory, the primary responsibility for making policy in the hands of electorally accountable policy-making officials such as Congress and the President.

The experiences of foreign regimes offered later nineteenth and early twentieth century Americans a model for civil service reform. Woodrow Wilson, writing in his 1885 "Notes on Administration," argued that "the task of developing a science of administration for America should be approached with a larger observance of the *utilities* [Wilson's emphasis] than is to be found in the German or French treatment of the subject" (Wilson, 1968b, p. 49). In this essay Wilson stated for the first time that "*administration* should be subservient to the *politics*" (Wilson's emphasis), a distinction that he would make more forcefully in his now famous 1887 essay "The Study of Administration" (Wilson, 1968a, p. 359).

The aim of Wilson's essay was to advocate a science of public administration and to delineate a distinction between politics and administration. According to Wilson, a science of administration would make government more businesslike and purify its organization [4]. Administration is a field of business that is removed from the "hurry and strife of politics" (Wilson, 1968a, p. 370). Administrative questions, for Wilson, are distinct from political questions because while political questions are policy questions, public administration is simply the "detailed and systematic execution of public law" (Wilson, 1968a, p. 372). Overall, in borrowing from Biuntschli and other German writers, Woodrow Wilson argued that administration was the detailed execution of general government policies and "lies outside the proper sphere of politics." Policies should be set by elected leaders and their appointees. Administration is the province of politically neutral, permanent officials selected for their expertise.

Wilson's distinction implied the need for bureaucratic efficiency and the existence of general principles of administration that were applicable in both liberal and authoritarian political systems. These management principles sought to drive a wedge between the bureaucratic power and that of elected officials and their appointees. Wilson stated, "If I see a monarchist dyed in the wool managing a public bureau well, I can learn his business methods without changing one of my Republican spots" (Wilson, 1968a, p. 379).

Whereas Wilson's essay had little influence until decades after his death [5], Frank J. Goodnow's 1900 *Politics and Administration* was perhaps the most influential book upon early twentieth century administrative thinking (Stillman, 1991). It sought to clarify the various functions of the state, which he described as politics and administration. Politics is defined as the "expressions of the state will" while administration is the "execution of these policies" (Goodnow, 1967, p. 18). However, while these are distinct functions, there is a need for a harmony between the expression and execution of the law because a popular government must be able to control the execution of the law if its will is to be expressed. Yet, while politics should control administration, there is a limit to how much politics should penetrate into administration lest the latter become inefficient.

The spoils system had produced a coordination of politics and administration, yet the spoils had two glaring deficiencies. One, it led to the impairing of administrative efficiency. Two, and far more important for Goodnow, the spoils was a threat to popular government and competitive elections because it supported the ruling party and kept it in power. The spoils system, a consequence of strong political parties and a decentralized administrative system, was a threat to democracy because "the party in control of the government offices had made use of them not merely to influence the expression of the popular will, but to thwart it when once expressed" (Goodnow, 1967, p. 131).

While Goodnow did recognize the importance of political parties in a popular government and sought to strengthen them in America, he rejected party (political) control over administration as the best way to harmonize the expression and execution of the popular will. Goodnow rejected perhaps the hallmark Jacksonian defense of spoils that it sustained strong parties and democratic control of the bureaucracy. Moreover, Goodnow also repudiated earlier claims that open competitive exams would end this corruption because these exams were a small part of the reform movement. The solution to preventing administration (party control of offices) from thwarting the political will was to remove it from political and party control:

> That it (popular government) shall not be lost in our case, depends very largely on our ability to prevent politics from exercising too great an influence over administration, and

> the parties in control of administration form using it to influence improperly the expression of the public will. (Goodnow, 1967, pp. 131–132)

The best way to assert a new harmony between the expression and the execution of the laws would be by creating a hierarchial and centralized administration with the President at the head to direct the operations of the government. Such a centralized system with superiors overseeing subordinates would limit the discretion of the latter and, thus, prevent them from acting politically.

While this model of organization sought to subordinate administration to politics, this subordination did not mean that politics should control administration. Instead, Goodnow makes it clear that this type of control is inefficient. There is a certain area of administration, moreover, that should be insulated from politics. These areas include the administration of justice; technical and scientific information gathering; as well as purely administrative (personnel?) management issues (Goodnow, 1967, pp. 78–82). These functions should be performed by politically neutral, tenured, and competent individuals who are to act in a semiscientific, quasi-judicial, and quasi-businesslike fashion (Goodnow, 1967, pp. 85, 87). Such efficient behavior would only be upset by politics.

Max Weber's writings on bureaucratic power in *Economy and Society* [6] were published after his death in 1920 and reiterated themes found in Wilson and Goodnow. Weber described the ideal type of bureaucracy as the technically most efficient type of organization for performing tasks (Weber, 1979, p. 214). In appealing to the language of efficiency, Weber argued that administrative organization, if it were to be efficient, must be hierarchically organized and staffed by technically competent experts enjoying life tenure. Moreover, civil servants would be subject to appointment by superiors, but these superiors would be removed from the direct supervision of the bureaucratic functions and tasks.

Central to the arguments of Wilson, Goodnow, and Weber, then, were that politics and patronage threatened the administrative efficiency of administration and that, in general, administrative and political questions were and should be distinct. The former should be addressed by technically competent civil servants insulated from politics. Thus, in these writings we see the emergence of a neutral competence ideology that stressed a politics/administration dichotomy in order to promote efficiency and limit the threats parties posed to popular government. The best way to augment the relationship between politics and government and to ensure that there was a coordination between the popular expression of the public will and its execution was through a centralized and hierarchial organization controlled from the top down. Weber, like Wilson and Goodnow, then, assumed the existence of a responsible political center or apex to the bureaucratic pyramid residing in elected officials.

In sum, articulation of a politics/administration dichotomy was meant to preserve political direction by elected policymakers while enhancing government integrity and expertise. Yet important parts of the crusade, particularly on the local level where most of the public sector existed, were a direct attack on political parties and the belief that the proper relationship among party, administration, and popular government was forged by the spoils system. Instead, the reformers believed that spoils damaged administrative efficiency and popular government and did little for the health of parties. Spoils, then, had to give way to the more important goals of technical expertise, administrative competence, and efficiency.

Overall, efforts to depoliticize the civil service and to distinguish between policy- and non-policy-making officials were grounded in attempts to reconcile bureaucratic power with the values of American representative democracy. Reforms sought to instill the value of neutral competency in the federal government as a check upon abuses of bureaucratic power that arose from party domination of the administration of government. Neutral competence ideology, along with the attendant coverage of the merit system to 90%-plus of the federal bureaucracy by World War II, did much to limit the political manipulation and activity of administration. However, the institution of the merit system alone was not enough; it only placed limits on some hiring decisions. It did little to prevent either the voluntary political activity of the workers themselves or the forced political activity of civil servants by their superiors. The Hatch Acts sought to address this problem.

The Hatch Acts were a series of laws passed in the late 1930s that placed numerous restrictions upon the political activities of government workers. While the previous reforms, such as the Pendleton Act, had supposedly done this, these new laws closed loopholes and extended the political ban well up the executive hierarchy (Van Riper, 1958, pp. 339–343). These laws, known as the Hatch Acts [7], effectively codified previous presidential orders by Cleveland, Hayes, and others, and they placed a ban upon certain political actions by civil servants. These acts were in many ways a Progressive Era reform that was inspired by the neutral competence ideology. They placed limits on the political activities of federal workers including bans upon running for office, campaigning for others, and raising or soliciting funds [8]. Violations of these prohibitions were to be penalized by the Civil Service Commission (CSC) through dismissal or other sanctions. The Hatch Acts, in their application to civil servants covered by the merit systems, precluded superior and perhaps policy-oriented political appointees from politically manipulating the administrative system. Effectively, the Hatch Acts, along with the merit system, aimed at creating a politically neutralized staff of workers who would be technically competent, efficient administrators.

III. PRE-HATCH ACT ENFORCEMENT OF NEUTRAL COMPETENCE: *CURTIS, WURZBACH,* AND FORCE POLITICAL CONTRIBUTIONS

The Supreme Court jumped on the bandwagon of civil service reform quickly, and even before the Pendleton Act was adopted several justices were articulating the language of neutral competence in their decisions. *Ex Parte Curtis* 106 U.S. 371 (1882) and *United States v. Wurzbach* 280 U.S. 397 (1929) represent the earliest decisions by the Supreme Court to enforce political neutrality and limits upon financial and campaign activity within the federal bureaucracy. Notable in both decisions, but especially in *Curtis*, is the appeal to a neutral competence logic that rejected spoils and party control of government. However, unlike in later cases where First Amendment issues were paramount, in neither of these cases were First Amendment claims crucial legal issues surrounding government restrictions upon political assessments and financial contributions.

At issue in *Curtis* was the constitutionality of an 1876 act that prohibited all members of the executive branch who had received Senate confirmation from "requesting, giving to, or receiving from, any other officer or employee of the government, any money or property or other thing of value for political purposes." Punishment was a misdemeanor and a fine not to exceed $500. Curtis was a federal employee who was convicted in district court of violation of this act for receiving money from employees. He appealed, contesting its constitutionality.

Chief Justice Waite wrote a majority decision that upheld the act. First, Waite argued that it was not a complete ban on the political solicitation of money for political purposes. He read it as only preventing federal employees from giving or receiving money from one another. The act left open the possibility that nonfederal employees or personnel could give money to individuals covered in this act. Specifically, the Court left in place most types of political assessments and other *legal* graft when it stated that the "managers of political campaigns, not in the employ of the United States, are just as free now to call on those in office for money to be used for political purposes as they ever were" (p. 373). For the Court the act simply prevented political superiors from demanding that subordinates unwillingly contribute.

The Court did not base its decision on the First Amendment rights of workers (as many of the later Hatch and patronage decisions would). Instead, the Court decided the case on the scope of the powers Congress had under Article I, Section 8 (the necessary and proper clause) and asked whether this act went beyond the bounds of proper legislative discretion. In holding that Congress did not exceed its discretion, the Court first cited a variety of laws and rules that had been adopted since 1789 that placed some limits on federal employees' accepting money for political purposes. Two main arguments were employed by the Court when inquiring into the legislative purpose of this act.

First, the Court held that its primary purpose was to promote the efficiency, integrity, and proper discipline of the federal service. Limits upon forced contributions freed workers from the fear of dismissal and thus promoted more efficient performance of duties. Second, the Court argued that a forced contribution system would serve to "furnish indirectly the money to defray the expenses of keeping the political party in power that happens to have for the time being the control of the public patronage" (p. 375). The Court, while noting the importance of political parties to republican government, also deferred to Congress and the contention that party control of the federal service was often dangerous to popular government when that control sought to prevent fair competition and when the party used the government to serve its own needs.

Note the language of the two main points of the Court's analysis of the act. One part of their decision was an appeal to the goals of administrative efficiency and political neutrality that the limits on contributions would serve, while the other was an appeal to the fear of party dominance of the government. Both claims in many ways echoed the rhetoric of the emerging neutral competence movement in their attack upon the spoils system and in damage spoils caused to a depoliticized administrative system.

Wurzbach was a 1929 decision that questioned the constitutionality of a 1925 Corrupt Practices Act that made it illegal for officers and employees of the United States to promote their candidacy or reelection in a party primary. Justice Holmes upheld the Act, contending that Congress could provide measures that would limit the political pressure that employees might face to contribute money if they were to retain employment. While Holmes's argument is brief, it also implicitly appeals to a neutral competence ideology in recognizing the need for a politically neutralized bureaucracy.

Wurzbach, in many ways, rested upon a logic similar to his opinion in *McAuliffe v. New Bedford* 155 Mass. 216 (1892), where Holmes had argued that public employees "may have a constitutional right to talk politics, but . . . no right to be a policeman." In making the distinction between a right and privilege to public office, Holmes contended that occupying a public office was no more than a privilege. Hence, certain rights, including those to engage in some political activities, may be curtailed in the interests of promoting reasonable control over government employees. The *McAuliffe* right/privilege distinction, as well as the dismissal of First Amendment rights in this decision and *Wurzbach*, served as a response to Bradley's dissent in *Curtis* and set the stage for the Court's future willingness to place limits upon the First Amendment rights of public workers in order to promote political neutrality.

Overall, these early decisions defined the terrain for future Court approaches to politics in the federal bureaucracy. There were appeals to the logic of efficiency, the fear of party dominance of the government, the need to insulate civil servants from political pressure if they were to perform their duties, and the claim that federal employment was merely a privilege such that First Amendment rights could be limited to the needs of administrative control. All these points were made by Wilson, Goodnow, and Weber, and they became important dicta in the rhetoric of neutral competence.

IV. THE HATCH ACT DECISIONS: LIMITS UPON EMPLOYEE POLITICAL ACTIVITY

Starting in 1939, Congress passed a variety of acts that sought to place limits upon the ability of the Roosevelt administration to use the federal bureaucracy for political/partisan purposes. The act, specifically Section 9, forbade employees and officers of the executive branch to take "any active part in political management or in political campaigns." Section 15 of the same act empowered the United States Civil Service Commission to enforce this act and to produce a list of activities that constitute an active part of the political management of a campaign. These activities were a codification of a variety of actions that had been listed in previous executive orders aimed at preventing persons in federal employment from interfering with elections or election results.

There have been two Supreme Court cases that challenged the political ban found in Section 9 of the Hatch Act. The first case, *United Public Workers v. Mitchell*, was decided in 1947; the other challenge, *United States Civil Service Commission v. National Association of Letter Carriers*, was decided in 1973. Both cases, in split decisions, upheld the Hatch Act.

United Public Workers grew out of a complaint by several members of a federal union who desired to engage in political activities including acting as poll watchers and serving as a ward chairman, a position with a variety of duties including distributing literature, organizing rallies, and hanging political banners. While much of the first part of *United Public Workers* addressed standing and jurisdiction issues that are not of concern here, the second half of the decision addresses the merits of the Hatch Act.

Justice Reed gave the opinion for the Court in a four-three decision. His opinion was jointed by Burton and Vinson, with Frankfurter offering a separate concurrence. Justices Black, Rutledge, and Douglas dissented. Reed opens up his opinion for the Court by addressing the First Amendment challenge that the act is an unconstitutional restriction on federal employees' free speech rights to engage in political activity. The Court confronts this claim head-on by stating that human rights are not absolutes and that "the interference with free expression is seen in better proportion as compared with the requirements of orderly management of administrative personnel" (p. 94). Several factors contribute to the need to limit the political activity of workers in order to promote good administrative management.

First, the Court notes how if political activity of federal workers hurts the civil service, its damage is no less than if the activity occurs after work hours. Second, the Court indicates how free speech rights have to be balanced against the need to protect a democratic society against the evils of political partisanship in the federal service (p. 96). Specifically, the Court, in citing public administration scholarship as authority [9], argues that there is a need to limit political activity in order to promote "political neutrality for public servants as a sound element for efficiency" (p. 97).

Elsewhere, the Court also notes how an "actively partisan governmental personnel threatens good administration" (p. 98), and that it would be absurd to think that Congress would not have the power to limit that political activity that is "offensive to efficiency" (p. 99). Finally, the Court stresses that party activity may hurt political neutrality and that, overall, partisan political activity is a threat to efficiency, political neutrality, and discipline (pp. 100–103).

Black's dissent, as well as the dissents by Douglas and Rutledge, significantly follows the arguments of the Court of Appeals, that held that the Hatch Act was overbroad in its scope and in its infringement of the First Amendment rights of workers. Black, for example, argues that the Hatch Act does not help promote clean democratic government but instead disenfranchises millions of individuals (pp. 111–113). However, Douglas takes on the supposed need to separate politics from administration in the federal service by arguing that perhaps it should be the higher levels of the administrative system and not the lower levels that ought to be politically neutralized (p. 112). His reason for that is that if partisan activity undermines the efficiency and confidence in the bureaucracy, then those who are most beholden to patronage (those in higher-level positions) should be limited in their activities. Yet even Douglas, despite his dissent, also cites public administration scholarship (p. 121, footnote 10) on the virtues of political neutrality. His real disagreement seems to lie not in the majority's appeal to efficiency and the evils of spoils but in the locus of the neutralization.

United Public Workers, while upholding the Hatch Acts, did so with only a four vote plurality. This margin left open the question of what a full Court would decide, and in 1973 a six-three decision did not support the Hatch Act's constitutionality [10].

United States Civil Service Commission v. National Association of Letter Carriers (Letter Carriers) was also a challenge to Section 9 of the Hatch Act. Here, six members of a union desired to campaign for candidates for public office. Part of their challenge to the act was to question the vagueness of section 9 that banned "political activity." The other part of their claim was to argue that decisions subsequent to *Mitchell* had eroded its holding such that the First Amendment rendered the ban on political activities as unconstitutional (pp. 553–554). The Court rejected all these claims. For our purposes, it is not necessary to examine all of the intricacies of the majority's decision. Instead, what should be noted is how *Letter Carriers*, like *Mitchell*, appealed to a neutral competence rhetoric to defend its arguments.

The majority rejected patronage and stated that "federal service should depend upon meritorious performance rather than political service, and that the political influence of federal employees on others and the electoral process should be limited" (p. 548). The basis of this claim rests in the majority's recounting the nineteenth century reforms directed against spoils and in their agreement that "partisan political activities by federal employees must be limited if the Government is to operate effectively and fairly" (p. 547). Political neutralization is a must if representative government is not to be eroded by the will of a party taking control of the government. Elsewhere in their decision, the Court also appeals to the language of efficiency and the needs of political neutrality for the good performance of administrative duties as other reasons why the Hatch provisions are reasonable restrictions upon the First Amendment rights of federal workers (p. 566).

In a brief dissent, Justice Douglas, Brennan, and Marshall make two arguments that would justify overturning the Hatch Act ban on political activity. First, the meaning of the act's restriction that no one shall take "an active part . . . in political campaigns" is so overbroad and vague that its lacks legal precision (p. 595). In noting that the Civil Service Commission's own rulings on this prohibition were voluminous, the dissent claims that it would lead to a chilling effect upon the exercise of free speech among federal employees. The second claim is that

Mitchell was no longer good law because that decision rested upon the logic that government employment was a privilege, not a right, and therefore employment could be conditioned upon the sacrifice of certain rights. Instead, the dissent noted recent decisions, specifically *Perry v. Sindermann* 408 U.S. 593, 597 (1972), that had eroded that right/privilege distinction. Limitation of one's First Amendment rights could not be a condition for federal employment especially if the requirements in the Hatch Act were not narrowly tailored and precise as to the activity prohibited.

The two Hatch Acts cases sought to neutralize the politics of the federal service by placing limits upon the political activity of federal workers. The Court's rationale in upholding these restrictions clearly appealed to the rhetoric of neutral competence, including the language of efficiency, the articulation of the evil effects of politics upon administration, and the need to limit party influence in government.

V. THE PATRONAGE DECISIONS: LIMITING PARTISAN HIRINGS

While the Hatch Acts decisions reinforced the politics/administration dichotomy by limiting the political activity of workers, two patronage decisions in 1976 and 1980 did the same by placing limits upon superiors in using political affiliation as a factor in hiring, firing, and promotion decisions. In these decisions the Court engaged in extensive debate concerning the merits of patronage with arguments over the supposed contributions of spoils to the maintenance of democracy, political parties, public accountability, and administrative control. These debates made significant reference to political science and public administration scholarship on these topics and, in addressing the merits of patronage, occurred within the rhetoric of the neutral competence.

Elrod v. Burns was a patronage hiring and dismissal controversy that grew out of the Daley machine in Chicago and Cook County, Illinois. In this case, several non-civil-service Republicans who were employees in the Sheriff's Office in Cook County were discharged (or threatened with dismissal) by the newly elected Democratic sheriff solely because they were Republicans. They filed suit in federal court, claiming that their First and Fourteenth Amendment rights had been violated. Specifically, they claimed that dismissal based upon party affiliation violated their right to free speech. The District Court dismissed their case for lack of demonstrable injury, the Court of Appeals reversed, and the latter decision was upheld by the Supreme Court in a five-three decision. Justice Brennan wrote the opinion for the Court, joined by Marshall and White. Stewart and Blackmun joined in a separate concurrence, with Powell, Rehnquist, and Burger in dissent.

Brennan begins his opinion by offering a history of the spoils system in America. In it he notes how the impetus for the Pendleton Act and civil service reform could be traced to the "corruption and inefficiency" of patronage employment (p. 354). Additionally, he notes how patronage is a threat to democracy and popular government because of the advantage it gives to one party in the electorial process:

> It is not only belief and association which are restricted where political patronage is the practice. The free functioning of the electoral process also suffers. Conditioning public employment on partisan support prevents support of competing political interests. . . . As government employment, state or federal, becomes more pervasive, the greater the dependence on it becomes, and therefore the greater becomes the power to starve political opposition by commanding partisan support, financial or otherwise. Patronage thus tips the electoral process in favor of the incumbent party, and where the practice's scope is substantial relative to the size of the electorate, the impact on the process can be significant. (p. 356)

According to Brennan, patronage hirings are a threat to the free speech rights of individuals. These free speech rights are crucial to the articulation of political discussion in America. Just as importantly, patronage hirings threaten democracy by damaging competitive elections and by making it easy for one party to manipulate government service to their unfair advantage.

Brennan's decision squarely confronted three traditional justifications given for spoils. One, patronage hiring practices have been defended as efficient because they create special incentives for employees to work, and they also make it easier for an employer and the public to control.

Brennan rejects this claim, arguing that constant replacement of workers after elections is hardly efficient, and there is also no indication that replacement workers will be more competent than the previous workers. Brennan also rejects the claim that patronage improves the public accountability of the federal service. He indicates that the elected officials, not civil servants, are the ones who are to be held accountable, and even if patronage does increase their public accountability, this gain in accountability is "at best marginal, a gain outweighed by the absence of intrusion on protected interests under the alternatives" (p. 366).

A second argument used to defend patronage is that it encourages the political loyalty of workers that is essential to the implementation of policies desired by the people who elected the government. In effect, the claim is that patronage is an important aspect of representative democracy and it ensures a linkage between the expression and the execution of the law. Brennan concedes this point in part, but says that patronage confined only to "policymaking officials" is needed to achieve this purpose. Individuals in non-policy-making positions have limited discretion and thus are in a limited position to obstruct the public will and implementation of laws.

Finally, a third defense of patronage is that it sustains political parties which are crucial to the democratic process. Brennan here indicates that while preserving parties and democracy is important, patronage is not the least restrictive way to serve this end. Brennan first notes how parties and the democratic process existed in America before the rise of patronage in the Jacksonian era. Second, echoing language reminiscent of Goodnow's, he again indicates how a party may use patronage to entrench itself in government and thwart the democratic process. In the Justice's words: "Thus, if patronage contributes at all to the elective process, that contribution is diminished by the practice's impairment of the same" (p. 370).

Overall, then, the majority in *Elrod* argues that patronage is inefficient, a threat to democracy, unnecessary to party maintenance, and a clear restriction on the rights of free speech of individuals seeking federal employment. However, the majority does not totally reject patronage hirings but rather the idea that the concerns of accountability, control, and efficiency that might flow from spoils can be "fully satisfied by limiting patronage dismissals to policy-making and non-policy-making positions" (p. 372). What is the line between policy and non-policy-making positions? While the Court notes difficulty in drawing a clean distinction, the majority suggest that consideration should be given to "whether the employee acts as an adviser or formulates the plans for the implementation of broad goals" (p. 368).

In dissent, Powell, Burger, and Rehnquist rejoin to Brennan's three arguments against spoils. While conceding that spoils may hurt government efficiency, these three justices cite several works in political science and public administration that defend patronage as important to democracy through its creation of strong parties that stimulate competition and make government accountable. Their argument notes the importance of patronage to supposed larger democratic goals that, when balanced against the free speech rights of individuals, take priority. A similar defense of patronage as crucial to party government and democracy would be repeated in the dissents of *Branti* and *Rutan*.

Branti v. Finkel 445 U.S. 507 (1979) was a New York case that grew out of the dismissal of Republican assistant public defenders by a newly appointed Democratic public defender. While the reasons for dismissal were really not different from those in *Elrod*, the Court took this case to clarify the distinction it had made between policy-making and non-policy-making positions, and to make a more exact argument when party affiliation might be used appropriately in hiring.

Stevens wrote the majority six-three opinion that held that the dismissals of the assistant public defenders was unconstitutional. Burger, Brennan, White, Marshall, and Blackmun joined in the decision while Stewart, Powell, and Rehnquist dissented. The majority in *Branti* reaffirmed their holding in *Elrod* and did not engage in any significant discussion of the merits or demerits surrounding spoils except in one footnote [11] referencing Brennan's discussion in *Elrod*. Instead, their main task was to refine the policy-making and non-policy-making distinction for party hiring. They did that by indicating that the real question was "whether the hiring authority can demonstrate that party affiliation is an appropriate requirement for the effective performance of the public office involved" (p. 518). This test was meant to clarify the policy-making criterion used in *Elrod*, but in many ways, as the dissent noted, it could be viewed as a strengthening of the ban on patronage hiring that would make perhaps thousands of dismissals based on party affiliation illegal. The holding suggested that perhaps even in policy-making positions party affiliation was not necessarily an appropriate requirement for the effective performance of duties and that it could not be considered.

In dissent, Stewart offered a spirited defense of the importance of party affiliation and patronage in hirings and contended that the majority holding sought to "constitutionalize[d] the civil service standard" by its continued "evisceration of patronage practices begun in *Elrod v. Burns*" (p. 505). According to Stewart, this decision represents an assault on a 200-year-old practice in American politics that has come to be used by elected officials to maintain the confidence and support of their subordinates.

The crux of Powell's dissent, for our purposes, rests in the defense of patronage. One, as noted, the dissenters argue that party affiliation is important for many public employers because it can be considered as one indicator of loyalty. Loyalty, they contend, is important to the administration of duties. Two, patronage appointments "help build stable political parties by offering rewards to persons who assume the tasks necessary to the continued functioning of political organizations" (p. 528). Political parties, Powell then argues, are necessary because they serve a variety of governmental interests including raising money to help "capture the attention of the electorate" (p. 528). This attention is crucial for educating the voters and delivering campaign messages to the public. Additionally, parties and patronage also become useful after campaigns end because they are governing devices that facilitate the "implementation of policies endorsed by the public" (p. 529).

A final argument directed in favor of patronage is that it facilitates political change. According to Powell, "The growth of the civil service system already has limited the ability of elected officials to effect political change" (p. 530) because many workers are insulated from political pressure and, thus, do not have to follow as faithfully the political directives as do those who serve in patronage positions. In sum, the dissenters argue that patronage serves an important governmental function in sustaining the strong parties that are necessary to electorial competition and in providing elected leaders with the control and discipline necessary to execute publicly supported policies.

The dissent in *Elrod* and *Branti*, then, represented an assault on the evolution of the civil service reform movement that the majority appeared to be constitutionalizing. It was a return to the Jacksonian spoils arguments that patronage was necessary to parties which sustain popular government and link the expression and execution of policies supported by the public. It appeared to represent an attack on the neutral competence ideology and sought to collapse the politics/administration dichotomy.

VI. THE JUDICIAL ZENITH AND RETREAT (?) FROM PATRONAGE LIMITATIONS: *RUTAN v. REPUBLICAN PARTY OF ILLINOIS*

A third patronage case was decided by the Supreme Court in 1990, and the five-four ruling in *Rutan v. Republican Party of Illinois* 110 S.Ct. 2729 (1990) revealed the most intense debate on the Court surrounding judicial assault upon patronage and spoils. In the majority was Brennan writing the decision, joined by Marshall, White, and Blackmun, with Stevens writing a separate concurring opinion. In dissent was the "Reagan" Court of Rehnquist, Scalia, O'Connor, and Kennedy.

The case grew out of a challenge to the Illinois governor's use of party affiliation when hiring, rehiring, transferring, and promoting individuals. They challenged this patronage practice, and the majority opinion on the Court struck it down as an unconstitutional infringement of the First Amendment rights of these individuals. Significantly, Brennan cited his decisions in *Elrod* and *Branti* and extended those rulings which had applied to patronage dismissals to include patronage hirings, transfers, promotions, and recalls after layoffs. Brennan again argued that the government interests in patronage were not vital enough to justify the limitation of the First Amendment rights of these workers.

More importantly, the majority used this decision to engage in a debate with the dissents from this case and *Branti* to justify the importance of limiting patronage in the governmental system. As in *Elrod*, Brennan argues that the preservation of the democratic process is not furthered by patronage. Moreover, given that civil service rules have already limited the number of patronage positions available in the last few years, the linkage between parties and patronage is now weak. Thus, "parties have already survived the substantial decline of patronage employment practices in this century" (p. 2737).

In dissent, Scalia launches a ferocious attack on the majority's antipatronage position by arguing that while the merit principle is clearly the "most favored" way to organize governments, neither is it the only way to do it nor does it enjoy exclusive constitutional protection (p. 2747). In referring to George Plunkitt in his discussion of patronage, Scalia describes spoils as part of the American administrative/political tradition, but he backs off from claiming that it is of "landmark status" or one of our "accepted political traditions" (p. 2748) [12].

Scalia's dissent is based upon two basic claims. First, he rejects the idea that the merit principle is the only constitutional way to organize the bureaucracy. Thus, the choice of which way to staff the government should be up to elected officials and not the courts. Second, Scalia will also defend patronage as having a rational basis as it supports strong parties, party government, and popular government. Clearly the second claim will be linked to his first and more important constitutional claim.

The primary constitutional line of attack that Scalia uses in his dissent is to argue that the strict-scrutiny standard used by the majority in this case, as well as in *Elrod* and *Branti*, to protect the rights of federal employees is inappropriate and ought to be rejected in favor of a balancing of interests test [13]. There are two parts to this claim for a new standard. First, Scalia argues that the restrictions on the speech of governmental employees have been held to be different from the restrictions that may be placed on that of the general citizenry. Second, if the government does have more latitude to act with regard to its own employees, then all the Court needs to ask is whether there is a rational basis for its regulations. Thus, when Scalia turns to the issue of spoils and patronage, his argument will be that so long as the government can show a rational basis on which patronage serves a reasonable governmental purpose, and this purpose outweighs the "coercive" effects on the employee, then the court should defer to Congress (p. 2752). In Scalia's words, "The whole point of my dissent is that the desirability of patronage is a policy question to be decided by the people's representatives" (p. 2752).

The second part of Scalia's dissent turns to showing how patronage does serve an important governmental interest. In presenting an argument in favor of patronage, Scalia states that "the Court simply refuses to acknowledge the link between patronage and party discipline, and between that and party success" (p. 2753). Scalia cites extensive political science and public administration literature that discusses how parties are important to American government and how strong parties provide challengers with the resources needed to take on an incumbent. Crucial to the formulation of a strong party, then, is patronage, which will entice and reward workers. Among other points in his discussion, Scalia indicates how parties, supported by patronage, will foster two-party competition, integrate excluded groups, and help build alliances. All of these functions, thus, are important to democracy and can be aided by patronage.

Scalia, then, in his dissent, does two important things. First, he seeks to place the justification for patronage on similar legal footing to that of the Hatch Act decisions (Note, 1991, 298). Use of patronage, as well as limits upon federal (public) employee free speech rights, would be limited in a balancing test if, on balance, an important governmental interest outweighed that of an individual. Thus, in blurring the patronage and Hatch Act cases Scalia is judicially connecting two bodies of law that had been hitherto separated. This linkage thus makes clear how two prongs of neutral competence ideology are being viewed by at least one or some members of the Court as resting upon similar constitutional if not policy grounds.

The second thing that Scalia does is to make a forceful argument for patronage that parallels Jacksonian defenses of spoils (Kannar, 1991, 1860). In effect, Scalia joins Rehnquist and Powell in earlier patronage cases (as well as Rehnquist, Kennedy, and O'Connor in the *Rutan* dissent) in rejecting much of the language of neutral competence and administration reform that had sought to eradicate spoils.

VII. CONCLUSION: THE FUTURE OF JUDICIAL ENFORCEMENT OF NEUTRAL COMPETENCE

Examination of Supreme Court assessment, Hatch Acts, and patronage decisions indicates that the Court has been a consistently strong defender of the politics/administration dichotomy. For the last 100 years the Court has deferred to Congress in its attempts to limit forced monetary contributions within the bureaucracy and to place limits upon the political activity of federal employees. The patronage decisions, on the other hand, represent a direct attempt by the Court to limit use of spoils in hiring, firing, and transfers. Together, these decisions constitute a rejection of the Jacksonian claims that spoils is necessary for strong parties, party government, and popular government. The Court has instead adopted the language and assumptions of the Progressive reform era in seeking to place administrative duties beyond the realm of politics. The Court's decisions have not only helped politically to neutralize the federal bureaucracy, but, along with other Supreme Court and lower court decisions, have done much the same in state and local governments [14].

One conclusion is that much of the success of the neutral competence movement is due not merely to legislative reforms but also to the efforts of the judiciary, which appear influenced by the rhetoric of the politics/administration dichotomy. A second conclusion is that the Court's support of neutral competence is mixed and may be eroding. As noted, members of the Court have generally been split on the Hatch and patronage decisions, with the liberals generally opposing Hatch restrictions but supporting the limits of patronage hirings. Conservatives, on the other hand, have supported Hatch restrictions but have been unwilling to limit the use of patronage in hiring practices. Hence, the Court's decisions in the last forty-five years have supported neutral competence even if particular justices have not consistently done so.

Justice Brennan was the ideological leader of three patronage decisions with Justice Rehnquist dissenting emphatically in all three. With Brennan's and Marshall's departure and the addition of Souter and Thomas to the Court, the slim five-four majority of *Rutan* could be in danger. This is especially true if Scalia's defense of strong party/patronage politics in the *Rutan* dissent is convincing to others on the Court.

Attacks on the Hatch Acts outside the Court occurred and intensified in Congress in 1990. A radical revision of the act which would have allowed federal employees to seek party offices and solicit party funds at their workplaces only narrowly failed to survive a presidential veto by one vote. President Bush justified his veto with concerns about the neutrality of the career service (Dowd, 1990). While for now it appears that the Hatch Act will survive, this attempt to alter it was the result of mounting criticism from unions, Republicans, Democrats, and academics (Martin, 1973; Herin, 1974) to lessen some of the restrictions upon the political activity of federal employees.

With a split Court and eroding legislative support, perhaps in time a majority of the Court may accept the logic of patronage and politics and become an ideological force that defends spoils as one legislative or executive prerogative in organizing state and federal bureaucracies.

NOTES

1. Justice Brennan wrote the opinion for the majority, joined by Justices White, Marshall, Blackmun, and Stevens. Stevens wrote a separate concurring opinion. Justice Scalia wrote the dissenting opinion, joined by Rehnquist, Kennedy, and O'Connor.
2. *Elrod v. Burns* 427 U.S. 347 (1976), and *Branti v. Finkel* 445 U.S. 507 (1980).
3. *United Public Workers v. Mitchell* 330 U.S. 75 (1947), and *U.S. Civil Service Commission v. Postal Workers* 413 U.S. 548 (1973).
4. Wilson, 363 (1968).
5. Van Riper, 1958, notes how Dorman Eaton, head of the New York Civil Service Reform League; Theodore Roosevelt; and F. J. Goodnow more successfully argued the need to keep politics and administration apart. Later, Max Weber and others clarified the distinction between politics and administration.
6. Reprinted as *Bureaucracy* in Weber (1979).
7. 5 U.S. Code 7324 (1988). The original versions of the Hatch Acts are listed as Act of August 2, 1939, ch. 410, 53 Stat. 1147, and Act of July 19, 1940, ch. 640, 54 Stat. 767.
8. The 1940 Hatch Act extended a similar ban on political activities to state and local workers receiving federal funds.
9. P. 97, footnote 32. It should be noted that the justices in *Elrod, Banti,* and *Rutan* expended a copious amount of space in their footnotes referencing public administration and political science literature that discusses neutral competence, spoils, and the latter's relation to strong party government, among other topics. Literally dozens of books and articles are cited.

10. Justice White wrote the opinion for the majority, which was joined by Burger, Stewart, Blackmun, Powell, and Rehnquist. Douglas dissented, joined by Marshall and Brennan.
11. 445 U.S. 507, at 513, footnote 8.
12. Brinkley, 1991, claims that Scalia thinks the Court ought to respect long-standing traditions that are not found in the constitutional text.
13. Johnson (1991, p. 422) discusses Scalia's claim that a lesser level of scrutiny should be applied to government management and operations including patronage.
14. There are literally thousands of cases that cite the Hatch Act and patronage cases as precedents. Among those Hatch decisions are *Oklahoma v. United States Civil Service Commission* 330 U.S. 127 (1947), which was a companion case to *Mitchell.* This case upheld the enforcement of the Hatch Act to state highway transportation employees who worked on projects receiving federal funds. *Smith v. Ehrlich* 430 F. Supp 818 (1976) and *Dingess v. Hampton* 305 F. Supp 169 (1969) upheld Hatch Act–like restrictions upon federally funded employees in the Legal Services Act (§ 1007 (a) (6), 42 U.S.C. § 2996 (a) (6) (Supp v. 1975)) and the Economic Opportunity Act of 1964 (5 U.S. C. § 1502 (a) (3)). Note also *Keefe v. Library of Congress* 777 F. 2d 1573 (1985), which upheld the provision of the 1970 Legislative Reorganization Act (§ 203, 2 U.S.C.A. § 166) that placed limits upon the partisan political activity of Library of Congress research aides. On the upholding of state and local government versions of the Hatch Act see, for example, *Perry v. Pierre* 518 F 2d, 184 (1975), *Lay v. Kingsport* 454 F 2d, 345 (1972), and *Reeder v. Kansas City Board of Police Commissioners* 733 F 2d, 543 (1984).

    Among the numerous patronage dismissal cases are a series of Puerto Rican cases in 1987 that sought to clarify the lines between policy-making and non-policy-making officials. These cases were a result of the change in administration following the 1984 Puerto Rican gubernatorial election. See, for example, *Hernandez v. Tirado v. Antau* 835 F 2d. 377 (1987), *Santiago-Correa et al. v. Hernandez-Colon* 835 F. 2d. 395 (1987), and *Vazques Rios v. Hernandez-Colon* 819 F 2d 319 (1987), where at 325 the court sought to draw a distinction between employees who happen to come into contact with confidential work versus those whose "jobs intrinsically place them in a confidential position relative to other policymakers or the policymaking process." Here, workers in the executive mansion who were not policymakers were dismissed for alleged political/patronage reasons and the court held that the dismissal violated the prohibitions outlined in *Elrod* and *Branti.*

    In *Jones v. Dodson* 727 F 2d. 1329 (1984) two Democrats were hired by a previous Democratic sheriff and fired by a new Republican. The court at 1336 overturned the dismissal, stating that *Branti* was meant to prevent "raw patronage" dismissal decisions.

    A list of pre-*Rutan* patronage litigation is outlined in Martin (1989).

REFERENCES

Brinkley, Michael, Despoiling the Spoils, *North Carolina Law Review 69*:719 (1991).

Dowd, Maureen, President Vetoes a Bill and Makes Threat on Second, *New York Times* June 16 (1990).

Goodnow, Frank, *Politics and Administration*, Russell & Russell, New York, 1967.

Heinen, Steven G., Political Patronage and the First Amendment: Rutan v. Republican Party of Illinois, *Harvard Journal of Law and Public Policy 14*:292–302 (1991).

Herin, Glen S., Patronage Dismissals: Constitutional Limits and Political Justifications, *University of Chicago Law Review 41*:297–328 (1974).

Hoogenboom, Ari, *Outlawing the Spoils*, University of Illinois Press, Urbana, 1961.

Johnson, Barry, Another Attempt to Eliminate Political Patronage, *Willamette Law Review 27*:405–428 (1991).

Kannar, George, Strenuous Virtues, Virtuous Lives: The Social Vision of Antonin Scalia, *Cardozo Law Review 12*:1845–1868 (1991).

Maranto, Robert, and Schultz, David, *A Short History of the United States Civil Service*, University Press of America, Latham, Md., 1991.
Martin, A., A Decade of Branti Decisions: A Government Official's Guide to Patronage Dismissals, *American University Law Review 39*:11–58 (1989).
Martin, Phillip, The Hatch Act in Court: Some Recent Developments, *Public Administration Review 33*:443–447 (1973).
Masters, Marick F. and Bierman, Leonard, The Hatch Act and the Political Activities of Federal Employee Unions: A Need for Policy Reform, *Public Administration Review 45*:518–526 (1985).
Rosenbloom, David, *Federal Service and the Constitution*, Cornell University Press, Ithaca, New York, 1971.
Stillman, Richard J., *Preface to Public Administration: A Search for Themes and Direction*, St. Martin's Press, New York, 1991.
Van Riper, Paul P., *History of the United States Civil Service*, Row, Peterson, Evanston, Ill., 1958.
Weber, Max, Bureaucracy, in *From Max Weber: Essays in Sociology* (Hans Gerth and C. Wright Mills, eds.), Oxford University Press, New York, 1979, pp. 196–240.
Wilson, Woodrow, The Study of Administration, in *The Papers of Woodrow Wilson* (Arthur Link, ed.), vol. 5, Princeton University Press, Princeton, N.J., 1968a, pp. 359–380.
Wilson, Woodrow, Notes on Administration, in *The Papers of Woodrow Wilson* (Arthur Link, ed.), vol. 5, Princeton University Press, Princeton, N.J., 1968b, pp. 49–55.

28
Bureaucracy and Justice: An Overview of Criminal Justice in the United States

Paul Knepper
Northern Kentucky University, Highland Heights, Kentucky

In the opening pages of *Presumed Innocent*, Scott Turow questions the ability of bureaucracy to dispense justice. Turow, who served for eight years as an assistant U.S. attorney in Chicago before becoming a bestselling novelist, speaks through Rusty Sabich, Chief Deputy Prosecutor of fictional Kindle County:

> It's not that I have grown uncaring. Believe me. But this business of accusing, judging, punishing has gone on always; it is one of the great wheels turning beneath everything we do. I play my part. I am a functionary of our only universally recognized system of telling wrong from right, a bureaucrat of good and evil. (Turow, 1987, p. 4)

In describing himself as a "bureaucrat of good and evil," Turow highlights the oxymoronic quality of the "justice bureaucracy": there is the idea of wise, compassionate human beings setting things right when individuals violate commonly held principles, and there is the image of cold-hearted functionaries endlessly processing cases to meet requisite quotas.

Without doubt, the machinery for apprehending, trying, and sanctioning lawbreakers constitutes a monumental bureaucracy in the United States. More than 1.7 million persons are employed by the 55,000 public agencies that make up American justice. These include 18,000 law enforcement organizations, 17,000 courts, 8,000 prosecuting attorneys offices, 5,700 correctional institutions, and 3,500 probation and parole authorities (Lindgren, 1992, p. 6). Prosecutors obtain in excess of 667,000 felony convictions in state courts each year (Langan, 1990, p. 2). More than 4.3 million persons are under some form of correctional supervision—an estimated one of every twenty-four male adults on a given day in 1990 (Jankowski, 1991, p. 1). Not surprisingly, government spending for justice activities increased almost twice as fast as spending for all activities between 1985 and 1990, 29% compared to 14% (Lindgren, 1992, p. 1).

There can also be no doubt that the administration of justice is government's chief function. "Justice is the first virtue of social institutions, as truth is of systems of thought," Harvard philosopher John Rawls observes. "A theory however elegant and economical must be rejected or revised if it is untrue; likewise laws and institutions no matter how efficient and well-arranged must be reformed or abolished if they are unjust" (Rawls, 1971, p. 3). Americans' fear of government's misuse of power led to adoption of the Bill of Rights at the nation's founding, and in recent decades, the suspicion that police and judges discriminate against certain groups has ignited urban violence and widespread protest.

Therefore, it is of great significance to explore the fit between bureaucracy and justice. Can bureaucratic organization deliver justice? The relationship between bureaucracy and justice will be examined by considering several related questions: How is the administration of justice structured? How did such a bureaucracy come into being? How does the bureaucracy operate? What problems arise with the administration of justice? What does the future hold for the justice bureaucracy?

I. THE STRUCTURE OF AMERICAN CRIMINAL JUSTICE

Before 1960 or so the term "criminal justice system" was rarely heard. Police, prosecutorial, court, and incarceral institutions were understood to carry out specific functions with little shared responsibility. But in 1967 the President's Commission on Law Enforcement and the Administration of Justice developed the *systems model* to depict the flow of cases from arrest to disposition. The model portrayed a unified network of public agencies devoted to dispensing justice in a rational, efficient manner (Walker, 1989, p. 21).

Since then, "criminal justice system" has come to refer to the process of identifying, trying, and punishing lawbreakers, although even a brief look at the process reveals little systematicness. To begin with, there is no single system. The administration of justice in the United States is splintered into federal, state, county, and municipal sets of agencies. Federal, state, and local governments duplicate police, prosecutorial, adjudicatory, and detention services. Little cooperation and coordination exist between governmental units that seem to be natural allies in the fight against crime. Police, prosecutors, jailers, and judges jealously defend their turf and compete for resources (Greene et al., 1990). Jurisdictions overlap, interests conflict, and domains of authority collide. Independence and idiosyncrasy prevail, prompting some observers to term this nation's response to crime the criminal justice *non*-system (Skoler, 1977).

Nevertheless, it is useful to classify criminal-justice agencies for heuristic purposes. Political scientists James P. Levine, Michael C. Musheno, and Dennis J. Palumbo divide the administration of justice into five clusters of agencies: lawmaking, law enforcement, prosecution, adjudication, and corrections (Levine et al., 1986, pp. 19–20).

A. Lawmaking

Legislative bodies at all levels of government make criminal-justice policy. These include the U.S. Congress, fifty state legislatures, and numerous county commissions and city councils. Through their power to make statutes, codes, and ordinances, these agencies define the substantive goals and procedural rules that other units must follow. They also attempt to influence the outcome of their policies. Through determinate sentencing laws, for example, lawmaking agencies try to structure the end result of the adjudication process (Travis et al., 1990).

Other groups, external to the public system, try to influence criminal-justice policymaking as well. Agenda setting enables interest groups to tip the scales of justice in their constituents' favor. National organizations, such as the National Rifle Association, the American

Bar Association, and the American Civil Liberties Union, influence crime policy through their lobbying efforts. Regional and local groups, including state bar associations and fraternal orders of police, participate in the agenda-setting process and, by means of professional codes, decide what laws will, and will not be, be enforced (Melone, 1985).

B. Law Enforcement

The nation's law enforcement agencies, the most visible members of the justice bureaucracy, include 12,200 local police departments, 3,100 sheriff's departments, 49 state police forces, and 1,500 special police forces (Reaves, 1992a, p. 2). Although some local police departments are quite large, most are very small, and about half employ fewer than ten sworn officers. Of sheriff's departments, nearly two-thirds employ fewer than twenty-five sworn officers, and a third employ fewer than ten (Reaves, 1992b, p. 1). Three-quarters of local departments serve populations of less than 10,000. However, about a fifth of all municipal police officers work in jurisdictions that serve 1 million or more residents (Reaves, 1992a, p. 3). The largest municipal police agency, the New York City Police Department, has more than 33,000 full-time employees.

Although local police retain responsibility for first response to incidents in urban areas, state and federal police duplicate other key activities such as patrol, traffic enforcement, and investigation. The size and organization of these departments vary considerably. The California Highway Patrol, the largest state police department, employs nearly 6,000 sworn officers, while the smallest, the North Dakota Highway Patrol, employs 115 troopers (Reaves, 1992a, p. 10). About half of the state police agencies conduct laboratory testing, fingerprint processing, training academy administration, and search-and-rescue operations. Nine agencies located within the Justice and Treasury Departments perform the bulk of federal law enforcement. These are the Federal Bureau of Investigation; the Drug Enforcement Agency; the U.S. Customs Service; IRS Criminal Investigation; Alcohol, Tobacco and Firearms Bureau; U.S. Secret Service; Postal Inspection Service; Immigration and Naturalization Service; and U.S. Marshals Service. The FBI, the most widely known federal law enforcement agency, investigates activities ranging from espionage to bank fraud in addition to common crimes defined by federal law (Walker, 1992, pp. 49–50).

C. Prosecution

Upon receiving arrest reports from law enforcement officials, state and federal prosecutors decide whether or not to proceed with criminal charges against suspects. State prosecutors are known by a variety of names: district attorney, county attorney, commonwealth's attorney, prosecuting attorney, and state's attorney. Since they are elected to office (to two- or four-year terms), they operate without oversight (Neubauer, 1992, pp. 103–117). In most prosecutorial districts chief prosecutors are aided by assistant prosecutors, that is, other attorneys who perform much of the case work. Nationwide about 2,300 chief prosecutors employ nearly 20,000 deputy attorneys (Dawson, 1992, p. 1). Public defender offices—government agencies employing attorneys to represent indigent criminal defendants—are located in about three-fifths of prosecutorial districts. Prosecutorial districts usually consist of a single county, although they may include two counties or more (Dawson, 1992, p. 4).

Federal prosecutors, called U.S. attorneys, must receive appointment to office from the President. One federal prosecutor resides within each judicial district. Since they are so numerous and typically identify with the law enforcement community, it is difficult for Washington officials to influence their day-to-day activities even though they are formally obliged to follow

Justice Department policies. Unlike local prosecutors, U.S. attorneys also represent the federal government in civil cases, such as traffic accidents involving a postal vehicle. Noncriminal matters amount to 40% of their work (Carp and Stidham, 1993, pp. 100–101).

D. Adjudication

The decision to prosecute triggers the adjudication process. One of the most important terms with reference to adjudication is "dual court system." This term implies that there are two independent systems—a set of fifty state court systems and one federal system—although there is significant overlap between the two systems [1].

The exact configuration of state courts varies considerably, but they may be divided into four tiers: *Trial courts of limited jurisdiction* are the most numerous; they constitute 90% of all courts in the United States. Known as justice of the peace courts, magistrate courts, municipal courts, city courts, county courts, and metropolitan courts (to list a few of the common names), these courts handle traffic violations, petty criminal cases, and ordinance violations, and they hold preliminary stages of felony cases (arraignments, bail hearings, and appointment of indigent counsel). *Trial courts of general jurisdiction* are major trial courts (although they have an appellate function as well in many states). Typically divided into districts or circuits following county and municipal boundaries, they hear matters not specifically delegated to inferior courts. The more common names for these courts are district, circuit, and superior courts. *Intermediate appellate courts* are located in about half the states (primarily the most populous) to relieve pressure on the highest courts. Often, these are the courts of last resort for appeals. *Courts of last resort*, most commonly called supreme courts, are the ultimate arbiters of state law. Most state supreme courts resemble the U.S. Supreme Court (Carp and Stidham, 1993, pp. 52–60; Neubauer, 1992, pp. 47–51).

The federal court system may be divided into trial courts, called "district courts"; intermediate appellate courts, known as "circuit courts of appeal"; and the nation's court of last resort, the U.S. Supreme Court. There are ninety-four federal judicial districts, generally one for each state, although larger states are divided into two or more districts. District court judges are assisted by 541 U.S. magistrates empowered to resolve minor cases and conduct preliminary stages of felony cases. The twelve circuit courts of appeal have jurisdiction over district court decisions. Appeals that are not resolved by the circuit courts or state supreme courts may end up before the U.S. Supreme Court, the highest appellate court in the nation. The U.S. Supreme Court functions as the final interpreter of the federal Constitution and as a national policymaker, exercising this prerogative in such decisions as *Gideon v. Wainright* (1963) and *Miranda v. Arizona* (1966) (Carp and Stidham, 1993, pp. 19–47; Neubauer, 1992, pp. 42–46).

E. Corrections

Individuals sentenced by the nation's criminal courts became subject to a variety of punitive organizations at the federal, state, and local levels. These authorities fall within one of two broad categories: institutional corrections and community corrections.

Institutional corrections consists of federal, state, and local facilities. The federal prison system, operated by the U.S. Bureau of Prisons, confines about 65,000 lawbreakers in six U.S. penitentiaries, thirty-five federal correctional institutions, fifteen federal prison camps, and nine metropolitan correctional/detention centers (Maguire and Flanagan, 1991, pp. 105–106). (About half of the federal prison population is serving time for violation of the Drug Abuse Prevention Act of 1970.) State corrections is generally organized into a separate department of corrections (with a cabinet-level director appointed by the governor) or a division within a larger state department. The state corrections chief has responsibility for maximum, medium, and minimum security institutions dispersed across the state. At 97,300 California has the largest prison population; North Dakota the smallest at 483 (Cohen, 1991, p. 2). State prisons, which confine felons, should not be confused with the nation's jails, which are administered by local governments for detention of those awaiting trial or misdemeanants. Nationwide there are about 3,300 jails. Texas has the largest number—275—but Los Angeles County is the jurisdiction with the largest jail population: the 8 jails within the county house nearly 23,000 inmates (Stephan, 1991, p. 4).

Community corrections consists of probation and parole authorities. Probation is a sentence given instead of a prison term and parole amounts to early release from prison. Probation is administered by hundreds of separate agencies with a variety of structures. In the most common plan probation is provided by a state agency organized into regional units, but counties retain control in many states. Currently there are approximately 2.6 million persons on probation (Jankowski, 1991, p. 2). Parole boards are organized within the corrections department in some states, function as independent agencies in others, and amount to consolidated probation-parole authorities in others. With nearly 300,000 adults on probation and 92,000 on parole, Texas has the largest community corrections population (Jankowski, 1991, pp. 2–3). There are about 60,000 probationers and 21,000 parolees under federal jurisdiction (Jankowski, 1991, pp. 2–3).

II. THE DEVELOPMENT OF THE JUSTICE BUREAUCRACY

In order to understand why the American way of criminal justice is so fragmented and decentralized, it is necessary to take a look at how the system developed. The roots of American criminal justice can be tracked to England, and specifically to the Norman kings, who formulated America's conception of justice administration.

A. The British Heritage

There was no crime in Anglo-Saxon England. There was wrongdoing, but there was no crime, because the idea of crime had not been invented. The Anglo-Saxons considered these harms personal matters to be settled through negotiation and reconciliation. The victim, or the victim's family, negotiated a settlement with the wrongdoer as compensation for the harm. Each citizen took responsibility for aiding neighbors victimized by wrongdoers (Goebel, 1976, p. 341). Justice was not expressed in written legal codes but was preserved in the memories of elder community members who ensured that matters were set right. They held local assemblies at regular intervals and "did justice to one another, finding the custom that applied to each case and adjusting it at need" (Cam, 1963, p. 12).

But after the Norman Conquest of England in 1066, things changed. William the Conqueror, the first Norman king of England, claimed title to all land, insisting that individuals enjoyed usage of land only by virtue of land rights granted by him. Furthermore, he proclaimed the basis of law to reside with the monarchy. The most significant judicial change, however, had to do with the doctrine of "the king's peace." In 1116 King Henry I, the son of William, issued the *Leges Henrici*, which established thirty judicial districts throughout the country and gave them authority over "certain offenses *against the king's peace*, arson, robbery, murder, false coinage and crimes of violence" [italics added] (Berman, 1983, p. 314). No longer were injuries between people considered personal wrongs but rather, public harms that demanded redressing the "injury" to the king. The Norman word for this breach of faith was *felony*, and for the wrongdoer, *felon*. Thus, serious harms in Norman England were called felonies because they represented "breaches of the fealty owed by all people to the king as guardians of the realm" (Berman, 1983, p. 314).

It was at this point that government "stole" conflicts away from individuals and initiated a monopoly over the criminal-justice process (Christie, 1977). The Norman kings formulated the modern conceptions of crime and criminal and, in the process, founded the criminal-justice bureaucracy. They replaced local systems of dispute resolution with a centralized system of law enforcement by Norman rulers. Within each shire (the early English equivalent of the county), the king appointed a *shire reeve* to enforce the king's peace (Walker, 1992, p. 5). By the early eleventh century, sheriffs had the responsibility of bringing enemies of the king to trial. The Normans also built castles to shut up foreign adversaries and domestic lawbreakers. A forerunner of the modern jail, the Norman stronghold held felons until trial, and until corporal punishment could be administered (Pugh, 1968, p. 11).

B. The Nineteenth Century

Early American justice was modeled loosely after the British. Prior to the nineteenth century, police, courts, and incarceral institutions were simple affairs. The earliest law enforcement officials were the sheriff and the constable. The sheriff, who was appointed by the colonial governor, collected taxes, conducted elections, maintained bridges and roads, and supervised the jail. The constable's office appeared as towns and cities grew up. It was the constable's job to organize the night watch in which townspeople had collective responsibility to guard by night against fires, animals, and suspicious persons (Walker, 1992, p. 6). Colonial courts adjudicated offenses against property, person, and morality, although real political power was retained by the governor, who performed executive, legislative, and judicial functions. They had both appellate and original jurisdiction. Similarly, colonial jails were small-scale institutions that operated somewhat like boarding houses. Detainees and petty offenders stayed in the jailer's house along with the jailer and his family, and they depended on handouts from friends or relatives (Freidman, 1973, pp. 32–49).

During the course of the nineteenth century, American criminal justice took on its decentralized character. The slave patrol, a distinctly American form of law enforcement, emerged within southern states to guard against slave revolts and capture runaway slaves, and it became the first police force in the South (Reichel, 1988). In the Northeast, municipal police forces appeared in response to urban riots. Boston experienced major riots in the 1830s that led to creation of the day watch in 1838 (Lane, 1975, pp. 26–38). New York's department, patterned after London's Metropolitan Police force, became the national model. American police departments borrowed uniformed patrols and militaristic organization. But unlike the British paradigm, American departments were immersed in machine politics, which led to corruption and entanglement in labor disputes (Richardson, 1965).

The growth of America's courts during this period was sporadic and unplanned. The Judiciary Act of 1789 established a federal court system with districts parallel to state boundaries. As circuit courts, superior courts, and courts of common pleas sprouted in the states, the distinction between trial and appellate courts sharpened. Gradually, courts of last resort in each state emerged. After the Civil War, state courts became more highly specialized than federal courts. City courts appeared, specifying their jurisdictions as city boundaries, along with courts claiming jurisdiction in certain types of disputes (probate, criminal) or over certain litigants (families, juveniles) (Friedman, 1973, pp. 122–126).

Jails made up America's incarceral system until 1790. In that year, the "penitentiary house" opened at Philadelphia's Walnut Street Jail. Walnut Street represented the first state prison, and it ushered in a new era founded on the principle that deprivation of liberty would be both punitive and reformative. Other states followed suit: New York (1796), New Jersey, (1797), Virginia (1800), and Kentucky (1800) (McKelvey, 1977). By 1870, 23 states had penitentiaries. Probation emerged in the midnineteenth century when John Augustus, a Boston shoemaker, paid fines for hundreds of drunks otherwise confined in jail. Augustus's efforts provoked Massachusetts to pass the first probation statute in 1878. Four states adopted similar legislation by 1900 (Lindner and Savarese, 1984).

C. The Progressive Era and After

The Progressive Era introduced reforms that gave American criminal system its contemporary shape. August Vollmer championed police professionalism while chief of the Berkeley, California, Police Department from 1905 to 1932. His reform agenda urged introduction of personnel standards, scientific management, and specialized units (vice, homicide) (Douthit, 1975). Pennsylvania introduced the first modern state police force, the Pennsylvania State Constabulary, in 1905. Other states created their own state agencies soon after. These state and local alterations were matched by the rapid development of federal law enforcement. The FBI, originally organized as the Bureau of Investigation in 1908, gained massive influence under the leadership of J. Edgar Hoover in 1924. Hoover capitalized on the nation's fears of a crime wave and dramatically increased the size and scope of the bureau's operations (Powers, 1987).

The progressives dramatically altered the nation's courts as well. Organizations such as the American Judicature Society and the American Bar Association worked to develop a unified court system. A dozen states streamlined their court systems with three- or four-tiered models during the early twentieth century. Further steps toward centralization followed with the federal judiciary taking the lead. In 1939 Congress established the Administrative Office of the United States Courts. This office gathered statistics on federal dockets and prepared judicial budgets. The federal government encouraged states to set up their own administrative offices by making funds available. North Dakota set up the first state administration office in 1927, and by 1977 every state had some form of central court administration in place (Carp and Stidham, 1993, pp. 65–78).

When the progressives turned their attention to the nation's prisons they conceived of the ideal of corrections. Embodied in the reformatory, this ideal stressed the prison as a means of rehabilitation rather than punishment. The nation's first reformatory, organized by Zebulon Brockway at Elmira, New York, opened in 1876. Eighteen more states across the East and Midwest opened reformatories before the movement ended in 1913 (Pisciotta, 1983). The federal government began building its own facilities during the first few decades of the twentieth century on the penitentiary plan. After the Three Prison Act of 1891, construction of federal prisons began at Atlanta and Leavenworth, and the Washington territorial prison at McNeil Island was renamed a federal prison. In 1907 the attorney general created the position of superintendent of prisons within the Justice Department, and in 1930 Congress established the Federal Bureau of Prisons (Keve, 1991).

III. THE JUSTICE BUREAUCRACY IN ACTION

No recital of the legal requirements of justice can explain the workings of a criminal-justice setup in which only a quarter of index crimes are cleared by police (Maguire and Flanagan, 1991, p. 445), less than a quarter of arrests result in formal felony complaints, and nine out of ten felony convictions are obtained through plea bargains (Langan, 1990, p. 1). The crucial decisions do not emerge in dramatic courtroom scenes, but through a series of quiet, mundane negotiations in hallways, lunchrooms, and corner offices. The day-to-day operation of justice is simply too complex for a formal description to be meaningful.

A. The Criminal Justice Wedding Cake

Samuel Walker, a professor of criminal justice, has developed a model of criminal justice process to account for the fact that there are fifty-one systems, and that within the same system, cases are treated differently. It consists of four layers. There is wide variation surrounding initial placement into a layer, but within each layer, there is a great degree of consistency. The model has been referred to as the "criminal justice wedding cake" (Walker, 1989, pp. 22–34).

The tiny layer at the top of the cake comprises celebrated cases. These cases are exceptions to ordinary case processing because they involve rich and famous defendants or victims. The trials of famous film stars, wealthy business leaders, and bizarre criminals attract great media attention. Another category of celebrated cases involves unknown defendants but landmark decisions. Americans are familiar with Ernesto Miranda not because he was rich or famous, but because of the mistake of a public official handling his case. What is significant about celebrated cases is that because of the attention these cases receive, outside observers assume the system ordinarily functions this way (Walker, 1989, pp. 26–27).

Felonies generally wind up in either the second or third layer depending on seriousness. Serious felony cases, or "real crimes," are dealt with in an adversarial manner; defendants are charged, prosecuted, convicted, and severely sentenced. The not-so-serious felonies, or "garbage cases," are treated with leniency. They are handled administratively. The distinction between the two results from judgments made by police and prosecutors about the case. They assess the complainant's credibility, the suspect's status, the legal seriousness of the charge, whether the suspect has a prior record, and the relationship between the victim and the suspect. Real crimes are thought to be committed by strangers (Walker, 1989, pp. 27–31). Consider the crime of rape, for example. Between 50% and 80% of rapes are committed by men who know their victims. Research in New York courts reveals that 60% of prior-relationship cases are dismissed and another 20% result in guilty pleas with virtually no punishment. Nearly all rapes by strangers go to trial. These distinctions are part of the routine administration of justice; they allow court officials to proceed with dockets swiftly and predictably (Vera Institute, 1981).

The fourth layer of the wedding cake, the misdemeanors, is a world unto itself. The volume of misdemeanor cases is staggering. The eight index crimes (murder/nonnegligent manslaughter, robbery, aggravated assault, burglary, larceny/theft, rape, motor vehicle theft, and arson) account for about a fifth of all arrests each year, and larceny/theft comprises roughly half of the total. The bulk of criminal cases, mostly public order offenses, must be disposed of in assembly-line fashion (Walker, 1989, pp. 31–34). These courts remain virtually untouched by the due process revolution; defendants are arraigned en masse and sentenced to extremely light sanctions with minimal assistance from—or completely without—an attorney. The "process is the punishment" in the sense that insistence on one's "rights" (a private attorney, numerous court appearances) costs more than the fine negotiated by plea bargain (Feeley, 1979).

B. Assembly-Line Justice

In myth, the prosecution and defense are adversaries. Wily attorneys convict the guilty and free the innocent with surprise witnesses, moving courtroom speeches, and shocking evidence. Judges referee the contest to ensure that the rights of defendants are preserved and the guilty receive their just deserts. In reality, prosecutors, defense attorneys, and judges form a group of courthouse regulars who process cases.

The courthouse work group refers to the idea that public defenders, prosecutors, and judges who work together on a daily basis develop an informal understanding about how cases should be handled. Rather than rivals, these are individuals who cooperate and compromise in order to achieve the common goal of disposing of cases quickly. They exist within each jurisdiction and process cases according to local customs related to plea bargaining and other less well known administrative routines (Eisenstein and Jacob, 1977; Clynch and Neubauer, 1981).

Courthouse work groups serve as the gatekeepers of national policy. In theory, trial courts are bound by the decisions of appellate courts. Decisions reached by the U.S. Supreme Court are supposed to be followed by every other court in the nation. Yet in practice, lower courts employ a variety of devices to neutralize top-down mandates. Courtroom work groups adjust case flow and the amount of punishment meted out to accommodate any externally imposed change. Mandatory sentencing schemes, pre-trial diversion, and other state or national policies are altered, accelerated, or thwarted by local cabals. There is no better example of this than the issue of ineffectiveness of counsel. In the 1984 decision of *Strickland v. Washington*, the U.S. Supreme Court established an "objective standard of reasonableness" as the proper criterion to be used in making a determination of the ineffectiveness of counsel. While Kentucky and Tennessee nominally adopted the new standard and hearing procedure, in practice they elevated the standard required to the older, and higher, "farce and mockery standard" established in *Powell v. Alabama* (1932) (Rhynhart and Thomson, 1990).

IV. PROBLEMS OF THE CRIMINAL-JUSTICE BUREAUCRACY

No understanding of the criminal-justice bureaucracy would be complete without some awareness of its problems. Some problems, such as those concerning the delivery of services, might be remedied with increased budgets, reorganization, improved communication, or other reforms. Others, however, are intractable. Unfortunately, the intractable problems number among the most profound.

A. No Victims Allowed

The American approach to criminal justice dispenses a strange form of justice. When one person (a lawbreaker) harms another (a victim), an abstract entity (the government) punishes the lawbreaker for a violation of an abstract concept (criminal law). A thief, for example, pays for his or her misdeed with time in confinement—not by returning the stolen articles—while the victim—the person who suffered the loss—receives no compensation. The objective is not to recover the stolen property but solely to identify the culprit and to confine his or her body. The victim has no formal role in American criminal procedure whatever (Van Ness, 1986, pp. 19–25).

There is the potential for conflict between victims and police because the police will not pursue allegations as the victim desires. The police require victims' cooperation for investigation and arrest, yet they have no obligation to meet victims' needs in return. Often, victims are frustrated by departmental regulations instructing police to treat property-crime complaints seriously only if they exceed a certain dollar amount. Victims may initiate complaints about an officer who follows standard procedure that jeopardize that officer's career. Similarly, the prosecutor's needs are at odds, or do not coincide with, the victim's. Above all else, the prosecutor's interest in the victim is to further the aims of law enforcement. The greatest portion of charges are dismissed because it is not in the prosecutor's interest to pursue them. Cases are rejected, charges dropped, and pleas negotiated for organizational interests, not victims' interests. When victims are given a voice in the adjudication process, such as the use of victim impact statements during sentencing, their wishes are utilized for sentencing the offender according to the state's needs, not the victim's needs. In practice, the victim's role in the administration of justice is as a tool, or weapon, for use against the defendant (Karmen, 1990, pp. 155–212).

Police, prosecutors, and judges have so little incentive to act in accordance with victims' needs because they are not accountable to them either legally or organizationally. Agencies look after their own interests. Official priorities are designed to meet legal mandates and organizational goals, and victims are viewed as an organizational resource to be drawn upon in the pursuit of these objectives. In everyday operations, whenever minor inconveniences to insiders (prosecutors, judges, attorneys) are weighed against major inconveniences to outsiders (victims, defendants, witnesses, jurors), insider interests prevail (Karmen, 1990, pp. 155–212).

B. Discretionary Justice

Discretion, the ability of a public official to decide whether or not, and in what manner, the law will be enforced, is unavoidable. At its most benign, discretion results in goal displacement. Police, prosecutors, and guards within the justice network substitute unofficial goals, like minimizing workloads and maximizing personal rewards, for the public goals of crime prevention and equal justice (Bayley and Bittner, 1989, pp. 90–95). At its most egregious, discretion allows hidden agendas to operate without interference.

One of the clearest examples of discretionary injustice involves racism in the imposition of the death penalty. Americans of African descent have constituted about 11% of the U.S. population since 1930, but nearly half the population on death row. Of the 4,000 legal executions that occurred between 1930 and 1990, 53% were black Americans. Blacks are executed for murder at a rate over five times that of whites; 1,640 blacks (or 48%) were executed for murder compared to 1,686 (or 50.8%) of whites. Even greater disparity is evident for rape. Of the 455 executions for rape between 1930 and 1990, 405 (89%) were of blacks and 48 (10.5%) were of whites. West Virginia, Louisiana, Mississippi, Oklahoma, and Virginia have never executed a white man for rape (Aguirre and Baker, 1990, pp. 135–140). The Supreme Court recognized this disparity in the landmark *Furman v. Georgia* (1972) decision. In a five-to-four decision the majority ruled that the death penalty had been invoked in a "freakish and wanton manner" in violation of the equal protection clause of the Fourteenth Amendment. Justice Potter Stewart observed that the death penalty had been imposed disproportionately on African Americans and other minority groups, and that selection bias based on race was constitutionally impermissible (*Furman v. Georgia* 408 U.S. 238).

What makes discretionary injustice so difficult to root out is that these decisions are relatively easy to cover up. Hidden agendas escape detection because illegitimate decisions are masked with legitimate decisions. While every decision is the product of a wide range of discretion, the official record of justice is carefully structured to reflect the operation of a well-oiled machine (Cavender and Knepper, 1992, pp. 396–397).

C. Accountability and Corruption

Who will guard the guardians? It's a troubling question without an immediate answer. Police, judges, and wardens are there when citizens break the law, but who is there when the justice officials themselves break the law? When the agencies that dispense justice violate the very laws they purport to uphold, the raison d'être for the institutions of justice is called into question.

Some instances of corruption may be attributed to individual acts of lawlessness. There is always the possibility that "one bad apple" might represent the extent of the corruption and this can be corrected with better personnel selection, tighter supervision, professional standards, internal review, or some other administrative device. Yet episodes of corruption occurring in the past few decades reveal that organized corruption also occurs. Multiple layers of a hierarchy, in addition to entire organizations, have been found to be steeped in abuse. At Arkansas's Cummins Prison Farm in the 1960s, Thomas Murton uncovered runaway abuses. Local businessmen exploited inmate labor; inmate "trustees" were allowed to sell liquor, operate gambling rings, and lend money; prison officials sold prison foodstuffs to local merchants for profit; inmates and others spent nights in shacks off prison ground with women; and about a hundred inmates were murdered as punishment and buried in a cow pasture on prison grounds (Murton and Hyams, 1969). In 1988 the Miami Police Department faced large-scale drug trafficking and worse. Over seventy-five Miami police officers were under investigation for criminal activities including drug dealing, robbery, theft, and murder. The FBI subpoenaed twenty-five officers in connection with a murder investigation and a conspiracy to sell police equipment; the elite Special Investigation section found $150,000 missing from its safe, and several hundred pounds of marijuana disappeared from the evidence room (Lyman and Potter, 1991, p. 140).

Episodes of official corruption such as these have led to greater activity by the courts. Court-mandated reforms in confinement standards and personnel practices have reached many jurisdictions recently. Over 500 jails in the United States were under court order to reduce crowding or improve conditions of confinement at the close of 1990 (Maguire and Flanagan, 1991, p. 85). Furthermore, since *Monroe v. Pape* (1961) resuscitated 42 U.S.C. Section 1983, it is possible for citizens to sue public officials for violations of civil rights. Section 1983 suits have led to a large number of successful damage suits against police, prison, and jail officials in recent years, amounting to nearly one-sixth of all civil cases in federal court. Section 1983 suits have forced many municipalities to establish contingency funds to cover lawsuits or purchase liability insurance (Barrineau, 1987).

V. THE FUTURE OF THE JUSTICE BUREAUCRACY

What will twenty-first-century justice look like? Predicting the future cannot be done with certainty, but emerging trends suggest that technology, privatization, and mediation will have even greater roles.

A. Technology

Numerous technologies have emerged within justice circles including electronic monitoring, DNA analysis, electronic surveillance, and automated criminal history records systems. In the criminal justice world of the 1990s fax machines relay arrest warrants, voice-activated cameras record courtroom testimony, motion-detection devices provide perimeter security for prisons, and the police conduct satellite-based visual surveillance. If criminal-justice agencies follow historical precedent, technology will loom larger in justice activities in the years to come.

This is because criminal justice officials have been slaves of technology. The police, for example, have adopted each new generation of weaponry, motorized patrol, communications equipment, and electronic gadgetry. A brief list of technological adaptations includes the call box

(1850), photography (1890), motorcycle patrol (1905), fingerprint identification (1911), patrol car (1915), polygraph (1923), teletype machine (1925), two-way radio (1929), sound spectrograph (1966), 911 communications (1968), hand-held radar (1970), automated fingerprint identification (1983), and remote video surveillance (1988). Police departments of the 1990s are buying 9mm semiautomatic weapons, microcomputer-based expert systems, and night-vision surveillance equipment. Clearly, law enforcement officers have more technology at their disposal today than ever before (Alpert and Dunham, 1988, pp. 23–25). But what has all this technology accomplished? Has the justice bureaucracy's reliance on technology brought about greater justice?

The short answer is probably not (Archambeault, 1987; Schlegel, 1988). To understand why, it is useful to look at a specific example: electronic monitoring. From its inception in the mind of a New Mexico judge inspired by *Spiderman* comics, electronic monitoring has experienced explosive growth. Since the first program began in Albuquerque in 1983, it has expanded to thirty-three states, with a threefold increase in 1988 alone (Corbett and Marx, 1991, p. 399). The system makes use of an electronic bracelet worn by the offender and a receiver-dialer placed in the offender's home to notify parole authorities of the offender's absence. While conventional wisdom praises this technology as a solution to the overcrowding crisis, several fallacies can be detected. Pronouncing electronic parole a success assumes that the United States has a coherent punishment strategy when in fact it does not. Documented failures expose a technology that is far from fail-safe, and even if the technology worked 100% of the time, human error would still cause failures. And surveillance technology, unlike the microchip, is not morally neutral. The increasing use of surveillance technology decreases the sanctity of a person's home, a significant value choice (Corbett and Marx, 1991).

Despite technology's inability to effect greater justice, it does meet significant bureaucratic goals and is therefore likely here to stay. New technology is synonymous with progress, and to oppose it is to be labeled backward and behind the times. Agency administrators seize technological improvements as a matter of careerism and survival, seeking to enhance their agency's reputation as a progressive, contemporary operation. Technological wizardry promises pure administrative efficiency. While legal judgments are viewed as subjective and imprecise, technological outputs carry the mystique of unbiased, accurate decision making. Performance criteria and organizational goals are more easily met by avoiding difficult human choices in favor of technical mandates. Also, technological "advances" enable justice agencies to plead for greater resources. Funding agents, as well as the public, are particularly willing to accept high-tech solutions to profound problems because they promise a quick—albeit expensive—fix (Corbett and Marx, 1991).

B. Mediation

Increased caseloads and dissatisfaction with the results of sanctions have led to mediation, or alternative dispute resolution programs. Mediation programs decide minor disputes for criminal and civil justice. By 1990 an estimated 700 programs were in operation, handling domestic conflicts, landlord/tenant matters, misdemeanors, and consumer/merchant disputes. Early speculation held that mediation would be limited to the private sector, but there is reason to believe that its use will expand in criminal law (Glick, 1993, pp. 161–167).

The Victim-Offender Reconciliation Project (VORP) is one kind of fast-growing mediation program. Since the first VORP opened in 1974 at Kitchener, Ontario, more than 200 others have appeared in the United States and Canada (Peachey, 1989). As originally developed, VORP functions as an organization outside the criminal justice network that works in cooperation with police and courts. In the mediation process the victim and offender meet face-to-face in the presence of a third-party facilitator. Mediators work to uncover facts, voice feelings, and reach agreements. So far, the majority of cases handled by VORPs have been property crimes, with burglary the common offense. But recently, a few VORP programs have begun to handle cases of violence with regularity (Umbreit, 1989).

Early evaluations indicate that victim-offender mediation is successful. Mediated restitution contracts are fulfilled in more than 80% of cases, and more than 90% of participants are satisfied with the outcome (Zehr, 1990, p. 164). Whether or not mediation grows or withers depends on criminal-justice institutions' ability to co-opt VORP programs. The American way of criminal justice is inherently geared toward punishing lawbreakers, and this emphasis undermines the goal of victim restitution. Since VORPs depend on court referrals, they operate at the behest of judges' commitment to alternative sentencing and diversion programs (Zehr, 1990, pp. 158–174).

C. Privatization

Privatization of the administration of justice is a growth industry. Private courts, private prisons, and private police operate alongside public agencies in nearly every jurisdiction across America.

Private policing, which has experienced the largest growth, is rapidly expanding. The nation's private police force has already outstripped public police. Security guards, or rent-a-cops, represent America's largest protective resource, outspending public law enforcement by 73%. Annual spending for private security in 1990 reached $52 billion compared to public law enforcement expenditures of $30 billion. Not surprisingly, security firms employ two-and-a-half times the work force. Private security agencies employed more than 1.5 million persons; public law enforcement agencies employed approximately 600,000 persons (Cunningham et al., 1991, p. 1). The growth of other privatization schemes, such as private prisons, may have peaked. In the United States private management firms operated sixty secure facilities for adult males by the end of 1991 (Thomas and Logan, 1991, p. 2). These facilities housed nearly 20,000 prisoners in a dozen states. Major private-prison companies, however, including Corrections Corporation of America and United States Corrections Corporation, have yet to show profits on prison ventures.

Yet the private sector's attachment to public criminal justice is here to stay. The U.S. corrections market is estimated to be $25 billion annually. The "market" consists of prison financing and construction, as well as a wide array of goods and services. Private companies sell everything from indestructible dishes to clog-proof toilets. Prison food and health services are two of the fastest growing niches (Lilly and Knepper, 1993). Recently, transnational firms have emerged in the United States, Canada, and England to sell punishment consulting and detention-related products in North American and European markets. World trends suggest that an international corrections-commercial complex exists in which a network of firms sell punishment schemes to Third World nations that are adopting Western style punishment institutions (Lilly and Knepper, 1992).

D. Continuous Expansion

The paradox of criminal justice in the 1980s was an *increase* in the prisoner population and—contrary to popular opinion—a *decrease* in crime. This paradox will likely be repeated in the 1990s: the justice bureaucracy is likely to expand during the next few decades even though crime will probably decrease.

During the 1980s the size of the justice bureaucracy increased significantly. The U.S. prison population more than doubled from 329,821 state and federal prisoners in 1980 to 710,054 in 1990. Between 1925 and 1974, the record high occurred in 1961, when 220,149 persons were incarcerated. Every year since 1975, new record highs have been set (Bureau of Justice Statistics, 1988, p. 4). Yet according to the two leading measures of crime, crime rates dropped during the same period. According to the FBI's *Uniform Crime Reports*, crime fell 4% between 1980 and 1988. The Bureau of Justice Statistics's *National Crime Survey* showed a 17% drop; the number of victimizations fell 10% for violent crime, 15% for personal thefts, and 18% for household crimes. In one year alone, the number of personal and household crimes fell by 1 million, while the nation's prison population jumped up 8% (Bastian, 1992, p. 2).

Some political leaders celebrated the paradox of falling crime rates and rising incarceration rates as evidence of the success of particular crime-reduction strategies. President Ronald Reagan, for example, told the nation in his 1985 Inaugural Address that the index crime rate had fallen two years in a row for the first time in twenty years as a result of aggressive law enforcement (Steffensmeier and Harer, 1991, p. 333). But a closer look at the nature of aggregate crime statistics offers a different explanation for the decrease. Crime is "age sensitive" (younger persons, particularly eighteen- to twenty-one-year-olds, commit relatively more crimes than other age groups), and therefore, shifts in the portion of younger or crime-prone individuals within the U.S population affect crime rates (Wilson, 1983, pp. 13–25). During the 1980s, the U.S. population was "aging out"—shifting toward proportionately fewer crime-prone individuals and toward more elderly or low-risk persons. When the age effect is purged statistically from crude crime rates, the decrease in crime vanishes, and 1980s age-adjusted rates show a period of relatively little change (Steffensmeier and Harer, 1987; 1991). In other words, changes in the age distribution in the U.S. population, not specific policies initiated in the 1980s, account for falling crime rates.

So why did the prison population double when crime remained stable? Fear of crime. Despite decreasing crude crime rates, the public is afraid of crime as ever before. The portion of U.S. citizens who are afraid to walk alone at night increased from 34% in 1965 to 40% in 1990 (Maguire and Flanagan, 1991, p. 184). The 1980s scenario will likely repeat itself during the 1990s so long as fear of crime remains high. Crime rates, particularly violent crime rates, will decrease even further as the baby boom generation passes into middle age (Steffensmeier and Harer, 1991, pp. 344–345). But the justice bureaucracy will continue to expand as a result of the public's willingness to spend more and more for criminal justice.

VI. BUREAUCRATS OF GOOD AND EVIL

Turow asked in his fiction what others have questioned in commentary and debate: whether in the daily struggle to clear dockets, sort files, log activities, type reports, and justify budgets, the assortment of agencies, departments, offices, units, and bureaus known as "the American criminal justice system" conduct any kind of activity that resembles justice. An overview of criminal justice in the United States reveals that "the system" was conceived by Norman kings of England in the eleventh century. From this point forward, government owned conflict between individuals and developed an administrative structure to manage these conflicts. Police, courts, and corrections diverged from their English counterparts during the nineteenth century and took on their modern shape during the Progressive Era. Today, the U.S. criminal-justice bureaucracy is monumental in size and expanding. A decentralized, fragmented network of government agencies carries out the administration of justice, but inefficiency is not the most serious challenge. The assembly-line method of case processing does promote a kind of efficiency. The more profound problems within contemporary criminal justice have to do with the fact that victims are slighted, discretion promotes injustice, and accountability remains an elusive goal. In the years to come, technology will likely play a larger part but probably will not bring about greater justice. Privatization may begin to erode the government's monopoly, but commercialization will benefit relatively few. Mediation projects hold the promise of a neighborhood-based means of conflict resolution but are in danger of being co-opted by government. Then and now, justice is up to the bureaucrats of good and evil.

NOTE

1. The following cases are discussed in the chapter: *Furman v. Georgia*, 408 U.S. 238 (1972), *Gideon v. Wainwright*, 372 U.S. 335 (1963), *Miranda v. Arizona*, 384 U.S. 436 (1966), *Monroe v. Pape*, 365 U.S. 167 (1961), *Powell v. Alabama*, 287 U.S. 45 (1932), *Strickland v. Washington*, 446 U.S. 668 (1984).

REFERENCES

Aguirre, Adalberto and Baker, David V., Empirical Research on Racial Discrimination in the Imposition of the Death Penalty, *Criminal Justice Abstracts 22*:135–153 (1990).

Alpert, Geoffrey P. and Dunham, Roger G., *Policing Urban America*, Waveland Press, Prospect Heights, Ill., 1988.

Archambeault, William, Emerging Issues in the Use of Microcomputers as Management Tools in Criminal Justice Administration, In *Microcomputers in Criminal Justice* (Joseph Waldron, ed.), Anderson, Cincinnati, Ohio, 1987.

Barrineau, H. E., *Civil Liability in Criminal Justice*, Anderson, Cincinnati, Ohio, 1987.

Bastian, Lisa D., Crime and the Nation's Households, 1991, in *Bureau of Justice Statistics Bulletin*, U.S. Department of Justice, Washington, D.C., 1992.

Bayley, David H. and Bittner, Egon, Learning the Skills of Policing, in *Critical Issues in Policing* (Roger G. Dunham and Geoffrey P. Alpert, eds.), Waveland Press, Prospect Heights, Ill., 1989.

Berman, Harold, *Law and Revolution: The Formation of Western Legal Tradition*, Harvard University Press, Cambridge, Mass., 1983.

Bureau of Justice Statistics, *Historical Statistics on Prisoners in State and Federal Institutions, Yearend 1925–86*, U.S. Department of Justice, Washington, D.C., 1988.

Cam, Helen, *Law Finders and Law Makers in Medieval England*, Barnes and Noble, New York, 1963.

Carp, Robert A. and Stidham, Ronald, *Judicial Process in America*, Congressional Quarterly Press, Washington, D.C., 1993.

Cavender, Gray and Knepper, Paul, Strange Interlude: An Analysis of Juvenile Parole Decision Making, *Social Problems 39*:387–399 (1992).

Christie, Nils, Conflict as Property, *British Journal of Criminology 17*:1–15 (1977).

Clynch, Edward J. and Neubauer, David W., Trial Courts as Organizations: A Critique and Synthesis, *Law and Policy Quarterly 3*:69–94 (1981).

Cohen, Robyn L., Prisoners in 1990, *Bureau of Justice Statistics Bulletin*, U.S. Department of Justice, Washington, D.C., 1991.

Corbett, Ronald and Marx, Gary T., No Soul in the Machine: Technofallacies in the Electronic Monitoring Movement, *Justice Quarterly 8*:399–414 (1991).

Cunningham, William C., Strauchs, John J., and Van Meter, Clifford W., Private Security: Patterns and Trends, *National Institute of Justice Research in Brief*, National Institute of Justice, Washington, D.C., 1991.

Dawson, John M., Prosecutors in State Courts, 1990, in *Bureau of Justice Statistics Bulletin*, U.S. Department of Justice, Washington, D.C., 1992.

Douthit, Nathan, August Vollmer, Berkeley's First Chief of Police, and the Emergence of Police Professionalism, *California Historical Quarterly 54*:101–124 (1975).

Eisenstein, James and Jacob, Herbert, *Felony Justice: An Organizational Analysis of Criminal Courts*, Little, Brown, Boston, 1977.

Feeley, Malcolm, *The Process is the Punishment*, Russell Sage Foundation, New York, 1979.

Friedman, Lawrence, *A History of American Law*, Simon and Schuster, New York, 1973.

Glick, Henry R., *Courts, Politics and Justice*, McGraw-Hill, New York, 1993.

Goebel, Julius, *Felony and Misdemeanor: A Study of the History of Criminal Law*, University of Pennsylvania Press, Philadelphia, 1976.

Greene, Jack R., Bynum, Tim S., and Cordner, Gary W., Planning and the Play of Power: Resource Acquisition Among Criminal Justice Agencies, in *The Administration and Management of Criminal Justice Organizations* (Stan Stojkovic, John Klofas, and David Kalinich, eds.), Waveland Press, Prospect Heights, Ill., 1990.

Jankowski, Louis, Probation and Parole 1990, in *Bureau of Justice Statistics Bulletin*, U.S. Department of Justice, Washington, D.C., 1991.

Karmen, Andrew, *Crime Victims: An Introduction to Victimology*, Brooks/Cole, Pacific Grove, Calif., 1990.

Keve, Paul W., *Prisons and the American Conscience: A History of U.S. Federal Corrections*, Southern Illinois University Press, Carbondale, Ill., 1991.

Lane, Roger, *Policing the City: Boston 1822–1885*, Atheneum, New York, 1975.

Langan, Patrick A., Felony Sentences in State Courts, 1988, in *Bureau of Justice Statistics Bulletin*, U.S. Department of Justice, Washington, D.C., 1990.

Levine, James P., Musheno, Michael C., and Palumbo, Dennis J., *Criminal Justice: Law In Action*, John Wiley, New York, 1986.

Lilly, J. Robert and Knepper, Paul, An International Perspective on the Privatization of Corrections, *Howard Journal of Criminal Justice 31*:174–191 (1992).

Lilly, J. Robert and Knepper, Paul, The Corrections-Commercial Complex, *Crime and Delinquency 39*: 150–166 (1993).

Linder, Charles and Savarese, Margaret, The Evolution of Probation, *Federal Probation 48*:3–10 (1984).

Lindgren, Sue A., Justice Expenditure and Employment, 1990, in *Bureau of Justice Statistics Bulletin*, U.S. Department of Justice, Washington, D.C., 1992.

Lyman, Michael and Potter, Gary W., *Drugs in Society*, Anderson, Cincinnati, Ohio, 1991.

Maguire, Kathleen and Flanagan, Timothy J., *Sourcebook of Criminal Justice Statistics 1990*, U.S. Department of Justice, Washington, D.C., 1991.

McKelvey, Blake, *American Prisons: A History of Good Intentions*, Patterson Smith, Montclair, N.J., 1977.

Melone, Albert P., Criminal Code Reform and the Interest Group Politics of the American Bar Association, in *The Politics of Crime and Criminal Justice* (Erika S. Fairchild and Vincent J. Webb, eds.), Sage, Beverly Hills, Calif., 1985.

Murton, Thomas and Hyams, Joe, *Accomplices to Crime: The Arkansas Prison Scandal*, Grove Press, New York, 1969.

Neubauer, David W., *America's Courts and the Criminal Justice System*, Brooks/Cole, Pacific Grove, Calif., 1992.

Peachey, Dean E., The Kitchener Experiment, in *Mediation and Criminal Justice: Victims, Offenders and Community* (Martin Wright and Burt Galaway, eds.), Sage, Newbury Park, Calif., 1989.

Pisciotta, Alexander W., Scientific Reform: The 'New Penology' at Elmira, 1876–1900, *Crime and Delinquency 29*:613–630 (1983).

Powers, Richard G., *Secrecy and Power: The Life of J. Edgar Hoover*, Free Press, New York, 1987.

Pugh, Ralph, *Imprisonment in Medieval England*, Cambridge University Press, Cambridge, 1968.

Rawls, John, *A Theory of Justice*, Belknap Press, Cambridge, Mass., 1971.

Reaves, Brian A., State and Local Police Departments, 1990, in *Bureau of Justice Statistics Bulletin*, U.S. Department of Justice, Washington, D.C., 1992a.

Reaves, Brian A., Sheriffs' Departments 1990, in *Bureau of Justice Statistics Bulletin*, U.S. Department of Justice, Washington, D.C., 1992b.

Reichel, Philip L., Southern Slave Patrols as a Transitional Police Type, *American Journal of Police* 7:51–77 (1988).

Richardson, James F., The Struggle to Establish a London-Style Police Force for New York City, *New York Historical Society Quarterly* 49:175–197 (1965).

Rhynhart, Frederick W. and Thomson, J. Michael, *Strickland* Standard Evaluation Using Kentucky and Tennessee Data: The New Flexible Federalism? Paper presented at the annual meeting of the Southern Criminal Justice Association, New Orleans, October, 1990.

Schlegel, Kip, Life Imitating Art: Interpreting Information From Electronic Surveillance, in *Critical Issues in Criminal Investigation* (Michael J. Palmiotto, ed.), Anderson, Cincinnati, Ohio, 1988.

Skoler, Daniel L., *Organizing the Non-System*, Lexington Books, Lexington, Mass., 1977.

Steffensmeier, Darrell and Harer, Miles D., Is the Crime Rate Really Falling? An 'Aging' U.S. Population and Its Impact on the Nation's Crime Rate, *Journal of Research in Crime and Delinquency* 24:23–48 (1987).

Steffensmeier, Darrell and Harer, Miles D., Did Crime Rise or Fall During the Reagan Presidency? The Effects of an 'Aging' U.S. Population on the Nation's Crime Rate, *Journal of Research in Crime and Delinquency* 28:330–359 (1991).

Stephan, James J., Jail Inmates, 1990, in *Bureau of Justice Statistics Bulletin*, U.S. Department of Justice, Washington, D.C., 1991.

Thomas, Charles W. and Logan, Charles H., The Development, Present Status, and Future Potential of Correctional Privatization in America, paper presented at the American Legislative Exchange Council Conference, Miami, March, 1991.

Travis, Lawrence, Latessa, Edward J., and Vito, Gennaro F., Agenda Building in Criminal Justice: The Case of Determinate Sentencing, in *The Administration and Management of Criminal Justice Organizations* (Stan Stojkovic, John Klofas, and David Kalinich, eds.), Waveland Press, Prospect Heights, Ill., 1990.

Turow, Scott, *Presumed Innocent*, Farrar Strauss Giroux, New York, 1987.

Umbreit, Mark S., Violent Offenders and Their Victims, in *Mediation and Criminal Justice: Victims, Offenders and Community* (Martin Wright and Burt Galaway, eds.), Sage, Newbury Park, Calif., 1989.

Van Ness, Daniel, *Crime and Its Victims*, InterVarsity Press, Downers Grove, Ill., 1986.

Vera Institute of Justice, *Felony Arrests*, Longman, New York, 1981.

Walker, Samuel, *Sense and Nonsense About Crime*, Brooks/Cole, Pacific Grove, Calif., 1989.

Walker, Samuel, *The Police in America*, McGraw-Hill, New York, 1992.

Wilson, James Q., *Thinking About Crime*, Vintage Books, New York, 1983.

Zehr, Howard, *Changing Lenses: A New Focus for Crime and Justice*, Herald Press, Scottsdale, Pa., 1990.

29
Termination and Bureaucracy: Ending Government Programs, Policies, and Organizations

Mark R. Daniels
Memphis State University, Memphis, Tennessee

I. INTRODUCTION

U.S. District Court Judge Ralph Thompson issued a decree in 1978 closing Oklahoma's Public Training Schools for dependent and neglected children. The decree called for widespread reform in Oklahoma's juvenile justice system, primarily through the process of deinstitutionalization, or placing children in the least restrictive environment. The state training schools were ordered closed, institutionalization as a juvenile justice policy was ended, and the policy of deinstitutionalization through community based treatment was to begin.

Twelve years later, despite Judge Thompson's order, over 1,000 dependent children were still institutionalized. But instead of being housed in state run "reform schools," these children were patients admitted to state operated and privately owned psychiatric hospitals, costing Oklahoma taxpayers approximately $40 million a year in Medicaid funds (Daniels, 1992, p. 2). According to psychologist Lois Weithorn, instead of "deinstitutionalized" these children were "trans-institutionalized" (*Newsweek*, 1989, p. 67), moved from one institutional setting to another. Although the public program of state training schools in Oklahoma ended, the policy of institutionalization—this time in psychiatric hospitals—continued.

How a terminated public policy, though ended in one program manifestation, can continue through a different program in a different bureaucratic location gives insight into the tenacity and resiliency of public policy in the face of organizational termination. The almost uncanny ability of public organizations and their policies to survive and prosper in the face of political and legal efforts aimed at their demise has led one author to ask, "Are government organizations immortal?" (Kaufman, 1976). And while public organizations and policies are human creations and are certainly not immortal, they certainly are hard to end, eliminate, terminate, kill. As with Dr. Frankenstein's monster, the creation eventually defies the creator.

The study of public policy has traditionally focused on formation, implementation, and evaluation. Surprisingly absent in the study of public policy is the phenomenon of termination.

Charles O. Jones has observed, "We know much more about how to get government going than we do about how to get it stopped" (Jones, 1984, p. 236). In this respect, much more research and investigation into termination are needed, especially in times of budget deficits, tax base shrinkage, and demands for more limited, streamlined government services. But how much do we already know about policy termination?

This chapter will review the most current literature on organizational and policy termination and will define and describe the reasons for, the types of, and the obstacles and steps to termination. Termination will be discussed as part of the overall process of public policy-making. Next, summaries of Herbert Kaufman's work in termination will be presented and discussed. Following this, case studies will provide examples of actual terminations: first, the case of Sunset legislation will be reviewed; and, second, the results of the termination of public training schools in the states of Massachusetts and Oklahoma will be compared. Finally, conclusions will be made about the need for and prospects of public sector terminations.

II. ORGANIZATIONAL AND POLICY TERMINATION: AN OVERVIEW

A. Definition

Public sector termination can be defined as "the deliberate conclusion or cessation of specific government functions, programs, policies, or organizations" (Brewer and deLeon, 1983, p. 385). This definition does not include changes in policy emphasis or jurisdiction, which may be organizational attempts to redirect activities and to justify existence, as policy termination. That termination is deliberate implies that it is rational: termination is premeditated behavior, with the intent of ending a particular public organization or policy. In this sense, it should be possible to identify and explain the circumstances leading up to and causing policy termination.

B. Termination and Policy Process Steps

According to Eugene Bardach, "Termination occurs—when it does occur—with either a bang or a very long whimper" (Bardach, 1976, p. 125). In the former case, public programs and policies end, after a lengthy resistance, with a shattering force. A lengthy political struggle finishes with an explosive ending. With the latter case, public programs and policies end after a long-term decline in the resources with which they are sustained. In either case, the key phrase in Bardach's quotation may be "when it [termination] does occur," referring to the reality that program or policy termination continues to be rare, even in the second decade of serious academic inquiry.

Policy-making is best described as a continuing process moving from perceiving problems needing a government response, to formulating, implementing, and evaluating the adopted policies (Brewer, 1978, p. 339; Jones, 1984, chapter 2). As part of the policy process, termination occurs at the very end, as a last step. Brewer and deLeon (1983) identify six steps in the policy-making process: initiation, estimation, selection, implementation, evaluation, and finally, termination. Jones (1984) similarly identifies seven steps in the policy-making process: getting problems to government; formulating proposals; legitimating programs; budgeting programs; implementing programs; evaluating programs; and last, conclusion/resolution/termination. In both cases, termination is seen as the final outcome of a political, but highly rational, policy process. Seen this way, termination is an integral part of the American political process.

Usually, however, termination has been treated as not so much an end as a beginning: a beginning to correct an errant policy or set of programs (Brewer and deLeon, 1983, pp. 385, 386;

deLeon, 1978), or to revise programmatic assumptions or components. Termination in both these treatments of steps is not so much a deliberate end to a policy or program as a revision or readjustment. Policy termination as previously defined in this chapter remains a rare phenomenon, and, one author observes, "It is precisely the rarity of the phenomenon that makes it important" (Bardach, 1976, p. 123).

C. Reasons for Termination

Peter deLeon examined numerous termination experiences and concluded that there are three main criteria, or reasons, leading to termination decisions (1983, pp. 634, 635): financial imperatives, governmental efficiencies, and political ideology. Huge budget deficits and tax revenue shrinkage lead to financial imperatives: programs are reduced wherever such cuts are deemed politically possible. Governmental efficiencies also revolve around cost and performance issues: is a program too costly in terms of service delivered? For example, the Comprehensive Employment and Training Act (CETA) was terminated when the excessive cost of training employable personnel was discovered. Finally, some programs are terminated without regard to financial imperatives or efficiencies and solely on the basis of political ideology. For example, President Nixon's opposition to the Office of Economic Opportunity and President Reagan's opposition to the Departments of Energy and Education were based upon ideological reasons.

In addition to the three reasons advanced by deLeon, a fourth can be advanced: a change in behavioral theory about how administrative, human, or social services should be delivered. For example, health research conducted during the 1950s demonstrated the behavioral benefits of deinstitutionalization to mental patients. Opponents of institutionalization often dramatized abuses in mental institutions in order to rally the public behind reform efforts and to create health services more appropriate and effective for treating mental illness (Bradley, 1976). Other health care reforms have also stressed organizational and policy termination (Behn, 1976; Daniels, 1992).

Finally, allowing for and tolerating program failure is a fifth reason for termination. Robert Biller suggests that termination is "critical to learning" (1976, pp. 136–139). That is, given the change and uncertainty that characterize modern postindustrial societies, and given policymakers' limited ability to forecast the future appropriateness or success of current policies, terminating policies that do not work is one way for policymakers to learn from their mistakes. Biller suggests that policy-making should be initially carried out on a trial basis, with "short time and money tethers," and that policies be corrected and adjusted according to feedback mechanisms. Although there are few examples of trial-type policy-making, the social experiments of the 1960s conform to this type of termination. For example, the New Jersey Negative Income Tax experiment tested an innovative approach to public assistance, representing a reform of the U.S. welfare system. The program was implemented on a sample population, ended after only a few years, and provided economists and social scientists with valuable data about welfare system alternatives.

D. Types of Policy Termination

The termination of public programs and policies has so far referred to the end of government functions and organizations in addition to programs and policies. At times, it is not possible to differentiate between a program and its government organization, or its government function. As an example, deLeon (1977, p. 10) points out the Social Security Administration (SSA) as an organization difficult to distinguish from its public funded government administered pension function, or from its social security payments program. Terminating the SSA as an organization also means terminating the function and program of public pension administration. Nonetheless, it is possible to distinguish among the terminations of public functions, organizations, programs, and policies.

A government function is defined by deLeon (1977, p. 10) as a service provided by the government which transcends organizations and policies. Functions are essentially those services which the public has defined as within the common interest, and which would not be delivered, or would be impossible to deliver, if not delivered by the government. Given that functions are tied to underlying assumptions about the role and responsibility of government, functions appear to be the most resistant to termination (deLeon, 1977, p. 11; Kaufman, 1976, p. 64).

Organizations are defined by deLeon as groups of employees that constitute a governmental institution (1977, p. 12), and the existence of organizations is closely tied to the government functions which they fulfill. Organizations are virtually immortal, but are easier to terminate than functions. When organizations are terminated, the function they perform is usually transferred to another organization (deLeon, 1977, p. 11; Kaufman, 1976, p. 64).

Policies are general approaches or strategies applied to the performance of government functions and are much more susceptible to termination because of four reasons identified by deLeon (1977, p. 13): First, organizations usually act in self-preservation and will sacrifice a policy in order to save the whole. Terminated policies can always be replaced with new policies which employ different approaches or strategies. Second, policies have fewer allies in the policy arena than do organizations. Organizations usually have stronger political supporters than do policies. Third, policies are easier to isolate and evaluate than organizations, which may have multiple policy objectives. Fourth, organizational critics usually focus their complaints against particular policies, which can be sacrificed in order to save the organization. Policy termination, as opposed to functional or organizational termination, has so far been the predominant level of analysis for policy termination analysts.

Finally, programs are the easiest targets to terminate. As operational manifestations of policies, programs are the primary focus of investigators and can easily be dropped and replaced with other, “more effective” programs if need be (deLeon, 1977, p. 14).

It may be useful to see these four types of policy termination as a hierarchy, arranged from the top down, from the most resistant to termination to the most susceptible to termination. Government functions are most resistant to termination, followed by organizations, policies, and finally programs, which are most susceptible to termination. What factors are behind a policy’s resilience to termination?

E. Obstacles to Policy Termination

Peter deLeon identifies six reasons why policy termination may be difficult (1977, pp. 17–28):

1. Intellectual reluctance: people do not like to consider that the underlying thinking behind a policy is flawed or is no longer relevant. People have a vested interest in the ideas behind policies. For this reason, there is an argument that terminators from outside the targeted program might implement termination more effectively than staff connected to the program (deLeon, 1982).

2. Institutional permanence: organizations and their policies are designed to endure beyond a single sponsor or bureaucrat. This bureaucratic strength works against termination efforts. A good example is the so-called sacred cow entitlement programs, such as social security or

veterans' benefits. Enacting legislation establishes these policies for generations of recipients, and termination is all but impossible (Wallerstein, 1976).

3. Systems adjustment: organizations and their policies are systems which respond to and change with their environment. In this case, an organization or a policy can always be one step ahead of termination. For example, killing off outdated military weapons systems occurs every year; however, though one system may die, another similar to it is reborn in its place (Lambright and Sapolsky, 1976).

4. Antitermination coalitions: significant political groups, some quite unsuspected, can arise in opposition to termination. Examples of these coalitions include the abolishment of the District of Columbia motorcycle squad and the formidable adversaries against termination who surprisingly emerged (Shulsky, 1976, pp. 183–197), and the abolishment of Miami's horse mounted police patrols (Ellis, 1983).

5. Legal obstacles: in a litigation prone political environment, the guarantee of due process may postpone termination indefinitely. When Commissioner Jerome Miller was closing the Massachusetts Public Training Schools, he anticipated the legal opposition and possible restraining order that would be brought by employees of the schools once layoffs were announced. He prevented this opposition and successfully closed the schools by continuing full employment, even though the students were removed from the schools and the employees had no work to perform (Behn, 1976, p. 153).

6. High start-up versus sunk costs: the notion that there are sunk costs which would be lost with termination often justifies the continuation of a suspect policy. Even though the District of Columbia's motorcycle squad was eliminated, twelve motorcycles were retained for ceremonial purposes, and these cycles soon found their way back to patrolling the streets in order to find something for the motormen to do when they were not escorting official limousines and motorcades (Shulsky, 1976, p. 197). Since the motorcycles were there, and the motormen were on payroll, the abolished patrol policy was rolled back.

The formidable obstacles against termination explain the dearth of termination studies, and the lack of generalization possible with the few extant termination cases. The most substantial effort to generalize about termination to date has been made by Herbert Kaufman in two book-length treatments (Kaufman, 1976; 1985).

III. KAUFMAN ON TERMINATION

Herbert Kaufman first explored the concept of organizational life cycles in *Are Government Organizations Immortal?* (1976), followed some years later by *Time, Chance, and Organizations* (1985). Kaufman views organizations as similar to, but not the same as, living organisms. And, like all living organisms, organizations should have a life cycle of "youthful vigor maturity, old age, and death" (Kaufman, 1985, p. 25). Death, or the termination of an organization, should be a natural consequence eventually resulting from the birth of an organization.

In his first study, *Are Government Organizations Immortal?*, Kaufman surveys ten of the eleven executive departments in existence in 1973 in the Executive Office of the President and compares the number of organizations listed in a 1923 Brookings Institution study of the federal administrative structure. Kaufman was examining the life cycles of the organizations: how many births over a fifty-year period, how many deaths, and the number of birthdays, or age, of the organization. He found that of the 175 organizations which existed in 1923, only 27 were terminated over a fifty-year period, or about 15%. Kaufman then examined the mortality rate of private organizations over the same fifty-year period by looking at business failure statistics and found that private organizations had a death rate over two times higher than the sampled government organizations. Why do government organizations have a greater life expectancy?

Kaufman suggests that the marginal change provided by an incremental government decision-making process insulates governmental organizations from a natural life cycle. Those deaths that did occur seemed, to Kaufman, to be attributable more to chance, or bad luck, than to any other factor. For most of the terminated governmental organizations studied by Kaufman, "overall, however, chance seems to have played a large part in their termination" (Kaufman, 1985, p. 55). The question, Are government organizations immortal? is asked as the conclusion of the study.

The immortality of organizations was further pursued in his later work, *Time, Chance, and Organizations*. In this study, Kaufman hypotheses that organizations die because "the inflows of energy and other resources necessary for them to keep their activities going, to keep their engines running, dry up" (Kaufman, 1985, p. 27). It is in this work that he advances his notion of organizational evolution. Organizational death is the failure of systems maintenance, the inability of an organization to evolve and adapt to new environmental conditions: organizations no longer adapt to their environment; fall behind the evolution of other, more successfully adapting organizations; and eventually go the way of the dinosaurs. Kaufman continues, however, to regard chance as playing a role in the termination of organizations: the timing of termination, not the existence of organizational death itself, appears to be random, left to chance, the luck of the draw.

Kaufman's work measures the resiliency of government organizations and suggests that much more study is needed before generalizations can be made about which organization, under what circumstances, and at what time, will become terminally ill. A hypothesis which Kaufman advances for testing is the "threshold test." According to this hypothesis, "organizations form out of a medium consisting of people, culture in the fullest sense, and energy; and the medium is enriched, or 'thickens,' as a result of the activities of organizations—even when organizations dissolve, for their contents return to the medium and are recycled to other organizations" (Kaufman, 1985, p. 141). Kaufman is making an organic comparison that as living things are formed out of the "dust" of the planet, so too are organizations formed out of the medium of people. The medium out of which living things formed becomes thicker when the number and complexity of the ingredients it comprises increase with time. With organizations, as the activities and interdependencies of people multiply and the levels of knowledge and skill rise, the medium that gives birth and sustenance to organizations becomes thicker. Are there indicators of thickness?

Kaufman proposes the following factors as indicators of the thickness of an organization's medium (Kaufman, 1985, pp. 144–146):

1. Organizational specialization: a high division of labor among organizations results in high interdependence and exchange.
2. Occupational specialization: a diverse, experienced work force, possessing occupational expertise, can move from one organization to another without difficulty.
3. Literacy and educational levels: the extent of educational expertise, coupled with support from educational institutions.
4. Cultural institutions and personnel: the extent that research centers and libraries support organizations and share collective knowledge.
5. Volume and speed of communication: the means of storing, retrieving, sharing, and communicating the collective knowledge of the organization.

6. Energy consumption per capita: technological advancement and a crowded and fertile organizational environment requires a high level of organizational energy.
7. Organizational density: the greater the number of organizations, the greater the chances of formation of complex combinations of organizations.

The thickness of an organization influences how healthy and resilient it is to terminal diseases: an organization's thickness determines its resistance to termination. As an organization is developing over its life cycle, that is, as its medium is becoming thicker, it develops an ever increasing resistance to termination. Termination potential may be greatest just after birth, while an organization's medium is beginning to develop thickness, or after maturity, when an organization's medium may become static and inflexible and incapable of integrating new inputs or of producing enough maintenance outputs.

Kaufman's termination studies are both empirical and speculative. His data in *Are Government Organizations Immortal?* were from a federal executive agency, and his conclusions were based upon statistical, summary analysis. In *Time, Chance, and Organizations*, however, Kaufman engaged in speculation about the nature of organizational existence and survival. Some reviewers expressed disappointment over what they perceived as the "speculative nature" (Hines, 1987) or the "overly sketchy comments" (White, 1987) of the book. In all fairness to Kaufman, however, his earlier work pioneered empirical inquiry into organizational termination, and it was from this work that hypotheses about the possible life cycles of organizations emerged. His work in *Time, Chance and Organizations* is an effort at theory building and is designed to encourage more empirical research into organizational termination.

Currently, two studies, both in the field of health care policy (Mueller, 1988; Daniels, 1992), have used some of Kaufman's termination theories. Muller's research found evidence supporting Kaufman's theory of longevity, and Daniels tested hypotheses which supported Kaufman's organizational medium theory. The results of both studies demonstrate the utility of Kaufman's termination theories.

IV. TACTICAL TERMINATION: THE CASE OF SUNSET LEGISLATION

A. A Brief History of Sunset

Sunset legislation is designed to terminate agencies and boards of state government automatically. Its intent is not so much to provide an immediate end to state agencies, but rather to require state legislators to conduct comprehensive program evaluation of existing boards and agencies (Common Cause, 1982, p. 3). Nonetheless, 6 years after the first state adopted Sunset legislation, a total of 271 boards and agencies were terminated, and numerous others were reorganized, recreated, or consolidated (Common Cause, 1982, p. 42). As of January 1989, a grand total of 325 state government entities were terminated (Kearney, 1990, p. 52).

Sunset legislation requires the periodic review of state agencies under the threat of automatic termination unless recreated through law. Since the enactment of the first Sunset law by Colorado in 1976, a total of thirty-six states have adopted Sunset laws (Common Cause, 1982, p. 1). The review cycle of state agencies and boards is specified by some Sunset laws and can range from every four to every twelve years.

Common Cause conducted the first comprehensive survey of the impact of Sunset legislation in 1982; they found that the benefits of Sunset included improvements in government performance through increased agency efficiency and public accountability; financial savings, with one-sixth of Sunset states reporting sizable savings; and legislative experience in conducting oversight, especially in linking oversight to the normal legislative process (Common Cause, 1982, pp. 12–24).

The most recent survey and analysis of the American states' experience with Sunset were conducted by Richard Kearney (1990, pp. 49–57), who reports that Sunset legislation has successfully terminated more than 325 government entities. More importantly, he notes, "State executive branches have been cleaned up through the deletion of nonfunctional, redundant, or unnecessary entities" (Kearney, 1990, p. 53). Ironically, however, Sunset has led to the creation of new government agencies. For example, Florida has terminated 90 agencies under Sunset since 1978 but has created 104 new agencies (Kearney, 1990, p. 53).

Evaluating the costs and benefits of Sunset is difficult in large part because of intangible variables that defy operationalization or measurement. Nonetheless, Kearney reports that eight states have compared the costs and benefits of Sunset and gives examples of three of these states. Over the 1980–1982 period, Connecticut reported costs of $201,500 against benefits of $518,000; Maryland saved $251,545 against costs of $82,500 in 1983; and Tennessee identified $105 million possibly saved since 1978.

Kearney also reported that although the majority of Sunset adopters have continued to use this process, twelve states have repealed or suspended the enabling legislation (Kearney, 1990, p. 55). Some of the states which eliminated Sunset review had relatively successful experiences with the process. For example, Montana terminated five agencies, Connecticut twenty-nine, Arkansas twenty-eight, Rhode Island seventeen, New Hampshire fifteen, and Illinois fifty agencies (Kearney, 1990, p. 55). Kearney hypothesizes that the states repealing or suspending Sunset may have developed alternative legislative oversight procedures or have been unable to maintain Sunset review because of low levels of legislative professionalism. Subsequent quantitative, comparative analysis of the Sunset dropouts confirms that, with the exception of Illinois, the dropouts are characterized by weak legislative capacity for the type of intensive evaluation and review required by Sunset (Kearney, 1990, p. 55). Part-time legislators with weak professional staff assistance are hard pressed to complete the evaluation and review involved in oversight of the Sunset process.

B. Sunset Legislation and the Adoption of New, Innovative Policies

A recent Sunset study advances and tests the theory that a government's capacity for adopting innovative policies is dependent upon its ability to terminate outdated organizations, policies, and programs (Daniels, 1993). As policies mature and grow old over time, they continue to address public problems that may have already been settled, have drastically changed in nature or intensity, or have possibly been surpassed in importance by new problems perceived to possess greater social importance and priority. Ending outdated policies releases economic and administrative resources that can be applied to new problems through innovative policies. As Brewer and deLeon observe, a current challenge facing most modern societies is how to adapt policy-making attitudes and habits developed during periods of high and sustained economic growth to the changing political and social demands resulting from the current period of economic stagnation (Brewer and deLeon, 1983, p. 387).

Is a government's capacity for adopting innovative policies dependent upon its ability to terminate outdated organizations, policies, and programs? In order to provide an answer to this theoretical question, several hypotheses involving the relationship between the adoption by state governments of Sunset legislation and the states' adoption of other public policies were tested.

However, little supporting evidence for this theory was found. The results of the study, however, provided additional insights about the nature of Sunset legislation.

States that are usually reluctant to adopt other new policies quickly, the "laggard states," are among the first states to adopt Sunset legislation. The relatively low legislative professionalism of these laggard states, and the inability of these legislatures to conduct oversight of public programs and agencies effectively, lead these legislatures to adopt Sunset as a means of strengthening their oversight function and of obtaining greater power over the administrative bureaucracy and the governor.

Ironically, it is also this low legislative professionalism that has led some of the Sunset adopting states to repeal or suspend Sunset. The substantial workload involved in reviewing agencies of state government is too much for part-time legislatures with little staff assistance.

C. The Future of Sunset Legislation

The experience of state governments with Sunset legislation has for the most part been successful. The states that have adopted Sunset have experienced improved administrative performance, accountability and efficiency, and financial savings and have been able to incorporate oversight into the normal legislative process. While some states have repealed Sunset, most did so in the early 1980s, and it appears that the remaining twenty-four Sunset states are content, for the time being, to retain it. Nonetheless, Kearney predicts that additional dropouts will occur (1990, p. 56).

Given the relative success of state governments, it is surprising that the federal government has not experimented with Sunset. Federal legislators may have been apprehensive about undertaking the sheer amount of increased administrative oversight connected with Sunset. Policy experts were not enthusiastic about the adoption of Sunset at the federal level. For example, deLeon gave a critical review of the limits of Sunset legislation, questioning whether or not Sunset is necessary, or whether performance evaluations of federal organizations and policies can be conducted objectively (deLeon, 1977). Behn (1977) recommended against federal adoption of Sunset, despite substantial support in the U.S. Senate.

Whatever the future holds for Sunset legislation, it has achieved many successes, has many supporters, and is an example of how organizations and policies can be terminated.

V. CLOSING THE MASSACHUSETTS AND OKLAHOMA PUBLIC TRAINING SCHOOLS: A CASE COMPARISON

One shortcoming of research conducted on policy termination is that it usually takes the form of a single case study which in some way is idiosyncratic. As Eugene Bardach observes, because "social science—and social scientists—thrive on generalizations rather than idiosyncracies, termination has never become "hot" as a topic of academic interest" (1976, p. 123). Bardach's ground-breaking symposium on policy termination published in the journal *Policy Sciences* in 1976 contained six essays, all of them case studies. It is difficult for researchers to find more than one government terminating a specific policy, to compare how governments terminate similar policies, or to make generalizations from similar studies. Are there similar policies which states have tried to terminate?

Starting in the 1960s, state governments began a trend and started to close state operated training schools. These were actually "reform" schools, intended for delinquent youth. For example, the Massachusetts Division of Youth Services removed nearly 1,000 delinquent youths from state training schools and placed them in an array of community based services (Behn,

1976). Reformers argued that closing the schools was supported by research which found that large juvenile facilities do not deter crime and often create violent and antisocial behavior among residents (Behn, 1976, pp. 156–158).

Oklahoma is another state which has recently experienced the termination of state training schools. By comparing the experiences of Massachusetts and Oklahoma, it is possible to avoid the "idiosyncrasy" of a single case study and attempt to make generalizations about the termination efforts of both states.

A. Closing the Massachusetts Public Training Schools

Robert D. Behn conducted a study of the termination of Massachusetts's Public Training Schools as a way of examining a successful effort at policy termination. His study was eventually published in the 1976 *Policy Sciences* symposium on policy termination, mentioned previously. Behn's primary research question was how Dr. Jerome G. Miller, commissioner of the Department of Youth Services, was able to accomplish what so few others have: terminate a government program.

Behn first identifies five survival tactics used by administrative agencies listed in a public administration textbook (Simon et al., 1950, chapter 19) and looks at how Dr. Miller was able to overcome these tactics and terminate the schools.

The first tactic is seeking the support of important extragovernmental groups. Commissioner Miller did not have any direct client or organized interest group to contend with. He did, however, have the employees to consider, and anticipating the confrontation that would result from layoffs, Miller decided to remove the youths from the schools but leave the employees on the payroll. Although forty-four employees were eventually terminated, Behn observes that "the willingness of Miller . . . to leave unproductive DYS employees on the payroll while the institutions were closed and the policy changes consolidated was essential to neutralizing the resistance of the employees" (1976, p. 153).

The second tactic is seeking legislative support. Miller received the legislative support of the House speaker, and though he received criticism for some administrative practices, there was never any legislative movement to reopen the schools (Behn, 1976, p. 154). When Miller found it difficult to obtain state funds from the legislature to pay in advance for the group home contracts, he circumvented the need for legislative support by instead accessing federal funds from the Law Enforcement Assistance Administration, administered through the governor's office (Behn, 1976, p. 155).

Seeking the support of superiors and other persons of prestige is the third survival tactic. One of the major supporters of school reform was the governor's spouse, Ms. Jesse Sargent. With the support of the governor, key staff members of the governor, and Jesse Sargent, Miller was able to rely on prestigious allies. At no time did Miller's superiors question his discretion or decision making.

The fourth tactic is seeking public support. Miller was successful in obtaining public support; as Behn notes, he "changed the political question from 'What do we do with these bad kids?' to 'What do we do with these bad institutions?' " (Behn, 1976, p. 157). He made sure that the public realized and understood the need for reform in the schools.

The fifth, and last, survival tactic is executive compromise and survival. Miller did not originally want to close the schools. Rather, he wanted to "replace the 'custodial model' of the reformatories with the 'therapeutic community model'—to 'humanize' the institutions" (Behn, 1976, p. 158). After his efforts to retrain the staff failed, Miller decided to close the institutions rather than deal with staff resistance to retraining. He put the staff in the unenviable position of either supporting the closing or defending the existing inhumane system. Once his efforts to retrain the staff failed, he eliminated the need for any compromise with the staff over reform issues by closing the schools.

Behn also studies how the termination of the schools was implemented. He refers to three problems of implementation identified by Pressman and Wildavsky (1973, chapter 5), changing actors, diverse perspectives, and multiple clearances, and examines how Commissioner Miller avoided them. First, the actors involved in closing the schools did not change, with "most of the major political figures . . . involved during the entire critical period" (Behn, 1976, p. 160).

Second, Behn believes that only one aspect of the diverse perspectives identified by Pressman and Wildavsky, "legal and procedural differences" (Behn, 1976, p. 161), was a real problem for Miller. There were many administrative rules and regulations, outside his span of control, which "prevented him from spending funds on the projects he desired and from assigning loyal personnel to the tasks he wanted done" (Behn, 1976, p. 161). For example, when faced with a shortage of funds for a special camping program at the Middlefield school, he named the program an "annex" of the Shirley school, located 70 miles away, and used funds from the Shirley budget for the Middlefield program. As Behn describes, "Miller employed as elastic and creative interpretations as possible" in order to ensure prompt and successful implementation (Behn, 1976, p. 162).

Third, Miller and his staff faced obstacles resulting from multiple clearances and approval requirements but circumvented barriers, went outside regular administrative channels, and used high-ranking executives to walk paperwork through the bureaucracy. While no criminal wrongdoing occurred, staff members admitted not following state procedures in the quest to implement reform (Behn, 1976, p. 163).

Behn concludes that closing the Massachusetts Training Schools was successful because Commissioner Miller did not separate the initiation of the policy of termination from the implementation, the actual "carrying out," of the policy. Miller skillfully negated the survival tactics of the status quo system of training schools and outmaneuvered the obstacles to termination by acting quickly and creatively.

In two later articles, Behn outlines a dozen "hints" for anyone planning a government termination.

Hint 1: Don't float trial balloons.
Hint 2: Enlarge the policy's constituency.
Hint 3: Focus attention on the policy's harm.
Hint 4: Take advantage of ideological shifts to demonstrate harm.
Hint 5: Inhibit compromise.
Hint 6: Recruit an outsider as administrator/terminator.
Hint 7: Avoid legislative votes.
Hint 8: Do not encroach upon legislative prerogatives.
Hint 9: Accept short-term cost increases.
Hint 10: Buy off the beneficiaries.
Hint 11: Advocate adoption, not termination.
Hint 12: Terminate only what is necessary. (Behn, 1978a, pp. 394–410).

This is based in large part on the successful Massachusetts experience closing the training schools (1978a) and offers generalized suggestions for closing any government facility (1978b). However, not all attempts at terminating state training schools have been as successful as Miller's in Massachusetts.

B. Closing the Oklahoma Public Training Schools

Abused and neglected by a mentally ill mother and an alcoholic father, Terry D. was taken away from his parents at age nine. After a series of unsuccessful placements in foster homes, he was declared by the state of Oklahoma to be a "dependent and neglected child" and was admitted to a state training (reform) school. In 1978, when Terry D. was fifteen years old, a class action suit was filed in Terry's behalf by Steve Nozick, deputy director of Legal Aid of Western Oklahoma.

Six years later, after a lengthy legal battle, the U.S. District Court decreed that deprived children or those needing psychiatric treatment cannot be placed in an institution for delinquents. Children like Terry D. would now be placed in neighborhood group homes, instead of reform schools.

Prior to the Terry D. case, half of the children held in the state detention centers or training schools had committed no crime (*Tulsa World*, 1990a, p. A4). The Terry D. case not only focused on the behavioral appropriateness of placing emotionally disturbed children with delinquents, but also alleged that physical abuse and improper medical practices occurred regularly.

The Terry D. case prompted the State of Oklahoma to reform its juvenile services system even before the 1984 decree. In 1982, the Oklahoma Legislature passed House Bill 1468, which included sweeping reforms in the juvenile system (*Tulsa World*, 1990a, p. A1). Simultaneously, five state training schools were closed. Legislative action called for community based services to replace the closed institutions.

Authorizing new programs through legislative initiative was not enough to implement these programs. Appropriation of funds was also needed to begin these reform programs, and, unfortunately, authorization occurred just prior to a severe recession in Oklahoma's economy. "Although the bill contained some innovative ideas for the juvenile justice system, a serious deficit really emerged," according to John Selph, a Tulsa county commissioner. According to Selph, "We closed the institutions, but the community-based program wasn't adequately supported or funded" (*Tulsa World*, 1990a, pp. A1, A4). Referring to the federal decree and the need for expanded juvenile services, Governor David Walters observed, "We blew up the juvenile justice system and never created a new one" (*Tulsa World*, 1989, p. A1). Without adequate funding for the authorized community based services, and with the closing of the state's training schools, the juvenile system was hard pressed to implement the Terry D. court decree. It was difficult to find placement within the juvenile system for emotionally disturbed dependent children. Because the training schools were closed, the state had to find a location to place dependent children.

Part of the Terry D. decision established that a court hearing and judgment—an adjudication—would be used to judge a child as "in need of treatment" (INT). Children are adjudicated INT because they are emotionally disturbed and cannot be treated adequately by the juvenile justice system (Beyer et al., 1990, p. 16). Once a judge hears evidence from medical witnesses that a child is emotionally disturbed, the child can be adjudicated INT, taken out of the juvenile justice system, and possibly committed to a psychiatric hospital. Some, but not all, INT children have committed crimes or have been considered delinquent. All INT children are in need of mental health treatment as a result of abuse, neglect, or emotional or mental illness.

The deinstitutionalization of deprived children, status offenders, and delinquents was a major factor in the increase of INT adjudications. Shortly after the 1984 INT adjudication decree by the court, a steady and then a dramatic increase occurred in INT children. In 1987, more children were committed to state custody as INTs than as delinquents.

Most INTs were sent to hospitals. Medicaid considers residential treatment, psychiatric hospital treatment, and treatment in the Central Oklahoma Juvenile Treatment Center (COJTC) and the Oklahoma Youth Center (OYC) as inpatient treatment and eligible for payment. In this regard, 65% of all INTs received inpatient Medicaid reimbursed psychiatric treatment. Of the remaining 35%, most were placed in group homes, with only a few placements in community or foster homes.

During 1982–1990, the number of individuals age twenty-one and under who received Medicaid financial psychiatric care increased 581% (DHS). Expenditures rose 1000% from slightly more than $4 million in 1982 to almost $40 million in 1990 (DHS).

Early in 1989, the U.S. District Court appointed a three member panel to advise the State of Oklahoma about the types of juvenile programs needed to comply with the Terry D. decree. The report listed thirty recommendations to bring the state's juvenile system into conformity with the Terry D. decree (Beyer, de Muro, and Schwartz, 1990, pp. iv–x). The total price tag of the recommendations was about $40 million, or about how much the state spends each year admitting INT children to psychiatric hospitals.

With the closing of the state training schools, and with the lack of adequate funding for community based services, increasing numbers of children found themselves adjudicated as INTs and committed to psychiatric hospitals and treatment centers. As the deputy director of the Oklahoma Department of Human Services explained, "They're just called something else and put in psychiatric hospitals instead of the training schools" (Miller, 1991). Despite the court's decision to terminate the training schools, the policy of institutionalization continued, this time through the use of admission to psychiatric hospitals.

What additional insights into policy termination result from the examination of Oklahoma's deinstitutionalization experience? First, intellectual reluctance was a hypothesis earlier advanced as an obstacle to termination. Here, the intellectual reluctance of the Oklahoma legislature to adopt or even consider children's mental health or juvenile justice reform resulted in using psychiatric hospitals as the new program manifestation of the policy of institutionalization. Unlike the Massachusetts experience, where training schools were closed under the initiative of the Department of Youth Services with alternative community based group homes (Behn, 1976), Oklahoma had no alternative programs to replace the dead training schools.

Abolishing inappropriate reform schools and saving taxpayers' money are desirable, but replacing an ineffective, costly policy with nothing is how Oklahoma's juvenile system became involved with psychiatric hospitals. A recent example is House Bill 1544, which calls for the elimination of the INT procedure and was introduced by Representative Linda Larason of Oklahoma City. Larason reported that her measure would save state Medicaid money and end inappropriate treatment (*Tulsa World*, 1991, p. A1). Although it passed ninety-four to four, a companion bill which required an annual state plan for mental health treatment of children failed. A federal judge may order an end to a program but cannot order legislation to replace one policy with another.

Second, the hypothesis of high start-up costs was earlier advanced as an obstacle to termination. Ironically, the costs of ending the training schools and funding psychiatric care and of incurring start-up costs and building community based group homes were the same: the only choice was whether to pay now or pay later, and Oklahoma decided to pay later, on the back end. Given that no effective alternative to the closed training schools was formulated by the legislature, the judiciary accessed the state's Medicaid funds through the INT adjudication procedure. "Reallocation of . . . money from the psychological services to prevention efforts would cut . . . costs considerably," explained Claudette Selph, executive director of the Parent-Child Center of

Tulsa (*Tulsa World*, 1990b, p. A4). She continued, "We're paying for it now—we're just paying for it on the back end."

Third, deLeon earlier hypothesized that organizations and their policies are dynamic systems which respond to and change with their environment. The state training schools defined the policy of the juvenile justice system: maintain a secure detention facility for dependent children who need long-term care and for whom foster parents cannot be found. Once the schools were ordered closed, psychiatric hospitals (another variation of a secure detention facility) were an easy organizational substitute, especially when funding could be obtained through Medicaid, without the vote of the legislature. The policy of institutionalization searched for another organization once the training schools were shut down.

Fourth, Kaufman's hypothesis about organizational thickness also helps one to understand the Oklahoma experience. The medium of the state training schools would score high on Kaufman's thickness indicators. Training schools are highly labor intensive: that is, the product is human service delivery to a captive population of dependent children. Training school personnel are usually highly educated: special education teachers, certified counselors, child care workers, psychologists, psychiatrists, administrative staff—all linked together through professional training offered by the state's several universities. The personnel of the training schools are paralleled within the state's many school districts and psychiatric hospitals and combined contribute to a high energy consumption: there is much employment activity in this field. As a medium, training schools score high on almost all of Kaufman's organizational thickness indicators.

The treatment of emotionally troubled children, be it by training schools, school districts, or psychiatric hospitals, is a crowded, dense environment which has given rise to complex organizations. Given the thickness of this organizational medium, it is not surprising that while a court order could terminate a particular program variation, that is, training schools, it could not terminate the medium within which these schools existed. The medium only strengthened the institutional based programs which remained operating after the training schools closed down. The personnel, the careers, the professions, and the degree and training programs connected with the training schools shifted over to the school districts and the psychiatric hospitals. Programs may come and go, but careers, professions, and an organization's medium last one or more human lifetimes.

Earlier, deLeon advanced the hypotheses of institutional permanence and antitermination coalitions as obstacles to termination. Perhaps an organization's medium and the medium's thickness may themselves possess a permanence which maintains a life of its own, beyond the realm of the termination of organizations and programs connected to it. Perhaps an organization's medium, if thick enough, is itself a type of antitermination coalition.

In sum, the termination of the training schools was accompanied by the continuation of the policy of institutionalization for four reasons: first, the intellectual reluctance of legislators to develop a parallel replacement policy; second, the misperceived high start-up costs of alternative programs, which in reality had the same cost as funding psychiatric care through Medicaid; third, the policy of detention, which was part of a dynamic system which searched for, and found, an alternative organization in psychiatric hospitals; and fourth, the medium within which institutionalized programs for the treatment of dependent children operated, which possessed an organizational thickness which was itself an obstacle to termination.

Whatever happened to Terry D.? "Everyone asks me where he is now," explained Steve Nozick, his attorney (*Tulsa World*, 1990c, p. A4). "I don't know. Several years after he became an adult, he was charged as an adult and spent time at McAlester [a state prison]. Predictably, he grew up as an emotionally disturbed kid. Abused kids commit crimes. It's tragic, but it happens to hundreds of kids."

The challenge facing the Oklahoma legislature, the officials at DHS, and the U.S. District Court is how many more hundreds of children will lead tragic lives in the absence of a coherent and comprehensive deinstitutionalized juvenile system. In Oklahoma's case, organizational termination ended with both a bang and a whimper. The program of training schools ended with an abrupt bang, but the policy of institutionalizing dependent children, now manifested by psychiatric hospitalization and detention, continues with a long whimper.

C. Comparing the Termination Experience

Comparing these two cases is a matter of extremes: the Massachusetts case presents a successful termination, while the Oklahoma case demonstrates the tenacity and resiliency of policy in the face of court ordered termination. In Massachusetts, the commissioner of DYS, an outsider newly appointed by the governor, led the movement to reform or close the training schools. His ability to rally public support and negate any organized resistance before it could form was a key factor in closing the schools. In Oklahoma, the school closings were ordered by a federal judge, and there were no key players who led the movement to close the schools. The absence of any termination leaders in Oklahoma led to a legislative vacuum wherein no alternative for the schools was formulated. Commissioner Miller not only closed the schools but made certain that legislation creating community based treatment centers would be enacted. The absence of public awareness or support for the school closings in Oklahoma prevented legislators from perceiving a constituency base for community based programs.

A comparison of these cases indicates the importance of administrative and political leadership during a termination attempt. In Oklahoma, the U.S. District Court relied upon outside experts to evaluate Oklahoma's youth services system and submit recommendations. Ironically, two of the researchers were from Massachusetts and one of them, Ms. Marty Beyer, was active in the research which precipitated the training school closings. Critical to Oklahoma's experience was the lack of attention to implementation of the new policy of deinstitutionalization: after the schools were closed, legislation for replacement programs was never enacted. The outside experts were hired only to advise the court and were not involved in the implementation of the recommendations.

Both cases demonstrated how existing policy-making theories can be operationalized to provide hypotheses for assessing termination efforts. Behn used theories developed by Herbert Simon and associates (Simon et al., p. 1950) and by Jeffrey Pressman and Aaron Wildavsky (1973). The Oklahoma study tested hypotheses developed from the work of Peter deLeon (1977) and Herbert Kaufman (1985). The repeated testing of theory is important for developing the research base of any field of scientific inquiry. Policy researchers should find encouragement in the theory testing in both these cases for the further advancement and testing of hypotheses in future termination studies.

VI. CONCLUSION

Given the moderate attention that has been given to termination studies, a fair amount of knowledge exists about the reasons and types of organization and policy terminations. Far from being an effort at reform or redesign, termination is the deliberate end of a government function, program, policy, or organization. An examination of termination studies indicates five reasons for termination: financial cutbacks, administrative efficiencies, changing political values or ideology, a change in theory about the delivery of government services, and program failure. A government function is most resistant to termination, followed by the organization itself, its policies, and its programs. Commonly mentioned obstacles to termination include intellectual reluctance, institutional permanence, systems adjustment, antitermination coalitions, legal obstacles, and high start-up versus sunk costs.

Herbert Kaufman's research on termination suggests that organizations have life cycles in a way that parallels, but does not duplicate, biological life cycles. Organizations are born, develop, and mature; become senior in age; and eventually die. Organizations have a much longer life span than biological organisms. Public organizations generally have a longer life than private organizations, primarily because of the small amount of change that occurs in incremental decision making. Kaufman's research raises many questions for further research, in particular, his theory about an organization's medium, which consists of people, culture, and energy. Future research could clarify how a medium forms and gives support to organizations, and which elements of a medium are most important to an organization's health, well-being, and life span.

Sunset legislation is an example of institutionalized termination and is currently successful in about half of American states. Most Sunset states have experienced improved administrative performance, accountability, efficiencies, and financial savings. However, some states have repealed their Sunset legislation because of the heavy workload involved in reviewing government agencies.

Comparing the cases of Massachusetts and Oklahoma and the termination of state training schools demonstrates the utility of existing theory in explaining the act of termination. Most significantly, comparing these cases reveals the importance of administrative and political leadership during the formation and implementation of termination.

In sum, while only a modest literature exists in the field of organization and policy termination, much progress has been made in explaining and understanding the phenomenon. This is a field ripe for further study, especially for the original, theory testing research demanded by dissertations.

REFERENCES

Bardach, Eugene, Policy Termination as a Political Process, *Policy Sciences, 7*(2):123–131 (1976).

Behn, Robert D., Closing the Massachusetts Public Training Schools, *Policy Sciences, 7*:(2):151–171 (1976).

Behn, Robert D., The False Dawn of the Sunset Laws, *The Public Interest 49*:103–118 (1977).

Behn, Robert D., How to Terminate a Public Policy: A Dozen Hints for the Would Be Terminator, *Policy Analysis, 4*(3):393–413 (1978a).

Behn, Robert D., Closing a Government Facility, *Public Administration Review, 38*(4):332–338 (1978b).

Beyer, Marty, DeMuro, Paul, and Schwartz, Ira, *Comprehensive Services for Oklahoma's Delinquent, Deprived, In Need of Treatment, and In Need of Services Children: Final Report*, Department of Human Services, State of Oklahoma, Oklahoma City, Oklahoma, 1990.

Biller, Robert P., On Tolerating Policy and Organization: Some Design Considerations, *Policy Sciences, 7*(2):137 (1976).

Bradley, Valerie J., Policy Termination in Mental Health: The Hidden Agenda, *Policy Sciences 7*(2):215–224 (1976).

Brewer, Garry D., Termination: Hard Choices, Harder Questions, *Public Administration Review 38*(3): 338–344 (1978).

Brewer, Garry D. and deLeon, Peter, *The Foundations of Policy Analysis*, The Dorsey Press, Homewood, Illinois, 1983.

Common Cause, *The Status of Sunset in the States: A Common Cause Report*, Common Cause, Washington, D.C., 1982.

Daniels, Mark R., Policy Termination, Innovation and the American States: A Comparative Analysis of Sunset Legislation, paper delivered at the Annual Meeting of the Midwest Political Science Association, Palmer House Hotel, Chicago, Ill., April 15–17, 1993.

Daniels, Mark R., Program Termination and Policy Continuation: Closing the Oklahoma Public Training Schools, paper delivered at the Annual Meeting of the Southeastern Conference on Public Administration, Montgomery, Ala., 1992.

deLeon, Peter, *The Sun Also Sets: An Evaluation of Public Policy*, The Rand Corporation, P-5826, Santa Monica, Calif., 1977.

deLeon, Peter, Public Policy Termination: An End and a Beginning, *Policy Analysis, 4*(3):369–392 (1978).

deLeon, Peter, New Perspectives on Program Termination, *Journal of Policy Analysis and Management* *2*(1):108–111 (1982).

deLeon, Peter, Policy Evaluation and Program Termination, *Policy Studies Review* *2*(4):631–647 (1983).

Department of Human Services, State of Oklahoma, Health Care Financing Administration Form HCFA 2082, 1982–1990.

Ellis, Carol L., Program Termination: A Work to the Wise, *Public Administration Review* *43*(4):352–357 (1983).

Hines, Samuel M., Organizations and Evolution: A Review of Herbert Kaufman's *Time, Chance and Organizations, Politics and the Life Sciences, 5*:266 (1987).

Jones, Charles O., *An Introduction to the Study of Public Policy*, Brooks/Cole Publishing, Monterey, Calif., 1984.

Katzenbach, Edward L., The Horse Calvary in the Twentieth Century: A Study of Policy Response, *Public Policy, 8*:120–149 (1958).

Kaufman, Herbert, *Are Government Organizations Immortal?* The Brookings Institution, Washington, D.C., 1976.

Kaufman, Herbert, *Time, Chance, and Organizations*, Chatham House Publishers, Chatham, N.J., 1985.

Kearney, Richard C., Sunset: A Survey and Analysis of the State Experience, *Public Administration Review* *50*(1):49–57 (1990).

Lambright, Henry W. and Sapolsky, Harvey M., Terminating Federal Research and Development Programs, *Policy Sciences* 7(2):199–214 (1976).

Miller, George A., Deputy Director of the Department of Human Services, State of Oklahoma, personal interview, March 12, 1991.

Mueller, Keith J., Federal Programs to Expire: The Case of Health Planning, *Public Administration Review, 48*(3):719–725 (1988).

Newsweek, Committed Youth, July 31, pp. 66–69, 72 (1989).

Pressman, Jeffrey L. and Wildavsky, Aaron B., *Implementation*, University of California Press, Berkeley, 1973.

Shulsky, Abram N., Abolishing the District of Columbia Motorcycle Squad, *Policy Sciences* 7(2):183–197 (1976).

Simon, Herbert A., Smithburg, Donald W., and Thompson, Victor A., *Public Administration*, Alfred A. Knopf, New York, 1950.

Tulsa World, Walters Dislikes DHS Juvenile Plan, February 14, p. A1, 1989.

Tulsa World, Lawyer Says Progress on Teen Justice in Peril, May 27, pp. A1, A4, 1990a.

Tulsa World, More Secure Space Needed, Panel Says, August 4, pp. A4, A14, 1990b.

Tulsa World, Location of 'Terry D.' Not Known, Says Attorney Who Filed Suit, December 11, p. A4, 1990c.

Tulsa World, One Children's Mental Health Bill Approved While Another Fails, March 13, p. A1, 1991.

White, Elliot, A Review of *Time, Chance, and Organizations: Natural Selection in a Perilous Environment, Politics and the Life Sciences, 5*:268 (1987).

Wallerstein, Michel B., Terminating Entitlements: Veterans' Disability Benefits in the Depression, *Policy Sciences, 7*(2):173–182 (1976).

30
Military Bureaucracy and Personnel Administration: The Case of the U.S. Air Force

Richard Hartwig
Texas A&M University—Kingsville, Kingsville, Texas

Like Caesar's Gaul, administration is divided into three parts: public administration, business administration, and, recently, administration of nonprofit organizations. Military administration is virtually invisible, occupying its own world, with its own specialized journals. It is all the more isolated since the advent of the all-volunteer military in the United States. It takes something like the Gulf War to focus attention on the existence and importance of military bureaucracies.

Military bureaucracies in the United States, although now shrinking (Callander, 1991; Marsh, 1991), are of the same order of magnitude as the federal civil service. Their personnel costs are approximately $150 billion per year. Attributes of military type rank-in-person systems are also seen in the Foreign Service, the Public Health Service, the FBI, the CIA, the Tennessee Valley Authority, and state and local police and fire departments. William Ouchi (1981) writes that the U.S. Army is a "Z" organization—similar in important respects to large Japanese businesses and IBM. (Ouchi's "Z" organization is characterized by long-term employment, slow evaluation and promotion, and job rotation.) If this is true, the applicability of the "military" model is widespread indeed.

Communication between civilian and military personnel administration is largely one-way. Military personnel specialists consult the private-sector literature on personnel assessment and other matters. However, they tend to neglect the literature in public administration. (Jeffries [1977, p. 329] notes that the military has adopted "business" techniques for planning and efficiency and that military organizations depend on the private sector for procurement and systems development.) Private and civilian public-sector analysts, on the other hand, usually ignore the military experience. Interaction patterns between military and private-sector specialists thus resemble those between Japanese and Anglo-American scholars in several fields. The Japanese learn from the English language literature, but the Anglos, being unable to read Japanese, are ignorant of the publications written only in that language.

The world of military bureaucracies is somewhat analogous to that of Japan in that it is physically isolated; it has a distinctive culture; and it speaks a language—punctuated with acronyms—which is largely unintelligible to outsiders. It is often assumed that military practice is so different from that of civil service systems that few lessons that can survive translation into the routines of civilians are to be learned. I disagree. Americans have been forced to learn from Japanese businesses, and we would do well to examine analogous organizational forms in the armed services with great care.

This chapter is meant to be an introduction to military organization theory and behavior for civilians. More specifically, it attempts to translate an important problem relating to the evaluation of military personnel into standard English. The problem is rating inflation, its causes, results, and cures. The following pages describe the history of the problem and U.S. Air Force attempts to effect a cure. Our focus will be the recent Air Force Officer evaluation System (OES), implemented in August 1988. (The less dramatic 1989 revision of the Air Force enlisted personnel evaluation system will not be examined here.) The implications of the Air Force experience extend well beyond the sphere of military organizations.

I. WALKING ON WATER

U.S. Air Force officers used to say that to get promoted, you had to be a "water walker." By the late 1980s, you had to be able to walk on water without getting your socks wet. By 1988, over 98% of Air Force officers received the highest possible numerical ratings on each of ten performance factors listed on the front side of their Officer Effectiveness Reports (OERs) [2] (see Appendix 1). The "word pictures" of the officers' job performance and career potential, on the back side of the OER form, were similarly inflated. They amounted to little more than carefully constructed strings of superlatives. According to Ginovsky this is nothing new: "The Air Force has fought and lost the battle against rating inflation for forty years. Since its creation in 1947, it has already tried six officer evaluation systems with twelve variations, all of which have seen gross inflation" (1988, p. 12).

The basic problem in the Air Force is the "up-or-out" system. With some exceptions, those who are twice passed over for promotion must leave the service.

How is a promotion board to decide whom not to promote if virtually all officers are "outstanding"? How do officers react to a personnel system that praises but does not always promote them? And what are the implications for the effectiveness of a force structure that may or may not promote the best and the brightest of each generation of Air Force warriors?

II. TOP DOWN AND BOTTOM UP

The centralized personnel evaluation systems in the armed forces are indispensable to the operations of the military. Since lateral entry is the exception rather than the rule, an illegitimate evaluation system can seriously damage a military service. The Air Force cannot advertise in *The New York Times* if it is losing pilots to the airlines and needs men to fly F-16s.

From the top down, a military personnel system is a way to provide an effective force structure. Each service needs to maintain morale, promote the best people, weed out the inadequate performers, train and retain specialists in various fields, and provide a potential career ladder for everyone. To do these things, each branch of the military has a central personnel agency. For the Air Force, it is the Military Personnel Center at Randolph Air Force Base, Texas. Personnel policies are set at this level, subject to direction from the Department of Defense.

The Officer Personnel Act (OPA) of 1947 established the promotion systems for the military services. The OPA set permanent limits on total grades and strength of field grade regular officers (majors and colonels)—which were adjusted by subsequent legislation. The crucial provisions of this law are the following:

1. Promotion by seniority and selection board
2. Accelerated ("below the zone") promotion for certain officers
3. Establishment of promotion lists
4. Promotion of regular officers at the 7, 14, and 21 year points for captains, majors, and lieutenant colonels
5. "Up-or-out" system for officers twice passed over for promotion

From the bottom up, the central fact of life for the career military officer is the promotion list. Promotion from second to first lieutenant and then to captain is almost automatic. Beyond this stage, the system becomes competitive. The Defense Officer Personnel Management Act (DOPMA) of 1981 provides that 95% of lieutenants may be promoted to captain, but only 80% of captains may be promoted to major. Of majors 70% can be promoted to lieutenant colonel, and 50% of lieutenant colonels may be promoted to full colonel (*Officer Ranks Personnel*, 1985, p. 88). (These guidelines are periodically adjusted and vary according to specializations.)

In theory, 27 of every 100 officers could be promoted to full-bird colonel, and expectations are high. It has been estimated, however, that only 19% of all officers even reach retirement age, because of career changes, injuries, illness, and other matters (Managing the Air Force, 1979–1980, p. 338). Expectations thus clash with reality.

The fundamental reality for military officers is that an outstanding series of evaluation reports is required for continued promotion. Evaluation reports have thus become a preoccupation—bordering on obsession—for the officer corps of all the services. In itself, ambition is not a problem. Competition is supposed to push up the best. Forced retirements for those not promoted are considered necessary to provide openings for the best and the brightest. But careerism has become a problem. Many argue that it is the opposite of leadership and seriously detracts from mission performance.

III. THE PERFECT SOLDIER

The promotion process for majors in the Marine Corps illustrates the difficulties facing all the military services. Promotion decisions are made by a central review board, composed of colonels. Decisions are made by ranking personnel folders, in which the fitness report is the central document. Over 90% of these majors have typically been ranked "outstanding" (the top rating) across the board. Yet, only 50% to 70% can be promoted to lieutenant colonel. Rating inflation forces the promotion board to find other ways to differentiate among officers. The Marine Corps Combat Readiness Evaluations System (MCCRES) has been used as one such discriminator. MCCRES was designed to improve training, but by the early 1980s, it had become a report card on commanders (Earl, 1984, p. 53). Some argue that this resulted in a zero-defects environment. Officers could not afford to take risks, even in training.

Since the promotion boards could not objectively tell who was excellent and who was not, they started to look for reasons *not* to promote. A common perception among junior officers was "One mistake and you're out!" Initiative was stifled as commanders increasingly resorted to micromanagement in order to prevent mistakes. Leadership suffered. Board members might also resort to the "old boy" network to discover in advance what officers were "really like." (This is evidently rare in the other services, which are much larger.)

The most important discriminator has been the indorsement level. (In military usage, "endorsement" begins with an *i* rather than with an *e*.) In the Marines, as in the Air Force until 1988, the initial rater would send a promising officer's fitness report up the line to progressively higher officers. An indorsement by a three-star general was a clear signal to promote. An equally "outstanding" officer whose fitness report was signed by a mere colonel was in deep trouble.

Historically, writing and evaluating fitness reports, or OERs, has been an exercise in hyperbole on the one hand, and subtlety on the other. The rater had to praise an officer elaborately, lest he damage the officer's career by comparison with those of other "water walkers." But at the same time, the responsible rater had to indicate whether or not the officer should be promoted. For example, a rater might praise a subordinate as being a "superlative" officer. This might make the ratee feel good. But in the lexicography of the Air Force, "superlative" is actually second best. "Outstanding" is the highest praise, having been used as such on an earlier OER form. The Air Force selection board member, who spent an average of two to three minutes on each folder, somehow had to interpret these hidden signals—which might not be there. The search for discriminators was carried to remarkable lengths. Hopgood (1985, pp. 60–61) writes that 1984 promotion boards for Marine Corps majors and colonels discussed such qualities as publications, general knowledge, hobbies, physical fitness (marathoner?), personal appearance (mustache?), civilian education (where?), and family problems—in addition to performance levels on duty, military education, and so on.

IV. PLUSES AND MINUSES

Strangely enough, even promotion systems which may distinguish among potential lieutenant colonels on the basis of having a mustache or running marathons have some virtues. In 1986, Captain Dale Hess, an Air Force personnel officer in Zaragoza, told the writer: "The grade inflation problem is insoluble, but it's not as bad as we think. The right people are getting promoted and the bad apples are being identified and gotten rid of (February 6, 1986)." If the basic objectives of the system are being accomplished, it might make little difference if evaluations do not operate the way they are supposed to. Moreover, grade inflation even has some virtues. Officers who are told they are magnificent performers begin to believe it and may increasingly act the part. Exaggerated ratings may thus improve morale. They also accidentally deal with a problem often ignored by evaluation system designers: the negative effect of mediocre evaluations on "lifers" who remain in an organization. Here, there is no problem, since only those who are to be expelled receive less than outstanding ratings. This system thus fosters the belief that military officers are an elite group, all of whom are above average. Finally, inflated ratings mean that raters and ratees do not have to undergo the painful process of officially criticizing and being criticized. One Navy E-9 (the top enlisted ranking) remarked in a graduate school class that he had made only one serious evaluation of his subordinates in his entire career. "There were buttons and teeth on the floor when I got done, but everybody knew exactly why they got their evaluation. Never again!"

Unfortunately, the vices of an inflated evaluation system are even greater than the virtues. Raters are forced to be dishonest to avoid unfairly penalizing their subordinates. They do so by not being specific, by saying that a ratee is responsible for hundreds of thousands of dollars of equipment, when he/she is simply running the motor pool. It also becomes harder to point out the really outstanding individual (Major Dennis Pruitt, Zaragoza, Spain, February 6, 1986). Marine Lt. Col. Earl (1985, p. 54) summarizes the costs of an inflated evaluation systems as follows:

1. Increasing cynicism among the officer corps regarding the performance evaluation system
2. An increasing tendency toward a "zero-defects" environment
3. Increasing micromanagement throughout the Corps
4. Increasing careerism
5. Increasing loss of personal integrity as the dishonesty of the current performance evaluation system "spills over" into other areas

By the mid-1980s, standards had deteriorated to the point that Air Force officers sometimes wrote their own OERs and had their superiors sign them. The escalation of indorsements up the line was such that many senior raters did not know the people they were recommending for promotion. The Officer Evaluation Report became more and more a record of performance rather than a means of evaluating performance. This pushed officers into a long series of peripheral activities which detracted from mission accomplishment. Doing one's job well was insufficient grounds for promotion. Higher education became one more method of "filling squares" on the evaluation form. In a recent Air Force major's promotion board, 86% of the potential selectees had master's degrees.

A related problem in the Air Force was the fierce competition for staff jobs rather than operational positions in the "wings," where the airplanes are flown. Headquarters staff jobs provided personal access to generals, whose OER endorsements were crucial for promotions—especially early, or "below-the-zone," promotions. Some commanders took advantage of the system, holding out their signature as a carrot to induce better performance or to recruit a leader for a pet organization (Erwine, 1988, p. 9). The scramble for distinguishing marks on one's record also led Air Force officers to complete their professional military education (Squadron Officer's School, Air Command & Staff College, and Air War College) ahead of schedule, often to the detriment of job performance. The inflated OER even caused legal problems for the Air Force. Officers who had been turned down for promotion and separated from the service would sometimes appeal to the civilian court system. After looking at the nearly perfect evaluation scores and the glowing "word pictures" describing an officer's performance, the courts would often uphold these appeals (Major Bruce Thieman, Air Command & Staff College, October 16, 1989).

Finally, an inordinate amount of time was spent in attempts to "game" the system and in seemingly trivial pursuits such as preparing an absolutely perfect official photograph for the selection folder. The haircut had to be just right; the ribbons had to be exactly one-half inch over the pocket of the uniform; and the body had to look trim and lean. The Navy requires a full-length, three-quarter-profile photograph, evidently to guard against promoting rotund personnel. One pear-shaped, but enterprising, officer solved this problem by lying on the ground in full dress uniform and having his picture taken by a friend on a roof.

V. HISTORY OF A DILEMMA

The Air Force Academy carried out a careful study of Air Force rating inflation between 1954 and 1969 (Brown, 1975). On a scale of 1 to 9, the average rating for second lieutenants was approximately 4.4 in 1954. By 1960, the average was 5.8. For colonels (the highest rank on the open OER) the average escalated from 7.2 to 8.2 during the same period. Average scores of all ranks fell sharply in 1961, after a revision of the OER form. Subsequently, however, the upward trend continued. By 1969, the average rating for second lieutenants was 8.2 and colonels were up to 8.5. It was obvious that the numerical ratings would soon be useless for differentiating among officers for purposes of promotion, assignment, or advanced schooling.

Relatively little has been written about the causes of rating inflation—perhaps because the answer is so obvious to military personnel. In all the military services, people take care of their own. Motivation and unit cohesion are extremely important, and the officer who "honestly" evaluates his subordinates may destroy both. With the advent of the up-or-out system, a single unfavorable evaluation could destroy a career.

Some argue that wars also play a role in fueling rating inflation. One colonel with experience in the Air Force Military Personnel Center noted that in the 1960s and early 1970s, large numbers of officers came home from their one-year tour in Southeast Asia with combat ribbons. New ribbons justified higher evaluation scores, which tended to become permanent unless performance declined (Colonel Gehagen, Lajes Field, The Azores, October 9, 1985). Pilots and navigators had special advantages. They often moved from one base to another and would accumulate four to five ribbons in a single combat tour. Promotion rates are approximately 5% higher for pilots, who continue to dominate the hierarchy of the Air Force, than for other personnel (in 1988, 31% of Air Force colonels and 58% of generals were pilots [Ginovsky, 1988b]).

One suspects that raters of personnel without combat experience inflated their ratings to enable their people to compete effectively with the Vietnam-era veterans. An additional complication is the competition among the major commands of the Air Force: Strategic Air Command (SAC) (bombers); Tactical Air Command (fighters); Military Airlift Command; and Space Command—which controls ICBMs. SAC is rumored to have had a twelve-man "gaming" team working to get its people promoted.

The Defense Officer Personnel Management Act of 1981 made the problem even more acute. Until 1981, an officer could retire at the rank of major; after DOPMA went into effect, retirement pay after twenty years became contingent upon promotion to lieutenant colonel. Pressure for top evaluations became even more intense as a result.

A. An Alexandrine Solution

By the early 1970s, the Air Force brass was fed up with rating inflation. They developed a 1-2-3 "forced distribution" mechanism. Only 22% of the officers could be ranked in the top bracket and only 28% in the second bracket. Half of the officer corps had to be placed in the lower half of the rating scale. According to one report, the new system resulted in a near mutiny when tested at Randolph Air Force Base, and the Military Personnel Center was outraged. But the Air Force is a hierarchical organization, and in 1974 the new OER was introduced anyway. In effect, the new OERs took power away from the promotion boards. They had to promote everyone in the 1 category, and could promote some of the 2s. But officers getting 3s lost all hope of eventually making lieutenant or full colonel rank. Large numbers of officers resigned their commissions. The new OER was also a severe blow to the pride, since Air Force officers tend to see themselves as top performers and had received top ratings in the past.

As usual, the officer corps dedicated its talents to gaming the system. Officers about to retire who had low "potential" would be given low ratings to save the quota of good marks for those who needed them. Officers up for promotion in a given year got the top ratings. The following year, their rankings would decline to leave 1 ratings for the new group, which was "in-the-zone" for promotion. Another common practice was to give low marks to personnel who had just transferred into a job. A third variant of the game was to change rating officers.

The forced-distribution OER was a disaster. The low scores stayed on the officers' records, and promotion boards could not tell what had caused them. Damage to morale and individual careers was not the only problem. It takes some two and one half years, 500 hours of flying time, and $7.5 million dollars to develop a fully qualified F-15 pilot (GAO, 1987, p. 2). Losing such a person simply because someone has to be ranked in the bottom half of the evaluation scale is inane.

The forced-distribution OER was progressively modified and then abandoned entirely in 1978, but the scars remained. The Form 707 OER which took its place was recognized as being inadequate. Having been burned in the past, however, the Air Force was reluctant to change until absolutely sure that any new evaluation system would be an improvement. Rating inflation thus continued unabated. By 1982, hyperinflation had set in; Air Force–wide evaluations for captains averaged 97.2% of a perfect score. The average score for majors was 98.8%; for lieutenant colonels, it was 98.3%. A single-point deviation from a perfect score could kill a career. Indorsement inflation became so prevalent that by 1985, a four-star general could not ensure a promotion with his signature alone (Erwine, 1988, pp. 12–13).

Faced with the total collapse of the system, a meeting of all four-star Air Force commanders (a "Corona") was convened. The generals informally decided to limit the number of OERs receiving a general's indorsement. Each general would sign only 30% of the OERs, his deputy 40%, and a colonel on his staff the remaining 30%, in effect reinstating something like the 1, 2, 3 system of the bad old days of 1974–1978. This time, however, letters were placed in the officers' personnel records indicating that the absence of a general's indorsement reflected not a decline in performance, but a policy change of the Air Force (Erwine, 1988, p. 13).

VI. BOUNDARIES OF CHANGE

Air Force personnel systems are constrained by congressional restrictions on the size and composition of the officer corps, by the "up-or-out" system, and by the related philosophy that an officer should be primarily a leader, a generalist, rather than a specialist.

Major William Anderson wrote in 1967 that the basic philosophy of the Air Force promotion system is sound, "provided the policies remain stable, the force size does not vary, and attrition can be planned and calculated" (Anderson, 1967, p. 8). Unfortunately, wars and the U.S. Congress have a tendency to change policies and force size. Moreover, the attrition rate for pilots is closely linked to economic cycles—in particular when the airlines are hiring—and cannot be predicted easily. A long lead time is required to fill gaps in the force structure since entry is only at the bottom of the system (with the exception of medical officers, attorneys, and a few other specialists). The basic personnel structure is thus rather static and is easily distorted by rapid change. In World War II, it was not unusual to encounter 25-year-old colonels. By 1967, the 38-year-old captain was the rule and not the exception (Anderson, 1967, p. 1). Today, the older captain is once again the exception, usually an officer who has previous service in the enlisted ranks. The Air Force personnel system is very flexible in terms of its ability to rotate people between jobs, but it is relatively inflexible when it comes to increasing or decreasing the number of personnel. The only quick way to increase the size of the Air Force is to mobilize the reserves.

The underlying philosophy of the U.S. Armed Forces (and the Foreign Service) is that an officer should be a generalist. The consummate generalist becomes a general, which is what each officer should aspire to. Historically, promotion decisions have been based on the individual's potential for broader responsibility, not simply on job performance. More responsibility requires a wide horizon, and officers were advised to engage in "career broadening." One could not become a colonel simply by flying an airplane. A variety of positions, and command responsibility in particular, was required for promotion. Promotion is imperative because of the up-or-out system. If an Air Force captain, for example, is passed over twice for promotion to major he/she must (1) take the severance pay and leave the service, (2) complete twenty years for retirement credit in the enlisted ranks, or (3) be selected for continuation as a captain.

The generalist, up-or-out philosophy has been widely criticized. Many pilots joined the Air Force because they wanted to fly. They have often been frustrated by having to take administrative positions in order to advance their careers. This is also a very expensive way to use trained pilots and navigators. It is even more expensive if they decide to fly the friendly skies with civilian airlines. The Army addresses this problem by using warrant officers as helicopter pilots and for other flying duties. (The warrant officer is a specialist who moves from grade one through four without having to "career broaden.") Warrant officers lack prestige, however, and this idea has been rejected by the Air Force.

The flying versus career broadening problem in the Air Force is compounded because pilots and navigators now face longer cockpit tours in the same type of aircraft—a by-product of the increased cost of training, the greater complexity of weapons systems, and a tendency toward greater specialization. It thus becomes harder to produce generalists. Beasley (1987, p. 114) writes: "The Air Force goals of the 'whole person,' and of having every officer strive to become a high-level leader, have been described in numerous surveys and research studies as costly, not 'mass-producible,' and unrealistic for the overall officer population."

The other services have similar problems. Grant (p. viii) writes that the Army loses money and valuable technical experience through the rapid promotion of enlisted men and that the traditional emphasis on a youthful Army is no longer appropriate in an environment where experience is increasingly important [2]. Beach (1987, p. 54) argues that the Navy's up-or-out system is disastrously expensive and is also wasteful of trained and able people. A Navy captain (equivalent to a full colonel in the Air Force) is often involuntarily retired at age fifty-two. As of 1987, his pension averaged $40,000 per year. Multiplied times his life expectancy of 27.1 more years, total retirement pay would be $1,084,000. Beach thus calculated that the 250 senior captains who retired in 1986 added about $271,000,000 to the national debt. This is all the more serious because the rapidly ballooning military retirement bill is not funded in the same way normal pension systems are: it comes out of current expenditures.

VII. REFORMING THE OER

A. The Old System

On the old form 707 OER (Appendix 1), the rater was asked to evaluate the officer on a six-category scale of ten performance factors. He/she was to give specific examples of accomplishment. The standard practice was to "firewall" these ratings, giving nearly all officers the highest rating of "well above standard" on all ten items. The back side of the form provided space for (1) an assignment recommendation, (2) an evaluation of potential, (3) the rater's comments, (4) the additional rater's comments, and (5) the indorser's comments. The key discriminator was the rank of the indorser. The top prize was a high-ranking general's recommendation to "promote ahead of contemporaries."

In the spring of 1987, the Air Force chief of staff expressed his dissatisfaction with the current OER system and announced a search for a new personnel evaluation form. General Welch indicated that extensive rating inflation made the current form less than useful as a source of feedback for officers and for determination of assignments. The OER was also failing to measure potential for promotion on the basis of performance. The system was differentiating among officers on the basis of nonperformance factors such as formal education and professional military education. The chief of staff also said, "Captains and majors should not worry about 'career-broadening' " (Dalton, 1987, p. 3).

Three groups were to study the options for a new system: (1) a "student group" of twelve majors at the Air Command and Staff College at Maxwell Air Force Base, (2) a commercial firm (Syllogistics Inc. and The Hay Group), and (3) a senior group of active-duty and retired officers at the Military Personnel Center. The first two groups produced published reports. Space limitations preclude a description/comparison of these recommendations.

B. Stairway to the Stars

A new personnel evaluation system has a profound impact on military organizations. A procedure such as the 1988 Officer Evaluation System describes in great detail the individual steps on a great stairway to the stars—the kinds of stars generals wear on the shoulder boards of their uniforms. Changes in the rules are analyzed meticulously by the officer corps. Subsequently, each military rank will march in nearly perfect lockstep up a stairway which becomes increasingly narrow as it ascends. Those who are pushed off will be those who did not match their performance or their politics to the new set of regulations and expectations.

The new OES emphasizes job performance over career potential for the lower officer ranks. The old OER structure was criticized for having attempted to achieve three major objectives by means of a single two-page form. The old Form 707 was supposed to provide feedback to the officer, document a record of performance, and provide the basis for promotion recommendations. Since these are partially conflicting objectives, it did all poorly (Ginovsky, 1988a, p. 12). In the current OES process, these three functions are separated.

Honest feedback on job performance is to be achieved by means of a handwritten performance feedback worksheet. This does not become part of the permanent record—except for appeal purposes. Feedback sessions are required for junior officers. Second, a formal Officer Performance Report (OPR) is to be written for all officers through the rank of colonel.

The new OPR form 707 (see Appendix 2) automatically eliminates the problem of numerical rating inflation. The rater simply indicates whether the officer being evaluated does or does not meet the standards of job knowledge, leadership, professional qualities, organizational skills, judgment, and communication skills. The real emphasis of the revised form is on the written descriptions of an officer's job, his/her impact on mission accomplishment, and the overall assessments of the rater and the additional rater. The senior rater is only to provide written comments if he/she does not concur with the evaluation of the first two officers. Descriptions/evaluations are to be factual and superlatives are to be avoided.

Raters *may* recommend an officer for military schooling in residence, as opposed to correspondence courses. This is a boost to one's career. However, raters may not make promotion recommendations, mention educational achievements, or refer to previous performance evaluations.

The major surprise in the new OPR is the absence of a "rate-the-rater" component, which had been recommended by both the Major's Group and the Syllogistics/Hay authors. In a rate-the-rater system, the promotion board can check the tendency of the senior rater to inflate his/her evaluations. "Outstanding" recommendations will be discounted if the general in question is overly free with them. A rate-the-rater element was successfully introduced into the Army OER system in 1979 [3].

The 1988 Air Force OPR Form 707B cannot differentiate statistically among officers, and it is questionable whether promotion boards can pick the best officers to promote on the basis of the brief paragraph on job performance. The key to the new system is a confidential promotion recommendation by the senior rater (Form 709, Appendix 3). This recommendation is made on a separate form, meant only for a particular promotion board. After the board meets, it is destroyed, so as not to prejudice future promotion boards. It is written only in years when an officer is eligible for promotion. The senior rater (reviewer) is normally a colonel—except when colonels are themselves being evaluated.

There are three categories of recommendation: "definitely promote," "promote," and "do not promote this board" (this time). An officer receiving a "definitely promote" is virtually assured of moving to a higher rank. Senior raters are allocated a fixed percentage of their ratees who may receive the highest recommendations. The percentage varies according to the rank of the officers being evaluated and the numbers of officers up for early promotion. For example, 65% of the captains being considered for major might be given "definitely promote" recommendations. Fractions are rounded downward, the excess being used to accommodate inequalities in talent among units. (Special procedures are used for nonline officers such as chaplains, judge advocates, and the various medical corps.) The bottom line is that promotions go to virtually all officers receiving "definitely promote," to some of those getting "promote," and to none of those who receive "do not promote this board" (*USAF Officers' Guide to the OES*, 1988).

The current OES procedures would seem to be a considerable improvement over what has gone before. To begin with, the dishonesty associated with rating inflation has been eliminated. Numerical inflation is solved by definition, since nearly all officers are rated "satisfactory" on the six performance criteria. Indorsement inflation is ended by the requirement that senior raters be colonels for the officer ranks of major and below (unless the officer works directly for a general). Officers being rated presumably get more accurate feedback on their performance, since the feedback form is separate from the promotion process. Officers should also be less distracted by peripheral activities such as premature military schooling, which were previously considered essential for promotion. Job performance and family life may improve as a result. Most promotion decisions ("definitely promotes") are now taken by people who know or have direct access to the officers in question.

The informal, closed process of deciding on promotion recommendations is largely up to the colonels in charge. Some of these colonels have convened miniature promotion boards at the base or wing level to decide on promotion recommendations to the official promotion boards. With group decision making, based on personal knowledge, fewer careers are likely to falter because of a single black mark by a superior.

The new OPR system also has the effect of pushing talent back to the wings, where the airplanes are flown. Headquarters staff jobs, with access to generals who sign OERs, used to be the route to a below-the-zone promotion. Since 1988, however, it has become dangerous to be part of an elite organization in which everybody is talented, since the allocations of "definitely promote" recommendations may not be significantly higher than for mediocre units.

VIII. CONCLUSIONS

What lessons can be learned from this history of people who both fly and walk on water? The first is the familiar one that personnel evaluations should focus on specific objectives. It is usually impossible to design a system which will simultaneously achieve multiple objectives. Wendell French claims that the purposes of motivation and behavior modification are mutually exclusive. McGregor writes that a supervisor's judicial role in evaluating and his advisory role in helping a subordinate achieve personal and organizational goals are in conflict (Hudson, 1986, p. 21). The new Air Force evaluation system has thus properly decoupled the objectives of providing feedback, evaluating performance, and recommending promotions. Each function is allocated its separate form and is separated in time.

Second, the Air Force experience underlines the importance of the distinction between evaluating performance and evaluating potential. The revision of the OER form reflects an attempt to reemphasize job performance. Nevertheless, the Air Force still emphasizes the philosophy of the generalist officer whose ultimate value is defined by his or her potential for promotion to positions of broader responsibility. It is a system which features job rotation, constant training, and competition for advancement. One result is a dynamic, flexible, and aggressive officer corps. Another is a tension between Air Force demands for mission accomplishment, in which a unit competes against a performance standard, and the individual's need for a satisfying and predictable career. The chief of staff may say that cockpit personnel should not have to worry about career broadening through the rank of lieutenant colonel, but this does not help the promotion boards if officers cannot be differentiated on the basis of performance.

Performance and potential require separate evaluation criteria (Hudson, 1986, pp. 35–36). The new system asks the promotion boards to emphasize performance for lieutenants and captains and increasingly to consider potential for majors and colonels. But beyond this, the tension between doing a good job and one's potential for greater things reflects underlying problems in the personnel system—problems which cannot be resolved by new OES forms. The basic question is whether the up-or-out system of generalist officers can be reconciled with increasing demands for specialization, economy, and job security.

A third lesson has to do with the relationship between personnel evaluation and the viability of an organization as a whole. Personnel appraisal is often seen as an isolated technique, with its own internal logic and rules. The key lesson of the Air Force experience is that impact on organizational effectiveness is the crucial aspect of personnel appraisal systems.

The 1974–1978 OER form was technically an improvement over what was used before, or has been used since. It successfully differentiated among officers. Yet, it was a total disaster from the perspectives of morale, officer retention, economy, and mission accomplishment. Half of the officers received ratings of "3" in the first year of the controlled OER and immediately saw their dying careers flash before their eyes. In a poignant article entitled "I Am a Three," Major Mark Wynn wrote, "One thing the previous system had was illusion. Many of us really did believe we could win eagles. A few hopeless cases even believed in stars" (1976, p. 44). It was not just eagles on the shoulder that they were likely to lose. Without twenty years in service, there would be only a lump sum retirement benefit, followed by a difficult transition to the civilian work force.

The link between evaluation and the retirement system is thus critical to an understanding of the pressures which fuel rating inflation in the military. Officer evaluation systems which do not address this issue are likely to fail.

A final lesson relates to power and authority in a hierarchical, military organization. If Air Force officers are ordered to fly into the face of death, they will do so without hesitation. But if they are ordered to write open evaluations which may damage the careers of their subordinates, they will most likely echo the famous phrase of Latin American creoles when confronted with a peremptory decree from the Spanish monarch: "Obedezco, pero no cumplo" (I obey, but I do not comply).

There are good reasons for such a response. The Syllogistics/Hay authors wrote, "There is a special relationship between an officer and his superior that is unique to military service" (1988, pp. III-62–63). This relationship is characterized not only by military discipline, but also by mutual loyalty and a sense of responsibility for the junior officer's career development—something that is fostered in all the services. The evaluation process threatens this bond, since an "honest" evaluation may ruin the junior officer's career [4].

The problem of loyalty is not unique to the military. Loyalty is the glue which holds good organizations together; distrust is a solvent which leads to disintegration. Absence of loyalty leads to personnel turnover, theft, lowballing, refusal to relocate, low motivation, poor teamwork, and low productivity. If these problems sound familiar, we may wish to investigate possible links to the personnel appraisal system in civilian, as well as in military, organizations.

ACKNOWLEDGMENTS

I appreciate the insights of Majors Dona Rosa and Bruce Thieman of the Air Command and Staff College at Maxwell Air Force Base and the courtesy and expertise of the Fairchild Library staff. My initial interest in this topic was stimulated by Masters in Public Administration students at Lajes Field, Azores; Zaragoza, Spain; Lindsey Air Base, Germany; Izmir, Turkey; and Moody Air Force Base and Kings Bay Submarine Base in Georgia.

NOTES

1. Interview with Major Donna Rosa of the Air Command and Staff College (ACSC), Maxwell Air Force Base, AL, August 28, 1987. Major Rosa is one of the authors of the "Officer Evaluation System Proposal," chartered by the Air Force Chief of Staff and carried out at the ACSC.
2. The percentages of white-collar jobs in the military enlisted ranks rose from 28% in 1945 to 47% in 1981 while the number of U.S. citizens between the ages of eighteen and twenty-one is projected to decline from 14.5 million in 1987 to 13 million in 1995 (Grant, pp. 35 and 37).
3. There is no official explanation as to why a rate-the-rater system was not chosen. The possibility of disapproval by the officer corps was probably important. It is also said that General Welch questioned the applicability of the system because of differences between the Army (which uses "rate-the-rater") and the Air Force. Army officers tend to stay within their own branch. AF officers rotate to different jobs and often work in highly technical organizations where the percentages of 1, 2, 3 ratings may not be meaningful. Major Thieman, ACSC, October 16, 1989.
4. The Air Force, the Navy, and the Coast Guard now protect the superior/subordinate relationship by not requiring the first rater to differentiate meaningfully among subordinates. The Marines have a closed evaluation form which is not shown to the ratee (Syllogistics/Hay, 1988, III-62–63).

APPENDIX 1
AF Form 707, August 1984
Officer Effectiveness Report

I. RATEE IDENTIFICATION DATA *(Read AFR 36-10 carefully before filling in any item)*

1. NAME *(Last, First, Middle Initial)*	2. SSN	3. GRADE	4. DAFSC
5. ORGANIZATION, COMMAND, LOCATION			6. PAS CODE
7. PERIOD OF REPORT FROM:	THRU:	8. NO. DAYS OF SUPERVISION	9. REASON FOR REPORT

II. JOB DESCRIPTION 1. DUTY TITLE:
2. KEY DUTIES, TASKS, AND RESPONSIBILITIES:

III. PERFORMANCE FACTORS *Specific example of performance required*	NOT OBSERVED	FAR BELOW STANDARD	BELOW STANDARD	MEETS STANDARD	ABOVE STANDARD	WELL ABOVE STANDARD
1. JOB KNOWLEDGE *(Depth, currency, breadth)*	O	☐	☐	☐	☐	☐
2. JUDGMENT AND DECISIONS *(Consistent, accurate, effective)*	O	☐	☐	☐	☐	☐
3. PLAN AND ORGANIZE WORK *(Timely, creative)*	O	☐	☐	☐	☐	☐
4. MANAGEMENT OF RESOURCES *(Manpower, materiel, fiscal;*	O	☐	☐	☐	☐	☐
5. LEADERSHIP *(Initiative, accept responsibility)*	O	☐	☐	☐	☐	☐
6. ADAPTABILITY TO STRESS *(Stable, flexible, dependable)*	O	☐	☐	☐	☐	☐
7. ORAL COMMUNICATION *(Clear, concise, confident)*	O	☐	☐	☐	☐	☐
8. WRITTEN COMMUNICATION *(Clear, concise, organized)*	O	☐	☐	☐	☐	☐
9. PROFESSIONAL QUALITIES *(Attitude, dress, cooperation, bearing)*	O	☐	☐	☐	☐	☐
10. HUMAN RELATIONS *(Equal opportunity participation, sensitivity)*		☐	☐	☐	☐	☐

AF FORM AUG 84 707 PREVIOUS EDITION WILL BE USED OFFICER EFFECTIVENESS REPORT

APPENDIX 1 (continued)

IV. ASSIGNMENT RECOMMENDATION: 1. STRONGEST QUALIFICATION:

2. SUGGESTED JOB *(Include AFSC)*:

3. ORGANIZATION LEVEL: 4. TIMING:

V. EVALUATION OF POTENTIAL:

Compare the ratee's capability to assume increased responsibility with that of other officers whom you know in the same grade. Indicate your rating by placing an "X" in the designated portion of the most appropriate block.

RATER ADDN RATER INDORSER | RATER ADDN RATER INDORSER | RATER ADDN RATER INDORSER | RATER ADDN RATER INDORSER

Lowest ← → Highest

VI. RATER COMMENTS

NAME, GRADE, BR OF SVC, ORGN, COMD, LOCATION	DUTY TITLE		DATE
	SSAN	SIGNATURE	

VII. ADDITIONAL RATER COMMENTS ☐ CONCUR ☐ NONCONCUR

NAME, GRADE, BR OF SVC, ORGN, COMD, LOCATION	DUTY TITLE		DATE
	SSAN	SIGNATURE	

VIII. INDORSER COMMENTS ☐ CONCUR ☐ NONCONCUR

NAME, GRADE, BR OF SVC, ORGN, COMD, LOCATION	DUTY TITLE		DATE
	SSAN	SIGNATURE	

APPENDIX 2
AF Form 707A, August 1988
Officer Effectiveness Report

I. RATEE IDENTIFICATION DATA *(Read AFR 36-10 carefully before filling in any item)*

1. NAME *(Last, First, Middle Initial)*	2. SSN	3. GRADE	4. DAFSC

5. PERIOD OF REPORT From: Thru:	6. NO. DAYS SUPERVISION	7. REASON FOR REPORT

8. ORGANIZATION, COMMAND, LOCATION	9. PAS CODE

II. UNIT MISSION DESCRIPTION

III. JOB DESCRIPTION 1. DUTY TITLE:
2. KEY DUTIES, TASKS, AND RESPONSIBILITIES:

IV. IMPACT ON MISSION ACCOMPLISHMENT

V. PERFORMANCE FACTORS	DOES NOT MEET STANDARDS	MEETS STANDARDS
1. Job Knowledge Has knowledge required to perform duties effectively. Strives to improve this knowledge. Applies knowledge to handle nonroutine situations.	☐	☐
2. Leadership Skills Sets and enforces standards. Motivates subordinates. Works well with others. Fosters teamwork. Displays initiative. Self-confident. Has respect and confidence of subordinates. Fair and consistent in evaluation of subordinates.	☐	☐
3. Professional Qualities Exhibits loyalty, discipline, dedication, integrity, and honesty. Adheres to Air Force standards. Accepts personal responsibility. Is fair and objective.	☐	☐
4. Organizational Skills Plans, coordinates, schedules, and uses resources effectively. Schedules work for self and others equitably and effectively. Anticipates and solves problems. Meets suspenses.	☐	☐
5. Judgment and Decisions Makes timely and accurate decisions. Emphasizes logic in decision making. Retains composure in stressful situations. Recognizes opportunities and acts to take advantage of them.	☐	☐
6. Communication Skills Listens, speaks, and writes effectively.	☐	☐

AF Form 707A, AUG 88 PREVIOUS EDITION IS OBSOLETE FIELD GRADE OFFICER PERFORMANCE REPORT

APPENDIX 2 (continued)

VI. RATER OVERALL ASSESSMENT

NAME, GRADE, BR OF SVC, ORGN, COMD, LOCATION	DUTY TITLE		DATE
	SSN	SIGNATURE	

VII. ADDITIONAL RATER OVERALL ASSESSMENT CONCUR ☐ NONCONCUR ☐

NAME, GRADE, BR OF SVC, ORGN, COMD, LOCATION	DUTY TITLE		DATE
	SSN	SIGNATURE	

VIII. REVIEWER CONCUR ☐ NONCONCUR ☐

NAME, GRADE, BR OF SVC, ORGN, COMD, LOCATION	DUTY TITLE		DATE
	SSN	SIGNATURE	

Instructions

All: Recommendations must be based on performance and the potential based on that performance. Promotion recommendations are prohibited. Do not consider or comment on completion of or enrollment in PME, advanced education, previous or anticipated promotion recommendations on AF Form 709, OER indorsement levels, family activities, marital status, race, sex, ethnic origin, age, or religion.

Rater: Focus your evaluation in Section IV on what the officer did, how well he or she did it and how the officer contributed to mission accomplishment. Write in concise "bullet" format. Your comments in Section VI may include recommendations for augmentation or assignment.

Additional Rater: Carefully review the rater's evaluation to ensure it is accurate, unbiased, and uninflated. If you disagree, you may ask the rater to review his or her evaluation. You may not direct a change in the evaluation. If you still disagree with the rater, mark "NONCONCUR" and explain. You may include recommendations for augmentation or assignment.

Reviewer: Carefully review the rater's and additional rater's ratings and comments. If their evaluations are accurate, unbiased, and uninflated, mark the form "CONCUR" and sign the form. If you disagree with previous evaluators, you may ask them to review their evaluations. You may not direct them to change their appraisals. If you still disagree with the additional rater, mark "NONCONCUR" and explain in Section VIII. Do not use "NONCONCUR" simply to provide comments on the report.

AF Form 707A, AUG 88 (Reverse)

U.S. GOVERNMENT PRINTING OFFICE: 1988-240-979:80756

APPENDIX 3
Sample AF Form 709, August 1988
Promotion Recommendation

I. RATEE IDENTIFICATION DATA *(Read AFR 36-10 carefully before filling in any item)*

1. NAME *(Last, First, Middle Initial)*	2. SSN	3. GRADE	4. DAFSC
5. ORGANIZATION, COMMAND, AND LOCATION			6. PAS CODE

II. UNIT MISSION DESCRIPTION

III. JOB DESCRIPTION 1. DUTY TITLE:

2. KEY DUTIES, TASKS, RESPONSIBILITIES:

IV. PROMOTION RECOMMENDATION

V. PROMOTION ZONE	VI. GROUP SIZE	VII. BOARD	VIII. SENIOR RATER ID
BPZ ☐ I/APZ ☐			

IX. OVERALL RECOMMENDATION	X. SENIOR RATER NAME, GRADE, BR OF SVC, ORGN, COMD, LOCATION	
DEFINITELY PROMOTE ☐	DUTY TITLE	
PROMOTE ☐		
DO NOT PROMOTE THIS BOARD ☐	SSN	SIGNATURE

Instructions

Review previous OERs, OPRs, Education/Training Reports, and Supplemental Evaluation Sheets. Discuss, if needed, the officer's performance with officials in the supervisory chain. Evaluate the officer's performance and assess his or her potential based on performance. Do not consider or comment on enrollment in or completion of professional military education or advanced academic education.

Provide an accurate, unbiased assessment free from consideration of race, sex, ethnic origin, age, religion, or marital status.

Provide the officer a copy of this report approximately 30 days prior to the board for which this report is prepared.

AF Form 709, AUG 88 *U. S. GOVERNMENT PRINTING OFFICE: 1988-201-372:80697 PROMOTION RECOMMENDATION

REFERENCES

ACSC OER Working Group, Officer Evaluation System Proposal, Air Command & Staff College, Air University, Maxwell AFB, Ala., 1987.

Anderson, William G., A Comparative Analysis of the Air Force Officer Promotion System, Air University, Maxwell AFB, Ala., 1967.

Beach, Edward L., Nobody Asked Me, But . . . , *U.S. Naval Institute Proceedings 13*:54–57 (1987).

Beasely, Dennis C., Blue Suit/Flight Suit/Grey Suit: The Rated Officer Dilemma, Air University, Maxwell AFB, Ala., 1987.

Blair, John D., Gilroy, Curtis L., and Phillips, Robert L., The All-Volunteer Army: Fifteen Years Later, *Armed Forces & Society 16*:329–350 (1990).

Callander, Bruce, Going: A Fifth of the Force, *Air Force Magazine 74*:36–39 (1991).

Dalton, Pat, Officer Effectiveness Report Being Reevaluated, *Air Force Times 23*:3 (1987).

Department of the Air Force, Air Force Regulation 39-62: The Enlisted Evaluation System (EES) (1989).

Department of the Air Force, Office of the Chief of Staff, Revised Officer Evaluation System (OES): Memorandum to All Air Force Officers (1988).

Department of the Air Force, Office of the Chief of Staff, USAF Officer's Guide to the OES (1988).

Earl, Robert L., Two Views on Performance Evaluation, *Marine Corps Gazette 68*:53–54 (1984).

Edwards, Mark R. and Sproull, Ruth J., Rating the Raters Improves Performance Appraisals, *Personnel Administrator* (August):77–82 (1983).

The Effect of DOPMA on Promotions, *Air Force Journal of Logistics 5*:10–11 (1981).

Erwine, Larry C., Officer Effectiveness Ratings—Facts or Fiction? Central Michigan University Integrative Project, MSA 685, January (1988).

General Accounting Office, Air Force Pilots: Developing and Sustaining a Stable, Combat-Ready Force,

Ginovsky, John, Air Force Takes Offensive Against Rating Inflation, *Air Force Times* July 25, pp. 12–13, 16 (1988a).

Ginovsky, John, GAO Foresees Fewer Pilots, Less Experience in 4 Years, pp. 4, 24 (1988b).

Grant, Bruce, The Army's Up or Out of Policy: A Cost Effective Approach to Manpower Utilization? Air Command and Staff College, Air University, Maxwell AFB, Ala.

Hardy, Allan C., and Harker, Keith B., U.S. Army Officer Perceptions of the New OER (DA Form 67-8), Naval Postgraduate School, 1982.

Hartwig, Richard, The Paradox of Malevolent/Benevolent Bureaucracy, *Administration and Society 22*: 206–227 (1990).

Hopgood, M. T. Jr., Oranges and Tennis Balls, *Marine Corps Gazette 69*:58–64 (1985).

Hudson, Billy W., The U.S. Air Force Officer Effectiveness Report as Promotion Selection Tool, Maxwell AFB, Ala., 1986.

Jefferies, Chris L., Public Administration and the Military, *Public Administration Review 37*:321–333 (1977).

Managing the Air Force, Air War College, 1979–1980.

Marsh, John O., Personnel: Active and Reserve Forces, *Annals of the American Academy of Political and Social Science 517*:94–105 (1991).

Maze, Rick, Hill Agrees to Let Military Exceed Personnel Ceilings, *Air Force Times 51*:17 (1991).

McGee, Michael L. and Malone, Dandridge M., Peer Ratings, *Army* (September):40–44 (1987).

Officer Ranks Personnel, H.Q., Department of the Army, Washington, D.C., Pamphlet 600-3, July 10, 1985.

Ouchi, William, *Theory Z*, Avon Books, Chicago, 1981.

Syliogistics, Inc. and The Hay Group, *Final Report: Air Force Officers Evaluation System Project*. Submitted to Directorate at Plans, Programs & Analysis, H.Q., Air Force Military Personnel Center, January 22, 1988.

West, Joe, February 18. 'Experience Holes' Feared in Officer Corps, *Air Force Times 51*(22):12 (1991).

Wynn, Mark, I Am a Three: Or How I Learned to Stop Worrying and Love the New OER System, *Air University Review 27*:43–46 (1976).

31
Public Bureaucracies in the Transition from Authoritarian to Democratic Regimes: Lessons from the Latin American Experience

Jorge I. Tapia-Videla
Wayne State University, Detroit, Michigan

I. INTRODUCTION

The dramatic political and socioeconomic changes that have taken place in the former Soviet Union and Eastern Europe in the last couple of years have called into question the usefulness and validity of many conventionally held views regarding the role and functions of both the state and the major actors in policy-making processes. The fall of authoritarian regimes in these countries has added impetus to discussions on how to promote and ensure the development of stable democratic systems in societies characterized by cycles of political instability, violence, and ethnic tensions through processes of planned systemic change and institution building.

The literature examining the transition to democracy phenomenon has centered its analysis on either broad questions of constitutional reform at the systemic level or the role played by, or assigned to, traditional institutions and actors such as the executives, legislatures, military, political parties, interest groups, or international factors. Little if any attention is given, however, to public bureaucracies and their potential for effectively influencing the content and direction of processes of change and innovation in the region in general and of public policy-making processes in particular.

It is our contention that the failure to examine public bureaucracies as major political actors prevents gaining an accurate understanding of broad patterns of political, economic, and social domination, control, and change. In addition, it reinforces the faulty and dangerous notion that public bureaucracies in formerly authoritarian regimes are sufficiently neutral instruments that there is little need to reevaluate their core values and behavior as they now serve new political masters.

Cross-cultural experience offers sufficient evidence that those engaged in building a democratic society—one that will emphasize the values of freedom and equality over order and efficiency, the cornerstone values for the old authoritarian regimes—must take a careful look at the workings of public bureaucracies. For in important ways democratic change rests in the system's ability to manage the conflicting goals of economic efficiency and rationality with the goal of legitimacy based on broad participation in public policy-making processes and equity in the distribution of and access to public services.

This chapter examines some of the pressing problems confronted by those attempting to build a democratic administrative state under conditions of rapid change and uncertainty [1]. More specifically, it focuses its analysis on the need for either improving or developing new institutional and social mechanisms for expanding the levels of democratic accountability and responsiveness of public bureaucracies as a necessary condition for strengthening democratic legitimacy.

In broad terms the experience of Latin America in this area illuminates both patterns of similarities and contrasts with the experience in the former Soviet Union and Eastern Europe [2]. In general terms, both regions have experienced periods of political history characterized by the presence of authoritarian political regimes; high levels of ethnic, social, and political tensions and conflict; explicit use of state coercion as a major mechanism for societal control; high levels of systemic instability; and progressive legitimation of a bureaucratic ethos that emphasizes the importance of a centrally controlled rationality—political as well as economic—used as guideline for achieving both societal change and economic growth. In this context, economic performance in most cases proved to be less than adequate for either ensuring self- sustained development or, at a minimum, being able to meet the basic needs of the populace. Finally, in both regions, attempts to impose formulas of societal change and control from the top failed and led to dramatic reversals in the composition of the dominant coalitions and the ideology inspiring their actions.

From our perspective, the most striking feature of the transitional experience in these regions is a paradox of sorts: starting from somewhat dramatically different polar extremes both regions confront in the transitional stage a set of problems requiring solutions that at first sight look strikingly similar in content and orientation.

In Latin America, the movement away from the authoritarian past is characterized by efforts to maintain or improve the neoliberal foundations of the economy while opening the political arena to ensure the participation of a traditionally marginalized citizenry that demands an equitable and prompt share of the benefits of economic growth. The challenge is how to reach a balance between the demands for improving the operations of a free market in the neoliberal tradition of capitalism and the need to reinstate and improve some of the traditional institutions and processes associated with the workings of a democratic welfare state—systematically undermined and vilified by the free-marketers as the source of all evils.

In the case of the former Soviet Union and Eastern Europe, the task is even more exacting: how to set the foundations of a free-market economy while opening the public policy arena to citizen participation. For the states, this problem will be compounded by conflicting goals, a weak base of legitimacy, and extreme economic constraints and political uncertainty. Is it possible to maintain some of the basic formal socioeconomic rights of the past while ensuring prompt and affordable access to basic economic goods in sufficient numbers and quality [3]? Have we learned how to nullify the traps of the Latin American model of redemocratization that have led to the establishment of systems of limited or restricted democracy and to the adoption of developmental paradigms devoid of substance and that at best can be viewed as projects of survival [4]?

At a minimum, the analysis of the transitional experience in Latin America suggests that the role played by public bureaucracies in the process of societal change needs to be closely examined whether one is interested in emphasizing the key values and practices associated with neoliberalism—free market, deregulation, privatization, dismantling of the old state apparatus, and so on—or whether one is interested in developing an administrative state that plays a key role as regulator and promoter of an equitable pattern of socioeconomic development. Clearly public bureaucracies play a central role as influential political actors in each and all phases of public policy-making processes—formation, implementation, and evaluation. Hence the need for paying close attention to questions that transcend the formal and somewhat traditional concerns about structural and procedural issues of the administrative state to go more directly to deal with questions of administrative accountability and responsiveness—at the core, the most important dimensions of a democratic administrative state [5].

Selecting the appropriate answer to this development riddle is not an easy one. The Latin American record has shown the complexities associated with both problems and solutions. In the long run, extremely low organizational potential and political willingness to effect substantive democratic changes have at best produced the façade of a weak and limited democracy operating on unstable economic foundations—the very conditions that have traditionally led to the old historical cycle of technocratic pyrotechnics so aptly described as the vicious circle of "Plus ça change, plus la même chose" [6].

In what follows I deal with a more limited set of issues: (a) the role, functions, and influence of the public administrative apparatus in Latin America, and (b) the problems associated with attempts to ensure acceptable degrees of accountability and responsiveness through institutionalized control mechanisms [7].

II. THE ADMINISTRATIVE STATE AND PUBLIC ADMINISTRATION IN LATIN AMERICA

Systemic instability in Latin American societies is greatly exacerbated by competing views about the legitimate scope and orientation of the state and by questions of inclusion or exclusion in the dominant coalition controlling the state. Without exception, the legitimacy of state intervention, and by extension the role played by the administrative apparatus, is questioned by important societal actors. The search for consensus and stability in an area characterized by sociopolitical conflict has led to the adoption of ideologies and models initially developed outside the Latin American context. This tradition—a distinctive feature of late development—has had a significant impact on the general patterns of Latin American development.

A. The Development of the Traditional Administrative State

Until the Great Depression in the 1930s the functions, size, and relative cost of the state apparatus remained fairly low and limited. The functions of the state were associated with the defense of territorial integrity, internal peace and order, and activities promoting capital accumulation and economic development—the latter viewed as primarily the responsibility of private entrepreneurs. The state played a largely subsidiary role.

Dominant groups were quick in grasping the advantages associated with controlling the administrative apparatus as mechanism for promoting their interests. The upper echelons of the public service were in the hands of personnel closely identified with the values and orientations of the groups in power. Use of mechanisms such as nepotism, spoils systems, social class, party membership, or loyalties was functional in ensuring a high degree of accountability and responsiveness to those in formal positions of power.

The public sector expanded as new services and initiatives were required by changes precipitated by industrialization, urbanization, commerce, emergence of new social groups and classes, and integration of national economies in the international market economy. The operation of public administration in the region reflected the tensions and conflicts found in the larger societal framework [8].

During this period, most countries in the region adopted organizational designs that first blended the corporatist tradition and the influences of European cameralism and, later, followed managerial ideologies promoting the mechanistic metaphor of bureaucratic administration [9]. Acceptance of the politics-administration dichotomy reinforced the legal tradition on which public management theory and practice was based. Problem solving at the societal level was defined as a question of legal and constitutional engineering. This tradition, still very much alive, permeated policy-making processes and the training of public servants. The faithful enforcement of the law became accepted as the hallmark of excellence in public service.

B. The Development of the Welfare Administrative State

Attempts to respond to the Great Depression through national economic policies based on import substitution models were to make the state the dominant force in the national economies. The state became the instrument for achieving a wide variety of new and conflicting goals ranging from regulating and promoting economic and social activities to ensuring social integration and equality. This incremental addition of functions in response to competing demands and values led to recurring policy conflicts and contributed to a pattern of weak systemic stability and legitimacy. While few disputed the role of the state as promoter of development, there were questions about its centrality, powers, size, cost, and efficiency on legal and ideological grounds.

Efforts to attain socioeconomic development gained momentum after World War II. The emergent welfare state incorporated value preferences—capitalism, liberal democracy, and the promise of rapid and sustained development—that gained a relative degree of political consensus and stability.

The welfare state is characterized by institutional developments with long-lasting consequences for the public administration. First, the achievement of economic development is predicated on the evolution of a modern and efficient public administrative apparatus. Organizationally, the welfare state expands the scope of its functions to include industrial, commercial, economic, financial, public health, social security, education, and welfare activities. The pattern of growth in the public sector is one of incremental aggregation. No integrated master plans existed before the launching of ambitious developmental policies and programs. The dramatic growth in the scope of state functions, size, cost, and relative power and influence is based on a rationality that is hard to decipher.

Second, the fragmented evolution of the public sector became an obstacle to attempts at tackling questions of development from a technical perspective. The uneasy coexistence of public policies and institutions established to respond to conflicting goals, with important differences in their levels of relative accountability and responsiveness, uneven professionalism and technical expertise, uncertain legitimacy, and considerable variation in resource availability, was further exacerbated by problems of jurisdiction and responsibility. The potential for exercising some degree of effective planning, control, and coordination by policymakers in general, and through public participation in particular, became minimal [10].

Third, the adoption of modern rational approaches to decision-making processes was to reinforce conceptions about the instrumental nature of both the organization and the management of the state. A technocratic ethos was set in place and with it the legitimation of the bureaucratic arena as the proper place for settling conflicts of interest [11].

Fourth, policymakers under the pressure for modernization, accepted the notion that the effectiveness of the public sector rested on a body of highly qualified personnel. The professionalization of the public service proved to have some major unintended consequences: (a) acceptance of the notion that professionalism ensures the development of a value neutral public service guided largely, if not exclusively, by technical rather than political considerations; (b) a public service that was unrepresentative of the general population; and (c) an administrative system that legitimized inequalities in services distribution and accessibility [12].

By the mid-1960s, the delicate foundation on which the welfare state was based began to crumble. The tentative and quite often implicit consensus behind many short-lived experiments on limited, formal democracy in the region was gone, and the era of the bureaucratic-authoritarian state had been inaugurated [13].

C. The Development of the Bureaucratic-Authoritarian Administrative State

The failure of the welfare administrative state to organize society for developmental purposes led key societal actors, particularly in the countries of the Southern Cone, to adopt models that mixed preexistent values and orientations with some new, modern components. Despite differences from one national experience to the next, some common ideological elements influenced the nature, organization and operations of the bureaucratic-authoritarian administrative state [14]:

1. Rejection of the liberal democracy formula for achieving self-sustained economic growth and the effective development of policies promoting national security;

2. The implementation of a new order based on a new state and a new modal pattern of relationship between the state and civil society. The new state, characterized by a high degree of exclusiveness, adopted corporatist formulas for reorganizing power relations.

3. A relationship between state and civil society that rested on a highly centralized, hierarchical, and technocratically founded system of authority. Political and social demobilization—achieved through the use of repression—was central to the effort to depoliticize the polity.

4. Rejection of the welfare administrative state of the past on both philosophical and technical grounds. An effort was made to develop a new administrative ethos that emphasized the virtues of the technocratic component of the corporativist ideology.

The subsidiary role of the state became a central tenet of the new model. The criticism of past public sector activities and performance led to a natural questioning of both their identity and their purpose. The deprecation of the notion of public service was reflected in the way rules governing the interface between public administration and the public were changed, through the capricious interpretation and enforcement of regulations, the legitimation of the idea that loyalty to the regime was more important than traditional merit, and ethical or moral criteria. Loyalty was secured by appointing military personnel to all levels of the bureaucracy [15] and through the extensive use of patronage practices.

5. The reorganization of the public sector characterized by three major features:

a. The privileged position assigned to top ranking bureaucrats—a group viewed as performing a depersonalized leadership function—promoting the efficient, economic, and effective operation of a neutral administrative apparatus. Their basic task was to design and implement the officially preferred strategy for development, and to protect the intellectual foundations of the technobureaucratic ideology on which the regime rested.

b. The ambitious scope of the reorganization effort. While in the past most reforms had been limited to a particular sector or group of public agencies, this time most reform programs had a comprehensive, global scope. The more pretentious the attempt by the regime to create a new order, the more comprehensive the administrative reform effort. The degree to which the ideology advocated by the regime permeated reform policies varied from one case to another, with the inclusiveness of the ideological dimension and the strength and commitment of both the regime and the dominant societal groups to the changes envisioned as necessary setting the framework for the scope and intensity of the reforms sought [16].

c. The acceptance of managerial ideologies stressing the instrumental nature of public administration. It was assumed that the relative degree of existing technological and professional capacity was homogeneously distributed within the system, and, what is more important, that the state had a high capacity to impose its will on both national and international actors.

The deepening of the international economic crisis of the late 1970s and the inability of the bureaucratic-authoritarian state to consolidate its legitimacy were to undermine the foundations of these regimes. Attempts to depoliticize politics and to solve societal questions through repression, ideological manipulation, and technocratic approaches proved ineffectual [17].

III. THE DEMOCRATIC ADMINISTRATIVE STATE AND THE QUEST FOR CONTROL OVER PUBLIC BUREAUCRACIES: THE UNFINISHED BUSINESS

The collapse of the authoritarian experiment brought forward a complex agenda of issues associated with establishing democracy in Latin America. Most analysts ignored the importance of the administrative foundations of the new state. The tone and content of the political discourse largely accepted old values and assumptions regarding the role and functions of public bureaucracies. At best, the old pattern of mechanical transfer of institutional and organizational schemes from abroad in the hope that they would take root reasserted itself.

The literature covers an extensive list of questions from traditional perspectives in both focus and subject matter. Key questions about democratic accountability and responsiveness of bureaucrats, or, more broadly, about the specific role and impact of public bureaucracies in the emergent democratic state have been largely ignored. The point is not minor, especially if one accepts the proposition that there is a connection between the nature of the political regime and the type of administrative state needed to achieve its objectives. In this context, issues of accountability and responsiveness are central to the relative success of democratic systems [18].

A. Bureaucratic Accountability, Responsiveness, an the Legitimacy Issue

The degree of legitimacy ascribed to both the state and its administrative apparatus is clearly the major factor that can either impede or promote effective levels of accountability and responsiveness. Most recent efforts in the region to elicit a consensus on what constitute the proper role, functions, and power of the state have opened to door to conflicts that threaten the stability of the new regimes. A similar situation occurs in areas that concern the rules or values that should govern relationships among the state, civil society, individuals, groups, and institutional relations. Questions about democratic values and behavior are difficult to answer on the theoretical or ideological plane and almost impossible to resolve in practice without a solid social and political consensus and legitimacy.

Attempts to prosecute gross violators of human rights offer a good example of the difficulties in attaining consensus even on presumably clear-cut policy issues. Over time the problem has become not one of political or democratic morality but rather one of political expediency. Politically it is easier to ignore justice and morality than to offend the military and put at risk the stability of the system: in a cruel paradox, the value of order becomes paramount to prevent the forces of order from overthrowing order.

This example illustrates the obvious: elected officials in the emergent democracies operate under severe pressure and constraints derived from internal and external factors, usually beyond the control of those in positions of formal authority—as in the debt crisis.

Accountability problems are complicated by the fact that it is often unclear for what and to whom bureaucracies are answerable, or how they are held accountable. Without clear lines of control and responsibility, the relative power of bureaucracies often seems to be out of control. The most extreme and consequential current case is that of the military. In most countries in the region the military operates in a vacuum of formal power—most of the time it seems to answer to no one but itself [19].

B. The Control Process in Latin America: Institutions and Processes [20]

1. *Accountability Processes Within the Executive Branch*

Latin American constitutional history shows a consistent preference for the adoption of presidential systems. The executive is clearly the most powerful branch of government. Usually the legislative branch is comparatively weak, while the judiciary, lacking power to exercise a full measure of judicial review over the acts of the other branches, has an extremely limited influence.

The executive branch is vested with an impressive array of formal powers that places the president at the center of the political arena. The president is called upon to carry out a number of roles that given him many opportunities to expand his ability to persuade and influence other significant actors in the political process. The office of the president has changed over time in response to changes brought by modernization processes. To respond to increasing levels of demands on their offices and be able to cope with the complexities of contemporary problems, presidents have strengthened the executive branch establishment. The bureaucratization of the office of the president reflects other changes that have taken place since World War II. The need for most presidents to secure office and govern with the support of political coalitions—often quite fragile in their composition and level of ideological and programmatic consensus—has set limitations on their ability to implement programs or to exercise leadership and control over the bureaucracy through the cabinet.

Presidents in Latin America have moved in the direction of strengthening those central staff agencies that in theory should help in keeping bureaucracies under control. Administrative reform efforts in the region have included attempts to improve the level of professionalism and effectiveness of agencies serving the president. Thus, the creation and periodic reforms of national offices for planning, budgeting, personnel, organization, and methods are aimed at providing the president with technically effective mechanisms to enhance his ability to govern—essential to executives operating under conditions of uncertainty and constraint. Supervisory direction and review, internal auditing, and the regular budgetary process have proved to be less than effective as control mechanisms. Reliance on hierarchical arrangements for exercising control over bureaucrats has been made difficult by built-in structural and procedural obstacles. Access to basic, reliable data, in a timely fashion, is rarely available to decision makers.

Over time, the relationships among the president, his cabinet—including all his department heads—appointed political officials serving at selected agencies, top ranking career bureaucrats, and other actors with influence in the public sector have evolved in unanticipated ways. Political factors have made ministerial cabinets unreliable as sources of political advice and control. The expansion of the civil service system, on the other hand, has limited the presidential exercise of patronage, or, alternatively, the removal without restraints of personnel who are either technically incompetent or politically unreliable. Long tenure in office by top ranking bureaucrats has in turn kept many presidents hostages to subordinates or advisers they cannot manage or control freely.

The level of professionalism of career bureaucrats has increased over the years through civil service mechanisms and specialized training. Their relative monopoly of technical skills and knowledge, their enhanced ability to build political ties and coalitions with actors outside the executive branch—including powerful international allies—their longevity in office, and the powers of their unions, have in the long run conspired to undermine the ability of the president to control the administrative apparatus of which he is formally in charge [21].

The problem is more general, though; for the raw material required for judging performance, accountability, and responsiveness is not available within the public bureaucracy or outside. In this sense, developments such as government by proxy or rampant privatization have further debilitated the ability of the executive to exercise decision-making powers effectively. Corruption and abuse of power take place regardless of whether those in office are career bureaucrats working for elected public officials or for a military junta. The dramatic growth in the number of powerful independent agencies and corporations responsible for carrying out important economic and social activities has complicated the control problem. All these agencies are beyond the formal control of presidential or ministerial authorities. Recent trends promoting further fragmentation of political power through devolution of functions to regional or local governments and decentralization of the authority and functions of central public administration have failed to deal with the issue of accountability as an important issue in itself [22].

Mechanisms of internal and external review and evaluation of executive actions are for the most part narrow in the scope of their jurisdiction and weak in terms of formal authority. Often, not even the budget process is fully used as a mechanism for providing policy guidance and supervisory direction and review.

Presidents, despite appearances to the contrary, have little capacity to exercise effective control over public agencies despite efforts to increase the technological capacity of their staff. To listen to officials of recent elected administrations is to hear roughly the same complaint: plans and electoral promises go up in smoke because of bureaucratic interference or sabotage [23].

Equally significant is the consistent failure to address accountability issues raised by the tendency to turn to outside organizations to perform a wide range of governmental functions and services. Under pressure of ideological and pragmatic considerations to shrink the scope of governmental functions and responsibilities, governments are increasingly moving to spend public funds to achieve public goals by using the talents and capacities of outside, nongovernmental organizations. The fact that government by proxy in the region has not reached considerable proportions still begs the question of how to allow maximum possible independence while assuring adequate accountability.

2. *Accountability Processes Within the Legislative Branch*

Legislatures in Latin America are comparatively weak in their formal powers to influence or control public bureaucracies. Recently, even in Costa Rica—the model democracy in Central America—the legislature has lost ground vis-à-vis the president in terms of capacity to influence policy-making processes and control bureaucracies [24].

Short terms in office and lack of substantive powers of oversight authority are further compounded by the lack of congressional staff support. Congressmen depend for their information largely on outside sources: for example, public bureaucrats, pressure group representatives, technical advisers from political parties, and colleagues serving in the legislature.

Iron triangles and issue networks are common features in the Latin American political landscape, especially in countries with some degree of social and political pluralism. In this context there are few incentives for congressmen to engage in oversight activities—there is more to be gained by cooperating than by fighting over issues with low potential for electoral rewards.

Case work is by far the most important dimension of the activities of most legislators. In countries where red tape and bureaucratic discretion have an important impact on influencing administrative outcomes, individuals rely on their representatives or senators to secure benefits to which they are entitled. Legislators, to be effective as case workers, must rely in turn on bureaucrats able to deliver decisions in individual cases.

While few studies have been conducted on the role played by legislatures in the budgetary process, evidence suggests that in Latin America there are few opportunities for Congress to play a significant role. Constraints on time, information, technical knowledge; weak formal powers; and the fragmentation of political parties exacerbate the inability of Congress to control bureaucracies by pulling the pursestrings. Too often, the budgetary process is an area formally dominated by the executive.

Few occasions present themselves for conducting public hearings or using other traditional legislative mechanisms available to their counterparts elsewhere. In balance, the potential for legislators to control public administration is debatable even in those legislatures considered to be strong by regional standards.

3. *Accountability Processes Within the Judicial Branch*

The judiciary is the weakest branch of government in the region as a whole. While a few have some measure of limited judicial review powers, in practice, the courts do not play an active role in deciding issues of administrative accountability or responsiveness. In countries lacking a constitutional tribunal, the courts have been called by default to decide on issues of constitutionality. The exercise of this limited power, however, is further constrained by practical considerations. To avoid being either politicized or caught in the middle of a fight between branches of government, courts tend to define problems as political in nature and hence beyond their jurisdictions—the basic rationale used for not questioning decisions made by military governments [25].

Traditionally questions of administrative control and accountability have been under the jurisdiction of either specialized administrative tribunals or general comptrollers offices—all outside the hierarchical control of the judiciary. Moreover, decisions made at this level are, in practice, outside the regular channels open for judicial review through the appellate court mechanism.

Thus, while the judicial branch plays an important role in adjudicating civil, criminal, and commercial law, they have a rather limited power to influence administrative accountability [26].

4. *Accountability Processes Through Other Control Mechanisms*

In Latin America there are many alternative instruments for accountability. Available data are insufficient to judge their relative effectiveness, though. Report essentially are descriptive, emphasizing their organizational and legal bases, or have strong normative overtones.

a. The Comptroller Office. Most countries in the region have established independent agencies for auditing public agencies. While neither their formal authority nor the scope of their functions can compare with those of their counterparts such as the U.S. General Accounting

Office or Britain's National Audit Office, their activities have substantial impact on the way public administration operates.

Over the years, the scope of their functions has expanded and gone beyond conventional auditing activities. As the major administrative court in the land, they have become important in both overseeing the operations of the civil service system and acting as a control mechanism on the activities of the executive branch. Not all sectors or activities in the public sector are either under their jurisdiction or subjected to the same depth of formal scrutiny, however. The major exception is the military; while formally the Office of the Comptroller General may have authority to operate in certain areas of military activities, others remain closed to any type of outside auditing or control—national security is usually being the rationale used for justification. The heavy reliance on legal approaches to questions of audit and administration has limited any policy analysis orientation or focus. In practice, these institutions are reluctant to be drawn into assessing policy implications.

Policy avoidance is defended on both pragmatic and theoretical grounds. In theory, it is argued, it is not proper for nonelected officials to judge political decisions. Their jobs is viewed as technically narrower: to see that the rule of law or proper procedures have been followed. Pragmatically, the reluctance obviously has to do with the fear of losing whatever degree of institutional independence they have achieved so far.

In either case, their activities can be construed as political—especially when they lend legitimacy to actions that otherwise might become, at a minimum, sources of political embarrassment or, worse, prevent the execution of a governmental policy or program the government may consider politically significant.

b. Publicity. Latin America has no tradition of using publicity as a mechanism for keeping public administration under control. On the contrary, secrecy has been a distinctive characteristic of the way government operates on a daily basis. Neither elected officials nor bureaucrats are required to justify decisions or actions publicly, and often they are prohibited by legislation or regulations from doing so.

The potential for eradicating the deeply ingrained tradition of governmental and administrative secrecy in the region is extremely limited. Secrecy is a particularly sensitive problem for the emerging democracies. Access to files and data dealing with human rights violations or repression under authoritarian rule, for example, continues to be controlled by the armed forces. No civilian authority is authorized either to see the materials or to verify that they have been destroyed. In fact, political expediency often prevents dealing with a subject closely linked to issues of criminal and civil responsibilities of members of authoritarian regimes. Sporadic attempts to introduce reforms aimed at expanding the scope of civilian control over the armed forces—even in those cases when their institutional prestige and standing have been at their lowest point—have proved to be largely ineffectual.

In general, the democratic ideal of ensuring an informed citizenry would require dramatic changes in this area of concern. In countries where the news media are controlled by either the government or some powerful economic interest group, there are limited opportunities for the average citizen to have access to timely, reliable, and objective information about governmental operations. More important, the trend in the region is for the people largely to rely on the electronic media for information about local, national, or international politics—and without exceptions the electronic media do the poorest job of them all.

c. Political Parties. Political parties in the region, and the party systems they help to create, show a great deal of variation in their capacities for ensuring the political control of bureaucracies. In one-party systems (Cuba, Mexico), the ruling party exercises an important role in the appointment and career mobility of professional bureaucrats—with only party loyalists making it to the top. Accountability and responsiveness to the party, however, may undermine the control monopoly sought by political officials in formal positions of authority. Inter- and intra-bureaucratic politics are a reflection of this built-in tension.

In multiparty systems, the degree of influence exercised by the ruling political parties depends on the role they play in the dominant coalition. Often, an informal quota system is built into the coalition formula, and the potential for exercising any meaningful control over the bureaucracy is severely limited, for the quota system provides some insulation to bureaucrats who feel protected by their party. The key to administrative advancement is party loyalty rather than adherence to either professional or democratic principles.

Political parties have reluctantly supported efforts to institutionalize control and accountability mechanisms placing limits on their freedom to use patronage and spoils practices or influence individual bureaucrats. Often, political parties are managed in ways that are not conducive to favoring the institutionalization of stricter control mechanisms. Party elites are usually more concerned about their ability to maintain control over the party apparatus than about using it as a potential mechanism for ensuring democratic practices—in actual practice, citizens have little opportunity to participate formally in key decision-making processes within their own parties.

d. Interest Groups. Well-organized groups have an important impact on public policy-making processes. In the administrative arena, the colonization of public agencies by outside interest groups is not unusual. Often it is difficult to determine who controls the policy agenda. Most bureaucracies are seen as mechanisms for promoting the interests of those in dominant positions of influence. Given the class orientation of most bureaucracies in the region, this development is hardly a surprise. Interest group influence and activities can provide additional insulation to bureaucrats unresponsive to the authority of elected public officials. Consistently administrative reform efforts have ignored this important problem, furthering the ability of outside groups severely to limit the maneuverability of the government in promoting innovation and change.

e. Public Participation. In different times and circumstances, public participation has been occasionally tried as a mechanism to empower people and to control unresponsive or unaccountable bureaucrats. Direct public participation is rarely found.

Unfortunately, most of the recent administrative reform plans have systematically ignored several points:

1. The potential for using public administration as a mechanism for securing inputs into the policy-making process from traditionally marginal sectors of society. In societies characterized by elitism and high levels of marginality, substantial numbers of the population participate in politics in extremely limited and largely symbolic ways.

In the past, attempts to ensure some degree of wider popular participation were undermined by factors such as the co-optation of the outsiders by the bureaucrats and the long-run apathy of participants who found limited input opportunities opened or found themselves lacking in technical skills or knowledge to judge the merits of the problem or its solution. Often, the inability of participants to effect change or wield influence through institutional channels has bred disillusionment, frustration, and open conflict [27].

2. The potential for using public administration as a mechanism to facilitate national and social integration. Despite appearances to the contrary, Latin American societies have failed to bridge historically deep and conflictive ethnic and racial cleavages, and the wide socioeconomic gap between the have and have-nots. In fact, twenty years of authoritarian rule has further exacerbated class and ethnic cleavages and the potential for open conflicts.

3. The need for improving the representative nature and composition of key political and administrative institutions. The public administrative apparatus offers an exceptional window of opportunity for creating the foundations of truly developmentally oriented regimes. The elitist nature of the administrative apparatus reinforces the class-oriented operations of a system that increasingly has become overly concerned with managing a precarious and unjust equilibrium.

4. The valuable lessons stemming from the examples of self-administration and participation provided by peasant and Indian communities in the region. The options for using public bureaucracies as mechanisms for expanding participation and representation in public policy-making processes—at the national or local levels—are being dramatically reduced.

Overall, the promise of public participation in policy-making processes as a mechanism of control remains open to question. The limited experience in the region shows the need to devise better ways for ensuring that participation is more than just an exercise in symbolic politics [28].

f. Training of Top Administrators and Public Managers. As suggested here, a key element in most administrative reform plans of the past was to strengthen the civil service system. The formation of the cadres of administrators—top ranking managers and middle-level career managers—has for the most part failed to ensure executive competence and a sense of commitment to the public interest. The systematic delegitimation of the state coupled with the undermining of the status of public service as led to the emergence of in-built limitations preventing both the recruitment and the retention of the "best and the brightest."

Judging from the opinions of regional experts on public personnel education and training, limited progress has been made in the last 10 years or so. Traditional problems such as technical incompetence, corruption, inefficiencies, and lack of an effective rapport between top bureaucrats and elected officials continue to plague the operations of a public sector burdened with crises affecting the very capacity to govern [29]. As in the past, many of the initiatives are still inspired by traditional paradigms that have proved to be largely irrelevant for coping with the problems of the region.

The overall effectiveness of regional initiatives in this area of concern will continue to be hampered by the lack of appropriate research in public administration and the unwillingness to resolve the incongruity between developmental needs and projected democratic reforms.

IV. CONCLUSIONS

Issues of democratic control over public bureaucracies are difficult to analyze because of the complexities of the region and of the actors and processes involved. These are further compounded by the lack of basic, reliable information about the public policy-making processes, in general, and of the politics of administrative accountability, in particular.

The review of available materials, however, has clearly identified areas of consensus and concern. Most analysts tend to agree on the important rolc played by public administration in public policy-making processes and the need for improving our ability to keep it under control. Also, there is a sense of frustration with the relatively low level of responsiveness of the government for developing the foundations of a democratic society while maintaining an adequate level of governmental effectiveness.

Whether such expectations can be met remains to be seen. The basic problem faced by public administrators is the lack of consensus about the type of values to be emphasized in building the democratic administrative state. Failure to define such questions imposes limits on the ability to create the conditions required to ensure a pattern of self-sustained development. Chances for effecting changes leading to effective accountability processes remain limited. At best, the tendency is to continue to tamper with traditional patterns of development. The enthusiasm generated by some experiences with the institution of the ombudsman, for example, tends to obscure that in order to be effective the institution requires precisely what is not there, namely, the existence of strong political institutions able and willing to prevent any group in society from claiming the right not to be accountable.

Consideration of the fact that the CIS countries and Eastern Europe face a similarly complex set of governability problems without the benefits of time and experimentation should stress the importance of comparing needs, prescriptions, and paradigms before committing scarce resources to concrete programs. Whether one likes it or not, the administrative dimension of the process of global change is important in that it has a long-lasting impact on public policy outcomes.

NOTES

1. The analysis is largely focused on the historical experience of countries in the Southern Cone—Chile, Argentina, Brazil, and Uruguay. A number of problems discussed in this chapter as well as many of its conclusions, however, are common to the region as a whole—hardly a surprise, considering the fact that the legitimacy of both the state and its major institutions has come under systematic questioning from powerful actors inside and outside their respective societies.
2. I do not claim any expertise on Soviet or Eastern European politics or administration. For descriptive purposes I have extensively relied on literature written by American specialists. The extent to which these materials are comprehensive or reliable has been a traditional area of controversy. It is interesting to note that in the case of the Soviet Union, often conceived as a bureaucratically run system, there is little information available in English on the subject of Soviet public administration under Communist rule. On this subject, see, among others, Lawrence C. Mayer, *Redefining Comparative Politics: Promise and Performance* (Newberry Park, London, New Delhi: Sage Publications, 1989), chapter 7. Publications consulted on the Soviet Union include, among others, Michael G. Roskin, *Countries and Concepts: An Introduction to Comparative Politics* (Englewood Cliffs, N.J.: Prentice-Hall, 1992), Leon P. Baradat, *Soviet Political Society* (Englewood Cliffs, N.J.: Prentice-Hall, 1992), Ferrel Heady, *Public Administration: A Comparative Perspective* (New York and Basel: Marcel Dekker, 1984), and Gordon B. Smith (ed.), *Public Policy and Administration in the Soviet Union* (New York: Praeger Publishers, 1980).
3. This list of pressing questions and dilemmas serve illustrative purposes; there is no doubt that the composition and ranking of problems faced by particular countries vary over time and with circumstances.
4. For a critical overview of the Latin American process of redemocratization, see Jorge Nef, "Policy Developments and Administrative Changes in Latin America," in O. P. Dwivedi and K. M. Henderson (eds.), *Public Administration in World Perspectives* (Ames, Iowa: Iowa State University Press, 1990), chapter 11.
5. As used in this chapter, the idea of "administrative state" recognizes that to an extent, all modern polities are "administrative states" since a number of important decisions—economic and social—are in the hands of administrators and of technicians. In general terms, an administrative state goes beyond the limited acceptance that administrators should be given the chance to share political power; in fact, the administrative state assumes the existence of a polity in which administrators are recognized as legitimate authority over a wide area of public policy issues and problems. The "democratic" dimension of the administrative state, however, stresses the importance of establishing effective mechanisms to ensure political and

administrative accountability and responsiveness as the required safeguards for preventing the development of raw administrative or technocratic rule.

6. Recent developments in Venezuela and Perú are good examples of the problem under discussion. Attempts to institutionalize political democracy under conditions of economic crisis, conflicting views about the legitimate role and functions of the state, and the administrative inability to deliver basic public services have further exacerbated the overall conditions of systemic instability.
7. The chapter relies extensively on Latin American sources and research conducted over the last five years. While an effort has been made not to present broad generalizations, one cannot avoid some degree of oversimplification while dealing with these highly complex and debatable issues. The literature on the subject is quite extensive and varied in scope and approaches. For an overview of issues, see, among others, Ronaldo Munck, *Latin America: The Transition to Democracy* (London: Zed Books Ltd., 1989), T. Cammack (ed.), *The New Democracies in Latin America* (London: Croom Helm, 1987), George A. Lopez and Michael Stohl, *Liberalization and Redemocratization in Latin America* (New York: Greenwood Press, 1987), Enrique Grossman et al., *La administración pública en tiempo de crisis* (Caracas: CLAD, 1986), Jacques Chonchol and I. Cherensky (eds.), *Crisis y Transformación de los Regímenes Autoritarios* (Buenos Aires: EUDEBA, 1985).
8. Differences in the overall pattern of systemic development were to influence the degree of stability, professionalism, and effectiveness of the different national public administrations. Countries like Chile were able to solve problems of national integration and legitimacy earlier than others in the region. The pattern of political and administrative development in Chile not surprisingly was different from the one found in Argentina and Perú in the same period.
9. For a discussion on the mechanistic metaphor see Gareth Morgan, *Images of Organization* (Newberry Park: Sage Publications, 1989), pp. 19–38.
10. For a general overview of these and related issues, see United Nations Development Programme, *Programa regional para América Latina y el Caribe: 1987–1991* (UNDP, DP/RLA/2).
11. Whether one is to receive a benefit depends, in effect, on the ability to influence the relevant administering agency. In the late 1960s in many countries, for example, it was easier to secure passage of legislation introducing agrarian reform policies than effectively to reform the agency responsible for its implementation.
12. Social security systems provide a good example. Most systems were established as preemptive policies aimed at co-opting either the emergent middle class or the modernized sector of the working force. During the populist era, the content of policies and programs was largely the by-product of pressure politics carried out in the best pluralist tradition. As a result, the number, quality, and accessibility of services provided are influenced by socioeconomic considerations. For a discussion about the relationship between service delivery systems and social class, see J. I. Tapia-Videla and C. J. Parrish, "Ageing, Development and Social Service Delivery Systems in Latin America: Problems and Perspectives," *Ageing and Society*, vol. 2 (London, 1982), pp. 31–55.
13. There are a number of interpretations dealing with the breakdown of the democratic regimes. Some analysts favor institutional or structural explanations, others emphasize social class or economic factors (late development and dependency), and so on. See, for example, Marcelo Cavarozzi, *Autoritarismo y Democracia, 1955–1983* (Buenos Aires, Argentina: Centro Editor, 1983), Federico G. Gil (ed.), *Chile at the Turning Point: Lessons of the Socialist Years, 1970–1973* (Philadelphia: ISHI, 1979), and Ronaldo Munck, *Latin America*.
14. While the chapter does not argue that all Latin American societies followed this type of development, it suggests that the model illuminates some of the ideological and organizational

elements that were to be present in many countries of the region—including those still adhering to some form of formal democracy. See, for example, David Collier (ed.), *The New Authoritarianism in Latin America* (Princeton, N.J.: Princeton University Press, 1979).

15. See Carlos Hunneus, "El ejército y la política en el Chile de Pinochet: Su magnitud y alcances." *Opciones*, 14, 1988, pp. 89–136.
16. For a general discussion regarding administrative reform, see, Ignacio Pérez Salgado and M. Váldez, "Balance de los movimientos de reforma administrativa en América Latina: Enseñanzas," in Gilberto Flores and Jorge Nef (eds.), *Administración Pública: Perspectivas Críticas* (San José, C.R.: ICAP, 1984), pp. 91–120; CLAD, "Decentralización político-administrativa en América Latina: Discurso político vs. realidad concreta. Informe Final" (Caracas, Venezuela: CLAD, 1989), and Sergio Baeza and Rodrigo Manubens (eds.), *Sistema privado de pensiones en Chile* (Santiago, Chile: Centro de Estudios Públicos, 1988).
17. See, among others, Aldo Ferrer, *Nacionalismo y orden constitucional* (México: Fondo de Cultura Económica, 1981), and Luis Macadar, "Enfoques sobre la instauración de modelos transnacionalizados en el Cono Sur," *Pensamiento Iberoamericano*, 56 (1984).
18. The relationships between bureaucracy and democracy, bureaucratic power and accountability, and bureaucrats and elected officials in democratic settings have been extensively studied in American and European social science literature. See, among others, Bernard Rosen, *Holding Government Bureaucracies Accountable* (New York: Praeger, 1989), B. C. Smith, *Bureaucracy and Political Power* (New York: St. Martin's Press, 1988), and Ronald Glassman et al., *Bureaucracy Against Democracy and Socialism* (New York: Greenwood Press, 1987).
19. Overall, whether via constitutional amendments, through legislation or on a de facto basis, the armed forces in the region have been placed beyond the formal control of civilian authorities. See Louis Goodman et al., *The Military and Democracy: The Future of Civil-Military Relations in Latin America* (Lexington: Lexington Books, 1990), and Thomas P. Anderson, *Politics in Central America: Guatemala, El Salvador, Honduras, and Nicaragua* (New York: Praeger, 1988), rev. ed.
20. This section relies on materials and ideas that the author has assembled over the years in interviews and exchanges with policymakers, administrators, and scholars in the region. The three major centers in Latin America publishing or distributing materials using nontraditional approaches to the study of public administration are the Insituto Centroamericano de Administración Pública (ICAP) in San José, Costa Rica; the Centro de Estudios de Estado y Sociedad (CES) in Buenos Aires, Argentina; and the Centro Latinoamericano de Administración para el Desarrollo (CLAD) in Caracas, Venezuela. Their materials are a must for those interested in questions of policy and administration in Latin America and the Caribbean.
21. It is not unusual to find career bureaucrats whose power and influence derive from contacts with influential members of international agencies or a major transnational conducting business in the country—often it is difficult to determine whose interests the bureaucrat is representing.
22. Despite the fact that the whole effort of decentralization rests on the assumption that present institutional arrangements are ineffective because of their lack of accountability and responsiveness, the final report of the international colloquium "Political and Administrative Decentralization in Latin America: Political Discourse vs. Reality" fails to mention either concept. CLAD, *Decentralización político-administrativa en América Latina: Discurso político vs. realidad concreta. Informe Final* (Caracas, Venezuela: CLAD, 1989).
23. While it is true that to some extent this has been a traditional ploy used by elected public officials all over the world to explain their failure to deliver on electoral promises, in Latin America without exception all newly elected administrations were shocked to discover how

tightly their hands were tied by an extensive and extremely sophisticated body of rules and regulations setting limits to their abilities for introducing innovation and change. Interviews with both elected and top ranking appointed political officials in the administrations of Presidents Alfonsín and Menem in Argentina and Aylwyn in Chile have consistently shown the importance of the negative impact that the "bureaucratic complex" inherited from the authoritarian past has on new administrations.

24. See, among others, Gregg L. Vunderink, "Neo-Liberal Costa Rica: The Closing of the Political Space," paper delivered at the Southwest Political Science Association (Fort Worth, Texas, March 1990), and Gary W. Wynia, *The Politics of Latin American Development* (New York: Cambridge University Press, 1990).
25. It is not unusual for newly elected governments to find a court system that is largely a creature of the old order in terms of personnel and ideological orientations and preferences. Often efforts to reform the judiciary become an extremely hard and difficult political battle for administrations trying hard to expand their base of political support. Not surprisingly, judicial reform takes second place to more pressing pressures and demands. In this sense, Argentina and Chile offer good examples.
26. Most experts writing on Latin American politics or public administration have traditionally ignored the courts as actors of much consequence.
27. It must be noted that these developments have taken place throughout the region regardless of the nature of the regime in power. Along these lines one finds striking similarities in countries as different as Cuba, the Sandinista Nicaragua, Chile—pre- and post-Pinochet—and Mexico as examples. See, among others, Lawrence S. Graham, *The State and Policy Outcomes in Latin America* (New York, Westport, and London: Praeger, 1990), Guy Poitras, *The Ordeal of Hegemony: The United States and Latin America* (Boulder, San Francisco, and Oxford: Westview Press, 1990), J. I. Tapia-Videla, "Ancianos y Políticas de Servicios en América Latina y el Caribe: Una Visión Histórica," in Elías Anzola et al., *La Atención de los Ancianos: Un Desafío para los Años Noventa* (Washington, D.C.: PAHO, 1994).
28. See, for example, Susan Eckstein (ed.), *Power and Popular Protest: Latin American Social Movements* (Berkeley: University of California Press, 1989).
29. See the documents presented at the Taller de expertos para el desarrollo de políticas y criterios técnicos para la modernización curricular de la formación de gerentes públicos en Iberoamérica (Bogotá, Colombia: UNDP/CLAD/ESAP, 1991).

32
Bureaucracy and Agricultural Policy Implementation in Venezuela (1958–1991)

Rita Giacalone
Universidad de Los Andes, Mérida, Venezuela

I. INTRODUCTION

Public policy implementation in Venezuela has been heavily affected since 1958 by the coexistence of the technocratic rationality of decision making at the centralized level with a pervasive clientelistic rationality within the bureaucratic apparatus in charge of executing decisions. In the specific case of agricultural policy, especially when it has to be implemented in rather isolated and backward rural areas, another type of element is also present and impinges on the way in which central decisions turn into concrete actions, that is, traditional power structures.

In this chapter we will analyze (1) the main characteristics of Venezuelan bureaucracy in the democratic period (1958–1991); (2) agricultural policy implementation during the same period, by means of the case of coffee policy in the Venezuelan Andes; and (3) the role of a clientelistic bureaucracy in the articulation of technical rationality and traditional structures.

II. BUREAUCRACY IN POST-1958 VENEZUELA

A quick profile of Venezuelan bureaucracy can be given through three adjectives: authoritarian, clientelistic, and incompetent. This may help explain why the word "bureaucrat" has a strong derogatory meaning for most Venezuelans. José A. Silva Michelena, in his pioneer study of the Venezuelan bureaucrats of the 1960s (Silva Michelena, 1967, p. 140), summarized the most common complaints about them: they did not perform a service in the community, they were technically incompetent, and they were not loyal to their organizations. The same author pointed out two sets of factors as responsible for this situation—the intrusion of family or party links on the appointment of bureaucrats and a poor organizational framework that allowed for excessive centralization, lack of coordination, and duplication of work, all at the same time. After all this, however, the author wondered whether these were not the same complaints made everywhere about bureaucrats and bureaucracy, even in industrialized countries like Canada and the United States.

Silva Michelena concluded his study with the affirmation that, in spite of all the negative feeling toward them, at the high and medium levels most bureaucrats were university graduates, with a progressive orientation toward their work, competent, and preoccupied with the advancement of their organizations. For him this could be explained by the fact that, after the fall of the military dictatorship of Marco Pérez Jiménez in 1958, a conscious effort had been made to replace bureaucrats at those levels with new people, usually younger and linked to the three political parties that constituted the post-1958 coalition government (Acción Democrática [AD], Comité de Política Electoral Independiente [COPEI], and Unión Republicana Democrática [URD]). At that moment, then, the clientelistic orientation of appointments was instrumental in allowing the entry into the bureaucracy of people with new ideas and a positive view of politics and job responsibility.

The fact that the new government initiated a program of modernization of Venezuela, on the basis of a highly rational plan adopted mostly from the example of the North Atlantic world community (Lombardi, 1982, p. 230), ensured that bureaucrats in charge of making decisions and implementing them at the top were, in general, in agreement with the main lines of that program. It would be at the end of the 1960s, when the coalition ended and the AD government had to resort to increasing repression to forestall the danger of a guerrilla movement and of ideological dissidence within its own party, that some of these bureaucrats began to express dissatisfaction with their jobs. And this dissatisfaction expressed itself by means of their propensity to change to jobs outside bureaucracy (Silva Michelena, 1967), rather than to give way to lousy work, irrational behavior, and so on.

After the work of Silva Michelena, most analysts of Venezuelan bureaucracy concentrated on the study of the decision-making process. In this area, positions range from that of R. Lynn Kelley (1970), for whom the private sector plays an important role at the level of decisions, to that of José Antonio Gil Yepez (1977; 1978), who posits that though the Venezuelan process of decision making has been pluralistic sometimes, the norm is inclined in the direction of a rather limited pluralism most of the time. Thus the Venezuelan democratic government would tend to behave in the same manner as authoritarian Latin American governments. In general, however, Diego Abente (1985) has aptly remarked that if these studies were inconclusive, the most important fact about them is that they are also "possibly obsolete," as most of them came out of data gathered before the mid-1970s, when a major transformation shook the whole Venezuelan society, affecting its bureaucracy.

Before discussing Venezuelan bureaucracy in the years after 1973, we want to add a few remarks on the general issue of bureaucrats and their behavior in Venezuela. The first is that the situation of the democratic governments after 1958 was rather similar to that recorded in nations that were then gaining their political independence. If the latter, as is the case of neighboring Trinidad and Tobago (Danns, 1978; Ryan, 1974), had to destroy the existing colonial bureaucracy and substitute a new one loyal to the political leaders of independence. Venezuelan governments had to impose bureaucratic institutions with a new overall modernizing program and democratic philosophy upon rather authoritarian structures. Here it was also necessary, as in the Trinidadian case, to achieve this by means of a change of personnel, and the need that this be loyal to the new regime and its modernizing program made almost imperative that party links were utilized as the norm for recruitment and promotion into the system. In fact, at the beginning of the democratic period party clientelism was a necessity for coalition politicians in order to secure the success of their socioeconomic and political projects.

The second remark we would like to make here relates to the question of the Venezuelan political system which has developed since 1958 and the place of party clientelism in that system [1]. The fall of the short democratic interregnum of 1945–1948, in the midst of successive military governments during most of the twentieth century, forced Venezuelan political leaders to emphasize the importance of control if the new democratic regime were to survive. As Daniel Levine (1977, p. 11) summarizes the idea, "Venezuelan political leaders . . . became convinced that their incapacity to control and channel . . . widespread conflict was what had opened the door for a military coup [in 1948]. They also learned that political leadership involves more than simple adherence to ideology and program—conciliation and bargaining became key political values." Coalition politics during most of the 1960s were part of this, but in addition negotiation among political elites was not possible if these elites did not gain a high level of control over the demands of their respective organizations. Without the availability of relatively abundant resources controlled by the Venezuelan state the consolidation of the democratic system could have been in trouble, but what interests us is that, though resources were under the control of the state, their distribution fell into the hands of the political parties, making them the big winners. New links were created and strengthened on the basis of the formation of party clientelistic networks, where the twin aspects of exchange and control could be clearly seen.

> In summary, the Venezuelan political system developed since 1958 has been based on the economic capacity of the state to subsidize democracy, providing the prebends necessary to maintain a certain consensus around the democratic system. In this process, the political parties have played a fundamental role. They have incorporated new popular sectors into the political system by means of enormous clientelistic networks, which are composed of a multiplicity of smaller networks. In this way, the political parties achieved an ample popular base for the political system at the same time that they diffused the conflict that could arise from electoral competition. (Giacalone and Hanes, 1992, p. 138)

An added element of interest to the situation of the bureaucrats is the fact that during most of its life the Venezuelan state has not depended on taxes. Thus most Venezuelans do not think they are entitled to "a certain quantity and quality of governmental performance" (Urbaneja, 1991, p. 172) as a community, and this makes it more necessary for them to resort to particularistic means to get preferential access to services or goods. Diego Bautista Urbaneja has stressed the strong presence of the party in government at all levels of state personnel, which means a big turnover in these employees after every election lost by the incumbent party. "Many bureaucrats owe their appointment to their party membership, not to merit. The Venezuelan citizen knows that, and the civil servant knows that the citizen knows, in a chain whose overall result is a further weakening of the sense of rights and duties in bureaucrats and citizens alike" (p. 172). Urbaneja also claims that, in general, if this has negatively affected the emergence of a professionalized civil service, what has developed is "an 'interrupted' technobureaucracy: if you have been an employee in the Agriculture Ministry for party reasons under an AD government and AD loses the elections, you are probably going to be removed and replaced. . . . But five years later, when AD next wins the elections, you are likely to be re-appointed to the Ministry of Agriculture, possibly in a higher position" (p. 175).

In 1973 and 1974 the boom in the international price of oil, the main export of Venezuela, produced sudden and impressive changes in the country. These changes affected everything, from eating habits to the structure of the state. To get an idea of the impact, let us remember that the current expenses of the central government rose 71.8% in the short term of two years, between 1972 and 1974 (Aranda, 1984, p. 248). A good part of this money went to a rapidly enlarging bureaucracy in order to man the programs and plans the government strove to put into operation. Some of these programs were part of a redistributive effort to make oil money available to most of the Venezuelan population through social policies (more health and education services, especially), but others were related to an enhanced presence of the state in the economic sphere. This presence was not new, as it had been part of the modernizing effort of the post-1958 coalition, but now the amount of resources available to the state turned this into the motor of economic life, introducing it in productive fields like aluminum smelters and oil production and distribution.

The consequences for Venezuelan bureaucracy were soon to become apparent: the rapid entry at all levels, high, medium, and low, or myriad persons exacerbated the problem of the lack of adequate human resources prepared for the jobs they were undertaking. One of the fields in which this was most notorious is, perhaps, public education at all levels, even at the national universities, where graduates without experience and even sometimes without good credentials had to be hired in order to respond to the massive entry of high school graduates. But here we will pay more attention to what happened in general with the bureaucracy of those programs that had a direct relationship to an economic field, such as agricultural programs.

One of the first important changes in the bureaucracy linked to agricultural policy was the division of encompassing agricultural boards into specialized boards for almost every area of interest, such as the Coffee and Cocoa National Board (Fondo Nacional del Café y del Cacao [FNCC]), created in 1959, splitting into a National Coffee Board (FONCAFE) and a National Cocoa Board in 1974, something that from the very beginning entailed the need to hire more bureaucrats for these new posts. Another important consequence was the availability of more money for agricultural policy, in accordance with the strategy of raising minimum prices for producers, subsidizing inputs like fertilizers and machinery, renegotiating and consolidating producers' debts, enlarging credits, and so forth. This fostered a situation in which, in an atmosphere of general optimism about the future of Venezuela, more bureaucrats, less well prepared than before and hired through the usual means of party patronage or family links, had in their hands larger amounts of money and practically free rein to implement governmental programs. This was due to the fact that organizations at the central level were subjected to so many rapid changes and pressing needs that they were unable to supervise the process of implementation adequately, especially at the local level.

Here it should also be noted that since 1958 bureaucracy had been seen as a field for social and economic advancement in a country where oil production was controlled until 1976 by foreign companies, and Venezuelans were usually relegated to rather subordinate positions within this most important industry of the country. Thus for the educated sons and daughters of an upward aspiring middle sector, mostly located in the urban centers, bureaucracy was the main channel for fulfilling their aspirations. After 1974 this trend intensified, and as the state became the motor of the economy, it also was increasingly seen as the element through which every Venezuelan could get a share of the oil riches of the country, by means of a public job, a scholarship, better health care, and so on. If the system had always accepted the fact that the entry or acquisition of any of these prebends resulted from the right party or family connections, now it became highly irrelevant whether or not you were qualified for whatever you were requesting. The state, in someway or another, owed it to you.

The relative ease with which positions were acquired, the feeling of a never-ending Venezuelan prosperity and of the right to partake of the oil money inclined bureaucrats to think that, once they were in the proper position, this could be used as the way to enhance their own private situation, both economically and socially. This could be summarized as a process by which practically all Venezuelan citizens had the notion that whatever the state was granting them was theirs by right, and in that manner state resources became "privatized" many times rather openly by bureaucrats. There were almost no complaints from outsiders as all thought that they were receiving their share of the oil money through different services, subsidized prices of food, and higher minimum wages, for example.

This reminds us of Crozier (1964), according to whom the main feature of modern industrial society is the development of large organizations, of which bureaucracy is just one. But in this development, these organizations clash with the resistance of the human resources available at a given moment within society. Crozier relates this resistance to characteristics of the cultural system in which organizations form and function. He concludes that what he calls "the pathology of organizations" is a product of "the relative incompatibility between the objectives that these seek (and which develop from a type of utilitarian rationality) and the means of social control determined by primary behaviors and values of the cultural system" (p. 18).

If we apply Crozier's concepts to Venezuelan bureaucracy in the post-1958 period, we can say that 1974 served in a way as a turning point, in the sense that what happened then and in the following years exacerbated primary behaviors and values that were probably part of the cultural systems before, but that now found an enlarged framework to develop. The kind of "amoralism" that permeated the system of recruitment and enrichment by way of public office was probably not new, but the fact that it was accessible to almost everybody and that most people were sharing in its benefits erased guilty feelings and responsibilities, with the due exceptions.

The oil prosperity of Venezuela lasted until 1979; then began a period of stagnation when many of the promises of the previous years were felt to be empty, and the feeling of optimism gave way to a feeling of demoralization. This increased as years passed and by the end of the 1980s manifested itself in riots at various Venezuelan urban centers in February 1989, and in a military coup attempt in February 1992 [2]. The overall situation had consequences for bureaucracy as well as for the rest of the institutions of the country. The propensity to use the state resources for their own benefit by members of the public service continued and was even considered necessary as many of the advantages and services offered by the state disappeared (subsidized food, subsidized transportation, facilities for free education, health care, etc.) little by little. But now the fight over the dwindling state resources made the question of this form of corruption a key one. It can be seen at the highest levels of the state apparatus with accusations and counteraccusations that involve even former presidents and their associates, but in fact permeates the bureaucracy at all levels.

If clientelistic links were usually approved practice and the use of a bureaucratic position to get rich did not seem to bother many people before, now there is a more crude form of fighting for appointments and preventing others from getting what one can not obtain. Morality permeates the pages of the daily journals and the discussions in Congress, bringing to the fore facts that for many years were not openly discussed but were widely known and, in general, accepted as norms. This is not to say that morality is not a value within the Venezuelan cultural system but that, in a way, with the impact of the relatively easy oil money of the 1970s, it was relegated to a secondary place. Venezuelans who had spoken against the negative aspects of that period at the time and others who had never spoken about them have now turned their attention to this question, which places a heavy strain on the fabric of the democratic political system of Venezuela, by threatening the role of the established political parties in it.

In the following section we will discuss the implementation of a specific agricultural policy, that of coffee, in a specific geographical area, the Venezuelan Andes (this covers three states: Mérida, Táchira, and Trujillo, near the border with Colombia), in the period 1958–1991, to establish the basis for exploring the role of a clientelistic bureaucracy in the implementation of technocratic decisions made at the central level in a medium permeated by strong traditional relationships and power structures.

III. COFFEE POLICY IMPLEMENTATION IN THE VENEZUELAN ANDES (1958–1991)

In the case of the Venezuelan Andes the incorporation of peasants in the new political system after 1958 was based on a policy that revolved around coffee, their main product in both the national and international markets since the second half of the nineteenth century. This policy was probably chosen by AD governments between 1959 and 1969 as an alternative strategy in an area where agrarian reform held little attraction since most peasants were small property owners (Powell, 1971). Moreover, the Andean region had been left out of the areas of peasant mobilization initiated by AD from 1936 on, and peasant federations created there after 1958 were usually dominated by COPEI (Powell, 1971, pp. 128, 202).

Coffee policy took some time to develop, and it followed the recommendations that came out of a series of official studies that concluded that the marketing system was taking most of the benefits out of the hands of small producers and placing them in the hands of intermediaries. Accordingly, incorporation of Andean peasants into a rapidly modernizing Venezuela was thought to rest on the possibility of changing this situation, returning benefits to the direct producers. This would help prevent increasing rural-urban migration and offer AD the possibility of challenging the COPEI domination in the region.

Official studies (Banco Agropecuario, 1968; Ministerio de Agricultura y Cría, 1967; 1974; Banco Central de Venezuela, 1978) were the basis for the decision to create a state monopoly of coffee marketing in 1974, once AD was back in power after a short COPEI interregnum. By then the government could profit from the experience obtained through the work of the National Board of Coffee and Cocoa (Fondo Nacional del Café y del Cacao [FNCC], between 1959 and 1973, and through the creation of a network of producer associations (PACCAS) sponsored by the state and the two main political parties (AD and COPEI).

In 1974 the Venezuelan government approved the establishment of a separate National Coffee Board (FONCAFE) as the only agency for selling or buying coffee and established minimum prices for each type and grade of coffee. This meant that whenever prices fell below the established minimum, the government would still pay producers that price. Similar decisions on minimum prices had been approved before (UNET-FONCAFE, 1987, pp. 115–116), but intermediaries benefitted from these prices when selling to the national coffee industry and to exporters. Now an agreement signed with the National Association of Coffee Industrialists (*torrefactores*) accepted that the only supplier for both the coffee industry and exports was FONCAFE, which would buy directly from producer associations.

This meant the development of a bureaucratic structure at different levels, in Caracas, and in San Cristóbal, Táchira State, but also a structure able to reach out to the small producers in order to control coffee marketing and make the presence of intermediaries impossible even in the most isolated Andean areas. (The organizing structure at the central level can be seen in FONCAFE, Memoria y Cuenta, 1985, p. 7). The whole marketing system was based on monopolistic control of coffee prices from the hands of producers to the hands of consumers (p. 118). The FONCAFE strategy regarding these producers' associations rested on financing them through credits and subsidized inputs (fertilizers, pesticides, etc.) in exchange for their role in gathering, grading (there are different qualities of coffee with different prices), and transporting coffee for sale inside and outside Venezuela.

The bureaucratic structure of FONCAFE at the local level was then built around a dual system: mixed enterprises of coffee producers and the state (PACCAs, from the Spanish initials of Productores Asociados para el Comercio de Café) and technical offices of FONCAFE. PACCAs were subjected to the strong presence and control of FONCAFE, for the National Board appointed the first vice presidents of their councils, vice presidents who were responsible for approving the day to day operations of the mixed enterprises, and their annual accounts. Many times PACCAs managers, who were paid employees of the enterprises, came from the ranks of former FNCC or FONCAFE employees (Zambrano, 1991). The central agency also had the power of periodically evaluating the administrative activities of mixed enterprises and of acting as a *comisario* for the annual assemblies PACCAs are supposed to hold. These responsibilities were in the hands of the Coordinating Office with Producers Associations, which was directly subordinate to the General Direction of FONCAFE, its Head-Manager. Regarding their importance in the Andean region it should be noted that of a total of 64 PACCAs at the national level in 1987, 21 were located in that region (UNET-FONCAFE, 1987, pp. 75–76; FONCAFE, Memoria y Cuenta, 1987, p. 53).

Technical offices were rather small and located throughout the Andean region, manned by agrotechnicians appointed by the Technical Coordinating Office of FONCAFE. This office had five Regional Nuclei, of which two corresponded to the Andean region (FONCAFE, Memoria y Cuenta, 1985, p. 7). By 1986 almost every state acquired its own decentralized office, directly linked to the General Direction of FONCAFE (FONCAFE, Memoria y Cuenta, 1986, p. 12). Though there is no reason to doubt that technicians obtained recruitment into the system by way of party or family connections, all had to have a certain technical competence. It fell to these offices to gather data on coffee production and to discover major problems, not only on technical questions such as control and prevention of coffee diseases, but sometimes on the socioeconomic conditions of small producers, whom they were supposed to help organize in their own associations. It is worth remarking here that technicians, usually linked to the government party, were seen not only as helping to improve coffee production but also as mobilizing agents of modernization among the most traditional, and usually illiterate, sectors of producers. Technical offices were important to producers by providing technical advice and helping them to fill out the necessary forms to qualify for credits granted at the central level by FONCAFE. These credits were larger than the usual annual lines of credit from PACCAs for ensuring the coffee harvest (advances for hiring of harvesters, food, fertilizers, etc.).

Let us see now how this structure functioned to implement coffee policy in the Venezuelan Andes. Previous to the creation of FONCAFE in 1974, in the Andean region of Venezuela there had been no organizations of coffee producers or other institutions responsible for the functioning of the commercial circuit of coffee (Morales, 1991). This was probably due to a combination of the geographical isolation of coffee producers in an area of difficult communications and the lack of a coherent state policy for the coffee sector before 1974. This meant that FONCAFE had to assure credit and technical expertise for the small producers, local offices to purchase the product, better road communication from these offices to the more centrally located PACCAs, managerial personnel linked to the decision-making body of the PACCAs. It also sometimes meant prodding individual producers with 3 to 100 hectores of land under coffee cultivation to organize themselves according to the legal model provided by the national government. Producers unwilling to associate with an institution sponsored by an AD government organized themselves into cooperatives, such as CRAM (Centro Regional de Acopio y Mercadeo) in Mérida and Táchira, with support from COPEI. Both types of organizations were recognized by the government as valid producers' associations able to buy coffee from producers, grade and store it, and channel it afterwards to the national coffee industry or to the ports according to the decisions and prices of FONCAFE. This coffee board received payments made by coffee industrialists and exporters and made this money available to PACCAs and cooperatives to pay back to producers. FONCAFE had the final authority on credits granted to producers and the appointment of technicians to local offices and of vice presidents to PACCAs.

PACCAs and cooperatives became points of articulation between producers and the state within the system of commercialization created in 1974. The system managed to secure uniform prices for each grade of coffee throughout Venezuela and access to credit and technical advice, but it produced extreme dependence of producers upon the state, PACCAs, and cooperatives. PACCAs mobilized the largest amounts of coffee, in comparison with cooperatives (UNET-FONCAFE, 1987, Cuadro No. 28), and they represented the most obvious case of state penetration. We will look in some detail at the problems encountered in implementing coffee policy over them.

The managers of PACCAs, usually coming from the previous FNCC or FONCAFE bureaucracy, became key members in the operations of the enterprise, mainly buying coffee according to a fixed classification which they interpreted, and recommending, or not, the granting of credits to specific producers. They obtained this degree of power in exchange for their expertise in marketing deals and their knowledge of how the bureaucratic apparatus functioned at the central level. Soon they became coffee producers and/or entrepreneurs who maintained fleets of trucks to take coffee to the industry of the ports. Employing their knowledge, they were able to buy land from producers who were giving up coffee cultivation or to form personal ties with established producers. In fact, PACCAs Councils tended to perpetuate themselves once elected, and managers with ten or twelve years on the job became practically the norm. First vice presidents appointed by FONCAFE remained blind to the fact that, for example, the PACCA of Santa Cruz de Mora, Mérida State, held only three assemblies in 15 years (PACCA Santa Cruz de Mora, 1990) instead of the annual events mandated by its statutes.

The main consequence of this behavior was that new power groups developed within the state monopoly of coffee trade at the level of certain PACCAs, usually the ones dominated by the largest producers. Declarations made by coffee producers and personnel from FONCAFE, as well as other local observers, recorded in Mérida and Caracas during the years 1988 to 1991 suggest different ways by which the system was used for personal enrichment: some producers complained about underclassification of coffee at the local offices, where producers could be paid a lower quality price for coffee which the PACCA sold later as first class [3]. Other producers made reference to fixing of the weighing of coffee in PACCAs. The main strategy, however, was linked to the mechanism of payment by FONCAFE to PACCAs. This was made through a quota system during the harvest period (October of one year to September of the following one), and for years the state delayed payments, especially after the fall of the international price of oil. Delays were a source of friction between PACCAs and producers but also a source of enrichment for the new power groups established in the points of articulation of the system. They could use state money to repay first their friends, and even political supporters, within the organization; they could also buy more coffee at a discount price through intermediaries from discouraged small producers and resell it to the same PACCA at full price. Large producers sometimes also bought from smaller ones the sale receipts that the local office gave them when they sold their coffee. Receipts were brought at a discount and redeemed in full.

An added element of conflict was the *remanente* ("the rest"). This was established by the government in 1976, when the international price of coffee was high but the government refused to let the price rise accordingly in the internal market, in order not to hurt national consumers. This mechanism tried to prevent the prevalent practice of smuggling coffee to neighboring countries, which was especially likely because of the proximity of the Andean producing region to the national border. The *remanente* was the difference between the international price of coffee and the national price to producers, and FONCAFE paid it to the producer in accordance with the total amount of coffee he sold in the year, regardless of whether that coffee was used for export or for the national industry. This was considered a populist measure by large producers, who usually prepared the best quality coffee for export, as the difference was paid to small producers as well. It was impossible to foresee how much coffee an individual producer would market every year, so the *remanente* was paid after the coffee year ended and regularly was delayed as the state became increasingly unable to continue subsidizing the system. This delay facilitated the same corrupt practices as the regular payment of coffee did.

Bureaucrats at the technical offices followed a different route. Usually they stayed out of this process of accumulation, though some turned into coffee producers thanks to credits granted by FONCAFE to technicians willing to create coffee farms employing the latest techniques in order to demonstrate their benefits to peasants. They were expected to act as poles of development within the context of small coffee producers. In practice the number of technicians who acquired land by means of these credits in the Andean region was small; some others managed to become producers by marrying the daughters of coffee producers. But in general the impression is that their relationships were usually with the small producers, while those FONCAFE bureaucrats in PACCAs Councils interacted with medium size and large producers. Accordingly, as the strength and ability of the state to redistribute oil riches to all were considerably reduced in the 1980s, the two groups moved in increasingly divergent directions.

After the first devaluation of the Venezuelan bolivar in 1983, brought about by the fall in oil prices and the problem of the increased burden of external debt, certain agricultural products, such as coffee, became internationally competitive. In 1986, the end of the quota system of the International Coffee Organization (FONCAFE, Memoria y Cuenta, 1986) made prices jump in the international market and produced the largest volume of coffee exports from Venezuela. Coffee, subsidized for producers and consumers for years, appeared to be able to hold its ground and produce benefits without support from the state. Or at least that was what the largest organized producers thought when they began pressing the government to alter its coffee policy. The "Manifesto of Santa Cruz de Mora," signed at the Andean town where one of the strongest PACCAs had developed, stated that FONCAFE had become a retarding element for coffee producers by delaying payment of their harvests and operating with capital that truly belonged to producers, who had generated it, and not to the state. That same year the Venezuelan Association of Coffee Producers (Asociación Venezolana de Caficultores [AVC]) joined in the fight against FONCAFE by asking that it be restructured. It is interesting that in the harsh exchange of accusations and counteraccusations between high officials of FONCAFE and those of the producers' associations each group blamed the other for using coffee money to undertake business dealings aimed at their personal benefit (*El Vigilante*, May 18, 1986; *Frontera*, June 11, 1986).

The demands of medium and large producers were four: (1) to transfer technical assistance from the central office to PACCAs; (2) to grant the latter the right to act directly in marketing, both nationally and internationally; (3) to allow PACCAs to enter the field of industry by processing the product; and (4) to create a financial organism devoted exclusively to the coffee sector (*El Universal*, Oct. 9, 1989). The producers wanted to diminish the role of FONCAFE and to transfer most of its activities to the PACCAs they controlled. The advantage of marketing without the intermediation and/or interference of FONCAFE was clear to them. Let us explain, however, that not all PACCA groups were in a position to attempt to deal with market forces by themselves, but the strongest PACCAs (Santa Cruz de Mora, Rubio, Sanare, Rio Claro) thought they could. Those were the ones that in 1990 were granted by the state the right to market coffee at the national and international levels, for they were the only PACCAs which had no outstanding debts with FONCAFE. The latter retained the right to market coffee from the other PACCAs and cooperatives, but it was only a question of time before they would acquire the same right (*El Universal*, Oct. 26, 1990, Jan. 25, and April 18, 1991: *El Nacional*, April 3, 1991). In fact at the beginning of 1992 the passing of the Law to Promote and Protect Free Competition meant the abolition of all the elements that remained under the control of FONCAFE, such as the fixing of minimum prices for producers. This occurred at the same time that a glut of international and national coffee markets has weakened prices and threatens to put an end to the hopes of large and medium producers (*El Universal*, August 18, 1992).

Before concluding this section we will explore the process by which, between 1986 and 1990, the Venezuelan government accepted the most important demands of the "Manifesto of Santa Cruz de Mora." Events at the national and local levels made this possible. At the national level, the producers encountered the sympathy of entrepreneurial sectors interested in effecting a readjustment of Venezuelan economic policy in accordance with the neoliberal economic trends in the world, while facing the resistance of the central bureaucratic apparatus. The fight had not ended when the election of December 1988 brought to government the same AD president, Carlos Andrés Pérez from Táchira State, who in 1974 had established FONCAFE and supported the agricultural policy that it represented. He reappointed as Head Manager the same person who had been in charge of the initial stages of the organization and echoed the populist language of the 1970s by claiming that giving up the coffee system of FONCAFE meant delivering small producers back into the hands of large producers. But this time the pervasive philosophy of the AD administration was running against this argument and in favor of giving the private sector free hands. This could be seen with the appointment as Minister of Agriculture of a person clearly linked to the interests of large international agroindustries. Soon the unavoidable clash between the Head Manager of FONCAFE and the Minister took place [4]. For a while, the Head Manager of FONCAFE was able to resort to his party and personal relations with the president and report directly to him, over the minister's head, but this was an unsustainable position. The final showdown occurred when the minister decided to back up accusations of corruption against the PACCA Santa Cruz de Mora, which obviously involved FONCAFE bureaucrats, intervened this PACCA and sent the case to the judicial system in 1991. Proof that came during the intervention period (1991–1992) weakened the position of the central office of FONCAFE, which could not prevent a major restructuring process that reduced its personnel from 450 to 200 (*El Universal*, August 18, 1992). It is perhaps ironic that this was accompanied by the ousting from power of one of the PACCA groups most active in promoting producers' demands.

At the local level, the same accusations that had been going around for years were now used by a group of medium and large producers to take up the banner against the incumbent Council of the PACCA Santa Cruz de Mora, taking the case to the newspapers and the national Congress. They managed to force the PACCA to call an Assembly and elect a new Council in October 1990, but the control of the PACCA Council over its organization manifested itself in the reelection of the same authorities. With this option eliminated, the opposition resorted to the Ministry of Agriculture and the judicial system. This shows the importance granted to the control of the producers' association in this time of scarcity of resources, especially as this PACCA had acquired the right to freely trade coffee in the national and international market. The opposition certainly felt that now positions of control were even more important to acquire access to opportunities for enrichment.

For bureaucrats of the technical offices the new changes practically meant the end of their relative autonomy among small producers. Credits have passed to other institutions that work for the whole agricultural sector and that only act as intermediaries between agricultural producers and private banks, while high rates of the latter's credits put them beyond the reach of small producers. Technical personnel have been reduced in numbers and merged with the broader group of technicians within the Ministry of Agriculture, thus losing most of their specialization, together with the resources that they formerly administered.

IV. CLIENTELISTIC BUREAUCRACY, TECHNICAL RATIONALITY, AND TRADITIONAL POWER STRUCTURES

The coffee policy developed through a series of technical studies made since 1958 and aimed at fostering the integration of small Andean coffee producers in a rapidly modernizing Venezuela by granting them the direct benefits of production ended by creating new channels of enrichment for medium and large producers, plus representatives of the coffee bureaucracy within producers' associations. The objective of freeing small producers from the hands of intermediaries was not achieved when a new breed of intermediaries formed around the points of articulation of relationships between the state and producers. The question is, How much of this intermediation was really new in the Andean region?

Before 1974, intermediation derived from the control of money resources that allowed merchants and larger producers to buy in advance the harvests of small producers indebted to them, take coffee to the industry and the ports, and negotiate a better price. Current intermediation in PACCAs is derived from the control of the know-how that FONCAFE bureaucrats provided but was made possible by their establishing relations with large producers who still had money plus traditional power.

It is interesting to see here how the traditional power structure manifested itself in the formation of cooperatives and PACCAs in the Andes. In the case of CRAM, when it was created, five of the seven posts of the Administrative Council were filled by representatives of the four groups (Uniones El Portón, San Isidro, La Macana y Chiguará) that had made the largest money contributions. In other words, the largest producers were those that in fact controlled the administration of the cooperative (CRAM, 1979). In the case of PACCA Santa Cruz de Mora, besides the 1,000 Class A shares bought by FONCAFE and the 622 Class B shares of the AVC, 128 producers acquired 378 Class B shares at the moment of its creation. Of these producers, three of the five that bought the largest number of shares (120 shares or 32% of the total) formed the first PACCA Council (PACCA Santa Cruz de Mora, 1976).

From the very beginning then, PACCAs and cooperatives in general remained in the hands of the traditional Andean power groups. In certain cases there could have been a certain displacement of COPEI elements by others more willing to work with AD governments, but large coffee producers seemed ready to employ the points of articulation of the coffee system to their own benefit regardless of the government color. A few accounts have pointed out instances when there have been movements of one or more large producers from one organization to another because of political or personal clashes, and when this occurred they took with them their clientele of small coffee producers. Sometimes the same happened with whole family groups (brothers, sons, cousins, and "compadres"). Another demonstration of the permanence of traditional power structures could be seen in the family names of many of the accusers and defenders of the incumbent Council of the PACCA Santa Cruz de Mora in 1990, in their declarations to the local press. Many of these were the names of families associated with merchant houses that made the first exports of coffee from the Andes at the end of the nineteenth century, before becoming themselves large coffee producers (Papparoni, Burguera, etc.) (Morales, 1991).

Why small producers remain faithful to traditional local loyalties could be explained by an observer with years of residence in the Andean region, who claims that

> they [small producers] prefer to make deals with a man from the same region that advances them money at a higher rate but whom they have at hand. . . , with whom they can speak, instead of receiving word from a lawyer and this is it. . . . They understand each other . . . and pay little by little or by whatever means. But they are afraid of the other [government credits] because they know it comes from an authority and they mistrust what they do not know. (Rivas, 1988)

Judging from these words by a former priest of a coffee town in the Andes we can see that fears of the unknown, including a modernizing state acting through a number of technicians usually from outside the coffee zones, could have determined, first, a certain initial reluctance to become indebted to FONCAFE, and, second, the fact that small producers with the chance to enter producers' associations did so respecting the traditional power structures already established around coffee production and commercialization. This way they used PACCAs and cooperatives for annual lines of credit to get their harvests ready, but not as agents of change. After all, their fathers and grandfathers had been receiving yearly advances of money and food in exchange for their coffee production from the fathers and grandfathers of the persons who now were in control of producers' organizations.

What then was the role of the coffee bureaucracy in this situation? In the case of the administrative personnel of FONCAFE, there was no resistance. Those at the central level seemed to be more interested in getting coffee to the industry, the ports, and the consumers at specified prices than in modernizing the traditional environment of Andean coffee production. Those involved in day to day operations of PACCAs participated in dealings with large producers, dealings that required that traditional structures not be altered.

The only resistance came from some of the technical offices of FONCAFE at the local level. There was not, however, any organized movement or support from the central coordinating office. It all seemed to depend on the view of the agrotechnician at a given spot. Some made a real effort to get the small producers to organize and fight for their rights, but usually what they finally obtained was that some small producers were able to use the opportunities provided by the system such as credits, to introduce technical innovations (for example, new varieties of coffee); in this way they improved themselves as individual producers, but not as a group. Where technical innovations were introduced among small producers with help from the agrotechnicians, these did not, in general, alter the previous power structure, though, of course, it is hard to foresee what consequences individual improvements will have over the long term.

This brings us to the question, Did a clientelistic bureaucracy impinge on the implementation of coffee policy in the Venezuelan Andes? The answer is quite inconclusive. In the case of those bureaucrats appointed to supervise PACCAs, they seemed more prone to endorse the idea that oil money was in fact theirs by right and that the state was a mere channel of upward mobility by putting them at the right spot. They were ready to privatize state resources to their own benefit, and, if this required that they associate with traditional power structures, they appeared unconcerned. In the case of technicians, they lacked the opportunities for economic mobility opened to the others and seemed more preoccupied with the modernizing and mobilizing function of coffee policy. Of course, it should be noted here that in both groups, administrative personnel of PACCAs and agrotechnicians, there were also exceptions to the general behavior of the group.

At this stage our research does not permit us to go beyond posing some questions regarding these differences in behavior. For example, had agrotechnicians had access to a situation where they could have become rich by using the resources of their posts, would they have acted differently? Was there any qualitative difference in the previous political or social formation of administrative personnel and agrotechnicians before entering the system that can help explain their different behavior? Was there any qualitative differences in the way they were recruited into bureaucracy? Were party links to AD stronger in any of the two groups?

Coffee policy after 1974 in Venezuela was rooted in a technocratically coherent line of thought that equated development with modernization and was based on a number of independent studies from diverse offices. The latter had adequately pinpointed the need to grant the small producer the full benefit of his work, by diminishing, and even eliminating, intermediaries who profited from the work of others. Implementation was the key to the fact that this latter objective could not be achieved. In this the clientelistic structure of bureaucracy played a part, but so did the persistence of traditional power structures. However, not all parts of that bureaucracy behaved in the same way or took the same position vis-à-vis implementation of coffee policy. This may help explain why today all large producers do not belong to the same traditional coffee families of the turn of the century, though the latter remain intermingled with the new breed born with the help of the coffee system created in 1974. And, at the same time, if small producers are still dependent and usually do not receive the full benefit of their efforts, they also can be said to be more modern in the sense that they have a better knowledge of the outside and have had the opportunity of establishing links with the state, by means of technical offices and bypassing of the local power structure.

One of the first comments that comes to mind when trying to place our results within the perspective of the literature on bureaucracy, especially on clientelistic bureaucracy in Latin America, can be related to the work by Merilee S. Grindle (1977), in which she studied both policy formulation and implementation in Mexico's staple commodities marketing agency (CONASUPO), between 1970 and 1975. One of her conclusions was "That the program itself ultimately proved less effective than hoped is mute witness to the strength and durability of traditional patron-client alliances and the constraints these place on the ability of bureaucrats to act as effective change agents" (pp. 162–163). We can say that in the case of coffee policy in the Venezuelan Andes the results point in the same direction.

Regarding bureaucracy itself, Grindle considers that in order to achieve certain personal and public goals bureaucrats enter into exchange relationships with others, relationships that affect the way in which they implement a given public policy (p. 10). According to her, whenever bureaucrats are "directly dependent on central office leadership for continued career mobility opportunities," they seem to keep as a priority the implementation of the central agency's objectives (p. 12). If we apply this to the FONCAFE bureaucracy that had to implement coffee policy in the Venezuelan Andes, we observe that it seems to apply to personnel in the technical offices of the organization, while the administrative personnel associated with PACCAs felt more independent of the central organization, as the possibility of personal enrichment opened new opportunities to them.

NOTES

1. For more detail on the political system and its clientelistic components see Powell (1971), Levine (1973), Blank (1973), Giacalone and Hanes (1992).
2. There are as yet no detailed analyses of these events. For more general information about them see *Revista SIC* (Caracas) marzo 1989 and marzo 1992.
3. Data used in this chapter were gathered as part of the research project *Socio-economic change and political control in Venezuela*, funded by the Conseio de Desarrollo Científico, Humanístico y Tecnológico (CDCHT) from the University of the Andes (ULA), Mérida, Venezuela. Field interviews with coffee producers, agrotechnicians, bureaucrats in producers' associations, and local observers from different parties took place between 1988 and 1991. We also consulted data on internal documents of FONCAFE and followed the discussions of coffee policy implementation through the national and local newspapers (*El Nacional* and *El Universal* from Caracas, and *Correo de Los Andes, El Vigilante*, and *Frontera* from Mérida).
4. Though FONCAFE is autonomous, administratively it reports to the Ministry of Agriculture.

REFERENCES

Abente, Diego, Policy Formation in Democratic Regimes: The Case of Venezuela, XIII International Congress of LASA, Albuquerque, New Mexico, 1986.

Aranda, Sergio, *La economia venezolana*, Editorial Pomaire, Caracas, 1989.

Ataroff, Michelle and Giacalone, Rita, *Aplicación de prueba piloto para un estudio integrado de los agroecosistemas cafetaleros de los Pueblos del Sur de Mérida*, CONICIT, Merida, 1988.

Banco Agropecuario, *El BAP y el café*, BAP, Caracas, 1968.

Banco Central de Venezuela, *Cacao-café-cana de azúcar-tabaco. Estudio integral del sector*, BCV, Caracas, 1978.

Blank, David E., *Politics in Venezuela*, Little, Brown, Boston, 1973.

Correo de los Andes, Mérida, 1988–1991.

CRAM, *Acta Constitutiva, Reglamento y Estatutos*, FONCAFE, San Cristóbal, 1979.

Crozier, Michael, *El fenómeno burocrático*, 2 vols., Amorrortu, Buenos Aires, 1964.

Danns, George K., *Leadership, Legitimacy and the West Indian Experience*, Institute of Development Studies, University of Guyana, Georgetown, 1978.

FONCAFE, *Memoria y Cuenta*, Caracas, 1984–1990.

Frontera, Mérida, 1988–1991.

Giacalone, Rita and Hanes, Rexene, The Military in a Subsidized Democracy: The Case of Venezuela, in *From Military to Civilian Rule* (C. P. Danopoulos, ed.), Routledge, London, 1992.

Gil Yepez, José Antonio, Entrepreneurs and Regime Consolidation, in *Venezuela: The Democratic Experience* (J. D. Martz and D. Myers, ed.), Praeger, New York, 1977.

Gil Yepez, José Antonio, *El reto de las élites*, Tecnos, Madrid, 1978.

Grindle, Merilee S., *Bureaucrats, Politicians, and Peasants in Mexico*, University of California Press, Berkeley, 1977.

Kelley, Lynn, The 1966 Venezuelan Tax Reform, *Inter American Economic Affairs 21*:1 (1970).

Levine, Daniel, Venezuelan Politics: Past and Future, in *Contemporary Venezuela and Its Role in International Affairs*, (R. D. Bond, ed.), New York University Press, New York, 1977.

Lombardi, John V., *Venezuela: The Search for Order, the Dream of Progress*, Oxford University Press, New York, 1982.

Lord, Peter P., The Peasantry as an Emerging Political Factor in Mexico, Bolivia and Venezuela, The Land Tenure Center, Madison, Wisc., 1967.

MARNR, *Los procesos agroeconómicos: Café*, Caracas, 1982.

Martz, John and Myers, David, eds., *Venezuela: The Democratic Experience*, Praeger, New York, 1977.

Ministerio de Agriculture y Cría, *El café en Venezuela*, MAC, Caracas, 1967.

Ministerio de Agricultura y Cría, *Estudio integral de la caficultura en Venezuela*, MAC, Caracas, 1974.

Morales, Ada F., Origine Historique et Fonctionnement des PACCAs dans les Pueblos del Sur de l'Etat de Merida, 47th International Congress of Americanists, New Orleans, 1991.

El Nacional, Caracas, 1988–1991.

Naim, Moisés and Pinango, Ramón, eds., *El Caso Venezuela: Una ilusión de armonía*, IESA, Caracas, 1985.

PACCA Santa Cruz de Mora, *Estatutos, Documento Constitutivo*, Mérida, 1976.

PACCA Santa Cruz de Mora, *Informe de la Junta Administradora 1/04/86 a 31/03/90*, Mérida, 1990.

Powell, John D., *Political Mobilization of the Venezuelan Peasant*, Harvard University Press, Cambridge, Mass., 1971.

Rivas, Eustorgio, Interview in Mérida, May 2, 1988.

Roseberry, William, *Coffee and Capitalism in the Venezuelan Andes*, University of Texas Press, Austin, 1983.

Ryan, Selwyn, *Race and Nationalism in Trinidad and Tobago*, ISER UWI, Mona, Jamaica, 1974.

Silva Michelena, José A., El burócrata venezolano, in *Cambio político en Venezuela. Exploraciones en Análisis y síntesis* (F. Bonilla and J. A. Silva Michelena, eds.), CENDES-MIT, Caracas, 1967.

UNET-FONCAFE, *Diagnóstico integral de la caficultura tachirense*, San Cristóbal, 1987.

El Universal, Caracas, 1988–1991.

Urbaneja, Diego Bautista, Politics and Society in Venezuela, in *Society and Politics in the Caribbean* (C. Clarke, ed.), Macmillan, London, 1991.

El Vigilante, Mérida, 1988–1991.

Zambrano, César, Interview in Canaguà, Mérida, March 26, 1991.

33
Bureaucracy and Development in the Brazilian Northeast, 1880–1964

Daniel Zirker
University of Idaho, Moscow, Idaho

The development of Northeast Brazil, a huge region of 1.5 million square kilometers (about 18% of the land surface of Brazil) and more than 40 million people, was the explicit administrative goal of a number of Brazilian public agencies between 1880 and 1964. It represented in some key respects an early and unique case in Latin America of an emphasis upon the bureaucracy as a central agent of regional and national development. Hence, it has provided a revealing insight into the role, functions, significance, and nature of the bureaucracy in twentieth-century Brazilian society.

Northeast Brazil has long had the largest concentration of poverty in the Western Hemisphere and is the site of periodic catastrophes, drought, and floods. It is not an exaggeration to say, as did Albert O. Hirschman in his classic work *Journeys Toward Progress*, that

> the very depth of misery and degradation into which a large part of its people are periodically plunged, have . . . made for a nation-wide consciousness that the overcoming of backwardness and suffering in the Northeast is one of the principal tasks of Brazil as a nation. (1973, 18)

The Northeast comprises three strikingly different geographical zones, the *litoral*, or tropical coastal zone, the *zona agreste*, or forested transitional zone, and the less-population *sertão*, or savannah plateau; only the last zone is subject to regular climatic catastrophe. Hence, the history of Northeast development administration, while periodically dominated by antidrought programs, tended to reflect a broad and experimental socioeconomic and political framework before 1964, often pitting different sectors of the socioeconomic elite, as well as competing bureaucracies, against each other in peaceful development initiatives, and later initiating a broad-based mobilization of rural and urban poor, further intensifying the competition between alternative development models. By the universal nature of the key administrative problems (see, for example, Aberbach and Rockman, 1987) that it raises, it is therefore a fecund study in comparative development administration.

The basic pattern that emerged over more than eighty years of Northeast Brazilian regional development administration prior to 1964 was paradigmatically bureaucratic, with the periodic creation of competitive agencies charged with overlapping functions and associated with competing elite (and, later, mass) sectors. By 1964, this distinctive bureaucratic pattern, while precluding the kind of unified regional development efforts evident in the Tennessee Valley Authority in the United States, or the Cassa per il Mezzogiorno in Southern Italy, nevertheless elicited (at least periodically) a maximum response from elite sectors acculturated to complacency and underdevelopment. The problems of Northeast Brazil, according to one observer, were analogous to those of a colony within a system of "internal colonialism" (Chaloult, 1978), and hence, as in a colony, federal authorities were confronted with the need to outflank the inevitable co-optation of bureaucratic agencies by local elites while nevertheless guaranteeing a modicum of loyalty among these same elites. Only during the one occasion that a Northeasterner became president of Brazil was a unified bureaucracy for the administration of regional development a political possibility. With Southern elites in the presidency, the impoverished Northeast was required to underwrite its own federal development administration. The answer to this dilemma, as in colonial history, came to be a unique pattern of bureaucratization: "divide-and-rule" was manifested in overlapping agencies and programs, as the following historical sketch will seek to clarify.

I. EARLY HISTORICAL BACKGROUND OF BUREAUCRATIZATION IN THE BRAZILIAN NORTHEAST

The formal development of the Northeast, and hence the gradual emergence of inchoate bureaucratic goals, began during the Brazilian Empire, 1822–1889. Interestingly, the sugar gentry, who had been the hegemonic economic elite in the region, lost a significant degree of their political autonomy with the growth of national authority during that period (Chaloult, 1978, p. 25). Considerable technical innovation had finally been introduced in the sugar industry, including agricultural techniques (e.g., the introduction of the plow) and refining and transportation technology. Also, the introduction of a new variety of sugarcane, 'Cayenne,' greatly increased productivity (Andrade, 1980, p. 69). Moreover, competition from cotton for regional export earnings was increasingly apparent (Andrade, 1980, p. 72). By the second half of the nineteenth century, cotton culture functioned without the use of slave labor, and this was especially significant in the sense that slave and wage labor had become increasingly competitive in the region (Andrade, 1980, pp. 74, 76).

The decline and abolition of slavery, in fact, had a determinate effect upon the administrative patterns that ultimately emerged in Northeast regional development programs. Slavery in Brazil had been in decline decades before its abolition in 1888, although its impact upon the economic system remained significant well after that date. By 1800 slaves constituted half of the Brazilian population (Merrick and Graham, 1979, pp. 318–319) and represented a separate, if captive, society, maintained in a state of servitude through a system of harsh and "militarylike" discipline (Stein, 1957). Slavery's predominance as a labor form in the production of export crops derived primarily from its adaptability to changing conditions (Merrick and Graham, 1980, p. 318), although the acquisition of a royal land grant sometimes depended upon the possession of slaves as a kind of proof of the ability to work the land (Stein, 1957, p. 55), hence implying the existence of a bureaucratic, or systemic, predisposition toward slavery. At any rate, as the export market declined in the eighteenth century, slavery became more urban (Merrick and Graham, 1980, p. 319), and by the midnineteenth century it had entered into decline, with the Northeast having both a smaller total slave population and a smaller percentage of the national total. With the decline of the slave population in the Northeast, a free labor force, most of whom were squatters, developed by the 1880s (Merrick and Graham, 1980, p. 71), and growing population pressures in the Northeast prevented most of the freed slaves from leaving their plantations after abolition. A great number of them therefore remained and were compelled by circumstance to work for low wages (Furtado, 1963, pp. 151–152). The pattern of exceptionally low agricultural wages typical of the region was thus established (Merrick and Graham, 1980, p. 88).

The catastrophic drought of 1877–1879 stimulated the first direct government support of Northeast regional development programs, and hence the establishment of a regional bureaucracy, in the following years. This drought followed a prolonged period of prosperity and population expansion in the province of Ceará which was based on the cotton boom of the previous decade, itself a result of the worldwide cotton shortage following the Civil War in the United States. The staggering loss of life from the drought—estimated at over 500,000 people dead of starvation (Hirschman, 1973, p. 22)—was accompanied by the officially sponsored migration of thousands of Nordestinos to the Amazon region (Furtado, 1963, p. 146; Hirschman, 1973, p. 28), according to one observer the basis of the subsequent rubber boom in the North (Hennessy, 1978, p. 111). Furtado contends, in this regard, that the extremely concentrated profits from the rubber boom, and the economic disadvantage of the Nordestinos who contributed to it, meant that "the great population shift of Nordestinos toward the Amazon was nothing more than an enormous waste of human beings at a period when the fundamental problem of the Brazilian economy was how to increase the supply of manpower" (Furtado, 1963, p. 148).

The form in which direct imperial aid to the region was allocated during and after the drought of 1877–1879 was significant only as a striking precedent, the first major case of Brazilian federal government aid to a beleaguered region. In practice, however, it turned out to be a relatively slow and initially apathetic response from local, provincial, and federal officials (Hirschman, 1973, p. 22), followed by a national outcry as the scope of the disaster became known, and finally a belated government intervention, in the form of an investigative commission. The recommendations of this commission initiated the bureaucratization of the problem that would fully emerge in the twentieth century. It called for an extensive program of public works, the building of large dams, and improved transportation facilities, all of which required the rapid development of new government agencies and increased the likelihood of the early emergence of basic bureaucratic foibles. One large dam, for example, the Quixadá, became famous as a glaring failure in the use of bureaucracy to foment development. As Hirschman noted, by its completion in 1906, "its very name had become a byword of government inefficiency and waste" (1973, p. 23). In fact, direct public assistance to the region—improvised job creation in the building of minor dams and public works—remained woefully inadequate while raising the spectre of corruption (Hirschman, 1973, pp. 22, 24) that was thereafter identified as the "indústria da seca," or "drought industry" (Daland, 1981, p. 239). Banditry, a regional phenomenon that is thought to have reinforced the archaic land-tenure and political patterns of the region after the 1920s, also increased dramatically after the drought of 1877–1879 (Hennessey, 1978, p. 118; Chilcote, 1972, p. 300).

Moreover, as with many of the subsequent droughts, this catastrophe accompanied a regional decline in the region's competitiveness on world markets (in sugar and cotton), which intensified the drought's pernicious effects on the agricultural work force (Merrick and Graham, 1980, p. 82). The political decline of the Northeast, moreover, was hastened by the growth of European immigration to the Center-South at a time when the fortunes of most Nordestinos had fallen to a new low. Roughly 4 million European and Japanese immigrants settled in the Center-South between 1880 and 1930 (Merrick and Graham, 1980, p. 318), bringing about a "major watershed" in Brazilian demographic history (Merrick and Graham, 1980, p. 321).

Severe fluctuations in the international price of sugar between 1890 and 1905 virtually eliminated the Northeast from effective competition in the international market and transformed the region into a producer of staples for the Center-South (Chaloult, 1978, p. 28; Oliveira, 1977, p. 62). The sugar-textile economy of the region increasingly stimulated subsistence agriculture among its unemployed and underemployed work force, who gradually resettled once again in the drought-vulnerable interior (Oliveira, 1977, p. 64). Meanwhile, the regional textile industry, with roughly the same number of workers in 1910 as that of Sao Paulo (Furtado, 1963, p. 264), became increasingly dependent upon foreign capital, which had the effect of "underdeveloping" it by such policies as the production of coarse cloth from high-grade cotton (Oliveira, 1977, p. 63). The urban labor market became an even less feasible alternative for a rural work force that was as vulnerable as ever to the effects of drought.

The formal bureaucracy of Northeast regional development, which effectively dates from the turn of the century, ironically achieved its institutionalization at about the same time that the region's two primary agricultural export commodities had been eliminated from the world market. Nathaniel Leff (1973, p. 245) argues that it was this nineteenth-century decline in sugar and cotton exports, coupled with the success of coffee exports, which established the Northeast/Center-South development disparities by the beginning of the twentieth century.

After a series of unsuccessful temporary commissions to explore government inefficiency in coping with the problem of recurrent droughts, the Inspetoria Federal de Obras contra a Sêca (Federal Inspectorate of Anti-Drought Works [IFOCS]) was formed in 1909, with headquarters in the national capital and direct subordination to the Minister of Public Works (Hirschman, 1973, p. 23). The formation of the agency was based in part on the successful irrigation program in the southwestern United States of the new Bureau of Reclamation (Hirschman, 1973, p. 25), although the outright corruption that had become a primary characteristic of Brazilian federal relief expenditures by the turn of the century was probably also a major consideration in the agency's creation (Hirschman, 1973, pp. 24–25). The first director of the IFOCS, Arrojado Lisboa, an engineer, divided the agency's limited resources between the construction of several large dams and a series of comprehensive scientific studies of the region (Hirschman, 1973, pp. 28–29); the latter would play an important role in development efforts in the following decade. In fact, these studies are thought to have constituted the agency's most important work during its first decade (Hirschman, 1973, pp. 29–30).

The primary influence of the IFOCS was the stimulation of what subsequently would be referred to as the "hydraulic approach" to Northeast regional development, the damming of rivers and building of reservoirs (Hirschman, 1973, p. 27; Burns, 1970, p. 351) which, in the estimate of Celso Furtado, ultimately constituted little more than direct subsidization of the huge Northeastern cattle estates (Furtado, 1965, p. 157). The central role within the agency accorded to scientists and engineers, in part a reaction to the political corruption associated with previous efforts, did not, however, lead to any immediate improvements in the federal drought relief program, as the drought of 1915 tragically illustrated (Hirschman, 1973, p. 29). Poverty and regional economic decline continued apparently unabated, and the IFOCS was compelled, by severe budgetary constraints, to drop its scientific studies of the region; in 1916 even the collection of river-flow data was suspended (Hirschman, 1973, p. 30).

The first Nordestino to become president of Brazil, Epitácio Pessôa, assumed office in 1919 and immediately focused government attention on the development of the Northeast. Chaloult contends that Pessôa "significantly integrated the Northeast into the national community," while conceding that the regional elite already had stronger interregional than regional ties (Chaloult, 1978, p. 29). This was reinforced by the *national* political prominence of Northeastern legislators in the Federal Congress in Rio de Janeiro, particularly significant given the inordinate influence of the state of Minas Gerais during the period. President Pessôa negotiated several large foreign loans in establishing a "special Fund for Irrigation Works and Cultivable Lands of the Northeast" (Hirschman, 1973, pp. 31–32) and made ample use of the studies that had been carried out 10 years earlier by the IFOCS, bringing back Arrojado Lisboa to head IFOCS once again and contracting three foreign engineering firms to begin work on a complex hydraulic development scheme for the region. By the end of his term in 1921–1922, federal expenditures on public works in the region, at least half of which had gone for the purchase of heavy earth-moving equipment, had reached about 15% of the federal government revenues, the equivalent of U.S.$150 million in 1963 value (Hirschman, 1973, pp. 30–31).

The impact of this extraordinary federal commitment to regional development upon the bureaucratization process was initially diffused, primarily because of the alacrity with which Pessôs's successor, Artur Bernardes, cut virtually all of the programs before they reached fruition. Hirschman argues that the commitment evinced by Pessôa stemmed from his realization that only a Northeastern president would undertake such a project, and that "it would be a long time before a Northeasterner would return to Catete Palace" (Hirschman, 1973, p. 32). The federal fiscal crisis, exacerbated by a dramatic plunge in coffee prices, led to a complete suspension of all public works in Brazil in 1925 (Hirschman, 1973, p. 34). As Josué de Castro (1966, p. 161) observed, "The expensive machinery brought from the United States by the previous administration was left to rust in the fields, alongside the sun-whitened skeletons of cattle dead from thirst." Development in the region had once again slowed to a crawl by 1930, a year of critical importance for the Brazilian *sistema*.

II. THE BUREAUCRACY AND THE ADVENT OF "DEVELOPMENTALISM"

The coup which placed Getúlio Vargas in the presidency in 1930 reflected a fundamental economic transformation of the national system (Flynn, 1979, p. 3), and this deeply affected the emergence of the bureaucracy involved with Northeast regional development. Vargas moved substantially away from the ideology of economic liberalism—and the important doctrine of government restraint (Skidmore, 1967, p. 34) that was practiced by the Empire and the "Old Republic"—in expanding state control of the economy during his fifteen-year dictatorship (Hewlett, 1980, pp. 37–38), although it is generally agreed that his administration had only a vague ideological framework (Lowenstein, 1944, p. 125; Young, 1967, p. 82). The political coalition that he established with the nascent middle class, the industrial work force, the new industrialists, and the landed oligarchy embraced a more nationalistic and domestically oriented industrialization strategy (Hewlett, 1980, p. 62; Furtado, 1972, p. 22), according to Furtado the product of a depressed coffee market, which made the continued importation of manufactured goods economically unfeasible (Furtado, 1972, pp. 24–24). The dramatic increase in state participation in the economy that accompanied this process led, in turn, to the emergence of a central government directly involved in capital accumulation (Evans, 1979, p. 85), and hence to an emphasis on "planning" as the central instrument of economic policy [1].

The political prominence of Northeasterners in Vargas's *golpe*, and the simultaneous occurrence of a serious drought in the Northeast (Dulles, 1967, p. 84), contributed to a significant increase in the political influence of the region in 1930. A prominent Northeastern politician, João Pessôa, Vargas's vice-presidential running mate and a nephew of former President Pessôa, was assassinated prior to the election (and subsequent coup) of 1930. This was highly instrumental in establishing widespread support for the coup, and later influenced the appointment of José Américo de Almeida, a writer and political lieutenant of Pessôa, to the important position of minister of transport and public works (Hirschman, 1973, p. 38), a crucial concession to the Northeast during a period of prolonged economic stagnation. The relatively recent suspension of Epitácio Pessôa's Northeast development program had focused national attention on the relationship between the inconsistency of government expenditures and the continuing underdevelopment of the region, moreover (Hirschman, 1973, p. 37) [2]. Although the development expenditures of the government rose after 1930 accordingly, the politics of the *getuliato*, particularly the policy of supporting the increased autonomy of Northeast regional elites (Roett, 1972, p. 18), and the establishment of a national sugar institute led to what Chaloult calls the "preservation of the pre-capitalist components of the Northeast agrarian sector" (Chaloult, 1978, p. 32). In essence the political power of the regional elites was augmented by the establishment of an overlapping development agency while the economy of the Northeast was increasingly subordinated to that of the South-Central region, a condition which caused a further deterioration in the tenuous economic condition of the Northeast's rural poor (Chaloult, 1978, p. 30).

The creation of the Sugar and Alcohol Institute (Instituto do Açucar e do Álcool [IAA]) is an important example of this pervasive pattern. The IAA was created in 1931 in response to the national crisis in sugar production, and it immediately established a system of production quotas and guaranteed prices which nominally favored the planters of the Northeast (Chaloult, 1978, p. 31). Despite the control of the IAA by Northeastern sugar growers, the quota system appears to have stabilized existing—and archaic—production techniques in the region (Oliveira, 1977, p. 67) and might even be said to have relinquished the region's predominance in that crop by stimulating the modernization of the South-Central sugar industry, which led to its eventual superiority (Chaloult, 1978, pp. 31–32). The Center-South region would be given major production quota increases in the 1950s, and by 1970–1971, the Northeastern state of Pernambuco had been reduced in its sugar production to 18.4% of the national total, while the South-Central state of São Paulo now produced 47.5% (Chaloult, 1978, p. 32).

The IFOCS, to be renamed the National Department of Anti-Drought Works (Departamento Nacional de Obras contra as Secas, or DNOCS) in 1945, received a major increase in funding in the early 1930s despite the profound effects of economic depression on national revenues. The agency's function as a coordinator of public works projects, primarily dam and road construction, made it the logical recipient of drought relief funds in 1932, when it received about 10% of the total federal revenues in response to the severe northeastern drought of that year (Hirschman, 1973, p. 39). The agency made a modest contribution to "hydraulic" and engineering progress in the region in the 1930s, quadrupling the total reservoir capacity, improving reservoir construction techniques, sinking wells in the Drought Polygon, building over 3,000 kilometers of highways and secondary roads (about half of which were constructed in 1932), and reducing the corruption associated with drought relief (Hirschman, 1973, pp. 39–40). Nevertheless, the bulk of its public works directly benefited the largest landowners, while—except in the provision of water supplies for several smaller cities—the agency never sank a single public well (Oliveira, 1977, p. 54).

One observer has noted, interestingly, that the IFOCS/DNOCS was always a national agency, empowered to counter the effects of drought wherever they might occur in Brazil, and "the fact that it has never carried out a single work *outside* of the Northeast is a result of its control by the regional oligarchy, and not an original intention or objective" (Oliveira, 1977, p. 51). The scientific and technical personnel of the agency had a long record of opposition to its policies, including Guimarães Duque's well-known 1930s analysis of conditions on the *sertão, Solo e Agua no Polígono da Secas* (*Soil and Water in the Drought Polygon*), in which the author recognized the socioeconomic basis of poverty in that zone, despite the continuing resistance of the agency to this dimension of the "drought problem" (Oliveira, 1977, pp. 50–51).

Francisco de Oliveira contended that the location of the headquarters of the IFOCS/DNOCS in the state of Ceará, where latifundia and cotton-cattle (rather than sugar) interests predominate [3], was not accidental: the agency, as he saw it, represented these elite interests (Oliveira, 1977, pp. 55–56). This representation, in his view, was both overt, in the sense of public expenditures generally supportive of specific economic interests, and covert, in the sense of contributing directly to high-level and widespread corruption. The presence of the former category was illustrated in the defining of the Drought Polygon coterminously with cotton-cattle zone—at a time when these producers were expanding their area of production at the expense of the sugar zone (Oliveira, 1977, p. 53). Subsequent and massive road-building programs in the *sertão* directly served the marketing of cotton, the only major economic activity requiring such roads in this zone. The construction of dams on large- and medium-sized properties, most of which were not publicly accessible, likewise illustrated these tendencies (Oliveira, 1977, p. 54).

Corruption associated with the agency tended to emerge, again according to Oliveira, as a function of belated government relief efforts in drought crises. The employment of these funds was apparently carried out frequently in the name of "phantom" work fronts and public works projects (Oliveira, 1977, p. 55). Another critique of the agency, offered by Stefan Robock in his 1963 Brookings Institution report on the region, questioned the validity of the hydraulic approach in dealing with the largely socioeconomic problems of the region (Robock, 1963, pp. 79–80). Robock recognized the earlier currency of engineering approaches to the problem, particularly in the academic milieu of the 1880s, but concluded that only a frankly economic approach could hope to address the more basic problems of poverty and low economic productivity in the region (Robock, 1963, p. 80).

The year 1945, and the end of the Getuliato, brought important changes to the institutional structures associated with the bureaucratization of Northeast regional development. The presidency of General Gaspar Dutra, which replaced Vargas's regime in that year, made some efforts—despite its fiscal conservatism—to increase effective federal expenditures for the development of the Northeast, the São Francisco River Valley (which cuts through the Northeastern *sertão*), and the Amazon (Flynn, 1979, p. 141). The IFOCS was renamed (DNOCS) in 1945 in a reorganization that was geared to increase the agency's reservoir-building and well-drilling record (Interior, 1976, p. 24). Furthermore, after more than a decade of observing the progress of the Tennessee Valley Commission in the United States, two agencies, the São Francisco Valley Commission (CVSF) and the São Francisco Hydroelectric Company (CHESF), were formed in 1948 to stimulate development along that largely Northeastern river, and this despite the absence of any serious droughts during this period (Robock, 1963, pp. 80–91) [4].

In what amounted to a classic bureaucratic pattern, according to Robock, the CVSF followed a "great policy of small services," including the provision of roads, infirmaries, small hospitals, and water and power facilities for small towns, but it was soon "captured" by elite political groups and subsequently lost much of its momentum (Robock, 1963, p. 83). The contrasting success of the CHESF, moreover, probably owes more to the practical limitations associated with the task of constructing and operating the huge Paulo Afonso hydroelectric dam—its principal mandate—than to an innate superiority in bureaucratic tactics, although the CHESF did evince a much higher degree of technical expertise among its personnel (Hirschman, 1973, pp. 56–57).

The drought of 1951 triggered a major shift in the pattern of federal expenditures for Northeast regional development, with the creation of the Northeast Development Bank (Banco de Nordeste do Brasil [BNB]), a new tactic designed to provide long-term credit for the development of agriculture, industry, and commerce in the region (Robock, 1963, p. 92; Chaloult, 1978, p. 33). Arguing that the federal antidrought policy in the Northeast required substantial revision, President Vargas expressed support for a broad-based socioeconomic development program for the region (Robock, 1963, pp. 92–93), a reflection of the advent of "developmentalism" (the strategic and ideological use of national development as a vehicle of political strategy) to Brazilian politics. The bank began functioning in 1954 with Fortaliza, the capital of Ceará, as its headquarters. Oliveira pointed to the significance of this siting as confirmation of the control already exercised over the new bank by the region's cotton-cattle oligarchy. It was one of the least industrialized Northeastern capitals at the time, and one of only two to be located within the Drought Polygon. Hence, he suggested that this was a sign that the BNB would soon be "captured" by this oligarchy, as he argues did, in fact, happen after the brief BNB presidency of Vargas adviser Rômulo de Almeida (Oliveira, 1977, p. 95).

The bank's original goals of long-term credit provision and collection of regional economic data, pursued during its first "stable" direction between 1956 and 1960, tended to exclude sugar production, apparently the product of its function as an overlapping agency with a competing clientele. This omission was rectified only after the creation of the Northeast Development Superintendency (SUDENE) in 1959 (Oliveira, 1977, p. 95) [5].

The 1950s heralded major changes in the national economic system, conditioning the process of development in the Brazilian Northeast. A major increase in the pattern of import-substitution industrialization in the Center-South, generally thought to have increased Brazil's economic and technological dependence upon industrialized countries (Ribeiro, 1967, p. 347), is often blamed for the growth of regional development disparities at that time, if only because of its contribution to the concentration of industry in the São Paulo area (Baer, 1979, pp. 195–196). The rapid spread of "developmentalism" as a guiding national outlook during the 1950s ironically tended to favor fast industrial growth in preference to long-term and nationalist development objectives (Hewlett, 1980, p. 65) and thus ultimately contributed to the growth of regional development disparities in Brazil. Finally, the major political pattern to emerge from this period, Brazilian *populism*, tended to reinforce archaic class and production relations while—apparently somewhat ambivalently—identifying the welfare of the peasantry as a major concern, demanding for it fair wages and other rights (Camargo, 1979, p. 120). Oliveira contends that the Northeastern sugar-textile political system rejected populism, except in a brief period during the 1950s, largely because of this apparent (though, again, not necessarily real) predisposition toward the peasantry, tending, rather, to elect antipopulist coalitions (Oliveira, 1977, p. 91).

III. POPULISM AND BUREAUCRACY: THE ORIGINS OF SUDENE

Developmentalism, recast in a less political and hence more acceptable vein, became the hallmark of the presidency of Juscelino Kubitschek, 1956–1960, and a "development euphoria," accompanied by the massive growth of bureaucratic entities, rapidly conditioned the national outlook (Robock, 1975, p. 28). The construction of Brasília epitomized a new national dedication to develop all of Brazil's potential (Flynn, 1979, p. 191), although this one project became Kubitschek's primary concern during the last two years of his presidency (Hirschman, 1973, p. 86), apparently limiting the administration's efficacy in other national development programs.

Furthermore, the nationalism implicit to Kubitschek's development scheme is thought to have facilitated the popular acceptance of a model that was not in the interests of the working classes (Flynn, 1979, p. 199). Kubitschek's careful alignment with the industrialists and the military, moreover, could not conceal his base as "essentially a politician of and for the middle class" (Flynn, 1979, p. 196). A crucial aspect of his restraint of elite and military reaction to his development program, according to Peter Flynn, was the absence in Brazil of a hegemonic fraction of the economic elite (Flynn, 1979, pp. 205–206), as well as the general and growing prosperity of the middle and elite sectors during this period. Meanwhile, the populist tendency of the regime appeared to move toward the incorporation of two groups that were not beneficiaries of the new progress, the peasantry and the urban poor (Camargo, 1979, p. 119).

The limited and elite-directed character of peasant participation in the new Brazilian populism was perhaps most evident in the Northeast, where relatively moderate *ligas camponesas*, or "pleasant leagues"—rural syndicates—achieved widespread notoriety in the late 1950s and early 1960s (Leeds, 1964, p. 191). The rapid rise to national political prominence of one moderately influential league organizer, Francisco Julião, who had declared himself to be a Catroite and a radical, was widely perceived in the press as an ominous political sign. Shepard Foreman contends that peasant political participation during this period was at best partial and fleeting, with the "extent of their participation far outweigh[ing] its significance (Foreman, 1975, p. 245). This could be attributed to the fact that the organization of the leagues was frequently controlled by regional political elites, particularly from the urban centers of the sugar zone (Flynn, 1979, p. 260; Leeds, 194, p. 194), and the league leaders, according to Leeds, "have almost exclusively been representatives of urban-centered interests and politics, even when agricultural products and landholding have been involved" (1964, p. 194). Thus it is thought by some observers that the growth of the leagues indicated in part the increasing pressure exerted by segments of the political elite for a larger regional share of national economic resources, particularly in view of the region's economic potential, largely based on its abundant and inexpensive labor supply (Oliveira, 1977, p. 114). Direct federal expenditures in the region had been steadily increasing since 1952.

The Northeast Development Superintendency (Superintendêcia do Desenvolvimento do Nordeste [SUDENE]) was created on December 15, 1959, through the promulgation of Law 3692, which empowered the new agency to study and propose plans for socioeconomic development in the region, supervise all programs of federal agencies in this enterprise, carry out projects assigned to it in the area of Northeast regional development, and coordinate technical assistance programs, both foreign and Brazilian, in the region (Interior, 1979a, p. 4). It could therefore be regarded as an extension of a pattern of federal commitment that was already extant, despite the break with bureaucratic and political precedent that the new agency represented.

IV. BUREAUCRATIC INNOVATION: THE EMERGENCE OF THE SUDENE

The establishment of the SUDENE conformed in its basic aspects with the creation of previous federal development efforts in the region: a serious drought in 1958 prompted another federal review of conditions in the region and ultimately led to the creation of yet another bureaucratic entity charged with ambiguous and (vis-à-vis other existing agencies) overlapping jurisdiction. This time, however, the team that was appointed to the task, the Working Group for the Development of the Northeast (Grupo de Trabalho para o Desenvolvimento do Nordeste [GTDN]), was largely composed of economists and was led by the young Northeastern economist Celso Furtado. Thus it produced two *socioeconomic* reports, the second of which remains the most influential and circumspect official analysis of the regional problems yet to emerge.

The second (revised) report of the GTDN opens with an expression of concern regarding the growing average income disparities between the Northeast and Center-South, already pronounced by 1956, and the inferior rate of economic growth in the Northeast (GTDN, 1967, p. 9), relegating the impact of periodic drought to a clearly subordinate status within the constellation of regional problems (GTDN, 1967, p. 67). It recommended the adoption of four basic policies as a way of beginning to address these problems directly: the stimulation of industrial investment in the region; the expansion and modernization of agriculture in the "humid zone," with a view to improving the urban food supply; the transformation of agriculture practices in the "semiarid" zones to initiate the use of more productive and drought-resistant techniques and crops; and the expansion of the agricultural frontier of the region to include the drought-free part of the state of Maranhão, with the long-term plan of relocating a significant part of the regional population to that area (GTDN, 1967, p. 14).

President Kubitschek was persuaded reluctantly to support the creation of the new bureaucratic agency after favorable public response to the report was noted, and after a three-hour meeting with Furtado. Prominent accounts of the agency's creation (e.g., Hirschman, 1973; Robock, 1963) disregard Kubitschek's initial resistance to its formation. An account in *Interior*, on the other hand, stresses the important of this encounter, citing Kubitschek's reluctant agreement, "I agree. It's difficult, but I agree" (1979a, p. 4). David E. Goodman (1972, p. 231) contended, however, "It is more appropriate to regard the creation of SUDENE as a direct response to the crisis engendered by the 1958 drought rather than as the logical outcome of intellectual argument and debate." Be that as it may, the passage of the directing legislation required 18 months of detailed and often acrimonious debate in the Brazilian Congress.

The commissioning of the SUDENE in late 1961, as an "autonomous" agency immediately subordinate to the Brazilian president, specified its largely technical and supportive role. The encouragement of administrative reform was one of its specified functions (Ministério Extraordinário, 1966, p. 14), as was the initiation of technical and "apolitical" planning, focusing upon the establishment of a Northeastern industrial infrastructure, originally a concession designed to reduce the resistance to the program of the regional political elite (Roett, 1972, p. 40; Oliveira, 1977, p. 116). Another important function of the new agency, one which tends to be disregarded in many interpretations (e.g., Hirschman, Robock, Roett) of this period, was its capacity to create mixed (governmental and private) corporations, which, according to Oliveira, represented one of the first major examples in the region of the state as producer (1977, p. 116). This was dependent upon a crucial section of the enacting legislation, Article 34/18, which was inserted only after lengthy debate and provided for a comprehensive program of tax incentives for industries willing to invest in Northeastern industrial development (Hirschman, 1971, p. 124).

Article 34/18, known after 1974 as the Northeast Investment Fund, or FINOR, became the SUDENE's central function after the military coup of 1964. Article 34 of the SUDENE legislation of 1961 originally allowed *Brazilian-owned* corporations to contribute up to 50% of their tax liability to an investment pool, administered by the SUDENE, to be used for approved industrial projects in which matching funds were already provided by direct investors. Amendment 18, passed in 1963, allowed foreign corporations operating in brazil to make use of this tax credit scheme (Goodman, 1972, pp. 235–236). Article 34 was authored by federal deputy Gileno Dé Carli, a representative of the Northeastern state of Pernambuco, after a fact-finding mission to

Italy, where he explored the tax-incentive program of the Southern Italian regional development agency, the Cassa per il Mezzogiorno (Interior, 1979a, p. 5; Almeida, 1979, p. 17).

In view of Brazil's highly concentrated and capital-intensive industrial structure, it has been argued that the value of 34/18 as a crucial stimulus to Brazilian industrial expansion into the Northeast (Goodman, 1972, p. 261) is seriously qualified by the character of the industries that resulted. They often had few direct economic ties with the Northeastern ambient (Goodman, 1972, p. 249) and tended to import technically trained labor, semiprocessed resources, and technology from the Center-South, while exporting their finished products to the more sophisticated markets of the Center-South. Furthermore, the geographically and economically concentrated industrial growth pattern in the Center-South was reflected in the pattern of industrialization that emerged in the Northeast, in which two states, Bahia and Pernambuco, received nearly 75% of the 34/18 investment funds before 1968 (while providing just 60% of the new industrial employment).

The cost of tax incentives for the stimulation of Brazilian regional industrialization increased significantly after 1968. The idea has been extended to other regions and economic sectors, often—in the view of one Brazilian analyst—at the expense of institutionalizing conflicting and even mutually neutralizing effects (Varsano, 1979, p. 30). Moreover, the cost of the program for the Northeast may have been prohibitively high. Oliveira argued that the Northeast Development Fund (Fundo de Desenvolvimento do Nordeste [FIDENE]) that was created by Article 34/18 became "the most powerful mechanism for the transference of bourgeois hegemony of the Center-South to the Northeast" (Oliveira, 1977, pp. 119–120) and was also an important step in "capturing" the political apparatus of the region (Oliveira, 1977, p. 119). He pointed to the origins of the primary political support for the SUDENE, mostly from Center-South politicians, and the manifest opposition to the agency from Northeastern congressmen (Oliveira, 1977, p. 116; Robock, 1963, p. 105), concluding that the SUDENE also represented a "flank attack" on the growing political consciousness of the popular classes of the Northeast (Oliveira, 1977, p. 113). Miguel Arraes, a governor of the Northeastern state of Pernambuco prior to his ouster in 1964, and then again after the restoration of democracy in 1985, noted that job creation, ostensibly one of the primary goals of Article 34/18, was ironically one of its weakest aspects (Arraes, 1969, p. 203).

Another range of basic objections to the SUDENE program related directly to wider concerns involving the growth of bureaucracies and was summarized by observers such as Stefan Robock, who noted the early expenditure of much-needed technical personnel in what was essentially a political struggle (Robock, 1963, p. 106), a problem that is endemic to bureaucratic agencies in general. The character of that particular struggle, moreover, created numerous subsidiary difficulties for a coordinating agency such as the SUDENE, and by 1964 virtually all of the agency's resources were being expended to prevent its political demise. A significant political opposition resisted the SUDENE's efforts to coordinate all formal development efforts in the Northeast, a key constituent of which was the major foreign assistance agency in the region, the United States Agency for International Development (USAID).

The interference of the USAID in the Northeast development process in the early 1960s, while extensively documented elsewhere (e.g., Roett, 1972; Levinson, and Onís, 1970; Parker, 1979; Oliveira, 1977), is important to recall at this juncture in at least two respects. First, it mirrored in its modus operandi the traditional Brazilian method of "containing" regional discontent through the bureaucracy and division and cooptation of regional political elites. In the early 1960s the Kennedy administration became worried by the image of widespread political unrest in Northeast Brazil [6], and chose shortly thereafter to use its foreign aid program to counter the efforts of the SUDENE. According to Roett, the USAID mission to the Northeast thereafter functioned as a drag on the efforts of the SUDENE, in the interests of relatively narrow political goals (Roett, 1972, pp. 173–174; Levinson and Onís, 1970, p. 291), thus conforming with what Roett characterizes as the general tendency of United States foreign aid at the time: the bureaucratic reinforcement of "stable" elites, often at the expense of national development objectives.

Second, the United States agency's interference in the SUDENE program stressed its government's distrust of *both* the SUDENE and the Brazilian federal government itself (Oliveira, 1977, p. 122). An Alliance for Progress mission to the region in late 1961, headed by former United States ambassador to Brazil Merwin Bohan, issued a set of recommendations for the "containment" of the peasant leagues in the region. These were only withdrawn at the insistence of the Brazilian federal authorities (Oliveira, 1977, p. 121). By 1962, the political section of the United States Embassy in Rio de Janeiro was insisting upon the implementation of a school-building program in the Northeast despite the active objections of the embassy's educational division, which argued—as did the SUDENE—that the region's critical teacher shortage made such construction actually counterproductive. The political section was thought to have won out by arguing that its purpose was to counter Communist subversion in the region, and that such a program would nevertheless provide a valuable presence in the area, and might even influence the outcome of the important 1962 elections in a critical state such as Pernambuco (Roett, 1972, pp. 74–75).

The resistance of the USAID to the SUDENE's development efforts apparently remained in effect until 1964, when the military intervention "stabilized" political change in the region, resulting in the removal of Northeast politicians such as Governor Miguel Arraes, and even the SUDENE's superintendent, Celso Furtado, a prominent economist who subsequently accepted a series of prestigious teaching positions in European and American universities. Broad-based and innovative experimentation in Northeast Brazilian development administration had essentially come to an end.

V. CONCLUSION

Giovanni Sartori has argued that "ideologies are the crucial lever at the disposal of elites for obtaining political mobilization and for maximizing the possibilities of mass manipulation" (Sartori, 1969, p. 411). The military coup that ended the postwar populist democratic period in Brazil introduced a new and malleable ideological focus, the Doctrine of National Security, which ultimately stressed a central concern with *demobilization* of peasants and urban poor, and hence undercut the cross-cutting and socially competitive administrative policies that had fueled change in the region. In the end, the ornate complex of regional development programs slipped into chronic dysfunction, SUDENE was crippled by military intervention, and the history of a unique 80-year period of overlapping development agencies was quietly revised [7]. It should be noted, however, that the process and politics of bureaucratization contributed directly to this outcome.

The eighty-five-year experiment in the bureaucratization of Northeast Brazilian regional development administration suggests a range of observations typical of bureaucracy in a variety of cultural and political settings. The following were especially underscored in this case: the tendency of successive regional development agencies to become closely identified with distinct elite groupings, and therefore to become tools—at least in the short term—for their preservation and enhancement; the critical development vacuum filled by bureaucracy in Northeast Brazil, and thus the exaggerated degree to which it came to affect society over time, suggesting the utility of this case in generalizing about the wider role of bureaucracy in society, or the bureaucratization of society; the critical effect of specific (often competing) policies, such as the hydraulic approach, in molding particular agencies, suggesting insights into the complex relationship between policy and administration; and, finally, the critical role that agencies can play in transforming policy and society, in other words, the politics of bureaucratization. Each of these deserves some elaboration by way of conclusion.

The association of successive development agencies in the Brazilian Northeast with distinct elite groupings, the defensive "nesting" process so often criticized in comparative development administration, tends to be typical precisely because the commitment to development is most likely to be found among elite sectors in a developing society; moreover, it is especially in this kind of setting where "there is a high reliance on the public sector for leadership" (Sharkansky, 1978, p. 38). In the case of Northeast Brazil, bureaucratization of the development process appears to have intensified the interelite competition that accompanied modernization, resulting in further stimulation of the process while effecting a condition that has been called, in a general sense, "depoliticizing politics" (Hummel, 1982, p. 205). Because the federal government emphasized varying agencies (and hence elite sectors) over time, an interelite competition, or "pluralism," ultimately developed, the object of which was—at least officially—regional development. Finally, it was in this protracted period of government-sponsored, interelite competition that a specific developmental elite emerged and was reinforced.

Key features of the complex role of bureaucracy in developing societies are also illustrated by the case of Northeast Brazil. The planning process increasingly came to represent one of the accepted venues for interagency competition, and although it seldom emanated from the best of intentions, the general rational for bureaucratic planning, the encouragement of "constructive change" (Berkley, 1984, p. 322), seems ultimately to have benefited the development process during certain junctures. Competition for federal revenues likewise became ingrained as a central feature of interelite competition, replacing overt violence to some extent. Bureaucracy thus increasingly filled a tutelary role, not only assuming political leadership, but serving as a teacher, for better or worse, of the most effective means of competition.

The central problem of Northeast Brazil, regional underdevelopment, was so intense and so obvious that policy tended to mold and shape agencies, rather than the more common reverse situation. Hence this case has offered interesting insights into the complex relationship between policy and administration. In such situations of extreme privation, policies come to be associated with groups (in this case, *elite* groups), and the agencies that are developed to implement them thus have limited options from the start. The implications of this for policy and administration are clear: such regional development plans (the TVA is one of the more familiar North American examples) can be expected to "lock" subsequent agencies into relatively narrow administrative options.

Despite this dynamic, however, a subtle and more pervasive effect that originates within bureaucracy itself can be said to affect society and appears to have been the most striking legacy of Northeast Brazilian development agencies. The depersonalization of politics within bureaucracy, in which "the public [is] replaced by the system and the citizenry by the corps of functionaries" (Hummel, 1982, p. 187), meant in the context of Northeast Brazil that all elite groups in the region would lose power, and that the centralized politics of bureaucratization would prevail. The Northeast regional development agencies represented an institutionalization of power, and as Hummel has noted in a general context, "Institutionalized power is simply not perceived by human beings as a power relationship. It is perceived as the background against which we act" (1982, p. 192). The most creative aspects of the interelite competition for development resources were eventually attenuated as this power struggle came increasingly to be masked by a technocratic bureaucracy. When the military government stepped into the Brazilian Northeast and formally ended federalism in 1964, the move was presented in the context of the Northeast regional development programs: this was "merely" a further rationalization of the system, it was argued. From a bureaucratic standpoint, the new military administrators were right.

The bureaucratization of development administration offers a unique opportunity to examine some of the most interesting parameters and sociopolitical effects of bureaucracy. The role of the bureaucracy in the Northeast became closely identified with particular, though not always crucial, projects, such as drought relief. In fact, the function of most agencies remained directly tied to reinforcing particular sectors of the elite, both with economic resources and with provision of ideological justifications, as Sartori might put it, for their respective survival. The politics of bureaucratization, moreover, in gradually masking and centralizing the power relations, eventually created a leviathan capable of swallowing elites. In this sense, examination of the bureaucracy over time in the Brazilian Northeast also represents an effective history of power relations in that region. This is the ultimate value of the study of bureaucracy.

NOTES

1. Ianni writes, "It was in this period that planning came to be a part of the thinking and practice of those governing, as the 'most rational' technique of organizing information, analyzing problems, making decisions and controlling the execution of economic-financial policies" (Ianni, 1979, p. 43).
2. Hirschman noted that in his 1930 campaign platform, "Vargas advocated specifically a return to the ideas of Epitácio Pessôa and pledged renewal of large-scale public works in the Northeast which had been victimized by the 'Dantesque combination of adverse climate and our disgraceful improvidence.' " According to Hirschman, this concern with the Northeast reflected a new national "mood" (1973, pp. 38–39).
3. The sertão runs to the coast in Ceará, and except for a humid sugar zone well in the interior, the state is largely (92%) in the Drought Polygon.
4. Hirschman noted "The originators of the São Francisco project were, if anything, more multi-purposeful than [those of] the TVA; since large stretches of the São Francisco Valley lacked roads, schools, health facilities, agricultural credit, industry and even people, they felt that their project should cover all of these facets" (1973, p. 53).
5. During the course of research in the BNB library in Fortaleza in 1981, I noted that a substantial collection of information relating to the production of sugar continued to be maintained.
6. Journalist Tad Szulc published several inflammatory articles in *The New York Times*, implying the imminent likelihood of the "Cubanization" of the region. Oliveira recalls the numerous American "observers," including Dr. Henry Kissinger, who made their appearance in Recife shortly thereafter (1977, pp. 120–121).
7. In 1981, when the author was engaged in research at the SUDENE library in Recife, the SUDENE Annual Reports for 1963 and 1964 had been "lost" from the library.

ACKNOWLEDGMENTS

The author would like to thank Prof. Ali Farazmand for his helpful comments and suggestions. The author would also like to thank the University of Idaho Research Council and the Martin

Institute for travel grants that facilitated this research. I would also like to thank the Killam Foundation at the University of Alberta.

REFERENCES

Aberbach, Joel D., and Rockman, Bert A., Comparative Administration; Methods, Muddles, and Models, *Administration and Society 18*:473–506 (1987).

Almeida, Rômulo de, Apresentação, in *Desenvolvimento Regional*, Editora Campus, Rio de Janeiro, 1979.

Andrade, Manuel Correia de, *The Land and the People of Northeast Brazil* (trans. Dennis V. Johnson), University of New Mexico Press, Albuquerque, 1980.

Arraes, Miguel, *Brazil: The Power and the People*, Penguin Books, Middlesex, England, 1969.

Baer, Werner, *The Brazilian Economy: Its Growth and Development*, Grid, Columbus, Ohio, 1979.

Berkley, George E., *The Craft of Public Administration*, 4th ed., Allym and Bacon, Boston, 1984.

Burns, E. Bradford, *A History of Brazil*, Columbia University Press, New York, 1970.

Camargo, Aspásia Alcântara de, Authoritarianism and Populism: Bipolarity in the Brazilian Political System, in *The Structure of Brazilian Development* (Neuma Aguiar, ed.), Transaction Books, New Brunswick, N.J., 1979.

Carvalho, Otamar de, *Desenvolvimento Regional: Um Problema Político*, Editora Campus, Rio de Janeiro, 1979.

Castro, Josue de, *Death in the Northeast*, Random House, New York, 1966.

Chaloult, Yves, *Estado, Acumulação e Colonialismo Interno*, Vozes, Petrópolis, Brazil, 1978.

Chilcote, Ronald, Protest and Resistance in Brazil and Africa: A Synthesis and a Classification, in *Protest and Resistance in Angola and Brazil: Comparative Studies* (Chilcote, ed.), University of California Press, Berkeley, 1972.

Daland, Robert, *Exploring Brazilian Bureaucracy: Performance and Pathology*, University Press of America, Washington, D.C., 1981.

Dulles, John W. F., *Vargas of Brazil: A Political Biography*, University of Texas Press, Austin, 1967.

Evans, Peter, *Dependent Development: The Alliance of Multinational, State, and Local Capital in Brazil*, Princeton University Press, Princeton, N.J., 1979.

Fishlow, Albert, Some Reflections on Post-1964 Brazilian Economic Policy, in *Authoritarian Brazil* (Alfred Stepan, ed.), Yale University Press, New Haven, Conn., 1973.

Flynn, Peter, *Brazil: A Political Analysis*, Westview Press, Boulder, Colo., 1979.

Foreman, Shepard, *The Brazilian Peasantry*, Columbia University Press, New York, 1975.

Furtado, Celso, *The Economic Growth of Brazil* (trans. Ricardo W. de Aguiar and Eric C. Drysdale), University of California Press, Berkeley, 1963.

Furtado, Celso, *Diagnosis of the Brazilian Crisis*, University of California Press, Berkeley, 1965.

Furtado, Celso, *Análise do Modelo Brasileiro*, Civilização Brasileiro, Rio de Janeiro, 1972.

Goodman, David E., Industrial Development in the Brazilian Northeast: An Interim Assessment of the Tax Credit Scheme of Article 34/18, in *Brazil in the Sixties* (Riordan Roett, ed.), Vanderbilt University Press, Nashville, 1972.

GTDN, *Uma Política de Desenvolvimento Econômico para o Nordeste*, 2nd ed., Ministério do Interior, SUDENE, Recife, Brazil, 1967, 1959.

Hennessy, Alistair, *The Frontier in Latin American History*, Edward Arnold, London, 1978.

Hewlett, Sylvia Anne, *The Cruel Dilemmas of Development: Twentieth-Century Brazil*, Basic Books, New York, 1980.

Hirschman, Albert O., Industrial Development in the Brazilian Northeast and the Tax Credit Scheme of Article 34/18, in *A Bias for Hope; Essays on Development and Latin America*, Yale University Press, New Haven, Conn., 1971.

Hirschman, Albert O., *Journeys Toward Progress: Studies of Economic Policy-Making in Latin America*, W. W. Norton, New York, 1973.

Holanda, Nilson, BNB . . . Um Banco Pioneiro (e Fiel à Missão qual Foi Destinado), *Interior 3*(21):15 (1977).

Hummel, Ralph P., *The Bureaucratic Experience*, 2nd ed., St. Martin's Press, New York, 1982.
Ianni, Octavio, *Estado e Planejamento do Brasil (1930–1970)*, 3rd ed., Editoria Civilização Brasileira, Rio de Janeiro, 1979.
Interior, Seca. Luta Contra um Problema Secular, *Interior 2*(9):24 (1976).
Interior, 5(29): (1979a).
Interior, Exportar. Uma Vocação Nordestina Prevista por Caminha, *Interior 5*(2):23 (1979b).
Leeds, Anthony, Brazil and the Myth of Francisco Julião, in *Politics of Change in Latin America* (Joseph Maier and Richard W. Weatherhead, eds.), Praeger, New York, 1964.
Leff, Nathaniel, Economic Development and Regional Inequality: Origins of the Brazilian Case, *Quarterly Journal of Economics, 86*:245 (1973).
Levinson, Jerome, and Onís, Juan de, *The Alliance That Lost Its Way: A Critical Report on the Alliance for Progress*, Quandrangle Books, Chicago, 1970.
Loewenstein, Karl, *Brazil Under Vargas*, Macmillan, New York, 1944.
Merrick, Thomas W., and Graham, Douglas H., *Population and Economic Development in Brazil: 1800 to the Present*, Johns Hopkins University Press, Baltimore, 1979.
Ministério Extraordinário para a Coordenação dos Organismos Regionais, *I Plano Diretor de Desenvolvimento Econômico e Social do Nordeste*, Divisão Documentação, SUDENE, Brazil, Recife, 1966.
Oliveira, Francisco de, *Elegia para uma Re(li)gião; Sudene, Nordeste. Planejamento e Conflitos de Classes*, Pas e Terra, Rio de Janeiro, 1977.
Parker, Phyllis R., *Brazil and the Quiet Intervention, 1964*, University of Texas Press, Austin, 1979.
Ribeiro, Darcy, Universities and Social Development, in *Elites in Latin America* (Seymour Martin Lipset and Aldo Solari, eds.), Oxford University Press, New York, 1967.
Robock, Stefan, *Brazil's Developing Northeast: A Study of Regional Planning and Foreign Aid*, The Brookings Institution, Washington, D.C., 1963.
Robock, Stefan, *Brazil: A Study in Development Progress*, Lexington Books, Lexington, Mass., 1975.
Roett, Riordan, *The Politics of Foreign Aid in the Brazilian Northeast*, Vanderbilt University Press, Nashville, 1972.
Sartori, Giovanni, Politics, Ideology, and Belief Systems, *American Political Science Review 63*:398–411 (1969).
Sharkansky, Ira, *Public Administration: Policy-Making in Government Agencies*, 4th ed., Rand McNally, Chicago, 1978.
Skidmore, Thomas, *Politics in Brazil, 1930–1964: An Experiment in Democracy*, Oxford University Press, London, 1967.
Stein, Stanley, *Vassouras: A Brazilian Coffee County, 1850–1900*, Harvard University Press, Cambridge, Mass., 1957.
Varsano, Ricardo, Incentivos Fiscais: Supressão ou Reformulação? *Rumos do Desenvolvimento 3*(16):30–33 (1979).
Young, Jordan M., *The Brazilian Revolution of 1930 and the Aftermath*, Rutgers University Press, New Brunswick, New Jersey, 1967.

34
Peruvian Population Policy Under Garcia

Lon S. Felker
East Tennessee State University, Johnson City, Tennessee

I. INTRODUCTION

Population policy in Peru has long been neglected. In the mid- to late 1980s, however, the Garcia Perez government initiated a number of policies in the area of family planning. Most of the programs embodying these policies took the form of public education, while others were related to health care. Regional seminars and meetings were organized in most of the provinces. Still, resources were scarce, and problems of security for government personnel became serious as the Shining Path guerilla movement spread. Even so, the Garcia Perez government's efforts could serve as a model for Latin American nation-states experiencing the severe problems of unbalanced urban growth and population development generated by the highest birth rates in the Andean region.

II. PERUVIAN POPULATION POLICY UNDER GARCIA

The government of President Alan Garcia Perez gave increasing attention to the problem of population growth in the course of the 1980s. Under previous governments, most notably those of the military juntas in power from 1968 to 1980, the high fertility rate in Peru was viewed variously as a sign of national strength, as a serious but not necessarily grave concern, or as a topic worthy of study, but not of immediate action. The Garcia government, largely working through preexisting organizations, began efforts to educate the public and extend family planning and health services to Peru's growing and increasingly impoverished population. The urgent need for planned growth was stressed by President Garcia in a number of public statements.

A. The Year 2000

Garcia linked the population issue to his oft-proclaimed concern for the Peru of the year 2000. In his end of the year address to the nation of December 20, 1986, the president of the Republic stated:

> The first point on which we must reflect refers to how many we wish to be, and this has called for a policy. I have already mentioned that to continue things as they are today, we will be about 30 million in the year 2000, more than 11 million living in Lima, and only 20 out of every 100 Peruvians will have work. [1]

The year 2000 has been used as a benchmark in various Peruvian projections of population growth since at least 1976. In that year a document was released by the government entitled "Lineamientos de Politica de Poblacion en El Perú." Prepared by the National Institute of Planning, the study presented three projections of the future population growth of the nation based on estimates taking into account (a) the situation without a population policy and without a structural change in the population, (b) the situation with a policy of structural change but without any explicit population policy, and (c) the situation with both structural change and an explicit population policy [2].

The projections resulting from these assumptions were of a year 2000 population of 32 million without a population policy (the estimated population for 1979 being 16 million) and, assuming said policy, a projected growth to 27.7 million [3].

> Following the census of July 12, 1981, the projections made in 1978 were revised, not only in the light of the new census data but also in conjunction with the results of the National Inquiry on the Prevalence of Contraception (1981), the National Inquiry of Fertility (1977–1978), and the National Demographic Inquiry (1974–1976). Three hypotheses were generated which reflected the median (or recommended) rate of growth, the "high" hypothesis and the "low" hypothesis. The median hypothesis was based on the assumed reduction in Peruvian fertility rates over the next forty-five years (58 percent, 1.3 percent a year). According to this hypothesis, the overall fertility rate would diminish to 5.38 in the period 1975–1980, and to 3.50 in the five-year period from 1995 to 2000, which was at that time the fertility rate of women in the Lima-Callao area. By the first quarter of the twenty-first century, this hypothesis projected an estimated fertility rate of 2.26. [4]

The "high" hypothesis assumed a lower rate of fertility decline over the same period: 50%, or 1.1% per year between 1980–2025. This would lead to a rate of fertility of 4 children per woman at the end of the century, and 2.4 in the period 2020–2025. The "low" hypothesis projected a much higher decline in fertility (64.3% or 1.4% per year), with a projected 3 offspring per woman in the period 1995–2000, and by 2020–2025 2.08 children, which would be the estimated rate of replacement—1 child per female [5].

Of course, mortality rates are an equally important factor in the calculation of the growth rate. The mortality rates for five-year periods beginning with 1980–1985 were calculated by means of a logistical curve. These took the form of calculations of the expected lifespan at birth. Table 1 shows the results of these calculations.

Life expectancy in Peru in 1983 was estimated at 58.6 years, which is higher than that of Bolivia (50.7) and Haiti (52.7), but lower than that of most of the more developed states of Latin America, such as Argentina and Uruguay (70 years). The anticipated higher life expectancy of

Table 1 Peru: Evolution of Mortality Based on Projections of Life Expectancy at Birth, Gross Rate of Mortality, and Rate of Infant Mortality, 1980–2025

Period	Life Expectancy at Birth (in years)			Gross Mortality (per 1,000)	Gross Infant Mortality (per 1,000)
	Total	Men	Women		
1980–1985	58.60	56.78	60.51	10.74	98.63
1985–1990	61.40	59.51	63.38	9.24	88.21
1990–1995	64.60	62.74	66.55	7.69	75.81
1995–2000	67.00	65.10	68.99	6.69	66.43
2000–2005	68.75	66.83	70.76	6.15	59.65
2005–2010	69.80	67.87	71.82	6.01	55.62
2010–2015	70.75	68.82	72.78	6.00	51.99
2015–2020	71.40	69.47	73.03	6.15	49.54
2020–2025	72.00	70.07	74.03	6.40	47.28

Source: Ine-Celade, Estimaciones y Proyecciones de Poblacion. Total del Pais: 1950–2025: Urbana y Rural; 1970–1995, *Boletin de Analisis Demografico,* No. 25, Lima, April 1983, and La Poblacion Del Peru 1980–2025: Su Crecimiento y Distribucion, *Boletin de Analisis Demografico*, No. 26, Lima, April 1984.

Peru in the year 2000 and after (67 years between 1995 and 2000 and 72 years in the period 2000–2025) was predicated on improvements in health care, control of infectious disease, and simply the general pattern of life extension observed in other countries of similar background to Peru, most notably Cuba, Mexico, Colombia, and Argentina [6]. Table 2 presents the fertility and mortality projections for all of the major nations of Latin America for the years 1984 and 2000.

As indicated in Table 2, the rate of growth, overall fertility rate (for the two five-year periods), and life expectancy for Peru were higher than those of both the Andean region and the average for Latin America. In the case of rate of growth, the difference is .28 for the Peru to Latin American difference, and .08 for the Peru to Andean region difference. The declines in the overall fertility rate and the extension of life expectancy had been premised on the assumptions of increased urbanization, increased education, and rising female status as constricting influences on the fertility rate as well as factors leading to longer life expectancy. The Peruvian projections to the year 2000 were predicated on similar logic.

For the preceding factors to become operative, however, it would require simply more than the "urbanization" of Peru's rural population. In fact, in and of itself, urban migration is not necessarily a sufficient determinant of lower fertility, as some studies have determined [7]. For Peru to hold its population growth to the point where it could keep pace with its food supply and employment expansion to the year 2000 would require a massive educational program, as well as a long-term effort at planning and related health initiatives. In the 1980s, the major vehicles for these policies were the public and private institutions that predated the Garcia administration.

B. The Peruvian National Council on Population

The educational program of the Garcia government was perhaps its most ambitious program. President Garcia cited certain population projections suggesting that with more education and parental responsibility, the Peruvian population could be held to 27 million, with 8 and not 11 million in Lima by the year 2000. With a government supported program in responsible

Table 2 Total Population and Indicators of Fertility and Mortality for the Years 1984 and 2000

Countries	Population (thousands) 1984	Population (thousands) 2000	Rate of Growth (per hundred) 1980–1985	Overall Rate of Fertility 1980–1985	Overall Rate of Fertility 1995–2000	Life Expectancy at Birth 1980–1985	Life Expectancy at Birth 1995–2000
Andean Region	92,300	132,205	2.52	4.41	3.44	62.85	67.85
Peru	19,198	27,952	2.60	5.00	3.50	58.60	67.00
Bolivia	6,200	9,724	2.68	6.25	5.50	50.74	59.44
Colombia	28,113	37,999	2.14	3.93	3.00	63.63	66.92
Chile	11,878	14,934	1.68	2.90	2.50	67.01	70.56
Ecuador	9,091	14,596	3.12	6.00	4.72	62.57	68.97
Venezuela	17,820	27,207	3.25	4.33	3.27	67.80	70.90
Atlantic area	169,321	225,453	2.10	3.74	2.90	64.70	68.31
Argentina	30,097	37,197	1.58	3.38	2.74	69.71	72.00
Brazil	132,658	179,487	2.22	3.81	2.91	63.41	67.48
Paraguay	3,576	5,405	3.00	3.00	4.85	65.11	67.85
Uruguay	2,990	3,364	2.70	2.76	2.38	70.34	72.34
Central America	25,615	40,175	2.95	5.21	4.20	63.43	69.72
Costa Rica	2,535	3,596	2.63	3.50	2.85	73.03	74.43
El Salvador	5,388	8,708	2.92	5.56	4.45	64.83	71.29
Guatemala	8,164	12,739	2.91	5.17	4.31	60.72	68.00
Honduras	4,231	6,978	3.38	6.50	5.00	59.91	67.79
Nicaragua	3,163	5,261	3.32	5.94	4.50	59.81	68.50
Panama	2,134	2,893	2.17	3.46	2.65	70.98	73.30
Mexico and the Caribbean	99,529	139,165	2.37	4.36	3.04	65.49	69.14
Cuba	9,966	11,718	0.62	1.98	2.10	73.45	74.66
Haiti	6,418	9,860	2.51	5.74	5.15	52.73	58.40
Mexico	77,043	109,180	2.59	4.61	3.00	65.73	69.56
Dominican Republic	6,102	8,407	2.32	4.18	2.81	62.58	68.10
Latin America	386,765	537,205	2.32	4.15	3.16	64.38	68.52

Source: Celade, America Latina: Paises segun Tases de Crecimiento, Pedriodo 1980–1985, *Boletin Demografica*, No. 32. Santiago de Chile, July 1983.

parenthood, coupled with the tacit approval of the Peruvian Catholic Church, Garcia hoped to attain a slower rate of population growth [8].

A major instrument in this policy was the National Council on Population (Consejo Nacional de Poblacion [CNP]). In the course of 1986 the CNP developed various departmental level programs under the general rubric of "Health, Population, and Development." The major thrust of these programs was the multisector coordination and participation of the community "as a dynamic element in the application of the population policy of the present government" [9].

To this end, public meetings were held in all the departments of Peru, leading to the formation of twenty-four departmental-level "commissions for the assistance of the national population policy," with these commissions presumably to form the major implementation mechanisms at the grass roots level. By September 1986, meetings had been held in the departments of: Ica, Huancavelica, Apruimace, Ayachucho, Cusco, Puno, Piura, Arequipa, Ancash, Junin-Pasco, and San Martin, and one interdepartmental meeting for Hural-Chancay.

Each of these meetings resulted in the commission mentioned earlier. Each was assisted by the regional development corporation of the region, termed CORDE in Peru (or Corporacion de Desarrollo), which is a system of central government sponsored and controlled (through central government provision of the development funds and personnel) public corporations at the regional level.

Another sponsor of these meetings was the organization known as Cooperacion Popular (COOPOP), together with the regional unit of the Department of Health for the particular state in which the meeting was held. In a number of cases, local universities participated. For example, in Arequipa the Universidad Católica Santa Maria was a cosponsor of the program held on August 18–19, 1986.

The format for these public meetings varied only slightly from department to department, probably reflecting the overall guidance of the Ministry of Health and the Council on Population. In a number of cases, the heads of both these units were present. Dr. David Tejada de Rivera, minister of health, and Dr. Edgard Ibarcena, president of the CNP, participated as initial speakers in many of the first-day sessions. The first day was normally devoted to an explanation of the national population policy by Dr. Tejada or Ibarcena, or another designated speaker. Also, the themes of the women's situation in Perú, health improvement, and the need for community participation in these issues were touched upon. The second day would be given over to work in groups. This, for example, was the pattern at the meeting in Ancash [10].

The participants at these meetings generally were made up of representatives of the health sector, the community of educators, and, in a number of cases, the Mothers' Clubs. At the Ancash meeting of August 28–29, 1986, 315 persons attended, of whom 104 were from the health sector, 51 were from the Mothers' Clubs, and 18 were educators. All of the provinces within the Department of Ancash were reported to be represented. In certain departments, those in very rural areas, the meetings drew heavily from the agrarian sector. In Junin-Pasco, for instance, the meeting of August 28–29 was composed of 171 participants, with large delegations from the peasant (*campesino*) communities, as well as a group from the urban migrants.

Given the differences in the composition of the participants, it is interesting to note the variation in the conclusions of the various working groups which were reported during the final days of these sessions. While the Ancash groups presented their conclusions around three central theses—health problems and how they should be addressed; how programs of health care and family planning might be implemented, and what are the most urgent measures needed for the successful development of the department—the Junin-Pasco groups, while not differing markedly in their conclusions regarding health care, took a somewhat different path in considering education and work.

Under the theme of education, the Junin-Pasco group concluded that changes in the public school curriculum were needed, specifically with regard to provision of instruction in family planning. Moreover, the group recommended, under the category of work, that "poles of development" should be established in the central region for purposes of encouraging economic development, with better incentives and assistance to rural communities at all levels for the purpose of preventing out-migration to urban areas [11].

It is striking that a meeting that comprised rural workers and urban migrants would focus on the need for enhanced public education in the area of population and family planning. In addition to enhanced curriculum, this group called for more training for the teaching staffs in family planning, something that was not noted in those meetings attended by many education groups.

Equally noteworthy is the Junin-Pasco group's attention to the problem of out-migration to the city, and to the need for concrete economic inducements to prevent large-scale out-migration.

The head of the CNP, Dr. Ibarcena, had stated that the council's policy was one of direct as well as indirect methods in the attainment of a national population policy. According to Dr. Ibarcena, the CNP was working through both public and private institutions to influence the size, distribution, and composition of the national population. He stressed that the council was striving to achieve an equilibrium between and among the growth, structure, and distribution (in geographic terms) of the population. In an interview in a popular Peruvian magazine (*Caretas*), Dr. Ibarcena stated:

> (W)e have not calculated demographic goals because we do not wish to influence the free decision and responsibility of persons and parents concerning the number and spacing of their offspring—as to who should nurture, educate and love—but rather to furnish them the educational and health services of the public and private sectors in order to contribute to the stability and security of the family, improving the quality of life. [12]

But an article in the same issue remarked that any government initiated population policy would have to overcome a history of inaction and indecision: "The population theme and that of demographic growth were not only ignored by the Velasco government, treated tangentially by that of Morales Bermudez and analyzed by that of Belaunde, but also nearly consigned to the category of policy miracles" [13].

Despite the lineaments of a population policy in existence since 1975, a 1985 Population Law, and the creation of the CNP and the National Institute on Population (a government-sponsored policy institute), the services of the Department of Social Security and those of the Ministry of Health, together with those of about twenty private agencies, had been sorely overtaxed. Only 2% of the population had access to the family planning services of the Department of Social Security, and only 4% to those of the Ministry of Health. The growth of the Peruvian population, one critic of the government's population policies concluded, "is vertigious and disorderly and obviously requires immediate and coordinated action" [14].

C. The Role of the Church

One positive factor in the population policy calculus was the entry of elements of the Peruvian Catholic Church into the ranks of those proposing concrete measures for family planning and responsible parenthood. The more progressive elements of the Lima clergy had quietly backed such efforts for years, recognizing their importance to the stability of the family and the society as a whole. In December 1986, the Church hierarchy took a more public stance on the problem, declaring its active support [15]. But the record of concrete efforts in assistance by organs of the Church was a mixed one, reflecting perhaps resistance within the national Church hierarchy to the concept of family planning and, more specifically, the dissemination of contraception information. The Peruvian Church was divided in respect to many population policy questions. The more conservative elements, following the prevalent thinking within the Vatican, had asserted themselves in the mid- and late 1980s. The rear-guard elements of the "liberation theology" school, although on the defensive, still had considerable popular support among the faithful within the *pueblos jovenes*. Despite its divisions, the Church demonstrated a willingness to come forward and give more than tacit support to family planning, a political coup for the Garcia administration's population policy.

D. Urban-Rural Demographic Imbalance

As reflected in Tables 1 and 2, the rate of growth in the Peruvian population in the period of the 1980s was high. According to the Centro Latino-Americana de Demografia (CELADE), the rate has been 2.6% and was higher than the average for the Andean region. During the same period (1980–1985), Cuba had a rate of 0.62; Uruguay, 0.70; and Argentina, 1.58. But this growth was not solely due to the high fertility rate. Given the total area of the country (1,285,215 square kilometers), the population density stands at 13.2 inhabitants per kilometer. This does not constitute overpopulation in simple terms. But when the fact that much of the land is rugged sierra, desertlike coastal plain, or *selva* (jungle), then these numbers warrant closer examination. But a more serious problem is the maldistribution of the population. In 1940 the urban population constituted only 35.4% of the total population. By 1961, this had climbed to 47.4%, and by 1972, 59.4%. In 1981, it was estimated that 64.8% of the population was urban, with a growth rate of 3.7 per hundred. This, when compared to the rural rate of 1.1 per hundred, was very high (see Table 3).

The rapid growth of the population had been accompanied by the processes of industrialization and urbanization. Table 3 suggests indirectly that these processes, occurring as they did over the preceding forty years, had been paralleled by the unequal growth of population in the city and the countryside. Although the total population grew at an annual rate of 2.3% over the period 1940 to 1981, the urban population grew at a rate of 3.8, while the rural sector population grew at a low 0.8% [16].

This disequilibrium in urban/rural population growth is not at all abnormal for Latin America, where many nations are experiencing unbalanced urban growth. In the case of Peru in the 1980s, the movement of population to the metropolitan Lima-Callao area contributed to a preexisting crisis in municipal service provision. As in other Latin American urban areas, the large immigrant population contributed to the growth of squatter settlements, usually through the simple process of a group of individuals banding together to set up crude dwellings on an area of

Table 3 Peruvian Population by Urban and Rural Area and Rates of Growth: 1940, 1961, 1972, and 1981 Censuses (Thousands)

Censuses	Total Absolute	Urban Absolute (Relative)	Rural Absolute (Relative)	Rates of Intercensus Growth (per hundred) Urban	Rural	Total
1940	7,080.0	2,506.0 (35.4)	4,573.7 (64.6)	3.2	0.8	1.8
1961	10,217.5	4,843.1 (47.4)	5,374.4 (52.6)	5.0	0.5	2.9
1972	13,954.8	8,284.5 (59.4)	5,670.2 (40.6)	3.7	1.1	2.7
1981	17,754.8	11,509.4 (64.8)	6,245.4 (35.2)	—	—	—
Increment 1940–1981	10,674.8	9,003.1 (15.7)	1,671.7 (15.7)	3.8	0.8	2.3

Source: Ine, National Censuses of 1940, 1961, 1972, and 1981: *La Poblacion del Peru*, 1980–2025. *Boletin de Analisis Demografico*, No. 26, April 1984.

vacant land. In the greater Lima area, where the climate is mild but the terrain is dry and desertous, this meant that many settlements existed without municipal water service, electric light, or sewer services. The health hazards of such an environment, the danger of infectious disease, and the general level of deprivation are all high. This danger has been demonstrated by the rampant cholera epidemic that has swept through Peru in the 1990s.

The municipal authorities had faced massive difficulties in coping with the demand for services, and private operators have moved into the water supply and other service provision markets, with not always satisfactory results. The ability of private providers to cope with the burgeoning population of the *pueblos jovenes* was limited by many factors, not the least of which was the highly restricted access to capital for small entrepreneurs.

Still, it should be noted that these squatter settlements had tended, if not forcefully evicted, to evolve into established housing areas, or *urbanizaciones*. This was due as much to the determination of the occupants as anything else. These highly organized communities band together and organize themselves to provide for water, sewage, and light, albeit not always by means approved of by the municipal authorities.

The most significant point about the development of the *pueblos jovenes* was that their very success begot imitation. The success of each new squatter community was a signal to others to attempt the same. Each new wave of rural-to-urban migrants contributed to the problems of congestion, unemployment, and sanitation in the cities.

The Garcia government's recognition of the problem, and of the need for planned growth of urban areas, was a significant achievement in itself, considering the hesitancy and uncertainty of previous administrations. Unfortunately, the government's population program could only reach a small proportion of Peru's people.

E. Rural Problems Contributing to Urban Population Imbalance

Without positive economic improvement, the rural peasantry found it exceedingly difficult to stay on the land. The young and mobile, having little to hold them, made their way to the city. This movement was, if anything, accelerated by the outbreak of the Sendero Luminoso (Shining Path) Maoist-inspired movement in Ayacucho province in the early 1980s. Refugees from Ayacucho and other areas affected by the insurrection and the Peruvian military's somewhat brutal tactics in combatting Shining Path poured into the cities.

There can be no doubt that Shining Path's terrorism and Khmer Rougesque tactics had a negative impact on Garcia's population containment strategies. Government health workers became assassination victims, and the Shining Path's control of major areas of the southern Andean area made it difficult to get the government's family planning message to a principal target population—the rural peasantry.

The social position of women, and rural and Amerindian women in particular, had definite consequences for the success of any family planning initiative. The close relationship between birth rates and the socioeconomic situation of women has been acknowledged in Peruvian population planning at least since the 1970s. The *Lineamientos* of the late 1970s remark that the Peruvian female's fertility rate (6.4) was more than double that of nations in which women had arrived at a position of equal rights and opportunities with men [17].

In this context, a key element in elevating women to social equality is literacy. This is equally important as a factor in successful implementation of family planning. As women achieve literacy, they have greater opportunity to acquire relevant information concerning contraception and health care.

But access to printed matter is as much a function of language as of literacy. If a significant population group is not only illiterate, but unable to speak or understand the language in which much of the family planning information is printed, then the problem of female literacy is doubly difficult to overcome. This is certainly true for the Quechua and Aymará speakers of Peru, who constitute a goodly percentage of the Amerindian populace. Despite the National Literacy Program and the Educational Reform initiated in the 1970s, it may be some time before the results begin to manifest themselves in terms of overall as well as female literacy. Table 4 indicates the urban/rural and male/female illiteracy rates for 1972 and 1981.

As Table 4 demonstrates, no substantial improvement in literacy among females can be deduced from the census data for the decade preceding the Garcia administration. It is difficult to find evidence that would suggest that literacy had been extended to significant segments of the Amerindian peasantry and, most especially, to the female populations having the highest fertility rates. This would suggest that in the short term, the government efforts in bringing family planning material to the attention of women focused extensively on social communication channels.

But any unbiased assessment of female status in the population question should take account of the views of Peruvian women. For societal norms and values, psychosocial roots of behavior and other related factors need to be addressed. Perhaps no government can truly alter long-standing sociocultural patterns, although some, such as that of Communist China, have attempted it. Educated Peruvian women speak of a *sociedad machista*, or male-dominated society. While the Garcia government never seriously addressed this issue, it certainly has been raised in family planning discussions and probably will continue to be raised in the future. Whether any Peruvian government will seriously address it is a matter of open conjecture.

F. An Assessment of Peruvian Population Policy

In the context of a growing concern for the Peru of the next century, and against a background of erratic urban growth and often violent rural unrest, the government of Alan Garcia gave population policy a higher priority than previous regimes. Building on the tentative efforts of previous governments, principally the attempt to include a demographic projection in the growth strategies of the military governments of the 1970s, and the first steps in 1982 to implement family planning programs, the Garcia government worked through the existing institutional machinery, the Consejo Nacial de Poblacion, the Instituto Nacional de Poblacion, as well as the Department of Social Security and the Ministry of Health, in order to implement its program.

Past efforts in this area had been marked by limitations in resources, and nothing in the Garcia government's efforts would suggest that resources were more abundant. While the

Table 4 Illiterate Population over Five Years of Age by Sex and Place of Residence: 1972 and 1981 (Thousands)

	1972		Percentage Female Illiteracy	1981		Percentage Female Illiteracy
	Males	Females		Males	Females	
Urban	429.4	749.4	63.5	382.9	679.9	63.9
Rural	927.2	1,480.4	61.4	1,263.5	1,098.1	63.5

Source: Ine, National Censuses of 1972 and 1981.

government succeeded in raising the awareness of unrestricted population growth as a serious national problem, it did not, in the long run, begin to counter the overwhelming problems contributing to population imbalance. The government agencies, councils, and ministries through which the population policies were implemented were beset not only by the shortage of funds, but also by the dangers of a national insurrection and attendant terrorism. To these might be added the barriers and pitfalls to be overcome in communications and in reaching the target populations with the family planning message and services. As a first serious effort, however, full marks should be accorded the Garcia administration. Even so, there remained much more to do.

One student of Peruvian population policy has called for increased efforts to evaluate family planning efforts as well as the implementation of a program of education for responsible parenthood, in order that these programs be placed on a solid basis for achieving their desired goals. Moreover, new initiatives in social communication should be undertaken to convey material on family planning and responsible parenthood [18].

A population policy in and of itself will not solve the massive social, economic, and political dilemmas of a nation such as Peru. Any such policy can only be collateral to more far-reaching development strategies. However, an effective population policy can be seen as a necessary, if not sufficient, policy for national development. Without one, the benefits of any economic growth will be diluted among too many to make an improvement in living standards. This has been the recent experience of much of the Indian subcontinent.

Under Garcia, Peru continued to be guided by the World Action Plan of the 1974 World Population Conference in Bucharest. All efforts to control population growth were to be informed by a respect for the parental right to determine the number and spacing of births "in [a] free, responsible and informed manner." Given Peruvian society's traditional respect for family privacy, this adherence to the Bucharest guidelines would seem warranted at the time.

As for future investigation of Peru's population policy, some examination of the Fujimori government's policies would make for an interesting and possibly enlightening comparison. The continuation of the Shining Path guerilla movement and the extension of the struggle into urban areas in the 1990s may greatly hinder the government's capacity to focus on population and family planning initiatives. The depressed economy has certainly had a debilitating impact on policy in this area as well.

NOTES

1. Text of the Presidential Message, *El Commercio*, Lima, Sunday, December 21, 1986, p. a-4.
2. Instituto Nacional de Planificacion, Republic of Perú, *Lineamientos de Politica de Poblacion en el Peru*, Lima, 1978, pp. 9ff.
3. Ibid.
4. Instituto Nacional de Estadistica (INE), *La Poblacion del Peru, 1980–2025: Su Crecimiento y Distribucion*, p. 1.
5. Ibid.
6. Ibid., p. 6.
7. M. B. Concepcion, Family Formation and Contraception in Selected Developing Countries: Policy Implications of WFS Findings, World Fertility Survey Conference 1980, pp. 197–260, vol. 1, World Fertility Survey, 1981.
8. *El Commercio*, p. a-4.
9. Reuniones Departmentales en Marcha, *Boletin Informativo del Consejo Nacional de Poblacion*, No. 8, September 1986, pp. 4–7.

10. Ibid., p. 5.
11. Ibid., p. 8.
12. "Edward Ibarcena, Presidente del Consejo Nacional de Poblacion," *Caretas*, no. 931, November 24, 1986, p. 47.
13. Kela Leon de Vega, "Los Chicos Crecen," *Caretas*, November 24, 1986, p. 46.
14. Ibid.
15. *Lima Times*, Sunday, December 12, 1986, p. 1
16. *La Poblacion del Peru: 1980–2025*, p. 20.
17. *Lineamientos*, p. 11.
18. Carlos Carbajal Chirinos, El Reto de la Poblacion, *Variedades*, no. 1815, Sunday, April 7, 1985, pp. 6–7.

35
Genesis of Public Administration and Its Early Development in Australia, 1788–1856

Habib M. Zafarullah
University of New England, Armidale, Australia

Australia was born a bureaucratic state in 1788 when the British government established a colony of settlement in the Antipodes and vested its entire administration in a group of officials appointed by and responsible to the Crown. This marked a departure from tradition, for previous efforts at colonization in different parts of the world had been undertaken by private companies or syndicates under charter of authority granted by the British government (McMartin, 1983, p. 4). The first Australian colony of New South Wales thus set a precedent in establishing and managing a colony.

Ostensibly, the principal objective of the authorities in London was to seek a place for the growing convict population which had been overcrowding the jails in England and other parts of the kingdom. Some historians believe that the real motives behind the founding of the settlement "were of much larger and more statesmanlike character" (Barton, 1889, p. 23). One fundamental reason was the loss of the American colonies; the other was the political necessity of stopping France from extending its empire to the Southern Hemisphere (Jenks, 1895, pp. 20–25). Whatever were the long-term political goals of the British government, the immediate objective—that of establishing a penal settlement—largely shaped the system of public administration that obtained during the first three decades of colonial life in New South Wales and its dependencies.

I. THE FORMATIVE PHASE: 1788–1823 [1]

Although the idea of establishing a military form of government in the new colony was abandoned after it had been considered by the British government, the kind of administration that emerged during the formative period was by and large military in character if not in purpose (Meston, 1927, p. 177). The nine governors/lieutenant governors who were in charge of governmental affairs in New South Wales from 1788 to 1823 were all military officers; their indoctrination and experience apparently influenced their mode of governing. Generally, they reflected leadership traits that bore marks of their military upbringing but each possessed a distinctive administrative style. Some were particular about petty details and reluctant to delegate responsibility; some were strict disciplinarians, while others were remiss. Some were authoritarian in their approach, while others were liberal and willing to share responsibility (McMartin, 1983, pp. 44–46).

A. The Role of Governor

As the representative of the Crown, the governor was the fountain of authority in the colony. His official instructions vested him with enormous powers; he was formally answerable only to the Home government. He was empowered to administer by decree—issuing proclamations that had the temporary force of law, pending final sanction of the Crown. He was authorized to make appointments from within the colony and to suspend any officer who failed to execute his duties with competency and integrity (O'Brien, 1947, p. 22; Bladen, 1898, pp. 54–55, 83). He granted land to colonists as well as to public functionaries, pardoned convicts unconditionally, or reduced the term of their sentences. Indeed, he was at the same time the leader of the community, its protector, lawgiver, and adjudicator, as well as the viceroy to uphold the paramountcy of the Crown.

Until 1823, there was no representative government in New South Wales. Though there existed a nominated Executive Council to advise the governor, he was not obliged to follow its advice or even to consult. However, as Jenks contends, "by affording the principal officials a constitutional opportunity of discussing together the general affairs of the colony and of tendering independent and collective advice, the institution of the Executive Council gave a powerful impulse to the spread of a wholesome public opinion" (Jenks, 1895, p. 155).

B. Centralized Administration

From the corps of civil officers, who accompanied Governor Phillip with the first fleet to the new settlement, evolved the future public service of New South Wales. Initially there were no departments; governmental functions were carried on by individual officers with the assistance of small groups of clerks (McMartin, 1983, p. 34). This establishment was distinct from the military corps, which was required to play an entirely different role—to assist the government to maintain law and order. The general administrative and developmental functions were vested in the civil officers. The emerging bureaucracy thus bore a distinct civilian character from the very beginning (McMartin, 1983, pp. 37, 40; Bladen, 1898, p. 21).

Because of the peculiarities of the situation, a centralized administrative structure developed. The line of authority was simple and clear, vertically apexing to the governor, from whom emanated all directions and commands. He was kept reasonably well informed of all that occurred at different levels of an uncomplicated hierarchy.

A key element of this centralized structure was the office of the Secretary to the Colony (initially Secretary to the Governor). In the early years, he helped the governor in the preparation of official orders and countersigned warrants of appointments. But soon his importance and responsibilities increased; he began to be involved in almost every aspect of government business (Bladen, 1898, p. 56). For all practical purposes, he gradually assumed the role of the most important functionary in the colony—the alter ego of the governor and his close confidant. He handled the bulk of the executive functions of the government, and his office became the repository of important documents and papers relating to convict and land administration, official dispatches, proclamations, and other colonial matters. The secretary together with the judge advocate and the commissary served as aides to the decision-making process (Watson, 1922, vol. 1, p. 267; 1922, vol. 4, p. 691; McMartin, 1983, pp. 59, 63–65).

By the early 1800s, the volume of work of the secretary had increased so much that it became necessary to have the services of a full-time permanent officer to take over his responsibilities and duties. But the Colonial Office ignored pleas for such an appointment (Watson, 1922, vol. 4, p. 537). And for the next two decades, the status of the governor's secretary remained unchanged although he acquired much prestige and importance in colonial affairs. Not only did the functions of his office expand but organizationally it increased in size [2].

The preeminent role of the secretary was acknowledged in 1820 when the British government appointed a colonial secretary and registrar of records and four years later acquitted him of the responsibilities of the secretary to the governor (Watson, 1922, vol. 2, p. 262). The office now acquired an independent status but remained close to the center of power in the colony. He was, among the civil officials, the highest paid and accorded precedence in the administrative hierarchy with powers of general superintendence, coordination, and control over the entire governmental machinery. He served as the channel of all official communication between the governor and other officials and colonists or between departments (Richardson, 1951, p. 24; McMartin, 1983, pp. 71, 138).

The Commissariat, during the first quarter century of settlement, also held an important position in the administrative structure. It was the forerunner of many latter-day departments such as the Treasury, Audit, Stores, and Transport. Directly responsible to the lords of Treasury in London, it handled the public accounts of the colony, kept records of all monetary transactions, stored and supplied provisions, and served as a public bank (McMartin, 1958b, pp. 215–216).

C. Administrative Procedures

For almost a decade and a half, however, administrative process remained disorganized: makeshift methods were utilized to run governmental business. Governor King made the first attempt to streamline the operations of public officers (Bladen, 1898, vol. 4, p. 258; Watson, 1922, vol. 2, pp. 623–625; vol. 3, pp. 36–37, 48). He established the practices of personally instructing each departmental head every morning on departmental administration, regularly circulating government and general orders among relevant officials, and publicizing the more important ones for the general information of the public (Watson, 1922, vol. 3, pp. 463, 632; McMartin, 1983, p. 59).

During Governor Macquarie's rule, more concrete steps were taken to improve administrative methods to cope with the increasing volume of business in the colony. The most notable improvements were made in records administration—files were classified by subject and both incoming and outgoing correspondence registered. The change became inevitable after frequent cases of frauds, misrepresentation, and mishandling of documents, but it became difficult to enforce the new procedures because of the lack of experience of most officers (Richardson, 1951, p. 66; McMartin, 1983, pp. 63, 65, 73; Watson, 1922, vol. 7, p. 782; see also Phillips, 1971).

The system of financial administration underwent some basic changes—methods were improved; colonial funds extended, classified, and placed under the management of trustees; and colonial revenue enhanced through increased duties (McMartin, 1983, p. 132). Audit administration, on the other hand, was still nascent; no specific officer or agency was entrusted to undertake the auditing of colonial accounts within the New South Wales. There were no Colonial Office instructions regarding audit, but governors did take the initiative in having departmental accounts audited in their own ways. It was not until 1822 that the Home government began to deal with colonial accounts through the Colonial Audit Office (McMartin, 1983, p. 182; Eddy, 1969, p. 155).

D. Discipline

The peculiar social and economic problems of settlement in the early years had negative influence on the developing bureaucracy. Government servants who were not precluded from engaging in free trade served as "a powerful inducement to officials to regard their public duty as secondary" (McMartin, 1983, p. 57). The participation of a number of senior officers in the military takeover after the disposition of Governor Bligh in 1808 posed questions of loyalty of public servants to the Crown-appointed governor. This had implications for discipline in the bureaucracy. The military interregnum was also responsible in creating a situation that lowered the morale of the service. There were few means to check dishonesty or ensure integrity among public servants (McMartin, 1983, pp. 57, 60).

In 1815, the secretary of state instructed Macquarie to prohibit public servants from engaging in trade and other pursuits of profiteering (Watson, 1922, vol. 9, p. 644). But Macquarie was hard-pressed to dissuade public servants from resorting to such practices. Because of the nature of its functions, the Commissariat provided its officers with opportunities to be dishonest and corrupt (Jenks, 1895, p. 42). But correcting such behavior proved difficult (Watson, 1922, vol. 2, pp. 632–636, 693–695; 1922, vol. 3, pp. 5, 18–22).

E. Staffing the Public Service

Two modes of recruitment developed during the period. According to the first, the higher officials were appointed by the Colonial Office in London, and they held office at the Crown's pleasure. As there were no specific rules to control such recruitment, patronage played an important role. The duties and responsibilities of these officials were defined by "commissions" that were granted them and which they carried to the colony. According to the second mode, recruitment mostly to subordinate positions was made locally by the governor subject to Colonial Office confirmation. These appointments often proved to be ad hoc as those holding them were often replaced by nominees from Britain.

As a result of the short supply of competent and interested persons to man public service positions, emancipated convicts were frequently appointed at small salaries, particularly during Macquarie's rule. This proved detrimental to efficiency (McMartin, 1983, p. 138). But Bigge, who made an extensive inquiry into the affairs of the colony during the time of Macquarie, deprecated the practice of employing ex-convicts and recommended their removal on the ground that it afforded them "an air of authority and presumption most unsuited to their condition" (Ritchie, 1970, p. 248).

But conditions and benefits of public employment were not lucrative enough to induce men of high intellectual or professional qualifications to choose a career in a distant land. Consequently, the recruitment requirements were such that people with minimum qualifications could enter the clerical branch of the service. The increase in governmental activities and the lack of capable hands made it imperative for the government to resort to "pluralism"—holding two or more positions by a single individual at the same time. Thus, magistrates were also called upon to undertake administrative duties in addition to their primary judicial functions, a practice that would continue for a long time (McMartin, 1983, pp. 75, 138).

Macquarie was not satisfied with the calibre of many public servants recruited in England. He complained that many of them were "totally unworthy to be employed in the several Situations to which their interest, unhappily not their merits, had promoted them" (Watson, 1922, vol. 9, p. 497). On the other hand, he favored the employment of emancipated convicts, for he was of firm conviction that they deserved preference over others because of the reformatory nature of the colony (Ellis, 1941, pp. 93–126; Watson, 1922, vol. 7, pp. 775–776).

Tenure of the higher public servants was contingent upon the Crown's pleasure but, invariably, it was guaranteed, and only gross misdemeanor and serious dereliction of duty could affect permanency. The governor was empowered to dismiss any public servant including those recruited in London (McMartin, 1983, p. 136; Jenks, 1895, p. 154).

F. Remuneration

Public servants were compensated for their efforts in a variety of ways. Some were solely remunerated by fixed salaries, others by fees. Some received both salaries and fees. Fringe benefits and allowances for domestic servants, free accommodation, rations, forage for horses, and the like, also formed part of the income of higher officials. On the other hand, many subordinate employees were paid for their services not in cash but in kind (McMartin, 1958a, pp. 45–80).

Advancement within the service was not regular; public servants obtained an increase in salary through solicitations and petitions. And while promotions, also infrequent, were primarily according to seniority, merit was also an important factor (Watson, 1992, vol. 12, pp. 495–497).

G. Developments in Tasmania

Until 1824, when Tasmania became a separate colony, it was a dependency of New South Wales and came under its administrative jurisdiction and control. Since its founding, the administration of the island settlement was looked after by four officers who were line functionaries of establishments located in Sydney. In 1804, separate "governments" were established in the southern and northern regions of the island. The former, with headquarters in Hobart, was administered by a lieutenant governor, but that in York Town (headquarters of the northern region) was under an administrator. Created "to prevent any overlapping of authority" (Jenks, 1895, pp. 150, 151, 153), both were under the direct control of the New South Wales governor.

The function of these "governments" encompassed judicial, ecclesiastical, medical, supply and provisions, survey, mineral exploration, shipping, and convict matters (Wettenhall, 1959, p. 48). But their operative procedures were "primitive"; supervision was ineffective; discipline was casual, and officials negligent or capricious in the performance of their duties. These shortcomings hampered development of the settlement although considerable efforts were made by early officials to build the basic physical infrastructure of the colony (Watson, 1922, vol. 1, pp. 263, 320).

Most appointments were made in either London or Sydney, but the expansion of governmental functions necessitated local recruitment to lower positions. But even these had to be sanctioned by the governor of New South Wales. Pressing circumstances, however, induced the local executive to "violate" such regulations. Macquarie relaxed the rules in 1817 and authorized the lieutenant governor to appoint (until approved by him) "properly qualified" persons to any vacancy provisionally. The remuneration of officers followed the pattern of the parent colony. Tenure of subordinate public servants was largely insecure, and free grants of land were made to induce settlers to enter the service (Fenton, 1884, pp. 33, 40, 51; Wettenhall, 1959, p. 56; Watson, 1922, vol. 2, p. 190).

By the early 1820s, the number of departments and extent of governmental functions increased considerably, resulting in difficulties in coordination and control. To improve the situation, this necessitated the amalgamation of the "governments" of the northern and southern regions. And to prevent various "forgeries, frauds and depredition," the Commissariat was removed from the control of the lieutenant governor and placed under the governor of New South Wales (Wettenhall, 1959, pp. 51, 67, 71; Wettenhall, 1967, pp. 6, 7; Meston, 1927, p. 178; Jenks, 1895, p. 75).

II. REFORM AND REORGANIZATION: 1823–1842

The Imperial Act of 1823 provided for a Legislative Council in New South wales basically to advise and assist the governor in the exercise of his powers, prerogatives, and responsibilities. However, composed of Crown nominees only, it had limited powers, as all laws and ordinances enacted by it had to be ratified by the British government. The arbitrary magistrates' tribunals had already been replaced by Courts of Quarter Sessions in 1823. Supreme Courts were created in New South Wales and Tasmania with jurisdiction over all categories of cases (Watson, 1922, p. 65).

Five years later, the New South Wales Legislative Council was enlarged and given control over customs revenue and expenditure, and the veto power of the governor was withdrawn. The judicial system was reformed with the introduction of English law and the establishment of Circular Courts. The jury system was extended to cover both criminal and civil matters. A significant development during the period was the emergence of the Executive Council. The governor was to act on its advice, but, at the same time, if he wished, he could override its opinion (Quick and Garran, 1901, p. 37; Jenks, 1895, pp. 150, 156).

But all these did little to change the basic format of public administration in New South Wales. Although the expansion of governmental functions necessitated the creation of new departments, they lacked uniformity in their structure and processes. There was also a shortage of staff to carry out their "specialised" functions properly. The Colonial Secretary's and the Surveyor General's Departments were the largest, each containing about a dozen clerks, but the other departments were all very small. Again, salaries which did not correspond to the duties resulted in wide disparities; recruitment principles were undefined; and "diversity did exist in departmental practices and procedures" (Melbourne, 1963, pp. 151–162; AONSW, 1827).

A. The Darling Reforms

In New South Wales the foundations of systematic public administration were laid during the tenure of Governor Ralph Darling (1825–1831). Indeed, historians have labeled him as "a generator of administrative change" (McMartin, 1959, p. 327). By the time he took over office, the administrative system was characterized by laxity and maladministration as a result of the absence of effective control, supervision, and coordination. As Darling himself observed: "Every department appeared to act for itself, without check or control: and indeed without any apparent responsibility . . . common routine and forms of Office were totally neglected" (quoted in Cell, 1970, p. 72; Rose, 1922, pp. 49–176; Blair, 1879, p. 334).

Consequently, each department developed "its own particular conception of its role and its style of official behaviour" (Watson, 1922, vol. 12, p. 149). Disorganization, short supply of capable personnel, and archaic administrative methods were stumbling blocks to good administration. It thus became difficult to handle the increasing tasks of government effectively.

Darling instigated a thorough overhaul of existing procedures. He outlined in detail the rules of business and the way public servants should behave. He also appointed numerous investigative bodies to look in to a variety of matters including salaries and qualifications of clerks. He gradually brought to an end the practice, initiated by Macquarie, of appointing convicts and emancipists as clerks, for he believed that the favor extended to them had "degraded the offices by placing individuals to them who had forfeited every claim of character." But because of the lack of enthusiasm among free settlers for public service jobs, convicts continued to be employed in various department. Nevertheless, upon directions from the Colonial Office in 1835, they were removed from every position of trust (Arthur Papers).

In 1827, Darling proposed the creation of a "civil service system" in New South Wales similar to the existing services in Ceylon and Mauritius—two other British colonies. He emphasized the need to recruit a "few well-educated young Gentlemen" in England for employment as writers in various departments. They should be provided with adequate opportunities of advancement, better salaries, and grants of land (Watson,1922, vol. 12, p. 365, vol. 13, pp. 76–79, vol. 18, pp. 106–109). Salary increases, he believed, should not be dependent entirely on length of service; rather "conduct and qualifications" of officers should be considered. Likewise, promotions should be based on "zeal and competence." The service, he proposed, should be divided into two distinct classes, namely junior or second class with a salary range of £200–250 and first class (£300–350).

Within a short time, Darling's ideas were, to some extent, realized. On the recommendations of a Committee on Salaries (1826) the service was classified on the basis of worth and duties of positions rather than incumbents' personal capabilities. This was probably the earliest attempt anywhere in the world to introduce position classification in public personnel administration. Fixed incremental salary scales were established and fees or allowances were not considered as part of salaries. Clerks were appointed on the basis of their performance in examinations, albeit nominal, followed by a period of probation (Jervis, 1952, pp. 150–151; Watson, 1922, vol. 13, pp. 568–569; McMartin, 1983, p. 180).

The Colonial Secretary's Department, in particular, was put on a sounder basis and its status as the principal executive department of the colony with coordinating and supervisory powers was further established. It underwent reorganization and each position was assigned a specific set of duties and responsibilities (Cell, 1970, p. 73). It served as a model for other departments not only in New South Wales but in other Australian colonies as well.

Generally, governmental business was simplified, the volume of interdepartmental correspondence reduced, the full working capacity of clerks utilized, progress of daily work monitored, penalties for absenteeism imposed, overtime discouraged and payments curtailed, and office hours strictly regulated. The importance of surveillance from above insofar as implementation of directives was concerned was especially emphasized (McMartin, 1983, pp. 154, 159, 163–164, 173; AONSW, 1831).

B. The Post-Darling Era

In 1837, a Board on Salaries and Classification of Clerks recommended further changes to personnel practices in order to induce capable young men to enter the service and "stimulate them to exertion of Ability and Zeal" so as to retain them permanently. Promotions were to depend on "merit alone" and increase in salaries on "good conduct and ability." These recommendations were followed up and more "comprehensive" examinations to assess candidates in handwriting, arithmetic, and English grammar introduced. The criteria for selection for clerkships were, in addition to performance in these examinations, "diligence, ability and good conduct" of candidates (McMartin, 1983, p. 164).

Earlier, the Colonial Office, in a bid to tighten up departmental administration, instructed governors in all the colonies at that time to review each position falling vacant in terms of its duties, responsibilities, and remuneration. They were also to consider the expediency of either abolishing or amalgamating positions and gradually replacing convict clerks. Hours of work were increased and punctuality in attendance demanded. And, to improve strained relationships then existing between the New South Wales governor and some senior public servants, those holding key positions in the hierarchy were required to support the governor with "cordiality and zeal" (Watson, 1922, vol. 24, pp. 471–472).

C. Tasmania: A Centralized Autocracy

With the establishment of Tasmania as an "independent" colony in 1825, the powers and functions of the lieutenant governor were increased. As the chief executive of the colony, he assumed full responsibilities of government and was vested with prerogatives similar to those conferred on the New South Wales governor. The Tasmanian governor now came under the direct control of the Colonial Office, although in certain matters (financial, for instance) he took orders from the lord commissioners of the Treasury (Watson, 1922, vol. 17, pp. 25, 264, 467). In 1828, a legislature with lawmaking powers similar to that of New South Wales was established.

In 1826, the Colonial Office classified the Tasmanian service into two categories—the regular members of the civil establishment and those who were in charge of convicts. As in the parent colony, higher officials were appointed in London through patronage. But the recruitment of minor public servants such as justices of the peace, coroners and constables, and convict supervisors was the discretion of the lieutenant governor, subject to confirmation in London (Townsley, 1961, p. 42). Important positions falling vacant had to be reported to the Colonial Office, which would then find replacements, and in this respect the recommendations of the lieutenant governor carried much weight (Watson, 1922, vol. 5, p. 197). But as Townsley observed, the lieutenant governor's "power of appointment was severely restricted and discretionary in character, though the exercise of such power depended upon how effectively he could impress the Secretary of State" (Townsley, 1951, p. 7). On the other hand, like that of the governor in New South Wales, of greater significance, was his power of dismissing public servants on disciplinary grounds.

During the rule of Arthur, the first lieutenant governor under the new governmental system, important administrative changes took place in the colony. The web of control centered on him, and a highly centralized bureaucratic structure emerged (Townsley, 1951, p. 8). For the maintenance of law and order, Arthur divided the colony into discrete districts and placed each under a stipendiary magistrate supported by an auxiliary staff. These magistrates, in effect, became the local organs of gubernatorial power. Periodic reports kept Arthur informed of developments in the periphery. As in New South Wales, the Colonial Secretary's Office served as the channel of communication between the lieutenant governor and the rest of the colony, and this further entrenched the centralized nature of public administration (Fenton, 1884, p. 67; Melville, 1835).

Following the New South Wales pattern, departments were reorganized and a code of conduct for public servants formulated. Hours of business were stipulated; punctuality in attendance and seriousness in carrying out duties inculcated; and acceptance of any form of payments by public servants, except those authorized, prohibited. Strict rules relating to the flow of correspondence among departments were also enforced (Forsyth, 1970, p. 53).

Arthur not only created his unique "model" of administration but also ensured its effective operation. He emphasized efficiency, abhorred laxity, and was cautious in the selection of personnel. He favored those who would comply with his orders without challenge. Consequently, he got rid of those he deemed unfit to operate his system and appointed, in their stead, his relatives and protégés. As Forsyth remarked, "He brought personal government as closely as possible it has ever been to its logical conclusion, the direction of all the affairs of a society by a single mind" (Forsyth, 1970, p. 53; see also West, 1852, p. 170). Of all the lieutenant governors of Tasmania, Arthur was the most criticized for his acts of patronage.

D. Victoria: Capricious Administration

In 1836, the settlement of Port Phillip in southern New South Wales was proclaimed and a civil authority established there. The general superintendence of the settlement was entrusted to a police magistrate, Captain William Lonsdale. He took orders directly from the governor in Sydney and reported back every month on the affairs of the settlement. His authority was limited as he served only as a local representative of the New South Wales government. He was supported by a small corps of functionaries as well as a military contingent which maintained law and order (Blair, 1879, p. 394).

With the arrival of Charles LaTrobe as lieutenant governor in 1839, the status of Port Phillip was upgraded. The control of all departments/offices in the settlement transferred to his hands. He was entrusted with the same kind and degree of powers as enjoyed by his counterpart in Tasmania. Soon the settlement had its own judicial system with a Court of Petty Sessions and Courts of Quarter Sessions; a clerk of peace and a commissioner of the Court of Requests were also appointed. Changes in other spheres were also notable. A Sub-Treasury, a Sub-Registry, and the office of a Deputy Sheriff were also created to handle the growing functions of government (Turner, 1973, pp. 155–156, 178).

Public administration during LaTrobe's time was almost paralytic. Departments were disorganized, and dereliction of duties, corruption, and dishonesty among officers were common. The Customs Department was a classic example of maladministration. The constant flow of people from the public service to the goldfields inhibited the working of departments, resulting in an enormous accumulation of undone business; efficiency fell and the finances remained unaccounted for (Watson, 1922, vol. 20, pp. 243, 363, 378, 707, vol. 21, pp. 297, 514–514). Many public servants were said to be "engaged in dummying"—acquiring property through unfair means (Gross, 1965, p. 65; Allen, 1882; Watson, 1922, vol. 24, pp. 107, 109; Serle, 1963, p. 116; Blair, 1879, p. 439; Turner, 1973, pp. 342–343).

LaTrobe's administrative style was "notoriously vacillating and pusillanimous," thereby weakening the authority of government. Patronage was excessive, and little credence was given to merit and competency as factors in recruitment. As it turned out, positions were indiscriminately created for his protégés, most of whom were said to be "incompetent" (Blair, 1879, pp. 394–395, 431, 440; Serle, 1963, p. 143).

E. South Australia: Dyarchical Administration

Unlike the eastern colonies, which originally began as convict settlements, South Australia was basically founded as a free colony. The purposes of government there, based on Wakefield's plan of colonization, were purported to be different. From the beginning, it was to cater to the needs of a free population rather than to maintain convicts and felons transported from Britain. But in realizing the plan, a peculiar form of administration emerged in the colony—one that served as a deterrent to effective administration.

The 1834 imperial statute of Britain (British Parliament, 1834) provided for the appointment of a governor as the Crown's representative and a three-member Council to advise him. As in the other colonies, he was responsible to the Colonial Office and was empowered to make laws and control the bureaucracy. But, at the same time, a resident commissioner was appointed to administer the survey, sale, and management of lands in the colony. He was responsible not to the governor or the Colonial Office but to the London-based Colonisation Commissioners appointed by the act. The latter were empowered to make appointments relating to land and immigration administration. Thus administrative authority was divided between the governor, who by implication was to rule the colony, and the resident commissioner, who acted independently of the governor and took orders from the Colonisation Commissioners.

This dyarchical form of administration caused enormous problems in the proper functioning of government. Although they were instructed not to interfere in each other's sphere of influence and administration, relations soon became strained. There was no unity of command or direction as many officials and departments simultaneously took orders from both. Neither "possessed authority of a constructive nature and [they] could achieve little save thwarting one another and delaying the progress of the colony" (Jenks, 1895, p. 130). The results were inimical to good administration: there emerged insubordination, indiscipline, inefficiency, indolence, corruption, and other forms of administrative ills (Price, 1924, pp. 97–98; Allen, 1882, pp. 129, 134–135; Hawker, 1967, p. 26).

Conditions of employment were bad. Salaries were meager and morale, consequently, low. This induced many public servants to undertake private business and spend most of their time in that pursuit (Price, 1924, pp. 100–103; Hawker, 1967, pp. 30–32; Pike, 1967, p. 226). Appointments were given to those who would undertake to purchase land proportionate to their salaries; indeed, many candidates for positions in the service were virtually forced to buy land and help realize Wakefield's colonisation theory (Price, 1924, p. 103; Blair, 1879, p. 469). Similarly, a promotion was, in effect, dependent upon an officer's capability of increasing his landholdings rather than on proven efficiency or length of service.

The administration was characterized by confusion and disorder. With the absence of a police force it became difficult to maintain discipline. Higher officials, inexperienced as they were, were "grossly inefficient." Accounts were not systematically recorded and work in most departments was in arrears (Pike, 1967, p. 98). As the second governor of the colony noted with disgust, the administration operated "with scarcely a pretension to system; every man did as he would and got on as he could." Little attention was paid to "official routine, propriety and principle" (SAA, 1839).

These circumstances led the British government to reconsider the dual system of government seriously. In 1838, the office of the resident commissioner was merged with that of the governor and a Legislative Council, to serve as an advisory body, was established (Jenks, 1895, p. 136). A process of reform was initiated by Governor Gawler. He espoused efficiency in administration and believed that inadequacy of salaries was an important deterrent to individual performance. He reorganized many departments, streamlined their procedures, and reformed financial administration; retrenched incompetent staff; and established a police force (Pike, 1967, pp. 235–243; Burges, 1978, p. 105; Blair, 1879, p. 469). He delegated powers over appointments and promotions to departmental heads and augmented staff by over 300% to carry out the expanding functions of government. But on other matters his policies "led to centralisation on a vaster scale" (Hawker, 1967, pp. 35–36; Blackett, 1911, pp. 146–147).

The governors who followed Gawler were equally committed to improving administrative performance, and the small bureaucracy was "converted . . . into an effective, smoothly functioning government machine" (SAA, Research Notes, p. 6). But retrenchment and cutbacks in expenditure were drastic. Many departments were also abolished and austerity in administration emphasized.

F. The Swan River Colony: Embryonic Administration

In Western Australia the administrative system originated in December 1828 when the Colonial Office appointed Captain James Stirling as civil superintendent of the Swan River Colony. In March 1831, his position was upgraded to that of governor and commander-in-chief. A Legislative Council with three other officials was also created to help in the administration of the colony. A corps of civil officers supported the governor (British Parliament, 1816–1830; CSAWA, 1929, p. 9; Crowley, 1959, p. 12; Crowley, 1960, p. 9; Battye, 1978, pp. 79–83).

Stirling was quick to organize his administration. In 1829, instructions and directives on departmental administration were issued and a Board of Counsel and Audit set up to manage public property. Office hours were stipulated and the procedure for transaction of business determined. Public servants were precluded from "idle and unnecessary conversation" with outsiders on official matters. A system of registering documents "of every description" was also introduced. These regulations were expanded five years later. Heads of departments were given wider responsibilities, and public servants were directed to devote their full time to their duties (Battye, 1978, p. 82; Bryan and Bray, 1935, p. 8).

As in other colonies, the colonial secretary emerged as the principal official with coordinating functions below the governor. The general supervisory powers, however, remained with the latter. Formally, he exercised the same sort of power and wielded the same degree of authority as his counterparts in the other colonies (CSAWA, 1929, pp. 11–12; Crowley, 1960, pp. 10, 25, 34). The bureaucracy grew at a slow pace, for the functions of government were not expansive; the population was not big enough to warrant a large administrative machine.

III. CONSOLIDATION AND REFINEMENT: 1842–1855

The year 1842 marked an important step in the political development of this remote branch of the British empire when the Australian colonies were granted representative government and given "free play to the[ir] growing democratic spirit" (Jenks, 1895, p. 162). The legislatures were expanded and given wider lawmaking powers and control over public finances of the colony (Lumb, 1965, p. 15). In 1850 the representative element in government was further enhanced in all the colonies except Western Australia. Port Phillip was separated from New South Wales, becoming a fully fledged colony, Victoria. As in other colonies, it now had a Legislative Council with two-thirds elected and one-third nominated members (Melbourne, 1963, pp. 376–380; Clarke, 1963, p. 106).

By 1855, all the colonial bureaucracies had grown enormously. This was particularly true for New South Wales [3]. The Colonial Office laid down new rules of recruitment that defined the process of appointing different categories of public servants in all colonies. Governors were empowered to fill lower ranks subject to confirmation, while the Colonial Office retained the authority to appoint higher officials. The essence of the new scheme was that the distribution of patronage was no longer the sole privilege of the Colonial Office and that governors could consider the claims of colonists for administrative positions. Promotions, as before, were to depend on merit rather than seniority alone (New South Wales, 1847, p. 607; McMartin, 1983, pp. 246–247).

Other rules streamlined conditions of service and the conduct of public servants. Duration of leave was curtailed and public servants were debarred from holding a seat in the legislature except by nomination. Stringent rules were also applied to stop embezzlement (Watson, 1922, vol. 22, p. 731; vol. 24, pp. 162–163, 635). The new regulations, even if rudimentary, sought to regularize public personnel administration of the colonies as early as 1842. It was a great step forward in administrative reform. But in actual practice, seldom were the rules followed.

In New South Wales, recruitment examinations were conducted by a board consisting of the clerk of the Executive Council, the auditor general, and the head of the department in which the position was to be filled. These examinations were designed to assess candidates' ability in handwriting, composition, arithmetic, orthography, and speed (New South Wales, 1872, p. 653).

A. Victoria: The Impact of the Economic Crisis

In Victoria, Charles Hotham, LaTrobe's successor, was bent upon improving the quality of administration even if that meant attacking "uneasy and discontented" public servants. The economic crisis of the early 1850s had important implications for public administration. Many departments were hard hit after the exodus of a large number of public servants to the goldfields. It became difficult for the government to manage the expanding affairs of the colony with the remaining personnel, who were either inexperienced or of poor quality. Those inducted from other colonies turned out to be novices or mediocre in clerical or other skills (Blair, 1879, p. 436; Serle, 1963, p. 143).

In spite of this exodus, the government adopted a policy of thorough retrenchment and stringent economy in administration to get over the impact of the crisis. The number of public servants was reduced by 16% and the total cost of running departments was slashed by over 26%. Many positions were either wholly abolished or merged with others. The Goldfields Commission, the most notorious of the departments, was reformed, and incompetent and corrupt officers were removed (Victoria, 1856–1857; Serle, 1963, p. 116). But overall, the situation in the bureaucracy was not markedly improved. The average public servant was obsessed with the performance of routine work and lacked initiative and drive, and "public interest" was said to be compromised at the alter of neglect, delay, and inefficiency. The organization of personnel in departments featured many inconsistencies and haphazard arrangements (*Weekly Herald*, 1856).

B. Tasmania: Attempts at Reform

Tasmania made a serious bid to reform its bureaucracy in the early 1850s and place it on a sounder basis. The 1851 Board of Classification of Clerks recommended the formulation of fixed rules of recruitment, promotion, salary increments, and retiring allowances. It proposed a fourfold vertical classification of the clerical staff—each with a fixed salary scale with annual increases and special bonuses for length of service. The board stressed the importance of a sound recruitment and promotion system so that "good and efficient officers may be secured" (Tasmania, 1852, p. 1). It proposed the appointment of a permanent committee of three members to superintend the recruitment and promotion processes. It was to conduct examinations to assess the capabilities of candidates, consider promotions, and adjudge the relative merit of candidates. This was the first time in Australia that some kind of central personnel authority had been envisaged in public administration and the idea even preceded the Northcote-Trevelyan proposals in Britain. The idea was in advance of its times and, understandably, was not adopted.

However, the recruitment of personnel in England was questioned by colonials on the ground that the system operated "injuriously and unsatisfactorily." On the other hand, they emphasized the appointment of locals (Tasmania, 1855, p. 160).

C. South Australia: Statutory Regulation of the Service

In 1852, South Australia became the first colony to enact public service legislation in Australia. On the recommendations of a Select Committee of the Legislative Council, the threefold classification introduced by Colonial Office regulations was retained. Entry into the service was to be through noncompetitive examinations to be conducted by a Board of Examiners. Advancement within a class was to be by seniority; promotion between classes, by merit (South Australia, 1852). Two years later, a superannuation scheme based on voluntary contribution and supplemented by government grant was established (South Australia, 1854). Other regulations debarred public servants from taking part in active politics or from openly criticizing governmental measures.

These statutory measures, however, could not improve the overall situation in public administration. The 1852 Act had its weaknesses; its application was limited to only a small number of public servants and salaries were not based on the importance of positions. Personal connection rather than merit influenced the recruitment process. Low salaries and insecure tenure led to alleged "slothfulness, inefficiency, cost and arrogance" among public servants (Hawker, 1967, pp. 67, 75, 88, 93–94; South Australia, 1855–1856).

IV. CONCLUSION

By the time responsible government was launched in 1855–1856, most of the Australian colonies had established administrative systems in operation. But personnel practices were not elaborately or even clearly defined in all. Molded to serve near-autocratic executives, the colonial bureaucracies had been administered without uniform rules or regulations. Each department was shielded from the others with its distinctive structural and personnel management patterns. The volume and nature of work performed by departments did not always justify costs, and performance was not in accord with the number of personnel.

Frauds and errors in financial administration were common even though a variety of methods were utilized to help in their detection. The centralized administrative structure, with all coordinating and some supervisory powers concentrated in the Colonial Secretary's Office in all colonies, created more problems than it solved; the result was procrastination in administration. Because of the short supply of competent personnel, pluralism, or the practice of appointing one person to several positions, flourished at all levels of administration.

The terms and conditions of service in public employment were much more liberal than those in private organizations; office hours were more flexible, tenure was comparatively secure, and retirement from service was normally accompanied by a healthy pension. But salaries were low. Political patronage often led to the appointment and promotion of poor calibre people, but, of course, there were exceptions. Some of those appointed on patronage turned out to be exceptionally gifted in the art of administration and helped establish the foundations of administrative systems upon which the superstructures were to be built later in the century.

NOTES

1. This section draws primarily from McMartin (1883), Cell (1970), Bladden (1898), Jenks (1895), and Watson (1922).
2. By 1817, there were eight on the establishment including the Secretary. Bigge Papers, appendix.
3. From 169 in 1806, it increased to 1760 in 1842 to 2581 in 1855; the number of departments increased from 9 to 31 in almost fifty years. McMartin (1983, appendix I, pp. 293–294).

REFERENCES

Allen, J., *History of Australia 1787 to 1882*, Mason, Firth and M'Cutcheon, Melbourne, 1882.

AONSW Colonial Secretary's Memorandum, May 21, 1831; Governor's Minute, October 10, 1827, 4/991. CSSB/2/1844.

Arthur Papers, Mitchell Library, A2164.

Barton, G. B., *History of New South Wales: Governor Phillip*, vol. 1, Government Printer, Sydney, 1889.

Battye, J. S., *Western Australia: A History from its Discovery to the Inauguration of the Commonwealth*, Facsimile ed., University of Western Australia Press, Nedlands, 1978.

Bigge Papers, Mitchell Library, Box 27, 6630.

Blackett, J., *History of South Australia*, Hussey and Gillingham, Adelaide, 1911.

Bladden, F. M., ed., *Historical Records of New South Wales*, Sydney, n.d.

Blair, D., *The History of Australasia*, McGready, Thomas and Niven, Glasgow, 1879.

British Parliament, *Papers: Colonies: Australia*, Vol. 3, No. 4, 1816–1830.

British Parliament, An Act to Empower His Majesty to Erect South Australia into a British Province or Provinces and to Provide for the Colonisation and Government Thereof. 4 and 5 William No. 4, 1834.

Bryan, C. and Bray, F. I., Peter Nicholas Brown: First Colonial Secretary of Western Australia, *Western Australian Historical Society Journal, 2*(18) (1935).

Burges, H. T., ed., *The Cyclopedia of South Australia*, Cyclopedia, Adelaide, 1907.

Calder, J. E., A Sketch of the Public Service: Fifty Years Ago, in *Scraps of Tasmanian History* (D. A. Davie, ed.), part 1, Calder, Hobart, 1975.

Cell, J. W., *British Colonial Administration in the Mid-Nineteenth Century: The Policy Making Process*, Yale University Press, New Haven, 1970.

Clarke, C. M. H., *A Short History of Australia*, New American Library, New York, 1963.

Crowley, F. K., *A Short History of Western Australia*, Macmillan, Melbourne, 1959.

Crowley, F. K., *Australia's Western Third: A History of Western Australia from the First Settlements to Modern Times*, Macmillan, London, 1960.

CSAWA, *Civil Service Journal*, Civil Service Association of Western Australia, Centenary Number, vol. 19, 1929.

Eddy, J. J., *Britain and the Australian Colonies, 1818–1831: The Technique of Government*, Clarendon, Oxford, 1969.

Ellis, M. H., Some Aspects of the Bigge Commission of Inquiry into the Affairs of New South Wales, 1819–1821, *Royal Australian Historical Society Journal [RAHSJ], 27*(2) (1941).

Fenton, J., *History of Tasmania*, J. Walch, Hobart, 1884.

Forsyth, W. D., *Governor Arthur's Convict System: Van Dieman's Land 1824–36*, Sydney University Press, Sydney, 1970.

Frost, A., *Convicts and Empire*, Oxford University Press, Melbourne, 1980.

Gross, A., *Charles Joseph LaTrobe*, Melbourne University Press, Melbourne, 1965.

Hawker, G. N., The Development of the South Australian Civil Service, 1836–1916, unpublished PhD Thesis, Australian National University, 1967.

Jenks, E., *History of the Australasian Colonies*, Cambridge University Press, Cambridge, 1895.

Jervis, J., Notes. *RAHSJ 38*(3) (1952).

Lumb, R. D., *The Constitutions of the Australian States*, 4th ed., University of Queensland Press, St. Lucia, 1965.

Martin, G., ed., *The Founding of Australia*, Hale and Iremonger, Sydney, 1978.

McMartin, A., The Payment of Officials in Early Australia, *Public Administration 17*(1) (1958a).

McMartin, A., The Treasury in New South Wales, 1786–1836, *Public Administration 17*(3) (1958b).

McMartin, A., Aspects of Patronage in Australia, 1786–1836, *Public Administration 18*(4) (1959).

McMartin, A., *Public Servants and Patronage*, Sydney University Press, Sydney, 1983.

Melbourne, A. C. V., *Early Constitutional Development in Australia: New South Wales 1788–1856*, University of Queensland Press, St. Lucia, 1963.

Melville, H., *The History of Van Dieman's Land, 1824–35*, Reprint, Horwitz-Grahame, Sydney, 1959.

Meston, A. L., The Growth of Self-Government in Tasmania, *Papers and Proceedings of the Royal Society of Tasmania*, (1927).

New South Wales, *Legislative Council Votes and Proceedings*, vol. 1, (1847).

New South Wales, Minutes of Evidence, Report of the SC on the Civil Service, *Legislative Assembly Votes and Proceedings*, vol. 1, 1872.

O'Brien, E., The Coming of the British to Australia, 1770–1821, in *Australia* (C. H. Grattan, ed.), University of California Press, Berkeley, 1947.

Phillips, M., *A Colonial Autocracy: New South Wales Under Governor Macquarie, 1810–1821*, Sydney University Press, Sydney, 1971.

Pike, D., *Paradise of Dissent: South Australia 1829–1857*, Melbourne University Press, Melbourne, 1967.

Price, A. G., *The Foundation and Settlement of South Australia, 1829–1845*, F. W. Preece, Adelaide, 1924.

Quick, J. and Garran, R. R., *The Annotated Constitution of the Commonwealth of Australia*, Angus and Robertson, Sydney, 1901.

Richardson, G. D., The Archives of the Colonial Secretary's Department of New South Wales, 1788–1856, M.A. Thesis, University of Sydney, 1951.

Ritchie, J., *Punishment and Profit*, Heinemann, Melbourne, 1970.

Rose, L. N., The Administration of Governor Darling, *RAHSJ 8*(2) (1922).

SAA, *Correspondence Book*, vol. 1, South Australian Archives, 1839.

SAA, Research Notes, The Civil Service in the Early Days, No. 108, South Australian Archives.

Serle, G., *The Golden Age: A History of the Colony of Victoria 1851–1861*, Melbourne University Press, Melbourne, 1963.

South Australia, An Act to Regulate the Salaries of Certain Clerks and Subordinate Officers of the Crown in South Australia, Act No. 9, 1852.

South Australia, An Act to Provide for the Retirement of Officers in the Civil Service, Act No. 21, 1854.

South Australia, Fifth Report of the SC on the Estimates, *Parliamentary Papers*, No. 158, 1855–1856.

Tasmania, Report of the Board on Classification of Clerks, *Legislative Council Votes and Proceedings*, No. 31, 1852.

Tasmania, Petition from the Public Service, *Legislative Council Votes and Proceedings*, First Session, 1855.

Townsley, W. A., *The Struggle for Self-Government in Tasmania, 1842–1856*, Government Printer, Hobart, 1951.

Turner, H. G., *A History of the Colony of Victoria from Its Discovery to Its Absorption into the Commonwealth of Australia*, vol. 1, Facsimile ed., Heritage, Melbourne, 1973.

Victoria, The Civil Service, *Victorian Parliamentary Papers*, vol. 2, No. C48, 1856–1857.

Watson, F., ed., *Historical Records of Australia*, Multiple Series/Volumes, Commonwealth Parliament, 1922.

Weekly Herald, July 11, 1856.

West, J., *The History of Tasmania*, vol. 1, Henry Dowling, Launceston, 1852.

Wettenhall, R. L., The Introduction of Public Administration into Van Dieman's Land, part 1, *Tasmanian Historical Research Association Papers and Proceedings, 7*(3) (1959).

Wettenhall, R. L., *Evolution of a Departmental System: A Tasmanian Commentary*, University of Tasmania, Hobart, 1967.

36
Political and Managerial Reform in a Small State: The Relevance of the 1980s

John Halligan
University of Canberra, Belconnen, Australia

The last two decades have been a period of intensive change in the public administrations of many countries. This period is differentiated from earlier decades by the pace and extent of change. Where once change was seen as incremental, piecemeal, and possibly of marginal or mixed impact, now it had become systemic, comprehensive, and sustained. Among those countries subject to reform, the relative significance and the overall intensity of change have varied. Some have been subject to protracted periods of experimentation, while others have experienced abrupt shifts in direction.

Two primary themes in these changes have centered on relationship between politicians and bureaucrats on the one hand and changes to the content and character of bureaucratic work on the other [1]. The first type of change essentially concerned the distribution of power within executive branches. They had become dominated by the bureaucracy for reasons that have been well documented, one popular characterization being that of the administrative state. In response to this condition and other pressures on government, political executives in recent decades sought to reassert themselves and to readjust their relationship with bureaucrats. The second trend is essentially about the content of and orientation toward bureaucratic work. There has been a marked swing to "management" internationally. This has been most explicit in countries where there has been an abrupt move from administration to management, but is evident in a range of countries which have been giving greater attention to management (Caiden, 1991).

A number of factors can be linked to reform (Garnett, 1980); fiscal conditions in particular assume greater prominence in the 1980s. The focus of this chapter is on the relationship between political and managerial factors. While there have been numerous studies of either political or managerial change, the combination of the two has not been carefully addressed. Of particular

An earlier version of this paper was presented to the session "Understanding Governance: The Work of the Eighties Reviewed," International Political Science Association XV World Congress, Buenos Aires, July 21–25, 1991. Ian Beckett, Center for Research in Public Sector Management, University of Canberra, assisted with the analysis of managerial and political change in other countries.

interest is thc relationship between the two types of change. The argument is that there are lessons to be learned from studying the interaction between the two and the actual mix of reforms.

In exploring these matters, there are two objectives: to consider how the two types of change are manifested and related in several countries, and to examine these questions more closely by considering whether one nation's experience, that of Australia, can illuminate the international experience. The chapter first reviews the literature in the light of the interests identified here. Political change is then examined in several countries as a prelude to the case study. This is followed by a comparison of the interaction between political and managerial change in several systems. The conclusions reflect on research agendas for the 1990s, bearing in mind the international experience of administrative reform in the 1980s.

I. STUDYING REFORM

How has the literature recognized these themes in administrative reform? The voluminous literature can be organized according to four broad categories: reviews of reform, analyses of either political *or* managerial change, and broader studies which encompass both. A number of studies of administrative reform in specific countries consider the political and managerial changes as part of more general reviews (Benda and Levine, 1988; Mascarenhas, 1990). There have been a few studies which address directly both political and managerial dimensions (Aucoin, 1990; Halligan and Power, 1992) (although other work has examined political and managerial traditions and approaches, e.g., Rosenbloom and Goldman, 1989; Halligan and Power, 1991). Much of the literature is otherwise compartmentalized, reflecting the inclination for specialist study of either political or managerial changes within executive branches.

Research on political change has concentrated on the interaction between politicians and bureaucrats (Aberbach et al., 1981; Peters, 1987). The major work on political-bureaucratic relations (Aberbach and Rockman, 1988a, p. 3; Aberbach et al., 1981) points to the historical dimension of changing bureaucratic and political roles. The convergence of political and bureaucratic roles featured in this work is one of the factors which have prompted politicians to seek a redefinition of the relationship with civil servants. Campbell (1988) recognizes such "counterweights" in his analysis of "three types of politically oriented officials."

The bureaucrat has also been depicted as unlikely to advocate major reform. The traditional conception of the bureaucrat was of the administrator who played a relatively passive role, in contrast to the proactive manager (Keeling, 1972). It was argued that "a preference for the quiet life . . . biases administrative decision making against radical change" and that "reactive and incremental rather than active policy" is more likely to result from behavior which emphasizes conciliation and consensus (Aberbach et al., 1981, pp. 13–14).

For whatever reason, research has indicated that new techniques and cultures have been introduced in order to expand political control over bureaucrats (Halligan and Power, 1992; Radin and Coffee, forthcoming).

There is also a separate literature on managerialism, although less readily discernible in the 1980s, with a few notable exceptions (Aucoin, 1988a; Metcalfe and Richards, 1987). The coverage of managerial change has since expanded greatly (e.g., the special issue of *Governance*, April 1990; Pollitt, 1990; Massey, 1992). The latter two works treat managerialism in the United States and United Kingdom, but ignore the interesting comparisons to be made with Australia and New Zealand, studies of which have been confined to a few writers, notably Hood (1990).

Managerialism has been the dominant feature of reform in a number of countries during the last decade. Aucoin captures a widely held conception that "managerialism, in contrast to the traditional bureaucratic ideal of 'administration', has developed in the public sector for the same reasons it has in the private sector, namely an increased concern with 'results', 'performance' and 'outcomes' " (1988a, p. 152; see also Halligan and Power, 1992; Peters, 1991). It has been manifested in different ways. In the United States, management has traditionally played a more distinctive role: "The managerialist ideology had long occupied a more prominent and accepted place in American than in British life" (Pollitt, 1990, p. 109). There were nevertheless important developments in the United States during the 1980s which Pollitt has treated as managerialist, but the major shift in orientation experienced by some executive branches was less apparent there. Its neighbor, Canada, also has long experience of management, which it has been developing since the Royal Commission on Government Organization (1962), although progress has been uneven. In contrast, in Australia, New Zealand and the United Kingdom, managerial change only surfaced in the 1980s, and received confirmation as significant in the second half of the decade [2].

Managerialism has received greatest acceptance in countries which have been subject to a distinctive change of direction (viz., Australia, New Zealand, and the United Kingdom), although it has received broad recognition elsewhere (e.g., Aucoin, 1990; Kooiman and Eliassen, 1987; Peters, 1991, pp. 393–394). Where its impact has been pronounced references have been made to new paradigms and to a watershed in public management (Aucoin, 1990; Power, 1990).

Studies that are more broadly or systematically cross-national and comparative may include classifications of reforms and general analyses which seek to develop propositions about reform (Caiden, 1991; Peters, 1991; Rowat, 1988; Olsen, 1988, 1991; March and Olsen, 1989). The conditions for change have not yet been well addressed in the literature. There is an extensive literature documenting the problems encountered in implementing reform in the past (Caiden, 1991; March and Olsen, 1989). Two central issues concern the scale of change and the basis of political changes in executive branches. Aucoin comes close to anticipating the linkage with managerial change by differentiating a "set of ideas" concerned with "the need to reestablish the primacy of representative government over bureaucracy" (1990, p. 115). He prefers to ground this directly in public choice theory, although it is not difficult to trace a history of experiments with reasserting the authority of the political executive (either the president or prime minister and cabinet) which predate the discovery of public choice in countries where it has been influential. Halligan and Power (1992) have argued that the intervention of the political executive is necessary where there is an attempt to effect major change (cf. also Hall, 1993).

II. POLITICAL CHANGE INTERNATIONALLY

Internationally, politicians have been seeking to regain or to extend their control of the bureaucracy in recent decades (Suleiman, 1985). This has involved redistributing power within the executive branch. As political executives experimented with various strategies for influencing the bureaucracy, an extended process of change often resulted. A number of countries experienced political change during the 1970s and 1980; two examples will suffice to illustrate.

In the United States, a number of developments from Nixon's term on assisted in enhancing the role of the presidency. For example, Carter's Civil Service Reform Act of 1978 was an important legislative lever for increasing the President's influence over personnel policy. It was not, however, until Reagan's time that the "centralization of executive decision making" and the "administrative presidency" were employed to best effect as part of a governance strategy (Hansen and Levine, 1988, p. 265). Benda and Levine observe, "The Reagan administration pursued a campaign to maximize presidential control over the federal bureaucracy that was more *self-conscious* in design and execution, and more *comprehensive* in scope, than that of any other administration of the modern era" (1988, p. 102). Of particular importance to these presidents was control over appointments (Benda and Levine, 1988, pp. 106, 108).

The United Kingdom is of particular interest because of the close link between political and managerial change. Prior to the election of Thatcher in 1979 there were a number of attempts to enlarge the influence of the political executive. It was not, however, until Thatcher exercised her authority over appointments and promoted management reforms for changing the Whitehall culture that it could be said that the political executive was beginning to regain the initiative. By the mid-1980s, Thatcher could be said to have had an impact which was associated with a general transformation of Whitehall culture in a managerialist direction.

A range of techniques and strategies have been employed for effecting a redistribution of power. These extend to undermining the bureaucracy and promoting political roles. They commonly focus on exercising influence over policymaking and the distribution of appointments. At the risk of oversimplification the tactics can be grouped under three headings: those which concentrate on demeaning the public relative to the private sector; those which focus on countering the influence of the public service by augmenting the resources of the politicians; and those concerned with seeking to control and direct the public service. In each case it is possible to distinguish a spectrum of responses.

The first approach has been the reevaluation of the worth and efficiency of the public service in terms of the private sector. A variety of behavior is apparent, ranging from favoring private sector techniques to favoring the private sector. At best the virtues of the private sector are extolled as part of a process of exhorting the bureaucracy to improve its performance and change its culture. At its crudest it simply involves public service bashing (e.g., Hennessy, 1988; Campbell, 1988; Levine, 1988).

The second set of tactics involves countering bureaucratic influence with political resources. There is a well-established tradition in some European countries of providing the political executive with special resources in the form of staff, the well-known examples being those of France and Germany. Other countries have adopted this type of practice by appointing new units or advisers to assist ministers. In Canada, for example, Mulroney augmented the resources of his personal office (Aucoin, 1988b). The Wilson Labour government regularized the practice of appointing advisers drawn from outside Whitehall, each cabinet minister being permitted to employ two "special advisers" who were to serve as temporary civil servants for the duration of the government (Hennessy, 1989, pp. 172–175, 188, 189). Under Health the Central Policy Review Staff (CPRS) was established as a nonpartisan organization which also offered a potentially centralizing influence. The Wilson government also established a Downing Street Policy Unit (Plowden, 1991). Australia has also concentrated on this route as a means for redistributing power within the executive branch. The important differences between systems revolve around the extent to which career civil servants are used instead of partisans.

The third type of technique is concerned with directly changing and controlling the public service. An array of administrative and statutory mechanisms have been developed to control the bureaucracy (Wilenski, 1986). Of particular importance has been the need to assume direction of policymaking and the role of the political executive in appointing top civil servants.

There is a consistent pattern in Westminster-derived systems of the political executive seeking top civil servants who will be responsive to its requirements. Mrs. Thatcher's intervention in the appointment of senior civil servants is well known. The Canadian political executive has also relied increasingly on being able to appoint preferred candidates from the civil service. There may also be more scope for appointing outsiders to senior positions (Bourgault and Dion, 1989, p. 127; Hennessy, 1988, pp. 190–191).

Studies of partisanship (Aberbach and Rockman's continuing work on senior officials in the U.S. civil service, 1988b) and the growing politicization in Germany offer insights into systems which have taken a different approach to influencing the bureaucracy. In some cases, countries which have already exhibited a considerable degree of politicization have become more politicized. As Derlien describes the German situation:

> Politicians have become more conscious of the political roles played by the civil service elite. More and more they tailor their patronage according to the limits set by existing statutes and conditions. They do so not in order to bring about a specific role understanding, but to reinforce civil servants' commitments to government policy. (Derlien, 1988, p. 76)

The response has been to extend further the level of partisanship among civil servants. Mayntz and Derlien comment, "The top civil service of the German Federal Republic has become steadily more politicized—in terms of a growing share of party members, and of the increasing importance of party membership for recruitment to top positions" (Mayntz and Derlien, 1989, p. 400).

III. A CASE STUDY IN POLITICAL CHANGE

The Australian case is of interest because there was an explicit phase of experimentation extending over fifteen years and the processes involved were rather more subtle if no less effective than some of the better-known international examples (Halligan and Power, 1992). The case first illustrates the choice made between two alternative paths to political control. The changes over the period are then grouped according to whether they directly enhanced the political executive or diminished the role of the senior public service, including by managerializing the public service (but note that there is some overlap between the two).

A. Use of Appointees

The key question was whether a partisan advisory structure—one that was based outside the bureaucracy—should be relied upon or whether it should extend into the bureaucracy, perhaps even forming, in the American style, the upper level of the departmental hierarchy.

A key advisor to Labor governments and disseminator of North American ideas within Australia, Peter Wilenski, has argued the need to reestablish ministerial control and increase responsiveness—an American concept—to government policies and priorities. This was part of a political framework which promised to increase "democracy"—by allowing the minister to have greater influence—and by expanding the accessibility and diversity of the public service and diminishing the role of the public servant. The essence of the argument was that the top positions were already politicized because the incumbents were involved in political decision making and a number of senior appointments were subject to political influences. Accordingly the role of public servants should be recognized by moving from covert to overt political appointments. Wilenski became the primary advocate of "a far more radical step . . . a move towards the United States system"—the appointment of senior public servants by the government (Wilenski, 1980, pp. 27–28; Wilenski, 1986).

This type of advice was influential in the framing of the Labor Party's 1983 election platform, with which it won government. The platform proposed a special division that would comprise all departmental heads (who made up the first division) and up to 5% of the second division. The appointments would be made by cabinet on the recommendation of individual ministers. In essence this scheme represented the most significant challenge to the tradition of public service neutrality since the formation of the federal government. The formulation specifically sought to place the control of policy direction in the hands of political appointees within the public service. It also meant a departure from the emerging convention, which was to develop the minister's office. Subsequently, the government chose not to take this path.

B. Enhancing the Political Executive

There was no simple linear process by which the political executives extended its influence; it involved oscillations as initiatives were successful or failed. At times it resembled a see-saw, as senior public servants and politicians skirmished over zones of influence. At stake was power at several levels. Of great importance was control over policy development, and to a lesser extent its implementation. It also extended to control over processes, such as coordination of policy and strategic direction, the budget, internal operations within departments, and external relationships. The extent to which each department was impregnable to, and independent of, "political" (i.e., partisan) influences was also contested.

For the purposes of this analysis three major areas of enhancing the political executive are discussed: the capacity and resources of the center—the prime minister and cabinet—and its effectiveness in establishing policy directions and priorities; ministerial resources, policy role, and departmental role; and the role of political appointments (Halligan and Power, 1992).

The effectiveness of the center in establishing policy directions and priorities for government was the first major area of change, and one which was to become more important as the complexity of government increased and the demands on it multiplied. The government's ability to determine political direction and priorities depends on its ability to function collectively, its organizational capacity, and the resources and the style of the prime minister (Campbell and Halligan, 1992a).

The consolidation of the public service and the reorientation of the government's priorities culminated in a set of far-reaching decisions following the 1987 election. The prime minister's capacity to influence the party's role in ministry making was enhanced by his third election win. He instigated a major reorganization of government (Halligan, 1987), the significance of which derived from the combination of administrative reorganization with major restructuring of the political executive. A new two-tier cabinet system ensured that all departmental interests had some representation through the portfolio minister but that tighter integration of the public service would also result.

Hawke entrusted substantial responsibility to cabinet ministers, while maintaining control over the direction of government through the cabinet system. His central agency, the Department of Prime Minister and Cabinet, became the center of a pattern of influence based on advice to the prime minister and a network of its emissaries distributed throughout the public service. The department was now the main source of top appointments in the public service, as a number of recent appointees reflected the "can do" philosophy that was highly compatible with top-down political management. It also maintained an important steering role over the public service (Campbell and Halligan, 1992b).

The second area was that of ministerial resources and policy roles. The ministerial adviser had been one of the most prominent additions to the executive branch over the last two decades. The political executive used advisers to increase its power by extending the scope of influence of the ministerial office. This might involve simply buttressing the minister's zone of influence by expanding his/her partisan penumbra. It commonly involved using partisans instead of bureaucrats for particular governmental processes, either those which operated on the margins of departments or as the gatekeeper for communications between ministers and bureaucracy. The ministerial adviser had been the primary mechanism for introducing a stronger partisan influence into the executive. This has been more pronounced with the Australian Labor Party because ministers had often favored persons who belong to the party.

The adviser could exercise a major influence on policy processes—if not necessarily on policy content—and this was important for providing a minister with the means for sustaining his or her authority. In terms of the redistribution of power between political and administrative systems, other considerations were important. By replacing bureaucrats as advisers in ministers' offices [3], they reduced the potential influence of the public service; by assuming responsibility for many of the political and policy processes that may have been conducted by public servants, they reduced the latter's role; by maintaining a political presence in departments and acting as the main communication link with the minister and other institutions, they contributed to the breakdown of barriers around departments and their autonomy.

The third area was that of appointments within the bureaucracy. Ministers have had the constitutional right to make departmental decisions, but in practice had left this to the old permanent heads. In recent times ministers have asserted their right to be directly involved in departmental administration. The appointment of senior officials was now influenced to a greater extent by the political executive. The preferences of ministers for senior staff might extend to positions within the Senior Executive Service as low as branch head.

Ministers can exercise considerable influence over senior appointments, but the extent to which this results in political appointments remains unclear, for the processes involved are subtle. Political appointments have extended to introducing partisans into the bureaucracy itself, the most celebrated examples occurring under a Labor government in the 1970s. The placement of partisans in strategic positions may occur, but ministers have not been prepared to engage in overt appointments. Despite intermittent public debate about politicization of the senior public service, there is little evidence to suggest that extensive use has been made of political appointments under Hawke. This may well derive from the realization that the political executive can command without resorting to extensive use of such appointments. In the early 1990s, all departmental secretaries and most members of the Senior Executive Service have been career public servants.

C. Dismantling the Mandarinate

The senior public service was widely perceived as being too elitist and insufficiently responsive. Hence the Royal Commission's proposition that the senior officialdom believes "that, independently of Parliament or the government, it is the guardian of 'the public interest' as opposed to sectional or vested interest, of continuity and stability in government administration, and of assumed social consensus about certain basic 'supra-political' values" (RCAGA, 1976, pp. 18–19). At least five types of measure have reduced the influence of senior public servants. Most have been introduced by the Labor government since 1983.

The first was to diminish their policy autonomy. At one time the senior public service had considerable independence in the policy process, often approaching that of a monopoly. In recent times, alternative sources of advice and assistance were increasingly relied upon by ministers. Ministerial staff served both as policy advisers and conduits for extragovernment policy proposals. Over time, the policy capacity of the ministerial office was strengthened. Policy became much more of a top-down process; the political directions emanated from cabinet, and the minister's office, not the department, was commonly the pivotal actor in the process.

A second method was to change the work of the senior public servant. The work assumed a greater managerial focus, reflecting the preference of the political executive for a public service which concentrated on achieving its objectives. In addition, the entry of new participants, specifically those sporting the imprimatur of ministers, meant that the role of the senior public servant became more limited. In a number of important respects the field has shrunk for senior public servants; the range of processes in which they participate has contracted. The "political" dimensions of the work, in particular, became less salient. The communications between minister and department were no longer shaped by public servants but by ministerial advisers as well. The relationships with interest groups were more circumscribed, and perhaps mediated by ministerial advisers.

A third tactic was to reduce the career autonomy of the senior public servant. Traditionally senior public servants had been part of the career system which enshrined permanency within the public service. An important means for expanding the influence of the political executive was to weaken and transform the officials' position. By altering the tenure of senior officials it was thought that a leveling process occurred, producing greater responsiveness. Two considerations were particularly important: altering the tenure of public servants (i.e., abolishing permanency) and providing for greater competition by increasing the opportunities for external entry. The notion of permanence was removed by redesignating the head of department as the departmental secretary and providing for fixed term appointments of up to five years. Otherwise secretaries of departments were to be subject to quinquennial reviews and to rotation among top positions.

The other break with the past was the abolition of the second division and what it represented. A Senior Executive Service (SES) was established in 1984 (Halligan, 1992); a central objective was that senior positions in the public service were to become more open and competitive by inviting applicants from within and outside the Australian public service to apply for all vacancies in the SES. A particular goal was to inject persons from the private sector into the public service. To facilitate the entry of outsiders, the opportunity for fixed-term engagements was provided. An important tactic for changing the traditional system then was to introduce new personnel by making lateral appointments to the public service.

New policies and procedures for handling displacement, redeployment, and retrenchment provided the basis of the fourth means for changing the bureaucracy. The Senior Executive Service was to operate as a servicewide, corporate entity. At this system level the quality of public service management was to be enhanced by greater movement of senior managers within the service. At the departmental level, there was to be greater opportunity for deploying senior staff. Under amended legislation there were greater powers to reduce the classification of inefficient staff and to retire an officer from the service because of inadequate performance. Another line of attack focused on promotions and promotion procedures. Appeals against promotions within the Senior Executive Service and upper middle management positions were abolished because such a right was regarded as inappropriate for managerial positions.

Reorganization provided the basis for further pressures on the senior service. By the middle of its second term, the Hawke government had its own appointees in most departments, although they were generally from within the Australian public service. With its extensive reorganization in July 1987, the political executive had the opportunity to appoint all department heads, thereby consummating the move toward firm control of senior appointments, and unequivocally demonstrating its preponderant position. Even though existing departmental secretaries were reappointed to the majority of the departments, the new structure in the government was able to exercise its judgment about all positions at the one time.

The impact at the senior executive level was immense. The 1987 reorganization reduced the number of departments and the new "megadepartments" required new senior management structures and fewer senior staff. Most departments were experiencing some form of reconstitution at the senior level as they sought to reflect new program and corporate structures in accordance with government objectives and cut-backs in staff numbers. Over the next three years 177 members of the Senior Executive Service who could not be located elsewhere within the service were retrenched. For these reasons the senior public service was under immense pressure to conform and adapt to the new managerial culture.

IV. RELATIONSHIP BETWEEN POLITICAL AND MANAGERIAL CHANGE

What is the relationship between political and managerial change in executive branches? Of particular interest here is the extent to which political change is a prerequisite for managerial reform [4]. The intervention of the political executive is essential for major reform to be implemented. Political change must necessarily precede other types of change (although the two may interact). An extension of this is that for managerial change to be sustained, a measure of longevity in office is required as well as a continuing commitment to reform. Also relevant is whether there is a relationship between the nature of the reform process and the reforms.

A. A Sequential Case

The Australian case is interesting because of how political and managerial changes were combined at one time and interacted in the process of reform. During the last two decades, there were two broad processes of change, one of which was first apparent in the 1970s but only achieved its greatest impact when linked with the other in the 1980s. The 1970s was essentially about political ascendancy over the bureaucracy, while the 1980s primarily concerned implanting the managerialist approach. In the 1970s politicians were confronting their relationship with the bureaucracy and the general condition of the public sector (e.g., large and overloaded). It was a period of experimentation with different mechanisms which facilitated the ascendancy of the political executive and its control of the public service. In the 1980s the focus broadened. The second stage involved the political executive becoming preoccupied with strengthening management in executive branches. But this was achieved by what has been termed political management: a combination of the political and managerial (Halligan and Power, 1991, 1992).

In the 1970s the reaction was to challenge the public servants' monopoly over advice to ministers and to question their indispensability to the processes of government. A number of initiatives were experimented with as they sought to strengthen the political executive. The result was a set of political mechanisms for influencing and directing the public service, as described previously, and which included improved capacity to set central directions and priorities, an expansion in the resources available to ministers, and more effective and diverse external policy advice. There were, however, limitations on the utility of these devices, and there were large gaps in the arrays of mechanisms. This enhancement of the political executive proceeded through several stages in the seventies and early eighties, as regimes at both the state and national levels experimented with flexing political muscles, before finally moving into a new phase in the 1980s when they embraced managerialist approaches to enforcing and maintaining control.

In the 1980s the focus broadened. In the second stage the political executive became preoccupied with strengthening management in the public service. The new framework was based on a coalition between political and management approaches. Although the piecemeal infiltration of managerial ideas had been occurring for some time, what was strikingly different was that managerial change was now seen in systemic and strategic terms.

Government of the 1980s benefited from the experimentation with various mechanisms for asserting the role of the political executive that had occurred in the 1970s. A range of tested political methods were now available and, providing they were effectively packaged, could serve to achieve political control of the executive branch. With the initial successes of state Labor governments in combining political reconstruction with managerialism in the early 1980s, an attractive model was available to a new Labor government in 1983. The managerial approach was crystallized as consensus rapidly emerged about the deficiencies of the public service. The intensification of fiscal austerity produced a need for tighter resource use which could not be satisfied by the process-oriented traditional approach.

A bipartisan view emerged that the management skills of the senior public service were both deficient and undervalued relative to policy and administrative skills. In addition, the emerging orthodoxy among many public administrators was that managerial approaches should be adopted. There were growing pressures within the public service for managers to have greater freedom from procedural constraints and for departments to be able to manage more independently of central agencies. These sentiments were reflected in various reports which saw the need to refashion the federal public service to reflect private sector modes of operating and to give prominence to management skills.

After its election in 1983, the Hawke Labor government accelerated the introduction of managerialism because it complemented its political agenda. Managerialism offered both a new approach for directing the public service and a rationalization for exerting greater ministerial control. The transformation of the public service to one in which management rather than administration supplied the official paradigm finally proceeded.

B. Other Sequences

In the Australian case there was a clear sequence in the phases: the political preceded and overlapped with the managerial, but the combination of the two was essential to ensure success. How does this compare with other countries? To what extent are there distinctive sequences?

The United Kingdom provides the closest pattern. There was early experimentation with various mechanisms for changing the balance of power within the executive branch, although the complex and entrenched interests of Whitehall were rather more resistant to change than Australian counterparts. Both countries chose to combine strong central direction with a program of financial management improvement. The strong contrast between Canberra and London was in the styles of the prime ministers. Thatcher sought to dominate, whereas Hawke's style was based more on cabinet and collective processes (Campbell and Halligan, 1992b). Both governments nevertheless produced a bureaucracy that was more attentive and responsive to the political executive without overtly and systematically politicizing it. But note that in both cases managerialism was really only confirmed as a serious force in the late 1980s after their respective 1987 elections. A third term allowed the governments' reform agendas to be sustained.

The Canadian pattern is rather curious. A form of managerialism was launched there in the 1960s, and they seem to have been dabbling with it ever since, with interludes of political intervention of various forms. Aucoin and Bakvis (1988, p. 31) account for the situation as follows:

> We discern a new philosophy of management emerging within the federal government. There is an important sense in which this philosophy has evolved gradually, especially

from the period of administrative reform initiated by the Glassco commission. But this evolution has not been without its reversals or discontinuities. At times it has produced or at least threatened to result in what one participant-observer has described as "a saturation psychosis," whereby, in the operating core of government, "we may be asking managers to invest too much of their time on implementing new techniques, leaving them insufficient time to operate the activities with which they have been charged."

One can also trace such elements in the U.S. context even though they are less explicit. There was clearly a concern with exercising greater control over the bureaucracy. Carter's Civil Service Reform Act in the late 1970s was an expression of that. According to Pollitt (1990, p. 88), the "Carter administration stressed its virtues in strengthening political control of the bureaucracy—an aim which is hard to reconcile with greater management freedom and delegation."

The New Zealand pattern differs from the others (Boston et al., 1991). The government lacked a reform program comparable to its Australian counterpart and was more a victim of acute economic conditions. The instruments of strong political control were not installed before the reform program was launched. Public service reform succeeded other changes. Central mechanisms, such as a prime minister's department, were belatedly and unsuccessfully attempted. Economic necessity demanded precipitous action in the mid-1980s, and the control of the reform program centered on the central agency, the Treasury, with the then-minister of finance being a major advocate of drastic reform. The reform agenda was substantially driven and dominated by the Treasury, an agency under the sway of public choice theory. This agenda outlived the government which facilitated its emergence: without the central infrastructure to support it the government was unable to sustain coherent political direction of the reform program.

C. Mixing Political and Managerial Change

There are indications that the excessive reliance on one or other of the two approaches may have deleterious effects. The excessive reliance on certain forms of political change tends to produce or extend politicization of the civil service. Certain forms of political change lower morale more than others. The excessive reliance on managerialism (e.g., compulsive change) may also be destructive. The wrong mix of managerial measures may have negative by-products. There is a further quandary: It is also possible to rely excessively on both. The following Australian case, which draws on Halligan and Power (1992, p. 67), illustrates some of the pitfalls.

The Australian state of Victoria was for some years clearly the *most* managerialist *and* also the *most* politically oriented executive branch. This had a number of consequences for its longer-term functioning. The Labor government attached much greater significance to political direction and control than it had to the other major ostensible objective of management reform—efficiency. The obsession with relying on political direction and avoiding bureaucratic mechanisms that had the potential to entrench roles for appointed officials placed greater demands on the political system than it was capable of meeting.

The inflated role of the political system produced an executive branch that was too permeable to external party influences. Although Labor leadership was highly sensitive to the need for effective collective decision making and corporate government, it was unable to contain the pressures within the party and the Labor movement in the longer term. The Victorian party was highly committed to power sharing and party influence on policy. It was also faction ridden, with the socialist left in the ascendancy.

On the managerial side, the Victorian government presided over the development of Australia's first senior executive service, performance pay, program budgeting, and experimentation with a range of managerialist techniques and practices. It failed, however, to follow through on change. The central management of change was neglected. Victoria did not develop something akin to the Commonwealth's Financial Management Improvement Plan; the program budgeting system never served as an effective means of cost control and the performance pay provision in the SES scheme was described as a "damp squib." In other words, there was a failure to follow through in the management of change by using standard bureaucratic devices for monitoring and maintaining direction.

The Victorian government was the first of the Australian executive branches to get the political management package together. Our analysis indicated that, regardless of the important contribution of the government in the development of political management, there were significant flaws in its mixture of the political and managerial.

This experience raises the question of the extent to which the political and managerial can be reconciled. They may combine effectively for exacting change, but the potential for instability remains substantial where they are not institutionalized. There may be a potentially volatile mix, for as Peter Aucoin observes, "The fundamental prescriptions of the two proceed from quite different premises about what constitutes public management. The coupling of the two thus must inevitably give rise to tensions, if not outright contradictions, in the implementation of these ideas" (Aucoin, 1990, p. 115).

V. CONCLUSIONS

The 1980s were notable for the triumph of managerialism. This was preceded and often accompanied by political change in a number of executive branches. In many countries traditional public administration has been irrevocably changed, and others are seeking to follow (Gore, 1993).

A major research agenda of the 1990s is digesting the reform movements which emerged in the 1980s. The failures and the successes will be more apparent. There will be opportunities to test whether those systems tempted by politicization will progress further down that track or retreat. This task may be complicated by those governments who seek to avoid being judged in political terms by proffering managerialist rationalizations for what are essentially political appointments. The fate of managerialism will be debated. Since its rise has been linked with economic conditions, the extent to which it will survive better times in a recognizable form remains to be seen. The various modes of managerialism will require careful analysis. Already there are some indications that the more extreme and narrow manifestations have been modified. Will a mature form of managerialism emerge? Or will it be the face of postmanagerialism which has to be properly identified?

The relationship between managerial and political change needs greater attention. This study has indicated the importance of the interaction between the two. The case study indicated that political change was required to allow major managerial change, but managerial change also allowed political change to be consummated. The role of political factors in establishing preconditions for managerial change and providing for effective implementation of reforms requires comparative research.

Propositions about what constitute successful reforms remain lacking. We have as yet too few estimates of the impact of reforms. This in part derives from the pace of change in some executive branches. The continuing turnover of senior executives and experimentation with corporate structures often mean that the researcher is confronting a moving target. Also, the extent to which some reforms looked to be durable only became apparent in some instances in the latter part of the 1980s.

Changes of these proportions are difficult to implement effectively, and countries had to work hard at sustaining their reform programs. For example, in the United Kingdom, the lack of real managerial change during Thatcher's first two terms has been documented and led to fresh endeavors to change the Whitehall culture, which included *The Next Steps* (Hennessy, 1988). Similarly, Australian reformers have had to maintain tight control over reform directions and have developed special mechanisms for guiding and sustaining the reform program (Campbell and Halligan, 1992b).

Over two decades ago, Peter Self lamented the condition of research on reform: "In seeking a framework for analysis, one looks in vain at much of the limited literature on administrative reform" (Self, 1978, p. 312). Since then new analyses have appeared to account for the intervening years of reform, but their application remains limited. As Olsen has commented, "So far, there is no comparative study of modernization efforts in a representative sample of countries" (Olsen, 1991, p. 136).

NOTES

1. Other significant changes can be identified: for example, external relations between the bureaucracy and the public have altered in important ways (e.g., modes of accountability), but these are less integral to the operations of the bureaucracy than the two previously identified.
2. There were earlier advocates of management. For example, the Royal Commission into Australian Government Administration (1976), although not primarily managerialist in orientation, recommended accountability management. For the United Kingdom there was the Fulton report.
3. But note that public servants have frequently been used as advisers.
4. A different type of argument, and one March and Olsen (1989) demonstrate, is that the prospects for reform are greater in certain types of system than others.

REFERENCES

Aberbach, Joel and Rockman, Bert, Image IV Revisited: Executive and Political Roles, *Governance 1*(1): pp. 1–25 (1988a).

Aberbach, Joel D. and Rockman, Bert A., Ideological Change in the American Administrative Elite, paper presented at the ECPR Joint Session, Rimini, Italy, April, 1988b.

Aberbach, Joel D., Putnam, Robert D., and Rockman, Bert A., *Bureaucrats and Politicians in Western Democracies*, Harvard University Press, Cambridge, Mass., 1981.

Aucoin, Peter, Contraction, Managerialism, and Decentralization in Canadian Government, *Governance 1*(1):144–161 (1988a).

Aucoin, Peter, Organizational Change in the Canadian Machinery of Government: From Rational Management to Brokerage Politics, pp. 283–308, in *Organizing Governance, Governing Organizations* (Colin Campbell, J. J., and Peters, B. Guy, eds.), University of Pittsburgh Press, Pittsburgh, 1988b.

Aucoin, Peter, Administrative Reform in Public Management: Paradigms, Principles, Paradoxes and Pendulums, *Governance 3*(1):115–137 (1990).

Aucoin, Peter and Bakvis, Herman, *The Centralization-Decentralization Conundrum: Organization and Management in the Canadian Government*, Institute for Research on Public Policy, South Halifax, 1988.

Beloff, Max and Peele, Gillian, *The Government of the UK: Political Authority in a Changing Society*, 2nd ed., Weidenfeld and Nicolson, London, 1985.

Benda, Peter M. and Levine, Charles H., Reagan and the Bureaucracy: The Bequest, the Promise, and the Legacy, in *The Reagan Legacy: Promise and Performance* (Charles O. Jones, ed.), Chatham House, Chatham, N.J., 1988, pp. 102–142.

Boston, Jonathan, Martin, John, Pallot, June, and Walsh, Pat, eds., *Reshaping the State: New Zealand's Bureaucratic Revolution*, Oxford University Press, Auckland, 1991.

Bourgault, Jacques and Dion, Stephane, Governments Come and Go, But What of Senior Civil Servants? Canadian Deputy Ministers and Transitions in Power (1867–1987), *Governance 2*(2):124–151 (1989).

Caiden, Gerald E., *Administrative Reform Comes of Age*, de Gruyter, Berlin, 1991.

Campbell, Colin, The Political Roles of Senior Government Officials in Advanced Democracies, *British Journal of Political Science 18*:243–272, 1988.

Campbell, Colin and Halligan, John, Central Agencies in Canberra and Ottawa, in *Comparative Political Studies: Australia and Canada* (M. Alexander and B. Galligan, eds.), Longman Cheshire, Melbourne, 1992a.

Campbell, Colin and Halligan, John, *Political Leadership in an Age of Constraint: Bureaucratic Politics under Hawke and Keating*, University of Pittsburgh Press/Allen and Unwin, Pittsburgh/Sydney, 1992b.

Campbell, Colin and Peters, B. Guy, eds., *Organizing Governance, Governing Organizations*, University of Pittsburgh Press, Pittsburgh, 1988.

Derlien, Hans-Ulrich, Repercussions of Government Change on the Career Civil Service in West Germany: The Cases of 1969 and 1982, *Governance 1*(1):50–78, 1988.

Garnett, James L., *Reorganizing State Government: The Executive Branch*, Westview Press, Boulder, Co., 1980.

Gore, Al, *From Red Tape to Results: Creating a Government That Works Better and Costs Less—Report of the National Performance Review*, Government Printing Office, Washington, D.C., 1993.

Governance, Special Issue on Managerial Reform, *3*(2) 1990.

Hall, Peter, Policy Paradigms, Social Learning, and the State, *Comparative Politics 25*(3):275–296 (1993).

Halligan, John, Reorganising Australian Government Departments 1987, *Canberra Bulletin of Public Administration 52*:40–47 (1987).

Halligan, John, Career Public Service and Administrative Reform: Australia, *International Review of Administrative Sciences 57*(3) (1991).

Halligan, John, A Comparative Lesson: The Senior Executive Service in Australia, in *The Promise and Paradox of Bureaucratic Reform* (Patricia W. Ingraham and David H. Rosenbloom, eds.), University of Pittsburgh Press, Pittsburgh, 1992.

Halligan, John and Power, John, A Framework for the Analysis of Recent Changes in Australian Executive Branches, in *Handbook of Comparative and Development Public Administration* (Ali Farazmund, ed.), Marcel Dekker, New York, 1991, pp. 91–99.

Halligan, John and Power, John, *Political Management in the 1990s*, Oxford University Press, Melbourne, 1992.

Hansen, Michael G. and Levine, Charles H., The Centralization-Decentralization Tug-of-War in the New Executive Branch, in *Organizing Governance, Governing Organizations* (Colin Campbell, S. J. and Peters, B. Guy, eds.), University of Pittsburgh Press, Pittsburgh, 1988, pp. 225–282.

Hennessy, Peter, Demystifying Whitehall: The Great British Civil Service Debate, 1980s Style, in *Organizing Governance, Governing Organizations* (Colin Campbell, S. J. and Peters, B. Guy, eds.), University of Pittsburgh Press, Pittsburgh, 1988, pp. 183–208.

Hennessy, Peter, Efficiency Unit, in *Improving Management in Government: The Next Steps*, Cabinet Office, London, 1988.

Hennessy, Peter, *Whitehall*, Secker and Warburg, London, 1989.

Hood, Christopher, De-Sir Humphreyfying the Westminster Model of Bureaucracy: A New Style of Governance? *Governance 3*(2):205–214 (1990).

Keeling, Desmond, *Management in Government*, George Allen and Unwin, London, 1972.

Kernaghan, Kenneth and Siegel, David, *Public Administration in Canada: A Text*, Methuen, Toronto, 1988.

Kooiman, Jan and Eliassen, Kjell, A., eds., *Managing Public Organizations: Lessons from Contemporary European Experience*, Sage Publications, London, 1987.

Levine, Charles H., Human Resource Erosion and the Uncertain Future of the U.S. Civil Service: From Policy Gridlock to Structural Fragmentation, *Governance 1*(2):115–143 (1988).

March, James G. and Olsen, Johan P., *Rediscovering Institutions: The Organizational Basis of Politics*, Free Press, New York, 1989.

Mascarenhas, R. C., Reform of the Public Service in Australia and New Zealand, *Governance 3*(1):75–95 (1990).

Massey, Andrew, *Managing the Public Sector: A Comparative Analysis of the United Kingdom and the United States*, Edward Elgar, Aldershot, 1992.

Mayntz, Renate and Derlien, Hans-Ulrich, Party Patronage and Politicization of the West German Administrative Elite 1970–1987—Towards Hybridization, *Governance 2*(4):384–404 (1989).

Metcalfe, Les and Richards, Sue, *Improving Public Management*, Sage, London, 1987.

Olsen, Johan P., Administrative Reform and Theories of Organization, in *Organizing Governance, Governing Organizations* (Colin Campbell, S. J. and Peters, B. Guy, eds.), University of Pittsburgh Press, Pittsburgh, 1988, pp. 233–254.

Olsen, Johan P., Modernization Programs in Perspective: Institutional Analysis of Organizational Change, *Governance 4*(2):125–149 (1991).

Peters, B. Guy, Politicians and Bureaucrats in the Politics of Policymaking, in *Bureaucracy and Public Choice* (J.-E. Lane, ed.), Sage, London, 1987.

Peters, B. Guy, *The Politics of Bureaucracy*, 3rd ed., Longman, New York, 1989.

Peters, Guy, Government Reform and Reorganization in an Era of Retrenchment and Conviction Politics, in *Handbook of Comparative and Development Public Administration* (Ali Farazmund, ed.), Marcel Dekker, New York, 1991, pp. 381–403.

Plowden, William, Providing Countervailing Analysis and Advice in a Career-Dominated Bureaucratic System: The British Experience, 1916–1988, in *Executive Leadership in Anglo-American Systems* (Colin Campbell and Wyszomirski, Margaret Jane, eds.), University of Pittsburgh Press, Pittsburgh, 1991.

Pollitt, Christopher, *Managerialism and the Public Services: The Anglo-American Experience*, Basil Blackwell, Oxford, 1990.

Power, John, ed., *Public Administration in Australia: A Watershed*, Hale and Iremonger, Sydney, 1990.

Radin, Beryl A. and Coffee, Joseph N., A Critique of TQM: Problems of Implementation in the Public Sector, *Public Administration Quarterly*.

RCAGA/Royal Commission on Australian Government Administration (Chairman: H. C. Coombs), *Report*, Australian Government Printing Service, Canberra, 1976.

Rosenbloom, David and Goldman, Deborah D., *Public Administration: Understanding Management, Politics, and Law in the Public Sector*, 2nd ed., Random House, New York, 1989.

Rowat, Donald C., Comparisons and Trends, in *Public Administration in Developed Democracies: A Comparative Study* (Donald C. Rowat, ed.), Marcel Dekker, New York, 1988, pp. 441–458.

Suleiman, E., *Bureaucrats and Policy Making*, Holes and Meier, London, 1985.

Self, Peter, The Coombs Commission: An Overview, in *Public Service Inquiries in Australia* (R. F. I. Smith and Patrick Weller, eds.), University of Queensland Press, St. Lucia, 1978, pp. 310–333.

Wilenski, Peter, Has the Career Service a Future? in *State Servants and the Public in the 1980s* (R. M. Alley, ed.), New Zealand Institute of Public Administration, Wellington, 1980, pp. 27–28.

Wilenski, Peter, *Public Power and Public Administration*, Hale and Iremonger, Sydney, 1986.

37
A Traditional Bureaucracy in Turbulence: Whitehall in the Thatcher Era

James B. Christoph
Indiana University, Bloomington, Indiana

Through most of its history the British civil service has been viewed as an institution that successfully blends stability and adjustability. Its development has not been strictly linear or wholly untroubled, but for the first eight decades of the twentieth century Whitehall enjoyed a respected position within the British political system and, it might also be argued, British society. Much of its reputation rested on its skill in combining elite intelligence with political neutrality, its adaptability to the changing of the partisans guard, its ability to serve the needs of ministers and broker consensus among interest and clientele groups, and its smoothness in governing its own affairs quietly and secretly.

The coming of Margaret Thatcher to the prime ministership in 1980 brought into play a set of forces that, if too recent to be called clearly transformational, seriously challenged deep-set civil service traditions and brought disruptions to Whitehall for which the name turmoil is not too dramatic. Serious inroads have been made into the national bureaucracy's accustomed self-government, its basic organization and personnel practices, and its relationship to individual ministers, the government of the day, and the public. Some observers have gone so far as to characterize these developments as hastening the end of British claims to a unique approach to bureaucracy, a change triggered by what one observer has called "the most radical shake-up in the British civil service for a century" (Plowden, 1992).

This chapter examines the nature, extent, and effects of this process by looking both at general developments and, through case studies, at two major change agents—the so-called Next Steps initiative and the impact on British bureaucracy of the country's involvement in European Community* (EC) institutions. The upsetting of entrenched Whitehall bureaucracy—of the world according to Heclo and Wildavsky (1981)—has been the result of both endogenous and

*There are numerous references in this chapter to the European Community (EC). On November 1, 1993, the European Community was officially renamed the European Union. Because it will be some time before the new name becomes well known, the more familiar older one is retained here.

exogenous factors: the highly publicized actions of Thatcher and those sharing her views to reshape administrative culture and the organization of British officialdom, and the less well-known changes permeating Whitehall as the result of Britain's changing the character of it international roles, most notably within the EC.

I. PRE-THATCHER REFORM EFFORTS

The modern British civil service (as contrasted to servants of the Crown) is the product of an evolution that goes back to the 1850s, when in reaction to the decentralized, noncareer, often inefficient, and sometimes nepotistic and politicized structure of British officialdom, the authors of the Northcote-Trevelyan Report proposed a new approach that stressed the creation of a single unified career service, recruited at an early age through competitive exams aimed at drawing the academically successful directly into the policy-making echelons of the service, to be promoted on merit and able to serve with equal skill ministers of whichever party controlled the government of the day (Fry, 1969; Hennessy, 1989). British governments did not accept these new organizational precepts immediately, but by the end of the nineteenth century a unified central civil service along Northcote-Trevelyan lines was in place. By the end of World War I, especially as the result of the efforts of the by-then powerful mandarin Sir Warren Fisher, a largely self-governing, self-contained elite institution, geared to the growth in the powers of the state and the increasing need for administrative competence, had emerged as a key element of the British constitution. Its main features were centralization and unification, with the Treasury serving as the enforcer of common financial and personnel policies across the system. It never lacked detractors, many of whom attacked it for social elitism, political conservatism, attachment to departmental interests at the expenses of general policy, and Machiavellian manipulation of transient ministers (Laski, 1939; Kellner and Crowther-Hunt, 1980). But the senior career service was viewed by the overwhelming majority of British politicians, down to the 1960s, as a subtle but effective instrument of governing whose dedication and policy adaptability contrasted favorably with those of other national bureaucracies, one which if occasionally in need of improvement still played its expected roles capably and managed to attract a steady supply of top talent.

There were sporadic efforts to reshape Whitehall prior to the advent of Margaret Thatcher and her ism. To those who continued to find Whitehall out of touch with the needs of a modern economy and society their fate was instructive. The most famous of these efforts was the Fulton Report of 1968. Set up by Labour prime minister Harold Wilson as one of his ventures touted to modernize the machinery of the state, the Fulton Committee's recommendations were concerned chiefly with introducing managerial specialization and efficiency to a civil service it regarded as the cozy preserve of generalists and dilettantes. Although some of Fulton's prescriptions (such as the establishment of a Civil Service College and transfer of part of the responsibility for Whitehall personnel from the Treasury to a new Civil Service Department) were set in motion by the Wilson and Heath governments of the late 1960s and early 1970s, the central recommendations that managerialism and specialization should be accented were blunted by a combination of lack of continuing prime ministerial interest in substantial reform and the resistance of those in control of the internal life of Whitehall.

II. THATCHER AS ENDOGENOUS CHANGE AGENT

The senior mandarins' ability to domesticate and survive the reformist urges of the 1960s and 1970s was not to continue unchallenged, however, for the agenda of the Thatcher governments beginning in 1979 included, along with making basic changes in the relationship of British governments to economic life, reformulating roles for the civil service. The prime minister's antipathy to Whitehall and its traditions was well-known (Hennessy, 1989; Young, 1989). She did not hesitate to blame the civil service for part of what she believed was wrong with Britain, starting with her belief that most of them were interventionists in the Keynesian tradition, consensualists in decision making, subtle weakeners of new ideas and ministerial initiatives, cosseted from the effects of the more dynamic and competitive parts of British life, and given to caution and compromise when what was needed were decisiveness, clear assumption of responsibility, enthusiastic support of top political initiatives, and toughness and consistency under pressure. In brief, her model for the public bureaucrat was the successful business entrepreneur, but one who instead of pushing new products would be more concerned with "rolling back the frontiers of the State." The Thatcher diagnosis, while overdrawn in places, was by no means off-target from the standpoint of her value system. To her, most permanent officials into whose hands new policies would be put were at once too powerful and too "wet," whereas to many of those officials, products of the years of consensus and close relation with ministers in policy-making, the prime minister was too ideological, inexperienced, and headstrong to fit smoothly into the familiar ways of getting things done (Christoph, 1984). Her views, if actively pursued and shared by her ministers, were bound to engender an environment of uncertainty and mutual hostility.

The course of the Thatcher governments' efforts to reshape Whitehall can be viewed as falling into two broadly distinct periods, with different strategic emphases. The first period, roughly coincident with her first two administrations (1979–1987), was marked by attempts to force the civil service to adopt new roles and outlooks in the context of a shrinking, but essentially familiar, organizational structure. The accent was on shaking up traditional bureaucratic complacency and inaction, on steps to make officials more managerial in outlook and businesslike in practice by introducing changes that took the senior civil service away from its historic roles of advising ministers, policy initiation, and consensus brokerage and toward "productivity," seen mainly as cheap and efficient administration of policies developed almost exclusively at the political level.

The second period, dating from the beginning of the third Thatcher government in 1987 and extending to the present, has been characterized by a continuation of some of the efforts of the earlier period but also by a much greater emphasis on reorganizing and restructuring the machinery of government through a process known as the Next Steps, after the key document of the period (Efficiency Unit, 1988), which has made profound changes in essential powers and relationships in Whitehall. Although it is doubtful that the events of the two periods derive from a single coherent, preordained strategy of sequential administrative reform, in retrospect they can be seen as parts of a comprehensive effort first to deconstruct and then to reconstruct the roles of public officials to fit the larger political and economic policy objectives.

The instruments employed in early Thatcher years can be divided into three broad categories. The first group centered around changes, mostly mandated from the political top, which might be termed *deprivileging* in that they were aimed at reducing the institutional, material, and socio-psychological status of regular civil servants, seen by Thatcher as reinforcers of smugness and barriers to efficient governing. By the end of the first Thatcher government the size of the civil service was reduced by over 100,000 jobs or almost one-fifth. The Civil Service Department, created by the Heath government as a way to free Whitehall from the heavy hand of the Treasury but viewed by the Thatcherites as a built-in lobby for bureaucrats, was abolished and its powers given back to the Treasury and to the Cabinet Office. Traditional channels for consultation (such as Whitley Councils) and third-party salary arbitration were abandoned, leading in 1981 to the first major strike by civil servants (at all levels) in British history and to a legacy of mistrust and insecurity in the closed world of "village Whitehall." A few outsiders were recruited directly into high official positions at super salaries, and first steps undertaken to make rigorous performance assessment central to salary and promotion decisions. At a minimum, these decisions signaled an intention to end time-honored personnel practices and to put civil service traditionalists off-balance and make them aware of the necessity of accepting new roles and standards of performance.

A second method purported to be aimed at making Whitehall into a more appropriate mechanism for the Thatcher agenda was *politicization.* Unlike either deprivileging or managerialism, it is a slippery concept whose actualization is difficult to establish conclusively. Nevertheless, in an atmosphere of psychological turmoil many civil servants saw it as a way of bringing them to heel by casting doubt on the much-revered image of a politically neutral permanent officialdom. A few well-publicized interventions by the prime minister in the appointment and promotion process early in her term, invoking a power that undoubtedly inheres in the office but traditionally had been reserved to senior mandarins, added to the disquiet brought on by efforts at deprivileging.

In one sense such fears turned out to be exaggerated. In a few cases where senior civil servants were passed over for appointment to permanent secretaryships at the instigation of Thatcher, the evidence did not show them to be Thatcherite Tories in either the partisan or the ideological sense. Instead, they were tipped as having caught the prime minister's attention for other reasons, notably as having the reputation of being tough, energetic, can-do, antiestablishment types. In another sense, however, fears of rising politicization were not allayed, as these interventions were seen by civil servants as linked to a more ominous development: the severe reduction in their independent advisory and policy generating roles.

From the onset the Thatcher forces made it plain that a value change in Whitehall was needed, in which the longstanding roles of senior civil servants which they had come to prize as their distinct contribution—joint policy direction with ministers, free expression of countervailing arguments in private discussions with political leaders, negotiation with clientele groups, control over their own internal governing processes, and so on—would be sharply diminished in favor of loyal acceptance of policies decreed by the party in power and with discovering better methods of implementing and selling them. Civil servants saw such developments as drawing them closer than ever before into public identification with the political agenda of the party in power, and concomitantly much less able to assert their traditional neutrality when a different party took power. Confided one civil servant when interviewed in the mid-1980s, "I sometimes think I see advice going to ministers which is suppressing arguments because it is known that ministers will not want them, and that for me is a betrayal of the civil service" (*Top Jobs in Whitehall*, p. 46). Some of these qualms may have been exaggerated, and might be viewed as simple resistance to the discomforts of change by complacent mandarins, but in the context of the other occurrences already described, "cue-taking civil servants could hardly be blamed for suspecting that the direction of their careers would depend on surviving political tests more palpable and tricky than the quieter in-house socialization requirements of the past" (Christoph, 1992, pp. 171–172).

A third key component of the Thatcher governments' efforts to remake the administrative sector was a heavy emphasis on *managerialism*. Whitehall had witnessed enthusiasm for upgrading the role of management before, in the recommendations of the Fulton Report of 1968, the brief interlude of Programme Analysis Review (PAR) in the Heath government of the early

1970s, and occasional surfacing of commitment to "managing by objectives" and increased prominence for specialists in an institution dominated by classically educated generalists (Fry, 1990; Gray and Jenkins, 1985). But prior to the 1980s the changes made in this direction were sporadic and gradual and, in the view of one branch of Whitehall's critics, effectively watered down by the traditional bureaucrats who still controlled the levers of organizational power (Kellner and Crowther-Hunt, 1980). Managerialism as a governing ideology really bloomed in the Thatcher decade, not only because the larger political environment was receptive to the values of business enterprise, but also because an activist prime minister busied herself with finding ways to introduce those outlooks into a heretofore resistant officialdom. Clear signals were given that in future the civil servants who would be looked at with favor would be those actively dedicated to "the effective management of men and resources," which to her meant chiefly increasing productivity and reducing costs, rather than those immersed in policy formulation or consensus brokering.

In the first week of her first term, the prime minister inserted foreign bodies into the workings of Whitehall by setting up a series of departmental task forces, headed by a successful private executive, Sir Derek (now Lord) Rayner. These teams, made up of a mix of outside businessmen and junior civil servants, undertook "scrutinies" of the efficiency of selected departmental activities and produced recommendations aimed at saving millions of pounds. The Rayner units' efforts to critique the conduct of administration and bring in money-saving ideas and staff from the outside soon became institutionalized in a permanent Efficiency Office, located in the Cabinet Office and close to the prime minister's inner circle. Managerialism also got a boost from the imposition on Whitehall in 1982 of a new set of techniques labeled the Financial Management Initiative (FMI) aimed at pinpointing individual officials' responsibility for the performance and budget of their unit. FMI was designed to heighten civil servants' awareness of the need to show, in the British term, "value for money" at the microlevel of operation. It was accompanied by increased stress on quantitative measures in defining and measuring objectives, which provided criteria for the assessment of individual performance in setting salaries. In their first half-dozen years of operation, the Rayner scrutinies and FMI embodied the rising commitment to managerialism in public administration. Like deprivileging and politicization, managerialism fitted neatly into New Right thinking concerning the state, providing the Thatcher forces with a popular label under which, as Christopher Pollitt has observed,

> the private-sector disciplines can be introduced to the public services, political control can be strengthened, budgets trimmed, professional autonomy reduced, public service unions weakened and a quasi-competitive framework erected to flush out the "natural" inefficiencies of bureaucracy. (1990, p. 49)

The changes brought to the civil service in the first two Thatcher governments were in many ways radical, certainly from the standpoint of defenders of Whitehall traditions. But in another sense they were less than transformational, as they assumed the continuation of a unified bureaucracy for which common policies were being prescribed. When incentives aimed at replacing advisory and policy concerns with management and delivery skills were developed, it was still thought that the carriers of such changes would be retrained civil servants operating in the familiar departmental pattern. At a minimum, a rising generation of officials, weaned on the ideology and incentives of new approaches and techniques, would soon be taking over even if "old Whitehall" continued to resist or dither.

III. THE NEXT STEPS PROGRAM: TOWARD THE BREAKUP OF WHITEHALL

The most sweeping attempt to reshape the structure of British administration in the postwar era is still taking form. The thinking behind the Next Steps program constitutes a definite break from the tradition stretching from the midnineteenth century to the Thatcher decade. Not only does it carry the earlier managerialist imperatives several steps further; it also reifies many of the precepts of public choice theory and what has been called the New Public Administration (Hood, 1990). The implementation of the program is in its early phases but already had led to major changes in constitutional, political, and administrative arrangements, some of which, if carried to their logical conclusions, have given rise to serious concern over the consequences, intended or not, for the government system as a whole. Because it has now become the centerpiece of bureaucratic reform in Britain, Next Steps deserves extended examination here.

The proximate origin of the program lay with the recognition in 1987 by the prime minister and her efficiency adviser (Sir Robin Ibbs, a former industrialist) that the introduction of responsible management norms and practices was not going fast or far enough. There was still insufficient commitment to new goals from individual civil servants at all levels, and incentives seemed to be lacking to bring them around (Plowden, 1992). The analysis advanced in the Ibbs report raised the previously heretical idea that in order to make officials think in managerial terms the time-honored concept of a unified career civil service would have to be severely modified (McDonald, 1992). Centralization and uniformity were seen as shackling the flexibility and thus the efficiency of individual managers. To quote a typical passage from the report:

> Recruitment, dismissal, choice of staff, promotion, pay, hours of work, accommodation, grading, organization of work . . . are all outside the control of most civil service managers at any level. The main decisions on rules and regulations are taken by the centre of the civil service. This means that they are structured to fit everything in general and nothing in particular. The rules are seen primarily as a constraint rather than as a support; and in no sense as a pressure on managers to manage effectively. (Efficiency Unit, 1988, paragraph 11)

The new system proposed by the Efficiency Unit, and endorsed by the prime minister on the day the report was published, centered on a radically different way of organizing the business of government. A central civil service would be retained but would now consist of a small core of officials engaged in the task of servicing ministers and managing the departments that would continue to "sponsor" particular policies and services. But new government organizations, to be called "agencies," would concentrate on the delivery of services, employ their own staffs, and be headed by a chief executive responsible (in "clearly defined" ways) to the minister in charge of the sponsoring department, as constitutional requirements of accountability preclude the creation of government units wholly severed from ministerial control. In the new two-tier arrangement policy objectives would remain the responsibility of the minister and a small core of civil servant advisers, but after that the agencies' managers were to have "as much independence as possible in deciding how these objectives are met. . . . The presumption would be that, provided management is operating within the strategic direction set by Ministers, it must be left as free as possible to manage within that framework" (Efficiency Report, 1988, paragraph 18).

This important break with civil service tradition was signaled by the establishment of chief executives (a title new to British government) to head the new agencies. Such positions were to be publicly advertised and open to outsiders as well as to those already holding career appointments in Whitehall. In line with managerial themes, but in contrast to longstanding Whitehall practice, chief executives were to be given limited-term contracts, usually five years, in many cases at advanced salaries and in every case supplemented by hefty bonuses for meritorious performance. The process by which each agency is set up culminates in the publication of a kind of contract called a framework document, which sets out such basics as the new agency's relationship with its sponsoring department, its general objectives, the resources provided to it, the outputs it is to achieve and how they will be measured, the conventions regarding answerability to Parliament about its activities, and so on. The objectives specified in the framework document may be general (e.g., for the Benefits Agency "ensuring that the correct amount of benefit are paid on time, with proper safeguards against fraud and abuse") or annual goals (e.g., for the Driving Standards Office reducing waiting time for driving tests to a national average of six weeks) (Plowden, 1992).

By mid-1992 seventy-five executive agencies had been carved out of regular ministries, carrying with them 291,000 civil servants, or more than one-half those employed at the national level. (Another twenty-six activities, engaging 66,600 civil servants, were declared to be candidates for near-future agency status.) The affected units ranged from tiny (fifty officials in the National Weights and Measures Laboratory in sixty in the Queen Elizabeth II Conference Centre) to large (63,100 in the Social Security Agency and 38,400 in the Employment Service). Of the seventy-five chief executives selected to head agencies, forty-six were chosen by open competition among career officials and twenty-nine were recruited from outside Whitehall. It was assumed that the agencies broken off from traditional Whitehall would either be engaged in highly technical activities, concerned with the routine delivery of services, or distant from central policy-making. In the classic sense of the term agencies would be engaged in "administration" and run by public managers, not involved in the "policy" side of government dominated by politicians and mandarins.

This distinction extends beyond the framework document to a new public management vocabulary. The key word, featured prominently in all the publications of the new agencies, is now "customer." In line with the emphasis on measurable performance, agency employees are expected to orient their behavior much less to the needs of ministers and more to the needs of customers, who may be either members of the general public (e.g., social security recipients) or government purchasers of their services (e.g., from the Central Statistical Office). Such a changing emphasis also reflects the Major government's enthusiasm for institutionalizing a set of "consumers' rights" against government, for example as embodied in the nascent Citizens' Charter.

The creation and rapid spread of the agency concept have given rise to considerable criticism, which has taken three principal forms. The first centers on problems of accountability and redress. The question of who can be blamed for mistakes made by the agencies supposedly is covered in the framework documents, but in practice there is already evidence of buck passing and avoidance of responsibility. The only vehicle currently available to a citizen or the Opposition wishing to challenge a decision by an agency is through the adversarial procedures of Parliament, which observers of British politics agree provide ample room for ministers to stonewall or, particularly in this case, put the blame on agency executives who cannot be made to answer themselves. Nor is there provision for redress, as the limited jurisdiction of British courts in administrative matters allows wide discretionary powers to the new chief executives.

A second criticism of the agency concept involves the extent to which their performance can be assessed in contrast to comparable previous performance by traditional departments. The Major government has made substantial claims to having improved service to their "customers" by meeting the measurable goals set out annually for each agency. Although it is early to be in a position to make firm assessments of agency performance, critics acknowledge that progress has been in reaching some short-term goals. But they argue that enthusiasm for the claims made for agency performance needs to be tempered for two reasons. One is that focusing on essentially quantitative indicators of effectiveness distorts the evaluation of bureaucratic performance by neglecting the condition of other, equally important but basically qualitative goals of the unit not amenable to easy measuring. The other reason why critics remain skeptical is that data comparing the performance of a unit prior to and after attaining data agency status are unavailable to outsiders, making them hostage to unconfirmable public relations packaging.

A third criticism is that the proliferation of agencies has severely fragmented the civil service without putting in its place a clear pattern or purpose beyond the more efficient delivery of services, with unfortunate consequences for the concept of public service. Thus Patrick Dunleavy (quoted in McDonald, 1992, p. 53) compares the impact of new agency with the condition of the U.S. federal government, whose departments are little more than "a congeries of bureaux and administrations loosely controlled by a central department administration" and based on no common administrative logic. William Plowden (1992) believes that increasingly there will be cultural as well as institutional gaps between the separate parts of what used to be a single institution that shared a broadly similar outlook as well as community. By separating the main service delivery from the central policy and advisory core of the bureaucracy, for better or worse the main reference of administrators will be outward—toward clients, competitors, suppliers, private sector bodies—rather than as before toward ministers, top mandarins, and a lifetime career in a supportive community. In Plowden's view the coexistence of two kinds of officials in a "unified but not uniform" bureaucracy—traditional career civil servants in advisory or policy posts and manager-implementers on short-term contracts—holds a potential for unstable disequilibrium. Because of the asymmetry of their reward systems and the unlikelihood of much lateral mobility between the two types of administration, talented Britons interested in a career in public service will have difficulty in deciding which stream holds more promise for them.

Of all the endogenous attempts to reshape British central bureaucracy, Next Steps is the most thoroughgoing and the most subversive of classic notions of Whitehall culture. Because the program is relatively new and still evolving, it is not possible to make firm judgments on its success in meeting declared objectives or the full extent of its impact on the larger British governmental system. It may be the change agent that is causing the most turbulence in the familiar patterns of Whitehall life, but it is not the only one, as an examination of new exogenous forces will show.

IV. EXOGENOUS FACTORS FOMENTING CHANGE

Although the chief shapers of the characters of British bureaucracy have been internal rather than external, from time to time there have been notable changes stimulated by the pressure of outside forces or shifts in Britain's role overseas. For at least two hundred years the extension and shrinking of the country's colonial empire came to be reflected in new administrative structures and relationships. The Colonial Office once was nearly the peer of the Foreign Office, only to be nudged aside in the decades of decolonization following World War II by the Commonwealth Office, which itself on the expiry of the Colonial Office in the 1960s was merged with the Foreign Office. A ministry like the Board of Trade took on a new complexion in the post-1945 world as a result of the "export-or-die" drives and the rise of international trade and tariff structures. The effects on the working of the Ministry of Defence of Britain's membership in NATO and related multinational organizations need no long exposition. UN membership has made claims on British interests and to some extent trained personnel. In these and similar cases, Whitehall had to make organizational adjustments to take into account new foreign relationships and commitments, in some cases losing unilateral control over policy areas once substantially its own.

Despite the increasing number and reach of such exogenous forces affecting British administration, it could be argued that few of them made a particularly strong impact on the dominant organizational patterns and culture of Whitehall. Wartime changes probably have been exceptions, but even in those cases the senior civil service tended to revert to an earlier status quo at the end of hostilities. And the nature of decision making in those earlier circumstances did not involve new multinational institutions with constitutional authority binding British governments. Thus British membership in the European Community marks a break in traditional patterns of handling exogenous forces, a condition that will cut even more deeply into national hegemony if the quickened economic and political integration associated with the 1991 Treaty of Maastricht should actually come into being by the turn of the century. Already the EC connection has posed problems for and stimulated changes in the way British bureaucracy operates. Acceptance by most British policymakers of the view that decisions vital to their country's well-being were being taken in Brussels and other sites of EC activity required new administrative arrangements, involving both structure and personnel, and called into question whether Whitehall's customary methods of reaching and coordinating decisions were tenable in dealing with EC matters.

V. THE EFFECTS OF THE EUROPEAN COMMUNITY CONNECTION

On entering the EC in 1973, Britain decided to follow the majority of member states in not having a separate ministry for EC affairs. Instead it opted for an arrangement by which EC work was to be parceled out to those departments already dealing with the relevant domestic policy areas, relegating the task of central policy coordination jointly to the Cabinet Office and the Foreign and Commonwealth Office (FCO) (Gregory, 1983; Bender, 1991; McDonald, 1992). The decision to locate the bulk of its EC work and contacts in preexisting departments was believed by the Heath government to offer special advantages. In the words of one observer, it "presented EC work as an extension of domestic policy-making, rather than as foreign policy"; it "distributed responsibility throughout Whitehall . . . in the hope of encouraging everyone to 'think European' "; and it diffused EC work, making it less politically obvious; thus "given the difficulties in both major parties over membership, it suited their leaders to avoid the easy target of a European ministry" (Gregory, 1983, pp. 130–131).

At the center, the FCO is engaged in the functions of receiving all written materials coming from and going to Brussels and distributing them to affected Whitehall ministries, of advising departments and the government on the EC implications of proposed policies and decisions, and of putting together the staff of UKREP, the group of departmental officials on secondment to the office of the UK ambassador to the EC. Gregory (1983) has pointed out that this role has led to the suspicion, especially among ministers, that the FCO now interferes in domestic policy-making, from which traditionally it has been insulated. Partly in reaction to those suspicions, the task of centrally coordinating EC policy was given to the European Secretariat of the Cabinet Office, a staff unit physically and politically close to Number 10 Downing Street, which acts to facilitate the resolution of differences among departments on EC policy questions and to keep a "watching brief" on areas of potential conflict.

The impact on British administration of twenty years of the EC connection has taken several forms. One development, familiar to students of policy communities everywhere, is that as a result of the creation of European units within a large number of ministries, and of the countless committee meetings, conferences with counterparts in the EC and in member countries, thousands of visits to Brussels, and secondments and exchanges of technical staff, there has been grown up in Whitehall a substantial if diffused cadre of Europe-wise civil servants on whom ministers and other public officials must depend in order to read signals coming from EC organs. This expanding group differs from many domestic policy communities because of the rather unique nature of the EC—possessed as it is of authority to override national governments in some circumstances but also very dependent on member states to agree to most of what it can do. The very way in which decisions are made in Brussels has required different skills and a different kind of political understanding of this growing cadre of civil servants from those typical of domestic decision making. Before British views can be officially presented in EC forums, agreement must often be reached by officials of dozens of home departments, many of which (such as Employment, Transport, and the Home Office) previously had little involvement in foreign-policy matters. This "revolution in coordination" (to quote a former UK ambassador to the Community) is changing the psychology of ministers and civil servants from one centered on a departmental world in which strong ministers prevail to one in which British positions now have to be hammered out first among a group of departments and then negotiated further at the EC level, where alliances rather than vetoes increasingly decide outcomes. As recently as ten years ago most ministers and senior bureaucrats could make decisions in comparative ignorance of what the EC was doing or planning to do in their fields, whereas today even fairly remote departments must have a collection of officials who know their way around Brussels and can interpret EC policies and politics for ministers and their advisers (Willis, 1980; Christoph, 1993). The growing frequency of EC Council decisions taken by majority votes rather than requiring unanimity has increased the need for British officials to know exactly what is going on in other EC countries before adhering to fixed positions.

Such changes in the traditional administrative style of a considerable part of Whitehall do not in themselves bring turbulence to that environment. Indeed they could be viewed as fairly normal adjustments to the need to expand the circle of decisions. There are, however, two related sets of developments that have caused greater uncertainty in this segment of the senior civil service, contemporaneously with the pressure for radical change imposed by the Next Steps ideology. One of these stems from the ambiguity about Britain's involvement with the EC shown by the top echelon of political leaders. The other relates to the effects on civil servants' roles and careers of having to function in the multinational cauldron of EC decision making.

Except for the brief period of the Heath government in the early 1970s, British governments and their supporting political parties have waxed and waned in their enthusiasm for the consequences of EC membership, especially those aspects most threatening to national sovereignty. The uncertainty of political support at the top has made some "high-flying" civil servants unwilling to be clearly identified with Whitehall Eurothusiasts or reluctant to do more than at most a tour of duty in Brussels. Many of them interviewed by the author in 1991 felt that until a group of key ministers consistently committed to European ideals came onto the scene, side by side with a cohort of top mandarins at home with EC questions, they would advise younger colleagues to hesitate before staking their future on EC-related assignments instead of the usual preferred routes of the Treasury or service in a minister's private offices (Christoph, 1993). Doubts about how fully civil servant entrants should make those kinds of commitments, or be tagged as overly European, add to the atmosphere of uncertainty now permeating Whitehall.

A second development with a potential for turbulence is the impact of contact with EC institutions on British civil servants' attitudes and expectations. With the increased frequency and intensity of contacts, especially with members of the EC Commission, British mandarins often find the socialization and cues normally given in Whitehall insufficient preparation for the style of administration prevailing in Brussels. They must now adjust both to the outlooks of their Continental counterparts, for whom the Whitehall model has little reality, and to the nature of the EC itself, an organization that when viewed from the perspective of British national government appears headless, porous, inefficient, unpredictable, and occasionally chaotic. It is true that the Civil Service College has introduced new courses aimed at reducing the unfamiliarity felt by Britons in dealing with their EC counterparts, but unfamiliarity with or irritation over non-British ways of proceeding continues to pose problems for British effectiveness in some multinational committees and offices. For example, one civil servant reported that unlike many of the Continentals, British officials are poor at conceptualizing on their own because they are not used to developing policies not already their minister's and hence tend toward passivity in wide-open discussions. Others felt that the British have brought to the EC a rationalist tradition that has improved its performance, but that their background has not prepared its mandarins for immersion in the more overtly politicized atmosphere of the Commission. To quote one interviewed senior official with almost twenty years of EC experience, Britons are "notably good as analysts and critics, able to give a proposal a quick, well-produced, well-coordinated response," but unlike the French they are much less skilled at setting the group's agenda in the first place or invoking European ideals at critical points of negotiation (cited in Christoph, 1993).

The process of adjusting to the new political and administrative world of the EC has been a two-way street for British officials. Among the outlooks the Britons interviewed believe their compatriots have brought, if not uniquely, certainly in heavy measure, to EC processes are a penchant for orderly presentation, a critical and often skeptical frame of mind in treating proposed innovations, a collective rather than an individualistic tradition of decision making, impatience with the more rhetorical and declamatory elements of the Continental tradition, and concern for financial probity.

But since Britons cannot do all the running in a multimember organization, or make converts to the Whitehall model of those coming from quite different administrative systems and cultures, they also have had to learn how to function in a bureaucratic world distinctly different from their own. Except for Britons recruited directly into the bureaucracy of the EC's main organs, most British civil servants on secondment or spending tours of duty in Brussels will return in due course to a longer career in Whitehall. Nor is there any assurance that officials working in EC units of Whitehall departments can make a lifetime career of such expertise in a system that continues to reward general qualities and flexibility more than specialization. (These returnees might logically be more attracted to the Next Step agencies, but in terms of agency subject matter they seldom qualify or are interested.) It is not surprising that one of the potential tensions for these individuals, and by extension for the service as well, involves the ease or difficulty with which they can be reabsorbed into an administrative culture so unlike that prevailing in the EC, especially if their careers depend on it.

We lack sufficient data to answer the question of how strong the impact of the accumulating EC experience of hundreds of senior officials has been on the norms and practices of Whitehall as these officials move from the relatively open, fluid, unashamedly politicized, specialized, and only semihierarchical life of the EC bureaucracy back to a distinctive national one still characterized by a heavy stress on team play, hierarchy, anonymity, and secrecy. One scenario would emphasize the pervasive effects of longstanding constitutional and political habits in suppressing or mitigating the importation of dysfunctional outside attitudes and behaviors. Returning civil servants, with a continuing career in mind, would thus be expected to reenter essentially the same administrative culture they drifted away from in their tour of duty, perhaps preserving some of their EC expertise but making use of it within the constraints of the older Whitehall model. A different scenario would focus on opportunities to transfer learned behavior and work attitude change in an environment already undergoing considerable flux. Because the Whitehall model is under attack and its force fading, it is said, it is increasingly possible to make a larger place at home for approaches and styles associated with bureaucratic decision making in the EC, especially greater openness, individual assumption of initiative and responsibility, a more casual attitude about hierarchy, greater acceptance of outsiders, and a franker public acknowledgment of the presence of political factors in administrative activity. The latter scenario clearly has appeal to those, like the author, who believe that European Community politics will be a dominant influence on British governmental structure in the years to come. If that turns out to be true, those used to functioning in a political culture akin to that of Brussels will be better equipped not only for multinational bureaucratic roles but also increasingly for those on the domestic front.

VI. CONCLUSIONS

The big changes made in Britain in the Thatcher and early Major years involved policy rather than institutions. Privatizing public holdings, reforming the National Health Service, reshaping educational choice, warring with trade unionism and local government authorities, embracing the main lines of the Single Europe Act, and so on, were actions that made Britain in the 1990s a far different place than it was when the Conservatives under Margaret Thatcher began their long stint in power in 1979. In general, institutional reform has lagged behind these dramatic policy changes. But it has been the argument of this chapter that unlike other traditional constitutional structures such as Parliament, the Cabinet, the courts, and political parties (even the prime ministership might not be an exception), in many ways it has been the British civil service which has undergone the greatest amount of formal and informal change, in its structure, powers, and attitudes.

The series of attempts to recast the character of the senior civil service reviewed earlier, centering around deprivileging, replacement of policy-making by managerialism, and introduction of elements of politicization, culminating in the major transformations of the Next Steps agenda, broke many of the links with traditions that had stretched, fairly unbroken, back to the Northcote-Trevelyan Report of the mid-Victorian period without replacing it with a new concept of the appropriate domain of public service. To reformers convinced that such a break was both necessary and healthy, the innovations of the 1980s provided an opportunity for reconstruction around seemingly more modern, efficient institutions. Even the presence of a certain amount of turbulence and uncertainty among the mandarins provided a sign that this time fundamental change rather than a series of palliatives was indeed occurring (Hennessy, 1989).

However one assesses the merits of the recent upheavals, problems remain for what remains of the old administrative class. So much attention has been paid to the creation of the new executive agencies as an exciting innovation that the proper role of those remaining in the core departments has been neglected (MacDonald, 1992, p. 203). Presumably they are to continue as a small network of policy advisers, but now removed from contact with or responsibility for policy implementation in areas for which they are technically responsible, a situation reminiscent of the still popular but simple-minded prescription that "policy" be separated from "administration" in complex societies.

Another type of change in bureaucratic culture appears to be taking root as a result of British civil servants' growing contacts with and experience in the different world of European

Community processes. Less dramatic than the impact of Thatcher on their world, and involving a smaller if still considerable fraction of career officials, the learning process associated with making the EC connection work for British administration is making a mark on this growing policy community within Whitehall. It is perhaps inevitable that such learning sits uneasily with more traditional bureaucratic values and habits, and thus infuses into an already uncertain environment another kind of challenge to a once stable, predictable, and unified institution.

REFERENCES

Bender, B. G., Whitehall, Central Government and 1992, *Public Policy and Administration 6*(1):13–20 (1991).

Chapman, Richard A., Concepts of the United Kingdom in Public Sector Reform: The Experience of the United Kingdom in the 1980s, *Public Policy and Administration 6*(2):1–19 (1991).

Christoph, James B., Rubbing Up or Running Down? Dilemmas of Civil Service Reform in Britain, in Donley T. Studlar and Jerold L. Waltman (eds.), *Dilemmas of Change in British Politics*, Macmillan, London, 1984.

Christoph, James B., The Remaking of British Administrative Culture: Why Whitehall Can't Go Home Again, *Administration & Society 24*(2):163–181 (1992).

Christoph, James B., The Effects of Britons in Brussels: The European Community and the Culture of Whitehall, *Governance 6*(4):518–537 (1993).

Efficiency Unit, *Improving Management in Government: The Next Steps*, Her Majesty's Stationery Office, London, 1988.

Fry, Geoffrey, *Statesmen in Disguise: The Changing Role of the Administrative Class of the British Home Civil Service 1853–1966*, Macmillan, London, 1969.

Fry, Geoffrey, The Fulton Committee and the "Preference for Relevance" Issue, *Public Administration 68*(3):175–190.

Gray, Andrew and Jenkins, William I., *Administrative Politics in British Government*, Wheatsheaf Books, Brighton, England, 1985.

Gregory, F. E. C., *Dilemmas of Government: Britain and the European Community*, Martin Robertson, Oxford, 1983.

Heclo, Hugh, and Wildavsky, Aaron, *The Private Government of Public Money*, 2nd ed., Macmillan, London, 1981.

Hennessy, Peter, *Whitehall*, Secker & Warburg, London, 1989.

Hood, Christopher, *Beyond the Bureaucratic State: Public Administration in the 1990s,* London School of Economics, London, 1990.

James, Simon, *British Cabinet Government*, Routledge, London, 1992.

Kellner, Peter, and Crowther-Hunt, *The Civil Servants*, Macdonald, London, 1980.

Laski, Harold J., *Parliamentary Government in England*, Viking, New York, 1938.

McDonald, Oonagh, *The Future of Whitehall*, Weidenfeld and Nicolson, London, 1992.

Plowden, William, Policy and Implementation, Politics and Management: Current British Attempts to Operationalise Some Old Distinctions, Paper for APPAM Fourteenth Annual Research Conference, Denver, Colorado, 1992.

Pollitt, Christopher, *Managerialism and the Public Services: The Anglo-American Experience*, Blackwell, Oxford, 1990.

Top Jobs in Whitehall: Appointments and Promotions in the Senior Civil Service, Report of a RIPA Working Group, Royal Institute of Public Administration, London, 1987.

Willis, Ruth, *Britons in Brussels: Officials in the European Commission and Council Secretariat*, Policy Studies Institute, London, 1982.

Young, Hugo, *The Iron Lady: A Biography of Margaret Thatcher*, Farrar Strauss Giroux, New York, 1989.

38
Public Bureaucracy in Korea

Bun Woong Kim
Dongguk University, Seoul, Korea

I. POLITICAL CULTURE AND BUREAUCRATIC ELITISM

Korean politics and administration manifest the historical stamp of Korean political culture, characterized by bureaucratic elitism and political-administrative centralism. The Korean political culture has been and still is influenced by the historical residues of Confucianism, Buddhism, and Taoism and by a high degree of ethnic homogeneity that disposes most Koreans, especially the masses, to a submissive authoritarian political psychology that tends to legitimize the moral authority of the upper strata.

Traditionally, Korean public policy has been exclusively viewed as the preferences and values of the governing elite solely. The nonparticipatory Korean masses have long been psychologically oriented toward powerful leadership by the elite and a centralized hierarchical bureaucracy. Thus, a highly centralized elitist administration typifies the recurrent institutional essence of Korean political tradition. Despite the trauma of Westernization in recent centuries, the core values of the Korean political culture have not been substantially altered by cross-cultural fertilization. Western patterns of liberal pluralistic ideals have had some acculturative impact upon the Korean elite; however, as yet the elite political culture remains highly authoritarian and still oriented toward exclusive decision making by a centralized elitist government (Kim, 1982).

Since the Republic of Korea's independence in 1945, the Western pluralist model has had a far-reaching impact on the establishment of the formal institutional framework of the Korean government. Beyond the formal structures, however, the impact has been minimal and bureaucratic elitism, perhaps more accurately stated as paralytic centripetalism, rather than democratic pluralism persists in public policy-making. We may ascribe this to the lack of sociocultural preconditions of pluralism. The authoritarian political tradition of Korea does not nurture such pluralistic prerequisites as (1) viable competition among individuals, elites, or groups; (2) opportunities for individuals and organizations to gain input access to the decision-making process; (3) organizational mediation between elites and masses; (4) viable instruments of mass participation in political decisions such as elections and other media of influence and access; (5) democratic consensus based on the "democratic creed." Korea's drift to authoritarian government therefore should be viewed in part as historical-cultural determinism and in part as the absence of the pluralistic prerequisites (Kim, 1985). The unusually cohesive Korean political structure, based on a remarkably homogenous society, does not condition environmental time-space for the fragmentation of power or the competitive balance of power between interest groups. The absence of natural cleavages is not consistent with an "equilibrium" model of diverse political groupings in balance.

The elite-mass class division of Korean society tends to support a political system maintained by domination and regulation, and not by pluralist interest group balancing. The high degree of political centralism or authority imposes elitist policy upon the different strata of the masses. Some other persistent ideological/ecological constraints in postwar Korean government also inhibit pluralistic prospects for political and socioeconomic development: (1) a narrow range of individual political freedom; (2) executive dominance of the bureaucracy, legislature, and judiciary; (3) limitations on the role and function of political parties; (4) increased role of the military in politics; (5) the security threat from North Korea; and (6) national planning for rapid economic growth.

The governing elite roles based upon the political passivity of the Korean masses may facilitate effective bureaucratic intervention in the economic and social areas but impedes the creation of autonomous centers of decision-making authority in the developmental process—the democratic/political area. The contemporary Korean polity has weak bureaucratic centers that are not capable of subjecting bureaucrats to political oversight. Recent Korean politics and administration manifest bureaucratic elitism and paralytic cetripetalism, which give little encouragement to the positive projection of democratic development.

Contemporary Korean administration has been affected by the turbulent history of ongoing constitutional development in Korea, which may be divided into five separate periods: (1) the Rhee administration under a presidential system (the First Republic, 1948–1960), led by Syngman Rhee; (2) the democratic administration under a parliamentary system (the Second Republic, 1960–1961), led by Chang Myon; (3) the Third and Fourth Republics (1961, 5–1979), led by Park Chung Hee; (4) the Fifth Republic (1980–1986), led by Jun Doo-Hwan; and (5) the Sixth Republic (1987–1992), led by Rho Tae-Woo. Except the Second Republic, all the republics have been under a presidential system.

Korea's recent move toward political democratization is expected to mature with its continued industrialization, a new popular consciousness, greater national self-confidence, proliferation of technocratic elites, and a new generation of democratic leadership. Koreans also face the challenge of permanently "civilianizing" their politics and government, calling upon all their talent to lead an increasingly complex economy and society. Korea's industry and business compete aggressively and impressively on the world stage. Korea has already made a historic commitment to greater democratization. Accordingly, there appears to be a general consensus among Koreans of various political persuasions that government institutions and administrative practices up to now have been inadequate to meet Korea's complex present and future demands. A drastic administrative reform will be a critical part of political democratization.

Korea now has the opportunity to match its socioeconomic progress with great politico-administrative reforms. If it succeeds in establishing a better administrative apparatus, it will have laid the groundwork not only for enduring democratic progress but also for enduring economic prosperity.

II. GOVERNMENT INTERVENTION AND ECONOMIC DEVELOPMENT

The decades of the 1980s and 1990s have been a critical period for assessing the Korean governmental role in economic development. During the period of the 1960s and 1970s, government economic intervention was praised as a success model by many scholars and practitioners. Over the last several years the efficiency of government intervention in the Korean economy has been intensively questioned and criticized because of the latent inefficiency of public intervention and the trend toward economic liberalization. Recently many scholars and practitioners have argued that government economic control should transform direct intervention to a free-market mechanism—that is, shrinking the governmental role through deregulatory reform, privatizing the public sector, and thus ensuring a greater reliance on private initiative and economic democracy.

For a quarter century Korea has achieved remarkable economic growth. From 1962 to 1985, the Korean economy grew at an average annual rate of 8.3%. The nation's per capita gross national produce (GNP) increased from $82 in 1961 to $6,790 in 1992. It is generally agreed that the sustained high growth in the Korean economy over this period was largely due to a significant shift in industrialization strategy from import substitution to export promotion in the early 1960s and the successful implementation of the outward-looking strategy thereafter. Among the diverse factors contributing to accelerated growth, government intervention was mostly attributed to the export-oriented policy.

Most Korean presidents and government elites feared the "waste" of competition and thus deepened their drive for favored government intervention in economic development. They were certainly strongly interventionist but envisaged administrative intervention as a means for encouragement of the outward-looking strategy and particularly for the central planning of the Korean economy. The components of the Korean administrators' interventionist role are traceable to their authoritarian bureaucratic elitism-specific patterns of socialization and administrative culture.

Until the advent of the Park administration in 1961, Korea suffered from a stagnant economy and political chaos. The administrative elites in the Park regime recognized the material benefits of unidimensional planned economic development in an atmosphere of circumscribed political liberties and were blessed by a hard-working literate population tired of poverty and political chaos. Thus, they engineered the drastic reshaping of the nation under the guise of single-minded national and presidential devotion to economic development. The bureaucratic elites produced an extreme degree of administrative centralization and collectivism.

Korean bureaucrats have depended on strong central regimes in which they dominate the policy-making process as well as policy execution. The policy-planning subculture of the bureaucratic elites has been characterized by (1) the "speed and flexibility" of policy response; (2) the "pragmatism" of choosing among all available instruments and tools without any ideological bias; and (3) the "particularism" of applying a certain policy to a limited number of clients in a specific situation. However, it appears that the development of interventionist administrative elites was desired in Korea because (1) resource utilization control required central planning and supervision and (2) rationally directed economic activity may produce enormous growth with stable or even reduced inputs of scarce raw materials. In sum, the ascendancy of bureaucratic elitism strengthened the administrative interventionist role in the Korean economy (Caiden and Kim, 1991).

III. DEMOCRATIZATION OF PUBLIC ADMINISTRATION

A. New Politics and Administrative Transformation

Democratic initiatives and administrative reforms are being adopted and pursued with varying degrees of zeal and energy in the present Sixth Korean Republic. Despite the dramatic political democratization underway in Korea, this has not been matched by a concurrent process of debureaucratization of public administration. Any genuine and enduring political transformation will require the consideration of both democratization and debureaucratization. Unfortunately in the Korean setting the two are not complementary.

We assume that, in Korea, political democracy is unlikely without government debureaucratization first. Demands for socioeconomic development have been and continue to be the rationale for the continuation of bureaucratic formalism as the main variable in Korea's administrative system. This fails to recognize the relationship between democracy and administrative reform. What is the value of political democratization if it cannot eradicate (or at least moderate) a rigidly authoritarian government regime and ensure social equity or public service betterment? The answer, from the experience of the last few decades, is clear. Democracy is a necessary ingredient of administrative reform, but it alone is not sufficient. Liberalization of the political economy and the deregulation or decentralization of public bureaucracy are ultimately needed to solidify the institutional structure of government so as to secure democratic ideals and values. This chapter reviews administrative reform strategies in the context of Korea's democratic initiatives in a period of rapid political transition.

A recent survey shows that the level of public support for democratization is higher than ever before. An overwhelming majority (78.8%) support more democracy in Korea. A relatively small minority (21.1%) do not agree. On the other hand, a few believe that less democracy is needed, and some (17.2%) think that Korea has achieved an optimal level of democracy (Shin et al., 1989).

Nevertheless, according to a recent survey by the Korean daily newspaper *Chosun Ilbo* and the Korea Gallup Poll, a majority of Koreans do not consider democratization to be one of the top problems facing national development. The urgent need for democratization ranks sixteenth (2.2%) on a list of eighteen priorities, after public safety (30.1%), economic stability (28.3%), housing (18.6%), traffic congestion (17.1%), political stability (14.2%), rural development (10.5%), pollution (8.3%), poverty (6.8%), labor disputes (4.7%), national unification (4.6%), student demonstrations (3.0%), political party behavior (2.8%), political party restructuring (2.4%), unemployment (2.1%), and the legitimacy of the preceding Fifth Republic (0.6%) (*Chosun Ilbo* March 6, 1990).

Socioeconomic stability is found to be the nation's top priority. Korea may be paying a high cost for turning to democracy. Since the birth of the Sixth Republic in February 1988, Korea has experienced political violence, corruption, labor unrest, student riots, and lawlessness. While radicals from the left scorn liberal democracy and pluralist capitalism, right-wing hardliners (and the conservative establishment) blame their leftist counterparts for the agony of political turmoil, for economic decline, and for a loss of social discipline. It is obvious that Korea's current democratization drive has been in the vortex of a left-right ideological dispute. Koreans today are deeply divided over the "bread and butter" issues of the Old Politics on the one hand and the noneconomic issues of the New Politics (i.e., participation, social equity, and pollution policies) on the other. Like other "newly industrializing countries," Korea has not yet resolved the issues of the Old and New Politics. Most important is the question of why Koreans give political democratization low priority. Our answer is that political democratization is impossible without administrative innovations and reforms. To transform authoritarian rule into democracy or to meet the demands and challenges of New Politics, public administration must be decentralized and debureaucratized.

A danger in contemporary Korea comes from the twin risks of populism and political paralysis when power is dispersed among many political parties in the National Assembly. The recent dramatic merger of the ruling Democratic Justice Party with two opposition parties to form a grand conservative coalition, the Democratic Liberal Party (DLP), may reduce the probability of populism and political paralysis.

We see a unique opportunity for DLP and the National Assembly to fashion a reform perspective which could result in a less authoritarian and centralized bureaucracy as a means of achieving political democratization and as a significant step toward full democracy. Certainly one ruling party now has the power to effect major change. The direction of that change will depend on the beliefs and attitudes of the members of the National Assembly and the president (Ahn, 1990).

B. Bureaucratization, Democratization, and Administrative Reform

Most newly industrializing nations must face the paradox of development administration that "effective administration is essential to accomplish development" (Bryant and White, 1982, p. 25). The troubling phenomenon is that strengthening administration may inhibit the course of political development in both political power and political institutions. Since the early 1960s government intervention in Korean economic development has been justified, as a model of success has overruled political development, reflecting a "bureaucratization of politics." A complementary equilibrium between bureaucrats and politicians concerning both policy-making and politics was never previously accomplished in Korean experience. A possible "Image III" (Aberbach et al., 1981) of the relationship between Korean politicians and bureaucrats could not be imprinted to all to suffice the expected/attempted in praxis.

In the governmental setting of the 1960s–1970s, the policy role of bureaucrats was exceptionally dominant over the interest aggregation of organized political forces. Bureaucratic policy-making was too strongly advocated to argue against its prevalent role images. Usually some innovative higher civil servants initiated a leading role in administrative reforms, although government bureaucracy is basically conservative and resistent to change. However, securing such a reformist innovation required that enlightened political leaders advocate such a policy. In fact, an effective combination of rank and file task elites with power elites also nurtured and encouraged bureaucratic politics as well as administrative reform (Lee, 1983).

The efficiency and inefficiency of strong government intervention in Korean economic development have been argued by scholars and practitioners. Whatever the validity of and rationale for the assessment, there is tacit agreement among Korean intellectuals that the components of the Korean government interventionist role are traceable to its authoritarian bureaucratic elitism, culturally pervasive in sociopolitics and administration. A consistent reliance on the centralized administrative elites nurtured a bureaucratization of politics, impeding the democratic pluralist setting then on trial (Kim and Bell, 1985).

Second, an alliance of the senior bureaucrats and the military-turned-politicians resulted in a "politicization" of bureaucracy after the military intervention of General Park's regime in politics. Various groups of former generals and colonels from the Second Republic (1961) to the Sixth Republic (1988–1992) have occupied key governmental positions as ministerial and agency heads, provincial governors, and heads of public enterprises and have also had a hold over the essential positions of viable ruling political parties.

A great deal of evaluation has been directed at the role of the Korean military in politics. The civil-military rule was credited with a significant positive role in socioeconomic development or industrialization (Kim, 1971). Even the linkage between the military regime and socioeconomic progress was pictured in the guardian model of a "Praetorian" military (Ro, 1987). The all-inclusive results of military political dominance have been criticized as an unnecessarily negative outcome for Korea's economic and political development, rather politically backward (Sohn, 1968; Kihl, 1982). In each perspective, militarized politicization of the bureaucracy was an undeniable phenomenon whether the political role of the military was beneficial to the socioeconomic sector or inhibitory to democratic political process.

Carrying the polarized conflict within current bureaucratic politics to its logical synthesis, a hybrid praxis oriented toward democratization must be pursued to resettle/restructure the extreme of bureaucratization of politics and politicization of bureaucracy. A possible synthesis—an integration of politics with administration—should be reexamined with an eye to a "hypothetical" convergence of the roles of Korean bureaucrats and politicians, in the context of backgrounds, structures, functions, group behaviors, and system dynamics. In this reciprocally synthesizing context, possible images and strategies of administrative reforms should be viewed and modeled in the process of political democratization.

Korea's ongoing move toward political democratization is expected to mature with its continued industrialized, a new popular consciousness, the upsurge of national self-confidence, the proliferation of technocratic elites, and a new generation of democratic leadership. Koreans also face the challenge of permanently "civilianizing" their politics and government, calling upon all their resources of talent to lead an increasingly complex economy and society. Korea's industry and business compete aggressively and impressively on the world stage. Today its scale of international trade ranks twelfth in the world. Koreans' per capita GNP now exceeds U.S. $6,000 and is expected to reach U.S. $10,000 in the mid-1990s. Korea has already made a historic commitment to greater democratization. Accordingly, there appears to be a general consensus among Koreans of various political persuasions that the form of government institutions and the administrative practices which have prevailed up to now are inadequate to meet Korea's complex present and future demands. Drastic administrative reform will be a critical part of political democratization.

Korea now has the opportunity to match its socioeconomic progress with great politico-administrative reforms. If it succeeds in establishing a better administrative apparatus, it will have laid the foundation not only for enduring democratic progress but also for enduring economic prosperity. Some broad generalizations about current Korean politics and administration are widely assumed: First, the simultaneous pursuit of political development and stability will invigorate democratic liberalization and inspire grater public participation in a gradual shift from "crisis politics" to "interest politics" (Ahn, 1987). Thus, the very process of political institutionalization will benefit Korea's liberal democracy.

Second, administrative reforms should be directed to deregulation, decentralization, popular participation, and more openness in the government, shifting from bureaucratic authoritarianism to democratic autonomy. Anticipating the structural-functional changes of the government, a more adequate institutional framework should be grounded on establishing a new tradition of peaceful political leadership succession, increasing citizen participation, revitalizing local autonomy, realigning governmental roles, and strengthening law and order (KDI, 1986).

Third, the current economic order and institutions should be reframed to enhance the quality of life and to bring about the social equity and justice that promote economic efficiency, provide equal opportunity, and enforce fair remuneration. To meet this objective a free market mechanism is required to keep a competitive spirit and to encourage private initiative through innovative entrepreneurship and establishment of liberalized principles.

Specifically, government policy should be directed to the prevention of concentration of economic power; promotion of fair competition, autonomy, and liberalization in the financial sector; privatization of public enterprises; modifications in land use and transactions; institutionalization of consumer protection; and encouragement of private sector initiatives (KDI, 1986; Yun, 1990).

The Korean experience in recent decades may prove the truth of the caveat "Democracy is unlikely to last without economic progress, but economic progress does not necessarily guarantee democracy." Here the public bureaucracy must play an intermediate role to balance growth in the economy in parallel with democracy. The crucial questions of administrative reform concerning this task are indeed; What and how?

Especially in this context, the constitution of the Sixth Republic is characterized by provision of intensified legislative/judicial control over the executive, revival of local self-government autonomy, liberalization of the economy, promotion of social equity, guaranteed freedoms of expression, assembly, organizing, and so forth (Cho, 1987). The Administration Seminar and Administrative Reform Committee Report recommend the very necessary administrative reform of Korea's national government to ensure the principles of political democratization, socioeconomic self-regulation, and administrative autonomy.

C. KAPA Perspectives

A historic international symposium, "Korean Republic Administration for Democratic Society," was held by the Korean Association for Public Administration (KAPA) in Seoul, August 24–25, 1988. The main focus was on how to innovate, revitalize, and reform Korean public bureaucracy to cope with the demands and challenges of political democratization and socioeconomic development. The following points summarize the perspectives of the KAPA conference.

1. Democratization requires administrative transformation. Administrative democracy in Korea should be preceded by political democratization.

2. Administrative decentralization is a necessity of political democracy. At the apex of government administration the presidency must be relieved of excessive routine administrative burdens as much as possible. A creative division of work between the president and the prime minister is necessary in order that the president may perform genuinely "political" functions. The prime minister's function of administrative integration should be enlarged. The prime minister should have the actual power to nominate cabinet members, a practice which has not yet been firmly empowered. National budgeting functions should be moved to the office of the prime minister from the Economic Planning Board.

3. The shadow of "dual control" which has plagued various administrative units invisibly must be cleared or eliminated to increase administrative rationality and to enhance morale among government officers and employees.

4. No pretext should hinder the implementation of local autonomy, including timing, financing, and diverse managing. Yet local self-government in Korea has not been revised since the military coup of 1961, though its constitutional base was reestablished with birth of the Fifth Republic, which followed the assassination of President Park in 1979.

5. Government regulation and control over autonomous entities—private universities, newspapers, broadcasters, commercial banks, R & D organizations, and social organizations—should be phased out in order to revitalize private sector initiatives.

6. Welfare administration must be enlarged and made more sophisticated in scale and quality to manage the demands of economic development in the last three decades.

7. To meet the changes and challenges of the international environment (the politics of Korea-U.S. trade relations, EC unification, Soviet perestroika in Asia and the Pacific, and the dramatic industrialization of ASEAN states) the inward-looking Korean bureaucracy must transform itself to a more adaptable machine for international competition.

8. Administrators should change their perceptions and behaviors from masters or "super-citizens" to civil servants and from partisan agents to neutral professionals. Neutrally competent public administration is required to provide honest government based on a merit system, laws, and policies. In the upper level of the public service, a more qualified leadership and a "passion for anonymity" are required for a mature strong democracy.

9. A new trust between government agencies and the people must be acculturated through the supremacy of the rule of law and citizen participation so that a new administrative process may exclude bureaucratic waste, fraud, and abuse, possibly nurturing the democratic politics of compromise and negotiation, policy responsiveness by broader participation and higher credibility, and social equity. For a more humane bureaucracy, people-centered administration must be sought.

10. Administrative centralization should be reexamined in a democratic context. Examples are monopolistic execution of discretionary power by the upper echelon of administration; the weak status of the civil service, which places politicians over bureaucrats; the policy that civil servants have no legal right to hold political party membership.

11. To facilitate the diversification of the pluralistic socioeconomic and political strata, the crucial task is to strengthen the natural bonds among citizens to promote individual freedom and social cooperation rather than constraining them through repressive control and domination. To check and correct the monopolistic/oligarchic policy-making the president and technocratic elites, the participatory policy roles of the National Assembly, political parties, interest groups, mass media, and citizens must be institutionalized to ensure more administrative rationality rather than mere "technoeconomic" rationality.

12. For advancing a "democratic welfare state" to achieve social equity by reducing disparities between social classes and regions, an effective social welfare system should be consolidated especially in relation to the issues of income distribution, public assistance, housing, poverty, unemployment, and urban-rural disparity.

13. Crucial civil servant law and ethical codes in Korea must be properly revised to prevent administrative corruption and dysfunction that may corrode public confidence, disrupt implementation of administrative activities, and cause serious conflicts between government agencies and the people. Both strategies to prevent administrative corruption and programs for civic education on administrative ethics-discipline-philosophy are required to achieve the development of a democratic society.

D. Administrative Reform Committee Report

The Administrative Reform Committee of the Sixth Republic submitted its final report on Government Reorganization and Administrative Reform to the president in July 1989. The ideals and values of the Committee Report are democratization; liberalization and progress on human rights, the free market mechanism, and private initiative; Two Koreas, South-North dialogue, and unification; internationalization; local self-government; socioeconomic development; social equity, welfare, and environmental protection; and administrative efficiency and effectiveness, that is, public productivity.

The following summary of the Committee Report transmitted to the president describes the challenges and policy responses in greater detail.

1. *Revitalizing Private Sector Initiative*

1. Delegation of government authority and functions to the private sector: According to the Ministry of Government Administration, government functions are divided into 145 macrobasic functions, 691 medium factor functions, 2,964 task functions, and 13.357 microunit functions. In order to reduce the administrative interventionist role and its costs in the political economy, functions that should be transferred to the private sector include market competition, civic campaigns, noncoercive public utilities, authorization and licensing of simple routine functions, and R&D and investigation functions.

2. Deregulation of control mechanism: Much attention is focused on how to reduce the costs and ease the burden of government control to promote the functional autonomy of the private market. Current administrative regulations number 3,618 (100%) procedures for the numerous forms of authorization (223, 6%), permission (592, 16%), patent licensing (48, 1%), validation (280, 8%), recommendations (396, 1%), registration (181, 5%), reporting (786, 22%), certification (377, 11%), confirmation (48, 1%), and others (1,047, 29%). In particular, 849 (23.5%) procedures must be deregulated to permit private sector autonomy (i.e., market competition control); to end overlapping supervision (i.e., automobile tests); to cut down on excessive discretion (i.e., grain sales permission); and to delegate regulation to local autonomy from central government (i.e., tourist business registration).

3. Privatization of government corporations: The current added value of public enterprises constitutes 9.1% of GNP and their combined fixed capital accounts for 15.6% of the nation's total fixed capital. Korea Telecom and Korea Electric Corporation produce 51% of the employment, 63.4% of the sales, and 33.6% of the capital of all government-owned corporations. The two big public corporations are to be privatized as part of the move toward a market-oriented economy.

2. *Administrative Decentralization*

4. Readjustment of central-local government functions: Total government functions are composed of central government 7,027 (66.3%) and its special local agencies 2,841 (19.0%), local self-government 1,503 (14%), and others (0.7%). Some 584 central government functions such as military manpower, labor disputes, civil defense, agricultural skills, and environmental protection should be delegated to local self-government.

5. Readjusting the boundaries of administrative regions, it is recommended that the "three-tier" administrative hierarchy of province-city or country-town (or township) be reduced to a two-tier system.

6. Regional administrative commissions are needed to coordinate interprovincial/intercity affairs for coping with the increasing administrative demands of transportation, communication development, and intense industrialization.

7. A Seoul metropolitan administration commission is needed to decentralize population, housing, pollution, sanitation, and public resources and utilities. Within the country as a whole, Seoul includes a large portion of the population (40.2%), households (35.8%), manufacturers

(57.1%), hospitals (47.0%), universities and colleges (44.7%), and automobiles (54.3%) on a relatively small land area (Seoul 0.6%, Seoul metropolitan 11.8%).

3. Reorganization of Central Government

8. The founding criteria of government agencies must be intensified, diversified, and specified in the Government Organization Law. The Emergency Management Office in the Office of Planning and Management can be integrated into the Section of General Affairs, and a new Policy Coordination Office is necessary.

9. Functional readjustment/or reallocation of the following organizations should be examined: Security Planning Agency (Korea CIA), Military Security Headquarters, Board of Audit and Inspection, Performance Evaluation Bureau, Office of Statistics and Fair Trade Office in the Economic Planning Board, Technology Policy and Development Office in the Ministry of Science and Technology, and Emergency Planning Committee of the National Security Council.

10. A new Civil Service Commission must be established in the Ministry of Government Administration to sustain the independent, neutral competence of public personnel administration.

11. The reorganization and evaluation of several ministries should be considered. These include Civil Defense Headquarters, National Police Headquarters, Fisheries Administration, Public Prosecutions Administration, National Silkworm Breeding Station, Office of Military Public Relations, and Office of College Education. There should be a separation of the Ministry of Culture and Information into two sections. The Minister of the National Unification should also be the Vice Premier of Unification Affairs. Integration of the Ministry of Trade and Industry with the Ministry of Energy and Resources is needed, as is the founding of a new Ministry of Industrial Trade and Commerce and a new Ministry of Construction and Housing, enlarged from the Ministry of Construction, and the Environmental Protection Agency.

12. The office functions of the following organizations should be enlarged and intensified: International Trade Commission, Office of Information Management in the Patents Administration, Office of Intellectual Property Protection, Small and Medium Industry Bureau, Social Insurance Bureau, National Institute of Health, Regional Labor Administration Offices, Seoul Metropolitan Transportation Commission, and Maritime and Port Administration. There should also be a leveling up of all sections to bureau level in the Ministry of Communications.

13. Reshuffle and revitalization of government committees: Among the current 403 Advisory and Administrative Committees, only 55 committees (13%) seem to be efficient and effective; 218 committees (54%) are supported by the national budget; and 54 committees (13%) have no policy outputs.

14. The discretionary power of an administrative decision making has to be delegated/decentralized downward to develop a "people-centered"/clientele-oriented administration.

15. The career structure of the civil service should be reexamined, especially in the following areas: application of position classification to the current rank system; promotion on the basis of merit performance; retirement; and salaries and compensation.

16. "Open" administration of both administrative information law and administrative procedure law should be pursued. Accordingly, both Government Archives and Record Service and the Government Computer Center in the Ministry of Government Administration must be enlarged.

E. Democratization Requires Administrative Reform

Administrative democracy in Korea must be preceded by political democracy. Korean public administration is now at a historic turning point because it is currently in a democratic context. Unfortunately it is true that Korean administrative reforms attempted so far have, to a large extent, been to legitimate political regime changes throughout the First to Sixth Republics. Most administrative transformations were led by ruling elites and did not come from the grass roots. Thus, those reforms did not reflect properly the values and ideals of administrative rationality and democracy, weakening public confidence in government bureaucracy. Both the KAPA perspectives and the Administrative Reform Committee strategies seem to be very valuable ingredients in the democratization/debureaucratization of Korean government. Nevertheless, it will be of no use if the people distrust government initiatives for democratic reform. Some argue that the Committee Report is undemocratic, unrealistic, and even irresponsible. Some critics wonder whether it has the capacity to change an authoritatively centralized system to a more democratic pluralist administration.

Koreans today seem more concerned with the New Politics of postmaterialism, participation, and social equity than with the Old Politics of materialism and the "bread and butter" economy. Naturally, the political values of democratization are often far more influential than socio-economic values of development. Korea now needs both change and stability; the key is how to manage the dynamic tension between the two. Korean public administration is at the margins of two great epochs, authoritarian and democratic. The bureaucracy can no longer be treated as a mere political tool for sustaining and securing the legitimacy of ruling power elites. Likewise, political democracy cannot be regarded as a catchy phrase for rationalizing the authoritarian oligarchy of bureaucratic elites. When political democracy and administrative democratization are in balance, Korea will move toward an advanced democratic society.

REFERENCES

Aberbach, J. D., Putnam, R. D., and Rockman, B. A., *Bureaucrats and Politicians in Western Democracies*, Harvard University Press, Cambridge, Mass., 1981, p. 9.

Administrative Reform Committee, Republic of Korea, *Report on the Administrative Reform*, July, 1989.

Ahn, Byung-Joon, Progress of Democracy in Korea: A Comparative Perspective, in *Progress in Democracy: The Pacific Basin Experience*, Ilhae Institute, Seoul, 1987, p. 20.

Ahn, Chung-Si, The State and Economy Under New Democracy: Korea's Democratic Transition in Comparative Perspective, a paper presented to the International Political Science Association Round-table, Seoul, Korea, May 22–24, 1990.

Bryant, C. and White, L. G., *Managing Development in the Third World*, Westview Press, Boulder, Colo., 1982, p. 25.

Caiden, Gerald E. and Kim, Bun Woong, *A Dragon's Progress: Development Administration in Korea*, Kumarian Press, West Hartford, Conn., 1991, pp. 138–139.

Cho, Suk-Choon, The New Constitution and the Reorganization of the Korean Central Government Agencies, *The Korean Journal of Policy Studies 2*:123–131 (1987).

Chosun, Ilbo, March 6 (1990).

Kihl, Young-Whan, Korea's Fifth Republic: "Domestic Political Trend," *Journal of Northeast Asian Studies, 1*(2):51–52 (1982).

Kim, Bun Woong, The Korean Political Psyche and Administration, in *Korean Public Bureaucracy* (Bun Woong Kim and Wha Joon Rho, eds.), Kyobo Publishing, Seoul, 1982, pp. 117–122.

Kim, Bun-Woong and Bell, David S., Bureaucratic Elitism and Democratic Development in Korea, in *Administrative Dynamics and Development: The Korean Experience* (Bun Woong Kim et al., eds.), Kyobo Publishing, Seoul, 1985, pp. 12–19.

Kim, C. I. E., The Military in the Politics of South Korea: Creating Political Order, in *On Military Intervention* (Morris Janowitz and Jacques Van Dorn, eds.), Rotterdam University Press, Idaho, 1971, pp. 361–368.

Korea Development Institute, *Korea Year 2000: Prospects and Issues for Long-Term Development*, KDI Press, Seoul, 1986, pp. 51–61.

Lee, Hahn-Been, Two Critical Combinations for Successful Administrative Reform, a paper presented at EROPA Tenth General Assembly and Conference, Seoul, Korea, October 16–22, 1983, pp. 4–8.

Riggs, Fred W., Bureau Power: Some Paradoxes for Northeast Asia, in *International Symposium on Socio-Political Changes and Administrative Responses Towards the 21st Century in Northeast Asia*, Korea Institute of Public Administration, Seoul, 1992.

Ro, Kwang-H., The Paertorian Military in South Korea: A Study of the Military in Politics, Proceedings of the 7th Joint Conference of the Korean Political Science Association and the Association of Korea Political Scientists in North America, Seoul, July 27–29, 1987.

Shin, Doh-Chull, Myung, Chey, and Kim, Kwang-Woong, Left-Right Polarization and Support for Democratization Among the Mass Public in Korea, in Korea Political Science Association (KPSA), *The Korean National Community and State Development*, KAPA, Seoul, 1989, p. 127.

Sohn, Jai-Souk, Political Dominance and Political Failure: The Role of the Military in South Korea, in *The Military Intervention: Case Studies in Political Development* (Henry Bienen, ed.), Russell Sage Foundation, New York, 1968, pp. 102–122.

Yun, Ke-Sop, Study on Privatization of Korean Public Enterprises, *Korean Social Science Journal 16*:48–60 (1990).

39
A Subordinate Bureaucracy: The Philippine Civil Service Up to 1992

Ledivina V. Cariño
University of the Philippines, Quezon City, Philippines

Under liberal democratic theory, the bureaucracy is the arm of the government of the day for concretizing its promises to the people. Staffed by persons appointed and promoted on the basis of expertise, it is a permanent body that serves each leadership competently and faithfully even if the incumbent's policies are the reverse of its predecessor's. It is neutral in political-party terms as well as in its ability to separate the demands of public office from the personal interests of its staff. It is the embodiment of rationality and efficiency.

But the theory has not delivered on its promise. The bureaucracy's neutral competence can degenerate into obsequiousness, a machine that questions no command. A civil service may so revere its procedures that responsiveness to even meritorious exceptions become unthinkable. Its performance may shield it from creativity so that experience may only evince trained incapacity.

Alternatively, the bureaucracy may discover power in its professionalism, neutrality, and rationality so that it orients services to itself and not to the people. In the name of efficiency, it may allocate goods and services on the basis of its own calculations, ignoring policy mandates or constituent demands. It may flaunt its control of resources to make citizens fearfully bow to its authority. It may allow access only to its favorites, so that its work is facilitated, and its performance rated highly, though the greater good not be attained.

The power emanating from its integral qualities as a bureaucracy may also push a civil service to attempt to be an equal partner or key member of the ruling leadership. As such it is not subordinate, as in the first case, nor is it a bureaucracy-for-itself, as in the second.

The theory did not anticipate the bureaucracy as a model of unthinking subordination, power manipulation, or political ascendancy. However, it did envision a mechanism for hewing it close to its original expectations. Through "overhead democracy" [1], the organization is made accountable to the political executive, which in turn answers to the electorate. This does not always describe reality either, but it is the law in most contemporary states.

The United States has propagated the liberal model in its technical assistance programs since the late 1940s. However, its own executive-bureaucracy relationship also does not adhere to the model. For instance, transients in the presidential office, not the permanent civil service, initiate and execute the major thrusts of each political leadership. The term "transients" may not convey the nature and clout of these professionals who enter and leave with each administration but who largely remain in Washington as consultants, lobbyists, and legislative staffers, never straying far from the corridors of power [2]. However, the civil service does not thereby become a conglomeration of anonymous nonentities, since its offices may form an "iron triangle" with like-minded legislators and lobby groups in pushing for their preferred policies in opposition to their nominal superior, the executive [3].

If the model does not work where it had originated, how does it fare where it is imported? The answer is complex. Not all countries qualify as democracies even under the most liberal definition of the term. Moreover, expertise as the basis for entry and retention is not assured. The executive is also not necessarily supreme, as civil servants may take part in coups, withhold information vital to policy, respond only to demands of favored groups, engage in corruption, or regard themselves as the principal definer of the public interest. Various bureaucracies, especially the people at their apex, have exercised such autonomous power at diverse times and places [4].

Since the liberal model is not adequate, then the interesting theoretical question is not why a bureaucracy is powerful but why and under what conditions it is subordinate. Moreover, since a democratic state is the implicit context of the theory, the contribution of the executive-bureaucracy relationship to the development of democracy is an important question. How a president and a civil service—cooperatively or antagonistically—use power to promote the general welfare or to enhance their private interests has important implications for the democratic development of the civil service and the nation.

This chapter studies the interactions of the executive and the civil service in this light. It focuses on the Philippine civil service, which has been subordinate to the executive throughout its existence. Executive-bureaucracy [5] relations in the Philippines from American colonization up to the end of the democratic period in 1972 will be first discussed. How the authoritarian government of Ferdinand E. Marcos unleashed the power potential of the civil service for his own purposes will be the second subject.

The next sections analyze the executive-bureaucracy relations from the start of redemocratization in 1986. The third section discusses what means the government of Corazon C. Aquino had used to remold the bureaucracy and how they had been strengthened or weakened by the civil service and other political forces. The succession of Fidel V. Ramos to the presidency through the regular electoral process and his initial relations with the civil service are the focus of the fourth part.

The final section offers reasons why Philippines executive-bureaucracy relations have been marked by presidential superordination and how that affects the role of the civil service and the executive as political instruments of a democratic society.

I. DEVELOPING A DOMINATED CIVIL SERVICE: FROM AMERICAN COLONIZATION TO THE EVE OF MARCOS'S COUP

Executive domination would have been the lot of the bureaucracy whichever protagonist won the disputed Philippine Islands on the eve of the twentieth century: the Spanish Crown, which had ruled it with an iron hand since 1521; the first independence movement in Asia, which culminated in the proclamation of the First Philippine Republic in June 1898; or the United States, which took over the colony in December 1898.

The Civil Service Act of 1900 introduced the values and methods favored by civil service reformers—recruitment by competitive examination, promotion by merit, permanence and neutrality despite changes in political leadership, and accountability of public office.

The United States used education along with its armed force as the major instrument of colonization. That emphasis gave rise to academic institutions of varying quality which became the source of Filipinos who used the bureaucracy as an avenue for social mobility. As such, many civil servants entered the bureaucracy with the required diplomas but without the expected competencies. The civil service tried to make up for such misfitting with training programs as up-to-date as any in the world. In addition, starting in the 1960s, the Civil Service Commission required graduate study in public administration before promotion to supervisory positions. Thus the Philippine civil service could be characterized as highly educated and well trained even though it continued to be deemed inefficient and ineffective.

Civil servants were supposed to uphold nonpartisanship, obedience to which was facilitated by two facts: (1) the Americans imposed swift and severe sanctions on persons caught violating civil service rules, and (2) the colony was effectively a one-party state throughout the American regime. The latter meant that despite party turnover in the United States and elections in the Philippines (since 1907), the bureaucracy did not have to contend with wide policy swings nor with new political personages after each election period.

The prohibition against party membership also cut off civil servants from the struggle of their compatriots for independence from America. Instead, they concentrated on technical assignments that did not solicit their views about the policy area. This was close to the classical bureaucratic role which civil servants carried over into independence. Although the presidency changed hands after every election, few policy shifts occurred since both parties adhered to similar political platforms and were dominated by practically the same elite families.

However, postwar politicians were less circumspect about making partisan demands. Thus the subtle circumventions of neutrality and antipatronage policies of the American period [6] became more open and widespread afterward.

The succession of one president by another took place with little upheaval, and the bureaucracy quietly accepted the new master each time. The latter appointed agency heads and as many aides as could be justified as "policy determining, highly technical or primarily confidential," qualities which exempted the appointee from civil service requirements. The new leadership could also hire less qualified political followers as "casuals," or emergency appointees.

A new president could summarily replace political transients and casuals. However, no wholesale turnout ever occurred since few Filipinos had no access to patrons on both sides of the political fence. Thus, practically everyone enjoyed security of tenure, up to the level of department undersecretary, giving any new government very little formal room to recruit its own people.

All presidents created offices directly under them to signal their main thrusts. In addition, they tried to get congressional authority for a general reorganization as soon as they took office. Most reorganization committees recommended the removal from the Office of the President of the favorite functions of his predecessor. They also proposed to create new offices (many for the same old programs) and to strengthen field operations; those served not so much to streamline or deconcentrate the bureaucracy as to open up new positions all over the country.

Reorganization allowed the executive to get rid of unsatisfactory employees or agencies without directly criticizing them, a culturally important face-saving device. However, dissatisfied agencies and bureaucrats fought the proposals in Congress, such that reorganizations became protracted and subject to horse-trading. Some proposals were never implemented because of presidential inaction in the face of bureaucratic recalcitrance [7]. Apparently, the subordinate bureaucracy could also win by tiring out a president.

Sometimes, civil servants played off the executive against Congress, and some managed to increase or modify their appropriations or enabling laws despite the absence of the president's support. This had implications on the executive-bureaucracy nexus:

> Along with the personalistic and fragmented party system, this beneficial alliance between individual administrators and legislators contributes to the paradoxical inability of the president, despite his ample constitutional authority as the chief executive, to direct, co-ordinate, and control the numerous agencies of the bureaucracy effectively. [8]

Bureaucratic subordination was thus incomplete. Yet few administrative officials used their power to put forward their own policy ideas except where these involved working conditions, such as reorganization programs and pay scales [9]. Most of their struggle was thus focused on personal demands or the internal problems of their own agencies. However, they did assist in actually writing up the bills and in following them up through the congressional mill.

Bureaucrats were also hardly disposed to change the ways of politics. In a survey of middle-level civil servants in the sixties, one-third mentioned helping in an electoral campaign—against civil service rules. Admitting little respect for politicians, about half asked for a dictator, or for that "bureaucratic utopia" where administrators instead of politicians ran the country [6]. Perhaps not a few of them hoped that this would see fruition when Ferdinand Marcos engineered a palace coup on September 21, 1972.

II. THE CIVIL SERVICE DURING THE DICTATORSHIP

When he became president in December 1965, Ferdinand Marcos strayed little from the conventions honored by previous chief executives relative to the treatment of the civil service. Like his predecessors, he removed a few casuals and built up the bureaucracy in the Office of the President. He also got congressional authority for a general reorganization. The proposals were completed in March 1972, but although they were produced by a joint legislative-executive commission, Marcos was not able to get Congress to approve them [11].

The stalled reorganization proposals became the first decree Marcos promulgated as a martial law dictator. This allowed him to hit back at two institutions he had denounced as stumbling blocks to his program of national greatness—the legislature and the bureaucracy. Amended eleven times within the first three years and many more times thereafter, the Integrated Reorganization Plan rapidly disintegrated and did not prove a good guide for making the civil service efficient nor organized for development, which were its professed aims. Agencies expanded and their number increased [12]. The reorganization's decentralizing thrust became once again an instrument for bureaucratic expansion rather than for bringing the government closer to the people.

Under martial law, personnel of public enterprises and regular agencies were made subject to the same law [13]. Because of this, unions of proprietary government corporations lost the right to strike. All benefits for employees thus became a gift from above, not the reward of a struggle waged by those below. Nevertheless, equal treatment of all employees never materialized. Those in public enterprises continued to enjoy higher wages in the guise of all kinds of allowances. In addition, a new division was forged between higher civil servants and the rest of the staff with the creation of the Career Executive Service and the wide gap between their salaries and those of all other employees.

Marcos proclaimed a "revolution from the center," arguing that a strong government was needed to lead the country toward economic emancipation, social justice, and participatory democracy. He encouraged the bureaucracy to nurture an image of itself as the source of societal direction [14]. To act as functional equivalents of the defunct legislature was close to the dream of Abueva's bureaucrats [15]. Yet it was political appointees rather than career officials who seized the opportunity to present their own policies.

As a buildup to his promised utopia, Marcos encouraged all civil servants to join the New Society Movement (Kilusang Bagong Lipunan [KBL]). In 1978, however, when he staged parliamentary elections, KBL was transformed into the ruling party. Civil servants who had joined a reform movement then found themselves pawns for electioneering.

Marcos also blurred the distinction between politicians and bureaucrats. Deputy ministers were chosen from his interim parliament, while career personnel were handpicked to run for political office. This made the peak of the bureaucracy the higher political levels, further encouraging partisan activity among government personnel.

Marcos's anticorruption rhetoric was stronger than that of most presidents. He had a succession of antigraft bodies and drives, all fading after much fanfare. However, laws became little more than expressions of access to the top, and corruption, already systemic, became even more centralized, an allocation to presidential kin and crony practically a feature of all transactions [16].

This was certainly not the promise of P.D. No. 6 (September 27, 1972), which authorized summary dismissals for erring public servants. Originally accepted by the public as a possibly potent weapon against pervasive corruption, it instead became instant punishment for uncooperative officials and a threat to dissenters within the ranks.

These changes weakened considerably the professions of neutrality and responsibility of the bureaucracy. Yet, the threat of, and actual recourse to, dismissals and worse punishments stifled criticisms and made the organization appear united behind the president.

Paradoxically, the bureaucracy gained strength as a democratic instrument in a few areas during the martial law period. Training programs included "Filipino ideology," a mixed bag of public service exhortations and exaltation of the president. While producing few Marcosistas, they did impress the need for nationalism and commitment upon some career personnel. However, they continued to see themselves as simple implementors who, while proud of their personal integrity and love of country, did not feel the need to encourage these norms in their staff, instill social commitment in their agencies, or get involved in wider political concerns [17].

Popular participation also blossomed during this period as pockets of the civil service became convinced that acting on the basis of citizen demands was a superior method of service delivery [18]. However, although the participatory rhetoric was encouraged since it enhanced the democratic image of the dictatorship, civil servants faced political and military censure when they truly believed it and acted accordingly.

Marcos's policies plunged the country into an economic crisis which became a crisis of legitimacy with the assassination of Senator Benigno Aquino, Jr., in 1983. At that point, even public school teachers, the most docile of public servants, participated in the widening national protests and practically invented the system of "mass leaves" to get around the strike ban.

Nevertheless, most of the bureaucracy stuck to their desks. Perhaps a majority were self-defined neutral civil servants who would obey any political leadership, regardless. However, a smaller group were "closet oppositionists" who sent to the opposition damning statistics and documents and who, by their invention of anti-Marcos jokes, painted themselves as captives and victims. They remained in the service not only because they regarded their work as valuable but also because there was little alternative employment in a shrunken economy.

The executive-bureaucracy struggle came to a head in the 1986 presidential campaign when the Civil Service Commission itself promoted political activity on behalf of the Marcoses. Many civil servants refused to enlist in the commission's move in the name of political neutrality. The CSC head then promptly redefined "political neutrality" as "loyalty to the government of the day" [19].

The break of the civil service with Marcos came when poll canvassers walked out in full view of a big television audience, after they became convinced that the official tally was being manipulated. Until then, fear and timidity had so ruled the bureaucracy that despite Marcos's efforts at politicization, it was probably more leadership-dominated than at any other period of its history.

III. THE BUREAUCRACY UNDER AQUINO

Corazon Aquino became president after a four-day "people's power" revolution in February 1986. Charged to redemocratize the country and remove the vestiges of the dictatorship, she presided over the restoration of traditional democratic institutions and processes. This included the ratification of a new constitution, the instauration of the legislature and the courts, and the peaceful transition of power to her successor, Fidel V. Ramos, in June 1992.

Part of the mandate of the Aquino government was the reform of political institutions, including the civil service. However, she resorted to Marcos's model of purges instead of the pre–martial law practice of accepting the civil service as is. Aquino's purge was complemented by a more drastic reorganization than any undertaken before. These were justified by the view that the bureaucracy was a major collaborator, not just a tool, of the dictatorship.

Summary dismissals, including those made in the guise of reorganization, were halted by 1989 by the combined forces of the courts, the Civil Service Commission, and the legislature. However, reorganizations continued to unsettle the bureaucracy up to the end of Aquino's term, partly because of frequent changes of cabinet officials, and partly because of a new Local Government Code that contracted the powers of some national offices.

The cabinet was revamped several times, each leaving a new wave of bureaucratic reorganization at its wake. De-Marcosification as a rationale weakened as many people prominently identified with Marcos were appointed to key political positions, were elected under the administration party, or joined it shortly afterward. Thus, punishment for being Marcosistas seemed to be meted out not to the most culpable persons but to the most vulnerable ones—lowly employees who had obeyed orders during the Marcos regime in order to keep their jobs.

Trimming the bureaucracy did not occur either. Despite the layoff of tens of thousands, civil servants actually increased as new positions were created and staffed by either new personnel or those recycled from other agencies.

Purging and reorganization did not occur without resistance or conflict. This was a new development; the martial law purges, though equally flawed, were acquiesced to quietly since resistance to the authoritarian leadership was dangerous. This was not expected under Aquino's government with her disavowal of undemocratic methods. Besides, the 1987 Constitution gave concrete support to employee organizations.

Thus, employees organized with the expectation that a government claiming to be democratic would not move against protest groups. This assumption was not totally correct, and few associations were able to protect their members from reprisal or to stop what they viewed as unfair treatment. This taught the lesson that mass actions would not necessarily work. Thus, many resorted to the old method of seeking concessions outside center stage. While those in organized demonstrations got the headlines, certain employee groups or agencies quietly negotiated salary increases or saved their positions or units; these became known only with the publication of their respective executive orders.

Nevertheless, a few positive results were won by groups with much more universal concerns. The most productive of these efforts were those where employee groups got the ear of the president or won the support of the Civil Service Commission, the Congress (especially the Senate), and the mass media.

Executive officials could be faulted for their resort to spoils and loyalty tests and their continued failure to appreciate the staff they had inherited. On the other hand, the instability of their status pushed many civil servants to greater inflexibility and noninnovativeness, for fear of making mistakes [20]. That lowered their worth further in the eyes of their new superiors—a vicious circle that hurt their cause as much as the assaults of those officials.

The bureaucracy continued not to distinguish itself as a source of policy ideas. Instead, policy proposals were worked out by the executive, with assistance from private-sector think tanks, advisers, or academics. The role of employees would be to put these proposals into bill form, if necessary. Many undertook this task despite reservations about the issue at hand. For instance, the standardization of salaries of civil servants was largely prepared by external consultants, with some assistance from insiders in the computations and fashioning as a bill. However, some of them privately pointed out its unfairness as it gave disproportionate increases to the top levels. Yet, they never articulated their reservations to their superiors.

The employees' inability to protect their collective interest could be traced to divisions within the bureaucracy itself. The changes in wages favored certain professional groups, political and administrative officials over the rank and file, the military over civilians. They also competed for scarce government allocations. Conflicts also arose over jurisdictional and substantial controversies—for instance, the Department of Labor versus the Department of Trade and Industry and the National Economic and Development Authority over the issue of a minimum wage hike for private-sector employees. However, they occurred with considerably less emotion, given the absence of strong commitment to their policy area.

The nature and frequency of corruption scandals suggest that the risk-benefits calculus had not been altered in favor of rectitude at both the political and bureaucratic levels. Many civil servants either had not turned their backs on opportunities for personal enrichment or still found it "part of their job" to obey superiors whose orders involved them in systemic corruption.

A few employee organizations documented corruption by top political and administrative officials in their agencies and released them to the mass media. Some of their exposés became the bases of legislative investigations, but produced little decisive executive action. Nor did employees or their organizations overcome harassment and threats from management despite a new Civil Service Commission supportive of civil service unionism.

On the whole, the bureaucracy engaged the Aquino government in more struggle than any other executive. Thus, civil service unions were resurrected by the purges and reorganization the Aquino government unleashed. Nevertheless, they have attracted attention disproportionate to their numbers, which remain small. However, the executive-bureaucracy interaction has also been shaped by the fact that the political system itself has changed considerably.

The legislature and media helped to air the grievances of the bureaucracy, whether it was summary dismissals, "bad-faith" reorganization, or political corruption. In addition, the Civil Service Commission had grown more independent of the executive and supported the bureaucracy in many issues.

Despite all these, however, the executive remained ascendant over the civil service. The popularity of Aquino, her hold on Congress, and the continued scarcity of alternative jobs have contributed to the continued dominance of the executive.

IV. THE SUCCESSION OF RAMOS

On June 30, 1992, Corazon Aquino turned over the presidency to Fidel V. Ramos to mark the country's first normal succession in twenty-seven years. She had directed her staff to begin the process of orderly transition only three days after her last State of the Nation Address and almost ten months before the election of her successor [21]. The transition process was formally directed by the president, but its vast requirements were handled largely by career civil servants. All agency transition committees were "composed of senior career officials of the department representing [its] major offices and units" [22]. A similar committee was convened at the cabinet and local government levels.

The transition process was explicitly in line "with the government's policy to protect and promote the career civil service" [23]. Among the required documents was a Red Book, which listed all positions open to political appointment, which complemented—and in so doing, hoped to protect—incumbents of Blue Book (career) positions, especially if the incoming officials could be impressed by the sheer number of jobs they could distribute that they would no longer disturb the career bureaucracy. More than providing information to the new officials, the process was also intended to communicate to the career personnel the executive's view of what they could be proud of, and what they could still contribute to the nation, thereby calming fears about the succession [24].

Ramos's call "for more private sector and less government," a leaner and better paid bureaucracy, a shift of decision-making powers to the provinces, and "the insulation of the career service from the corrosive political patronage" is reminiscent of the guiding principles of his predecessor's Presidential Commission on Government Reorganization. However, he campaigned on at least three thrusts which might prove different. First, he put more stress on the principle of command responsibility. Second, he pledged a "more professional and more meritocratic" bureaucracy; he explicated this as calling for more generalists, a move that could buck the trend for specialization in vogue since the early 1960s. Both of these could be traced to his military socialization. However, the third concern, the "bigger representation of employees in policy-making bodies in government agencies and not simply in matters relative to employee welfare," squared more with the Ramos of People Power fame. Coupled with the desire for people empowerment, it signaled the possibility of a president's broadening the compass of participation both inside and outside government [25].

Aside from the transition, the civil servants became engulfed, like the rest of the nation, in the election process, which featured the longest ballot ever: six candidates for president, an equal number for vice president, and the selection of twenty-four senators, one representative, and a host of local officials. While the bureaucracy as a whole was not recruited to campaign for administration candidates, politicians recruited them while their parties traded accusations about the use of public funds and personnel for political process. Career Executive Service officers did not challenge a candidate's enumeration of:

> complaints from civil servants . . . (about) attempts of higher officials to enlist their personnel . . . as *hakot* (forced participants) to rallies, *tagasundo* (greeters) at airports, and soon, [to] bring their reluctant voters to the precincts. [26]

in his speech at their convention. Nevertheless, the situation was more comparable to the pre–martial law years than to the Marcos period. In 1992, any campaigning undertaken by civil servants was an accommodation to specific political patrons or direct superiors, not obedience to a directive from the president or the Civil Service Commission.

Nevertheless, the response of the civil service to Ramos the candidate was not enthusiastic. He was not the front-runner in straw polls of major government offices. Moreover, his hold on the Career Executive Service officers eroded from 47% to 27% when he did not appear in person in their convention to discuss his plans for the bureaucracy. Of the six presidential candidates, the only one who did so, Jovito Salonga, got 16% at its start and 46% afterward [27]. Yet, both Ramos and Salonga avowed a commitment to the merit system and greater participation of the civil servants in governance. An analyst thought Salonga's advantage lay in having "patiently answered the participants' queries," coupled with "his very clear understanding of the workings of the bureaucracy, of the officials' doubts and fears regarding the transition period, and his emphatic commitment to uphold professionalism and careerism in the government service" [28]. The fact that candidate Ramos did not seek such rapport with civil servants could indicate that like many political leaders, Ramos relegated the bureaucracy to one of the minor links a president has to forge, perhaps assuming its subordination to be automatic.

Along with unearthing a possible irritant between the new president and the bureaucracy, the CESO convention was also instructive for the fears and demands expressed there by civil servants. They centered on issues related to the sourcing of appointees to (career) executive positions, the apprehension about courtesy resignations (the polite version of purges) and reorganization, professionalism, incentives, and control of corruption. All these issues were internal to the bureaucracy and, except for corruption, centered on their tenure and welfare. No bigger policy issues were raised, not even concerns about the role of government, decentralization, or the public-private balance, extrabureaucratic concerns already mentioned in the forum by the candidates.

President Ramos followed the pre–martial law presidential tradition when he assumed office in 1992. This is true both in his policy of attracting all politicians to his fold as well as accepting the bureaucracy largely as is. He even retained some of his predecessors' cabinet officials and most of his department heads and kept transients and career officials who did not submit courtesy resignations (as a pre-1972 political appointee would have). No purges are in sight. However, like all presidents before him, he also asked the Congress for authority to conduct a general reorganization of the bureaucracy. This could wake up the unions, which had been quiet since his installation.

V. EXPLAINING THE CONTINUED DOMINATION OF THE BUREAUCRACY

The current subordination of the Philippine bureaucracy to the executive is likely to continue. At the period of succession, the civil service acquiesced to being used for political purposes and sought only a president who was more understanding of its needs. In both the transition and electoral processes, it had not tried to put forward policy ideas, worrying only about its tenure security and benefits.

Four types of regimes—American colonialism, postindependence democratic governments, then authoritarianism, and now redemocratization—nurtured executive domination for their own specific reasons. Commencing at the dawn of the twentieth century, the Philippine merit system experiment—with the executive firmly directing the bureaucracy—antedated all but three States of the Union. It was promoted as a guileless manifestation of the American effort to propagate the ideals of its civil service reformers. However, it also cannot be gainsaid that an apolitical, competent machine suited the colonial power well, since it removed a big educated and professional group from political agitation and demands for independence and taught them to regard American colonialism as benevolent.

Adherence to ideals of public administration as the country emerged from the ravages of war also formally justified the continuation of a dominated bureaucracy after independence. Besides, at that time, development was regarded as a politically neutral, value-free, and technical goal. Under both regimes, efficiency was sought over commitment; having set the goals, the executive needed only to drill the civil service on methods and techniques. However, the unintended politicalization effected by corruption and partisanship made the bureaucracy less a tool of the people than an instrument for itself and for its executives.

The Marcos dictatorship tried to upgrade the bureaucracy from subordinate to partner by encouraging civil servants to get involved in policy and party matters. It also fostered—along with Marcos's personality cult—ideological training in democracy, social justice, and love of country. These values, while not genuinely desired by the government, linked some civil servants with the underprivileged in society and also developed their greater sense of accountability, allowing them to move away from the dictatorship. Yet, the leader, assisted by transient and career civil servants, ignored his own propaganda and set aside justice and equity for plunder and self-enrichment.

A regime of double-speak and force cowed its supposed collaborator as it did the rest of the society. While a few career officials enjoyed the favors of power and others developed some integration with the masses, the rest became even more acquiescent.

Believing the civil service to be indeed Marcos's collaborator and partner, the redemocratizing government of Aquino tried to bring the executive-bureaucracy relationship back to the status quo ante. Like its pre-1972 predecessors, it treated the bureaucracy as a subordinate, eschewing Marcos's invitations to coequality. Moreover, it practiced *ressentiment politics*, making decisions based on its anger against persons and institutions identified with the old order [29].

However, executive domination since 1986 was moderated by the commitment to political rights: pledges to uphold due process and transparency, rights of association and criticism, and sensitivity to public opinion went along with summary dismissals, "bad faith" reorganization, and weaknesses in enforcing ethical and performance norms. The leadership's frequent use of slogans of popular empowerment also emboldened civil servants to organize, baptizing as a variant of empowerment their own attempts to resist executive decisions.

Thus, under Aquino, the struggle between the executive and the civil service became more pronounced. Militant sections of the bureaucracy did not only concentrate on issues of wages, benefits, and positions but also championed the more public-interested demands for integrity in the use and management of funds and personnel. Nevertheless, these changes did not manage to make the executive less dominant over the bureaucracy.

Since four types of political regimes have not changed the kind of executive-bureaucracy relationship obtaining in the Philippines, one must identify other characteristics of the political system and the culture which tend to nurture and support that pattern.

An important factor is an authoritarian culture, which the bureaucracy reinforces in its hierarchical line of command. Thus civil servants accept, as they did when they were children, power holders and their orders without argument. This is accompanied by a strong sense of shame and losing face, which makes employees risk-averse and unwilling to make mistakes. The result is a reactive organization that waits for executive directives instead of suggesting its own thrusts and approaches.

Also, inured in a system of dyadic relations and factional power plays [30], civil servants have found it more advantageous to fight for themselves or their immediate groups than to mobilize and unite so that the whole bureaucracy can be reformed. After all, this strategy has won exemptions from pay scales and modified reorganization plans.

These tendencies are reinforced in a hardly growing economy marked by job scarcity, which puts a premium on unquestioning obedience to superiors. Complaints, criticisms, and collective action put one's employment on the line and produce an unacceptable risk for the bulk of the bureaucracy.

Besides, the struggle is taking place within an inegalitarian economic and social structure that has remained unchanged despite upheavals in the system of government. With executives maintaining policy continuity whatever the political system, it is unrealistic to expect bureaucrats—with their intimate knowledge of the workings of politics and avowal of "neutrality"—to present antielite proposals. Besides, many civil servants enjoy the patronage of the economic dominants, and as socially mobile individuals, are unlikely to go against the interests of the class to which they aspire to belong.

Factors associated with the executive also influence the struggle with the civil service. The colonial governors-general and postindependence presidents have had ample powers as well as strong personalities. The 1987 Constitution, wary of dictatorship, has clipped the presidency's formal authority, but the presidencies of Aquino and Ramos continued to be "more equal" than the other two branches of government. This could be traced not only to their respective personalities and consensual tendencies, but also the centrifugal orientation of the political system, where institutions and persons accommodate the wishes of any person who happens to be at its head.

Before 1972, legislators were independent patrons of civil servants and their partners against the executive, helping them stall decisions, get advantages for their agencies, or go against merit system norms even when the president tried to enforce them. They were silenced by the authoritarian leader and became his satellite patrons instead. Under Aquino, legislators were liberated to complete the triangle with the civil service and the presidency again. This was evident in the swiftness with which they passed laws protecting the bureaucracy and, in effect, clipping the powers of the president in that domain. However, Congress has not been immune to the abuse and corruption it is attempting to check in the civil service and the executive. Besides, the presidency's informal power over the purse—controlling as it does the release of funds for congressional pork barrel and other projects—has served to limit any legislator's fancied coequality with the executive.

Presidential superordination is further supported by the bureaucracy's reputation of corruption and inefficiency. Instead of making themselves indispensable with top performance, many employees reacted to purging and reorganization with work slowdown and continuation of disvalued activities like corruption and absenteeism. Thus, while it was able to win sympathy and support from media, Congress, and the general public where it was perceived as unjustly treated by the executive branch, it dissipated such support when it manifested ineffectiveness, laziness, and corruption instead.

Under Aquino, the political leadership had to deal with an increasingly militant membership that slowly moved out of narrow bread-and-butter issues into concerns—shared with the executive and the citizenry—regarding the norms of public office. That forced the executive to clarify and refine its policies on the civil service. However, that struggle dealt more with methods of performance than their substantive goals and directions, reinforcing the view of the bureaucracy as simply a technical arm of the state.

That orientation to methods and to the internal concerns of the civil service has been encouraged by Ramos's return to the conventions of normal succession followed by all governments before Marcos's coup. Such an orientation has led in other countries to the development of a bureaucracy-for-itself, where a civil service becomes its own major constituency, to the disregard of presidential directions or popular demands. This has happened in Thailand [31], Bangladesh [32], and Saskatchewan, Canada [33]. In all these cases, however, the bureaucracy had strong links with dominant social forces and could count on their support in the struggle against the executive.

In the Philippines, on the contrary, the civil service is facing a former general who is supported by the business elite, and it may not even get the backing of legislators, who are even now scrambling to get into the good graces of the executive. Thus, it would be safer to predict that the self-concern of the bureaucracy would make it even more an apolitical body, more malleable to the desires of the new executive.

As an expert body which was slowly imbibing the values of listening and responding to the demands of the majority, the bureaucracy could have become a force the executive had to reckon with, a body which insisted on its commitment to social justice, due process, and public accountability. A simple acquiescent instrument worried only about its wages and working conditions will not serve that purpose. The democratic development of the nation would be served more appropriately by a struggle which forces both protagonists to clarify their vision for the society and their respective roles in it.

NOTES

1. Emmette Redford, *Democracy in the Administrative State*, Oxford University Press, New York, 1969.
2. James Pfiffner, Political Appointees and Career Executives: The Democracy-Bureaucracy Nexus in the Third Century, *Public Administration Review, 4*(1):57–65 (January–February 1987).
3. Fred W. Riggs, The Survival of Presidentialism in America: Para-Constitutional Practices, *International Political Science Review, 9*(4):247–278 (1988).
4. See, for instance, discussions of the bureaucracies of Thailand, Turkey, Pakistan, and Latin America in Fred W. Riggs, *Thailand: The Modernization of a Bureaucratic Polity*. East-West Center Press, Honolulu, 1966; Clarence E. Thurber and Lawrence S. Graham (eds.), *Development Administration in Latin America*, Duke University Press, Durham, N.C., 1973, and Khrishna K. Tummala (ed.), *Administrative Systems Abroad*, University Press of America, Lanham, New York and London, 1982.
5. "Executive," or "political leadership," refers here to a country's head of government and his/her principal political officials or cabinet. It is equivalent to "government of the day," "X's administration," or "Y's government." Chief executive" or "president" refers to the individual at the apex of leadership. "Bureaucracy" or "civil service" is the set of civilian agencies that make up the administrative system.
6. Onofre D. Corpuz, *The Philippines*, Prentice-Hall, Englewood Cliffs, N.J., 1965.

7. See, for instance, the fate of the Government Survey and Reorganization Commission (1954–1956) in Leandro A. Viloria, *U.S. Technical Assistance on Public Administration in the Philippines: Establishing a Management Improvement Program.* College of Public Administration, University of the Philippines, Manila, 1969.
8. Jose V. Abueva, Administrative Culture and Behavior of Middle-Level Civil Servants in the Philippines, in (Edward W. Weidner, ed.), *Development Administration in Asia*, Duke University Press, Durham, N.C., 1970, 167–168.
9. Leandro A. Viloria, *U.S. Technical Assistance on Public Administration in the Philippines: Establishing a Management Improvement Program.* College of Public Administration, University of the Philippines, Manila, 1969; Abelardo G. Samonte, WAPCO: A Case Study of Administrative Reform in the Philippines, in *Administrative Reforms in Asia* (Hahn-Been Lee and Abelardo G. Samonte, eds.), Eastern Regional Organization for Public Administration, Manila, 1970, 48–75; and Amelia P. Varela, *Administrative Culture and Political Change.* Occasional Paper No. 88-2, Publications Office, College of Public Administration, University of the Philippines, 1988.
10. Jose V. Abueva, Administrative Culture and Behavior of Middle-Level Civil Servants in the Philippines, in *Development Administration in Asia* (Edward W. Wiedner, ed.), Duke University Press, Durham, N.C., 1970, 168.
11. Perla A. Segovia, Administrative Reorganization, Institutional Development and Management Improvement, *Philippine Journal of Public Administration 21*(3–4): (July–October 1977).
12. This was most marked in public enterprises, which increased from 75 to about 250 during the fourteen-year period of dictatorship. The bureaucracy itself doubled in this period—from 569,000 in 1973 to 1.3 million in 1985. See the Presidential Commission on Government Reorganization, *Principles and Policy Proposals, Book I.* Provisional Report, PCGR, Manila, 1986.
13. Presidential Decree No. 807, Providing for the Organization of the Civil Service Commission in Accordance with the Provisions of the Constitution . . . , October 6, 1975.
14. Office of the President, "Transition Management Plan," undated, ca. December 1991.
15. Jose V. Abueva, Administrative Culture and Behavior of Middle-Level Civil Servants in the Philippines, in *Development Administration in Asia* (Edward W. Weidner, ed.), Duke University Press, Durham, N.C., 1970, 168.
16. Ma. Concepcion P. Alfiler, Administrative Measures Against Bureaucratic Corruption: The Philippine Experience, *Philippine Journal of Public Administration, 23*(3–4):323–349 (July–October 1979), and Belinda A. Aquino, *Politics of Plunder: The Philippines Under Marcos*, Great Books and University of the Philippines-College of Public Administration, Manila, 1987.
17. Josefina G. Tayag, Ideology and Public Administration: The Philippine Experience, Unpublished D.P.A. dissertation, College of Public Administration, University of the Philippines, March 1989.
18. Frances F. Korten and Robert Y. Siy, Jr., *Transforming a Bureaucracy: The Experience of the Philippine National Irrigation Administration*, Ateneo de Manila University Press, Quezon City, 1989.
19. Jesus Borromeo, Remarks at the Symposium on Political Neutrality, College of Public Administration, University of the Philippines, 1985.
20. Patricia Santo Tomas, Remarks given in the Roundtable Discussion on Bureaucracy and Public Accountability, sponsored by the Philippine Social Science Council, Philippine National Science Society and Pi Gamma Mu, Quezon City, May 3, 1988.
21. Sobrepeña, Aniceto, Interview by the author. May 29, 1992.

22. Office of the President, "Transition Management Plan," undated, December 1991, 2.
23. Office of the President, "Transition Management Plan," undated, December 1991, 7.
24. Sobrepeña, Aniceto, Interview by the author, May 29, 1992.
25. Fidel V. Ramos, The Bureaucracy Under a Ramos Administration, condensation of speech read before the National Convention of the Career Executive Service Officers, *The Public Manager 4*(4):6 (April 1992); and Face to Face: Government Must Have a Pro-Poor Bias (interview), *Philippine Daily Globe*, May 10, 1992, 11.
26. Jovito R. Salonga, The Civil Service and the Salonga Presidency, condensation of speech read before the National Convention of the Career Executive Service Officers, *The Public Manager 4*(4):4 (April 1992).
27. Salonga Tops Execs' Mock Election, *The Public Manager 4*(4):1,3 (April 1992).
28. The Convention That Almost Never Took Place, *The Public Manager 4*(4):8 (April 1992).
29. Juan J. Linz, The Breakdown of Democratic Regimes: Crises, Breakdown and Reequilibrium, in *The Breakdown of Democratic Regimes* (Juan J. Linz and Alfred Stepan, eds.), The Johns Hopkins University Press, Baltimore, 1978, 42.
30. Carl H. Lande, *Leaders, Factions and Parties: The Structure of Philippine Politics*, Southeast Asian Studies, Yale University, New Haven, 1965.
31. Fred W. Riggs, *Thailand: The Modernization of a Bureaucratic Polity*, East-West Center Press, Honolulu, 1966; and Chai-Anan Samudavanija, The Bureaucracy, in *Government and Politics of Thailand* (Somsakdi Xuto, ed.), Oxford University Press, Singapore, 1989, 75–108.
32. Mohammad Mohabbat Khan and Habib Zafarullah, Public Bureaucracy in Bangladesh, in *Administrative Systems Abroad* (Krishna Tummala, ed.), University Press of America, Lanham, New York, 1978, 158–187.
33. Seymour Martin Lipset, Bureaucracy and Social Change, in *Reader in Bureaucracy* (Robert Merton et al., eds.), The Free Press, Glencoe, Ill., 1952, 221–232.

40
Interrelationship of Sociopolitical Structure and Public Administration in India

R. B. Jain
University of Delhi, Delhi, India

The interrelationship of the state and society has been an important theme in the evolution of political thought in the past half century. That the state is deeply embedded in society and that societal variables do affect the autonomy and performance of the state are now accepted facts. Whether it is the system theorists, or the dependency theorists, or the ecologist interpreters of public administration, all seem to agree that in any society interactions among the state, its sociopolitical structures, and its administrative framework ultimately determine its policy outcomes. Such interactions not only help pattern societal preferences, but also pave the way to political and administrative developments in the context of divisiveness within and between classes, ethnic and religious segments, interest groups, and linguistic differences. The literature on comparative public administration is replete with the emphasis on interaction and interrelationship between an administrative system and its external environment and the impact of sociocultural values on bureaucratic behavior, the processes of political and administrative change, and vice versa [1]. While scholars have concentrated more on the study of the state's capacity to bring about socioeconomic change through the evolution of a pattern of political and administrative institutions, little attention has been paid to understanding the impact that the sociopolitical structures in any society have on its political or administrative development.

This chapter is concerned with an analysis of the sociopolitical structure in a complex and developing society, that of India, with a view to discerning the interrelationships among its social and political structures, continuing policy changes, and administrative development. The attempt is to show that although a highly heterogeneous and complex social system with traditional, diversified religious-cultural values creates enormous pressures on its public administrative system, it does not necessarily stifle administrative development. The need is to coordinate policy and administrative changes in a manner that not only responds to the growing socioeconomic compulsions of the society, but also enables its people to participate in the politicoadministrative processes. Ideally such an analysis and similar findings on the context of other developed and developing societies would be helpful in building up a theory of societal context and administrative development.

I. THE INSTITUTIONAL STRATEGIES

India was one of the first of the British colonies to gain independence from the yoke of an imperial power. After attainment of freedom in 1947, the challenge before the political leadership was to frame a well-conceived strategy of change, development, and nation building, and to forge instrumentalities thereof—both mobilizational and institutional. To attempt to achieve a modicum of economic and political development in the aftermath of partition, through a democratic political system, while undertaking at the same time reconstruction of a hardened social structure—not only deeply rooted in the age-old traditions, but highly fragmented—was indeed a formidable task. The four basic objectives of socioeconomic and political development uppermost in the minds of political leaders at that time were (a) creation of a stable democratic polity; (b) laying the foundations of a self-reliant economy for rapid growth; (c) attainment of social justice through the elimination of discrimination based on class, caste, sex, and religion and eradication of poverty; and (d) rebuilding of the dilapidated administrative structure to be able to withstand the pressures generated by the growing demands and aspirations of expectant masses.

The leadership in India responded by channeling the processes of change through the creation of a state system based on Western liberal democratic ideology of freedom and equality, incorporating the parliamentary system of government, reconciling it with the concept of economic planning, and reforming the administrative machinery to enable it to respond to the growing exigencies and requirements of a social system divided by a variety of sociocultural identities.

Although the framing of a new political setup with its institutions, structures, and rules of the game has proved to be a matter of incalculable difficulty for many of the new nations of Asia and Africa, India presented a striking contrast. Not only was an elaborate state system created with speed, but the democratic structure it established was institutionalized in considerable detail. This had been possible because of both antecedent agreement on fundamentals and continuing diffusion of these agreements in the generation that followed independence. Even as early as 1928, the Motilal Nehru Committee had framed a complete draft spelling out the features of (free) India's polity. It recommended, among other things, a parliamentary form and federal structure of government and an exhaustive list of fundamental rights. These recommendations found overwhelming support among the members of the Constituent Assembly in the late 1940s.

However, decision making on India's institutional strategy was not wholly a product of agreements that were reached during the national movement. The framers did consider the emerging framework anew. Certain occasions did occur when the members of the Constituent Assembly ran into serious disagreements. But debate was avoided at most opportunities. Viable compromises were sought on fundamental provisions such as the federal structure of the country, the importance of the judiciary in interpreting the constitution, and the role of "due process"; the question of a proper balance between the personal liberties of the citizen and the integrity of the nation, between the right to property and the goal of social and economic development, between the need for centralization and the extent of decentralization to lower levels of the polity, between the right to equality and the question of special rights and privileges of minorities and tribal religious groups [2] and so on.

In order to prevent the country from falling into pieces, certain restraints on the power of some institutions and the freedom of individuals were introduced. For example, the central government was armed with effective powers against the constituent states. Similarly, preventive detention to strengthen the government's hand came to be accepted as a necessary provision despite its restrictions on the most fundamental rights of a democratic citizen. It was dubbed a "necessary evil." Again, while defining the relationship between Parliament and the courts, due consideration had to be given to the need to arm the state with powers to reduce social and economic disparities; consequently the "due process" clause was modified to suit Indian conditions [3]. Efforts were also made to elicit the maximum consensus in order to lay down a strong foundation for the nation. What emerged, as a result, was a federal structure of parliamentary government with a cabinet form of executive at the national and state levels directed to liberal democratic goals of individual freedom and social justice in the fulfillment of which government was assigned a positive role. The institutional structure that came into being was essentially modernist in character but with important departures from the Western model designed to facilitate national integration and social assimilation [4].

The Indian leadership, in fact, borrowed the Western liberal philosophy and Indianized it according to unfamiliar and unique Indian practices and attitudes. Grant of "special privileges" to the backward groups in society and the "Scheduled Castes and Tribes" was an innovation designed to help the economically and socially weaker sections of the community. Similarly, the linguistic diversity of the country was given constitutional support through the granting of legal status to all the major regional languages. The system also provided for flexible methods of adaptation to changing social needs and demands by making the amendment procedure relatively easy to effect. This was a deviation from strictly orthodox federal practices.

A political system, though a subsystem of the society, is supposed to perform the overall and overriding function of looking after the society and managing it to the extent that this can be done at a conscious, corporate level. It is necessary, therefore, that a maximum number of members of a society participate in the exercise of this function. Certain groups may be legally or actually deprived of the right to participate in the process, while even many who have the right to participate may not choose to do so unless it be made mandatory for them. The extent of the formal right of participation in the political process which is concerned with the total whole, the actual facilitation of the exercise of such a right, and the actual exercise of the right, thus, may be taken as determining the degree of political development which a society has achieved when compared to other societies or to itself in a former stage. This particular aspect of making maximum possible opportunities available for free participation of people in public affairs was the one on which the edifice of a democratic system was built in India.

The arena of power in India has not been limited to a ruling oligarchy or an aristocracy of birth; it has increasingly spread to the society as a whole by drawing new sections into its ambit. This is what differentiates the Indian political system both from the European systems where, during the phase of rapid industrialization and social change, political participation was confined to the upper classes of society; and from the revolutionary experiments of both communist and noncommunist varieties, where barring intraparty feuds and military coups, political competition was generally not allowed to interfere with the process of development. In India, politics is neither suppressed nor confined to a small aristocracy. On the contrary, it provides the larger setting within which decision making in regard to social and economic development takes place [5].

The launching of the new governmental organization and the inauguration of the Indian Republic in January 1950 did not complete the process of institutionalization. The emergence of further consensus on the political system involved new developments in the institutional layout of the country and important modifications of the formal structure of authority. The creation of a

National Planning Commission within the political structure was one among such developments directed toward the attainment of planned economic growth. The commission was entrusted with the task of formulating "Five Year Plans," enunciating the social and economic priorities of the nation, and suggesting a general model of economic development. The states were reorganized on a linguistic-cultural basis to integrate heterogeneous communities into a nation, yet at the same time given an opportunity to maintain and promote their own regional language and culture. The dream of achieving unity in diversity was actually pursued. The launching of community development programs and the establishment of the Panchayati Raj institutions were other measures within the framework of the Indian political process that were undertaken to secure democratic decentralization for the purpose of social and economic development at the grass-roots level and in relation to the processes of nation building. A continuous process of administrative reform was initiated, first through an assessment of the administrative machinery by some inside and outside observers and later through the creation of a number of specific committees and a high powered Reform Commission to suggest necessary administrative changes; such changes were continuously monitored by a permanent Department of Administrative Reform [6].

Despite indigenous and foreign criticism, the story of Indian polity since independence has been one of remarkable stability. Except for a brief aberration, the state of emergency in 1975–1977, the forty years of independence have seen remarkable performance of democratic elections, reasonably efficient political and administrative institutions, and basic political stability.

II. EVOLUTION OF THE ADMINISTRATIVE STATE

A. The Inheritance

At independence, India inherited from the British a monolithic, strictly hierarchical administrative structure, with the line of command running unimpeded from the viceroy and governor-general in Delhi to the farthest village, but with certain well established traditions [7]. The purpose of such a system was to keep the interest of the British power in India dominant, make sure that the government got the revenge it needed, and, in terms of peace and security, maintain law and order.

The system of administration that had evolved in India from the time of Warren Hastings and Lord Cornwallis from imperial rule until independence had five distinguishing features: (a) the district as the basic unit of administration, and the office of the district collector as a prototype of a "District-Maharajah" "the alter-ego of the vice-regal authority" controlling, directing, and coordinating all administrative activity in his district; (b) centralization—as the recognized principle of administration both territorially and functionally and centralization of decision making in almost all policy areas—public finance, legal and judicial systems, education, health, and even public works; (c) the steel-frame of administration—a strong institution of a single dominating civil service, with the Indian Civil Service (ICS) an elite generalist service, occupying the top position among other allied and subordinate services down the levels of central and provincial hierarchies; (d) a system of elaborate rules and regulations designed by the British as a means of maintaining control over the decision-making power of their large number of Indian subordinates, who had varying levels of training, outlooks, and goals, and who were dispersed far from the administrative centers; and (e) a system of Secretariat and Executive offices—a split system prevailing at both the central and provincial levels, ostensibly separating questions of policy from those of administration [8].

Such a system of administration suited the British. This was the status quo regime. It maintained and preserved broadly the structure of society in India as it then existed, particularly the large proportion of rural society. It did not concern itself with any radical or specific socioeconomic changes. The Impact of the administration on the large proportions of Indian citizens was minimal. Thus, when the time for transfer of power came in 1947, the administrative system was not appropriately prepared to handle the massive developmental and postindependence tasks [9].

B. The Impact of Independence

The period since independence has witnessed most changes in the administrative system. As mentioned earlier, the attainment of independence brought in its wake momentous problems, simultaneously needing multiple revolutions: first, the transition from a colonial system of government to a full-fledged parliamentary democracy with a federal structure of government and commitment to a welfare state; second, the transformation of a semisubsistence economy into a modern industrial community to solve the problems of poverty, unemployment, and want; third, a social revolution changing a caste-ridden stratified society into a progressive community oriented to social justice; and fourth, a technological revolution to shine the light of modern science on the crusted traditional ways of a conservative people. The broad strategies adopted by the Indian leadership, to usher into a new era, were (a) the political integration of the country; (b) the framing of a new Republican Constitution; (c) the adoption of adult franchise; (d) a system of rule of law and independent judiciary; (e) a policy of a mixed economy and democratic socialism for agroindustrial growth; (f) a policy of equal opportunity and protective discrimination for furthering social justice; and (g) a policy of nonalignment in foreign affairs. All these strategies have led, since then, to a number of veritable changes in the policy process and the administrative system. But some of the old problems still persist in one form or the other while the processes of modernization and socioeconomic changes over the last four decades have given rise to a new set of problems pertaining to policy and administration.

C. The Constitutional Imperatives

The pattern of administrative development in India was largely guided by the imperatives of the Republican Constitution, which came into force on January 26, 1950. The structure of administration not only had to respond to the system of parliamentary government and the principle of federalism enshrined in the Constitution, but was also expected to implement the new policy goals inherent in a number of its provisions relating to socioeconomic dispensations. Some of these are discussed in the following sections.

1. *Federalism: The Administrative Implications*

Indian federalism has retained the earlier principle of centralization of the British era in the structure of administration; it has vested imposing powers and responsibilities in the Union government. The emergency powers contained in the Indian Constitution enable India, under certain circumstances, to transform itself into a unitary state. Under emergency provisions, the Union Executive and the Parliament can direct a state government in the use of its powers or assume all of its powers, the Union Executive acting for the state executive and the Union Parliament enacting legislation as if it were the state legislature.

Apart from the fact that the central government has the constitutional right to modify the distribution of powers between the center and the states under certain circumstances, the central government also has vast powers over the collection and distribution of revenues, which make the state heavily dependent on the central government for financial support. Although the constitution provides for the devolution of revenue to the states under Article 275, the Union Government under Article 282 has the power to make grants to the states for any public purpose, even though the purpose is one for which Parliament cannot normally legislate. Under this provision, the central government allocates vast amounts of development funds to the state as part of Five Year Plans drawn up by the National Planning Commission, an advisory body of the central government, putting additional responsibility on its administrative structure. However, despite these centralized trends, each state has a personality of its own and can no longer be treated by the central government as merely a piece of territory for administrative purposes. The number, territorial size, and composition of states have changed many times since independence in response to the demands of the people of various regions.

2. *Fundamental Rights and the Directive Principles of State Policy: The Administrative Imperatives*

The Indian constitution is committed to providing fundamental changes in the socio-economic order through its provision on fundamental rights and Directive Principles of State Policy. While the fundamental rights guarantee for each citizen certain substantive and procedural protection against the state, the Directive Principles of State Policy, although not enjoying legal force through the courts, provide direction to the nation "to promote the welfare of people by securing and promoting as effectively as it may a social order in which justice, social, economic, and political, shall inform all the institutions of national life" [10]. Taken together, these provisions have meant a number of mandatory obligations that are required to be observed by administrative personnel in the discharge of their functions and the emergence of a large number of different types of administrative institutions at all levels to carry out the purposes and aspirations of a new nation.

Thus for example the right of equality under Article 16 of the Constitution guarantees equal protection before the law, provides for equal opportunities in public employment, abolishes untouchability, and prohibits discrimination in the use of public places on the grounds of religion, race, caste, sex, or place of birth. At the same time it protects the rights of minorities and provides protective discrimination for the downtrodden and the backward class of the population, the so-called Scheduled Castes and Scheduled Tribes, as mentioned in the Constitution. The administrative implications of such constitutional provisions are far-reaching; for example, they impose additional administrative costs to implement preferences for members of Scheduled Castes and Scheduled Tribes. In recent years, such provisions have led to some important public controversies. Not only have there been allegations of lowering of administrative standards due to the inductment of candidates with questionable capabilities; there have been public riots in some states as a result of perceived reverse discrimination [11].

3. *The Public Services*

Perhaps India is the only country whose public services have been accorded constitutional status, and their rights and privileges have been safeguarded. Article 311 of the Constitution provides a safeguard to a public employee's right to be served with a notice to show cause before he can be dismissed from the service on charges of misconduct, inefficiency, or corruption.

Such legal and constitutional guarantees, which were intended to protect civil servants from arbitrary actions and unjust administrative decisions, have come to be used as the "guardian" of corrupt and incompetent bureaucrats [12]. Such legal guarantees have now been somewhat diluted with the recent Supreme Court decision in the case of the *Union of India vs. Tulsi Ram Patel* (1985) [13]. The Supreme Court has upheld the government's claimed right to dismiss any employee without a formal inquiry and a reasonable opportunity to defend himself. All that the authority concerned has to do is to write down the charges warranting the termination of his services.

But the most unique feature of the provisions of the Indian Constitution is Article 312, pertaining to the creation of all India Services, which retain the same prestige and status once accorded to the old ICS. The special characteristic of these services is that although officers are recruited and trained by the Union government, they serve both the Union and the state governments and occupy top policy-making and executive positions in both the central and the state governments. Moreover, they cannot be dismissed, removed, or reduced in rank, except for cause and only with the approval by the Union Public Service Commissions.

Apart from the all-India Services, the Constitution also provides for Central Services for the Union Government and State Services for the state governments. While the all-India and Central Services are recruited by the Union Public Service Commission, the State Services are recruited by the State Public Service Commission. The commissions have been established as constitutional agencies to protect the services and the merit system from political interference.

4. *The Statutory Authorities*

The other independent bodies for various administrative purposes provided in the Constitution are (a) the Election Commission to conduct elections for various legislative bodies and all elective offices under the Union and the states; (b) the Finance Commission, appointed every five years for determining the principle of distribution of revenues between the central and state governments; (c) the office of the Comptroller and Auditor General to audit accounts of the Union and the state governments; and (d) the Scheduled Caste and Scheduled Tribe Commissioners to look after the welfare of the Scheduled Castes and Scheduled Tribes in India. The independent and impartial working of these bodies has been ensured partly by the methods of their appointment and conditions of their services, and partly by the fact that the expenses of these offices are the first charge on the Consolidated Fund of India and are not subject to the vote of the Parliament.

This is a brief summary of how the various constitutional provisions have influenced the growth of the administrative machinery. Given the sociopolitical background at independence, the Constitution makers did well to specify the principles on which the foundations of a new administrative state were to be laid.

III. THE INDIAN SOCIAL STRUCTURE

Institutional strategies alone are not enough for conceiving a process of change, development, and nation building. Social structures and environmental factors do affect the state and the administrative system, and hence the development of the polity. The significance of those factors is multiplied all the more in the pluralist society of India, where the nation shares loyalties with a variety of other sociocultural identities. These identities have contributed both to the process of its development and to its decay. While they have played a major mediating role between politics and society, translating group loyalties into focal points of political solidarity, at the same time they have given rise to a number of fissiparous and separatist tendencies within the political and administrative framework, weakening its overall capacity for development.

A. The Demographic Characteristics

Among the many social variables that have affected the Indian administrative system, a tremendous growth in population, despite an aggressive and extensive family planning campaign, has been the most crucial factor [14]. From 251 million in 1921, India's population more than doubled by 1971, reaching 540 million. The census of 1981 and 1991 reported India's population at 685.48 and 846 million respectively, which is expected to exceed 1 billion by the end of the twentieth century at the present annual rate of increase of approximately 2.1%. The annual rate of population growth has increased from 1.1% between 1921 and 1931 to 2.2% between 1961 and 1971, to an average of 2.4% between 1971 and 1981, and 2.1% between 1981 and 1991.

In the 1950s, the urban population in India rose from 61.9 million to 77.8 million, an increase of 0.43% in the proportion of urban population to total population. By 1981, India's cities had grown by about 100 million persons at an annual rate of increase of 3.8%. The census of 1971 placed urban population at about 24% of the total. The urban population stood at 25.7% of the total (1991). Cities such as New Delhi, Bombay, Calcutta, Madras, Bangalore, and Hyderabad have experienced population explosions over the period through 1981. The percentage of urban population as a whole has been consistently increasing.

The Indian population of almost 850 million people is divided by religion, sex, language, caste, dress, and even food habits. These divisions have been further compounded by the gap between the rich and the poor, the English-speaking elite and the vernacular mass, and the urban and rural. In its diversity and continental size, India shares more of the characteristics of the European Community than the more integrated multiethnic and unified polities of the United States [15]. India contains all of the major world religions, it is subdivided into myriad castes, it has fifteen official languages and a thousand dialects and tribal tongues. Politically and administratively, these diverse groups are organized into twenty-five states and seven union territories. The process of mobilization and social change in the last forty years has heightened the sense of awareness of the political and administrative subsystem. That the system has been sustained over these years, has withstood those challenges, and has not disintegrated amply highlights the two-way interrelationship between the sociopolitical structures of a society and its political and administrative development. Whereas such factors have led to political and administrative decay in most developing societies, in India these have provided potential for administrative resilience and growth.

As a result of the dramatic growth in the population and an increase in nationalization, a large segment of the population has become increasingly dependent upon certain services provided by the government. Urbanization has been related to industrialism, and these combined with population growth have placed heavier demands on transportation, communication, financial utility, education, medical, health, and other services. Planning of population growth and development of adequate and appropriate human resources have put additional burdens on the administrative system.

> Government has become more intensively involved in regulating, planning, stimulating and even undertaking directly economic and commercial activities in many significant areas. The government of India's commitment to the abolition of poverty through socialism and a variety of social services for minorities and the economically disadvantaged classes have further accelerated the demands on government apparatus,

> and have penetrated more and more sectors of the citizen's life. Citizens' increased dependence upon the activities and initiative of the government in all spheres of life has further increased public employment. [16]

Table 1 indicates clearly the growth of public employment at the central government level in India.

The expansion of government has brought in its wake an inevitable increase in bureaucracy and public employment at all levels, particularly at the lower levels of organization. Government employment has expanded not only because of the radical changes taking place in the nature and growth of government functions, but also because of the fact that in a country which cannot afford unemployment insurance the creation of lower posts has often been used to placate the massive unrest of the educated unemployed youth, particularly at the levels of state administrations. All these developments have added to the cynicism and disenchantment that generally prevail in the public mind about the efficacy of the public management system as a whole.

Although overstaffing the public service imposes a financial burden on the state, undermines morale, and presents a major obstacle to efficient management, and expanding regular government employment does not help solve the shortage of productive employment opportunities in the economy, most developing countries do not find any other alternative to growing unrest due to unemployment. For short-term unemployment relief, temporary public works (or food-for-work programs) are preferable, in terms of both costs and returns. However, they result in indiscriminate additions to line agency payrolls that are likely to become permanent [17].

Another characteristic of the public employment in India is reflected in Table 2, which shows the distribution of central government employees by ministries and departments during the growth decades of 1961 to 1980. During these twenty years, central governmental manpower increased from 1,986,577 (regular staff) in 1961 to 3,321,072 in 1980, a growth of 1,334,495 employees or 67.2%.

Table 1 Growth of Central Government Employment, 1953–1980

Year	Employment* (000)	Year	Employment* (000)
1953	1561	1967	2746
1954	1613	1968	2793
1955	1692	1969	2807
1956	1792	1970	2851
1957	1839	1971	2921
1958	1914	1972	NA
1959	1989	1973	NA
1960	2025	1974	NA
1961	2094	1975	NA
1962	2156	1976	NA
1963	2349	1977	NA
1964	2536	1978	3477
1965	2637	1979	NA
1966	2710	1980	3678

*Includes regular and nonregular employees.
N.A. indicates figures not available.
Source: O. P. Dwivedi and R. B. Jain, *India's Administrative State*, Gitanjali Publishing House, New Delhi, 1985, p. 19.

Table 2 Distribution and Growth of Central Government Employees* by Ministries and Departments, 1961, 1971, and 1980

Departments/Ministries	31 March 61 1961	31 March 71 1971	31 March 80 1980	Growth 1961–1980 Numerical	%
Agriculture & Irrigation	29290	20227	25445	–3845	—
Atomic Energy	4417	14492	23292	18875	422.2
Cabinet Secretariat	2093	7271	195**	–1898	90.68
Commerce & Civil Aviation	—	—	8209	8209	—
Communications	241599	385560	532524	290295	120.2
Defense (Civilian)	279177	473728	515319	236142	84.6
Education & Culture	4830	11966	8776	3946	81.63
Electronics	—	—	682	682	—
Energy	1561	5351	6639	5078	325.30
External Affairs	3448	4023	4884	1436	41.64
Finance	86833	118956	158023	71190	82.0
Health & Family Welfare	8194	15437	19518	11324	138.2
Home Affairs	29357	77759	237207	207850	708.0
Audit & Accounts	38007	51091	22772	17765	46.7
Industry	12233	13540	69849	57616	471.0
Information & Broadcasting	9274	15234	20204	10930	117.8
Labour	4145	10336	9664	5519	133.14
Law, Justice & Company Affairs	2024	2784	3602	1578	77.36
Petroleum and Chemicals	—	316	502	502	—
Planning	1519	1633	5975	4458	293.36
Railways	1146921	1373634	1553229	406308	35.4
Rural Reconstruction	945	—	1591	646	68.3
Shipping and Transport	10293	5536	5769	–4757	–46.2
Space	—	—	9439	9439	—
Steel Mines & Coal	6299	10294	11911	5612	89.1
Supply & Rehabilitation	15874	14257	14402	–1472	–9.3
Science & Technology	9962	11542	17992	8030	80.6
Tourism & Civil Aviation	10742	14684	17570	6828	83.6
Works & Housing	25936	34395	39261	13325	51.4
Social Welfare	—	1049	578	578	—
Other Departments	1604	3562	6049	4445	277.1
TOTAL	1986577	2698657	3321072	1334495	67.2

*Only regular employees included.
**In 1977, the Department of Personnel and Administrative Reforms was separated from the Cabinet Secretariat and merged with the Ministry of Home Affairs, reducing the number of employees.
Source: The table has been compiled from the statistical data available from the reports of the various ministries/departments of the Government of India. O. P. Dwivedi and R. B. Jain, *India's Administrative State*, Gitanjali Publishing House, New Delhi, 1985, pp. 28–29.

The most dramatic growth is concentrated in four ministries (communications, which includes the post office, telegraph and telephones; civilian defense; home affairs; and railways), which accounted for 85.5% of the total increase. These four growth sectors reflect the conscious public policy decisions made by India to enhance services in these areas. Obviously, maintenance of law and order, transportation, and communications are priority items for the government.

The expansion of public bureaucracy has been accompanied by a proliferation in the number of regulations, some of which are virtually impossible to administer and make the processing of transactions cumbersome. The expanding sphere of the role of governments has placed the bureaucracy in a monopolistic position and has enhanced the opportunities for greater administrative discretion. For example, during the first two decades of the postindependence period, legislation output increased by more than three times compared to that of any period preceding the attainment of independence. During this period about sixteen hundred statutes, including twenty-one constitutional amendments, more than one hundred regulations, one hundred president's acts, and one hundred and fifty ordinances, were enacted. In addition, an average of about five thousand rules were being issued every year [18]. Executive regulations together with increased bureaucratic discretion provide opportunities and incentives for corruption, since regulations governing access to goods and services can be exploited by civil servants in extracting "rents" [19]. Thus in many developing countries, public bureaucracies have become uncontrolled and unaccountable centers of power pursuing their own interests through the institutionalization of systematic extortion and bribery. Under conditions of uncertainty and with a government which acts as the nation's largest employer, producer, regulator, and even consumer, both the public and civil servants have come to accept government inefficiency and ineffectiveness as part of the natural order of things [20].

B. The Caste System

The social system in India is organized around caste structures and caste identities, which are as old as Indian civilization. The tribal, linguistic, religious, regional, and caste loyalties; the fundamental characteristics of the social infrastructure of Indian society, have made a deep impact on the working of the political and administrative system and have affected the processes of development. Caste is undoubtedly an all-India phenomenon in the sense that there are everywhere hereditary endogamous groups which form a hierarchy. Caste, being the important organizational structure, has hampered developmental processes and proved to be the most important cause of backwardness and economic inequality. In its original form the system was associated with social hierarchy based on occupations, but later on it became a negative feature of society when its basis became "birth" and not occupation. The caste system in India, as it has emerged, stratified the society socially, corrupted it politically, and weakened it economically.

After independence the caste system grew further; regionalism had taken the shape of caste consciousness and caste mobilization. "Politicization of the caste system" [21] became the new trend in Indian politics. In the process not only the Hindus of the upper class but the outcasts, the so-called untouchables, also came to play an important role. In order to ameliorate the conditions of this section of the society, the state in India devised the means of according special privileges to the Scheduled Castes and Tribes and backward classes as these communities were described in the Constitution. These concessions were given to these communities for a limited transitional period only. But the measure became a long-term phenomenon. Even after forty years of independence these special concessions in the shape of reservations to political and administrative offices and in educational institutions have not been withdrawn; they have rather increased day by day. While such output responses of the state system helped in initial development and brought about the desired social change, at the same time they created additional tensions hampering the process of development. This wrong method for a right purpose has not only widened the gap between the communities, but has also led to the emergence of certain vested interests who are not ready to give up these privileges, even after their full nourishment. The lower caste dilemma is still there, and it has created further discontent and conflicts in the society. The "Son of the Soils" theory inherent in the *Mulki* rule in some states in India and the issue of reservation tend to aggravate caste animosities and generate social upheavals and violence, as has been amply demonstrated by the disturbances that have recently (1988, and later in 1990–1991) occurred in Gujarat, Andhra Pradesh, and Karnataka. It needs to be made clear that the reservation system that is being resisted is not what has been conceded to the Scheduled Castes and Scheduled Tribes. It is the expanding base of reservations among the so-called backward castes that threatens to produce a backlash. The vested interest in backwardness that the system of reservation has created might further lead to a realignment of communities on lines that can only perpetuate the present division.

C. Impact of Religion

Apart from the caste system, another major social factor that affects political and administrative development is religion. All the major religions of the world, Hinduism, Buddhism, and Sikhism, are represented in India. The vast majority of the population, almost 83%, are, however, Hindus, while Muslims constitute 12% of the total, the third-largest concentration of Muslims in the world. The major source of conflicts in the society has been between these two major and important religions—Hinduism and Islam. All other religions practically have no role except in a limited context, for instance, Christianity in Kerala or Eastern border areas and Sikhism in Punjab. The roots of the Hindu-Muslim resentment are deep and can be historically traced back to the Muslim period. During the last few centuries, however, the Hindus and Muslims had learned to live together and shared in the development of social and cultural traditions. The political evolution of India under the British revived the old animosities, which gave rise to alienation and hostility and the demand for a separate state of Pakistan. This issue paralyzed the nationalist struggle under Mahatma Gandhi. It resulted in a deep schism in Indian society leading to the division of the country and led to an outbreak of violence and bloodshed. From time to time even after independence such communal riots have frequently occurred in various parts of India. In the recent past the incidence of such events has again increased, putting great strains on the administrative system. Apart from the loss in terms of lives, communal riots cause widespread destruction of property and adversely affect economic activities. Communal tension of the Hindu-Muslim variety already has a long and sordid history. It has been further compounded by the developments in Punjab during the last ten years. These developments have injected into the situation the potential for a Hindu-Sikh confrontation, which fortunately has not so far occurred. Because of the possibilities of such conflicts in the societies, the administrative machinery has to keep itself in readiness to combat fanatic violence, terrorist activities, and mindless destruction of lives and property. This explains the growth in the number of paramilitary and police forces and other intelligence security agencies that have come to dominate the administrative system in India—the Central Reserve Police Force, the Border Security Force, the Industrial Security Force, the VIP Security Commandos, and so on. Not only these have created problems of deployment and administrative coordination; they have also been a cause of resentment and tensions between the central government and the governments of the states. The developmental capacities of the administration have certainly received some setbacks but have not been completely destroyed.

D. Bureaucratic Dysfunctionism

Apart from the proliferation of law enforcement, social structure in India also tends to encourage bureaucratic dysfunctionism [22].

In a way, of course, the structural characteristics of Indian bureaucracy correspond to the Indian culture and the social milieu in which it operates. Complex as it is, the Indian culture is itself a product of the influences of flourishing folk cultures, the subcultures of castes and classes, and the urban culture of an English-educated middle class. It is an amalgam of various traits, traditions, attitudes, and outlooks that draw on the three dominant religions: Hinduism, Islam, and Christianity. The coexistence of a large number of religious groups makes India unique. Thus, an understanding of the Indian bureaucracy must include a study of its symbolic relationship with the Indian culture. The importance of caste determines the social outlook in India. An official's behavior will, therefore, also be culturally determined. In spite of his participation in a depersonalized system, his behavior must necessarily be culture bound or he risks social disapproval. This aspect of the problem was commented on some time ago by a noted scholar:

> An administrative system influenced by such traditional loyalties will tend toward an ascriptive rather than achievement-oriented pattern of recruitment. And that is why a person who asks favours from officers belonging to his caste does not consider his act unethical. Similarly when a government official "fixes" applications and licenses in utter disregard to merit but in accordance with family and caste loyalties he is obeying a law of social conduct more ancient than that of the upstart state. Moreover, in any traditional society, the family forms the common interest group "par excellence". . . . Since family in this usage includes uncles, cousins, nephews, grandparents and other near and distant relatives, a great deal of pressure to "fix" jobs for them or to find some other source of income to support them is not uncommon. . . . Moreover, these relatives . . . would like to take advantage of his position in securing jobs, procuring permits, etc., while he is still influential. They do not consider the exploitation of relatives' official status as something bad or unethical. [23]

The orientation of officials in India is not merely based upon personal, economic, and social conditions or caste, but also on what is often termed "ethnoexpansionism." This involves the assumption that one's own ways are per se superior to all other ways and that the circumstances one enjoys should be desired by all men. The concept of ethnoexpansionism is of particular value to the analysis of the cultural content of Indian bureaucracy. When the upper castes assume bureaucratic office, their aim is not merely to expand their ranks through favoritism, but also to invest their caste values with a quality that they consider will be acceptable to other groups, castes, and communities.

E. Secularism, Casteism, and Religious Values

Secularism has been a characteristic distinguishing India's composite culture. As a policy of the government after independence, secularism, as Nehru conceived, was designed to safeguard the peace and security of the minorities, renunciation of revivalism and obscurantism of religion, and recognition of differences and nonconformities in socioreligious affairs. The state in India, as the Constitution provides, is neutral in matters of religion but provides opportunity for all religions to flourish, subject to "public order, morality and health." Yet religion has been a dominating factor and a force in the politico-administrative culture in India, despite the fact that the "new culture of science and technology has had a healthy impact of intermingling the different communities and religions" [24].

The Indian culture, which has been a history of unity and synthesis, of reconciliation and growth, of harmony and assimilation, of fusion of old traditions and new values, has several contradictory forces within its fold. The forces of progress and regress have simultaneously worked on Indian culture. At the same time, it has been dominated by an individualistic ethos, a stratified society, and the theories of *dharma* and *karma*, the institutions of castes based on occupations, and the inequalities in the social system due to the caste hierarchy. All these cultural factors not only have been reflected in the political processes, but also find their expression in the development of administrative policies. The most appropriate example of such a policy is the Reservation system in the public services in India and the preferential treatment of some of the specified communities sanctioned by some of the constitutional provisions to which we have already referred. The kinds of tensions and conflicts often leading to violence that these have created in the social fabric of the nation are too well known to be repeated. At the same time, such practices have brought dissension to the administrative system. A number of developmental policies and programs of the government have even been influenced in their conception and implementation through these cultural imperatives [25]. Not only political processes have been affected by these forces; in many cases bureaucratic functionaries belonging to the so-called high castes have felt constrained to visit places inhabited by the so-called low caste citizenries in the course of their official dealings [26].

F. Authoritarian Character of Indian Bureaucracy: The Cultural Context

Although the present traits of authoritarian behavior in the Indian bureaucracy have been traced to the British days of colonialism, when most Britishers, whatever their convictions about authority relations at home, showed a high degree of authoritarianism in their behavior toward the Indian subordinate whether he was the despised clerk or the illiterate worker [27], some scholars have tried to examine the linkages between patterns of social relations and authority patterns in Indian organizations, both governmental and nongovernmental. The available evidence of superior-subordinate relations in India indicates that the parental type in general and the assertive superior in particular dominate authority relations in Indian organizations. Many Indian top managers, particularly in the governmental hierarchies, are relatively authoritarian in their relationships with lower management and labor. Along with cases of paternalism, that is nurturance, this element of assertiveness in superior behavior is not only a characteristic of top management but also a feature of all authority relations at all levels in any organization—governmental or nongovernmental [28].

An explanation of the linkage between the individual behavior in organizations and the wider culture has also been sought in the concept of national character. “A man brings to his work attitudes and modes of behaviour which have evolved from his life experience” [29]. Thus in India, it has been suggested that the expectation is that a highly controlling superior has a positive effect on the presumed existence of a basic or a modal Hindu personality, in which security for the individual is associated with dependence upon superiors. However, it seems likely that in a country like India, with its great variety of regional, linguistic, caste, class, and religious differentiations, there are many national characters, rather than a modal personality. Even if it assumed that in complex societies with their wide range of social differentiation, the family ties and early childhood experiences with authority are relatively uniform, the concept of national character tends to ignore the influence of other social relationships outside the period of early childhood which individuals enter into throughout their latency and adolescence periods and which are highly differentiated along class, caste, and rural-urban dimensions [30].

It has thus been argued that the administrative and management culture prevalent in India today reflects the family atmosphere and the way people live at home. India is a hierarchical society, where the father has all the answers. Nobody can question him. This is also carried to the work environment, where the boss is always right. The rigid nature of ties in the family is reflected in the controls that people adopt at the office, where countless forms having no substance are required to be completed. The system does not tolerate flexibility. People are actually taught not to question but only to remember and to follow. This is the reason why many functionaries in administration tend to have low self-esteem vis-à-vis their superiors. The superior at work expects loyalty not to the project, but to himself. He actually destroys another person's self-esteem because that is how he can maintain the status quo. That is why information in the Indian administrative system flows in one direction only. The junior person's views are invariably ignored. People thus tend to be docile and in awe of the hierarchical structure. Anyone who takes a different approach is termed an oddball. This is precisely the reason why it is often contended that the technology which is presently being introduced in India belongs to the 1990s, while the country's administrative setup is still in the 1920s [31].

G. The Linguistic Multiplicity

Another element of social infrastructure which has made inroads in the nation-building process in India and has affected public administration is linguistic multiplicity, which is unique in many respects than in comparison to many other countries of the world, such as Canada, Belgium, Russia, and Switzerland. Their example is, however, irrelevant in understanding the language problem in India. According to the linguistic survey published in 1927, there were 179 languages and 544 dialects in the erstwhile Indian subcontinent, which in 1981 grew into 1,018 languages. Despite the multilingualism prevailing in India, the last phase of the Indian national struggle for independence witnessed the demand for one national language. But the emergence of a neat and acceptable formula of a single national language has not been easy. The state in India recognized linguistic multiplicity when it accorded legal status to fourteen languages of India listed in the Eighth Schedule of the constitutional document (later amended to include fifteen languages) and recognized Hindi to be the national language. Such provisions, however, did not satisfy many leaders, especially in the Eastern and Southern parts of the country. The politicians recognized, propagated, and exploited the economic importance of a language's being the official one. It was argued that any section of the society belonging to the official language group was also able to capture most of the job opportunities in the country. This created strong subregional movements directed against the officially recognized national language. The language problem became a live political issue. Hindi became the scapegoat in the larger politics of state autonomy. Many a time it led to violent outbreaks in the country and unprecedented acts of self-immolation and the like. The linguistic configuration was thus responsible for the creation of more regional diversities and many more states as subunits of the political system, expanding the tendencies of a vast administrative machinery and leading to further drains on the already limited state resources and delays in the implementation of public policies. Linguistic differences have also prevented the growth of a consistent national policy on language and education. This has in turn led to lowering of educational standards and a greater strain on human resource development.

H. The Social Classes: Urban/Rural Dichotomy

As has been indicated earlier, the social structure in India consists of powerful status groups based on religion, caste, and language. Although a class system has also begun to emerge in India, it remains tenuous. The slow process of industrialization and urbanization has led to a highly uneven pattern of class growth. Status groups continue to cut across class lines. As a result, the development of class identities and political mobilization based upon class appeals has been inhibited [32]. India's urban-based class structure is small when compared to the rural society. The 15 million industrial workers in the organized sector of the economy make up only 10% of the total work force of 100 million. Of these, only 3%, or 5 million, work in large modern factories. The industrial work force, moreover, not only is small; its portion of the total labor force has also remained remarkably stable over the past several decades.

Rural India contains 71% of the population, and some 70% of the labor force is engaged in agriculture. Despite the land reforms of the late 1940s and early 1980s, the distribution of land ownership in rural India has been grossly unequal. In the early 1970s, over 95% of India's rural households owned less than 20 acres of land; 43% owned less than 5 acres; and 24% owned no land at all, with the percentage of landless labor increasing. The disparities in land ownership are revealed in the fact that 30% of rural families held 70% of the cultivable land [33].

In comparison, the size of the urban population represents a consumer market larger than the entire European Community. These changes in the rural/urban population and the emerging class structure have meant the evolution of new administrative policies, strategies, and institutions. In the past forty years, there has been a proliferation of a number of administrative institutions, authorities, and agencies both at the center as well as in the states to cater to the strategies of integrated rural development, and the needs of growing urban metropolises, incredibly crowded, lacking in adequate housing, transportation, water, electricity, sewage, and sanitation facilities. The administrative strategies evolved have ranged from technological and scientific innovations in the field of agricultural production to the establishment of institutions of democratic decentralization and a host of specified agencies for catering to the needs of specified target groups of small, marginal, and landless farmers and the weaker sections of the society, such as women, tribal groups, the backward classes, and the poorest of the poor. In the urban areas, new agencies for regulating industrial development, large, medium, and small scale, and a host of institutions for providing a number of services for urban life have come into operation. Because of a growing concern for environmental degradation a number of regulatory agencies have come into being to protect the environment from further degradation, although with little success. All these developments have further meant keen political competition among various segmented social groups and cultural communities based on language, religion, region, and caste, creating additional pressures on the administrative systems. The existence of multifarious agencies with conflicting and overlapping jurisdictions has not only highlighted the problems of unified direction, control, and coordination, but raised afresh the basic issues of centralization and decentralization and the relative autonomy of various units of administration.

I. Social Justice and Alleviation of Poverty

Among the most important policy changes that have affected Indian public administration has been the issue of social justice and alleviation of poverty. To what extent have the new strategies, institutions, and concepts of rural/urban development been able to realize the fundamental objective of alleviating poverty and achieving a modicum of social justice?

At the time of independence, in 1947, the leaders of free India thought that they would be able to achieve a just and equitable social and economic order in a short time and that poverty would be eliminated before long. Forty years later, the political economy of the country, at least in the sphere of social justice and poverty eradication, appears to have done badly. According to a World Bank report, a third of the world's poor still live in India and 40% of India's population lives below a minimal poverty line. Over the Sixth Plan period, according to Government of India reports, there has been a drop of 11% in poverty, which stands at 37%. The projected estimate in the drop of the poverty ratio after the Seventh Plan period is another 11%, leading to 26%, and will further drop to 5% by the end of the century. Poverty persists because neither economic growth nor targeted development spending has been sufficient to help the truly poor. Another factor is that poverty is concentrated in the countryside and growth in the cities.

Both official and unofficial studies have found that subsidies of all kinds—not only agricultural inputs, but also food, education, and medicine—go disproportionately to the better off. Even in the antipoverty programs, some 15.2% of the beneficiaries are the nondeserving, not counting the money squandered by the corrupt. One of the reasons for the persistence of this phenomenon is the excessive centralization in the administration of such programs, and the noninvolvement of people at the grass-roots level in the implementation of such schemes. Although the green revolution has created pockets of rural prosperity, real farm incomes have stagnated for thirty years while nonagricultural incomes have more than doubled. One poverty expert has calculated that even if incomes were to grow at a speeded-up 1% a year, halving the poverty rate by trickle down alone would take thirty-five years.

The strategies of poverty eradication programs count on faster economic growth through a technology-led second green revolution, a drop in the population growth rate, and redistribution. The latest budget (1993–94) has allocated a sum of Rs. 50,600 million (approx. $1688 million) for anti-poverty programs, only .25% of the total outlay of Rs. 1,31,3230 million. Yet these projects, which consist of mass employment schemes (Jawahar Rozgar Yojana) and other welfare programs are intended to serve only about 2.736 million families, a small fraction of the poor [34].

Although it is true that social injustice has not grown and poverty has not increased since India became independent, at the same time there is no evidence that India has moved toward a more egalitarian or poverty-free society. Perhaps the objective of social justice might have been unrealistic, but as one scholar has put it,

> The uneven distribution of economic power and benefits through manipulation of the polity has created major distortions and problems for the political economy. The issue doesn't seem to pose any serious threat to the state and the administrative system. The poor do not press hard enough upon the state which has been effectively under the control of an elite. Poverty at best remains only a moral problem of the Indian political economy. It pricks the sentiments and the conscience of the liberal middle class elite, but does not pose great political challenge to the state. After forty years of independence, social inequalities and poverty still remain the major blight on the nation's political economy. [35]

IV. POLICY OF PLANNED ECONOMY AND ADMINISTRATIVE DEVELOPMENT

In pursuance of the objectives of a welfare state and rapid economic growth, India had adopted Five Year Plans as a major instrument of public policy and the principle of "mixed economy" as the guiding ideology for planned developmental efforts. The planning objectives and social premises were derived from the Directive Principles of State Policy set out in the Constitution. Attempts to formulate and implement development plans have been accompanied by a vast expansion of various administrative planning institutions and agencies and phenomenal growth of public services for developmental purposes. In the process, administration has become more and more hierarchical giving rise to problems of coordination at the horizontal level. Although the various plan documents also provide directions and strategies for developing administrative capabilities and effecting administrative reforms to meet the challenges posed by the policy of planned socioeconomic development, efforts to achieve greater administrative decentralization and a larger measure of planning have not been able to bridge the large and ever-growing gap between planning and implementation.

The strategy of planned economic growth and the consequent formulation and implementation of plan policies have put tremendous strain and responsibilities on the administrative system. The success of developmental plans and policies depends to a significant degree upon the effectiveness and capability of the administrative machinery. The structural and organizational problems of administration posed by planning start with the establishment of the planning machinery itself; its location; defining its powers, functions, and responsibilities; defining its work vis-à-vis the other administrative departments; establishing effective channels of communication with the political organization; establishing units for supervision and evaluation of execution; establishing relations with the state and regional level organizations, the private sector, interest groups, trade unions, cooperatives, and so on. All these pose structural problems. The availability of qualified efficient personnel with development orientation poses problems not only of human resources, but also of behavior, attitude, and a distinct administrative culture for development [36]. In many ways the process of planning has also made a deep impact on the character and functioning of the traditional administrative units and institutions. Two specific aspects need discussing: institutional development and the impact of planning on traditional administration.

A. The Institutional Development

The new institutions that have been established as a result of the adoption of planning are (a) the National Planning Commission, an expert advisory body at the center responsible for formulating plans, assessing resources, providing for all technical and statistical details needed in planning activities, determining the nature of machinery need for implementation of plans, and from time to time and appraising the progress achieved in the execution of each stage of the plan. The National Development Council, a kind of supercabinet consisting of the chief executives of all the states of the Indian Union, has emerged as an apex body to promote national cooperation between the center and the states. In almost all central government ministries and organizations planning cells have been established to assist in the formulation of plan projects and targets in each substantive area. Similarly planning boards and state planning departments have come into being at the levels and various state governments for the preparation of state plans and their integration in the national plan.

Because of various historical and political factors, the planning system in India continues to be highly centralized. The unsatisfactory performance of centralized planning has led to demands for decentralization. The increased scope of plan activities at lower levels, recent development strategy emphasis on area development, and adoption of a target group development approach tend to make the argument for decentralization stronger. The issue is not so much whether to decentralize, as how and what to decentralize [37]. However, efforts to establish planning machinery at substate levels, although under way for some time, have been halfhearted, with the result that no worthwhile organization for plan formulation has emerged at these levels.

Deficiencies have been particularly marked with respect to the machinery for project planning and establishing linkages between projects. The successful operation of decentralized planning within a framework of multilevel planning requires appropriate organizations at these levels, which must be staffed with personnel of requisite technical expertise, especially for preparing sound projects and working out linkages among them [38].

As a sequel to the Directive Principles of State Policy provided in the Constitution and with a view to involving people in the process of plan formulating and implementation, a scheme of community development programs, Panchayati Raj institutions, Block Development officers, and a host of village level workers were introduced in the decade of the fifties and sixties in various state governments. But in the majority of cases, these institutions have been virtually languishing as a result of government indifference and in some cases the tacit hostility of political leadership at the state level. The so-called experiments in district planing introduced since 1969 were reduced to a mere collection of felt needs or of disaggregated departmental figures. The late attempts to strengthen district and block level planning in the early 1980s were not very successful. The execution of plans has greatly suffered because of the absence of appropriate and adequate implementing machinery. A suggestion has recently been made to amend the Constitution to give more powers and funds to district level administration, so that the concept of district planning becomes a reality [39].

B. Impact of Planning on Traditional District Administration

The planning system has placed a heavy burden and responsibilities on the district as a traditional unit of administration and its head, the district officer or deputy commissioner, the various designations such officers have been known by in India. Different patterns of administration exist in different regions. A common model of administration which may permit flexibility for adjustments due to regional variations needs to be developed [40]. The question whether the district collector, who has traditionally been performing the law and order and revenue collection functions, should be associated with developmental functions has been continuously debated since independence. The impact of the British legacy, namely, the centralization of decision making, the system of rules, the generalist concept of services, has further affected the pattern of behavior of the district officials. This pattern is characterized by inflexible adherence to and dependence upon rules, a focusing of decision-making upward, and its reverse, a lack of delegation of authority and a generalized rigidity that prevent the organization from adapting readily to changing demands upon it. It is further complicated by situational elements such as administrative involvement in development programs, in the context of a developing society itself; and by particular Indian components as well. Notable among the particular Indian components are the tendency for any group of people to divide into small groups on the basis of particularistic ties, heightening a lack of trust and reluctance to delegate authority, a tendency encouraged by the ideology of the caste system, to think of human reactions in hierarchical terms; and a tradition of deference to authority [41].

The compulsion of planned socioeconomic development has no doubt changed the pattern and complexion of the administrative system from the British framework of a stable order to that of a system of continuous strain, both politically and administratively, "adopting *ad hoc*— and frequently unsuccessful remedies to a procession of deeper, more intricate, and apparently less easily alleviated crises" [42]. The administrative system, to say the least, has been unsteady throughout India and at present is at its lowest ebb in efficiency and integrity. Commenting on this change in the temper and values of administration, a former official who has been a part of the administrative machinery in both preindependence and postindependence periods has observed:

> The British administration in India governed too little and did not concern itself enough with changes in the social and the economic order. Perhaps the Indian governments have governed too much. This may well have been inevitable, part of the temper of times, since India gained independence. When the idea of a welfare state was the generally accepted norm, India had also a great deal to make up to come abreast with other nations of the world. . . . Where the life of the community, or at least its vital growth and development depends so heavily on the administrative machine, any inefficiency or erosion in standards has a snowballing influence and gathers speed in geometric progression. India has indeed been caught up in the problem of governing less but effectively, or taking in more ineffectively. Each difficulty, whether economic or social, has tended to produce more rather than less government but the country has by no means turned the corner towards ensuring reasonable standards of prolonged good management. [43]

V. POLICY OF INDUSTRIAL DEVELOPMENT AND THE PUBLIC SECTOR

Another major policy issue confronting the government today is the issue of "liberalization" for industrial progress and the role of the public sector in India's economic development. The policy of a "mixed economy" adopted by the government in the spring of the Indian Republic has led to the establishment of almost 200 public sector projects at the central level and approximately 700 at the state level, each representing an investment worth approximately U.S. $25 million. However, a majority of these enterprises have failed to come up to expectations. Many have incurred heavy and continuing losses and far from contributing to the resources available for development have become a drain on the public exchequer. Such a phenomenon has been attributed to the growth and persistence of bureaucratic culture rather than commercial culture in the management of these enterprises; backseat driving by the ministries leading to the constriction in the autonomy of managers of public sector enterprises which is so necessary for decision making: lack of manpower planning and training of executives; and lack of development of marketing techniques. Some of these shortcomings were noticed at the very outset. The company form of public enterprise was thought of precisely to provide management autonomy. But while the "form" was there, the reality of "autonomy" was missing [44].

The government at present is trying to remove some of the unwarranted advantages which accrue to public sector undertakings, "the most over fed part of an under nourished economy." About half of the public sector plants are working at 75% of capacity and more than a fifth at less than 20% of capacity. Although policymakers have not yet openly advocated "privatization" as the possible remedy, public monopolies in such areas as oil refining, power generation, and telecommunication equipment have been opened to private competition.

The policy of industrial controls and licensing was considered necessary in the early stages for fulfilling the objectives of planning and for ensuring that scarce resources were allocated to priority projects. The system, which one economist calls "command capitalism," was originally intended to make India self-reliant, egalitarian and labor-intensive. Although some measure of self-reliance was achieved at the cost of the other two objectives, it has led to the emergence of a parallel black market economy and corruption, which far from promoting rational allocation of resources have only led to the growth of the luxury sector. It has been estimated that "black " or "untaxed" money amounts to at least 20% of gross domestic product, with perhaps another 15% generated by smuggling.

The policy of delicensing has made little headway in either bringing out technological developments and qualitative improvement in India's indigenous industrial products or expanding the export market of locally produced high-tech, industrial electronic, and software products. The missing link in the economic policy has been the marketing of indigenous products abroad. The recent policies of tax cuts and delicensing have only meant relief for the rich without any lowering of price, improvement in quality, or safeguarding of the consumer's interest. No wonder a majority of big businessmen have never been as happy as in the present regime, despite the unpopularity that the government might have earned with some because of the highly publicized pursuit of highly placed tax evaders. Whether the recently enacted Consumers Protection act 1987 would have the necessary teeth to compel big business to think about the interest of the poor consumers remains to be seen.

A. Social Structure and Small-Scale Industries

India's industrial policy has been largely governed by the Industrial Policy Resolutions of 1948 and 1956, which laid the pattern of industrial growth through a division of industrial sectors reserved exclusively under the public sector, or those sectors which were left open for private investments and others where both the public and private sectors could continue to expand. Notwithstanding these resolutions, the Industrial Policy Statement of 1980 aimed at promoting an economic federation with an equitable spread of investment and the wide dispersal of returns over small but growing institutions. Prompted by the growing number of small-scale entrepreneurs and the so-called bullock capitalists who had emerged in the various progressive states in India [45], the government had used indirect measures that have the effect of marginalizing private capitalism in class politics and making it dependent on the state. Government policies toward capital have promoted its involution, that is, the multiplication of more smaller enterprises. The ideological justification was readily found in Mahatma Gandhi's "ideology of cottage and labour intensive industries by self-employed workers." Promoting small-scale industry in order to enhance employment, economic development, and competition has accelerated the propensities of India's small business and commercial classes [46]. The Industrial Policy Statement of 1980 gave a predominant place to small-scale sectors and widened the scope of such industries to include those having an investment from 1 million rupees to 2 million rupees. Since then there has been a tremendous growth in the sector of small-scale industries as is clear in Table 3.

Table 3 Growth of Small-Scale Industries

S. No. Item	1977–78	1978–79	1979–80	1980–81
1. Number of Units (thousands)	663	723	798	862
2. Production (rupees/millions)	1,40,000	1,57,900	1,90,600	2,80,800
3. Employment (thousands)	5,890	6,380	6,975	7,100
4. Exports (rupees/millions)	8,448	9,535	10,435	11,010

Source: Ram Kumar Vepa, *Small Industry Development Programme*, Indian Institute of Public Administration, New Delhi, 1983, p. 2.

A number of backward areas were identified for purposes of location of such industries. The Industries Development and Regulation Amendment Act of 1984 provides for reservation of certain selected items for exclusive production by small-scale sectors. As a result of such a shift in Indian industrial policy, a number of administrative institutions have been established at the central and state levels. These organizations and agencies provide a comprehensive range of consultancy services and technical, managerial, and marketing assistance. A new form of organization known as the Small Scale Industries Development Corporation has also come into being in almost all the states with the National Small Industries Corporation as an apex body. Thus the shift in industrial policy as a result of the emerging social and class structure has prompted the establishment of new forms of administrative organizations in the administrative system. It is still too early to attempt an assessment of their efficacy as instruments of development.

VI. CONCLUDING REFLECTIONS

The foregoing analysis has sought to reflect upon the linkages of sociopolitical structure, policy changes, and public administration in the complex developing society of India. It has outlined, although briefly, the kind of changes in administrative institutions, structures, style, and culture that have taken place in the country since independence. Many of these outcomes have been the direct consequences of the changing sociopolitical structures and the emerging cultural values in the society.

Although one can discuss specific administrative changes occurring at particular points of time caused by certain sociopolitical exigencies or sudden policy changes, the emerging pattern and style of public administration in India have been the product of the totality of the sociopolitical environment that has operated in the country so far.

Basically, there have been a number of visible changes in the administrative system and style since the British period [47]. The district as the fundamental unit of administration has undergone a metamorphosis both in terms of importance and in the position and status of its chief executive. The importance of both the district and the district officer has weakened and disintegrated as a result of the vast expansion of governmental activities. The demands put forward by the local political leadership and in recent times the emergence of self-styled social and political workers with the right type of political connection at the center and at times with the support of antisocial elements, have become a source of constant harassment to the authority of the district officers, with the result that administration suffers much at the delivery point and at the cutting edge.

Along with the decline of the district as a level of administration, there has been a simultaneous decline in the strength and morale of the main public service—the so-called steel frame of the British administration. Although the Indian Administrative Service still maintains its dominant position despite the various attempts by the Administrative Reform Commission and the Pay Commission to water it down, its position and prestige in general have suffered, because of the various sociopolitical factors discussed in this chapter. Public and political reactions, values, judgments, and even sentiments and prejudices have affected the performance and morale of public bureaucracy in India. There seems to be at present a strong reaction and suspicion against the power of the bureaucracy, and the constant hammering that it has received at the hands of politicians has earned it the name of a "villain" among the public, who regard it as a great impediment to the attainment of the socioeconomic millennium promised to them by politicians. Ethical values of politicians, businessmen, and bureaucrats have gone down so low that there is no aspect of public life today which is free of the incidence of corruption or black money. The dual personality which each of these possesses has enabled each to preach moral values in public but not to hesitate to throw off professional and individual morality when out of the public eye [48].

The increased authority for "licensing" and "control and regulating," particularly in the industrial sector, has opened large areas and umpteen opportunities for corruption, bribery, and affluence through ill-gotten wealth. Although at no time in the recent history of India has the public ever believed that the administration was clean, nevertheless there were times when suspicion was very low. All through these years, and particularly in the later period, corruption has almost become the way of life. A sort of cynicism seems to prevail that one has got to live with it. In the process, the one section of society which has suffered immensely is the poor citizen. He is devoid of proper means through which to be heard, or even put forward his complaint or grievance for any effective or speedy redress. The record of central and state governments in the postindependence period on the question of providing services which are "sensitive, courteous and satisfying" has been, to say the least, dismal. Even with the vast bureaucracy, the treatment of the rank and file employees as compared to their high-ranked colleagues leaves much to be desired. The way they are huddled in dingy rooms overcrowded with dilapidated furniture, accumulated dust on files, cobwebs on the corners and *almirahs*, no proper sanitary or water arrangements, all these and much more speak of the prevailing duality in the administrative architecture and culture in India.

The officers' excessive dependence upon notations entered by the junior clerks on every file, the outdated administrative procedures and formalism, the excessive delay in forwarding an application, and the infinite time taken to pass the final order, the uncertainty in the application of rules or regulations with the bending of regulations for selective applications, the methods of flattery and encouraging subservience for obtaining service from the administrators, the lubrication required in the form of payment to powerful political or bureaucratic functionaries, the sight of an untidy, dirty, and unclean public office with dust and vermin and betel leaves' red stains, have all become a part of administrative culture in India. Coupled with the excessive "secrecy" and "mystique," such situations do not encourage any citizen even to attempt to seek what is legally due to him, thereby generating a sense of indifference, apathy, and resignation, which makes people prefer to use the services of the so-called "intermediaries" on "payment" and get the work done rather than face the ordeal himself and be frustrated. In the government system of today's India, the hallowed traditions of continuity, hierarchy-based status, and distance-based authority have become so important that the overall work ethic is usually one of apathy and indifference. Performance is at the level of the lowest common denominator. There is no concern for the common man, his time, his difficulties, his inconvenience in coming to the office again and again. It is taken for granted that the lower hierarchy of employees have become insensitive and unresponsive to their duties. Those on the other side of the public counter or officials' table find any exception to these norms surprising.

One of the crucial problems emerging from the complex social structures and environmental factors has been the lack of proper coordination and control in the implementation of a number of decisions and policies at various levels of public administration. Because of the existence of a multiplicity of public agencies—judicial, state and local, and of different character—some autonomous, semiautonomous and departmentally controlled and simultaneously working in the same sector or area, and/or for the same clientele as target groups, these agencies have often worked at cross-purposes. The net effect has been that not only have administrative efforts been counterproductive, but the citizen at large has suffered from the utter confusion and the plurality of jurisdiction that overwhelms him in his dealings with the administration. Inadequate systems of "control and coordination" in the processes of policy formulation and implementation, a proper balance between the needs for a centralized uniform policy and decentralized implementation, an adequate system of rapid consultation and communication among the vertical hierarchies and horizontal authorities, and the creation of an effective delivery system to the different social and target groups are the emerging administrative imperatives born of the compulsions of a complex heterogeneous social system. Despite the creation of a number of specialized agencies such as the Departments of Plan-Implementation or Coordination at the center and state levels, this aspect of public administration has not visibly improved. There seems to be an impending necessity of new technological tools and administrative strategies, if the capability of the system in this respect is to be improved substantially.

The preceding analysis of the interrelationships of the sociopolitical structure and administrative system in India may appear to be highly critical about the negative impacts created by these factors, but it is neither intended to undermine the achievements and performance of the Indian administrative system nor to suggest that administrative performance and inefficiency are incompatible with a complex sociopolitical structure. The administration in India has been a fine machine, capable of rendering some excellent performance in the sphere of policy-making and implementation. It has over the years sustained the working of the most populous democracy with the largest politically conscious people anywhere in the world. It has been able to maintain its strength and achieve a strong industrial base for the nation through a system of planned development. There has absolute growth in terms of literacy, education, scientific and technical knowledge, and even relative prosperity. A modicum of balance between the conflicting demands, aspiration, and influences of different classes, castes, religions, and linguistic groups has been sought. The bureaucracy in India has responded well in times of crisis, particularly when it has been given clearly defined objectives and unambiguous priorities. All these are a ray of hope for further improvement in the style and operations of the administrative system in India.

Despite the tremendous increase in public employment, growth of public enterprises, proliferation of administrative agencies, and enormous burden of public expenditure as a result of the growing socioeconomic demands made on the system, the process of administrative development in India has been a continuous one while the administrative system has at times shown signs of strains due to constant pressures, largely generated by the weight of its own structure and continuous policy changes. The system has certainly acquired some resilience to withstand and bear such pressures. That public administration in India has not disintegrated, despite dysfunctionalism, pathologies, and negative consequences of a growing bureaucratic apparatus, lends adequate support to our hypothesis that a complex sociopolitical structure in a developing society need not always inhibit the processes of administrative development.

NOTES

1. For a detailed discussion on the interpretation of the ecological aspects of public administration see Ferrel Heady (ed.), *Public Administration: A Comparative Perspective*, Marcel Dekker, New York, 1984.
2. See Rajni Kothari, *Politics in India*, Orient Longman Ltd., New Delhi, 1972, pp. 100–108.
3. Ibid.
4. Ibid.

5. For a collection of essays on this subject see John K. Pulparampil (ed.), *Indian Political System: A Reader in Continuity and Change*, N. V. Publications, New Delhi, 1976, pp. 452–453.
6. See, for example, the Reports of A. D. Gorwala and Paul H. Appleby on the Reform of Public Administration in India in the 1950s, and the various Reports of Administrative Reforms Commission in the late 1960s and early 1970s. For a detailed discussion on this topic see R. B. Jain, *Contemporary Issues in Indian Administration*, Vishal Publications, New Delhi, 1976, chapter XII.
7. This section is based on the author's study, R. B. Jain and O. P. Dwivedi, Policy Developments and Administrative Changes in India, in *Public Administration in World Perspective* (R. B. Jain and O. P. Dwivedi, eds.), Iowa State University Press, Ames, 1990.
8. Richard P. Taub, *Bureaucrats Under Stress*, University of California Press, Berkeley, 1969, p. 156.
9. E. N. Mangat Rai, *Patterns of Administrative Development in Independent India*, University of London, London, 1976, p. 30.
10. Constitution of India, Article 37.
11. R. B. Jain, Reverse Discrimination: A Dilemma in Quest for Social Justice and Equal Opportunity, *Indian Journal of Public Administration, 27*:181–198, (January-March 1981); and Myron Weimer, Preferential Policies, *Comparative Politics 16*:35–52 (October 1983).
12. For details see O. P. Dwivedi and R. B. Jain, Bureaucratic Morality in India, *International Political Science Review 9*(3):205–214 (1980).
13. 3 SCR 398, AIR 1985, SC 1414.
14. This section draws partly from the author's earlier joint study; see O. P. Dwivedi and R. B. Jain, *India's Administrative State*, Gitanjali Publishing House, New Delhi, 1985.
15. See Robert A. Hardgrave, Jr., and Stanley A. Kochanek, *India: Government and Politics in a Developing Nation*, Harcourt Brace Jovanovich, San Diego, p. 4, 1986.
16. Dwivedi and Jain, *India's Administrative State*, pp. 16–17.
17. Seluck, Ozgediz, *Managing the Public Service in Developing Countries: Issues and Prospects*, World Bank, Washington, D.C., Staff Working Paper No. 583, 1983.
18. R. C. S. Sarkar, Role of Government Departments in the Legislative Process, *Journal of Constitutional and Parliamentary Studies*, New Delhi, *21*:1 (1968).
19. A. O. Krueger, The Political Economy of Rent Seeking Society, *The American Economic Review 64*(3):291–303 (1974).
20. David J. Gould and Jose A. Aonaro-Reyes, *The Effects of Corruption on Administrative Performance: Illustrations from Developing Countries*, World Bank, Washington, D.C., 1983.
21. See Kothari, *Politics in India*.
22. For a lengthier discussion on this topic see R. B. Jain and O. P. Dwivedi, Administrative Culture and Bureaucratic Values in India, a paper presented at the 5th Conference on Public Policy and Administrative Studies, University of Guelph, Guelph, April 22, 1988.
23. O. P. Dwivedi, Bureaucratic Corruption in Developing Countries, *Asian Survey 72*:48 (1967).
24. Ramashray Roy, *Bureaucracy and Development: The Case Study of Indian Agriculture*, Manas Publications, New Delhi, 1975.
25. B. P. Singh, Political Culture and Public Administration in the National Value System: The Indian Scenario, *The Indian Journal of Public Administration 27*:1043–1054 (October-December 1981).
26. See Rajni Kothari, *Caste in Indian Politics*, Orient Longmans, New Delhi, and Miriam Sharma, *The Politics of Inequality, Competition and Control in an Indian Village*, Hindustan Publishing Co., Delhi, 1979.

27. B. B. Misra, *Administrative History of India, 1854–1947*, Oxford University Press, Bombay, 1979.
28. Sudhir Kakar, Authority Patterns and Subordinate Behaviour in Indian Organizations, *Administrative Sciences Quarterly 16*(3):298–307 (1971).
29. Harry Levinson, *The Exceptional Executive*, Cambridge University Press, Cambridge, pp. 17–19, 1968.
30. Kakar, Authority Patterns, p. 304.
31. See Sam Pitroda, Work Culture Kills Self-Esteem, *The Statesman*, New Delhi, January 19, 1988, p. 4.
32. Hardgrave and Kochanek, *India*, p. 11. For a detailed analysis of the class structure in Indian society, see Lloyd I. Rudolph and Susanne H. Rudolph, *In Pursuit of Lakshmi: The Political Economy of the Indian State*, The University of Chicago Press, Chicago, 1987, pp. 26–35.
33. Hardgrave and Kochanek, *India*, pp. 18–19.
34. For a detailed study of poverty in India, see Atul Kohli, *The State and Poverty in India: The Politics of Reform*, Cambridge University Press, Cambridge, 1987.
35. V. A. Pai Panandiker, Preference for Political Stability, *The Hindustan Times*, August 22, 1987.
36. Keshav C. Sharma, Development Planning and Development Administration, *International Review of Administrative Sciences 34*:121–129 (1968); and S. R. Maheshwari, Administering the Planning System, *Indian Journal of Public Administration, 30*:603–512 (July-September 1984).
37. Kamta Prasad, Planning in India: Some Basic Issues Relating to Operational and Strategic Aspects, Presidential Address to the 66th Annual Conference of Indian Economic Association, Bangalore, 1983.
38. Ibid.
39. See Autonomy for Districts Urged, a statement made by Dr. Kamta Prasad as reported in *The Hindustan Times*, June 23, 1988. The 73rd and 74th Constitutional Amendment Acts of 1993 have given constitutional status to Panchayati Raj institutions and urban local self governments in India.
40. In a series of meetings with the district collectors, former Prime Minister of India Rajiv Gandhi urged that the district administration be revitalized and the role of district officers properly delineated. See Proumilla Kalhan, Fresh Briefs for Collectors, *The Hindustan Times*, June 20, 1988.
41. Taub, *Bureaucrats*, p. 161.
42. Rai, *Patterns*, p. 5.
43. Ibid, p. 6.
44. P. R. Dubhashi, Administrative Reform: The Current Context, Lecture at the Indian Institute of Public Administration, 1985. (Published as a paper by IIPA, 1985.)
45. The term "bullock-capitalist" has been coined by Lloyd Rudolph and Susanne Rudolph to refer to the small to medium-sized self-employed independent agricultural producers who displaced large landowners in the agrarian power constellation and became small producers using labor-intensive technologies that promote employment. See Rudolph and Rudolph, *In Pursuit of Lakshmi*, pp. 49–54.
46. Ibid, p. 27.
47. This section draws some of the arguments from the author's earlier study; see Jain and Dwivedi's Policy Developments.
48. Dwivedi and Jain, *India's Administrative State*, pp. 122–123.

41
Bureaucracy and Rural Development in Bangladesh

Habib M. Zafarullah
University of New England, Armidale, Australia

Mohammad Mohabbat Khan
University of Dhaka, Dhaka, Bangladesh

Because Bangladesh is primarily an agrarian economy, rural development has occupied an important place on the public policy agenda of successive governments since independence. Unfortunately, however, one regime after another, in the guise of bolstering the "national interest," has utilized its own rural development policies to further its political interests. The bureaucracy in such a design served as an accomplice.

During the last twenty years, moves by each regime to formulate policies, plans, and programs to alleviate rural poverty have followed a unique model—that of reform without consensus. Such a key national policy as rural development was designed rather capriciously by the regime without involving the target group—the rural populace—or, for that matter, the mainstream opposition political forces. There was little or no effort to reconcile conflicting interests, to sort out the fundamentals of the policy, or to tie rural development policy with macropolicies to serve both the principles of economic rationalism and social equity.

Each successive regime unhesitatingly discarded the policy of its predecessor without reviewing its rationale, extraneous and endogenous factors relating to its success or failure, or its immediate or potential long-term impact on the target population, on the one hand, and the national economy, on the other. Instead, it lost no time in coming up with its own framework of rural development, one that would work to its advantage.

The lack of a consensus-based policy meant that the rural population was compelled to acquiesce to the fancies of the ruling clique without getting any opportunity to interact with the policymakers and plead its own case. A review of rural development policies of the last twenty years, therefore, displays not-so-impressive performance insofar as they have contributed to alleviating rural poverty by meeting the basic needs of the people.

I. PAST DEVELOPMENTS

By exploring the history of local government vis-à-vis rural development in preindependent Bangladesh, we may be able to discern how the past influenced perceptions about development and how these shaped institutions at the grass roots to help attain the major goals of rural uplift. It will also permit us to fathom the role of the bureaucracy in such developmental initiatives.

The region which now comprises Bangladesh has always been an administered polity. Local government institutions began working at the grass roots during ancient times in India. Two institutions known as *headman* and *panchayat* simultaneously operated at this level. They were primarily responsible for maintaining law and order in the countryside but, to some extent, were also involved in social and economic development of the villages. The headman, who was not elected by the people, invariably belonged to the dominant elite stratum in the village. He wielded significant influence over village affairs because of his role as the only contact point between the villagers and the higher governmental authorities. The panchayats, on the other hand, were elective bodies but, nonetheless, were controlled by representatives of the upper castes and quite often by the headmen.

During the Mughal rule, the panchayati system virtually weakened as some of its functions were taken over either by the headman, who now played the role of law enforcer, or by a class of intermediaries who served as links between the tax administration and the taxpayers.

With the advent of the British, there emerged a new form of local governmental system whose central thrust was to reap the maximum benefit from colonial rule. The focus was on the improvement of law and order and the optimization of revenue collection. The entire system operated within a bureaucratic fabric. The viceroy, as the representative of the Crown in England, played the key role in overseeing, directing, and guiding all activities that permeated all strata of Indian society.

At the local level, institutions were not allowed to develop spontaneously; rather, they were imposed from above at the behest of the central government. Until the 1880s, no significant changes were perceptible in local governance. The same old headmanship was continued with a changed nomenclature and the panchayat, which was no longer a representative body, was catapulted to the next higher level—the union—but with no effective powers. A plan by Lord Ripon, the viceroy, proposing significant changes in 1882 was never fully operationalized. According to this plan, local government was to facilitate devolution of authority in administration and to decentralize revenue administration. There were to be two local government bodies: an elected union committee and a partially representative local board. The centrally appointed officials were expected to play a crucial role in the working of the local board. Ostensibly, this plan would provide for political education of the masses to enable them to identify, understand, and solve their own problems at the local level.

In effect, a new layer in the local government system, not included in the plan, appeared above the two proposed local level bodies. Being an entirely nonrepresentative institution, it usurped all local government powers and forced the lower two bodies to be wholly dependent on it. In a similar vein, the Royal Commission upon Decentralization (1907–1909), although publicly affirming democratization in local government, recommended central control of local bodies.

Thus it is clear that the trend in local government in undivided India was to encroach upon the local affairs of the colonial rulers and to assert their dominance in local administration in both the urban and rural areas. As one keen observer of local government comments, "The Indian local self-government . . . was in many ways a democratic facade to an autocratic structure" (Tinker,

1954, p. 70). Local developmental activities in the rural areas were always directed and controlled by the bureaucracy through nonrepresentative institutions that indubitably abhorred people's participation. Native politicians were hardly, if ever, associated with local developmental initiatives.

After the British left in 1947, Pakistan (of which Bangladesh was a part until 1971) continued the old system for twelve years. Existing union and district boards functioned as before with the bureaucracy playing the dominant role in development. The Basic Democracy (BD) system introduced in 1959 not only perpetuated bureaucratic dominance but created mechanisms to enlarge and intensify such dominance further.

Basic Democracy introduced a four-tier local government structure consisting of the union, *thana*, district, and divisional councils. To provide a semblance of democracy, the union council was made a representative institution; the rest were all under the control of civil servants largely responsible for administrative coordination and supervision of the affairs of the respective councils below them. As Tepper (1966, p. 107) observes: "A powerful district council remain[ed] the primary agent of administration, and an even more powerful government at higher levels c[ould] easily view the union councils as convenient administrative adjuncts." Clearly, the bureaucratic input in governance at the grass roots was substantial.

The 1960s was a buoyant period in developmental activities in the rural areas in erstwhile Pakistan (1947–1971). Several programs were initiated at the behest and supervision of the government of the time. These basically were designed to build the physical infrastructure of the countryside: construction of roads and culverts, irrigation schemes, embankments, markets, and the like. All these came under the ambit of the Rural Works Programme (RWP), which was geared to generate employment for the rural poor. Another significant strategy was to create consciousness among the rural farming community to initiate and sustain a vigorous cooperative movement. While its scope was nationwide, its focal point was a specific rural area (for details, see Zafarullah, 1978).

We have discussed the system of local government that developed during the British and Pakistan periods. Now let us turn our attention to the cycle of development in Bangladesh since independence in 1971. Four distinct but interrelated phases can be identified, each providing a specific model of local governance.

A. The First Political Regime (1972–1975)

After taking over the reins of government in 1972, the democratically elected political regime of the Awami League dissolved the local government system that the new nation had inherited from Pakistan. Contrary to popular expectations that had counted on the political leadership to introduce democracy at the local level, the government, in essence, resurrected the system which it itself had discarded as unworkable because of its antidemocratic attributes. What emerged was a reincarnated basic democracy system with only slight modifications in composition and functions of the lowest rung of the local government structure (GOB, 1973a). In the higher tiers of the structure, the practice of nominations to fill positions on the local bodies was introduced. For all practical purposes, the administration of public affairs in all these tiers was wholly assigned to centrally appointed officials—the circle officer in the *thana*, the subdivisional officer in the *mahukuma*, and the deputy commissioner in the *zilla*.

The pattern of administration at the local level was in no way dissimilar to the national standard. It was highly centralized with the prime minister concentrating all powers in his hands. Yet, not being satisfied with the magnitude of his authority and to assert his position in government further, he unilaterally and capriciously replaced the parliamentary form of government by a strong presidential type that would ensure his hold over the entire political and administrative structure (Khan and Zafarullah, 1988a, p. 173).

An offshoot of this changeover was to redesign the local government structure; all *mahukumas* (subdivisions) were converted into *zillas* (districts) and placed under powerful governors who were to take order from the president and be responsible to him. A web of strong central control was woven with this "reform." However, before it could be implemented, the regime itself was liquidated by a military coup.

B. The First Military-Turned-Civilian Regime (1975–1982)

After a series of coups and countercoups, General Ziaur Rahman (Zia) was installed as the de facto ruler of the country. He moved swiftly and systematically to consolidate his hold over state power, and one of the key strategies he pursued was ingraining and widening of his political base in the rural areas where the majority of the population lived. He began a process of providing alternative policies pertaining to governance, the economy, and society.

An early move of the regime was to restructure the local government system (LGS), especially in the rural areas. A three-tier LGS replaced the existing one that had been lying dormant for some years. The new LGS covered the *zilla*, the *thana*, and the union. A *parishad* or council, displaying many of the attributes of a body corporate, was provided for each tier, but it was only at the lowest level (i.e., the union) where the representative element was wholly incorporated. The other two higher bodies were made quasi-representative with room for both elected and appointed members (Zafarullah and Khan, 1989).

All appointed members on the *zilla* and *thana parishads* were public officials of various nation-building departments working at the two levels. Although regulations provided for the *zilla* and *thana parishads* to oversee and control the affairs of the locality under their jurisdiction, in reality they were made to work within strict central control. The officials nominated to serve on the *parishads* were appointed by the ministries under which they were placed and took orders from their administrative overlords and reported back to them. They hardly permitted the elected members to play their designated roles. Indeed, the *zilla parishad* was never constituted in the manner provided for in the Local Government Ordinance of 1976 (GOB, 1976). During the tenure of the regime, it remained under the total control of the national bureaucracy.

To concentrate its power at the grass roots further, the regime introduced the *swanirvar gram sarkar* (SGS) in 1980 as the fourth tier of the LGS. This microgovernmental system actually amalgamated two programs—the *swanirvar andolan* (movement for self-reliance) and *gram sarkar* (village government)—which had been successfully experimented with by private initiatives and initially without any support from the government (Khan and Zafarullah, 1980). The former aimed at achieving a breakthrough in agricultural production together with reducing population growth. *Gram sarkar*, on the other hand, was an administrative arrangement to organize the people at the grass roots better, mobilize development activities, and utilize indigenous resources more fully (Khan and Zafarullah, 1981).

The SGS consisted of one *gram prodhan* (village chief) and eleven members, including two women. They were chosen through consensus by the *gram shava* (village assembly) composed of all adult members of a village. The specific functions of the SGS included increasing food production, eradicating illiteracy, reducing population growth, stimulating the rural cooperatives movement, and maintaining law and order.

The SGSs died rather prematurely without being allowed to work for any considerable length of time. They were abolished by the succeeding regime, which came to power through another coup d'état in early 1982. But, even during their existence, these grass-roots governments were influenced and controlled by the bureaucracy and used for narrow partisan purposes. In effect, they were used to serve as the underpinning for the Bangladesh Nationalist Party (BNP)—the political party launched by Zia in the late seventies (Zafarullah and Khan, 1989).

C. The Second Military-Turned-Civilian Regime (1982–1990)

The regime of General H. M. Ershad introduced significant changes in the area of local government. These were apparently to "bolster" rural bodies, to take government "nearer" to the people through local institutions, and to "facilitate people's participation" in administration and development (Siddiqui, 1992, p. 152). On paper, the new LGS looked extremely novel by Bangladesh standards. It had all the elements of a contemporary model in local governance—democracy, decentralization, and participation. The colonial tradition of designating the district as the center of local administration and development was finally discarded.

The new scheme transformed the *thana* into the *upazila*. It became the centerpiece of the reform, for it was at this level that all development activities were to be conceived, planned, and implemented. Its affairs were controlled by the *upazila parishad*, consisting of an elected chairman and representatives (the chairmen) of union *parishads* within the *upazila*. Others on the *parishad* included three women and one man nominated by the national government from among residents of the *upazila*, members of the national bureaucracy located in the *upazila*, and the chairman of the *upazila* central cooperative association (Khan and Zafarullah, 1988b; Siddiqui, 1992, p. 153).

It was thus a mixture of both elected and nominated members, but the former apparently had greater control over *upazila* administration as, unlike the official elements, they enjoyed voting power. In reality, however, officials, who represented various line ministries at that level, influenced decision making by dint of their expertise, experience in administration, and better academic backgrounds. They dominated proceedings of *upazila* meetings and in the majority of cases easily prevailed over the elected representatives.

The *upazila* chairman was assigned the responsibility of coordinating development activities, initiating new plans and programs, and supervising project implementation. But, in reality, he depended on the counsel and recommendations of the bureaucrats, on whom he had little administrative control. It was the *upazila nirbahi* (executive) officer (UNO) who served as the principal functionary and in that capacity had overall control over his colleagues from the various ministries. The major reason for his being so powerful was the responsibility granted him to appraise their performance and report to the government (Khan and Zafarullah, 1988b, p. 15).

During the tenure of this regime, the *zilla parishad* never became a truly representative body. It performed only perfunctory functions. Its only function worth mentioning was coordination of development activities in *upazilas* under its territorial jurisdiction, and in that it was under the total domination of bureaucrats (Siddiqui, 1992, p. 161).

D. The Second Political Regime, 1991–Present

In the winter of 1990, the nine-year-old autocratic regime was toppled by a mass upsurge. This was followed by free and fair elections that returned the BNP to power. One of the earliest moves of the new regime was to abolish the existing LGS. The abolition was prompted not by any rational administrative or economic reason but by political factors; the new leadership, which was instrumental in leading the movement against the previous regime, was determined to get rid of almost everything done by its adversary. The prime minister and other key ministers minced no words in censuring the existing LGS lock, stock, and barrel. They were not prepared to let the system continue even with modifications; rather they were keen to see it replaced by a system of their own making.

A Local Government Structural Review Commission (LGSRC) was appointed to devise a new LGS. Its principal recommendations included the resurrection of the SGS model—to make the village the focal point of local governance by encouraging people's participation at the grass roots (GOB, 1992). But subsequent legislation did not reflect the main thrust of the report of the LGSRC. The idea of a *gram shava* was rejected and the government decided on a two-tier arrangement. At the top the local government structure was to be the *zilla parishad* at the district level and at the bottom the union *parishad.*

Between these two tiers, at the *thana* (previously *upazila*) level, all the nation-building departments of the national government are to be located to provide basic support services for development in the rural areas. Here lies the crux of the problem. Although the union *parishad* has been assigned the responsibility of rural development, the very presence of national civil servants at the *thana* and their direct involvement in infrastructure building, service delivery, and regulatory administration will have the effort of thwarting the initiative of the local people in development.

In sum, from independence till the fall of the second military-turned-political regime in 1990, the LGS in Bangladesh has remained in the clutches of the bureaucracy. Decentralization, people's participation, and local democracy have remained myths and have never been fully realized. The underlying goals of rural development policies have remained largely unaccomplished. This is evident from the fact that each national five-year plan is followed by another which either points out the shortcomings of the previous plan or the failures of the preceding regime in implementing all or parts of it. In many ways, the bureaucracy is largely blamed for all the follies and mishaps in development policy execution.

II. RURAL DEVELOPMENT POLICIES IN BANGLADESH

The national five-year plans of the country provide the broad outlines of policy relating to rural development. Since 1972, there have been four such plans and one shorter plan that have evinced the priorities of the regime formulating them. There have been several shifts in policy directions but these have not always proved to be meaningful. Later we enumerate the salient features of each plan vis-à-vis rural development.

A. The First Five-Year Plan

The First Five-Year Plan (1FYP) (1973–1978) was broadly aimed at reducing poverty and achieving social justice in the rural areas. To achieve these objectives, the 1FYP "visualized a need for restructuring rural institutions to meet the problems of the organization of rural people, utilization of resources and development of a local planning system" (GB, 1984, pp. 208–209).

Keeping this broad strategy in perspective, the 1FYP called for undertaking programs in four sectors. First, it proposed the reorganization of cooperative institutions to ensure proportional representation of poor groups in their management. The government contemplated protecting the poorest of the poor by broadening the base of cooperatives. The existing two-tier cooperative framework of the Integrated Rural Development Programme (IRDP) was to be utilized for this purpose. Second, each local government body was to be entrusted with the planning, implementation, and coordination of development activities within its jurisdiction. Such bodies were also to ensure people's participation in local level development. Third, the development of rural infrastructure (i.e., roads, bridges, drainage and irrigation canals, embankments and sluice gates, huts and bazaars, and training institutions) was to come under the purview of the RWP. The building and maintenance of rural infrastructure would generate employment for the rural poor, the planners believed. Finally, the land reform program was premised on lowering the ceiling on landholding, on the one hand, and on securing the rights of sharecroppers through compulsory registration of tenancies, on the other.

The Food for Work Programme (FWP), IRDP, and the Area Development Programme (ADP) were the basic modes through which rural poverty was to be alleviated under the 1FYP. These three programs were not operationalized simultaneously but at different times during the plan period because of unanticipated problems such as the floods and famine of 1974 (GOB, 1973).

It has been observed that the primary condition for any form of fundamental change in the rural economy was wanting. Thus, all three programs suffered considerably as a result of inherent constraints in the 1FYP (GOB, 1985, p. 209). FWP worked to the advantage of the rural well-to-do rather than creating short-term employment opportunities for the poor. The IRDP vastly expanded its activities, but even this could not contribute much in the way of developing organizations for small farmers and the landless poor. Likewise, ADP experienced both institutional and managerial inadequacies which resulted in sluggish implementation of projects.

The landholding system was another deterrent to the equitable distribution of the benefits of development projects among the poor. The existing local government bodies were nonrepresentative in character and were largely dominated by the rural rich.

The rural development policy goals outlined by the 1FYP could not be fully achieved, and employment and investment growth remained unrealized because of a "short-fall in domestic and external resources, inadequate institutional support, lack of skilled manpower . . . inflation and recession" (GOB, 1980, chapter 1, p. 2).

B. Two-Year Approach Plan

The military-turned-civilian regime of Ziaur Rahman launched the Two-Year Approach Plan (TYAP), which, for all practical purposes, reflected the social and economic priorities of the regime. TYAP's main focus was to generate a higher economic growth rate than that of the 1FYP. This was to be reached by containing the plummeting poverty level, improving income distribution, and, as a corollary, facilitating "social justice" (GOB, 1978, p. 29). The anticipated success of the plan centered on increasing job opportunities and enhancing productivity. One of its strategies to accomplish its objectives was effective utilization of local resources and mass mobilization through institutional arrangements and revitalization of the local government system (Khan and Zafarullah, 1980, p. 2). Like its predecessor, however, the TYAP failed to serve its purpose.

C. Second Five-Year Plan

By appreciating the "overwhelming problems of poverty, unemployment, illiteracy and malnutrition of the [rural] masses," the Second Five-Year Plan (2FYP) (1980–1985) proposed a "comprehensive" rural development approach for Bangladesh. This policy document outlined a new strategy to accelerate economic growth in the rural areas. It was to have as its pivot a new goal—"self-reliance"—to be attained through people's participation in nation building and developmental activities within the framework of a new form of grass-roots democratic institution—*gram sarkar* (GOB, 1980, chapter 2, p. 5).

The major thrust of the policy was the organization of the rural poor within an expanded program of rural development (GOB, 1985, p. 209–210). A new institution replacing the existing IRDP was created to oversee the Annual Development Plan, which was geared to achieve "all-round" development by encompassing many areas of activity—agriculture, irrigation, flood control, roads, livestock, fishery, health, education, and so on.

A "new" strategy for rural development was developed during the later part of the plan period. This strategy had three components: (a) development of physical infrastructure; (b) agricultural irrigation, minor drainage, and flood control works; and (c) a production and employment program (PEP).

It was claimed by the government that the most notable program during 2FYP was the RWP, as it was based on a decentralized "participatory" planning and implementation notion. It was further asserted that local bodies at different levels identified, planned, approved, and executed local level projects with the involvement of the people. But, as before, the performance of RWP remained a delusion. Indeed, the RWP had achieved very little to ameliorate the conditions of the rural poor aside from providing them with temporary job opportunities. The infrastructure developed by the program did lead to an increase in agricultural production, but its long-term beneficiaries turned out to be rich farmers who had access to both the means of production and resources (GOB, 1989, p. 111).

The cooperatives program continued with the two-tier system as before. During the middle of the plan period efforts were made to develop "appropriate" rural institutions for the landless and disadvantaged women largely because of the inherent limitations of the primary tier in the cooperatives system.

The two-tier cooperatives system bypassed many small and marginal farmers. Most of the benefits of *Krishak Samabaya Samity* (KSS) and *Upazila* Central Cooperatives Association (UCCA) were reaped by well-to-do farmers, and the landless were virtually excluded from the process. The *Bhumiheen Samabaya Samity* (BSS) and *Mahila Samabaya Samity* (MSS), which were especially created to serve the landless and disadvantaged women, respectively, made insignificant progress. Both the KSS and UCCA became increasingly dependent on the government's financial support and failed to become self-reliant (GOB, 1989, p. 111). Though the cooperative system covered all the *upazilas* in the country and contributed to agricultural production, its effectiveness and desired impact on the well-being of the farming community in terms of its potential for diffusing innovation left a lot to be desired (GOB, 1989, p. 111).

D. Third Five-Year Plan

The Third Five-Year Plan (3FYP) (1985–1990), noted that regardless of past initiatives toward rural development, landlessness, unemployment, illiteracy, and malnutrition continued to characterize the rural scene. Endemic poverty was the crux of these problems.

The nation's policymakers searched for new strategies to get rid of rural poverty. Thus, the 3FYP unequivocally reiterated the problems and specifically formulated a new policy concerning rural development. It sought to raise at least 10% of the rural poor above the poverty line. Rural pauperization was to be prevented by fulfilling basic physical infrastructure and social service needs. By expanding productive sectors the employment compass was to be enlarged and income opportunities enhanced. The rural poor were to be offered better access to the means of both farm and nonfarm production through their own organizations. More importantly, through participation the rural poor were to be given greater latitude to share local resources (GOB, 1985, p. 216).

Adoption of an enterprising strategy and a clearly formulated policy became imperative to attain these objectives. It was argued that by solely concentrating on agricultural development and infrastructure building it would be difficult to make any appreciable dent on poverty. In the past, emphasis on these two sectors alone was the cause of the failure to generate enough employment and income opportunities. The demand therefore was to complement the agriculture and infrastructure sectors with new openings for employment generation for the poor, thereby giving them an equitable share of the gains of development.

The rural development programs outlined by the 3FYP were similar to those of the 2FYP. Development of the rural physical infrastructure would concentrate on the construction of feeder roads, bridges, and culverts, and development of rural growth centers (RGCs). To boost agricultural productivity, minor irrigation projects were to be launched, the supply and distribution of fertilizers and seeds augmented, and credit facilities improved.

The Production and Employment Programme (PEP) was to be given special impetus during the plan period. PEP was conceived as a package program with interrelated components: institutions, technology and training, credit, other inputs, and marketing. The target was to organize 10,770 BSS/MSS/informal groups with about 250,000 members. This target was exceeded by almost 70% during the plan period as 367,000 members constituted 16,090 organizations (GOB, 1990a, section V–F, p. 4). In the area of capital formation through shares and savings the targets of Tk. 93 million [1] could not be reached, as there was a shortfall of about 11%. Out of a target of Tk. 4,680 million, only 5.56% could be distributed as credit to members of cooperative societies and informal groups for undertaking income generating enterprises. Recovery of loans varied widely between 36% and over 90%. Against a target of 106,000, only 81,000 was imparted with skill development training (GOB, 1990a, section V–F, p. 4).

E. Fourth Five-Year Plan

Like previous plans, the current Fourth Five-Year Plan (4FYP) (1990–1995) restates the problems of rural poverty and emphasizes the need to pursue a policy of "employment-led growth" to create more jobs in both the farm and nonfarm sectors. The specific objectives of the 4FYP are directed to a reduction of rural poverty by increasing gainful employment and income opportunities by expanding productive sectors. Technology and skills for productive purposes are to be improved, and access for the poor to the means of production is to be ensured. Agricultural development is to be facilitated by expanding the irrigation program. Basic infrastructure building is to continue as before, and women are to be actively involved in rural development. Rural institutions are to be further developed to play a vital role in this respect (GOB, 1990a, Section V–F, 6).

This strategy, bearing striking resemblance to the one suggested by the 3FYP, is based on two premises. First, rural development programs, to increase employment and income opportunities, must reach the landless, small farmers and informal groups. And, second, the programs' aim should be to increase labor productivity.

III. PUBLIC INSTITUTIONS AND RURAL DEVELOPMENT

In the implementation of the rural development policies and plans of the Bangladesh government, several public organizations are now involved. They include ministries, attached departments, training institutes, and autonomous bodies that are either directly or indirectly charged with the implementation of rural development programs throughout the country.

There are a number of ministries at the highest level of the administrative hierarchy that are entrusted with development functions in the rural areas. Most directly relevant among them is the Ministry of Local Government, Rural Development and Cooperatives (MLGRD&C), which regulates local administration and associated developmental activities in the countryside. As a component of the national secretariat system, the MLGRD&C formulates public policies relevant to its basic goals; undertakes policy and administrative planning; evaluates plan implementation; frames legislation, rules, and regulations; regulates expenditure; coordinates activities under its control; and so forth.

It has two divisions, one looking after local government and administration and the other rural development and cooperatives. Each of these two divisions is under the administrative direction of a senior civil servant known as the secretary. Broadly, his responsibilities are fourfold:

1. Advising the minister on policy and administrative affairs
2. Overseeing routine operations of the division
3. Supervising the staffing and organizational process of the division
4. Managing the financial aspects of the division

The secretary is assisted by a number of joint, deputy, senior assistant, and assistant secretaries in that order. A total of 247 people are employed by the MLGRD&C, of whom 61 are members of the Bangladesh Civil Service—the higher bureaucracy in the country (GOB, 1991, p. 6).

The Local Government Division has three departments under it. Two of these—the Local Government Engineering Bureau and the Public Health Engineering Department—undertake infrastructure-building activities. The Rural Development Division is supported by the Department of Cooperatives. These departments employ a further 14,561 people, 677 of them higher civil servants (GOB, 1991, p. 16).

Some of the major functions of the Local Government Division pertaining to the rural areas are overseeing the administration of local governmental affairs; regulating, financing, and inspecting local authorities and rural police; supplying water and developing water sewerage facilities; managing hatcheries; and coordinating the rural works program. The Rural Development and Cooperatives Division, on the other hand, is basically and more directly concerned with the formulation and implementation of plans relating to rural development; cooperative activities, including banking, marketing, and farming; agricultural credit; small and cottage industries; and training and education. An important function of the division is to administer the Integrated Rural Development Program throughout the country (GOB, 1990b, pp. 67–68).

There are several autonomous public corporations which are controlled by the MLGRD&C. Some of them perform municipal or public utility functions while others are more directly involved in rural development. Two rural development academies undertake research and consultancy functions, while the Rural Development Board is involved in rural project implementation.

The Bangladesh Rural Development Board (BRDB) replaced the old IRDP, which was launched in 1965. It is a statutory body corporate created in 1982 (GOB, 1982a) to

1. Promote village-based primary cooperative societies with a view to enabling them to be autonomous, self-managed and financially viable vehicles for increasing production, employment generation, and rural development

2. Encourage functional cooperatives for generating income and employment for the rural poor
3. Arrange for effective training of members of the managing committees of village-based primary cooperative societies and model farmers in agriculture and rural development activities.

Over the years, the BRDB has expanded its operations throughout the countryside. One of its primary functions is the organization of cooperatives, and until 1991 it successfully organized 66,669 cooperatives of farmers at the lowest level. These farmers' cooperatives, known as *Krishak Samabaya Samity* (KSS), are also provided with credit for crop production and the purchase of irrigation equipment (BRDB, 1991, p. 2). Marketing is another area covered by the BRDB. The marketing program has been designed "to safeguard the interests of farmers" (BRDB, 1990, p. 6).

The irrigation management program (IMP) is another component of the BRDB model. Basically, its purpose is to ensure the capacity utilization of minor irrigation equipment available to farmers.

Among the many poverty alleviation programs of the BRDB, the Production and Employment Program (PEP) is one of the most important. PEP aims to organize "assetless" people into several viable economic groups so that they are capable of accumulating their own capital through thrift deposits. Under PEP, they are provided training on awareness raising, leadership development, skill development, project planning and management, accounts keeping, and so forth. Credit is provided by BRDB for income generating activities to create both short- and long-term self-employment opportunities in the rural areas (BRDB, 1990, p. 34).

Rural development workers of various kinds and categories are provided continuous training by BRDB. Training programs have been designed "to improve [the] skill and living standard of the [rural] people," and these encompass cooperative management, modern agricultural techniques, family planning, health, and nutrition.

In addition to the MLGRD&C, several other line ministries are involved in developmental activities in the rural areas. These include Agriculture; Education; Environment and Forest; Fisheries and Livestock; Food; Health and Family Welfare; Irrigation, Water Development and Flood Control; and Land. Their officials are located at the *zilla* and *thana* levels and they operate in the same manner as the MLGRD&C.

IV. THE BUREAUCRATIC ELEMENT IN RURAL DEVELOPMENT

The administration of rural development in Bangladesh is essentially steered by central control and bureaucratization. Both are so intricately linked that one complements the other. As we have seen before, the degree of control of the central or national government has always been conspicuous. The tendency of all regimes—political, military, or pseudo-military—has been to keep a firm grip on LGS and its activities. Local democracy has been a facade, and the political party in power has unabashedly utilized the LGS to further its political interests at the cost of people's welfare. The electoral process has been nakedly manipulated by it with the support of the governmental machinery to win elections for its candidates. "Decentralization," "people's participation," and "local level planning" have been words especially chosen by political leaders and government functionaries either in making election pledges or in persuading the people to support them in their "crusade" against poverty, illiteracy, malnutrition, and the like.

A. Central Control

The spectrum of control of the national government over local governance has always been expansive. Its ramifications have been wide. Its implications for local participation and development have been deleterious. The LGS framework devised by successive governments at the national level has had built-in instruments to ensure the dominance of the national government. This has been particularly evident in local government finance. Economic management at the local level is almost entirely under the control of the higher bureaucracy.

During the second military-turned-civilian regime, the development fund of an *upazila* was largely financed by the national government. Each *upazila* was provided a bloc grant that was to be spent according to guidelines formulated by the national government. There was no scope for an *upazila* to drift from this stringent measure even if it meant better utilization of funds given its peculiarities and needs. Noncompliance could lead to suspension of grants, and that would have meant disaster for the *upazila*. Because local bodies lacked the means to raise revenue on their own initiative and build a sound resource base at their level, they had to depend on the national government for funds.

In the case of specific programs like PEP, the several line ministries have played a domineering role. BRDB is not alone in providing direction and assistance to this program. Officials from the Agriculture, Fisheries, Livestock, Land, Public Health, Engineering, and Health Departments are directly involved in providing PEP groups training, extension materials, inputs, and advice relating to income generating activities, family planning aids, and so on, and it is in this situation that the bureaucracy enjoys an upper hand in program implementation and evaluation. More often than not, the bureaucrats from these departments have provided their own solutions to problems without consulting the target groups (CPA, 1992).

The several projects under BRDB depended so much on financial grants from the government that whenever the release or disbursement of funds was delayed, those had to be severely cut in size and scope (BRDB, 1990, p. 26).

Intensive inspections of field projects of the Upazila Central Cooperatives Associations (UCCA) have been regularly carried out by senior officials of BRDB. Reports based on these inspections were further assessed by the central bank (BRDB, 1990, pp. 27–28). UCCAs have frequently aired their displeasure with such bureaucratic meddling in their affairs (CPA, 1992).

B. Administrative Decentralization

Decentralization, from a political perspective, never materialized in Bangladesh. There has only been a redistribution of administrative powers. Officials of line ministries at the local level have been entrusted with the discharge of special functions. These officials have little or no discretion to make decisions pertaining to local governance. Under the *upazila* system, the representatives of the national government frequently bypassed the elective council in taking orders from and reporting to their superiors in the capital. Indeed, there was a kind of dyarchy or dual administration in operation at the *upazila*. One was represented by the *upazila parishad* and the other by officers of the several line ministries, either in combination or in isolation. As one writer argues, this form of decentralization cannot serve any useful purpose, for the LGS is unable to free itself from the clutches of the bureaucracy and make significant breakthroughs in development (Mawhood, 1985).

The Committee for Administrative Reorganization/Reform (CARR) (1982) was explicit about the form of decentralization that should be practiced in Bangladesh. It was emphatic about a policy of nonintervention by the national government and argued for strengthening the governing capability of local institutions. It recommended effective authority for local representative bodies to decide on local issues (Khan, 1986). In spite of this assertion by the committee, the *upazilas* were not delegated enough powers to work independently of the national government. As before, the bureaucrats at the center continued to dominate local administration and the implementation of the rural development policies and plans of the government.

C. Policy Formulation

The Planning Commission is the premier staff agency of the government. It undertakes the preparation of national plans (annual, five-year, and perspective) for the economic and social development of the country. It assists other agencies of the government in designing development projects and serves as the central coordinating body in project implementation. It advises the government on policy issues and sets the broad parameters of social and economic development (Islam, 1977, pp. 41–42).

During the first political regime, a bold attempt was made to free the planning machinery from the control of career civil servants. The top echelons of the Planning Commission were manned by economists from outside the governmental structure. These nonbureaucrats applied a different approach in centralized planning which was a complete break with past traditions and was not appreciated by the bureaucracy. As the first vice chairman of the Planning Commission himself noted:

> There was a lack of effective co-operation with the members of the civil service and the bureaucracy; the bureaucracy and the administrative ministries were not eager to accept the procedures of planning or to grant the Planning Commission its leading role in the process of economic policy-making. (Islam, 1977, p. 6)

It was not long before these academics were forced to leave the Planning Commission. They were replaced by the members of the generalist civil service who, for all practical purposes, reversed the planning exercise devised by the professional economists (Zafarullah, 1987, p. 469). This practice of bureaucratic dominance over the planning process continues.

D. Local Level Planning

CARR had also envisioned an LGS that should be supported by a decentralized planning and budgetary process. But the nature of control by the national government has thwarted this. Its directives clearly dictated the terms of utilizing financial resources granted to *upazilas*. The development plans of *upazilas* were largely prepared and implemented by the bureaucrats. Such plans could not be prepared in isolation in response to local needs; rather it had to be in consonance with the current national five-year plan and plans of specific ministries. Here lay the essence of the problem. In endeavoring to keep harmony with these plans, an *upazila* had to compromise its specific needs with no meaningful results.

As part of the local planning process, the national government specified the use of committees in project management. Three such committees were important—a project selection committee, a project evaluation committee, and a tender committee. While the idea of collegiality in administration is generally considered rational, in the case of local level planning in Bangladesh, such committees turned out to be the domain of civil servants. The people who were to be either actively involved in the planning process or consulted were actually shunned by these committees. If they were at all involved or consulted, it was done only to provide a feel of popular participation in local development. Moreover, selection of development projects was considerably influenced by the rich rural elites, who indubitably served the interests of the regime. They took advantage of whatever local government autonomy they could muster to further their own interests, often at the expense of community welfare (Blair, 1989, pp. 233–241). The local poor people's most active role in development was as hired day laborers and nothing more than that (Khan and Zafarullah, 1988b).

Bureaucrats located at higher levels such as the district, divisions, and the national secretariat frequently made on-site surveys of *upazila* project areas and reported on the status of development projects to concerned authorities such as the MLGRD&C and the Cabinet Division. Obviously, their reports were taken seriously and an *upazila* often strictured for either deviating from the prescribed rules or performing below expected "standards." This sort of exercise gave the bureaucrats enough leverage to control the LGS in the country.

Among the locally stationed national bureaucrats, the planning and finance officer played the dominant role in the local level planning process. Indeed, he was the financial manager of the *upazila*—preparing the budget, authorizing development and nondevelopment expenditures, and monitoring and evaluating project implementation (GOB, 1982, annex II). In performing his duties he was required to consult his other colleagues, who represented various line ministries, but not always did they see eye to eye on every issue. Actually, the intrabureaucratic tensions of the national bureaucracy were also evident at the local level.

E. Ineptitude of Local Politicians

One reason why bureaucratization has had firm roots in Bangladesh is the imbalance between political and administrative development. Like most developing countries, Bangladesh seriously suffers as a result of the overdeveloped nature of its bureaucratic apparatus vis-à-vis political institutions. Even after so many years of independence, democratic institutions are yet to take firm shape. Most politicians are still to learn the fundamentals of democracy and respect basic democratic values. This is particularly true at the local level, where politicians are uneducated and have little or no understanding of the formal political process, let alone development administration and its associated paraphernalia. Bureaucrats take advantage of politicians' lack of education and administrative experience and, by capitalizing on their "ingenuity," "expertise," "knowledge," level of "confidence," and social and economic backgrounds, they become intransigent and overbearing in everything they do. Most politicians, aware of their limitations, give way to bureaucratic dominance.

V. CONCLUSION

This chapter has shown that a number of serious problems and unfavorable tendencies have undermined the development of local self-governing institutions in Bangladesh and their role as catalysts of rural development. In the past, successive regimes dominated local governance, leaving the local people little scope for participation. Such dominance has always been driven by political considerations. Both Zia and Ershad utilized local government bodies to mobilize public support for their regimes, and, in this, they were effectively bolstered by the bureaucracy. The absolute dependence of local bodies on the national government for financial support provided the ground for the bureaucracy to interfere in local government affairs. The local councils were dominated by a triumvariate of locally "elected" politicians (most belonging to the ruling party), local rich elites, and the bureaucracy.

Bureaucratization of rural development may have produced some gains for Bangladesh. In the absence of an enlightened political elite, the bureaucracy, in spite of all its dysfunctions, has made some contribution to rural development in this impoverished nation. But that does not justify the continuation of the existing bureaucratic approach. In today's world, the concerted involvement of the community in nation-building activities is considered consequential. It is the people who should decide what is good for them and their immediate environs. As trusted delegates, legislators are expected to promote the interests of their electorates. And bureaucrats, as public employees paid for their services from the taxpayers' money, are counted on to serve the people selflessly and earnestly.

NOTE

1. The taka (Tk.) is the currency of Bangladesh. One U.S. dollar is roughly equivalent to Tk. 38.

REFERENCES

Blair, H. W., ed., *Can Rural Development Be Financed from Below: Local Resource Mobilization in Bangladesh*, University Press, Dhaka, 1989.

BRDB, *Annual Report 1989–90*, BRDB, Dhaka, 1990.

BRDB, *Annual Report 1990–91*, BRDB, Dhaka, 1991.

CPA (Center for Public Affairs), *Preliminary Survey of Some Rural Development Projects of the BRDB*, CPA, Dhaka, 1992.

GOB (Government of Bangladesh), *Presidential Order No. 22*, Bangladesh Government Press (BGP), Dhaka, 1973a.

GOB, *The First Five Year Plan 1973–78*, Planning Commission, Dhaka, 1973b.

GOB, *The Local Government Ordinance 1976*, BGP, Dhaka, 1976.

GOB, *The Two Year Approach Plan 1978–80*, Planning Commission, Dhaka, 1978.

GOB, *The Second Five Year Plan 1980–85*, Planning Commission, Dhaka, 1980.

GOB, *The Bangladesh Rural Development Bocrd Ordinance 1982*, BGP, Dhaka, 1982a.

GOB, *Local Government Ordinance 1982*, GBP, Dhaka, 1982b.

GOB, *The Third Five Year Plan 1985–90*, Planning Commission, Dhaka, 1985.

GOB, *Mid-Term Review of the Third Five Year Plan*, Planning Commission, Dhaka, 1989.

GOB, *The Fourth Five Year Plan 1990–95*, Planning Commission, Dhaka, 1990a.

GOB, *Allocation of Business Among the Different Ministries and Divisions 1990*, Cabinet Division, Dhaka, 1990b.

GOB, *Statistics of Civil Officers and Staff of the Government of the People's Republic of Bangladesh 1991*, Public Administration Computer Centre, Dhaka, 1991.

GOB, *Report of the Local Government Structural Review Commission*, BGP, Dhaka, 1992.

Islam, N., *Development Planning in Bangladesh*, C. Hurst, London, 1977.

Khan, M. M., Process of Decentralization in Bangladesh, *Community Development Journal, 21*: (1986).

Khan, M. M. and Zafarullah, H. M., Rural Development in Bangladesh: Policies, Plans and Programs, *Indian Journal of Public Administration, 26*:779–784 (1980).

Khan, M. M. and Zafarullah, H. M., Innovations in Village Government, *Asian Profile, 9*:447–453 (1981).

Khan, M. M. and Zafarullah, H. M., Entrenched 'Strong Man' Rule: The Governmental System in Bangladesh, in *The Changing Shape of Government in the Asia-Pacific Region* (J. W. Langford and K. L. Brownsey, eds.), Institute for Research on Public Policy, Halifax, Nova Scotia, 1988a, pp. 171–198.

Khan, M. M. and Zafarullah, H. M., *The Decentralized Planning Process in Bangladesh*, Asian Institute of Technology, Bangkok, 1988b.

Mawhood, P., *Local Government in the Third World*, John Wiley, Chichester, England, 1985.

Siddiqui, K., ed., *Local Government in South Asia: A Comparative Study*, University Press, Dhaka, 1992.

Tepper, E., *Changing Patterns of Administration in Rural East Pakistan*, Maxwell School, New York, Syracuse University, 1966.

Tinker, H., *The Foundations of Local Self-Government in India, Pakistan and Burma*, Athlone Press, London, 1954.

Zafarullah, H. M., Experiences in Rural Development: An Institutional Analysis of the Comilla Projects, *The Dhaka University Studies, 28*:174–189 (1978).

Zafarullah, H. M. and Khan, M. M., The Politics of Rural Development in Bangladesh, *Asian Journal of Public Administration, 11*:3–24, 1989.

42
Bureaucracy in the Ottoman-Turkish Polity

Metin Heper
Bilkent University, Ankara, Turkey

In the Ottoman-Turkish political evolution (from 1299 to the present) both government and civil bureaucracy went through significant changes. An early classification among the political institutions of the Ottoman Empire was that by Lybyer (1913), which distinguished the "Ruling Institution" from the "Moslem Institution": the former was made up of the sultan and his household, the civil bureaucracy, and the military; the latter consisted of the religious bureaucracy. The "executive" and "administrative" functions were carried out, at least during the earlier centuries, by the civil and religious bureaucracies, respectively (İnalcık, 1954). According to another classification (Karpat, 1968, p. 72) the latter together formed the "men of pen," who were distinguished from the "men of sword," or the military. In the Republican Turkey (1923 to the present), the "general civil service" comprised officials and employees of the central government, including judges, foreign service personnel, teachers and professors in public schools and universities, and the administrative and clerical staff of the ministries (Kingsbury and Aktan, 1955, p. 22).

The present chapter is an analysis of the place of the higher civil servants in the Ottoman and the Republican Turkish polities. The bureaucratic elite in question were primarily involved in "politics" rather than in "administration." The higher bureaucrats, in fact, considered themselves as a group quite different from the middle and lower bureaucrats. Midhat Pasha, grand vizier during the late 1860s, referred to the middle and lower echelons of bureaucracy as "ordinary functionaries and secretaries" (Pakalın, 1940, p. 41). And one author referred to the higher civil servants of the Republican period as "high cadre" (Atay, 1969, p. 365). Certainly, higher bureaucrats in both the Ottoman Empire and Republican Turkey were far superior to the rest of civil servants by virtue of the education they received (Berkes, 1964; Mardin, 1969a; Dodd, 1965).

During the Ottoman period, higher civil servants generally carried the title of "pasha." Before the *Tanzimat* (Reform) period, starting in 1839, that title was given to the governors of the provinces, the viziers of the capital, and the officials immediately below in rank. After 1839, the officials in the first four (of nine) grades of the civil (and military) hierarchy had the title of pasha (Deny, 1936, pp. 1030–1031). Republican Turkey retained that title for officers only (and that for a while). During the Republican period, the higher civil service comprised permanent secretary, general director, chairman of ministerial boards of inspection, and other officials in similar advisory and controlling positions in the highest ranks (Dodd, 1965, p. 269; Roos and Roos, 1968, p. 27).

I. THE INITIAL INSTITUTIONALIZATION PATTERN AND ITS DEGENERATION, CIRCA 1299–1789

The Ottoman and Turkish higher civil servants' aloof attitude toward their subordinates was a replica of their relations with social groups, and, later, with politicians. The Ottoman-Turkish polity and its social structure developed out of a nucleus of *ghazi* [1] traditions and in the process adopted Islam. The group of *ghazis* that eventually formed the state had come into contact with Islam when they were placed on both sides of the Islam-Byzantium frontiers. They had, however, even during those earlier centuries preserved the autonomous norms of a ruling tradition (Wittek, 1965, pp. 17–18). Later, this tradition was reinforced when the Ruling Institution was served almost exclusively by converts to Islam having the status of slaves of the sultan (İnalcık, 1973).

Although initially young "Turks" were recruited, gradually Christian boys, specially levied and educated, constituted the backbone of the civil and military bureaucracies. From among the brightest among them, a group was selected to be trained in the Palace School (*Enderun*), established by Mehmet the Conqueror (1451–1481) shortly after the fall of Constantinople in 1453. There they received an intensive training lasting as long as twelve years. Eventually a chosen few were given responsible positions in the civil bureaucracy. Others were destined to serve in the military (Miller, 1941; Toynbee and Kirkwood, 1927; Gibb and Bowen, 1950). Such a recruitment pattern and the special education which the recruits went through made them faithful servants of the sultan: "[The civil bureaucrats and the members of the military were] entirely devoted to the will and commandments of the Grand Signor, that is, one who does blindly all that he orders, and if possible, all that he thinks" (Miller, 1941, p. 70).

Thus during this earlier period in the Ottoman-Turkish political evolution bureaucrats supported an absolute system of government with power concentrated at the apex of the polity, that is, in the sultan. This concentration of powers was considered necessary in order to preserve harmony through providing justice. An old maxim repeated in Turkish political literature from *Kutadgu Bilik* in the eleventh century to the *Gülhane* Rescript of 1839 indicated the need for upholding justice: "A ruler can have no power without soldiers, no soldiers without money, no money without the well-being of his subjects, and no popular well-being without justice" (İnalcık, 1964, p. 43).

As a prop to the institutionalization pattern delineated here a fief, or *timariot*, system had been established. The state held the legal ownership of the land where the fiefs worked, leaving only the right of usufruct to the distinguished members of the cavalry. The cavalry obligated the villagers, part of the *reaya* (subject people who paid taxes but had no part in government), to cultivate land or to go through a military drill and be part of a cavalry unit which joined the sultan's army in time of war. The merchants and craftsmen were rigidly organized into guilds. Istanbul had not existed as a Muslim city before its fall in 1453, and the conquerors found there no ancient Islamic society with its inner structure already full-grown, and, therefore, no natural leaders in ancient families with an inherited social prestige (Hourani, 1968, p. 47).

This particular social structure ruled out the flourishing of any autonomous local aristocracies. And members of the polity other than the sultan were essentially salaried functionaries of the state with no feudal privileges. They did not usually own any significant amount of land; after their death their riches would be seized by the state. The sultan monopolized all of the economic resources (Heper, 1980).

The system that emerged was essentially a closed system, save for limited interactions with other systems through war, and as such was primarily an indigenous system with no trace of Westernization or the democratization processes. The concept of the "Ottoman way" was thus developed; in included a belief in the superiority of the system. At the time it *was* superior, particularly in military terms to the systems around it. The awareness of this fact led to an overconfidence in the system itself and to an undue effort to keep it intact. Thus was developed the concept of *nizam*, roughly meaning "preservation of order."

However, as soon as the Ottoman Empire was consolidated into its quasi-medieval structure (circa the second part of the sixteenth century), destructive forces began to work within it. In the first place, fundamental transformations that took place in the pattern and volume of production and trade, and of precious metal stocks, and the resultant price increases in Europe, played a fundamental role in the disintegration of the socioeconomic structure of the empire. In the process, handicrafts declined; industry could not flourish. The ensuing adverse trade relations led to financial difficulties. Second, the wars that the empire engaged in toward the end of the sixteenth century and thereafter no longer provided war booty and, in the last analysis, led to financial losses (Shaw, 1976, pp. 171–174).

As a consequence the fief system was eliminated, and the taxing rights were sold to private parties—the so-called tax-farmers. This was followed by the emergence of *ayan*, or local notables. The resultant compartmentalization of power and politics between the center and the periphery loosened the grip of the sultans on the economic resources of the empire, with an accompanying slackening of their control on the bureaucracy.

Consequently two cardinal principles of the military were abandoned: the prohibition against marriage before retirement on pension and the prohibition against engaging in any craft or trade (Gibb and Bowen, 1950, p. 182). Concerning the civil component of government, first, the initiation of policy was gradually transferred from the sultan to the Grand Vizierate. During the seventeenth century, the grand viziers' official residence, which in time came to be known as the Sublime Porte, became the real center of government. The Imperial Divan still met, but only occasionally and for purely ceremonial matters (Lewis, 1961, p. 372). Second, with the degeneration of training (Toynbee and Kirkwood, 1927, p. 26) and with the introduction of nepotism into the ranks of the civil bureaucracy, that institution developed political orientations not in keeping with the political philosophy of the earlier period: there was a growth in caprice in government. During this period of change, the Ottoman "government became decidedly less 'constitutional' than it had been" (Gibb and Bowen, 1950, p. 199).

During the early Ottoman centuries the civil bureaucracy was a relatively insignificant component of the government. During the period of disintegration it benefited from the disintegration of power at the apex. At the time civil bureaucratic elite became part of the ruling oligarchy comprising the military, religious, and civil bureaucracies; they shared with the other members of the oligarchy norms deriving from neotraditionalism and Islam. A set of bureaucratic norms in the form of Westernization goals was to develop only when the civil bureaucratic elite began to make contacts with the West from the eighteenth century on. In the latter set of norms could be found the seeds of a bureaucratic ruling tradition.

II. THE EMERGENCE OF A BUREAUCRATIC RULING TRADITION AND THE REACTIONS TO IT, CIRCA 1789–1909

The period of nearly a century extending from the accession of Sultan Selim III (1789) to the First Ottoman constitutional period (1876–1879) is a crucial era for the emergence and development of the bureaucratic ruling tradition (Findley, 1980; Findley, 1989). During this period efforts were made to curb the disintegration process that had started two centuries earlier; in the process the civil bureaucratic elite became the leading component of government. During the last quarter of the nineteenth century and the first decade of the following century, however, the civil bureaucracy and the worldview it represented came under severe attacks.

From the end of the eighteenth century it was conceived as appropriate to diverge from the old order, which had degenerated anyway, in order to save the empire (Shaw, 1971). The new worldview admitted the superiority of European countries, at least in some respects, and of the need to adopt first some "techniques" and later full "technologies" from those countries.

In accordance with the new strategic decision to abandon a static concept of society, an effort was made to free the polity from any ready-made formula, which would impede its ability to effect the changes deemed necessary. From this point on the public policies and programs were to be complimentary neither to basic Islamic formulae nor to the "will" of the ruler in its old sense; the only criterion in promulgating such policies and programs was going to be "reason" (Berkes, 1964, pp. 132–133).

It was really the civil bureaucratic elite who in the process assumed the policy-making function. The sultan was responsible for promulgation of policy decisions, but more and more they were developed by the advisory councils of the quasi-autonomous ministries and departments and by advisory councils outside and above the ministries or departments. All these agencies were gradually staffed by a new generation of civil servants different in their outlook and with a new sense of responsibility (Lewis, 1961, p. 99).

The rise to prominence of the civil bureaucratic elite was a consequence of the efforts of Sultan Mahmut II (1807–1839) to relegate into a secondary position the other powerful groups in the polity. The first move along these lines was against provincial notables who had deprived the central ruling bodies of some of their economic resources. In 1812, immediately after the conclusion of the peace treaty with Russia, Mahmut II began to suppress such notables. He crushed them by military means, often using one against the other, or deprived them of their titles and leases so that they were forced to submit. It was then decided to entrust public services in the provinces exclusively to salaried civil servants appointed by the central government. The tax-farming system was abolished in 1831, and the central administration appointed revenue collectors (*muhassıls*) directly attached to the central government (Shaw and Shaw, 1977, pp. 1–54; Lewis, 1961, p. 61).

Once the provincial notables were to a large extent suppressed, Mahmut II could make his move against the Janissaries, the cream of the military. After much maneuvering he was able to get rid of them in 1826. He also entrusted to the civil bureaucracy the administration of *evkaf*—the charitable foundations and endowments which constituted the chief repository of ecclesiastical economic power (Chambers, 1964, p. 317).

The economic resources so retrieved came to a great degree under the control of the civil bureaucracy. The objective was to develop a bureaucracy able to save the empire through political formulae based on "reason." The newly created military, known as *Nizam-ı Cedit*, or New Order, was expected to support the civil bureaucracy in the latter's mission in question. The military bureaucracy was rendered subordinate to the military [2].

Contacts of the bureaucracy with the West had started long before Sultan Selim III's reign when some bureaucrats were sent to Western capitals on fact-finding missions. More organized contacts with the West followed in the late eighteenth and early nineteenth centuries. Early borrowings from the West were in the area of the military. Then, as the earlier assumption of Ottoman supremacy was abandoned, the Sultans began to send regular diplomatic missions instead of ad hoc envoys to the major Western capitals.

In the capital, what may be considered as the first institution of education for the new group of higher civil servants was the Translation Chamber, established by Mahmut II in 1833 when, after the Greek revolt in the late 1820s, he gave up his reliance on Greek interpreters and replaced them with Moslems. The Moslems were to master French in the Translation Chamber. The establishment of this chamber was soon followed by founding of several schools to provide training for bureaucratic careers. The basic goal was to train "enlightened statesmen" (Onur, 1964, pp. 45–46).

The civil servants who received education in the said chamber and the schools viewed themselves as a group apart from social groups, as from the sultan. In their opinion, they were the only group fit to administer the empire (Mardin, 1962, pp. 179ff., 182–183, 187–188). They were known as "the group of high officials belonging to the Reşit Pasha school" (Pakalın, 1940, p. 59) [3]. The members of this group considered themselves as the servants of the state, not of the sultan (Mardin, 1957a, p. 13). They assumed that the policies developed by them and freed from Islamic traditions would be best for the empire. Grand Vizier Âli Pasha, of this group of bureaucrats known as the Old Ottomans, justified the measures he had taken in order to stay on top by saying that he could not trust other people (Mardin, 1955, p. 10).

In order to ensure the continuity of their pattern of rule the Old Ottomans developed the idea of "institutions replacing individual rulers." Reşit Pasha argued that consistency and intelligent administration could only be obtained if "institutions" were established and if these institutions were endowed with a ruling tradition [4]. Such an approach was diametrically opposed to the councils of a certain Sarı Mehmet Pasha, who in the eighteenth century had argued that the Ottoman Empire could be saved only if competent sultans could be had (Wright, 1935).

In their efforts to realize the autonomy of the civil bureaucracy the Old Ottomans resorted to heavy-handed policies. Such methods found their opponents in the persons of the Young Ottomans. Some members of the civil bureaucracy broke camp in the 1860s with the grand viziers of the decade (Âli and Fuat Pashas) and started agitating for the introduction of some sort of a liberalization process. They put particular emphasis on "representation": Âli was . . . [in the Young Ottomans' view] the symbol and apex of a tyrannical bureaucracy. Namık Kemal [a leading critic of the Old Ottomans] wrote with effective irony about the peasant who visiting Istanbul and seeing many fine houses, thinks there must be many Sultans. There are many Sultans, the peasant is told, but they lack the title. They are ministers" (Davison, 1963, p. 223).

It is significant, however, that the Young Ottomans had only a rationalist democracy in mind. According to Namık Kemal "the government could limit individual rights and liberties only by laws conforming to abstract good" (Berkes, 1964, p. 211). According to the Young Ottomans' version of representative principle the good of the country was to be decided not by a handful of bureaucrats but by a larger group of intelligentsia.

The bureaucratic ruling tradition espoused by the Old Ottomans experienced even more difficult years during the era of Abdülhamit II (1876–1909). The strategic decision of the Hamidian era was to a great extent abandon Westernization and replace it with "Islamic civilization" (Berkes, 1964, pp. 261–262, 268). The neotraditionalism in question rejected both the secular policies of the Old Ottomans and "liberal" policies of the Young Ottomans. One reflection of this new approach was the emphasis placed on religion under the banner of Pan-Islamism, formulated to hold the empire together through Islamic solidarity.

Abdülhamit II tried hard to render the civil bureaucracy subservient to him. For instance, he allowed no grand vizier to become entrenched in office until he found men he trusted. During the six years after he prorogued the Parliament in 1977, there were sixteen tenants of the Grand Vizierate. In the eyes of Abdülhamit II, "meritorious bureaucracy" was "loyal bureaucracy" (Pears, 1917, p. 106).

However, even during this period, bureaucratic orientations acquired during the Old and Young Ottoman times were not entirely abandoned. As Lewis (1961, pp. 194–195) has noted, "The government of Turkey was still the accepted and recognized prerogative of an elite of professionals who retained all the rights and duties of politics, including that of opposition."

In the persistence of such political orientations among the bureaucratic elite secularly oriented high schools played a crucial role. Among such high schools the Civil Service School, or *Mülkiye*, continued to be an intellectual center. Even under the pressure of the Hamidian regime it remained a "forcing ground of new ideas" (Lewis, 1961, pp. 180–181). Of the many forces which contributed to the revolution of 1908, as a consequence of which Abdülhamit II was removed from his throne and the Second Constitutional Period inaugurated, a Western type of education and Western liberal ideas among the Ottoman intelligentsia have been considered important (Kazamias, 1966, p. 99). Among others, some of the high officials had become rallying points for discreet opposition against Abdülhamit II (Hourani, 1968, p. 59).

It must be noted that although the earlier political orientations persisted during the Abdülhamit era, the members of the civil bureaucracy who had such orientations were largely precluded from holding influential positions. Nevertheless, as indicated, the ruling tradition of the earlier decades was not altogether abandoned. It is true that during the Young Turk period (1908–1918) [5] that followed the Abdülhamit era, the military spearheaded Westernization efforts. The civil bureaucracy, however, was not entirely out of the political scene.

III. CONSOLIDATION OF THE BUREAUCRATIC RULING TRADITION, CIRCA 1909–1950

The leaders of the Young Turk era were, according to Berkes (1964, p. 329), "Turks who had broken with tradition through education." This description of those leaders unequivocally shows the strategic decision of this period: again it was a decision to resort to Westernization. In fact, this was the period during which the ground was prepared for the early Republican secularizing reforms.

In 1916 a bill was passed with the aim of doing away with the quality of modern laws and *Şeriat* (Islamic Canon Law). The bill also provided for taking away from Sheikhulislam (the highest religious official) the administration of those primary schools which operated with the income of the pious foundations. The new Marriage Act introduced civil marriage instead of the religious one. The Koran was translated into Turkish, despite great protest from the religious community (Sugar, 1964, p. 134).

On the whole, the military spearheaded the efforts at secularization. From the late Abdülhamit II era, because of the significance attached to increasing military threats from abroad, emphasis had been placed on higher military schools. The military schools far outnumbered the schools from which the civil functionaries came (Ramsaur, 1957, p. 18). Besides their greater numbers, the military schools were better in quality than the civil schools: "In the Empire the best schools, teachers, and equipment had been provided for the officers; the officer corps had hence become Westernized early" (Sugar, 1964, p. 162). The military thus assumed leadership of the secularization process. In fact, during the early years of the Young Turk era the officers dismissed "[p]alace-oriented pashas and reactionary and useless functionaries" (Lewis, 1961, p. 238; Pears, 1919, p. 244), whom they despised (Whitman, 1919, pp. 162–163).

However, as a whole, the civil bureaucracy continued to play a significant role. Despite the militaristic trappings of the Young Turk government, internal policies of that government necessitated paying increased attention to the civil bureaucracy. For one thing, the policy of developing a "national economy" [6] made it imperative that a governmental machinery for "economic planning and control" be developed (Sugar, 1964, p. 160). Still more significantly, the objective of progress involving "cultural" change [7] made the involvement of the civil bureaucracy in carrying out "progressive" policies indispensable:

> It is noteworthy . . . that as early as the Young Turk Revolution of 1908, the part played by Enver the Soldier appears to have been spectacular rather than genuinely dominant, and that the movement was directed and sustained behind the scenes by Talat Bey, [originally] a Salonican telegraphy clerk and Javid Bey, a financier of Jewish extraction—that is by Turks who had received their training in two non-military branches of Western technical achievement. (Toynbee and Kirkwood, 1927, p. 39)

In fact, the contribution of civil functionaries to the Young Turk movement had begun during the last years of the Abdülhamit II era. Junior bureaucrats—schoolteachers, telegraph clerks, and junior administrators—had joined camp with the military in the movement against the regime (Ahmad, 1969, pp. 1–13; Rustow, 1964, p. 361). During the Young Turk period, special attention was given to these lower echelons as part of the socialization activities of the Committee of Union and Progress—the political organ of the Young Turk movement (Szyliowicz, 1966, p. 269).

Consequently, as already noted, the civil bureaucracy were not altogether out of the political scene; to a certain extent, they participated in the politics of the Young Turk era (İnal, 1951). As a continuation of the political ideology of the Young Ottomans [8], the Young Turks championed, at least in their early years, liberal political norms. In the face of Islamic resistance, however, the movement soon reverted to heavy-handed policies, to effect an "enlightened despotism" (Yalman, 1956, p. 55).

With this reorientation, the ruling tradition of the military and civil bureaucracies was again revived. In the process, the intellectuals of the Young Turk movement further elaborated on the earlier concepts. One such intellectual was a certain Ahmet Rıza, a bureaucrat. He aimed at awakening Turkish people through education. Rıza introduced a concept which implied invariable relations between "things." Since such a law could only be conceived by experts, it was necessary to leave politics to the latter (Mardin, 1969b, pp. 6–7). Another intellectual of the period was Abdullah Cevdet. The core of Cevdet's thought, too, consisted in the idea of educating the people, who were to be guided by the elite (Mardin, 1969b, pp. 12, 16).

In these ideas one can easily see the seeds of various concepts later encountered in the bureaucratic ruling tradition of the early Republican era (1923 to the present). The new strategic decision of the early Republican period was "wholesale" acceptance of "Western civilization"—a total transformation of the social, economic, and political life of the nation.

However, as a contemporary author has noted, Atatürk believed that only after "cultural" awakening could the Turkish nation attempt economic development (Karaosmanoğlu, 1968, p. 116). The transformation was to be total in a cultural sense (Mardin, 1971). It was still to be selective Westernization, but borrowing from the West was no longer to be hindered by Islamic traditions.

By far the most significant step in the formation of the leading cadre of the Republic was what is often referred to as "Angora Reform"—to solidify the hold of Atatürk and his close associates on the dominant intellectual group in Turkish society. Atatürk believed that reason and scientific method could create an almost unlimited future of material progress (Ward, 1942, pp. 51–52). Thus, if an elite could be trained with a secular and rational bent of mind, such a group could lead Turkey to prosperity and esteem (Frey, 1965, pp. 40–42).

The new political cadre of the early years of the Turkish Republic emerged from a small group composed of Atatürk and his close associates. These intellectual-political leaders, however, comprised a tiny group in terms of the polity proper. Even if the new political-"cultural" goals aimed at transforming some "superstructure" institutions only, the implementation of the ensuing policies would have necessitated the services of a bureaucracy. For this purpose, out of the three institutions, initially the military was utilized to a great extent. However, once the War of Independence (1919–1922) was over, the military was played down and more attention was paid to the civil bureaucracy. The new approach made it necessary, of course, that the religious bureaucracy be suppressed to a large extent.

On the other hand, what emerged from the war was a civil bureaucracy with a dual loyalty: "Alongside national young bureaucrats . . . [there were] bureaucrats from the Sublime Porte. The nationalist wing of the bureaucracy always found the Sublime Porte wing in opposition to itself in the reformist movements" (Avcıoğlu, 1969, p. 155). Consequently, first, some purges were made, and second, steps were taken to gain the loyalty of the remaining former bureaucrats, who had to be employed because of a lack of qualified personnel. However, as the civil bureaucratic cadres were less than satisfactory for carrying out the Westernization policies, a new breed of civil servants had to be created (Heper, 1980–1981).

As a result, a long-range program of educating a new generation of civil servants loyal to the Republican ethics was adopted (Atay, 1969, p. 448). Consequently, the new schools of higher learning, according to Atatürk, were intended to be not merely the training ground of high officials and legal specialists but, more important, the basis of a new jurisdiction consistent with revolutionary ideals and in harmony with the social needs of Turkey (Wortham, 1931, p. 207).

The formal education offered in these schools was conducive to an extremely elitist political attitude. It aimed at creating graduates who were intellectually superior, well versed in normative-theoretical formulations (Kazamias, 1966, pp. 135, 147, 151, 220ff.). As a result of this pattern of education and the specific mode of modernization—Westernization with an emphasis on only selective institutions—reformism soon acquired a static meaning (Selek, 1968, p. 713). For instance, when in 1945 a land reform bill was proposed:

> [T]he deputies in the Assembly binded into two groups as soon as the debate on the law started—one in favor of the law, the other opposed to certain parts, namely to the drastic expropriation aspects of the law. . . . The first group was composed mostly of intellectuals and government officials who adopted a social-intellectual approach to land reform. The second group, composed mostly of deputies with some personal interests involved, adopted a technical viewpoint. (Karpat, 1959, p. 119)

Gradually the civil bureaucracy's place in the polity was solidified. The civil bureaucracy was organized as a career civil service. Special laws and regulations protected the bureaucracy from arbitrary interference by the political executive. A civil servant who was denied promotion or removed from an attractive post remained in the service and could seek promotion and reinstatement by appeal to the Council of State (the Turkish version of France's Conseil d'Etat). The latter council was composed of civil servants and as such provided a secure bulwark against unfair treatment. The civil bureaucracy was also made a close system through the seniority rule and an educational caste system. Initial entry was governed by educational qualifications; thereafter, seniority played a significant role. Lateral entry was insignificant (Eren, 1963, p. 36; Chambers, 1964, pp. 308–309). The civil bureaucrats, secure in their jobs, enjoyed relatively high salaries. During the war years, their salaries were reinforced with assistance in kind—coal, clothing, sugar, fat, rice, and the like (Karpat, 1959, pp. 129–130).

The bureaucratic ruling tradition reached its zenith in the late 1930s, when the civil bureaucracy adopted the principles Atatürk and his associates had developed and when its place was reinforced in the polity and society. At the same time, however, forces were preparing the doomsday of the happy marriage between the bureaucratic and political elites of the 1930s. While the ruling elite had assumed "an integrated and classless society" to be raised "to the level of contemporary civilization" through populist and nationalist and to a lesser extent *étatist* policies, their nondoctrinaire and ambivalent economic approach allowed the strengthening of certain social and economic interests in society.

The new economic groups had no ambition to capture political office so long as the political-bureaucratic elite satisfied themselves with reforms that did not unfavorably affect the economic interests of these new groups. When this came to an end, the new groups decided to capture the government. They were aided by an emerging liberal intelligentsia opposed to the repressive policies of the 1940s (Frey, 1965, p. 282). With the coming of power to the Democratic Party in 1950 a new era started.

IV. THE BUREAUCRATIC RULING TRADITION ON TRIAL, 1950 TO THE PRESENT

The Democrats wished to break the shackles that had been imposed upon the polity by the bureaucratic elite; they were opposed to the latter's prescriptive and largely static Westernization and rather cautious economic policies (Heper, 1991, p. 679). The Democrats made a distinction between those Westernizing reforms "accepted by the people" and those not (Tunaya, 1962, p. 223). They made concessions on religious matters (Reed, 1954, p. 281). Concerning the economy, they wanted to speed up the processes toward more liberal economic policies. The intellectual-bureaucratic reaction against the Democrats was primarily a reaction to the new concept of state, which was perceived as contrary to the earlier bureaucratic ruling tradition: the intellectual-bureaucratic elites thought that politics was no longer used "to promote the interests of the nation as a whole," but to promote the ends of "a privileged few." Second, because of concessions on the Westernization reforms, "irrational" was preferred to "rational." Intellectualism was abandoned; politics was no longer based on "reason."

Under the shield of autonomy granted to them in 1946, university professors had largely initiated the intellectual-bureaucratic reaction. Four basic ideas had been given special emphasis: (1) action should be guided by ideas, (2) ideas should be intellectually respectable, (3) politics should not be a process of providing benefits to certain social groups, and (4) the civil bureaucracy should be given a more prominent place in Turkish polity [9]. Professors' most willing audience were civil bureaucrats (Berkes, 1965, pp. 89ff.).

As would be expected, the Democrats reacted negatively to these ideas. When a law was passed to restrict academic freedom, a faculty member from the School of Political Science (*Mülkiye*) of Ankara University asked a deputy (an old family friend) why he had sponsored that bill; the deputy's answer was "I can't stand the ideas you spread in that faculty. I wanted to put a stop to them" (Roos, 1960, p. 17). A similar statement was made by the then prime minister

Adnan Menderes, too (Aksoy, 1957, p. 11). At the time the government passed three separate laws to restrict academic freedom.

Even if the civil bureaucrats did not play as active a role as the university staff members, they, too, in their own way tried to keep alive the bureaucratic ruling tradition. Despite the fact that the DP governments dismissed some key bureaucrats, reduced the economic status of the civil bureaucracy, and avoided the usual bureaucratic channels as much as possible [10], the bureaucratic elite asserted their right to rule, that is, to contribute substantially to the making of critical decisions. "Unshakenly confident of . . . [their] higher responsibilities to the nation" they did not look with favor at the efforts to make them more responsive to closer public scrutiny (Bent, 1969). Imbued with a paternalistic philosophy (Eren, 1963, p. 170), they complained that the new political elite dragged politics down into the streets (Yalman, 1956, p. 227). In response to a survey question this author put to them, thirty-four of the thirty-six civil servants, who held the highest bureaucratic posts in the 1945–1960 period, agreed (in 1969) that "what Turkey needs more than anything else is experienced and informed people significantly contributing to public policy-making," and, needless to say, they considered themselves as best fitting that definition (Heper, 1976, p. 516).

Not unlike the civil bureaucratic elite at the time, the military, too, took democracy as a discourse at a higher level of rationality. As a consequence, the 1961 Constitution, drawn up in the wake of the 1960 military intervention, legitimized the de facto political influence of the bureaucratic intelligentsia. Article 4 stipulated, "The nation shall exercise its sovereignty through the authorized agencies as prescribed by the principles laid down in the Constitution." The 1924 Constitution had simply stated that the nation would exercise its sovereignty through the Grand National Assembly. The authorized agencies included the newly created Constitutional Court and National Security Council; the Council of State, which had new powers; the Turkish Radio and Television agency, which had autonomy and independence from the government; and the universities, which were now granted full academic freedom. The Constitution allowed incomplete political participation, and it designated certain bureaucratically staffed agencies as the watchdogs of the political regime (Heper, 1985, pp. 85, 88–89).

The political elite, however, had no sympathies with the regime the 1961 Constitution aimed at institutionalizing in Turkey. Celal Bayar, president of the republic from 1950 to 1960, declared that the Constitution was no more than a constitutional legitimation of the bureaucracy and the intellectuals (Mardin, 1973, p. 186). Süleyman Demirel, several times prime minister after 1965, repeatedly complained that the country could not be governed with the 1961 Constitution (Heper, 1985, p. 89). The Justice Party governments of the late 1960s and the Nationalists Front governments of the 1970s continually challenged the jurisdictions of the Council of State and the Constitutional Court.

The bureaucratic elite's response was that of engaging in "negative politics"; the bureaucracy on one side and the government and parliament on the other became hostile powers (Heper, 1977, pp. 80–82). The bureaucratic elite also attempted to promote the idea of state capitalism, feeling that they needed a new kind of legitimation (Karpat, 1973, p. 91).

Significant social and structural changes caused by economic development, rural immigration, and urbanization in a milieu now infused with "liberalism" [11] led to ideological polarization and political fragmentation. In such an environment, the bureaucratic elite could not keep their ground. Particularly from 1973 on, what Kalaycıoğlu (1988, p. 166) calls "amoral partyism" increased by leaps and bounds. From 1973 to 1980 Turkey was governed by coalition governments, their members each heavily engaged in unrestrained patronage and nepotism. Never before in Turkish political development had civil servants been reshuffled to the extent they were during this period (Heper, 1979–1980, pp. 105–106). While in the 1962–1974 period the average number of years that a director general of a state economic enterprise kept his office was 3.5 years, for the 1974–1980 period the corresponding figure was 1.7 years (Tutum, 1980, p. 290). In addition, the more critical posts were usually filled by ideologically committed militants or even by outright partisan roughnecks. Even the most sensitive agencies, such as the police and security services, were not immune from such penetration of the civil bureaucracy by the political parties (Karpat, 1981, pp. 38–40; Çulpan, 1980, p. 3; Tutum, 1976, p. 29).

Thus, when the military intervened in September 1980 they no longer viewed the bureaucratic elite as the upholders of the norms that held the community together and, thus, tried to inject into politics some degree of rationality [12]. In fact, in the eyes of the military the bureaucratic intelligentsia now had rather low status. General Kenan Evren, head of the junta, accused those in the civil bureaucratic ranks of having subscribed to "reactionary ideas" and "perverted ideologies."

Initially, the military took action against those civil servants who had committed administrative acts falling under the category of "punishable offense." Extremist governors and mayors were replaced with more moderate officials or by retired officers. Later, measures were taken against many other officials, too. Several civil servants were retired or simply relieved of their duty. The military also took action against the Council of State and universities. Constraints were placed on the jurisdiction of the Council of State. Through the newly established High Board of Education the military wished to rationalize the promotions and appointments in universities and see to it that the curricula at the universities would not challenge the normative bases of the Republic. There were also some efforts to streamline the bureaucracy structurally so as to make it more efficient and effective, that is, turn it into a legal-rational bureaucracy. The latter approach to bureaucracy was an upshot of the fact that, unlike the earlier one, the military intervenors of the 1980–1983 period had, particularly in economic matters, a less étatist orientation.

In this last respect, the post-1983 Motherland Party governments went even further and adopted a liberal economic policy [13]. The earlier policy of import substitution was replaced by an export-oriented one. From now on an emphasis on market forces rather than regulation from above was to carry the day. The relevant objectives concerning the bureaucracy were twofold: reducing the scope of the bureaucracy in politics and rendering the bureaucracy more efficient and effective. For this purpose four policies were adopted: privatization of state economic enterprises, simplification of bureaucratic procedures and other organizational reforms, decentralization at the localities, and reduced bureaucracy at the center.

Concerning the first three objectives the Motherland Party governments scored only limited success. Although privatization of the state economic enterprises was a cornerstone of those governments' programs, little progress could be made in that direction. Even with regard to those enterprises that were profitable, the buyers expected the state to provide watertight guarantees. In order to make those in the red more competitive, subsidies made to them from the general budget were reduced to a minimum. In response, the enterprises constantly raised the prices of their goods and services. They could do this with impunity as they continued to have a near-monopoly in their respective markets.

In respect to reform of bureaucratic procedures and organization, the overriding goal was to encourage the exercise of initiative. This could take place, it was reasoned, if everybody knew what he was supposed to do. Thus, efforts were made to define function, authority, and responsibility better. The purpose was to achieve an improved division of labor and coordination among the various bureaus and to encourage the delegation of authority. However, officials were reluctant to change their administrative styles. For instance, they resisted delegation of authority.

The governments also tried to make civil servants more enthusiastic about their work, and for this purpose the following measures were adopted: application of a merit principle for the more successful functionaries (for example, promotions by jumping echelons and paying of bonuses), increases in supplementary payments, more frequent pay increases, and greater flexibility in moving people through set civil service positions. The Motherland Party governments were also keen to facilitate the citizens' dealing with the bureaucracy; thus they sought to simplify procedures where the citizens had face-to-face interaction with government officials. These efforts to make easier citizens' relations with the bureaucracy met with some success. Where the elaborate rules and regulations had to be left intact, the governments urged the officials emphatically to be as helpful to the people as possible. The governments' success in making the officials more enthusiastic about their work and be more helpful to citizens were less than satisfactory. Here, too, the officials could not easily shed their traditional behavior patterns. And, on the whole, they could not adapt themselves to the policy shifts in many areas introduced by the Motherland Party governments. The governments' response to this state of affairs was twofold—decentralization at the localities and debureaucratization at the center.

Decentralization at the localities primarily concerned municipalities. At the major urban centers, two-tiered municipal systems consisting of a metropolitan municipality and a number of district municipalities were established. The tutelage powers of the Ministries of Interior and Public Works and Resettlement over the metropolitan municipalities were greatly curtailed. The resources at the disposal of the municipalities were greatly bolstered.

Decentralization vis-à-vis the municipalities in the major urban centers, however, stopped at the level of metropolitan municipality; it did not extend to the district municipalities. The district mayors felt that they would have been more effective if they had had greater autonomy. In their turn the officials at the metropolitan level regarded the district mayors as novices who should first go through a period of training.

The attitude of the metropolitan municipality toward the district municipalities reflected the traditional attitude of the center toward the periphery. Later, even the limited decentralization in question was not maintained intact. Primarily as a reaction to the high level of inflation that Turkey experienced from the mid-1980s on, the central government cut back on its lending to the municipalities. In addition, as a consequence of some alleged irregularities at municipalities the central government expanded its oversight of them.

It follows that in the late 1980s the Motherland Party governments became unwilling to delegate authority to localities. This did not mean that they were ready to reinstate the traditional bureaucrats at the center in power and status. In fact, Prime Minister Turgut Özal and his close entourage gave short shrift to counsel from the traditional civil servants. Despite their so-called liberal revolution, Özal governments felt no compulsion to convert the public bureaucracy into a legal-rational one. Instead, during this decade too, political elites tried to turn the bureaucracy into a virtually subordinate arm of government. And now they were even more successful.

Their first tactic was a further politicization of the public bureaucracy. They placed their followers in a number of important agencies. Civil service posts were made less secure; many functionaries were obliged to work on a contract basis. Certain higher civil servants in critical agencies were purged. Within the existing agencies some autonomous units were created; they were headed by persons brought from outside. Some functions were transferred from an existing agency to a newly created one. The latter, too, were led by officials appointed from outside the bureaucracy. What used to be autonomous agencies were brought under the closer control of the government.

Those portions of the bureaucracy not considered fit for the implementation of new policies and consequently left to their own devices now began to function in a more cumbersome manner than before. Citizens, including members of weighty social groups, faced a bureaucratic labyrinth that showed strong signs of pathology. A bureaucracy that at times had been the most significant element of the center now became either extremely politicized or deadwood. This was basically a consequence of the historical rift between the center and the periphery and the inability of the bureaucratic and political elites to develop a harmonious relationship among themselves and of their inability to effect a transition from virtually complete bureaucratic domination to virtually complete political domination.

NOTES

1. *Ghazis* had been a community of marching warriors that formed the seed of the Ottoman state.
2. Mahmut II created the Office of *Serasker* (commander of the army), which became the nucleus of the future civilian War Ministry. Through it the civil bureaucracy was able to contain the power of the military until the Young Turk revolution in 1909 (Chambers, 1964, p. 316).
3. As grand vizier, Reşit Pasha played an important role in the initiation of the *Tanzimat* (Reform) period in 1839, which continued until 1876.
4. Although Reşit Pasha was a protégé of Sultan Mahmut II, he at times complained of the narrowmindedness of the latter (Mardin, 1957b, p. 10).
5. The reforms in questions were carried out after 1913, when the Committee of Union and Progress came into power.
6. It was during this period that the first conscious efforts were made to formulate a national economic policy. However, economic policy was largely derived from the political goal of "Turkification." Against the interests of a minority economic elite consisting entirely of Christians and Jews—so-called Levantines—the economic policies of this period were directed toward creating Turkish-Moslem entrepreneurs (Avcıoğlu, 1969, pp. 127–133).
7. Largely limited to certain life-styles borrowed from the West.
8. For the links between the Young Ottomans and the Young Turks, see Mardin (1969).
9. These views were expressed by, inter alia, Savcı (1955a; 1955b), and Soysal (1962). On the close relationship between the school and political socialization of civil servants in Turkey, see Heper and Kalaycıoğlu (1983).
10. A stronger emphasis was placed on state economic enterprises; the upper echelons of these enterprises were staffed by personnel relatively sympathetic to the DP politicians, and every effort was made to provide these personnel with comfortable incomes.
11. While stacking the bureaucratic agencies against the political ones the 1961 Constitution also enlarged the scope of individual rights and liberties; the bureaucratic elite had wished to have such safeguards against "the absolutism of majority."
12. On the bureaucracy during the interregnum of 1980–1983, I draw upon Heper (1984).
13. For the period from 1983 to the present I essentially draw upon Heper (1989), Heper (1990a), and Heper (1990b).

REFERENCES

Ahmad, Feroz, *The Young Turks: The Committee of Union and Progress in Turkish Politics, 1908–1914*, At Clarendon Press, Oxford, 1969.

Aksoy, Muammer, Üniversite Hadisesi ve Başbakan, *Forum*, February 15 (1957).

Avcıoğlu, Doğan, *Türkiye'nin Düzeni. Dün, Bugün, Yarın*, Bilgi Yayınevi, Ankara, 1969.

Atay, Falih Rifki, *Çankaya: Atatürk'ün Doğumundan Ölümüne Kadar Bütün Hayat Hikayesi*, Doğan Kardeş, Istanbul, 1969.

Bent, Frederick T., The Turkish Bureaucracy as an Agent of Change, *Journal of Comparative Administration, 1*:47–64 (1969).

Berkes, Niyazi, *The Development of Secularism in Turkey*, The McGill University Press, Montreal, 1964.

Berkes, Niyazi, *Batıcılık, Ulusçuluk ve Toplumsal Devrimler*, Yön Yayınları, Istanbul, 1965.

Chambers, Richard L., [Turkey:] The Civil Bureaucracy, in *Political Modernization in Japan and Turkey* (Robert E. Ward and Dankwart A. Rustow, eds.), Princeton University Press, Princeton, N.J., 1964.

Çulpan, Refik, Bürokratik Sistemin Yozlaşması, *Amme İdaresi Dergisi 13*:31–45 (1980).

Davison, Roderic, *Reform in the Ottoman Empire, 1856–1876*, Princeton University Press, Princeton, N.J., 1963.

Deny, J., Pasha, in *Encyclopedia of Islam* (M. T. Huntsma et al., eds.), 1936.

Dodd, C. H., The Social and Educational Background of Turkish Officials, *Middle Eastern Studies, 1*:268–276 (1965).

Eren, Nuri, *Turkey Today and Tomorrow. An Experiment in Westernization*, Praeger, New York, 1963.

Findley, Carter V., *Bureaucratic Reform in the Ottoman Empire: The Sublime Porte, 1789–1922*, Princeton University Press, Princeton, N.J., 1980.

Findley, Carter Vaughn, *Ottoman Civil Officialdom: A Social History*, Princeton University Press, Princeton, 1989.

Frey, Frederick W., *The Turkish Political Elite*, The M.I.T. Press, Cambridge, Mass., 1965.

Gibb, H. A. R. and Bowen, Harold, *Islamic Society and the West: A Study of the Impact of Western Civilization on Moslem Culture in the Middle East*, Part I, Oxford University Press, London, 1950.

Heper, Metin, Political Modernization as Reflected in Bureaucratic Change: The Turkish Bureaucracy and a "Historical Bureaucratic Empire" Tradition, *International Journal of Middle East Studies, 7*:507–521 (1976).

Heper, Metin, Negative Bureaucratic Politics in a Modernizing Context: The Turkish Case, *Journal of South Asian and Middle Eastern Studies 1*:65–84 (1977).

Heper, Metin, Recent Instability in Turkish Politics: End of a Monocentrist Polity? *International Journal of Turkish Studies, 1*:101–113 (1979–1980).

Heper, Metin, Center and Periphery in the Ottoman Empire with Special Reference to the Nineteenth Century, *International Political Science Review 1*:81–105 (1980).

Heper, Metin, Transformation of Charisma into a Political Paradigm: "Atatürkism" in Turkey, *Journal of the American Institute for the Study of Middle Eastern Civilization 1*:65–82 (1980–1981).

Heper, Metin, Bureaucrats, Politicians and Officers in Turkey: Dilemmas of a New Political Paradigm, in *Modern Turkey: Continuity and Change* (Ahmet Evin, ed.), Leske and Budrich, Opladen, Germany, 1984.

Heper, Metin, *The State Tradition in Turkey*, The Eothen Press, Walkington, England, 1985.

Heper, Metin, The Motherland Party Governments and Bureaucracy in Turkey, 1983–1988, *Governance 2*:457–468 (1989).

Heper, Metin, The State and Debureaucratization: The Turkish Case, *International Social Science Journal 126*:605–615 (1990a).

Heper, Metin, Turkey, in *Public Administration in the Third World: An International Handbook* (V. Subramaniam, ed.), Greenwood Press, New York, 1990b.

Heper, Metin, The State and Bureaucracy: The Turkish Case in Historical Perspective, in *Handbook of Comparative and Development Public Administration* (Ali Farazmand, ed.), Marcel Dekker, New York, 1991.

Heper, Metin and Kalaycıoğlu, Ersin, Organizational Socialization as Reality-Testing: The Case of the Turkish Higher Civil Servants, *International Journal of Political Education, 6*:175–198 (1983).

Hourani, Albert, Ottoman Reform and the Politics of Notables, in *Beginnings of Modernization in the Middle East* (William R. Polk and Richard L. Chambers, eds.), The University of Chicago Press, Chicago, 1968.

İnal, Mahmud Kemal, *Osmanlı Devrinde Son Sadrazamlar*, Milli Eğitim Basımevi, Istanbul, 1951.

İnalcık, Halil, [Turkey:] The Nature of Traditional Society, in *Political Modernization in Japan and Turkey* (Robert E. Ward and Dankwart A. Rustow, eds.), Princeton University Press, Princeton, N.J., 1964.
İnalcık, Halil, *The Ottoman Empire: The Classical Age, 1300–1600* (trans. Norman Itzkowitz and Colin Imber), Weidenfeld and Nicolson, London, 1973.
Kalaycıoğlu, Ersin, Political Culture and Regime Stability: The Case of Turkey, *Journal of Economics and Administrative Studies 2*:149–179 (1988).
Karaosmanoğlu, Yakup Kadri, *Politikada 45 Yıl*, Bilgi Yayınevi, Ankara, 1968.
Karpat, Kemal H., *Turkey's Politics: The Transition to a Multi-Party System*, Princeton University Press, Princeton, N.J., 1959.
Karpat, Kemal H., Land Regime, Social Structure and Modernization in the Ottoman Empire, in *Beginnings of Modernization in the Middle East* (William R. Polk and Richard L. Chambers, eds.), The University of Chicago Press, Chicago, 1968.
Karpat, Kemal H., Structural Change, Historical Stages of Modernization and the Role of Social Groups in Turkish Politics, in *Social Change and Politics in Turkey* (Kemal H. Karpat, ed.), Brill, Leiden, 1973.
Karpat, Kemal H., Turkish Democracy at Impasse: Ideology, Party Politics and the Third Military Intervention, *International Journal of Turkish Studies 2*:1–143 (1981).
Kazamias, Andreas M., *Education and the Quest for Modernity in Turkey*, The University of Chicago Press, Chicago, 1966.
Kingsbury, Joseph B. and Aktan, Tahir, *The Public Service in Turkey. Organization, Recruitment and Training*, Institute of Administrative Sciences, Brussels, 1955.
Lewis, Bernard, *The Emergence of Modern Turkey*, Oxford University Press, London, 1961.
Lybyer, A. H., *The Government of the Ottoman Empire in the Time of Suleiman the Magnificent*, Harvard University Press, Cambridge, Mass., 1913.
Mardin, Şerif, Âli Paşa ve Hürriyet, *Forum*, October 15 (1955).
Mardin, Şerif, Yeni Osmanlıların Hakiki Hüviyeti: Tanzimat Bürokrasisi, *Forum*, July 1 (1957a).
Mardin, Şerif, Tanzimat Fermanının Mânası: Yeni Bir İzah Denemesi, *Forum*, November 15 (1957b).
Mardin, Şerif, *The Genesis of Young Ottoman Thought: A Study in the Modernization of Political Ideas*, Princeton University Press, Princeton, N.J., 1962.
Mardin, Şerif, Power, Civil Society and Culture in the Ottoman Empire, *Comparative Studies in Society and History 11*:258–281 (1969a).
Mardin, Şerif, *Continuity and Change in the Ideas of the Young Turks*, Robert College, Istanbul, 1969b.
Mardin, Şerif, Ideology and Religion in the Turkish Revolution, *International Journal of Middle East Studies, 2*:197–211 (1971).
Mardin, Şerif, Center-Periphery Relations: A Key to Turkish Politics? *Daedalus 102*:169–190 (1973).
Miller, Barnette, *The Palace School of Muhammad the Conqueror*, Harvard University Press, Cambridge, Mass., 1941.
Onur, Vedad, *Tanzimat Devrinin Büyük ve Unutulmaz Devlet Adamları*, Ziraat Bankası, Ankara, 1964.
Pakalın, Mehmed Zeki, *Son Sadrazamlar ve Başvekiller, Cilt I*. Ahmet Said Matbaası, Istanbul, 1940.
Pears, Sir Edwin, *Life of Abdülhamid*, Constable, London, 1917.
Pears, Sir Edwin, *Forty Years Under Abdulhamid*, Henry Holt, New York, 1919.
Ramsaur, Ernest Edmonton Jr., *The Young Turks: Prelude to the Revolution of 1908*, Princeton University Press, Princeton, N.J., 1957.
Reed, Howard A., Revival of Islam in Secular Turkey, *The Middle East Journal 8*:267–282 (1954).
Roos, Noralou P. and Roos, Leslie L., Changing Patterns of Turkish Public Administration, *Middle Eastern Studies 5*:28–36 (1968).
Ross, Irwin, From Atatürk to Gürsel—What Went Wrong in Turkey, *New Leader* December 5 (1960).
Rustow, Dankwart A., [Turkey:] Military, in *Political Modernization in Japan and Turkey* (Robert E. Ward and Dankwart A. Rustow, eds.), Princeton University Press, Princeton, N.J., 1964.
Savcı, Bahri, Türkiye'de Demokratik Savaşın Şekli Prensipleri, *Forum* January 15 (1955b).
Savcı, Bahri, İktidar Savaşı Yapmadan İktidar, *Forum,* July 1 (1955b).
Selek, Sabahattin, *Anadolu İhtilâli*, İstanbul Matbaası, Istanbul, 1968.

Shaw, Stanford J., *Between Old and New: The Ottoman Empire Under Sultan Seim III, 1789–1807*, Harvard University Press, Cambridge, Mass., 1971.

Shaw, Stanford J., *History of the Ottoman Empire and Modern Turkey. Volume I: Empire of the Gazis: The Rise and Decline of the Ottoman Empire, 1280–1808*, Cambridge University Press, Cambridge, 1976.

Shaw, Stanford J. and Shaw, Ezel Kural, *History of the Ottoman Empire and Modern Turkey. Volume II: Reform, Revolution, and Republic: The Rise of Modern Turkey, 1808–1975*, Cambridge University Press, Cambridge, 1977.

Soysal, Mümtaz, Yanlış Reçete, *Yön*, February 28 (1962).

Sugar, Peter F., [Turkey:] Economic and Political Modernization, in *Political Modernization in Japan and Turkey* (Robert E. Ward and Dankwart A. Rustow, eds.), Princeton University Press, Princeton, 1964.

Szyliowicz, Joseph S., Political Participation and Modernization in Turkey, *Western Political Quarterly 19*:266–285 (1966).

Toynbee, Arnold J. and Kirkwood, Kenneth P., *Turkey*, Charles Scribner's and Sons, New York, 1927.

Tunaya, Tarık Zafer, *İslamcılık Cereyanı. Meşrutiyetin Siyasi Hayatı Boyunca Gelişmeşi ve Bugüne Bıraktığı Meseleler*, Baha Matbaası, İstanbul, 1962.

Tutum, Cahit, Yönetimin Siyasallaşmasi ve Partizanlık, *Amme İdaresi Dergisi 9*:9–32 (1976).

Tutum, Cahit, Türk Personel Rejiminin Sorunlarına Genel Bir Bakış, *Amme İdaresi Dergisi 13*:95–107 (1980).

Ward, Barbara, *Turkey*, Oxford University Press, New York, 1942.

Whitman, Sidney, *Turkish Memoirs*, Heinemann, London, 1919.

Wittek, Paul, *The Rise of the Ottoman Empire*, Luzac, London, 1965.

Wortham, H. E., *Mustapha Kemal of Turkey*, The Holme Press, London, 1931.

Wright, I., Walter Livingston, *Ottoman Statecraft: The Book of Counsels for Vezirs and Governors of Sarı Mehmet Pasha*, Princeton University Press, Princeton, N.J., 1931.

Yalman, Ahmet Emin, *Turkey in My Time*, University of Oklahoma Press, Norman, Okla., 1956.

43
Bureaucracy, Bureaucratization, and Debureaucratization in Ancient and Modern Iran

Ali Farazmand
Northern Kentucky University, Highland Heights, Kentucky

I. INTRODUCTION

Iran has one of the longest traditions of bureaucracy and civilization in the world. Beginning around 8,000 years ago, Iranian bureaucracy grew first in the city-state of Susa and then as the major institution of governance and administration under the Elamite and Persian empires. It continued its influence as a dominant institution of governance and power through centuries under the Islamic Khalifate and the following Safavid and Ottoman empires, but began to decline during the eighteenth and nineteenth centuries. The rise of bureaucracy and the bureaucratic state in modern Iran began in the 1920s. Therefore, bureaucracy has played a formidable role in modern Iranian society, politics, and economics, as it did during the ancient time. Bureaucratization is a political and administrative phenomenon, and it has an ancient origin, though the modern concepts of bureaucracy and bureaucratization are eighteenth century concepts (Argyriades, 1991; Farazmand, 1989). To Weber (1947), bureaucratization is a political phenomenon, and it is inevitable in modern society, for bureaucracy is a rational organization of modern administration and government. Its instrumentality is indispensable to rulers and governments around the world.

This chapter analyzes Iranian bureaucracy in modern time with reference to the ancient Persian Empire. First a historical perspective on Iranian bureaucracy is given as the context. Then, the phenomenon of bureaucratization in Iran from the 1920s to the 1970s is discussed. This is followed by an analysis of the bureaucracy and the Iranian revolution of 1978–79 with the changes that have taken place in the postrevolutionary bureaucracy in Iran. Finally, a conclusion is provided along with a brief comparative discussion of bureaucratization and debureaucratization in pre- and postrevolutionary Iran. This chapter is drawn primarily from my previous works as well as my forthcoming book on the history of Iranian bureaucracy and public administration (see Farazmand, 1982; 1989; 1991a; 1991b; forthcoming), plus a number of select sources, some of which are cited in the text and others that are not.

II. HISTORICAL BACKGROUND

Bureaucracy has played a key role in Iranian society, politics, and administration for over 8,000 years. The earliest experience of state tradition and administrative functions on a massive scale began around 6000 B.C. in Susa. As one of the oldest sites of ancient civilization, Susa began political life first as a city-state rival to Sumer in the Mesopotamia, then as the capital of one of the oldest empires of antiquity, Elam. Bureaucracy under the long history of the federated Elamite Empire developed significantly and played a major role in the Iranian society and the empire (Cameron, 1968; Ghirshman, 1954; Mallowan, 1965).

The Elamite language—with a written alphabet developed simultaneously with that of the Sumerian—and the prosperous economy of the federal empire contributed considerably to the bureaucratic development of Iran. Subsequently, a growing class of professional bureaucrats emerged in ancient Iran. Susa was one of the key centers of both civilization and bureaucratic systems of government in the ancient world for a long time, even after the fall of the Elamite Empire to the Medes in 600 B.C. Among the major administrative achievements of Elamite Iran were the development and management of a gigantic system of underground irrigation, *ganats,* an Iranian invention that turned an arid country into an agricultural land; the invention and development of the written Elamite language and its extensive use in the bureaucracy; and the construction and maintenance of numerous public works and enterprises such as roads, bridges, cities, towns, communication centers, and economic/commercial centers (Cameron, 1968; Farazmand, 1991a; 1991b; Ghirshman, 1954).

Bureaucracy was highly instrumental in the administration of the intergovernmental relations of the federal state of Elam for almost 2,500 years. Indeed, the foundations of the bureaucracy and administrative state of the following Persian Empire were laid under the Elamite empire (ibid.).

The elevation of bureaucracy and bureaucrats under the powerful Median Empire, which conquered Assyria in 612 B.C. as well as many kingdoms eastward and was planning to annex Babylon, was another significant step toward the professionalization of the bureaucracy and its increased power in society. Bureaucracy flourished under the Medes, who were masters of statecraft, and Iranians began to gain a reputation as "excellent administrators." The arrival of the Aryans, a young, energetic group of people of Indo-European origin, on the plateau during the second migration wave at the turn of the first millennium B.C. eventually changed the entire structure of Iranian civilization. They were also destined to change not only the political history of the Near East but world civilization by conquering the known world of antiquity in a single generation. They established an administrative system that was managerially efficient and politically effective, and their military power was second to none. Initially, the Medes crafted expertise in statehood through a well-disciplined and organized bureaucracy; then they transferred their achievements to their Persian cousins. The concept of "state" was for the first time adopted officially by the Aryans, who "turned that concept into a reality" (Ghirshman, 1954, p. 127). This was particularly true under the Achaemenid Empire of Persia.

The world-state Persian Empire of the Achaemenids inherited a rich legacy of effective and efficient administration with the professional bureaucracy of the Elamite and Medes. When Cyrus the Great subdued the Median Empire, he found an efficient bureaucracy and administration already established, experienced, and developed. But the empire Cyrus founded required a different organization (ibid.). Bureaucracy in the Persian Empire formed one of the key pillars of governance and administration, along with the military organization, the royal court, and the nobility. The organization of the empire into forty-six *satrapies*—vast territories with major kingdoms and nations—which stretched to India in the east and Egypt, Eastern Europe, and the Greek world in the West was one of its major innovations. Wherever the Persian army went, the bureaucracy followed and quickly established itself as an effective and efficient instrument of administration and governance (Farazmand, forthcoming; Frye, 1975; Olmstead, 1948).

The Persian bureaucracy during the 200-plus years under the Achaemenids became highly professionalized, and bureaucrats enjoyed high prestige, power, and privileges in society throughout the empire. The administrative reforms of Darius the Great signified a new development in the direction of professionalization of Iranian bureaucracy and administration. Cyrus the Great was a genius military and political leader; his successor Darius was also a great administrator. Close attention to a sound economy and an efficient administrative system prompted him to reorganize and reform the legal, financial, communication, and managerial systems of the administration of his vast empire. It was a turning point in the administrative history of the Near East, and indeed in the ancient world. Bureaucracy was both large and further professionalized, with numerous languages used in different parts of the empire, although the Elamite and Aramaic languages continued to play the key role in the system as the official languages of the bureaucracy, along with Old Persian as the language of the Court (ibid.).

The subsequent fall of the empire to Alexander did not make the Persian bureaucracy weak. Indeed, it was totally adopted by the new occupiers, and the Persian administrative system continued. The later rise of the Parthian Empire with its decentralized system of administration was not favorable to the professionalized and centralized system of bureaucracy and administration of the earlier time, yet bureaucracy continued to flourish under the new system, which found powerful allies among the great nobles of the Seven Families, who actually governed the Parthian Empire for well over 400 years (240 B.C.–227 A.D.). Romans learned a great deal from the Iranian bureaucracy during this period of both hostility and peaceful interaction (ibid.).

Iranian bureaucracy was further perfected in the long period of the Sasanid Empire (227–651 A.D.), in which purification of the Persian culture, administration, and society was rigidly enforced. The bureaucracy regained the powerful position it had enjoyed before, and it found high status of both professionalization and power in society and politics. The Sasanid state in general and its bureaucracy became the models for many generations of empires and governments to follow. The Persian Sasanids perfected the art of statehood and bureaucratic administration, a professional legacy that has been inherited not only in modern Iran but in many other parts of the region (ibid.; Eisenstadt, 1963; Frye, 1963).

After the fall of the Persian Empire to the conquering Islamic forces the Persian bureaucracy continued to play the dominant role as the major institution of governance under the new empire. The conquering Arabs adopted the entire Persian state and administrative system, for they had little or none of their own. Consequently, Persianization of the Islamic Empire—particularly of the Abbasid Khalifate—was a phenomenon of historical significance. This tradition of Persian administrative/bureaucratic hegemony continued during the Salgugh Empire, as well as in the following Ottoman Empire, which subdued the Khalifate and ruled most of the Middle East and part of Eastern Europe for almost a millennium. The Ottomans adopted the Persian bureaucratic system and made some changes in it as time passed (Farazmand, 1991b, forthcoming; Frye, 1963).

Persian bureaucracy emerged powerful once again during the sixteenth century under the powerful Safavid Empire, which revived the ancient Sasanid traditions of state, culture, and glory for over two centuries. The merit system was reinforced, along with the religious and political criteria for selection and promotion, and the bureaucracy assumed huge responsibilities in implementing gigantic public works and managing large public enterprises (Savory, 1980).

However, Iranian bureaucracy fell into a declining path as instability and chaotic succession followed the Safavids. The feudalistic system of monarchy under the decentralized and despotic two hundred year regime of the Qajars was detrimental to the revival, development, and refinement of Iranian bureaucracy so rich in the past. While the West was emerging from the Middle Ages and flourishing in economy and administration, Iran was struggling to maintain its integrity and existence; she was sandwiched between the main power contenders of Russia, Britain, and France throughout the nineteenth century. Despotism also weakened Iran internally. So, the bureaucracy declined; efforts toward reform also failed in this period.

III. BUREAUCRATIZATION OF IRAN (1920s–1970s)

The rise of the modern bureaucracy and the bureaucratic state in Iran began in the 1920s, after the fall of the Qajar dynasty through a military coup d'êtat by Colonel Reza Khan, who subsequently established the Pahlavi dynasty in 1924. A series of administrative reforms changed the structural system of economy, politics, and administration. The bureaucracy was reorganized on two pillars; the ancient Persian bureaucratic and administrative system and the modern Western concepts of organization and management. A new civil service law was adopted, and significant reforms in the judiciary and the executive bureaucracy were implemented, all on a secular basis. Rural Iran was for the first time penetrated by the state and was bureaucratized to some extent through the establishment of the rural police or *gendarmerie*, an armed rural bureaucracy that reinforced the power of the local landed aristocracy or feudal landlords. In urban areas as well, the bureaucratization of society was pursued along with other measures that were taken to alter Iranian economy and society, but the political system remained autocratic and dictatorial.

The second wave of bureaucratization in Iran began with the agrarian and administrative reforms of rural and urban areas in the 1960s. This period signified a turning point in the history of Iranian administrative and socioeconomic structures. Through the agrarian reform, with the three stages of land reform implementation into the 1970s, the semifeudal system of economy and society in rural Iran, where about 70% of the population lived, was transformed into a capitalistic system integrated with international capital. Capitalism in Iran flourished under the direct control of the autocratic state. This was accomplished through the bureaucratization of rural and urban Iran. State bureaucracy replaced the local independent feudal powers who had until the 1960s ruled rural Iran (Bill, 1972; Farazmand, 1982, 1989; Halliday, 1979).

A. The Power Position of the Bureaucracy

The power position of the bureaucracy in Iran grew dramatically as the society became thoroughly bureaucratized. The bureaucratic state and the Pahlavi regime became the same. After the rise of autocracy in Iran in the 1950s, the Shah with the advice of the Americans and other Western powers was forced to implement a number of reforms and to institutionalize the whole society. This was also the period of institution building which the Western social scientists had prescribed as a strategic approach to national development in the third world (Huntington, 1968).

In Iran, the bureaucratic state became the institution of power and the only foundation of legitimacy of the regime. This was because the Shah was considered by most Iranians an American Shah who did not represent the Iranian people and their aspirations for independence. Thus the regime relied almost solely on the bureaucratic state—military, security, and civilian. The regime and the bureaucratic state were identified with each other; a challenge to the state was considered a direct challenge to the regime and was not tolerated. Consequently, the power of the bureaucracy became pervasive in all spheres of Iranian life (Afkhami, 1985; Cottom, 1979; Farazmand, 1989; Razi, 1987).

The nature of the Iranian bureaucratic state is well described by Fred Halliday (1979, p. 63), who explains it in terms of five characteristics: "It is capitalist, it is developing capitalist, it is dictatorial, it is a monarchic form of dictatorship, and it is in a certain sense dependent on the advanced capitalist countries. . . . The state has become, to a considerable degree, dependent on the support it receives from the U.S. and other developed capitalist world generally."

The Iranian bureaucracy was the central arm of the government and the Pahlavi regime and was by nature antiparticipatory, hegemonistic in behavior, dominant politically and culturally, and stifling in terms of human development as it impeded Iranian individual effort to grow personally. The bureaucracy was also extremely elite oriented and promoted extreme inequality economically and socially. It was also extremely politicized and centralized. "Extreme centralization and politicization, however, appeared as the dominant factors—traits which helped the White Revolution in its first decade and debilitated it in the second" (Afkhami, 1985, p. 58).

One of the most powerful bureaucracies of Iran during the 1960s and 1970s was the Ministry of Agriculture and Rural Development (MARD), a gigantic organization in charge of agrarian/rural reforms. Emerging from the agrarian reforms of the White Revolution of the Shah in the early 1960s, MARD with its many affiliated agencies—some of which were huge in size and power themselves—was elevated to an extremely high position of prestige, power, and influence in administration, policy, and politics. During the 1960s and early 1970s, MARD was pervasive in all aspects of rural Iran and its leadership at both the central and the regional level acted as minikings throughout Iran. Even the governors-general of the provinces were not immune from the influence of this gigantic bureaucracy, which expanded its organizational domain well beyond its original scope of mission and activities. By the early 1970s it was involved in comprehensive plans and projects such as huge economic development zones or poles, regionalization of Iranian economy and agriculture, administration of rural and urban projects, assumption of huge enterprises in both agriculture and industry, and more. MARD district administrators also became so powerful in rural areas that they were characterized as minikings and system maintainers at the local levels.

The power of the bureaucracy in general and the MARD bureaucracy in particular was enhanced by many ways: through its discretion to dispense money through contracts and purchases; its establishment and maintenance of powerful alliances with private businesses; and its role as the facilitative institution through which the growing number of huge multinational corporations and agribusinesses operated in Iran. Other factors that added to the power of the bureaucracy included the lack of effective budgetary control over its operation, and lack of significant judicial control over its administration (in fact, the judiciary often reinforced bureaucratic power at the expense of the society and the people). Consequently, "payoffs to bureaucrats became a common way of influencing public policy and administrative behavior" (Farazmand, 1989, p. 42). The power of the bureaucracy was further enhanced by the lack of free news media. The notorious secret police, SAVAK, had absolute control over the media and of any form of free expression in Iran. Despite the pervasive power the bureaucracy and bureaucratic state exercised in Iran, it was by no means an autonomous state. It was subservient to the regime and to the Shah. The bureaucracy was dependent on the Shah, but dominated the rest of the society. The latter gave the bureaucratic state partial autonomy: for as long as the bureaucracy did not pose a threat to the regime, it was left to act autonomously in relation to the rest of the society.

B. The Goals and Functions of the Bureaucracy

No distinction could be made between the goals and functions of the Iranian bureaucracy and those of the political system under the Pahlavi regime. The bureaucracy was the key instrument of system maintenance and regime enhancement. And no change could be made in the bureaucracy and administrative system without a significant alteration in the political system. The "organizational framework of Iranian politics hinged upon the bureaucracy" (Afkhami, 1985, p. 57).

Thus the overriding goal of the bureaucracy was to enhance the Pahlavi regime and the personal interests of the Shah. Its second major goal was to enhance the process of capitalist development and capital accumulation in the interest of the both domestic big bourgeoisie and international capital. The third goal was to legitimize the social system of capitalism and its social relations in Iran. Still other goals included the formulation, development, and presentation to the Shah of policies and programs that would promote the preceding goals.

But one of the most important goals of the bureaucracy was to enhance its own power and to dominate the society. In this regard, it was also successful: The degree of "formalism and bureaucratism was so pervasive that no political, economic, or social affairs of the country could be run without the exercise of bureaucratic power" (Farazmand, 1989, p. 45). Formalism allowed the regime and the state to announce policies and goals in vague and unclear ways, whereas the bureaucracy implemented or chose not to implement policies or decisions that were counter to the goals of the regime and to those of its own elite.

C. The Bureaucratic Elite

The bureaucracy was dominated by a highly powerful elite who were members of both political and economic elite circles at the national and regional levels. As a well integrated web system, the elite structure in Iranian prerevolutionary society was both complex and rigid. The complexity was a result of its diverse and differentiated components drawn from various segments of the society—military, political, social, economic, and administrative. The complexity enabled the regime to promote rivalry among the members of the elite at all levels—inner circle, general, and specific—and to divide and rule without much difficulty.

The inner circle constituted the top, strategic elite of all sectors involved; they were the backbone of the regime and their number was less than one thousand, and indeed, by one account, about four hundred (Bill, 1972). Next was the general elite, which included a larger membership from economic, political, social, administrative, and military strategic groups or families. Here, the so-called Thousand Families constituted the core, but the membership of the general elite was much larger. Members of the general elite often served in an interlocking web or network of positions highly sensitive to the regime's survival, maintenance, and enhancement.

The administrative or bureaucratic component of this general elite was also very powerful, along with the military and security components. The particular or specialized elites were found in different sectors or organizations, urban and rural. These were the key administrative officials who had specialized roles and functions. Finally, resembling the national general and inner circle elites, the local elites were also indispensable to the regime. Among all these elites, the bureaucratic elite was the integrating component; it provided the rigidity of the structure and, hence, was a formidable force for system integration and domination (Farazmand, 1989). Thus, the structural complexity and rigidity of the Iranian elite provided the regime with the best combination of instrumentality of rule, governance, and control. The result was the elimination of any possibility of the rise of an independent elite capable of challenging the status quo and the regime. Since the real power was held by the royal family and the Shah, the Iranian political and economic elite was reduced to a "Second Stratum" (Zonis, 1971), lacking autonomy and independence. The regime monopolized all power, and alienated all peoples of Iran, including the entire elite, both the strategic inner circle and the general elites. Consequently, dissatisfaction with and resentment toward the regime grew rapidly during the late 1960s and 1970s. And when the regime's challengers began organized activity, many members of the elites, including some administrators, joined them. This problem of regime legitimacy erosion was accentuated and aggravated during the revolution of 1978–79, when many members of the political, administrative, bureaucratic, and economic elites also joined the antiregime challengers and revolutionaries (Farazmand, 1989; Razi, 1987).

The power of the bureaucratic elite was therefore crucial to the integration of the system and the regime in Iran for a long time, for, as an instrumental rationality, it provided the complexity and flexibility as well as the structural rigidity to deal with challengers. The bureaucracy and bureaucratization of Iran under the Shah were highly instrumental in maintaining the Pahlavi regime, in providing some legitimacy, in enhancing the regime and the Shah's power, in promoting capitalism and capitalist development in rural and urban Iran, and in facilitating domestic and international capital accumulation in Iran. It was also instrumental in transforming rural Iran into a capitalistic system, and in replacing the rural feudal power of the landlords with the centralized power of the bureaucratic state. This resulted in significant repression of the rural people, widening the gap between rich and poor throughout Iran, and resulted in a displacement of more than 12 million rural population to urban areas, where they found their situation even worse than before. During the revolution of 1978–79 these large numbers of rural migrants played a significant role by joining the antiregime demonstrators in the streets; they fueled the revolution.

IV. THE REVOLUTION OF 1978–79 AND THE BUREAUCRACY

The revolution of 1978–79 in Iran was one of the most significant revolutions the world witnessed during the last three centuries. It was a general uprising in which all segments of all classes participated. Since the regime had alienated even its closest power elites, they also joined the antiregime movement. The result was a general uprising by almost all Iranians, who included a wide range of the opposition, none of which was able to bring down the regime alone. Consequently, all opposition groups and forces of regime challengers from the left to the right, from the most secular to the most religious, were united by necessity together under the religious leadership of Ayatullah Khomeini, who had from the 1960s never stopped his opposition to the regime and never compromised with it. He gained the confidence of millions of Iranians who aspired to overthrow the regime but were not able to do it alone.

Therefore, the rise of the religious leadership in the Iranian revolution and the subsequent introduction of the Islamic Republic Government in Iran are phenomena that are relatively unique in modern history. The survival and continuity of Iranian government under the new Islamic Republic have dashed many of the earlier hopes of the previous regime's supporters as well as other contenders for power in postrevolutionary Iranian politics. Many have tried to bring the new regime down, but have failed to do so.

The revolution and the Islamic Republic government have impacted the Iranian bureaucracy in many ways. There have been significant changes in the bureaucracy and its behavior and structure. Generally, these effects may be characterized by the phenomena of debureaucratization, institutionalization, and rebureaucratization.

V. DEBUREAUCRATIZATION OF IRAN: 1979–82

During the revolution, there was a general populist idea that the bureaucracy of the old regime was an oppressive machine and that must be destroyed or totally reformed. There was also a popular attitude that the established bureaucracy must be ignored and decisions made spontaneously and implemented immediately. There was no patience with red tape, and popular actions prevailed throughout the revolution and for several years afterward.

Thus, the process of debureaucratization of Iran began in several ways. First, the bureaucratic elites were immediately replaced: some had already left the country, others were fired, and still others were forced to retire. Bureaucratic rules and regulations were bypassed by revolutionary committees in all organizations as well as in every neighborhood in rural and urban Iran. Employee councils replaced hierarchical authorities, and administrative action was guided by revolutionary and popular demands and decisions which were implemented promptly. Religious, political, and revolutionary criteria established standards for administrative and managerial actions.

In rural and urban areas, thousands of local and regional revolutionary organizations sprung up during and after the revolution, staffed by volunteers from all occupations who provided their services and expertise to promote justice, to help provide services to the poor, and to carry out major development projects and other public works such as building highways, roads, bridges, hospitals, public baths, clinics, libraries, schools, colleges, and irrigation systems. Organizations such as the Reconstruction Crusaders, Housing Foundation, Land Distribution Committees, and War Refugees Foundation were among the most successful and popular bodies born during the revolution which have operated in the antibureaucratic manner and have had a remarkable record of achievements in Iran.

The debureaucratization of Iran altered the structure of the bureaucracy by either taking over the old machinery and operating it in a revolutionary manner or ignoring it altogether by creating new structures on an antibureaucratic basis. Democratization of workplace organizations in public, private, and nonprofit sectors was a major development. Hence public bureaucracy was a major battleground for employee political and democratization activities.

Democratization and debureaucratization phenomena were not, however, without cost. A degree of anarchy and lack of organizational discipline also pervaded the bureaucracy. Structurally, several changes also took place in the bureaucracy through the newly enacted legislative mandates of the Parliament, which created an Administrative Justice Office and a Supreme Council of revolutionary representation and heavily politicized the administrative system in general. In short, the phenomenon of debureaucratization along with the Islamization of the Iranian administrative system during 1979–82 had significant impacts on bureaucracy and public administration in Iran.

A. INSTITUTIONALIZATION AND REBUREAUCRATIZATION: 1983 TO THE PRESENT

The period since 1983 marks a major shift in the direction of moderation, a relaxation of radical positions in domestic and international affairs, and a standardization of social arrangements and governmental activities. The containment of terrorism and the military defeat of the opposition groups from left to right so characteristic of the first period strengthened the trend toward institutionalization, stabilization, and long-term planning by the government. While religious ideology and Islamization of the society and the bureaucracy were emphasized, "unity of all

Islamic groups and individual citizens" was called for all the time by the revolutionary leader Ayatullah Khomeini (quoted in Farazmand, 1991a, p. 758). The first Five Year Plan of the new government was ratified and adopted by the Parliament, which called for recruitment and return of thousands of professional experts for rebuilding the society and the administrative system. The merit system was given high value, but loyalty to the revolution and the Islamic government was of utmost importance in recruitment, selection, and maintenance of the work force. While nonreligious members of the bureaucracy were given some recognition, this was done only so long as they did not oppose the new regime. This new development was characteristic of all organizations in the public and private sectors, except the bona fide religious organizations.

The major changes that took place in the bureaucracy were structural, behavioral, and attitudinal in nature. Structurally, a gradual standardization, routinization, and bureaucratization replaced the previous debureaucratization. The bureaucracy was reorganized along more or less traditional bureaucratic lines, although spontaneity and Islamic requirements dominated the process and operation of the new system. Other major changes were the institutionalization and solidification of the religious representation as a special elite force of executive policy and political decision makers at the top of each agency, ministry, organization, and foundation in the country. This new cadre of religious elites has acted as strategic patronage appointees in the bureaucratic agencies, where they have been performing the job of system and regime maintenance, regime enhancement, and coordination with other related agencies. They have provided effective organizational leadership, harmony, and stability to the new system of administration and the bureaucracy. As time has passed, their appreciation for merit and professionalism has grown significantly, and they have been highly open-minded and receptive to expert advice.

Another major development has been the institutionalization of many organizations, committees, and other types of administrative bodies with subsequent consolidation and reorganization. Consolidation of many organizations into large administrative bodies has been followed in some cases by a degree of bureaucratization and formalization of the administrative system. This has resulted in some satisfaction among bureaucrats who have gained some recognition, but to dissatisfaction and disenchantment among the clients and citizens who have to deal with the bureaucracy and find that a lot of the problems of the old bureaucracy have returned (see Farazmand, 1991b, chapter 55, for details).

Still another change has affected the status of women in the work force. Conflicting proposals and legislative mandates have affected educated women in the bureaucracy. Opposing calls for their service and simultaneous encouragement to them to take more time to raise their children and thus create jobs for men have been a source of anxiety for many female members of the bureaucracy. Reform legislation has given women more rights equal to those of men in many respects. Recent legislation seems to have been in the right direction, recognizing the realities of the place of women in the work force and in various occupations in society.

Still another change relates to the control of bureaucracy and administration. Unlike in the past regime, under which there was no effective legislative and other means of control over the bureaucratic state (Binder, 1962; Farazmand, 1989; Zonis, 1971), significant oversight and control have been exercised over the bureaucracy and administrative system in postrevolutionary Iran. This oversight and control arise from the generally pluralistic nature of the Iranian polity, the media, the powerful Parliament, the independent judiciary, and a host of religious and political organizations throughout the society. The bureaucracy is controlled, but bureaucracy by nature has many ways to protect itself and to escape control from outside. This is a commonly observed problem even in the most democratic and advanced societies of the West.

Another major change in the bureaucracy has been a relative shrinking of its gigantic size. A number of public enterprises—nationalized industries and corporations—have been turned over to the private sector, and many others have been contracted out to the private sector. This has been a global trend, of course, and Iran has pursued this policy in order to attract foreign investment and credits, but also to promote managerial efficiency. The fact is that the huge Iranian bureaucracy is hard to manage efficiently and the lack of a sufficiently trained personnel and managerial cadre has made it very difficult for the government to manage the administrative system properly.

The trend toward institutionalization of revolutionary organizations and rebureaucratization of the administrative system in postrevolutionary Iran has had a significant impact on citizens, on bureaucrats, and on the government in general. The citizens seem to have been a little disappointed to see many bureaucratic practices of the past return. Frustration over how to deal with the rules of the old bureaucratic machinery while talking and feeling revolutionary has been a major problem expressed by people. On the other hand, the relative revival of morale and motivation among bureaucrats has been a major source of improved performance in the organizations of the administration. Such improvements may be found mostly in professional lines of administration.

The government has been caught between the necessity for a stable and institutionalized system of administration managed with high efficiency, on the one hand, and response to popular revolutionary demands. The dilemma is to maintain high responsiveness to the revolutionary and equitability demands of the people, particularly the lower and middle class, on the one hand, and to manage the public's business of running a huge public sector with efficiency. This dilemma is still a source of problems that have not been resolved. Maintaining political and religious responsiveness and efficiency is a challenge for the new Islamic government in Iran, a challenge likely to continue for a long time. On top of this dilemma is the forceful implementation of Islamization of the bureaucracy and administrative system, as well as the other institutions of the government and society. Islamization of the bureaucracy began during the first stage of debureaucratization, but it seems to have been well established and will continue to characterize Iranian bureaucracy in the future. Studies are needed to determine its impact on the performance of bureaucrats and administrators.

VI. SUMMARY AND CONCLUSION

Iran has had one of the longest traditions of bureaucracy in the world. Born in the city-state of Susa about 8,000 years ago and developed as an institution of the Elamite Empire during the fifth and first millennia, bureaucratization of the Iranian administrative system and professionalization of the bureaucracy reached their peak during the Median Empire as well as during the more than a millennium history of the world-state Persian Empire, with some exceptions under the Parthians. The fall of the empire to the Islamic conquerors in 651 did not end the rich Iranian traditions of bureaucracy, state, and administration. To the contrary, the Iranian bureaucracy and administrative system were adopted totally by the new rulers of Islam, and Persianization of the Islamic empire continued until the revival of the Iranian Salgugh Empire, only to be strengthened further under the powerful Safavid Empire in the sixteenth and seventeenth centuries. The Persian reputation for being excellent administrators was maintained until the eighteenth and nineteenth centuries, when Persia experienced a political, military, and administrative decline and was subjected to the influence and interference of Britain, France, and Imperial Russia.

The rise of modern bureaucracy and bureaucratization of Iran began during the 1920s with the rise of the Pahlavi regime. Iranian bureaucracy was based on the two pillars of the ancient system and modern concepts of institutionalization and management borrowed from the West. The first wave of bureaucratization occurred in the 1920s under Reza Shah's reform programs. But by far the most comprehensive process of bureaucratization in Iran occurred during the 1950s, 1960s, and 1970s. Bureaucratization of Iran and the bureaucracy in this period were political and administrative phenomena aimed at three broad objectives: transforming the Iranian countryside from a semifeudal system of society and economy into capitalism and its social relations with international capital; serving as the key instrument of capital accumulation and of facilitating capitalist development in Iran; acting as the key instrument of the bureaucratic state, providing the regime with a basis of legitimacy and rule; and working as an instrument of system maintenance and regime enhancement.

Bureaucratization of Iran meant more effective repression and displacement of the Iranian people. The powerful position of the bureaucracy and the bureaucratic elite permeated the society, and, since any challenge to the bureaucratic state was considered a challenge to the regime itself, the bureaucracy became the most repressive instrument of political, economic, and administrative domination in Iran. Since all powers were monopolized by the regime and the Shah, the second-stratum political and bureaucratic elite of Iran was also alienated.

The Iranian Revolution of 1978–79 as a general uprising by almost all Iranians from all strata led to the fall of the Pahlavi regime and the long tradition of monarchy in Iran. Subsequently, the Iranian bureaucracy and administrative system experienced severe debureaucratization with significant positive and negative consequences. Survival, stabilization, and institutionalization of the postrevolutionary Iranian government under the Islamic Republic brought fundamental changes in the bureaucracy and the administrative system.

The impact of debureaucratization was followed by a process of effective institutionalization and consolidation of the governmental institutions, and by a gradual process of rebureaucratization. Although the goals of system maintenance and regime enhancement seem to have been achieved effectively by the new developments, the managerial efficiency of the gigantic public sector bureaucracy has suffered. It seems that the remaining nonbureaucratic organizations of the revolutionary period have been more efficient and effective than the rebureaucratized ones.

This problem is now being attacked by the recent governmental policies of reprivatization, denationalization, and contracting out. These policies have serious negative as well as positive consequences that cannot be ignored by a postrevolutionary government with the mission of representing and serving the oppressed and providing economic justice. While rebureaucratization appears to have reemerged and the bureaucracy to have regained some power in society, Iran is far from being a bureaucratic state, and there are far more effective mechanisms of control over the bureaucracy than under the previous regime. The bureaucratization of prerevolutionary Iran and the dominance of the bureaucratic state under the Pahlavi regime were politically and administratively compatible with Weber's (1947) assertion of the role of bureaucracy in modern capitalist society, and of its role as a power instrument serving rulers, whether democratic or dictatorial. The repressive role of the bureaucracy in Iran was also a major contributor to the fall of the regime in 1978–79. The postrevolutionary bureaucracy of Iran has gone through major changes, but it has not attained even part of the power it used to enjoy. However, its growing position of power under the Islamic Republic and the increasing bureaucratization of the polity may pose threats or challenges to the new regime. It would be a prudent policy to avoid bureaucratization, contain bureaucratism, and promote more participatory, antibureaucratic institutions and administrative bodies in society, rural and urban. This would have the positive effects of system and regime enhancement for the Islamic Republic as well as promoting democratic values and self-management among the Iranian people. There are many desirable alternatives to bureaucratization, and many ways to promote debureaucratization.

REFERENCES

Afkhami, Gholam R., *The Iranian Revolution: Thanatos on a National Scale,* The Middle East Institute, Washington, D.C., 1985.

Argyriades, Demetrios, Bureaucracy and Debureaucratization, in *Handbook of Comparative and Development Public Administration* (Ali Farazmand, ed.), Marcel Dekker, New York, 1991, pp. 567–585.

Bill, James, *The Politics of Iran: Groups, Classes, and Modernization*, Charles Merril Press, Columbus, Ohio, 1972.

Binder, Leonard, *Political Development in a Changing Society,* University of California Press, Los Angeles, 1962.

Cameron, George, *History of Early Iran*, Greenwood Press, New York, 1968.

Cottam, Richard, *Nationalism in Iran*, University of Pittsburgh, Press, Pittsburgh, 1979.

Eisenstadt, S. N., *The Political Systems of Empires*, The Free Press, New York, 1963.

Farazmand, Ali, Bureaucratic Politics Under the Shah: Development or System-Maintenance?, Ph.D. dissertation, the Maxwell School, Syracuse University, New York, 1982.

Farazmand, Ali, *The State, Bureaucracy, and Revolution in Modern Iran: Agrarian Reforms and Regime Politics*, Praeger, New York, 1989.

Farazmand, Ali, Bureaucracy and Revolution: The Case of Iran, in *Handbook of Comparative and Development Public Administration* (Ali Farazmand, ed.), Marcel Dekker, New York, 1991a, pp. 755–767.

Farazmand, Ali, State Tradition and Public Administration in Iran in Ancient and Contemporary Perspectives, in *Handbook of Comparative and Development Public Administration* (Ali Farazmand, ed.), Marcel Dekker, New York, 1991b, pp. 255–270.

Farazmand, Ali, *State and Bureaucracy in Persia (Iran): 5,000 Years of Public Administration*, Praeger, Westport, Conn.

Frye, Richard, *The Heritage of Persia*, The World Publishing Company, New York, 1963.

Frye, Richard, *The Golden Age of Persia*, Harper & Row, New York, 1975.

Ghirshman, R., *Iran: From the Earliest Time to the Islamic Conquest*, Penguin Books, New York, 1954.

Halliday, Fred, *Dictatorship and Development*, Penguin Books, New York, 1979.

Huntington, Samuel P., *Political Order in a Changing Society,* Yale University Press, New Haven, Conn., 1968.

Mallowan, M. E. L., *Early Mesopotamia and Iran,* Thames and Hudson, London, 1965.

Olmstead, A., *History of the Persian Empire: The Achaemenid Period*, University of Chicago Press, Chicago, 1948.

Razi, Hosein G., The Nexus of Legitimacy and Performance: The Lessons of the Iranian Revolution, *Comparative Politics 19*:453–469 (1987).

Savory, R., *Iran Under the Safavids*, Cambridge University Press, Cambridge, 1980.

Weber, Max, *The Theory of Social and Economic Organization* (trans. A. M. Parsons and T. Parsons), The Free Press, New York, 1947.

Zonis, M., *The Political Elite of Iran*, Princeton University Press, Princeton, N.J., 1971.

Index